INTERNATIONAL BUSINESS

Environments and
Operations

SIXTH EDITION

INTERNATIONAL BUSINESS
ENVIRONMENTS AND OPERATIONS
SIXTH EDITION

JOHN D. DANIELS
Indiana University

LEE H. RADEBAUGH
Brigham Young University

ADDISON-WESLEY PUBLISHING COMPANY
Reading, Massachusetts • Menlo Park, California • New York
Don Mills, Ontario • Wokingham, England • Amsterdam • Bonn
Sydney • Singapore • Tokyo • Madrid • San Juan • Milan • Paris

Sponsoring Editor: Beth Toland
Development Editor: Cindy Johnson
Map Development Editor: Christine O'Brien
Illustrators: Maryland CartoGraphics, Inc.
Managing Editor: Mary Clare McEwing
Production Supervisor: Sarah Hallet
Production Services: The Book Department, Inc.
Technical Art Consultant: Richard Morton
Copy Editor: Barbara Pendergast
Text Design: Margaret Tsao
　　　　　　　 Meredith Nightingale
Cover Design: Richard Hannus
　　　　　　　 Meredith Nightingale
Manufacturing Supervisor: Roy Logan

Library of Congress Cataloging-in-Publication Data

Daniels, John D.
　　International business : environments and operations / John D.
Daniels, Lee H. Radebaugh.—6th ed.
　　　　p.　　cm.
　　Includes bibliographical references.
　　ISBN 0-201-57100-5
　　1. International business enterprises.　2. International economic
relations.　3. Investments, Foreign.　I. Radebaugh, Lee H.
II. Title.
HD2755.5.D35　1991
658.1'8—dc20

91-22710
CIP

Reprinted with corrections, May 1992.

3 4 5 6 7 8 9 10-DO-95949392

_____ PREFACE

A Changing World

The publication of the sixth edition of an international business text in 1992 is especially significant to us. It marks the five-hundredth anniversary of Columbus's first voyage to the Americas, an event that led to perhaps the most dramatic change in the history of international commerce. It also marks the target and rallying date for full economic unification within the European Community (EC), an evolutionary event that promises to change the future conduct of international commerce. Although these changes are perhaps unparalleled, change is the essence of international business. In fact, we often hear the comment that international business must be interesting because of the rapid changes in our global environment. If this is so, then international business has been especially interesting since the publication of our fifth edition in 1989! Consider some of the changes that have taken place since then:

- The Berlin Wall came down. Both the USSR and Yugoslavia broke apart.

- The former communist bloc countries underwent varying degrees of political and economic transformation. Most of these countries, even Albania, increased their openness to the West.

- The German Democratic Republic and the Federal Republic of Germany merged, as did Democratic Yemen and the Arab Republic of Yemen.

- Burma, Czechoslovakia, and Kampuchea became, respectively, Myanmar, the Czech and Slovak Federal Republic, and Cambodia.

- Privatization occurred in places that one would not have predicted.

- South Africa freed Nelson Mandela and began dismantling its apartheid laws, largely as a result of international economic pressures during the same period.

- Iraq and Iran ended their long war.

- Iraq invaded Kuwait, was weakened by a near-global trade embargo, and was removed by a United Nations force.

v

- Oil prices reached an all-time high and then fell back to previous levels.

- Members of the General Agreement on Tariffs and Trade negotiated fruit-lessly for freer world trade, while freer regional trade negotiations moved forward, especially among EC members and a North American group including Canada, the United States, and Mexico.

- The Panama Canal closed for the first time.

- Environmental issues came to the forefront, particularly with a globally celebrated Earth Day, some major oil spills, and rising concerns about the fairness of international trade among countries with diverse environmental standards.

- Japanese stock prices took their sharpest downturn but then recovered.

- Italy and Japan solicited foreign workers due to acute labor shortages.

Revising a text in this dynamic setting was both exhilarating and challenging. Since the first edition, we have agreed that we would start with a "zero budget," that is, planning anew rather than depending on what we had written before. At the same time, we have agreed that our text should have strong theoretical underpinnings that are less likely to change, regardless of international occurrences. We are fortunate that these give our text a continuity and backdrop against which we are able to explain recent global changes that are likely to be familiar to students. They also allow us to approach the multitude of environmental changes with a clear sense of their place in the text.

To guide us in the preparation of this sixth edition, we queried people who have taught international business courses in a variety of institutions. We asked them how their course was changing and what topics should be added, deleted, or emphasized to a different degree in our presentation. We asked how we could better present the material and what additional enhancements would be helpful in teaching the course. We were gratified that so many professors took the time to give us constructive suggestions.

Although there were too many suggestions to detail here, the major ones for the text can be summarized as follows:

- Update examples and cases.

- Simplify the presentation by using more tables and figures.

- Help students identify where places are geographically.

- Speculate more about the future.

And for the Instructor's Manual:

- Improve the section on audiovisual materials.

- Strengthen the multiple-choice test bank.

- Add true-false and discussion questions.

- Add creative learning activities that instructors may use.

We have addressed all these points and more in the sixth edition.

Our Approach to the First Course in International Business

With each new edition we started with the same question: What should be taught in a first course in international business when some students will thereafter have little or no classroom exposure to the subject and others will use the course as background for more specialized studies in the area? We continue to feel strongly that introductory students should be exposed to all the essential elements of international business. But what are these essential elements? From our queries we found a near consensus that our coverage should continue to be as broad as possible. The pervasive feeling is that the field will continue to evolve too rapidly to know for sure what the future essentials will be. It is far better, our respondents reasoned, to risk covering too much than to risk the omission of emerging issues and approaches that may well turn out to be essentials by the time students enter the workplace.

The sixth edition is by necessity longer than the fifth edition because of the inclusion of newly relevant topics. Nevertheless, we have monitored length by tightening the style and minimizing repetition from earlier editions.

We essentially have maintained the order of presentation from the last edition but have made some changes in the order of chapters. We believe the following topics present a systematic introduction to international business:

- An overview of current international business patterns, with an emphasis on what makes international patterns different from domestic ones.

- The social systems within countries as they affect the conduct of business from one country to another.

- The major theories explaining international business transactions and the institutions influencing the activities.

- The financial forms and institutions that measure and facilitate international transactions.

- The dynamic interface between nation-states and the firms attempting to conduct foreign business activities.

- The alternatives for overall corporate policy and strategy that accommodate global operations.

- The concerns and management of international activities that fall largely within functional disciplines.

Our approach throughout the text is to emphasize the managerial viewpoint rather than that of the social science disciplines from which international business draws its theoretical underpinnings. For example, as we talk about trade policy, we discuss not only the effects of different policies on national objectives, but also the courses of action that companies and industries can and do take to influence policy and to react to whatever policy is undertaken. We feel that the student who can evaluate courses of action in light of the theoretical foundations of the business world will be well prepared to operate in the rapidly changing global business environment.

New Features and Topics

In response to the suggestions we received, we have added the following new features and topics to the sixth edition:

Maps   A large number of maps throughout the text and a 16-page full-color atlas will help students locate areas discussed in the course. We feel strongly that geographic literacy is an asset to the international business person; therefore, we have selected maps that will improve students' understanding of geographic data. A poll conducted by the Gallup Organization for the National Geographic Society and published in 1988 asked respondents in nine countries (Canada, France, Italy, Japan, Mexico, Sweden, the United Kingdom, the United States, and the former West Germany) a number of questions, including the location of sixteen seemingly not-too-difficult places on a world map (the United States, Canada, Mexico, Central America, Italy, the United Kingdom, France, West Germany, Sweden, Egypt, South Africa, Vietnam, the USSR, Japan, the Pacific Ocean, and the Persian Gulf). Although the Swedes emerged as the geographic champs, they averaged only 70 percent or 11.6 correct answers. Respondents from the United States ranked sixth among respondents from the nine countries taking the test, with an average of only 54 percent or 8.6 correct answers. Not surprisingly, within each nationality group, people with more formal education scored better. Regardless of nationality, people were better able to locate places closer to them than more remote places. For example, respondents in Sweden scored higher than those from the United States in locating the six European countries on the list; but U.S. respondents scored better than Swedes in finding the United States, Canada, Central America, Mexico, and the Pacific Ocean.

The Gallup/National Geographic Poll also indicated possible differences among countries in educational philosophy, such as emphasis on rote memorization of information versus knowledge of tools to find information. For example, Swedes scored higher than any other group on factual geographic information, such as locating countries without an index and knowing population figures. However, U.S. respondents placed more emphasis than any other nationality on tool skills, including the importance of using computers and knowing how to interpret maps, such as estimating distances from map scales. We feel both skills and geographic knowledge are important, and we have included maps in this edition to support both. The maps within the chapters are aimed primarily at finding locations. The full-color map section includes geopolitical maps and other maps that are concise but rich sources of information.

Regrettably, we cannot present maps from all national perspectives; however, students should be aware that maps do differ among countries. An obvious difference is in the portrayal of disputed territories. Less obvious is the tendency to put one's own country toward the middle, east to west, of a flat map projection. People also divide global segments differently. For example, in the United States one is taught that the Western Hemisphere is divided into two continents at the border between Panama and Colombia. But Panamanians are taught that North and South America are divided between Costa Rica and Panama. In most other Latin American and Caribbean countries, one is taught that the entire Western Hemisphere is made up of only one continent, America, with several subcontinental segments. Most people within these countries refer to everyone living therein as Americans and to people from the U.S.A. in particular as either *estadounidenses* or *norteamericanos,* Spanish for United Statesians and North Americans, respectively. We hope the addition of maps to the sixth edition will introduce a greater awareness of international differences as they build a greater geographical awareness.

New Cases We have always planned to include current and interesting cases in our revisions, but they are especially important for this sixth edition since so much has changed in the world since the last edition. Eleven cases, or one quarter of the total included, are entirely new, and the rest of the cases have been updated to reflect new information. The case listing on pages xv–xviii identifies the new cases we have added.

Looking to the Future Each chapter now concludes with a section titled, "Looking to the Future." These sections contain likely future scenarios of which students should be aware and are provided to bridge the gap between the text discussion and the events students read about in current periodicals. They emphasize the dynamic nature of international business and may be useful tools for classroom discussion as well.

New Topic Coverage In addition to updates and more current examples, each chapter also contains new topics that are critical for understanding international business. The following is a sampling of the additions and changes we have made:

- Integrated coverage of the legal environment (Ch. 2).
- Body language and country clusters that share cultural attributes (Ch. 3).
- Expanded treatment of international product life cycle (Ch. 4).
- Problems of the Uruguay Round and of multilateral negotiations within GATT (Ch. 5).
- Buy vs. build decision, now integrated into direct investment discussion (Ch. 6).
- Mathematical demonstration of purchasing price parity and the effect of interest rates on exchange rates (Ch. 8).
- Countertrade added to the discussion of barter and compensatory trade (Ch. 7).
- More coverage of the IMF and monetary considerations of the EC (Ch. 8).

- Deregulation of equity markets added to a completely revised chapter on financial markets (Ch. 9).

- Changes in the Second World, integrated throughout the text and reflected in a completely rewritten chapter (Ch. 10).

- Europe 1992 examined closely in a new chapter on regional economic integration (Ch. 11).

- North American free trade zone (Ch. 11).

- International efforts toward pollution control and the environment (Ch. 11).

- Extraterritoriality, ethics and standards, and the Foreign Corrupt Practices Act expanded (Ch. 12).

- Protection of intangible assets (Ch. 13).

- Export financing coverage consolidated with other export considerations (Ch. 14).

- Growing importance of nonequity and partial-equity arrangements reflected in strategic alliances (Ch. 15).

- Environmental scanning added to country evaluation discussion (Ch. 16).

- New sections on hetarchies and keiretsus (Ch. 17).

- International branching considerations (Ch. 18).

- Global cash management (Ch. 20).

- Career considerations of foreign assignments and strategies for expatriates (Ch. 21).

Improvements to Pedagogy (Why Students Learn Well from This Book)

While providing greater breadth and depth of coverage than many other introductory texts, we have taken care not to overwhelm students. In this new edition we have simplified language and sentence structure so that the material is as easy to understand as possible. We have added many new charts and tables to clarify prose discussions. Captions now accompany all figures to help students understand each figure's key message.

Integrated Case Methodology   One pedagogical technique we have carried over is the use of short cases to introduce and conclude each of the 21 chapters. This concept has been very well received for its effectiveness. The opening cases are designed to accomplish two objectives: (1) to build students' interest so that they are motivated to read what follows, and (2) to introduce problems and situations that will be further explained by theories and research findings presented in the chapter that follows. For instance,

Chapter 10 begins with a case dealing with the negotiations and adjustments that led to an early joint venture in the former Soviet Union, the opening of a McDonald's restaurant. The enterprise is one about which almost all students have some familiarity and interest. Elements of the case are then used as examples within the chapter to illustrate the conditions for international business in historically planned economies (HPEs) and to point out what companies may do to operate within HPEs.

The closing cases are designed to serve a different purpose: to present situations that require students to analyze possible courses of action based on what they have learned in the chapter. In other words, the beginning cases enhance interest and the recall of essential facts; the ending cases enhance the development of critical reasoning skills by asking students to apply the essential facts to business decision making.

Real-World Examples   We have also continued the use of extensive real-world examples throughout the text to illustrate approaches that individuals, companies, industries, and countries have taken in specific situations. These examples not only enliven the presentation but also provide a practical and concrete counterpoint to the general discussion that helps students understand key concepts.

Study Support   To further emphasize key ideas (and to encourage students not to direct their study efforts too much to the illustrative data), we continue to include the margin notes that we pioneered in our fourth edition. These notes outline the major points of each section. They have been fully revised for the sake of emphasis and clarity. We also highlight new terms as they are introduced and include them in a greatly expanded glossary. Chapter objectives and bulleted chapter summaries recap major points and are additional study aids.

An ample number of endnotes to aid students and instructors in digging deeper on different subjects complete each chapter. Three indexes to chapter materials—subject, author, and company—are carryovers from earlier editions, and we have added a new index of places keyed to the full-color map section. The indexes, like the notes at the end of each chapter, reflect the up-to-date and worldwide content found in the new edition.

Instructor Supplements

Professor Arvind Jain of Concordia University has assumed primary responsibility for the sixth edition's Instructor's Manual. As an adopter of several previous editions, Dr. Jain has worked closely with us throughout our revision process. His participation has enabled work on the text and the manual to proceed simultaneously, yielding better integration and pedagogical consistency between the two. His energy and teaching insights greatly enhance the supplementary teaching materials.

Tests   The large multiple-choice test bank continues to be a key component of the Instructor's Manual. This bank has been edited from a student perspective and revised to reflect the text's content changes. Misleading words and phrases, negative questions, "all of the above" questions, "none of the above" questions, and all of the trivia-type questions have been eliminated. Discussion questions that can be used for essay exams or for class discussions and true-false questions have been added. Computerized test-preparation software for use with the test bank is also available.

Visuals   Four videotape segments presenting current excerpts from "Mac-Neil/Lehrer Business Reports" are available to adopters free of charge from Addison-Wesley Publishing Company. These news reports will bring the changing business environment into the classroom.

The audiovisual resource section of the Instructor's Manual has been reorganized for more efficient use. In addition, it has been greatly enhanced to provide more information on films and videotapes and to suggest multiple sources for purchase, rental, or loan. This section in each chapter now discusses the use of relevant films and videos and how they relate to chapter coverage.

Lecture Support   The Instructor's Manual now includes suggestions for games, exercises, and projects suitable for classroom use and describes key articles useful in preparing for lectures or discussion. End-of-chapter cases are discussed in detail, and each chapter has several transparency masters, including additional exhibits not found in the student text. We hope you will find the Instructor's Manual for the sixth edition to be a significant improvement and a big help in developing the course.

Electronic Color Transparencies   A selection of transparency masters from the Instructor's Manual are available on diskette. Using Harvard Graphics and a color printer, an instructor can output color acetates to use in class. The diskette is provided to faculty free upon adoption and may be requested by writing to: Beth Toland, Addison-Wesley Publishing Company, One Jacob Way, Reading, MA 01867.

International Business Newsletter   This newsletter, featuring interviews with scholars of international business, point-counterpoint views, and other articles of interest will be published twice annually (January and August) for adapters of Addison-Wesley international business textbooks. The first issue will be available January 1992.

Student Supplements

Two new supplementary products from Addison-Wesley can be used with our text to enhance student case work and projects.

PC Globe   An interactive microcomputer-based atlas and geography data base, PC Globe is available exclusively from Addison-Wesley Publishing Company at a reduced price for business and economics students. Students can use the data base to research foreign locations and cultures and to build their knowledge of geography.

The Economist Yearbook   An annual country-by-country compilation of developments in business, economics, agriculture, and politics, the concise edition of *The Economist Yearbook* is a useful tool for case analysis and country-based research.

Acknowledgments

Few textbooks succeed to a sixth edition. We are gratified that this text, representing over eighteen years of our collaborative efforts, is one of the successful ones. We believe that our ability to reach a sixth edition is due largely to three factors: (1) the continued updating to parallel the rapidly changing world and the evolving field of international business, (2) the clarity of the presentation, refined over the long life of the book, and (3) the interest and efforts of a large group of academicians and students who continue to give us critical feedback on content and pedagogy.

We have been fortunate from the first edition to have had colleagues who would make the effort to critique draft materials, react to coverage already in print, advise on suggested changes, and send items to be corrected. Since it is the cumulative efforts of several editions that have brought us to a sixth edition, we would like to acknowledge everyone's efforts. However, many more individuals than we can possibly list have helped. To those individuals who must remain anonymous, we offer our sincere thanks.

Since 1989, however, several people have taken part in our market research and have helped us keep tabs on the changing nature of the international business course. We would like to thank them for their help.

> Yohannan T. Abraham, Southwest Missouri State University
> Aaron Andreason, University of Montana
> S. Alexander Billon, University of Delaware
> Eugene Blackmum, Cerritos College
> James Boyle, Glendale Community College
> Alena Bullock, Brookdale Community College
> Charles Cambridge, California State University, Chico
> Frank Cancelliere, Long Island University-C. W. Post Campus
> Richard Dutton, University of South Florida
> Bert Faulhaber, Ball State University
> James Gaertner, University of Texas, San Antonio
> Yezdi H. Godiwalla, University of Wisconsin, Whitewater
> Robert Hamilton, Temple University

Joseph Hill, East Carolina University
Thomas Jackson, University of Vermont
Chip Miller, University of Montana
Herman S. Napier, University of Arkansas
Arvind Phatak, Temple University
Bradley Roof, James Madison University
Lloyd Russow, University of Toledo
Charles Snow, Auburn University
Fred Truitt, University of Washington

Special thanks go to the faculty members who gave detailed comments for the planning and preparation of this edition.

Jean Boddewyn, City University of New York
Jeffrey T. Doutt, Sonoma State University
Eldridge T. Freeman, Jr., Chicago State University
Miriam K. Lo, Mankato State University
Paul Marer, Indiana University
Mark E. Mendenhall, University of Tennessee at Chattanooga
Moonsong David Oh, California State University, Los Angeles
Lucie Pfaff, College of Mt. St. Vincent
George Sutija, Florida International University
William A. Stoever, Seton Hall University
John Thanopoulos, University of Akron
Heidi Vernon-Wortzel, Northeastern University

Finally, we would like to thank the typists and graduate students who were extremely helpful to us in the preparation of this edition and without whom we could not have made the necessary changes. A few were so helpful that we cannot let them remain nameless: James Claus, Sheldon Holsinger, Melanie Hunter, Derek Jarvis, Philip Lee, Christine Nelson, Crissan Pierce, and Stephen Schiltz.

Both of us come from diverse functional backgrounds and represent a gamut of opinions on the proper role of business and government in international affairs. In order to develop better coherence among the chapters, we read, criticized, and contributed to each other's sections. John D. Daniels was charged with Chapters 1, 3, 4, 5, 6, 10, 12, 13, 15, 16, 17, 18, and 21; Lee H. Radebaugh was charged with Chapters 2, 7, 8, 9, 11, 14, 19, and 20. We welcome your comments and suggestions for the next edition.

Bloomington, Indiana   J.D.D.
Provo, Utah   L.H.R.

CASES IN THE SIXTH EDITION

(New cases are asterisked.)

CHAPTER 1   The *Stars Wars* Trilogy   **5**

An account of how different locations affected the production and distribution of the film.

Disneyland Abroad   **31**

The reasons and methods of setting up theme parks in Japan and France.

CHAPTER 2   *The *Taipan*'s Dilemma   **39**

Excellent look at the impending change in Hong Kong's status.

Bata, Ltd.   **77**

The dilemmas facing a Canadian MNE considering investing in the Czech and Slovak Federal Republic and deciding what to do about South Africa.

CHAPTER 3   **Parris-Rogers International (PRI)**   **83**

Shows how deep-seated cultural values impacted a British firm's operations in Saudi Arabia.

John Higgins   **114**

Examines to what extent U.S. expatriate managers should adapt to Japanese ways in a U.S.-Japanese joint venture.

CHAPTER 4   **Sri Lankan Trade**   **125**

Illustrates the application of trade theories to Sri Lankan governmental policies.

The Cashew   **158**

Analyzes changing world market factors and alternatives for continued competitiveness of Indian producers.

CHAPTER 5   **Automobile Imports**   **165**

The dynamics of competition and trade policies in the U.S. market.

Steel Imports   **193**

A look at alternatives steel-producing firms can take in the face of changing global competition.

CHAPTER 6   **Bridgestone Tire Company**   **201**

Examines why a Japanese firm acquired Firestone in the United States.

Electrolux Acquisitions   **226**

The transition from local to global competition in the electrical appliance industry.

CHAPTER 7   *__Foreign Travels, Foreign-Exchange Travails__*   **235**

A first-hand account of the complexity of exchange rate calculations.

The Mexican Peso   **259**

An illustration of factors that influence the value of a currency and of government policies in the face of currency weakness.

CHAPTER 8   *__The Japanese Yen__*   **265**

The Japanese yen as an example of how exchange rates are determined.

Caterpillar and the Fluctuating Dollar   **293**

Corporate strategy in the face of a dollar that is changing in value.

CHAPTER 9   **Hypothetical Script for Collapse**   **301**

Scenarios illustrating how a bank failure in Hong Kong can ripple throughout the world.

LSI Logic Corp.   **334**

Strategies employed by a high-tech company to gain access to funds on global capital markets.

CHAPTER 10   *__McDonald's__*   **343**

A detailed look at the issues involved in doing business in a historically planned economy that focuses on a Russian/Canadian joint venture.

__Taurus Hungarian Rubber Works__   **379**

Issues for businesses in the historically planned economies in Eastern Europe in transition to market economies.

CHAPTER 11   **Incident: Ford in Europe—The Early Years**   **389**

Ford's strategy for organizing in Europe in order to take advantage of the common market.

   ***A North American Free Trade Area**   **423**

Timely case on a controversial subject.

CHAPTER 12   **MNEs in Canada**   **431**

Illustrates the love-hate relationship when a significant part of a country's economy is controlled by foreign firms.

   Foreign Real-Estate Holdings in the United States   **456**

Discusses whether restrictions should be placed on foreign ownership.

CHAPTER 13   **ARAMCO**   **463**

Illustrates how the power of oil firms has shifted in response to changing economic and political situations.

   ***PepsiCo in India**   **494**

A "classic" case about competitive factors influencing the outcome of negotiations.

CHAPTER 14   ***Sunset Flowers of New Zealand, Ltd.**   **505**

A view of the uncertainties faced by exporters, regardless of home country or size.

   Black & Decker   **532**

B & D's strategy for coordinating worldwide production to cut costs.

CHAPTER 15   **Grupo Industrial Alfa**   **537**

A Mexican firm's use of alliances with foreign companies to improve its competitive situation.

   NPC   **566**

The process by which a U.S. firm tried to gain access to some German technology.

CHAPTER 16   **Ford Motor Company**   **573**

Shows the process of allocating sales and production efforts among countries.

   Mitsui in Iran   **602**

The risk factors in the Middle East and their implications for a Japanese/Iranian joint venture.

CHAPTER 17   Nestlé   **609**

*One of the world's most international companies and the problems
and methods of managing the spread of operations.*

Westinghouse   **643**

*Analyzes the problems of finding a suitable organization structure
for an internationally significant company with an extreme of
product diversity.*

CHAPTER 18   Marks & Spencer   **655**

A highly successful British retailer stumbles in its foreign expansion.

Source Perrier   **689**

*Examines alternatives for a French firm's growth in the
U.S. market.*

CHAPTER 19   *Daimler-Benz   **699**

International accounting in the European Community.

The Coca-Cola Company   **727**

*The development of an accounting procedure manual for a
global company.*

CHAPTER 20   *Olivetti's Foreign-Exchange Risk-Management   **731**

*How one company manages its exposure to significant
foreign-exchange risk.*

*Hewlett-Packard in Europe: A Cash-Management
Strategy   **756**

Global cash management techniques and issues.

CHAPTER 21   Dow's International Management Development   **761**

*Illustrates how a company has successfully developed human
resources to complement its global objectives.*

The Office Equipment Company   **797**

*Demonstrates the different qualifications, training, and
compensation needs for potential candidates to head a U.S. firm's
operations in El Salvador.*

CONTENTS

PART 1
BACKGROUND   **3**

Chapter 1   International Business: An Overview   **4**

   Case   The *Star Wars* Trilogy   **5**

           Introduction   8
           Types of International Business   10
           The External Environment   13
           Influences on Trade and Investment Patterns   18
           Recent World Trade Patterns   21
           Recent Direct Investment Patterns   26
           Looking to the Future   29
           Summary   30

   Case   **Disneyland Abroad**   **31**

PART 2
COMPARATIVE ENVIRONMENTAL FRAMEWORKS   **37**

Chapter 2   The Legal, Political, and Economic
Environments Facing Business   **38**

   Case   The *Taipan*'s Dilemma   **39**

           Introduction   43
           The Legal Environment   43
           The Political Environment   45
           The Economic Environment   52

Political-Economic Synthesis   56
Adapting to Foreign Environments   57
The Classification of Economies   58
Key Economic Issues in Industrial and
   Developing Countries   62
North-South Dialogue   72
External Influences on Development   73
Looking to the Future   75
Summary   76

Case   Bata, Ltd.   77

**Chapter 3   The Human and Cultural Environments
               Facing Business**   **82**

Case   Parris-Rogers International (PRI)   83

Introduction   87
Types of Variables   88
Physical Attributes   89
Behavioral Attributes   90
Reconciliation of International Differences   104
Looking to the Future   112
Summary   113

Case   John Higgins   114

**PART 3
THEORIES AND INSTITUTIONS:
TRADE AND INVESTMENT   123**

Chapter 4   International Trade Theory   124

Case   Sri Lankan Trade   125

Introduction   128
Mercantilism   130
Absolute Advantage   132
Comparative Advantage   136
Factor-Proportions Theory   140
The Product Life Cycle   142
Determination of Trading Partners   147
Independence, Interdependence,
   and Dependence   148
Why Companies Trade   153

Looking to the Future   155
Summary   156

Case   **The Cashew**   **158**

Chapter 5   **Governmental Influence on Trade**   **164**

Case   **Automobile Imports**   **165**

Introduction   168
The Rationale for Governmental Intervention   169
Forms of Trade Control   178
The Role of GATT   186
Meshing Protection and International Strategy   189
Looking to the Future   191
Summary   191

Case   **Steel Imports**   **193**

Chapter 6   **Foreign Direct Investment**   **200**

Case   **Bridgestone Tire Company**   **201**

Introduction   204
The Meaning of Foreign Direct Investment   205
The Relationship of Trade and Factor Mobility   207
Direct Investment Motivation   211
Market-Expansion Investments   211
Resource-Seeking Investments   217
Multiple Motives   220
Buy-versus-Build Decision   221
Advantages of Direct Investors   222
Looking to the Future   224
Summary   224

Case   **Electrolux Acquisitions**   **226**

PART 4
WORLD FINANCIAL ENVIRONMENT   **233**

Chapter 7   **Foreign Exchange**   **234**

Case   **Foreign Travels, Foreign-Exchange Travails**   **235**

Introduction   238
Terms and Definitions   239

How the Foreign-Exchange Market Works   244
Convertibility   250
Exchange Restrictions   251
Compensatory Trade   253
The Uses of the Foreign-Exchange Market   256
Looking to the Future   257
Summary   258

Case   The Mexican Peso   259

Chapter 8   The Determination of Exchange Rates   **264**

Case   The Japanese Yen   265

Introduction   268
The International Monetary System   268
The Determination of Exchange Rates   276
Forecasting Exchange-Rate Movements   283
Business Implications of Exchange-Rate Changes   289
Looking to the Future   291
Summary   291

Case   Caterpillar and the Fluctuating Dollar   293

Chapter 9   Financial Markets for International Operations   **300**

Case   Hypothetical Script for Collapse   301

Introduction   303
Local Debt Markets   304
Eurocurrencies   306
International Bonds   310
Offshore Financial Centers   312
Equity Securities   314
International Banks   319
Nonbanking Financial Services Firms   327
Development Banks   329
Looking to the Future   332
Summary   333

Case   LSI Logic Corp.   334

**PART 5
THE DYNAMICS OF INTERNATIONAL BUSINESS-
GOVERNMENTAL RELATIONSHIPS   341**

Chapter 10   Business with Historically Planned Economies   342

Case   **McDonald's   343**

Introduction   347
Business Volatility   350
Transformation to Market Economies   354
Factors Affecting Business Expansion   362
Trade Restrictions   367
Methods of Doing Business with HPEs   369
Looking to the Future   372
Summary   377

Case   **Taurus Hungarian Rubber Works   379**

Chapter 11   Regional Economic Integration   388

Case   **Incident: Ford in Europe–The Early Years   389**

Introduction   391
Regional Economic Integration   392
The European Community   394
Latin American Cooperation   403
Eastern European Integration   406
Asian Integration Efforts   408
African Cooperation   409
Commodity Agreements   410
Other Multilateral Institutions   416
Looking to the Future   420
Summary   421

Case   **A North American Free Trade Area   423**

Chapter 12   The Impact of the Multinational   430

Case   **MNEs in Canada   431**

Introduction   435
Evaluating the Impact of the MNE   435
Economic Impact of the MNE   438
Political and Legal Impact of the MNE   445

Operational Impact of International Business
   Activities   453
Looking to the Future   454
Summary   454

Case   **Foreign Real-Estate Holdings in the United States**   **456**

Chapter 13   **International Business Diplomacy**   **462**

Case   **ARAMCO**   **463**

Introduction   467
Needs and Alternatives for Fulfillment   468
Negotiations in International Business   471
Home-Country Involvement in Asset Protection   478
Multilateral Settlements   480
Consortium Approaches   482
External Relations Approaches   484
Protection of Intellectual Property Rights   488
Looking to the Future   491
Summary   492

Case   **PepsiCo in India**   **494**

International Business Environments: An Atlas
follows page 484

PART 6
CORPORATE POLICY AND STRATEGY   **503**

Chapter 14   **Global Sourcing, Production, and
Export Strategies**   **504**

Case   **Sunset Flowers of New Zealand, Ltd.**   **505**

Introduction   508
Global Sourcing   511
International Manufacture   516
Export Strategy   521
Looking to the Future   530
Summary   531

Case   **Black & Decker**   **532**

Chapter 15   **Strategic Alliances**   **536**

Case   **Grupo Industrial Alfa**   **537**

Introduction   540

Some Variables Affecting Choice   541
Licensing   544
Franchising   551
Management Contracts   554
Turnkey Operations   556
Custom Contracts   557
Improving Access to Foreign Technology   558
Shared Ownership   559
Managing Foreign Arrangements   563
Looking to the Future   564
Summary   564

Case   NPC   566

Chapter 16   Country Evaluation and Selection   **572**

Case   Ford Motor Company   573

Introduction   575
Scanning for Alternatives   577
Influential Variables   578
Return on Investment: Country
    Comparison Considerations   582
Some Tools for Comparing Countries   588
Investment Proposal Evaluation   596
Divestment Decisions   598
Looking to the Future   599
Summary   600

Case   Mitusi in Iran   602

Chapter 17   Control   **608**

Case   Nestlé   609

Introduction   613
Location of Decision Making   614
Organizational Structure   620
Planning   628
Business Research   631
Corporate Culture   634
Reports   635
Control in Special Situations   639
Looking to the Future   641
Summary   642

Case   Westinghouse   643

Appendix: Problems of International Data   649

**PART 7
FUNCTIONAL MANAGEMENT, OPERATIONS,
AND CONCERNS**   **653**

Chapter 18   Marketing   **654**

Case   Marks & Spencer   655

Introduction   659
Market Size Analysis   659
Pricing   671
Promotion   676
Branding   680
Distribution   682
Looking to the Future   687
Summary   688

Case   Source Perrier   689

Chapter 19   Multinational Accounting and Tax Functions   **698**

Case   Daimler-Benz   699

Introduction   702
Factors Influencing the Development of Accounting
   Around the World   704
Harmonization of Differences   707
Transactions in Foreign Currency   709
Translation of Foreign Currency
   Financial Statements   711
Taxation   715
Taxation of Foreign-Source Income   716
Non-U.S. Tax Practices   721
Looking to the Future   725
Summary   725

Case   The Coca-Cola Company   727

Chapter 20   The Multinational Finance Function   **730**

**Case   Olivetti's Foreign-Exchange
         Risk-Management   731**

Introduction   732
Organization of the Finance Function   733
Internal Sources of Funds   735
Global Cash Management   736
Inflation and Foreign-Exchange
   Risk Management   743
Key Issues in Foreign-Exchange
   Risk Management   747
Financial Aspects of the Investment Decision   753
Looking to the Future   754
Summary   755

Case   **Hewlett-Packard in Europe:
A Cash-Management Strategy   756**

Chapter 21   **Human Resource Management**   **760**

Case   **Dow's International
Management Development   761**

Introduction   763
Management Qualifications and Characteristics   764
Foreign Managerial Transfers   767
Management Recruitment and Selection   778
Management Training   780
Labor Market Differences   781
Labor Compensation   783
Comparative Labor Relations   785
International Pressures on National Practices   789
Multinational Ownership and
   Collective Bargaining   790
Looking to the Future   793
Summary   795

Case   **The Office Equipment Company   797**

GLOSSARY   **G-1**

COMPANY INDEX AND TRADEMARKS   **I-1**

NAME INDEX   **I-6**

MAP INDEX   **I-14**

SUBJECT INDEX   **I-18**

INTERNATIONAL BUSINESS
Environments and Operations
SIXTH EDITION

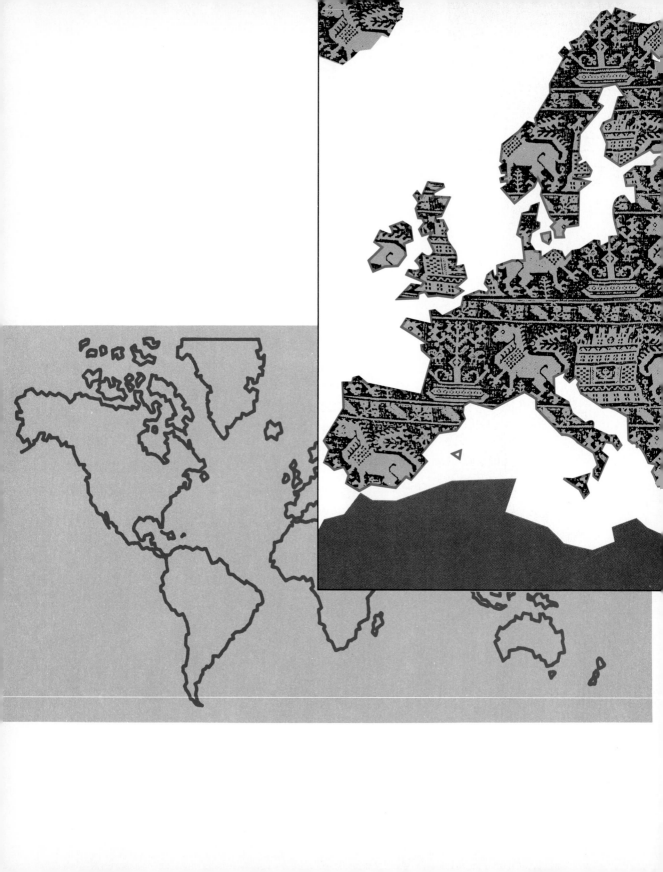

PART 1
BACKGROUND

Whether we are managers actively engaged in decision making within an internationally competitive environment or citizens interested in regulating international business to achieve our own objectives, it is useful to know why international business takes place, what advantages accrue to firms operating internationally, what makes this business different from purely domestic operations, and how these operations relate to a country's overall international economic position.

Chapter 1 sets the stage for a more detailed examination of the above considerations. The chapter begins by defining the field, explaining why the growth has been so great in recent years, and relating the field to both the functional areas of business (for example, marketing, finance, and management) and the basic disciplines (such as geography, law, and economics). The chapter continues with an explanation of the multiple forms by which international business may take place. The last sections in Chapter 1 examine recent trends in world trade and investment by product and geographic area and provide a brief explanation of the factors that cause changes to take place.

CHAPTER **1**

INTERNATIONAL BUSINESS: AN OVERVIEW

The world is a chain, one link in another.
MALTESE PROVERB

Objectives

- To define international business and emphasize differences between business within domestic and international contexts.

- To illustrate reliance on external disciplines (e.g., geography, history, political science, law, economics, and anthropology) because of their impact on the conduct of international business.

- To define and discuss basic terms relating to international business.

- To introduce different means (e.g., exporting, licensing, and investing) a firm can use to accomplish its global objectives.

- To relate major events changing trade and investment patterns.

- To describe changing composition of world trade and investment in terms of countries and products.

Y ou have probably seen *Star Wars, The Empire Strikes Back,* or *Return of the Jedi.* But you might not know that these three films constitute the most successful sequence ever produced. Few films enjoy success when rereleased. Those that have been successful, such as Walt Disney's *Pinocchio,* are generally rereleased only at seven-year intervals. Yet the 1977 film, *Star Wars,* was successfully rereleased five times by 1987. The intergalactic aspect of the trilogy is obvious. Less obvious, though, are the international dimensions, right here on planet earth, that contributed to the films' triumphs.

The deal to produce *Star Wars* was international from the start. George Lucas, the American producer, had written short summaries of two films he wished to make. He took his ideas to every studio in Hollywood, and each one turned him down. In desperation, he used his last $2000 to buy a ticket to the Cannes (France) Film Festival, in the hope of gaining some backing. There he made an agreement with a Hollywood studio for production of *American Graffiti* and *Star Wars.*

When the time came to film *Star Wars,* cost data were obtained from several technically capable interior facilities. The contract was awarded to a studio outside London. The lower wages of British technicians more than offset the additional costs of transporting personnel from the United States to Great Britain. By the time *The Empire Strikes Back* and *Return of the Jedi* were filmed, the labor cost differentials were no longer significant, but it was convenient to stay on at the English studios, since personnel were working so well together.

Not everything was filmed in England, however. The films' success was due largely to the fact that the extraterrestrial locales appeared authentic. At times the technicians used plates filmed elsewhere to go behind interior scenes shot in England. For instance, in *Star Wars* the Alliance leaders plot the destruction of the Death Star from the secret Rebel base on the planet Yavin. The background for Yavin was in fact the ancient Mayan ruins of Tikal in Guatemala. At other times it was necessary to film on location because of action taking place within rather than in front of scenery. For the scenes in which R2-D2 and C-3PO crash on the desert planet Tatooine, are captured by Jawas, and are sold to a local moisture farmer and his nephew (Luke Skywalker), the filming actually took place on the Sahara Desert in Tunisia. At the beginning of *The Empire Strikes Back* the Rebel force is held up in a hideout on the ice planet Hoth. In reality this was a place above the Arctic Circle in Norway.

In addition to the logistics of filming real actors in different locations, these scenes had to be combined with the miniature effects, which were made at a specially constructed monster factory in California. As shots were completed for *The Empire Strikes Back,* videocassettes had to be transported 6000 miles. Because of transportation and communications advances,

C A S E

THE

STAR WARS

TRILOGY[1]

global collaboration in film making has become commonplace. These advances enable us to see more realistic-looking scenes than were possible only a few years before *Star Wars*.

The actors were primarily U.S. and U.K. nationals. Carrie Fisher, Harrison Ford, and Mark Hamill, who played Princess Leia Organa, Han Solo, and Luke Skywalker, respectively, were all from the United States. Alec Guinness, who played Ben (Obi-Wan) Kenobi, and Anthony Daniels, who played C-3PO, were both from the United Kingdom. Lord Darth Vader could be characterized as a binational—the actor, David Prowse, is British; however, James Earl Jones, an American, did the voice because of Prowse's strong Devon farmer's accent.

The distribution of the films has been truly international. The expectation of receiving both domestic and foreign income is necessary to justify the risky investment in a high-cost film. About 40 percent of the revenues have come from outside the United States; however, there have been some formidable obstacles. For example, most communist countries prohibited entry before they began their economic and political reforms. Some other countries, such as Haiti and Mali, have such poor economies that few people can afford to see the films. Even if attendance could be generated, the moviegoers would pay in their local currencies, which are gourdes and francs, respectively. Since the governments are also poor, especially in ownership of other currencies, they would be hard-pressed to convert the gourdes and francs to a currency that the producers could use. The film distributors have made separate agreements with each country that shows one of the *Star Wars* trilogy so that revenues will come back to Lucasfilm Ltd., the producer, in U.S. dollars.

Almost everywhere the films have been screened, they have received high public acceptance. This has been due at least in part to good reviews and shrewd marketing, yet many films that share these attributes still fail to become international hits. What these films did, which was probably the critical factor in their success, was to portray universal themes. The noted French anthropologist Claude Levi-Strauss has studied widespread cultures and observed common threads in their myths, tragedies, and fairy tales. He attributed this commonality to the fact that the mind classifies by opposing absolutes, such as good versus evil. Another explanation may be that there is a bit of the child in all of us, all over the world, and as George Lucas said, "*Star Wars* is a movie for children." Yet the success of this trilogy has been more marked in some countries than in others. In Denmark, for example, revenues have been less than stellar, probably because the Danes simply do not like science fiction.

The films' widespread acceptance should not lead one to conclude that the films and their promotion were identical everywhere. The language dubbing of dialogue and/or the placement of subtitles is a costly but standard process necessary to appeal to a mass clientele who do not understand well the original language in films. Subtitles were necessary everywhere, in fact, for the characters speaking languages of foreign planets. These languages were drawn from combinations of obscure earthly dialects. In *Return of the Jedi,* for example, Jabba the Hutt's language was taken from an Inca-Indian dialect, and the Ewoks' was taken from a combination of five languages that included Mongolian, Tibetan, and Nepali.

Another standard but costly process involves review and approval by censors, without which the showing of a film may be either prohibited altogether or restricted to only part of the target audience. The *Star Wars* trilogy was no exception. Although intended for children, censors in a number of countries found some scenes too violent for youthful audiences. In Sweden, for example, Lucasfilm had to cut out the sequence of *Return of the Jedi* in which a monster swallows its victims and lets them die slowly and painfully during a thousand-year dinner.

Promotional techniques varied from country to country because experienced distributors knew what would most likely attract film patrons. The stars were hustled to Australia to sit for newspaper, radio, and television interviews. In Japan the advertisements were more action oriented than elsewhere. In Spain *The Empire Strikes Back* was entered into the Madrid Film Festival, which gave it national recognition and acceptance.

There has been no need to alter the films technically since 35-millimeter projection has become the worldwide standard for theatrical showings. For television, however, there are no worldwide standards—for example, an Italian TV set cannot pick up French programs. As revenues from television transmission are crucial for the success of films, high-quality, expensive conversions must be done for each television transmission system where sales are to be made.

One of the big revenue sources for the *Star Wars* trilogy has been the sale of worldwide rights to such firms as Coca-Cola, Procter & Gamble, and the Atari Division of Warner Communications to produce and sell Star Wars products, ranging from bubble gum and books to wallpaper, piggy banks, and underpants. By the tenth anniversary of the premier of *Star Wars,* the retail sales of these products were more than $2.6 billion. The companies that have been given rights have themselves sometimes depended heavily on foreign operations. For example, more than $400 million in *Star Wars* merchandise has been sold in the United Kingdom. Rather than selling directly abroad themselves, some of the companies have made separate subcontracts with foreign firms to produce and sell particular products in the foreign countries. They have also produced abroad for the U.S. market. Take one company, the Kenner Division of General Mills. Its All Terrain Armored Transport accessories are manufactured in Hong Kong, the *Return of the Jedi* action figures, in Taiwan, and the Laser Pistol, in Macao. The Chewbacca Bandoleer Strap is assembled in Mexico from parts that are made in the United States.

INTRODUCTION

The goals of private business are to increase or stabilize profits. Success is influenced by
• Foreign sales
• Foreign resources
Government business may or may not be profit-motivated.

The Field of International Business

International business includes all business transactions that involve two or more countries. Such business relationships may be private or governmental. In the case of private firms the transactions are for profit. Government-sponsored activities in international business may or may not have a profit orientation.

In order to pursue any of its international objectives, a company must establish international operational forms, some of which may be significantly different from those used domestically. The choice of forms is influenced not only by the objective being pursued, but also by the environments in which the firm must operate. These environmental conditions also affect the means of carrying out business functions, such as marketing. At the same time, a company operating internationally will, to a lesser degree, affect the environment in which it is operating. These relationships are illustrated in Fig. 1.1.

Figure 1.1
International Business: Operations and Influences
The conduct of international operations depends on companies' objectives and the means with which they choose to carry them out. The operations affect, and are affected by, the national and competitive environments that are encountered.

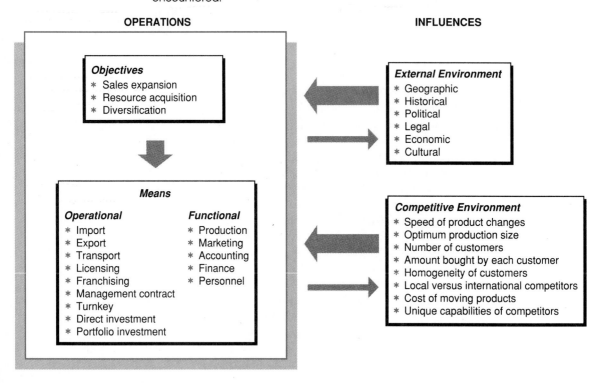

Motivation for International Business

There are three primary motivations for firms to pursue international business: to expand sales, to acquire resources, and to diversify sources of sales and supplies.

Sales Expansion Sales are limited by the number of people interested in a firm's products and services and the customers' capacity to make purchases. Since the number of people and the degree of their purchasing power are higher for the world as a whole than for a single country, firms may increase their sales potential by defining markets in international terms.

Ordinarily, higher sales mean higher profits. If, for example, each sales unit has the same markup, more volume means more profits. Lucasfilm, for example, receives a percentage of the sales made by companies marketing *Star Wars* merchandise; thus Lucasfilm's revenues increase with each additional toy that Parker Kenner, the British arm of Kenner, sells in the United Kingdom. In fact, profits per unit of sales may increase as sales increase. *Star Wars* cost approximately $10 million to produce; as more people see the film, the average production cost per viewer decreases.

International sales are thus a major motive for firms' expansion into international business. Many of the largest firms in the world derive over half of their sales from outside their home country—such firms include BASF from Germany, Electrolux from Sweden, IBM from the United States, Michelin from France, Nestlé from Switzerland, Philips from the Netherlands, and Sony from Japan.[2]

Resource Acquisition Manufacturers and distributors seek out products and services as well as components and finished goods produced in foreign countries. Sometimes this is to reduce their costs: for example, Lucasfilm used studios in the United Kingdom in the filming of *Star Wars,* and Kenner manufactures its Laser Pistol in Macao. The potential effects on profits are rather obvious. The profit margin may be increased, or cost savings may be passed on to consumers, thereby permitting more people to buy the products. Sometimes foreign procurement is employed to acquire some unique capability not readily available within one's own country, such as the use of the Arctic snow fields for filming *The Empire Strikes Back.* Such a strategy may allow firms to improve their product qualities or at least differentiate them from their competitors, thus increasing their market share and profits.

Diversification Companies usually prefer to avoid wild swings in their sales and profits, so they seek out foreign markets and procurement as a means of achieving this end. Lucasfilm has been able to smooth its yearlong sales curve somewhat because the summer vacation period (the main season for children's film attendance) varies between the Northern and Southern Hemispheres. It has also succeeded in arranging important television contracts during different years in different countries. Many other firms take advantage of the fact that the timing of business cycles differs among countries. Thus while sales decrease in one country that is undergoing a recession, they increase in another that is experiencing recovery. Finally, by obtaining supplies of the same product or component from different countries, a firm may be able to avoid the full impact of price swings or shortages in any one country.

TYPES OF INTERNATIONAL BUSINESS

When conducting international business, companies must choose among different operational forms (see Fig. 1.1). In making their choices, they should consider their own objectives and resources as well as the environments in which they operate. The following discussion introduces the major operating forms, which also correspond closely to the categories in which countries keep records of aggregate international transactions.

Merchandise Exports and Imports

Merchandise exports and imports are usually
- *A country's key international economic transaction*
- *A company's first international operation*
- *Continued even when companies diversify their methods of operating*

Merchandise exports are tangible goods sent out of a country; **merchandise imports** are tangible goods brought in. Since these goods visibly leave and enter, they are sometimes referred to as *visible* exports and imports. The terms *exports* and *imports* are frequently used in reference only to *merchandise* exports or imports. In the opening case, the Jedi action figures are merchandise exports for Taiwan when they are sent to the United States and merchandise imports for the United States when they arrive.

The exporting and importing of goods is the major source of international revenue and expenditure for most countries. Among companies engaged in some form of international business, more are involved in importing and exporting than in any other type of transaction.

Importing and/or exporting is usually, but not always, the first type of foreign operation a firm undertakes. This is because at an early stage of international involvement these operations usually entail the least commitment and the least risk to a firm's resources. For example, firms may be able to export by using excess capacity, thus limiting the need to invest more capital. In addition, firms may be able to use the services of trade intermediaries who, for a fee, will take on the export-import functions, thus eliminating the need for trained personnel and a department to carry out foreign sales or purchases.

Exporting and importing are typically not abandoned when firms adopt other international business forms. Although they may sometimes cease, they usually continue, either by business with other markets or to complement the new types of business activities.

Service Exports and Imports

Services are earnings other than those derived from goods.
- Examples are travel, transport, fees, royalties, dividends, and interest.
- They are very important for some countries.
- They involve many special international business forms.
- The firm often enters licensing and franchising agreements after experience with merchandise trade.

Service exports and imports are international earnings other than those derived from goods sent to another country. Receipt of these earnings is considered a service export, whereas payment is considered a service import. Services are also referred to as *invisibles*. International business comprises many different types of services.

Travel, Tourism, and Transportation   When prints of *Return of the Jedi* were sent from the United States to be shown in Japan, they traveled internationally as did the *Star Wars* actors when they went to Australia to publicize the film. Earnings from transportation and foreign travel can be an important source of revenue for international airlines, shipping companies, reservations agencies, and hotels. On a national level, such countries as Greece and Norway depend heavily on revenue collected from carrying foreign cargo on their ships. The Bahamas earns much more from foreign tourists than it earns from exporting merchandise.

Performance of Activities Abroad   **Fees** are payments for the performance of certain activities abroad—for example, banking, insurance, rentals (e.g., the *Star Wars* film), engineering, and management services. Engineering services are often handled through **turnkey operations,** which are the construction under contract of operating facilities that are transferred to the owner when the facilities are ready to begin operations. Fees for management services are often the result of **management contracts,** arrangements under which one firm provides management personnel to perform general or specialized management functions for another firm.

Use of Assets from Abroad   **Royalties** are payments for the use of assets from abroad, such as trademarks, patents, copyrights, or other expertise under contracts known as **licensing agreements.** Royalties are also paid for **franchising,** a way of doing business in which one party (the franchiser) sells an independent party (the franchisee) the use of a trademark that is an essential asset for the franchisee's business. In addition, the franchiser assists on a continuing basis in the operation of the business, such as by providing components, managerial services, or technology.

Firms often move to foreign licensing or franchising after successfully building exports to a market. This move usually involves a greater international commitment than the early stages of exporting do. The greater involvement occurs primarily because the firm has to send qualified technicians to the foreign country to assist the licensee or franchisee in establishing and adapting its production facilities for the new product.

Investments

Key features of direct
investment are
- Control
- High commitment of
  capital, personnel, and
  technology
- Access to foreign
  markets
- Access to foreign
  resources
- Higher foreign sales
  than exporting (often)
- Partial ownership
  (sometimes)

Direct Investments   Foreign investment is the ownership of property abroad, usually in a company, for a financial return. **Direct investment** is a subset of foreign investment that takes place when control follows the investment. Control can come from a small percentage of the equity of the company being acquired, perhaps even as little as 10 percent. The ownership of a controlling interest in a foreign operation is the highest type of commitment to foreign operations. Not only does it imply the ownership of an interest abroad, it usually involves the transfer of more personnel and technology between countries than when there is no controlling interest in the foreign facility. Because of the high level of commitment, direct investment usually (but not always) comes after a firm has acquired experience in exporting or importing. Direct investment operations may be set up in order to gain access to certain resources or access to a market for the firm's product. Kenner, for example, uses its Mexican direct investment to assemble the Chewbacca Bandoleer Strap because this provides access to a resource, cheap labor for the product's manufacture. Kenner also has direct investments in Europe, which have been made as a means of gaining markets in the countries where the production occurs.

When two or more organizations share in the ownership of a direct investment, the operation is known as a **joint venture.** In a special type of joint venture, called a **mixed venture,** a government is in partnership with a private company.

For U.S. firms as a whole, sales from output produced abroad through direct investment are many times greater than sales from U.S. production that is sent abroad as merchandise exports.[3] Today most of the world's largest firms have substantial foreign direct investments encompassing every type of business function, such as extraction of raw materials, growing of crops, manufacture of products or components, selling of output, and handling of various services.

Key components of port-
folio investment are
- Noncontrol of foreign
  operation
- Financial benefit, e.g.,
  loans

Portfolio Investments   **Portfolio investment** can be either debt or equity, but the factor that distinguishes portfolio from direct investment is that control does not follow this kind of investment.

Foreign portfolio investments are important for nearly all firms with extensive international operations. They are used primarily for financial purposes. Treasurers of companies, for example, routinely move funds from one country to another to get a higher yield on short-term investments. They also borrow funds in different countries.

Importance of Different Forms   For most companies the two most important forms of foreign business activity are merchandise trade and direct investment. These forms also have the biggest impact on regulations governing the private flow of business among countries, and that is why we emphasize these two types of activities in this chapter. Other forms, such as licensing and turnkey projects, are also important and may even be the most important for individual companies and countries. We shall investigate these other forms from an operational standpoint in later chapters.

Multinational Enterprise

A firm that has a world-wide approach to markets and production is also known as an MNE or TNC. It is usually involved in nearly every type of international business practice.

The **multinational enterprise,** or MNE, has a worldwide approach to foreign markets and production and an integrated global philosophy encompassing both domestic and overseas operations. The true MNE will usually utilize most of the operating forms that we have discussed. Because of the difficulty of ensuring whether a firm has a "worldwide approach," narrower operational definitions emerge. For example, some might say that a firm must have production facilities in some minimum number of countries or be of a certain size in order to qualify as an MNE. The term **multinational corporation,** or MNC, is also common in the literature of international business and is often used as a synonym for MNE. We prefer the MNE designation because there are many internationally involved companies, such as accounting partnerships, that do not use a corporate form.

Another term sometimes used interchangeably with MNE, especially by the United Nations, is **transnational corporation,** or TNC. This term is used also to refer to a company owned and managed by nationals in different countries. To avoid confusion, we shall use TNC only in its latter meaning throughout the text.

Some writers separate MNEs into two categories. The **global company** is one that integrates operations from different countries, such as designing a product or service with a global market segment in mind or making different parts of a product in different countries. The **multidomestic company** is one that allows each country's operations to be very independent.

THE EXTERNAL ENVIRONMENT

Drawing on Other Disciplines

Managers in the worldwide environment must understand
• Social science disciplines
• All functional business fields

The external environment is the aggregate of conditions outside the company that influence the success of its practices. Inasmuch as international business operates within the broad context of the world environment, its managers must have a working knowledge of the basic social sciences, including geography, history, political science, law, economics, and anthropology.

A knowledge of *geography* is important because it helps managers to determine the location, quantity, and quality of the world's resources and their availability for exploitation. The uneven distribution of resources gives rise to the production of different products and services in different parts of the world. In our *Star Wars* example, these differences led to the filming of some scenes in Tunisia and others in Norway. Geographical barriers such as high mountains, vast deserts, and inhospitable jungles affect communication and distribution channels for companies in much of the world's economy. Human population distribution around the world and the impact of human activity on the environment exert a strong influence on international business relationships.

An understanding of *history* provides managers with a systematic recording of the evaluation of ideas and institutions. Looking at the past gives international businesspeople a clearer understanding of the functioning of international business activities in the present. History is, after all, the accumulation of human experience that determines how we live today. Technical and institutional developments have expanded the scope of business. For example, the creation of the three *Star Wars* films could not have occurred in the same way at an earlier period. Likewise, transactions that are not now feasible may be possible in the future, and others may be carried out in different ways.

Politics has played and will continue to play an important role in shaping business worldwide. *Political science* describes the relationships between business and national political organizations and, in turn, helps to explain behavior patterns of governments and business firms in areas of potentially conflicting interests. The political leadership in each country controls whether and how international business will occur. The prohibition of *Star Wars* distribution in Cuba is an example of a political decision that adversely affected international business. The 1990 agreement for PepsiCo's Pizza Hut to start operations in the former Soviet Union is an example of a more open political policy, *glasnost*, that positively affected international business.

Each country has its own laws regulating business. Agreements among countries set international law.

Domestic and international *law* largely determines what the manager of an international company can or cannot do. This includes domestic laws in both the home and host countries that regulate such matters as taxation, employment, and foreign exchange transactions. For example, when *The Empire Strikes Back* was shown in Japan, Japanese law determined how Japanese revenues would be taxed and how revenues could be exchanged from yen to U.S. dollars. U.S. law, in turn, determined how and when the earnings from Japan would be taxed in the United States. International legal agreements between the two countries temper how the earnings are taxed by both nations. Only by understanding the treaties among nations and the laws for each country where operations may take place can companies such as Lucasfilm determine where they might operate profitably abroad.

An appreciation of *economics* gives a manager the analytical tools to determine (1) the impact of an international company on the economy of the host and home countries and (2) the effect of a country's economic policies on the international company. Economic theory also explains why nations exchange goods and services with each other, why capital and people travel from one country to another in the course of business, and why one country's currency has a certain price relative to another's. For example, the decision by Lucasfilm to use British studios was economic. Economics provides a framework for understanding why, where, and when one country can produce goods or services less expensively than another. The decision not to distribute the *Star Wars* films in such places as Haiti was economic, based on a belief that there was insufficient economic wealth to provide a large enough market. The decision to distribute in France was also economic, based not only on the fact that France's economy was more prosperous, but also on an expectation that the French francs earned from moviegoers would buy enough U.S. dollars to make the showings profitable.

Through the study of *anthropology,* managers may better understand the values, attitudes, and beliefs people have concerning themselves and their environment, thus improving their ability to function in different societies. Recall that Lucasfilm had to cut scenes from *Return of the Jedi* to get permission for children's viewing in Sweden.

Functional Adjustments to the Environment The previous discussion is intended as an introduction. National differences in geography, history, political science, law, economics, and anthropology affect how a company conducts its operations. Yet the amount of adjustment required is related to the degree of dissimilarity between the home and foreign countries and is also a function of the number of different foreign environments in which the company is operating. We shall examine these external environmental influences in greater detail in subsequent chapters.

A company's specific functional adjustments (for example, how it markets, produces, staffs its operations, and maintains its accounts) depend largely on the environment. Recall our *Star Wars* case: Lucasfilm had to use different promotion methods for different countries. It undoubtedly had to deal with different labor and accounting regulations for its production in the United Kingdom as well. We shall also examine specific functional adjustments in greater detail in subsequent chapters.

The Competitive Environment

Each company and each industry has a different competitive environment, which may vary from one country to another. As a result, some firms may be better able to take advantage of foreign opportunities than others. Some firms may also have to deal much more with foreign competition than others within their domestic markets. The most appropriate form of international business opportunity, such as exporting versus licensing, may differ among firms and products, as well as among the countries in which the business is undertaken. Some of the most important factors are shown in Fig. 1.1 and will be discussed in later chapters. Some trends that are affecting the nature of international competition are briefly explained in the following section.

Shrinkage of Time and Space   A traditional difference between international and domestic business is that international forms usually encompass greater distances. Greater distance usually increases operating costs and makes control more difficult, but distance problems are less severe than they used to be because advances in communications and transportation have come at an accelerated rate. Today, scheduled air service from New York to London takes only three and a half hours and there is almost instantaneous fax and telephone transmission. As recently as 1970 there was no commercial transatlantic supersonic travel, no fax machines, and no overseas direct-dial telephone service. In fact, one usually had to go in person to the telephone company and wait sometimes for hours while operators tried to complete an international connection. Compare these recent changes with those in earlier periods. The far-flung production and distribution of the three *Star Wars* films make William Shakespeare's words "All the world's a stage, and all the men and women merely players" seem prophetic. During Shakespeare's lifetime (1564–1616), most people traveled no more than a few miles from where they were born. The time and cost of moving people or goods from one country to another was so great that sections of the world were isolated from each other. Many products that were commonplace in one area were either unknown or very rare in another. The New World was still being explored (and Australia had not yet been discovered by Europeans), and such products as tobacco and potatoes were not introduced into England until after Shakespeare's birth. (One may ponder what the Italian diet must have been before Marco Polo reputedly brought pasta from Asia and the Spaniards introduced tomatoes from South America.) European powers were still fighting to make or break trade monopolies with the Far East so that they could reap the profits from such exotic luxuries as tea. Communications between areas were very slow, although the Dutch did introduce the first airmail service during this period, via pigeon. It was not until four years after Shakespeare's death that the *Mayflower* sailed from Plymouth, England, to Massachusetts, a trip that took over three months. Another two and a half centuries passed before Jules Verne fantasized that people might encircle the globe in only 80 days.

Business is becoming more global because
• Transport is quicker
• Communications enable control from afar

Expansion of Technological and Geographic Frontiers   So much that we take for granted today results from the cumulative penetration of technological and geographic frontiers over many decades. Besides the technology to make films, other technology had to be developed in order for the *Star Wars* producers to make and sell the films. More distant production locations could be used only because videotapes made in the English studio could be transported to California in a day and because actors could travel quickly to locations around the world. Without the transport innovations of the twentieth century, production would have taken so long that the actors might have aged noticeably before the films were completed. Communications developments such as telephone transmission via satellites have not only speeded up interactions, they have allowed people in one country to control operations elsewhere.

Institutional Developments   What we now take for granted is also the result of cumulative institutional developments by business and government that let us effectively apply technological innovations. While the ability to distribute films in foreign countries, for example, is due in part to transport advances, it is also related to the evolution of institutional arrangements. Take Lucasfilm's sales to Chile, for example. As soon as the films arrive in Chilean customs, a bank in Santiago would likely collect a distribution fee in pesos from the Chilean distributor and make payment to Lucasfilm in dollars at a bank in the United States. If businesses were still conducted as they were in the era of early caravan traders, Lucasfilm would probably have had to accept Chilean merchandise, such as copper or wine, in payment for the films. The merchandise would have been shipped back to the United States and sold before Lucasfilms could have received a usable income. Although such barter transactions still do take place, they are not the most common means for making international payments. Barter transactions are usually cumbersome, time consuming, risky, and expensive. The relative ease with which most producers today can get paid for goods and services sold abroad is due to the development of a host of innovations. These include money to replace barter, clearing arrangements to convert one country's currency into another's, insurance to cover damage en route and nonpayment by the buyer, and bank credit agreements.

There are innumerable other institutional arrangements that have facilitated the conduct of international business. One involves the transport of mail. The first international postal agreement, between France and part of what is now Germany, was enacted during Shakespeare's lifetime. Today you can send a letter to any place in the world by buying stamps denominated in your own country's currency, regardless of how many countries the letter must pass through en route. Lucasfilms could buy U.S. postage stamps for a letter sent to its Chilean distributors even though the letter might be routed on an Argentine airline that made stops en route in Colombia and Peru. Imagine what it would be like if separate payment and shipment had to be arranged for each country through which a letter passes.

Development of Global Competition   Firms today are able to respond to many foreign opportunities more quickly than ever before. News in one place is transmitted almost simultaneously elsewhere, resulting in more rapid diffusion of new product information and consequently more sales in foreign countries. Firms can also shift production more quickly from one country to another because of their foreign experience and because goods can be transported efficiently from most places. Likewise, companies can separate component and/or product manufacture among countries to take advantage of cost differences. Recall from the opening case that Kenner carried out the

Institutional arrangements
- Are made by business and government
- Ease flow of goods
- Reduce risk

Most large firms operate internationally because
- New products become global quickly
- Firms can produce in different countries
- Domestic firms face international competitors

more automated part of its Chewbacca Bandoleer Strap production in the United States and the more labor-intensive production in Mexico. Some Japanese and South Korean firms are now producing part of their product lines at home and part in the United States, then exporting from each production location.

Because companies can respond to foreign market and production opportunities, competition has become more global. Firms that hitherto operated only domestically with domestic competitors are now facing increased competition from foreign firms and from domestic firms that operate internationally. When they do not recognize and respond to new global competition, the results can be catastrophic. A good example is Mesta Machine, one of a handful of U.S. firms that supplied equipment to the U.S. steel industry when the United States dominated steel output worldwide. The firm overlooked technical advances by foreign equipment manufacturers and ignored the rapid growth of foreign markets. Suddenly Mesta found itself in competition with overseas rivals that could offer lower prices, faster delivery, and the technology demanded by the foreign and U.S. steel industry. Mesta responded too late and went bankrupt.[4]

INFLUENCES ON TRADE AND INVESTMENT PATTERNS

Economic Conditions

Economic conditions affect year-to-year trade volume, but trade tends to fluctuate more than the economy does.

Changes in worldwide affluence have affected the total value of world trade and investment, the types of products involved, and the proportionate value of international business accounted for by individual countries. Definitive figures on the changes in historic world output are unavailable, but indications are that international trade has remained a fairly constant percentage of gross world product (GWP) over a long period. This does not mean that trade and production will be related in exactly the same way every year. During economic booms, as in much of the 1970s, trade tends to grow more rapidly than production. Conversely, a slow economic growth rate, as in the early 1980s, causes trade to increase more slowly than production. In the late 1980s, trade and production both grew at about the same moderate rate. The reason for this cyclical relationship is that consumers and government policymakers consider many foreign goods marginal and thus curtail imports as the economy slackens. Producers may also attempt to export only when they have surpluses and will add capacity to serve foreign markets only if the foreign demand is sustained for a long period of time.

Rising affluence increases the percentage of trade in manufactures and lessens the percentage in agriculture.

Changing world affluence has affected the types of products and their relative importance in world trade. In the mid-nineteenth century, Ernst Engel, a German political economist and statistician, observed that as family incomes increase, the percentage spent on food tends to decrease, whereas the percentage spent on other items tends to remain fairly constant or increase. This is true even though the absolute amount spent on food increases due to substitution of more expensive food items. When the human body has reached the limit of its intake capacity, food purchases are replaced by non-food items. This trend has decreased the proportion of world trade and investment accounted for by agricultural products and increased the proportion accounted for by the manufacturing sector. In addition to traditional goods and services, the world mass market now has access to commodities that once were luxuries, such as watches and foreign travel.

Technology   Rapid technological changes in this century have created new products, displaced old ones, and altered the relative positions of countries in world trade and investment. The most obvious examples of change are new products, such as jets, computers, and transistor radios, which make up a large portion of international business. Products that existed in earlier periods have increased their share in world trade because of technological changes in the production process, as with automobiles, or because new uses have been found for them, as with soybeans and fish meal. Other products have been at least partially displaced by substitutes, such as artificial fibers for cotton, wool, and silk and synthetic rubber and synthetic nitrate for the natural products. Still other products have experienced reduced growth in demand because technology has resulted in methods of conservation. Thinner tin cans and copper wiring that can carry more telephone messages simultaneously have moderated demand for these metals. Because most technical advances have emanated from the most industrialized (richer) countries, firms from these countries control a greater share of the trade and investment in the manufacturing sector, which has been the major growth area. As a result, many of the poorer countries have had a proportionately smaller share of international business.

The main effects of technology are
- *Changes in products traded*
- *Changes in trading countries*
- *Increased trade share of industrial countries*

Wars and Insurrection

Military conflicts disrupt traditional international business patterns as participants divert their transportation systems and much of their productive capacity to the war effort. In addition, political animosity and transport difficulties may interfere with trading channels. For example, Iraq's international trade fell sharply after its 1990 invasion of Kuwait as other countries either severed trade relations or disrupted supply lines. The composition of trade changes because of a shift from consumer goods to industrial goods that can be used in meeting military objectives. International investment is disrupted because foreign-owned plants are frequently destroyed or expropriated. There is little capital available to move abroad, and even if there were, uncertainties and political regulations would prevent it.

Military conflicts
- *Change what is produced*
- *Increase international business risk*
- *Have a growing global effect on business*

Increased global interrelationships lend far-reaching impact to today's military conflicts. A particularly notable example was the worldwide oil price increases resulting from Iraq's invasion of Kuwait. Even national disturbances may have widespread international implications. The Chilean disruptions in the early 1970s, for example, had a substantial effect on world copper production and usage. The civil war within Lebanon resulted in a shift in international banking from Beirut to Bahrain and Cyprus.

Political Relationships

Political and Economic Blocs   A bloc is a group of nations united by treaty or agreement for mutual support or joint action in a variety of areas. As a result of the political schism after World War II between the communist and noncommunist countries, only a very small percentage (about 5 percent) of total world trade was conducted between the two blocs. Direct investment between the groups was negligible because of restrictions by communist countries on private ownership, particularly foreign ownership. Many of the communist countries, however, are in the process of instituting market economies and are building affiliations to the noncommunist countries, especially in Western Europe. Consequently, many observers are optimistic that business between the two groups will increase substantially.

Since the 1950s several groups of countries have banded together and removed most trade restrictions among themselves. The most notable example is the European Community (EC), which is scheduled to remove all trade barriers among member countries by the end of 1992. Because of the greater ease of trade among members, a greater percentage of the members' total trade is being conducted within the group. Because of the growth generated within the EC, the members' portion of total world trade has grown. This growth rate, along with the access to larger markets within the community, has also been a major attraction to foreign investors. The EC's successes have influenced other countries to seek membership in trading blocs of their own, such as the proposed North American bloc including Canada, Mexico, and the United States.

Multinational Agreements   In recent years governments have signed a number of international accords and agreements affecting world business. These multinational agreements have resulted from the realization that countries are increasingly interdependent and that a degree of consistency and uniformity is needed in order to assure a flow of goods and services internationally. Included among the many agreements are the International Monetary Fund (IMF), which has altered currency regulations; the International Civil Aviation Organization (ICAO), which sets air safety and international safety and procedural standards; and various international patent and trademark conventions, which delineate certain property rights for companies operating internationally. In addition to these multilateral activities, many countries have signed bilateral tax agreements that prevent international

Some possible effects of blocs are
- An increased portion of international business among member countries
- A decreased portion of business with non-member countries
- Stimulation of international business

Key features of multinational agreements are
- Promotion of consistent and uniform rules
- Exchange of concessions
- Promotion of economic growth

firms from being taxed on the same earnings by both their home and foreign countries. Without these provisions against double taxation, few foreign investments would be economically feasible.

The General Agreement on Tariffs and Trade (GATT), in which most countries are participants, provides a forum for negotiating mutual reductions in trade restrictions. Through tariff conferences, restrictions have been reduced on most items in world trade, and countries have agreed on procedures to simplify the conduct of international trade. However, negotiations among GATT members broke down in late 1990, thus leading to uncertainty on the future role of this organization.

Another development has been the emergence of international agencies, such as the World Bank, the Asian Development Bank, and the Inter-American Development Bank, which give loans and assistance for government-guaranteed projects. In some cases these resources have been an alternative to governmental or private capital. In others the funds have been used to finance social programs and infrastructure development, such as housing and highways, for which alternative funds would not be forthcoming. In these latter cases the agency loans have undoubtedly stimulated trade and direct investment by enabling countries to buy necessary equipment from abroad and allowing them to build the infrastructure needed for the efficient conduct of business activities.

RECENT WORLD TRADE PATTERNS

Since world trade is unevenly distributed by area and product, it is useful to examine its overall patterns and trends. Such an examination is helpful for understanding, in a broad sense, where world business opportunities are located.

Divergent Growth Rates

Reasons for divergent growth rates include
• Faster-growing trade in manufactures
• Rising prices of oil exports
• Rapid industrialization of NICs

Economic Level of Countries   One of the most common ways of classifying countries is by their level of economic or industrial development. The high-income countries (Western Europe, the United States, Canada, Australia, New Zealand, and Japan) are usually referred to as industrial, developed, or First World countries. The communist countries and those undergoing transition from communism have been known as centrally planned economies (CPEs), non-market economies (NMEs), or Second World countries, regardless of whether they have high or low incomes. One still encounters all these terminologies; however, the terms Second World countries and historically planned economies (HPEs) are presently more descriptive because some former CPEs are in transition from their historic economic systems. Other countries are referred to as developing countries, less-developed countries (LDCs), or Third World countries. One should be aware that there is considerable disagreement on where to place certain countries within these categories, particularly countries undergoing changes in their economic systems or in their income levels. For example, it is common to find a country listed as a First or Second World country in one set of statistics compiled by an international agency and as a Third World country in another. This lack of uniformity underscores the rapid pace of change in many countries today and the fact that useful in the aggregate, these labels do not depict the complexity of a given country's economic status. Unfortunately, because of these inconsistencies, some of our statistics and discussions may not be totally consistent either.

Although there is a lack of accurate historic trade figures for the HPEs, most estimates have put their share of world trade at only about 10 percent. Where more accurate figures on world trade are available, we find that LDCs have a very low share (see Fig. 1.2), primarily because of their heavy dependence on agricultural products and raw materials for their export earnings. Because of the economic and technical factors discussed earlier, earnings from these types of exports have not kept pace with earnings from manufactured goods. In manufactured production the developed countries have advantages in world markets because of their technology and their ability to reduce costs through large-scale production. In many cases the LDCs have insufficient domestic production or resource capacity to supply their own needs, much less those of other areas.

In spite of these obstacles, there has been a turnaround in the trade position of some LDCs thanks to three major factors. Foremost has been the ability of oil-exporting countries to raise the price of petroleum exports substantially, especially during the 1970s, when the price of oil exports increased more than 1200 percent.[5] Prices fell after 1981, but not nearly as much as they had risen. Further Persian Gulf hostilities could lead to further price rises. A second factor has been the rapid industrialization of a number of LDCs, such as Brazil and Taiwan, now sometimes referred to as newly industrialized countries (NICs). A third factor has been the easier access to industrial countries' markets for LDCs' manufactured products. At the United Nations Conference on Trade and Development (UNCTAD) in 1964, developing countries began to pressure the industrial nations to give preference to manufactured exports from developing countries. By the end of the 1970s every industrial country had policies allowing LDC manufacturers easier access than industrial manufacturers. In spite of this turnaround for some LDCs, most LDCs have been able neither to export petroleum nor to industrialize rapidly. For them, there has been a downward trend in share of world trade.

Given the difficulties experienced by the LDCs, it is not surprising that nine of the ten largest exporters and nine of the ten largest importers are industrial countries (see Table 1.1). The only exception is the former Soviet Union, an HPE. Six countries are members of the EC and conduct a large portion of their trade among themselves, there being far fewer restrictions among EC members than between the EC and other countries.

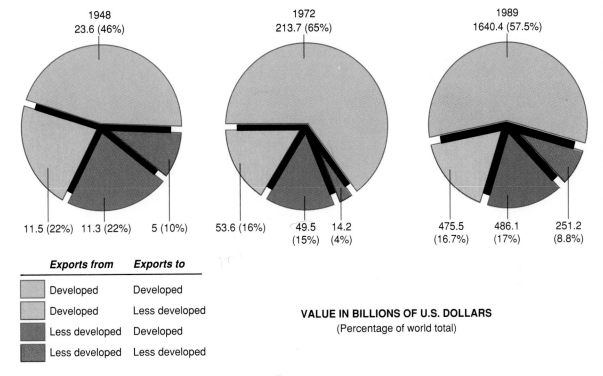

Figure 1.2
Value of World Trade Between Developed and Less-Developed Areas,
Selected Years
Between 1948 and 1972, LDCs' export share declined substantially; however, their position has improved somewhat since then. *Source: Statistical Yearbook, 1968* (New York: United Nations, 1969), pp. 398–399; *Statistical Yearbook, 1973* (New York: United Nations, 1974), pp. 402–409; *Direction of Trade Statistics Yearbook, 1990* (Washington, D.C., International Monetary Fund, 1990), p. 7; and *Direction of Trade Statistics Annual, 1970–74* (Washington, D.C., International Monetary Fund, n.d.), pp. 8–35.

Since the turn of the century the portion of U.S. exports
• Has increased in Asia and Canada
• Has decreased in Europe and Latin America
Recent shifts in U.S. trade partners are linked to
• Petroleum trade
• Foreign policy changes
• Asian industrialization

Twentieth-Century Changes in U.S. Trading Partners   The major change in U.S. export markets during this century has been the decline in the relative importance of Europe as a trading partner. Before the turn of the century more than 80 percent of U.S. exports were sent to Europe, by the 1920s the figure had dropped to about 50 percent, and by the 1990s it was about 30 percent. The biggest gain in exports has been to Asia. Exports to Asia have grown from less than 1 percent at the turn of the century to over 30 percent now, making Asia a larger export market for U.S. products than Europe.[6] Canada is the largest importer of U.S. products.

For U.S. imports, the big losers in proportionate share in this century have been Europe and Latin America. Purchases from Europe, which constituted about half of U.S. imports at the turn of the century, have been between

TABLE 1.1 | MAJOR EXPORTING AND IMPORTING COUNTRIES (billions of dollars, 1990) Nine of the ten largest exporters and importers are industrialized countries; the Soviet Union is classified as an historically planned economy.

Exports		Imports	
Germany*	421	United States	515
United States	394	Germany*	356
Japan	286	France	234
France	216	Japan	234
United Kingdom	185	United Kingdom	224
Italy	170	Italy	182
Netherlands	134	Netherlands	127
Canada	131	Soviet Union‡	121
Belgium-Luxembourg	118	Belgium-Luxembourg	120
Soviet Union‡	103	Canada	119

Source: GATT as reported in *Globe & Mail* (Toronto) March 30, 1991.

*Figures combine trade for the former Federal Republic of Germany and the former German Democratic Republic.

‡Because of difficulties in determining a realistic conversion value, the figures are at best only rough estimates. The country has subsequently split into nations known collectively as the Commonwealth of Independent States.

20 and 30 percent per year since the early 1920s. Purchases from Latin America made up about 30 percent of U.S. imports until 1960; since then the figure has fallen steadily and is now about 15 percent. The major gains in import share over this century have been from Canada and Japan. The growth for Canada has been fairly steady, from about 5 percent early in the century to about 20 percent currently. Japan also accounts for about 20 percent of U.S. imports, but its growth has been very recent. Japan and Canada are the largest exporters to the United States. The proportion of imports coming from Asia has grown from a turn-of-the-century figure of about 15 percent of total U.S. imports to about 35 percent now.

Since 1970 the relative importance of U.S. trading partners has shifted considerably, due primarily to three factors: shifts in petroleum trade, foreign policy changes, and greater industrialization of certain Asian countries. Because of increased revenues from oil sales, Mexico, Saudi Arabia, and Venezuela have become more important markets. The People's Republic of China, the former Soviet Union, and Egypt have become more prominent because of foreign policy changes. Increased income from industrialization in Thailand, South Korea, Taiwan, and Malaysia has been responsible for their purchasing a larger share of total U.S. exports. The United States brings in a larger portion of its imports from Mexico and Norway because they became new oil suppliers and from Japan, Taiwan, South Korea, and Singapore because of their new industrial production capabilities. The biggest losers in export share to the United States since 1970 have been Canada and Germany.[7]

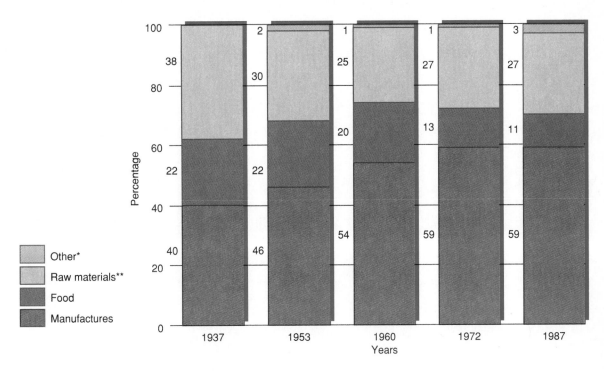

Figure 1.3
World Trade by Major Product Category for Selected Years in Percentage of Total World Trade
Manufactures account for the largest portion of world trade. *Sources:* W. S. Woytinski and E. S. Woytinski, *World Commerce and Governments* (New York: Twentieth Century Fund, 1955); *United Nations Statistical Yearbook, 1973* (New York: United Nations, 1974), p. 56; *International Trade Statistics Yearbook, 1987,* Vol. I (New York: United Nations, 1989), p. 1098.

*Includes such things as live animals and products not classified by reporting countries.
**Includes agricultural raw materials, fuels, minerals, and chemicals.

Trade by Product Category

Although figures on global trade by product category are always a few years old before they are compiled and published, we can nevertheless discern some trends.

Figure 1.3 shows growing importance of manufactured goods in world trade up to 1972. Since then the categories, although fluctuating from one year to another, have remained fairly stable in relation to each other. The U.S. imports and exports show similar dependence on manufactured products.

As shown in Fig. 1.4, the First World countries account for the majority of world exports in every category except fuels. The Second World countries account for a small portion of world trade in all categories. The Third World countries have improved their world export share in chemicals, machinery, and other manufactures during recent years.

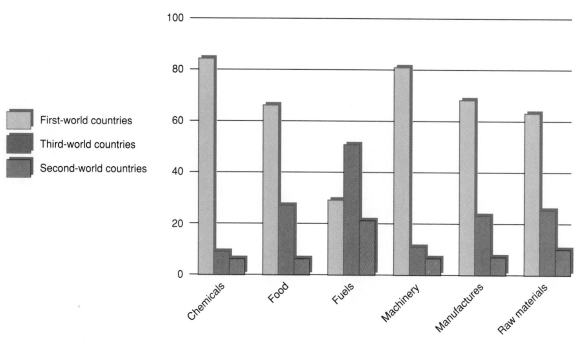

Figure 1.4
World Exports by Type of Country (major product categories, 1988)
First World countries lead in exports of all product categories except fuels. *Source: International Trade Statistics Yearbook, 1988, Vol. I. (New York: United Nations, 1990), p. 1102.*

RECENT DIRECT INVESTMENT PATTERNS

Move to Direct Investment

Until the emergence of international firms, all private foreign investments were portfolio investments rather than direct investments. The push to direct investment began in the 1920s, but even then, portfolio movements were about double the direct ones. During the Depression of the 1930s it became obvious that portfolio investors, especially those from the United States who were the main suppliers of foreign capital, had chosen foreign projects unwisely. Direct investments fared much better and their value recovered somewhat in the late 1930s.[8] Since World War II, direct investment by U.S. firms has grown substantially. Direct investment by firms from other industrial countries grew slowly for a number of years after World War II. During this time, firms from those countries were busy rebuilding their domestic markets and were short of funds to invest on the outside. Since about 1965, their direct investment positions have expanded rapidly.

Direct Investor Description

In direct investment,
- Almost all ownership is by firms from industrial countries
- LDC ownership is starting to increase

Country of Origin   One way of describing investors is to look at the origin of investment by area. More than 95 percent of the value of direct investment ownership is estimated to be in industrial countries.[9] Table 1.2 summarizes the information from industrial countries and illustrates that nearly all recent investment has emanated from just seven countries. The proportion of global value originating in the United States has been falling, whereas the proportion originating in the United Kingdom and Japan has been increasing.

There has been some recent growth in direct investment from the developing countries. There are now several hundred LDC direct investors that own several thousand foreign investments. Most of this movement has been from the developing countries that have experienced recent industrialization, such as Hong Kong, Singapore, Mexico, Brazil, and Argentina.[10]

At the end of 1989 foreign direct investment in the United States was valued at $401 billion. About 30 percent of it originated in the United Kingdom, 17 percent in Japan, and 15 percent in the Netherlands. LDC direct investments make up a substantially higher (10 percent) portion of the direct investment within the United States than the LDC ownership in total world direct investment.[11] Foreign direct investment within the United States has been growing more rapidly in the past few years than the flow of direct investment from the United States to foreign countries; thus at the end of 1989 the value of direct investment within the United States was about 7 percent more than the value of direct investment by U.S. interests in foreign countries. These foreign direct investment figures are based on book values (the costs when the investments were made) rather than market values (what the investments would be worth if sold). Since the growth of U.S.-owned direct

TABLE 1.2 | FOREIGN DIRECT INVESTMENT OUTWARD FLOW BY INDUSTRIAL COUNTRY (cumulative flow, U.S. $ billion) Note the decline in share for the United States and the gain for the United Kingdom and Japan.

Country	1961/70	%	1971/80	%	1981/88	%
United States	46,822	66.3	134,354	44.4	121,230	21.6
United Kingdom	7,398	10.5	55,112	18.2	120,520	21.4
Japan	1,438	2.0	18,052	6.0	93,672	16.7
Germany	4,091	5.8	23,130	7.7	47,745	8.5
France	2,641	3.7	13,940	4.6	40,556	7.2
Netherlands	2,692	3.8	27,829	9.2	36,926	6.6
Canada	1,483	2.1	11,335	3.7	29,437	5.2
Other*	4,011	5.8	18,554	6.2	71,549	12.8
Total	70,576	100.0	302,306	100.0	561,635	100.0

Source: OECD, *International Direct Investment and the New Economic Environment,* The Tokyo Round Table (Paris: OECD, 1989), p. 60.
*Refers to other OECD (industrial) countries.

investment took place earlier, its current market value is estimated to be much greater than the market value of foreign direct investment in the United States.

Economic Sector of Investment   Between 1929 and 1973 U.S.-owned direct investment shifted toward manufacturing and away from mining and services (see Fig. 1.5a). Although the same type of historical data are not readily available for non-U.S. direct investment, estimates indicate that U.S. and non-U.S. investment composition are very similar. Since the early 1970s composition has not changed appreciably for manufacturing. The petroleum sector has decreased in importance, due largely to a growing reluctance on the part of many countries to allow foreign ownership of mineral rights. The category "other" has recently grown most rapidly, due largely to the growth of such service industries as finance and insurance.

The composition of U.S. direct investment abroad varies between developed countries and LDCs. The book value at the beginning of 1990 showed that manufacturing comprised 45 percent of the investment in developed countries but only 32 percent in LDCs. Petroleum and insurance investments comprised a higher portion of the investment in LDCs than in developed countries.[12] This divergence is due partially to circumstance, since oil investments have to be made where the oil is found. The insurance investments are located primarily in Bermuda, where there are regulatory and tax advantages. Economic conditions are also a major factor, since the developed countries are the main markets for manufactured goods and are large enough to allow for efficient production. The divergence is lessening, since manufacturing investments have been growing more rapidly than petroleum investments in LDCs.

At the beginning of 1990 the value of foreign direct investment in the United States was distributed in the following sectors: manufacturing, 40 percent; wholesale trade, 14 percent; petroleum, 9 percent; real estate, 9 percent; and other, 28 percent.

Location of Investment   The major recipients of direct investment are industrial countries, accounting for about three quarters of the world value.[13] This pattern parallels the outward flow of direct investments owned by U.S. enterprises. At the beginning of 1990 U.S. ownership abroad was about $373 billion, of which a little less than a quarter was located in LDCs. Figure 1.5b shows that Europe has a growing share of U.S. direct investment, whereas Canada and Latin America have declining shares. The portion in Latin America has been declining for a longer period; in the 1920s, nearly half was located there.

There are two primary reasons for the U.S. interest in developed countries. First, more investments have been market seeking (that is, producing in

---

Highest growth has been in services and manufacturing because
- *There has been faster growth in world consumption*
- *There are less stringent ownership regulations than in some other sectors*

Highest percentage of investment is
- *Petroleum within LDCs*
- *Manufacturing within industrial countries*

Investments occur most in industrial countries because they have
- *The biggest markets*
- *The least perceived risk*

LDC-owned investment is largely regional.

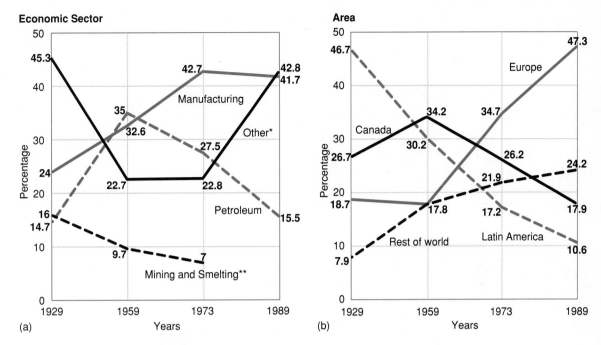

Figure 1.5
Changing Pattern of United States Direct Investment Abroad in Percentages (by value)
The largest portion of U.S. direct investment abroad is in manufacturing and in Europe. *Source: Survey of Current Business,* various issues.

*Includes transportation, trade, utilities, and other service industries.
**Mining and smelting is included in "other" for 1989.

a country in order to sell the output there), and the developed countries have more income to spend. Second, political turmoil in many LDCs has discouraged investors.

When direct investment originates in developing countries, most of it has gone to countries within the region where the parent firm is located—for example, Malaysian investments in Thailand. There is some evidence, however, that these investors are beginning to develop footholds in more distant industrial countries, such as South Korea's Pohang Iron & Steel, which makes metal sheets in the United States.[14]

LOOKING TO THE FUTURE   Companies must make decisions today about an uncertain future. If a company waits to see what happens, it is already too late, since investments in research, plant, and training may take many years to complete. The companies that guess right on what the future will bring are the ones that will make investments to produce and sell the type of goods and services at a price that customers will be willing to pay. They can produce and sell them in conformity with the rules of the societies where they are operating. But it is not always possible to guess correctly. By postulating different ways that the future may evolve, companies may be better able to avoid unpleasant surprises, even though they are uncertain as to which of the multiple environments they will face. Given the importance of the future, we shall end each chapter with scenarios that present foreseeable ways in which areas may develop.

SUMMARY

- The cumulative penetration of technological and geographic frontiers, coupled with institutional development, has resulted in a global competitive environment marked by the use of foreign countries as production bases and sales outlets and by a rapid international diffusion of new products and processes.

- Because of its broad global environment, a number of disciplines (geography, history, political science, law, economics, and anthropology) are useful to help explain the conduct of international business.

- When operating abroad, companies may have to adapt their methods of carrying out business functions. This is because the environment may dictate the appropriate operational method and because the business forms used for foreign operations may be different from the domestic ones.

- Among the forms of international business are trade in goods and services, transportation, licensing, franchising, turnkey projects, management contracts, and direct and portfolio investments.

- Multinational enterprises (MNEs) take a worldwide approach to markets and production. They are sometimes referred to as multinational corporations (MNCs) or transnational corporations (TNCs).

- The major factors causing changes in world trade and investment patterns are economic conditions, technology, wars and insurrections, and political relationships.

- Most world trade and direct investment are accounted for by the developed or industrial countries. They are the major importers of all product categories

and the major exporters of all except fuels. Over 95 percent of direct investment originates in industrial countries, which also receive about 75 percent
of direct investment.

 ■ A long-term trend has been the increased portion of trade and investment
accounted for by the manufacturing sector.

C A S E
DISNEYLAND
ABROAD[15]

In 1984 Tokyo Disneyland completed its first
year of operations after five years of planning
and construction since the Walt Disney Corporation entered into an agreement with the Oriental
Land Company in Japan. More than 10 million
people (9 percent from other Asian countries)
visited the park, spending $355 million. This
was $155 million more than had been expected,
largely because the average expenditure per visitor was $30, rather than the estimated $21 per
visitor. Tokyo Disneyland thus became quickly
profitable. Growth continued, so that by 1990
more than 14 million people visited the park,
a figure slightly larger than the attendance at
Disneyland in California and about half the
attendance at Walt Disney World in
Florida.

The Tokyo park is in some ways a paradox.
Although such firms as Lenox China and Mister
Donut had to adapt to Japanese sizes and tastes,
Tokyo Disneyland is nearly a replica of the two
parks in the United States. Signs are in English,
and most food is American-style. The management of the Oriental Land Company demanded
this because they wanted visitors to feel they
were getting the real thing and because they had
noted that such franchises as McDonald's have
enjoyed enormous success in Japan as Japanese

youth have embraced American-style culture.
Yet, a few changes were necessary, such as the
addition of a Japanese restaurant.

The timing of the Tokyo Disneyland opening
coincided with a rise in income and leisure time
among the Japanese. A Disney executive said
that a similar rise in income and leisure had
contributed to the successful opening of the first
park near Los Angeles.

That the park is nearly identical to the ones in
the United States masks the fact that there have
been numerous operational adjustments. Probably the most important were in the methods of
promotion. Whereas Disney uses its own staff to
prepare advertising in the United States, it has
relied on outside agencies within Japan to adapt
to cultural differences. Even within Japan there
are differences. For example, ads outside of
Tokyo are more informational, whereas those in
Tokyo, where the park is well known, rely more
on a fun image.

Disney provided no financing for the Tokyo
operation. Disney provided master planning, design, manufacturing and training services during
construction, and consulting services after completion of the facility. Disney received fees
for its efforts during the construction phase, and
it now receives a 10 percent royalty from admis-
sions and 5 percent from merchandise and food
sales.

The success of Tokyo Disneyland led the company to consider expansion into Europe. In 1985
it announced that it had narrowed its locational

choice to two countries, Spain and France, for a park scheduled to open in 1992. Since the park was estimated to provide about 40,000 permanent jobs and would draw large numbers of tourists, the two countries openly courted Disney. Disney, in turn, was likened to Scrooge McDuck, as it openly played one country against the other in an attempt to get more incentives. Spain offered two different locations and 25 percent of the cost of construction, and claimed it could attract 40 million tourists a year. The French guaranteed 12 million customers a year, the number Disney estimated as the break-even point, and agreed to extend the Paris railway to the park's location (thus linking the park to the rest of Europe) at a cost of about $350 million. In addition, the French government offered 4800 acres of land at about $7500 per acre, a cheap price for the area, and loaned 22 percent of the funds needed for financing. Disney finally signed an agreement with the French government in 1986 because of the more central location of Paris (109 million people live within a six-hour drive of the French theme park), the large number of tourists who visit Paris throughout the year. and the availability of flat land near Paris. (The four Disney theme parks are depicted on Map 1.1.)

The negotiations resulted in Disney's agreement to own at least 16.7 percent, but not more than 49.9 percent, of Euro Disney, which included satellite investments around the park for hotels, shopping centers, campgrounds, and other facilities. The total investment by 1992 has been estimated at between 2.4 and 3.0 billion U.S. dollars. Disney opted for a 49 percent stake. Disney's confidence was due in part to the fact that 2.5 million Europeans visited the U.S. parks in 1990. Remaining shares were sold through an international syndicate of banks and securities dealers, with 50 percent going to investors in France, 25 percent in Britain, and the remainder elsewhere in Europe.

If Disney had opted for a Spanish location, the park would have been much more like the ones in the United States, where visitors are out-side for almost all amusements. But Disney had learned from the Tokyo experience that colder weather does not necessarily impede attendance. Nevertheless, the colder climate in the Paris area requires more indoor shows, strategically located fireplaces, a glass dome over the teacup ride, protected waiting lines, and more focus on technology and historical themes. Because of French individualism, Disney has had to relax some of its U.S. grooming codes and has admitted that it may have to alter its no-alcohol policy for this park.

In spite of the economic benefits that the park is expected to bring, many people in France have feared that the park is just one more step toward the replacement of the French culture with that of the United States. A best-selling book denounced the French governmental concessions. Critics have called Euro Disneyland "a cultural Chernobyl"; Disney's chairman was pelted by eggs in Paris; and one magazine, *le Nouvel Observateur,* showed a giant Mickey Mouse stepping on the rooftops of Parisian buildings. Yet, the late actor Yves Montand summed up the feelings of young French when he said, "T-shirts, jeans, hamburgers—nobody imposes these things on us. We like them." Walt Disney Productions sought to head off criticism by explaining in the French press that Disney was of French descent, with an original name of D'Isigny rather than Disney. Disney also agreed to make French the first language in the park, although relying heavily on visual symbols. Disney has built an attraction, Discoveryland, based on the science fiction of France's Jules Verne, and a movie theater featuring European history. The park is also emphasizing that Pinocchio was Italian, Cinderella was French, and Peter Pan flew in London. But the "cultural invasion" is not entirely one way. In 1990 Disney announced plans for a large-scale shopping center adjacent to Walt Disney World to be anchored by Japanese and European department stores.

Disney's success in Japan and expansion into France has not gone unnoticed by competitors. By 1990 theme parks were either under way or

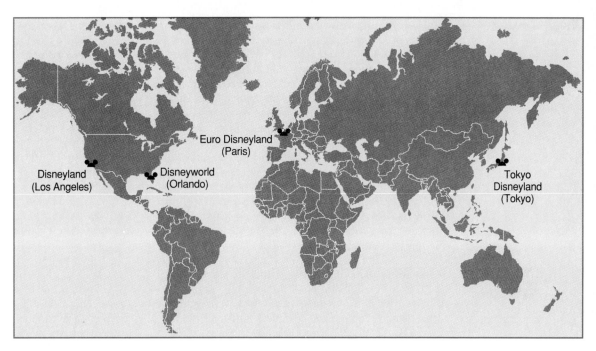

Map 1.1
Disney's Four Theme Parks
All four parks are easily reached from highly populated areas within high-income
countries. The Japanese and French locations are less suitable for year-long,
outside activities than are the locations in the United States.

in planning stages all over Japan and Europe.
Japanese parks include Space World, Sesame
Place, and Santa Land. Among the many European parks are Busch Gardens and Universal
Studios. This competitive expansion has raised
questions about the future success of Disney's
foreign theme parks, especially the one in
France. The head of MCA's recreational group,
the parent of Universal Studios, said, "We're
going to kick Disney's butt all over Europe."

Questions

1. What do you think motivated Disney to set
   up parks abroad, and what might be the pros
   and cons from the standpoint of the Walt Disney Corporation?
2. Why do you suppose Disney decided to take
   no ownership in the Japanese operation and

then a maximum allowed ownership in
France?
3. Other than the points mentioned in the case,
   what other operating adjustments might be
   necessary to ensure success of the foreign
   operations?
4. In response to a question about the possibility
   of opening a Disneyland in Russia, Roy E.
   Disney, vice chairman of the Walt Disney
   Corporation, indicated that the company was
   not in a position to create a park there in the
   near future. What might be the pros and cons
   of constructing a park in the former Soviet
   Union? Might Disney set up other parks
   abroad elsewhere? If so, where? What types
   of operating forms should Disney consider?
5. What might Disney do to face its competitive
   threats abroad?

Chapter Notes

1. We wish to acknowledge the cooperation of Robert M. Greber, Chief Executive Officer, and Susan Trembly, Publicity and Advertising Assistant, at Lucasfilm Ltd. for granting interview information. In addition to the interview data, the case relied on data from the following sources: Sid Adilman, "Star Wars' Heralds Dawn of Canadian Paycable Amid Ad Blitz for Blockbuster Pix," *Variety,* January 19, 1983, p. 2; Louise Sweeney, "Returns from 'Jedi': Marketing a Megahit," *Christian Science Monitor,* June 30, 1983, pp. B7–8; "$2 Mil. for 'Star Wars' on Aussie TV," *Variety,* March 10, 1982, p. 43; Timothy White, "Slaves to the Empire," *Rolling Stone,* July 24, 1980, pp. 33–37; Jean Vallely, "The Empire Strikes Back," *Rolling Stone,* June 12, 1980, pp. 31–34; Gillian MacKay, "George Lucas Launches the Jedi," *McClean's,* Vol. 96, May 30, 1983, pp. 42–44; Gerald Clarke, "Great Galloping Galaxies!" *Time,* Vol. 121, May 23, 1983, pp. 62–65; Conrad Phillip Kottak, "Social-Science Fiction," *Psychology Today,* Vol. 106, February 1978, pp. 12–18; "Fun in Space," *Newsweek,* May 30, 1977, pp. 60–61; Aljean Harmetz, "Showing of 'Star Wars' Trilogy Set," *New York Times,* February 28, 1985, p. 20; *Variety,* June 3, 1987 ("Star Wars," 10th Anniversary issue); Anne Thompson, "Hollywood Goes Global," *San Francisco Chronicle: Datebook,* April 22, 1990, p. 35; and Geraldine Fabrichant, "U.S. Movies, Like Wine, Now Must Travel Well," *Herald Times,* Bloomington, Ind., June 26, 1990, p. 11.

2. "The Stateless World of Manufacturing," *Business Week,* May 1, 1990, p. 103.

3. The sales from the direct investment were estimated at 108 percent in the U.S. Department of Commerce Benchmark Study. See Ned G. Howenstine, "Gross Product of U.S. Multinational Companies, 1977," *Survey of Current Business,* February 1983, p. 25.

4. Thomas F. O'Boyle, "Rise and Fall," *Wall Street Journal,* January 4, 1984, p. 1.

5. *1981 Yearbook of International Trade Statistics,* Vol. 1 (New York: United Nations, 1983), p. 1224.

6. Christopher L. Bach, "U.S. International Transactions, Fourth Quarter and Year 1989," *Survey of Current Business,* Vol. 70, No. 3, March 1990, p. 49.

7. Robert T. Green, "Internationalization and Diversification of U.S. Trade: 1970 to 1981," Department of Marketing Administration Working Paper 83/84-5-1 (Austin: University of Texas, Graduate School of Business, October 1983), pp. 3–7.

8. John H. Dunning, "Capital Movements in the 20th Century," *Lloyds Bank Review,* April 1964, pp. 20–21.

9. See, for example, "TNCs in World Development," *The CTC Reporter,* No. 26, Autumn 1988, pp. 7–8; and U.S. Department of Commerce, *International Direct Investment: Global Trends and the U.S. Role* (Washington, D.C.: International Trade Administration, 1988), p. 96.

10. Louis T. Wells, Jr., "Guess Who's Creating the World's Newest Multinationals," *Wall Street Journal,* December 12, 1983, p. 26.

11. "Foreign Direct Investment in the United States: Detail for Position and Balance of Payments Flows, 1989," *Survey of Current Business,* Vol. 70, No. 8, August 1990, pp. 41–46.

12. *Ibid.,* p. 48.

13. "TNCs in World Development," *loc. cit.*

14. Wenlee Ting, "The Emerging Challenge of the NIC Multinationals: Technology, Marketing and Operations." Paper presented to the Academy of International Business Annual Meeting, San Francisco, December 1983, pp. 2–3.

15. Data were taken from Michael Dobbs, "Mickey Mouse Storms the Bastille," *Across the Board,* Vol. 23, No. 4, April 1986, pp. 9–11; *Moody's Industrial Manual,* Vol. 2,

1987, p. 5942; "Bonjour, Mickey," *Fortune,* Vol. 113, No. 2, January 20, 1986, p. 8; Peter Lewis, "Disney Advances on Europe," *Maclean's,* Vol. 98, No. 27, July 8, 1985, p. 42; Terry Trucco, "How Disneyland Beat All the Odds in Japan," *Advertising Age,* Vol. 55, No. 57, September 6, 1984, pp. 14–16; David J. Jefferson, "Nation's Oldest Theme Park Changes with the Times," *Wall Street Journal,* May 14, 1990, p. B2; Robert Neff, "In Japan, They're Goofy About Disney," *Business Week,* March 12, 1990, p. 64; Yumiko Ono, "Theme Parks Boom in Japan as Investors and Consumers Rush to Get on the Ride," *Wall Street Journal,* August 8, 1990, p. B1; Stewart Toy, Mark Maremont, and Ronald Grover, "An American in Paris," *Business Week,* March 12, 1990, pp. 60–64; Robert Wrubel and Phyllis Feinberg, "Breaking Out of the Mousetrap," *Financial World,* Vol. 157, No. 3, January 26, 1988, pp. 20–22; Joann S. Lublin, "Walt Disney Co. Is Planning to Slip European Investors a Mickey," *Wall Street Journal,* September 13, 1989, p. C1; Carlo Wolff, "Investors Predicting European Disneyland to Spur French Boom," *Hotel & Motel Management,* September 25, 1989, p. 24; Albert Axebank, "Mickey-Disney Team Takes Moscow by Storm," *Journal of Commerce,* October 18, 1988, p. 1A; John Marcom, Jr., "Le Défi Disney," *Forbes,* Vol. 143, February 20, 1989, pp. 39–40; "Shares in Euro Disneyland," *Wall Street Journal,* October 6, 1989, p. A7; Rhonda L. Rundle, "Walt Disney Plans Huge Development Near Theme Parks," *Wall Street Journal,* March 14, 1990, p. B9; and Steven Greenhouse, "Playing Disney in the Parisian Fields," *New York Times,* February 17, 1991, p. F1.

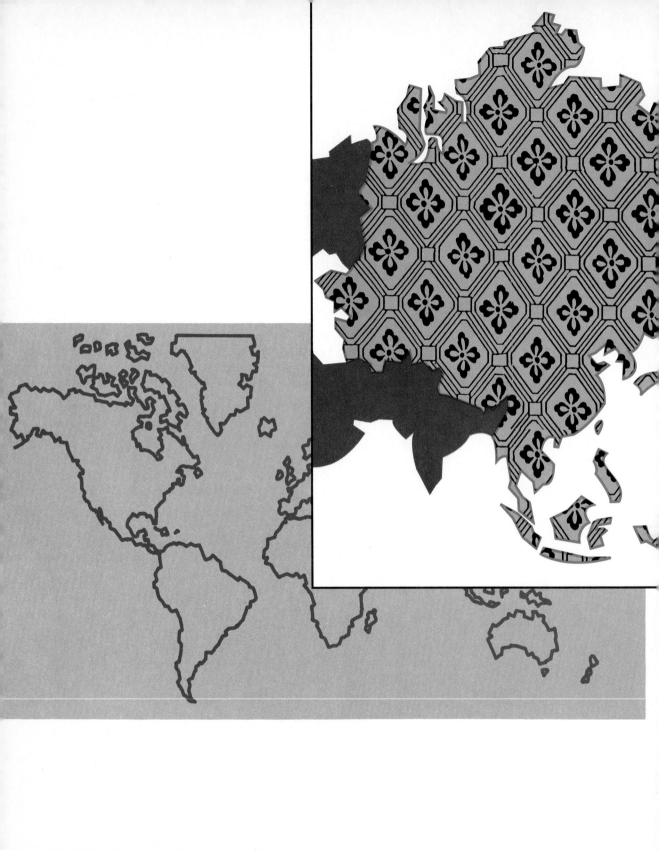

PART **2**

COMPARATIVE ENVIRONMENTAL FRAMEWORKS

The firm operating internationally is affected by and has an immense impact on the environments in which it operates. International business today is conducted among organizations within virtually every conceivable value and institutional framework. Chapter 2 explores first the major types of legal systems used within and among countries. Then the chapter examines the relationship between countries' economic and political philosophies and systems. Next, the adjustments and relations to these economic and political systems by international firms are discussed. Finally, the chapter examines national differences generated by varying levels of economic development. Chapter 3 analyzes the major physical and behavioral human variations among nations that influence the conduct of business. The chapter concludes with recommendations and caveats for companies coming into contact with alien societies.

CHAPTER 2

THE LEGAL, POLITICAL, AND ECONOMIC ENVIRONMENTS FACING BUSINESS

Half the world knows not how the other half lives.
ENGLISH PROVERB

Objectives

- To identify the major legal systems in the world and to describe how they affect business.

- To describe the major political ideologies in theory and practice.

- To discuss different economic systems in theory and practice.

- To describe some important problems facing different countries.

- To evaluate the role of the foreign firm in different political and economic systems.

Mr. David Gledhill, *taipan,* or top manager, of Swire Group, is faced with important strategic dilemmas as 1997 fast approaches and Hong Kong's relationship with China remains uncertain. The Swire Group (which had 1988 sales of HK$ 25.1 billion) is one of the three major *hongs,* or family-controlled business empires, that are so prominent in Hong Kong. The other two are Jardine Matheson (which had 1988 sales of HK$ 14.8 billion) and Hutchison Whampoa (which had 1988 sales of HK$ 12.9 billion). All three began as British-owned China traders that started operations in the 1800s, primarily selling opium to and buying tea from China. The *taipans* of each of the three *hongs* report to the family owners—the Swire Group to the Swires, a wealthy London-based family; Jardine Matheson to the Keswick family of London; and Hutchison Whampoa to Mr. Li Ka-Shing, its Chinese owner.

All three *taipans* are faced with the same dilemma: How much do they need to diversify out of Hong Kong by 1997? Jardine Matheson made the first major outward move by shifting its registered office to Bermuda in 1984. Even though the *hongs* have done an excellent job of diversifying out of Hong Kong, they still depend greatly on the economy of Hong Kong and thus need to come to some sort of accommodation with China.

The Swire Group is an interesting company. It is a corporate organization with international interests in all aspects of trade—from transport and its associated industries to manufacturing and insurance. It was started in 1816 in Liverpool, England, by John Swire, but the Asia business really flourished under the control of John's son. Swire began business in China under the name *Taikoo,* which means "great and ancient," a term by which it is still known today. Many of its products still carry the *Taikoo* name. Although the Swire Group has operations all over the world, its major operations are in Hong Kong.

CASE
THE
TAIPAN'S
DILEMMA[1]

What is the dilemma facing Swire over Hong Kong, and why is 1997 such a key date? Although until 1685 Westerners were restricted to Macao, the Portuguese enclave 75 miles south of Canton (see Map 2.1), there was substantial interest in China trade. William Jardine and James Matheson, two Scottish traders, realized the value of trading opium grown in India for tea grown in China. In 1839 a dispute between the British and the Chinese culminated in the first Opium War, which was resolved in August 1842, giving Britain control of Hong Kong in perpetuity, allowing Westerners greater access to China, and permitting Western merchants to operate under their own laws in specific Chinese ports, such as Xiamen and Shanghai. In 1860 Kowloon (Nine Dragons), the tip of the peninsula just north of Hong Kong Island, was also ceded to the British in perpetuity. However, in 1898 the New Territories, which comprises 90 percent of the land area of Hong Kong, was leased to Britain for 99 years, with the lease

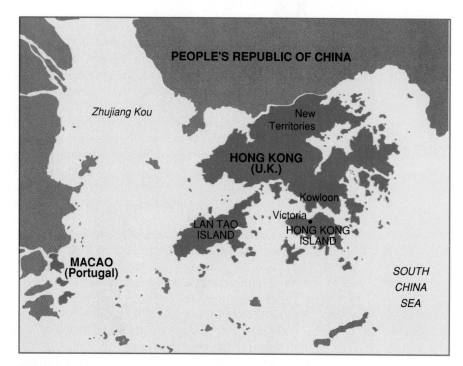

Map 2.1
Hong Kong
Hong Kong, situated at the mouth of the Pearl River, is a free market economy surrounded by (and closely integrated with) China.

ending in 1997. The New Territories, separated from Kowloon by Boundary Street, extends from Kowloon to the Chinese border.

Until 1982, little attempt was made to solve the problem of the 99-year lease. However, real estate in Hong Kong tends to sell on a 15-year-lease basis, and 1982 was only 15 years from 1997. The nervousness on the part of the Hong Kong business community led to talks between the British and Chinese governments to determine the status of the community after 1997. At that time, Hong Kong was officially a British colony, presided over by a governor appointed by the Queen of England for a term typically of five years. The governor holds all final executive and administrative powers, but is advised by the Executive Council and legislates through the Legislative Council. In essence, Hong Kong is ruled bureaucratically by the governor and his civil servants. The British Parliament monitors the efforts of the governor, hoping to preserve the rights of the people of Hong Kong but without permitting them a direct vote.

The talks between British Prime Minister Margaret Thatcher and the Chinese government resulted in the change to take place in 1997. After prolonged negotiations, the British and Chinese signed the Sino-British Joint Declaration on the future of Hong Kong. The People's Republic of China (PRC) will assume control over Hong Kong on July 1, 1997, the date when Hong Kong becomes a Special Administrative Region of China. The key phrase adopted by the negotiators is "one country, two systems," referring to the political and economic structures that exist in Hong Kong and China. Hong Kong is supposed to retain its separate political and economic status for 50 years after the 1997 switch. Thus China could continue with its centrally planned economy, and Hong Kong could maintain the exemplary free-wheeling, free-market economy that has flourished so successfully there over the years.

The hopes and dreams of Hong Kong were shattered on June 4, 1989, by the massacre at Tiananmen Square in Beijing. That event triggered significant instability in Hong Kong, increasing the exodus of some of the best and brightest of Hong Kong—along with their wealth—to Canada, Australia, and any other countries that would accept them. In order to keep key services from shutting down due to the loss of managers, Britain offered British passports to 225,000 people, thus allowing them to stay in Hong Kong until the colony reverts to China. Many Hong Kong natives did whatever they could to get passports from Western nations as a hedge against the future. If things did not turn out as expected after 1997, they reasoned, they could use their foreign passports and leave. The Chinese, however, closed the loophole by stating that everyone with multiple passports would have until midnight, June 30, 1997, to decide which passport they would use. Point, counterpoint.

Given the political instability facing Hong Kong, why don't firms just leave? What is the attraction? Hong Kong, a newly industrializing country (NIC) and one of the four tigers of Asia (the others being Singapore, Taiwan, and South Korea), has experienced significant growth in the past few decades. It is now one of the financial and manufacturing centers of Asia and is the entrepôt (export/import intermediary) for China. Hong Kong is the largest trader and investor with China and is China's window to the world. Hong Kong basically has no agricultural industry or raw materials. Even without the treaty of 1984, China could have taken over Hong Kong by simply turning off the water or refusing to ship the food that it supplies to Hong Kong.

Given that Hong Kong needs to import most of its food, water, and raw materials, it has developed a strong export strategy. Because of the tremendous volume of trade that flows through Hong Kong, it has the second largest port in the world. It is estimated that 75 percent of Hong Kong's manufactured goods are made for export. Key exports for Hong Kong include textiles, plastics, electronics, and watches and clocks. Hong Kong's major market for finished goods is the United States, and its major market for parts and semimanufactured goods is China. Because of low wages in China, Hong Kong companies are now having most of their labor-intensive work done in China rather than Hong Kong. Still, Hong Kong managers are ideally qualified to work with the Chinese because they understand the Chinese culture better than Westerners do.

Another major strength for Hong Kong is the role of the government—which is largely one of absence. Hong Kong's government policy has been termed "positive noninterventionism." Factor prices, such as wages, are set by the market rather than by government-mandated minimum wages, and taxes and subsidies are not a part of Hong Kong business life. Government ownership of goods and services is confined to law and order, postal services, the supply of water, and airport services. The government, however, owns the land in Hong Kong and sells it through public auction. Its conservative land policies have kept the price of land in Hong Kong very high.

Political and economic uncertainties may have discomforted the local Hong Kong residents, but foreigners—led by the Japanese—are investing huge sums in Hong Kong. Although foreign investors are nervous about the future, they are betting that the Chinese government will not do anything to interfere with the important role that Hong Kong plays in its economy.

In spite of the fear triggered by Tiananmen Square and subsequent events, there are three reasons why China might not disturb Hong Kong. First, China tends to honor its treaties. Second, many feel that China's treatment of Hong Kong will be perceived as a model for eventual unity with Taiwan. Third, Hong Kong is important to China. It is estimated that two thirds of the foreign investment that went into China over the decade 1977–1987 came from Hong Kong. In addition, 25–30 percent of China's foreign exchange earnings come from Hong Kong. In spite of this, there is fear that China might crack down on Hong Kong or restrict its free-wheeling economy in order to shift importance to Shanghai, China's key business center.

In addition to the threat from China, Hong Kong faces other threats, including increasing trade restrictions in markets where its firms sell and increasing competition from other Asian nations, such as the other three tigers, and the Philippines, Malaysia, Thailand, and Vietnam. Given these challenges, Hong Kong will likely undergo a political and economic transformation in the coming decades.

The corporate response to the threat from China is more problematic. As mentioned above, Jardine Matheson responded to the threat by moving its corporate headquarters to Bermuda, even though its operating divisions are still located primarily in Hong Kong. It is diversifying its operations outside of Hong Kong and China in order to hedge its future. Doing that is more difficult for a firm such as the Swire Group, since a large portion of its earnings come from Cathay Pacific and from properties located in Hong

Kong. It is in its best interest to work with rather than avoid China. The *taipan* does have a dilemma.

INTRODUCTION

Each of the countries where MNEs operate is characterized by different legal, political, and economic frameworks, diverse levels of economic development, and a variety of economic conditions. To each of an infinite number of situations the MNE brings a frame of reference based on its own domestic experience as well as on lessons from foreign settings. If the firm is to be successful, management must carefully analyze the interaction between corporate policies and the legal, political, and economic environment in order to maximize efficiency. The purpose of this chapter is to provide managers with background on the legal, political, and economic systems that they are likely to encounter and information that they need to consider as they make strategic decisions about operations in different countries.

THE LEGAL ENVIRONMENT

One of the dimensions of the external environment that influences the operations of business is the legal system. Managers must be aware of particular legal systems in the countries where they operate as well as the legal relationships that exist between countries.

Kinds of Legal Systems

The three types of legal systems are
● Common law
● Civil law
● Theocratic law

Legal systems usually fall into one of three categories: common law, civil law, and theocratic law. The United States and the United Kingdom are examples of countries that operate in a **common law system,** although the United States also has a Uniform Commercial Code that regulates business and has the properties of a civil law system. Common law is based on tradition, precedent, and custom and usage, and the courts fulfill an important role in interpreting the law based on those characteristics. Because the British are the originators of common law in the modern setting, the former colonies of Britain are also common law countries.

The **civil law system,** also called a codified legal system, is based on a very detailed set of laws that are organized into a code. These statutes or codes are the basis of doing business. Over 70 countries, including Germany, France, Japan, and the USSR, operate on a civil law basis.[2]

Thus a basic difference between the two systems is that common law is based on the courts' interpretation of events, whereas civil law is based on the facts and how they are applied to the law. An example of the difference generated between the two systems is in contract law. In a common law country, contracts tend to be very detailed with all contingencies spelled out. In a civil law country, however, contracts tend to be shorter and less specific because many of the issues covered in a common law contract are actually included in the civil code.

The best example of the **theocratic law system** (a system based on religious precepts) is Muslim law, which is followed to some degree in 27 countries. Muslim law is based on Islam, and it tends to govern all aspects of life, even though the legal portion is just a small part of the doctrine. Islamic countries often have legal systems that are a blend of Islamic law and common or civil law systems. Their legal systems are often a unique blend based on previous colonial ties and Islamic principles.[3]

National laws affect the way that critical elements of the management process are performed.[4] Those laws can relate to business within the country or business between and among countries. The major categories of legal influence are:

National laws also regulate business between and among countries.

1. business, or contract, law—the protection of patents, trademarks, and copyrights; accounting standards

2. the general legal environment—environmental law, health and safety standards

3. the establishment of business

4. labor law

5. antitrust and cartels

6. prices

7. taxes

The managers of MNEs must become cognizant of the legal system in every country in which they operate. The usual recourses are to employ a variety of local legal firms or to work with an international law firm that has offices worldwide. The challenge is to understand the relevant legal rules of the game and then determine how flexible to be in adhering to those rules. Competent local legal counsel is essential in understanding local legal systems.

International Law

International law governs the relationship between sovereign nations.

The concept of **international law** can be so broad as to encompass any laws that influence international transactions or so narrow as to refer only to treaties that govern the relationships between sovereign nations. The relationships between countries involve the flow of goods, factors of production (such as intermediate goods, raw materials, labor and management), and capital. These flows are influenced by national law as well as international treaties. Multilateral treaties such as those that result from the negotiations of the General Agreement on Tariffs and Trade, and bilateral treaties such as the Free

Trade Agreement between the United States and Canada, are treaties of friendship, commerce, and navigation. They address the following issues:

Bilateral treaties address problems and disputes between nations and individuals within those nations.

1. the entry of individuals;

2. the entry of goods (export and import tariffs and nontariff barriers);

3. the entry of ships and cargoes;

4. the entry of capital;

5. the acquisition of property;

6. the protection of persons and property (such as protection from nationalization and expropriation and protection of patents, trademarks, and copyrights); and

7. the transfer of funds.[5]

Thus treaties not only make international trade easier, they can help resolve problems and disputes between nations and individuals within those nations.

A nation can spread its legal influence by requiring that firms headquartered in that nation abide by home country national law in all countries where the firms operate. This principle of **extraterritoriality,** is the source of a great deal of international ill will.

Extraterritoriality occurs when governments apply their laws to companies' foreign operations.

A good example of the issues facing companies that operate internationally is the case of Hong Kong. Hong Kong's legal system is based on British common law, but 50 years after July 1, 1997, when Hong Kong systems are abolished, business will operate on the basis of Chinese law, which is currently undergoing significant reform. During the 50-year period when Hong Kong is classified as a Special Administrative Region, there will be a degree of uncertainty in the legal system as the transition from Hong Kong to Chinese law proceeds. Firms that are not familiar with either system will have a difficult time planning their operations.

THE POLITICAL ENVIRONMENT

The role of the political system is to integrate the society.

The role of the economic system is to allocate scarce resources.

Two major aspects of any society that have an enormous impact on the way business is conducted are the political and economic systems. The **political system** is designed to integrate the society into a viable, functioning unit. The **economic system** is designed to allocate scarce resources among competing users, and it is concerned with the control and coordination of resources and the ownership of property. In contemporary societies it is very difficult, if not impossible, to separate political systems from economic systems. In our discussion, however, the two systems will be discussed independently, and a synthesis will follow.

Ideology is the systematic body of constructs, theories, and aims that constitute a sociopolitical program.

An **ideology** is the systematic and integrated body of constructs, theories, and aims that constitutes a sociopolitical program. Most modern societies are **pluralistic,** meaning that different ideologies coexist within the society because there is no official ideology accepted by all. The ideologies may be

Pluralistic societies are those in which a variety of ideologies coexist.

very similar, with only minor differences, or they may be very different. The ultimate test of any political system is its ability to hold a society together in spite of pressure from divergent ideologies. This is a major problem in the 1990s in the Eastern European countries and the Soviet Union, where ethnic/ideological conflicts are threatening to break apart many nations, particularly Yugoslavia, the Czech and Slovak Federal Republic, and the USSR.

Political ideologies are many and varied, so it is difficult to fit them neatly into a continuum representing degrees of citizen participation in decision making. Figure 2.1 is a rough schematic of the various forms of government. The two extremes in a theoretical sense are democracy and totalitarianism. From these two extremes various degrees of participation have evolved. Changes are continuing to occur very rapidly in the world today, and many

Figure 2.1
The Political Spectrum *Source:* Endpaper ("Democracy/Totalitarianism") from *American Democracy in World Perspective* by William Ebenstein, C. Herman Pritchett, Henry A. Turner and Dean Mann, © 1967 by Harper & Row Pub. Co. Reprinted by permission of the publisher.

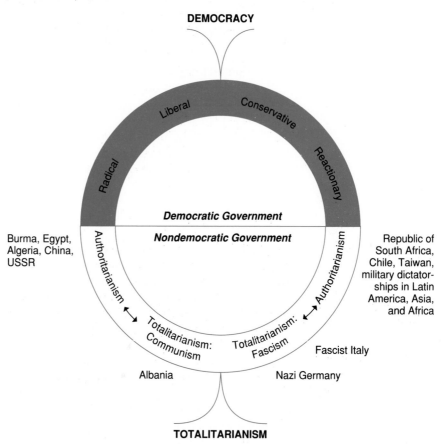

of the authoritarian regimes are being replaced by different types of democracies. Using Fig. 2.1 as a framework, the USSR could be viewed as moving away from totalitarianism and toward democracy. (Whether this burgeoning transition will be successfully completed remains, of course, much in doubt.) Another example of movement along the continuum can be seen in the United Kingdom. Under Margaret Thatcher, the democratic government took a decidedly conservative turn. As yet another example of change, many of the Latin American dictatorships of the 1970s and 1980s (such as Brazil and Panama) gave way to more democratic forms of government.

Democracy

Democratic systems involve wide participation of citizens in the decision-making process.

The ideology of pure **democracy** derives from the ancient Greeks, who believed that citizens should be directly involved in the decision-making process. According to this ideal, all citizens should be equal politically and legally and should enjoy widespread freedoms. In reality, the complexity of society increases with the population, and full participation becomes impossible. As a result, most modern nations that espouse democracy actually practice various forms of **representative democracy.**

In representative democracy, majority rule is achieved through periodic elections.

The following features characterize contemporary democratic political systems:

1. freedom of opinion, expression, press, and organization;
2. elections in which voters decide who is to represent them;
3. limited terms for elected officials;
4. an independent and fair court system that has high regard for individual rights and property;
5. a relatively nonpolitical bureaucracy and defense infrastructure;
6. a relative openness of the state.[6]

Totalitarianism

In a totalitarian state participation in decision making is restricted to only a few individuals.

If democracy is at one end of the spectrum, then totalitarianism is at the other end. In a totalitarian state a single party, individual, or group of individuals monopolizes political power and neither recognizes nor permits opposition. In such a regime, the opportunity to participate in decision making is restricted to a few individuals.

Theocratic totalitarianism is best exemplified by the Moslem countries in the Middle East.

Secular totalitarianism is often enforced through military power and based on worldly rather than religious concepts.

Three major forms of totalitarianism exist today. The form most familiar to Westerners is communism, but there are other forms as well. Iran and the sheikdoms of the Middle East have a form of government that could be called **theocratic totalitarianism. Secular totalitarianism** is found in many Latin American countries, as well as in Iraq, Egypt, and Taiwan. Latin American governments routinely fluctuate between wary democracy and military dictatorship, although in recent years democracy has been gaining.

Communism is a very complex ideology in which the political and economic systems are virtually inseparable. According to Karl Marx, economic forces determine the course taken by a society. He predicted that the capitalist societies would eventually be overcome by two types of revolutions—political and social. The completion of the political revolution would precede and ignite the social revolution, a long-range transformation based largely on economic inequities. Political revolution would result in what Marx called a dictatorship of the proletariat (the working class), which in theory would remain in power for only a short time to smooth the transition during the social revolution. The government would be responsible for organizing society into different groups in order to obtain as much input as possible into the decision-making process. Then, as the social revolution approached completion, the dictatorship would disappear and full communism would take its place. In fact, Marx's predictions have not materialized, and by the 1990s communism has been discredited in many parts of the world. Communism is on the ropes, but its demise is far from certain.

Contemporary Political Systems

All contemporary forms of government differ from the theoretical forms upon which they are built. Although pure democracy does not exist in modern nations, various forms of representative government are seen in which citizens vote for individuals to represent them and make collective decisions. Voting eligibility may be based on attainment of a certain minimum age, as in the United States, or on racial classifications, as in South Africa.

One form of democracy is parliamentary government, an excellent example of which is seen in the United Kingdom. The United Kingdom is divided into geographic districts, and a representative is elected to represent each district in the House of Commons. Elections must be held at least every five years. After a general election, the monarch asks the leader of the party with the majority of seats in the House of Commons to form a government. The leader of the majority party becomes the prime minister and selects a cabinet. The party with the second-largest number of seats becomes the opposition; other parties can align with either the majority or the opposition party. The members of each party select the person to lead the party. The person thus becomes either the prime minister or the leader of the opposition.[7]

The French model involves the direct election of a president who sits for seven years and selects a premier and a Council of Ministers upon the recommendation of the premier. A Parliament comprised of a National Assembly elected by the people and a Senate selected by indirect suffrage is responsible for legislation.[8] This form of government, like the American system, has a separation between the executive and legislative branches.

In most democratic countries, multiple political parties may participate in the election process. Many democracies have only a few dominant parties, so it is not difficult for them to form a government. In Italy, there are so many political parties that the government in power is usually a minority government that has formed a coalition with several minority parties. Whenever a vote of no confidence is taken, a new coalition must be formed before a new government can be formed. Israel and Germany are other modern democracies in which governments are formed through coalitions. In the 1990 German elections, for example, the Christian Democrats and Christian Social Union grabbed only 43.8 percent of the vote, so Helmut Kohl was forced to put together a coalition government. It was also the first time since World War II that East and West Germans voted for one government, and 74.5 percent of the eligible East Germans voted.

Mexico has a single dominant party democracy.

In some democracies there is a single dominant party that controls political power. Mexico, for example, is a democracy that has been ruled by one political party, the Institutional Revolutionary Party (PRI), for nearly 60 years. Its members are Mexico's elite, people who are the most educated and experienced in government. The PRI does not have a particularly ideological thrust; it is mainly interested in keeping the country together.

Even casual observation reveals that contemporary communism differs markedly from theoretical communism. In reality, the political revolutions predicted by Marx resulted in a permanent rather than a transitory dictatorship. Marx's concept of democratic centralism gave way to totalitarian or autocratic centralism, with no general participation in decision making—especially by those with opposing viewpoints.

Many totalitarian countries are moving toward democracy—especially in Eastern Europe.

The political winds began to change, however, in many of the communist countries. In 1989 tumultuous events in China and Eastern Europe shocked the world. When the Chinese initiated significant economic reform in the 1980s, the people began to demand greater political freedom. In spite of the desire of the government to maintain absolute political control, the people went to the streets, and a massacre occurred on and around Tiananmen Square in Beijing on June 4, 1989.

The hopes for political reform in China were shattered, but the standard was picked up in Eastern Europe. Beginning with the fall of the Berlin Wall in late 1989, totalitarian governments in Eastern Europe fell one by one. With little democratic infrastructure in place, the transition from totalitarian to democratic government is far from certain. In the case of East Germany, however, the communist government was simply disbanded as West and East Germany united.

The beginnings of political reform came even to the USSR. Mikhail Gorbachev's initiatives involved political as well as economic change. It is impossible to predict what the ultimate structure of the Soviet Union will be because by the early 1990s the opening of the political process and the surfacing of limited dissent were literally tearing the Soviet Union apart. Many of the 15 Soviet republics, especially Russia and the Baltic republics, were agitating for independence from the Kremlin. Many have compared the political situation of the USSR to the political situation in the United States when the Constitution was drafted over 200 years ago.[9] Unfortunately, the Soviet Union will probably be unable to resolve its problems of centralization versus local autonomy without violence.

Another nation still evolving along the political spectrum is Poland. In the presidential election in 1990, one candidate espoused a strong presidency, whereas the other espoused a parliamentary form of government. As a new constitution was to be drafted in 1991, the winner of the election would clearly have an impact on the type of democratic form of government that Poland would adopt.[10]

Measures of Freedom

The events of 1989 and 1990 continued a trend that had gained momentum in the early 1980s. According to a study by Freedom House, by 1975, most Third World democracies had disappeared. The number of countries espousing Marxism had expanded from 6 at the end of the 1960s to 17 at the beginning of the 1980s. Since 1980, however, no additional countries became Marxist, and by the end of 1988, 38.3 percent of the world's population lived in free countries.[11] Since the late 1970s, when the Freedom House survey became established, there have been "30 transitions from military or one-party domination to formal civilian, elected rule, as well as 10 reversions to military rule."[12] The transition from totalitarianism to democracy was taking hold.

Political freedom is the right to participate freely in the political process.

Civil liberty is the freedom to develop one's own views and attitudes.

In the Freedom House survey countries are categorized as "free," "partly free," and "not free." The groupings are based on two major factors: political rights, which enable people to participate freely in the political process, and civil liberties, which involve "the freedom to develop views, institutions, and personal autonomy apart from the state."[13] People are considered free if they can choose the nature of the political system and the leaders of their country. (See Map 2.2.)

The following paragraph summarizes the 1989–1990 *Survey:*

60.7 percent of the world's population lives in countries that are free or partly free.

> The *Survey* classified 61 countries as free, 44 as partly free, and 62 as not free. It found that 38.87 percent of the world's people lived in countries rated free; 21.85 percent in those rated partly free; and 39.28 in those found not free. However, while 60.72 percent of the world's population was living in free societies or those with a relatively high degree of freedom (the highest number since the *Survey* began), the free or freer countries were almost uniformly liberal democracies, societies with institutional safeguards for the preservation of political rights and civil liberties and juridical mechanisms for self-correction and redressing injustices. Such institutional safeguards were not present in the 62 not-free countries, nor to an appreciable extent in the new but as yet undefined political and socioeconomic order emerging in much of Eastern Europe. Moreover, existing democracies and the delicate process of reform in partly free nations were threatened by a myriad of political, social and economic factors.[14]

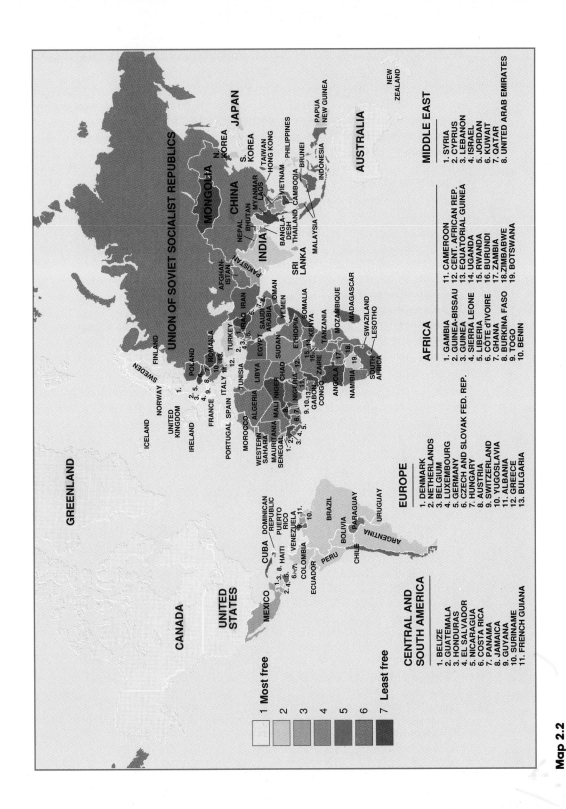

Map 2.2
Political Systems
Freedom is a continuum from most free (elections, choices, broad governance and civil rights) to least free (military or foreign control, low self-determination, lack of decentralized political power).

51

THE ECONOMIC ENVIRONMENT

Economic systems are usually categorized as capitalist, socialist, or mixed. It is possible, however, to classify them according to method of resource allocation and control (**market economy** or **command economy**) and type of property ownership (**private ownership** or **public ownership**). Expanding this concept to include mixed ownership and control results in the taxonomy shown in Fig. 2.2. For example, Hong Kong would most likely fit in block A, whereas the People's Republic of China would probably fit in block I, although it might be in the upper left-hand corner of block I. The United States might fit in block D, although it would be in the upper part of that block.

The ownership of the means of production range from complete private ownership at one extreme to complete public ownership at the other extreme. In reality, the extremes do not actually exist anywhere. The United States, for example, is considered to be the prime example of **private enterprise,** yet the government owns some means of production, and it actively produces in such sectors of the economy as education, the military, the postal service (which is quasi-public sector), and certain utilities. The Soviet Union, which espouses public ownership of the means of production, allows peasant farming on a small-scale, private basis. Most countries lie somewhere in the mixed category, which is very broad and includes varying degrees of public and private ownership. Similarly, the control of economic activity takes place on a continuum from market to command economies, with the actual situation

In a market economy, resources are allocated and controlled by consumers, who "vote" through buying goods.

In a command economy, resources are allocated and controlled by government decision.

In private enterprise, individuals own the resources.

In public ownership, the government owns the resources.

Figure 2.2
Interrelationships Between Control of Economic Activity and Ownership of Factors of Production

CONTROL / OWNERSHIP	Private	Mixed	Public
Market	A	B	C
Mixed	D	E	F
Command	G	H	I

Control ownership
A. Market-Private
B. Market-Mixed
C. Market-Public

Control ownership
D. Mixed-Private
E. Mixed-Mixed
F. Mixed-Public

Control ownership
G. Command-Private
H. Command-Mixed
I. Command-Public

lying somewhere in between. Tremendous economic change is currently taking place, especially in the centrally planned economies.

Market Economy

The market mechanism involves an interrelationship of price, quantity, supply, and demand.

In a market economy, two societal units are very important: the **individual** and the **firm.** Individuals own resources and consume products, while firms use resources and produce products. The market mechanism involves an interaction of price, quantity, supply, and demand of resources and products. Labor is supplied by the household if the firm offers an adequate wage. Products are consumed if the price is within a certain range. A firm bases its wages on the quantity of labor available to assume a job. Resources are allocated as a result of the constant interplay between households and firms, as well as the interplay between households and between firms, such as when the input of one firm is the output of another. The key factors that make the market economy work are **consumer sovereignty** and the freedom of the enterprise to operate in the market. As long as both units are free to make decisions, the interplay of supply and demand should ensure proper allocation of resources.

Consumer sovereignty is the freedom of consumers to influence production through choice.

The market economy has been highly successful in most industrial countries, especially the United States. Even here, however, a perfect market economy does not exist because of the influence of three factors: **large corporations, labor unions,** and the **government.** The large corporation can reduce market pressures somewhat by exerting control over the purchase of resources or the sale of products. Because of the large size of the firm and the relative smallness of each individual shareholder, there is a wide gap between ownership and control of decision making. Decisions may or may not be strictly motivated by the market. The rise in entrepreneurial activities has challenged some of the assumptions of the large firm and injected some dynamism into the economy.

Large corporations, labor unions, and the government limit freedom in a free market.

Labor unions evolved in response to the power exerted by the owners and managers of business over the labor market. Tremendous benefits in terms of salaries, fringe benefits, work conditions, and bargaining power have been won by the unions, but market forces have been seriously disrupted. Many unions control entry into the work force and restrict the freedom of workers to change occupations in response to supply and demand. Government policies continue to shape the U.S. economy. Fiscal and monetary policies have a direct effect on employment, production and consumption of goods and services (for example, the military), and the growth of the money supply. As will be pointed out in Chapter 5, the government also intervenes in the free flow of goods internationally through protectionist measures.

Centrally Planned Economies

In centrally planned economies, the government tries to coordinate the activities of the different economic sectors. In the extreme form of central command, goals are set for every enterprise in the country; the government determines how much is produced, by whom, and for whom. The assumption is that the government is a better judge of how resources should be allocated than is the economy in general or the consumer in particular.

At the heart of a centrally planned economy is its blueprint, generally a five-year plan. Based on this overall plan, specific targets are set each year for each sector of the economy. The governmental plan attempts to coordinate all sectors, since the output of one firm becomes the input of another. A centrally planned economy must rely on the accuracy of government targets instead of on market prices to allocate resources properly. The Soviet Union was the foremost example of a planned economy.

Mixed Economies

No economy is purely market determined or centrally planned. The United States and the Soviet Union (prior to recent reforms) represented opposite ends along the spectrum of mixed economies. In practice, however, what we call mixed economies generally have a higher degree of government intervention than is found in the United States and a greater degree of reliance on market forces than is found in the Soviet Union. Government intervention can be regarded in two ways: actual government ownership of means of production and government influence in economic decision making. Ownership is easy to quantify statistically, but since influence is a matter of policy and custom, it is difficult to measure precisely.

Many industrial countries such as Germany and Sweden have relatively low levels of government ownership but a strong tradition of social welfare. The United Kingdom also has a strong welfare system supported by taxes, although the government is involved more heavily in corporate ownership than the Swedish and German governments are.

Sometimes, the role of government in the economy can cause some serious problems. In 1990, Faul Gardini, the chairman of Ferruzzi Finanziaria S.p.A., the second-largest private company in Italy, resigned. One of his companies, Montedison, had formed a joint venture in chemical production with E.N.I., the state-controlled energy company. Montedison tried to cut costs by selling unprofitable plants and laying off workers, while E.N.I. was hesitant to cut workers because of likely political ramifications. When Gardini decided that it was impossible for him to make market-oriented decisions in a political environment, he quit.[15]

Another illustration of state intervention is found in Japan, a nation often called "Japan, Inc." At the close of World War II, Japan, unlike many

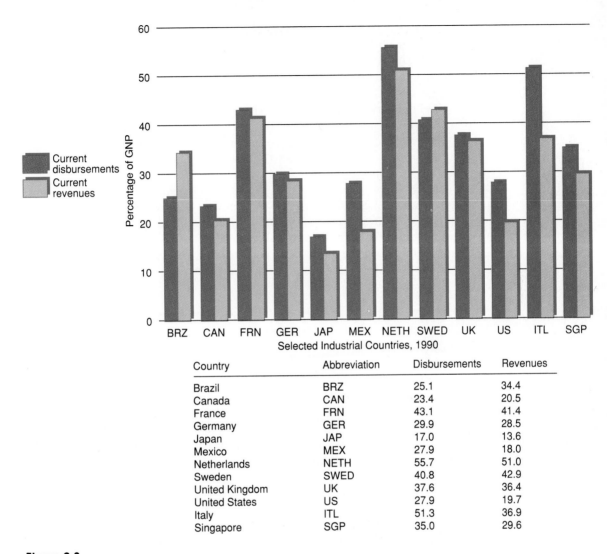

Country	Abbreviation	Disbursements	Revenues
Brazil	BRZ	25.1	34.4
Canada	CAN	23.4	20.5
France	FRN	43.1	41.4
Germany	GER	29.9	28.5
Japan	JAP	17.0	13.6
Mexico	MEX	27.9	18.0
Netherlands	NETH	55.7	51.0
Sweden	SWED	40.8	42.9
United Kingdom	UK	37.6	36.4
United States	US	27.9	19.7
Italy	ITL	51.3	36.9
Singapore	SGP	35.0	29.6

Figure 2.3
Central Government Disbursements and Revenues as a Percentage of GNP of Selected Countries
Source: World Development Report, 1990 (New York: Oxford University Press, 1990), pp. 198–201.

Japan's MITI has given strategic direction to investment and production priorities.

countries, such as France and Italy, decided to leave investment in the private sector rather than nationalizing key sectors and industries. Japanese policy-makers focused more on setting targets and using fiscal incentives to direct investment flows. The Ministry of International Trade and Industry (MITI) was organized to guide industrial development through "strategic planning and authority (both formal and informal) over investment and production priorities."[16]

MITI seemed to be more concerned with developing a vision than with setting up a blueprint for the economy. During MITI's early years in the 1950s and 1960s, a policy of protectionism was invoked so that industries could achieve economies of scale free of outside competition. During the 1960s, however, MITI implemented selective liberalization that involved MITI-inspired industrial reorganizations. These reorganizations led to the creation of industries, such as automobiles and steel, that became formidable world competitors. Structural adjustment to the oil price increase of the 1970s was also inspired and encouraged by MITI as it forced companies to become more energy efficient.

> Free-market countries differ greatly in size of government revenues and expenditures relative to GNP.

Two indicators of the role of government in capitalist societies are central government disbursements and revenues as a percentage of gross national product. Figure 2.3 compares data from several countries. Note the wide divergence among countries, with Japan showing the lowest percentages and the Netherlands the highest. As noted earlier, however, Japan's influence in the economy extends beyond actual expenditures.

POLITICAL-ECONOMIC SYNTHESIS

Except for the discussion on communism, we have made no attempt to link an economic philosophy with a particular political regime, nor a particular political philosophy with any of the economic systems discussed in the previous section. In general, a totalitarian political regime encompasses public ownership of the means of production and a command economy. Prior to the late 1980s, the countries that took this approach were the East European nonmarket economies, such as the USSR, Poland, Yugoslavia, Hungary, Albania, Bulgaria, and East Germany; many African countries, such as Libya, Zambia, Ethiopia, Mozambique, and Angola; Cuba; and China.

> Totalitarian societies are often marked by command economies and public ownership.

There are many examples of totalitarian regimes and mixed (primarily capitalistic) economies, especially among the secular totalitarian countries. Some Middle Eastern examples include Jordan, Saudi Arabia, Bahrain, and Kuwait. African examples include Cameroon, Gabon, Kenya, and Zaire.[17]

> Democratic governments usually mix best with private ownership and control of resources.

Many observers think that a democratic form of government is complemented best by private ownership of the means of production and a market economy. Their rationale is that the voter is considered to be rational and to understand self-interest in the same way that the consumer understands self-interest and prefers to make independent choices. Japan, the United States, Switzerland, Germany, Canada, Colombia, Ecuador, Argentina, and South Korea all have this combination of political and economic systems.

> Democratic socialists believe that elected governments should own and control economic resources.

Democratic socialists, however, take a different view. They believe that since economics and politics are so closely connected, the voters should rely on their elected government to control the economic system; that is, the part of the economy not owned by the government should be regulated by the government. The rationale for democratic socialism is that in order to have a democratically controlled economy and the economic security necessary for liberty, the economy must be owned or regulated by a welfare-oriented government. Radical democratic socialists advocate government ownership of all resources. More moderate democratic socialists support a mix of state-owned firms, cooperatives, small-scale private firms, and "freelancers" (e.g., journalists and artists).[18] Some countries that fit this model are Austria, Denmark, France, Greece, Israel, Portugal, Sweden, Egypt, and Zimbabwe.[19]

Clearly, numerous combinations of political and economic systems are possible. Speaking generally, perhaps the greater the tendency toward political totalitarianism, the greater the reliance on government intervention in ownership and control of the economy. However, most democratic countries have also experimented with different degrees of intervention in the economic system. The extremes are tending to converge to a more even mix of public-private interaction in ownership and control. In the case of the industrial countries, the emphasis seems to be on control rather than on ownership.

The extremes in political economic interaction are converging in mixed economies.

Most countries that have significant central planning and government ownership and control of resources are privatizing. Governments find that it is increasingly difficult to manage the economy and provide adequate support for public companies. Those companies often operate under political rather than business guidelines, and resources are not used as efficiently as they might be in the private sector. Governments that have huge budget deficits quite often point to the drag on the economy induced by inefficient public enterprises.

Privatization is occurring in most countries with significant government ownership.

ADAPTING TO FOREIGN ENVIRONMENTS

Most foreign firms face the challenge of adjustment. For example, a firm based in the United States is accustomed to the legal, political, and economic systems of that country and has devised ways to survive profitably in that particular environment. Upon entering another country for the first time, the firm needs to answer questions such as:

Firms need to resolve key questions as they enter different political and economic systems.

1. What is the country's political structure?

2. Under what type of economic system does the country operate?

3. Is the firm's industry in the public or private sector?

4. If it is in the public sector, does the government also allow private competition in that sector?

5. If it is in the private sector, is it moving toward public ownership?

6. Does the government view foreign capital as being in competition or in partnership with public or local private enterprises?

7. In what ways does the government control the nature and extent of private enterprise?

8. How much of a contribution is the private sector expected to make in helping the government formulate overall economic objectives?

The questions appear simple, but owing to the dynamic nature of political and economic events, the answers are complex. Many foreign firms are still investing in Hong Kong, even though the conditions that will exist after 1997 are very uncertain. Hong Kong firms such as Swire are investing outside of Hong Kong because of the same uncertainty. Firms attempting to invest in Eastern Europe and the Soviet Union are experiencing enormous difficulties because the environment in those countries is very different from anywhere else in the world, and the changes taking place there are so rapid and unpredictable.

Foreign firms must be aware of their own experiences and how those experiences have helped shape their managerial philosophies and practices. In addition, firms must determine how the new environment differs from their more familiar domestic environment and decide how managerial philosophy and practice must be changed to adapt to the new environment.

THE CLASSIFICATION OF ECONOMIES

There is no uniform classification of countries, and even the existing classifications are changing because of changes in political and economic systems. Table 2.1 identifies the classifications provided each year in the *World Development Report*.

Countries have traditionally been classified as belonging to the First World, Second World, or Third World. The First World countries have high-income economies. The First World includes the industrial world and some of the high-income oil-producing states. The Second World countries have centrally planned economies, which are in a state of flux. According to the World Bank, the Second World countries have low- and middle-income economies. It is difficult to know how to refer to centrally planned economies (CPEs), because most of them are in various stages of transition to a market economy. The World Bank has decided to refer to them as historically planned economies (HPEs), so the Second World is being phased out and many countries are being classified as Third World.

The Third World countries, also known as developing countries, also have low- and middle-income economies. With only a few exceptions, the low-income countries are found in Asia, Africa, and Latin America. Middle-income countries are much more widespread geographically, and a majority of Latin America's population lives in middle-income countries. African nations tend to be more concentrated in the lower-middle-income categories, and Latin American nations tend to be more concentrated in the upper-middle-income categories. A combination of upper-middle-income countries and high-income countries make up the NICs (newly industrialized countries). Although the World Bank has not issued a comprehensive list of NICs, the designation generally includes Argentina, Brazil, China, Hong Kong, Hungary, India, Israel, the Republic of Korea, Mexico, Poland, Portugal, Romania, Singapore, Taiwan, and Yugoslavia.

Second World countries are now considered to be low- and middle-income countries.

Developing countries are located primarily in Africa, Asia, and Latin America.

TABLE 2.1 | WORLD BANK CATEGORIES

Country Groups

I. High-Income Economies (25 countries)

1988 Per Capita GNP of $6000 or more
OECD Countries
Saudi Arabia
Israel
Singapore
Hong Kong
Kuwait
United Arab Emirates

II. Middle-Income Economies (54 countries)

1988 Per Capita GNP of more than $545 but less than $6000

Upper-Middle-Income Economies (37 countries)
1988 Per Capita GNP Between $2200 and $6000

Lower-Middle-Income Economies (17 countries)
1988 Per Capita GNP Between $545 and $2200

III. Low-Income Economies (42 countries)

1988 Per Capita GNP of $545 or less

IV. Nonreporting Nonmember Economies (9 countries)

Albania
Bulgaria
Cuba
Czechoslovakia (now the Czech and Slovak Federal Republic)
German Democratic Republic (now part of Germany)
Democratic People's Republic of Korea
Mongolia
Namibia
Union of Soviet Socialist Republics

Analytical Groups

I. Oil Exporters

Countries for which exports of petroleum and gas account for at least 30 percent of merchandise exports

Algeria, Bahrain, Brunei, Cameroon, Congo, Ecuador, Egypt, Gabon, Indonesia, Iran, Iraq, Kuwait, Libya, Mexico, Nigeria, Norway, Oman, Qatar, Saudi Arabia, the Syrian Arab Republic (Syria), Trinidad and Tobago, United Arab Emirates, and Venezuela

II. Severely Indebted Middle-Income Countries

Argentina, Bolivia, Brazil, Chile, Congo, Costa Rica, Côte d'Ivoire, Ecuador, Honduras, Hungary, Mexico, Morocco, Nicaragua, Peru, Philippines, Poland, Senegal, Uruguay, and Venezuela

TABLE 2.1 (continued)

III. OECD Members

Geographic Regions (Low-Income and Middle-Income Economies)
I. Sub-Saharan Africa

All countries south of the Sahara except South Africa

II. Europe, Middle, East, and North Africa

Includes eight developing countries in Europe

III. East Asia

All the low- and middle-income countries of East and Southeast Asia and the Pacific, east of and including China and Thailand

IV. South Asia

Bangladesh, Bhutan, India, Myanmar, Nepal, Pakistan, and Sri Lanka

V. Latin America and the Caribbean

Notes: OECD (Organization for Economic Cooperation and Development) includes Australia, Austria, Belgium, Canada, Denmark, Finland, France, Germany (now comprised of West Germany and the German Democratic Republic), Greece, Iceland, Ireland, Italy, Japan, Luxembourg, Netherlands, New Zealand, Norway, Portugal, Spain, Sweden, Switzerland, Turkey, United Kingdom, United States; Greece, Portugal, and Turkey are classified as middle-income economies rather than as high-income economies in the World Bank statistics, even though they are OECD countries.

These lists include only countries with populations of 1 million or more.

Source: World Development Report, 1990 (New York: Oxford University Press, 1990), pp. x and xi.

TABLE 2.2 | BASIC INDICATORS (1988)

	Population (millions)	Life Expectancy at Birth	Distribution of Gross Domestic Product (percent)		
			Agriculture	Industry	Services
High Income	784.2	76	3	31	56
OECD	751.1	76	3	31	56
Low Income	2884.0	60	33	36	32
Middle Income	1068.0	66	12	40	50
Upper	326.3	68	N/A	N/A	N/A
Lower	741.7	62	18	39	44

Source: World Development Report, 1990 (New York: Oxford University Press, 1990), pp. 178–182.

Key Economic Indicators

As countries shift from low-income to industrial market economies, they also shift from agriculture to manufacturing to services.

Table 2.2 provides comparative indicators for the different country groupings. As countries move from low- to high-income economies, the distribution of gross domestic product (GDP) shifts in emphasis from agriculture to industry to services.

The geographical distribution of wealth is even more dramatically illustrated in Fig. 2.4. The world's wealth is located primarily in the high-income

Figure 2.4

Per Capita GNP by Major Country Category Source: World Development Report, 1990 (New York: Oxford University Press, 1990), pp. 202–203.

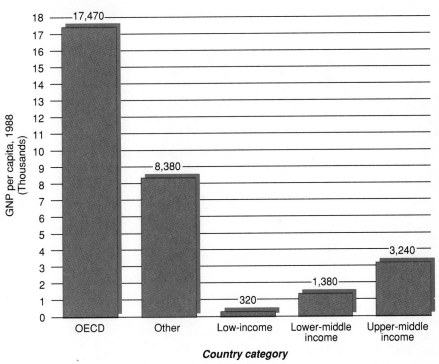

Country category	GNP per capita, 1988
High-income (25)	$17,080
OECD (19)	17,470
Other (6)	8,380
Developing (96)	750
Low-income (42)	320
Middle-income (54)	1,930
Lower-middle-income (37)	1,380
Upper-middle-income (17)	3,240

countries. The low- and middle-income countries, where the vast majority of the population lives, are underrepresented in per capita income.

KEY ECONOMIC ISSUES IN INDUSTRIAL AND DEVELOPING COUNTRIES

A variety of cultural, legal, political, and economic factors influence the management of the MNE. The impact of these factors varies considerably from country to country. Obviously, the environment in a developing country such as China is very different from that of an industrial country such as Germany.

Even though there is great disparity among the developing countries, they share many common problems and characteristics. Some of the most frequently mentioned problems are inflation, external debt, weakening currencies, shortage of skilled workers, political instability, economic instability, overreliance on the public sector in economic development, war and insurrection, mass poverty, rapid population growth, weakening commodity prices, and reliance on imported oil.

Six key issues are
- Economic growth
- Inflation
- Trade strategy
- Payments imbalances
- Country debt
- Poverty

We cannot discuss in this chapter every problem of concern to industrial and developing countries, nor can we address the issues specific to historically planned and transitional economies that will be covered later. We will, however, discuss six economic factors that could influence management decisions: economic growth, inflation, trade strategy, payments imbalances, country debt, and poverty. We will close with some comments on the dialogue between industrial and developing countries known as the North–South dialogue.

Economic Growth

Developing countries have exhibited stronger growth but investment is risky.

The MNE would prefer that every country in the world have political stability, low rates of inflation, and high rates of real growth. Even if the firm does not expand market share in each market, it would be able to increase revenues at the same pace as the general economy. Developing countries provide large market potential and exhibit strong economic growth overall, but investing there tends to be riskier than in the industrial countries. Figure 2.5 illustrates real growth in GDP between industrial and developing countries during the periods 1973–1980, 1980–1989, and the year 1989. Although growth in developing countries has been slightly better than it has been in the industrial countries, the two have essentially kept pace with each other.

Economic growth has been strong in East Asia and South Asia.

Growth in recent years has been especially strong in East Asia and South Asia. (See Fig. 2.5.) There is tremendous market size and growth in Asia. The relatively slower growth in the industrial countries is a troublesome sign because these countries tend to ignite growth for the rest of the world.

The French and British are selling off many state-owned enterprises.

An interesting trend in the 1980s was the increasing privatization of business. The initiatives taken during the 1960s and 1970s to absorb industry into the public sector were not very successful in the industrial or developing

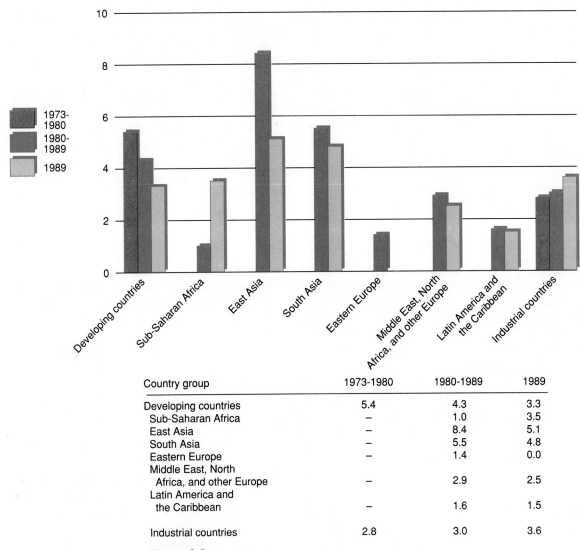

Country group	1973-1980	1980-1989	1989
Developing countries	5.4	4.3	3.3
Sub-Saharan Africa	–	1.0	3.5
East Asia	–	8.4	5.1
South Asia	–	5.5	4.8
Eastern Europe	–	1.4	0.0
Middle East, North Africa, and other Europe	–	2.9	2.5
Latin America and the Caribbean	–	1.6	1.5
Industrial countries	2.8	3.0	3.6

Figure 2.5
Real Rate of Growth of GDP *Source: World Development Report, 1990* (New York: Oxford University Press, 1990), p. 8.

countries. For example, during the 1980s, a number of British state-owned companies were sold to individual shareholders as part of Prime Minister Thatcher's movement to private sector ownership of firms. A center-right coalition in France, headed by Jacques Chirac, defeated the socialists in 1986 and began to sell off many of the companies that had been taken over by the government when François Mitterrand was first elected president.

Severe internal and external debt has been an incentive to speed the privatization effort. In Argentina, the government sold two major state-owned enterprises in 1990. The first was the national telephone company, where the government sold 60 percent of its ownership interest to private investors. The second was its national airline, Aerolineas Argentinas, which was sold to Iberia, the Spanish airliner. The government retained a 5 percent interest, sold 10 percent to the employees, and sold the rest to Iberia. It was able to get rid of the fiscal responsibility for the airliner as well as eliminate $2.01 billion in foreign debt paper as part of the sale. Similar trends have emerged in other developing countries, principally in Africa, which have found that state socialism does not generate enough economic growth.

The rate of growth of per capita GDP in developing countries has been falling.

Figure 2.6 provides a measure of the growth of per capita GDP in the developing regions for three different time periods. Except in Asia, the rate of growth in those regions as measured by per capita GDP has been falling in recent time periods.

Inflation

Inflation is an important part of the economic environment (see Chapter 8) because of its effect on interest rates, exchange rates, the cost of living, and general confidence in a country's political and economic system. For example, fear of inflation in Japan and Germany accounts for the unwillingness of those countries to stimulate their economies in order to achieve more rapid economic growth. The magnitude of inflation seen in many developing countries is incomprehensible to most people in the industrial world. During the period 1980–1988, inflation increased in Argentina by 290.5 percent, in Brazil by 188.7 percent, in Bolivia by 482.8 percent, in Peru by 119.1 percent, and in Israel by 136.6 percent.[20] By the end of the 1980s, inflation in Brazil was 1000 percent per annum.

Inflation has been rapid in Brazil, Bolivia, Peru, and Israel.

In highly inflationary environments, it is difficult for firms to plan for the future and run profitable operations. Companies must change prices almost daily in order to maintain a sufficient cash flow to replace inventory and keep the firm operating. Accurately forecasting inflation is difficult, so firms end up underpricing or overpricing products, which results in a shortage of cash flow or a price that is too high to maintain market share.

Inflation of the magnitude seen in Bolivia, Argentina, or Brazil also creates problems for firms that deal in international markets. If the exchange rate depreciates at the same pace as inflation, then the prices that foreigners pay for exports of the inflationary country will not really change. But if the exchange rate does not change as much as inflation is forcing companies to raise their prices, the local companies will soon find that they cannot compete in world markets.

Inflation weakens the value of a currency and destabilizes a country politically.

Inflation causes political destabilization. If the government tries to control it by controlling wages, the real income of the population declines and frustration sets in. If the government decides to do nothing, the country risks having the economy deteriorate to the point that real incomes fall anyway. To institute fiscal rigor when the government is in a fragile position in the

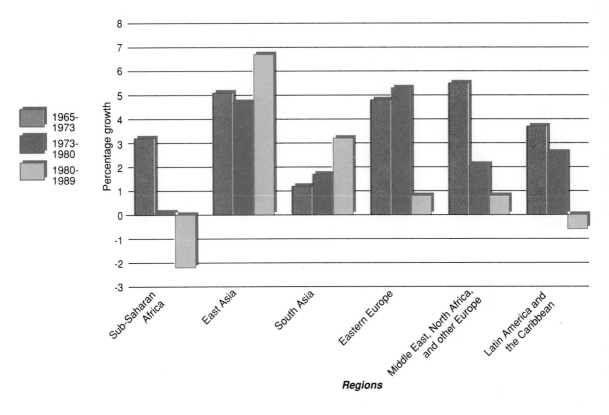

Regions	Growth of real per capita GDP(percent)		
	1965-73	1973-80	1980-89
Sub-Saharan Africa	3.2	0.1	-2.2
East Asia	5.1	4.7	6.7
South Asia	1.2	1.7	3.2
Eastern Europe	4.8	5.3	0.8
Middle East, North Africa, and other Europe	5.5	2.1	0.8
Latin America and the Caribbean	3.7	2.6	-0.6

Figure 2.6
Growth of Real Per Capita GDP by Developing Region, Selected Periods
Source: World Development Report, 1990 (New York: Oxford University Press, 1990), p. 11.

first place is very difficult. In spite of the problems created by inflation, inflationary countries can still offer strong profits for traders and investors. Brazil has been able to fuel its economic growth largely through inflation and to soften the impact of inflation through special fiscal policies. Its large market and relatively strong per capita income have created good opportunities, in spite of the uncertainty and instability.

TABLE 2.3 | INFLATION, 1971–1990 (in percent)

	Average 1971–80[1]	1981	1982	1983	1984	1985	1986	1987	1988	1989	1990
Industrial countries[2]	8.7	10.1	7.5	4.9	4.7	4.1	2.3	2.9	3.2	3.8	3.5
United States	7.8	10.4	6.1	3.2	4.4	3.5	2.0	3.6	4.1	4.7	4.9
Japan	9.0	4.9	2.7	1.9	2.3	2.0	0.6	0.1	0.7	1.3	1.0
Germany, Federal Republic of	5.1	6.3	5.3	3.3	2.4	2.2	−0.2	0.2	1.2	2.8	2.4
Other industrial countries[2]	10.6	12.7	11.0	8.1	6.7	6.1	4.2	4.1	4.0	4.6	3.9
Developing countries[3]	20.5	25.8	25.2	32.4	38.2	39.7	31.1	40.5	67.1	45.5	18.1
By region											
Africa	14.1	20.8	13.1	17.9	20.8	13.3	14.4	15.0	18.8	15.1	11.8
Asia	10.5	10.4	6.4	6.7	7.3	7.1	9.1	9.8	14.6	10.0	6.8
Europe	13.8	23.6	33.1	22.8	25.4	25.5	24.8	30.3	49.3	50.3	35.5
Middle East	13.5	15.1	12.9	12.0	14.4	17.0	18.2	19.3	18.8	14.6	13.5
Western Hemisphere	39.8	60.8	66.8	108.6	133.0	144.9	87.8	130.0	277.6	154.9	34.2

[1]Compound annual rates of change. Excluding China.

[2]Averages of percentage changes for individual countries weighted by the average U.S. dollar value of their respective GNPs over the preceding three years.

[3]Percentage changes of geometric averages of indices of consumer prices for individual countries weighted by the average U.S. dollar value of their respective GDPs over the preceding three years.

As shown in Table 2.3, inflation in developing countries dropped steadily during the 1980s, with the exception of the years 1987–1988. The drop between 1989 and 1990 was especially large.

Trade Strategy

Different countries have very different trade strategies. Investments by MNEs in industrial countries typically are established to service local markets, which also tend to be relatively free to exports and imports. Developing countries, however, often have adopted specific strategies to encourage exports or impede imports. MNE management must understand a country's attitude toward trade, since it may affect the type of investment undertaken. Countries such as Korea, Hong Kong, and Singapore have developed policies that encourage firms to produce for the export market. Other countries, such as Argentina and the Philippines, have established trade barriers and incentives to favor production for the domestic market.

Explanations for why firms trade and why governments intervene in trade are discussed in Chapters 4 and 5. There are some interesting facts on macroeconomic performance of countries grouped by their trade orientation. Countries that are strongly export oriented tend to have a higher average percentage growth in real GDP, a higher average percentage growth in per capita GNP, a larger percentage of gross domestic savings relative to GDP, and a larger percentage growth in manufactured exports than do other countries. They also tend to exhibit lower rates of inflation.[21]

Payments Imbalances

The balance-of-payments performance for developing countries has been mixed in recent years.

Table 2.4 highlights the current account balances (exports minus imports of goods, services, and unilateral transfers) of different categories of countries during the period 1981–1990. The performance in the developing countries has been mixed. Overall, the deficit improved until the mid-1980s, and it has fluctuated over the last half of the decade. It has definitely improved in the Asian region, however.

The industrial countries as a group did not do very well, largely because of the performance of the United States. The U.S. deficit on its current account of $156.6 billion in 1990 was partially offset by the surpluses in Japan and

TABLE 2.4 | SUMMARY OF PAYMENTS BALANCES ON CURRENT ACCOUNT, 1981–1990[1]
(in billions of U.S. dollars)

	1981	1982	1983	1984	1985	1986	1987	1988	1989	1990
Industrial countries	−15.8	−19.5	−18.0	−57.3	−51.1	−17.5	−44.6	−59.0	−67.0	−74.5
United States	6.9	−8.7	−46.3	−107.1	−115.1	−138.8	−154.0	−135.3	−139.3	−156.6
Japan	4.8	6.9	20.8	35.0	49.2	85.8	87.0	79.5	84.0	93.5
Germany, Federal Republic of	−3.6	5.1	5.3	9.9	16.6	39.3	45.0	48.5	49.7	51.2
Other industrial countries	−23.9	−22.8	2.1	4.9	−1.7	−3.8	−22.7	−51.6	−61.4	−62.6
Developing countries	−49.1	−83.4	−62.4	−31.4	−26.0	−42.2	1.4	−19.1	−19.4	−26.0
By region										
Africa	−22.1	−21.3	−12.2	−8.0	−0.6	−9.6	−5.3	−9.5	−7.8	−8.4
Asia	−18.6	−16.5	−14.2	−4.2	−14.0	3.9	21.6	10.0	8.8	5.6
Europe	−13.9	−8.0	−5.8	−3.0	−3.1	−2.0	1.0	3.5	1.4	−1.3
Middle East	48.5	5.0	−19.4	−13.7	−3.6	−17.2	−3.8	−11.7	−10.4	−6.2
Western Hemisphere	−43.0	−42.5	−10.9	−2.5	−4.7	−17.3	−12.0	−11.5	−11.5	−15.8

[1]Including official transfers.

[2]Covers estimated balances on current transactions only in convertible currencies of the USSR and nonmember countries of Eastern Europe.

[3]Reflects errors, omissions, and asymmetries in reported balance of payments statistics on current account, plus balance of listed groups with countries not included.

[4]Staff estimates of the difference between the beginning-of-year and end-of-year "float," that is, the value of those exports that have not yet been recorded as imports (usually because the goods are in transit or because of delays in the processing of the documentation). The estimates should be viewed only as rough orders of magnitude.

The United States has a huge current account deficit, and Japan and Germany have huge surpluses.

Germany. The huge U.S. deficit has been a constant source of contention between the United States and the rest of the world. Since a country's balance of payments must always be stable, the United States has been able to offset its current account deficit with an inflow of capital from abroad. Foreign governments and individuals have continued to invest in the United States because of relatively high real interest rates, political stability, a strong local economy, and general confidence in the political and economic system of the United States. In addition, in the early 1980s U.S. firms began to invest more in the United States than abroad, thereby reducing the outflow of foreign direct investment. As a result, the United States has been buying foreign products and selling the strength and stability of the U.S. economy. Some feel that this heavy reliance on foreign capital has made the United States the world's largest debtor. However, the money has flowed in as a result of economic opportunity in a way significantly different from that of other large debtor nations.

Some would argue that a current account surplus is evidence of a mercantilist government policy, where a government favors exports over imports. Countries with surpluses tend to be fairly satisfied with their situation. In recent years, however, countries with large surpluses such as Taiwan and Japan, have been pressured to open their markets and stimulate consumption in order to reduce the surplus. Countries with deficits have been under pressure to increase exports and correct fundamental economic imbalances in order to slow down imports and bring the trade deficit up to a more even balance.

National Debt

One of the consequences of the rapid increase in the cost of oil during the 1970s was the equally rapid increase in debt as developing countries sought assistance from private or government institutions in other countries to finance oil imports and other products necessary for development. Debt in the developing countries increased from less than $100 billion in 1970 to $1336.6 billion in 1990.[22] The two largest borrowing regions were Latin America and Africa.

The largest debtor regions are Latin America and Africa.

Figure 2.7 identifies the major developing country debtors. Note the tremendous size of the debt in countries such as Brazil and Mexico. It is interesting to note that in 1986 South Korea was in third place, whereas it dropped to tenth place in 1988. A major problem with debt is that countries have a difficult time paying it off. The debt service ratio, the ratio of interest payments plus principal amortization to exports, is quite high, especially in the western hemisphere. This suggests that countries are not able to use as much of their export earnings as they would like for economic development. An increasing share of those earnings is going to service their debt.

As debts rise, crises are inevitable. The first crisis occurred in the international banking community in Poland in the 1970s. At that time it appeared that Poland would have to default (not pay its obligations), and many experts were unsure what impact this would have on the international financial community. The next crisis came in August 1982, when Mexico, with nearly four

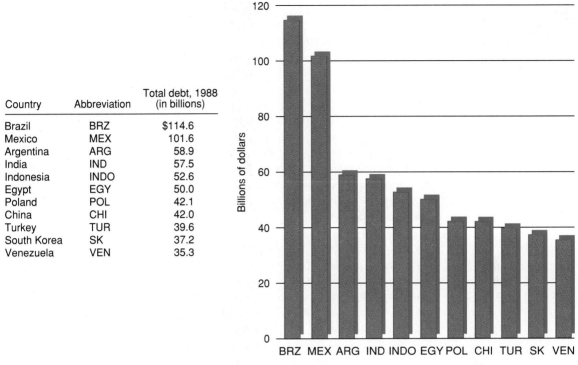

Country	Abbreviation	Total debt, 1988 (in billions)
Brazil	BRZ	$114.6
Mexico	MEX	101.6
Argentina	ARG	58.9
India	IND	57.5
Indonesia	INDO	52.6
Egypt	EGY	50.0
Poland	POL	42.1
China	CHI	42.0
Turkey	TUR	39.6
South Korea	SK	37.2
Venezuela	VEN	35.3

Figure 2.7
Third World Debtors (in billions of dollars) *Source:* Morgan Guaranty Trust Co., "Brazil Will Press for Concessions Won by Mexico," published in *Wall Street Journal*, Jan. 9, 1987, p. 24. *World Report, 1990*, pp. 218–219.

times the debt of Poland, could not fulfill its debt-service obligations. As a result, it was forced to reschedule principal and interest payments. When a country reschedules debt, it changes the interest rate of the loan and/or the timing of the payments of principal and interest. Most of the large debtors, especially Brazil and Argentina, were in the same position and had to go through reschedulings at the same time.

In 1987 the crisis, especially among the Latin American debtors, reached critical proportions. Brazil declared a moratorium on interest and principal payments to commercial creditors—basically a suspension of payments—arguing that it could not afford the $5 billion in annual interest payments, an amount that was 12 percent of its federal budget.[23] As a result of the high degree of uncertainty in Latin American loans, many banks set aside large reserves in case the loans could not be repaid. Banks establish reserves by reducing earnings and increasing the reserve account. This allows them to reduce earnings a little each year, especially in profitable years, rather than waiting for a major default and reducing earnings all at once. This reduction in earnings is problematic because it also reduces the banks' lending ability and financial strength.

Latin countries also were trying to create novel ways to reduce the debt

Banks have set aside reserves against developing country loans.

Debt-equity swaps are one way that developing countries are trying to solve their debt problems.

The IMF provides economic advice to help countries solve debt problems and get new loans.

pressure by, for example, converting debt into equity. A debt-equity swap is based on a foreign lender's exchanging its dollar debt in a developing country for real assets in that country, such as equity in a local business.

An example of a debt for equity swap is the sale of Aerolineas Argentinas to Iberia mentioned before. Iberia is paying $260 million in cash and assuming $2.01 billion in debt paper for its 85 percent interest in Aerolineas Argentinas.

The International Monetary Fund has played a crucial role in helping the debtor nations restructure their economies. In country after country the IMF has recommended strong economic restrictions as a precondition for receiving loans from the IMF. These loans are almost a prerequisite for persuading the international commercial banks to reschedule their loans. Restrictions have involved a combination of export expansion, import substitution, and a drastic reduction in public spending. In Mexico, for example, the government deficit was running at an estimated 17.6 percent of GDP in 1982, and the IMF gave the government a target of 5.5 to 6.5 percent, a substantial reduction in government spending.[24]

In many developing countries, these radical requirements have touched off heated debate and have sorely tested the political stability of the governments in power. Once the IMF sets targets, it monitors those targets periodically as a precondition to releasing funds. The private international banks often use the results of this monitoring to determine their policies.

MNE management is concerned about the high debt situation because it is difficult to operate in that type of environment. Imports are often curtailed, and hard currency is difficult to obtain. In addition, governments might institute a variety of macroeconomic measures to control debt, including slowing down economic growth, which would have a negative impact on sales opportunities for firms.

Poverty

The 1990 issue of the *World Development Report* focused on poverty. In spite of the rapid growth in the world over the past three decades, especially in income, consumption, and some broader measures of well-being, over 1 billion people in the developing countries live in poverty. The poverty line is only $370 per year. Even on broader issues of well-being conditions are significantly worse in the developing countries than they are in the high-income countries. For example, life expectancy in Sub-Saharan Africa is only 50 years, whereas it is 80 years in Japan.

Table 2.5 identifies some broad measures for poverty in the developing world. Africa and developing Asia are significantly worse off than Latin America. The mortality and life-expectancy rates are not significantly different, but the gross numbers and percentage of the population below the poverty line are much worse.

The World Bank emphasizes two strategies for improving the lot of the poor:

Strategies for eliminating poverty include
- Efficient labor-intensive growth
- Provision of adequate social services

1. Efficient labor-intensive growth based on appropriate market incentive, physical infrastructure, institutions, and technological innovation.

2. Adequate provision of social services, including primary education, basic health care, and family planning services.[25]

The first strategy implies a significant role for the MNE. Because of the low wage rates in the developing countries, there should be plenty of opportunities for low-end manufacturing as education and skill levels improve. Governments may assist in infrastructure development and provide incentives for firms to locate in their countries in order to encourage economic development.

TABLE 2.5 | HOW MUCH POVERTY IS THERE IN THE DEVELOPING COUNTRIES? THE SITUATION IN 1985

Region	Extremely Poor			Poor (including extremely poor)			Social Indicators		
	Number (millions)	Headcount Index (percent)	Poverty Gap	Number (millions)	Headcount Index (percent)	Poverty Gap	Under 5 Mortality (per thousand)	Life Expectancy (years)	Net Primary Enrollment Rate (percent)
Sub-Saharan Africa	120	30	4	180	47	11	196	50	56
East Asia	120	9	0.4	280	20	1	96	67	96
China	80	8	1	210	20	3	58	69	93
South Asia	300	29	3	520	51	10	172	56	74
India	250	33	4	420	55	12	199	57	81
Eastern Europe	3	4	0.2	6	8	0.5	23	71	90
Middle East and North Africa	40	21	1	60	31	2	148	61	75
Latin America and the Caribbean	50	12	1	70	19	1	75	66	92
All developing countries	633	18	1	1,116	33	3	121	62	83

Note: The poverty line in 1985 PPP dollars is $275 per capita a year for the extremely poor and $370 per capita a year for the poor.

The headcount index is defined as the percentage of the population below the poverty line. The 95 percent confidence intervals around the point estimates for the headcount indices are Sub-Saharan Africa, 19, 76; East Asia, 21, 22; South Asia, 50, 53; Eastern Europe, 7, 10; Middle East and North Africa, 13, 51; Latin America and the Caribbean, 14, 30; and all developing countries, 28, 39.

The poverty gap is defined as the aggregate income shortfall of the poor as a percentage of aggregate consumption. Under 5 mortality rates are for 1980–1985, except for China and South Asia, where the period is 1975–1980.

Source: Hill and Pebley 1988, Ravallion and others (background paper), and United Nations and World Bank data 1989.

Source: World Development Report, 1990 (New York: Oxford University Press, 1990), p. 29.

NORTH-SOUTH DIALOGUE

In 1964, in Geneva, the first session of the United Nations Conference on Trade and Development (UNCTAD) was held, leading to what is now called the North-South dialogue. (The North refers to the industrialized countries and the South to the developing countries.)

None of the pronouncements emanating from the session was particularly new, but the collective resolve of the developing countries (i.e., the South) appeared to be stronger than ever.

Since 1974 various meetings focusing on specific problems have been held in order to continue the North-South dialogue. In particular, the developing countries have expressed concern in the following areas: stabilization of export earnings and commodity prices, reduction of trade barriers in the developed countries, increased aid, debt moratorium, and additional private investment. Their basic concern is how to transfer wealth from the developed to the developing countries. Even though each side has moderated its position, a wide discrepancy remains between what the developing countries want and what the developed countries are willing to give.

UNCTAD V, held in Manila, in 1979, may have started a new era of cooperation and understanding in the dialogue. The four main areas of emphasis in the conference were: (1) trade and financial-flow aspects of the relationships between developed and developing countries, (2) emphasis on growing interdependence among different parts of the world economy, (3) efforts to bring socialist countries into the dialogue on economic issues, and (4) emphasis on trade liberalization and concern about expanding protectionism.[26] Unlike the conflict-ridden earlier sessions of UNCTAD, the mood seemed to be one of cooperation.

The UNCTAD VI meeting, held in Yugoslavia, in 1983, focused on the problems of debt and protectionism. At that meeting, the developing countries identified the following points as the key focus for the discussions:

1. automatic debt relief,
2. an increase in world liquidity through the IMF,
3. greater aid and private bank lending to developing nations,
4. freer access for developing country exports to the markets of the rich.[27]

The meeting was not as fruitful as the developing countries had hoped, however. The industrialized countries acknowledged that protectionism hurts the developing countries and agreed to open access to their markets more as the recovery took hold. But they also encouraged the richer developing countries to do the same for their poorer neighbors. This suggestion met with some resistance from the developing countries, which felt that they needed barriers to support their own infant industries. The industrial countries also opposed discussions of increasing liquidity because they viewed the World Bank and the International Monetary Fund (IMF) as better suited to deal with those issues. UNCTAD originally was organized to deal with commodity issues,

The North-South dialogue has focused on
- Stabilization of earnings and prices of commodity exports
- Reduction of trade barriers and better access to markets
- Increased aid
- A moratorium and partial forgiveness of debt
- Increased private investment
- Increased world financial liquidity

whereas the World Bank and IMF were geared toward financial issues. In addition, the industrial countries have greater control over the World Bank and the IMF than they do over UNCTAD. The industrial North in effect seemed to say that the developing South would see a lot of its problems disappear as the impact of the recovery "trickled down" to the developing countries.

UNCTAD VII, held in Geneva, in 1987, decided to focus more on promoting development, growth, and international trade. Three objectives in particular were established by the managing director of UNCTAD: (1) to establish in each country growth-oriented structural adjustment programs, (2) to acquire financing appropriate to the situation of overindebtedness, and (3) to put into place a universal, growth-oriented adjustment effort.[28] A major accomplishment at the meeting was a final agreement on the establishment of a common fund for commodities. The fund will be used to help develop new markets for commodities produced by commodity-dependent countries and to help the countries diversify. This is significantly different from what was originally envisioned in 1977.

Most recently, UNCTAD has called for a significant reduction in the debt of the 15 biggest debtors. UNCTAD recommends that the banks write off one third of the debt of those 15 debtor nations. That suggestion is favored by the debtor nations, but is not very popular with the banks.[29]

EXTERNAL INFLUENCES ON DEVELOPMENT

Multilateral Institutions

The IMF also provides financial support for countries with balance-of-payments problems.

The road to development is complex, and it is difficult for the developing countries to meet the challenges alone. The International Monetary Fund (IMF) and World Bank are instrumental in the development process. The IMF provides financial support for countries suffering severe balance-of-payments problems, a group that includes most of the developing countries. As noted earlier, this financial assistance, although multilateral, comes with strings attached. Countries are often forced to make substantial and politically unpopular concessions for IMF support. At times, countries have felt that IMF financing entails too much loss of sovereignty.

The World Bank provides development financing for projects.

The World Bank also provides financing to low-income developing countries, especially in infrastructure development, such as transportation, communications, and power. The World Bank tends to take a more active role in helping countries modify their basic economic policies in return for aid. Such changes would also bring the countries' policies more in line with that of the IMF.

The Multinational Enterprise

In the 1970s numerous books and articles were published describing the impact of the MNE on developing countries. MNEs were accused of causing a

In general, MNEs are not as great an influence on developing countries as once thought.

variety of problems, including the destruction of the nation-state. This charge seems unjustified for several reasons: (1) a shift in bargaining power toward the nation-state; (2) a dispersion of multinationals to include home countries other than the United States, thus eliminating the United States as the sole source of economic influence; (3) the development of multinationals by developing countries themselves; (4) the emergence of more multinationals, including a larger number of smaller, more flexible enterprises; and (5) greater flexibility on the part of multinationals in adapting to local situations.[30]

One of these points deserves elaboration. The number of Third World multinationals, usually based in the rapidly developing middle-income countries, has increased dramatically in recent years. These MNEs are located primarily in three types of developing countries: resource-rich ones (such as OPEC members); labor-rich and rapidly industrializing ones (such as Hong Kong, Taiwan, and South Korea); and market-rich, rapidly industrializing ones (such as Brazil, Mexico, and the Philippines).[31] Hyundai Motor and Goldstar are examples of two Korean MNEs. Governments in these countries tend to be committed to international business activities. MNEs from the developing countries also tend to be more readily accepted in sister countries since they are "part of the group" and are perceived to be less threatening than MNEs from the industrialized countries.

A humorous description of the MNE appeared several years ago in the *Economist*:

> It fiddles its accounts. It avoids or evades its taxes. It rigs its intra-company transfers prices. It is run by foreigners, from decision centers thousands of miles away. It imports foreign labour practices. It doesn't import foreign labour practices. It underpays. It competes unfairly with local firms. It is in cahoots with local firms. It exports jobs from rich countries. It is an instrument of rich countries' imperialism. The technologies it brings to the third world are too old fashioned. No, they are too modern. It meddles. It bribes. Nobody can control it. It wrecks balances of payments. It overturns economic policies. It plays off governments against each other to get the biggest investment incentives. Won't it please come and invest? Let it bloody well go home.[32]

Developing countries need access to the capital and technology of MNEs.

Many developing countries are finding that they need to provide a better climate for foreign investment in order to have access to the capital and technology of the industrial country MNEs as a key part of their industrial strategy. For years, Mexico would not allow majority ownership for most new investment, but the debt problems of the early 1980s caused them to pass new legislation in order to attract more capital. They found that incurring debt was not the best route, and as a result began, in 1984, to improve the investment climate and restore the confidence of foreign investors in the hopes of attracting more capital. In addition, in 1990, the Mexican government entered into talks with the United States to establish a free-trade agreement that would also include Canada and would become the largest trading bloc in the world.

MNEs have a great deal to offer developing countries in terms of capital, technology, managerial expertise, and access to world markets. As the oil companies have learned, however, they need to be increasingly flexible about the way profits are to be earned. As will be discussed in Chapter 15, licensing agreements, production agreements, management contracts, and joint ventures are sometimes taking the place of wholly owned direct investments. As host countries improve their basic operating environments to attract investment and the MNEs adjust their operating strategies to these environments, development will increase and profits will be earned.

LOOKING TO THE FUTURE The major changes in the future will involve important political and economic developments. It is clear from the events of the late 1980s and early 1990s that totalitarianism is being challenged—but is fighting back—throughout the world. Significant political instability will be the rule rather than the exception in countries with shifting political ideologies. In the Soviet Union and China, the pressures for political liberalization will continue, although the price is likely to be significant human loss. A new generation of leaders may have to rise up to lead these countries into the twenty-first century.

Economically, the same type of liberalization will take place in the centrally planned economies. Those countries, however, will probably opt for a form of democratic socialism rather than a pure laissez-faire capitalist system such as that found in Hong Kong. Transforming a centrally planned economy into a market economy is a difficult and painful process. There will be high levels of unemployment and economic stagnation in the transition. Those conditions may induce political instability, and it is impossible to predict the outcome. Nevertheless, Eastern Europe will need technical and managerial help and will have to turn more to the West to obtain it.

The challenges for the industrial countries will be to open markets to trade and services while continuing to liberalize goods trade without raising protectionist barriers against the developing countries. The slow growth of the early 1990s will lead to greater trade pressures and protectionism and could threaten the atmosphere of cooperation that developed in the 1980s. The industrial countries of the West will be constantly challenged by the industrial and emerging nations of Asia, and the competitive balance of power may continue to shift to Asia. That puts even greater pressure on the industrial countries of the West to innovate in product and process technology in order to remain competitive.

The developing countries will continue to grapple with political and economic instability, inflation, balance-of-trade deficits, and high debt service. They are in a difficult and almost insolvable position. Their growth and development will have a significant effect on the industrial countries as markets and as a source of production of intermediate and final products.

SUMMARY

- The role of the political system is to integrate the society; the role of the economic system is to allocate scarce resources.

- Most complex societies are pluralistic; in other words, they encompass a variety of ideologies.

- In democracies there is wide participation in the decision-making process, whereas in totalitarian states only a relative few may participate. Totalitarian regimes can be communistic, theocratic, or secular. Totalitarian regimes are beginning to accede to greater participation in the decision-making process.

- Most democracies have multiple political parties, whereas some, such as Mexico, have one dominant political party.

- The economic system determines who owns and controls resources. In a market system individuals allocate and control resources; in a command economy the government allocates and controls resources. A command economy is compatible with a totalitarian political system; a market economy is compatible with a democracy.

- A multinational enterprise (MNE) that enters a country needs to determine the nature of the political and economic system and how it can fit into that system.

- There are three major world economies: The First World is made up of the market industrial economies; the Second World consists of the centrally planned economies; and the Third World is comprised of the developing countries. The centrally planned economies are undergoing significant economic change.

- Developing countries are divided into low-income (per capita GNP of $545 or less) and middle-income (per capita GNP of $545 to $6000) categories. Middle-income developing countries are divided into lower-middle-income and upper-middle-income categories.

- As countries become more prosperous and their economies shift from low-income to high-income categories, the distribution of Gross Domestic Product (GDP) shifts in emphasis from agriculture to industry to services.

- Some of the greatest problems facing the developing countries are inflation, external debt, weakening currencies, a shortage of skilled workers, political instability, war and insurrection, mass poverty, rapid population growth, weakening commodity prices, and reliance on imported oil. Developing countries have exhibited strong growth, but they are riskier places of investment than the industrial countries.

- Inflation today is not as rampant as it was during the 1970s, but it is still severe in some countries, such as Argentina, Brazil, and Israel.

- The trade strategy of countries ranges from strongly outward oriented (such as Hong Kong and Korea) to strongly inward oriented (such as Argentina and India).

- Many of the large debtor nations have had to restructure their loans because of their inability to meet principal and interest payments.

■ The UNCTAD meetings focus on growth and solving the problem of indebtedness. The International Monetary Fund (IMF) is concerned with stabilizing exchange rates and helping countries overcome their problems of indebtedness. The World Bank is concerned with providing capital for Third World development.

C A S E
BATA, LTD.[33]

In 1990, the management of Bata, Ltd. had a critical decision to make concerning the possibility of reinvesting in Czechoslovakia (now the Czech and Slovak Republic). This may not seem like a major concern at first, but there is significant history between Bata and Czechoslovakia. As war swept across Europe in 1939, Tom Bata, Sr., was faced with a difficult situation. His father, the ninth generation of a family of shoemakers in Czechoslovakia, had built a worldwide shoe network in 28 countries, using machinery and the mass-production technology of the 1920s. Tom was left with the responsibility of panding that empire during a period of great uncertainty worldwide. Because of the invasion of the Nazis and the uncertain future that occupation held, Bata took 100 Czech families and emigrated to Canada to preserve his father's business.

Since that time, Bata's decision has been ratified through strong growth worldwide. Bata, Ltd. is a family-owned business whose production facilities produce over 300 million pairs of shoes annually, generating over $3 billion in revenues through sales in 6000 Bata-owned retail outlets and 125 independent retailers in 115 nations. Its 85,000 employees work in over 90 factories and five engineering facilities, as well as the retail operations mentioned earlier. Bata's influence is so pervasive that it makes and sells one out of every three shoes manufactured and sold in the noncommunist world. In fact, the word for shoe in many parts of Africa is "bata."

Bata, Ltd. is run as a decentralized operation that is free to adjust to the local environment, within parameters. Tom Bata travels extensively to check on quality control and to ensure good relations with the governments of the countries where Bata, Ltd. operates.

Although Bata, Ltd. has factories in more than 90 countries and operations of one form or another in over 100, it does not own all of those facilities. Where possible, it owns 100 percent of the operations. In some countries, however, the government requires less-than-majority ownership. In India, for example, 60 percent of the stock of the local Bata operations trades on the Indian stock exchange, and in Japan, Bata, Ltd. owns only 9.9 percent of the operations. In some cases, Bata, Ltd. provides licensing, consulting, and technical assistance to companies in which it has no equity interest.

Bata, Ltd.'s strategy for servicing world markets is instructive. Some MNEs try to lower costs by achieving economies of scale in production, which means that they produce as much as possible in the most optimal-sized factory and then service markets worldwide from that single production facility. Bata, Ltd. tries to service its different national markets by producing in a given market nearly everything it sells in that market. Part of the reason for this strategy is that Bata, Ltd. can achieve economies of scale very quickly because it has a fairly large volume in the countries where it produces.

This may seem difficult to believe, especially since Bata, Ltd. has production facilities in some African nations where it is the sole industry. Bata, Ltd., however, believes that it can achieve economies of scale very easily because it is a labor-intensive operation. Bata, Ltd. also tries to get all of its raw materials locally. This is not possible in some cases, especially in some of the poorer developing countries. Nevertheless, it tries to have as much value-added as possible in those countries.

Another of Bata, Ltd.'s policies is that it prefers not to export production; rather, it chooses local production to service the local market. Obviously, that rule is not fixed, since the company produces in only 90 countries but has distribution in over 100. Sometimes Bata, Ltd. becomes entangled with local governments when it imports some raw materials but does not export. Then it has to adjust to the local laws and requirements for operation.

Bata, Ltd. avoids excessive reliance on exports partly because of the risk. For example, if an importing country were to restrict trade, Bata could possibly lose market opportunity and market share. In addition, Mr. Bata noted the benefit to the developing country of not exposing itself to possible protectionism:

> We know very well what kind of a social shock it is when a plant closes in Canada. Yet in Canada we have unemployment insurance and all kinds of welfare operations, and there are many alternative jobs that people can usually go to. In most of the developing countries, on the other hand, it's a question of life and death for these people. They have uprooted themselves from an agricultural society. They've come to a town to work in an industry. They've brought their relatives with them because working in industry, their earnings are so much higher. Thus a large group of their relatives have become dependent on them and have changed their lifestyle and standard of living. For these people it is a terrible thing to lose a job. And so we are very sensitive to that particular problem.

Bata, Ltd. operates in a variety of different types of economies. It has extensive operations in both the industrial democratic countries and the developing countries. It has been soundly criticized (as have been most MNEs) for operating in South Africa and thus tacitly supporting the white minority political regime, and it has also been censured for operating in totalitarian regimes, such as Chile. Bata counters by pointing out that the company has been operating in Chile for over 40 years, during which time a variety of political regimes have been in power.

Although Bata's local operations have not been nationalized very many times, the company has had some fascinating experiences. In Uganda, Bata's local operations were nationalized by Milton Obote, denationalized by Idi Amin, renationalized by Amin, and finally denationalized by Amin. During that time the factory continued to operate as if nothing had happened. Mr. Bata's explanation for finally being left alone is that, "Shoes had to be bought and wages paid. Life went on. In most cases, the governments concluded it really wasn't in their interest to run businesses, so they cancelled the nationalization arrangements."

Despite Bata, Ltd.'s ability to operate in any type of political situation, Mr. Bata prefers a democratic environment. He feels that while both democratic and totalitarian regimes are bureaucratic, a democracy holds the potential to discuss and change procedures, whereas under totalitarianism it is sometimes wise to remain silent.

Bata, Ltd. has a multifaceted impact on a country. The basic strategy of the company is to provide footwear at affordable prices for the largest possible segment of the population. The product, footwear, is a necessity rather than a luxury. The production facilities are labor intensive, so jobs are created, which increases consumers' purchasing power. Although top management may come from outside of the country, local management is trained to assume responsibility as quickly as possible. Because the company tries to get most of its raw materials locally, suppliers are usually developed. Since Bata, Ltd. likes to diversify its purchases, it usually develops more than one supplier for a given product, which leads to competition and efficiencies.

Typically Bata, Ltd. brings in its own capital resources at the start-up of a new operation, but it is also skillful in utilizing international capital markets. More than once Bata, Ltd., used the resources of the International Finance Corporation (IFC), a division of the World Bank that provides development financing for private-enterprise projects in developing countries. One of Bata's most recent attempts at IFC financing was to expand a tannery in Bangladesh. The importance of getting IFC support is that Bata, Ltd. would be much more likely to attract other debt and equity capital once it had received IFC approval. All of the five previous Bata projects supported by the IFC had been successful, and the loans had been paid back.

The South African dilemma presented unique challenges for Bata management, however. South Africa, whose population ranks just below those of Nigeria, Egypt, and Ethiopia, has long been considered a good place to invest because of its large market size. South Africa's per capita GNP is the largest in Africa. The country's main attraction has been the incredibly high rate of return that companies can earn, owing largely to low labor costs and mineral wealth. The relatively large market still allows firms to achieve economies of scale in production while exploiting the low labor costs.

But the situation deteriorated rapidly in the early 1980s. The system of apartheid, which has resulted in a political, social, and economic separation of blacks, coloreds, and whites, has characterized South Africa for decades, and change has been slow. Government opposition has begun to unite around the concept of one man, one vote. Black nationalists will settle only for total voting rights, whereas the white government refuses that concept at all costs. Rioting has left many dead and has heightened the uncertainty of South Africa's political future. Most of the fighting has been between rival black factions. The African National Congress (ANC), led by Nelson Mandela, opposes capitalism and has stated that it would nationalize all industry, whether domestic or foreign-owned. The ANC is beginning to back down from that stand, but reluctantly. The rival Inkatha movement is more

open to free-enterprise capitalism. South Africa's 0.8 percent per capita GNP growth during 1980–1988 was significantly below that of the average of 2.3 percent for upper-middle-income developing countries. In addition to a relatively stagnant economy and political strife, pressure has come from foreign firms and governments. A number of U.S. firms, including Apple Computer, Coca-Cola, Ford, International Harvester, General Motors, IBM, Honeywell, and Warner Communications, have sold or significantly reduced their investments in South Africa. In 1984, only seven U.S. companies had pulled out of South Africa. In 1985, forty pulled out; in 1986, fifty left; and by mid-1987, thirty-three firms had already withdrawn. U.S. investment in South Africa had dropped in half between 1982 and 1986. Even the U.S. consulate in Johannesburg had lost faith in the future of South Africa, noting that South Africa was on its way to becoming "just another African country: chronic debtor, import-starved . . . a repressive regime unable to manage its own domestic constituency in any positive way."

The Canadian attitude toward South Africa was also negative. Canada's government issued very conservative voluntary guidelines on new investments in South Africa. As a result, Bata finally decided to leave South Africa in 1986. It did not identify the buyer or the sales price. The company denied that apartheid was the reason for pulling out. Company personnel stated that "it really was a business decision that took into account all of the factors with respect to investment in South Africa at the present time." Under the terms of the sale, the Bata company name and trademark will no longer be used in South Africa, and all ties with Canada will be broken. Apparently, the new buyer gave assurances that the jobs of the workers, most of whom are black, would be preserved. As the South African economy began to turn the corner in the late 1980s and the De Klerk government begins to dismantle apartheid and pave the way for a solution to the political impasse, Bata management must be rethinking their decision.

The problem of Czechoslovakia is different. Sometimes investment decisions are an affair of the heart. Even though the Communist government took over Bata's operations in 1945, Bata is interested in possibly starting up operations again in Czechoslovakia. The problem is, who owns the plants? The Czech government would like some kind of compensation for the factories, but Bata feels that the factories are still his. Some experts feel that Bata will eventually receive an equity investment in the huge facilities in exchange for managerial expertise, marketing help, and capital. It is estimated that it would take as much as $100 million to modernize the plants, which currently employ 85,000 people and turn out 100 million pairs of shoes a year.

Questions

1. Why do you think that a developing country might allow Bata, Ltd. to operate locally?
2. Do you agree with Bata's assessment of the riskiness of exporting? How do you think the developing countries might react to that assessment?
3. Explain why Bata, Ltd.'s operations might be less susceptible to serious political influence than some other types of companies.
4. What problems do you think that Bata might encounter in starting up operations and operating profitably in the Czech and Slovak Republic again? What should Bata do?

Chapter Notes

1. The major sources for the case are as follows: William H. Overholt, "Hong Kong: A Look at the Coming Decade," *Pacific Rim Business Digest*, October 1990, pp. 5–10; David E. Sanger, "As Hong Kong's Elite Leave, Investors from Japan Arrive," *New York Times*, 29 May 1990, p. A1; Pete Engardino, "In Asia, the Sweet Taste of Success," *Business Week*, 26 November 1990, p. 96; *Culturgram: Hong Kong* (Provo, Utah: Brigham Young University, January 1988); "The Dragon's Embrace," *Economist*, 26 August 1989, pp. 51–52; David Lethbridge, ed., *The Business Environment in Hong Kong*, 2d ed. (Oxford: Oxford University Press, 1984); Swire Pacific Limited *Annual Report*, 1988; *The Swire Group* (Hong Kong: Swire Group Public Relations Hong Kong, November 1989).

2. Michael Litka, *International Dimensions of the Legal Environment of Business* (Boston: PWS-Kent, 1988), p. 4.

3. *Ibid.*

4. Richard N. Farmer and Barry M. Richman, *Comparative Management and Economic Progress* (Homewood, Ill.: Richard D. Irwin, 1965), pp. 238–255.

5. Litka, *op. cit.*, pp. 22–23.

6. Robert Wesson, *Modern Government—Democracy and Authoritarianism*, 2d ed. (Englewood Cliffs, N.J.: Prentice-Hall, 1985), pp. 41–42.

7. *Europa Yearbook*, 1989, pp. 2679 and 2692.

8. *Europa Yearbook*, pp. 1013–1018.

9. Michael Barone, "Playing Politics, Soviet Style," *U.S. News and World Report*, 15 January 1990, pp. 38–41; "Is the Soviet Union Next?" *U.S. News and World Report*, 15 January 1990, pp. 31–37; "Soviet Union," *Business Week*, 29 October 1990, p. 51; Carroll Bogert, "The Congress of Futility," *Newsweek*, 29 October 1990, p. 50.

10. Gail E. Schares and Lynne Reaves, "Poland Isn't Just Picking a President, It's Picking a Future," *Business Week*, 5 November 1990, p. 74.

11. Marc F. Plattner, "Democracy Outwits the Pessimists," *Wall Street Journal*, 12 October 1988, p. A20.

12. R. Bruce McColm, *Freedom in the World: Political Rights & Civil Liberties 1989–90* (New York: Freedom House, 1990), p. 1.

13. *Ibid.*, pp. 19 and 20.

14. *Ibid.*, p. 4.

15. Clyde Haberman, "Chairman of Top Italian Company Resigns," *New York Times,* 23 November 1990, p. C1.

16. *World Development Report,* 1984 (Washington, D.C.: World Bank, 1984), p. 67.

17. "Freedom House Comparative Survey of Freedom for 1987," *Freedom at Issue,* January–February, 1987, p. 33. This survey has an interesting matrix that plots political systems on one axis and economic systems on the other. Examples of countries are included in each cell in the matrix.

18. John R. Freeman, *Democracy and Markets: The Politics of Mixed Economies* (Ithaca, N.Y.: Cornell University Press, 1989), p. 7.

19. *Ibid.*

20. *World Development Report, 1990* (New York: Oxford University Press, 1990), pp. 202–203.

21. *World Development Report, 1987,* p. 84.

22. *World Development Report, 1990,* p. 225.

23. Jeffrey Ryser, Stephen Baker, and Elizabeth Weiner, "The Debtors' Revolt Is Spreading in Latin America," *Business Week,* December 28, 1987, pp. 88–89.

24. "Will Mexico Make It?," *Business Week,* October 1, 1984, pp. 74–77.

25. *World Development Report, 1990,* p. 138.

26. Mahmud al Burney, "A Recognition of Interdependence: UNCTAD V," *Finance & Development,* September 1979, p. 18.

27. Paul Lewis, "Aid and Trade Are in the Air at North–South Talks," *New York Times,* June 12, 1983, p. 8F.

28. "Conditions in Global Economy Prompt Renewed Focus on Growth," *IMF Survey,* July 27, 1987, p. 233.

29. "A Debtor's Dream," *Economist,* 10 September 1988, p. 81.

30. Paul Streeten, "Multinational Revisited," *Finance & Development,* June 1979, pp. 39–42.

31. David A. Heenan and Warren J. Keegan, "The Rise of Third World Multinationals," *Harvard Business Review,* January/February 1979, pp. 102–103.

32. "Controlling the Multinationals," *Economist,* January 24, 1976, p. 68.

33. The material for the case was taken from the following sources: Dean Walker, "Shoemaker to the World," *Executive,* January 1981, pp. 63–69; Gary Vineberg, "Bata Favors Free Trade but Tempers Asia Stance," *Footwear News,* Vol. 39, No. 24, June 13, 1983, pp. 2ff; Ira Breskin and Gary Vinesbert, "Parent Bata Looks After Far Flung Footwear Family," *Footwear News,* Vol. 39, No. 23, June 6, 1983, pp. 1ff.; Ira Breskin, "Globe-Trotting Bata, Ltd.: A World Bank Customer," *Footwear News,* Vol. 38, No. 38, October 4, 1982, p. 23; "After Sullivan," *Economist,* June 13, 1987, p. 71; Elizabeth Weiner and Steve Mufson, "All Roads Lead Out of South Africa," *Business Week,* November 3, 1986, pp. 24–25; Jonathan Kapstein, John Hoerr, and Elizabeth Weiner, "Leaving South Africa," *Business Week,* September 23, 1985, pp. 104–112; Robert Collison, "How Bata Rules Its World," *Canadian Business,* September 1990, pp. 28–34; Peter C. Newman, "The Return of the Native Capitalist," *Macleans,* 12 March 1990, p. 53.

CHAPTER **3**

THE HUMAN AND CULTURAL ENVIRONMENTS FACING BUSINESS

To change customs is a difficult thing.
LEBANESE PROVERB

Objectives

- To demonstrate how human-cultural environments are examined and to show some of their principal limitations.

- To highlight human physical characteristics peculiar to different countries and to show the effects these characteristics have on efficiency of business practices worldwide.

- To examine major customs that differentiate business practices from country to country.

- To present guidelines for multinational firms that operate internationally.

When Prime Minister Margaret Thatcher made an official visit to Saudi Arabia, the first such visit ever by a British head of government, she deferred to Islamic custom on appropriate attire for women. She wore a long-sleeved, ankle-length dress throughout the day. During her talks with King Khalid, she wore a net veil over her face. This deference was a symbolic gesture to demonstrate her sensitivity to the Saudi culture, which helped to gain acceptance of her proposals to Saudi officials.

A year before Mrs. Thatcher's visit, Parris-Rogers International, a British publishing house, sold its floundering Bahraini operations, which had been set up to edit the first telephone and business directories for five Arab states on or near the Arabian peninsula, plus the seven autonomous divisions making up the United Arab Emirates. (A map of the region is shown in Map 3.1.) Like many foreign firms, PRI was drawn to the Middle East because of the burgeoning business brought on by rising oil prices. Whereas Prime Minister Thatcher had protocol officers to advise her when she visited Saudi Arabia, PRI had no such guidance. The ensuing lack of understanding and failure to adapt to a different culture contributed directly to PRI's failure.

Because most of the oil-rich states have had an acute shortage of local personnel, great numbers of foreign workers have been hired, and they now make up a large portion of the work forces in those states. In Saudi Arabia in 1990, for example, 75 percent of the work force was foreign-born. Thus when PRI could not find sufficient qualified people locally, it filled four key positions through advertisements in London newspapers. Angela Clarke, an Englishwoman, was hired as editor and researcher, and three young Englishmen were hired as salesmen. The four new-hires left immediately for Bahrain. None had visited the Middle East before; all expected that they could carry out business in their accustomed way.

C A S E
PARRIS-ROGERS
INTERNATIONAL
(PRI)[1]

The salesmen, hired on a commission basis, expected that by moving aggressively they could make the same number of calls as would be normal in Great Britain. They were used to working about eight hours a day, to having the undivided attention of potential clients, and to restricting most conversation to the specifics of the business transaction.

What the salesmen found instead was that there was less time to sell because the Moslems were required to pray five times a day and because the work day was reduced even further during Ramadan, the ninth month of the Muhammadan year observed as sacred with fasting from dawn to sunset. Appointments often began after the scheduled time. When the salesmen finally got in to see Arab businessmen, they were often expected to go to a café where the Arabs would divert the conversation to idle chitchat. Whether in a café or in the office, the drinking of coffee or tea seemed to take precedence over the business

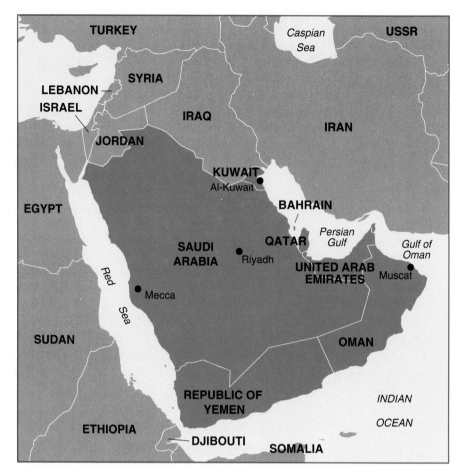

Map 3.1
PRI's Business Contract in the Middle East
PRI's contract included Bahrain, Kuwait, Oman, Qatar, Saudi Arabia, and the
United Arab Emirates (Abu Dhabi, Ajman, Dubai, Fuzaira, Ras al-Khaimah, Sharjah,
and Umm al-Qaiwain).

matter. It seemed further to the salesmen that the Arabs placed little importance on the appointments, since they frequently diverted their attention to
friends who joined them at the café or in the office.

Angela Clarke was paid a salary instead of a commission, so PRI bore
all of the expense resulting from her work being thwarted in unexpected
ways. PRI had based its government contract prices for preparing the telephone directories on its English experience. In Bahrain, however, the preparation turned out to be more time-consuming and costly. In the traditional
Middle Eastern city there are no street names or building numbers. Ms.

Clarke had to do a census of Bahraini establishments, identifying each with such prepositions as "below," "above," or "in front of" some meaningful landmark, before getting to the expected directory work.

Angela Clarke encountered other problems because of her status as a single woman. She was in charge of the research in all 13 states and had planned to hire freelance assistants in most of them. Yet because she was a single woman Saudi authorities denied her entry to Saudi Arabia. Her visa for Oman took six weeks to process each time she went there. These experiences were particularly frustrating for her because both Saudi Arabia and Oman sometimes eased the entry of single women when their business was of high local priority. In the states that she could enter, Ms. Clarke sometimes was required to stay only in hotels that government officials had approved for foreign women. Even there she was prohibited from eating in the dining room unless accompanied by the hotel manager. Her advertisements to hire assistants were met by personal harassment and obscene telephone calls.

PRI's salesmen never adjusted to work in the new environment. Instead of pushing PRI to review its commission scheme, they tried to change the way that the Arab businessmen dealt with them. For example, after a few months they refused to join their potential clients for refreshments, and they showed their irritation at "irrelevant" conversations, delays, and interruptions from outsiders. The Arab businessmen responded negatively. In fact, PRI received so many complaints from them that the salesmen had to be replaced. By then, irrevocable damage had been done to PRI's sales.

Angela Clarke fared better, thanks to her compromises with Arab customs. She began wearing a wedding ring and registering at hotels as a married woman. When traveling, she ate meals in her room, conducted meetings in conference rooms, and had all incoming calls screened by the hotel operators. To avoid arrest by decency patrols, she wore long-sleeved blouses and below-the-knee length skirts in plain blue or beige. When PRI left the area, Angela Clarke stayed on to work for a Japanese bank in Bahrain. Still, in spite of her compromises, her inability to enter Saudi Arabia caused PRI to send in her place a salesman who was not trained to do the research.

The rapid growth and intrusion of foreigners into the region has created adjustment problems for the foreigners and for the local societies as well. On the one hand, foreign workers provide needed skills to fuel the increasingly complex economy; on the other hand, Middle Easterners fear that their presence will erode deep-seated values and traditions. In many cases, foreigners are expected to conform; in others, they are allowed to pursue their own customs in isolation from the local populace. For example, according to traditional Islamic standards, most Western television programming is immoral. Foreigners, however, in some places are permitted to acquire unscramblers to view Western television fare; local people may not.

Moreover, women soldiers from the United States were allowed to work in the same hangars with male Saudi Air Force crews during the liberation of Kuwait from Iraq; however, the women were not permitted to jog or drive anywhere or to show bare arms and legs outside military areas.

The Saudi government also has had second thoughts about some of the culture's double standards. At one time, for example, male and female hotel guests were allowed to swim in the same pools in Saudi Arabia. This permission was rescinded, however, because Saudis frequent the hotels and could be corrupted by viewing "decadent" behavior. When Angela Clarke and the salesmen first arrived in Bahrain, there were prohibitions on the sale of pork products, including imported canned foods. This prohibition was later modified, but grocers had to stock pork products in separate rooms in which only non-Muslims could work or shop.

These dual and changing standards for foreigners and citizens make adapting difficult for foreigners. This situation has been further complicated because the Middle East is going through a period of substantial, but uneven, economic and social transformation. This was well described as follows:

> Changes that in other countries have been spread out over several generations are being accomplished in a few short years. Diesel trucks and jet airplanes are replacing camel caravans, but the camel has not yet been discarded. Modern architecture and broad, tree-lined avenues are replacing mudbrick houses on twisting streets, but mudbrick buildings are still evident. Nomads (Bedouins) are beginning to drive from place to place; but it is common to see a pickup truck or a Mercedes parked beside a traditional tent.[2]

As contact increases between Arabs and Westerners, there will be increased cultural borrowing and meshing of certain aspects of traditional behavior. This meshing is apt to come slowly, perhaps more slowly than many think. A noted anthropologist summarized the Americans' misconception of change by the Saudis:

> We tend to think of them as underdeveloped Americans—Americans with sheets on. We look at them as undereducated and rather poor at anything technological. All we have to do is to make believers out of them, get them the proper education, teach them English, and they will turn into Americans.[3]

In fact, when Saudi students who have spent time abroad return home, they revert to traditional behavior. Likewise, foreigners, after completing an assignment in Saudi Arabia, return to their traditional behaviors. While U.S. troops were deployed in Saudi Arabia, an American female soldier said, "I'm thankful I'm not a Saudi woman. I just don't know how they do it." At the same time, a female Saudi doctor said, "It is so strange. I am glad not to be an American woman. Women are not made for violence and guns." These behaviors and attitudes indicate how deeply rooted both Saudi and Western traditions are.

INTRODUCTION

A business employs, sells to, buys from, is regulated by, and is owned by people. Therefore an international company must consider differences in groups of people or societies in order to predict and control its relationships and operations. The PRI case illustrates how human differences give rise to different business practices in various parts of the world. When doing business abroad, a company should determine whether the usual business practices in a foreign country differ from its home country experience or from what its management ideally would like to see exist. If customs differ, international management must then decide what, if any, adjustments are necessary to operate efficiently in the foreign country.

Some differences, such as those regarding acceptable attire, are discerned easily, whereas others may be more difficult to perceive. For example, people in all cultures have culturally ingrained responses to given situations. They expect that people from other cultures will respond the same way as those in their own culture do and that people in similar stations or positions will assume similar duties and privileges. All of these expectations may be disproven in another culture. In the PRI case, for example, the British salesmen budgeted their time and regarded drinking coffee and chatting about nonbusiness activities in a café as "doing nothing," especially if there was "work to be done." The Arab businessmen, on the other hand, had no compulsion to finish at a given time, viewed time spent in a café as "doing something," and considered "small talk" a necessary prerequisite for evaluating whether they could interact satisfactorily with potential business partners. Because of their belief that you "shouldn't mix business and pleasure," the Englishmen became nervous when friends of the Arab businessmen intruded. Yet the Arabs felt that "people are more important than business" and saw nothing private about business transactions.

In truth, it is impossible to learn all the differences in cultural norms between one's own country and a foreign place of business. Managers can, however, pinpoint those cultural areas that have been noted to cause the greatest operational problems and become better prepared to note more subtle differences as well.

Even when a company successfully identifies the differences in the foreign country where it intends to do business, must it alter its customary or preferred practices to be successful there? There is no easy answer. Although the PRI case illustrates the folly of not adjusting, international companies nevertheless have sometimes been very successful in introducing new products, technologies, and operating procedures to foreign countries. Sometimes these introductions did not run counter to deep-seated attitudes, and in some cases the local society is willing to accept behaviors from foreigners that it would not accept from its own citizens. For example, an American female executive said, "I do business comfortably in Japan. I don't find myself subjected to the same kind of sexism that, they tell me, is prevalent in other areas of Japanese life. I am treated as an American businessperson. . . . Most people overseas are well aware of the differences between Americans and themselves."[4]

The Nation-State as Proxy of Society

The nation-state is a useful proxy of society because
- Boundaries are cause and effect of national differences in norms
- Laws fall primarily along national lines

There is no universally satisfactory definition of a society, but in international business, the concept of the nation-state provides a workable shorthand, since basic similarity among people is both a cause and an effect of national boundaries. The laws governing business operations apply primarily along national lines. This does not mean that everyone in a country is alike, nor does it suggest that each country is unique in all respects. There are, however, certain physical, demographic, and behavioral norms characteristic of each country that may affect a firm's methods of conducting business in that country.

In using the nation-state as a point of reference, it is important to remember that much greater variation exists within some countries than within others. Geographic and economic barriers in some countries may confine people's movements from one region to another, thus limiting their interactions. In addition, decentralized laws and government programs may enhance regional separation. Furthermore, linguistic, religious, and ethnic differences within a country usually preclude the fusing of the population into a homogeneous state. India, for example, is much more diverse than Denmark for all the reasons just given.

Limitations of country-by-country analysis occur because
- Not everyone in a country is alike
- Variations within some countries are great
- Commonalities link groups from different countries

Of course, nationality is not the only way of grouping people. Everyone belongs to various other groups—for example, those based on profession, age, religion, and place of residence. There are many commonalities that might in some ways link groups from different countries more closely together than groups within a country. For instance, people in urban areas differ in certain attitudes from people in rural areas; and managers have different work-related attitudes than production workers, regardless of the country examined.[5] Therefore, if we compare countries, we must be careful to examine relevant groups. If, for example, a firm is interested in predicting how a group of British scientists and a group of French scientists might work together, it would be more appropriate to see whether there are differences in the two groups' approaches to solving problems rather than whether British and French problem-solving approaches in general are different. The common occupational bond might make scientists in the two countries more similar to each other than to nonscientists within either of the countries.

TYPES OF VARIABLES

There are too many human variables and too many different types of business functions for us to have an exhaustive cause-effect discussion in one chapter. Depending on how we classify physical and behavioral variables and the business activities that they might influence, we can easily arrive at thousands of direct relationships.[6] This chapter concentrates on just a few of the variables that have been found to influence business practices substantially. While within this and subsequent chapters we can describe a few of the effects that these variables may have on the process of management, we must let the reader anticipate the full range of possible adjustments. The latter part of the chapter highlights alternative approaches for determining and dealing with differences that exist in foreign countries as well as the changes that may occur in international firms themselves as they come in contact with new human environments.

PHYSICAL ATTRIBUTES

Variation

Differences in dominant characteristics can influence conduct of business.

Although each country comprises people whose physical attributes vary widely, there are usually some dominant characteristics. The variations are due largely to genetics and become less noticeable as people migrate and intermarry. Even in the absence of mixing with other groups, gene frequency (and thus physical characteristics) may change over a period of time because of natural selection as humans adapt to the changing physical environment. There is also some evidence that the cultural environment, including the social norms and responses, may affect physical attributes, such as infant stress later affecting adult height.[7]

International businesspeople must grasp the sometimes subtle differences that may influence the conduct of business. For example, the susceptibility in a given population to certain diseases may affect the market for pharmaceutical products. But neither the market for automobiles nor the accounting practices of pharmaceutical firms would be affected by this tendency.

Appearance

Businesspeople must consider societies' self-stereotypes.

Appearance is among the most noticeable of human variations. While most differences in appearance are readily apparent, there are a host of subtle variations that may be overlooked by nondiscriminating outsiders. For example, Asians complain that Western films and advertisements frequently depict Orientals' national backgrounds incorrectly. For example, they may identify a Chinese person as a Japanese or a Korean as a Thai.

An individual's size would seem to be an obvious difference. However, one U.S. company unsuccessfully attempted to sell men's slacks in Japan based on U.S. tailoring patterns. Before the company discovered the sizing error, a competitor, who cut clothing to fit the slimmer Japanese customer, had preempted the market. In another case, a U.S. firm had good initial sales for its brassieres in Germany but then witnessed a rapidly declining demand. Initially, the decline was attributed to higher labor costs, which had to be passed on to consumers. Additional research, however, revealed that there were size variations between German and U.S. women. This difference was complicated by the buying behavior of German women who tended not to try on merchandise in the store nor to return it because of discomfort. Instead, they simply did not make repeat purchases. As a result, there was an initial lack of necessary feedback.

Physical differences must be taken into consideration in such business functions as product changes, machinery height, and selection of advertising message. Also, idealized traits have an impact. People often adopt culture-wide stereotypes, largely reflecting wishful thinking. For example, U.S. advertisements typically depict individuals who are younger and thinner than the majority of the people toward whom the product is aimed. In Germany, the tall Nordic type is the ideal, though most Germans are actually no taller than the average Polish or French person.[8]

BEHAVIORAL ATTRIBUTES

Businesspeople agree that cultural differences exist, but disagree on what they are.

Culture consists of specific learned norms based on attitudes, values, and beliefs, which exist in every society. Visitors remark on differences; experts write about them; and people managing affairs across countries find that results cannot be fully explained by economic models.[9] Great controversy surrounds these differences because there is an acknowledged problem of measuring variances.[10] Culture cannot be isolated easily from such factors as economic and political conditions and institutions. An opinion survey, for example, may reflect a short-term response to temporary economic conditions rather than the basic values and beliefs that will have longer-term effects on how business can be managed. Different cultures may share values, but may order them differently if it becomes necessary to trade off the achievement of one for another. This is illustrated by a question posed to groups of Asian and U.S. businessmen: "If you were on a sinking ship with your wife, your child, and your mother who could not swim, which one would you save if you could rescue only one?" In the United States about 60 percent chose the child and about 40 percent the wife, with none choosing the mother. All of the Asians chose the mother.[11] Although this example is outside the realm of business, it illustrates that different nationalities may prioritize objectives differently. Businesspeople must be very tentative about proclaiming existing differences and appropriate reactions.

Despite these problems, considerable research conducted in recent years indicates that some aspects of culture are significantly different across national borders and have a substantial impact on how business is conducted normally in different countries. There recently has been an upsurge in studies comparing business operations in industrial countries, whereas previously most interest was in primitive areas where little international business occurs. One of the common means of research has been the reliance on trained experts, usually cultural anthropologists, to relay their observations of a national character. This method was used extensively during World War II, for example, to predict how the enemy would react to different situations. Another method is to compare carefully paired samples of organizational practices from two or more countries. The following discussion highlights some of the major findings of such research.

Group Affiliations

Affiliations can be
- Ascribed
- Acquired
- A reflection of resources and position

All countries' populations are commonly subdivided into groups, and individuals belong to more than one group. Affiliations determined by birth are known as **ascribed group memberships;** these include differentiations based on sex, family, age, caste, and ethnic, racial, or national origin. Among **acquired group memberships** (those not determined by birth) are religion, political affiliation, and professional and other associations. The type of membership often reflects individuals' place in the social-stratification system (the class or status position) as well. Every society has stratification, such as valuing people in managerial and technical positions more than production workers.

Performance capability is viewed most highly in some societies.

Competence versus Group Affiliation   In some societies, such as in the United States, peoples' acceptance for jobs and promotions is based primarily on performance capabilities. This does not mean, of course, that there is no discrimination against people in the United States because of their sex, race, or religion. However, the belief that competence should prevail is valued sufficiently highly that recent legislative and judicial actions have aimed at instituting that value. This value is far from universal. In many cultures, competence is of secondary importance, and the belief that it is right to place some other criterion ahead of competence is just as strong in those cultures as the belief in competence is in the United States. Whatever factor is given primary importance—be it seniority, gender, or some other factor—will largely influence eligibility for certain positions and compensation.[12]

Egalitarian societies place less importance on ascribed group membership.

The more egalitarian, or open, a society is, the less difference ascribed group membership will make in access to rewards. Sometimes membership rigidity actually extends to legal proscriptions. In South Africa, for example, blacks, whites, and coloureds still are eligible only for certain jobs, in spite of recent progress in dismantling apartheid laws. In other cases, memberships prevent large groups of people from getting the preparation that would equally qualify them. In countries with poor public education systems, elite groups send their children to private schools while other children receive inferior public education.

Country-by-country atti-
tudes vary toward
● Male versus female
  roles
● Importance of youth
  versus older age
● Family versus nonfam-
  ily ties

Importance of Different Group Memberships   Although there are count-
less ways of defining group memberships, three of the most significant ways
are in terms of gender, age, and family. An international comparison reveals
how widespread the differences are and how important they are to business
considerations.

Gender-based Groups

There are strong country-specific differences in attitudes toward males and
females. The Chinese show an extreme degree of male preference. Because
of governmental restrictions on family size and the desire to have a son to
carry on the family name, the practices of aborting female fetuses and killing
female babies are widespread.[13]

Recall the case at the beginning of this chapter and the fact that the female editor for PRI could not get permission to enter Saudi Arabia. Saudi
Arabians exhibit an extreme example of behavioral rigidity related to gender.
Separation is maintained at even a greater level than in most other Islamic
countries. Schools are separate as is most social life. Only about 10 percent
of women work outside the home, and when they do, they remain separate
from men. Women are legally prohibited from driving cars and are socially
restricted from riding in a taxi without a male relative. Most of the jobs for
women are in professions with little or no male contact, such as teaching or
providing medical treatment to other women. When women do work in integrated organizations, the Saudis put partitions between them and male employees.

Even among countries in which women constitute a large portion of the
working population, there are vast differences in the types of jobs regarded
as "male" or "female." In Uruguay, over 40 percent of administrative and
managerial positions are filled by women, compared to less than 5 percent in
Spain.[14]

Culturally mandated male and female behaviors may carry over to other
aspects of the work situation as well. For example, Molex, a U.S. manufacturer of connectors, which has a manufacturing facility in Japan, invited its
Japanese workers and their spouses to a company dinner one evening. Neither wives nor female employees appeared. To comply with Japanese standards, the company now has a "family day," which the women feel
comfortable attending.[15]

Age-based Groups

Age involves some curious variations. Many cultures assume that age and
wisdom are correlated, and these countries usually have a seniority-based
system of advancement. Until the 1980s in the United States, retirement at

age 60 or 65 was mandatory in most companies, and relative youthfulness has been a professional advantage. This esteem for youthfulness does not, however, carry over to the U.S. political realm, where there are relatively high minimum-age requirements for many posts as well as no mandatory retirement age.

Family-based Groups

In some societies, especially Mediterranean and Latin American countries, the family constitutes the most important group membership. An individual is accepted largely on the basis of the social status or respectability of his or her family rather than on the basis of individual achievement. Because family ties are so strong, there also may be a compulsion to cooperate closely within the family unit but to be distrustful of links involving others. Within Greek businesses, for example, workers in family restaurants cooperate and mobilize their efforts to attain success much more effectively than workers in large organizations where people are from many different families.[16]

Barriers to employment on the basis of age or sex are undergoing substantial changes in many parts of the world. Thus statistical and attitudinal studies even a few years old may be unreliable. One of the changes has involved the growing number of women and men in the United States employed in occupations previously dominated by the other sex. During the 1980s, for example, the proportion of male secretaries, telephone operators, and nurses rose substantially, as did the proportion of female architects, bartenders, and bus drivers. During the same period in Japan the percentage of females working increased about 10 percent, whereas the number of women in management positions more than doubled.[17]

Local attitudes may force hiring by local norms or opinions.

Some Effects on International Business Hiring Practices   Even if individuals have the qualifications for a certain position and there are no legal barriers to hiring them, social obstacles may prevent them from being hired. Other workers, customers, local shareholders, or governmental officials may oppose certain groups, making it even more difficult for them to succeed.

Class structures may be so rigid within one type of group that they are difficult to overcome in other contexts. One U.S. firm set up a plant in Taiwan without realizing the strength of the class structure, which is built largely on the military hierarchy. The U.S. managers hired the person they considered most qualified to head the organization. In practice, however, this individual consistently deferred to a subordinate who had outranked him during their military experience. In many African countries the tribal relationship is still very important. To attract workers in some rural areas, it may be necessary to get permission from tribal chiefs by compensating them.

Importance of Work

In industrial countries most people work long after they have satisfied basic necessities.

There are different motives for work in different places.

People work for a number of reasons. Most people in industrial societies could satisfy their basic needs for food, clothing, and shelter by working fewer hours than they do. What motivates them to work more? The reasons for working and the relative importance of work among human activities may be explained largely by the interrelationship of the cultural and economic environment of the country in which one lives. The differences in motivation help to explain management styles, product demand, and levels of economic development.

Attitudes toward work may change as economic gains are achieved.

Protestant Ethic   Max Weber, a German sociologist, observed near the turn of the century that the predominantly Protestant countries were the most economically developed. Weber attributed this fact to the attitude toward work held by most of the inhabitants of those countries, an attitude he labeled the **Protestant ethic.** According to Weber, the Protestant ethic was an outgrowth of the Reformation, when work was viewed as a means of salvation. Adhering to this belief, people preferred to transform productivity gains into additional output rather than into additional leisure.[18] Although few societies today retain this strict concept of work for work's sake, leisure is valued more highly in some societies than in others. On average, the Japanese take less leisure than people in any other industrial country, due largely to high commitments to their employers.[19] In the United States, another country where incomes probably allow for considerably more leisure than most people take, there is still much disdain, on the one hand, for the millionaire playboy who contributes nothing to society and, on the other hand, for the person who lives on welfare. People who are forced to give up work, such as retirees, complain strongly of their inability to do anything "useful." This view may be contrasted with those that predominate in some other societies, such as rural India, where living a simple life with minimum material achievements is still considered a desirable end in itself.

In industrial countries today, and in most of the rapidly developing countries as well, personal economic achievement is considered commendable. Some observers note that many economies, in contrast, are characterized by limited economic needs that are an outgrowth of the culture. If incomes start to rise, workers in these economies tend to reduce their efforts, and thus personal income remains unchanged.[20] Other observers, however, have argued that this may be a very short-lived phenomenon, and that expectations rise slowly on the basis of past economic achievement. Most of us believe we would be happy with just "a little bit more"—until we have that "little bit more," which then turns out to be not quite enough.

People are more eager to work if
• Rewards for success are high

Belief in Success and Reward   One factor that influences people's attitude toward working is the perceived likelihood of success and reward. The concepts of success and reward are closely related. Generally people have little

- There is some uncertainty of success

enthusiasm for efforts that seem too easy or too difficult, in other words, where the probability of success or failure seems almost certain. For instance, few of us are eager to run a foot race against either a snail or a race horse because the outcome in either case is too certain. Our highest enthusiasm occurs when the uncertainty is high—in this instance, probably when racing another human of roughly equal ability. The reward for successfully completing an effort, such as winning our imaginary foot races, may be high or low as well. People will usually work harder at any task when the reward from success is high compared with the reward from failure.

The same tasks performed in different countries will have different probabilities of success and different rewards associated with success and failure. In cultures where the probability of failure is almost certain *and* where the perceived rewards of success are low, there is a tendency to view work as a necessary evil. This attitude may exist in harsh climates, in very poor areas, or in subcultures that are the object of discrimination. At the other extreme, there is also little enthusiasm for the work itself in areas such as Scandinavia, where the tax structures and public policies redistribute income from high earners to low earners. There, the probability of success is high and rewards tend to be high and similar regardless of how hard one works. The greatest enthusiasm for work exists where high uncertainty of success is combined with the likelihood of a very positive reward for success but not for failure.[21]

Work ethic is related to habit.

Work as a Habit   Another factor in the trade-off between work and leisure is that the pursuit of leisure activities may itself have to be learned. After a long period of sustained work, people may have problems deciding what to do with free time. This insight helps to explain the continued drive for greater achievement seen in some societies that already have considerable material achievements. One study that attempted to determine why some areas of Latin America developed a higher economic level and desire for material achievement than others attributed differences to the fact that some Spanish settlers worked themselves rather than using slave or near-slave labor. In such areas as Antioquia in Colombia, the Spanish settlers who labored themselves developed a work ethic and became the industrial leaders of the country.[22] Clearly, when comparing the importance of work from one country to another, the effects of habit cannot be overlooked. An international firm may thus find it easier in some societies than in others to motivate its work force with shorter work weeks or longer vacation periods.

High-need achievers want
- Personal responsibility
- To take calculated risks
- Performance feedback

Lower-need achievers prefer smooth social relationships.

High-need Achievement   The **high-need achiever** is a person who will work very hard to achieve material or career success, sometimes to the detriment of developing smooth social relationships or spiritual achievements.[23] Three attributes distinguish high-need achievers:

1. They like situations that involve personal responsibility for finding solutions to problems.

2. They set moderate achievement goals for taking calculated risks.

3. They want concrete feedback on performance.

The average manager's interest in material or career success varies substantially from one country to another, which explains situations in which the local manager reacts in ways that the international firm may neither expect nor wish. For instance, a purchasing manager with a high affiliation need may be much more concerned with developing an amiable and continuing relationship with suppliers than in reducing costs and speeding delivery. Or in some countries the local managers may place such organizational goals as employee and social welfare ahead of the foreign firm's priorities for growth and efficiency.

Need Hierarchy   Maslow's **hierarchy of needs** is a well-known motivation theory,[24] which is shown schematically in Fig. 3.1. According to Maslow, people try to fulfill lower-order needs sufficiently before moving on to higher ones. People will work to satisfy a need, but once it is fulfilled it is no longer a motivator. This fulfillment is not an all-or-nothing situation, but because lower-order needs are more important, they must be nearly fulfilled before triggering a higher-order need to be an effective motivator. For instance, the most basic needs are physiological, including food, water, and sex. These

Figure 3.1
Need-Hierarchy Comparisons
The hierarchy on the right illustrates a wider social bar (3) and a narrower self-actualization bar (5) than the one on the left. Workers represented by the hierarchy on the right require more social needs to be fulfilled before triggering a self-esteem need (4) as a motivator. These workers would be less motivated by self-actualization than those workers represented by the hierarchy on the left.

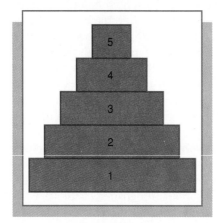

Maslow's needs

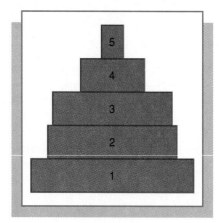

Large, social, and small
self-actualization needs

needs may have to be nearly satisfied (say, 85 percent satisfied), before triggering a safety need. The safety need, centering around a secure physical and emotional environment, may have to be only 70 percent satisfied before triggering the social need (acceptance by peers and friends). After the social need is sufficiently satisfied, a person may be motivated by an esteem need, the self-image from receipt of recognition, attention, and appreciation for one's contributions. The highest order need, self-actualization, refers to self-fulfillment or becoming all that is possible for one to become. The relative fulfillment requirements are shown by the horizontal bars in Fig. 3.1.

The ranking of needs differs from country to country.

Maslow's theory is helpful for differentiating the reward preferences of employees in different countries. In very poor countries, most workers may be so deprived that a firm can motivate them simply by providing enough food and shelter. Elsewhere, other needs will have to be addressed to motivate workers. Observers have noted that people from different countries attach different importance to various needs and even rank differently some of the higher-order needs. One of the most extensive studies compared countries on what was called a masculinity-femininity dimension and found that employees in the Netherlands and the Scandinavian countries placed more importance on social needs and less on self-actualization than did employees in such countries as the United States, Austria, and Switzerland. In other words, in Scandinavia and the Netherlands group-centered motivation methods may have a more positive impact on employees than individual job-enrichment methods, which are strong motivations in the United States. Evidence that national differences exist among needs is also exhibited through tests on individualism and uncertainty avoidance.[25]

Importance of Occupation

The perception of "best" jobs varies somewhat by country.

In every society, certain occupations are perceived to bring greater economic, social, or prestige rewards than others. This perception will determine to a great extent the numbers and qualifications of people who will seek employment in a given occupation as individuals compete for high-reward jobs. Although overall patterns are universal (e.g., professionals are ranked ahead of street cleaners), there are some indications of national differences. For instance, physicians tend to be ranked higher than university professors in the United States, probably because of the importance people in the United States attach to financial rewards. The rank is reversed in Japan, probably because of the importance the Japanese attach to education and clean occupations.[26] The reluctance of educated people to dirty their hands or associate directly with operative workers has sometimes made it difficult to find lower-level managers in Latin America. To generalize, in the Latin American culture there are a class of leisure, a class of people who work with their minds, and a third class of people who work with their hands.[27] The importance of business as a profession is also predictive of the degree of difficulty that an international firm may have in hiring qualified managers. In many countries, people with the desired educational qualifications prefer to work in governmental posts rather than in business. Therefore, the international firm in such a situation may have to undertake more training programs because it must hire relatively uneducated people.

Another international difference involves the desire to work for an organization as opposed to being one's own boss. For example, the Belgians and the French, more than most people of other nationalities, prefer, if possible, to go into business for themselves, and thus Belgium and France have more retail establishments per capita than most other countries. Psychological studies also show that French and Belgian workers place a greater importance on personal independence from the organizations employing them than do workers in many other countries.[28]

Jobs with low prestige usually go to people whose skills are in low demand. In the United States, for example, such occupations as babysitting, delivering newspapers, and carrying groceries traditionally have been done largely by teenagers, who grow out of the jobs through additional age and training. In most less-developed countries these are not transient occupations; rather, they are filled by adults who have very little opportunity to move on to more rewarding positions. (In the United States, as well, there is rising concern that low-paying menial jobs are becoming more permanent, thus perpetuating income disparities.)

Self-Reliance

There are national varia-
tions in the preference for
autocratic versus participatory leadership and in
attitudes of self-determination versus fatalism.

Superior-Subordinate Relationships   In some countries an autocratic style of management is preferred; in others a consultative style prevails. Studies on what is known as power-distance show that in Austria, Israel, New Zealand, and the Scandinavian countries the consultative style is strongly preferred, but in Malaysia, Mexico, Panama, Guatemala, and Venezuela the autocratic style is favored. There is a significant correlation between national preferences for autocratic leadership and the incidence of autocratic political leadership.[29] Clearly, it may be easier for organizations to initiate worker-participation methods in some countries than in others.

Trust   Although trust is difficult to measure, various studies indicate that national groups differ in the degree to which individuals trust others.[30] The greater the people's trust, the greater their eagerness and ability to establish rapport with others. Where trust is high, both managers and subordinates prefer participative to authoritative decision making; they actually tend to function this way. Certainly one of the factors leading to acceptance of new products, as in the United States, is the individuals' trust that they will not be cheated by the manufacturer and that they will be protected by the legal system. Acceptance in dealing with a new firm may be similar. People of some nationalities have high levels of trust and get right to the point in a business discussion. Conversely, people of other nationalities may spend more time in preliminary discussion before getting down to business. This difference, although partially a consequence of cultural formalities, is also affected by the need some groups have to seek more cues before deciding whether to trust others in a business relationship. In some parts of the world nearly all transactions among individuals are carried out by cash rather than check as an assurance of payment. In this type of environment, it is difficult to raise funds through the sale of company shares, since people prefer to place their funds in visible assets they can control themselves.

Degree of Fatalism   If people believe strongly in self-determination they may be willing to work hard to achieve goals and to take responsibility for performance. A belief in fatalism, on the other hand, may prevent people from accepting a basic cause-effect relationship. Religious differences play a part: Conservative Christian, Buddhist, Hindu, and Moslem societies tend to view occurrences as "the will of God." In Pakistan, chemistry texts must say "$H_2 + O$, by the grace of God, $=$ water."[31] In such an atmosphere it is difficult to persuade personnel to plan ahead. Even getting workers to cooperate in accident or damage prevention—by checking tire pressure, for example—may be hard. Studies show that there are national differences even among managers in fairly developed societies.[32]

Individual versus Group   In many countries people respect personal achievement; in fact, they compete openly with each other within the work place in order to gain a greater share of compensation or prestige rewards. With this in mind, at a meeting of his professional staff in Japan, a U.S. design engineer singled out an individual to credit him for his performance on a project. Rather than motivating the employee or others to perform well, the individual praise created embarrassment for people at the meeting. In Japan, collective effort is valued and the Japanese are reluctant to single out individuals.[33]

We have already noted that the degree of importance of the family unit as a group varies from one society to another. There are also differences in what is conceived to constitute a family. In some countries, the typical household includes only the nuclear family (a husband, wife, and minor children). For most people in the world, however, the same household may contain a vertically extended family (several generations) and/or a horizontally extended one (aunts, uncles, and cousins). This difference has a number of effects on business. First, material rewards from an individual's work may be less motivating in such societies, because these rewards are divided among more people. Second, geographic mobility is reduced, because with relocation more people in a family would have to find new jobs. Purchasing decisions may be more complicated because of the interrelated roles of family members. Even where the extended family does not live together, mobility may be reduced because people prefer to remain near relatives. Security and social needs also may be met more extensively at home rather than in the work place.

Communications

All languages are complex and reflective of environment.

A common language within countries is a unifying force.

Language   Linguists have found that even very primitive societies have complex languages that reflect the environment in which people live. Because of varying environments, it is often difficult to translate directly from one language to another. For example, people living in the temperate zone of the Northern Hemisphere customarily use the term *summer* to refer to the months of June, July, and August, whereas people in tropical zones may use the term to denote their dry season, which varies substantially in time of year from one country to another. Some concepts simply do not translate. For instance, in Spanish there is no word to refer to everyone who works in a business organization. Instead, there is one word, *empleados,* which refers to white-collar workers, and another word, *obreros,* which refers to laborers. This distinction reflects the substantial class difference between the groups. Another interesting difference between English and Spanish, which undoubtedly reflects attitudes, is that a clock "runs" in English but "walks" in Spanish.

Languages such as English, French, and Spanish have such widespread acceptance (they are spoken prevalently in 44, 27, and 20 countries, respectively) that native speakers are generally not very motivated to learn other languages. (See the Languages map in the full-color map section of this book.) Commerce and other cross-border associations can be conducted easily with other nations that have the same official language. When a second language is studied, it is usually chosen because it will be useful in dealing with other countries. English and French have traditionally been chosen because of commercial links developed during colonial periods. France has recently begun subsidizing French language training in Eastern Europe and the former Soviet Union because of the possible advantage to its commerce.[34] In countries that do not share a common language with other countries (e.g., Finland and Greece) there is a much greater need to study a second or multiple languages in order to function internationally. But English, especially American English, is being added to languages worldwide. Some 20,000 English words have entered the Japanese language; the Russian word for tight denim pants is *dzhinsi* (pronounced "jeansy"); the French call a self-service restaurant *le self;* and Lithuanians go to the theater to see *moving pikceris.*[35]

Even within the same language there may be substantial differences. The terms *corn, maize,* and *graduate studies* in the United Kingdom, correspond to *wheat, corn,* and *undergraduate studies,* respectively, in the United States. They are among the approximately 4000 words used differently between the two countries. Although the wrong choice of words is usually just a source of brief embarrassment, a poor translation may have tragic consequences. Inaccurate translations have been blamed for structure collapses at construction sites in the Middle East.[36] In contracts, correspondence, negotiations, advertisements, and social gatherings, words must be chosen carefully.

Language also may reflect the internal cohesion of a country. In some countries, such as Japan and Portugal, almost everyone speaks the same native language. In about half the countries of the world, however, different groups speak different languages, and the groups may be very difficult to unify. In some cases, the official language of the country is actually spoken by only a minority of the inhabitants. This is true in India and Zaire, where, nevertheless, the most power has accrued to those few people who speak the official language.[37]

Silent language includes such things as color, distance, time, and status cues.

Silent Language   Of course, formal language is not our only means of communication. We all exchange messages by a host of nonverbal cues, and these cues form a **silent language.**[38] Colors, for example, conjure up meanings that are based on cultural experience. In most Western countries black is associated with death, yet white in parts of the Far East and purple in Latin America have the same connotation. To be successful, the color of products and their advertisements must match the consumers' frame of reference.

Another example of silent language is distance between people during conversation. Our sense of appropriate distance is learned, and it differs from one society to another. In the United States, for example, the customary distance for a business discussion is five to eight feet; for personal business it is eighteen inches to three feet.[39] When the distance is closer or greater than is customary, we tend to feel very uneasy. A U.S. manager conducting business discussions in Latin America may constantly be moving backward to avoid the closer conversational distance to which the Latin American official is accustomed. At the conclusion of the session, each party may feel an unexplainable distrust of the other.

Punctuality is another area in which cultural differences may create confusion. In the United States, participants usually arrive early for a business appointment. For a dinner at someone's home, guests arrive on time or a few minutes late, and for a cocktail party, they may arrive a bit later. In a foreign country, the concept of punctuality may be radically different. A U.S. businessperson in Latin America, for example, may consider it discourteous if the Latin American manager does not keep to the appointed time. Latin Americans may find it equally discourteous if the U.S. businessperson arrives for dinner at the invited time.

Cues concerning a person's relative position may be particularly difficult to grasp. A U.S. businessperson, who tends to place a greater reliance on objects as prestige cues, may underestimate the importance of a foreign counterpart who does not have a large private office with a wood desk and carpeting. A foreigner may react similarly if U.S. counterparts open their own garage doors and mix their own drinks.

Body language (the way in which people move their bodies, touch, and walk) differs from country to country. Few gestures are universal in meaning. For example, the "yes" of a Greek, Turk, or Bulgarian is indicated by a sideways movement of the head that resembles the negative shake used in the United States and elsewhere in Europe. In some cases, one gesture may have several meanings. For instance, the joining of the index finger and thumb to form an "O" means O.K. in the United States, money in Japan, and "I will kill you" in Tunisia.[40]

Cues are perceived selectively and differ among societies.

Perception and Processing   We perceive cues (features indicating the nature of things) selectively. We may identify by means of any of our senses (sight, smell, touch, sound, and taste) and in various ways within each sense. For example, through vision we can sense color, depth, and shape. The cues that we use to perceive things differ from one society to another. The reason is partly physiological—for example, genetic differences in eye pigmentation enable some groups to differentiate colors more finely than others—and partly cultural—for example, a relative richness of vocabulary can cause people to notice very subtle differences in color.[41] Differences in vocabulary reflect cultural differences: There are more than 6000 different words in Arabic for camels, their body parts, and the equipment associated with camels.[42]

Regardless of societal differences, once people perceive cues, they process them. Information processing is universal in that all societies categorize, plan, and quantify. In terms of categorization, we bring objects together according to their major shared function. Something to sit upon is thus called a chair in English, whether it is large or small, made of wood or plastic, upholstered or not. The languages of all societies have future and conditional tenses; thus all societies plan. All societies have numbering systems as well. But the specific ways in which societies go about grouping things, dealing with the future, and counting differ substantially.[43] For example, in United States telephone directories, the entries are organized by last (family) names, whereas in Iceland they are organized by first (given) names. Icelandic last names are derived from the father's first names; thus Jon, the son of Thor, is Jon Thorson, and his sister's last name is Thorssdottir (daughter of Thor).[44]

Idealists settle principles first.

Pragmatists
- Settle small issues first
- Want specific measurable achievements

Evaluation of Information   In spite of vast differences within countries, there are national norms that govern the degree to which people will try to resolve principles before they try to resolve small issues or vice versa. In other words, people will tend toward either **idealism** or **pragmatism.** From a business standpoint, the differences manifest themselves in a number of ways. The idealist sees the pragmatist as being too interested in trivial details, whereas the pragmatist considers the idealist too theoretical. Labor, in a society of pragmatists, tends to focus on very specific issues, such as a pay increase of one dollar per hour. In a society of idealists, labor tends to make less precise demands and to depend on mass action, such as general strikes or support of a particular political party, to demonstrate its principles.[45]

Ethics and Etiquette

There is no universally accepted moral behavior.

Behavior that is considered normal in our native culture may be unacceptable in another society. Practices that are accepted in one place may be considered immoral in another. An advertisement showing a man and woman in close contact is acceptable in a Western country but must be changed in many Asian countries to fit a moral context in which even holding hands in public is taboo. U.S. motion picture exports illustrate different moral conceptions based on different attitudes toward punishment for crimes, body exposure, sexual explicitness, and violence.

Questions of etiquette surround the practice of gift giving. If a Western businessperson visiting a counterpart in the Far East fails to bring a small but thoughtful gift, that official not only may consider it a breach of etiquette, but also may conclude that the foreign businessperson is not very interested in the meeting. Likewise, some foreign managers, unaware that invitations into private homes are not customary, may similarly feel injured when an invitation is not forthcoming.

In many places it is customary to make payments to governmental officials in order to obtain their services or to obtain governmental contracts. While these payments are not part of coded regulations and may even be condemned officially, they are so well embedded in local custom and precedent that they nearly have the prescribed enforcement of common law. In Mexico, for example, it is common for companies to give tips once a month to the postman. Otherwise, the mail simply gets lost.[46] The going rate of payment is rather easily ascertained and is usually graduated on the basis of ability to pay. It is a fairly efficient means of taxation in countries that pay civil servants poorly and do not have the means of effectively collecting income taxes. Still, many of these payments are considered bribes and are frequently viewed by home country constituents as so unethical that home country laws are enforced against practices in foreign operations.

There are so many behavioral rules that businesspeople cannot expect to memorize all of them for every country where business relations might occur. Wide variations exist even in form of address, and it is difficult to know whether to use the given or the surname, which of several surnames to use, and whether a wife takes the husband's name.[47] Fortunately, though, there are up-to-date guide books that have been compiled geographically based on the experience of many successful international managers.[48] Furthermore, one may consult with knowledgeable people at home and abroad, from governmental offices or in the private sector.

RECONCILIATION OF INTERNATIONAL DIFFERENCES

Cultural Awareness

Problem areas in cultural awareness are
● Things learned subconsciously
● Stereotypes
● Societal subgroups

Where cultural differences exist, businesspeople must decide whether and to what extent they should adapt home-country practices to the foreign environment. But before making that decision, managers must be aware of what the differences are. As we discussed early in the chapter, this is not an easy task. There is much disagreement about the differences, and no foolproof method exists for building greater cultural awareness.

In any situation, some people are more prone to say the right thing at the right time while others unintentionally offend. Most people are more aware of differences in things that they have learned consciously, such as table manners, than in things that they have learned subconsciously, such as methods of approaching problem solving. Nevertheless, there is general agreement that awareness and sensitivity can be improved. In this chapter we have presented a framework of human cultural factors that have been noted to require special business adjustments on a country-to-country basis. By paying special attention to these factors, businesspeople can start building awareness.

Reading about and discussing other countries and researching how people from other countries regard the home culture can be very instructive. The opinions presented must be measured carefully. Very often they represent unwarranted stereotypes, an accurate assessment of only a subsegment of the particular country, or a situation that has since undergone change. By getting varied viewpoints, businesspeople can judge assessments of different cultures better. One may observe the behavior of those people who are well accepted or those with whom one would like to be associated in a given society in order to emulate their behavior.

The person who moves to a foreign country frequently encounters **culture shock,** "a generalized trauma one experiences in a new and different culture because of having to learn and cope with a vast array of new cultural cues and expectations, while discovering that your old ones probably do not fit or work."[49] People working in a very different culture may pass through stages. First, like tourists, they are elated with "quaint" differences. Later, they may feel frustration, depression, and confusion—the culture shock phase—and their usefulness in a foreign assignment may be greatly impaired. Fortunately, most people's culture shock begins to ebb after a month or two as optimism and satisfaction improve.[50]

Grouping Countries

Some countries are more similar to one another than they are to other countries, usually because they share many attributes that help mold their cultures, such as language, religion, geographic location, ethnicity, and level of

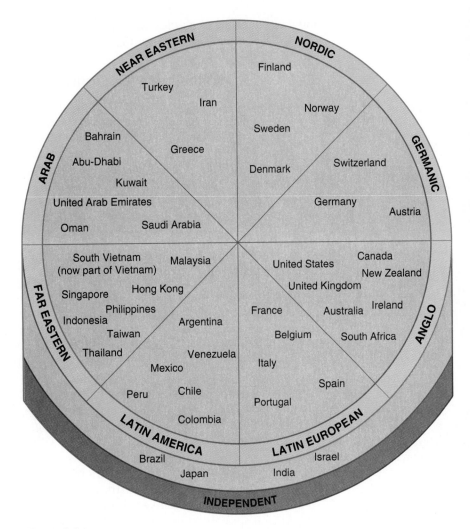

Figure 3.2
A Synthesis of Country Clusters
Not all countries have been studied extensively in terms of common attitudinal variables that may affect the efficient conduct of business differently from one country to another. However, it has been noted that, of the countries that have been studied, some can be grouped because of having attitudes that closely resemble each other. *Source:* Simcha Ronen and Oded Shenkar, "Clustering Countries on Attitudinal Dimensions: A Review and Synthesis," *Academy of Management Review,* Vol. 10, No. 3, 1985, p. 449.

economic development. Figure 3.2 groups countries on the basis of attitudes and values from a large number of cross-cultural studies. One should expect fewer nuances when moving within a cluster than when moving from one cluster to another, such as a Peruvian versus a Thai company doing business in Colombia.[51] Such clusters must be used with caution, however. They deal only with overall similarities and differences among countries, and one may easily be misled when considering specific business practices to use abroad.

Fitting Needs to the Company Position

Not all companies need to have the same degree of foreign cultural awareness. Nor must a particular company have a consistent degree of awareness during the course of its operations. Since companies usually increase foreign operations over a period of time, they may expand their knowledge of cultural factors in tandem with their expansion of foreign operations. (Refer to Fig. 3.3 for an illustration of relative needs.) The further a firm moves from domestic operations on any one of the four axes shown, the more effort needs to be placed on building awareness of cultural differences. Ordinarily, there is no need for a company to tackle multiple functional adjustments in multiple dissimilar countries simultaneously.

On Axis A in Fig. 3.3, foreign operations near the center are focused on achieving a limited functional objective. For example, in a purely market-seeking operation, such as exporting from the home country, the company must be aware of cultural factors that may influence the marketing program. Consider advertising, which may be affected by the real and wishful physical norms of the target market, the roles of group membership in terms of status and buying decisions, and the perception of different words and images. A company undertaking a purely resource-seeking international activity can ignore the effects of cultural variables on advertising, but must consider factors that may influence supply, such as methods of managing a foreign labor force. With multifunctional activities, such as producing and selling a product in a foreign country, the added functions warrant concern with a wider array of cultural relationships. At the far extreme are operations that are integrated across various countries. In these situations, a firm must consider the cultural differences between its home country and a foreign country, and the distinctions among the various foreign countries involved.

Axis B shows that the more countries in which a firm is doing business, the more cultural nuances it must consider. Think of the adjustments a manager from corporate headquarters who visits the company's foreign distributors would undergo. The more countries visited, the more cumbersome the trip would be and the more predeparture training time would be needed.

The relationship between the similarity between countries and the relative need for cultural adjustment is shown on Axis C. For example, a U.S. firm starting business in Australia will find greater similarity to its cultural experiences than if it were starting a new business in Japan.

A company may handle foreign operations on its own or it may contract another firm to handle them, as shown on Axis D. The risk of making operating mistakes because of misunderstanding may be effectively reduced if operations are turned over to another firm. If the firm contracts with another domestic firm experienced in the foreign country, it can avoid direct dealings

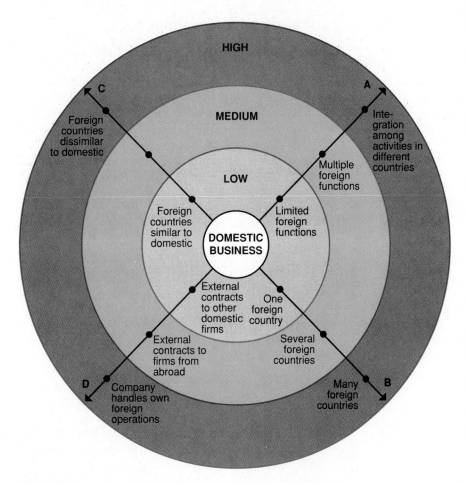

Figure 3.3
Cultural Awareness Needs Related to Foreign Operations
The farther out a company moves from the center of the axis along any of the
dimensions (A, B, C, or D), the more it needs to understand cultural differences.
When moving outward on more than one dimension (especially on all four), the
need for cultural awareness becomes even more pronounced.

with the foreign environment. If the business is contracted to a foreign firm,
then the company must understand the cultural nuances that may influence
the relationship between the two companies, such as the means of negotiating an agreement or the ordering of objectives for the operation. As a company gains experience in the foreign country, its managers normally learn to
operate efficiently there and may then consider internalizing activities that
had previously been contracted to another firm.

Dangers of Polycentrism

Polycentrists are overwhelmed by national differences and risk not introducing workable changes.

In organizations characterized by **polycentrism** control is decentralized so that "our man in Rio" is free to conduct business in what he thinks is "the Brazilian way." Taken to the extreme, a polycentric individual or organization is "overwhelmed by the differences, real and imaginary, great and small, between its many operating environments."[52] Since most discussions of foreign business focus on uniquenesses encountered abroad and the attendant problems that the firms have experienced, it is understandable that many managers would develop a polycentric view. This is, however, an overly cautious response. In reality, it is uncertain whether companies' practices abroad are any more prone to failure than those at home.

If a company's views are too polycentric, the company may shy away from certain areas or may avoid transferring intact home-country practices or resources that may, in fact, work well abroad. For example, American Express assembled its worldwide personnel managers for an exchange of views. The complaints from the overseas managers centered on certain corporate directives that they claimed did not fit "their" country. The impression was created that foreign operations were so unique that each overseas office should develop its own procedures independently. Further talks, however, revealed that the complaints really were focused on one particular personnel-evaluation form. If the company were to delegate the proposed control, as these overseas managers were suggesting, it would risk not introducing some of its other standard forms and procedures abroad. Furthermore, it would risk duplication of efforts, which might have been more costly than trying to administer the ill-suited evaluation directives. The additional discussions also generated comments for the first time from the personnel managers in U.S. domestic offices who had received the same corporate instructions. They indicated that they had as many problems with the personnel form as their foreign counterparts had. Thus the problem, originally attributed to environmental differences, was seen to be universal.

If an international firm is to compete effectively with local firms, it must usually perform some functions in a distinct way. Polycentrism, however, may lead to such extensive delegation or to such extensive imitation of proven host-country practices that innovative superiority is lost. Furthermore, control may be diminished as operations for each country move separately in order to foster local rather than worldwide objectives.

Dangers of Ethnocentrism

Ethnocentrists overlook national differences and
• Ignore important variables
• Think change is easily introduced

Enthnocentrism is the belief that one's own group is superior to others. The term is used in international business to describe the firm or individual who is so imbued with the belief that what worked at home should work abroad that environmental differences are ignored. Ethnocentrism may fall into three categories. In the first category, important variables are overlooked because a

- Believe home-country objectives should prevail

manager has become so accustomed to certain cause-effect relationships in the home country that differences abroad are ignored. To combat this type of ethnocentrism, managers can refer to checklists of human variables in order to assure themselves that all the major factors are at least considered. In cases of the second type, a firm recognizes both the environmental differences and the problems of change but is focused on achieving home-country rather than foreign or worldwide objectives. This type of operation may result in diminished long-term competitive viability because (1) the company does not perform as well as competitors, and (2) it develops opposition to its practices. In cases of the third type of ethnocentrism, managers recognize differences but assume that the introduction of changes is both necessary and easily achieved. The problems accompanying this type of attitude will be discussed in the next section.

Change Agent or Changed Agent?

International firms often follow hybrids of home and foreign norms.

Between the extremes of polycentrism and ethnocentrism are hybrid business practices that are not exactly like the international company's home operations and not exactly like those of the typical host-country firm. These hybrids are the most common means of reconciling differences. When the host-country environment is substantially different, the international firm must decide whether to get people in the host country to accept something new (in which case the firm will be acting as a change agent), or to make changes in the firm itself.

Managers must expect to find their own value system challenged.

Value System   It is much easier to adapt to things that do not challenge our value system than to things that do. We can usually be flexible about whether we eat our salad before or after the main course, but we would probably think twice before exposing more of our bodies or paying bribes to government officials, actions that would require some moral adjustment if we do not do these things in our own country.

The more a change upsets important values, the more resistance the firm will experience.

A Spanish textile factory opened in a community of Guatemala and tried to install training methods, work hours, and a host of other production "improvements" commonplace in more developed areas. Not only did people refuse to work, but soldiers had to protect the factory from the community. The management retracted and gave in on those things that were most important to the potential workers. These included a four-hour period between shifts so that male workers could attend to agricultural duties and female workers could do household chores and nurse their infants. The laborers were willing to work Saturday afternoons in order to compensate for production lost during shift breaks.[53] The important lesson of this is that the more a change disrupts basic values, the more the people affected will resist it. When changes do not interfere with deep-seated customs, accommodation is much more likely. By giving in on matters that were most important to the workers, the foreign firm was able to secure an effective and committed work force.

Fortunately, neither international firms nor their representatives are always expected to adhere to the national norm by people in the host society. For example, many practices that are considered "wrong" in Western culture are either customary elsewhere or only recently abolished and liable to be reinstated. These practices include chattel slavery, polygamy, concubinage, child marriage, and the burning of widows.[54] Although foreigners are not expected to participate in these practices, the exposure may be so traumatic to them that the foreigners cannot perform their duties efficiently.

The Society for Applied Anthropology, whose members advise agencies on instituting change in different cultures, has adopted a code of ethics to protect foreign cultures with which they come into contact. Among the considerations is whether a project of planned change will actually benefit the target population. This respect of other cultures is itself a Western cultural phenomenon that goes back at least as far as St. Ambrose's fourth-century advice, "When in Rome, do as the Romans do." Elsewhere there has been no such compulsion to adjust. Because the definition of what is a benefit depends itself on cultural value systems, this code is a challenge to implement.

Cost-Benefit of Change   A firm must consider its sometimes conflicting objectives of cost minimization and sales maximization along with its resources. We have noted, for example, that international firms tend to introduce the same or only slightly altered products into foreign markets instead of designing products that would be best suited for maximum acceptance in those markets. This may be the right decision, even though it is costly to convince people to buy "the next best thing" and even though sales are not maximized. The cost of designing and producing a new product may raise the price of the "best thing" too much, and the firm may lack the resources to make large-scale product changes.

The cost of making change may exceed the benefit gained.

Resistance to Too Much Change   When Sears, Roebuck decided to open its first retail store in Spain, a main problem arose with suppliers. Sears tried to deal with its Spanish suppliers in much the same way as it deals with U.S. suppliers. Among the many new policies that Sears tried to introduce immediately were payments by check, firm delivery dates, standard sizes, no manufacturer's labels, and larger orders. Suppliers balked or continued to do things their old way, claiming forgetfulness.[55] Acceptance by suppliers may have been easier to obtain if Sears had made fewer demands at one time, phasing in its other policies over a period of time.

Resistance to change may be lower if the number of changes is not too great.

Participation   One way of avoiding undue problems if changes are to be introduced is by promoting participation. By discussing in advance the possibility of change, the firm may ascertain how strong resistance might be, stimulate the recognition of a need for improvement, and temper fears of adverse consequences among individuals who might otherwise feel that they have no say in their own destinies. Managers sometimes think that delegation

People are more willing to implement change when they are involved in the decision.

and participation are unique to highly developed countries in which people have educational backgrounds that enable them to make substantial contributions. Experience with economic development programs, however, indicates that participation in even the most undeveloped communities of the world may be extremely important. Two of the most successful development programs on record are the Vicos project in Peru and the Etawah project in India.[56] Unlike some other development programs, these projects relied heavily on participation by the people of the communities. This is in spite of preferences in both countries for authoritarian leadership.

Reward Sharing   Sometimes a proposed change may have no foreseeable benefit for the people whose support is needed to ensure its success. Production workers, for example, have little incentive to shift to new work practices unless they see some benefits for themselves. A U.S. firm manufacturing electrical appliances in Mexico moved workers easily from radio to black-and-white television production. When the firm introduced color televisions, however, product defects inexplicably increased. The company learned that the workers were eager to turn out high-quality black-and-white sets because they or their friends might be consumers. The expensive color sets, however, were so far beyond their means that workers had no incentive to be careful in production. The firm's solution was to develop a bonus system for quality.

Opinion Leaders   By discovering the local channels of influence, an international firm may locate opinion leaders to help speed up the acceptance of change. In Ghana, government health workers frequently ask permission and seek the help of village witch doctors before inoculating people or spraying huts to fight malaria. This achieves the desired result without destroying important social structures. Opinion leaders may emerge in different places, such as among youth in a rapidly changing society. An interesting use of this concept in Mexico involved sending low-level workers rather than supervisors to the parent plant in the United States. These workers returned as heroes among their peers and were emulated when they demonstrated new work habits.

Timing   Many good ideas are never applied effectively because they are ill timed. Change brings uncertainty and insecurity: A labor-saving production method creates resistance because people fear losing their jobs. Fewer impediments will occur if the labor-saving methods are introduced when there is a labor shortage rather than a surplus, regardless of what management says will happen to employment. Attitudes and needs may change slowly or rapidly, so keeping abreast of these changes helps in determining timing.

Learning Abroad   The discussion thus far has centered on the interaction between the international firm and the host society. The interaction is, of course, a two-way street. The firm not only affects the relationship but is also

People are more apt to support change when they see personal or reference-group rewards.

Managers seeking to introduce changes should first convince those who can influence others.

Firms should time change to occur when there is likely to be least resistance.

International firms
• Change some things abroad

- Change themselves when encountering foreign environments
- Learn things abroad that they can apply at home

affected by it. It may change things abroad or alter its own activities to fit the foreign environment; it may also learn things that will be useful in its own home country or in other operations.

The national practices most likely to be scrutinized for possible use in other countries are those found in the countries that are doing best economically.[57] For example, in the nineteenth century, when Britain was the economic leader, interest focused on the British cultural character. Then, at the turn of the century, attention was diverted to Germany and the United States. More recently, attention has shifted toward Japan and South Korea as business theorists and practitioners debate whether some of their business practices can be adopted successfully elsewhere. Whether a company is importing or exporting business practices, one must consider the same factors when questioning whether and how change can be introduced.

LOOKING TO THE FUTURE

Contact across cultures is becoming more widespread than ever before. Advances in transportation and communications, along with rising personal incomes, are allowing greater freedom of travel. Global competition is growing, and thus many of the same international companies compete more against each other in many different parts of the world. These factors lead to a leveling of cultures. More-similar products are demanded and more-similar methods are used to produce them globally. Many small cultural groups are being absorbed into more-dominant national ones, and in recent years, many regional languages have become extinct. Some observers predict that if there is to be rapid educational and technological advancement, cultural change is inevitable.[58]

There are four scenarios of future international cultures:
- Smaller cultures will be absorbed by national and global ones.
- Subcultures will transcend national boundaries.
- Organizations will become more similar worldwide but people in organizations will hold on to cultures.
- Cultural identities will be mobilized for separatism.

On the other hand, there is evidence of emerging subcultures within countries because of the influx of people from other countries. There are also religious sects and ethnic groups that retain traditional ways rather than assimilate completely. There is also evidence that some groups accept new ideas, products, and technologies more readily than others. All of these factors might lead to future problems in defining culture along national lines. The distinct subcultures within a country may have less in common with each other than with subcultures in other countries, such as the Inuits in Arctic lands and the Kurds of the Middle East that transcend borders.

There is a third possibility that cultures will converge in some, but not all, respects. Clearly, organizations are becoming more similar internationally in what they produce and in what technologies they use. However, people within the same organizations are continuing to hold onto their national differences as strongly as ever.[59] In other words, some tangibles are becoming more universal; but the ways in which people cooperate, attempt to solve problems, and are motivated may not become more universal.

A fourth possibility is that cultural identities will continue to be used to mobilize national identity or liberation, such as through religious separatism in Iran, the independence movement among the Basques, or even "Buy British" campaigns. Such activities may retard or even prevent the homogenization of cultures.[60]

SUMMARY

- International firms must evaluate their business practices to ensure they they take into account national norms for physical and behavioral characteristics.

- A given country may encompass very distinct societies. People may also have more in common with similar groups in foreign countries than with people from different groups in their own country.

- There are notable group differences in such physical variations as skin color, height, weight, and form of the body; color, abundance, distribution, balding, and graying of the hair; blood type; and resistance and susceptibility to certain diseases. Businesspeople must consider the effects that these variances and wishful stereotypes may have on their practices.

- Societal culture includes norms of behavior based on attitudes, values, and beliefs. Businesspeople agree that there are national differences but disagree as to what these differences are.

- Group affiliations based on sex, family, age, caste, religion, political preference, associations, and ethnic, racial, or national origin often reflect a person's degree of access to economic resources, prestige, social relations, and power. An individual's affiliations may determine his or her qualifications and availability for given jobs.

- Most people work far more than is necessary for the satisfaction of their basic needs for food, clothing, and shelter. The relative importance of work is determined largely by the interrelationship of the cultural and economic environment. The explanations for the motivation to work include the Protestant ethic, the belief that work will (or will not) bring success, habit, the need for achievement, and the fulfillment of higher-order needs.

- Occupations bring different economic, social, and prestige rewards in different countries. People gravitate to jobs for which they perceive high rewards. The many differences from one society to another result in varied attitudes toward working for government, business organizations, or oneself.

- National groups differ in the degree to which individuals trust others, in attitudes toward nature and fate, in whether they prefer an autocratic or a participative working relationship, and in their cooperative group memberships, especially family-based ones.

- We communicate through formal language, through silent language based on culturally determined cues, and through observance of prevailing moral imperatives and etiquette. We evaluate much information on the basis of our own cultural backgrounds. The failure to note subtle distinctions can result in much misunderstanding in cross-national dealings.

■ People working in a foreign environment should be sensitive to the dangers of excessive polycentrism or of ethnocentrism.

■ In deciding whether to act as a change agent in a foreign land or to develop new practices to fit the native population, an international firm should consider the cost and benefit to the firm of each alternative, the importance of the change to both parties, the possibility of participation in decision making, the way rewards of change may be allocated, the identity of opinion leaders, and the right timing.

■ There is usually more interest in studying and possibly adopting business practices from those countries that are showing the most economic success. Cultural factors may determine whether or not they can be successful in another society.

■ Controversy exists over whether and to what purpose national cultures are converging as they come into greater contact with each other.

C A S E
JOHN HIGGINS*

Leonard Prescott, vice president and general manager of Weaver-Yamazaki Pharmaceutical of Japan, believed that his executive assistant, John Higgins, was losing his effectiveness in representing the U.S. parent company because of his extraordinary identification with the Japanese culture.

Weaver Pharmaceutical, with extensive international operations, was one of the largest U.S. drug firms. Its competitive position depended heavily on research and development (R&D). Sales activity in Japan had begun in the early 1930s through distributorship by Yamazaki Pharmaceutical, a major producer of drugs and chemicals in Japan. World War II disrupted sales, but Weaver resumed export sales to Japan in 1948 and captured a substantial market share. To prepare for increasingly keen competition

from Japanese producers in the foreseeable future, Weaver decided to undertake local production of some of its product lines. In 1953 the company began preliminary negotiations with Yamazaki, which culminated in the establishment of a jointly owned and operated manufacturing subsidiary in 1954. (Japan is shown in Map 3.2.)

Through the combined effort of both parents, the subsidiary soon began to manufacture sufficiently broad lines of products to fill the general demands of the Japanese market. Importation from the United States was limited to highly specialized items. The company conducted substantial research and development on its own, coordinated through a joint committee of both parents to avoid unnecessary duplication of efforts. The subsidiary had turned out many new products, some of which were marketed successfully in the United States and elsewhere. Weaver management considered the Japanese operation to be one of the most successful of its international ventures. It felt that the company's future

---

*The case is reprinted from *Stanford Business Cases 1963* with the permission of the publishers, Stanford University Graduate School of Business, 1963 by the Board of Trustees of the Leland Stanford Junior University. This is a condensed version of the original by M. Y. Yoshino.

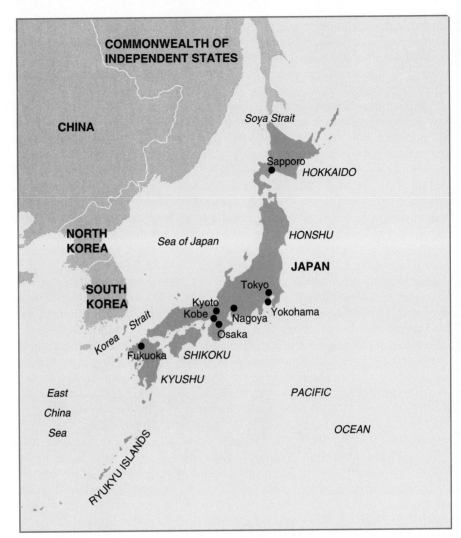

Map 3.2
Map of Japan
As a nation consisting of islands, Japan's relative historical isolation has led to less cultural borrowing than one finds in most other countries.

prospects were promising, especially since steady improvement was occurring in Japan's standard of living.

The subsidiary was headed by Shozo Suzuki, who as executive vice president of Yamazaki and also president of several other subsidiaries limited his participation in Weaver-Yamazaki to de-

termination of basic policies. Daily operations were managed by Prescott, assisted by Higgins and several Japanese directors. Though several other Americans were assigned to the venture, they were concerned with R&D and held no overall management responsibilities.

The Weaver Company had a policy of moving

United States personnel from one foreign post to another with occasional tours in the international division of the home office. Each assignment generally lasted for three to five years. Since there was a limited number of expatriates, the personnel policy was flexible enough to allow an employee to stay in a country for an indefinite period of time if he or she desired. A few expatriates had stayed in one foreign post for over ten years.

Prescott replaced the former general manager, who had been in Japan for six years. Prescott was experienced at international work, having spent most of his 25-year career with the company in jobs with international responsibilities. He had served in India, the Philippines, and Mexico and had spent several years in the home-office international division. He was delighted to be challenged to expand the Japanese operations. After two years there, Prescott was pleased with the progress the company had made and felt a sense of accomplishment in developing a smoothly functioning organization.

He became concerned, however, with the notable changes in Higgins's attitude and thinking. Prescott felt that Higgins had absorbed and internalized the Japanese culture to such a degree that he had lost the U.S. point of view. He had "gone native," resulting in a substantial loss of his administrative effectiveness.

Higgins was born in a small Midwestern town; after high school he entered his state university. Midway through college he joined the army. Because he had shown an interest in languages in college, he was given an opportunity to attend the Army Language School for intensive training in Japanese. After fifteen months he was assigned as an interpreter and translator in Tokyo. While in Japan, he took further courses in Japanese language, literature, and history. He made many Japanese friends, fell in love with Japan, and vowed to return there. After five years in the army, Higgins returned to college. Because he wanted to use the language as a means rather than an end in itself, he finished his college work in management rather than in

Japanese. He graduated with honors a year and a half later and joined Weaver. After a year in the company training program he was assigned to Japan, a year before Prescott's arrival.

Higgins was pleased to return to Japan, not only because of his love for Japan, but also for the opportunity to improve the "ugly American" image abroad. Because of his language ability and interest in Japan, he was able to intermingle with broad segments of the Japanese population. He noted that U.S. managers had a tendency to impose their value systems, ideals, and thinking patterns upon the Japanese, believing that anything from the United States was universally right and applicable. He felt indignant about these attitudes on numerous occasions and was determined to remedy them.

Under both Prescott and his predecessor, Higgins's responsibilities included troubleshooting with major Japanese customers, attending trade meetings, negotiating with government officials, conducting marketing research projects, and helping with day-to-day administration. Both managers sought his advice on many difficult and complex administrative problems and found him capable.

Prescott mentally listed a few examples to describe what he meant by Higgins's "complete emotional involvement" with Japanese culture. The year before, Higgins had married a Japanese woman who had studied in the United States and graduated from a prestigious Japanese university. At that time, Higgins had asked for and received permission to extend his stay in Japan for an indefinite period. This seemed to Prescott to make a turning point in Higgins's behavior.

Higgins moved to a strictly Japanese neighborhood, relaxed in a kimono at home, used the public bath, and was invited to weddings, neighborhood parties, and even Buddhist funerals. Although Weaver had a policy of granting two months' home leave every two years with paid transportation for the employee and his family, Higgins declined his trips, preferring to visit remote parts of Japan with his wife.

At work, Higgins had also taken on many

characteristics of a typical Japanese executive. He spent a great deal of time listening to the personal problems of his subordinates, maintained close social ties with many of the men in the organization, and had even arranged marriages for some of the young employees. Consequently, many employees sought Higgins's attention to register their complaints and demands with management. These included requests for more liberal fringe benefits in the form of recreational activities and acquisition of rest houses at resort areas. Many employees also complained to Higgins about a new personnel policy, installed by Prescott, that involved a move away from promotion based on seniority to one based on superiors' evaluations of subordinates. The employees asked Higgins to intercede on their behalf. He did so and insisted that their demands were justified.

Although Prescott believed it was helpful to learn the feelings of middle managers from Higgins, he disliked having to deal with Higgins as an adversary rather than as an ally. Prescott became hesitant to ask Higgins's opinion because Higgins invariably raised objections to changes that were contrary to the Japanese norm. Prescott believed that there were dynamic changes taking place in traditional Japanese customs and culture, and he was confident that many of Higgins's objections were not tied to existing cultural patterns as rigidly as Higgins seemed to think. This opinion was bolstered by the fact that many of the Japanese subordinates were more willing to try out new ideas than Higgins was. Prescott further thought that there was no point in a progressive U.S. company's merely copying the local customs. He felt that the company's real contribution to Japanese society was in introducing new ideas and innovations.

Recent incidents had raised some doubts in Prescott's mind as to the soundness of Higgins's judgment, something Prescott had never questioned before. For example, there was a case involving the dismissal of a manager who in Prescott's opinion lacked initiative, leadership, and general competency. After two years of con-

tinued prodding by his superiors, including Prescott himself, the manager still showed little interest in self-improvement. Both Higgins and the personnel manager objected vigorously to the dismissal because the company had never done this before. They also argued that the man involved was loyal and honest and that the company was partially at fault for having kept him on for the last ten years without spotting the incompetency. A few weeks after the dismissal, Prescott learned accidentally that Higgins had interceded on behalf of the fired employee, resulting in Yamazaki Pharmaceutical's taking him on. When confronted, Higgins simply said that he had done what was expected of a superior in any Japanese company.

Prescott believed these incidents suggested a serious problem. Higgins had been an effective and efficient manager whose knowledge of the language and the people had proved invaluable. On numerous occasions, his friends in U.S. firms said they envied Prescott for having a man of Higgins's qualifications as an assistant. Prescott also knew that Higgins had received several outstanding offers to go with other companies in Japan. Prescott felt that Higgins would be far more effective if he could take a more emotionally detached attitude toward Japan. In Prescott's view, the best international executive was one who retained a belief in the fundamentals of the home [U.S.] point of view while also understanding foreign attitudes. This understanding, of course, should be thorough or even instinctive, but it also should be objective, characterized neither by disdain nor by strong emotional attachment.

Questions

1. How would you contrast Higgins's and Prescott's attitudes toward the implementation of U.S. personnel policies in the Japanese operations?

2. What are the major reasons for these differences in attitude?

3. If you were the Weaver corporate management person responsible for the Japanese operations and the conflict between Higgins and Prescott had come to your attention, what would you do? Be sure first to identify some alternatives and then to make your recommendations.

Chapter Notes

1. Most data were taken from an interview with Angela Clarke, a protagonist in the case. Additional background information came from Kenneth Friedman, "Learning the Arabs' Silent Language: Interview with Edward T. Hall" [the noted anthropologist quoted in the case], *Bridge,* Spring 1980, pp. 5–6; Samira Harfoush, "Non-Traditional Training for Women in the Arab World," *Bridge,* Winter 1980, pp. 6–7; "British Premier Visits Saudi Arabia," *New York Times,* April 20, 1981, p. A2; Karen Elliott House, "Modern Arabia," *Wall Street Journal,* June 4, 1981, p. 1; David Ignatius, "A Saudi Job Offers Hordes of Foreigners a Chance to Prosper," *Wall Street Journal,* March 20, 1981, p. 1; The Economist Intelligence Unit, *Country Profile: Saudi Arabia, 1986–87* (London: Economist Intelligence Unit, 1986), p. 11; James Le Moyne, "Army Women and the Saudis Shock One Another," *New York Times,* September 25, 1990, p. A1; and Geraldine Brooks, "Mixed Blessing," *Wall Street Journal,* September 11, 1990, p. A1.

2. Eve Lee, "Saudis as We, Americans as They," *Bridge,* Winter 1980, pp. 6–7.

3. Hall in Friedman, *loc. cit.*

4. Lorna V. Williams, "Women in International Business," *American Way,* February 18, 1986, p. 51.

5. Marshall H. Segall, *Cross-Cultural Psychology: Human Behavior in Global Perspective* (Monterey, Calif.: Brooks/Cole, 1979), p. 143; and Luis R. Gomez-Mejia, "Effect of Occupation on Task Related, Contextual, and Job Involvement Orientation: A Cross-Cultural Perspective," *Academy of Management Journal,* Vol. 27, No. 4, 1984, pp. 706–720.

6. Richard N. Farmer and Barry M. Richman, *Comparative Management and Economic Progress,* rev. ed. (Bloomington, Ind.: Cedarwood Publishing, 1970), pp. 20–21, for example, list 15 behavioral variables relating to each of 36 business functions. George P. Murdock listed 72 cultural variables in "The Common Denominator of Culture," in *The Science of Man in the World Crises,* Ralph Linton, ed. (New York: Columbia University Press, 1945), pp. 123–142.

7. S. Gunders and J. W. M. Whiting, "Mother-Infant Separation and Physical Growth," *Ethnology* 7, No. 2, April 1968, pp. 196–206, and Thomas K. Landauer and J. W. M. Whiting, "Infantile Stimulation and Adult Stature of Human Males," *American Anthropologist,* Vol. 66, 1964, p. 1008.

8. James F. Downs and Herman K. Blebtreu, *Human Variation: An Introduction to Physical Anthropology* (Beverly Hills, Calif.: Glencoe Press, 1969), p. 197.

9. Ian Jamieson, *Capitalism and Culture: A Comparative Analysis of British and American Manufacturing Organizations* (Farnborough, England: Gower Press, 1980), Chapter 1.

10. Nancy J. Adler and Jill de Villafranca, "Epistemological Foundations of a Symposium Process: A Framework for Understanding Culturally Diverse Organizations," *International Studies of Management and Organization,* Winter 1982–1983, pp. 7–22.

11. James A. McCaffrey and Craig R. Hafner, "When Two Cultures Collide: Doing Business Overseas," *Training and Development Journal,* Vol. 39, No. 10, October 1985, p. 26.

12. Harry C. Triandis, "Dimensions of Cultural Variation as Parameters of Organizational Theories," *International Studies of Management and Organization*, Winter 1982–1983, pp. 143–144.

13. "China's Gender Imbalance," *Wall Street Journal*, June 7, 1990, p. A12.

14. *Women at Work* (Geneva, Switzerland: International Labour Office, 1988, no. 1).

15. Kenneth Dreyfack, "You Don't Have to Be a Giant to Score Big Overseas," *Business Week*, April 13, 1987, p. 63.

16. Triandis, *op. cit.*, p. 146.

17. "The Job Market Opens Up for the 68-Cent Woman," *New York Times*, July 26, 1987, p. E6; Christine L. Williams, *Gender Differences at Work* (Berkeley: University of California Press, 1989); and Urban Lehner and Kathryn Graven, "Quiet Revolution," *Wall Street Journal*, September 6, 1989, p. A1.

18. Max Weber, "The Protestant Ethic and the Spirit of Capitalism," and Kember Fullerton, "Calvinism and Capitalism," both in *Culture and Management*, Ross A. Webber, ed. (Homewood, Ill.: Richard D. Irwin, 1969), pp. 91–112.

19. "Work and Play," *Wall Street Journal*, April 13, 1990, p. A6; and James R. Lincoln, "Employee Work Attitudes and Management Practice in the U.S. and Japan: Evidence from a Large Corporate Survey," *California Management Review*, Vol. 32, No. 1, Fall 1989, p. 92.

20. J. H. Boeke, *Economics and Economic Policy of Dual Societies* (New York: Institute of Pacific Relations, 1953), pp. 39–41.

21. Triandis, *op. cit.*, pp. 159–160.

22. Everett E. Hagen, *The Theory of Social Change: How Economic Growth Begins* (Homewood, Ill.: Richard D. Irwin, 1962), p. 378.

23. David C. McClelland, *The Achieving Society* (Princeton, N.J.: Van Nostrand, 1961); David C. McClelland, "Business Drives and National Achievement," *Harvard Business Review*, July–August 1962, pp. 92–112; M. L. Maehr and J. G. Nicholls, "Culture and Achievement Motivations: A Second Look," *Studies in Cross Cultural Psychology*, in Neil Warren, ed. (London: Academic Press, 1980), Vol. 2, Chapter 6.

24. Abraham Maslow, *Motivation and Personality* (New York: Harper, 1954).

25. Geert Hofstede, "National Cultures in Four Dimensions," *International Studies of Management and Organization*, Spring–Summer 1983, p. 68; for an earlier comparison among countries, see Mason Haire, Edwin Ghiselli, and Lyman Porter, *Managerial Thinking* (New York: Wiley, 1966), pp. 90–103.

26. Donald Treiman, *Occupational Prestige in Comparative Perspective* (New York: Academic Press, 1977), especially Appendix C.

27. Robert R. Rehder, *Latin American Management Development and Performance* (Reading, Mass.: Addison-Wesley, 1968), p. 16.

28. Hofstede, *op. cit.*, pp. 54–55.

29. Hofstede, *op. cit.*, pp. 50–57.

30. See, for example, Geza Peter Lauter, "Sociological-Cultural and Legal Factors Impeding Decentralization of Authority in Developing Countries," *Academy of Management Journal*, September 1969, Vol. 12, No. 3, pp. 367–378; Richard B. Peterson, "Chief Executives' Attitudes: A Cross-Cultural Analysis," *Industrial Relations*, May 1971, Vol. 10, No. 2, pp. 194–210; G. Katona, B. Strumpel, and E. Zahn, "The Sociocultural Environment," in *International Marketing Strategy*, H. B. Thorelli, ed. (Middlesex, England: Penguin Books, 1973).

31. Mary Williams Walsh, "Heaven Only Knows What Comes Next in Pakistani Science," *Wall Street Journal*, September 13, 1988, p. 1.

32. L. L. Cummings, D. L. Harnett, and D. J. Stevens, "Risk, Fate, Conciliation and

Trust: An International Study of Attitudinal Differences among Executives," *Academy of Management Journal,* September 1971, p. 294, found differences among the United States, Greece, Spain, Central Europe, and Scandinavia.

33. McCaffrey and Hafner, *op. cit.,* p. 26.

34. "Language Lessons," *Wall Street Journal,* August 9, 1990, p. A6.

35. Vivian Ducat, "American Spoken Here—and Everywhere," *Travel & Leisure,* Vol. 16, No. 10, October 1986, pp. 168–169; Bill Bryson, *The Mother Tongue: English and How It Got That Way* (New York: Morrow, 1990).

36. Christian Hill, "Language for Profit," *Wall Street Journal,* January 13, 1977, p. 34.

37. Vern Terpstra and Kenneth David, *The Cultural Environment of International Business,* 3rd ed. (Cincinnati: South-Western, 1991, pp. 22–34.

38. This term was first used by Edward T. Hall, "The Silent Language in Overseas Business," *Harvard Business Review,* May–June 1960, and included five variables (time, space, things, friendships, and agreements).

39. *Ibid.*

40. Emmanuelle Ferrieux, "Hidden Messages," *World Press Review,* July 1989, p. 39.

41. For a survey of major research contributions, see Harry C. Triandis, "Reflections on Trends in Cross-Cultural Research," *Journal of Cross-Cultural Psychology,* March 1980, pp. 46–48.

42. Benjamin Lee Whorf, *Language, Thought and Reality* (New York: Wiley, 1956), p. 13.

43. Segall, *op. cit.,* pp. 96–99.

44. Tony Horwitz, "Iceland Pushes Back English Invasion in War of the Words," *Wall Street Journal,* July 25, 1990, p. A8.

45. E. Glenn, *Man and Mankind: Conflict and Communication Between Cultures* (Norwood, N.J.: Ablex, 1981).

46. William Stockton, "Bribes Are Called a Way of Life in Mexico," *New York Times,* October 25, 1986, p. 3.

47. Peter Gosling, "Culture and Commerce: What's in a Name?" *Southeast Asia Business,* No. 6, Summer 1985, pp. 30–38.

48. A list of recent books appears in Katherine Glover, "Do's & Taboos," *Business America,* August 13, 1990, p. 5.

49. Philip R. Harris and Robert T. Moran, *Managing Cultural Differences* (Houston: Gulf, 1979), p. 88, quoting Kalervo Oberg.

50. Adrian Furnham and Stephen Bochner, *Culture Shock* (London: Methuen, 1986), p. 234.

51. Ben L. Kedia and Rabi S. Bhagat, "Cultural Constraints on Transfer of Technology Across Nations: Implications for Research in International and Comparative Management," *Academy of Management Review,* Vol. 13, No. 4, October 1988, pp. 559–571.

52. Hans B. Thorelli, "The Multi-National Corporation as a Change Agent," *The Southern Journal of Business,* July 1966, p. 5.

53. Manning Nash, "The Interplay of Culture and Management in a Guatemalan Textile Plant," *Culture and Management,* Ross A. Webber, ed., pp. 317–324.

54. Bernard Lewis, "Western Culture Must Go," *Wall Street Journal,* May 2, 1988, p. 18.

55. "Problems of Opening a Retail Store in Spain," *Wall Street Journal,* March 27, 1967, p. 1.

56. Conrad M. Arensberg and Arthur H. Niehoff, *Introducing Social Change: A Manual for Americans Overseas* (Chicago: Aldine, 1964), pp. 123–125.

57. Ian Jamieson, "The Concept of Culture and Its Relevance for an Analysis of Business Enterprise in Different Societies," *International Study of Management and Organization*, Winter 1982, pp. 71–72.

58. Peter Blunt, "Cultural Consequences for Organization Change in a Southeast Asian State: Brunei," *Academy of Management Executive*, Vol. 2, No. 3, Fall 1988, p. 239.

59. J. D. Child, "Culture, Contingency and Capitalism in the Cross-National Study of Organizations," in *Research in Organizational Behavior*, L. L. Cummings and B. M. Staw, eds. (Greenwich, Conn.: JAI Publishers, 1981), Vol. III, pp. 303–356; Andre Laurent, "The Cross-Cultural Puzzle of International Human Resource Management," *Human Resource Management*, Vol. 25, No. 1, pp. 91–102.

60. Lourdes Arizpe, "On Cultural and Social Sustainability," *Development*, Vol. 1, 1989, pp. 5–10.

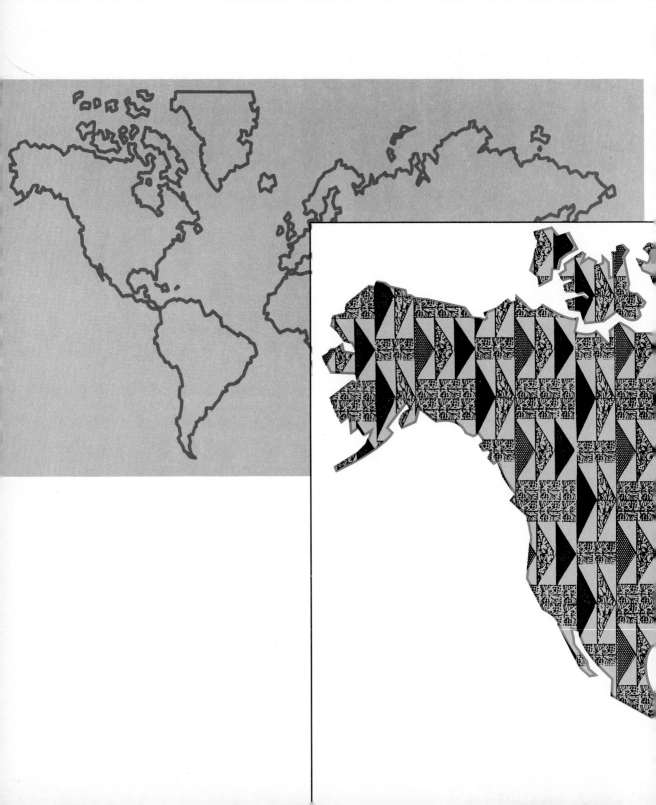

PART **3**

THEORIES AND INSTITUTIONS: TRADE AND INVESTMENT

Why do trade and investment take place? What are the governmental institutions that enhance or retard trade and factor mobility? What would happen if there were no institutions? These are the major questions considered in this part.

Chapter 4 considers the question of why foreign trade takes place, first through the development of the theory of international trade from the standpoint of nations. The advantages and disadvantages of specialization resulting from trade are then discussed. Finally, the chapter examines advantages for firms involved in foreign trade, and introduces the behavioral and legal impediments to trade.

Chapter 5 presents the arguments against a free flow of trade among countries and the mechanisms by which nations regulate both the inward and outward flow of goods across their borders. Included is a discussion on the role of GATT and on the alternatives companies may consider when they face import competition.

Chapter 6 is concerned with still another essential aspect of the field of international business: the reasons behind foreign direct investment. There is a separate analysis of direct investment to seek foreign markets and to obtain foreign supplies. The close relationship between trade and investment is also examined. Finally, the chapter discusses the advantages of direct investors over firms without direct investment.

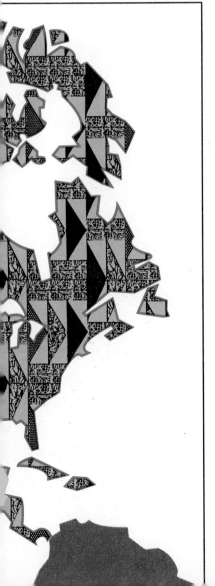

CHAPTER **4**

INTERNATIONAL TRADE THEORY

*A market is not held
for the sake of one person.*
AFRICAN (FULANI) PROVERB

Objectives

- To explain what trade patterns would exist if trade could move freely.

- To discuss how global efficiency can be increased through free trade.

- To point out the underlying assumptions of trade theories.

- To introduce prescriptions for targeting trade patterns.

- To explore how business decisions determine what trade takes place.

Sri Lanka, which means resplendent land, is an island country of more than 16 million people off the southeast coast of India. Lying just above the equator, it is 270 miles long and 140 miles across at its widest points (see Map 4.1). It has a hot tropical climate with two monsoon periods, yet the central mountain region is cool enough to experience frost. Known as Ceylon from the early sixteenth century until 1972, Sri Lanka is in many ways typical of most developing countries. It has a low per capita income (about $420 per year), a high dependence on a few primary products for earning foreign exchange, insufficient foreign exchange earnings to purchase all of the desired consumer and industrial imports, and a high unemployment rate. In many other ways, though, Sri Lanka is atypical of developing nations. By various measurements comparing the quality of life among countries, Sri Lanka ranks fairly high. Its 87 percent literacy rate is one of the highest in Asia, and its standards of nutrition, health care, and income distribution are among the highest in the Third World. Its life expectancy of 71 years is one of the highest in the developing world, and its recent population growth rate of 1.5 percent per year is one of the lowest.

Although Sri Lanka did not become independent until 1948, it has a long recorded history of international trade. By the middle of the third century B.C., special quarters of its capital were set apart for "Ionian merchants." King Solomon sent his galleys to Sri Lanka to purchase gems, elephants, and peacocks to woo the Queen of Sheba. Sinbad and Marco Polo sailed there. Sri Lanka sent ambassadors to Claudius Caesar in the Roman Empire and later established trade links with China. One by one the European powers came to dominate the island in order to acquire products unavailable in their own countries. The Portuguese, for example, sought such products as cinnamon, cloves, and cardamom, and the English developed the island's economy with tea, rubber, and coconuts, replacing rice as the major agricultural crop.

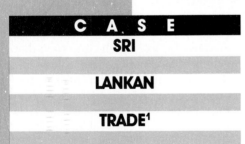

C A S E

SRI

LANKAN

TRADE[1]

Since its independence, Sri Lanka has looked to international trade policy as a means of helping to solve such problems as (1) foreign exchange shortage, (2) overdependence on one product and one market, and (3) insufficient growth of output and employment.

Foreign exchange is needed for buying imports. Advances in international communications and transportation have contributed to rising Sri Lankan expectations, which in turn have translated into preferences for foreign products or for foreign machinery to produce them. These desires have grown more rapidly than foreign exchange earnings have.

Sri Lanka also has been concerned about its overdependence on a single export product and market. Until 1975 more than half of Sri Lanka's export earnings were from tea. This made Sri Lanka vulnerable in two ways. First, world demand for tea has not grown as rapidly as that for many other products, particularly manufactured ones. Therefore, tea has not offered as

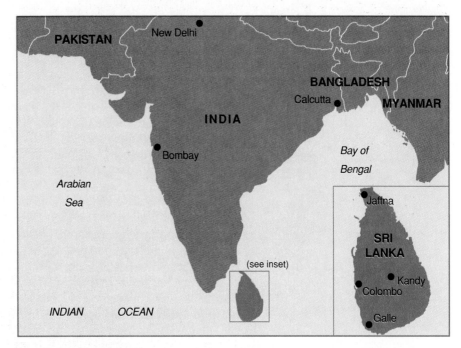

Map 4.1
Map of Sri Lanka
The island nation of Sri Lanka lies off the southeast coast of India.

viable a means of increasing economic growth, employment, or foreign exchange earnings as some other products. Second, tea prices can fluctuate substantially because of bumper crops or natural disasters in any tea-exporting country. For example, the wholesale price of tea has changed by as much as 90 percent from one year to the next. This makes planning for long-term business or government projects very difficult. Because Sri Lanka is a former British colony, many Sri Lankans also have been concerned that the country cannot be politically and economically independent as long as trade is so centered on the British market. At the time of independence, for example, one third of Sri Lankan exports went to the United Kingdom. Sri Lanka was thus potentially vulnerable to British political demands and economic downturns.

Because of these varied but interrelated problems Sri Lanka has attempted since independence to earn more foreign exchange by exporting more of its traditional commodities. In addition, Sri Lanka has sought to diversify its production. From independence in 1948 until 1960, Sri Lanka made little attempt to change its export dependence on tea, rubber, and coconuts to pay for imported food and industrial goods. From 1960 until a change of government in 1977, the emphasis was on the restriction of imports in order to encourage local production, which would thus save foreign exchange. Since then the focus has been on the development of new industries that can export a part of their production and thus earn more foreign exchange. Whether the diversification has been for import substitution or export development, the intended outcome has been to create growth and jobs by using unemployed people and other unemployed resources. By moving to new products, the country expects to be less dependent on the tea market and on sales of that product into the traditional British market.

The decision to develop exports of nontraditional products raises the questions of what those products should be and how to get firms to produce them for foreign markets. In 1977 the newly elected government in Sri Lanka was determined that assistance should be given only to those industries that would give Sri Lanka the best potential advantage in world markets. The government took numerous steps to ease restrictions on imports in order to judge where competitive advantages lay. Authorities reasoned that the industries that could survive import competition were the most likely to become competitive in export markets.

Governmental authorities were not satisfied to sit back and wait for imports to determine the whole future industrial thrust, however. They felt that some entirely new industries might have to be assisted. Additionally, there was a desire to make some short-term export gains in order to develop credibility for the export development program. The export development division of the Ministry of Industries was instrumental in creating a methodology to identify appropriate products for development and promotion.

An obvious way of selecting product groups was to identify nontraditional products that were already being exported in small amounts, since this ability to export indicated potential growth. The export development division also sought to find other products for which Sri Lanka might have a potential advantage in competing abroad. They first identified products that would have a high need for semiskilled and skilled labor because: (1) labor costs in Sri Lanka were low, (2) the labor force was fairly well educated, and (3) unemployment and underemployment were high. The division narrowed that group of products to include only those for which Sri Lanka had indigenous raw materials for production and packaging. This was deemed to be an important competitive indicator because it would be costly to import materials that would then have to be processed before being reexported. Finally, the division examined market conditions where Sri Lanka was most apt to be able to sell. This examination was based on an analysis of demand in two types of markets: (1) those where Sri Lanka had special market concessions and therefore would experience minimal trade barriers and (2) those that were geographically close to Sri Lanka and could be served with minimum transport costs.

Seventeen products emerged and were ranked by export potential and expected benefits for the country. The leading items were:

- processed tea (packaged teabags and instant tea)
- ready-made garments (shirts, pajamas, and dresses)

- chemical derivatives of coconut oil
- edible fats
- bicycle tires and tubes
- other rubber products such as automobile tires and tubes

Other items included canvas footwear, passionfruit juice, canned pineapple, ceramicware, seafood (lobsters and shrimp), handicraft items, and gems.

This identification of the most likely competitive industries encouraged some businesspeople to consider investments in new areas. Additionally, the government established industrial development zones. Companies that produced in and exported their production from the zones could qualify for up to a 10-year tax holiday plus another 15 years of tax concessions, depending on the size of the investment and the number of employees. They could also bring in goods and components without paying import taxes on them at the time of import. The import tax was deferred until the ensuing products were sold domestically. If the items were reexported, there was no import tax.

The first manufacturers to take advantage of the incentives were textile and footwear producers who had special access to the U.S. and European markets. Since then the products have become more diverse. Such operations as the production of PVC film, carpets, and data entry have been approved.

Sri Lanka continues to have a shortage of foreign exchange. As imports have entered Sri Lanka more easily and as incomes have risen, consumers have demanded even more foreign products. As a result, Sri Lanka has restricted large consumer items but has allowed smaller items, such as watches, to enter freely because of a belief that they would otherwise be smuggled in.

The move to establish new export industries is accomplishing many of its objectives. Manufacturing has grown as a portion of total exports and tea has fallen. There has also been a dispersion of Sri Lankan export markets, with such countries as the United States, Saudi Arabia, Germany, and India gaining in importance. Whereas one third of exports once went to Britain, no single country now accounts for as much as 15 percent of Sri Lankan sales.

INTRODUCTION

Trade policy focuses on the questions

- What products to import and export
- With whom to trade
- How much to trade

In the introductory case, Sri Lankan authorities, like authorities in all countries, wrestled with the problems of what, how much, and with whom the country should import and export. Once they made decisions, officials enacted trade policies to achieve the desired end results. These policies, in turn, affected business: They influenced what products companies might be able to sell in Sri Lanka from both Sri Lankan and foreign sources. The trade policies

TABLE 4.1 | EMPHASIS OF MAJOR THEORIES

Theory	Description of Natural Trade			Prescriptions of Trade Relationships			
	How much is traded?	What products are traded?	With whom does trade take place?	Should government control trade?	How much should be traded?	What products should be traded?	With whom should trade take place?
Mercantilism	—	—	—	Yes	X	X	X
Neomercantilism	—	—	—	Yes	X	—	—
Absolute advantage	—	X	—	No	—	X	—
Country size	X	X	—	—	—	—	—
Comparative advantage	—	X	—	No	—	X	—
Factor proportions	—	X	X	—	—	—	—
Product life cycle (PLC)	—	X	X	—	—	—	—
Country similarity	—	X	X	—	—	—	—
Dependence	—	—	—	Yes	—	X	X

Some theories explain
trade patterns in the ab-
sence of government in-
terference.

Some theories explain
what government actions
should strive for in trade.

also affected what companies could produce in Sri Lanka for sale in either the domestic or the foreign market. Although Sri Lankan officials set policies to conform to the country's unique conditions and objectives, they relied on a body of trade theory shared by officials around the world.

Whereas some theories precede events (e.g., Einstein's theory of relativity was a necessary antecedent to the atomic experiments that followed several decades later), international trade was practiced long before any trade theories had evolved. Sri Lankan trade, for example, predated recorded trade theories by more than 1500 years.

Two types of trade theories have emerged. The first type deals with the natural order of trade: That is, it examines and explains what trade patterns would exist if trade were allowed to move freely among countries. Theories of this type pose questions of how much, which products, and with whom a country will trade in the absence of restrictions among nations. Not all of these theories consider all of these questions; their focuses are shown in Table 4.1 under the heading "Description of Natural Trade." Note that two of these theories are also prescriptive: That is, they posit that a system of unrestricted trade should prevail. (They are marked "no" for the question "Should government control trade?") Some other theories of the first type are merely descriptive: That is, they explain what does or will happen but do not judge the result. The second type of theory prescribes governmental interference with the free movement of goods and services among countries in order to alter the amount, composition, and direction of trade. These theories are marked "Yes" under the question "Should government control trade?" in Table 4.1.

Since no single theory explains all natural trade patterns and since all prescriptions are relevant to some of the actions taken by governmental policymakers, this chapter examines a variety of approaches. However, the subject of governmental interference in trade is so broad that an entire chapter is devoted to discussion of many of the specific arguments and methods (see Chapter 5). Both the descriptive and prescriptive theories have considerable impact on international business. They provide insights about favorable market locales as well as potentially successful products. The theories also increase understanding about the kinds of government trade policies that might be enacted and predict how they might affect competitiveness.

MERCANTILISM

According to mercantil-
ism, countries should ex-
port more than they
import.

Why has Sri Lanka been so dependent on primary rather than manufactured products? Perhaps the answer lies in **mercantilism,** the trade theory that formed the foundation of economic thought from 1500 to 1800,[2] and premised that a country's wealth was measured by its holdings of treasure, usually in the form of gold. According to mercantile theory, governments should export more than they import, and if successful, they would receive the value of their trade surpluses in the form of gold from the country or countries that ran deficits. Nation-states were emerging during the period 1500–1800, and gold served to consolidate the power of central governments. The gold was invested in armies and national institutions that served to solidify people's primary allegiances to the new nation with a lessening of bonds to such traditional units as city-states, religions, and guilds.

But how could a country export more than it imported? Trade was conducted largely by governmental monopolies. Restrictions were imposed on most imports and many exports received subsidies. Colonial possessions, such as Sri Lanka under British rule, were used to support this trade objective first by supplying many commodities that the mother country might otherwise have had to purchase from a nonassociated country. Second, the colonial powers sought to run trade surpluses with their own colonies as a further means of obtaining revenue. They did this not only by monopolizing the colonial trade but also by preventing the colonies from manufacturing. Thus the colonies had to export less-valued raw materials and import more-valued manufactured products. Mercantile theory was intended to benefit the colonial powers, and the imposition of regulations based on this theory caused much discontent in the British colonies and was a background cause of the American Revolution.

As the influence of the mercantilist philosophy weakened after 1800, the colonial powers seldom acted to limit the development of industrial capabilities within their colonies, but institutional and legal arrangements continued to tie the trade of colonies to their industrialized mother countries. Sri Lanka, like the many other countries that have attained independence since World War II, began with a production structure and trade pattern that closely resembled those seen during the heyday of mercantilist economic influence. Efforts to alter this pattern are discussed later in this chapter in the section on independence, interdependence, and dependence.

A favorable balance of trade is not necessarily a beneficial situation.

Some of the terminology of the mercantilist era has endured. The term **favorable balance of trade,** for example, is still used to indicate that a country is exporting more than it is importing. An **unfavorable balance of trade** is indicative of a trading deficit. Many of these terms are misnomers: For example, the word *favorable* implies benefit, whereas *unfavorable* suggests disadvantage. In fact, it is not necessarily beneficial to run a trade surplus, nor is it necessarily disadvantageous to run a trade deficit. If a country is running a surplus, or favorable balance of trade, for the time being it is receiving goods and services from abroad of less value than it is sending out.[3] In the mercantilist period the difference was made up by a transfer of gold, but today the difference usually is made up by granting credit to the deficit country. If that credit is not repaid in full, the so-called favorable trade balance actually may turn out to be disadvantageous for the country with the trade surplus.

A country that practices neomercantilism attempts to run an export surplus to achieve some political or social objective.

In recent years the term **neomercantilism** has been used to describe countries that apparently try to run favorable balances of trade in an attempt to achieve some social or political objective. For instance, a country may try to achieve full employment by producing in excess of the demand at home and sending the surplus abroad. Or a country might attempt to maintain political influence in an area by sending more merchandise to the area than it receives from it.

ABSOLUTE ADVANTAGE

According to Adam Smith, a country's wealth is based on its available goods and services rather than on gold.

So far we have ignored the question of why countries need to trade at all. Why can't Sri Lanka (or any other country) be content with the goods and services produced within its territorial confines? In fact, many countries, following mercantilist policy, did try to become as self-sufficient as possible by producing goods locally.

In his 1776 book, *The Wealth of Nations*, Adam Smith questioned the mercantilists' assumption that a country's wealth depends on its holdings of treasure.[4] He said instead that the real wealth of a country consists of the goods and services available to its citizens. Smith developed the theory of **absolute advantage,** which holds that different countries can produce different goods more efficiently than others. Based on this theory, he questioned why the citizens of any country should have to buy domestically produced goods that they could purchase more cheaply from abroad.

Smith reasoned that if trade were unrestricted, each country would specialize in those products for which it had a competitive advantage. Each country's resources would shift to the efficient industries because the country could not compete in the inefficient ones. Through specialization, countries could increase their efficiency because: (1) labor could become more skilled by repeating the same tasks; (2) labor would not lose time in switching from the production of one kind of product to another; and (3) long production runs would provide incentives for the development of more effective working methods. A country then could use the excess of its specialized production to buy more imports than it could have otherwise produced. But in what products should a country specialize? Although Smith believed the marketplace would make the determination, he thought that a country's advantage would be either natural or acquired.

Natural Advantage

Natural advantage refers to climate and natural resources.

A country may have a **natural advantage** in the production of a product because of climatic conditions or because of access to certain natural resources. The climate may dictate, for example, what agricultural products can be produced efficiently. Sri Lanka's efficiency in the production of tea, rubber, and coconuts, for example, is due largely to advantageous climatic conditions.

Sri Lanka imports wheat and dairy products. If Sri Lanka were to increase its production of wheat and dairy products, for which its climate is less suited, it would have to use land now devoted to the cultivation of tea, rubber, or coconuts, thus decreasing the output of those products. At the same time, the United States could produce tea (perhaps in hothouses) but at the cost of diverting resources away from products such as wheat for which its climate is naturally suited. Both countries can trade tea for wheat and vice versa more cheaply than they could become self-sufficient in the production of both. Moreover, the more diverse the climates of two countries, the more likely it will be for them to have natural trade advantages with one another.

Most countries must import ores, metals, or supplies of fuel from other countries whose natural resources are plentiful. No one country is large enough or sufficiently rich in physical resources to be independent of the rest of the world except for short periods. Sri Lanka, for example, exports natural graphite but must import its supply of natural nitrates. Another natural resource is soil, which, when coupled with topography, is an important determinant of the type of products to be produced most efficiently in different areas.

The variation in natural advantages in different places also helps to explain where certain manufactured or processed products might be best produced, particularly if transportation costs can be reduced by processing an agricultural commodity or natural resource prior to exporting. Recall that Sri Lankan authorities sought to identify industries that could use its primary commodities such as tea. The processing to make instant tea would likely save bulk and transportation costs on tea exports. To make canned liquid tea could add weight, however, thus lessening the internationally competitive edge.

Acquired Advantage

Acquired advantage refers to technology and skill development.

Most of the world's trade today consists of manufactured goods and services rather than agricultural goods and natural resources. The production location of these goods is due largely to an **acquired advantage,** commonly referred to as product or process technology. An advantage in product technology refers to an ability to produce a different or differentiated product. Denmark, for example, exports silver tableware, not because there are rich Danish silver mines but because Danish companies have developed distinctive products. An advantage in process technology refers to an ability to produce a homogeneous product more efficiently. Japan, for example, has exported steel in spite of having to import iron and coal, the two primary ingredients necessary for steel production. A primary reason for Japan's success is that its steel mills encompass new labor-saving and raw-material-saving processes.

Resource Efficiency Example

The idea of absolute advantage in international or domestic trade can be explained by picturing two countries (or regions within one country) and two commodities. In this example, we assume the countries are Sri Lanka and the United States and the commodities are tea and wheat. Since we are not yet considering the concepts of money and exchange rates, we shall treat the cost of production in terms of the resources needed to produce either tea or wheat. This is a realistic treatment in that real income depends on the output of goods associated with the resources used to produce them.

We start with the assumption that Sri Lanka and the United States each have the same amount of resources (land, labor, and capital) that can be used to produce either tea or wheat. Let us say that 100 units of resources are available in each country (shown in Fig. 4.1). In the case of Sri Lanka we assume that it takes 4 resources to produce one ton of tea and 10 resources per ton of wheat. In the United States it takes 20 resources per ton of tea and 5 resources per ton of wheat. Sri Lanka is thus more efficient (that is, takes fewer resources to produce) than the United States in the production of tea, and the United States is more efficient than Sri Lanka in the production of wheat.

Consider a situation in which the two countries have no foreign trade. If Sri Lanka and the United States were each to devote half of their resources to the production of tea and half to the production of wheat, Sri Lanka would

Figure 4.1
Production Possibilities with Absolute Advantage

ASSUMPTIONS

Sri Lanka
1. 100 resources available
2. 10 resources to produce a ton of wheat
3. 4 resources to produce a ton of tea
4. Uses half of resources per product when there is no foreign trade

United States
1. 100 resources available
2. 5 resources to produce a ton of wheat
3. 20 resources to produce a ton of tea
4. Uses half of resources per product when there is no foreign trade

PRODUCTION	Tea	Wheat
Without Trade:		
Sri Lanka (Point A)	12½	5
U.S. (Point B)	2½	10
Total	15	15
With Trade:		
Sri Lanka (Point C)	25	0
U.S. (Point D)	0	20
Total	25	20

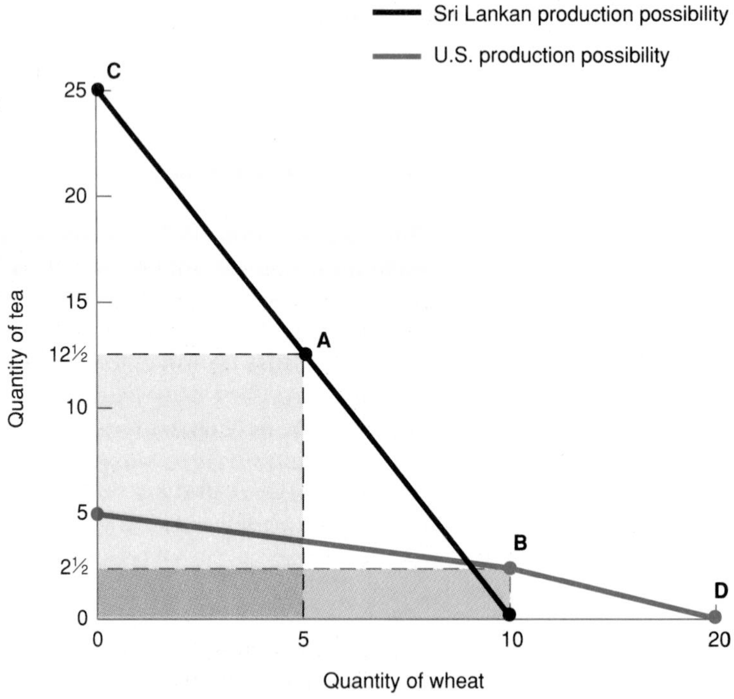

— Sri Lankan production possibility
— U.S. production possibility

be able to produce 12½ tons of tea and 5 tons of wheat (point A in Fig. 4.1), whereas the United States could produce 2½ tons of tea and 10 tons of wheat (point B in Fig. 4.1). Since each country has only 100 resources, neither country can increase the production of wheat without decreasing the production of tea or vice versa. Without trade the combined production of the two countries would then be 15 tons of tea (12½ plus 2½) and 15 tons of wheat (5 plus 10). If each of the two countries were to specialize in the commodity for which it had an absolute advantage, Sri Lanka could then produce 25 tons of tea and the United States 20 tons of wheat (points C and D in Fig. 4.1). We can see then that by specialization the production of both products can be increased (from 15 to 25 tons of tea and from 15 to 20 tons of wheat). By trading, the two countries can have more tea and more wheat than would be available to them without trade.

Theory of Country Size

Bigger countries have several differences from smaller countries. They

- Tend to trade a smaller portion of output or consumption
- Have more varied resources
- Have higher transport costs for foreign trade
- Can handle large-scale production

The theory of absolute advantage does not deal with country-by-country differences in specialization; however, some recent research based on country size helps to explain how much and what type of products will be traded.

Variety of Resources   The **theory of country size** holds that because countries with large land areas are more apt to have varied climates and natural resources, they are generally more nearly self-sufficient than smaller countries. Most of the very large countries such as Brazil, China, India, the United States, and the former Soviet Union import much less of their consumption and export much less of their production than small countries such as Iraq, the Netherlands, and Iceland.[5] Although this relationship generally holds true, there are exceptions. Albania, for example, is a small country for which trade is a small percentage of national income because of its stringent restrictions on trade.

Transport Costs   Although the theory of absolute advantage ignored transport costs, these costs affect large and small countries differently. Normally, the farther the distance, the higher are the transport costs, and the average distances for trade are higher for large countries. Assume, for example, that the normal maximum distance for transporting a given product is 100 miles because, beyond that distance, prices increase too much. Most of the production and market in the United States are more than 100 miles from the Canadian or Mexican borders. In the Netherlands, however, almost the entire production and market are within 100 miles of its border. Transportation costs thus make it more likely that small countries will trade.

Scale Economy   Although land area is the most obvious way of measuring countries' size, countries also may be compared on the basis of their economic size. Countries with large economies and high per capita incomes are more likely to produce goods that use technologies requiring long production runs because these countries develop industries to serve their large domestic markets. These same industries tend to be competitive in export markets as well.[6]

COMPARATIVE ADVANTAGE

The Logic

Gains from trade will occur even in a country that has absolute advantage in all products because the country must give up less-efficient output to produce more-efficient output.

What happens when one country can produce all products at an absolute advantage? In 1817 David Ricardo examined this question and expanded on Adam Smith's theory of absolute advantage to develop the theory of **comparative advantage.** Ricardo reasoned that there may still be gains from trade if a country specializes in those products that it can produce more efficiently than other products without regard to absolute advantage.[7] While this may initially seem incongruous, a simple analogy should clarify the logic of this theory. Imagine that the best physician in a particular town also happens to be the best medical secretary. Would it make economic sense for the physician to handle all the administrative duties of the office? Definitely not. The physician can earn more money by devoting all of his or her professional energies to working as a physician, even though that means having to employ a less skillful medical secretary to manage the office. In the same manner, a country will gain if it concentrates its resources on the production of the commodities that it can produce most efficiently. It will then buy, from countries with fewer natural or acquired resources, those commodities that it has relinquished. Like the physician, the country will concentrate its efforts on the production of those commodities for which comparative efficiency is greatest.

Production Possibility Example

In the following example we assume that the United States is more efficient in the production of both tea and wheat than Sri Lanka. The United States thus has an absolute advantage in the production of both products. In this example it takes Sri Lanka 10 resources to produce either a ton of tea or a ton of wheat, whereas it takes the United States only 5 resources to produce a ton of tea and 4 resources to produce a ton of wheat (see Fig. 4.2). As in the earlier example of absolute advantage, we once again assume that each country has a total of 100 resources available. If each country uses half of its resources in the production of each product, Sri Lanka can produce 5 tons of tea and 5 of wheat (point A on Fig. 4.2). The United States can produce 10 tons of tea and 12½ tons of wheat (point B on Fig. 4.2). Without trade, neither country can increase its production of tea without sacrificing some production of wheat or vice versa.

Although the United States has an absolute advantage in the production of both tea and wheat, it has a comparative advantage only in the production

ASSUMPTIONS

Sri Lanka
1. 100 resources available
2. 10 resources to produce a ton of wheat
3. 10 resources to produce a ton of tea
4. Uses half of resources per product when there is no foreign trade

United States
1. 100 resources available
2. 4 resources to produce a ton of wheat
3. 5 resources to produce a ton of tea
4. Uses half of resources per product when there is no foreign trade

PRODUCTION	Tea	Wheat
Without Trade:		
Sri Lanka (Point A)	5	5
U.S. (Point B)	10	12½
Total	15	17½
With Trade (increasing tea production):		
Sri Lanka (Point C)	10	0
U.S. (Point D)	6	17½
Total	16	17½
With Trade (increasing wheat production):		
Sri Lanka (Point C)	10	0
U.S. (Point E)	5	18¾
Total	15	18¾

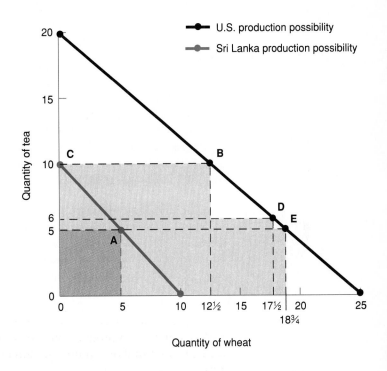

Figure 4.2
Production Possibilities with Comparative Advantage

of wheat. This is because its advantage in wheat is comparatively greater than its advantage in tea. By using the same number of resources the United States can produce 2½ times as much wheat as Sri Lanka but only twice as much tea. Although Sri Lanka has an absolute disadvantage in the production of both products, Sri Lanka has a comparative advantage (or less of a comparative disadvantage) in the production of tea. This is because Sri Lanka is half as efficient in tea and only 40 percent as efficient in wheat production.

Without trade the combined production would be 15 tons of tea (5 in Sri Lanka plus 10 in the United States) and 17½ of wheat (5 in Sri Lanka plus 12½ in the United States). By opening up trade the production of tea, wheat, or a combination of the two can be increased. If we increase the production of tea without changing the amount of wheat that could have been produced before trade, the United States could now produce all 17½ tons of wheat by using 70 resources (17½ tons times 4 per ton). The remaining 30 U.S. resources could be used for the production of 6 tons of tea (30 resources divided by 5 per ton). These are shown as point D in Fig. 4.2. Sri Lanka would use all of its resources in the production of 10 tons of tea (point C in Fig. 4.2). The combined wheat production has stayed at 17½ tons, but the tea production has increased from 15 to 16 tons.

If we increase the production of wheat while leaving tea production the same as it was before trade took place between the two countries, Sri Lanka could use all its resources on the production of tea, yielding 10 tons (point C on Fig. 4.2). The United States could produce the remaining 5 tons of tea by using 25 units of resources. The remaining 75 units of U.S. resources could now produce 18¾ tons of wheat (75 divided by 4). These are shown as point E in Fig. 4.2. Without sacrificing the tea available before trade, wheat production has increased from 17½ to 18¾ tons.

If the United States were to produce somewhere between points D and E in Fig. 4.2, both tea and wheat production would increase over what was possible before trade took place. Whether the production targets are for an increase of tea, wheat, or a combination of the two, both countries can gain by having Sri Lanka trade some of its tea production to the United States for some of the United States' wheat output.

Some Assumptions Behind the Theories

Full employment is not a valid assumption.

Full Employment   Our physician/medical secretary analogy assumed that the physician could stay busy full-time practicing medicine. If we relax this assumption, then the advantages of specialization are less compelling. The physician might, if unable to stay busy full-time with medical duties, perform secretarial work without having to forgo the physician's higher income. The theories of absolute and comparative advantage both assume that resources are fully employed. When countries have many unemployed resources, they may seek to restrict imports in order to employ idle resources even though they are not employed efficiently then.

Countries' goals may not be limited to efficiency.

Efficiency Objective   A second assumption of the physician/medical secretary analogy is that the individual who can do both medical and office work is interested primarily in maximization of profit or maximum efficiency. Yet, there are a number of reasons why physicians might not choose to work full-time at medical tasks. They might find administrative work relaxing and self-fulfilling. They might fear that a hired secretary would be unreliable. They might wish to maintain secretarial skills in the somewhat unlikely event that administration, rather than medicine, commands higher wages in the future. Countries as well often pursue objectives other than output efficiency: They may fear overspecialization because of the vulnerability created by changes in technology and price fluctuations.

Two Countries, Two Commodities   For the sake of simplicity, Ricardo originally assumed a very simple world comprised of only two countries and two commodities. Our example made the same assumption. Although this is unrealistic, it does not diminish the usefulness of the theory. Economists have applied the same reasoning to demonstrate efficiency advantages with multiproduct and multicountry situations.

Transport Costs   Neither the theory of absolute advantage nor that of comparative advantage considered the cost of moving products from one country to another, but this is not a serious limitation. Although specialization might reduce the number of resources necessary for producing goods, resources are also needed to move the goods internationally. If it costs more resources to transport the goods than are saved through specialization, then the advantages of trade are negated.

Resources are neither as mobile nor as immobile as the absolute and comparative advantage theories assume.

Mobility   The theories of absolute and comparative advantage assume that resources can move freely from the production of one good to another domestically but that they are not free to move internationally. Neither of these assumptions is completely valid. The misplaced textile worker in New England, for example, might not move easily into an aerospace job in California. Rather, this worker would very likely have difficulty working in such a different industry and might have trouble moving to a new area. Contrary to the theories, there is some mobility of resources internationally, although not as much as there is domestically. To cite an example, in recent years a significant number of Sri Lankan workers have been employed in the Middle East.

Services   The theories of absolute and comparative advantage deal with commodities rather than services; however, an increasing portion of world trade is in services. This fact does not render the theories obsolete, however, because resources must go into the production of services as well as commodities. For instance, the United States trades services for commodities and services for services because of relative national capabilities. Some services that the United States sells extensively to foreign countries are education (e.g., foreign students attending universities in the United States) and credit card systems and collections. Yet the United States is a net importer of shipping services. For the United States to become more self-sufficient in international shipping might result in the diversion of resources from their more efficient use in higher education or in the production of competitive products.

FACTOR-PROPORTIONS THEORY ▮▮▮▮▮▮▮▮▮▮

In their theories of absolute and comparative advantage, Smith and Ricardo showed how output could be increased if countries specialized in the products for which they have an advantage. Their theories did not, however, help to identify which types of products would most likely give a country an advantage. They assumed that the workings of the free market would lead producers to the goods that they could produce more efficiently and away from the goods that they could not produce efficiently. About a century and a quarter later, two Swedish economists, Eli Heckscher and Bertil Ohlin, developed the **factor-proportions theory,** which held that differences in countries' endowments of labor relative to their endowments of land or capital would explain differences in factor costs. They proposed that if labor were abundant in relation to land and capital, labor costs would be low and land and capital costs high. If labor were scarce, then the price of labor would be high in relation to the price of land and capital. These factor costs would lead countries to excel in the production and export of products using their abundant, and therefore cheaper, factors of productions.[8]

Land–Labor Relationship

On the basis of the factor-proportions theory, Sri Lankan authorities reasoned that they were likely to have a competitive advantage for products using large numbers of semiskilled workers. Labor was a production factor that they had in abundance.

The factor-proportions theory appears logical on the basis of a casual observation of worldwide production and exports. In countries where there are many people relative to the amount of land—for example, Hong Kong and the Netherlands—land prices are very high. Neither Hong Kong nor the Netherlands, regardless of their climate and soil conditions, excels in the production of goods requiring large amounts of land, such as sheep or wheat. These products are found in countries such as Australia and Canada where land is abundant relative to the number of people. Casual observation of manufacturing in relation to the labor–land proportions also seems to substantiate the theory. In Hong Kong, for example, the most successful industries are those in which technology permits the use of a minimum amount of land relative to the number of people employed; there, clothing production is housed in multistoried factories in which workers share minimal space. Hong Kong does not compete in the production of automobiles, which requires much more space per worker.

Labor–Capital Relationship

When labor is abundant in relation to capital, cheap labor rates and export competitiveness in products requiring large amounts of labor relative to cap-

Production factors are not homogeneous, especially labor.

ital would be expected. The opposite would be anticipated when labor is scarce. India, Iran, and Tunisia, for instance, excel in the production of handmade carpets that differ in appearance as well as production method from the carpets produced in the United Kingdom and the United States made by machines purchased with cheap capital.

U.S. imports have high intensity of less-skilled labor.

U.S. exports are labor intensive compared with U.S. imports.

Studies examining the labor-to-capital relationship have shown that export competitiveness is sometimes surprising, however. For example, Wassily Leontief found that in the United States, those industries that were more successful exporters had a higher labor intensity than those that faced the most import competition.[9] Because of the presumption that the United States has abundant capital relative to labor, this surprising finding is known as the **Leontief paradox.** Several possible explanations have been proposed for this finding.

One of the most plausible is that the Heckscher-Ohlin theory assumes erroneously that production factors are homogeneous. Labor skills are, in fact, very different within and among countries, since different people have different training and education. Training and education require capital expenditures that do not show up in traditional capital measurements, which include only plant and equipment values. By modifying the Heckscher-Ohlin theory to account for different labor groups and the capital invested to train these groups, the factor-proportions theory seems to hold. If we look at labor not as a homogeneous commodity but rather by categories of labor, we find that the industrial countries actually have a more abundant supply of highly educated labor (to which a high capital expenditure has been made) than of other types. Industrial country exports embody a higher proportion of professionals such as scientists and engineers; thus they are using their abundant production factors. LDC exports, on the other hand, have a high intensity of less-skilled labor.[10]

Different Production Methods

The factor-proportions analysis becomes more complicated when the same product might be produced by different methods, such as with either high inputs of labor or high inputs of capital. Canada produces wheat in a capital-intensive (high level of machinery per worker) way because of its abundance of low-cost capital relative to labor. In India, on the other hand, the same wheat is produced by using many fewer machines because there is abundant and cheap labor. Where there is more than one way of producing the same output, it is the relative input cost in relation to output that determines which country can produce the same product more cheaply. The fact that products can be produced in different ways is another possible explanation of the Leontief paradox in that the U.S. industries facing the most competition because of cheap foreign labor are the ones that have responded most intensively by substituting machines for labor.

THE PRODUCT LIFE CYCLE

According to the PLC theory, the production location for many products moves from one country to another depending on the stage in the products' life cycle.

Another theory attempts to explain world trade in manufactured products on the basis of stages in a product's life.[11] Briefly, the theory of **product life cycle (PLC)** states that certain kinds of products go through a cycle consisting of four stages (introduction, growth, maturity, and decline) and that the location of production will shift internationally depending on the stage of the cycle. These four stages are on a continuum rather than fully differentiated from each other. Nevertheless, the major changes are highlighted in Table 4.2, and we shall describe each stage in terms of its major characteristics.

Stage 1: Introduction

The introduction stage is marked by
- Innovation in response to observed need
- Export by the innovative country
- Evolving product

Innovation, Production, and Sales in Same Country New products are usually developed because there is a need and a market for them. Since there is generally more ready observation of nearby market conditions, the development is more apt to be in response to domestic than to foreign needs. In other words, a U.S. firm is most apt to develop a new product because of observed needs in the U.S. market, a French firm because of perceived needs in the French market, and so on. To illustrate how this works, producers in both the United States and France observed the need for longer-term food preservation as more women worked outside the home and had less time for food shopping. The prevalence of large kitchens and cheap electricity in the United States encouraged U.S. innovators to develop frozen food which could be stored in large freezer compartments. U.S. producers thus became leaders in the frozen-food industry. In France, however, large freezer compartments were impractical, so French producers led in the development of forms of food packaging (such as boxed milk) that would eliminate the need for refrigeration. Once a research and development group has created a new product, that product could theoretically be manufactured anywhere in the world, even though its sales are intended primarily for the market where consumer needs were first observed. In practice, however, the early production generally occurs in a domestic location because the company wishes to use its excess capacity and because it is useful for the company to locate near the intended consumers in order to obtain rapid market feedback and to save transport costs.

Location of Innovation Since the early manufacturing and sales of new products occur primarily in countries that make product innovations, it is useful to know where new products are developed. Indications are that during the last few decades nearly all of the world's technology has emanated from the developed countries and that during most of that period the United States has been the leading innovator.

TABLE 4.2 | INTERNATIONAL CHANGES DURING A PRODUCT'S LIFE CYCLE Overall, production and sales in LDCs grow in relative importance during a product's life cycle.

	Life Cycle Stages			
	Introduction	**Growth**	**Maturity**	**Decline**
Production location	• in innovating (usually industrial) country	• in innovating and other industrial countries	• multiple countries	• mainly in LDCs
Market location	• mainly in innovating country, with some exports	• mainly in industrial countries • shift in export markets as foreign production replaces exports in some markets • fast-growing demand	• growth in LDCs • some decrease in industrial countries • overall stabilized demand	• mainly in LDCs • some LDC exports • overall declining demand
Competitive factors	• near-monopoly position • sales based on uniqueness rather than price • evolving product characteristics	• number of competitors increases • some competitors begin price-cutting • product becoming more standardized	• number of competitors decreases • price is very important, especially in LDCs	• price is key weapon • number of producers continues to decrease
Production technology	• short production runs • evolving methods to coincide with product evolvement • high labor and labor skills to capital input	• capital input increases • methods more standardized	• long production runs using high capital inputs • highly standardized • less labor skill needed	• unskilled labor on mechanized long production runs

A number of reasons account for the dominant position of industrial countries, especially the United States. The primary ones are high incomes, which permit risking expenditures on research that may or may not yield gainful results, competition, demanding consumers, and the availability of scientists and engineers. In the United States scientific achievements are regarded with a particular awe, dramatized by such adjectives as "wonder," "miracle," and "magic" when referring to new products, and a sizable contingent of consumers generally believe that "new" is better than "old."

Once a company develops a competitive advantage through innovation, it is increasingly necessary to continue making improvements in order to stay competitive. The improvements may come in the product itself or in the method of manufacturing or distributing the product.[12]

Although the United States has had a leading position in the origin of product innovations, there is evidence that the U.S. share of new products has been declining and that Japan may now be the world's leading innovator.[13] There is also evidence from a recent study of ten major trading nations that innovation is the main source of their competitive strengths. But since innovations can be imitated, there is a need to continually develop new innovations in order to stay in the forefront.[14] For the purpose of explaining the PLC theory, however, we shall continue to use the United States as an example.

Exports and Labor   Although most sales are for the domestic market during the introduction stage of a product cycle, a small part of the production may be sold to customers in foreign markets who have heard about the new product and actively seek it. These foreign customers are most likely to be found in countries with similar market segments. In the case of the U.S., these would be other industrial countries because similarities in income levels create similar market segments.

At this stage the production process is apt to be more labor intensive than it will be in later stages. Because the product is not yet standardized, it is necessary to produce it by a process that permits rapid changes in product characteristics as dictated by feedback from the market. This implies high labor input as opposed to automated production, which is more capital intensive. A second factor influencing the early labor intensity is that process technology (the capital machinery necessary to produce a product on a large scale) usually develops later than product technology. It is only when sales begin to expand very rapidly (Stage 2) that there is an incentive to build machinery capable of producing the product on a large scale. At the introductory stage, sales growth may be too uncertain to warrant the high development costs of the new process machines.

The fact that the United States excels in the development of new products that are generally made in labor-intensive ways helps us to understand the Leontief paradox, which showed that the United States generally exports labor-intensive products. Since U.S. labor rates are known to be among the highest in the world, how can the United States compete? According to one view, this ability stems from the monopoly position of original producers, which allows them to pass on costs to consumers who are unwilling to wait for possible price reductions later on. There is much evidence of this behavior based on eventual price decreases of products such as calculators and videocassette recorders. Another explanation is that although U.S. labor is paid a high hourly wage, its education and skill levels make it adept and efficient when production is not yet standardized. When production becomes highly automated, the U.S. labor force becomes less competitive because unskilled labor may be quickly trained to perform highly repetitive tasks efficiently.

Interestingly, the United States enjoys its best manufacturing export advantage in those industries in which production workers are most highly paid, such as aerospace. The least competitive advantage is in the industries with lower wage rates, such as clothing.[15]

Stage 2: Growth

Growth is characterized by

- Increases in exports by the innovating country
- More competition
- Increased capital intensity
- Some foreign production

If sales begin to grow after a product is introduced, there is an incentive for competitors to break the monopoly position. They can often do this by making slight product changes, thereby overcoming the protection conferred through patents. At the same time, demand is likely to be growing substantially in foreign markets, particularly in other industrial countries. In fact, demand may be sufficient to justify the capital expenditure to produce in some foreign markets in order to reduce or eliminate transport charges and tariffs.

Either the innovator or the new entrant may begin producing abroad, but the output at this stage is likely to stay almost entirely in the foreign country with the new manufacturing unit. Let us say, for example, that U.S. production had a monopoly that has been broken by Japanese output. The Japanese output will be sold mainly in Japan because: (1) there is growth in the Japanese market; (2) unique product variations are being introduced for Japanese consumers; and (3) Japanese costs may still be high owing to production start-up problems.

Because sales are growing rapidly in many markets, there are greater incentives at this level for the development of process technology. However, product technology may not yet be well developed because of the number of product variations introduced by different competitors who are trying to take a leadership position by gaining market share. Thus the production process may still be characterized as labor-intensive during this stage, but it is becoming less so. The original producing country will increase its exports in this stage but face the loss of certain key export markets for which local production has commenced.

Stage 3: Maturity

Maturity includes

- Decline in exports from the innovating country
- More product standardization
- More capital intensity
- Increased competitiveness of price factor
- Production starts in LDCs

In Stage 3, maturity, worldwide demand begins to level off, although it may be growing in some countries and declining in others. In the mature stage of production there is often a shakeout of producers so that product models become highly standardized, making cost a more important competitive weapon. Longer production runs become possible for foreign plants, which in turn reduce per unit cost. The lower per unit cost enables sales to increase more in LDCs.

Since markets and technologies are widespread, the innovating country no longer has a production advantage. In fact, there are incentives to begin moving plants to LDCs where unskilled but inexpensive labor can be used effectively on standardized (capital-intensive) work processes.

Stage 4: Decline

Decline is characterized by
- Concentration of production in LDCs
- Innovating country becoming net importer

As a product moves to the declining stage, those factors occurring during the mature stage continue to evolve. The markets in industrial countries decline more rapidly than in LDCs as affluent customers spend disposable income on ever-newer products. By this time, market and cost factors have dictated that almost all production is situated in LDCs, which export to the declining market in industrial countries.

Verification and Limitations of PLC Theory

In recent years there have been a number of attempts to verify the PLC theory. Studies have found behavior to be consistent with the predictions of the PLC model for certain consumer durables, synthetic materials, and electronics.[16]

The PLC model seems to hold for many industries, but there are many other types of products for which this behavior would not be expected.[17] The first such type includes those products that, because of very rapid innovations, have extremely short life cycles, which makes it impossible to achieve cost reductions by moving production from one country to another. For example, product obsolescence occurs so rapidly for many electronic products that there is little international diffusion of production. The second type is the luxury product for which cost is of little concern to the consumer. The third type of product is one for which international transportation costs are so high that there is little opportunity for export sales, regardless of the stage within the product life cycle. The fourth type of product is one in which a firm can use a differentiation strategy, such as advertising, in order to maintain consumer demand without competing on the basis of price.[18]

Regardless of the type of product, there has been an increased tendency on the part of MNEs to introduce new products at home and abroad almost simultaneously as they move from multidomestic to global strategies. In other words, instead of merely observing needs within their domestic markets, companies develop products and services to serve observable market segments that transcend national borders. In so doing, they eliminate the leads and lags that are assumed to exist as a product is diffused from one country to another. Furthermore, companies are increasingly producing abroad simply to take advantage of production economies rather than in response to growing foreign markets. Singer, for example, produces certain sewing machine models in Brazil to sell in export markets, not to supply sewing machines to Brazil.

DETERMINATION OF TRADING PARTNERS ▮▮▮▮▮▮▮

Country Differences

Most trade theories emphasize differences among countries:
- *Climates*
- *Factor endowments*
- *Innovative capabilities*

Thus far in this chapter, the theories to explain why trade takes place have focused on the differences among countries. These theories tend to explain most of the trade among dissimilar countries, such as trade between an industrial country and an LDC or trade between a temperate country and a tropical one. On the basis of these theories we would expect that the greater the dissimilarity among countries, the greater the potential for trade. For example, great differences in climatic conditions would lead to greatly differentiated agricultural products. Countries that differed in labor or capital intensities would differ in the types of products they could produce efficiently. And national differences in innovative abilities would affect how production of a product would move from one country to another during the product's life cycle. A number of factors help to explain why a country trades more with one partner than with another.[19] The most important factors are described in this section.

Country-Similiarity Theory

Most trade today occurs among apparently similar countries.

When we observe actual trade patterns, we see that most of the world's trade occurs among countries that have similar characteristics. Most trade occurs among industrialized countries, which have highly educated populations and are located in temperate areas of the globe. Thus, overall trade patterns seem to be at variance with the traditional theories that emphasize country-by-country differences.

The fact that so much trade takes place among industrial countries is due to the growing importance of acquired (product-technology) advantage as opposed to natural advantage in world trade. The **country-similarity theory** holds that, having developed a new product in response to observed market conditions in the home market, a producer will then turn to markets that are perceived to be the most similar to those at home. In other words, consumers in industrial countries will have a high propensity to buy high-quality and luxury products, whereas consumers in lower-income countries will buy few of these products.[20]

Although the markets within the industrial countries might have similar demand characteristics, there are differences in how these countries specialize in order to gain acquired advantages. For example, the British have excelled for some time in biochemistry and applied engineering, the Germans in synthetics chemistry, and the French in pharmacology. It is also known that substantial country-to-country differences exist in apportionment of R&D expenditures, thus giving rise to the development of different technical and product capabilities in different industrial countries.[21] Furthermore, those domestic industries for which there is intense competitive rivalry are likely to be the ones that innovate faster and develop international advantages.[22]

Pairs of Trading Relationships

Although the theories regarding country differences and similarities help to explain broad world trade patterns, such as between industrial countries and LDCs, they do little to help us understand specific pairs of trading relationships. Why, for example, will a particular industrial country buy more from one LDC than another? Why will it buy from one industrial country rather than another? Although there is no single answer to these questions that will explain all product flows, the distance between two countries explains more of these world trade relationships than any other factor. This is especially true for products for which the transport cost is high relative to the production cost.

Cultural similarity, as expressed by language and religion, also helps to explain much of the direction of trade. Apparently importers and exporters find it easier to do business in a country that they perceive as being similar. Likewise, much of the trade between specific industrial countries and LDCs is explained by historic colonial relationships. Importers and exporters find it easier to continue business ties than to develop new distributorship arrangements in countries where they are less experienced.

INDEPENDENCE, INTERDEPENDENCE, AND DEPENDENCE

No country is completely dependent or independent, though some are closer to one extreme or the other.

The concepts of independence, interdependence, and dependence help to explain world trade patterns and countries' trade policies. They form a continuum, with independence at one extreme, dependence on the other, and interdependence somewhere in the middle. There are no countries located at either extreme of this continuum; however, some tend to be closer to one extreme than the other.

Independence

Too much economic independence means doing without certain goods, services, and technologies.

In a situation of **independence,** a country would have no reliance on others for any goods, services, or technologies. Since all countries engage in trade, however, no country has complete economic independence from other countries, and all thus have at least some access to goods and services produced in a foreign country. The most recent instance of economic near-independence was seen in the Tasaday tribe, found by hunters on the island of Mindanao in the southern Philippines in 1971. Although some scientists have called the Tasadays a hoax, many others believe that the tribe may indeed have been the last group on earth to live in virtual isolation. A less extreme example is Albania, which experienced near-isolation from the end of World War II until the death of dictator Enver Hoxha in 1985.[23] Their isolation from other societies brought certain advantages to the Tasadays and Albanians: They did not have to be concerned, for example, that another society might cut off their supply of essential foods or tools. Of course, for both societies the price of their independence was having to do without products that they could not produce themselves.

In most countries, governmental policy has focused on achieving the advantages of independence without paying too high a price in terms of consumer deprivation. China and India, for example, have pursued economic independence much more vigorously than have Brazil and Mexico, with different results in different periods.[24] Earlier in this chapter we showed that large countries typically depend much less on foreign trade than do small countries, but even in large countries consumers could suffer through policies designed to promote more independence. The degree of suffering would, of course, depend on the type of product: The elimination of coffee or tea imports into the United States would probably involve less of a hardship than the cessation of foreign purchases of certain essential metals, such as manganese, cobalt, and chromium. In between are products that could be produced domestically, but at a much higher price. No country today seeks complete independence, but most try to forge their trade patterns so that they are minimally vulnerable to foreign control of supply and demand.

Interdependence

Interdependence is mutual dependence.

One way of limiting one's vulnerability to foreign changes is through **interdependence,** or the development of trade relationships on the basis of mutual need. France and Germany, for example, have highly interdependent economies. Each depends about equally on the other as a trading partner, and thus neither is likely to cut off supplies or markets because the other could retaliate effectively.

Dependence

Too much dependence causes a country to be vulnerable to events in other countries.

In recent years, many developing countries have decried their **dependence,** realizing that they are too dependent on the sale of one primary commodity and/or too dependent on one country as a customer and supplier. Because LDC economies are small, they tend to be much more dependent on a given industrial country than the industrial country is dependent on them. Mexico, for example, depends on the United States for over 60 percent of its imports and exports, whereas the United States depends on Mexico for less than 5 percent of its imports and exports. Mexico can thus be much more adversely affected by U.S. policies than the United States can be affected by Mexican policies. This sort of dependence by an LDC on an industrial country has led to a widespread belief that dependence will retard the LDC's development.[25] Fear of dependency has led many LDCs to try to change their production and trade patterns, as reflected in the opening case on Sri Lanka.

Figure 4.3 shows that in 21 of the 22 industrialized countries (all except Iceland) the leading export accounts for less than 25 percent of total export earnings. Among the developing countries, however, 57 percent are dependent on one commodity for at least 25 percent of their export earnings. A selected list of high-commodity dependencies by LDCs is given in Table 4.3.

The developing countries are also more dependent on one trading partner than are industrial countries (see Fig. 4.4). The trading partner on whom the developing country typically depends is almost always an industrial country (some examples are shown in Table 4.4). Only one of 22 industrial countries (Canada) conducts over half its trade with one partner (the United States) and only 23 percent of industrial countries depend on their leading trading partner for over 25 percent of their exports. Seventy-five percent of LDCs depend on their leading trading partner for more than 25 percent of their exports.

Although theorists and policymakers wishing to lower dependency have proposed a number of different approaches, they all propose that LDCs intervene in the foreign trade markets. As shown in the introductory case, Sri Lanka has attempted to diversify its exports by developing nontraditional products that its policymakers believe can ultimately be competitive in world markets.

Trade Strategies Among Developing Countries   In earlier discussions we emphasized that most LDCs depend on the export of primary products. The manufactured goods they export are usually mature products requiring high inputs of unskilled or semiskilled labor. While these distinctions are true in an overall sense, they nevertheless obscure some differences among groups of developing countries. For those countries that do export manufactured goods, the type of good and country can be placed into one of three categories. Countries in the first group—Hong Kong, Singapore, Taiwan, South Korea, Israel, Portugal, and Greece—lack natural resources and have concentrated on exporting mature labor-intensive products. They have all emphasized marketing, design, and information about foreign markets as a means of becoming competitive. Countries in the second group—Yugoslavia, Argentina, Brazil, Mexico, and Turkey—have natural resources, which they can use for further processing into manufactured goods, and domestic markets that are large enough to support scale economies. These countries have had success in exporting capital goods, chemicals, and other intermediaries. Countries in the third group—India, Pakistan, Egypt, and Indonesia (large poor nations)—have developed exports of standardized intermediate goods such as textiles, plywood, and cement that are not typical labor-intensive commodities.[26]

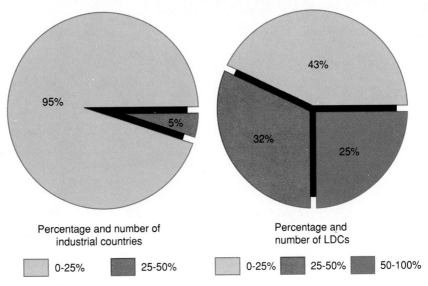

Percentage and number of industrial countries

Percentage and number of LDCs

0-25%   25-50%   0-25%   25-50%   50-100%

Figure 4.3
Dependence on Leading Commodity for Export Earnings
Among 22 industrial countries, none receives over half and only one receives
between 25 and 50 percent of export earnings from its leading export
commodity. Among 28 LDCs, seven receive over half and nine receive between
25 and 50 percent of their export earnings from their leading export commodity.
Source: Commodities are based on compilation of three-digit Standard Industrial Trade
Classifications in *1986 Yearbook of International Trade Statistics,* Vol. I (New York: UN
Department of International Economic and Social Affairs, 1988) for all countries for which
1985 data are reported.

**TABLE 4.3 | SELECTED LDC DEPENDENCE ON ONE COMMODITY
FOR EXPORT EARNINGS**

LDC	Commodity	Percent of LDC's Exports
Colombia	Coffee	59.9
Cuba	Sugar	77.1
Gabon	Petroleum	76.1
Ghana	Cacao	58.3
Jamaica	Base metal ores	65.3
Liberia	Crude materials (non-petrol)	90.3
Macao	Clothing	56.8
Mali	Cotton	55.7
Mauritania	Iron ore	49.1
Niger	Uranium and Thorium ores	83.2
Rwanda	Coffee	71.5
Sierre Leone	Semiprecious stones and crude materials	70.4
Somalia	Live animals	89.7

Source: 1987 Yearbook of International Statistics, Vol. 1 (New York: UN Department of International Economic and Social Affairs, 1989).

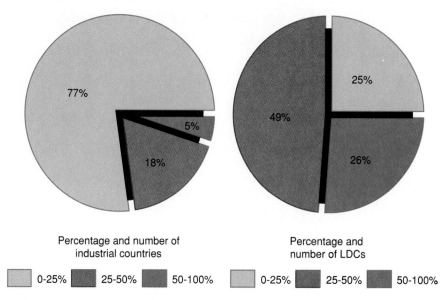

Percentage and number of   Percentage and
industrial countries   number of LDCs

▢ 0-25%	■ 25-50%	■ 50-100%	▢ 0-25%	■ 25-50%	■ 50-100%

Figure 4.4
Dependence on Major Export Partner
Among 22 industrial countries, one receives over half and four receive between
25 and 50 percent of their export earnings from their major trading partner.
Among 85 LDCs, 22 receive over half and 42 receive between 25 and 50 percent
of export earnings from their major trading partner. *Source: 1988 Yearbook of
International Trade Statistics,* Vol. I (New York: UN Department of International Economic
and Social Affairs, 1990).

TABLE 4.4 | SELECTED LDC DEPENDENCE ON ONE TRADING PARTNER

LDC	Export Market	Percent of LDC's Exports
Afghanistan	USSR*	59.4
Brunei Darussalam	Japan	61.2
Central African Republic	France	44.1
Mauritius	United Kingdom	43.5
Mexico	United States	64.7
Somalia	Saudi Arabia	86.5

*Now, the Commonwealth of Independent States.

Source: 1987 Yearbook of International Trade Statistics, Vol. 1 (New York: UN Department of
International Economic and Social Affairs, 1989).

_____ **WHY COMPANIES TRADE** ▬▬▬▬▬▬▬▬▬▬▬

Most theories are based on a national perspective, but trade decisions are usually made by companies.

Incentives to export include

- Use for excess capacity
- Reduced production costs per unit
- Increased markup
- Spread of sales risk

Incentives to import include

- Cheaper supplies
- Additions to product line
- Reduction of risk of nonsupply

Most trade theories approach the issue from a national perspective; that is, they begin with a question such as, "Why should Sri Lanka trade?" Regardless of the advantages that countries may gain by trading, trade ordinarily will not begin unless businesses within the country perceive that there are opportunities for exporting and importing. Since companies have a limited number of resources, they must decide whether to exploit those resources domestically or internationally. Only if they see that the international opportunities might be greater than the domestic ones will they divert their resources to the foreign sector. To understand why trade takes place, it is therefore useful to understand the trade advantages accruing to individual businesses.

Export Opportunities

Excess Capacity Use   Companies frequently have immediate or long-term output capabilities for which there is inadequate domestic demand. This may be in the form of known reserves of natural resources or product-specific capabilities that cannot be easily diverted to the production of other goods for which there might be an adequate domestic demand.

As shown earlier in this chapter, small countries tend to trade more than large countries. One reason is that process technology may allow a firm to produce efficiently only on a large scale, larger than the demand in the domestic market. Take automobile production, for example. Volvo has a much greater need to export from the small Swedish market than General Motors does from the large U.S. market.

Cost Reduction   Studies have shown that a company can generally reduce its costs by 20–30 percent each time its output is doubled, a phenomenon known as the **experience curve**.[27] For instance, if we assume a 20 percent cost reduction and an initial cost of $100 per unit, the second unit produced will cost $80, the fourth $64, and so on. The reduction may come about because of several factors: covering fixed costs over a larger output, increasing efficiency because of the experience gained producing large quantities of units, and making quantity purchases of materials and transportation. Therefore, it is obvious that the market leader may garner cost advantages over competitors. One way a company can increase output is by defining its market in global rather than domestic terms.

More Profitability   A producer might be able to sell the same product at a greater profit abroad than at home. This may happen because the competitive environment in the foreign market is different, possibly because the product is in a different stage of its life cycle abroad. Thus a mature stage at home may force domestic price cutting, whereas a growth stage abroad may make price reductions unnecessary there. Greater profitability also may come about because of different government actions at home or abroad that affect profitability—for example, differences in the taxation of earnings or differences in regulations on prices.

Risk Spreading   By spreading sales over more than one country market, a producer might be able to minimize fluctuations in demand. This may come about because business cycles vary from country to country and because products might be in different stages of their life cycles in different countries. Another factor in spreading risk through exportation is that a producer might be able to develop more customers, thereby reducing its vulnerability to the loss of any single or few customers.

Import Opportunities

The impetus for trade involvement may come from either the exporter or the importer. In either case, there must be both a seller and a buyer. Impetus may come from an importer because a firm is seeking out cheaper or better-quality supplies, components, or products to be used in its production facilities. Or a firm may be actively seeking new products that have been developed abroad in order to complement its existing lines. This will give the company more to sell; it might also enable the importer to use excess capacity in its own distribution sales force.

If international procurement of supplies and components lowers costs or improves the quality of finished products, the procuring company may then be better able to combat import competition for the finished products. Or the procuring firm may be able to compete more effectively in export markets itself. The automobile industry exemplifies global competition that depends on subcontractors, including foreign ones, to reduce production costs.[28]

An importer, like an exporter, might be able to spread its operating risks. By developing alternative suppliers, the firm is less vulnerable to the dictates or fortunes of any single supplier. For example, many large steel customers in the United States, such as the automobile industry, have diversified their steel purchases to include European and Japanese suppliers. This strategy has reduced the risk of supply shortages for the U.S. automobile industry in case of a strike among steelworkers in the United States, but at the same time, it has contributed to the problems of the steel industry within the United States.

Trade Impediments

Trade impediments include
- Lack of knowledge about opportunities
- Lack of information on trade mechanics
- Fears about risks
- Trade restrictions

In spite of the advantages that may accrue for firms engaging in importation or exportation, many factors can impede a firm's entry into trading relations, and these in turn affect the full realization of trade among countries. First, a firm's management may have imperfect knowledge of markets in foreign countries and thus be unable to take advantage of the avenues open to the firm. Or a producer might be aware of potential demand in foreign countries but nevertheless not know the mechanics of exporting and distributing in foreign markets. The process of exporting, after all, involves a whole new set of terminology and institutions. Finally, a company might perceive that exporting or importing is too risky. A potential exporter, for example, may fear that payment will not be forthcoming, that payment will be in a currency that cannot easily be used, or that the competitive environment abroad is too unknown or disorderly. A potential importer may lack the resources to seek out global resources or may fear that supplies are too uncertain given the greater distance between countries and the perceived problems (whether accurate or not) of more strikes and unrest abroad.

Governmental policies might either enhance or retard the movement of trade. Policies to improve imperfect knowledge about the foreign environment might positively increase trade. Direct restrictions on the importation or exportation of goods are obvious barriers. It is safe to say, though, that all governments have policies that both enhance and retard trade. In the Sri Lankan case at the beginning of the chapter, the government sought to remove some marketing imperfections by helping to identify industries likely to be competitive internationally. At the same time, however, Sri Lanka set direct import restrictions on a number of products.

LOOKING TO THE FUTURE   If present trends continue, factor endowment (land, labor, and capital) relationships will continue to evolve. The population growth rate is much higher in LDCs, especially sub-Saharan Africa, than in developed countries. Two possible consequences include a continued shift of labor-intensive production activities to LDCs and agricultural production away from densely populated areas. At the same time, the finite supply of natural resources may lead to price increases for these resources (except for short respites). This may work to the advantage of LDCs because supplies in industrial countries have been more fully exploited.

Some trade theories and current policymakers hold that a **laissez-faire** trade policy (one with minimum government influence) should prevail. Yet governments are seldom neutral in their effects on trade competitiveness. Many countries have recently tried to better their trade advantages by altering the quality and quantity of their resource inputs and by targeting sectors in which to develop acquired advantages. These approaches are exemplified by the economic and trade successes of Japan, Taiwan, and South Korea. South Korea, for example, has been transformed in a fairly short time from a poor agricultural country to a net exporter of key manufactured products. To achieve this transformation, the South Korean government took an active role in targeting key sectors (especially steel, automobiles, and consumer electronics) to ensure that they obtained needed capital. In the case of steel, the government created a state-owned company. The government gave incentives for firms to acquire foreign technology, to improve on it, and to train workers in quality control procedures. In addition, the government invested heavily in education in order to improve the input quality of employees. Not only did South Korea increase the educational attendance rate, it also increased the proportion of scientists and engineers in higher education.[29]

Given the success of some Asian countries, the future will likely bring greater global governmental efforts to improve trade advantages. In turn, there will likely be controversy regarding the fairness of competition between government-supported and laissez-faire industries. There will be further discussions on the appropriateness of transferring successful trade policies from one country to another. For example, the collective approach that works so well in Japan, Taiwan, and South Korea may not be appropriate for individualistically oriented societies such as the United Kingdom and the United States.[30]

Four factors are worth monitoring because they could cause product trade to become a less significant portion of total and international business in the future. First, the protectionist sentiment is growing, and this could prevent competitively produced goods from entering foreign countries. Second, as economies grow, efficiencies of multiple production locations also grow; thus country-by-country production may replace trade in many cases. Third, flexible small-scale production methods using robotics may enable even small countries to produce many goods efficiently for their own consumption, thus eliminating the need to import them. Fourth, services are growing more rapidly than products as a portion of production and consumption within industrial countries; consequently, product trade may become a less important part of countries' total expenditures. Furthermore, many of the rapid-growth service areas, such as home building and dining out, are not easily tradeable, thus trade in goods plus services could become a smaller part of total output and consumption.

The move to multiple production facilities in different countries has already led to a more rapid growth of international business through direct investment than through trade. For example, U.S.-based firms have held their global market share much better in recent years than has U.S. output. This is because they have served foreign markets increasingly from their overseas production units. At the same time, such non–U.S.-based firms as Honda are serving the U.S. market increasingly from their U.S.-located production units.[31] This growing mobility of companies is likely to create further distinctions between the competitiveness of countries and the competitiveness of companies headquartered therein.

SUMMARY

- Trade theory is useful because it helps to explain what might be produced competitively in a given locale, where a company might go to produce a given product efficiently, and whether governmental practices will interfere with the free flow of trade among countries.

- Some trade theories deal with the question of what will happen to international trade in the absence of governmental interference; others prescribe how government should interfere with trade flows in order to achieve certain national objectives.

■ Mercantilist theory proposed that a country should try to achieve a favorable balance of trade (export more than it imports) in order to receive an influx of gold. Neomercantilist theory also seeks a favorable balance of trade, but its purpose is to achieve some social or political objective.

■ Adam Smith developed the theory of absolute advantage, which holds that consumers will be better off if they can buy foreign-made products that are priced more cheaply than domestic ones.

■ According to the theory of absolute advantage, a country may produce goods more efficiently because of a natural advantage (e.g., raw materials, climate) or because of an acquired advantage (e.g., technology or skills).

■ The theory of country size holds that because countries with large land areas are more apt to have varied climates and natural resources, they are generally more nearly self-sufficient than smaller countries. A second reason for their greater self-sufficiency is that their production centers are more likely to be located at a greater distance from other countries, thus raising the transport costs of foreign trade.

■ The comparative advantage theory holds that total output can be increased through foreign trade even though one country may have an absolute advantage in the production of all products.

■ Some of the assumptions of the absolute and comparative trade theories that have been questioned by policymakers are that full employment exists, that output efficiency is the major objective, that there are no transport costs among countries, that resources move freely within countries, and that resources are immobile internationally.

■ The factor-proportions theory holds that the relative factor endowments in a country of land, labor, and capital will determine the relative costs of these factors. These costs, in turn, will determine what goods a country can produce most efficiently.

■ The theory of product life cycle (PLC) states that many manufactured products will first be produced in the countries in which the products were researched and developed. These are almost always industrialized countries, with the United States accounting for the largest share in recent years. Over the life of the product, production will tend to become more capital intensive and will be shifted to foreign locations.

■ According to the country-similarity theory of trade, most trade today takes place in manufactured goods among industrial countries because there are more-similar market segments among these countries.

■ LDCs have been increasingly concerned that they are overly vulnerable to events in other countries because of their high dependence on one export product and/or one trading partner. As they try to become more independent of the external environment, however, they face the risk that their own consumers may have to pay higher prices or do without some goods.

■ Although most trade theories deal with country-to-country benefits and costs, it is usually at the firm level that trading decisions are made. Companies may seek trading opportunities in order to use excess capacity, lower production costs, or spread risks. They may not engage in foreign trading activities, however, because of ignorance of opportunities or how to take advantage of them or because they consider foreign operations too risky.

C A S E
THE
CASHEW[32]

The cashew tree is best known today for its nuts, which account for about 20 percent of the value of nuts produced worldwide—a value about equal to that of almonds or hazelnuts.

The fruit of the tree (known as the cashew apple), however, drew first attention. The Tupi Indians of Brazil first harvested the cashew apple in the wild. They later introduced it to early Portuguese traders, who in turn propagated the plant in other tropical countries. But attempts to grow the tree on plantations proved unsuccessful because the cashew was vulnerable to insects in the close quarters of plantations. Instead, some of the abandoned plantation trees propagated new trees in the wild where they thrived in the forests of India, East Africa, Indonesia, and Southeast Asia.

Several factors inhibited early use of the cashew nut. First, cashew fruit matures before the nut, so the fruit is spoiled by the time the nut can be harvested usefully. Second, the processing of cashew nuts is tedious and time consuming. In the 1920s, however, a processing industry developed in India, and the nuts became more valuable than the fruit because they became so popular among Indian consumers. India maintained a virtual monopoly on cashew processing until the mid-1970s. This monopoly

was due to a combination of three factors: First, India was the largest producer of wild cashews; second, early demand occurred in India, meaning that any other country would have to incur added transport charges in order to reach the Indian market; and third, and most importantly, the Indian workers were particularly adept at the process technology.

Cashew nut processing was performed in a very labor-intensive manner, requiring manual dexterity and low labor rates. The nut is contained beneath layers of shell and thin skin. To remove the shell, the nut must be placed in an open fire for a few minutes and then tapped (while still hot) with a wooden hammer. If the nut is broken in the tapping, its value decreases considerably. Once the shell is removed, the nut is placed in an oven for up to ten hours, after which the skin is removed by hand while the nut is still warm. Removal is done without fingernails or any sharp objects that can mark or break the surface. The nuts are then sorted and graded into 24 different categories by the size of the pieces. The highest-quality grade typically sells for about four times the price of the lowest grade, which is sold almost entirely to the confectionery industry.

Through the years several factors began to threaten India's prominence as a cashew producer. First, as demand for the nuts grew in the United States and the United Kingdom, a shortage developed. Since the nuts were grown in the wild and were unsuited to plantation growth,

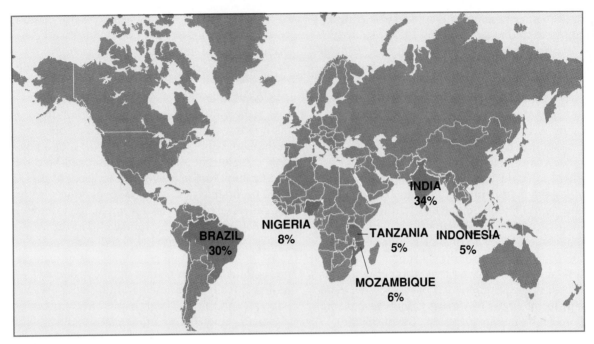

Map 4.2
Location of World's Cashew Nut Production
The major cashew-producing areas are all in the tropics. This map shows the location of the six largest producers. *Source:* Percentages refer to share of world cashew nut production as shown in *FAO Production Yearbook*, Vol. 42, 1988.

India turned to East Africa, especially Mozambique, Tanzania, and Kenya, for supplies. Those countries were experiencing high unemployment and were at first eager to sell the raw nuts. Nevertheless, by the late 1980s India was still the largest nut producer (see Map 4.2).

By the 1950s India was no longer the world's major consumer, and the East African countries began to realize that they might be able to bypass India by processing the raw nuts themselves. Cashew-processing methods were well known, so there was no technological obstacle. There was another barrier, however, that blocked early competition from East Africa. The Indian labor force worked on homemade handicrafts as children, and as a result, by the time they were employed in cashew processing, they could perform delicate hand operations effi-ciently. Without this training, the East Africans were at a fatal disadvantage.

Although the Africans' inability to compete granted a reprieve to the Indian industry, it put them on notice that they were vulnerable to supply cutoffs. The Indian Council for Agricultural Research, the International Society for Horticultural Sciences, and the Indian Society for Plantation Crops expanded their efforts to increase India's production of raw nuts. Concomitantly, three different companies developed mechanical equipment to replace hand processing. The Sturtevant Tropical Products Institute developed a method now used by a London equipment manufacturer, Fletcher and Stewart, which cracks the shells with a steel plate. Oltremare Industria of Italy and Widmer and Ernst of Switzerland both developed shell-cutting machines. Equipment was sold to East African countries and to Brazil in the 1970s. These countries decreased their raw-nut exports to India in order to maintain supplies for their own processing.

Two factors have kept India's hand-processing industry afloat. First, the machinery breaks many nuts, so Indian processors still face little competition in the sale of higher-grade cashew nuts. At any time, however, newer machinery might solve the breakage problem, again threatening the approximately 200 Indian processors and their 300,000 employees. Furthermore, there is increased competition for the lower-grade output. The second factor responsible for the enduring Indian industry is that their processors have been able to obtain more raw nuts as Indian raw-nut production has increased. Pesticide technology now makes cashew tree plantations feasible, thus increasing the number of trees per acre. Furthermore, Indian experimentation in hybridization, vegetative propagation, and grafting and budding techniques promises to increase the output per tree to five times what it was in the wild.

The Indian processors have been vulnerable to two more threats. One is political, the other technological. First, because India could no longer compete as well in its traditional North American and European markets for lower-grade nuts, a larger portion of those nuts was sold during the 1980s in the USSR, which became India's largest cashew nut customer in terms of tonnage. The USSR bought the nuts at a price above world market levels, and its buying habits were believed to have a political motive. By buying large quantities at a high price, the Commonwealth of Independent States (CIS) might acquire considerable political influence in India, especially in the Kerala area where the processing industry is centered. If the CIS continues to develop friendlier relations with Western countries and continues its internal political and economic problems in the 1990s, there is an increasing possibility that these sales might decline drastically.

Second, there has been a potential for an excess cashew nut supply, which can result from plantation techniques and improved technology in India and elsewhere. To find outlets for a possible nut glut, the All-India Coordinated Spices and Cashew Nut Improvement Project has centered on finding new markets for products from the cashew tree. The cashew apple, for example, is available in far greater tonnage than the cashew nut. It has been discarded in the past because processors could get either fruit or nut but not both, and the nuts have been considered more valuable. Experimentation is going on to harvest both the fruit and the nut. The fruit is also being studied for commercial use in candy, jams, chutney, juice, carbonated beverages, syrup, wine, and vinegar. A second area of research is in the use of cashew nut shell liquid, which was once discarded as a waste product and is now used extensively in industrial production of friction dusts for formulation in brake linings and clutch facings. Thus far, however, the extraction of cashew nut shell liquid has been too costly to make it fully competitive with some other types of oils.

Questions

1. What trade theories help to explain where cashew tree products have been produced historically?
2. Might India lose its competitive advantage in future cashew nut production? Why or why not?
3. If you were an Indian cashew processor, what alternatives might you consider to maintain future competitiveness?

Chapter Notes

1. Data for this case were taken from *1983 Commodity Yearbook* (Jersey City, N.J.: Commodity Research Bureau, Inc. 1983), p. 340; "The Business Outlook: Sri Lanka," *Business Asia,* February 6, 1981, p. 48; "Sri Lanka Investment: Inside or Outside the Free Trade Zone?" *Business Asia,* April 24, 1981, pp. 134–135; P. Murugasu, "Selecting Products for Export Development," *International Trade Forum,* October–December 1979, pp. 4–7; International Monetary Fund, *Direction of Trade Statistics Yearbook 1982* (Washington, D.C.: IMF, 1982), p. 345; "United States Congress Speaks on Sri Lanka," bulletin issued by the Embassy of the Democratic Socialist Republic of Sri Lanka, Washington, April 1979; Lucien Rajakarunanayake, "Sri Lanka: Patterns of Serendipity" (Washington, D.C.: Embassy of Sri Lanka, May 1975); Colin de Silva, "Sri Lanka, the 'Resplendent Isle,'" *New York Times,* February 14, 1984, Sec. xx, p. 9; *World Development Atlas, 1989* (Washington, D.C.: International Bank of Reconstruction and Development, 1989), p. 9; and Sarath Rajapatirana, "Foreign Trade and Economic Development: Sri Lanka's Experience," *World Development,* Vol. 16, No. 10, October 1988, pp. 1143–1158.

2. The mercantilist period is not associated with any single writer. A good coverage of the philosophy of the era may be found in Eli Heckscher, *Mercantilism* (London: George Allen & Unwin, 1935).

3. For a discussion of the problems in running a trade surplus, see Maria Shao, William J. Holstein, and Steven J. Dryden, "Taiwan's Wealth Crisis," *Business Week,* No. 2993, April 13, 1987, pp. 46–47.

4. The book has been reprinted by various publishers. For the specific references of this chapter the edition used was Adam Smith, *The Wealth of Nations* (New York: The Modern Library, n.d.).

5. Stephen P. Magee, *International Trade* (Reading, Mass.: Addison-Wesley, 1980), pp. 10–12.

6. G. C. Hufbauer, "The Impact of National Characteristics and Technology on the Commodity Composition of Trade in Manufactured Goods," in *The Technology Factor in International Trade,* Raymond Vernon, ed. (New York: Columbia University Press, 1970), pp. 145–231.

7. David Ricardo, *On the Principles of Political Economy and Taxation,* originally published in London in 1817, has since been reprinted by a number of publishers.

8. Bertil Ohlin, *Interregional and International Trade* (Cambridge, Mass.: Harvard University Press, 1933).

9. W. W. Leontief, "Domestic Production and Foreign Trade: The American Capital Position Re-examined," *Economia Internationale,* February 1954, pp. 3–32.

10. See, for example, Anne O. Krueger, "Trade Policies in Developing Countries," in *Handbook of International Economics,* Vol. 3, Ronald W. Jones and Peter Kenen, eds. (Amsterdam: North-Holland, 1984), pp. 519–569; and Bela Balassa, *The Newly Industrialized Countries in the World Economy* (New York: Pergamon, 1981), Chap. 7.

11. Raymond Vernon, "International Investment and International Trade in the Product Life Cycle," *Quarterly Journal of Economics,* May 1966, pp. 190–207; Paul Krugman, "A Model of Innovation, Technology Transfer, and the World Distribution of Income," *Journal of Political Economy,* Vol. 87, April 1979, pp. 253–266; David Dollar, "Technological Innovation, Capital Mobility, and the Product Cycle in North-South Trade," *American Economic Review,* Vol. 76, No. 1, pp. 177–190.

12. Robert B. Reich, "The Real Economy," *The Atlantic Monthly,* Vol. 267, No. 2, February 1991, pp. 35–52.

13. See, for example, Paul Streeten, "Technology Gaps between Rich and Poor Countries," *Scottish Journal of Political Economy,* November 1972, Vol. XIX, No. 3, pp. 213–230; and Theresa Tellez, "Science, Technology and the Matter of Choice," *Science and Public Affairs,* October 1973, p. 55, for LDC estimates. Estimates of the U.S. portion are from National Science Foundation studies reported in Victor K. McElheny, "U.S. Science Lead Is Found Eroding," *New York Times,* March 14, 1976, p. 1. For more recent country-by-country comparisons of R&D expenditures, see Barnaby J. Feder, "Europe's Technology Revival," *New York Times,* May 21, 1984, p. D1 +; William J. Broad, "Novel Technique Shows Japanese Outpace Americans in Innovation," *New York Times,* March 7, 1988, p. 1 +.

14. Michael E. Porter, *The Competitive Advantage of Nations* (New York: The Free Press, 1990).

15. Daniel J. B. Mitchell, "Recent Changes in the Labor Content of U.S. International Trade," *International Labor Relations Review,* April 1975, pp. 355–375.

16. For good summaries of the studies to test the theory as well as recent tests, see James M. Lutz and Robert T. Green, "The Product Life Cycle and the Export Position of the United States," *Journal of International Business Studies,* Winter 1983, pp. 77–93; and Alicia Mullor-Sebastian, "The Product Life Cycle Theory: Empirical Evidence," *Journal of International Business Studies,* Winter 1983, pp. 95–105.

17. Ian H. Giddy, "The Demise of the Product Life Cycle in International Business Theory," *Columbia Journal of World Business,* Spring 1978, pp. 90–97.

18. This has been argued as a factor enabling industrial countries to charge high prices to LDCs while purchasing LDC manufactured products at the lowest possible prices. See Frances Stewart, "Recent Theories of International Trade: Some Implications for the South," in Henry Kierzowski, ed., *Monopolistic Competition and International Trade* (Oxford: Oxford University Press, 1984).

19. For a good overview of studies on this subject as well as an empirical analysis, see Rajendra K. Srivastava and Robert T. Green, "Determinants of Bilateral Trade Flows," *Journal of Business,* Vol. 59, No. 4, October 1986, p. 623–639.

20. Stefan B. Linder, *An Essay on Trade Transformation* (New York: Wiley, 1961).

21. Michael J. Thomas, "The Location of Research and Development in the International Corporation," *Management International Review,* No. 1, 1975, p. 39.

22. Michael E. Porter, "The Competitive Advantage of Nations," *Harvard Business Review,* Vol. 90, No. 2, March–April 1990, p. 78.

23. Kenneth MacLeish, "Stone Age Cavemen of Mindanao," *National Geographic,* August 1972, pp. 219–249; Seth Mydans, "In Mindanao: Ancient Tribe or a Hoax from the 1970's," *New York Times,* December 7, 1987, p. 6; Robin Knight, "Albania Peeks Out, Never Forgetting 'Life Is Earnest,'" *U.S. News & World Report,* Vol. 102, No. 18, May 11, 1987, p. 36.

24. Bela Balassa, "The Cambridge Group and the Developing Countries," *The World Economy,* Vol. 8, No. 4, September–October 1985, pp. 201–218.

25. For a very good survey of the literature (pro and con) on this point, see José Antonio Ocampo, "New Developments in Trade Theory and LDCs," *Journal of Developing Economics,* Vol. 22, No. 1, 1986, pp. 129–170.

26. Hollis Chenery and Donald Keesing, "The Changing Composition of Developing Country Exports," in Sven Grassman and Erik Lundberg, eds., *The World Economic Order: Past and Prospects* (London: Macmillan, 1981), pp. 82–116.

27. See, for example, Boston Consulting Group, *Perspective in Experience* (Boston: Boston Consulting Group, 1970); and Robert D. Buzzell, Bradley T. Buzzell, Gale Sultaw,

and Ralph G. M. Sultaw, "Market Share: A Key to Profitability," *Harvard Business Review,* Vol. 58, No. 1, 1975.

28. Ulli Arnold, "Global Sourcing—An Indispensable Element in Worldwide Competition," *Management International Review,* Vol. 29, No. 4, 1989, p. 22.

29. Alice H. Amsden, "Asia's Next Giant," *Technology Review,* May–June 1989, pp. 47–53.

30. G. C. Lodge and E. F. Vogel, *Ideology and National Competitiveness* (Boston: Harvard Business School Press, 1987).

31. Robert Kuttner, "One Big, Happy Global Economy? Not Yet, Friend," *Business Week,* October 15, 1990, p. 18; and Masaaki Kotabe, "Assessing the Shift in Global Market Share of U.S. Multinationals," *International Marketing Review,* Vol. 6, No. 5, 1989, pp. 20–35.

32. Data for this case were taken from "L'Anacarde ou Noix de Cajou," *Marches Tropicaux,* June 13, 1980, pp. 1403–1405; R. J. Wilson, *The Market for Cashew Nut Kernels and Cashew Nutshell Liquid* (London: Tropical Products Institute, 1975); J. H. P. Tyman, "Cultivation, Processing and Utilization of the Cashew," *Chemistry and Industry,* January 19, 1980, pp. 59–62; Jean-Pierre Jeannet, "Indian Cashew Processors, Ltd.," ICH Case 9-378-832 (Boston: Harvard Business School, 1977); Jean-Pierre Jeannet, "Note on the World Cashew Nut Industry," ICH Case 9-378-834 (Boston: Harvard Business School, 1977); and "Meanwhile, Back in Mozambique," *Forbes,* Vol. 11, No. 16, November 16, 1987, p. 110.

CHAPTER **5**

GOVERNMENTAL INFLUENCE ON TRADE

A little help does a great deal.
FRENCH PROVERB

Objectives

- To evaluate the rationale for governmental policies to enhance and/or restrict trade.

- To examine the effects of pressure groups and trade-offs among groups on trade policies.

- To compare the protectionist arguments used in developed versus developing countries.

- To study the potential and actual effects of governmental intervention on the free flow of trade.

- To give an overview of the major means by which trade is restricted.

- To show that governmental trade policies create business uncertainties.

The beginning of 1991 marked nine years since Japan began its "voluntary" limitation of automobile exports to the United States. Had Japan not voluntarily limited the exports through negotiations with the United States, the United States would certainly have imposed even more restrictive sanctions. Different groups have disagreed whether the Japanese automobile imports should have been limited, whether the agreements have served the objectives for which they were intended, and whether new controls should be placed on the importation of vehicles. How did this situation develop?

Between 1979 and 1980, just prior to the first voluntary limitations, the foreign share of the new-car market in the United States increased from 17 percent to 25.3 percent. Clearly, the U.S. automobile firms and their workers were in trouble. By the end of 1980, 193,000 of the 750,000 members of the United Auto Workers (UAW) were unemployed.

There was considerable disagreement as to the exact cause of the automobile import problem and on how best to alter the competitive situation. Managers of the U.S. automobile firms and officials of the UAW spoke out in favor of restricting imports. This was a milestone because the automobile industry and its union had long been supporters of free trade and had in the past publicly opposed import restrictions on such products as steel.

Although imports were rising at the same time that sales by U.S. firms were declining, factors other than imports were contributing to the problems of the U.S. automobile industry. U.S. consumers had historically preferred Detroit's major product—large cars with rear-wheel drive. The dramatic increase in gasoline prices during 1979 and 1980 was unexpected and led to a rapid switch in demand. At the same time, the number of consumers demanding cars at all was decreasing as a general recession and unprecedentedly high interest rates reduced car sales drastically.

CASE
AUTOMOBILE
IMPORTS[1]

The U.S. automakers were not holding their own in sales of the small cars that they had been producing for several years. Japanese producers, the primary automobile exporters to the United States, were evidently as surprised as Detroit was by the sudden shift in demand. The Japanese lacked capacity to fill U.S. orders quickly, yet many buyers were willing to wait six months for delivery of a Honda rather than purchase a U.S.-manufactured model. The reasons for the American preference for Japanese automobiles were debatable. Some argued that price differences created by labor-cost differences were the cause. Those who accepted this view largely favored the taxing of imports in order to raise their prices. Yet, on the basis of canvassing 10,000 U.S. households, the Motor and Equipment Manufacturers Association found that imports strongly outranked U.S. small cars in perceived fuel economy, engineering, and durability. People who accepted these results were opposed to limiting imports.

The initial arguments for protecting or aiding the U.S. auto industry were based on two premises: (1) that the costs of unemployment are higher than the increased costs to consumers of limiting imports, and (2) that U.S. production could become fully competitive with imports if actions were taken to help it overcome its temporary problems. The first premise is based on such factors as personal hardship for people displaced in the labor market; diminished purchasing power, which adversely affects demand in other industries; and the high taxes that would be needed to support unemployment insurance and food stamps. A *New York Times* poll showed that 71 percent of Americans felt that it was more important to protect jobs than to have access to cheaper foreign products. The second premise is based on such factors as the historical competitive capability of the U.S. producers, the possibility of scale economies of U.S. production, and the much higher productivity possible with new plants.

Protectionists have argued that the restraints worked. The U.S. auto industry recovered by 1984, when it announced record profits. In fact, however, the turnaround was also due in part to recovery from the recession. For whatever reason, General Motors (GM), Ford, and Chrysler were able to invest heavily in more automated plants and to trim inventory costs.

Opponents of protection blamed the problems on poor management decisions and maintained that consumers and taxpayers should not be expected to reward the companies by footing the bill to see them through what was a crisis of their own making. According to antiprotectionists, any assistance, even short-term, would result in at least one of the following consequences: higher taxes because of subsidies to companies, higher prices for foreign cars (which are preferred by many consumers), or the necessity of buying domestic cars (which many perceived as inferior). Some antiprotectionists felt that government assistance in limiting imports would result in foreign retaliation against U.S. industries that are more competitive with foreign production—Japan, for example, might curtail purchases of U.S.-made aircraft.

The antiprotectionists have argued that the industry's recovery was primarily due to an increased U.S. demand for more expensive (and more profitable) cars. Some analysts claimed that this was a natural phenomenon of the market, since gasoline prices went down again. Others alleged that it was an outgrowth of the import restrictions, which gave U.S. consumers little choice except to buy more expensive cars. Because Japanese producers were not able to increase their U.S. profits by selling more cars, they did so instead by selling more luxurious models and raising prices. During the three years of the original export restraints, the price of the average Japanese import increased by $2600, and a Wharton Econometrics study attributed $1000 of this to import restraints. In the meantime, the prices of U.S.-made cars increased by 40 percent. These price increases made both U.S. and Japanese producers more profitable.

Although the Japanese have continued their restraint on sales, they have increased their allocation from 1.68 million units of imports in 1982 to 2.3 million units in 1990. Since their imports have been less than their allocations for the last several years, protectionists have argued that the restrictions have become meaningless. The effect on U.S. employment has been minimal as producers have turned to more automated means of production. The high profits increased the bargaining power of U.S. automobile production workers so that they increased their earnings relative to other production workers. This has stimulated even further automation.

Since restrictions were first placed on Japanese automobile imports, the question of which firms and which production to protect has become more complicated. Clearly, the UAW has been primarily interested in maintaining jobs. UAW representatives were instrumental in helping to convince Japanese firms to set up U.S. operations, primarily to assemble vehicles. (The operations are shown in Table 5.1.) The UAW wants much more, though; it is pushing to have more parts made in the United States. In 1990 the UAW president estimated that only 38 percent of parts were made in North America and that Japanese firms were keeping the higher-skilled and higher-paid production jobs in Japan. The UAW has also proposed legislation to force U.S.-owned companies to "invest at home and produce vehicles covering the full range of market segments." This push for "local content" runs counter to some of the policies being pursued by those U.S. auto firms that are trying to produce "global" cars in order to obtain maximum economies of scale and buying specific parts that can be produced more cheaply in other countries (such as die-cast aluminum parts in Italy). The Ford Escort, for example, which was assembled in the United States, Britain, and the former West Germany, contained parts from many countries. Furthermore, many of the cars sold under the Big Three automakers' brand names have been made abroad by other companies, a fact unknown to most U.S. consumers. These cars include the Ford Festiva made by Kia Motors in South Korea, GM's Pontiac LeMans made by Daewoo Motors in South Korea, and Chrysler's Dodge and Plymouth Colt and Vista made by

**TABLE 5.1 | JAPANESE AUTOMOBILE INVESTMENTS
IN THE UNITED STATES**

Year	Firm
1982	Honda
1983	Nissan
1984	Toyota*
1987	Toyo Kogyo (Mazda)
1988	Mitsubishi†
1988	Toyota
1989	Subaru-Isuzu‡

*joint venture with GM for New United Motors Manufacturing
†joint venture with Chrysler
‡joint venture between the two firms

Mitsubishi Motors in Japan. The competitive situation is complicated by the fact that GM owns 36.7 percent of Isuzu Motors, Ford owns 25 percent of Mazda, and Chrysler until recently owned 24 percent of Mitsubishi. In addition, Japanese-owned operations in the United States, such as Honda and Mazda, are now exporting parts and finished vehicles to Japan.

In the meantime, the UAW has been concerned that the import restraints on automobiles largely affect only Japan and only assembled vehicles. Ford announced that it would spend $500 million to produce 130,000 Mazda cars per year in Mexico for sale in the United States.

INTRODUCTION

All countries seek to influence trade. Each has

- Economic, social, and political objectives
- Conflicting objectives
- Pressure groups

The preceding case shows why and how automobile imports into the United States were restricted. This is not an atypical situation: No country in the world permits an unregulated flow of goods and services across its borders. Restrictions commonly are placed on imports and occasionally on exports. Direct or indirect subsidies frequently are given to industries to enable them to compete with foreign production either at home or abroad. In general, governmental influence is exerted in an attempt to satisfy economic, social, or political objectives. Action to increase automobile workers' employment is an example of such an objective. Often, there are conflicting objectives (e.g., increased employment versus lower consumer prices of automobiles) and much disagreement as to the likely employment effects of trade policies (e.g., employment increases for auto workers versus possible decreases for workers in other industries if foreign countries retaliate against U.S. trade policies by restricting their imports of some U.S.-made products).

Not surprisingly, any proposal for changes in trade regulations results in heated debates among individuals and interest groups who believe that they will be affected. Of course, the interest groups that are most directly affected are most apt to speak up. People whose livelihood depends on U.S. automobile production (workers, owners, suppliers, and local politicians) perceive the losses from import competition to be very great. Workers see themselves as being forced to take new jobs in new industries, perhaps in new locales. They may experience prolonged periods of unemployment, reduced incomes, and insecure work and social surroundings. People threatened in this way are liable to become a very strong pressure group. Workers in an industry that is affected only indirectly by retaliation, such as the aircraft industry, do not readily perceive the same threat and are less vocal. Neither do consumers perceive the threat, although they must pay higher prices for both foreign and domestically made cars. Although the aggregate costs certainly are great, they are so diffused throughout society that consumers are not likely to join together to protest import limitations very vigorously.

THE RATIONALE FOR GOVERNMENTAL INTERVENTION

Unemployment

The unemployed can form an effective pressure group for import restrictions.

Import restrictions to create domestic employment

- May lead to retaliation by other countries
- Are met by less retaliation if implemented by small countries
- May decrease export jobs owing to price increases for components
- May decrease export jobs owing to lower incomes abroad

Pressure groups are a real challenge to governmental policymakers and businesspeople. There is probably no more effective pressure group than the unemployed because no other group has the time and incentive to write letters in volume to congressional representatives or to picket.

One problem with restricting imports to create jobs is that other countries might retaliate. The most cited example occurred in 1930 when the United States raised import restrictions to their highest level ever. In a matter of months, other countries countered with their own restrictions, and the United States lost rather than gained jobs as its exports diminished.[2] In recent years, new import restrictions by a major country have almost always brought quick retaliation. When automobile imports from Japan were restricted, for example, Japanese pressure groups forced import restrictions on American orange juice.

Two factors may mitigate the problems of retaliation. First, there may be less tendency to retaliate against a small country (in terms of economic power) that places barriers on imports. Thus a small country may be able to increase employment more easily by means of imposing trade barriers. Second, if redistribution because of retaliation decreases employment in a capital-intensive industry but increases it in a labor-intensive industry, employment objectives may be achieved.

Even if there is no retaliation, the net number of jobs gained for the economy as a whole through producing domestically is bound to be smaller than the number of people who would be employed in the newly protected industry. That is because many people would otherwise be employed in handling the imports. In the case of the United States, for example, it is estimated that 194,000 jobs are directly related to the imported-car industry. These include such workers as employees of importers, dealers, and distributors of foreign cars and workers in U.S. plants that make foreign-car parts.[3]

Imports may also help create jobs in other industries that may form pressure groups against protectionism. Take the apparel industry in the United States. Such firms as Warnaco and Liz Claiborne joined retailers to protest textile import restrictions because they needed foreign-made variety and quality to compete against global companies. Or take Caterpillar Tractor, one of the largest exporters in the United States. It buys crankshafts from Germany and Japan to cut costs enough to be competitive in foreign markets.[4] Imports stimulate exports less directly by increasing foreign income and foreign-exchange earnings, which are then spent on new imports by firms and individuals in the foreign country.

Costs of import restrictions include
- Possibly higher prices
- Possibly higher taxes

They should be compared with costs of unemployment.

If import restrictions do result in a net increase in domestic employment, there will still be costs to some people in the domestic society through higher prices or higher taxes. The first three years of Japan's voluntary export restraint are estimated to have cost the United States $160,000 per job saved.[5] If protection seems permanent, the domestic industry may lag behind in technical and product development as well.

Higher prices or higher taxes must be compared with the costs of unemployment resulting from freer trade. It may be preferable to find some means by which individuals are compensated for their losses and by which they move to new employment. These tasks are challenging: First, it is hard to put a price tag on the distress suffered by people who must either be out of work or change jobs, or move; second, it is difficult for working people to understand that they may be better off financially if part of their taxes go to help support people whose positions were lost because of imports; and finally, it may be equally difficult to convince people to accept handouts in lieu of their old jobs.

A complicating factor is that potentially displaced workers are frequently the ones who are least able to find alternative work. In the garment industry, for example, sewing and cutting jobs are being transferred in great numbers from industrial to developing countries. Canada is an industrial country that has been losing these jobs. Forty-one percent of its sewing and cutting workers speak English as a second language; and the record of retraining these immigrants has thus far not been very successful.[6]

Many countries assist workers who are affected adversely by imports. Assistance is provided in the form of supplements to unemployment benefits, and workers often spend the funds on living expenses in the hope that they will be recalled to their old jobs. Some observers argue that too little is done in the way of retraining and relocation.

Infant-Industry Argument

The infant-industry argument says that production becomes more competitive over time because of
- Gaining economies of scale
- Efficiency of workers

One of the oldest arguments for protection from imports was presented as early as 1792 by Alexander Hamilton. The logic of the **infant-industry argument** for protection is that although the initial output costs for an industry in a given country may be so high as to make it noncompetitive in world markets, over a period of time the costs will decrease to a level sufficient to achieve efficient production. Two factors account for the lowering of costs over time. The first one is economies of scale. Because of high fixed costs, a company may have to reach a certain level of output and sales to bring about a reduction of total unit costs to the level of the competition, assumed in this case to be foreign competition. The second one is the learning curve. Initial production may be costly because of the inexperience of workers and managers, but as they gain experience, their output will grow and the unit costs of production will decrease. Proponents of the infant-industry argument hold that the domestic infant industry should be guaranteed a large share of the domestic market so that adulthood is ultimately reached.

While it is reasonable to expect costs to decrease over a period of time, they may not go down sufficiently. There are therefore some problems in using trade protection as a means of obtaining international competitiveness for a domestic industry. The first is the difficulty of identifying those industries that have a high probability of reaching adulthood. Examples of industries that grew to be competitive because of government protection are certainly available—automobile production in Brazil and Korea is a good example. In many other cases, however (e.g., automobile production in Argentina and Australia), the industries remain in an infantile state even after many years of operation. If infant-industry protection is given to an industry that does not reduce costs sufficiently, chances are that the owners, workers, and suppliers will constitute a formidable pressure group that may effectively prevent the import of a cheaper competitive product.

Even if policymakers can ascertain which industries are likely to reach productive adulthood, it does not necessarily follow that governmental assistance should be given to them. There are, of course, many examples of entrepreneurs who endured early losses in order to gain future benefits, and policymakers may argue that assistance should be given only if the entry barriers to new firms are very high. Some segment of the economy must absorb the higher cost of local production during infancy. Most likely the consumer will pay higher prices; however, a government may subsidize the industry so that consumer prices are not increased, in which case the taxpayer absorbs the burden. For the infant-industry argument to be fully viable, future benefits should exceed early costs.

The automobile-import case at the beginning of this chapter raises interesting questions about the infant-industry argument. We have all heard of second childhood, but is the automobile industry in the United States in its second infancy? Can this U.S. industry overcome some of its present disadvantages? Or does the automobile industry, like people, go around only once? In other words, has the absolute or comparative advantage shifted to other countries, thus precluding U.S. ability to compete effectively in the future? If efficiency can be achieved, who should incur the short-term costs: investors, taxpayers, or consumers?

Industrialization Objectives

Countries seek protection to promote industrial production because

- It brings faster growth than agriculture
- It brings in investment funds

In recent years many countries have sought protection to increase their level of industrialization. Their reasons are:

1. An emphasis on industrialization will increase output more than an emphasis on agriculture.

2. Inflows of foreign investment in the industrial area will promote growth.

- It diversifies the economy
- It brings more price increases than primary products

3. Diversification away from traditional agricultural products or raw materials is necessary to stabilize trade fluctuation.

4. The prices of manufactured goods tend to rise more rapidly than the prices of primary products.

Industrial countries are generally better off economically than nonindustrial countries. Since the Industrial Revolution in England in the late eighteenth century, a number of countries have developed an industrial base while largely preventing competition from foreign-based production. This, for example, was the experience of the United States, Japan, and the former Soviet Union. As in the infant-industry argument, the premise here is that importing cheaper products from abroad would prevent the establishment of domestic industry if free-market conditions were allowed to prevail. The industrialization argument differs from the infant-industry argument in that proponents argue that objectives will be achieved even if domestic prices do not become competitive on the world market.

Marginal Agricultural Returns In many developing countries there are frequently surpluses of population engaged in agriculture. This is particularly true in economies such as India or Egypt, which have little additional arable land available. What this means is that large numbers of people may be able to leave the agricultural sector without greatly affecting the country's agricultural output. If these surplus workers can be employed in the manufacturing sector, their output is likely to contribute a net gain to the economy because so little agricultural production is sacrificed in the process. If the cost of the domestically produced manufactured product is higher than an imported one, sales of the imported product must be restricted to ensure survival of the domestic industry. This will result in either higher prices or taxes; nevertheless, real output should rise in the economy.

When a country shifts from agriculture to industry

- Output increases if the marginal productivity of agricultural workers is very low
- Demands on social and political services in cities may increase
- Development possibilities in the agricultural sector may be overlooked

Shifting people out of agriculture is not without risk. One problem is that individuals' expectations may be raised and left unfulfilled, thus leading to excessive demands on social and political services. Indeed, one of the major problems facing poor countries today is the massive urban migration of people who cannot be easily absorbed. There is no work for them either (1) because the industrialization process has proceeded too slowly or (2) because they lack the rudimentary skills and work habits necessary for employment in manufacturing. A second problem is that agriculture may in fact be a better means of effecting additional output than industry. Not all poor countries are utilizing their lands fully, nor is industrial development the only means of economic growth. Such countries as the United States, Canada, and Argentina grew rapidly during the nineteenth century, in large part through agricultural exports, and they continue to profit from such exports. Australia, New Zealand, and Denmark maintain high incomes along with substantial agricultural specialization. A third problem is that if protection is to be given to manufacturing enterprises, policymakers must decide on which type so that the additional consumer prices and taxes are minimized. A fourth problem is that too much of a shift from rural to urban may reduce agricultural output in developing countries, thus further endangering their self-sufficiency. Interestingly, most of the world's agricultural production and exports come from the so-called industrial countries.

If import restrictions keep out foreign manufacturers, foreign firms may invest to produce in a restricted area.

Promoting Investment Inflows   Import restrictions are a major impetus for direct investment movements, particularly those regulating the purchase of foreign-produced manufactured products. The influx of foreign firms may hasten the move from agriculture to industry as well as contribute to growth by adding to the stock of capital and technology per worker employed. It may also add to employment, which is an especially attractive benefit from the standpoint of most policymakers.

Diversification   Export prices of most primary products undergo great fluctuations. Whether due to such uncontrollable factors as weather affecting supply or business cycles abroad affecting demand, price variations can wreak havoc on economies that are dependent on the export of primary products. This is particularly true when an economy depends very heavily on a few commodities for employment of its population and for its export earnings. For example, the Côte d'Ivoire's exports fell by a quarter over two years when cocoa and coffee prices plummeted.[7] Because a large number of developing countries depend heavily on just one primary commodity, they frequently can afford foreign luxuries one year but be unable to afford replacement parts for essential equipment the next.

A greater dependence on manufacturing is, however, no guarantee of stable export earnings. The gross national product of most less developed countries (LDCs) is small; consequently, a change may simply shift dependence to one or two manufactured products from one or two agricultural ones. The basic risk of having all of one's eggs in one basket has not been removed.

Terms of trade for LDCs may deteriorate because

- Demand for primary products grows more slowly
- Production cost savings in primary products will be passed on to consumers

Terms of Trade   **Terms of trade** refers to the quantity of imports that a given quantity of a country's exports can buy. The prices of raw materials and agricultural commodities have not risen as fast as the prices of finished products. As a result, over a period of time it will take more primary products to buy the same amount of manufactured goods. Further, the demand for primary products does not rise as rapidly, so most LDCs have become increasingly poorer in relation to developed countries. This condition supposedly warrants the protection of emerging manufacturing enterprises that replace traditional products.[8] The declining terms of trade for LDCs have been explained in part by lagging demand for agricultural products and by changes in technology that have saved on utilization of raw material. A further explanation sometimes offered is that, because of competitive conditions, savings due to technical changes that lower production costs of primary products are largely passed on to consumers, whereas cost savings in manufactured products go to higher profits and wages.[9]

Import Substitution Versus Export Promotion   By placing restrictions on imports a country may produce goods for local consumption that it formerly imported. This is known as **import substitution.** In recent years many countries have questioned whether import substitution is the best way to develop new industries through protection. If the protected industries do not become efficient, consumers may have to pay high prices or taxes for an indefinite period of time to support them. In addition, since capital equipment and other supplies usually must be imported, foreign-exchange savings are minimal. These countries have witnessed the rapid growth of countries such as Taiwan and South Korea, which have achieved a favorable balance of payments and rapid economic growth by promoting export industries, a process known as **export-led development.** For these reasons, some countries are now trying to develop industries for which export markets should logically exist, such as the processing of raw materials that they are currently exporting. This change affects international companies' operating in these countries, too: They are increasingly required to export from the countries where they are producing, whereas formerly they could sell all their outputs in each country where they produced.

In reality, it is not easy to distinguish between the two types of industrialization, nor is it always possible to develop exports. Industrialization may initially result in import substitution, yet export development of the same products may be feasible at a later date. The fact that a country concentrates its industrialization activities on products for which it would seem to have a comparative cost advantage does not guarantee that exports can be generated. There are a variety of trade barriers, to be discussed later in this chapter, that are particularly problematic to the development of manufacturing exports from nonindustrialized countries.

Relationships with Other Countries

Another reason countries restrict trade is that they are concerned with their economic or political positions relative to other countries.

Balance-of-Payments Adjustments   Since the trade account is a major component within the balance of payments for most countries, governments make numerous attempts to modify what would have been an import or export movement in a free-market situation.

Trade influence differs from the other means of balance-of-payments adjustment (deflation of the economy or currency devaluation) primarily because of its greater selectivity. This may be either an advantage or a disadvantage compared to other adjustment mechanisms. If a country is running

---

Margin notes:

Industrialization should emphasize either
- Products to sell domestically or
- Products to export

Trade restrictions may have an uneven effect on industries, but a country can choose to restrict the least essential imports.

a deficit, for example, either a devaluation or a domestic deflation can make domestically produced goods and services less expensive than foreign ones. This has a widespread effect on both imports and exports as well as on such service accounts as tourism. Because of the breadth of industries affected, fairly small changes relative to other countries' prices may substantially affect payments balances. Furthermore, this minimizes the burden of adjustment on any single industry. Direct trade influence may, however, allow a country to choose the types of products or services to be affected. For example, the importation of luxury items may be curtailed, whereas no change may be made in rules or prices governing imports of needed foodstuffs.

Export restrictions may
- Keep world prices up in a monopoly situation
- Be extremely costly to prevent smuggling
- Lead to substitution

Price-Control Objectives   A few countries hold monopoly or near-monopoly control of certain resources. To maintain control and pursuant high prices, strict export regulations are enforced. South Africa and Colombia pay high prices to prevent diamonds and emeralds, respectively, from flooding world markets. Australia, for example, has for over 50 years prohibited the export of Merino rams, considered the top-quality wool producers in the world. Unfortunately, this type of policy encourages smuggling and requires high prevention costs. Brazil lost its world monopoly in natural rubber after a contrabandist brought rubber plants into Malaysia and now has practically no world sales. A second problem is that if prices are kept too high, substitutes may be developed. For example, the high price of Chilean natural nitrate led to the development of a synthetic, and high sugar prices in the mid-1970s led to the development of a corn-derivative substitute.

Export restrictions may
- Keep domestic prices down by increasing domestic supply
- Give producers less incentive to increase output
- Shift foreign production and sales

A country may also limit exports of a product that is in short supply so that domestic consumers may buy the good at a lower price than if foreign purchasers were allowed to bid the price up. In recent years, Argentina has done this with wheat and the United States with hides and soybeans. The primary danger in these policies is that the lower prices at home will not entice producers to expand domestic output, whereas foreign output is expanded. This may lead to long-term market loss.

Import restrictions may
- Prevent dumping; be used to put domestic producers out of business
- Get other countries to bargain away restrictions
- Get foreign producers to lower their prices

Countries also fear that foreign producers will price their exports so artificially low that they drive domestic producers out of business, resulting in a costly dislocation for displaced workers and industries from other countries. If entry barriers are high for new domestic firms, the surviving producers may even be able to extract monopoly profits or withhold supplies to help other industries in their own countries. Thus far there is a lack of evidence that monopoly prices result from displacement of domestic producers. For example, low import prices have eliminated most U.S. consumer electronics production, yet in the United States the prices for consumer electronics are among the lowest in the world.[10] Nevertheless, there have been allegations that Hitachi, the only producer of a key chip, delayed deliveries to Cray Research, the leading U.S. supercomputer producer, to give Japanese computer makers an advantage.[11] The ability to price artificially low abroad may result from high domestic prices due to a monopoly position at home or from home-government subsidy or sponsorship policies.

The underpricing of exports (usually below cost or below the home-country price) is often referred to as **dumping,** and most countries have legislation to prevent imports of dumped products. This legislation is usually enforced only if the imported product disrupts domestic production. If there is no domestic production, then the only host-country effect is a subsidy to its consumers. Home-country consumers or taxpayers seldom realize that they are in effect subsidizing foreign sales. The U.S. antidumping legislation is extremely controversial. A foreign firm can be fined if it makes less than an 8 percent profit on its export price. Or it can be fined if its export price is as little as a half percent below its domestic price, even though currency-value fluctuations may account for a much greater difference.[12]

Price control is also the objective when trade restrictions are used as a means of forcing other countries to bargain away restrictions of their own. In 1988, for example, the United States passed the so-called Super 301 clause in its trade act, which permitted a threat of trade retaliation in negotiations to get other countries to reduce import barriers for U.S. exports. Within two years the United States used the clause successfully against Brazil and Japan, but unsuccessfully against India.[13] The danger in this mechanism is that each country may escalate restrictions rather than bargain them away.

A final price argument for governmental influence on trade is the **optimum-tariff theory,** which holds that a foreign producer will lower its prices if a tax is placed on its products. If this occurs, benefits shift to the importing country. For example, assume that an exporter has costs of $500 per unit and is selling to a foreign market for $700 per unit. With the imposition of a 10 percent tax on the imported price, the exporter may choose to lower the export price to $636.36 per unit, which, with a 10 percent tax of $63.64, would keep the price at $700 for the importer. The exporter may feel that a price higher than $700 would result in lost sales, thus a profit of $136.36 per unit instead of the previous $200 per unit is still better than no profit at all. An amount of $63.64 per unit has thus shifted to the importing country. As long as the foreign producer lowers its price by any amount, some shift goes to the importing country and the tariff is considered to be an optimum one. There are many examples of products whose prices did not rise as much as the amount of the imposed tariffs; however, it is very difficult to predict if exporters will reduce their profit margins.

Fairness   All countries regulate how their companies can produce. The standards they impose—such as requirements for worker safety or the disposal of wastes—reflect the social and environmental values of their citizens. Since standards vary from one country to another, the costs incurred by producers vary as well. Some industries affected by import competition—for example, the U.S. television and steel industries—reason that their own governments should protect them because foreign producers do not have to adhere to the same stringent requirements that raise production costs.[14] For example, one of the biggest differences in standards exists between the United States, which has enacted clean-air legislation, and Eastern Europe, which has few laws regulating pollution.[15] Some argue that cost differences therefore do not necessarily reflect differences in efficiency; rather, they reflect differences in social and environmental values.

In protecting essential industries, countries must

- Determine which businesses are essential
- Consider costs and alternatives
- Consider political consequences

Political Objectives   Much governmental action on trade is not based on economic reasoning. A major consideration is the protection of essential domestic industries during peacetime so that in wartime the country is not dependent on foreign sources of supply. This argument for protection has much appeal in rallying support for barriers to the importation of foreign-produced goods. However, in times of real crisis or military emergency, almost any product could be considered essential. Because of the high cost of protecting an inefficient industry or domestic substitute, the **essential-industry argument** should not be (but frequently is) accepted without a careful evaluation of costs, real needs, and alternatives. Once an industry is afforded protection, the protection is difficult to terminate. On the basis of this argument, the U.S. government subsidizes domestic production of silicon so that domestic chipmakers will not have to depend entirely on foreign suppliers.[16]

Defense arguments are also used to prevent exports, even to friendly countries, of strategic goods that might fall into the hands of potential enemies.[17] This policy may be valid if a country assumes that there will be no retaliation that prevents it from securing even more essential goods. Even if this assumption is made, it is possible that the importing country may simply find alternative sources of supply or develop a capability of its own. Closely akin to this strategy is the policy of restricting exports of raw materials that could be sold competitively because of fear that essential supplies will become depleted.

Trade controls on nonstrategic goods also may be used as a weapon of foreign policy to try to prevent another country from easily meeting its economic and political objectives. A good example was the international cessation of trade with Iraq after its invasion of Kuwait. Iraq's loss of oil exports was a severe economic loss amounting to 43 percent of the combined gross national products of Iraq and Kuwait. But there were also costs to the countries imposing the sanctions. Oil prices rose, hurting poor countries especially. The United States, formerly the largest exporter to Iraq, lost sales of $1.29 billion a year, which was concentrated within those firms doing business in Iraq. NRM-Steel, for example, had already produced equipment for an export order, and the trade freeze reduced its earnings by about 20 percent.[18]

There are many other examples of governments influencing trade for political reasons: Aid, credits, and purchases are frequently tied into a political alliance or even to votes within international bodies. Most major powers buy at higher than world prices from certain LDCs in order to maintain their influence on those countries. The United States did this with sugar-producing countries; France, with citrus producers. In country-to-country negotiations, government officials may even trade off some of the economic advantages of their own nations' firms in order to gain political advantages.

FORMS OF TRADE CONTROL

The previous discussion centered on the end objectives sought by governmental influence on trade. Attaining any of the objectives depends in great part on groups at home who pressure for actions they believe will have the most positive (or least negative) influence on them. Since the actions taken on foreign trade by one country will have repercussions abroad, retaliation from foreign governments looms as another potential obstacle to the achievement of the desired objectives. The choice of instruments to achieve trade goals is therefore important, since domestic and foreign groups may respond differently to them. One of the ways the types of influence may be understood is to distinguish between (1) those that influence quantity movements by directly influencing prices and (2) those that affect quantity movements directly. Another common distinction is between tariff barriers and nontariff barriers. Tariff barriers influence prices, and nontariff barriers may affect either price or quantity directly.

Figure 5.1 illustrates how either type of barrier affects both the price and the quantity sold, but in a different order and with a different impact on producers. Parts (a) and (b) both have downward sloping demand curves and upward sloping supply curves. In other words, the lower the price, the higher the quantity demanded; the higher the price, the larger the supply made available for sale. The intersection of the S and D curves illustrates the price (P_1) and quantity sold (Q_1) without governmental interference. By raising the price from P_1 to P_2 in (a), the amount that consumers are now willing to buy will fall from Q_1 to Q_2. Producers are unwilling to sell more because the increase in price goes to taxes rather than to them. Part (b) shows a restriction in available supply; therefore, a new supply curve (S_1) is imposed. The quantity now sold falls from Q_1 to Q_2. At the lower supply, the price rises from P_1 to P_2, which reflects the intersection of the D and S_1 curves. The major difference in the two approaches is that producers raise prices in (b), which helps compensate for their decrease in quantity sold. In (a), producers decrease the quantity they sell *and* they are unable to raise their prices because the taxes have already done this.

Tariffs

Tariffs may
• Be on goods entering, leaving, or passing through a country

The most common type of trade control is the **tariff,** or **duty,** a governmental tax levied on goods shipped internationally. If collected by the exporting country, it is known as an **export tariff;** if collected by a country through which the goods have passed, it is a **transit tariff;** if collected by the im-

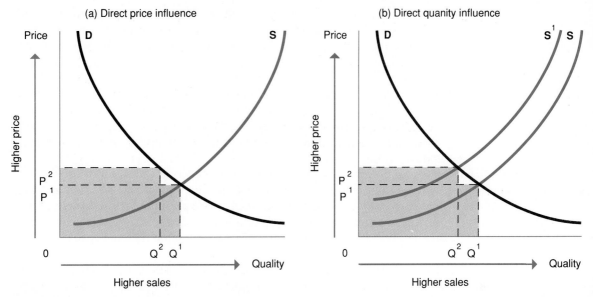

Figure 5.1
Comparison of Trade Restrictions
In (a), the tax on imports raises the price, which decreases the quantity demanded. In (b), the quantity limits on imports decrease supply available and raise prices. This price rise in (b) is charged by producers.

- Be for protection or revenue
- Be per unit or per value

porting country, it is an **import tariff.** The import tariff is by far the most common.

Import duties serve primarily as a means of raising the price of imported products so that competitively produced domestic goods will gain a relative price advantage. A duty may be classified as protective in nature even though there is no domestic production in direct competition. For example, if a country wishes to reduce the foreign expenditures of its citizens because of balance-of-payments problems, authorities may choose to raise the price of some foreign products, even though there is no close domestic substitute, in order to curtail consumption temporarily.

Tariffs also serve as a means of governmental revenue. Although of little importance to the large industrial countries, the import duty is a major source of revenue in many LDCs because governmental authorities there may have more control over ascertaining the amount and nature of goods passing across their frontiers and collecting a tax on them than they do over determining and collecting individual and corporate income taxes. Revenue tariffs are most commonly collected on imports; however, many nations that export raw materials use export duties extensively. New Caledonia's tariff on nickel is an example of such a tariff. Transit duties were once a major source of revenue for countries, but they have been nearly abolished through governmental treaties.

A tariff may be assessed on the basis of a tax per unit, in which case the duty is known as a **specific duty.** It may also be assessed as a percentage of the value of the item, in which case it is known as an **ad valorem duty.** It is not uncommon for both a specific duty and an ad valorem duty to be charged on the same product, in which case it is known as a **compound duty.** A specific duty is easier to assess because it is not necessary for customs officials to determine a value on which to calculate a percentage. During normal periods of price rises, the specific duty will, unless changed, become a smaller percentage of the value and therefore be less restrictive to imported goods.

One of the major tariff controversies concerns industrial countries' tariff treatment of manufactured exports from developing countries that are seeking to diversify and increase earnings by adding manufactured value to their raw materials exports. Raw materials frequently can enter developed markets free of duty; however, once processed, those same materials usually have a tariff assigned to them. Since an ad valorem tariff is based on the total value of the product, nonindustrial countries have argued that the **effective tariff** on the manufactured portion is higher than would be indicated by the published tariff rate. For example, a country may charge no duty on coffee beans but may assess a 10 percent ad valorem tariff on instant coffee. If $5 for a jar of instant coffee covers $2.50 in coffee beans and $2.50 in processing costs, the $0.50 duty is effectively 20 percent on the manufactured portion, since the beans could have entered free of duty. This has made it more difficult for developing countries to find markets for their manufactured products. In addition, many of the products that developing countries are best able to produce are the ones that in industrial countries are produced by employees who are ill equipped to move easily to new employment. The result is the formation of pressure groups to keep these products out. A further problem is that, although developing countries' products have preferential import restrictions, the most successful LDC exporters reach thresholds at which they lose preferential status. For example, Taiwan, Singapore, Hong Kong, and South Korea no longer have preferential treatment in the United States. The special treatment came about as a result of LDC pressures in UNCTAD and is known as the Generalized System of Preferences (GSP).

Another controversy concerns who bears the brunt of paying tariff costs. Some critics have claimed that in the United States the payment falls mainly on the poor. This claim is illustrated by the following examples:

- Mink furs are duty free. With the money a mother saves on her mink, perhaps she can afford to buy her child a polyester sweater, which carries a 34.6 percent tariff.

- Lobster is duty free. With the savings, struggling parents may be able to afford infant-food preparations, which carry a 17.2 percent tariff.

- Orange juice carries a 36 percent tariff, but Perrier is assessed only 0.4 cent per liter. (If the Customs Service reclassifies Perrier as benzene, then it can enter duty free.)

- Fresh broccoli carries a 25 percent tariff, but, happily, truffles are duty free.

- Footwear valued at not more than $3 a pair with rubber or plastic outer soles and uppers is tariffed at 48 percent. If valued at more than $12, the tariff is only 20 percent.[19]

Unfortunately, we do not know whether the preceding examples are selective or typical. Furthermore, price is only one type of burden on the poor. For example, the tariff on broccoli is imposed to ensure employment of migrant workers who plant and harvest the crops. A similar tariff on truffles would not help their employment inasmuch as the United States lacks sufficient quantities of the wild fungi, truffles, to make harvesting commercially viable.

Nontariff Barriers: Direct Price Influences

Governmental subsidies may help firms be competitive.

- Subsidies to overcome market imperfections are least controversial.

- There is little agreement on "unfair" subsidies.

- There has been a recent increase in export-credit assistance.

Subsidies   Although countries sometimes make direct payments to producers to compensate them for losses incurred by selling abroad, governments most commonly provide other types of assistance to firms to make it cheaper or more profitable for them to sell overseas. For example, most countries offer their potential exporters an array of services, including the provision of information, sponsorship of trade expositions, and establishment of contacts for businesses overseas.[20] These types of service subsidies are frequently more justifiable than tariffs from an economic standpoint, since they are designed largely to overcome market imperfections rather than to create them. Furthermore, there are economies to be gained by disseminating information widely and other countries are not likely to complain about such types of assistance. On the other hand, some observers may contend that users should be the only ones to share the costs. At any rate, export assistance is apt to result in less opposition than the imposition of import restrictions.

Other types of subsidies are more controversial, and producers frequently assert that they face unfair competition from subsidized exports. What exactly constitutes a subsidized export? On this point there is little agreement. Does Canada subsidize exports of fish because it gives grants to fishermen to buy trawlers? Did Britain subsidize steel when the government-owned steel company had severe losses? Did the United States block some automobile imports because the state of Pennsylvania made numerous concessions to convince Volkswagen to locate its plant there?[21] Recent questions also have been raised about various governments' support of research and development and tax programs that directly or indirectly affect export profitability.

Some other forms of government assistance to exportation warrant mention, including foreign aid and loans. These forms are nearly always "tied"—that is, the recipient must spend the funds in the donor countries, making some products competitive abroad that might otherwise be noncompetitive. Tied aid is especially important in winning contracts to supply telecommunications, railways, and electric-power projects. One study estimates that about one third of capital goods traded worldwide are financed through tied-aid packages.[22] Most industrial countries also provide repayment insurance for their exporters, thus reducing the risk of nonpayment for overseas sales. Another scheme has been combining aid with loans so that the rate on paper does not look as low to competitor nations as it really is.

Customs Valuation   Customs officials used to have fairly wide discretion in determining the value of an imported product for affixing an ad valorem duty. If, for example, the invoice value of a shipment was $100, customs officials might instead use the domestic wholesale or retail price or even an estimation of what it would cost if the product were produced domestically. This meant that they might charge a duty on a value much higher than the $100. This discretion was permitted to prevent exporters and importers from declaring an arbitrarily low price on invoices in order to avoid incurring as high a tariff as would otherwise be imposed. In practice, however, the discretionary powers were sometimes used as an arbitrary means of preventing the importation of foreign-made products by assessing the value too high.

Most industrial countries have now agreed on a sequence of techniques for assessing values. Customs officials must first use the invoice price. If there is none or if its authenticity is doubtful, they must then assess on the basis of the value of identical goods and then on the basis of similar goods coming in at about the same time. If these techniques cannot be used, they may compute a value based on final sales value or on reasonable cost.

Another customs-valuation problem can be traced to the fact that so many different products are traded. It is easy (by accident or on purpose) to classify a product so that it will require a higher duty. With over 13,000 categories of products a customs agent must use discretion to determine if silicon chips should be considered as "integrated circuits for computers" or as "a form of chemical silicon." A few examples should illustrate the problems that companies can encounter. The U.S. Customs Service had to determine whether sport utility vehicles, such as the Suzuki Samurai and Land Rover, were cars or trucks. They assessed the 25 percent truck duty instead of the 2.5 percent duty on cars. Procter & Gamble's Duncan Hines Muffin Mix operation had to suspend production for seven weeks while awaiting an eventual favorable ruling that the topping brought in from its Canadian plant should not be classified as sugar. Nike had to pay almost $9 million in back fees when the U.S. Customs Service ruled that its Air Jordan shoes should be assessed a synthetic rather than a leather shoe duty.[23]

Other Direct Price Influences   Countries frequently use other means to affect prices, including special fees (e.g., for consular and customs clearance and documentation), the requirement that customs deposits be placed in advance of shipment, and the establishment of minimum prices at which goods can be sold after they have customs clearance.

Nontariff Barriers: Quantity Controls

Quotas   The most common type of import or export restriction from a quantity basis is the **quota.** From the standpoint of imports, a quota most frequently limits the quantitative amount of a product allowed to be imported in a given year. The amount frequently reflects a guarantee that domestic producers will have access to a certain percentage of the domestic market in that year. For many years, the sugar-import quota of the United States was set so that U.S. producers would have about half the home market. In this case the quotas were allocated further by country on the basis of political considerations rather than price. Consumer prices of imported sugar equaled the price of more expensive domestically produced sugar, since lowering the consumer price on imports could not increase the quantity of imports sold. This sort of restriction of supply will usually increase consumer prices because there is little incentive to use price as a means of increasing sales. In the case of import tariffs the gains from price increases to consumers are received in the form of government revenue in the importing country. In the case of quotas, however, the gains are most likely to accrue to producers or exporters in the producing country as added per unit profits.[24] Windfall gains could accrue to middlemen in the importing country if they bought at a lower world-market price and then sold at the higher protected domestic price. Further problems arise when quotas are allocated among countries, because officials must ensure that goods from one country are not transshipped through a second country's quota. Such a situation occurred when the United States claimed that Chinese-made garments had illegally reached U.S. customs as Macao-made garments.[25]

Import quotas are not necessarily intended to protect domestic producers. Japan, for example, maintains quotas on many agricultural products not produced in Japan. Imports are allocated as a means of bargaining for sales of Japanese exports as well as to avoid excess dependence on any one country for essential food needs, which could be cut off in case of adverse climatic or political conditions.

Export quotas may be established to assure that domestic consumers will have a sufficient supply of goods at a low price, to prevent depletion of natural resources, or to attempt to raise an export price by restricting supply in foreign markets. To restrict supply, some countries have banded together in various commodity agreements, whereby they have restricted and allocated exports by producing countries of such commodities as coffee and oil so that prices are raised to importing countries.

A specific type of quota that prohibits all trade is known as an **embargo.** Like quotas, embargoes may be placed on either imports or exports, on whole categories of products regardless of destination, on specific products to specific countries, or on all products to given countries. Although embargoes are generally imposed for political purposes, the effects may be economic in nature. For example, the United States imposed an embargo on Nicaragua between

1984 and 1990 because of political animosity with the Sandinista party in power. But the effects on Nicaragua were economic: Nicaragua had difficulty getting supplies, particularly replacement parts for machinery that had been made in the United States, and Nicaragua could not easily sell its banana crop that previously went primarily to the United States.

According to "buy-local" practices,

- Governmental purchases give preference to domestically made goods
- Government sometimes legislates preference for domestically made goods

"Buy-Local" Legislation   If governmental purchases are a large portion of total expenditures within a country, the determination of where governmental agencies will make their purchases is of added importance in international competitiveness. Most national governments give preference to their own producers in the purchase of goods, sometimes in the form of content restriction (i.e., a certain percentage of the product for governmental purchase must be of local origin) and sometimes through price mechanisms. For example, a governmental agency may be able to buy a foreign-made product only if the price of the foreign product is some predetermined margin below that of a domestic competitor. Sometimes the preference for local products is more subtle: For example, the Nippon Telegraph and Telephone Public Corp. (NTT), a Japanese quasi-government telecommunications monopoly in the world's second-largest telecommunications market, purchases only a very small portion of its equipment from foreign sources. Foreign firms claim that they have superior technology and prices, but in practice they have been excluded from the market.[26]

There is an abundance of legislation worldwide that simply prescribes a minimum percentage of domestic value that must be encompassed in a given product for it to be sold legally within the country. In the introductory case on automobile imports, the local content proposed for cars sold in the United States would be, if implemented, such a type of legislated protection. Among those implemented already in other countries are Mexico's requirement on automobile components and Brazil's requirement on electronics.

Other types of trade barriers include

- Arbitrary standards
- Licensing arrangements
- Administrative delays
- Reciprocal requirements
- Service restrictions

Standards   Countries commonly have set classifications, labeling, and testing standards in a manner that allows the sale of domestic products but inhibits the sale of foreign-made products. These standards are sometimes ostensibly for the purpose of protecting the safety or health of the domestic populace. However, the Big Three automobile producers have recently pushed for fuel-economy legislation that would require each automaker to boost economy, averaged across all models, by the same percentage. Such a proposal, if passed, would be burdensome for Japanese producers, whose fuel-economy averages already far exceed those of the Big Three.[27]

Specific Permission Requirements   Many countries require that potential importers or exporters secure permission from governmental authorities before conducting trade transactions, a procedure known as a **licensing arrangement.** To gain a license, a company may have to send samples abroad in advance. The requirement for licenses not only may restrict imports or exports directly by denial of permission, but also may result in further deterrence of trade because of the cost, time, and uncertainty involved in the process. Similar to a licensing arrangement is a **foreign-exchange control.** For instance, in order to import a given product an importer in an exchange-control country must apply to governmental authorities to secure foreign exchange to pay for the product. Once again, the failure to grant the exchange, coupled with the time and expense of completing forms and awaiting replies, constitutes an obstacle to the conduct of foreign trade.

Administrative Delays   Closely akin to specific permission requirements are intentional administrative delays on entry, which raise uncertainty and the cost of carrying inventory. For example, France required that all imported videotape recorders arrive through a small customs entry point that was both remote and inadequately staffed. The resultant delays effectively kept Japanese recorders out of the market until there was a negotiated "voluntary export quota" whereby Japan limited its penetration of the French market.[28] Peruvian customs officials routinely take months to clear merchandise and then charge customs storage fees that amount to a high portion of the import's value.

Reciprocal Requirements   In recent years there has been an upsurge in requirements that exporters effectively take merchandise in lieu of money. Colombia, for example, paid for buses from Spain's ENESA with coffee, and China purchased railroad engineering services from Italy's Tecnotrade with coal.[29] Since these transactions often require exporters to find markets for goods outside their lines of expertise, many firms avoid this type business. These barter transactions are often referred to as **countertrade,** or **offsets.**

Restrictions on Services   Trade restrictions are usually associated with governmental interference in the international movement of goods. In addition to earnings from the sale of goods abroad, many countries depend substantially on revenue from the foreign sale of such services as transportation, insurance, consulting, and banking. These services account for about 30 percent of the value of all international trade.[30] There have been reports of widespread discrimination by countries favoring their own firms. Among the complaints have been that Japanese airlines get cargo cleared more quickly in Tokyo than do foreign carriers; that Argentina requires automobile imports to be insured en route with Argentine firms; that Germany requires models for advertisements in German magazines to be hired through a German agency (even if the advertisement is made abroad); that Spain restricts the dubbing of foreign films, forcing people to read subtitles; and that Germany prohibits its insurance brokers from helping German clients to arrange insurance abroad.[31]

THE ROLE OF GATT

The most important trade-liberalization activity in the post–World War II period has been through the General Agreement on Tariffs and Trade (GATT), which began in 1947 with 23 members and now has more than 100 members. GATT has given the world a basic set of rules under which trade negotiations take place and a mechanism for monitoring the implementation of these rules.

Most-Favored-Nation Clause

To belong to GATT, nations must adhere to the **most-favored-nation (MFN)** clause. MFN means that if a country, such as the United States, grants a tariff reduction to one country—for example, a cut from 20 percent to 10 percent on wool sweaters from Australia—the United States would grant the same concession to all other countries of the world. The MFN applies to quotas and licenses as well. Although MFN was initially intended to be unconditional, countries have always made exceptions to it.[32]

The most important exceptions are as follows:

1. Manufactured products from developing countries have been given preferential treatment over products from industrial countries.

2. Concessions granted to members within a trading alliance, such as the European Community (EC), have not been extended to countries outside the alliance.

3. Nations that arbitrarily discriminate against products from a given country are not necessarily given MFN treatment by the country whose products are discriminated against.

4. Nonsignatory countries are not always treated in the same way as those that grant concessions.

5. Countries sometimes stipulate exceptions based on their existing laws at the time of signing a GATT agreement.

6. Exceptions are made in times of war or international tensions.

The first exception provides that most industrial countries grant tariff preferences to developing countries under the Generalized System of Preferences (GSP). Under the second exception, the United States and Israel agreed in 1985 to remove all tariffs on each other's products without giving the same benefits to other countries. Under the third exception, the United States does not grant MFN treatment to a number of countries in the former communist bloc. Under the fourth exception, only countries signing GATT's Government Procurement Code (nondiscrimination against imports in government procurement) are granted automatic permission to bid on public works contracts open to foreign bids. Under the fifth exception, Switzerland excludes agricultural trade. Finally, under the last exception, the United Kingdom suspended MFN treatment to Argentina as a result of the two countries' being at war in the South Atlantic.

GATT-Sponsored Rounds

GATT's most important activity has been the sponsoring of "rounds" or sessions named for the place where the round begins, which have led to a number of multilateral reductions in tariffs and nontariff barriers for its membership. The process of granting reductions is across the board: In other words, countries may agree to lower all tariff rates by a given percent, but not necessarily the same percent by all countries, over some specified period of time. Given the thousands of products traded, it would be nearly impossible to negotiate each product separately and even more difficult to negotiate each product separately with each country separately. Nevertheless, each country brings to the negotiations certain products that it considers exceptions to its own across-the-board reductions. That a series of negotiations have resulted in vast tariff reductions indicates not only that countries are committed to work jointly toward freer trade but also that tariffs are the easiest trade barrier to tackle.

The Tokyo Round, for example, resulted in an overall reduction in tariffs, including a reduction between the United States and the EC by 35 percent each way, and a reduction of 40 percent by Japan on U.S. imports into Japan. In spite of these tariff reductions, the primary thrust of the negotiations involved grappling with the increasingly important and complex nontariff barriers, especially in five specific areas: industrial standards, government procurement, subsidies and countervailing duties, licensing, and customs valuation. In each of these five areas, conference members agreed on a code of conduct for GATT nations.[33]

The Agreement on Industrial Standards provides for treating imports on the same basis as domestically produced goods. Similarly, the Agreement on Government Procurement calls for treating bids by foreign firms on a nondiscriminatory basis for most large contracts.

The Agreement or Code of Conduct on Subsidies and Countervailing Duties recognizes domestic subsidies as appropriate policy tools whose implementation, however, should avoid any adverse impact on other countries. Export subsidies are prohibited, the only exception being agricultural products. This agreement also spells out procedures regarding the possibility of using countervailing duties against a second country if the first country believes its domestic firms are being harmed by the second country's subsidy.

The Licensing Code commits members to simplify their licensing procedures significantly and to treat both foreign and domestic firms in a nondiscriminatory manner.

The Customs Valuation Code calls for either c.i.f. or f.o.b. valuation (invoice value with or without transportation and insurance included) and bans certain types of valuation methods, such as basing valuation on the selling price of a product in the importing country. The specific procedures were discussed earlier in the chapter in the section on customs valuation.

GATT as Monitor

There is general agreement that tariff-reduction agreements are difficult to enforce. There are simply too many subtle means that countries use to circumvent the intent of negotiations. Furthermore, there is one important area on which participants have been unable to agree: the use of temporary safeguards against severe domestic disruptions caused by expanding imports. GATT still allows safeguard measures that can reverse the injurious effects of increases in imports that, in turn, result from trade-liberalization moves. In such a situation the injured nation may cancel a previously negotiated action that liberalized trade as long as the country feels that this move is necessary to prevent further injury, particularly in the form of increased unemployment in the affected industry.

In practice, very few safeguards have been imposed under the new GATT rules. However, there have been a number of "voluntary" limitations on exports, such as the example of Japanese limits on auto exports to the United States discussed in the opening case. A voluntary restraint can circumvent GATT agreements because neither the importing country nor the exporting country complains to the GATT Council in Geneva (the organization's ruling body), and GATT can do nothing without a complaint.

What can GATT do if there are complaints? First, it investigates to determine whether the allegations are valid. If the complaints are valid, then countries may pressure the offending party to change its policies. In extreme cases, other GATT members could rescind MFN treatment from the violating country; however, such a measure has not become necessary. The mutual commitment to cooperate has been sufficient to gain widespread compliance with GATT directives. For example, the United States eliminated custom-user fees after the GATT Council investigated complaints from Canada and the EC; and Japan lifted quotas on eight processed-food products, which had raised complaints in the United States.

GATT Limitations

The Office of the U.S. Trade Representative estimated that only about two-thirds of the 1989 world trade of $3730 billion was covered by GATT regulations; i.e., one-third of trade is in products that countries make exceptions to their across-the-board reductions in restrictions. About half the noncovered trade consists of services, such as financial services, which remain highly protected in many countries. Two other areas of importance are agricultural products and textiles and apparels.[34]

The Uruguay Round began in 1986 and disbanded without an agreement by its target date at the end of 1990. Although by 1992 the negotiations were underway again, the experience of the four years of GATT Uruguay Round negotiations exemplifies the growing difficulty of reducing trade restrictions through globally oriented trade agreements. At the core of the problem are the facts that the less-sensitive concessions have already been made and that attention has moved toward services and away from products. Other problems include the fact that talks become more cumbersome as more countries become signatories of GATT and the growing expectation on the part of industrial countries that LDCs should also make trade concessions. For example, the United States has urged Europe to remove barriers to the freer flow of agricultural products; and Europeans have urged the United States to remove its dumping legislation, its safeguards against imports that might violate U.S. patent protection, and its textile-import limitations. These are all areas of such high domestic sensitivity that politicians seem unlikely to yield to international pressures during negotiations. The area of services is so complex that there is as yet little agreement even on how to commence negotiations. Trade in many services involves the potential movement of people internationally, such as in construction and the professions. One immediately encounters immigration issues and difficult licensing requirements and opinions over qualifications.[35]

MESHING PROTECTION AND INTERNATIONAL STRATEGY

When facing import competition, firms can
- Try to get protection
- Make domestic output competitive
- Move abroad

Governmental actions concerning trade are usually examined in terms of their effects on such broad objectives as balance of payments, income distribution, employment, and tax receipts or on such narrow objectives as decreasing steel imports versus increasing citrus exports as a trade-balancing measure. The very fact that changes in governmental actions may substantially alter the competitiveness of facilities in given countries creates uncertainties about which businesses must make decisions.[36] These decisions affect companies that are facing import competition as well as those whose exports are facing protectionist sentiment.

Foreign Competition and U.S. Automakers

Take the case at the beginning of this chapter on foreign automobile competition in the United States. A U.S. company facing the competition had a number of options, including: (1) pushing for import restrictions or other forms of governmental assistance; (2) effecting internal adjustments, such as cost efficiencies, product innovations, or improved marketing; (3) moving production to a lower-cost country and exporting to the United States; and

(4) concentrating on market niches where there is less import competition. Clearly, there are substantial costs, as well as considerable uncertainty as to outcome, associated with any one of these options.

The U.S. automobile industry was successful in lobbying for the first option. The U.S. firms also pursued the second option by instituting various cost-saving measures. Ford estimated its cost level in 1984 to be $4 billion a year less than in 1979.[37] Cost breakthroughs are not always feasible, however, and when they do occur, the innovations may be short-lived as foreign competitors respond with like improvements. The benefit of moving production abroad (option 3), such as Ford's sourcing in Mexico, could be negated if the United States afterward prohibited importation from the foreign plant. The likelihood of import restrictions in such a situation would be inversely related to the number of producers following this option. In other words, because Ford, Chrysler, and GM all went to foreign sourcing, there is no strong coalition to push for import controls on foreign-produced components, except from labor. The Big Three auto firms have also followed the fourth option. Each has made arrangements for foreign companies to supply small cars for them so that they can concentrate more of their production efforts on the larger cars, for which there is less foreign competition. A company should attempt to assess the costs and probabilities of each alternative before embarking on a program.

The potential protection of the U.S. auto industry also created problems for firms that were planning to export to the U.S. market. They could lobby against the protection, try to devise process or product technologies that would overcome the restrictive measures, or locate their production in the United States. As was the case for domestic producers, each of these options involved costs and risks. As was the situation with U.S. auto firms, Japanese auto firms followed each of the alternatives to some extent. They lobbied with the Japanese government to take steps to counter U.S. actions. They developed allies, such as associations of foreign-car importers, to lobby on their behalf in the United States. They continued efforts to reduce costs in case tariffs were imposed. They developed capabilities for adding more luxury items so that profits might not diminish if quotas were imposed. They also negotiated arrangements to produce outside Japan, such as in Mexico and the United States, in case sanctions would be taken only against Japanese output.

Approaches to the International Environment

From the preceding discussion it is clear not only that firms may take different approaches to counter changes in the international competitive environment but also that their attitudes toward protectionism are influenced by the investments that they have made already to develop their international strategies.[38] Companies that depend primarily on trade (whether market seekers or resource acquirers) and those that have integrated their production among different countries are most apt to lose with increased protectionism. Companies with single or multi-domestic production facilities (such as production in the United States to serve the U.S. market and production in Mexico to serve the Mexican market) are most apt to gain through protectionist measures.

LOOKING TO THE FUTURE   Problems of reducing trade restrictions globally will most likely continue in the foreseeable future. Governmental reactions will likely be to focus on bilateral and regional agreements, rather than the global ones envisioned by GATT. The United States, for example, typifies the non-global approach with its already existing bilateral agreements on textile quotas with 41 different countries and its current implementation of a North American free-trade area.

Some additional arguments for protectionism may likely gain importance in the foreseeable future and also give rise to more bilateral agreements. One of these involves nations' equal access to one another's markets on a product-by-product basis. This argument has erupted within the United States within recent years and is sometimes referred to as a strategic-trade policy.[39] Briefly, the argument is that in industries where increased production will greatly decrease cost, either from scale economies or learning effects, producers who lack equal access to a competitor's market will have a disadvantage in gaining enough sales to be cost competitive. This has been argued, for example, in the semiconductor, aircraft, and telecommunications industries, especially in relation to governmental procurement policies, production and export subsidies, and import restrictions. One may envision the use of bilateral agreements and retaliation to bring about a so-called level playing field.

Although the above trends seem to indicate a growing difficulty in bringing about the freer movement of trade, there are other indications for optimism on trade growth. Even with fewer globally negotiated concessions, the global trading system is not apt to fall apart. Trade has been growing rapidly and should continue to do so. One factor is the movement in many countries to privatize formerly government-owned companies and to open up import markets so that domestic companies must operate more efficiently by having to compete. These movements have been especially important in Eastern Europe and in the newly industrialized countries of Asia. Even such highly protected countries as Mexico, Brazil, and Argentina have begun liberalizing imports.[40]

SUMMARY
- Despite the potential resource benefit of free trade, no country permits an unregulated flow of goods and services.
- Given the possibility of retaliation and the fact that imports as well as exports create jobs, it is difficult to determine the effect on employment of protecting an industry.

- Policymakers have not yet solved the problem of redistribution of income through changes in trade policy.

- The infant-industry argument for protection holds that without governmental prevention of import competition, certain industries would be unable to pass from high-cost to low-cost production.

- Because industrial countries are generally more advanced economically than nonindustrial ones, governmental interference is often argued to be beneficial if it promotes industrialization.

- Direct influence on trade is used as a more selective means of solving balance-of-payments disequilibrium than resorting to either changes in currency values or internal price adjustments.

- Trade controls are used to control prices of goods traded internationally. Such controls include protection of monopoly positions, prevention of foreign monopoly prices, greater assurance that domestic consumers get low prices, and requiring foreign producers to lower their profit margins.

- Much of the interference in the free flow of goods and services internationally is motivated by political rather than economic concerns, including maintaining domestic supplies of essential goods and preventing potential enemies from gaining goods that would help them achieve their objectives.

- Many nonindustrial countries are seeking export markets within the industrialized world for their manufactured products but argue that the effective tariffs on their products are too high.

- Trade controls that directly influence price and secondarily influence quantities include tariffs, subsidies, minimum price laws, arbitrary customs valuations, and special fees.

- Trade controls that directly affect quantity and secondarily affect price include quotas, "buy-local" regulations, licensing, foreign-exchange controls, arbitrary standards, administrative delays, and requirements to take goods in exchange.

- The General Agreement on Tariffs and Trade (GATT) is the main negotiating body through which countries have multilaterally reduced trade barriers and have agreed on simplified mechanisms for the conduct of international trade. However, recent experience indicates that further trade liberalization on a global basis will be harder to achieve.

- The development of an international strategy will greatly determine whether firms will benefit best from protectionism or from some other form of countering international competition.

C A S E
STEEL
IMPORTS[41]

In 1984 the United States instituted steel-import quotas. In 1989 these were extended until March 31, 1992, so that foreign steel supplies could increase from 19.1 percent to 20.26 percent of the overall U.S. market. This overall quota necessitated negotiations for separate voluntary restraint agreements (VRAs) with each country supplying steel. How did this situation come about?

At the end of World War II, the U.S. steel industry was the most powerful in the world, and it seemed that no one could challenge its su-

premacy. By 1950, U.S. raw steel production accounted for 47 percent of the world's supply. By the early 1980s, however, this share fell to about 10 percent, where it has since stabilized. Not only has the U.S. world share of production fallen, the United States has become a net importer of steel. (See Map 5.1 for the major sources of U.S. imports.) Steel companies in the United States have argued that import figures understate the inroads of foreign competition because so much additional steel enters in finished products such as automobiles and pipes. Steel jobs in the United States fell by more than 200,000 in the 1980s.

Worldwide, several factors are important for understanding the evolving competitive situation. One involves additional capacity created in

Map 5.1
Major Sources of U.S. Imports
Note that five major producing areas account for 79% of the imported steel in the United States. *Source:* U.S. International Trade Commission, *Monthly Report on the Status of the Steel Industry,* March 1989.

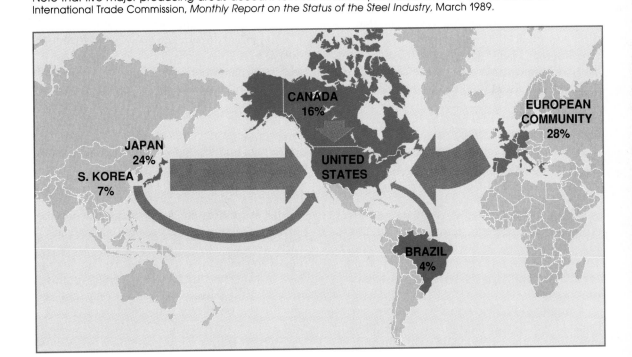

countries that are relatively new to steel production. Many developing countries consider domestic mills essential for achieving their industrialization objectives, and they view steel output in terms of security and prestige considerations. These countries have been able to increase capacity because the technology, except for certain specialty steels, has become widespread and easily attainable. Because of the high priority placed on steel, many countries have been willing to forgo other development projects in order to build mills or have received financial assistance from outside for construction. Since the early 1970s the largest capacity increase has been among Third World countries; they have a substantial, growing excess capacity. In the 1980s Brazil and South Korea's worldwide ranks moved from 10th and 18th to 6th and 8th, respectively. Excess capacity in the United States, Europe, and Japan led steelmakers in all three areas to effect capacity cuts.

Given the high fixed costs of steel production, a second factor affecting steel competition is that much of the world's production has been government-owned. Some observers argue that these firms will continue operating regardless of whether they cover their short-term costs. Because of employment pressures in countries such as France, it has been politically very difficult to cut back production more rapidly in the state facilities. Export markets have been used as an instrument of maintaining more output. The state-owned companies in such countries as Spain and Argentina have reported record losses, but continued exporting at low prices. In addition to direct ownership, it has been argued that governmental assistance through tax incentives, reorganization schemes, provision for long-term, low-interest loans, and waiving of environmental requirements have placed U.S. steel producers at a disadvantage vis-à-vis some foreign producers.

A number of other factors have contributed to the ability of foreign steel producers to compete effectively in the United States. One such factor is technology: Although U.S. firms claim that their newest plants are as advanced as any, the average age of plants in some countries is much below that of U.S. plants, so these plants are more productive on average. For example, it is generally recognized that the useful life of a coke oven is 25 years; however, in 1982, 41 percent of U.S. ovens exceeded that age as compared with only 2 percent in Japan. In 1958 it took Japanese workers nearly 36 man-hours to produce a ton of cold-rolled sheet steel, which U.S. steelmakers could turn out in 12 man-hours. Japanese productivity caught up with that in the United States in 1975; by 1983 it exceeded U.S. productivity by 25 percent. American firms once guaranteed their workers pay increases that exceeded increases in productivity in order to gain a "no-strike" clause in labor contracts. This caused steelworkers to earn more than U.S. production workers in any other manufacturing sector. The plight of the industry, however, caused U.S. companies not to grant any increases between 1982 and 1988, and in 1987 the contract between labor and USX, the largest U.S. steel producer, actually called for wage cuts.

Another factor concerns production location. Most U.S. mills were built decades ago in the corridor of states bordering the Great Lakes. This location minimized transportation costs for raw materials and for finished steel to be shipped to industrial users in this same corridor. Today, however, if a firm wants to use cheaper iron from Brazil and to sell to the expanding industrial and population base in the South and West, these locations may no longer be optimal. Japan, the largest steel exporter to the United States, situates its production largely at deep-water ports. The Japanese industry now has an estimated cost advantage on purchases of raw materials even though they are imported. Despite these advantages, Japan is increasingly importing steel from Taiwan and South Korea, both of which have, on average, lower labor rates and newer plants than Japan. South Korea's Pohang Iron & Steel is now considered the world's most efficient steelmaker. In addition, the average South Korean steelworker earns only one third the salary of a Japanese steelworker.

Regardless of the source of competition, there is a general agreement that there must be major new investment and restructuring of the U.S. steel industry if it is to align its costs with those of imported steel. The steel industry in the United States has argued the difficulty of making this investment because of poor earnings records and the poor outlook of recent years. The lack of funds has been contested by critics who pointed to U.S. Steel's (now USX) acquisition of Marathon Oil when it apparently lacked funds for technological improvements. The USX chairman responded, "Rebuild steel mills to do what? Sit and rust again?" Critics have also blamed industry managers for spending funds for years on hopelessly obsolete (now being retired) plants rather than targeting outlays to viable facilities.

Six competitive responses appear to offer some hope for the future of the steel companies in the United States. The first has been a move to so-called minimills, such as those owned by Nucor, which have specialized products, the latest technology, and proximity to markets. These plants are competitive, and their combined capacity and sales were about 25 percent of the U.S. market by the end of the 1980s. Furthermore, they have recently been moving toward the premier products, such as sheet steel for the auto industry. The second response has been a move by foreign steel firms, such as Nippon Kokan and Kobe Steel of Japan, to buy into the U.S. industry or form joint ventures with U.S. firms, thus infusing funds and technology while not competing so directly with U.S. firms. The third has been a move by U.S. producers to buy semifinished steel from abroad, thus cutting costs at an important level of production. For instance, Korea's Pohang has a joint venture in the United States with USX, to which hot-rolled coils are shipped from Korea. The fourth has been a move to merge firms in the industry in order to gain administrative scale economies, to complement production, and to phase out less competitive plants while maintaining a full product line. An example of this was the Republic Steel-LTV merger plan. The fifth is to phase out nonsteel activities and older steel facilities to concentrate on efficient steel operations. Both Bethlehem and Inland have been following this approach. The sixth is to diversify out of steel. The business of both Armco and USX is now primarily nonsteel related, and USX discussed the possibility in 1990 of getting out of steel altogether. Relatedly, the big five Japanese steelmakers are all diversifying from steel.

In spite of these moves, the steel industry in the United States continues to push for stringent protection. Many steel customers in the United States have complained that the quotas, when coupled with steel-capacity cuts, meant higher prices, delayed deliveries, and inability to get steel of the needed specifications. Caterpillar has complained of being burned because of short supply. Handy & Harman's Indiana Tube Corporation has even considered moving its production abroad to overcome the supply problem.

Questions

1. Should the United States seek to maintain a steel industry even if it could not become cost competitive with foreign steel?

2. Should foreign producers be allowed to export steel to the United States at a price below their cost?

3. Can the United States again become cost efficient in the production of steel vis-à-vis foreign competition?

4. What types of governmental assistance might the United States give to the steel industry to help it compete more effectively with foreign steel? What are the advantages and disadvantages of each option?

5. Contrast the differences and similarities of the U.S. steel situation with those of the automobile case at the beginning of the chapter.

Chapter Notes

1. The data for the case were taken from "U.S. Trade Agency Facing Crucial Decision on Detroit's Plea for Auto Import Curbs," *Wall Street Journal,* November 7, 1980, p. 29; "Car Wars," *Wall Street Journal,* February 15, 1980, p. 1; "Japan Asks Its Car Firms to Limit Exports to U.S. and Start American Production," *Wall Street Journal,* February 13, 1980, p. 2; "U.S. Autos Losing a Big Segment of the Market—Forever?" *Business Week,* March 24, 1980, pp. 78–85; "7 of 10 Americans Agree," *New York Times,* November 6, 1980, p. A23; Leslie Wayne, "The Irony and Impact of Auto Quotas," *New York Times,* April 8, 1984, p. F1 + ; "Brock Vows to End Import Quotas on Japanese Cars," *Wall Street Journal,* May 3, 1984, p. 29; Morgan O. Reynolds, "Unions and Jobs: The U.S. Auto Industry," *Journal of Labor Research,* Vol. 7, No. 2, Spring 1986, pp.103–126; Rachel Dardis and Jia-Yeong Lin, "Automobile Quotas Revisited: The Costs of Continued Protection," *The Journal of Consumer Affairs,* Vol. 19, No. 2, Winter 1985, pp. 277–292; Owen Bieber, "Are Japan's U.S. Auto Plants Unfair?" *New York Times,* May 13, 1990, p. F13; United States General Accounting Office, *Foreign Investment: Growing Japanese Presence in the U.S. Auto Industry* (Washington: GAO/NSIAD-88-111, 1988); Doran P. Levin, "Honda Blurs Line Between American and Foreign," *New York Times,* March 14, 1990, p. A1 ff; "Mazda Motor Corp.," *Wall Street Journal,* July 26, 1989, p. 23; Joseph B. White, "Automobiles," *Wall Street Journal,* November 7, 1989, p. B1; Melinda Grenier Guiles, "GM Puts 'Captive Imports' to New Test," *Wall Street Journal,* September 16, 1988; and Yumiko Ono, "Tokyo to Keep Its Restraints on Car Exports," *Wall Street Journal,* January 18, 1990, p. A14.

2. James J. Kilpatrick, "How Not to Create Jobs," *Nation's Business,* March 1983, Vol. 77, No. 1, p. 5.

3. John Andrew, John Helyar, and Bill Johnson, "Silver Lining," *Wall Street Journal,* February 29, 1984, p. 1.

4. *Ibid.,* p. 19; Peter Truell, "Textile Makers Demanding More Protection Threaten Hopes for Seamless U.S. Trade Policy," *Wall Street Journal,* May 16, 1990, p. A20; and Eduardo Lachica, "Alliance of Textile and Apparel Makers Splits as Senate Mulls Import-Quota Bill," *Wall Street Journal,* July 13, 1990, p. A10.

5. Robert W. Crandell, "Import Quotas and the Automobile Industry: The Costs of Protectionism," *Brookings Review,* Summer 1984, pp. 8–16.

6. Alexander Dagg, "Keeping the Jobs at Home," *Globe and Mail* [Toronto], July 3, 1990, p. 18.

7. Roger Thurow, "Ivory Coast's Reliance on Commodities Topples It from Its Role-Model Pedestal," *Wall Street Journal,* May 9, 1989, p. A16.

8. Peter F. Drucker, "The Changed World Economy," *Foreign Affairs,* Vol. 64, No. 4, Spring 1986 discusses recent occurrences. Lloyd G. Reynolds, "Economic Development in Historical Perspective," *American Economic Review,* May 1980, p. 92, surveys an earlier period.

9. Supportive of the premises are Raul Prebisch, *The Economic Development of Latin America and Its Principal Problems* (New York: United Nations Department of Economic Affairs, 1950); Charles P. Kindleberger, *The Terms of Trade: A European Case Study* (New York: Wiley, 1956), and W. Arthur Lewis, *Aspects of Tropical Trade, 1883–1965* (Stockholm: Almquist and Wiksells, 1969). Nonsupportive are M. June Flanders, "Prebisch on Protectionism: An Evaluation," *Economic Journal,* June 1964; Theodore Morgan, "The Long-Run Terms of Trade between Agriculture and Manufacturing," *Economic Development and Cultural Change,* October 1959; and Gottfried Haberler, "Terms of

Trade and Economic Development," in *Economic Development of Latin America*, H. Ellis, ed. (New York: St. Martin's Press, 1961).

10. Mark M. Nelson, "U.S. Is Wary of EC Import Regulations," *Wall Street Journal*, June 29, 1989, p. B1.

11. John Diebold, "Beyond Subsidies and Trade Quotas," *New York Times*, November 2, 1986, p. F3.

12. James Bovard, "No Justice in Anti-Dumping," *New York Times*, January 28, 1990, p. F13.

13. Peter Truell, "U.S. Won't Seek Trade Retaliation Against India," *Wall Street Journal*, June 13, 1990, p. A6; and Clyde H. Farnsworth, "U.S. Likely to Forego Sanctions Against India," *New York Times*, June 14, 1990, p. D2.

14. John M. Culbertson, "The Folly of Free Trade," *Harvard Business Review*, No. 5, September–October 1986, pp. 122–128.

15. Barbara Rosewicz and Richard Koenig, "Sweeping Change," *Wall Street Journal*, May 25, 1990, p. A1 ff; and "Cleaning Up East Germany," *Wall Street Journal*, June 5, 1990, p. A18.

16. Hazel Bradford and Evert Clark, "When the Pentagon Wants Something America Doesn't Have," *Business Week*, No. 2970, October 27, 1986, p. 46.

17. Eduardo Lachica, "U.S., South Korea Reach Agreement on Sale of Aircraft," *Wall Street Journal*, September 10, 1990, p. C17; and John Maroff, "U.S. Export Ban Hurting Makers of New Devices to Code Messages," *New York Times*, November 19, 1990, p. A1 ff.

18. Karen Pennar, "Will the Embargo Work? A Look at the Record," *Business Week*, September 17, 1990; and Eugene Carlson, "Enterprise," *Wall Street Journal*, August 29, 1990, p. B2.

19. James Bovard, "Our Taxing Tariff Code—Let Them Eat Lobster!" *Wall Street Journal*, March 28, 1990, p. A12.

20. F. H. Rolf Seringhaus, "The Impact of Government Export Marketing Assistance," *International Marketing Review*, Vol. 3, No. 2, Summer 1986 offers a detailed discussion of the effects.

21. Robert B. Reich, "Beyond Free Trade," *Foreign Affairs*, Vol. 61, No. 4, Spring 1983, p. 786.

22. Clyde H. Farnsworth, "U.S. Will Tie Aid to Exports in Bid to Curb the Practice," *New York Times*, May 16, 1990, p. C1, referring to a study by the National Foreign Trade Council; Peter Truell, "Bush to Ask Limits for Export Aid by Other Nations," *Wall Street Journal*, September 13, 1989, p. A2; and Robert Letovsky, "The Export Finance Wars," *Columbia Journal of World Business*, Vol. 25, Nos. 1 & 2, Spring/Summer 1990, pp. 25–35.

23. Shoba Purushothaman, "Customs Classification Codes Confuse Importers, Who Cry 'Trivial Pursuit,'" *Wall Street Journal*, September 27, 1988, p. 38; Eduardo Lachica, "U.S. Designates Suzuki Samurai as Truck Import," *Wall Street Journal*, January 5, 1989, p. A3; and David Rogers, "Customs Service Puts Its Foot Down on Nike," *Wall Street Journal*, April 18, 1990, p. B6.

24. Joan Berger, "Tariffs Aren't Great, but Quotas Are Worse," *Business Week*, No. 2989, March 16, 1987, p. 64.

25. Eduardo Lachica, "U.S. Threatens to End Textile Pact with Macao," *Wall Street Journal*, November 1, 1990, p. A6.

26. Michael Berger, "Phone Market: Japan Keeps Hanging Up on the U.S.," *Business Week,* March 11, 1985, p. 67; and Jacob M. Schlesinger, "Japan's NTT Loosens Its 'Family' Ties," *Wall Street Journal,* May 21, 1990, p. A6.

27. Neal Templin, "Fuel-Economy Law That Would Stymie Japanese Is Sought by U.S. Auto Makers," *Wall Street Journal,* December 5, 1989, p. A10.

28. "Japan to Curb VCR Exports," *New York Times,* November 21, 1983, p. D5.

29. "New Restrictions on World Trade," *Business Week,* July 19, 1982, p.119.

30. John Templeman, Bill Javetski, Jeffrey Reyser, and Barbara Buell, "The New Trade Talks Look Jinxed," *Business Week,* No. 2965, September 22, 1986, p. 47; and Phedon Nicolaides, "Economic Aspects of Services: Implications for a GATT Agreement," *Journal of World Trade,* Vol. 23, No. 1, February 1989, pp. 125–236.

31. Laura Wallace, "Rising Barriers," *Wall Street Journal,* October 5, 1981, p. 1; Nina Darnton, "Spain Restricting the Dubbing of Foreign Movies," *New York Times,* June 4, 1984, p. C11; Chris Best, "Free Trade in the International Insurance Industry," *Risk Management,* August 1986, p. 12; J. J. Boddewyn and Iris Mohr, "International Advertisers Face Government Hurdles," *Marketing News,* May 8, 1987, p. 20; and Joan M. Feldman, "The Dilemma of 'Open Skies,'" *New York Times Magazine,* April 2, 1989, pp. 31–32 ff.

32. Gary C. Hufbauer, "Should Unconditional MFN Be Revised, Retired, or Recast?" in *Issues in World Trade Policy,* R. H. Snape, ed. (New York: St. Martin's Press, 1986), pp. 32–55; Frieder Roessler, "The Scope, Limits and Function of the GATT Legal System," *The World Economy,* Vol. 8, No. 4, September 1985, pp. 287–298.

33. Ann V. Morrison, "Tokyo Round Agreements Set Rules for Nontariff Measures," *Business America,* Vol. 9, No. 14, July 7, 1986, pp. 11–13.

34. Clyde H. Farnsworth, "Winners and Losers in Trade Talks," *New York Times,* November 29, 1990, pp. C1–C2.

35. Clyde H. Farnsworth, "U.S., Despite Dispute, Will Go to Trade Talks," *New York Times,* November 14, 1990, p. C1 ff; and Paul Magnusson, "The GATT Talks: Forget the Darn Deadline," *Business Week,* November 19, 1990, p. 51.

36. For a good discussion of alternatives when faced with import competition, see Ingo Walter and Kent A. Jones, "The Battle Over Protectionism: How Industry Adjusts to Competitive Shocks," *Journal of Business Strategy,* Vol. 2, No. 2, Fall 1981, pp. 37–46.

37. "Ford Posts Record Net in Quarter," *New York Times,* April 27, 1984, p. D1.

38. For a discussion of MNE changes in their lobbying effort for protectionism, see Giles Merrill, "Coping with the 'New Protectionism': How Companies Are Learning to Love It," *International Management,* Vol. 41, No. 9, September 1986, pp. 20–26.

39. Lindley H. Clark, Jr., "How 'Managed Trade' Would Really Work," *Wall Street Journal,* November 9, 1989, p. A16; Ravi Sarathy, "The Interplay of Industrial Policy and International Strategy: Japan's Machine Tool Industry," *California Management Review,* Vol. 31, No. 3, Spring 1989, pp. 132–160; and David B. Yoffie and Helen V. Milner, "An Alternative to Free Trade or Protectionism: Why Corporations Seek Strategic Trade Policy," *California Management Review,* Vol. 31, No. 4, Summer 1989, pp. 111–131.

40. Brink Lindsey, "Trade Crisis? What Trade Crisis?" *Wall Street Journal,* March 7, 1990, p. A18.

41. Data for this case were taken from "Basic Problems," *Wall Street Journal,* September 30, 1983, p. 1 + ; Thomas F. O'Boyle and J. Ernest Beazley, "U.S. Steel Bid Stirs

Debate Inside Firm," *Wall Street Journal,* February 3, 1984, p. 25; Thomas F. O'Boyle, "Forging a Link," *Wall Street Journal,* December 20, 1983, p. 1; "The Rebirth of Steel," February 16, 1984, p. 34; Donald F. Barnett and Louis Schorsch, *Steel: Upheaval in a Basic Industry* (Cambridge, Mass.: Ballinger, 1984); "It's a No-Win Situation for Both Sides at USX," *Business Week,* No. 2981, January 19, 1987, p. 55; J. Ernest Beazley, "Big Steel's Push to Extend Import Quotas Draws Debate," *Wall Street Journal,* December 30, 1987, p. 2; Rick Wartzman and Carol Hymowitz, "Uneasy Revival," *Wall Street Journal,* November 4, 1988, p. 1; Clare Ansberry, "USX, Kobe Steel to Form Venture for a New Plant," *Wall Street Journal,* October 20, 1989, p. A4; Clare Ansberry, "Industry Focus," *Wall Street Journal,* October 17, 1989, p. A6; James Brooke, "Brazil Shakes Up Its Steel Industry," *New York Times,* May 28, 1990, p. 23; Peter Truell, "Economy," *Wall Street Journal,* December 13, 1989, p. A2; Jacob Schlesinger, "Nippon Steel, in a Diversification Move, to Make, Sell Notebook-Sized Computers," *Wall Street Journal,* September 11, 1990, p. B4; and José A. Mendez and Gerard Berg, "The Effects of Steel Import Restraints on U.S. Exports, Imports and Domestic Sales in Steel-Consuming Industries," *Journal of World Trade,* Vol. 23, No. 4 (1989), pp. 35–44.

CHAPTER 6

FOREIGN DIRECT INVESTMENT

Who moves picks up, who stands still dries up.
ITALIAN PROVERB

Objectives

- To explain why direct investments are viewed differently by investors and governments than portfolio investments.

- To demonstrate how foreign direct investment may be acquired.

- To evaluate the relationship between foreign trade and international factor mobility, especially direct investment.

- To classify the major types of direct investment motivation.

- To illustrate the circumstances that lead companies to seek foreign supplies through their foreign direct investments.

- To show how and why government actions influence the movement of direct investment.

- To introduce the advantages of direct investors.

The Bridgestone Tire Company is the largest tire producer in Japan, with 50 percent of the Japanese market. During the 1970s its sales grew sixfold. Between 1978 and 1987 it grew from the fifth-largest to the third-largest tire company in the world, a position that it still holds. Although most of the company's sales efforts have been geared toward the Japanese market, foreign sales have been increasing. Part of these foreign sales have been indirect because Bridgestone is a major supplier to Japanese automobile firms. Since they are part of the original equipment on exported Japanese automobiles, Bridgestone tires arrive in foreign markets where the company makes little or no export effort. Direct exports are also important. By the mid-1980s, Bridgestone's top management believed that it was essential to grow outside of Japan, assuming that by 1990 or 1995 there would be few major tire companies in the world. The prediction of industry consolidation proved correct, as shown in Map 6.1. Management also believed that it would be difficult to sustain growth in Japan because it is hard to exceed 50 percent of the market.

In 1987 Bridgestone announced it would expand its truck and bus tire plant in Tennessee in order to produce about 2 million passenger tires a year by 1990. This was seven years after the company's president stated that the firm's first priority would be the establishment of a manufacturing investment in the United States. Probably the major factor influencing this priority was the firm's high direct and indirect export sales to the United States. By 1987 one out of every ten new cars sold in the United States carried Bridgestone tires. These sales gave Bridgestone a solid indication that it could compete against firms with established U.S. sales and manufacturing facilities. Some dealers carried Bridgestone tires as replacements as well; however, Bridgestone had only 2 percent of this larger market. Bridgestone

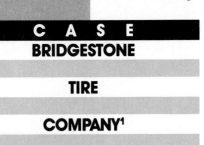

CASE
BRIDGESTONE
TIRE
COMPANY[1]

became more confident about its ability to manage and control an automobile-tire manufacturing investment in the highly competitive U.S. market. Part of this confidence derived from the company's success with foreign manufacturing facilities in four developing countries, its success in Australia after buying out Uniroyal there, and its success with U.S. truck-tire manufacturing after buying a Firestone facility in 1982.

Then, in 1988, Bridgestone surprised analysts by buying Firestone's tire operations for $2.6 billion. This gave them five North American plants supplying about 40 percent of the tires for North American vehicles built by Ford and 21 percent of those built by General Motors as well as plants in Portugal, Spain, France, Italy, Argentina, Brazil, and Venezuela. Although Bridgestone remained the world's third-largest tire company, the acquisition put them very close to the two largest firms, Goodyear and Michelin. Michelin's purchase of Uniroyal Goodrich in 1989 pushed them clearly into the number-one position.

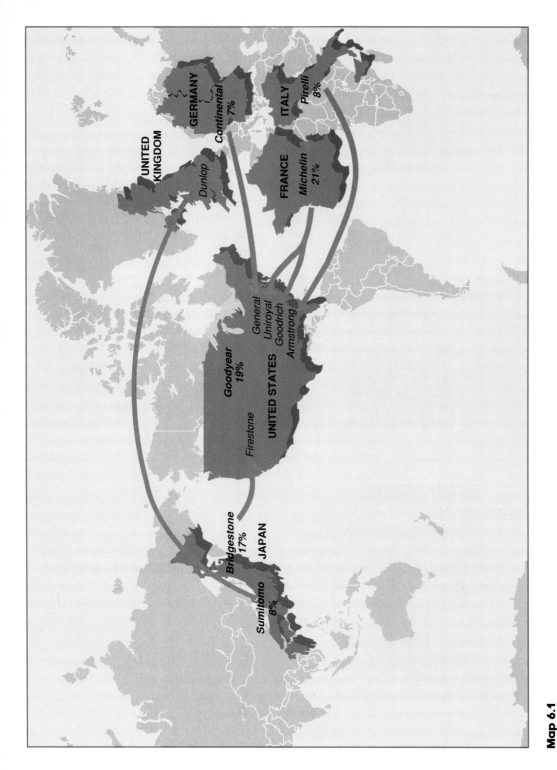

Map 6.1
Major Global Tire Producers and Their Recent Foreign Acquisitions

These percentage figures are for 1990 global market share. The arrows indicate the direction of recent acquisitions.

But why should Bridgestone manufacture automobile tires in the United States? Why not continue exporting, since sales had grown by this means? Several factors had a potential negative impact on Bridgestone's export activities to the United States. The first of these was government-imposed restrictions. Although imports of replacement tires comprised a very small part of the U.S. market, these imports could be restricted if sales of U.S.-made tires were to go down. More probable could be action taken against imports of Japanese automobiles, thus jeopardizing the sale of original-equipment tires. The possibility of import restrictions already had led four major Japanese automakers to begin some U.S. production, and all opted for U.S.-made tires once their plants were operating. Toyota, by the way, bought 40 percent of Bridgestone's original-equipment tires. Finally, because of Japan's huge trade surplus with the United States, the United States could conceivably place overall restrictions on the import of Japanese products.

Exports might also be imperiled if Japanese costs went up in relation to American costs. Because of high transportation costs for tires, which are bulky relative to their value, it is usually difficult to ship tires over large distances except as part of original vehicle equipment. Bridgestone's overseas shipping expenses ranged between $3 and $12 per tire, depending on size. U.S. producers even depended on multiple U.S. plant locations in order to minimize transport costs. It was generally conceded that a one-plant firm in the United States could not maintain sales on both the East and West coasts. Bridgestone's ability to overcome the high transport costs was due largely to the low value of the yen relative to the U.S. dollar. Since most of Bridgestone's costs were in yen, a fall in the yen resulted in lower costs in terms of U.S. dollars; thus Bridgestone could absorb the international transport costs. When the yen strengthens, Bridgestone's dollar costs go up. By mid-1986 the strong yen put the competitive sales price below Bridgestone's break-even point. The yen strengthened even more in 1987 and 1988, making it even more difficult to serve the U.S. market by exporting to it. However, the strong yen meant that Bridgestone would likely pay less in yen for an investment in the United States.

But why buy Firestone rather than starting up a new automobile tire facility? Probably the major factor was an expectation of overcapacity in the industry brought on in large part by the increased use of radial tires, which last longer. Firestone had already secured sales. An acquisition would add less capacity to a glutted market than a start-up operation would. Nevertheless, by the early 1990s U.S. overcapacity kept U.S. tire prices and industry prices low. Bridgestone found that the Firestone operations were less efficient than had been anticipated. On top of that, Firestone lost the General Motors account. Although Bridgestone reorganized U.S. operations and invested heavily to modernize Firestone facilities, U.S. losses in the early 1990s were about equal to profits in Japan.

INTRODUCTION

Foreign sales are increasingly being made from foreign-controlled production facilities; this is called **foreign direct investment (FDI).** No one explanation or theory encompasses all the reasons for this increase.[2]

The preceding case illustrates the multiplicity of factors influencing the decision of one firm to produce in a foreign country. Before deciding to invest in the United States, Bridgestone faced a sequence of decisions. One of the first was whether or not to serve foreign markets. Bridgestone was content with the Japanese market as long as it could expand rapidly within that market. However, once the company had acquired a large and fairly stable share of a maturing market, it had to consider either product diversification or geographic diversification in order to sustain growth.[3] Either type of diversification would involve the risks that arise from operating in new arenas. Bridgestone chose to diversify geographically because its managers believed its competitive advantage was more specific to the production of tires than to knowledge of the Japanese market. For example, Bridgestone spent more on R&D than Goodyear, the world's largest tire manufacturer, when Bridgestone began expanding heavily abroad. The high level and concentration of R&D expenditures has led Bridgestone to make notable breakthroughs in both product and process technologies.[4] Bridgestone first entered foreign markets through exporting and was successful. Nevertheless, management felt that it could not sustain an export market to the United States because of the high transport cost of tires, the possibility of U.S. government import restrictions, preferences by final or industrial consumers for a U.S.-made product, and an uncertain cost structure created by the changing yen–dollar relationship. Bridgestone still might have chosen to license its technologies and/or its name to producers already in the U.S. market, which would have generated revenues without the risk of operating in an alien environment. By this time, though, the perceived risk of operating in the United States was minimal because of Bridgestone's growing foreign experience and the likelihood that it could sell output to Japanese automakers with whom the company had experience. There were also competitive reasons for Bridgestone's not licensing. The company felt that it must be located in growth markets if it were to survive the expected shakeout in the industry. The transfer of technology to other tire producers eventually might undermine Bridgestone's ability to compete in other markets.

The Bridgestone case also illustrates that a direct investment may be acquired in alternative ways. Neither the motives nor the methods for acquiring direct investment as illustrated in the case are conclusive. This chapter will further examine these various motives and methods.

The growth of foreign direct investment has resulted in a heightened interest in three other questions:

1. What effect does the investment have on national economic, political, and social objectives?

2. Should a firm choose to operate abroad by some form other than direct investment, such as licensing?

3. What is, or should be, a firm's pattern of investment in terms of where to operate abroad?

These questions will be discussed from an introductory standpoint in this chapter. Then they will be explored more thoroughly in subsequent chapters.

THE MEANING OF FOREIGN DIRECT INVESTMENT

The Concept of Control

Direct investment usually implies at least 10 or 25 percent ownership.

In Chapter 1 we saw that for direct investment to take place, control must follow the investment. The amount of ownership share necessary for control is not clear-cut. If stock ownership is widely dispersed, then a small percentage of the holdings may be sufficient to establish control in managerial decision making. On the other hand, even a 100 percent share does not guarantee control. If a government dictates whom a firm hires, what the firm must sell at a specified price, and how earnings will be distributed, then one could say that control has passed to the government. These are all decisions that governments frequently do impose on foreign or domestic investors operating within their confines. But it is not only governments that may jeopardize the stockholders' control. If some resource needed for the firm to operate is not regulated by the firm's owners, then those who control the resource may exert substantial influence on the firm. Because of the difficulty of identifying direct investments, governmental offices have had to establish arbitrary definitions, usually indicating ownership of either 10 or 25 percent of the voting stock in a foreign enterprise as minimum for an investment to be considered direct.

The Concern over Control

When foreign investors control a firm, decisions of national importance may be made abroad.

Governmental Concern   Why should anyone care whether an investment is controlled from abroad? Many critics are concerned that the national interest will not be best served if a multinational firm makes decisions from afar on the basis of its own global or national objectives. For example, General Motors (GM) owns 100 percent interest in Vauxhall Motors in the United Kingdom. The control of Vauxhall by GM in this direct investment means that GM's corporate management in the United States is concerned directly with and makes decisions about personnel staffing, export prices, and the retention versus payout of profits in Vauxhall. The British public also is concerned in this case because decisions that directly affect the British economy are being made (or at least can be made) in the United States. The British government, on the other hand, owns slightly less than 1 percent of GM. Since this is not enough for control, the British government does not expend time and effort in making management decisions for GM. Nor is the U.S. populace concerned that vital GM decisions will be made in Britain. This does not mean that noncontrolled investments are unimportant, however. They may substantially affect a country's balance of payments and they may play an important part in a firm's financial management and strategy. These points will be discussed in depth in later chapters.

When investors control an organization, they
- Are more willing to transfer technology and other competitive assets
- Usually use cheaper and faster means of transferring assets

Investor Concern   Control is also very important to many investors who are reluctant to transfer certain vital resources to another domestic or foreign organization that can make all its operating decisions independently. If valuable patents, trademarks, and management know-how are transferred, they can then be used to undermine the competitive position of the original holders. This desire to deny rivals access to competitive resources is referred to as the **appropriability theory.**[5] In the introductory case, for example, Bridgestone was hesitant to transfer either product technology, such as its Super-Filler radials, or process technology, such as its mold changeover methods, to other companies. Bridgestone's management is well aware of how acquired technology can be used to catch a leader. Between the end of World War II and 1979, much of Bridgestone's technology came from Goodyear, which held a noncontrolling interest in Bridgestone. Another reason for control is to ensure that decisions serve global as opposed to national objectives.

Operating costs may also decrease when control is retained. This is because (1) the parent and subsidiary are likely to have a common corporate culture, (2) a company can use its own managers who understand its objectives, (3) protracted negotiations with another company are avoided, and (4) possible problems of enforcing an agreement are evaded. This self-handling, as opposed to contracts with other companies, is often referred to as **internalization.**[6]

This desire for control does not imply that the control of foreign operations is always preferable. There are many circumstances in which assets are transferred to noncontrolled entities, such as the transfer of trademarks and technology through licensing agreements.

Methods of Acquisition

Direct investments usually, but not always, involve some capital movement.

Direct investment has traditionally been considered an international capital movement that crosses borders when the anticipated return (accounting for the risk factor and the cost of transfer) is higher overseas than at home. Although most direct investments involve some type of international capital movement, an investor may transfer many other types of assets. Such organizations as Westin Hotels have transferred very little capital to foreign countries. Instead, Westin has transferred managers, hotel cost controls, and reservations capabilities in exchange for equity in foreign hotels. An example of a direct investment made completely by transferring nonfinancial resources instead of capital was the Plessey (British) acquisition of Airborne Accessories Corporation in the United States. Plessey had two assets that were vital to Airborne Accessories: technology and established sales capabilities outside the United States. Plessey offered the owners notes in exchange for the ownership. Although the interest and principal on these notes was to be paid strictly out of the earnings of the acquired company, the owners reasoned that this interest was a higher return than they could get by continuing to own and manage Airborne themselves.[7]

Aside from committing nonfinancial resources, there are two other means of acquiring assets that do not involve international capital movements in a normal sense. First, if a business earns funds in a foreign country, these may be used to establish an investment. For example, if a firm exports merchandise but holds payment for those goods abroad, the settlement could be used to acquire an investment. In this case the company merely has exchanged goods for equity. Although this is not a method used extensively for initial investment, the use of retained earnings is a major means of expanding abroad. Initially a firm may transfer assets abroad in order to establish a sales or production facility. If the earnings from the facility are used to increase the value of the foreign holdings, direct investment has increased without a new international capital movement. The second means is by trading equity between firms in different countries. For example, Naarden in the Netherlands acquired a share of Flavorex in the United States by giving the Flavorex owners stock in the Naarden Company.

In several of the preceding examples a firm in one country acquired an interest in an ongoing business operation in another country. Alternatively, the investors could have established an entirely new company abroad. In either case the investors' ownership of voting shares might have been less than 100 percent. If it were less, the remainder could be (1) widely rather than narrowly held and (2) owned by private rather than by governmental sources.

THE RELATIONSHIP
OF TRADE AND FACTOR MOBILITY

Both finished goods and production factors are partially mobile internationally.

Whether capital or some other asset is transferred abroad initially to acquire a direct investment, the asset is a type of production factor. Eventually, the direct investment usually involves the movement of various types of production factors as investors infuse capital, technology, personnel, raw materials, or components into their operating facilities abroad. Therefore, it is useful to examine the relationship of trade theory to the movement of production factors.

The Trade and Factor Mobility Theory

Chapter 4 explained that trade often occurs because of differences in factor endowments among countries. A country such as Canada, with abundant arable land relative to its small but educated labor force, may cultivate wheat in a highly mechanized manner. This wheat may be exchanged for handmade sweaters from Hong Kong, which require abundant semiskilled labor and little land.

Historical treatises on trade assumed that the factors of production were nearly immobile internationally and that trade could move freely. In actuality, there are many natural and imposed barriers that make both finished goods and production factors partially mobile internationally. Factor movement is an alternative to trade that may or may not be a more efficient allocation of resources. If the factors of production were not free to move internationally as assumed by early economic theorists, then trade would ordinarily be the most efficient way of compensating for differences in factor endowments. If neither trade nor the production factors could move internationally, a country would often have to forgo consuming certain goods. Alternatively, countries could produce them differently, which would usually result in decreased worldwide output and higher prices. We can only speculate on the astronomical cost of coffee if it were produced, say, in hothouses in Arctic regions. In some cases, however, the inability to utilize foreign production factors may stimulate efficient methods of substitution, such as the development of new materials as alternatives for traditional ones or of machines to do hand work. The development of synthetic rubber and rayon was undoubtedly accelerated because wartime conditions made it impractical to move silk and natural rubber, not to mention silkworms and rubber plants.

Substitution

There is pressure for most abundant factors to move to an area of scarcity.

Whenever the factor proportions vary widely among countries, there are pressures for the most abundant factors to move to countries of greater scarcity so that they can command a better return. Thus in countries with an abundance of labor relative to land and capital, there is a tendency for laborers in that country to be unemployed or poorly paid; if permitted, these workers will gravitate to countries with relatively full employment and higher wages. Likewise, capital will tend to move away from countries where it is abundant to those where it is scarce. Mexico is thus a net recipient of capital from the United States, and the United States is a net recipient of labor from Mexico.

If finished goods and production factors were both completely free to move internationally, then the comparative costs of transferring goods and factors would determine the location of production. A hypothetical example as shown in Fig. 6.1 should illustrate the substitutability of trade and factor movements under different scenarios.

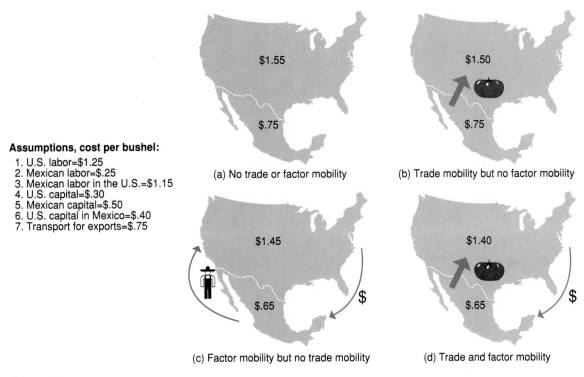

Assumptions, cost per bushel:
1. U.S. labor=$1.25
2. Mexican labor=$.25
3. Mexican labor in the U.S.=$1.15
4. U.S. capital=$.30
5. Mexican capital=$.50
6. U.S. capital in Mexico=$.40
7. Transport for exports=$.75

(a) No trade or factor mobility

(b) Trade mobility but no factor mobility

(c) Factor mobility but no trade mobility

(d) Trade and factor mobility

Figure 6.1
Comparative Costs Based on Trade and Factor Mobility Assumptions: Tomatoes in the United States and Mexico
The least expensive costs are when trade and production factors are both mobile.

Assume: (1) that the United States and Mexico have equally productive land available at the same cost for growing tomatoes; (2) that the cost of transporting tomatoes between the United States and Mexico is $0.75 per bushel; and (3) that workers from either country pick an average of two bushels per hour during a 30-day picking season. The only differences in price between the two countries are due to variations in labor and capital cost. The labor rate in the United States is assumed to be $20.00 per day, or $1.25 per bushel; in Mexico it is assumed to be $4.00 per day, or $0.25 per bushel. The cost of capital needed to buy seeds, fertilizers, and equipment costs the equivalent of $0.50 per bushel in Mexico and $0.30 per bushel in the United States.

If neither tomatoes nor production factors can move between the two countries (see Fig. 6.1a), then the cost of tomatoes produced in Mexico for the Mexican market would be $0.75 per bushel ($0.25 of labor plus $0.50 of capital), whereas those produced in the United States for the U.S. market would be $1.55 per bushel ($1.25 of labor plus $0.30 of capital). If trade restrictions on tomatoes were eliminated between the two countries (Fig. 6.1b), the United States would import from Mexico because the Mexican cost of $0.75 per bushel plus $0.75 of transportation cost to move them to the United States would be less than the $1.55 cost of growing them in the United States.

Consider another scenario in which neither country allows the importation of tomatoes but in which both countries allow certain movements of labor and capital (Fig. 6.1c). An investigation shows that Mexican workers can enter the United States on temporary work permits for an incremental travel and living expense of $14.40 per day per worker, or $0.90 per bushel. At the same time, U.S. capital can be enticed to invest in Mexican tomato production provided that it receives a payment equivalent to $0.40 per bushel, less than the Mexican going rate but more than it would earn in the United States. In this situation, Mexican production costs per bushel would be $0.65 ($0.25 of Mexican labor plus $0.40 of American capital). U.S. production costs would be $1.45 ($0.25 of Mexican labor plus $0.90 of travel and incremental costs plus $0.30 of American capital). Note that each country would be able to reduce its production costs (Mexico from $0.75 to $0.65 and the United States from $1.55 to $1.45) by bringing in abundant production factors from abroad.

With free trade and the free movement of production factors (Fig. 6.1d), Mexico would produce for both markets by importing capital from the United States. According to the above assumptions, that would be a cheaper alternative than sending labor to the United States. In reality, neither production factors nor the finished goods that they produce are completely free to move internationally. Some slight changes in imposing or freeing restrictions can greatly alter how and where goods may be produced most cheaply.

In the case of the United States, in recent years there has been more legal freedom for capital to flow out than for labor to flow in. As a result, there has been an increase in U.S.-controlled direct investment to produce goods that are then imported back into the United States. In fact, capital moves globally more easily than does labor. Furthermore, technology, particularly in the form of more efficient machinery, is generally more mobile internationally than labor. The result is that differences in labor productivity and cost explain much of trade and direct investment movements.

Complementarity of Trade and Direct Investment

Factor mobility via direct investment often stimulates trade movement due to a need for

- Components
- Complementary products
- Equipment for subsidiaries

In spite of the increase in direct investments to produce goods for re-import, firms usually export substantially to their foreign facilities; thus FDI is not usually a substitute for exports.[8] Many of these exports would not occur if overseas investments did not exist. In these cases, factor movements stimulate rather than substitute for trade. One reason for this phenomenon is that domestic operating units may ship materials and components to their foreign facilities for use in a finished product. For example, the Mexican government has required that automobiles sold in Mexico be assembled there. Chrysler therefore put an investment in Mexico to which parts are shipped from the United States. Yet the quantity of parts from the United States has varied as Mexico has changed requirements for local parts.[9] The foreign subsidiaries or affiliates also may buy capital equipment or supplies from home-country firms because of their confidence in performance and delivery or to achieve maximum worldwide uniformity. A foreign facility may produce part of the product line while serving as sales agent for exports of its parent's other products. Bridgestone, for instance, continued to export its automobile tires from Japan for several years while using the sales force from its U.S. truck-tire manufacturing operations to handle the imports.

DIRECT INVESTMENT MOTIVATION

Businesses and governments are motivated to engage in direct investment in order to
- Expand markets
- Acquire supplies or resources

Governments may additionally be motivated to gain political advantage.

The reasons that firms engage in direct investment ownership are no different from the reasons for their pursuit of international trade. They are:

1. to expand markets by selling abroad, and
2. to acquire foreign resources (e.g., raw materials, production efficiency, knowledge).

When governments are involved in direct investment, an additional motive may be to attain some political advantage. These three objectives in turn may be pursued by any one of three forms of foreign involvement. One of these, the sale of services (e.g., licensing or management contracts), often is avoided either for fear of loss of control of key competitive assets or because of greater economies from self-ownership of production. The following discussion will concentrate on the remaining two forms: trade and direct investment. We will emphasize why direct investment is chosen in spite of the fact that most firms consider it riskier to operate a facility abroad than at home.

MARKET-EXPANSION INVESTMENTS

Transportation

Transportation increases cost so much that it becomes impractical to ship some products.

Early trade theorists usually ignored the cost of transporting goods from one place to another. More recently, location theorists have considered total landed cost (cost of production plus shipping) to be a more meaningful way of comparing where production should be situated. When transportation is added to production costs, some products become impractical to ship over a great distance. In the opening case, we showed that one of the factors influencing Bridgestone's decision to invest in the United States was the high cost of transporting tires relative to the production price of tires. Numerous other products that are impractical to ship great distances without a very large escalation in the price quickly come to mind: A few of these products and their investing companies include newspapers (Thompson Newspapers, Canadian), margarine (Unilever, British-Dutch), dynamite (Nobel, Swedish), and soft drinks (PepsiCo, U.S.). For these firms, it is necessary to produce abroad if they are to sell abroad. When firms move abroad to produce basically the same products that they produce at home, their direct investments are known as **horizontal expansions.**

Excess domestic capacity
- Usually means exporting rather than direct investment
- May be competitive through variable cost pricing

Lack of Domestic Capacity   As long as a company has excess capacity at its home-country plant, it may be able to compete effectively in limited export markets in spite of the high transport costs. This could be because the fixed operating expenses are covered through domestic sales, thus enabling foreign prices to be set on the basis of variable rather than full cost. Such a pricing strategy may erode as foreign sales become more important or as output nears full plant capacity utilization. This helps to explain why firms, even those with products for which transport charges are a high portion of total landed costs, typically export before producing abroad. Another major factor is that companies want to get a better indication that they can sell a sufficient amount in the foreign country before committing resources for foreign production. Finally, they may want to learn more about the foreign operating environment by exporting to it before investing in production facilities within it. Once they have experience in foreign production, they are more apt to shorten the export-experience time before they produce abroad.

This reluctance to expand total capacity while there is still substantial excess capacity is not unlike a domestic expansion decision. Internationally as well as domestically, growth is incremental. To understand this process, it is useful to draw a parallel of how growth may take place domestically. The simplest example is the firm that makes only one product. Most likely, this firm will begin operations near the city where its founders are already residing and will begin selling in only the local or regional area. Eventually, sales may be expanded to a larger geographic market. As capacity is reached, the firm may build a second plant in another part of the country to serve that region and save on transportation costs. Warehouses and sales offices may be located in various cities in order to assure closer contact with customers. Purchasing offices may be located close to suppliers in order to improve the probability of delivery at low prices. In fact, the company may even acquire some of its customers or suppliers in order to reduce inventories and gain economies in distribution. Certain functions may be further decentralized geographically, such as by locating financial offices near a financial center. As the product line evolves and expands, operations continue to disperse. In the pursuit of foreign business it is not surprising that growing firms eventually find it necessary to acquire assets abroad.

In large-scale process technology, large-scale production and export usually reduce unit landed costs by spreading fixed costs over more units of output.

In small-scale process technology, country-by-country production usually reduces unit landed costs since transportation is minimized.

Scale Economies   Transportation costs must be examined in relation to the type of technology used to produce a good. The manufacture of some products necessitates plant and equipment that use a high fixed-capital input. In such a situation, especially if the product is highly standardized or undifferentiated from competitors, the cost per unit is apt to drop significantly as output increases. Products such as ball bearings, alumina, and semiconductor wafers fall into this category. Such products are exported substantially because the cost savings from scale economies overcome the added transport expenses to get goods to foreign markets.

The needed scale of production must be considered in relation to the size of the foreign market being served. For example, many European firms have production facilities in both the United States and Canada. They are more apt to sell the U.S. output only in the United States because of the large market, whereas much of the Canadian output is sold in their home countries to gain large-scale production.[10]

Products that are more differentiated and labor intensive, such as pharmaceuticals and certain prepared foods, are not as sensitive to scale economies. For these types of products, transportation costs may dictate smaller plants to serve national rather than international markets.[11] David's Cookies, for example, first entered the Japanese market with ingredients mixed in the United States. However, because there was little cost reduction obtained by mixing bigger batches of batter, David's switched to Japanese ingredient preparation to overcome the transport cost incurred when exporting.[12]

Trade Restrictions

If imports are highly restricted,

- Companies often produce locally to serve the local market
- Firms are more prone to produce locally if market potential is high in relation to scale economies

We have shown that for various reasons there are numerous ways in which a government can make it impractical for a firm to reach its market potential through exportation alone. The firm may find that it *must* produce in a foreign country if it is to sell there. For example, Mexico announced that within five years locally produced microcomputers would have to comprise 70 percent of the market. Although many producers questioned whether the same prices and quality could be maintained as when they exported, they nevertheless were reluctant to abandon a growing market.[13] Such governmental pronouncements are not unusual. They undoubtedly favor large companies that can afford to commit large amounts of resources abroad and make foreign competitiveness more difficult for the smaller firms, which can afford only exportation as a means of serving foreign markets.

How prevalent are trade restrictions as an enticement for making direct investments? There is substantial anecdotal evidence of firms' decisions to locate within protected markets, yet studies of aggregate direct investment movements are inconclusive regarding the importance of trade barriers.[14] A possible explanation for the fact that some studies have not found import barriers to be an important enticement is that the studies have had to rely on actual tariff barriers as the measure of restrictions. This reliance overlooks the importance of nontariff constraints, indirect entry barriers, and potential trade restrictions. In the opening case, Bridgestone reacted to these latter impediments to trade rather than to the actual existence of tariffs on tires. Almost certainly import barriers are a major enticement to direct investment, but they must be viewed alongside other factors, such as the market size of the country imposing barriers.

For example, import trade restrictions have been highly influential in enticing automobile producers to locate in Mexico. Similar restrictions by Central American countries have been ineffective because of their small markets. However, Central American import barriers on products requiring lower amounts of capital investment and therefore smaller markets (e.g., pharmaceuticals) have been highly effective at enticing direct investment.

Consumer-Imposed Restrictions

Consumers sometimes prefer domestically made products because of
- Nationalism
- A belief that their own products are better
- A fear that foreign-made goods may not be delivered on time
- A compatibility between these products and local preferences

Government-imposed legal measures are not the only trade barriers to otherwise competitive goods: Consumer desires also may dictate limitations. For example, consumers may prefer buying domestically made goods, even though they are more expensive. They also may demand that merchandise be altered so substantially that scale economies from exporting are infeasible. The reasons for preferring domestically made products may include nationalism, a belief that foreign-made goods are inferior, or a fear that service and spare parts will not be easily obtainable for imported wares.

Nationalism   The impact of nationalistic sentiments on investment movements is not assessed easily; however, some evidence does exist. There have been active campaigns at times in many countries to persuade people to buy locally produced goods. In the United States, for instance, attempts have been made to boycott Polish hams, Japanese Christmas ornaments, and French wines. Some U.S. manufacturers have promoted "made in the USA" to appeal to consumers in areas that have been hit with import competition.[15] Fearful that adverse public opinion might lead to curbs on television imports, some Japanese firms announced the establishment of production plants in the United States.[16]

Product Image   The link between product image and direct investment is clearer than the one just discussed between nationalism and direct investment. The image may stem from the merchandise itself or from beliefs concerning after-sales servicing. In tests using commodities that were identical except for the label of country origin, consumers were found to view products differently on the basis of product source.[17] Although there are examples of eventual image changes, such as the general improvement in the image of Japanese products that occurred concomitantly with the decline in image for U.S. products, it may take a long time and be very costly for a company to try to overcome image problems caused by manufacturing in a country that has a lower-image status for a particular product. Consequently, there may be advantages to producing in a country with an already-existing high image.

Delivery Risk   Many consumers fear that parts for foreign-made goods may be difficult to obtain from abroad. Industrial consumers often prefer to pay a higher price to a producer located nearby in order to minimize the risk of nondelivery due to distance and strikes. For instance, Hoechst Chemical of Germany located one of its dye factories in North Carolina because the textile industry in that region feared that delivery problems would plague the cheaper German imports.

Product Change   Often a company must alter a product to suit local tastes or requirements, and this may compel the use of local raw materials and market testing. Test marketing and altering a product at a great distance from the production is most difficult and expensive. Coca-Cola, for example, sells some drinks (made from local fruits) abroad that are not available in the United States. It is definitely much cheaper to make these drinks overseas.

The need for product alteration has two other effects on company production. Initially, it means an additional investment; as long as an investment is needed to serve the foreign market anyway, management might consider locating facilities abroad. Next, it may mean that certain economies from large-scale production will be lost, which may cause the least-cost location to shift from one country to another. The more the product has to be altered for the foreign market, the more likely that the production will be shifted abroad. Two of the factors influencing the decision of Volkswagen to set up U.S. production facilities, for example, were the ever-increasing safety requirements set by the U.S. government and the desire for new options by U.S. consumers, which were different from those needed to sell in other parts of the world. But these changes were not sufficient to garner a large share of the U.S. market, and Volkswagen announced the closing of its U.S. assembly operations in 1987.[18]

Following Customers

Companies can keep customers by producing abroad when those customers produce abroad.

There are many examples of companies that sell abroad indirectly: That is, they sell products, components, or services domestically that become embodied in a product or service that their domestic customer then exports. Bridgestone, for example, sold tires to Toyota and Honda, which in turn exported fully assembled cars (including the tires) to foreign markets. In these situations the indirect exporters commonly follow their customers when those customers make direct investments. Bridgestone's decision to make automobile tires in the United States was based partially on a desire to continue selling to Honda and Toyota once those companies initiated U.S. production.

Bridgestone's truck-tire investment was in turn instrumental in Yasuda Fire & Marine Insurance Co.'s decision to establish a U.S. investment in order to provide workman's compensation insurance to Bridgestone's operations in the United States.[19]

Following Competitors

In oligopoly industries, competitors tend to make direct investments in a given country at similar times.

Within oligopoly industries (those with few sellers), several investors often establish facilities in a given country within a fairly short time period.[20] Much of this concentration may be explained by internal or external changes, which would affect most oligopolists within an industry at approximately the same time. For example, in many industries, capacity-expansion cycles are similar for most firms. Thus the firms would logically consider a foreign investment at approximately the same time because their domestic capacity would be approached at approximately the same time. Externally, they might all be faced with changes in import restrictions or market conditions that indicate a move to direct investment in order to serve consumers in a given country. In spite of the prevalence of these motivators, much of the movement by oligopolists seems better explained by defensive motives.

Much of the research done in game theory shows that people often make decisions based on the "least-damaging alternative." The question for many firms is, "Do I lose less by moving abroad or by staying at home?" Let's say that some foreign market may be served effectively only by an investment in the market, but the market is large enough to support only one producer. One way of facing this problem would be for competitors to set up one joint operation and divide profit among them; however, antitrust laws might discourage or prevent this. If only one firm decides to establish facilities, it will have an advantage over its competitors by garnering a larger market, spreading its R&D costs, and making a profit that can be reinvested in other areas of the world. Once one firm decides to produce in the market, competitors are prone to follow quickly rather than let the firm gain advantages. Thus the decision is based not so much on the benefits to be gained, but rather on the greater losses sustained by not entering the field. In most oligopoly industries (e.g., automobiles, tires, petroleum), this pattern emerges and helps to explain the large number of producers relative to the size of the market in some countries.

Closely related to this is the decision to invest in a foreign competitor's home market to prevent that competitor from using high profits obtained therein to invest and compete in other parts of the world.

Changes in Comparative Costs

The least costly production location changes because of inflation and increased wage rates.

A company may export successfully because its home country has a cost advantage. The home-country cost advantage depends on the price of the individual factors of production, the size of operations, transportation of finished goods, and the productivity of the combined production factors.

None of these conditions affecting cost is static; consequently, the least-cost location may change over time. Recall in the opening case that a factor affecting Bridgestone's decision to locate in the United States was the fact that Japanese costs (measured in dollars) grew much faster than those in the United States, owing largely to a rise in the value of the yen relative to the dollar.

The concept of shifts in comparative costs of production is closely related to that of resource-seeking investments. A firm may establish a direct investment to serve a foreign market but eventually import into the home country from the country to which it was once exporting. Some of these concepts will be discussed in the following section on resource-seeking investments.

RESOURCE-SEEKING INVESTMENTS

There is a cartoon showing Santa Claus speaking to his elves. The caption reads, "I'm sorry to report that after the first, I'll be moving operations to Taiwan."[21] This cartoon is consistent with the popular image of direct investments motivated by cheap foreign labor used to make imported products. While this does take place, the explanation overlooks some of the costs of producing abroad. For example, Lionel Trains moved from the United States to Mexico but had so many problems with training and communications that it moved back home after a few years. Furthermore, there are cost advantages from direct investment that are not fully encompassed in the popular labor-oriented image.

Vertical Integration

In vertical integration, raw materials, production, and marketing are often located in different countries.

Most vertical integration is supply-oriented.

Vertical integration involves the control of different stages as a product moves from raw materials through production to its final distribution. As products and their marketing become more complicated, there is a greater need to combine resources located in more than one country. If one country has the iron, a second has the coal, a third has the technology and capital for making steel and steel products, and a fourth has the demand for the steel products, there is a great interdependence among the four and a strong need to establish tight relationships in order to ensure the continuance of the production and marketing flow. One way of adding assurance to this flow is by gaining a voice in the management of one of the foreign operations by investing in it. Most of the world's direct investment in petroleum may be explained by this concept of interdependence. Since much of the petroleum supply is located in countries other than those with a heavy petroleum demand, the oil industry has become integrated vertically on an international basis.

Certain economies also may be gained through vertical integration too. The greater assurance of supply and/or markets may allow a firm to carry smaller inventories and spend less on promotion. It may also permit considerably greater flexibility in shifting funds, taxes, and profits from one country to another.

Advantages of vertical integration may accrue to a firm by either market-oriented or supply-oriented investments in other countries. There are examples of both: Of the two, however, there have been more examples in recent years of supply-oriented investments designed to obtain raw materials in other countries than vice versa. This is because of the growing dependence on LDCs for raw materials and the lack of resources by LDC firms to invest substantially abroad. This movement of capital and technology to LDCs is consistent with a theory that holds that factor mobility is most efficient when the more mobile factors, such as capital, move so as to be combined with the less mobile ones, such as natural resources. Without the capital movement the natural resources otherwise might not be exploited efficiently.[22]

Rationalized Production

In rationalized production, different components or portions of a product line are made in different parts of the world. The advantages are

- Factor cost differences
- Long production runs

The challenges are

- Satisfying governments that local production takes place
- Higher risk of work stoppage
- Record keeping

Companies increasingly produce different components or different portions of their product line in different parts of the world—**rationalized production**—to take advantage of the varying costs of labor, capital, and raw materials. An example of rationalized production is the more than 1800 plants in Mexico, known as *maquiladoras*, which are integrated with operations in the United States. Semifinished goods can be exported to Mexico duty free, as long as they will be reexported from Mexico. Once the labor-intensive portion of the production is accomplished in Mexico—such as sewing car seats for General Motors or building television cabinets for Panasonic—duties in the United States are charged only on the amount of value added in Mexico.[23]

Many companies shrug off the possibility of rationalized production of parts because of the risks of work stoppages in many countries because of strikes or a change in import regulations in just one country. An alternative to parts rationalization is the production of a complete product in a given country, but only part of the product range within that country.[24] A U.S. subsidiary in France, for example, may produce only product A, another subsidiary in Brazil only product B, and the home plant in the United States only product C. Each plant sells worldwide so that each can gain scale economies and take advantage of differences in input costs that may affect total production cost differences. Each may get concessions to import because of demonstrating that jobs and incomes are developed locally.

A possible different advantage of this type of rationalization is smoother earnings when exchange rates fluctuate. Take the value of the Japanese yen relative to the U.S. dollar. Honda produces some of its line in Japan, which is then exported to the United States. Honda also produces some of its line in the United States, which is then exported to Japan. If the yen strengthens, Honda may have to cut its profit margin to stay competitive with exports to the United States. But this cut may be offset with a higher profit margin on the exports to Japan.[25]

Access to Production Factors

A company may establish a presence in a country in order to improve its access to knowledge and other resources.

The concept of seeking abroad some input not easily or inexpensively available in the home country closely resembles vertical integration. Many foreign firms have offices in New York in order to gain better access to what is happening within the U.S. capital market or at least to what is happening within that market that can affect other worldwide capital occurrences. The search for knowledge may take other forms as well. It may be a U.S. pharmaceutical firm in Peru conducting research not allowed in the United States. It may be C.F.P. (French), which bought a share in Leonard Petroleum to learn U.S. marketing in order to compete better with other U.S. oil firms outside the United States. It may be McGraw-Hill, which has an office in Europe to uncover European technical developments.

The Product Life Cycle Theory

The product life cycle theory shows that

- New products are produced mainly in industrial countries
- Mature products are more likely to be produced in LDCs

In Chapter 4 we explained the **product life cycle (PLC) theory** in relation to trade and production location.[26] This theory shows how, for market and cost reasons, production of many products moves from one country to another as a product moves through its life cycle. During the introductory stage production occurs in only one (usually industrial) country. During the growth stage production moves next to other industrial countries, and the original producer may decide to invest in the foreign facilities to earn profits there. In the mature stage, when production shifts largely to developing countries, the same firm may decide to control those operations as well.

Governmental Investment Incentives

Governmental incentives may shift the least-cost location of production.

In addition to placing restrictions on imports, countries frequently encourage direct investment inflows by offering tax concessions or a wide variety of other subsidies. Such incentives are offered by many central governments. Direct-assistance incentives include tax holidays, accelerated depreciation, low-interest loans, loan guarantees, subsidized energy or transport, and the construction of rail spurs and roads to serve the plant facility.[27] These incentives affect the comparative cost of production among countries, enticing companies to invest there to serve national or international markets.

Political Motives

Governments take ownership in or give incentives to direct investors to

- Gain supplies of strategic resources
- Develop spheres of influence

Sometimes trade is undertaken to serve political motives. During the mercantilist period, for example, European powers sought colonies in order to control the colonies' foreign trade and extend their own sphere of influence. With the passing of colonialism, some have sought to accomplish many of the old colonial aims by establishing company control of vital sectors in the economies of LDCs.[28] For instance, if a U.S. firm controls the production of a vital raw material in an LDC, it can effectively prevent unfriendly countries from gaining access to the production. It may also be able to hold down prices to the home country, prevent local processing, and dictate its own operating terms. Observers have pointed out, for example, that Great Britain, France, Italy, and Japan established national oil companies with governmental participation (B.P., C.F.P., E.N.I., and J.P.D.C., respectively) in order to lessen their reliance on U.S. multinational petroleum firms, which might give preference to the United States in the allocation of supplies.[29] In the process of gaining control of resources, much political control is transferred to the industrial nations.

Governmental encouragement of MNE expansion to other developed countries may be aimed toward gaining greater control over vital resources. Japan, for example, is highly dependent on foreign sources for certain foodstuffs, lumber, and raw materials; therefore, Japanese governmental agencies have assisted national companies that undertake foreign investments in these sectors in order to protect supplies in Japan.[30]

The control of resources is not necessarily the political aim for encouraging direct investors. During the early 1980s, for example, the U.S. government instituted various incentives designed to increase the profitability of U.S. investment in Caribbean countries unfriendly to Cuba's Castro regime. The reasoning was that the incentives would lure more investment to the area, causing the economies of the friendly nations to strengthen. This would in turn make it difficult for unfriendly leftist governments to gain control.

Where there is governmental ownership and control of companies, not all of these governmental enterprises have become multinational. There are simply too many objectives for government ownership other than control over foreign economies. Even if the governmental enterprise has foreign facilities, it does not necessarily mean that political motives just described prompted the investment.[31] The firm may simply be acting in terms of any of the rational economic motives discussed earlier in the chapter.

MULTIPLE MOTIVES

A combination of factors, rather than one, usually explains a direct investment.

Although previous discussions within this chapter have categorized investments by separate motives, in reality most decisions to invest abroad, such as the Bridgestone case at the beginning of the chapter, are based on multiple motives. Another such combination of influences may be illustrated by Brazilian automobile investments.

As the automobile became a mature product, there were many opportunities for saving labor costs by moving operations to a country with cheap labor, such as Brazil. One problem, however, is that economies of large-scale operations are needed to reduce the total cost of the vehicles. As long as car imports were permitted by Brazil, the U.S. and European producers could serve the Brazilian market more cheaply by exporting than by manufacturing a low volume in Brazil for that market. To move *all* operations to Brazil would be too costly and would so disrupt domestic operations that the imposition of some type of home-government sanctions would become inevitable. However, in the next stage, the Brazilian government required local production as a requisite for serving the Brazilian consumer. Consequently, Ford, GM, Chrysler, Volkswagen, Daimler Benz, Saab-Scandia, Alfa Romeo, and Fiat established production facilities. The car companies built plants because the Brazilian market was deemed too important to lose and too important to let competitors have to themselves. Output became high, and Brazil is now a major exporter, even sending components back to home countries.[32]

Political motives for investment are seldom isolated from economic motives. To encourage companies to invest abroad, governments must consider the objectives of the potential investors. During the early 1980s, for example, U.S. policymakers reasoned that many U.S. firms might find it advantageous to tap cheap labor sources in the Caribbean, thereby strengthening the economies of countries unfriendly to Castro's Cuba. Consequently, various incentives were enacted to improve the profitability of U.S. investors in the Caribbean, such as allowing certain Caribbean output to enter the United States virtually free of restrictions. Investors, acting purely on economic motives, helped to achieve governmental objectives.

BUY-VERSUS-BUILD DECISION

There are advantages and disadvantages to the alternatives of acquiring an interest in an existing operation or constructing new facilities. The MNE must consider the alternatives carefully.

Reasons for Buying

The advantages of acquiring include
- Avoidance of start-up problems
- An easier financial situation
- Not adding capacity in market

A major motive for seeking acquisitions is the difficulty of transferring some resource to a foreign operation or acquiring that resource locally for a new facility. One particularly difficult resource is personnel, especially if the local labor market is tight. Instead of paying higher compensation rates than competitors to entice employees away from their old jobs, the buy-in approach gains not only labor and management but also a whole organizational structure through which these personnel may interact. Acquisitions also may be a means of gaining the goodwill and brand identification important for mass consumer products, especially if the cost and risk of breaking in a new brand are high. If a company must depend substantially on local financing rather than on the transfer of capital, it may be easier to gain access to local capital through an acquisition. For one thing, local capital suppliers may be more familiar with an ongoing operation than with the foreign enterprise. Second, an existing company may sometimes be acquired through an exchange of stock, thus circumventing home-country exchange controls.

In other ways acquisitions may reduce costs and risks as well as provide quicker results. A firm may be able to buy facilities, particularly those of a bankrupt operation, for less than it would cost to build plants at current construction costs. If an investor fears that a market does not justify added capacity, such as in the Bridgestone situation, acquisition avoids the risk of depressed prices and lower unit sales per producer that might result from new facilities. Finally, by buying a company an investor avoids the high expenses caused by inefficiencies during the start-up period and gets an immediate cash flow rather than tying up funds for the period of construction.[33]

Reasons for Building

Firms may choose to build if
- No desired firm is available for acquisition
- Acquisition will carry over problems
- Acquisition is harder to finance

While the advantages just mentioned are possible through acquisitions, a potential investor will not necessarily be able to gain them. Since foreign investments frequently are made where there is little or no competition, it may be difficult to find a company to buy. In addition, local governmental restrictions may prevent the purchase of firms for fear of lessening competition or dominance by foreign enterprises. Those firms that can be acquired may create substantial problems for the investor: personnel and labor relations may be both poor and difficult to change, ill will rather than goodwill may have accrued to existing brands, or facilities may be inefficient and poorly located in relationship to future potential markets. Finally, local financing may be easier rather than harder to obtain if a firm builds facilities, particularly if the investor plans to tap development banks for part of its financial requirements.

ADVANTAGES OF DIRECT INVESTORS

Most successful domestic firms, especially those with unique advantages, invest abroad.

Direct investment makes firms more successful domestically.

Are companies big because they are multinational or are they multinational because they are big? Such a "chicken-and-egg" type question has hounded direct investment theorists: On one hand, there is evidence that very successful domestic firms are most likely to commit resources to direct investments; on the other hand, ownership of foreign direct investment appears to make firms more successful domestically.[34]

Monopoly Advantages Prior to Direct Investment

One explanation for direct investment is that investors perceive a monopoly advantage over similar companies in the countries to which they go. The advantage is due to the ownership of some resource that is unavailable at the same price or terms to the local firm. The resource may be in the form of access to markets, patents, product differentiation, management skills, or the like. Because of the greater cost usually incurred by transferring resources abroad and the perceived greater risk of operating in a different environment, the firm will not move unless it expects a higher return than at home and a higher return than the local firm abroad.[35]

Certain monopoly advantages may accrue to large groups of firms and explain their relative ability and willingness to move abroad. One such observation has been made in reference to the cost and access to capital. When the capital component is an integral part of a new investment, the company that can borrow in a country with a low interest rate has an advantage over the company that cannot. Prior to World War I, Great Britain was the largest source for direct investment because of the strength of sterling and the resulting lower interest rates on borrowing sterling funds. From World War II until the mid-1980s, the strength of the U.S. dollar gave an advantage to U.S. firms. More recently, this advantage has shifted to Japanese firms.[36]

Related to this is the relative power of different currencies in terms of the plant and equipment they will purchase. During the two and a half decades immediately following World War II, the U.S. dollar was very strong, and it was perhaps overvalued in later years. As a result, by converting dollars to other currencies, U.S. firms could purchase a greater output capacity in foreign countries than they could after the dollar began to slide downward in 1971. The reverse was true for firms from such countries as Japan and the former West Germany, which invested more heavily in the United States during the late 1970s and mid-1980s when the yen and mark increased their purchasing power.

Currency values do not, however, provide a strong explanation of direct investment patterns. There was a two-way investment flow between the United States and the former West Germany and the United States and Japan when the dollar was weak as well as when the dollar was strong. Then, in the first half of the 1980s, U.S. companies were not increasing investment abroad significantly, whereas foreign companies were investing heavily in the United States in spite of the strong dollar. The major reasons were high real interest rates in the United States and a relatively strong U.S. economy. In the late 1980s, when the dollar was weak again, there were record flows of direct investment both to and from the United States.[37] The currency-strength situation therefore only partially explains direct investment flows and must be viewed along with other multiple motives for direct investment.

Advantages after Direct Investment

Firms with foreign investments
- Tend to be more profitable
- Tend to have more stable sales and earnings

In order to support large-scale expenditures (such as expenditures for R&D) that are necessary to maintain a domestic competitive viability, companies frequently must sell on a global basis. To do this, they often must establish direct investments abroad. The advantage accruing to more internationally oriented firms by spreading out some of the costs of product differentiation, R&D, and advertising is apparent in a comparison of their profitability with that of other firms. Among industry groups and groups of similar size that spent comparable amounts on advertising and R&D and had similar capital intensity, the more internationally oriented firms in almost every case earned more than the other firms.[38]

Economies in different countries are in different stages of the business cycle at different times. Companies that operate in these different economies are known to be able to reduce fluctuations in year-to-year sales and earnings more than firms operating only in a domestic environment,[39] thereby effectively reducing their operating risks.

LOOKING TO THE FUTURE   In the near future, as in the recent past, direct investment should continue to grow more rapidly than trade or gross national products. The reasons for this growth should remain the same as those described in the chapter, but resource-seeking investments might grow more rapidly than market-seeking investments. The reasons are that trade restrictions on products continue to be reduced, thus making the use of least-cost production facilities more practical, and companies have more experience in manufacturing abroad and thus perceive less risk in integrating global production.

FDI in services may also grow in relative importance because of the difficulty of removing protectionist barriers on service trade, because service providers (such as investment bankers, advertising agencies, and insurance firms) need to react quickly to the overseas needs of their clients, and because service firms need to provide a full geographic range of activities to clients who are global.

The triad areas of Western Europe, North America, and Japan should continue to be the major sources and recipients of direct investment because of the wealth of the companies based there and the outlook for economic growth within these regions. The special trading relations being developed between Canada and the United States and among the members of the European Community should further stimulate this growth. The former Eastern bloc of nations should get much more attention now that regulatory changes permit some foreign ownership for the first time in the post–World War II era and as potential investors become more optimistic about risk and opportunities there. Among LDCs, regulatory changes should also be a factor. Such countries as Argentina, Brazil, and Mexico are privatizing many state companies and are allowing levels of foreign investment that have until very recently been prohibited. These moves should stimulate their receipt of FDI as well.

SUMMARY

■ Direct investment is the control of a company in one country by an organization based in another country. Because control is difficult to define, arbitrary minimum ownership of the voting stock is used to define direct investment.

■ Governments are concerned about who controls enterprises within their confines for fear that decisions will be made contrary to the national interest.

■ Firms often prefer to control foreign production facilities because (1) the transfer of certain assets to a noncontrolled entity might undermine their competitive position, and (2) there are economies of buying and selling with a controlled entity.

■ Although a direct investment usually is acquired by transferring capital from one country to another, capital is not usually the only contribution made by the investor or the only means of gaining equity. The investing firm may supply technology, personnel, and markets in exchange for an interest in a firm located abroad.

■ The factors of production and finished goods are only partially mobile internationally. Moving either of them is one means of compensating for differences in factor endowments among countries. The cost and feasibility of transferring production factors internationally rather than finished goods will determine which alternative results in cheaper costs.

■ Although a direct investment may be a substitute for trade, it also may stimulate trade through sales of components, equipment, and complementary products. Foreign direct investment may be undertaken to expand foreign markets or to gain access to supplies of resources or finished products. In addition, governments may encourage direct investments for political purposes.

■ The price of some products increases too substantially if they are transported internationally; therefore, foreign production is necessary to tap foreign markets.

■ Companies usually try to delay establishing foreign production as long as they have excess domestic capacity.

■ The degree to which scale economies lower production costs influences whether production is centralized in one or a few countries or dispersed among many countries.

■ Since most direct investments are intended for selling the output in the country where the investments are located, governmental restrictions that prevent the effective importation of goods are probably the most compelling force causing firms to establish their direct investments.

■ Consumers may feel compelled to buy domestically made products even though these products are more expensive. They also may demand that products be altered to fit their needs. Both of these considerations may dictate the need to establish foreign operations to serve foreign markets.

■ Direct investment sometimes has chain effects: When one company makes an investment, some of its suppliers follow with investments of their own, followed by investments by their suppliers, and so on.

■ In oligopoly industries, companies from the same industry often invest in a foreign country at about the same time. This occurs sometimes because they are responding to similar market conditions and sometimes because they wish to negate competitors' advantages in the markets.

■ Vertical integration is needed to control the flow of goods across borders from basic production to final consumption in an increasingly interdependent and complex world distribution system. It may result in lower operating costs and enable firms to transfer funds among countries.

■ Rationalized production involves the production of different components or different products in different countries to take advantage of different factor costs.

■ The least-cost location of production may change over time, especially in relation to stages of the life cycle of a product. It also may change because of governmental incentives that effectively subsidize production.

■ Governments may encourage their firms to invest abroad in order to gain advantages over other countries.

■ Most investments are made because of interrelated multiple motives.

■ There are possible advantages and disadvantages to the alternatives of direct investment by buy-in as opposed to start-up operations.

■ Monopolistic advantages help to explain why firms are willing to take what they perceive to be higher risks of operating abroad. Certain countries and currencies have had such advantages, which helps to explain the dominance of firms from certain countries at a given time.

■ Foreign investment may enable firms to spread certain fixed costs vis-à-vis domestic firms. It also may enable firms to gain access to needed resources, to prevent competitors from gaining control of needed resources, and to smooth sales and earnings on a year-to-year basis.

C A S E
ELECTROLUX
ACQUISITIONS[40]

Electrolux, the world's largest manufacturer of electrical household appliances, once pioneered the marketing of vacuum cleaners. However, not all products bearing the Electrolux name have always been controlled by the Swedish firm. For example, Electrolux vacuum cleaners were independently sold and manufactured in the United States from the 1960s until 1987. The Swedish firm also manufactures Eureka vacuum cleaners.

Electrolux pursued its early international expansion largely to gain economies of scale through additional sales. The Swedish market was too small to absorb fixed costs as much as the home markets for competitive firms from larger countries. When additional sales were not possible by exporting, Electrolux still was able to gain certain scale economies through the establishment of foreign production. Research and development expenditures and certain administrative costs thus could be spread out over the additional sales made possible by foreign operations. Additionally, Electrolux concentrated on standardized production to achieve further scale economies and rationalization of parts.

Until the late 1960s, Electrolux concentrated primarily on vacuum cleaners and building its own facilities in order to effect expansion. Throughout the 1970s, though, the firm expanded largely by acquiring existing firms whose product lines differed from those of Electrolux. The compelling goal was to add appliance lines to complement those developed internally. Its profits have enabled Electrolux to go on an acquisitions binge. Electrolux acquired two Swedish firms that made home appliances and washing machines. Electrolux management felt that it could use its existing foreign-sales networks to increase the sales of those firms. In 1973 Electrolux acquired another Swedish firm, Facit, which already had extensive foreign sales and facilities. Electrolux acquired vacuum-cleaner producers in the United States and in France; to gain captive sales for vacuum cleaners, the company bought commercial-cleaning service firms in Sweden and the United States. Electrolux also bought a French kitchen-equipment producer, Arthur Martin, along with a Swiss home-appliance firm, Therma, and a U.S. cooking-equipment manufacturer, Tappan.

Except for the Facit purchase, these acquisitions all involved firms with complementary lines that would enable the new parent to gain certain scale economies. However, not all of the acquired firms' products were related, and Electrolux sought to sell off unrelated businesses. In 1978, for example, Electrolux bought a diverse Swedish firm, Husqvarna, because of its kitchen-equipment lines. Electrolux was able to sell Husqvarna's motorcycle line but could not get a good price for the chain-saw facility. Reconciled to being in the chain-saw business, Electrolux then acquired chain-saw manufacturers in Canada and Norway, thus becoming one of the world's largest chain-saw producers. The firm made approximately 50 acquisitions during the 1970s.

In 1980 Electrolux announced a takeover distinguished from those of the 1970s. It offered $175 million, the biggest Electrolux acquisition to date, for Granges, Sweden's leading metal producer and fabricator. Granges was itself a multinational firm (1979 sales of $1.2 billion) with about 50 percent of its sales outside of Sweden. The managing directors of the two firms indicated that the major advantage of the takeover would be the integration of Granges' aluminum, copper, plastics, and other materials into Electrolux's appliance production. Many analysts felt that the timing of Electrolux's bid was based on indications that Beijerinvest, a large Swedish conglomerate, wished to acquire a nonferrous-metals mining company. Other observers thought that Electrolux would have been better off to continue international horizontal expansion, as it had in the 1970s.

Since the Granges takeover, Electrolux has resumed its acquisition of appliance firms. It bought Italy's Zanussi to become Europe's top appliance maker with 23 percent of that market. In 1986 it acquired White Consolidated Industries, the U.S. manufacturer of such appliance brands as Frigidaire, White-Westinghouse, Kelvinator, and Gibson. This made Electrolux the largest appliance maker in the world; however, this lead was short-lived, as Whirlpool acquired a controlling interest in the appliance business of Philips, a Dutch giant.

Meanwhile, other producers were growing through consolidation as well. Maytag, for example, acquired such brands as Magic Chef, Admiral, and Norge and then combined European operations with Hoover. The Electrolux president, Anders Scharp, said that industry consolidation would not allow for much more growth through acquisition of household-appliance firms. Further Electrolux acquisitions would concentrate on outdoor products and commercial appliances. One wonders whether Electrolux can continue making so many acquisitions because its sales have been increasing much more rapidly than its profits. The company has had a penchant for buying poor-performing firms cheaply and then spending heavily to turn them around.

Electrolux and its competitors were becoming global appliance producers even though this traditionally has been an industry in which companies have sold little outside their home countries. The varying sizes of kitchens from one country to another complicated international standardization of models, but Electrolux was betting that life-styles in the industrialized nations would be increasingly similar. If they were right, the company could take advantage of economies of scale in technical breakthroughs and designs. In 1990 Electrolux admitted its difficulty in streamlining operations. Within Europe alone it had 40 different brands of refrigerators selling 120 basic designs with 1500 variants, and the company was adding models to hit specialty niches. Meanwhile, Whirlpool has been adding its name (Philips/Whirlpool) to appliances sold in Europe through its acquired operations there. The plan is to drop the Philips brand name once European consumers accept the Whirlpool name.

Questions

1. How do Electrolux's reasons for direct investment differ from those of Bridgestone at the beginning of the chapter?
2. How has Electrolux's strategy changed over time? How have these changes affected its direct investment activities?
3. What are the main advantages and possible problems to a company of expanding internationally primarily through acquisitions as opposed to building its own facilities?
4. Should Electrolux have taken over Granges?
5. What will be the future global competitive situation in household appliances and how does that fit with the Electrolux strategy?

Chapter Notes

1. Data for the case were taken from Edward Noga, "Bridgestone," *Automotive News*, April 20, 1981, p. E10; Edward Noga, "Bridgestone Tries U.S. Market," *Advertising Age*, April 6, 1981, p. 85; David Pauly, "Bridgestone Tire: Made in Japan," *Newsweek*, August 11, 1980, pp. 62–64; Mike Tharp, "Bridgestone, Japan's Tire Giant, Now Seeking International Role," *New York Times*, November 21, 1980, p. D4; "Japan: Why a Tiremaker Wants a U.S. Base," *Business Week*, January 14, 1980, p. 40; Bernard Krisher, "A Different Kind of Tiremaker Rolls into Nashville," *Fortune*, Vol. 105, No. 6, March 22, 1982, pp. 136–145; Zachary Schiller and James B. Treece, "Bridgestone May Try an End Run around the Yen," *Business Week*, No. 2983, February 2, 1987, p. 31; Roger Schreffler, "Bridgestone's New Rolling Thunderbolt, *Automotive Industries*, Vol. 165, No. 12, December 1985, p. 55; Jonathan P. Hicks, "A Global Fight in the Tire Industry," *New York Times*, March 10, 1988, p. 29; Jonathan P. Hicks, "Decreasing Demand and Global Competition Propel Consolidation," *New York Times*, February 11, 1990, p. F8; Zachary Schiller and Roger Schreffler, "So Far, America Is a Blowout for Bridgestone," *Business Week*, August 6, 1990, pp. 82–83; Gregory Stricharchuk, "Bridgestone Corp. Combines Operations in North America into Single Company," *Wall Street Journal*, August 2, 1989, p. A4; and Zachary Schiller and Roger Schreffler, "Why Tiremakers Are Still Spinning Their Wheels," *Business Week*, February 26, 1990, pp. 62–63.

2. Some surveys of the considerable number of explanations may be found in Jean J. Boddewyn, "Foreign and Domestic Divestment and Investment Decisions," *Journal of International Business Studies*, Vol. XIV, No. 3, Winter 1983, pp. 23–35; A. L. Calvet, "A Synthesis of Foreign Direct Investment Theories and Theories of the Multinational Firm," *Journal of International Business Studies*, Spring–Summer 1981, pp. 43–60; John H. Dunning, "Toward an Eclectic Theory of International Production," *Journal of International Business Studies*, Spring–Summer 1980, pp. 9–31; Robert Grosse, "The Theory of Foreign Direct Investment," *Essays in International Business*, No. 3, December 1981, pp. 1–51; M. Z. Rahman, "Maximisation of Global Interests:

Ultimate Motivation for Foreign Investments by Transnational Corporations," *Management International Review,* Vol. 23, No. 4, 1983, pp. 4–13; Alan M. Rugman, "New Theories of the Multinational Enterprise: An Assessment of Internalization Theory," *Bulletin of Economic Research,* Vol. 38, No. 2, 1986, pp. 101–118; and T. A. Corley, "Progress in Multinational Studies at Reading and Elsewhere, 1981–86" (Reading, England: University of Reading Department of Economics, Discussion Papers in International Investment and Business Studies, No. 120, 1989).

3. For a discussion on the effect of growth change on growth alternatives, see Briance Mascarenhas, "Strategic Group Dynamics," *Academy of Management Journal,* Vol. 32, No. 2, June 1989, pp. 333–352.

4. Krisher, *op. cit.,* p. 141; Schreffler, *loc. cit.*

5. This desire to hold a monopoly control over certain information or other proprietary assets has been noted by such writers as M. Casson, "The Theory of Foreign Direct Investment," Discussion Paper Number 50 (Reading, England: University of Reading International Investment and Business Studies, November 1980); Stephen Magee, "Information and the MNC: An Appropriability Theory of Direct Foreign Investment," in *The New International Economic Order,* Jagdish N. Bhagwati, ed. (Cambridge, Mass.: M.I.T. Press, 1977), pp. 317–340.

6. Alan M. Rugman, *Inside the Multinationals: The Economics of Internal Markets* (New York: Columbia University Press, 1981); David J. Teece, "Transactions Cost Economics and the Multinational Enterprise," *Berkeley Business School International Business Working Paper Series,* No. IB-3, 1985.

7. "Plessey Co. Acquires Airborne Accessories for $8.9 Million Notes," *Wall Street Journal,* February 21,1968, p. 6.

8. Masaaki Kotabe, "Assessing the Shift in Global Market Share of U.S. Multinationals," *International Marketing Review,* Vol. 6, No. 5, 1989, pp. 20–35.

9. Stephen Baker, "A Free-for-All for Carmakers South of the Border," *Business Week,* October 16, 1989, p. 32.

10. Masaaki Kotabe and Glenn Omura, "Sourcing Strategies of European and Japanese Multinationals: A Comparison," *Journal of International Business Studies,* Spring 1989, pp.113–133.

11. Yves Doz, "Managing Manufacturing Rationalization within Multinational Companies," *Columbia Journal of World Business,* Fall 1978.

12. Clyde Haberman, "Made in Japan: U.S. Cookie," *New York Times,* February 17, 1984, p. B6.

13. Lawrence Rout, "Mexico Limits U.S. Makers of Computers," *Wall Street Journal,* February 1, 1982, p. 31.

14. Studies that found import barriers to be an important enticement include Sanjaya Lall and N. S. Siddharthan, "The Monopolistic Advantages of Multinationals: Lessons from Foreign Investment in the U.S." *The Economic Journal,* Vol. 92, No. 367, September 1982, pp. 668–683; T. Horst, "Firm and Industry Determinants of the Decision to Invest Abroad," *Review of Economics and Statistics,* August 1972, pp. 258–266; John H. Dunning, *American Investment in British Manufacturing Industry* (London: Allen and Unwin, 1958); and D. Orr, "The Determinants of Entry: A Study of the Canadian Manufacturing Industries," *Review of Economics and Statistics,* Vol. 57, 1975, pp. 58–66. Those not finding import barriers to be important include R. E. Caves, M. E. Porter, A. M. Spence, and J. T. Scott, *Competition in the Open Economy: A Model Applied to Canada* (Cambridge, Mass.: Harvard University Press, 1980); and B. Balassa, "Effects of Commercial Policy on International Trade, the Location of Production and Factor

Movements," in *The International Allocation of Economic Activity,* Bertil Ohlin, ed. (New York: Holmes & Meier, 1977).

15. Kenneth Dreyfack, "Draping Old Glory around Just about Everything," *Business Week,* No. 2970, October 27, 1986, pp. 66–67.

16. "Toshiba Plans to Build Color-TV Plant in U.S.," *Wall Street Journal,* April 5, 1977, p. 43, and "Mitsubishi U.S. Unit to Assemble TV Sets in Irvine, California, Plant," *Wall Street Journal,* April 14, 1977, p. 7, shows two examples of responses to nationalistic advertisements by Zenith.

17. Philippe Cattin, Alain Jolibert, and Coleen Lohnes, "A Cross-Cultural Study of 'Made in' Concepts," *Journal of International Business Studies,* Vol. XIII, No. 3, Winter 1982, pp. 131–141; Robert D. Schooler, "Bias Phenomena Attendant to the Marketing of Foreign Goods in the U.S.," *Journal of International Business Studies,* Spring 1971, pp. 71–80; A. Nagashima, "A Comparison of Japanese and U.S. Attitudes toward Foreign Products," *Journal of Marketing,* January 1970, pp. 68–74.

18. "Why VW Must Build Autos in the U.S.," *Business Week,* February 16, 1976, p. 46; and John Templeman, "What Ended VW's American Dream," *Business Week,* October 7, 1987, p. 63.

19. Steven P. Galante, "Japanese Have Another Trade Barrier: Limiting Business to Compatriot Firms," *Wall Street Journal,* April 12, 1984, p. 36.

20. Edward B. Flowers, "Oligopolistic Reactions in European and Canadian Direct Investment in the United States," *Journal of International Business Studies,* Fall–Winter 1976, pp. 43–55; Frederick Knickerbocker, *Oligopolistic Reaction and Multinational Enterprise* (Cambridge, Mass.: Harvard University, Graduate School of Business, Division of Research, 1973). For opposing findings, see Lall and Siddharthan, *loc. cit.*

21. "Salt and Pepper," *Wall Street Journal,* December 15, 1983, p. 31.

22. K. Kojima, *Direct Foreign Investment: A Japanese Model of Multinational Business Operations* (London: Croom Helm, 1978).

23. Brian O'Reilly, "Business Makes a Run for the Border," *Fortune,* Vol. 114, No. 4, August 18, 1986, pp. 70–76; Dudley Althaus, "Manufacturing in Mexico," *Dallas Times Herald,* September 21–27, 1987, p. 1 + ; and Stephen Baker, David Woodruff, and Bill Javetski, "Along the Border, Free Trade Is Becoming a Fact of Life," *Business Week,* June 18, 1990, pp. 41–42.

24. Doz, *loc. cit.*

25. Sarkis Khoury, David Nickerson, and Venkatraman Sadanad, "Exchange Rate Uncertainty and Precommitment in Symmetric Duopoly: A New Theory of Multinational Production," *Recent Developments in International Banking and Finance,* Vols. IV, V, 1991.

26. Raymond Vernon, "International Investment and International Trade in the Product Cycle," *Quarterly Journal of Economics,* May 1966, pp. 191–207.

27. Robert Weigand, "International Investments: Weighing the Incentives," *Harvard Business Review,* Vol. 61, No. 4, July–August 1983, pp. 146–152.

28. Among the many treatises on this subject is Carlos F. Diaz Alejandro, "International Markets for Exhaustible Resources, Less Developed Countries and Transnational Corporations," in *Economic Issues of Multinational Firms,* Robert G. Hawkins, ed. (New York: JAI Press, 1977).

29. M. Y. Yoshino, *Japan's Multinational Enterprises* (Cambridge, Mass.: Harvard University Press, 1976), pp. 53–57.

30. Terutomio Ozawa, "Japan's Resource Dependency and Overseas Investment," *Journal of World Trade Law,* January–February 1977, pp. 52–73.

31. For a good discussion of differences in European government-owned enterprises, see Renato Mazzolini, *Government Controlled Enterprises* (New York: Wiley, 1979).

32. Lewis H. Diugid, "Brazil to Supply Pinto Power," *Washington Post*, October 1, 1972, p. H7; "The Brazilian Motor Vehicle Industry," *Notes on International Business Research*, No. 10 (Cambridge, Mass.: M.I.T. Press, August 1975).

33. Joann S. Lublin, "Japanese Increasingly View Takeovers as Faster, Cheaper Way to Enter Europe," *Wall Street Journal*, July 21, 1989, p. A12.

34. Mascarenhas, *loc. cit.*; Yui Kimura, "Firm-Specific Strategic Advantages and Foreign Direct Investment Behavior of Firms: The Case of Japanese Semiconductor Firms" (Niigata, Japan: International Management Research Institute, International University of Japan, 1988).

35. Stephen H. Hymer, *A Study of Direct Foreign Investment* (Cambridge, Mass.: M.I.T. Press, 1976); and Alan M. Rugman, "Internationalization as a General Theory of Foreign Direct Investment: A Re-Appraisal of the Literature," *Weltwirtschaftliches Archiv*, Band 116, Heft 2, 1980, pp. 365–379.

36. Robert Z. Aliber, "A Theory of Direct Foreign Investment," in *The International Corporation*, Charles P. Kindleberger, ed. (Cambridge, Mass.: M.I.T. Press, 1970), pp. 28–33; Robert Johnson, "Distance Deals," *Wall Street Journal*, February 24, 1988, p. 1.

37. Louis Uchitelle, "Overseas Spending by U.S. Companies Sets Record Pace," *New York Times*, May 20, 1988, p. 1+; and "Investing Abroad Is Paying Off Big for U.S. Companies," *Business Week*, November 6, 1989, p. 34.

38. John D. Daniels and Jeffrey Bracker, "Profit Performance: Do Foreign Operations Make a Difference?" *Management International Review*, Vol. 29, No. 1, 1989, pp. 46–56.

39. Joseph C. Miller and Bernard Pras, "The Effects of Multinational and Export Diversification on the Profit Stability of U.S. Corporations," *Southern Economic Journal*, Vol. 46, No. 3, 1980, pp. 792–802; Alan M. Rugman, "Foreign Operations and the Stability of U.S. Corporate Earnings: Risk Reduction by International Diversification" (Vancouver, Simon Fraser University, 1974); A. Servern, "Investor Evaluation of Foreign and Domestic Risk," *Journal of Finance*, May 1974, pp. 545–550.

40. Background data on Electrolux may be found in "Why Electrolux Wants a Materials Supplier," *Business Week*, February 18, 1980, pp. 78–79; "Company Briefs," *Wall Street Journal*, October 19, 1979, p. 5; Alan L. Otten, "Electrolux, a Big Success in Appliances, Is Helped by Decentralized Operations," *Wall Street Journal*, June 4, 1980, p. 16; "Electrolux to Proceed with Granges Offer, Providing Sweden Acts," *Wall Street Journal*, June 18, 1980, p. 29; "Electrolux Suspends Its Purchases of Stock in TI Group of Britain," *Wall Street Journal*, February 21, 1984, p. 38; Sharon Tully, "Electrolux Wants a Clean Sweep," *Fortune*, Vol. 114, No. 4, August 18, 1986, pp. 60–62; and "On a Verge of a World War in White Goods," *Business Week*, November 2, 1987, pp. 91–94; "Electrolux Shifts the Focus of Its Acquisition Program," *Wall Street Journal*, March 22, 1988, p. 27; James P. Miller, "Whirlpool Plans Brand Recognition Effort in Europe," *Wall Street Journal*, January 1, 1990, p. A12; "Have Europe's Top Acquirers Added Shareholder Value?" *Mergers & Acquisitions*, March–April 1989, pp. 60–68; and William Echikson, "Electrolux, in Bid for European Unity, Seeks Common Refrigerator for Continent," *Wall Street Journal*, August 21, 1990, p. C13.

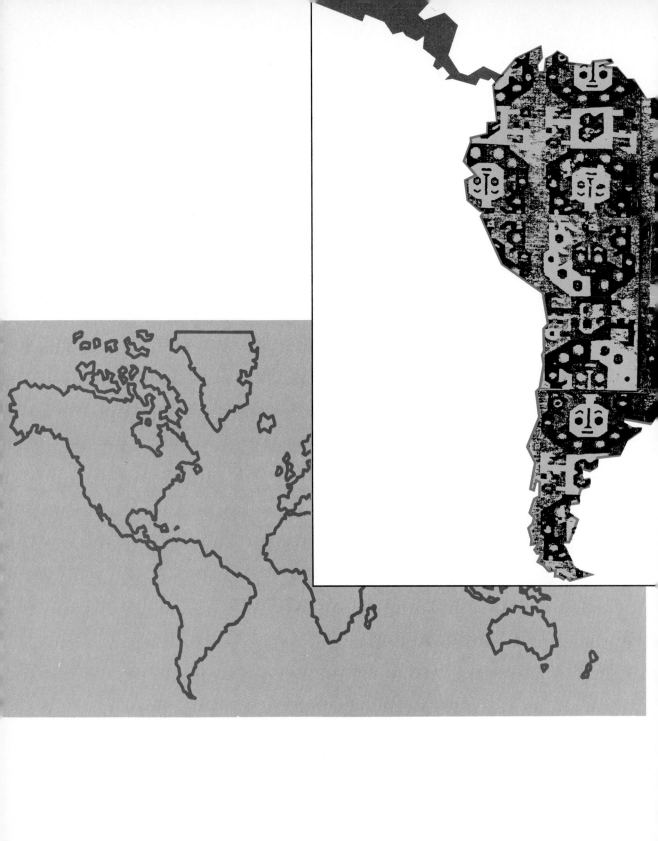

P A R T **4**

WORLD
FINANCIAL
ENVIRONMENT

A company that operates internationally must work within the framework of diverse financial systems and still measure and report its worldwide performance in terms of some common frame of reference. Because different nations have distinct currencies, transactions among countries must be conducted in more than one currency.

Chapter 7 considers why foreign exchange transactions take place, defines the terms used in international currency transactions, and explains how the foreign exchange markets work. The chapter also discusses convertibility and the mechanisms countries use to restrict foreign exchange transactions.

Chapter 8 explains how different currencies' values are determined. The emphasis is on the exchange rate arrangements that exist within the international monetary system, the theories that explain the determination of exchange rates, the methods used to forecast exchange rate movements, and the effects that values and movements have on business operations.

A company operating internationally faces a more diverse group of financial institutions than is found domestically. These institutions and their scopes and limitations are described in Chapter 9. There is a particular emphasis on the interrelatedness of institutions globally and on the high debt of many developing countries.

CHAPTER **7**

FOREIGN EXCHANGE

All things are obedient to money.
ENGLISH PROVERB

Objectives

- To discuss the terms and definitions of foreign exchange.

- To describe how the foreign-exchange market works for immediate and long-term transactions.

- To explain the role of convertibility in transactions.

- To illustrate how countries control limited supplies of foreign exchange through licensing, multiple rates, import deposit requirements, and quantity controls.

- To describe how the foreign-exchange market is used in commercial and financial transactions.

$\mathbf{I}$ was traumatized by exchange rates long ago. It was in 1936, to be exact, when I had a course in international finance with the redoubtable Prof. Jacob Viner. I could never understand why the exchange rate on the British pound was $4.88, whereas the rate on the French franc was 20 to the dollar. If the pound was $4.88, why wasn't the franc $0.05? Or if the franc was 20 to the dollar, why wasn't the pound 0.205 to the dollar? I just didn't know which country was up. So I gave up thinking about the subject for a long, long time.

When I can't avoid the subject it still baffles me. For example, I do some work on the Israeli economy. Now, when Americans say that the exchange rate went up they mean that the dollar rose relative to other currencies. But when the Israelis say that the exchange rate went up they mean that other currencies rose relative to the shekel. Baffling! Maybe it's because they read from right to left.

My allergy to exchange rates really hurts when I have to meet a foreign currency hand to hand, as was seen on a recent trip to Israel and France.

From Shekels to Francs   Leaving Israel to fly to Paris (see Map 7.1) I had a handful of leftover shekels. I decided to exchange them for francs. Going from the exotic shekel to the romantic franc without passing through the humdrum dollar made me feel like a sophisticated jet-setter.

I received 279 francs, which somehow seemed enough for taxi fare from Charles de Gaulle Airport to my Paris hotel. I also got a printout saying that the rate was 0.39. Since I thought that the shekel was worth about 50 cents and the franc about 20, it seemed reasonable enough that a figure like 0.39 should appear somewhere, although I wouldn't have bet on doing the algebra right the first time.

C A S E
FOREIGN TRAVELS,
FOREIGN-EXCHANGE
TRAVAILS*

Five hours later I am speeding along in a French taxi and the taximeter is clicking off two francs at an even more furious pace, alongside a sign saying "No checks accepted." I worry about whether my 279 francs are going to survive this race, at the same time trying to remember whether I should multiply the francs by 0.2 or by five to get them into my native currency.

To my relief, the taxi and the meter slow down as we enter the XVI Arrondissement, and the meter says only 132 when we stop in front of the hotel. "One hundred and sixty," says the driver. (All this is a blur in my mind now, and I'm not sure what language we were using. I suppose English.) "Why?" I ask. "Luggage," he explains. I am so annoyed and angry about this, as well as by his general manner, that I determine to give him no tip. I had barely reached the sidewalk, however, when I realized that I had only 19 francs left. I had

*Herbert Stein, "Foreign Travels, Foreign-Exchange Travails," *The Wall Street Journal*, 27 August 1990, p. A10.

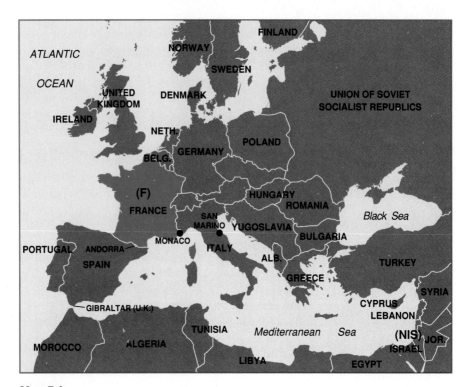

Map 7.1
France and Israel
The French franc (F) and the Israeli shekel (NIS)—the source of the foreign-exchange travails from the perspective of a traveler used to the U.S. dollar.

given the driver 260. But he assured me that I was mistaken. He showed me that in one pocket he had a lot of money, which was his, and in the other pocket he had a little, which was what had been mine. Before we could pursue the subject he drove off.

The receptionist in the hotel was philosophical. She explained that the event was not uncommon and there was nothing I could do about it.

So there my wife and I were on a Sunday afternoon, Ascension Day, in a small hotel, sans restaurant, in a quiet part of Paris, having had no dinner and with about $2 in francs, after tipping the bellman. I asked the receptionist, who for some reason reminded me of *A Tale of Two Cities,* whether she could cash a traveler's check. She could, and the rate was 4.9. She saw my surprise and explained that the rate had gone down (this was three days after the invasion of Kuwait) but maybe it would go up next week. She was still philosophical. "It's only a few centimes," she said. Later in a calmer mood I figured out that 4.9 is 2 percent less than five.

All the money amounts are trivial. This story is not about amounts; it is about confusion, mental anguish, humiliation. It is about states of mind, which is, after all, what economics is all about.

Armed with $50 worth of francs we set out to find a light supper. Fortunately, French restaurants, brasseries, and bistros all have menus posted outside, so you can review your options before committing yourself. Even with $50 my options were not great. But the second time around the Place I realized the solution to my problem was the brasserie whose menu welcomed credit cards. There I would not have to worry about running out of francs and someone else would have to figure out how much my bill was in dollars. (When I did get my credit-card bill at home my franc expenditures had been translated into dollars at a rate more favorable to me than any I encountered in Paris.)

The next morning we went to the bank to change money. There was the usual bulletin board with exchange rates in two columns—*Vente* and *Achat.* Which was I, buying or selling? I was selling dollars and buying francs. The bank was selling francs and buying dollars. I knew that whichever it was, I was going to get the smaller amount. And even the smaller amount was 5.2 with some more decimals, much more than *La Tricoteuse* at the hotel had paid. In fact, the rate was 5.27719 francs to the dollar. I cashed only $50 because I still had the money I had exchanged at the hotel. Also, hadn't I learned that when the oil price rose the dollar did too, because people had to pay for oil in dollars? Probably I would get a better rate the next day.

The net I received was 234.21. The commission and value-added tax had eaten up 29.61 francs. Later, I figured out the net rate had been 4.6842, almost 5 percent less than I had gotten from *La Tricoteuse,* whom I had unjustly maligned.

We now had almost 500 francs and started out to spend them. Our first stop was a fruit stand. Have you ever tried to calculate in your head what is the price in cents of two oranges when they cost 35.75 francs per kilo and you do not have access to scales? Or how much money you should give the cashier when you are not immediately sure whether *quinze* is 15 or 50? You hold out a handful of change and let her pick what she wants. She seems honest.

Having managed to get rid of quite a few francs, we undertook to get more the next morning. I proposed to *La Tricoteuse* that she should sell me some, but she declined. I think she had an agreement with the bank next door not to do any banking during hours when the bank was open. At the bank I discovered that, contrary to my speculation about the price of oil, the dollar had declined from 5.27719 francs to 5.22027. But we had learned about the commission, which was a constant, so by buying $200 worth we reduced (raised?) the net price to 5.072.

Now we were really flush with francs, and I had a sudden insight into the truth of monetarism. The idea is that individual behavior is significantly governed by the possession of a certain kind of asset, called "money." Here I was with dollar currency, traveler's checks, credit cards, and checks on an account in an internationally known bank. With a call to my broker I could get a telegraphic transfer of a large amount of money from a money-market fund. Compared to my total liquid assets, the amounts of French currency I ever held were minute. But the difference between feeling that I had little French currency and feeling that I had much was significant. When I felt that I had little I tried to hold on to it, fearing to find myself in a place or time when it would be indispensable to me. When I felt that I had much I was quite prepared to get rid of it, lest I have it "left over" at some point, or have to trade it in at a great loss. I had demonstrated that money matters. How much it matters I leave to econometrics.

Dishes or Riches?   Feeling flush with francs we presented ourselves on the day before we were to leave Paris at a very expensive restaurant for lunch. As soon as I looked at the menu my franc anxiety returned. I had never seen such prices. I began a hasty and not reassuring estimate of how many francs were in my wallet and my wife's pocketbook. There was nothing on the menu to indicate that credit cards were accepted. I couldn't see any money passing at other tables or even anyone signing checks. Presumably the waiter knew without being told whose lunch was to be charged to the duc de Guermantes. But he would know that I wasn't the *duc* of anything. For one thing, I had had to borrow a coat and tie from the checkroom to get admitted in the first place. I wondered how many hours of dishwashing it would take to work off 500 francs. When the check came I inquired, appearing as confident as I could, whether they took credit cards. The answer was affirmative, and I was rich again.

That left us with an unexpectedly large amount of francs. Even after some splurging I had some to turn in at the bank at the airport, where I sold at 5.77 to the dollar francs that I had bought at an average price of 4.9787. I was glad to get rid of them. Now I could stop thinking about centimes and resume thinking about trillions of dollars in the budget or the GNP.

INTRODUCTION

There is a fundamental difference between making payment in the domestic market and making payment for goods, services, or securities purchased abroad. In a domestic transaction only one currency is used, whereas two or more currencies may be used in a foreign transaction. For example, a U.S. company that exports $100,000 worth of textile machinery to a Zurich textile producer will ask the Swiss buyer to remit payment in dollars unless the U.S. firm has some specific use for Swiss francs. (If the firm has a Swiss subsidiary, for instance, it may wish to make the funds acquired available to this subsidiary and would accept payment in Swiss francs.)

Assume that the situation just described is not the case and that you are a U.S. importer who has agreed to purchase a certain quantity of French perfume and to pay the French exporter 20,000 francs for it. How would you go about paying? First, you would go to the international department of your local bank to buy 20,000 French francs at the going market rate. Let's assume that the dollar/franc exchange rate is FF 5 = $1. Your bank then would debit your demand deposit by $4000 plus transactions costs and give you a special check payable in francs made out to the exporter. The check then would be sent to the exporter, who would deposit it in a Paris bank. The bank in turn would credit the exporter's account with 20,000 francs, and the transaction would be complete.

> Foreign exchange includes currencies and other instruments of payment denominated in other currencies.

The special checks and other instruments for making payment abroad are referred to collectively as foreign exchange. It is sometimes difficult to understand and relate to different currencies. As we saw in the opening case, dealing in foreign exchange is almost like using Monopoly money. It is hard to develop a context or feeling for the currency. As illustrated in the opening case, the first step in understanding foreign exchange is to understand the basic terms and key markets.

As an extension to the case, we need to understand the global and national context in which exchange rates are set. Then, we need to see how foreign exchange is used in international transactions and the nature of risks and risk aversion strategies adopted by MNEs. These issues will be developed in several different chapters.

To be effective, MNEs as well as small import and export firms must understand exchange rates. The exchange rate can influence where a wholesaler or retailer buys products from and sells products to an end consumer as well as where a manufacturing firm acquires raw materials or components and produces products. In addition, the rate of exchange affects the location of capital that a firm needs to access in order to expand.

TERMS AND DEFINITIONS

> An exchange rate is the number of units of one currency needed to acquire one unit of a currency of another country.

An **exchange rate** can be defined as the number of units of one currency that must be given to acquire one unit of a currency of another country. It is the price paid in the home currency to purchase a certain quantity of funds in the currency of another country. For example, on November 30, 1990, it took only $0.19773 to purchase one French franc. The exchange rate, then, is the link between different national currencies that makes international price and cost comparisons possible.

> The spot rate is the exchange rate involved for immediate delivery.

If the rate is quoted for current foreign-currency transactions, it is called the **spot rate.** The spot rate applies to **interbank transactions** for delivery within two business days or immediate delivery for over-the-counter trans-

The interbank market is the foreign-exchange market between and among banks.

The forward rate is the rate quoted for future delivery.

The spread in the spot market is the difference between the bid (buy) and offer (sell) rates quoted by the foreign-exchange trader.

actions that usually involve nonbank customers. If the rate is quoted for delivery of foreign currency in the future, it is called the **forward rate.** The forward rate is a contractual rate between the foreign-exchange trader and the trader's client.

The Spot Market

Since most foreign-currency transactions take place with foreign-exchange traders, the rates are quoted by the traders, who work for foreign exchange brokerage houses or commercial banks. That is one of the confusions identified in the opening case. The rates are quoted by the trader, not the buying or selling party. Whether the traders quote prices in the spot or the forward market, they always quote a bid (buy) and offer (sell) rate. The bid is what the trader is willing to buy foreign exchange for, and the offer is what the trader is willing to sell foreign exchange for. The spread in the spot market— the difference between the bid and offer rates—is the margin on which the trader earns a profit on overall transactions. Thus the rate quoted by a trader for the British pound might be $1.9420/10. This implies that the trader would be willing to buy pounds at $1.9410 and sell them for $1.9420. Obviously, the trader would want to buy low and sell high.

The direct quote is the number of units of the domestic currency needed to acquire one unit of the foreign currency.

The indirect quote is the number of units of the foreign currency needed to acquire one unit of the domestic currency.

As just noted in the example, the pound is quoted by the trader, a U.S. bank in this case, at the number of U.S. dollars for one unit of the foreign currency (the British pound). This is also known as the direct, or normal, quote. If the rate were quoted in terms of the number of units of the foreign currency for one unit of the domestic currency, it would be known as the indirect quote, or reciprocal, because it is the inverse of the direct quote. For example,

$$\frac{1}{\$1.9420} = 0.54129 \text{ British pounds (£) per U.S. dollar (\$).}$$

U.S. terms represent the direct quote.

European terms represent the indirect quote.

Both the direct and indirect quotes are used. In the United States it is common to use the direct quote for domestic business. This is often referred to as **U.S. terms** (or the American system). For international business banks often use **European terms** (or **Continental terms**), which would be the indirect quote. The rate quoted for the French franc earlier was the direct rate. The indirect rate at that same time was 5.0575 francs per dollar. It is customary to use the U.S. dollar as the **base currency** for international transactions; the other currency in the transaction would be the **quoted currency.** Most large newspapers, especially those devoted to business or with business sections, quote exchange rates on a daily basis. The *Wall Street Journal,* for example, provides the direct and indirect rates for 50 different currencies in every issue, as shown in Table 7.1. The rates are the selling rate of Banker's Trust for interbank transactions of $1 million and more. In addition to the spot rates of each of those currencies, the forward rates are provided for the

TABLE 7.1 | EXCHANGE-RATE QUOTES The exchange rates provided here are the direct and indirect spot rates for 50 key currencies and the direct and indirect forward rates for six of the currencies. The rates are the offer rates for very large transactions.

EXCHANGE RATES

Friday, November 30, 1990

The New York foreign-exchange selling rates below apply to trading among banks in amounts of $1 million and more, as quoted at 3 p.m. Eastern time by Bankers Trust Co. Retail transactions provide fewer units of foreign currency per dollar.

Country	U.S. $ equiv.		Currency per U.S. $		Country	U.S. $ equiv.		Currency per U.S. $	
	Fri.	Thurs.	Fri.	Thurs.		Fri.	Thurs.	Fri.	Thurs.
Argentina (Austral) . . .	.0001896	.0001981	5275.00	5047.00	**Jordan** (Dinar)	1.5603	1.5603	.6409	.6409
Australia (Dollar)	.7745	.7715	1.2912	1.2962	**Kuwait** (Dinar)	%	%	%	%
Austria (Schilling)	.09492	.09438	10.54	10.60	**Lebanon** (Pound)	.001439	.001439	695.00	695.00
Bahrain (Dinar)	2.6532	2.6532	.3769	.3769	**Malaysia** (Ringgit) . . .	.3699	.3711	2.7035	2.6950
Belgium (Franc)					**Malta** (Lira)	3.3784	3.3784	.2960	.2960
Commercial rate . . .	.03232	.03216	30.94	31.09	**Mexico** (Peso)				
Brazil (Cruzeiro)	.00714	.00748	160.00	133.67	Floating rate	.0003409	.0003409	2933.00	2933.00
Britain (Pound)	1.9420	1.9375	.5149	.5161	**Netherlands** (Guilder) . .	.5917	.5884	1.6900	1.6995
30-Day Forward . . .	1.9340	1.9293	.5171	.5183	**New Zealand** (Dollar) . .	.6100	.6085	1.6393	1.6434
90-Day Forward . . .	1.9190	1.9137	.5211	.5225	**Norway** (Krone)	.1708	.1704	5.8550	5.8700
180-Day Forward . . .	1.9003	1.8947	.5262	.5278	**Pakistan** (Rupee)	.0460	.0460	21.72	21.72
Canada (Dollar)	.8576	.8591	1.1660	1.1640	**Peru** (Inti)	.00000229	.00000229	436109.90	436109.90
30-Day Forward . . .	.8546	.8562	1.1702	1.1680	**Philippines** (Peso)	.03704	.03704	27.00	27.00
90-Day Forward . . .	.8500	.8514	1.1765	1.1745	**Portugal** (Escudo)	.007582	.007551	131.90	132.44
180-Day Forward . . .	.8429	.8442	1.1864	1.1845	**Saudi Arabia** (Riyal) . .	.26734	.26734	3.7406	3.7406
Chile (Official rate) . . .	.003113	.003114	321.20	321.18	**Singapore** (Dollar) . . .	.5806	.5831	1.7225	1.7150
China (Renmimol)	.191205	.191205	5.2300	5.2300	**South Africa** (Rand)				
Colombia (Peso)	.001912	.001912	523.00	523.00	Commercial rate . . .	.3964	.3992	2.5225	2.5048
Denmark (Krone)	.1741	.1730	5.7450	5.7810	Financial rate	.2882	.2907	3.4700	3.4400
Ecuador (Sucre)					**South Korea** (Won) . . .	.0013996	.0013996	714.50	714.50
Floating rate	.001147	.001147	871.50	871.50	**Spain** (Peseta)	.010521	.010471	95.05	95.50
Finland (Markka)	.27875	.27747	3.5874	3.6040	**Sweden** (Krona)	.1783	.1775	5.6100	5.6324
France (Franc)	.19773	.19675	5.0575	5.0025	**Switzerland** (Franc) . . .	.7828	.7794	1.2775	1.2830
30-Day Forward . . .	.19755	.19646	5.0620	5.0900	30-Day Forward . . .	.7826	.7793	1.2778	1.2832
90-Day Forward . . .	.19689	.19598	5.0790	5.1025	90-Day Forward . . .	.7818	.7785	1.2791	1.2845
180-Day Forward . . .	.19587	.19495	5.1055	5.1295	180-Day Forward . . .	.7805	.7776	1.2812	1.2860
Germany (Mark)	.6676	.6638	1.4980	1.5065	**Taiwan** (Dollar)	.037383	.037392	26.75	26.74
30-Day Forward . . .	.6672	.6636	1.4987	1.5070	**Thailand** (Bahi)	.03998	.03998	25.01	25.01
90-Day Forward . . .	.6661	.6626	1.5012	1.5091	**Turkey** (Lira)	.0003593	.0003610	2783.00	2770.00
180-Day Forward . . .	.6639	.6605	1.5062	1.5141	**United Arab** (Dirham) . .	.2723	.2723	3.6725	3.6725
Greece (Drachma) . . .	.006489	.006452	154.10	153.00	**Uruguay** (New Peso)				
Hong Kong (Dollar) . . .	.12819	.12825	7.8010	7.7970	Financial	.000673	.000673	1485.00	1485.00
India (Rupee)	.05534	.05534	18.07	18.07	**Venezuela** (Bolivar)				
Indonesia (Rupiah) . . .	.0005353	.0005353	1868.01	1868.01	Floating rate	.02018	.02018	49.55	49.55
Ireland (Punt)	1.7825	1.7740	.5610	.5637	**SDR**	1.42677	1.44017	.70088	.69436
Israel (Shekel)	.5044	.5047	1.9825	1.9813	**ECU**	1.36439	1.37890	. . . .	. . . .
Italy (Lira)	.0008891	.0008838	1124.75	1131.50					
Japan (Yen)	.007541	.007496	132.60	133.40					
30-Day Forward . . .	.007544	.007500	132.56	133.33					
90-Day Forward . . .	.007543	.007499	132.57	133.35					
180-Day Forward	.007537	.007497	132.68	133.39					

Special Drawing Rights (SDR) are based on exchange rates for the U.S., Germany, British, French, and Japanese currencies. Source: International Monetary Fund.

European Currency Unit (ECU) is based on a basket of community currencies. Source: European Community Commission.

%-Not quoted.

Source: The Wall Street Journal, 3 December 1990, p. C10.

British pound, the Canadian dollar, the French franc, the German mark, the Japanese yen, and the Swiss franc.

The cross rate is an exchange rate computed from two other exchange rates.

A final important definition for the spot market is the **cross rate,** which is an exchange rate computed from two other rates. Since most foreign-currency transactions are denominated in terms of U.S. dollars, it is common to see two nondollar currencies related to each other in the cross rate. To simplify this discussion, we will use the European quotes of the Swiss franc and German mark and figure the cross rate with the Swiss franc as the quoted currency and the German mark as the base currency. In Table 7.1 the spot rates for German marks (DM) and Swiss francs (SwF) on Friday, November 30, 1990, were:

DM 1.4980 per U.S. dollar   and   SwF 1.2775 per U.S. dollar.

The cross rate would be:

$$\frac{\text{SwF } 1.2775}{\text{DM } 1.4980} = \text{SwF } 0.8528 \text{ per DM},$$

which means that one German mark equals 0.8528 Swiss francs. It is common to see the cross rate quoted as 85.28. The *Wall Street Journal* now publishes a cross-rate table along with the dollar-exchange rates. Table 7.2 identifies the cross rates for several key currencies. The columns provide the direct quotes for each currency, and the rows provide the indirect quotes.

TABLE 7.2 | KEY CURRENCY CROSS RATES (LATE NEW YORK TRADING NOV. 30, 1990) The rows reflect the direct quote, and the columns reflect the indirect quote. Assuming a U.S. dollar perspective and using the *row* for U.S. dollars, the direct dollar quote for British pounds is $1.9435 per pound. Using the *column* for U.S. dollars, the indirect dollar quote for Japanese yen is 132.53 yen per dollar.

	Dollar	Pound	Swiss Franc	Guilder	Yen	Lira	Deutsche Mark	French Franc	Canadian Dollar
Canada	1.1650	2.2642	.91229	.88996	.00879	.00104	.77822	.23042	. . . .
France	5.0560	9.826	3.9593	2.9944	.03815	.00449	3.3774	. . . .	4.3399
Germany	1.4970	2.9094	1.1723	.88659	.01130	.00133	. . . .	.29608	1.2850
Italy	1125.0	2186.4	880.97	668.27	8.489	. . . .	751.50	222.51	963.7
Japan	132.53	257.57	103.782	78.490	. . . .	.11780	88.530	26.212	113.78
Netherlands	1.6885	3.2816	1.3222	. . . .	.01274	.00150	1.1279	.33396	1.4494
Switzerland	1.2770	2.4818	. . . .	.75629	.00964	.00114	.85304	.25257	1.0961
United Kingdom	.51454	. . . .	.40293	.30473	.00388	.00046	.34371	.10177	.44168
United States	. . . .	1.9435	.78309	.59224	.00755	.00089	.66800	.19778	.85837

Source: Telerate

Source: The Wall Street Journal, 3 December 1990, p. C10.

German and Swiss managers keep track of the cross rate, since they trade extensively with each other and any material shifts in the cross rate could signal a change in prices of goods. For example, assume that a German exporter sold a product costing DM 100 to a Swiss importer for SwF 85.28 as shown in the cross-rate example. If the cross rate were to move to SwF 0.870 per DM, the German exporter and Swiss importer would have to make some interesting decisions. If the exporter kept the price to the importer at DM 100, the importer would now have to come up with SwF 87 to buy the product. The exporter could lower the price to DM 98.0 so that the product would still cost SwF 85.28. If the exporter decided to keep the price at DM 100, the Swiss importer would have two options: (1) increase prices to reflect the higher cost of the import and thus keep profit margins the same as before, or (2) keep prices the same and end up with a smaller profit margin due to the higher cost of the product. If the product were especially price sensitive, neither the exporter nor the importer would want to see the price rise in Switzerland.

The Forward Market

As noted above, the spot market is for foreign exchange traded within two business days. However, some transactions may be entered into on one day but not completed until sometime in the future. For example, the French exporter of perfume might sell perfume to the U.S. importer with immediate delivery but not require payment for 30 days. The U.S. importer has an obligation to pay francs in 30 days, so he or she may enter into a contract with a trader to deliver dollars for francs in 30 days at a forward rate, the rate today for future delivery.

The forward spread is the difference between the spot and forward exchange rates.

Thus the forward rate is the rate quoted by foreign-exchange traders for the purchase or sale of foreign exchange in the future. As was noted in Table 7.1, there is a difference between the spot rate and the forward rate known as the **spread** in the forward market. In order to understand how spot and forward rates are determined, you should first know how to calculate the spread between the spot and forward rates.

In the example below we compute the points, or the difference between the spot and forward rates, for 90-day contracts for the Canadian dollar and the Japanese yen quoted in U.S. terms:

	Canadian dollars	Japanese yen
Spot	$0.8576	$0.007541
90-day forward	0.8500	0.007543
Points	− 76	+ 2

The spread in Canadian dollars is 76 points; because the forward rate is less than the spot rate, the Canadian dollar is at a **discount** in the 90-day forward market. The spread in Japanese yen is only 2 points, and since the forward rate is greater than the spot rate, the yen is at a **premium** in the forward market.

The premium or discount can also be quoted in terms of annualized percent. Use the following formula to determine the annualized percentage.

$$\text{Premium (discount)} = \frac{F_0 - S_0}{S_0} \times \frac{12}{N} \times 100,$$

where F_0 is the forward rate on the day the contract is entered into, S_0 is the spot rate on that day, N is the number of months forward, and 100 is used to convert the decimal to percent amounts (e.g., $0.05 \times 100 = 5\%$).

Using Canadian dollars,

$$\text{Discount} = \frac{0.8500 - 0.8576}{0.8576} \times \frac{12}{3} \times 100 = -3.54\%,$$

which means that the Canadian dollar is selling at a discount of 3.54 percent under the spot rate.

Forward markets do not exist for all currencies in all countries. For example, in Table 7.1, there is no forward market in the United States for the Brazilian cruzeiro. This is because a forward contract in cruzeiros generally is not available in the interbank market. Given the high rate of inflation in Brazil, there is an excess of cruzeiros, and it would be practically impossible for the interbank market to balance off its purchases of cruzeiro contracts with its sales of cruzeiro contracts. The market is too thin (i.e., does not have enough transactions) to warrant the forward market in the interbank market. However, banks in Brazil are permitted to provide forward contracts for exporters, usually for a period of up to 180 days. The bank quotes usually reflect interest-rate differentials.

HOW THE FOREIGN-EXCHANGE MARKET WORKS

Basic Spot and Forward Markets

With a basic understanding of exchange rate quotations, we can now examine how foreign exchange is traded.

The majority of foreign-exchange transactions are carried out by commercial banks, with the rest conducted by foreign-exchange brokers. **Brokers** are specialists who facilitate transactions between banks and replace direct contact between banks.

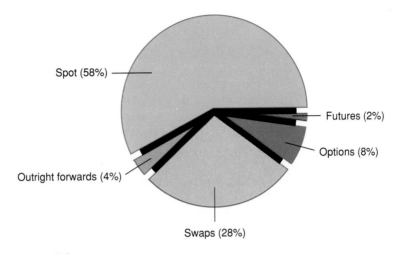

Spot (58%) ——

—— Futures (2%)

—— Options (8%)

Outright forwards (4%)

Swaps (28%)

Figure 7.1
Foreign-Exchange Markets, 1989
Most foreign-exchange transactions in 1989 were in the spot market (58 percent).
Outright forwards and swaps (which combine a spot and forward transaction)
closely followed with 32 percent of the transactions. *Source:* Federal Reserve Bank of
New York.

A swap is an exchange of
currencies in the spot
market with the agree-
ment to reverse the transaction in the future.

As noted in Fig. 7.1, 58 percent of all foreign-exchange trading in the
United States is conducted in the spot market, primarily the interbank market.
The next-largest category is the **swap** market. A swap is a simultaneous
spot and forward transaction. For example, a U.S. firm might need British
pounds for 30 days, so it enters into a spot transaction to exchange dollars
for pounds and enters into a simultaneous forward transaction to exchange
the pounds for dollars in 30 days when the need for British pounds is completed.

The other major foreign-exchange transactions are outright forwards,
options, and futures. The outright forward is a forward contract that is not
connected to a spot transaction. For example, a firm might be receiving British pounds in 90 days and thus enter into a forward contract to trade pounds
for dollars in 90 days. An option is the right to trade foreign currency. It is a
relatively new instrument that is gaining in importance. A firm that buys an
option pays a brokerage fee and a premium to have the right to buy or sell
foreign currency within a certain time period. For example, let's assume that
a firm enters into an option to buy Japanese yen at 130 yen per dollar
($0.00769 per yen). The firm would have to pay the premium and the bro-
kerage fee for the right to enter into the option. If the rate is 140 yen per
dollar ($0.00714) when the firm wants to buy the yen, it would not exercise
the option, because it would not cost as much to buy the yen at the market
rate as it would at the option rate. If the market rate is 120 yen per dollar

($0.008), the firm would exercise the option, since it would be cheaper to buy at the option rate than it would be to buy at the market rate. The option provides the firm some flexibility, but the firm must also pay the brokerage fee and the premium whether it exercises the option or not.

The futures contract is similar to the forward contract in that it specifies an exchange rate in advance of the future exchange of currency. The futures contract is not as flexible as a forward contract, because the futures contracts are for specific amounts of currency and for specific maturity dates, whereas forward contracts can be tailor-made to fit the size of the transaction and the maturity date. Forward contracts depend on a client's relationship with the bank of the trader, but the futures contract is entered into by anyone through a broker on the exchange floor.

International Transactions   The foreign-exchange market is based on the economic law of supply and demand. Sometimes governments intervene to control the flow of currency by having their central banks buy or sell currency in the open market. However, the central action in the foreign-exchange market revolves around the commercial banks in the major money centers of the world. In the 1989 New York Federal Reserve survey, it was determined that 82 percent of the foreign-exchange transactions were interbank; the remaining 18 percent were divided between the futures and options market, financial customers, and nonfinancial customers.

> The world's communication networks are now so good, and so many countries have fairly unrestricted markets that we can talk of a single world market. It starts in a small way in New Zealand around 9:00 A.M. New Zealand time, just in time to catch the tail end of the previous night's New York market. Two or three hours later, Tokyo opens, followed an hour later by Hong Kong and Manila and then half an hour later by Singapore. By now, with the Far East market in full swing, the focus moves to the Near and Middle East. Bombay opens two hours after Singapore, followed after an hour and a half by Abu Dhabi, with Jeddah an hour behind, and Athens and Beirut an hour behind still. By this stage trading in the Far and Middle East is usually thin and perhaps nervous as dealers wait to see how Europe will trade. Paris and Frankfurt open an hour ahead of London, and by this time Tokyo is starting to close down, so the European market can judge how the Japanese market has been trading by the way they deal to close out positions. By lunch-time in London, New York is starting to open up, and as Europe closes down, so positions can be passed westward. During the afternoon in New York, trading tends to be quiet. The problem is that there is nowhere to pass a position to. The San Francisco market, three hours behind, is effectively a satellite of the New York market. Very small positions can be passed on to New Zealand banks, but the market there is extremely limited.[1]

According to the Federal Reserve Bank of New York, the daily foreign-exchange volume conducted in London was $187 billion, compared with $129 billion in New York and $115 billion in Tokyo (see Fig. 7.2). The Lon-

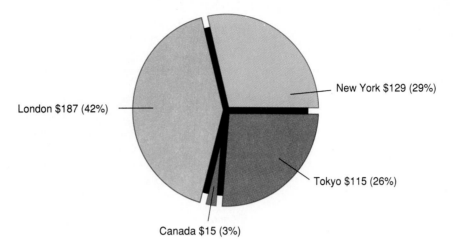

London $187 (42%)

New York $129 (29%)

Tokyo $115 (26%)

Canada $15 (3%)

Figure 7.2
Daily Average Foreign-Exchange Volume, 1989 (in billions of U.S. dollars)
The largest market in the world for dealing in foreign exchange in 1989 was
London, closely followed by New York and Tokyo. *Source:* Federal Reserve Bank of
New York.

don market is pivotal because of its central position in trading hours vis-à-vis
the rest of the world and its greater transaction opportunities. London trading
increased to $187 billion in 1989 from $90 billion daily in 1986, $49 billion
daily in 1984, and $25 billion daily in 1979.[2]

Daily foreign-exchange trading in the United States increased from $26
billion in 1983 to $50 billion in 1986 and $129 billion in 1989. As noted in
Fig. 7.3, the most actively traded currencies in the United States in order of
importance were the German mark, the Japanese yen, the British pound, and
the Swiss franc.

> Most foreign-currency
> transactions are handled
> by traders in the commer-
> cial banks.

Most transactions are handled in the interbank market. Even in interbank dealings, the majority of the transactions are done by traders in the
home offices of the major money center banks. Typically these traders are
responsible for a single currency, and they end up dealing with the traders of
that currency worldwide. Each money center bank, such as Chase Manhattan
or Manufacturers Hanover Trust, has a trading room where the currency traders are housed, allowing them contact with each other as well as with the
major traders worldwide.

Sometimes the bankers go through brokers instead of working directly
with traders of other banks. A few major brokers and several minor ones in
the United States deal in foreign-exchange transactions. These brokers typically try to link traders of different banks in foreign-exchange transactions.
Brokers sometimes work the corporate market as well, but that is rare in
comparison with their major area of specialty.

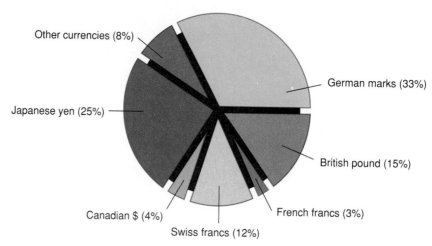

Figure 7.3
Daily Foreign-Exchange Trading in the United States, 1989
The most-traded currency in the United States in 1989 was the German mark, closely followed by the Japanese yen. Even though Canada is the United States' largest trading partner, only 4 percent of the foreign-exchange volume was in Canadian dollars. *Source:* Federal Reserve Bank of New York.

Even though the money center banks trade most of the foreign exchange in the world, companies that are not located in these money centers still can go through regional or local banks for foreign-currency transactions. However, their banks generally work through a money center bank as demonstrated in Fig. 7.4.

Specialized Markets

Certain specialized institutions and markets deal in futures and options and offer some variety from the banking sector: the International Monetary Market (IMM) in Chicago, the London International Financial Futures Exchange (LIFFE), and the Philadelphia Stock Exchange (PSE). As noted in Fig. 7.4, a customer operates in these three markets through a broker.

The IMM deals primarily in the futures contracts, which are contracts for forward delivery of currencies for specific amounts with a specific maturity date.

The International Monetary Market   The International Monetary Market (IMM) was opened in 1972 by the Chicago Mercantile Exchange to deal primarily in futures contracts for the British pound, the Canadian dollar, the West German mark, the Swiss franc, the Japanese yen, and the Australian dollar. These contracts are for specific amounts and have a specific maturity date. For example, a futures contract in Japanese yen is set by the IMM at 12.5 million yen. If you wanted to buy futures for 100 million yen, you would have to buy eight yen contracts from a broker. The contract sizes for the other

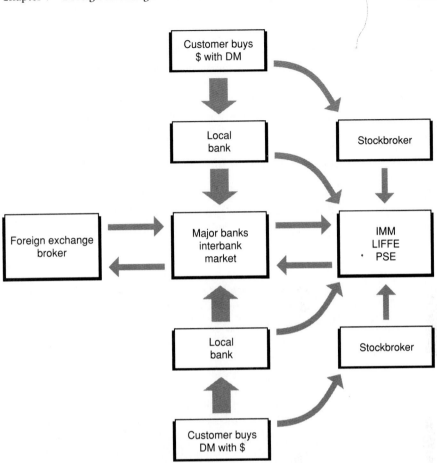

Figure 7.4
Structure of Foreign-Exchange Markets
Corporate clients deal in foreign exchange through their banks or through
securities brokers. Banks deal heavily in the interbank market and through foreign-
exchange brokers. Note: As will be described below, the International Money Market
(IMM) Chicago trades foreign-exchange futures and DM futures options, the London
International Financial Futures Exchange (LIFFE) trades foreign-exchange futures, and the
Philadelphia Stock Exchange (PSE) trades foreign-currency options. *Source:* K. Alec
Chrystal, "A Guide to Foreign Exchange Markets." *Bulletin* (Federal Reserve Bank of St.
Louis, March 1984), p. 9.

currencies are 125,000 deutsche marks, 100,000 Canadian dollars, 62,500
British pounds, 125,000 Swiss francs, and 100,000 Australian dollars. The
"Futures Prices" section of the *Wall Street Journal* provides quotes of the con-
tracts each day.

Although the contracts have a fixed maturity date, there is a ready market for the contracts at the IMM. Brokers make deals on the trading floor

rather than over the telephone as is the case with the forward markets for banks. Futures contracts at the IMM also tend to be small relative to the transactions normally encountered in the interbank market. The IMM limits how much the futures prices can vary from one day to the next, whereas there are no such restrictions in the banking market. Finally, the IMM requires a margin, or deposit, equal to about 4 percent of the contract to be made by the purchaser of a contract.

The London International Financial Futures Exchange   The London International Financial Futures Exchange (LIFFE), which opened in September 1982, deals in futures contracts in British pounds, German marks, Swiss francs, and Japanese yen in fixed contract sizes. The market also deals in Eurodollars, which are dollars banked outside of the United States, and should provide an alternative to the interbank market in Europe for foreign-exchange risk protection.

The Philadelphia Stock Exchange   The Philadelphia Stock Exchange (PSE) represents a fairly recent concept in foreign-exchange trading, that of **options.** As described above, an option is a contract specifying the right to buy or sell foreign exchange within a specific period (American option) or at a specific date (European option).

Each option is for a specific value of currency. For example, each Australian dollar option is for 50,000 Australian dollars. The PSE offers foreign-exchange options for the Australian dollar (50,000 Australian dollars), the British pound (31,250 pounds), the Canadian dollar (50,000 Canadian dollars), the German mark (62,500 marks), the Japanese yen (6,250,000 yen), and the Swiss franc (62,500 francs). Many foreign-exchange experts feel that the options market in foreign exchange will expand and become more important as transactions costs decrease. As noted earlier, options provide more flexibility than do futures or forwards, but at a relatively high cost.

CONVERTIBILITY

The difficulty involved in exchanging one currency for others is a measure of its **convertibility.** For example, although it is easy to convert U.S. dollars into Russian rubles, it is virtually impossible to convert rubles into dollars. Therefore, the U.S. dollar is considered freely convertible, but the Russian ruble is considered inconvertible.

Convertibility has essentially two parts. Most countries today have nonresident, or external, convertibility. For example, all nonresidents with deposits in French banks may at any time exchange all of their franc deposits for the currency of any other country. In other words, a U.S. exporter to France can be paid in francs and be assured that those francs can be converted to dollars or some other currency. However, not all countries permit nonresident convertibility. In the case of the Soviet Union, a foreign firm like Pizza

Hut may generate significant ruble profits in the Soviet Union, but it may not be able to convert those profits into dollars and ship them out of the country. Lack of currency convertibility is a major problem for foreign firms attempting to invest in the Soviet Union.

In 1982 many foreigners with dollar deposits in Mexico had those deposits converted into pesos by the Mexican government because of an acute shortage of foreign exchange. In that case, as in the Soviet Union, not even nonresidents could enjoy convertibility status. In Western Europe, the trend toward convertibility was accelerated in 1958 when fourteen countries agreed to establish external convertibility for their currencies, meaning that nonresidents of these countries as well as all exporters from these countries were free to use the proceeds of their overseas sales anywhere in the world.

Full convertibility means that the government allows both residents and nonresidents to purchase unlimited amounts of any foreign currency with the domestic currency. In 1989, 31 countries were free from payments restrictions, defined as basically "official actions directly affecting the availability or cost of exchange, or involving undue delay." Another 32 countries had currencies with restrictions on payments for capital transactions but not for payments on current transactions, one country had a currency with restrictions on current transactions but not for capital transactions, and 83 countries had restrictions on both current transactions and capital transactions.[3] Each government determines the convertibility of its own currency.

Hard currencies are usually fully convertible. They are also relatively stable in value or tend to be rather strong in comparison with other currencies. They are desirable assets to hold.

In the absence of full convertibility, there is often a **black market,** which is essentially a parallel market with the official market and is usually outside of the sanction and control of the government. However, not all parallel markets are black markets. For example, South Africa has a commercial rate and a financial rate; both are sanctioned by the government, but the rates are very different, as noted in Table 7.1.

A hard currency is a currency that is usually fully convertible and strong or relatively stable in comparison with other currencies.

A black market is a free market for a currency that operates outside of the control of the government.

EXCHANGE RESTRICTIONS

Some governments impose various exchange restrictions to control access to foreign exchange. Some of the devices they use are import licensing, multiple exchange rates, import deposit requirements, and quantity controls.

Licensing

Licensing occurs when the government requires that all foreign-exchange transactions be regulated and controlled by it through application.

Governmental **licenses** fix the exchange rate by requiring all recipients, exporters, and others who receive foreign exchange to sell it to the central bank at the official buying rate. The central bank of a country, which is the institution usually empowered to establish monetary policy, or some other government agency rations the currency it acquires by selling it at fixed rates to those needing to make payment abroad for goods considered essential. The test of essentiality is made by the government or some agency acting for the government, such as the central bank. An importer may purchase foreign exchange only if that importer has obtained a license for the importation of the goods in question. For example, purchases of raw materials and basic foodstuffs would likely be regarded by the government of a developing country as essential; thus foreign exchange would be sold to importers of these commodities.

In New Zealand, for example, imports were controlled through an Import Licensing Schedule until 1988. However, only about 18 percent of New Zealand's imports were affected by the schedule. In Colombia, imports are subject to one of four different import systems: (1) freely importable goods, requiring only registration; (2) goods subject to prior approval and requiring an import license; (3) goods included in the prohibited import list; and (4) goods requiring special import-export arrangements for their importation.[4]

Multiple Exchange Rates

A multiple exchange rate is where a government sets different exchange rates for different transactions.

Another way to conserve foreign exchange is to allow more than one rate of exchange: This is known as a multiple exchange-rate system. Interestingly, multiple exchange-rate arrangements have been rather common. In the 1989 IMF survey on exchange-rate arrangements, 28 countries used more than one exchange rate for imports, 32 used more than one rate for exports, and 35 used a different rate for exports and imports.[5] There are several ways to determine a multiple exchange rate, but some countries, such as Jamaica, require a premium or discount on foreign-exchange transactions in specific industries or with specific countries. Therefore, if the government wants to discourage imports, it can establish a very high exchange rate for the transactions it does not favor, thereby making the imports very expensive.

Import Deposit Requirement

An import deposit requirement takes place when the government requires a deposit prior to the release of foreign exchange.

Advance import deposits are another form of foreign-exchange control. In 1989 in Colombia, "an advance exchange license deposit had to be lodged at the official rate for exchange certificates at least 20 calendar days prior to an application for an exchange license. The rate of deposit was 95 percent of the value of the exchange license."[6] According to the 1989 IMF report on exchange arrangements, 19 IMF-member countries used advance import deposits of one form or another to force companies to think carefully about the wisdom of importing and to allow the government time to plan its foreign exchange flows.

Quantity Controls

In quantity controls, the government limits the amount of foreign exchange that can be used in a specific transaction.

Governments may also limit the amount of exchange for specific purposes. These types of control, called **quantity controls,** are often used in conjunction with tourism. In Chile, for example, the limit for Chilean tourists going abroad in 1989 was the equivalent of U.S. $1000 per trip for travel to Latin American and Caribbean countries and U.S. $3000 per trip for travel to other countries. For travel by land to adjacent countries, 20 percent of the allowance is provided in the form of foreign exchange, and the rest is provided in money orders.[7]

COMPENSATORY TRADE

Compensatory trade is often used when firms have difficulty getting access to hard currency in payment for products sold or services rendered.

Sometimes countries have so much difficulty generating enough foreign exchange to pay for imports that even licensing doesn't work; they need to come up with creative ways to get the products they want. Although this shortage of foreign exchange is associated primarily with the historically planned economies and developing countries, it can also impact industrial countries. Canada and Australia, for example, found that they had to enter into special agreements with McDonnell-Douglas to pay for the military aircraft that it wanted to purchase. As a result, firms and governments are often forced to resort to creative ways of settling payment, many of which involve trading goods for goods as part of the transaction. The term **compensatory trade** refers to any one of a number of different arrangements in which goods and services are traded for each other, either on a bilateral or multilateral basis. More specifically, it is defined as "any contractual commitment imposed as a condition of purchase, by the importer on the exporter, with the intention of creating quid pro quo benefits for the former."[8] Although it is nearly impossible to determine the extent of compensatory trade arrangements, an estimated 20 to 30 percent of international trade is tied in some form of compensatory trade.[9]

Barter

Barter is the trade of goods for goods.

Barter, the oldest form of compensatory trade, occurs when goods are traded for goods of equal value without any flow of cash. Although there are many problems in negotiating a barter agreement, there are examples of it: PepsiCo agreed to swap Pepsi syrup and bottling equipment for Russian vodka, and Occidental Petroleum arranged sales of fertilizer plants and pipelines to the Soviet Union in exchange for ammonia. In the past, Argentina has shipped wheat and frozen meat to Peru and received iron ore pellets in exchange. Indonesia bartered some of its oil for a sorely needed steelmaking complex from West Germany.[10] Figure 7.5 illustrates how a barter transaction might be structured.

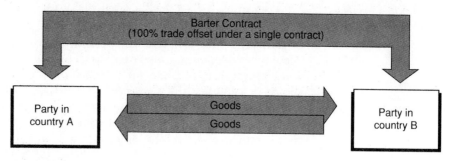

Figure 7.5
Model of a Barter Transaction *Source:* Pompiliu Verzariu, *Countertrade, Barter, Offsets* (New York: McGraw-Hill, 1985), p. 26.

A barter variation is when goods are traded for goods which are sold for cash rather than consumed.

A slight variation of barter trade includes goods and money. One example is when Mitsui, one of the largest Japanese trading companies, bought tanning material in the Soviet Union and shipped it to Argentina in exchange for plastic products. Mitsui marketed these products in the United States for cash.

Countertrade

In offset or countertrade, goods and services are sold for cash with the condition that the seller help the buyer earn foreign exchange through different means.

Another type of compensatory trade, called **offset trade** or **countertrade,** is becoming increasingly important. Countertrade exists "when reciprocal and contingent exchanges of goods and services are specified by contract and each flow of deliveries is valued and settled in monetary units."[11] A good example of how a firm might have to deal with offset involves McDonnell Douglas and the sale of F-18A fighter aircraft to the government of Canada. The sale of aircraft to Canada in 1980 was to net McDonnell Douglas nearly $3 billion, a significant amount of money for one sale. Over the eight-year period involved in the delivery dates, this would result in average imports for Canada of several hundred million dollars per year. Given the weakness of the Canadian dollar in relation to the U.S. dollar at the time of the sale, this was bound to concern the Canadian government. As a result, the negotiations for the sale of the aircraft involved not only the technical capabilities of the F-18s and the attendant costs, but also the industrial benefits that McDonnell Douglas could promise the Canadian government.

The Canadian offset program covers a period of 15 years with a three-year grace period. The total program commitment of $2.9 billion must be covered from the following three areas: aerospace and electronics (minimum 60 percent), advanced technology (minimum 6 percent), and diversified activities (maximum 40 percent). The aerospace and electronics area is the most important of the three, and it involves designated production, co-production, technology transfer, and joint R&D. The diversified activities portion of the offset commitment involves investment/technology development, export development, and tourism development.

Evidence Account Transaction

Figure 7.6 shows how a complex transaction such as the F-18A sale to Canada might be structured. This type of transaction is sometimes known as an **evidence account transaction** because it requires adherence to certain contractual obligations. As noted, it involves the primary exporter, the importing government, and other secondary exporters and importers.

Whether firms become involved in the complexities of offset trade depends mainly on the strength of demand for their products, alternative sources of supply, and foreign exchange problems in the buying country. However, offset trade results primarily from foreign exchange shortage and is a good example of how firms and governments can compensate for the shortage through creative business transactions.

Figure 7.6
Model of an Evidence Account Transaction *Source:* Pompiliu Verzariu,
Countertrade, Barter, Offsets (New York: McGraw-Hill, 1985), p. 32.

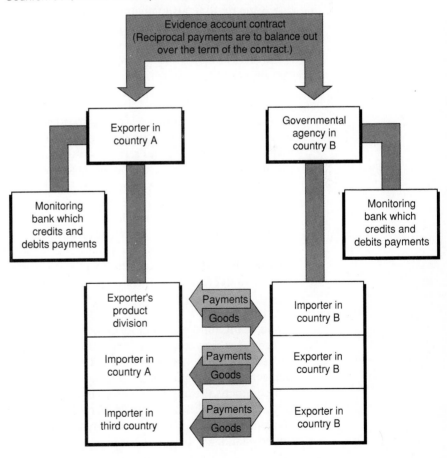

_____ **THE USES OF THE FOREIGN-EXCHANGE MARKET** ▬▬▬▬

The major uses of foreign exchange are: commercial transactions, making the market, arbitrage, and risk bearing/risk reduction.

Banks collect foreign exchange, lend foreign exchange, and buy and sell foreign exchange.

So far, we have defined the key terms and concepts involved in foreign exchange. Now we will discuss the four major uses of foreign exchange: commercial transactions: making the market, arbitrage, and risk bearing or risk reduction.[12]

The major facilitators of these transactions, as mentioned earlier in the chapter, are the international departments of the commercial banks, which perform three essential financial functions: (1) collections, (2) lending, and (3) the buying and selling of foreign exchange. The collection function involves the bank in serving as a vehicle for making payments between its own resident customers and foreign nationals.

The purchase and sale of foreign exchange are undertaken by a commercial bank for many purposes. For instance, travelers going abroad or returning from a foreign country will want to purchase or sell foreign currency. Residents of one country wishing to invest abroad also would need to purchase foreign currency from a commercial bank.

Suppose that a Canadian exporter is to receive payment from a U.S. importer in U.S. dollars, and the exporter wishes to use the funds to make payment for raw materials purchased in Norway. The bank in this case simultaneously serves as a collector and acts as a dealer in a foreign exchange.

Commercial Transactions

The focus in this book is more on commercial transactions—that is, those transactions that involve the buying and selling of foreign exchange to facilitate the trade of goods and services—than it is on financial transactions. Thus GM of Canada may have to convert U.S. dollars into Canadian dollars when parts or components that it produces in Canada are shipped to the United States. A U.S. parent company might receive Canadian dollar dividends from its Canadian operations that it must convert into U.S. dollars. A Canadian company might borrow Swiss francs and convert them into Canadian dollars to use for expansion of operations in Canada. Some of these transactions are financial in nature, but they relate to the commercial side of the business.

Making the Market

"Making the market," another important use of foreign exchange, refers to transactions between brokers and traders at banks or directly between the traders at different banks. Normally these transactions are undertaken to provide sufficient foreign-exchange balances for the banks to conduct their normal commercial transactions as well as to balance their positions in foreign exchange so that they are not overbought or oversold in a currency. As mentioned earlier, 82 percent of the daily transactions in foreign exchange in the United States are between banks. These transactions obviously are part of making the market rather than commercial transactions.

Arbitrage

Arbitrage is the buying and selling of foreign exchange at a profit due to price discrepancies.

Arbitrage is the process of buying and selling foreign exchange at a profit due to price discrepancies between markets. For example, one could sell U.S. dollars for Swiss francs, Swiss francs for German marks, and German marks for U.S. dollars, the goal being to end up with more dollars at the end of the process. Assume that a trader converts $100 into SwF 150 (Swiss francs) when the exchange rate is SwF 1.5 = $1.00. The trader then converts the francs into DM 225 (German marks) at an exchange rate of DM 1.5 = SwF 1.00, and then finally converts the marks into $125 at an exchange rate of DM 1.8 = $1.00. Thus arbitrage yields $125 from the initial sale of $100.

Interest arbitrage involves investing in interest-bearing instruments in foreign exchange and earning a profit due to interest-rate and exchange-rate differentials.

Interest arbitrage involves investing in debt instruments in different countries. For example, a trader could take $1000 and invest it in the United States for 90 days, or take the $1000, convert it into British pounds, invest the money in Great Britain for 90 days, and then convert the pounds back into dollars. The investor would pick the highest-yielding alternative at the end of 90 days.

Risk

Speculators take positions in foreign exchange with the major objective of earning a profit.

Foreign-exchange transactions can also be used to speculate for profit or to protect against risk. Both types of transactions are related to risk but in different ways. **Speculators** are important actors in the foreign-exchange market because they spot trends and try to take advantage of them. They can become an important source of the supply of and demand for a currency. Speculation is taking an open position in a foreign currency for a profit. In speculation, for example, an investor would hold German marks in anticipation of the strengthening of the mark against other currencies. If the mark strengthens, the investor earns a profit; if the mark weakens, the investor incurs a loss.

On the side of protection against risk are foreign-exchange transactions designed to **hedge** against a potential loss due to an exchange-rate change. For example, a U.S. parent company expecting a British pound dividend in 90 days could enter into a forward contract to hedge the dividend flow. It could go to the bank and agree to deliver pounds for dollars in 90 days at the forward rate. That eliminates the risk and uncertainty of an unfavorable shift in the exchange rate by locking in a specific forward rate for the dividend flow.

LOOKING TO THE FUTURE   Most of the future dimensions to foreign exchange will be covered in the next few chapters as we discuss the context in which exchange rates are determined and the nature of the international financial system. However, there are a few key future issues that can be drawn from this chapter.

First, it is clear that significant strides have been made in the development of foreign exchange markets in recent years, and those strides will continue in the future. The speed at which transactions are processed and information is transmitted globally will certainly lead to greater efficiencies and opportunities in the trading of foreign exchange. Ten years ago, there was little discussion of options, for example, but in the past four years, the percentage of total transactions accounted for by options has doubled. Similar growth in this new market will take place in the next decade as transactions costs come down and firms can use options more effectively.

In addition, the banks and securities firms will continue to find creative ways to help firms use the foreign exchange markets more efficiently at less risk. This will be very important in helping to expand international transactions.

Third, exchange restrictions hamper the free flow of goods and services, but these restrictions should diminish as governments gain greater control over their economies. The regional integration in Europe, which will be discussed in a future chapter, has led to discussions of a common European currency, which will allow cross border transactions in Europe to progress more smoothly. As Mexico attempts to cooperate with the United States and Canada in a free trade agreement, its government will be forced to slow down inflation and stabilize the Mexican currency in order to allow trade to flow more smoothly.

Finally, it is doubtful that different forms of countertrade or offset transactions will disappear as alternatives to currency. Since even some industrial countries are forced to enter into creative purchasing agreements in order to get access to key products, firms will have to learn to package transactions in order to help countries conserve scarce foreign exchange.

SUMMARY

- A major distinction between domestic and international payments for goods and services is that more than one currency is used for international transactions.

- An exchange rate is the value of one currency in terms of another. A spot exchange rate is the rate quoted for current transactions, whereas the forward rate is a rate quoted by a foreign-exchange trader for a contract to receive or deliver foreign currency in the future.

- The difference between the spot and forward rates at the time of a contract is the forward spread. The foreign currency is selling at a discount if the spread is negative and at a premium if the spread is positive.

- Most foreign-exchange transactions take place through the traders of commercial banks, with the majority of the transactions occurring in the spot market rather than the forward market. Also, most of the foreign-exchange transactions are interbank transactions rather than between banks and non-banking institutions.

- The International Monetary Market (IMM) is a specialized market that deals in futures contracts in the British pound, the Canadian dollar, the German mark, the Swiss franc, the Japanese yen, the Mexican peso, the French franc, and the Dutch guilder. Other specialized markets include the London International Financial Futures Exchange (LIFFE) and the Philadelphia Stock Exchange (PSE).

■ A convertible currency can be freely traded for other currencies. Some countries' currencies are partially convertible in that residents are not allowed to convert to other currencies but nonresidents are.

■ Some governments control access to their currencies through import licensing, multiple exchange rates, import deposit requirements, and quantity controls.

■ The four major uses of foreign exchange are: commercial transactions, making the market, arbitrage, and risk bearing or risk reduction.

C A S E
THE MEXICAN PESO[13]

On August 31, 1976, the Mexican peso was cut loose from its exchange rate of 12.5 pesos to the dollar, which was established in 1955. From 1955 to 1976 the exchange rate had been maintained artificially through a variety of mechanisms. Import controls and market intervention were used extensively to allow the peso to appear stabler than it was, thereby frustrating firms operating in Mexico. Many companies established manufacturing operations in Mexico only to find that the government eventually would phase out their ability to import needed raw materials and components.

During the 1970s pressure began to build for a change in the value of the currency. Tourism, a major source of foreign exchange, began to taper off because of rising prices resulting directly from general inflation in the economy. (See Map 7.2.)

Mexico began importing more than it was exporting, which resulted in an outflow of pesos to buy the excess imports. Exporters to Mexico did not want to hold onto pesos, preferring instead to convert them into dollars. To give so many

dollars in order to buy back the pesos would have depleted Mexico's holdings of dollar reserves severely if Mexican authorities used these existing reserves to make the conversion. Instead Mexico chose to maintain its level of reserves by increased short-term external borrowing of dollars, which would eventually result in principal and interest payments that could rob Mexico of what little foreign exchange it could gather.

Because of these and other pressures, officials agreed to devalue the peso on August 31, 1976, to 20.5 pesos to the dollar in the hope that this devaluation would absorb some of the excess supply of pesos in the market and allow the economy to stabilize. Even though devaluation was the initial solution to the problem, the government also considered establishing more elaborate foreign-exchange controls so that spot transactions could be allocated according to governmental priorities. Finally, Mexico decided on devaluation rather than the establishment of an elaborate bureaucracy to administer the foreign-exchange controls.

Unfortunately, the solution to the problem was short-lived. From 1976 to mid-1981 the peso held its postdevaluation level, but inflation and other forces that had created the problems leading up to the 1976 devaluation reemerged.

Year	Pesos (Mex$) per dollar EOY
1970	12.5
1975	12.5
1976	12.9
1977	22.7
1978	22.7
1979	22.8
1980	23.3
1981	26.2
1982	96.5
1983	143.9
1984	192.6
1985	371.7
1986	923.5
1987	2,209.7
1988	2,281.0
1989	2,641.0
1990	2,945.4

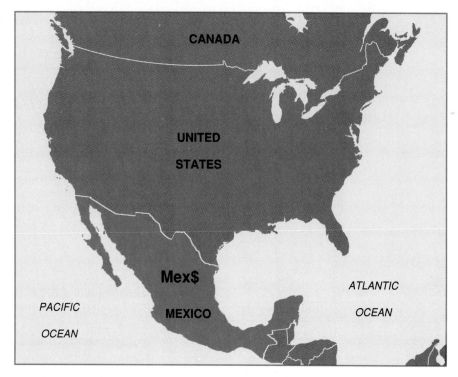

Map 7.2
The Mexican Peso
The Mexican peso held firm from 1955 to 1976, but the devaluation of 1976 was simply a prelude of things to come, as illustrated in this map.

Imports again exceeded exports, tourism fell steadily, foreign credit became tight and expensive, and world oil prices and demand softened considerably. The Central Bank of Mexico steadfastly maintained that a relatively modest devaluation of 15–20 percent would correct the imbalances in the economy, and officials appeared to be in no hurry to make any changes.

Meanwhile, the situation worsened. In the absence of capital controls, wealthy Mexicans spent their money abroad on consumer durables and investments that would shelter them against another possible devaluation. With the government continuing to exude confidence up to the last hour, a devaluation of over 40 percent was announced on February 17, 1982, bringing the new rate to 38.50 pesos to the dollar. At the same time the government announced that it hoped to keep the exchange rate to a level of 38–43 pesos during the rest of the year. In an interesting move, a subsequent devaluation was announced on February 26, 1982, to 47.25 pesos, rendering obsolete the prediction of slightly a week earlier.

The two devaluations were not successful. In August 1982, after another devaluation, the government decided to establish two exchange rates: a preferential rate and a free-market rate. The official rate was only 49 pesos, unfortunately, and the free-market rate shot up to 105 pesos.

In September 1982 the government nationalized all private banks and instituted currency controls. In addition to these rules, the government established a fixed priority list for determining who would get foreign exchange.

A preferential rate of 50 pesos was established for imports of basic foods and capital goods needed to produce food, intermediate products and capital goods needed to keep industry functioning, and capital goods for industrial expansion.

Importers faced obstacles in getting foreign exchange, even when they were high enough on the priority list to be eligible for foreign exchange. However, the controls did recognize the contribution of exports to the generation of foreign exchange. For materials imported and incorporated in export products the preferential rate could be used even if such materials were not on the preferential list if the exported product generated more foreign exchange than the cost of the import.

During the 1980s, the peso continued to weaken. Fueled by inflation that averaged a low of 59.2 percent in 1984 and a high of 159.2 percent in 1987, the peso fell to a year-end rate of 143.9 pesos per dollar in 1983 and 2281 pesos per dollar in 1988.

During 1988 there were two exchange markets in Mexico: the controlled market and the free market. Transactions in the controlled market included (1) merchandise export receipts (with some exceptions); (2) payments by in-bond industries for wages, salaries, leasings or rents, and the purchase of Mexican goods and services, other than fixed assets; (3) royalties for the use of foreign technologies and patents; (4) payments of principal, interest, and related expenses resulting from financial and suppliers' credits by the public and private sectors; (5) payments for imports with some exceptions; (6) expenses in relation to the Mexican foreign service and contributions regarding Mexico's membership in international organizations; and (7) other transactions specifically authorized by the Secretariat of Finance and Public Credit.

Those who wished to convert pesos in the controlled market could use a retail exchange rate that was determined between the participant and the banks, or at the "equilibrium exchange rate," which was determined for the controlled market each day at a fixing session at the Bank of Mexico in which the major banks exchanged bids for purchases and sales of foreign exchange. For example, on December 30, 1988, the equilibrium exchange rate in the controlled market for the U.S. dollar was Mex $2281 per U.S. $1, and the buying and selling rates in the same market were Mex $2241 and Mex $2273 per U.S. $1, respectively. On the same date in the free market, the buying and selling rates for the dollar were Mex $2270 and Mex $2330, respectively. In the free market, there were no limitations to the access to, ownership, or transfer of foreign exchange.

The Bank of Mexico provided an instrument for forward cover of foreign exchange for the repayment of certain foreign-debt obligations. Since 1987, the Bank of Mexico also began to operate a short-term foreign-exchange risk coverage market through which commercial and financial operations are covered against exchange fluctuations. The scheme applies only to the U.S. dollar, and the coverage is based on the equilibrium exchange rate prevailing on the date of the contract.

In 1988 there were also a variety of import controls and controls on access to foreign exchange. In the controlled market, importers could acquire foreign exchange for the full value of merchandise already imported and for which payment had not yet been made. Full advance payment for all imports was also allowed, if the value of the goods did not exceed U.S. $10,000 or if the payment was made through a letter of credit. For purchases in excess of U.S. $10,000, only 20 percent advance payment was allowed.

In July 1988 Carlos Salinas de Gortari was elected President in Mexico, and he took office on December 1. At that time, he speeded up the process of economic liberalization by liberalizing trade and foreign investment and by embarking on an ambitious privatization program. It soon became obvious that the centerpiece of his economic program was the control of inflation. Consumer price increases fell to 19.7 percent by 1989 year-end, and they were expected to rebound to nearly 30 percent by 1990 year-end. However, Salinas continued to work to control inflation, and many experts predicted inflation below 20 percent by the end of 1991 and possibly single digits thereafter. As a commitment to those policies, the government extended the Pact for Stabilization and Economic Growth (PECE) through the end of 1991.

The Pact relies on continued price controls and a decline in the rate of daily peso slippage. In order to reduce inflation induced by higher-priced imports, the government decided to formally devalue the peso by P0.8 per day. However, that slippage was reduced to P0.4 per day at the end of 1990. The feeling in Mexico was that the peso was overvalued and that exports were becoming increasingly difficult. However, strong oil revenues and the repatriation of capital into Mexico were helping to keep the peso in line. This inflow of capital nearly eliminated the difference between the official and free-market exchange rates by the end of 1990.

The controlled exchange rate was expected to reach about Mex $2951 by the end of 1990, and many experts were predicting major changes in the exchange rate in 1991. Given that 64.2 percent of Mexico's exports are to and 68.2 percent of its imports are from the United States, it made sense for the Mexican government to tie its currency to the U.S. dollar. The key to a parity with the dollar is the elimination of inflation. A total freeze in the peso/dollar exchange rate was expected to be announced during the third quarter of 1991, together with a new currency unit (a New Peso) worth 1000 old pesos and a maxi-devaluation of about 24 percent that would produce a fixed new parity of four new pesos per dollar. If inflation could be controlled, that would allow the new exchange rate to remain at four new pesos to the dollar for the foreseeable future and the elimination of a controlled/free-market differential.

Questions

1. At the end of 1990, there were no forward quotes for the Mexican peso and no futures or options quotes either. Why do you think that was the case then? Is it still the case today? Why or why not?
2. Why did the Mexican government establish a controlled foreign-exchange market, and why did that market differ from the free market?
3. What problems do you think that you would face as a business trying to operate in two different foreign-exchange markets?
4. What were some of the ways that the Mexican government has tried to control access to foreign exchange in the past?
5. Why do you think that the government has tried to eliminate foreign-exchange controls? What are the keys to success in those efforts?

Chapter Notes

1. Julian Walmsley, *The Foreign Exchange Handbook* (New York: Wiley, 1983), pp. 7–8.
2. Federal Reserve Board of New York.
3. International Monetary Fund, *Exchange Arrangements and Exchange Restrictions Annual Report, 1989* (Washington, D.C.: IMF, 1989), pp. 568–572.
4. *Ibid.,* p. 109.
5. *Ibid.*
6. *Ibid.,* p. 110.

7. *Ibid.,* p. 97.

8. *Ibid.,* pp. 23–24.

9. Pompiliu Verzariu, *Countertrade, Barter, Offsets* (New York: McGraw-Hill, 1985), flyleaf.

10. The illustrations in this section are from *Wall Street Journal,* May 18, 1977, p. 1.

11. Verzariu, *op. cit.,* p. 27.

12. K. Alec Chrystal, "A Guide to Foreign Exchange Markets," *Bulletin* (St. Louis, Mo.: Federal Reserve Bank of St. Louis, March 1984), pp. 11–16.

13. Richard Moxon, "The Mexican Peso," in Robert S. Carlson, H. Lee Remmers, Christine Hekman, David K. Eiteman, and Arthur I. Stonehill, eds., *International Finance Cases and Simulation* (Reading, Mass.: Addison-Wesley, 1980), pp. 22–23; "Acme Do Mexico, S.A.," a case by Ingo Walter, Graduate School of Business, New York University, 1983; "Mexico Lists Priority Items for Imports," *Wall Street Journal,* 20 September 1982, p. 28; Lawrence Rout, "Mexican Firms May Be Able to Get Dollars . . . ," *Wall Street Journal,* 3 September 1982, p. 3; Lawrence Rout, "Mexicans Start Picking Up the Pieces after Last Week's 30% Devaluation," *Wall Street Journal,* 23 February 1982, p. 30; Lawrence Rout, "Mexico Seeking to Hold Peso at 38 to Dollar," *Wall Street Journal,* 22 February 1982; Lawrence Rout, "Mexico Ponders the Peso's Problems," *Wall Street Journal,* 28 January 1982, p. 27; "Mexico Eases Down the Peso," *Business Week,* 31 August 1981, p. 79; "Business Outlook Mexico," *Business Latin America* (New York: Business International Corporation, 10 December 1990), pp. 400–402; "Mexico Prolongs PECE, Reduces Devaluation Pace," *Business Latin America* (New York: Business International Corporation, 19 November 1990), pp. 365–366; The Economist Intelligence Unit, *Mexico Third Quarter 1990* (London: The Economist Intelligence Unit for Business International Corporation, 1990); International Monetary Fund, *Exchange Arrangements and Exchange Restrictions Annual Report 1989* (Washington, D.C.: IMF, 1989).

CHAPTER **8**

THE DETERMINATION OF EXCHANGE RATES

A fair exchange brings no quarrel.
DANISH PROVERB

Objectives

- To describe the International Monetary Fund and its role in the determination of exchange rates.

- To discuss the major exchange-rate arrangements under which the currencies of the world function.

- To identify the major determinants of exchange rates in the spot and forward markets.

- To explain what the balance of payments is and how it affects exchange rates.

- To show how to forecast exchange-rate movements.

- To explain how exchange rates influence business decisions.

As explained by the IMF and illustrated in Map 8.1, "The currency of Japan is the Japanese yen. The authorities of Japan do not maintain margins in respect of exchange transactions, and exchange rates are determined on the basis of underlying demand and supply conditions in the exchange markets. However, the authorities intervene when necessary in order to counter disorderly conditions in the markets. The principal intervention currency is the U.S. dollar. . . . Authorized banks may freely carry out spot and forward exchange transactions with their customers, nonresident banks, and among themselves. Forward exchange contracts may be negotiated against foreign currencies quoted on the Tokyo exchange market and in other major international foreign-exchange markets. There are no officially set rates in the forward market, and forward exchange transactions are based on free-market rates. There are no taxes or subsidies on purchases or sales of foreign exchange."

Thus the yen is very different from the peso described in the previous chapter. It is a floating currency that is not subject to the same types of controls as the Mexican peso.

The yen was trading at 251 yen per dollar as recently as 1985. As noted in Table 8.1, by mid-1985 the dollar began its long slide against the yen, and by the end of 1988 it was worth only 125.85 yen. However, 1989 and early 1990 were a period of weakening of the yen against the dollar. The dollar rose to 132.05 yen at the end of the first quarter of 1989, 144.1 at the end of the second quarter, 139.3 at the end of the third quarter, and 143.45 at the end of the fourth quarter.

These moves in late 1989 went against conventional wisdom. Most economists felt that the yen would move to 100 yen per dollar by the end of 1989, but a number of domestic and international problems tempered

C A S E
THE JAPANESE YEN[1]

that enthusiasm in 1989. A stock scandal including many of Japan's top political and business leaders (the Recruit Scandal), the massacre in Tiananmen Square in China, and the proposed unification of East and West Germany led to a weakening of the yen. In addition, there was a great deal of confidence in the U.S. government's ability to manage its economy. As noted in Table 8.1, however, there was a huge gap in dollar-denominated and yen-denominated securities, driving up the demand for dollars.

Part of the difference in interest rates was explained by the difference in consumer prices, but investors could still get a relatively higher real return on investment in securities in the United States.

There were clearly some trouble spots in the Japanese economy. The stock market began a decline in late 1989, and inflationary pressures were beginning to rise. In early 1990 there was an open debate between the Ministry of Finance and the Bank of Tokyo over what the interest-rate policy should be. That debate drove the stock market down even further and shook investors' confidence in the Japanese government's ability to manage the economy and, therefore, the exchange rate.

Year	Yen(¥) per dollar at year end
1970	357.65
1975	305.15
1980	203.0
1981	219.9
1982	235.0
1983	232.2
1984	251.1
1985	200.5
1986	159.1
1987	123.5
1988	125.85
1989	143.45
1990	134.4

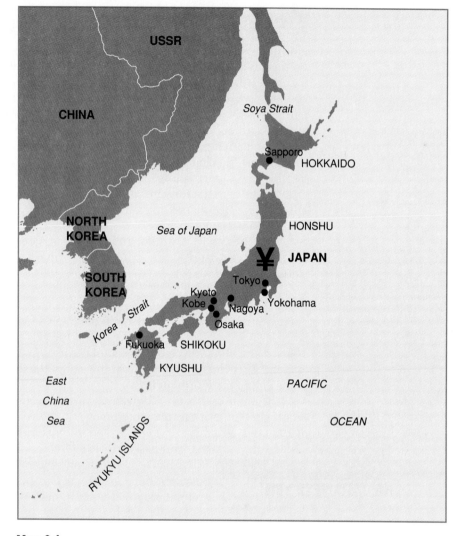

Map 8.1
Japan and the Japanese Yen
The Japanese yen has strengthened significantly against the U.S. dollar since World War II. Although the yen fluctuates against the dollar on a daily basis, the year-end exchange rate in yen per dollars is indicative of the movement in the value of the yen over time.

Even though Japan had enjoyed the world's largest current-account surplus (excess of exports over imports), that surplus had fallen by one third since 1987 due to the huge outflow of Japanese capital. Since prices on Japanese assets, especially land and buildings, have risen dramatically in recent years, Japanese investors have found that they can get a better yield

TABLE 8.1 | **JAPAN/WORLD DATA** Consumer prices and government bond rates tend to be lower in Japan than in the industrial countries in general and the United States in particular.

Data Classifications	1985	1986	1987	1988	1989
Yen/dollar year-end					
exchange rate	200.50	159.10	123.50	125.85	143.45
Consumer prices*:					
World	10.1	7.2	9.2	13.1	17.0
Industrialized countries	4.1	2.4	3.0	3.4	4.5
Developed countries	35.3	27.0	35.3	57.0	77.8
United States	3.6	1.9	3.7	4.0	4.8
United Kingdom	6.1	3.4	4.1	4.9	7.8
Germany	2.2	−0.1	0.2	1.3	2.8
Japan	2.0	0.6	0.0	0.7	2.3
Government bond rates:					
United States	10.62	7.68	8.38	8.85	8.50
United Kingdom	10.62	9.87	9.48	9.36	9.58
Germany	6.87	5.92	5.84	6.10	7.09
Japan	6.34	4.94	4.21	4.27	5.05

*Consumer prices reflect the change in the consumer price index over the prior year.

on their money outside of Japan. Thus the Japanese invested $26 billion overseas in 1989, up 21 percent from 1988. Their export of capital actually exceeded their current-account surplus.

As the fear of inflation began to rise in Japan, the natural response would have been to increase interest rates. The governor of the Bank of Japan decided to increase interest rates in December 1989, but the furor that ensued caused him to delay any further increases. Given that interest rates in the United States were also high at the time due to inflationary concerns, the demand for yen fell and the demand for dollars rose, increasing the price of the dollar in terms of yen. Although the yen was falling, the Japanese government couldn't figure out how to deal with it. In the first three months of 1990, the Bank of Japan used 17 percent of its foreign-exchange reserves to sell dollars for yen, hoping to prop up the yen. The United States contributed to this effort by selling dollars for yen, but it didn't want to push the dollar down too much for fear of losing the battle against inflation. Both Japan and the United States tried to convince the governments of other countries, such as Germany and Britain, to go along, but the U.S. government wanted those countries to use their own currencies rather than U.S. dollars. However, the market realized that intervention would not solve the problems, and that the solution lay in interest-rate policy.

By the end of summer 1990, many analysts were predicting that the yen would be at 160 yen to the dollar by the end of 1990. However, the U.S. economy began to weaken, and interest rates came down as the government tried to avoid a recession. The Gulf crisis momentarily strengthened the dollar against the yen, but the economic fundamentals were more important. As yen interest rates rose and dollar interest rates fell, the demand for the dollar fell, and so did the price. By the end of 1990, the yen was hovering at 130 yen per dollar, after experiencing a high of 124.33 in the previous 12 months and a low of 159.79.

INTRODUCTION

As discussed in the preceding chapter, an exchange rate represents the number of units of one currency needed to acquire one unit of a currency of another country. The definition seems simple, but how is that exchange rate initially determined, and what causes it to change? This chapter takes a closer look at exchange rates and how they are determined. In addition, it focuses on some of the key management decisions that are influenced by exchange-rate changes. Management must make decisions about the sourcing of raw materials and components, the location of manufacturing and assembly, and the location of final markets. Exchange rates can exert a strong influence on any of these decisions.

THE INTERNATIONAL MONETARY SYSTEM

The International Monetary Fund

The Depression, economic isolation, and trade wars of the 1930s were followed by the global conflict of World War II. Toward the close of World War II in 1944, the major Western governments met to determine what international institutions were needed to bring relative economic stability and growth to the free world. As a result of the meetings, the **International Monetary Fund (IMF)** and World Bank were organized.

The IMF was organized to promote exchange-rate stability and facilitate the international flow of currencies.

The IMF was signed into existence in the United States in 1945 by 29 nations; the agreement now includes 151 countries. The IMF's major objectives are to promote exchange stability, maintain orderly exchange arrangements, avoid competitive currency devaluation, establish a multilateral system of payments, eliminate exchange restrictions, and create standby reserves.

The **Bretton Woods** system, named after the location of the 1944 conference, operated under a principle of fixed exchange rates by which each member country established a par value for its currency based on gold and the U.S. dollar. This **par value** became a benchmark by which the country related its currency to the currencies of the rest of the world. Currencies were allowed to vary within 1 percent of par value (extended to 2.25 percent in December 1971), depending on supply and demand conditions. Further moves from par value and formal changes in par value (through devaluation or revaluation) were made with the IMF's approval.

Par value is the benchmark value of a currency initially quoted in terms of gold and the U.S. dollar.

Because of the strength of the U.S. dollar during the 1940s and 1950s, member currencies were denominated in terms of gold and dollars. By 1947 the United States held 70 percent of the international official gold reserves. Because of this, governments bought and sold dollars rather than gold. It was understood, although not formalized, that the United States would redeem gold for dollars, and the two became fixed with respect to each other. The dollar thus became the benchmark of the world trading currency.

The Board of Governors is the highest authority of the fund, and it is comprised of a representative of each member country. The number of votes that a country gets depends on the size of its quota. Although the Board of Governors is the ultimate authority in key matters, it delegates day-to-day authority to a 22-person Board of Executive Directors. This Board tends to operate by consensus, even though the strength of each vote is based on the size of the quota.

When a country is selected by the Board of Governors to join the IMF, it is assigned a quota related to its national income, monetary reserves, trade balance, and other economic indicators. The quota, which determines a country's voting power and other issues, can be paid in Special Drawing Rights and the country's currency.

Problems with Liquidity   The problem with the system as envisioned by the IMF was that, in practice, rigidity replaced stability. Countries did not allow an exchange-rate alteration to occur until a crisis developed. It became more and more evident that, as the world's reserve currency, the dollar was in a difficult position. As other countries' economies began to strengthen, it appeared that gold and internationally acceptable currencies (initially known as the **official reserves**) could not handle the reserve requirements of a country. The freer flow of goods and capital put increasing pressure on a country's reserve assets. Also, the growing accumulation of dollars outside of the United States during the 1960s threatened to wreck the stability of the system of fixed exchange rates. The problem was that governments became increasingly uneasy about the currency (i.e., the dollar) component of their reserves. Thus they tended to want to replace these currencies with gold. As trade increased, the ratio of reserves to trade decreased sharply.[2]

Special Drawing Right (SDR) was

- A unit of account developed by the IMF
- Designed to increase world liquidity

Currencies making up the SDR "basket" are the U.S. dollar, the German mark, the Japanese yen, the French franc, and the British pound.

To help increase international reserves during the period when the United States was expected to be able to reduce its balance-of-payments deficit, the IMF created the **Special Drawing Right (SDR).** The SDR is a unit of account that was created by the IMF and distributed to nations to expand their official reserves base. Brazil, for example, could trade some of its SDRs to the United States for dollars. The first SDR allocation was made in 1970. Initially, the SDR was denominated in gold, then by a basket of 16 currencies. On January 1, 1981, the IMF began to use a simplified basket of 5 currencies for determining valuation: the U.S. dollar (40 percent); the German mark (19 percent); and the Japanese yen, French franc, and British pound sterling (13 percent each). These specific weights were chosen because they broadly reflected the relative importance of the currencies in international trade and payments, which in turn are based on the value of the export of goods and services by the countries issuing these currencies.

The SDR has not taken over the role of gold or the dollar as a primary reserve asset, but it has become a **unit of account.** This means simply that the SDR has become a benchmark, or reference point, for a variety of transactions. The IMF uses the SDR rather than a specific national currency in most of its official reports. In addition, several countries base their currency on the value of the SDR or a combination of the SDR and another currency.

The SDR has become a unit of account (benchmark) for official IMF transactions.

Evolution to Floating Exchange Rates   As just mentioned, the IMF's initial system was a system of fixed exchange rates. Because the U.S. dollar was the cornerstone of the international monetary system, its value remained constant with respect to gold. Other countries could change the value of their currencies against gold and the dollar, but the value of the dollar remained fixed.

Partly because of the inflationary pressures that began to build in the United States in the mid-1960s, the traditional U.S. trade surplus began to shrink. Continued outflow of private and governmental long-term capital, coupled with the diminishing trade surplus, caused an increasing deficit in the balance of trade and capital. As it became apparent that 1971 would see the first U.S. balance-of-trade deficit in the twentieth century, it was clear that something had to be done.

On August 15, 1971, President Nixon announced a new economic policy that included the suspension of exchanging gold for dollars and the institution of an import surcharge. These moves were an attempt to force the other industrial countries to the bargaining table in hopes of restructuring the world monetary order. The Smithsonian Agreement of December 1971 resulted in an 8 percent devaluation of the dollar, a revaluation of some other world currencies, a widening of exchange-rate flexibility (from 1 to 2.25 percent on either side of par value), and a commitment on the part of all countries to reduce trade restrictions, thus allowing goods and services to flow according to supply and demand.

Exchange flexibility was widened from 1 percent to 2.25 percent on either side of par value in 1971.

This restructuring of the international monetary system did not last. World currency markets remained unsteady during 1972, and the dollar was devalued again by 10 percent in early 1973. Major currencies began to float against each other instead of relying on the Smithsonian Agreement.

Because the Bretton Woods Agreement was based on the system of fixed exchange rates and par values, the IMF had to change its Article of Agreement in order to permit floating exchange rates. The Jamaica Agreement of 1976 provided the amendment to the original Articles of Agreement that permitted greater flexibility in exchange rates. There was some concern that the world monetary system would collapse under the freedom of flexible exchange rates, so the agreement reiterated the importance of pursuing exchange stability.

The Jamaica Agreement resulted in greater exchange-rate flexibility.

Exchange-Rate Arrangements

The Jamaica Agreement formalized the break from fixed exchange rates. As part of this move, the IMF permitted countries to select and maintain an exchange arrangement of their choice, as long as they properly communicated their arrangement to the IMF. Each year the IMF receives information from the member countries and classifies each country into one of three broad categories:

1. currencies that are pegged to a single currency or to a composite of currencies;

2. currencies whose exchange rates have displayed limited flexibility compared with either a single currency or group of currencies; and

3. currencies whose exchange rates are more flexible.[3]

There are three major IMF categories for exchange-rate systems.

Table 8.2 identifies the countries that fit in each category. Note that the countries in each category are subject to change each year. In 1983, for example, there were 38 countries pegged to the U.S. dollar, compared with only 31 in 1985 and 28 by mid-1990; there were 33 countries in the more-flexible category in 1983, compared with 48 in mid-1990.

Pegged Rates   Countries that fit in this category **peg,** or fix, the value of their currency with zero-fluctuation margins (in this case, of countries that peg to a single currency) or very narrow margins of 1 percent or less in the case of pegs to the SDR or other composite currency. Countries in the "other-composite" subcategory have selected a basket of currencies that is different from the SDR. An example of this is the Swedish krona:

In the pegged-rate system, countries fix the value of their currency to another currency or composite of currencies.

> In managing the exchange rate of the krona, the Sveriges Riksbank (the central bank) is guided by a trade-weighted index based on a basket of 15 currencies of Sweden's most important trading partners. In constructing the index, the Swedish authorities established two criteria to be met by each country and currency included in the basket: (1) the country had to account for at least 1 percent of Sweden's total foreign trade (exports minus imports) during the previous five-year period, and (2) each currency had to be quoted daily on the foreign-exchange market in Stockholm. The weights are proportional to Sweden's foreign trade with each of the countries whose currencies are included in the index, with the exception that the weight of the U.S. dollar has been doubled and that of the other currencies adjusted accordingly. To take account of changes in average trade shares, the weights are adjusted each year (on April 1) on the basis of trade statistics for the last five calendar years.[4]

In 1989 the three most important currencies in the basket were the U.S. dollar (22.8 percent), the deutsche mark (16.0 percent), and the pound sterling (11.7 percent).

Limited Flexibility   As shown in Table 8.2, the "limited-flexibility" category of arrangements is divided into two subcategories. In the first subcategory,

TABLE 8.2 | EXCHANGE-RATE ARRANGEMENTS AS OF JUNE 30, 1990 The United States dollar tends to be an important benchmark for countries in the pegged and limited-flexibility categories, and it is an independently floating currency.

| | CURRENCY PEGGED TO | | | |
U.S. Dollar	French Franc	Other Currency	SDR	Other Composite
Afghanistan	Benin	Bhutan (Indian rupee)	Burundi	Algeria
Angola	Burkina Faso	Kiribati (Australian dollar)	Iran, I.R. of	Austria
Antigua & Barbuda	Cameroon		Libya	Bangladesh
Bahamas, The	C. African Rep.	Lesotho (South African rand)	Myanmar	Botswana
Barbados	Chad		Rwanda	Cape Verde
Belize	Comoros	Swaziland (South African rand)	Seychelles	Cyprus
Djibouti	Congo		Zambia	Fiji
Dominica	Côte d'Ivoire	Tonga (Australian dollar)		Finland
Dominican Rep.	Equatorial Guinea			Hungary
Ethiopia	Gabon			Iceland
Grenada	Mali			Israel
Guyana	Niger			Jordan
Haiti	Senegal			Kenya
Iraq	Togo			Kuwait
Jamaica				Malawi
Liberia				Malaysia
Nicaragua				Malta
Oman				Mauritius
Panama				Morocco
Peru				Mozambique
St. Kitts & Nevis				Nepal
St. Lucia				Norway
St. Vincent				Papua New Guinea
Sudan				Poland
Suriname				Romania
Syrian Arab Rep.				Sao Tome & Principe
Trinidad and Tobago				Solomon Islands
Yemen, Republic of				Somalia
				Sweden
				Tanzania
				Thailand
				Uganda
				Vanuatu
				Western Samoa
				Zimbabwe

FLEXIBILITY LIMITED IN TERMS OF A SINGLE CURRENCY OR GROUP OF CURRENCIES			MORE FLEXIBLE		
Single Currency	Cooperative Arrangements		Adjusted According to a Set of Indicators	Other Managed Floating	Independently Floating
Bahrain	Belgium		Chile	China, P.R.	Argentina
Qatar	Denmark		Colombia	Costa Rica	Australia
Saudi Arabia	France		Madagascar	Ecuador	Bolivia
United Arab Emirates	Germany		Portugal	Egypt	Brazil
	Ireland			Greece	Canada
	Italy			Guinea	E. Salvador
	Luxembourg			Guinea-Bissau	Gambia, The
	Netherlands			Honduras	Ghana
	Spain			India	Guatemala
				Indonesia	Japan
				Korea	Lebanon
				Lao P.D. Rep	Maldives
				Mauritania	New Zealand
				Mexico	Nigeria
				Pakistan	Paraguay
				Singapore	Philippines
				Sri Lanka	Sierra Leone
				Tunisia	South Africa
				Turkey	United Kingdom
				Vietnam	United States
				Yugoslavia	Uruguay
					Venezuela
					Zaire

Source: International Monetary Fund, *International Financial Statistics* (Washington, D.C.: IMF, October 1990), p. 22.

"flexibility limited vis-à-vis a single currency," the exchange rates fluctuate within a 2.25 percent margin. In all four cases the U.S. dollar is the benchmark for the currencies. The 2.25 percent margin is consistent with the Smithsonian Agreement signed in 1971, which increased the flexibility in the par value system from 1 percent to 2.25 percent.

The other subcategory, "cooperative agreements," refers to the **European Monetary System (EMS).** The EMS was created in 1979 as a means of creating exchange stability within the members of the European Community (EC). The major reason for this movement was to facilitate trade among

The EMS is a system of limited flexibility where countries agree to hold their values within limits of member countries.

the members of the EC by minimizing exchange-rate fluctuations. The EMS is a series of exchange relationships determined by the Council of Economics and Finance Ministers, and the Committee of Central Bank Governors of the EC that link the currencies of most EC members through a parity grid. A central exchange rate is determined for the currency of each country participating in the EMS by the use of a **European Currency Unit (ECU).** The ECU is similar to the SDR in concept, except that the basket includes the currencies of all countries in the EC, including those not actually part of the EMS.

However, the ECU is different from the SDR in that it is being discussed as the common currency of the EC. Corporations can use the ECU for accounting purposes, and there are ECU bonds and EC traveler's checks.

Once the central exchange rate is determined for the currency of each country in the EMS, a parity exchange rate is determined for each pair of countries. For example, there would be a parity rate for the French franc and German mark, for the Italian lira and French franc, and so on. With the exception of the Italian lira and British pound, which are permitted a fluctuation of 6 percent, bilateral rates are allowed to deviate from the central parity rates by only 2.25 percent before the respective central banks must intervene to protect the integrity of the central rate.

The tenth country to join the EMS was Britain, in 1990. Prime Minister Margaret Thatcher's main reservations about joining the EMS were that Britain would have to engage in a very restrictive monetary policy sponsored by the Bundesbank (the German Central Bank) and that significant unemployment would follow. British interest rates in 1990 climbed to 15 percent, strengthening the pound against the dollar and most major European currencies. This position of strength allowed Britain to join the EMS by the end of the year.

As Europe approaches even greater economic integration, there is some talk of establishing a European Central Bank and a single currency instead of separate national currencies coordinated by the EMS. This would result in the elimination of the "cooperative-arrangements" category, but as of the end of 1990, there was no guarantee that such a move would take place.

Frequent changes in the value of a currency or total freedom to float according to supply and demand are the hallmarks of "more flexibility."

More Flexibility   The final major category of exchange arrangements is called "more flexible." In countries whose currencies float independently, government intervention occurs only to influence but not neutralize the speed of movement of the exchange-rate change as we saw in the introductory case on Japan. The leaders of the major industrial countries meet periodically to discuss common economic issues, and exchange-rate values are often on the agenda. The Plaza meeting of the G-7 in 1985 was where the governments announced that the dollar had been strong too long, and this declaration caused the dollar to begin its slide. However, there were strong economic fundamentals that contributed to the dollar's fall, not just the intervention of these governments. In 1991 the G-7 countries were to meet to discuss the weakness of the dollar and decide whether or not they would intervene to prop up the dollar.

The currencies in the "independently floating" subcategory are of prime importance in the world economy. In 1988, for example, the four major currencies that comprised the official holdings of foreign exchange of the member countries of the IMF were the U.S. dollar (63.3 percent), the deutsche mark (16.2 percent), the Japanese yen (7.2 percent), and the pound sterling (3.1 percent).[5]

In the "other-managed-floating" subcategory, governments usually set rates for short intervals, such as a week at a time, and buy and sell the currency at that rate for that period. Mexico is an example of a country that is in this category. As discussed in the previous chapter, the Mexican government determined in 1990 that it would let the value of the Mexico peso slide by 0.4 pesos per dollar per day. The basic determination of the amount of the change was the inflation differential between Mexico and the United States and the desire on the part of the Mexican government to not allow imports to have an inflationary impact on the Mexican economy.

The final subcategory, currencies that are "adjusted according to a set of indicators," includes the Malagasy franc of Madagascar. The Malagasy franc's exchange rate "is managed flexibly with reference to a basket of several currencies. The weight assigned to each currency in the basket is based on the distribution of Madagascar's trade during 1973–1980. There is no single intervention currency, although the majority of transactions take place in French francs and U.S. dollars. In accordance with the movement in the basket, the Central Bank of Madagascar adjusts the Malagasy franc exchange rates on a daily basis against ten currencies which it quotes."[6]

Parallel Markets   As shown in Table 8.2, only 23 of the 151 countries of the IMF that reported their exchange-rate arrangement have currencies that are floating independently.

Many of the other countries control their currencies fairly rigidly. Some of them license their exchange, as noted in Chapter 7, so that residents and nonresidents alike do not enjoy full convertibility. In many of these cases a black market parallels the official market. The less flexibility there is, the likelier there is to be a black market. However, even Mexico, a country in the "other-managed-floating" category, has a black market for its currency. In these countries, the black market is aligned more closely with the forces of supply and demand than is the official market. The black market exists because the government buys dollars for less than the market thinks they are worth. In economic theory, if the government's official rate for the currency is overvalued, the black market tends to undervalue the same currency. The true economic value is probably somewhere in between.

The black, or parallel, market closely approximates real supply and demand for a currency.

The Role of Central Banks

Each country has a central bank responsible for the policies that affect the value of its currency on world markets. The central bank in the United States is actually the Federal Reserve System (the Fed), a system of twelve banks, each representing a region of the United States. The New York Federal Reserve Bank handles the system's intervention in the foreign-exchange markets. Intervention policies are determined by the Federal Open Market Committee. However, the Fed does not act independently of the rest of government; in particular, the Secretary of the Treasury is legally responsible for stabilizing the exchange value of the dollar.[7]

In spite of the unique nature of the central bank system in each country there is some semblance of international cooperation through the **Bank for International Settlement (BIS)** in Basel, Switzerland. One of the functions of the BIS is to act as a central banker's bank. It gets involved in swaps and other currency transactions between central banks in the major industrial countries. In addition, central bankers can gather there to discuss monetary cooperation. As mentioned earlier in the chapter, the European Community has been discussing establishing one exchange rate in Europe to replace individual national currencies, but that would require a central bank in Europe to help establish monetary policy and intervene in currency markets.

Central banks often control the value of their currencies through intervention.

THE DETERMINATION OF EXCHANGE RATES

As noted earlier, exchange rates are either freely floating or fixed to something. The following sections explain how rates change under three major types of exchange-rate systems: freely fluctuating, managed fixed, and automatic fixed. In addition, the roles of purchasing-power parity, the Fisher Effect, and other factors related to the relationships between currencies are discussed.

Major Types of Exchange Systems

Freely Fluctuating   To understand the law of supply and demand as it relates to foreign exchange, we will use a two-country model involving the United States and Japan. Figure 8.1 illustrates the concept of equilibrium in the market and then a movement to a new equilibrium level as situations change. The demand for yen in this example is a function of U.S. demand for: (1) Japanese goods and services and (2) yen-denominated financial assets. An example of the former would be the U.S. demand for yen to buy

Demand for a country's currency is a function of the demand for goods, services, and financial assets of that country.

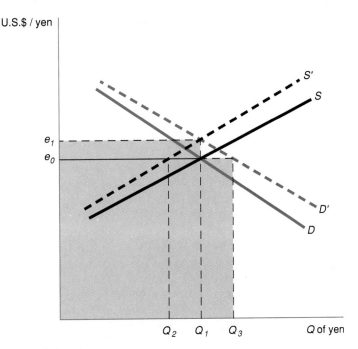

Figure 8.1
Equilibrium Exchange Rate
Due to relatively high inflation in the United States, the demand for yen rises but the supply for yen falls, increasing the value of the yen in terms of U.S. dollars.

Japanese-made autos. An example of the latter would be U.S. demand for yen to buy Japanese securities. The supply of yen (which is tied to the demand for dollars in this illustration) is a function of Japanese demand for: (1) U.S. goods and services and (2) dollar-denominated financial assets. Initially, the supply of and demand for yen in Fig. 8.1 is at the equilibrium exchange rate e_0 (for example, $0.00667 per yen, or 150 yen per dollar) and the quantity of yen Q_1.

Assume that there is a drop in demand for U.S. goods and services by Japanese consumers because of, say, relatively high U.S. inflation. This would result in a reduction in the supply of yen in the foreign-exchange market, causing the supply curve to shift to S'. Simultaneously the increasing prices of U.S. goods might lead to an increase in demand for Japanese goods and services by U.S. consumers, which would lead to an increase in demand for yen in the market, causing the demand curve to shift to D', and finally leading to an increase in the quantity demanded and an increase in the exchange rate. Thus the new equilibrium exchange rate will be at e_1 (for example,

$0.00769 per yen, or 130 yen per dollar). From a dollar standpoint we could say that the increase in demand for Japanese goods would lead to an increase in supply of dollars as more consumers tried to trade their dollars for yen, and a reduction in demand for U.S. goods would result in a drop in demand for dollars. This would result in a reduction in the price of the dollar, indicating a weakening or depreciation or devaluation of the dollar.

Managed Fixed Exchange Rate   In the preceding example, Japanese and U.S. authorities allowed changes in the exchange rates between their two currencies to occur in order to reach a new currency equilibrium. In fact, however, one or both of the countries might not want exchange rates to change. For example, assume that the United States and Japan decide to manage their exchange rates. The U.S. government might not want its currency to weaken, because its businesses would have to pay more for Japanese products, which would lead to more inflationary pressure in the United States. The Japanese government might not want the yen to strengthen because it would mean unemployment in its export industries. But how can the governments keep the values from changing when the United States is earning too few yen? Somehow the shortage between yen wanted and yen available must be alleviated.

Governments buy and sell their currencies in the open market as a means of influencing price.

In a managed system, the Federal Reserve of New York holds foreign-exchange reserves, which it has built up through the years for this type of contingency. It could sell enough of its yen reserves (make up the difference between Q_1 and Q_3) at the fixed exchange rate to maintain the exchange rate. Or the Japanese central bank might be willing to accept dollars so that U.S. consumers can continue to buy Japanese goods. These dollars would then become part of the Japanese foreign-exchange reserves.

The fixed rate can continue as long as the United States has reserves and/or as long as the Japanese are willing to add dollars to their holdings. Unless something changes the basic imbalance in the currency supply and demand, though, the Federal Reserve Bank of New York will run out of yen and the Japanese central bank will stop accepting dollars because it fears that it holds too many. At this point it would be necessary to change the exchange rate so as to lessen the demand for yen.

Devaluation occurs when the government reduces the value of the currency relative to a foreign currency.

Once a government decides that intervention will not work, it must adjust the value of its currency. If the currency is freely floating, the exchange rate will seek the correct level according to the laws of supply and demand. However, a currency that is pegged or fixed to another currency or to a group of currencies usually is changed on a formal basis with respect to its reference currency or currencies. This formal change is termed more accurately a devaluation or revaluation, depending on which direction the change takes. If the foreign-currency equivalent of the home currency falls (or the home-currency equivalent of the foreign currency rises), then the home currency has

Revaluation takes place when the government strengthens the value of the currency relative to a foreign currency.

devalued in relation to the foreign currency. The opposite would happen in the case of a revaluation.

Automatic Fixed Rate System   As in the managed system just discussed, let us assume that the countries have agreed to maintain fixed rates by setting their domestic money supply on the basis of the amount of reserves held by the central bank and by denominating their currency value in terms of the reserve asset. Historically, the major reserve asset has been gold. In the latter part of the nineteenth century, most countries were on a gold standard.

Consider the Japanese situation in which the United States has a shortage of yen. Under an automatic fixed rate system the United States hypothetically would now sell gold to get the needed yen. However, unlike the managed system just described, there would be automatic adjustments to prevent the United States from running out of gold. As the United States sold off some of its gold, its money supply, which is tied to the amount of gold, would then fall. This would lead to higher U.S. interest rates as well as lower U.S. investment, followed by increased unemployment and lower prices. Meanwhile, the increase in gold in Japan would be having an opposite effect. The higher interest rates in the United States than in Japan and the decrease in U.S. prices relative to Japanese prices would cause an increase in the supply of yen in the United States as funds flowed in for investments and to purchase U.S. goods and services. This would result in a strengthening of the dollar and a weakening of the yen.

Thus, although the law of supply and demand can determine exchange rates in an open market, many governments intervene in the market to impact exchange rate movements. Although the automatic fixed rate system is possible, it is not as widely seen as the freely fluctuating and managed exchange rate systems.

Purchasing-Power Parity

If home-country inflation is lower than that of the foreign country, the home currency should be stronger in value.

Purchasing-power parity (PPP) is the key theory that explains the relationships between currencies: In essence, it claims that a change in relative inflation must result in a change in exchange rates in order to keep the prices of goods in two countries fairly similar. Figure 8.1 illustrates this point. According to the PPP theory, if Japanese inflation, for example, were 3 percent and U.S. inflation were 6 percent, we would expect the value of the dollar to fall by the difference in the interest rates. That means that the dollar would be worth fewer yen than was the case before the adjustment, and the yen would be worth more dollars than before the adjustment.

In order to relate inflation to exchange-rate changes, the following formula can be used:

$$\frac{e_t - e_0}{e_0} = \frac{i_{h,t} - i_{f,t}}{1 + i_{f,t}}$$

where

e is the exchange rate quoted in terms of the number of units of the home currency for one unit of the foreign currency,

i is the rate of inflation,

h represents the home country (in these examples, the U.S.),

f represents the foreign country (in these examples, Japan),

o represents the base period, and

t represents the end of a period.

The anticipated future exchange rate would equal

$$e_t = e_0 \left(\frac{1 + i_{h,t}}{1 + i_{f,t}} \right)$$

For example, assume that the consumer price index in the United States went from 100 to 106 and the consumer price index in Japan went from 100 to 103 at a time when the exchange rate at the beginning of the period was 160 yen to the dollar, or $0.00625 per yen. Using the formula given above,

$$i_{h,t} = \frac{106 - 100}{100} = .06$$

$$i_{f,t} = \frac{103 - 100}{100} = .03$$

$$e_t = .00625 \left(\frac{1 + .06}{1 + .03} \right)$$

yields $0.00643 per dollar, or 155 yen per dollar. Thus the yen yields more dollars and the dollar is worth less yen when inflation in the United States is higher than in Japan.

The PPP theory is very useful in explaining the relationship between exchange rates, but it is not perfect. We need to make assumptions about the equilibrium exchange rate at a starting point and recognize that currencies are rarely related accurately in a two-country world. When several currencies are involved, it is difficult to use prices to determine an equilibrium rate. Also, exchange rates are essentially a function of traded goods, whereas inflation relates to all goods whether traded or not. Throughout the period since 1973, when the world essentially shifted to a floating-rate regime, those rates have not conformed to the PPP theory very accurately. In 1986, for example, the market exchange rate for the Japanese yen was 168 yen per dollar. However, the exchange rate equalized for PPP should have been 223, a difference of 24.2 percent. The West German mark was 12.5 percent weaker than it should have been, and the British pound was 19.3 percent stronger than it should have been against the U.S. dollar.[8] In 1990 the dollar/yen exchange rate fluctuated from a high of nearly 160 yen per dollar to a low of 120 yen per dollar, and yet comparative inflation did not change that much during the year. U.S. tourists also complained about how expensive it was to travel in Europe in comparison with the United States, demonstrating that purchasing-power differences existed in Europe and the United States. Finally, although relative rates of inflation may be helpful over the long run, there are many other factors that influence exchange rates, as will be seen below.

Interest Rates

To relate interest rates to exchange rates, we must first relate interest rates to inflation. This is accomplished through the Fisher Effect, which postulates that the nominal interest rate r in a country is determined by the real interest rate R and the inflation rate i as follows:

If the nominal interest rate in the home country is lower than that of the foreign country, we would expect the home country's inflation to be lower so that real interest rates would be equal.

Fisher Effect $(1 + r) = (1 + R)(1 + i)$

According to this theory, if the real interest rate is 5 percent, the rate of inflation in the United States is 2.9 percent, and the rate of inflation in Japan is 1.5 percent, then the nominal rates of interest would be computed as follows:

United States	$r = (1.05)(1.029) - 1 = 8.045$ percent
Japan	$r = (1.05)(1.015) - 1 = 6.575$ percent

Thus the difference in interest rates between the United States and Japan is a function of the difference in their inflation rates. If the inflation in the countries were the same (zero differential) but interest rates in the United States were 10 percent and in Japan were 6.575 percent, investors would place their money in the United States where they could get the higher real return.

The bridge from interest rates to exchange rates can be explained by the **International Fisher Effect (IFE).** According to the IFE, the interest-rate differential is an unbiased predictor of future changes in the spot exchange rate. An unbiased predictor is one that is neither consistently above nor below the actual future spot exchange rate. That does not mean that the interest-rate differential is an accurate predictor, just that it is unbiased.

The International Fisher Effect implies that the currency of the country with the lower interest rate will strengthen in the future.

Using Japan and the United States as an example, the IFE states that if nominal interest rates in the United States are higher than those in Japan, the value of the dollar should fall by that interest-rate differential in the future. The fall in the value of the dollar indicates a weakening or depreciation of the dollar. Remember from the Fisher Effect that nominal interest rates are higher in the United States than in Japan because inflation is also higher.

Thus if inflation is lower in Japan than in the United States, the dollar is expected to be weaker as well. That flows from the discussion that accompanies Fig. 8.1, in which consumers would demand Japanese goods rather than U.S. goods, causing an increase in demand for yen and a contraction in supply of yen. This would lead in turn to a strengthening of the yen or a weakening of the dollar.

Forward rates are determined primarily by interest-rate differentials.

The interest-rate differential is also the most important factor in the determination of forward exchange rates. For example, if exchange rates between the United States and Japan were to remain constant but the interest rates in the United States were significantly greater than the interest rates in Japan, investors would always invest in the United States. In theory, the forward rate would be the rate that exactly neutralizes the difference in interest rates between the United States and Japan. If U.S. interest rates are higher than Japanese interest rates, the forward exchange rate for the U.S. dollar would be lower than the Japanese yen by the interest-rate differential so that the yield in dollars on the U.S. investment would equal the yield in dollars of the yen investment converted at the forward rate.

Thus the forward rate allows investors to trade currencies freely for future delivery at no exchange risk and without any differential in interest income. If a difference were to exist, traders would take advantage of this and earn income until the difference were eliminated.

Although the interest-rate differential is the critical factor for a few of the most widely traded currencies, the expectation of future spot rates is also very important. Normally, a trader will automatically compute the forward rate through the interest-rate differential and then adjust it for future expectations where necessary. Some forward rates are quoted strictly on future expectations rather than on interest-rate differentials. This is especially true for currencies that are not traded very widely and for which total convertibility does not exist.

Other Factors

Other key factors are confidence and technical factors, such as the release of economic information.

A variety of other factors could cause exchange rates to change. One important determinant in a world of political and economic uncertainty is that of **confidence.** During times of turmoil, people prefer to hold currencies that are considered safe-haven currencies. During the early 1980s the U.S. dollar was considered a safe-haven currency, and this perception was an important source of its strength. In 1990, after Iraq invaded Kuwait, the dollar strengthened a little because of the safe-haven concept, but weaker economic fundamentals eventually forced the dollar down. When the Mexican peso began to slide in the early 1980s, local investors transferred large amounts of pesos out of Mexico via dollar transfers until the Mexican government clamped down. The investors had no confidence in the peso and preferred to hold dollar balances outside of Mexico.

In addition to the basic economic forces and confidence in leadership, exchange rates are influenced by a number of **technical factors,** such as the release of national economic statistics, seasonal demands for a currency, and a slight strengthening of a currency following a prolonged weakness or vice versa. For example, in late 1990, the following comment followed a moderate strengthening of the dollar in a period of dollar weakness: "Many traders and currency analysts insist that sentiment about the dollar remains bearish and argue that buying spurts seen recently were simply a correction before selling resumes. But the dollar's downward momentum has clearly slowed. Buyers tend to snap the dollar up whenever it falls too far too fast, causing violent trading action at lower levels and indicating that a bottom may be forming, traders contend."[9]

FORECASTING EXCHANGE-RATE MOVEMENTS

In the previous section we looked at the general law of supply and demand, showed how governments intervene to manage exchange-rate movements, and explained how inflation and interest rates can be important determinants of exchange rates. In this section we survey data that can be monitored in order to get an idea of what will happen to exchange-rate values.

Managers need to be concerned with the timing, size, and direction of an exchange-rate movement.

As the preceding discussion elaborates, a variety of factors influence exchange-rate movements. Managers must be able to analyze these factors in order to have a general idea of the timing, size, and direction of an exchange-rate movement. However, prediction is not a precise science, and many things can cause the best of predictions to differ significantly from reality.

For freely floating currencies, the law of supply and demand determines market value. However, very few currencies in the world are freely floating; most are managed to a certain extent, which implies that governments need to make political decisions on the value of the currency. Assuming that governments use a rational basis for managing the value of their currencies (an assumption that may not be realistic in all cases), managers can monitor some of the same indicators that they follow in order to try to predict values.

The following factors have been identified as ones that should be monitored when analysts are trying to predict an exchange-rate change or a free-market movement in rates:

1. balance-of-payments statistics,

2. interest-rate differentials,

3. inflation differentials,

4. governmental fiscal (expenditures) and monetary policies (growth in the money supply) that are important indicators of inflation,

5. the trend in exchange-rate movements,

6. an increase in the spread between official and free-exchange rates,

7. the politics of the exchange-rate change,

8. business cycles,

9. changes in international monetary reserves, and

10. governmental policies that treat symptoms rather than causes.[10]

Most of these factors have been discussed already in one form or another as major determinants of exchange rates. Others are fairly obvious. However, it is important to understand how balance-of-payments statistics are determined and how they can be used to help forecast exchange-rate changes.

The Balance of Payments

The balance of payments summarizes the international transactions between domestic and foreign residents.

A country's **balance of payments** summarizes international transactions between domestic and foreign residents. A more comprehensive definition follows:

> The balance of payments is a statistical statement for a given period showing (a) transactions in goods, services, and income between an economy and the rest of the world; (b) changes of ownership and other changes in the economy's monetary gold, special drawing rights, and claims on and liabilities to the rest of the world; and (c) unrequited transfers and counterpart entries that are needed to balance, in the accounting sense, any entries for the foregoing transactions and changes which are not mutually offsetting.[11]

The concept of double-entry accounting holds true in the balance of payments. This implies that each transaction has two entries of equal value that must be accounted for. Debit entries have a negative arithmetic sign, and credit entries have a positive arithmetic sign. The debit entries reflect payments by domestic to foreign residents, and credit entries reflect payments by foreign to domestic residents. Although this appears simple, transactions are not recorded as they are in elementary accounting. In balance-of-payments statistics, export data may come from customs records, and the payment may come from a different source. In addition, errors may occur in recording transactions and many items must be estimated, such as expenditures by tourists. Thus the balance-of-payments statistics include an account called "Errors and Omissions," which is used to balance the total debits and credits.

Table 8.3 provides balance-of-payments data for the United States. Notice that the United Nations keeps balance-of-payments data in SDRs but also provides a conversion rate at the bottom of the table.

TABLE 8.3 | U.S. BALANCE-OF-PAYMENTS STATISTICS The current account deficit has fallen since 1986, due largely to the increase in exports.

Aggregated Presentation: Transactions Data, 1982–1989 (in billions of SDRs)								
	1982	**1983**	**1984**	**1985**	**1986**	**1987**	**1988**	**1989**
A. Current Account, excl. Group F	**−6.58**	**−41.81**	**−101.97**	**−110.80**	**−113.23**	**−111.30**	**−94.38**	**−82.71**
Merchandise: exports f.o.b.	191.12	188.84	214.64	212.97	190.43	193.31	237.58	282.40
Merchandise: imports f.o.b.	−224.33	−251.88	−324.54	−332.69	−313.88	−316.60	−332.31	−370.85
Trade balance	−33.21	−63.05	−109.90	−119.72	−123.45	−123.28	−94.73	−88.45
Other goods, services, and income: credit	127.65	126.90	147.55	152.72	143.84	151.22	156.75	186.29
Reinvested earnings	*1.12*	*6.66*	*8.07*	*18.56*	*15.27*	*26.40*	*11.32*	*16.81*
Other investment income	*74.57*	*65.67*	*75.75*	*68.63*	*60.41*	*54.32*	*68.82*	*80.59*
Other	*51.96*	*54.57*	*63.73*	*65.52*	*68.17*	*70.51*	*76.61*	*88.90*
Other goods, services, and income: debit	−92.69	−96.48	−127.38	−128.67	−120.20	−128.31	−145.47	−169.41
Reinvested earnings	*2.17*	*−.09*	*−2.82*	*1.17*	*1.87*	*−1.27*	*−4.90*	*−2.66*
Other investment income	*−51.88*	*−48.97*	*−63.04*	*−63.36*	*−59.04*	*−62.50*	*−73.74*	*−93.92*
Other	*−42.97*	*−47.42*	*−61.52*	*−66.48*	*−63.03*	*−64.53*	*−66.84*	*−72.83*
Total: goods, services, and income	1.75	−32.63	−89.73	−95.67	−99.80	−100.37	−83.45	−71.56
Private unrequited transfers	−1.29	−1.20	−1.73	−2.04	−1.59	−1.43	−1.33	−1.24
Total, excl. official unrequited transfers	.45	−33.83	−91.46	−97.71	−101.39	−101.80	−84.79	−72.80
Official unrequited transfers	−7.03	−7.97	−10.52	−13.08	−11.83	−9.50	−9.59	−9.91
Grants (excluding military)	*−4.99*	*−5.91*	*−8.40*	*−10.99*	*−10.00*	*−7.79*	*−7.73*	*−8.00*
Other	*−2.05*	*−2.06*	*−2.12*	*−2.09*	*−1.83*	*−1.70*	*−1.86*	*−1.91*
B. Direct Investment and Other Long-Term Capital, excl. Groups F through H	**−6.64**	**−1.73**	**38.20**	**71.53**	**62.72**	**25.99**	**68.59**	**59.44**
Direct investment	14.78	10.79	21.91	1.42	5.87	2.14	30.43	22.40
In United States	*12.57*	*11.20*	*24.73*	*18.88*	*28.71*	*36.17*	*43.50*	*47.67*
Abroad	*2.22*	*−.41*	*−2.82*	*−17.46*	*−22.84*	*−34.03*	*−13.07*	*−25.26*
Portfolio investment	−.94	4.38	28.56	62.42	61.28	24.51	30.04	35.04
Other long-term capital								
Resident official sector	−6.04	−4.36	−4.16	−1.02	−.41	−1.16	.33	1.73
Disbursements on loans extended	*−7.81*	*−7.64*	*−7.58*	*−5.84*	*−6.06*	*−3.75*	*−4.30*	*−3.02*
Repayments on loans extended	*3.45*	*4.29*	*3.97*	*4.23*	*4.81*	*5.54*	*7.40*	*4.76*
Other	*−1.68*	*−1.01*	*−.56*	*.59*	*.84*	*−2.95*	*−2.77*	*−.01*
Deposit money banks	−14.45	−12.54	−8.11	8.72	−4.02	.50	7.80	.27
Other sectors	—	—	—	—	—	—	—	—
Total, Groups A plus B	−13.22	−43.54	−63.78	−39.26	−50.50	−85.30	−25.79	−23.27
C. Other Short-Term Capital, excl. Groups F through H	**−16.54**	**31.20**	**40.74**	**29.29**	**11.99**	**40.57**	**6.16**	**9.75**
Resident official sector	6.51	5.24	1.39	−1.37	−.32	−1.47	−.19	.81
Deposit money banks	−24.14	27.65	26.47	24.11	22.80	35.67	2.98	7.67
Other sectors	1.09	−1.69	12.88	6.56	−10.49	6.37	3.37	1.27
D. Net Errors and Omissions	**31.41**	**8.43**	**23.46**	**15.71**	**9.78**	**1.10**	**−7.14**	**27.59**
Total, Groups A through D	1.65	−3.91	.43	5.74	−28.73	−43.63	−26.77	14.06

TABLE 8.3 (continued)

	Aggregated Presentation: Transactions Data, 1982–1989 (in billions of SDRs)							
	1982	1983	1984	1985	1986	1987	1988	1989
E. Counterpart Items	−.13	−.43	−.59	1.24	1.46	.97	−.48	1.32
Monetization/ demonetization of gold	−.03	−.26	−.23	−.04	−.20	.12	−.17	.09
Allocation/cancellation of SDRs	—	—	—	—	—	—	—	—
Valuation changes in reserves	−.11	−.17	−.36	1.28	1.66	.85	−.31	1.23
Total, Groups A through E	1.52	−4.34	−.16	6.97	−27.27	−42.66	−27.25	15.39
F. Exceptional Financing	—	—	—	—	—	—	—	—
Security issues in foreign currencies	—	—	—	—	—	—	—	—
Total, Groups A through F	1.52	−4.34	−.16	6.97	−27.27	−42.66	−27.25	15.39
G. Liabilities Consituting Foreign Authorities' Reserves	2.87	5.02	2.64	−2.12	28.46	36.64	29.91	5.78
Total, Groups A through G	4.39	.68	2.48	4.85	1.19	−6.03	2.66	21.16
H. Total Change in Reserves	−4.39	−.68	−2.48	−4.85	−1.19	6.03	−2.66	−21.16
Monetary gold	.03	.25	.23	.05	.21	−.12	.17	−.11
SDRs	−1.24	−.04	−.95	−.88	−.22	−.39	.09	−.41
Reserve position in the Fund	−2.32	−4.14	−.97	.90	1.29	1.59	.76	.36
Foreign-exchange assets	−.86	3.25	−.78	−4.91	−2.46	4.94	−3.68	−21.00
Other claims	—	—	—	—	—	—	—	—
Credit from the Fund and Fund administered resources	—	—	—	—	—	—	—	—
Conversion rates: U.S. dollars per SDR	1.1040	1.0690	1.0250	1.0153	1.1732	1.2931	1.3439	1.2818

Source: International Monetary Fund, *Balance of Payments Statistics* (Washington, D.C.: IMF, May 1990), p. 22.

Types of Transactions

The current-account balance contains merchandise trade, services, and unilateral transfers.

Current Account   The **current-account balance** is very important because it summarizes the real transactions that occur in a country. The current-account balance includes merchandise trade; other goods, services, and income; and unrequited transfers. The **merchandise trade balance** is critical because of the sheer volume of transactions that takes place. The export of merchandise is a credit because it results in the receipt of payment from abroad. An import is a debit because it results in making payment to the seller abroad. The balance of trade is important, because it is the most basic measure of a country's transactions with the rest of the world. Even though the U.S.

has a large balance-of-trade deficit, it has been improving steadily since 1986. A merchandise import or export involves an exchange where a buyer in one country and a seller in another country exchange something of equal value. However, an unrequited transfer (or unilateral transfer) occurs when consideration is provided to only one party, such as aid to a drought-stricken country.

The key transactions accounted for in the services account are travel and transportation, tourism, fees and royalties, and income on investments. U.S. tourists going abroad result in a debit entry because they are transferring funds abroad to pay for the vacation. Income received from a foreign investment is treated as a credit, much like merchandise exports, because the income results in receipt of payment from foreign sources.

Direct and portfolio investments are major forms of long-term capital flows.

Long-term Capital   The major categories in long-term capital are direct investment, portfolio investment, and loans. The direct investment category reflects U.S. investment abroad and foreign investment in the United States. Foreign investment in the United States has grown steadily since 1985, and it reflects the inflow of cash that offsets the outflow from the balance-of-trade deficit. Note that a balance is given for the current account and long-term capital in Table 8.3 (Total, Groups A & B). That balance is often referred to as the **basic balance** because it measures the long-term international economic stability of a country. Supposedly it indicates productivity, factor endowments, buyer preferences, international competition, perception of the economy as a haven for investment, and the like. Although the basic balance is negative for the United States, it has been improving since 1987.

Short-term Capital   The short-term capital account represents funds that flow as a result of real transactions, such as the payment for exports and imports, as well as the flow of long-term capital transactions, such as the outflow to pay for direct investments or the inflow to recognize the receipt of investment income. In addition, it also represents speculative flows that exploit short-term interest rates and flows that respond to, say, political uncertainty.

Other Items   The category in Table 8.3 called "net errors and omissions" was defined earlier as the amount necessary to make the debits equal the credits. The items below the line (including categories E to H) represent official financing in the balance of payments. Counterpart items relate to certain changes within the official reserves and need not be discussed in detail here. Category G in Table 8.3 refers to claims that foreign official agencies have on the assets of the country. Category H is changes in the reserve position of the country. It does not represent the actual reserves, just changes in their value.

Major balances in the balance of payments are merchandise trade, current account, and the basic balance.

Surplus and Deficit   The terms **balance-of-payments deficit** and **balance-of-payments surplus** are often mentioned in the press. As was noted earlier, the balance of payments must always be in balance because of the concept of double-entry accounting. Thus the idea of a surplus or deficit must refer to a specific component of the balance of payments. The balances most often cited are the merchandise trade balance in particular and the current-account and basic balances.

Understanding these different balances can be difficult. Japan was hard to understand in mid-1990, because it had the biggest current-account surplus in the world, a growth rate of 5 percent, and an inflation rate one-half that of the industrial countries, but it still had a weak yen and a declining stock market. The problem was that its basic balance was in trouble. The current-account surplus was more than offset by an outflow of capital, and some suggested that the purchasing-power parity value of the yen was closer to 170–200 yen per dollar. The United Kingdom was in the most trouble of the industrial countries, because its current-account deficit was exacerbated by an outflow of capital, so that its basic balance was 10 percent of GNP, the largest of the industrial world. The current-account deficit of the United States was offset by the inflow of capital, but that is an unstable solution in the long run. Germany was in the best situation of all, because it had a huge current-account surplus, like Japan, but a low outflow of capital, so that its basic balance was the largest in the world. This suggests that the German mark should remain strong over the long run, whereas the yen and dollar are basically unstable, and the British pound should eventually weaken.[12]

If there is a material surplus or deficit in the balances just mentioned, there are three major ways to correct the situation: (1) disrupt trade and capital flows, (2) correct internal economic imbalances, and (3) force or allow the exchange rate to change. It would be illogical to assume that market forces are the sole determinants of trade and capital flows. Governments can and do provide incentives and disincentives in response to their own objectives and pressure from lobbyists. Even at a given level of governmental intervention, disequilibrium still can occur, leading to even more intervention. Disrupting trade and capital flows is a cosmetic solution to disequilibrium and requires specific identification of the determinants of the surplus or deficit and the policies to achieve equilibrium. Chapter 5 discussed many ways to restrict trade and capital flows, such as subsidies, tariffs, quotas, and restrictions on the repatriation of dividends. Earlier in this chapter and in Chapter 7, we showed how governments can intervene to support their currencies by buying and selling foreign exchange, using multiple exchange rates, and so on.

Ways to correct an imbalance in the balance of payments:
- Disrupt trade and capital flows
- Correct internal economic imbalances
- Force or allow the exchange rate to change

The second major way to restore equilibrium is to correct internal economic imbalances. As noted earlier, inflation is one of the major sources of a deficit in the balance of payments. Inflation can be reduced through strict monetary and fiscal policies, high interest rates, and wage and price controls.

However, this approach can lead to an economic slowdown and unemployment, both of which are very unpopular politically. Exports can also be diversified through industrialization and by shifting resources to products that are more competitive in export and import markets. Import-competing industries, where economically feasible, also can be encouraged.

In the final analysis it may be impossible to stave off a change in the exchange rate in order to try to restore equilibrium in the balance of payments. Many countries consider their balance of trade a key factor in determining whether to change the value of their currency. Analysts feel that a depreciation will make domestic products less expensive in international markets, thereby leading to an increase in exports. Simultaneously, the depreciation will make imports more expensive, resulting in a reduction in demand and thus a reduction in imports.

In looking at balance-of-payments data, especially the balance of trade, it is important to understand what is really causing a surplus or deficit. The United States has been beset with significant balance-of-trade deficits in recent years. Interestingly, imports as a percentage of GNP have not changed significantly since 1980, when imports were 10.5 percent of GNP. In 1988 they were 9 percent of GNP, and in 1989 they were 9.7 percent of GNP. However, exports as a percentage of GNP dropped steadily from 10.0 percent in 1980 to 6.7 percent in 1986. In 1988 they were only 6.6 percent of GNP, and in 1989 they were 7.5 percent of GNP. Economic growth in the United States has exceeded that of many other nations, especially the industrial countries that trade with the United States, so imports have climbed along with economic growth. The growth in imports is thus a factor in both the increase in the U.S. economy and an increase in market share in the U.S. economy. Coupled with the drop in exports as a percentage of GNP and the fact that the economies of the United States' major importers have been soft, it is obvious that the United States has some real problems. It would be too simplistic to assume that a weakening of the dollar would solve all of the trade problems of the United States.

BUSINESS IMPLICATIONS OF EXCHANGE-RATE CHANGES

Market Decisions

On the marketing side, exchange rates can affect demand for a company's products at home and abroad. A country such as Mexico may force down the value of its currency if its exports become too expensive owing to relatively high inflation. Even though inflation would cause the peso value of the Mex-

A depreciation of a currency could help imports become more expensive and exports become less expensive.

ican products to rise, the devaluation means that it takes less foreign currency to buy the pesos, thus allowing the Mexican products to remain competitive.

One interesting ramification of a peso depreciation is the impact of the cheaper Mexican goods on exporters from other countries. For example, the cheaper Mexican goods flooding the market in Argentina might take away market share from Italian exporters, thus affecting the Italian economy.

A good example of the marketing impact of exchange rate changes is the problem that Japanese car manufacturers were having selling to the United States in 1986 and 1987 due to the sharp rise in the value of the yen. As the dollar fell 47 percent against the yen in the 16 months ending in December 1986, Japanese car companies found that their cost advantage had disappeared, prices had to be increased, and profit margins had to be trimmed in order to remain competitive. In addition, Korean cars were making inroads due to the low costs and prices of Korean products. Thus a currency depreciation could result in foreign products becoming so expensive in a country like the United States that U.S. products soon would pick up market share from imports. The key is whether or not the percentage of devaluation exceeds the relative increase in inflation.

When a currency changes in value, exporters and importers need to decide whether or not to change prices.

In the case of Japan, the strengthening of the Japanese yen in the latter part of 1990 was advantageous to the Japanese in one sense—the cost of imports. Oil prices skyrocketed in late 1990 as Iraq invaded Kuwait, and oil is priced in dollars. Because the yen was rising against the dollar, the stronger yen offset the higher cost of oil.

Production Decisions

Production decisions also could be affected by an exchange-rate change. A manufacturer in a country with high wages and operating expenses might be tempted to locate production in a country such as Argentina (where the austral is rapidly losing value) because a foreign currency could buy lots of australs, making the initial investment relatively cheap. Another reason for locating in a country such as Argentina is that goods manufactured there would be relatively cheap in world markets. However, a firm could accomplish the same purpose by going to any country whose currency is expected to remain weak in relation to that of the parent-country currency. The attractiveness of a weak-currency country must be balanced with the potential problems of investing there.

Firms might invest in weak-currency countries because they are
- Relatively cheap for initial investment
- A good base for inexpensive exports

Financial Decisions

The final business area where exchange rates make a difference is in finance. The areas of finance that are most affected are the sourcing of financial resources, the remittance of funds across national borders, and the financial statements. There might be a temptation to borrow money where interest rates are lowest. However, we mentioned earlier that interest-rate differentials

Exchange rates can influence the sourcing of financial resources, the remittance of funds, and the reporting of financial results.

often are compensated for in the money markets through exchange-rate changes.

In the area of financial flows, a parent company would want to convert local currency into the parent's own currency when exchange rates are most favorable so that it can maximize its return. However, countries with weak currencies often have currency controls, making it difficult to manage the flow of funds optimally.

Finally, exchange-rate changes also can influence the reporting of financial results. A simple example can illustrate the impact that exchange rates can have on income. If the Mexican subsidiary of a U.S. company earns 100 million pesos when the exchange rate is 200 pesos per dollar, the dollar equivalent of income is $500,000. If the peso depreciates to 300 pesos per dollar, the dollar equivalent of income falls to $333,333. The opposite would occur if the local currency appreciates against the parent currency.

LOOKING TO THE FUTURE   The international monetary system has undergone significant reform in the past two decades. As the historically planned economies undergo a transition to market economies, they will feel significant pressure on their exchange rates. High rates of inflation and weak demand for those currencies will lead to major devaluations—certainly a key factor affecting the Russian rouble in March and April of 1991.

The European Monetary System should continue to strengthen, and national economic policies will be coordinated more closely as the Europeans move closer to a common currency. However, the weaker economies of some of the new entrants into the EC will continue to plague harmonization and the problems arising during the reunification of Germany will keep the German mark from soaring too high against the currencies of the other EC members.

Some of the most interesting changes in currency values will take place in the "more flexible" category. Countries in the "adjusted according to a set of indicators" and "other managed floating" categories need to gain greater control over their economies in order to move to the "independently floating" category. Countries in the latter category are under constant pressure to control inflation and to keep from being tempted to intervene in the markets.

Firms will face constant pressure to understand the factors influencing particular exchange rates and to adjust corporate strategy in anticipation of rate movements. Their job will only get easier if exchange rate volatility diminishes.

SUMMARY   ■ The International Monetary Fund (IMF) was organized in 1944 to promote exchange stability, maintain orderly exchange arrangements, avoid competitive currency devaluation, establish a multilateral system of payments, eliminate exchange restrictions, and create standby reserves.

- The Special Drawing Right (SDR) was instituted by the IMF to increase world liquidity.

- The currencies of countries that are members of the IMF are divided into three categories: those that are pegged (fixed in value) to a single currency or to a composite of currencies, those that have displayed limited flexibility compared with either a single currency or a group of currencies, and those that are more flexible.

- Many countries that strictly control and regulate the convertibility of their currencies have a parallel, or black, market that maintains an exchange rate more indicative of supply and demand than is the official rate.

- The Bank for International Settlements (BIS) in Switzerland acts as a central banker's bank. It facilitates discussion and transactions among the central banks of the world.

- The demand for a country's currency is a function of the demand for that country's goods and services and financial assets denominated in that currency.

- A central bank intervenes in currency markets by creating a supply for its currency when it wants to push the value of the currency down or creating a demand for its currency when it wants to strengthen its value.

- A devaluation of a currency occurs when formal governmental action causes the foreign-currency equivalent of that currency to fall (or that currency's equivalent of the foreign currency to rise). A depreciation occurs with a change in the same direction that is permitted by the government but not formally acted on as such.

- The major factors that determine the value of a currency are purchasing-power parity (relative rates of inflation), real interest rates (nominal interest rates reduced by the amount of inflation), confidence in the government's ability to manage the political and economic situation of the country, and certain technical factors that are a result of trading.

- The major determinant of the forward exchange rate is the interest-rate differential between currencies.

- The major factors that managers should monitor when trying to predict the direction, magnitude, and timing of an exchange-rate change are the balance-of-payments statistics, the country's reserve position, relative rates of inflation, interest-rate differentials, trends in spot rates, and the forward exchange rate. Also, they must look at the political situation.

- A country's balance-of-payments statement summarizes all international transactions by government, business, and private residents during a specified period of time (usually one year).

- In the system of double-entry accounting, each transaction, as represented by a debit or credit, is offset by an entry that represents the financing or settling of the transaction.

- The major balances in the balance of payments that require close monitoring are the merchandise trade balance, the balance on goods and services, the current-account balance, and the basic balance (the current-account balance plus long-term capital flows).

- Exchange rates can affect businesses in three major ways: market decisions, production decisions, and financial decisions.

C A S E

CATERPILLAR AND THE FLUCTUATING DOLLAR[13]

Caterpillar, one of the world's largest heavy-equipment manufacturers, has been beset by two major problems: competition from Komatsu Ltd. of Japan and a fluctuating U.S. dollar. The 30 percent strengthening of the dollar against the yen in 1989 and early 1990, as noted in Fig. 8.2, made Japanese goods less expensive in the United States and third-country markets, giving Komatsu a substantial competitive advantage, and in early 1990, for the second time since 1981, Caterpillar executives tried to plot a strategy on how to cope with the strong dollar.

Caterpillar concentrates in the worldwide production and sale of heavy equipment and engines. (See Map 8.2.) It manufactures products in wholly owned or affiliated plants in the United States, Brazil, Canada, France, the United Kingdom, Australia, Belgium, Indonesia, India, Italy, Japan, and Mexico. It also has contract manufacturers in the United States, Finland, Norway, South Korea, the United Kingdom, and Germany. Products are manufactured under license in eight countries, and parts warehouses and distribution facilities are located in the United States as well as in nine foreign locations. Parts and components are shipped worldwide for final assembly in combination with other parts and components manufactured or purchased locally.

The Dollar Prior to the 1980s   As noted earlier in the chapter, the U.S. dollar operated under a fixed exchange-rate system until 1973. As Fig. 8.3 shows, the two dollar devaluations of 1971 and 1973 resulted in a dollar exchange rate that was considerably below that of the pre-1971 era. The effective exchange rate, which is the value of the dollar against its major trading partners weighted for the importance of trade with them, reached a low point in 1973 and again in late 1978 and early 1979.

Several reasons account for the weakening dollar in the 1970s. An overvalued dollar and relatively strong U.S. economy, especially in the late 1960s, led to a growth in imports, a weakening of exports, and a balance-of-trade deficit. This deficit was magnified by the rise in oil prices and a worldwide recession in the mid-1970s. As the world began to recover from the recession later in the 1970s, the U.S. economy rebounded quickly, leading to strong demand for imports and increasingly wider trade deficit.

However, the deficit began to turn around in 1978 and 1979 as the declining dollar finally began to take hold. In particular, there was a marked increase in the exports of U.S.-manufactured goods as foreign customers continued to purchase these products because of sustained economic growth abroad, especially in Western Europe and Japan.

The Dollar in the Early 1980s   In 1980 the dollar began a substantial turnaround.

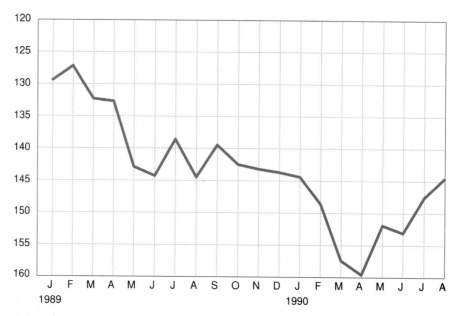

Figure 8.2
The Value of the Yen Per U.S. Dollar
The yen weakened substantially against the dollar in 1989–1990 before beginning
to strengthen.

Higher U.S. interest rates attracted marginal capital from abroad. The trend continued in 1981 as a tight monetary policy resulted in higher interest rates and as the current account continued to improve. Several factors were credited for the strength: relatively low inflation in the United States, relatively high nominal interest rates, the perception of the United States as a safe haven from world crises, a strong U.S. stock market, and demand for dollars by multinational corporations.

The strong dollar had good points and bad points both domestically and abroad. It was hurting U.S. exporters but helping U.S. importers. Foreign exporters liked the strong dollar because it gave them cheaper access to the U.S. market and helped them to compete with U.S. companies abroad. On the other hand, the strong dollar was sapping many of the industrial

economies. The huge federal budget deficit in the United States kept interest rates high, which created a strong incentive for European investors to invest in the United States rather than in Europe. These capital inflows helped offset the trade deficit outflows, so the dollar stayed strong. However, high interest rates kept the European countries from lowering their interest rates to stimulate their weak economies. These countries feared that lower interest rates would force even more of their capital to the United States and thus strip their countries of capital needed for investment.

The developing countries had difficulties because their debt burdens were denominated largely in dollars. High interest rates increased the amount of interest that needed to be paid, and the strengthening dollar meant they had to come up with more of their own currencies to

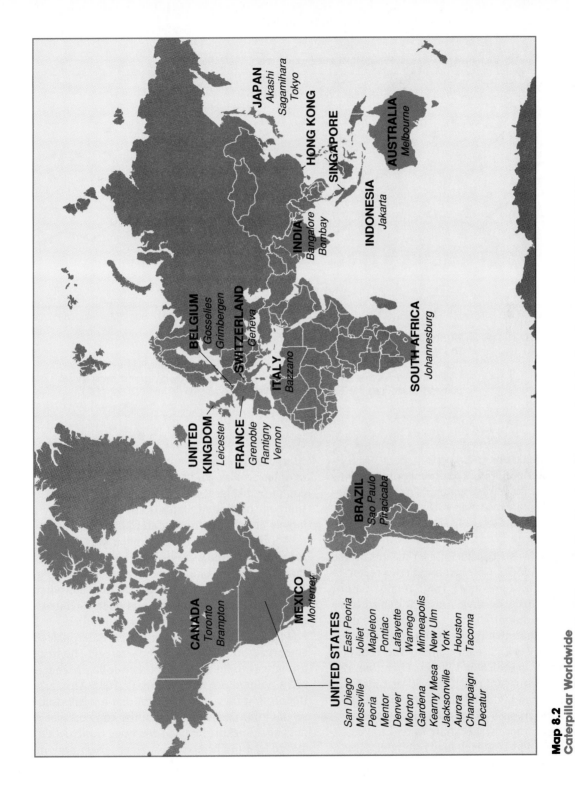

Map 8.2

Caterpillar Worldwide

The map identifies all Caterpillar marketing headquarters, manufacturing locations, and distribution centers worldwide (excludes Caterpillar machinery made by contract manufacturers or made under license).

U.S. nominal effective exchange rate against 15 industrial country currencies, 1980-1982=100

Figure 8.3
The Value of the U.S. Dollar
The dollar weakened substantially in the early 1970s. It strengthened in the early 1980s, then it weakened again and moved up and down against most major currencies toward the end of the 1980s.

purchase the dollars to pay off the debt. Both industrial and developing countries found that the strong dollar made raw materials imports (especially oil) more expensive.

Caterpillar's Problems   During this period of the rising dollar, Caterpillar experienced severe competitive pressures. Traditionally, Caterpillar has relied extensively on U.S. export of components and products to service world markets. More than two thirds of Caterpillar's employees work at U.S. plants, and 81 percent of its assets are in the United States. Therefore, the strong dollar made it difficult for Caterpillar to compete. In addition, Komatsu was challenging Caterpillar seriously in the United States and other markets for market share due to the cost advantage and weak exchange rate which the Japan-based company enjoyed. By 1980,

Komatsu, with a 40 percent price advantage over Caterpillar, grabbed over 17 percent of all equipment sold. Komatsu increased its market share in the United States from 15 to 25 percent, largely at the expense of Caterpillar.

Another problem for Caterpillar was that some of its major markets were experiencing serious difficulty. Collapsing oil prices and soaring Third World debt made it difficult for Caterpillar to sell machinery to mining and energy-related projects, especially in developing countries.

To tackle these and other issues, Caterpillar embarked on a three-pronged strategy. The first prong was to lobby for a weaker dollar. Management pointed out in Caterpillar's 1985 Annual Report that they were hopeful that a weak dollar would "ultimately strengthen the competitiveness of U.S. exporters, cut the huge trade deficit, and reduce the protectionist fever which now infects Congress."

The second prong of Caterpillar's strategy was to cut costs. This was accomplished initially by closing plants and laying off workers. Employment was reduced 40 percent (35,000 workers) to a level of 53,000 workers. Factory space was reduced by one third through the closing of nine plants.

The third prong of the strategy, related to the strong dollar and the desire to cut costs, led Caterpillar to become involved in contract manufacturing and expanded production capability abroad. Contract manufacturing has given Caterpillar more flexibility in responding to swings in the economy. Caterpillar began producing abroad specifically to take advantage of the strong dollar, even though its changes were not as significant as those found in other U.S. companies. At the time, many independent distributors in the United States were buying Caterpillar products abroad at cheap prices, importing them into the United States, and undercutting Caterpillar in its own market. So management decided to have foreign manufacturers make Caterpillar-brand products and also to replace U.S. suppliers with foreign ones. Foreign production of Caterpillar's own products jumped from 19 percent in 1982 to 25 percent in early 1987; sourcing of parts overseas increased four-fold during the same time period.

The Weakening U.S. Dollar   In the fall of 1985, however, the dollar began to weaken. As noted in Fig. 8.3, the fall was steep, but not uniform. Against some currencies, notably those of the Asian NICs (newly industrialized countries), the dollar remained fairly stable; against some of the OECD (Organization for Economic Cooperation and Development) countries, however, the fall was fairly pronounced. The major concerns seemed to be the continuing large U.S. trade deficit, concerns about possible trade protectionism in the United States, the large federal budget deficit, and strong pressures on several currencies in the European Monetary System, especially the German mark.

Although the dollar was falling, U.S. exports were not increasing dramatically, largely because of weakness in other industrial economies and the fact that foreign competitors were willing to absorb the difference in smaller profit margins. In addition, imports continued to climb due to the strong U.S. economy and the reluctance of importers to raise prices and thus lose market share. However, most experts were looking for a gradual improvement in the trade balance in 1988 as the weak dollar began to take hold.

The Dollar in the Late 1980s   The problem is that the dollar began to strengthen again in 1989, especially against the Japanese yen, and Caterpillar was not ready. Many U.S. companies built more overseas factories, increased their purchases of Japanese parts and components, and used financial hedging strategies to lessen the impact of a fluctuating—especially strengthening—dollar. Overseas investments of U.S. companies increased 24 percent in 1988, 14 percent in 1989, and were expected to increase by 13 percent in 1990. Caterpillar, however, has basically remained an exporter, the second largest in the United States behind Boeing.

Because of this strong U.S. production strategy, Caterpillar has resorted to lobbying the government for help by demonstrating the significant advantage that Japanese companies have in the U.S. and abroad when the dollar is so strong. Although the Japanese government tried to shore up the yen in early 1990, the U.S. government was not trying hard to weaken the dollar due to other concerns. Caterpillar led the assault on the government in 1985, and that lobbying helped tilt the decision in late 1985 to drive the dollar down. Caterpillar management hoped that its lobbying efforts in 1990 would have a similar effect.

During the mid-1980s, Caterpillar decided to modernize its plants, so it established its Plant With A Future program, or PWAF. Although Caterpillar management eventually hopes to cut costs by 19 percent with the new modernization, it will take several years, and the decline in the yen would be difficult to offset with productivity changes. Thus Komatsu has lots of room to discount prices and offer special bargains, whereas Caterpillar is really boxed in by the strong dollar. As pointed out by Caterpillar's chairman and CEO, "Our No. 1 competitor virtually got a 25 percent price increase without changing one yen on price."

Questions

1. What are the major factors that have influenced the value of the dollar over the past twenty years?

2. What are the key factors that you would monitor if you wanted to have a clear idea of the future direction of the dollar? Be sure to explain how those particular factors might influence the dollar.

3. Evaluate the strengths and weaknesses of Caterpillar's strategy to counteract the strong U.S. dollar.

4. What are the potential implications of that strategy as the dollar began to weaken by the latter part of 1990?

Chapter Notes

1. Most information for the case came from the following sources: International Monetary Fund, *Exchange Arrangements and Exchange Restrictions Annual Report, 1989* (Washington, D.C.: IMF, 1989), p. 261; "Economists on Currencies," *Euromoney*, May 1990, p. 145; Mike McNamee, "Only Higher Rates Can Halt the Yen's Big Slide," *Business Week*, p. 82; "The Japanese Paradox," *The Economist*, 7 April 1990, p. 77; Steven H. Nagourney, "Yen for Trouble," *Barron's*, 26 March 1990; *International Financial Statistics*, October 1990.

2. "The Institutional Evolution of the IMF," *Finance & Development*, September 1984, p. 8.

3. International Monetary Fund, *International Financial Statistics* (Washington, D.C.: IMF, November 1990), p. 22.

4. International Monetary Fund, *Exchange Arrangements and Exchange Restrictions Annual Report 1989* (Washington, D.C.: IMF, 1989), p. 462.

5. George S. Tavlas, "International Currencies: The Rise of the Deutsche Mark," *Finance & Development*, September 1990, p. 38.

6. International Monetary Fund, *Exchange Arrangements and Exchange Restrictions Annual Report 1989, op. cit.*, p. 294.

7. Julian Walmsley, *The Foreign Exchange Handbook* (New York: Wiley, 1983), pp. 84–90.

8. *International Economic Conditions* (Federal Reserve Bank of St. Louis, August 1987), p. 1.

9. Candace Cumberbatch, "Any Fed Easing of Credit Isn't Likely to Damage Dollar Much, Traders Say," *Wall Street Journal*, 29 October 1990, p. c11.

10. David K. Eiteman and Arthur I. Stonehill, *Multinational Business Finance*, 5th ed. (Reading, Mass.: Addison-Wesley, 1989), pp. 164–165.

11. International Monetary Fund, *Balance of Payments Statistics* (Washington, D.C.: IMF, 1984), p. XIV.

12. "The Japanese Paradox," *The Economist*, 7 April 1990, p. 77.

13. Data for the case were taken from Hans H. Helbling, "International Trade and

Finance under the Influence of Oil—1974 and Early 1975," *Federal Reserve Bank of St. Louis Review,* May 1975, p. 13; *Wall Street Journal,* February 27, 1978, p. 1; *Wall Street Journal,* April 21, 1978, p. 1; *Federal Reserve Bulletin,* April 1981, p. 270; various issues of *Survey of Current Business;* "Strength of the Dollar Is Explained by a Mix of Economics, Psychology," *Wall Street Journal,* December 14, 1983, p. 33; "The Super-dollar," *Business Week,* October 8, 1984, pp. 164–174; various issues of the Caterpillar Annual Report; Alex Kotlowitz, "Weaker Dollar Isn't a Boon for Caterpillar," *Wall Street Journal,* February 20, 1987, p. 6; Harlan S. Byrne, "Track of the Cat," *Barron's,* April 6, 1987, p. 13; Barry Stavro, "Heavy Equipment," *Forbes,* January 12, 1987, p. 146; Robert L. Rose, "Caterpillar Sees Gains in Efficiency Imperiled by Strength of Dollar," *Wall Street Journal,* 6 April 1990, p. A1; Kevin Kelly, "A Weakened Komatsu Tries to Come Back Swinging," *Business Week,* 22 February 1988, p. 48; Robert L. Rose, "Caterpillar's Fites Says Dollar's Rise Hurts U.S. Firms," *Wall Street Journal,* 9 March 1990.

CHAPTER **9**

FINANCIAL MARKETS FOR INTERNATIONAL OPERATIONS

*They were bowing to you when borrowing,
but you are bowing to them when collecting.*
RUSSIAN PROVERB

Objectives

- To show different ways in which firms can acquire outside funds for normal operations and expansion.

- To examine local debt markets, the Eurocurrency and Eurobond markets, and equity markets worldwide.

- To discuss the functions of the international banking community in facilitating the flow of funds.

- To highlight the role of development banks and similar institutions.

Scene 1: On December 2, 1991, a small Hong Kong (see Map 9.1) lending company, Global Vista Finance Co., quietly closes its doors. For months it had aggressively plunged most of its $7 million in borrowed money into the Hong Kong real-estate market, which is now collapsing.

The next day, crowds of depositors begin to form outside the main office of a middle-sized Hong Kong bank, Gresham Bank Ltd. It had enjoyed a tidy business of borrowing money from bigger banks and re-lending it at high interest rates to little, unregulated firms like Global Vista. Suddenly, business was no longer so tidy. Gresham was discovering that other banks were refusing to lend it any more cash.

Scene 2: While there is no central bank in Hong Kong, an informal agreement among banks calls for the huge $30 billion Eastern Imperial Bank of Hong Kong to bail out a sister bank that gets into trouble. After lengthy negotiations that result in a hefty interest rate for a line of emergency credit to little Global Vista, Eastern Imperial comes to the rescue. As it does so, however, Eastern Imperial suddenly finds that it is having trouble. Many depositors, worried about the possibility that Eastern Imperial could have major exposure in loans to real-estate developers, begin moving their money elsewhere. Where Eastern Imperial looks for new sources of cash, it finds that other major banks are demanding higher-than-usual rates of interest.

Scene 3: Huge sums of money begin to move electronically around the world as banks, big investors, multinational companies, and Arab governments shift their dollars to safe havens, primarily to major banks in New York. By December 6, banks in places considered less safe in a crisis—Panama, Singapore, the Bahamas, and Canada—have become shaky.

Scene 4: The first U.S. bank to falter is the $15 billion Heartland National Bank of Chicago. It is a relatively healthy, conservatively run bank with a number of prosperous branches in Illinois. But it is owned by the now-shaky Eastern Imperial Bank of Hong Kong. This connection is extremely unsettling to Heartland National's largest depositors—three major money funds—which begin yanking millions out of the bank on December 8. The Federal Reserve Bank of Chicago moves quickly to inject new funds.

Scene 5: The following day the $3 billion Transamericana Investment Bank of London runs out of funds. It had been a major lender of Eurodollars to credit-hungry Latin American countries. After 24 hours of often-heated discussion, Transamericana can obtain no more credit from the consortium of eight private banks that owns it (one U.S., one Swiss, one German, and four Latin American banks and Eastern Imperial of Hong Kong). The central bank of Switzerland has agreed to pro-

C A S E

HYPOTHETICAL SCRIPT

FOR COLLAPSE*

*John J. Fialka, "Script for Collapse," *Wall Street Journal,* 10 November 1982, p. 1. Reprinted by permission of *The Wall Street Journal,* Dow Jones & Company, Inc., 1982. All rights reserved.

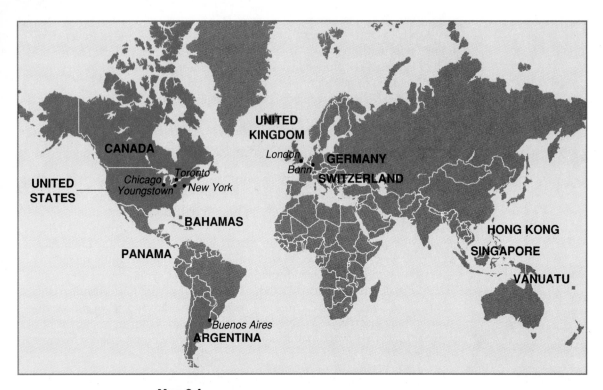

Map 9.1
The Global Script for Collapse
The interlocking nature of the world's banking system shows how instability in Hong Kong could ripple through institutions in countries around the world: Canada, the United States, Britain, Switzerland, Germany, the Bahamas, Panama, Argentina, Singapore, and Vanuatu.

vide one eighth of the needed bailout funds, but its counterparts in the United States, Germany, and Great Britain say that they have no legal or moral commitment. The Latin American central bankers say that they are strongly behind the bank but that they have no funds to back it up with. So Transamericana fails.

Scene 6: On December 11, Hector Aquinas-Marx, the finance minister of Argentina's new Socialist-Labor government, assembles a group of foreign bankers and announces that Argentina is repudiating its $55 billion of foreign debt. This is a profound shock to the bankers, who, for one thing, thought that Argentina had borrowed only $40 billion. As Mr. Aquinas-Marx explains, Argentina's rationale for the move is rather simple. For weeks it had been unable to obtain the new loans necessary to make interest payments on its old loans. The mishandling of the Transamericana failure, he says, is the last straw. From now on, Argentina, which has a small trade surplus, will pay for what it needs with cash. "We never needed you anyway," Mr. Aquinas-Marx tells the foreign bankers. "It was you who needed us."

Scene 7: On December 12, gloom spreads through the world banking community as banks begin to fall like bowling pins following the Argentina announcement. There is gloom in the New York headquarters of Megabank, a $54 billion institution that had pioneered the lending to Argentina. Megabank had parceled out pieces of the Argentine debt to dozens of other banks throughout the country and had lent $1 billion itself.

But there is joy in Megabank's currency-trading office in Zurich. There Rennie Zitz, a 23-year-old trader, has made Megabank more than $1 billion by holding a "short position" in Swiss francs for several weeks. He had borrowed the currency and sold it, then reaped an enormous profit by later buying an equal number of francs back after the Swiss currency dropped sharply against the dollar.

The dollar went up because some Swiss investors were converting their Swiss bank accounts to dollars and then wiring the money to New York, where they would be protected by the Federal Deposit Insurance Corporation (FDIC). Swiss banking regulators did not spot Mr. Zitz's transaction because he had booked it through Megabank's branch on the South Pacific island of Vanuatu, an office consisting of one clerk, one desk, and a telex machine.

Scene 8: On December 13, Youngstown (Ohio) Hope & Trust Bank joins the mounting pile of bank corpses in the United States. Neither its officers nor the federal banking authorities have been able to repair the damage caused by a run on the bank when it became known that Youngstown had participated in Megabank's lending foray into Argentina.

But Joe Lunchpail, a shop foreman at Youngstown Tube & Prong, goes to the bank anyway. He feels sure that he can rescue the $898.42 in his checking account because the bank is insured by the FDIC. Sure enough, the man from the FDIC is there, and Mr. Lunchpail takes his cash home to bury it in a dry place under one corner of his garage. With a sense of great relief, he flips on his Japanese TV set and opens a can of Dutch beer to sip as he watches the evening news report of the economic chaos that seems to be going on elsewhere. Then he learns that Youngstown Tube & Prong is closing. There is no longer an export market for prongs.

INTRODUCTION

This hypothetical case is meant to demonstrate the interdependence of capital markets and industrial growth worldwide. It may seem farfetched to assume that events in Hong Kong could influence a steelworker's job in Ohio, but stranger things have happened. Economic problems in Brazil and Mexico certainly have had a strong influence on the activities of the large multinational banks.

The small firm involved only tangentially in international business may be concerned only about the functions of the foreign-exchange section of its commercial bank. The larger MNE investing and operating abroad cares about access to capital in local markets as well as the large global capital markets. These capital markets and the institutions set up to make them run are primarily in the private sector. However, banks in some countries are owned by the government, and some lending institutions, such as the World Bank, are either government-owned or receive most of their funding from governments.

This chapter examines the financial markets and institutions that allow firms to grow globally and service customers around the world. Initially, the focus will be primarily on the markets themselves, especially the Eurocurrency, Eurobond, and equity markets. In the section on banking, we discuss the institutions and the services. Then we concentrate on the financial institutions distinct from banks that make the securities markets work. We close with a discussion on development banks and their contribution to corporate finance.

LOCAL DEBT MARKETS

Firms have learned to be creative in gaining access to local credit markets.

As corporations expand across foreign frontiers, they must adjust to local debt markets, both short term and long term. Since each country has different business customs, firms need to abandon strict operating procedures developed in other countries. When Caterpillar Tractor went to Brazil for the first time, it was accustomed to operating through one bank for all of its transactions. Very quickly, however, it became clear that the tight credit market in Brazil required different operating procedures. So Caterpillar opened accounts in several banks, allowing it to tap several different credit sources. Caterpillar liked this so much that it exported its Brazilian policy back to the United States, which allowed it to gain access to funds from many different banks.

Commercial paper is an IOU backed by standby lines of credit.

In the United States it is customary for U.S. companies needing cash to sell **commercial paper,** a form of IOU backed up by standby lines of bank credit, which are the lines of credit that the companies can gain access to if they need to use them to settle their IOUs. When U.S. subsidiaries of foreign corporations began to issue such paper, the market required that the paper be guaranteed by the parent company. Some giants, like Shell Oil, did not need to rely on their parent, because they were large enough and had a good enough reputation to gain access to capital on their own, but most companies did.

Even though domestic and international markets are becoming more and more like a single market—at least in the case of the industrial countries—

Local credit markets depend on internal political and economic pressures.

local markets still depend a great deal on internal political and economic pressures. In Latin America, for example, high inflation has created problems for a number of firms. In some countries, efforts to control inflation have curtailed the money supply and thus the availability of funds.

In Italy, foreign banks entered the market to provide financing for local firms, and most experts consider the foreign banks more efficient, competitive, and innovative than their Italian counterparts. However, they lack the branch network of the Italian banks and the strong banker–customer relationships that are necessary in the highly regulated Italian market. As a result, many of the large foreign banks, such as Lloyds, Chemical Bank, and Hongkong and Shanghai Bank, are leaving the local market to the local banks.[1]

Spain's preparations for entry into the European Community (EC) revolutionized the local credit market. Before 1981 the only source of medium-term financing was from capital markets outside of Spain. When loans were denominated in currencies other than the Spanish peseta, the borrowers were exposed to a foreign-exchange risk when they had to pay off their loans. However, several changes in Spanish banking laws in 1981 opened up the local peseta financial market. The major source of influence was the international banks, long accustomed to creative financing.[2]

Foreign companies sometimes are treated differently from domestic companies when it comes to access to the credit markets. In Brazil in the early 1980s, for example, subsidiaries of foreign-owned companies were excluded from local credit markets, because they wanted those subsidiaries to bring in hard currency from abroad.[3]

Sometimes, however, foreign companies can get access to credit differently than local firms because of their access to hard currency. Firms can enter into back-to-back loans during periods when interest rates are high or credit is frozen. A back-to-back loan is one that involves a company in Country A with a subsidiary in Country B, and a bank in Country B with its branch in Country A. The example below of a U.S. food company operating in Italy shows how the Italian subsidiary can gain access to Italian loans by having its U.S. parent provide dollars for the U.S. subsidiary of an Italian bank. Under that condition, the Italian bank will lend money to the Italian subsidiary of the U.S. parent. An example of a back-to-back loan by a U.S. food company operating in Italy is as follows:

Firms can enter into back-to-back loans during periods when interest rates are high or credit is frozen.

> A dollar deposit is made in the U.S. with a branch of a leading Italian bank. At the same time, the equivalent amount in lira is lent by the bank to the company's Italian sub as a seven-year loan. The loan will be repaid in full to the bank at the end of the loan period. Once the loan is terminated, the parent will withdraw its deposit plus interest. The subsidiary pays Italian prime. Every six months, the exchange rate is adjusted if it varies more than 5 percent from the contracted rate. Thus, the subsidiary shoulders the exchange risk.[4]

If a U.S.-based MNE decides to use foreign credit markets to finance foreign operations, it must take into consideration interest-rate differentials and exchange-rate risks. As noted in Chapter 8, interest rates differ from country to country, primarily because of inflation differentials. In Brazil in 1989, the consumer price index rose by more than 1000 percent, which was reflected in high interest rates and a rapidly devaluing currency. If the Brazilian subsidiary of a U.S. company decided to borrow in dollars at lower interest rates rather than pay the high interest rates on Brazilian currency loans—if they were even available—it would be exposed to an exchange-rate risk. If the Brazilian currency were to devalue against the dollar (which it certainly did during the period of high inflation), the Brazilian subsidiary would have to come up with more Brazilian currency to purchase dollars to pay the principal and interest.

From these illustrations it is obvious that MNEs need to weigh several factors as they look at the local credit markets: (1) availability of funds, (2) cost due to interest rates and foreign-exchange risk, and (3) local customs and institutions. Because situations and events are dynamic, corporate treasurers must be able to react quickly.

Three factors that MNEs need to consider as they access local credit markets include
- Availability of funds
- Cost due to interest rates and foreign-exchange risk
- Local customs and institutions

EUROCURRENCIES

The Eurocurrency market is an important source of debt available to the MNE. A **Eurocurrency** is any currency that is banked outside of its country of origin. Eurodollars, which constitute a fairly consistent 65–80 percent of the market, are dollars banked outside of the United States. Dollars held by foreigners on deposit in the United States are not Eurodollars, but dollars held at branches of U.S. or other banks outside of the United States are Eurodollars. Similar markets exist for Euro-Japanese yen (Euro-Yen), Euro-German marks (Euro-Deutsche marks), and other currencies, such as British pounds, Swiss francs, and French francs.

A Eurocurrency is any currency banked outside of its country of origin.

The Eurocurrency market is worldwide. Large transactions take place in Asia (Hong Kong and Singapore), the Caribbean (the Bahamas and the Cayman Islands), and Canada, as well as in London and other European centers. However, London is the key center for the Eurocurrency market, given that nearly 20 percent of all Eurocurrency transactions in 1989 took place in London. Luxembourg is the center for Euro-Deutsche mark deposits, with Brussels and Paris the centers for Euro-Sterling deposits.[5]

London is the key center of the Eurocurrency market.

The major sources of Eurodollars are: (1) foreign governments or individuals who want to hold dollars outside of the United States; (2) multinational corporations with cash in excess of current needs; (3) European banks with foreign currency in excess of current needs; and (4) the reserves of countries such as Japan, Taiwan, and Germany that have large balance-of-trade surpluses. The demand for Eurocurrencies comes from individuals, firms, and governments that require funds for operating capital, investment, and the payment of principal and interest on debt. Eurocurrencies exist partly for the convenience and security of the user and partly because of the cheaper lending rates for the borrower and better yield for the lender. The security issue arose because some governments feared currency controls in the United States and decided that they wanted to hold their U.S. dollars offshore.

Eurocurrency Expansion

The fractional reserve is the percentage of Eurodollar deposits that banks hold rather than lend out.

The key to Eurocurrency expansion is the **fractional reserve concept.** The total size of the Eurocurrency market is much greater than the actual cash deposited. Once a Eurocurrency (assume dollar) deposit is made in a London bank, the bank may use that asset as a basis for making a dollar-denominated loan to someone else. The fraction of the original deposit not loaned out is called the *fractional reserve.* Since there are no reserve requirements on Eurocurrency deposits, it is up to the individual bank to determine how much protection it requires in the form of reserves. The expansion occurs when the initial loan is spent, deposited in another bank, or used as a basis for another loan.

Even though there are no specific Eurocurrency controls, banks are subject to solvency rules, and Eurocurrency assets and liabilities are a part of the overall assets and liabilities of the bank that are subject to capital ratios and capital provisions. In some cases, such as in Britain with the Bank of England, liquidity is monitored very closely; a Central Bank can issue more of its own currency to ease a liquidity crisis, but it would be hampered by a liquidity crisis caused by another currency.

Market Size

The Eurocurrency market is large—$6.1 trillion by September 1989.

The size of the market is difficult to determine and depends on whether the gross or net size is being discussed (the net size eliminates transfers between banks). Gross liabilities usually are just over twice the net size of the market. In 1971 the total gross Eurocurrency market size was about $150 billion. As Fig. 9.1 shows, the market grew to $4.561 trillion by March 1988. It was estimated that the market reached $6.1 trillion by September 1989.[6] Figure 9.2 illustrates that the dollar portion of the Eurocurrency market has remained over 70 percent for most of the past decade, although the importance of the dollar has diminished in recent years, especially as the dollar has fallen in value. By 1988 the dollar portion had slipped to less than 70 percent. As the dollar rises in value, however, the dollar portion of Eurocurrencies will also rise.

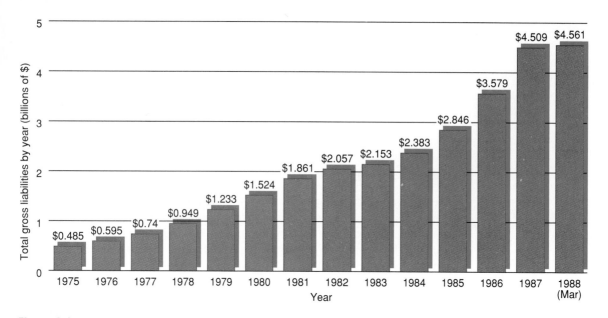

Figure 9.1
Eurocurrency Market Size (Total Gross Liabilities)
The Eurocurrency market has increased steadily since 1975 and is expected to exceed $8 trillion by the end of 1991. *Source:* The Federal Reserve Bank of St. Louis, *International Economic Conditions,* various issues.

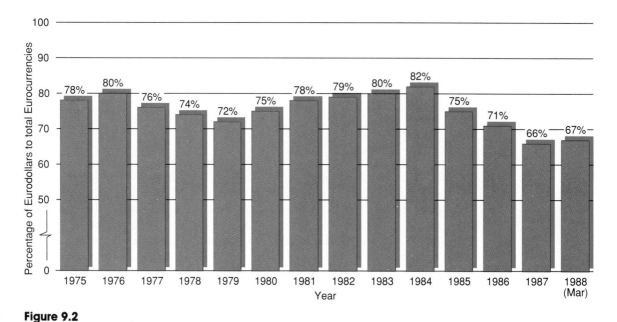

Figure 9.2
Percentage of Eurodollars to Total Eurocurrencies
The U.S. dollar is the major share of the Eurocurrency market, although it has lost importance since 1985 when the dollar began to fall against the currency of most industrial countries. *Source:* The Federal Reserve Bank of St. Louis, *International Economic Conditions,* various issues.

Eurocurrency Market Characteristics   The Eurocurrency market has several interesting characteristics:

1. It is a wholesale rather than retail market, which means that transactions tend to be very large. Public borrowers such as governments, central banks, and public-sector corporations tend to borrow most of the funds. Also, nearly four fifths of the Eurodollar market is interbank, which means that the transactions take place between banks.

2. The market is essentially unregulated.

3. Deposits are primarily short term. Most of the deposits are interbank, and they tend to be very short term. This leads to concern about risk, since most Eurocurrency loans are for longer periods of time.

4. The Eurocurrency market exists for savings and time deposits rather than demand deposits. That is, institutions that create Eurodollar deposits do not draw down those deposits into a particular national currency in order to buy goods and services.

5. The Eurocurrency market is primarily a Eurodollar market (see Fig. 9.2).

In addition to ordinary deposits in the Eurocurrency market, there are also certificates of deposit (CDs) available in dollars, sterling, and yen. Although CDs are available in units of $100,000, most are traded in multiples of $1 million or more. The CDs are usually quoted at a discount at a fixed interest rate, but they can also be quoted at floating interest rates.

The Eurocurrency market has short- and medium-term characteristics. Short-term Eurocurrency borrowing has a maturity of less than one year. However, it is also possible to borrow at maturities exceeding one year. Anything over one year is considered a **Eurocredit.** These Eurocredits may be loans, lines of credit, or other forms of medium- and long-term credits, including **syndication,** in which several banks pool resources to extend credit to a borrower.

A major attraction of the Eurocurrency market is the difference in interest rates as compared with domestic markets. Because of the large transactions and the lack of controls and their attendant costs, Eurocurrency deposits tend to yield more than domestic deposits, and loans tend to be relatively cheaper than in domestic markets. Figure 9.3 illustrates these differences in interest rates. Traditionally, loans are made at a certain percentage above the **London Inter-Bank Offered Rate (LIBOR),** which is the interest rate banks charge one another on loans of Eurocurrencies. The interest rate above LIBOR, which is characterized in Fig. 9.3 as the Eurocurrency borrowing rate, depends on the credit-worthiness of the customer and must be large enough to cover expenses and build reserves against possible losses. The unique characteristics of the Eurocurrency market allow the borrowing rate usually to be less than it would be in the domestic market. Most loans are made on variable-rate terms, and the rate-fixing period is generally six months, although it could also be one or three months. Because of the variable nature of the interest rates, the maturities can extend into the future.

Key characteristics of the Eurocurrency market:

• Wholesale rather than retail
• Virtually unregulated
• Savings and time rather than demand deposits
• Primarily dollar-based

A Eurocredit consists of loans that mature in one to five years.

Syndication occurs when several banks pool resources to make a large loan in order to spread the risk.

LIBOR is the interest rate that banks charge each other in Eurocurrency transactions.

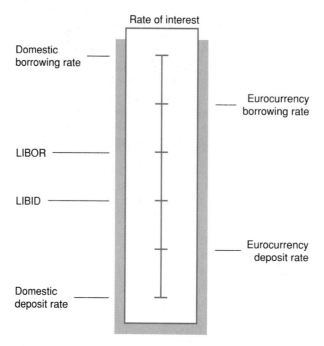

Figure 9.3
Interest-Rate Differentials
The Eurocurrency borrowing rate is typically less than the domestic borrowing rate due to lower costs and larger transactions.

The LIBID is the bid rate that corresponds to the LIBOR, and the difference between the LIBOR and the LIBID is usually about one eighth of a percentage point. The rate one earns on deposits in the Eurocurrency is usually less than the LIBID, but it is often more than can be earned in the domestic market.

INTERNATIONAL BONDS

Many countries have very active bond markets available to domestic and foreign investors. One good example is the United States: In mid-1980s, given the high real interest rates, relative political and economic stability, and governmental desire to finance its high budget deficits with borrowing, the U.S. market was attractive to foreign investors. The repeal of the withholding tax on interest in the United States in 1984 also eliminated a major roadblock for foreign investors taking U.S.-issued bonds.

Foreign Bonds and Eurobonds

Foreign bonds are sold outside of the country of the borrower but in the currency of the country of issue.

Eurobonds are sold in countries other than the currency of issue.

The international bond market can be divided into foreign bonds and Eurobonds. **Foreign bonds** are sold outside of the borrower's country but are denominated in the currency of the country of issue. For example, a French corporation floating a bond issue in Swiss francs in Switzerland would be floating a foreign bond. A **Eurobond** is usually underwritten, or placed in the market for the borrower, by a syndicate of banks from different countries and placed in countries other than the one in whose currency the bond is denominated. If the French firm floated a bond issue in German marks in Switzerland, Luxembourg, and London, the issue would be a Eurobond.

The Eurobond Market

Although the Eurobond market is centered in Europe, it has no national boundaries. Unlike most conventional bond issues, Eurobonds are sold simultaneously in several financial centers through multinational underwriting syndicates and are purchased by an international investing public that extends far beyond the confines of the countries of issue.

Occasionally, Eurobond issues may provide currency options, which enable the creditor to demand repayment in one of several currencies and thereby reduce the exchange risk inherent in single-currency foreign bonds. More frequently, however, interest and principal on the bonds are payable in U.S. dollars. Over the last several years the Eurobond market has become a market for dollar-denominated obligations of foreign as well as U.S. borrowers that are purchased by non-U.S. investors.

Eurobonds are sometimes issued in different currencies and are convertible into common stock.

In an effort to broaden investor appeal, corporate borrowers increasingly have shifted from straight debt issues to bonds that are convertible into common stock. The option of conversion rests with the holder of the convertible issue. For the nonresident investor, one of the main attractions of a convertible issue is that it usually offers a larger current return than does the dividend of the underlying stock.

In the past decade, the Eurobond market has grown explosively, due to a variety of reasons—primarily the deregulation of markets. The weakening of the dollar in 1985 also caused a shift out of dollars toward Euro-Yen and Euro-Deutsche mark issues. The control of inflation in the industrial countries also has resulted in a big demand for financial assets, allowing companies to issue bonds in unprecedented quantities and in a variety of currencies. The major benefits of the Eurobond market are that it is relatively unregulated, its income is essentially untaxed, and there appears to be greater flexibility in making issues than is the case in purely national markets. In addition, it is an important step toward a fully integrated European capital market. The yen is potentially the largest source of funds for the Eurobond market, because of the huge trade surpluses that Japan has enjoyed in recent years.

The European Currency Unit (ECU) has become an interesting "currency" of lending in the Eurobond market. The ECU, which is based on a basket comprised of the currencies of the EC, accounts for nearly 10 percent of all international bond issues.[7] It is attractive in that it allows borrowers to diversify into different currencies and allows them to use cash flows from different countries where it has operations to pay back the investors. Corporate borrowers include Citicorp, PepsiCo, Peugeot, Olivetti, and Toyota.[8]

Although the Eurobond market grew by 20 percent in 1989 over 1988 to $212.7 billion, it still remained below the U.S. bond market at $275.0 billion but above the Japanese bond market at $80 billion. The Eurobond market is very important because of its ability to place issues more cheaply and efficiently than domestic markets. In 1989 private corporate borrowers raised their share in total borrowing to 58.8 percent of the market, up from 38.1 percent in 1985. The other major borrowers are governments, private banks, and supranational agencies (such as the different agencies of the European Community). In terms of currency, the largest volume of Eurobond denominations is clearly dollars, followed by sterling, deutsche marks, yen, and ECU's. To illustrate the magnitude of difference in the different currencies, in the 11 months to end-November 1989, new issues in the Eurodollar market stood at $115.3 billion, whereas in the Euro-Sterling market, the next-largest market, they stood at only $19.7 billion.[9]

The major challenge facing the Eurobond market in the future is the deregulation of capital markets. As domestic markets deregulate, there is the possibility that the Eurobond market may become increasingly unnecessary.[10] In the early part of 1990, the Eurobond market fell to half its level in the previous year, so perhaps the problems of the market were beginning to take hold. A major contributor was the collapse of the Japanese stock market in early 1990 and the hesitancy of the large Japanese securities firms to enter the Eurobond market. However, there was no way of knowing if the slowdown in early 1990 was a temporary or a permanent condition.

OFFSHORE FINANCIAL CENTERS

So far we have alluded to the major financial centers of the world. The countries with large markets, such as the major OECD countries, have large domestic financial markets. This does not mean that they have large financial markets that deal in foreign currencies, however; neither does it mean that they have large offshore centers.

Center Characteristics

Offshore financial centers are cities or countries that provide large amounts of funds in a currency other than their own. These centers provide an alternate, and usually cheaper, source of funding for MNEs so that they don't have to rely strictly on their own national markets. Generally these markets in these centers are regulated in a different, and usually more flexible, way than are the domestic markets. The centers have one or more of the following characteristics as well:

1. There is a large foreign-currency (Eurocurrency) market for deposits and loans (e.g., London).

2. The market of the center is a large net supplier of funds to the world financial markets (e.g., Switzerland).

3. The market of the center is an intermediary or pass-through for international loan funds (e.g., Bahamas, Cayman Islands).

4. The center has economic and political stability.

5. There is an efficient and experienced financial community.

6. The center has good communications and supportive services.

7. There is an official regulatory climate favorable to the financial industry, in the sense that it protects investors without unduly restricting financial institutions.[11]

Offshore financial centers can be operational or simply accounting centers.

These centers can be considered as operational centers where extensive banking activities are carried out; or booking centers, where little actual banking activities take place but where transactions are recorded in order to take advantage of low (or no) tax rates and secrecy. London is an example of an operational center, and the Cayman Islands is an example of a booking center. Although there are many offshore financial centers, the seven most important ones are London, the Caribbean (servicing especially Canadian and U.S. banks), Switzerland, Singapore, Hong Kong, Bahrain (for the Middle East), and New York.

Specific Centers

Key offshore financial centers are in London, the Caribbean, Panama, Hong Kong, Singapore, and Bahrain.

London is a crucial center because it offers a variety of services and has a large domestic as well as offshore market. The Caribbean centers (primarily the Bahamas, Cayman Islands, and Netherlands Antilles) are essentially offshore locations for the New York banks. Switzerland has been a primary source of funds for decades, offering stability, integrity, discretion, and low costs. Singapore has been the center for the Asian dollar market since 1968, thanks to a variety of government regulations that have facilitated the flow of funds, its strategic geographic location, and its strong telecommunications links with the rest of the world. Hong Kong is critical because of its unique status vis-à-vis the United Kingdom and China and its geographic proximity to the rest of the Pacific Rim. However, Singapore is beginning to take over much of Hong Kong's business because of insecurity concerning the 1997 takeover of Hong Kong by China. Bahrain, an island nation in the Persian Gulf, is the financial center of petrodollars (dollars generated from the sale of oil) in the

Middle East. Even though oil prices had a period of weakness in the mid-1980s, a tremendous amount of revenue is generated by the oil producers. In addition, the increase in prices that accompanied the Gulf conflict in 1990–1991 should increase the flow of petrodollars again.

EQUITY SECURITIES

In addition to the debt instruments in the local debt markets as well as the Eurodollar and Eurobond markets, the equity-capital market is another source of financing. The three largest international stock exchanges in the world in terms of market capitalization are the Tokyo, New York, and London stock exchanges. Market capitalization is the total number of shares of stock listed on the stock exchange times the market price per share. Prior to 1987 the New York market was by far the largest in the world. In 1984 Wall Street controlled 55 percent of the world's equity market, three times as much as Tokyo and eight times as much as London.[12] From 1984 to 1986, however, the gap narrowed quickly. By 1986 the market capitalization of U.S. equities was down to 43 percent of the world total, whereas the Japanese had increased from 20.1 percent to 29.1 percent. The soaring yen and rapid increase in Japanese equity prices caused Tokyo to surpass New York in the spring of 1987 to become the world's largest equity market.[13] As noted in Table 9.1, the Japanese continued to hold the lead in 1989.

> The three largest stock markets in the world are in Tokyo, New York, and London.

The U.S. market is important for U.S. and foreign companies looking for equity capital. A partial explanation for the popularity of the U.S. market is the size and speed of offerings. For example, the large pension funds in the United States can take large blocks of stock at relatively low transaction costs. In the past few years, pension-fund managers have looked at foreign stocks

TABLE 9.1 | GLOBAL STOCK-MARKET CAPITALIZATIONS (Total Market Value in U.S. $ Billions) The largest stock markets in the world are in Tokyo, New York, and London.

Country	1989	1984	1980
Japan	4,102	617	357
United States	3,027	1,714	1,391
United Kingdom	823	219	190
Germany	362	78	71
France	339	40	53
Canada	290	116	113

Source: Deloitte, Haskins & Sells, *Review* (New York: DH&S, 14 September 1987), p. 2; *Euromoney*, May 1990, p. 80. Source for both tables, Morgan Stanley Capital International.

as a good form of portfolio diversification. Many companies go to the United States because the depth and breadth of the market enable them to raise funds there easily. In a study of the 300 stocks traded the most internationally, only two Japanese stocks and six U.S. stocks were listed in the top 50. This reflects the depth and liquidity of the markets in both Japan and the United States and the fact that Japanese and U.S. companies can raise most of their capital in their own countries rather than having to rely on foreign markets.

Deregulation

The major event in international equity markets in recent years was the "big bang," the deregulation of the British stock market which occurred in London on October 27, 1986. Prior to that time, the City of London (the financial district in London) operated on two different sides. The first side was the domestic front, home to the U.K. financial firms that controlled the U.K.'s financial system. Custom and regulation basically kept the domestic side from keeping up with financial services developed elsewhere.

The other side was the Eurocurrency market, which was dominated by foreign institutions. The British government's abolition of exchange controls in 1979 blurred the differences between the domestic and international sides of the City of London. However, the big bang resulted in a dismantling of the trading system, a liberalization of Stock-Exchange membership requirements, and an opening of the market to foreign competition.[14] These changes have resulted in a significant liberalization of one of the largest capital markets in the world.

The deregulation of stock markets worldwide, especially in London, has led to a modernization of the exchanges through the introduction of new technologies and the competition of other exchanges and financial services firms from other countries.

One side effect of deregulation has been the modernization of stock exchanges around the world. New technologies are being employed by nearly every major exchange worldwide, and the exchanges are beginning to link together in various ways, such as in listing and trading securities in each other's markets. Both the Stockholm and Amsterdam stock exchanges have announced formal links with U.S. exchanges, primarily in the Midwest. There are similar links between Amsterdam and Tokyo and between London and the United States. These are just a few examples of dozens of linkages that exist and are being planned worldwide.[15]

The stock-market crash of 1987 demonstrated how closely linked the different stock markets are.

The stock-market crash of October 1987 resulted in the nearly simultaneous collapse of stock prices around the world, illustrating how global the stock markets had become. Since the markets are not open at the same time around the world, global events occur sequentially as markets open and react to information. In a study of the globalization of securities, it was found that market events are more important than individual industry events in affecting stock prices. The authors also predicted that global investors armed with the same information would minimize the dominance of any particular national stock market over international markets.[16]

It is interesting to note that most stock markets fell in 1990, with the exception of Hong Kong, which rose 4.7 percent over the previous year. However, the Bank of Japan and the Ministry of Finance engineered a fall in the Japanese stock market that resulted in a drop of 40 percent in 1990. Their feeling was that stock prices had climbed too high and that too much growth was built on high stock prices and high land prices. The U.S. stock market was down only 5.3 percent in 1990. For much of the 1980s, the Nikkei index in Japan was roughly 10 times the Dow Jones Industrial Average (DJIA), but that relationship had grown to 14 to 1 by the end of 1989. At the end of 1990, the Nikkei was trading at around 24,000, whereas the DJIA was trading at around 2600, illustrating how much the Nikkei had really fallen in a relative sense in 1990.[17]

The Euroequity Market

The Euroequity market is the market for shares sold outside of the national boundaries of the issuing company.

Another significant event in the past decade is the creation of the Euroequity market. The **Euroequity market** is the market for shares sold outside of the national boundaries of the issuing company. Prior to 1980 few companies thought of offering stock outside of the national boundaries of the headquarters. Since then, hundreds of companies from all over the world have issued stock simultaneously in two or more countries.

London's stock market issues more foreign shares as a percentage of total shares than any other stock market.

Table 9.2 shows global stock markets in a slightly different light than Table 9.1. In Table 9.2, stock markets are ranked by equity turnover of foreign stocks. Thus the London Stock Exchange is ranked first in equity turnover of foreign stocks, even though it is ranked only third in terms of total turnover as well as the market value listed in Table 9.1.

TABLE 9.2 | INTERNATIONALLY ORIENTED STOCK EXCHANGES The London Stock Exchange trades the largest volume of foreign stocks of any exchange in the world, followed by New York and Tokyo.

Exchange*	A Total Equity Turnover U.S. $ Billion	B Foreign Sector Turnover as % of A
1. London	462,410	29.96
2. New York	1,542,845	4.37
3. Tokyo	2,434,953	0.83
4. Germany	330,399	4.86
5. AMEX	44,401	16.17
6. France	114,002	3.71
7. Brussels	10,569	27.45

*Ranked by equity turnover of foreign stocks.
Source: "How the Heavyweights Shape Up," *Euromoney*, May 1990, p. 62.

In the list of 300 stocks traded most actively in the Euroequity market, Japanese and U.S. stocks dominate the list with 68 and 44 entries, even though they are not among the top 50 as mentioned above. Companies of 22 different countries are listed in Euroequity markets, with Japan and the United States followed by the United Kingdom (26), France (25), Canada (23), the Netherlands (19), Germany (15), and Sweden (13).[18]

Japanese and U.S. companies rely on foreign exchanges less than do companies from other countries.

In some cases, such as with Yamanouchi Pharmaceutical of Japan, firms list on only one foreign exchange and nowhere else. Yamanouchi lists in London. In other cases, firms list on many different exchanges. Deutsche Bank of Germany lists its stock on eight different exchanges, including London, Tokyo, Paris, Brussels, and different exchanges in Germany.[19]

The most popular way to get international listings is to issue an **American Depository Receipt (ADR)** in the United States or be included in the SEAQ International system. An ADR is a negotiable certificate issued by a U.S. bank in the United States to represent the underlying shares of stock of a foreign corporation, which are held in trust at a custodian bank in the foreign country. ADRs are traded like a share of stock, with the ADR representing some multiple of the share of the underlying stock. The issuance of an ADR allows U.S. investors to invest in a foreign company without the foreign company having to go to the trouble of listing in the United States and being subject to all of the rules and regulations of the Securities and Exchange Commission.[20] SEAQ International is London's screen-based on-line quotation system and is the leader in the trading of international equities. It currently has no direct competitors, although there are some systems that are trying to come on line as serious competition.[21]

The ADR is a negotiable certificate issued by a U.S. bank and representing shares of stock of a foreign corporation.

It is interesting to note in Table 9.2 how different the stock exchanges are in terms of international participation. Nearly 30 percent of total equity turnover in London involves foreign equities, whereas less than 1 percent of the total equity turnover in Tokyo does. London trades twice as many foreign equities as does the New York Stock Exchange, seven times more than Tokyo, and 8½ times more than all eight German exchanges combined.[22] London's geographical location, the existence of the large financial infrastructure, the availability of SEAQ International, and more liberal disclosure standards make London an ideal place for the center of the Euroequity market.

The top five foreign issuers of securities on the New York Stock Exchange in 1989 were Royal Dutch Shell, Schlumberger, SmithKline Beecham, Alcan Aluminum, and British Petroleum. Five of the top ten listers used ADRs rather than direct securities. The top five listers on SEAQ International were Deutsche Bank, Siemens, Royal Dutch Shell, Mannesmann, and Volkswagen. The Germans are heavily represented in the top securities listed on SEAQ International.[23]

In spite of the growth of Euroequities, most trades take place in the domestic markets. The New York Stock Exchange is allowing after-hours trading and hopes to have 24-hour trading in place by the year 2000. In 1979 the NYSE market share of reported U.S. trading in listed stocks was close to 90 percent, but its share had dropped below 70 percent in 1990. The move to 24-hour trading is an attempt to regain market share. However, some experts feel that they want to trade the security of a company when that company's home market is open so that they can see what is driving the price of the stock.[24] It will be interesting to watch the development of a 24-hour market as the decade progresses.

Other Exchanges

Equity markets are being established in developing countries, but few companies are listed and extensive trading does not take place.

In most developing countries, the financial system is bank-oriented and strongly controlled by the government. However, equity markets can make a significant contribution to corporate development and can be a source of funding for MNEs that want to locate in those countries and get access to local capital. Equity markets are an important tool for economic development, they can help mobilize investment funds, and they can lower the cost of capital for firms. However, there are also a number of problems in the development of equity markets in developing countries. The major costs are the inevitability of market cycles, causing difficulties in raising capital; interest-rate fluctuations; intermediation costs (the costs of establishing, maintaining, regulating, and using the markets); the need for additional regulation; the loss of some control by the government over the financial system; possibilities of speculation and dishonest activities; and inefficient allocation of resources from a national perspective.[25]

In spite of the problems identified above, there are a number of emerging markets in the developing countries. There are three levels of emerging markets:

- established markets, such as Greece, Spain, Mexico, and Brazil, that have been in existence for a long time, although their volume has not been tremendous;
- emerging markets, such as Hong Kong and Singapore, that have arisen because of special situations; and
- markets, such as South Korea, that were specifically organized more recently to foster or accelerate economic growth.[26]

Even though these markets are growing and contributing to economic growth, they are not major players in the international equities market. Of the top 20 exchanges in the world that deal in foreign securities, only Kuala Lumpur, Malaysia, and Hong Kong are in developing countries. The stock markets in most emerging markets simply do not do enough volume in enough securities to attract the needed capital. The high rates of inflation and uncertain returns that are present in many of the emerging markets also cause problems in attracting capital.

INTERNATIONAL BANKS

An essential aspect of the growth of international business has been the increase in international banking services. Firms would have been unable to expand as they have without the timely flow of money and other resources provided by the international banks. Not only do banks facilitate the flow of existing corporate resources, they also provide debt financing from local and international markets. A Canadian bank, for example, could loan funds to a Canadian corporation that is attempting to acquire a U.S. business, or it could provide that financing through the Eurodollar market. Because of the entrance of commercial banks into investment-banking activities and vice-versa, it is difficult to separate commercial banks from other financial-services firms. However, these latter firms, such as Goldman Sachs and Nomura Securities, will be discussed after the section on banking.

Leading World Commercial Banks

Japanese banks are the largest in the world in terms of capital and assets.

U.S. MNEs are among the world's largest, but U.S. banks are not. Table 9.3 illustrates that the only U.S. bank in the top ten in 1988 was Citicorp, which ranked third, but even it was not on the top-ten list in 1989. The top-ten was dominated by the Japanese in both years. Prior to 1988 *The Banker* ranked banks according to asset size, but in 1988 it shifted to capital, consistent with the recommendations by the Bank for International Settlements. According to the new BIS requirements, banks doing cross-border business must have

TABLE 9.3 | RANKINGS OF TOP-TEN BANKS IN THE WORLD BY CAPITAL BASE The top-ten banks in the world are dominated by the Japanese and Europeans.

Ranking	1989	1988
1	Sumitomo[1]	Nat West
2	Dai-Ichi Kangyo[1]	Barclays[3]
3	Fuji[1]	Citicorp[5]
4	Crédit Agricole[2]	Fuji
5	Sanwa[1]	Crédit Agricole
6	Mitsubishi[1]	Sumitomo
7	Barclays[3]	Dai-Ichi Kangyo
8	Nat West[3]	Mitsubishi
9	Deutsche[4]	Ind. Bank of Japan
10	Ind. Bank of Japan[1]	Sanwa

[1]Japanese   [2]French   [3]U.K.   [4]German   [5]U.S.
Source: The Banker, July 1990, p. 68 and July 1989, p. 41.

capital equal to at least 8 percent of their assets by March 1993. The definition of capital includes permanent shareholders' equity and disclosed reserves.

The strong emergence of the Japanese banks is startling. Using the old asset measurement to rank order international banks, there was only one Japanese bank in the entire list in 1980, and it was number ten; that same bank was first in the world in 1987. In 1980 Citicorp was number one, Crédit Agricole was number three, and Banque Nationale de Paris was number four. In terms of asset size, the Japanese would still hold seven of the top ten places in 1989, with the other three going to Crédit Agricole (seven), Banque Nationale de Paris (eight), and Citicorp (ten). The strength of the yen and Japan's large trade surpluses have boosted the power of Japanese banks worldwide.

Table 9.4 shows the country representation of most of the top banks in the world in 1989. It is interesting to note how many of the largest 1000 banks are in the United States, even though they don't rank in the top ten in terms of capital. In fact, Citicorp is the only U.S. bank in the top 25 in the world.

Structure of International Banking

MNEs find that their banks offer a variety of services worldwide through a variety of different operational modes. The major way that banks become involved in cross-border operations is through **correspondent** relationships. In correspondent relationships, banks in different countries facilitate international financial transactions for each other's clients. For example, a bank in Country A may ask its correspondent in Country B to remit funds from an importer in Country B to an exporter in Country A. A bank may have several correspondent banks in the different countries where it wants to do business, or it may operate through a key bank.

Banks may also increase their influence abroad through establishing **branches.** A branch is a legal form of operation that is an extension of the parent bank. It is not a separate corporation where the parent owns stock, like a subsidiary. A branch is used to gain access to local capital or Eurocurrencies, and it is often established to eliminate relying on correspondent relationships. Branches are also being used to gain access to local clients. The bank that has the largest global spread is Citicorp, the large U.S. bank that placed twelfth in *The Banker's* 1989 list of top-1000 banks. Citicorp has total assets of over $207 billion, offices in 90 countries, and is expanding even yet. It is the only bank that has offices in each OECD country where foreign banks are allowed to establish offices, and it has the broadest network of any bank in Europe. The total number of domestic and overseas branches, offices, subsidiaries, and affiliates is almost 3300.[27]

Some banks also have entered into more formal relationships with banks at home and abroad in order to service clients better. A **consortium bank,** for example, occurs when several banks from different countries pool their

Banks get involved in international banking through correspondent relationships, establishing branches or subsidiaries abroad, or setting up consortium banks with banks in other countries.

TABLE 9.4 | COUNTRY REPRESENTATIVE OF THE TOP BANKS IN THE WORLD IN 1989 Even though the U.S. banks are not among the top 25 in the world, there are more large U.S. banks among the top 1000 than in any other country.

Country	Number of Banks
United States	222
Japan	112
Italy	108
Germany	82
Spain	35
United Kingdom	32
Switzerland	30
France	28
Austria	20

Source: The Banker, July 1990.

resources to form another bank that engages in international transactions. This enables the banks to draw on the strengths of their partners, such as foreign-currency deposits, branches in different countries, or expertise in specific types of banking transactions.

Domestic U.S. banks can also establish **Edge Act corporations** in different cities in the United States in order to get involved in international transactions. By law, a bank is allowed to establish an Edge Act company in different cities outside of its home state, as long as the Edge Act bank is involved in international and not domestic banking activities.

A final major type of operation for U.S. banks is the **International Banking Facility.** IBFs were created in the United States to allow U.S. banks to engage in Eurodollar-type operations. There are currently IBFs in 20 states, at 150 banks and 328 agencies and branches, mostly in New York. Although the dollar deposits in the IBFs are not exactly Eurodollars, they are almost identical in terms of interest rates, etc. The IBFs have lower costs due to the absence of reserve requirements and state income taxes. U.S. companies can obtain access to IBF funds through their foreign subsidiaries, and they must prove that the funds are being used to support international operations. The IBFs are not exactly separate physical facilities but are simply an accounting separation of activities engaged in by international banks.[28]

An International Banking Facility can be created in the United States to allow U.S. banks to engage in Eurodollar-type transactions.

Important Dimensions of International Banking

International banks must face a wide variety of issues, and a large number of key developments have taken place in recent years; we will focus here on the following areas that have an impact on MNEs and their operations world-

Three important areas in international banking are the expansion of services, market access and changing market conditions, and profitability.

wide: the expansion of services, market access and changing market conditions, and profitability.

Expansion of Services   The market for financial services has virtually skyrocketed for banks in recent years. The major functions that are especially suited for the international banks are:

1. export and import financing;
2. foreign-exchange trading;
3. debt and equity financing in domestic and Euromarkets;
4. international cash management, especially electronic funds transfer across national borders;
5. financial engineering for corporate clients; and
6. the supply of information and advice to clients.

Although there are at least these six areas in which banks can offer services for corporate clients, banks do not necessarily excel in every area. Where they cannot provide services themselves, they must operate through correspondent banks at home and abroad. For example, many of the regional banks in the United States attempt to provide export and import financing and foreign-exchange trading for their local clients, but they usually work through large money center banks to effect the trades.

Banks also attempt to establish niches where they feel they can develop a comparative advantage. Bankers Trust, for example, established the following strategy in 1983: "Bankers Trust will combine the on-balance-sheet capability of a commercial bank with the intermediary skills and entrepreneurial spirit of an investment bank. We want to accomplish what we believe to be the challenge of the 1980s—worldwide merchant banking."[29] Bankers Trust sold off lines of business that were not compatible with those objectives and has been very successful in the investment-banking market. BT managers feel that their success is in combining corporate banking functions with investment banking in the Eurodebt and equity markets as well as in foreign exchange and other financial services.

Foreign-exchange trading is a key service provided by the large international banks. In 1990, *Euromoney* identified Citicorp as the best foreign-exchange house in the world in the 1980s. It trades actively in 50 different international money centers in 90 different currencies. In 1988 its net income from foreign exchange was double that of the nearest competitor. Its offices worldwide allow it to gather information about foreign-exchange movements more effectively than any other bank.[30]

Debt and equity financing blurs the line between commercial and investment banking. A commercial bank lends money to its clients and often makes syndicated loans as well, where it arranges a loan involving many different banks, both foreign and domestic. The top four banks in syndicated loans are Citicorp, J. P. Morgan, Chase Manhattan, and Manufacturers Hanover—all U.S.-based banks. Syndication involves one of the lead banks structuring a loan that involves several other banks—often from different countries. The loans can be advertised, or they can be by invitation only.

An investment bank provides funding for corporations by helping them raise funds in both debt and equity markets. In the United States, commercial banks are not allowed to engage directly in equity securities, so the large investment companies, such as Goldman Sachs, are not bank related. Most of the leaders in the Euromarkets are investment banks, which will be discussed in the next section. Bankers Trust, however, is an example of a U.S. commercial bank that has also developed a successful investment-banking strategy and is very active in Eurodollar and Eurobond issues. It does so through BT Securities, which is separate from its commercial banking operations.

Multinational banks allow faster transfer of funds through electronic means.

International cash management has exploded in growth in recent years because of the introduction of **electronic data interchange (EDI).** EDI provides for the movement of money and information electronically, cutting down on the paper flow and speeding up the transaction time of data transfers. Banks are a key element in this process, but this service was not developed adequately until the early 1970s; prior to that, transfers of funds between European countries could take several days to several weeks, even when cable transfers were used.

SWIFT is a cooperative arrangement of banks worldwide to transfer funds instantaneously.

In an effort to eliminate the time lag in carrying out international money transfers by mail or telex, a number of banks organized the **Society for Worldwide Interbank Financial Telecommunication (SWIFT)** in 1973. SWIFT has grown from an initial membership of 239 banks in 15 countries to over 1200 banks in more than 50 countries. SWIFT services primarily involve processing transactions such as customer transfers, foreign-exchange confirmation, bank transfers, and documentary credits. A special-message text language allows banks to "talk" to each other by computer in a common language. This added capability greatly facilitates information transfers.[31]

CHIPS is a clearing mechanism for domestic and foreign currency transactions in the United States.

Another important institution is the **Clearing House Interbank Payment System (CHIPS),** an international electronic check-transfer system that moves money between major U.S. banks, branches of foreign banks, and Edge Act subsidiaries of out-of-state banks. The system handles a large volume of transactions per day and most of the foreign-exchange trade and Eurodollar transactions. CHIPS has speeded up the settling of its transactions to the close of each business day rather than the next business day as was the custom.[32]

Financial engineering is the creative design of financial instruments (derivatives) by international banks to hedge underlying assets, like bonds and stocks.

Financial engineering is a term that has surfaced in recent years as a result of the creative design of financial instruments by the international banks. Since the stock-market crash of 1987, there has been significant volatility in the financial markets. Foreign exchange, bonds, equities, and commodities are underlying transactions that have seen big swings in prices and returns, especially over the past few years. As a result, banks have developed the derivatives market, a market designed to protect underlying transactions. Examples of derivatives are forward contracts, futures, options, and swaps. Vanilla derivatives are simple uses of the derivatives to hedge exposure. However, banks have developed complex, custom-tailored derivatives and applied them to unique situations for the firms. Thus the financial-engineering dimension of commercial and investment banks is one of creativity and flexibility. It has become an important element in the strategy of large banks such as Bankers Trust and Citicorp.

Market Access and Changing Market Conditions   We will examine three important aspects of market access: the lack of access foreign banks have to certain markets, such as Japan and Korea; the opening of Europe by the end of 1992; and the changes taking place in the U.S. market.

Many countries do not allow equal access to their markets by foreign banks.

A report by the U.S. Treasury identified several countries that have significant barriers to entry of their financial markets by foreign financial-services firms. In Japan, for instance, the regulation of interest rates gives Japanese banks an edge over foreign banks and allows them to operate on narrower profit margins abroad. In addition, operating restrictions, the close ties between Japanese banks and Japanese corporations, and lack of clarity over banking regulations make it difficult for foreign firms to operate.[33]

South Korea is another country that has restricted the entry of foreign banks. Foreign banks are hindered by "discriminatory restrictions on their ability to establish head offices and branches, obtain local-currency funding, raise capital, and engage in trust business."[34]

The key is that banks want access to different markets in order to service their clients better. However, governments may restrict access to their local markets in order to preserve the competitive position of local banks. Canada has recently lifted most of its restrictions on foreign banks, but it still does not allow foreign banks to establish branches.

The European Community has established December 31, 1992, as the date on which they hope to eliminate a series of barriers on the free flow of goods and services in order to establish one common market. An important aspect of the liberalization efforts relates to financial services. The EC has told foreign banks that they would be given reciprocal national treatment in the EC member nations. This means that foreign banks would be given the same privileges as EC banks as long as EC banks are given similar treatment in those foreign countries.[35]

The deregulation of the banking industry in Europe should result in the merger of smaller banks and the establishment of large pan-European banks to compete with Japanese and U.S. banks.

The opening of the different country markets in the EC is having enormous consequences in Europe. Currently, each country has a myriad of laws that restrict competition by foreign banks. However, with the elimination of barriers in 1992 many of those protected banks are likely to be eliminated by competition. For example, European banks on average have half the deposits per capita of U.S. banks but 20 percent more branches. Because of the barriers, many of the European banks have remained inefficient and noncompetitive.

A wave of mergers and acquisitions is taking place in European banking, and many experts believe that Europe will soon be dominated by 15 pan-European banks, with Citicorp the only foreign bank with significant position in the market. Citicorp currently has 18,000 employees in 21 countries in Europe, and it is growing to position itself well in Europe after 1992. Japanese banks are also attempting to position themselves well, but the Europeans may end up with a significantly better position in the next decade.[36] At the present time, 10 of the top 25 banks in the world are European, not counting Hong-kong & Shanghai Bank. Hongkong & Shanghai Bank recently decided to move its headquarters from Hong Kong to Britain because of the uncertainty surrounding the 1997 takeover of Hong Kong by China. Although as much as 80 percent of the bank's profits come from Hong Kong, it will be considered a European bank, the fifteenth-largest in the world.[37]

The large U.S. market is in the process of opening up—to U.S. banks. More than 260 foreign banks are operating in the United States, and their share of the market has grown from 14 percent in 1982 to 21 percent in 1989. Japanese banks control about 25 percent of the banking market in California. Japanese banks in particular have been taking significant amounts of corporate business away from U.S. banks. They are able to lend money at much lower rates and are able to respond much more quickly and creatively than their U.S. competitors.

The possible deregulation of the financial market in the United States should allow U.S. banks to become more competitive with the Japanese.

U.S. banks have made serious strategic errors in the past decade, but much of their comparative disadvantage is created by the banking environment in the United States. "U.S. banks are hobbled by structural impediments that include barriers to forming national networks, rigorous reporting requirements, and disadvantageous tax and accounting standards."[38] Because of the U.S. aversion to bigness in banks, there are legal barriers that prohibit U.S. banks from establishing interstate branches and from offering securities and insurance products. However, these prohibitions are being challenged, and many feel that U.S. banks must be allowed the same privileges as European banks if they are to remain competitive. A major fear is that the changes going on in the financial-services industry might relegate U.S. banks to third place behind the Japanese and Europeans if significant changes are not made in the U.S. financial-services industry. However, the problems that have resulted from the deregulation of the savings and loan industry have made many in Congress question the wisdom of changing controls over commercial banks.

Profitability   Although the Japanese banks are the biggest in terms of assets and the most valuable in terms of stock-market capitalization, they are definitely not the most profitable. As noted in Table 9.5, most of the most-profitable banks in the world are U.S. and European.

In 1989, however, the earnings of a number of large international banks fell as a consequence of a new round of massive losses on Latin American

TABLE 9.5 | MOST-PROFITABLE BANKS The Japanese banks are the largest in the world, but the European and U.S. banks are the most profitable.

	Real Profitability Index*
Wells Fargo/U.S.	1.239
BankAmerica/U.S.	1.217
Banco Bilbao Viscaya/Spain	1.214
Skandinaviska Enskilda Banken/Sweden	1.192
NCNB/U.S.	1.175
National Australia Bank/Australia	1.167
Security Pacific/U.S.	1.161
First Chicago/U.S.	1.126
Paribas/France	1.125
Abbey National/Britain	1.125

*Based on return on equity adjusted for onetime tax benefits, differing capital ratios, inflation, and tax rates.

Source: William Glasgall, "Happy Days Aren't Here Again," *Business Week,* 2 July 1990, p. 80.

Poor loans, especially to developing countries, are among the problems affecting the profitability of international banks.

loans. The banks were affected by loans to developing countries because many of them are holding loans on which no principal and interest are being paid. New banking regulations in the United States require banks to identify the amount of their nonaccrual loans at the end of each quarter. A **nonaccrual loan** is one for which principal or interest is 90 days past due or for which payment of interest or principal is determined to be doubtful. The nonaccrual concept relates to domestic as well as foreign loans, and many banks have had as many problems with domestic loans as with foreign loans.

As a result of massive difficulties in collecting on loans to the developing countries, the major U.S. banks have gradually been building huge loan-loss reserves in order to protect themselves from a major default. The first major protective move came in 1987 when Citicorp added $3 billion to its loan-loss reserves, thereby boosting its reserves to 25 percent of Latin American loans and 100 percent of its nonperforming loans.[39] In 1989 J.P. Morgan & Co. added $2 billion to its reserves, representing 100 percent of its portfolio of medium- and long-term developing-country debt. Most banks' reserves have hovered in the 25 percent range, but in recent years international banks have been increasing their reserves to the 35–50 percent range. Having reserves of that size allows the banks to hedge against a default in a given year.[40]

The new BIS requirement that banks must have a capital/asset ratio of at least 8 percent by March 1993 is causing some banks to try to add to their capital base through profitability. Banks in each country are affected by different circumstances. In the United States, risky real-estate dealings and the problems of leveraged buy-out loans are added to the Latin American debt situation as sources of pressure on profits. In addition, the Japanese banks that are competing in the United States and operating on such thin margins are making it difficult for U.S. banks to increase margins and enhance profits.

The Japanese banks have been hurt by conditions in both Japan and the United States. An example is the stepping down of the Chairman of Sumitomo Bank in Japan in 1990. The leadership change was a function of several factors. Although the direct factor was a stock-manipulation scandal, Sumitomo was heavily involved in the runup of the stock and securities markets in Japan in the latter half of the 1980s. From the beginning of 1985 to the end of 1989, the Nikkei index in Japan rose 237 percent, and property values in Japan's three major cities rose an average of 126 percent. Thus the banks began to get involved in both of those high-growth markets in order to fatten profit margins. However, the collapse of the stock market in 1990 and the tapering off of property values severely hurt the Japanese banks.[41] As the banks move back into traditional project and retail lending, their margins will fall even more, making it difficult for them to achieve the 8 percent capital/assets ratio by 1993. As the leveraged buy-out market in the United States becomes even riskier, Japanese banks are pulling out from financing many of the buy-outs of U.S. firms.[42] This should help the margins of the Japanese banks but cause problems for firms that will have more difficulty borrowing money to effect an LBO.

NONBANKING FINANCIAL SERVICES FIRMS

So far we have discussed debt and equity markets available to MNEs as well as the international banks that provide financial services. But there are a number of other financial-services firms in addition to banks that provide financial services for MNEs. Sometimes the distinction between banks and financial-services firms that deal in the securities markets (both debt and equity) is unclear because of differences in different countries' regulations. For example, the United Kingdom does not require a separation of commercial and investment banking, whereas both Japan and the United States do. As Table 9.6 shows, there is only one British firm among the twenty-five largest securities and financial-services firms. This is so primarily because U.K. banks can engage in both commercial and investment banking.

Some nations require separate commercial banking and securities functions, others do not.

Firms often behave very differently abroad than they do at home. Thus Japanese and American commercial banks are heavily involved in securities work abroad, although that is prohibited at home.

In looking at Table 9.6, note the importance again of the U.S. and Japanese firms. In 1980 Nomura ranked twentieth in the Eurobond lead manager league tables and was relatively small in the United States and Europe. However, the speed with which it has attacked the world markets since 1986 is amazing. Nomura, the most powerful financial institution in Japan, is expected to become the largest in the world during the 1990s.[43] *Euromoney* iden-

The Japanese and U.S. securities firms are now the largest in the world.

TABLE 9.6 | THE WORLD'S 25-LARGEST SECURITIES FIRMS* The world's largest securities firms are dominated by the U.S. and Japanese securities firms.

Rank 1989	Rank 1988	Company (Country)	Capital	Change From 1988	Assets	Net Income
1	2	Salomon (U.S.)	$12,848	21%	$90,636	$470
2	1	Nomura Securities (Japan)	10,892	0	28,810	N.A.†
3	3	Merrill Lynch (U.S.)	10,048	3	52,297	−217
4	5	Shearson Lehman Hutton (U.S.)	8,966	10	50,356	110
5	4	Daiwa Securities (Japan)	7,743	6	24,687	N.A.†
6	6	Nikko Securities (Japan)	6,560	5	18,512	410
7	7	Yamaichi Securities (Japan)	6,405	4	16,150	N.A.†
8	8	Dean Witter‡ (U.S.)	4,432	31	16,840	166
9	9	Goldman Sachs (U.S.)	4,018	45	40,546	N.A.
10	11	Hees International (Canada)	3,669	17	4,605	215
11	10	Morgan Stanley (U.S.)	2,764	14	28,812	443
12	13	CS First Boston (U.S.)	1,783	−4	21,709	N.A.
13	20	New Japan Securities (Japan)	1,716	50	4,444	N.A.†
14	14	Nippon Kangyo Kakumaru (Japan)	1,557	5	3,625	N.A.†
15	—	Kokusai Securities (Japan)	1,557	6	3,080	N.A.†
16	15	Paine Webber (U.S.)	1,523	4	15,479	52
17	17	Bear Stearns (U.S.)	1,451	3	22,941	172
18	16	Kleinwort Benson (U.K.)	1,347	3	15,200	84
19	22	Prudential-Bache‡ (U.S.)	1,322	10	10,318	N.A.
20	21	S.G. Warburg (U.K.)	1,300	14	17,831	108
21	18	Sanyo Securities (Japan)	1,278	6	3,179	N.A.†
22	19	Wako Securities (Japan)	1,254	6	2,601	N.A.†
23	23	Morgan Grenfell (U.K.)	891	5	10,678	57
24	—	Okasan Securities (Japan)	762	6	2,538	N.A.†
25	25	Kidder Peabody‡ (U.S.)	742	−8	10,820	N.A.

Note: Capital is defined as owner's equity, reserves, minority interest, preferred stock, and long-term debt. Assets are calculated net of custody securities and securities purchased under agreement to resell.

*Ranked by capital as determined by Worldscope; figures are based on each company's 1989 fiscal-year results. (In millions of U.S. dollars at December 31, 1989, exchange rates; percentage change based on home currency)

†Year-end changed to March; 12 months not available

‡Subsidiary, listed for comparative purposes

Source: "The Global Giants," *The Wall Street Journal Reports,* 21 September 1990, p. R30.

tifies it as the firm that has had the greatest impact on capital markets in the 1980s. It is currently the lead manager of all international issues in the world, and four of the top five lead managers are Japanese securities firms.

One of the remarkable things about the Japanese securities firms is their profitability. Although Table 9.6 does not contain profits data for the Japanese firms due to a change in fiscal year-end in that survey, there are good data for 1988. In 1988 the estimated profits of the six largest U.S. securities firms were $1.9 billion, but the four largest Japanese firms listed profits of $3.9 billion. In the fall of 1989 the 50 largest U.S. financial institutions had a combined market capitalization of $95 billion, whereas the 13 largest Japanese financial institutions had a combined market capitalization of $500 billion. This gives the Japanese firms tremendous financial leverage for the future.[44]

DEVELOPMENT BANKS

Although MNEs tend to go to private capital markets for financing, there is also a significant amount of funding available from development banks. The funds are usually directed for specific types of projects, so the firms have to qualify for those projects. However, these development banks can provide funding as well as guarantees for projects that might grant the firms access to funds in the private capital markets.

The World Bank

The World Bank provides development financing for the developing countries of the world.

The "World Bank" is the **International Bank for Reconstruction and Development (IBRD)** and the **International Development Association (IDA).** The IBRD has two affiliates, the **International Finance Corporation (IFC)** and the **Multilateral Investment Guarantee Agency (MIGA).** The Bank, the IFC, and the MIGA are sometimes referred to as the "World Bank Group."[45]

International Bank for Reconstruction and Development   The IBRD was organized in 1945 along with the IMF to aid in rebuilding the world economy. It is owned by the governments of 151 countries, and its capital is subscribed by those governments; it provides funds to borrowers by borrowing funds in the world capital markets and from the proceeds of loan repayments as well as retained earnings. At its founding, the bank's major objective was to serve as an international financing facility to function in reconstruction and development. With the Marshall Plan providing the impetus for European reconstruction, the bank was able to turn its efforts toward the developing countries.

The IBRD lends money to governments for convertible currency for infrastructure development.

Generally, the IBRD lends money to a government for the purpose of developing that country's economic infrastructure, such as roads and power-generating facilities. Funds are directed toward developing countries at more advanced stages of economic and social growth. Funds are lent only to members of the IMF, usually when private capital is unavailable at reasonable terms. Loans generally have a grace period of five years and are repayable over a period of fifteen or fewer years.

The projects receiving IBRD assistance usually require importing heavy industrial equipment, and this provides an export market for many U.S. goods. Generally, bank loans are made to cover only import needs in foreign convertible currencies and must be repaid in those currencies at long-term rates.

An example of an IBRD loan is a $30 million loan to the Dominican Republic, approved in 1989.

> The government will be assisted in formulating and implementing an effective and comprehensive strategy for the development of new industrial free zones and the expansion of existing ones; reducing unemployment, increasing foreign-exchange earnings, and strengthening backward linkages with the domestic economy; alleviating scarcity in term financing; and improving the capacity of institutions involved in financing, regulating, and promoting free zones. Cofinancing, in the amount of $1.4 million, is expected.[46]

The World Bank has special operational emphases, including environmental and women's issues. Given that the Bank's primary mission is to support the quality of life of people in developing member countries, it is easy to see why environmental and women's issues are receiving increasing attention. On the environmental side, the Bank is concerned that its development funds are being used in the recipient countries in an environmentally responsible way. Internal concerns, as well as pressure by external groups, are leading to significant research and projects relating to the environment.

The women's issues category, specifically known as Women in Development (WID), is part of a larger emphasis on human resources. The importance of improving human capital and improving the welfare of families is perceived as a key aspect of development. The WID initiative was established in 1988, and it is oriented to increasing women's productivity and income. Bank lending for women's issues is most pronounced in education; population, health, and nutrition; and agriculture.

IDA provides infrastructure loans for the poorest countries in the world.

International Development Association   The IDA was formed in 1960 as a part of the World Bank Group to provide financial support to LDCs on a more liberal basis than could be offered by the IBRD. The IDA has 137 member countries, although all members of the IBRD are free to join the IDA. IDA's funds come from subscriptions from its developed members and from the earnings of the IBRD. Credit terms usually are extended to 40 to 50 years with no interest. Repayment begins after a ten-year grace period and can be paid in the local currency, as long as it is convertible. Loans are made only to the poorest countries in the world, those with an annual per capita gross national product of $480 or less. More than 40 countries are eligible for IDA financing.

An example of an IDA project is an $8.3 million loan to Tanzania approved in 1989 to implement the first stage in the longer-term process of rehabilitating the country's agricultural-research system. Cofinancing is expected from several countries as well as another multilateral lending institution.[47]

Although the IDA's resources are separate from the IBRD, it has no separate staff. Loans are made for the same types of projects as those carried out by the IBRD, but at easier and more favorable credit terms.

As mentioned earlier, World Bank/IDA assistance historically has been for developing infrastructure. The present emphasis seems to be on helping the masses of poor people in the developing countries become more productive and take an active part in the development process. Greater emphasis is being placed on improving urban living conditions and increasing productivity of small industries.

International Finance Corporation   The IFC was established in 1956. There are 133 countries that are members of the IFC, and it is legally and financially separate from the IBRD, although the IBRD provides some administrative and other services to the IFC. The IFC's main responsibilities are: (1) to provide risk capital in the form of equity and long-term loans for productive private enterprises in association with private investors and management; (2) to encourage the development of local capital markets by carrying out standby and underwriting arrangements; and (3) to stimulate the international flow of capital by providing financial and technical assistance to privately controlled finance companies. Loans are made to private firms in the developing member countries and are usually for a period of seven to twelve years.

IFC activities are oriented primarily toward helping the private sector in developing countries.

The key feature of the IFC is that its loans are all made to private enterprises and its investments are made in conjunction with private business. In addition to funds contributed by IFC, funds also are contributed to the same projects by local and foreign investors.

IFC investments are for the establishment of new enterprises as well as for the expansion and modernization of existing ones. They cover a wide range of projects, such as steel, textile production, mining, manufacturing, machinery production, food processing, tourism, and local development finance companies. Some projects are wholly locally owned, whereas others are joint ventures between investors in developing and developed countries. In a few cases, joint ventures are formed between investors of two or more developing countries. The IFC has also been instrumental in helping to develop emerging capital markets.

The Multilateral Investment Guarantee Agency (MIGA)   The MIGA was established in 1988 to encourage equity investment and other direct investment flows to developing countries by offering investors a variety of different services. The MIGA offers guarantees against noncommercial risks; advises developing member governments on the design and implementation of policies, programs, and procedures related to foreign investments; and sponsors a dialogue between the international business community and host governments on investment issues.[48] Because the MIGA is so new, its real contribution to the promotion of investment flows is still unclear.

Regional Development Banks

During the seventies and eighties, there was a dramatic increase in the number of development banks, and they have become an important source of financing for the developing countries, especially the riskiest developing countries. Although many of the development banks are national in scope, there are also a number of regional development banks. In Europe, the most important regional development bank is the European Investment Bank, which offers funds for private and public industrial and infrastructure projects in Europe and to over 70 nations associated with the European Community. Latin America has five active regional development banks: (1) the Andean Development Corp., (2) the Caribbean Development Bank, (3) the Inter-American Development Bank, (4) the Central American Bank for Economic Integration, and (5) the Banco Latinoamericano de Exportaciones. There are a number of other similar development banks in Africa and Asia.

> There are regional and national development banks that attempt to finance the same types of activities as does the World Bank.

An example of a regional development bank is the **InterAmerican Development Bank (IDB).** The IDB was organized in 1959 to give countries in the Western Hemisphere (principally the United States and Latin America) the same types of services the World Bank provides. However, the IDB projects are wider in scope and tailored for member countries. Loans are made from ordinary capital resources to private and public entities of the 44 member nations. These loans are generally made at favorable rates of interest and are repayable in the currencies lent. Procurement sources of goods and services are limited to those countries that contribute funds to the IDB.

The cumulative sectorial breakdown of IDB loans is as follows for 1961–1988: 27 percent for energy projects; 21 percent for agriculture and fisheries; 15 percent for industry and mining; 13 percent for transportation and communications; 11 percent for environmental and public health; 4 percent for education, science, and technology; 4 percent for urban development; and 5 percent for other projects. The largest borrowers are Brazil, Mexico, and Argentina.[49]

LOOKING TO THE FUTURE The difficulty in describing global capital markets is the speed of change. As world trade increases and global interdependence rises, the velocity of financial transactions also must increase. The next two decades should use the rise in importance of the German mark and the Japanese yen relative to the U.S. dollar. In addition, the Japanese financial institutions will continue to strengthen their position among the biggest and best of the global financial-services firms at the expense of the Europeans and Americans. However, the changes taking place in Europe should result in a consolidation of European financial institutions and the establishment of formidable competitors to the largest Japanese and U.S. financial-services firms. In addition, a liberalization of the financial-services industry in the United States should help to strengthen the position of U.S. banks vis-à-vis those of different countries.

Even though national financial markets are deregulating at a rapid pace, there will still be a strong need for Eurocapital markets. The high degree of competition in those markets should be very healthy for MNEs, because the financial-services firms will be forced to develop new financial products at cheaper prices in order to maintain their market share. This will result in new financial instruments to finance growth as well as to protect the underlying debt and equity instruments issued by the corporate clients of the banks and securities firms. Although there are some mixed signals on the future of the Eurobond market, there is no doubt about the future of equity trading. The current existence of a global equity market means that traders can trade on stock markets virtually 24 hours a day. However, the traders typically take place in the securities of a market when that market is open. The globalization of markets will expand when trades in the securities of market A take place 24 hours a day, whether that market is open or not (which is what we are moving toward). As information technology expands, as we see stock exchange listing requirements standardize, and as accounting standards become more harmonized, we will see the global trade of securities increase dramatically.

SUMMARY

- Local debt markets, which vary dramatically from country to country owing to local business customs and practices, are important sources of funds for MNEs.

- A Eurocurrency is any currency that is banked outside of its country of origin. The dollar comprises the bulk of the Eurocurrency market and is referred to as the Eurodollar.

- Eurodollars are expanded through the fractional reserve concept, whereby a bank reserves only a fraction of each Eurodollar deposited and loans the remainder of the deposit, thus "creating" more Eurodollars.

- A Eurobond is a bond issue sold in a currency other than that of the country of issue. A foreign bond is one sold outside of the country of the borrower but denominated in the currency of the country of issue.

- Offshore financial centers such as London, Switzerland, the Caribbean, Singapore, Hong Kong, Bahrain, and now New York City, deal in international transactions that are not regulated in the same way as domestic markets.

- Most industrial countries and some developing countries have stock exchanges in which equity capital can be raised by firms. However, the three major international equity markets for the sale and purchase of securities by individuals from many countries are in New York, Tokyo, and London.

- The Japanese stock market has overtaken the U.S. stock market as the largest in the world. This occurred as a result of the strengthening yen and rising Japanese securities prices.

- Many corporations are beginning to list their securities on stock exchanges in different countries in order to raise capital.

- Because of the strong Japanese yen and large Japanese trade surpluses, the Japanese banks are achieving international dominance.

- The major operational modes used in international banking are branches, consortia, correspondents, and Edge Act corporations.

- International banks are faced with a number of challenges, such as providing adequate financial services, dealing with market access and changing market conditions, and increasing profitability.

- U.S. and Japanese securities and financial-services firms dominate world markets. The Japanese brokerage houses now do the greatest volume in the Eurobond market.

- The World Bank Group includes the International Bank for Reconstruction and Development (IBRD), the International Development Association (IDA), the International Finance Corporation (IFC), and the Multilateral Investment Guarantee Agency (MIGA). These multilateral lending institutions are designed to provide financial support for LDCs on a private as well as public basis. The IFC is especially active in providing debt and equity financing in private-sector projects.

C A S E
LSI LOGIC CORP.[50]

In the late 1970s, Wilfred Corrigan, the British-born chairman and president of Fairchild Camera & Instrument Corp., sold Fairchild to Schlumberger Ltd. Approximately one year later, in November 1980, he started LSI Logic Corp., a manufacturer of custom-made microchips based in Malpitas, California. Although Mr. Corrigan's idea of custom-made microchips sounded unconventional at the time, he was able to use his record at Fairchild to convince some U.S. venture capitalists in January 1981 to invest nearly $7 million in the new firm.

The company had only four employees at this point, but since Corrigan had solved two key issues—the nature of the product and the initial infusion of cash—there was a solid foundation for growth. Corrigan now had to decide how LSI Logic should service its customers worldwide, and how and where it would raise capital to keep expanding.

Global Strategy Mr. Corrigan learned from his experience at Fairchild that a producer of mi-

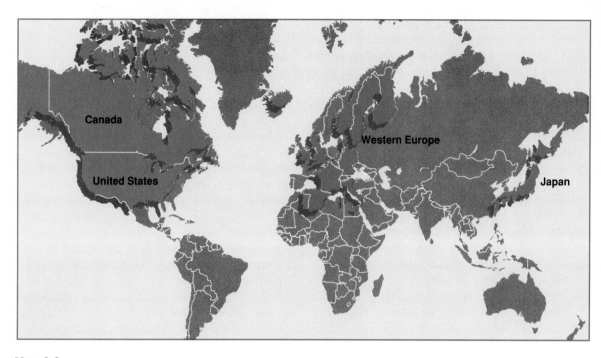

Map 9.2
The Triad Strategy
LSI Logic's global business and financing strategy included the three major markets in the world: Asia (specifically Japan), North America, and Europe.

crochips had to think globally in terms of the location of production and the consumer. He quickly decided that in order to be successful, he needed to concentrate on being in three key geographic areas—Japan, the United States, and Europe (illustrated in Map 9.2). He called this his "global triad strategy." The key organizational strategy was to establish firms incorporated in the producing and consuming countries that would be jointly owned by LSI Logic and local investors. However, LSI Logic would hold a controlling interest in the firm. Although the operations in each country would be relatively independent of each other, they would still be linked by technology, money, and management. This would allow the synergy of interdependence to take place, but it would also permit local freedom in meeting the demands of the market.

Initial European Thrust   Once Corrigan got operations under way, he began to look for more cash. The key was to find the right amount, at the right price, with the least number of problems. In February 1982, slightly more than a year after U.S. venture capital gave the company a start, LSI Logic turned to Europe in search of venture capital. It was found in a European investing community hungry for U.S. high-tech stock, so it was able to raise $10 million, mostly—but not exclusively—in Britain. That offering brought LSI Logic an average of $7 a share, compared with only $0.90 per share when it was set up only a year earlier.

At this point LSI Logic was growing rapidly. In May 1983 Corrigan took the firm public in the United States and raised over $162 million, an average now of $21 a share. That was a significant improvement over its European experience and demonstrated the size of the appetite in the United States for new high-tech companies.

The Japanese Strategy   In spite of the success in Europe and in the United States, Corrigan still had not been able to complete the third part of his triad—Japan. However, Corrigan learned that Nomura Securities, the largest brokerage house in Japan (and subsequently the world), had purchased large blocks of LSI stock for its clients in Japan. Encouraged by this information, Corrigan traveled to Japan to meet with Nomura officials and try to decide what LSI Logic's next move should be. As a result of the visit and discussions, Corrigan decided that the time was right for starting operations in Japan. Following the strategy he had used elsewhere, Corrigan established a Japanese subsidiary of LSI Logic (called LSI Logic Corp. K.K.) in which the parent company owned 70 percent, and 25 local Japanese investors owned 30 percent. The investors were not small operations, however. Nippon Life Insurance Company, the third-largest insurance company in the world, just behind Prudential and Metropolitan Life, became a major shareholder in the new venture. The new investment was just right for LSI Logic. Not only did Corrigan now have access to the Japanese consumer market, but he also had access to the Japanese capital market. As a Japanese company, LSI Logic Corp. K.K. and its manufacturing affiliate, Nihon Semiconductor Inc., could now establish lines of credit with Japanese banks. In order to help LSI Logic penetrate the capital markets better and to develop more of a local image in Japan, Corrigan hired Keiske Awata, a senior executive of NEC Corp. who was working

outside of Japan at the time. Mr. Awata gave a Japanese image to LSI Logic in Japan and helped open the right doors to the financial world. LSI Logic was able to get a local line of credit at only 6 percent, compared with 9 percent in the United States at the time.

Second European Thrust   Now that business in Japan was under way, Corrigan turned his attentions again to Europe. He was planning to set up a new European company and he needed to decide on its structure. The company could be set up as a branch of the U.S. parent that would use U.S. capital and be totally controlled and protected by the parent, or it could be set up as a European company. Corrigan decided to do the latter, so he used Morgan Stanley & Co., the large U.S.-based securities firm, to set up LSI Logic Ltd. The parent company retained an 82 percent stake in the new company, and the rest was sold to European investors in a private offering. One of the investors was the venture-capital arm of five West German banks. Corrigan was convinced that by setting up a European company, he was able to get more money by selling shares at a higher price than would have been possible otherwise and that LSI Logic Ltd. was better placed to service European customers than a branch of the parent company would have been.

Convertible Bonds   In 1985 and again in 1987, Corrigan returned to European capital markets, but this time LSI floated a bond issue. The first issue of $23 million was put together by Swiss Bank Corp., one of the largest banks in the world. The second issue, a bond issue with securities convertible into common stock, was floated by Morgan Stanley and Prudential-Bache Capital Funding. There were two main attractions to the Eurobond market for LSI Logic: a decent price (lower interest rates than would have been offered in the United States), and a quicker time frame. Since LSI didn't have to worry about all of the listing regulations of the Securities and Exchange Commission in the United States, it was able to get the offering together faster and out to the investing public.

Although significant amounts of funds were raised in foreign markets (over $200 million since 1982), there was no real exchange risk. LSI Logic operations worldwide were earning revenues that could be used to pay off the financial obligations. In addition, LSI Logic subsidiaries had access to local credit markets because they were organized as local corporations rather than branches of a foreign corporation.

Questions

1. What were the different ways that LSI Logic used international capital markets? Discuss specifically the nature of the instruments (i.e., local, foreign, Euro, etc.).
2. Why did it use those markets rather than just the U.S. market?
3. How did its organizational strategy fit with its capital-acquisition strategy?

Chapter Notes

1. "Italy," *Financing Foreign Operations* (New York: Business International Corporation, June 1990), p. 10.
2. "A New Credit Market in Pesetas," *Business Week,* 15 June 1981, p. 102.
3. Rodrigo Briones, "Latin American Money Markets," in *International Finance Handbook,* Abraham M. George and Ian H. Giddy, eds. (New York: Wiley, 1983), p. 4.9.4.
4. "Italy," *Op. cit.,* p. 13.
5. "The Euromarkets," *Financing Foreign Operations* (New York: Business International Corporation, May 1990), p. 1.
6. *Ibid.*
7. *Ibid.,* p. 2.
8. *Ibid.*
9. Paul Keller, "The Pursuit of the ECU," *Euromoney,* January 1990, p. 77.
10. "Markets into the 1990's," *Euromoney* Supplement, March 1990, pp. 1–3.
11. Maximo Eng and Francis A. Lees, "Eurocurrency Centers," in *International Finance Handbook,* Abraham M. George and Ian H. Giddy, eds. (New York: Wiley, 1983), p. 3.6.3 and 3.6.4.
12. "Why the Big Apple Shines in the World's Markets," *Business Week,* July 23, 1984, p. 101.
13. Barbara Buell, William Glasgall, Richard A. Melcher, and Jonathan B. Levine, "The Tidal Wave That's Sweeping International Finance," *Business Week,* July 13, 1987, p. 57.
14. "Flinging Open the Doors of Change," *Euromoney* Supplement, August 1986, p. 2.
15. "Big Bang Rumbles across Europe," *The Banker,* May 1987, p. 82.
16. George M. Von Furstenberg and Bang Nam Jeon, "International Stock Price Movements: Links and Messages," *Brookings Papers on Economic Activity,* by William C. Brainard and George L. Perry, ed. (Washington, D.C.: The Brookings Institution, 1:1989), pp. 163–165.

17. Paul Wiseman, "Economic Shocks Jolt Tokyo Harder," *USA Today,* 15 August 1990, p. 1; *Wall Street Journal,* 26 December 1990, pp. C1 and C11; Marcus W. Brauchli and Clay Chandler, "Battered Nikkei," *Wall Street Journal,* 23 August 1990, p. 1.

18. "How the Heavyweights Shape Up," *Euromoney,* May 1990, p. 56.

19. *Ibid.*

20. David K. Eiteman and Arthur I. Stonehill, *Multinational Business Finance,* fifth ed. (Reading, Mass.: Addison-Wesley, 1989), pp. 280–282.

21. Simon Brady, "London's Lead Looks Impregnable," *Euromoney,* May 1990, p. 70.

22. "How the Heavyweights Shape Up," p. 62.

23. *Ibid.,* p. 66.

24. Jeffrey M. Laderman, "Stock Around the Clock," *Business Week,* 2 July 1990, pp. 30–32.

25. Bryan Lorin Sudweeks, *Equity Market Development in Developing Countries* (New York: Praeger Publishers, 1989), pp. 38–43.

26. Vitrang R. Errunza, "Emerging Markets: A New Opportunity for Improving Global Portfolio Performance," *Financial Analysts Journal,* September–October 1983, pp. 51–52.

27. "The Widest Global Presence," *Euromoney* Supplement, January 1990, p. 7.

28. "The Euromarkets," *Op. cit.,* p. 3.

29. "Banks of the Decade," *Euromoney* Supplement, January 1990, p. 2.

30. "Better than the Roll of a Dice," *Euromoney* Supplement, January 1990, p. 10.

31. "Banking Tomorrow—Communications," *The Banker,* October 1984, pp. 73–77.

32. "CHIPS: Goodby to Next-Day Settlements," *Business Week,* March 23, 1981, p. 98.

33. Eduardo Lachica, "Canada, Europe Said to Ease Entry in Finance Markets," *Wall Street Journal,* 12 December 1990, A6.

34. *Ibid.*

35. *Ibid.*

36. Craig Forman, "Europe's Banks Grapple with Sea Change," *Wall Street Journal,* 17 May 1990, p. A12.

37. Cynthia Owens and Craig Forman, "Hongkong Bank to Form a Parent Based in Britain," *Wall Street Journal,* 18 December 1990, p. A11.

38. Robert Guenther and Michael R. Sesit, "U.S. Banks Are Losing Business to Japanese at Home and Abroad," *Wall Street Journal,* 12 October 1989, p. A1.

39. G. Christian Hill, Richard B. Schmitt, Peter Truell, and Robert Guenther, "BankAmerica Raising Reserve $1.1 Billion; Manufacturers Hanover Mulls Similar Step," *Wall Street Journal,* 9 June 1987, p. 3.

40. Robert Guenther, "Morgan Adds $2 Billion to Reserve for Loans to Developing Nations," *Wall Street Journal,* 22 September 1989, p. A3.

41. Marcus W. Brauchli, "Exit of Sumitomo Chief Marks End of Era," *Wall Street Journal,* 15 October 1990, p. A12.

42. Michael R. Sesit, "Japanese Banks Retreat from U.S. Buy-Outs," *Wall Street Journal,* 5 September 1990, p. C1.

43. "The Greatest Impact on the Capital Markets," *Euromoney* Supplement, January 1990, p. 6.

44. "Has the U.S. Got the Bottle for a Fight?" *Euromoney,* January 1990, p. 50.

45. *The World Bank Annual Report, 1989* (Washington, D.C.: The World Bank, 1990, p. 3.

46. *Ibid.*, p. 148.

47. *Ibid.*, p. 143.

48. *Ibid.*, p. 3.

49. "Regional Development Banks," *Financing Foreign Operations* (New York: Business International Corporation, November 1989), p. 14.

50. Sources for case: Udayan Gupta, "Raising Money the New-Fangled Way," in "Global Finance & Investing: A Special Report," *Wall Street Journal,* September 18, 1987, p. 14D; Nick Arnett, "LSI Lands Former NEC Chief to Head Affiliated Company," *Business Journal—San Jose,* January 14, 1985, p. 17 (1); "LSI Gets a Circuit-Supply Pact," *Wall Street Journal,* January 6, 1987, p. 7.

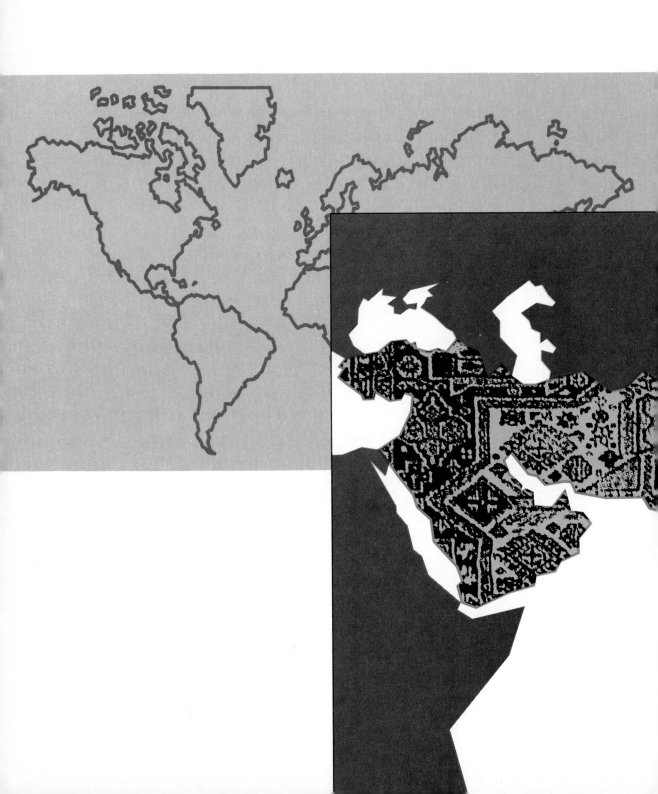

PART 5

THE DYNAMICS OF INTERNATIONAL BUSINESS— GOVERNMENTAL RELATIONSHIPS

The environment of international business is constantly changing as nations deviate from prior political–economic orientations, alter their external relationships with other countries, and modify their attitudes and policies concerning international business. Firms must adapt to the changing environment. In addition, they have specific strengths that may help them deal more effectively with governments in some periods than in others.

Chapter 10 discusses business with historically planned economies (HPEs) by emphasizing both optimistic and pessimistic views of future opportunities. The chapter stresses the variety of likely opportunities among HPEs and diverse opportunities for firms depending on nationality, size, and product line.

Chapter 11 deals with regional economic integration agreements, in terms of both theory and practice, then discusses international commodity agreements and describes major international agencies promoting economic cooperation. The dynamics of economic cooperation is emphasized throughout the chapter.

Although the international mobility of production factors and finished goods by multinational firms may allow the world's consumers to use some products that would otherwise not be available and to consume others at a lower cost, all countries seek to influence factor mobility. Chapter 12 analyzes the economic and noneconomic motives and methods by which nation-states seek to influence the flow of direct investment. Chapter 13 examines the approaches by which international firms and governments may deal with one another in order to satisfy the objectives of each and to attempt to strengthen the bargaining position relative to that of the other party.

CHAPTER **10**

BUSINESS WITH HISTORICALLY PLANNED ECONOMIES

Whether you buy or not, you can always barter a little.
RUSSIAN PROVERB

Objectives

- To demonstrate the historical volatility of commerce between market and historically planned economies.

- To assess the market transformation process from central planning.

- To survey the major problems inherent in expansion of business between market and historically planned economies.

- To describe the various methods and opportunities for commerce between the market countries and those with a history of planning.

Some historians trace the origin of the hamburger to Russia. Supposedly, sailors brought a dish made up of raw ground beef and hot spices to the port of Hamburg, where the recipe was altered, cooked, popularized, and given its name. Hamburgers eventually went from Hamburg to England and then to North America. If this historical account is accurate, then when McDonald's opened its first Moscow establishment in 1990, the hamburger's round-trip journey was complete.

The process of the Russian entry for McDonald's was a long one. George A. Cohon, president of McDonald's Canadian subsidiary, first made contact with Soviet officials during the 1976 Olympics in Montreal. This began lengthy negotiations, during which Cohon traveled to Moscow about once every three weeks until a protocol agreement was signed in 1987. This protocol agreement came about shortly after the former USSR enacted legislation to permit joint ventures with Western firms. Thereafter, progress was swift. A formal agreement was signed in 1988, and Cohon was able to reduce his traveling to only "about one trip a month." In the meantime, McDonald's opened restaurants in Hungary and Yugoslavia, which provided some operating experience in communist countries.

These moves were highly compatible with McDonald's growth strategy. By the mid-1980s the company was growing more rapidly outside the United States than within, and company executives reasoned that the pattern must continue if rapid growth objectives were to be met. In essence, the U.S. market for McDonald's had become nearly saturated. The figures seem like hyperbole: McDonald's controlled almost 20 percent of the U.S. fast-food market. It accounted for 32 percent of all hamburgers and 26 percent of all french-fry sales by U.S. commercial restaurants. The company used 7.5 percent of the entire U.S. potato food-crop, was the world's largest owner of retail real estate, and accounted for about 5 percent of all Coca-Cola sales in the United States. It was estimated that 7 percent of the entire U.S. work force had at one time worked for McDonald's, and that McDonald's was the first employer for one out of every fifteen U.S. workers. Slightly more than half of the U.S. population lived within a three-minute drive to a McDonald's unit. The company had to look abroad, and by 1987 about 30 percent of McDonald's restaurants were located outside the United States. They were in 51 countries and in such far-flung locations that communist countries seemed the logical next frontier.

CASE
McDONALD'S[1]

McDonald's Russian joint venture is between its Canadian subsidiary and the Moscow City Council. McDonald's has a 49 percent interest, the maximum then allowed by local law. (Since 1990 foreigners may own a 99 percent joint venture interest.) The minority ownership has not proved a problem since local law requires at least a three quarters majority vote to approve important decisions. In effect, the representatives from McDonald's and the Moscow City Council must come to an agreement on virtually any major decision.

Between the signing of the joint venture agreement and the 1990 inauguration, much planning and other work had to be completed. In actuality, most of the joint ventures in the former Soviet Union never manage to become operative. When the Moscow restaurant opened, an American legal specialist on joint ventures in Moscow estimated that although about 1400 joint venture agreements had been signed with Western firms since enactment of the 1987 law, only about 50 were actually operating. He also reckoned that only about 100 others had a real prospect of reaching a successful implementation.

The procurement of supplies has proved to be a major hurdle for foreign investors in the former USSR, and McDonald's experience was no exception. For McDonald's the supply problem was created partly by the rigid bureaucratic system, partly by shortages, and partly by the fact that available supplies did not meet McDonald's standards. In spite of having the Moscow City Council as the majority owner in the venture, and in spite of having backing from some strong Kremlin ties, the venture continually ran into negative responses, such as, "Sorry, you're not in my five-year plan," when attempting to obtain such materials as sand or gravel to build the restaurant. The company had to negotiate to assure that it would be allocated, in the central plan, sufficient sugar and flour, which are both in short supply. For some products in sufficient supply, such as mustard, there were regulations that prevented manufacturers from deviating from present recipes in order to comply with McDonald's needs. For many other supplies, local plants were required under strict allocation regulations to sell all output to existing Soviet companies, leaving no opportunity to produce extra products for McDonald's. McDonald's buyers were sickened by the conditions in slaughterhouses within the former USSR. Yet another problem was that some supplies simply were not produced or consumed in the former USSR, such as iceberg lettuce, pickling cucumbers, and the Russet Burbank potatoes that are the secret behind McDonald's fries.

McDonald's had to scour the country for supplies, making contracts, for example, for milk, cheddar cheese, and beef. In addition, the company undertook several approaches to ensure ample supplies of the quality it needs. The company brought in seed potatoes and pickling cucumber seeds from the Netherlands to grow on a collective farm under the supervision of a McDonald's hired agronomist from planting to harvest. The company brought in bull semen to improve the quality of cattle, taught the farmers how to raise leaner beef by castrating their cattle a month later than usual and slaughtering them a month earlier. They trained farmers in the former Soviet Union to harvest and pack produce without bruising it. Yet McDonald's had to import some supplies: mustard from Canada, tomato paste from Portugal, apples from Bulgaria, and packaging material and sesame seeds from several locations.

McDonald's built a $40 million food-processing center about 45 minutes away from the first restaurant. The center is capable of making 1 million buns per week and uses 23,400 gallons of milk, 127,740 cheese slices, 17,715 gallons of sauce, and more than 5200 gallons of pickles per week. Since distribution is as much a cause of shortages as production, McDonald's carries supplies in its own trucks. Because McDonald's is concentrating on long-term development, adequate supplies are critical. People in the former USSR are accustomed to waiting in long lines, even though there is no assurance that there will be anything left to buy after the wait. Adequate supplies are, therefore, a way for McDonald's to differentiate itself.

A major hindrance for foreign investors in the former Soviet Union is the shortage of hard currency. McDonald's was not successful at negotiating the conversion of its ruble profits, but it did not expect to repatriate its earnings and investment quickly. Since the joint venture agreement is for 20 restaurants, most of the profits for many years will have to be reinvested to finance the expansion. Nevertheless, McDonald's has done several things to increase convertibility possibilities and to minimize its hard-currency expenditures. To begin with, many of the furnishings were brought in from Yugoslavia so that some already blocked dinars could be used as part of its investment. McDonald's was able to negotiate a hard-currency royalty payment of 5 percent of sales; however, the subsequent weakening of the ruble has resulted in fewer U.S. dollars when converting its ruble profits. The Russian partner has arranged barter transactions for imported supplies. The second restaurant to be opened in Moscow will accept only hard currency, and this currency can be used to convert ruble profits earned in other restaurants. The processing center exports apple pies to European countries and plans to supply food to other restaurants and hotel facilities in Moscow, which have foreign joint venture partners. These payments will be in hard currencies as will be rentals in an office building McDonald's is planning to construct.

McDonald's placed one small help-wanted ad and received approximately 27,000 applicants for its 605 positions. The company sent six managers from Moscow to its hamburger university outside Chicago for six months' training and sent another 30 restaurant managers for several months' training in Canada or Europe. After training, they instructed new employees. The company translated manuals and videotapes into Russian so that trainees could learn everything from how to wash windows and mop floors to assemble a Big Mac (pronounced *"Beeg Mek"* in Moscow). Since McDonald's wants to be in the former Soviet Union for the long haul, an important part of training has been to teach employees to be very polite to customers by smiling and saying "May I help you?" and "Thank you for coming." These courtesies are not common in the former Soviet Union. The company pays wages to most workers that are about average by local standards; however, managers can earn much more if they prove themselves. In the United States McDonald's has an aversion to labor unions; however, it helped organize a work collective for the Russian staff in order to comply with the nation's labor laws. In contrast to North America, McDonald's placed a laundry room within its restaurant where uniforms are washed by machine and ironed by hand. This helps assure a standard of cleanliness not usually present in the former Soviet Union, especially since few homes have appliances for washing and drying and because soap is in short supply.

One problem McDonald's did not encounter was attracting sufficient customers. Based on its Hungarian experience, where the company cut its advertising after an unusually heavy response, McDonald's did no advertising prior to its Moscow opening. However, television covered the upcoming event extensively. When the doors opened for the Moscow restaurant, it was almost impossible to accommodate the crowds despite the fact that the 700 indoor seats made this the largest McDonald's anywhere in the world. (There are another 200 outside seats that could not be used for the opening because of the cold January weather.) An estimated 30,000 people were served the first day, eclipsing the previous record of 9100 for one day in 1988 in Budapest, Hungary. The crowds arrived even though the price of a Big Mac, french fries, and soft drink were equivalent to the average pay for four hours of work. In contrast, one could get lunch at a state-run or private-sector cafe for between 15 and 25 percent of what it cost at McDonald's. In spite of such crowds, a Russian engineer was quoted as saying, "We only stood in line for 45 minutes. I've never seen such fast service." Overall response has since been so high that McDonald's has limited sales to ten Big Macs per customer in order to minimize the scalping of hamburgers outside the restaurant.

Given the prices and having to line up outside in the January cold, why were sales so high? Savings rates in the former Soviet were very high, primarily because of insufficient available goods and services to purchase. There was thus a pent-up demand, especially for any type of Western product that could be bought for rubles. The store's location on busy Pushkin Square was another advantage. Having the Moscow City Council as a partner was certainly helpful. About this, Cohon said, "In one way, doing business is easier in Russia. The state owns all the land, so if you want a corner on their equivalent of Park Avenue, all the state has to say is: here's the address."

What will be the future of McDonald's in historically planned economies? The managing director of McDonald's Development Corp. said, "We'll do one store, one country at a time, and plans will be made as we grow and develop." After observing the success of Pizza Hut's restaurant in China, McDonald's has since opened a 500-seat restaurant in Shenzhen, China, near Hong Kong. McDonald's knew that the cost for a meal there in relation to customers' incomes would be even higher than in Moscow; however, Pizza Hut had served to capacity even though one of its pizzas cost about two weeks' salary for the average worker.

The ability to expand by franchising might be limited. McDonald's movements into Hungary, Yugoslavia, the former Soviet Union, and China have all been through its direct ownership in joint ventures. The president of McDonald's international division explained two franchising problems: The first is that franchisers look for individuals with entrepreneurial track records, and in these countries, it's hard to find that; the second is that it is difficult to find people who can afford to buy a franchise.

INTRODUCTION

The demolition of the Berlin Wall and the overthrow of European communist dictatorships in 1989 brought renewed Western interest in the possibility of conducting business in countries that had heretofore been considered off limits. The countries that sparked this interest were those that had been commonly called communist, nonmarket economies (NMEs), centrally planned economies (CPEs), Second World countries, or the Eastern bloc. (This latter term was political rather than geographic; that is, East-West trade referred to business between communist and noncommunist countries rather than between the Eastern and Western Hemispheres.) The changes were so unforeseen and have occurred (and continue to occur) so rapidly that one risks making statements that will quickly become obsolete. Nevertheless, because of the changes taking place within many of these countries, the old terminology no longer seems appropriate for them. At the same time, there has been a growing realization that some other countries also have had strong elements of fairly recent central planning, even though they have not usually been grouped with the CPE countries. Although old terms and classifications will continue to be used, there is clearly a need for a new and more meaningful terminology.

The term **historically planned economies (HPEs)** refers to countries that since World War II have adhered for some time and to some degree to some type of Marxist-Leninist political principles, have undertaken a centrally planned approach to economic development, and have maintained certain economic conditions associated with CPEs. Among HPEs, countries differ in whether their political bodies have or have not made a commitment to become a market economy. For example, the Czech and Slovak Federal Republic, Hungary, and Poland have made such a commitment, but Bulgaria, Romania, and China maintain that a combination of central planning and market economy is possible.[2] Countries also differ in how far they have moved to date. Algeria, for example, has already moved far from its earlier CPE doctrines and policies; Poland has made a commitment to transform to a market economy, but has not yet had time to complete the change; China has embarked on some reforms, while adhering to communistic and centrally planned principles; and Cuba has committed neither to a market transformation nor to reforms. Table 10.1 and Map 10.1 summarize these differences.

But why do these changes bring renewed Western interest in business with HPEs? The answer is partly political. Along with reforms and transformation has come a thawing of Cold War tensions that brings with it the hope

TABLE 10.1 | CLASSIFICATIONS OF HISTORICALLY PLANNED ECONOMIES (HPEs) HPEs vary in their commitments to transform and in their historical trading relations with each other.[a]

	Location	Commitment to Transform	Member of COMECON
Afghanistan	Asia	T	No
Albania	Europe	N	No[e]
Algeria	Africa	T	No
Angola	Africa	R	No
Benin	Africa	T	No
Bulgaria	Europe	R	Yes
Cambodia	Asia	N	No
Chile	S. America	T	No
China (People's Republic of)	Asia	R	No
Commonwealth of Independent States (formerly USSR)	Europe–Asia	R[c]	Yes
Congo	Africa	R	No
Cuba	N. America	N	Yes
Czech and Slovak Federal Republic	Europe	T	Yes
Ethiopia	Africa	T	No
German Democratic Republic (GDR)	Europe	T[b]	Yes
Guinea	Africa	T	No
Hungary	Europe	T	Yes
Korea (Democratic Republic of)	Asia	N	No
Lao People's Democratic Republic	Asia	R	No
Madagascar	Africa	T	No
Mongolia	Asia	R	Yes
Mozambique	Africa	T	No
Myanmar (formerly Burma)	Asia	R	No
Nicaragua	N. America	T	No
Poland	Europe	T	Yes
Romania	Europe	R	Yes
Somalia	Africa	R	No
Tanzania	Africa	T	No
Vietnam	Asia	R	Yes
Yemen (Democratic Republic of)	Asia	R[d]	No
Yugoslavia	Europe	T[c]	No

Key: Commitment to transform
  T = in transition to or now primarily a market economy
  R = committed to reforms while largely maintaining central planning
  N = committed to central planning or unsure of making reforms

[a]Paul Marer was extremely helpful in identifying and classifying countries through his first-hand experience and consulting work at the World Bank.

[b]The GDR became a part of the Federal Republic of Germany in 1990, but shares many characteristics with the transitional and committed countries.

[c]The CIS and Yugoslavia have strong regional differences in commitments on reformation or transition. In Yugoslavia, for instance, Slovenia and Croatia are now independent and prefer a transformation, but other regions do not.

[d]The Democratic Republic of Yemen joined with the Arab Republic of Yemen to become the Republic of Yemen in 1990, but shares characteristics with reforming countries.

[e]Albania was a COMECON member until 1961.

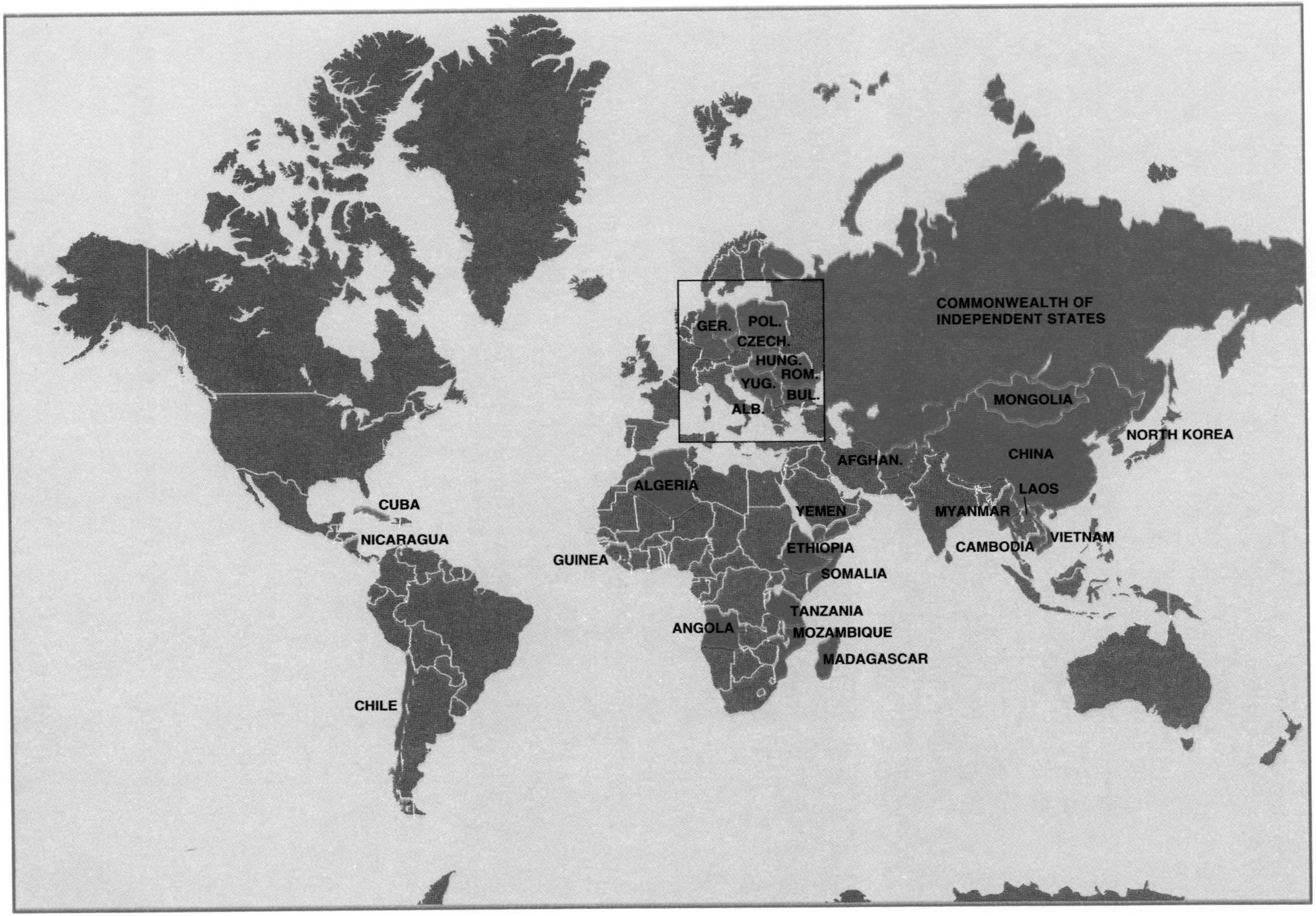
COMMONWEALTH OF
INDEPENDENT STATES
GER.
POL.
CZECH.
HUNG.
ROM.
YUG.
BUL.
ALB.
MONGOLIA
NORTH KOREA
CHINA
LAOS
AFGHAN.
ALGERIA
CUBA
YEMEN
MYANMAR
NICARAGUA
VIETNAM
CAMBODIA
ETHIOPIA
GUINEA
SOMALIA
TANZANIA
ANGOLA
MOZAMBIQUE
MADAGASCAR
CHILE

Map 10.1
Historically Planned Economies
Some historically planned economies are located in areas other than Europe. They vary in their commitments to transform and in their historical trading relations with each other.

Western interest in business with HPEs has been renewed because of

- Improved political relationships
- Prospects of economic growth

that governmentally imposed barriers to business relationships will soon break down. And the answer is partly economic. Most of the HPEs experienced slow economic growth during the 1970s and 1980s; consequently, the outlook for expanded commercial activities seemed bleak. The reforms and transformation offer hope of rejuvenated economic growth and increased business opportunities.

Most of the recent optimism has centered around business possibilities in European HPEs and China, which will be the areas emphasized in this chapter. The interest in the former is because of the level of development, and the interest in the latter is because of population size and economic growth. These conditions help to explain why McDonald's, in the opening case, has entered Hungary, Yugoslavia, the CIS, and China, but not Mongolia. Although European HPEs have per capita incomes of only about one tenth those in Western industrial countries, these incomes are still about ten times those in such African HPEs as Somalia and Mozambique. Furthermore, even though the per capita incomes of European HPEs closely resemble those of some Latin American developing countries, the European HPEs share some characteristics more favorable to rapid economic development than most Latin American countries. These include more highly educated populations and more equality of incomes and social-status levels. China is a special case. Although its per capita income is only about a quarter of those in European HPEs, China's growth rate during the 1980s was much higher, rivaling the growth rates of its publicized East Asian neighbors. Furthermore, it is hard to ignore an economy with so many people. Even if the Chinese could afford to eat at McDonald's only once in a lifetime and McDonald's were to operate at a 15,000-customer-per-day capacity, it would take over 200 years to serve the present population.

Yet, in spite of perceived greater opportunities, entry into the HPEs is not without costs and risks. In the opening case, McDonald's Russian operations have necessitated a number of adjustments. These include the participation in long and complex negotiations, development of export sales to overcome foreign-exchange shortages, the taking of ownership (as opposed to franchising) to compensate for the lack of entrepreneurs with investment funds, the selection of a partner with political clout rather than food or distribution experience, the creation of supplies that heretofore did not exist, the training of employees to be customer-oriented in spite of pent-up demand, and the acceptance of a much longer time horizon to repatriate profits to the parent.

BUSINESS VOLATILITY

Risk to Business

Western business with HPEs has been compared to a "light switch"; it turns on and then off.[3] The McDonald's case is an example of business volatility created by changing political attitudes. McDonald's began negotiation of entry into the former USSR in 1976 without significant progress until the former USSR enacted joint venture legislation in 1987, whereupon negotiation and start-up came quickly. Changes sometimes have been in response to unpopular actions by HPEs (such as the Soviet invasion of Afghanistan), to cooperation against a common enemy (such as the alliance against Germany in World War II), or to the ascendancy of different political decision makers in the East or those in the West who hold different philosophies about business interactions with dictatorships and/or countries with central planning (for example, President Reagan's trade sanctions against Nicaragua).

Volatility in East-West trade has occurred when
• HPE actions changed
• Different U.S. decision makers were in power
Trade volatility makes businesspeople reluctant to expend resources.

Although the post-1989 period has been marked by more congenial relations between most HPEs and the Western industrialized countries, there are still risks of future sanctions. In 1991 the Soviet military opened fire against protestors in Lithuania, and China convicted human rights advocates in the Tiananmen movement for "counterrevolutionary propaganda." Had these events occurred under a different scenario, the U.S. reaction might have been different. For example, had a strong human rights advocate, such as Carter, been the U.S. president at a time when the United States was not being supported by the former Soviet Union and China for its military actions to liberate Kuwait, the "light switch" might have been put on "off" or "dim."

The change in decision makers sometimes has been the result of elections, but not always. Within the United States there have always been differences of opinion about economic sanctions. These have occurred within Congress, among White House administrations, and between the legislative and executive branches of government. The differences have been characterized as: "There are theological positions on both sides. To the hawks, any trade helps the Russians and zero is already too much. To the doves, trade leads politics, and more trade will improve relations."[4] After the 1989 changes in European HPEs, the U.S. Congress eased, but nonetheless, maintained strategic export controls to the former Soviet bloc and disallowed subsidiaries of U.S. firms to trade with Cuba.[5] Apparently, there is still considerable opinion that (1) the threat from certain HPEs still exists, (2) nonthreatening HPEs will transfer technology to threatening nations, and/or (3) HPEs can be coerced into further liberalization.

Within the ideology of a restrictive trade position, three different motives sometimes have been pursued. The first is a defensive or punitive one, focusing on controls to weaken an unfriendly country economically and militarily in a type of economic warfare. The second is to try to remedy a situation through the withholding of trade, such as trying to coerce the former Soviet Union into allowing the emigration of more Jews to Israel. The third is to make a public declaration in order to register displeasure over certain activities, for example, the shooting down of a Korean passenger plane by the former Soviet Union.[6]

Within the ideology of a more liberal trade position in the United States it is argued that (1) restrictions merely penalize U.S. exporters and help firms from other Western countries, (2) the benefits to HPEs from getting more U.S. products is of limited strategic benefit to them anyway, and (3) closer economic ties will lessen political tensions.

It is not only the policies of Western countries that cause shifts in East-West business relations. Communist countries also have altered their attitudes and practices substantially. In both the former Soviet Union and the People's Republic of China, for example, changes in leadership and planning cycles have resulted in wide swings in how much each country depends on foreign business, with whom the foreign business occurs, what products are involved, and what forms of business are allowed.

Most companies prefer to invest their capital and human resources in endeavors that are expected to continue for a long period of time. Because there is still considerable uncertainty about the future of political relations with some HPEs, some firms hesitate to commit their resources to development of business with HPEs. On the one hand, Western businesses have witnessed increased peaceful political interactions. On the other hand, they also realize that past experience shows how rapidly business can change because of politics and how it can continue to fluctuate over time.

Examples of Change, Especially in the United States

The twentieth century opened with peaceful trading operations between the United States and what was then Russia. The two countries were neither allies nor enemies, so there was no official governmental effort to expand or restrict the volume of trade. When the two countries became allies in World War I, U.S. exports to Russia jumped more than eighteenfold, due largely to war-related credits. When the Bolsheviks came to power, Soviet foreign trade became a state-controlled monopoly, credits nearly disappeared, and U.S. exports to the country became negligible. A formal trade agreement between the countries in 1935 resulted in the Soviet Union's becoming the biggest customer for the United States during the Depression. In 1939 the German-Russian nonaggression pact and subsequent invasions of Poland and the Baltic states led to the imposition of certain U.S. export embargoes, which were dropped in 1941 when the two countries again became allies and major trading partners. Between 1947 and 1953, in the early Cold War period, trade between the United States and the USSR became almost nonexistent.[7] Trade has climbed since 1953, but with substantial year-to-year changes because of political relationships and agreements. The most notable agreements were special wheat sales and growth in credit, which caused exports to jump in the 1970s.

U.S. trade with the East European countries, China, and Cuba fell to nearly zero after communist takeovers. With leadership changes in Eastern Europe and China, their trade with the United States has increased. Table 10.2 shows recent U.S. trade with major HPEs, indicating that China is by far

TABLE 10.2 | U.S. TRADE WITH SELECTED HISTORICALLY PLANNED ECONOMIES (in thousands of dollars, 1989 and first half of 1990) Note that U.S. trade with all HPEs combined is only about 3 percent of total U.S. imports and exports, and that China accounts for the overwhelming portion of that trade.

	Imports		Exports	
	1989	January–June 1990	1989	January–June 1990
Afghanistan	3,821	2,818	4,776	2,464
Albania	2,815	1,742	5,287	3,468
Bulgaria	57,331	23,277	180,733	19,177
Cambodia	314	112	34	34
China	11,859,172	6,503,077	5,775,478	2,471,841
CIS (formerly USSR)	690,891	435,636	4,262,336	2,405,780
Cuba	0	77	2,629	718
Czech and Slovak	82,117	36,908	51,287	29,338
East Germany	134,825	60,926	92,893	52,733
Hungary	326,694	168,722	119,305	66,789
Laos	821	64	341	8
Mongolia	1,088	673	30	14
North Korea	533	0	16	30
Poland	362,862	186,704	411,228	148,607
Romania	348,201	115,512	155,312	265,660
Vietnam	0	0	10,493	5,238
TOTAL	13,871,482	7,536,248	11,072,178	5,471,900
Total, U.S. Imports from and Exports to the world	468,012,021	237,052,966	349,432,947	188,478,272

Note: Because of rounding, figures may not add to the totals shown.

Source: Compiled from official statistics of the U.S. Department of Commerce in 63rd Quarterly Report to the Congress and the Trade Policy Committee, *Trade Between the United States and the Nonmarket Economy Countries During April–June 1990* (Washington: United States International Trade Commission, November 1990), pp. 5, 7.

the dominant HPE trading partner with the United States. Overall, U.S. trade with all HPEs comprises only about 3 percent of total U.S. exports and imports.

Exports from other Western industrialized countries have followed varied patterns, reflecting once again the diverse political relationships. For example, in the critical period from 1948 to 1953, when U.S. exports to communist countries fell so sharply, the exports of Canada, the United Kingdom, and Sweden to the Eastern bloc took sharp declines as well, whereas the exports of Austria, Finland, France, and West Germany shot upward. When the United States cut exports in response to the former Soviet's invasion of Afghanistan, exports from Canada and the United Kingdom increased substantially to the former Soviet Union and Eastern Europe.[8]

TRANSFORMATION TO MARKET ECONOMIES

As we have already discussed, historically planned economies differ greatly in terms of the commitment and progress they have made toward achieving the goal of transforming their centrally planned economies into market economies. At one extreme is the former German Democratic Republic (GDR), which has been reunited with and in fact is being absorbed into the German Federal Republic. At the other extreme is Cuba, whose leader, Fidel Castro, in reference to the political liberalization and other changes within Eastern Europe, said, "We are witnessing sad things in other socialist countries, very sad things. We are astonished at the phenomena that we see."[9] These differences are important when assessing whether and when a country might become a market economy. It is likely that in the foreseeable future HPEs will be at different points along the continuum. The nearer countries are to the central-planning end of the continuum, the more Western business managers will encounter situations traditionally associated with business in CPEs.

It is also important to realize that attaining a market economy is not necessarily a panacea for economic success; in fact, most of the world's LDCs would qualify as market economies. Economic development is a very complex process, and there have been very few successes in the twentieth century. In essence, the HPEs vary widely in terms of factors that may affect their growth, with or without a high degree of transformation. These factors include educational attainment, endowments of natural resources, national cohesiveness, access to investment capital, industrial structure already in place, experience in entrepreneurial endeavors, and infrastructure development. For companies contemplating East-West commercial activities, the countries' development potentials should be examined along with their prospects for transformation.

Models of Successful Market Economies

Countries in the process of transforming their economies obviously aspire to become economic successes, not to join the ranks of the LDCs. There is considerable debate within HPEs as to which model to emulate. The **social market economies** of northern Europe are characterized by heavy governmental spending and high taxation to pay for such social services as health care, education, subsidized housing for the poor, and unemployment benefits. The **consumer-directed market economy,** as seen in the United States, involves minimal government participation while promoting growth through

Some HPEs want to
- Become market economies
- Make reforms within a central planning system
- Stay as they are

Three models of market economies are
- Social
- Consumer-directed
- Administratively guided

the mobility of production factors, including high employment turnover. An **administratively guided market economy,** as exemplified by Japan, requires a great deal of cooperation among government, management, and workers to achieve growth and full employment with low job turnover on a nonmandated basis. But regardless of model differences, there are a number of factors common to all the successful market economies.

All successful market economies share characteristics.

First, the successful market economies are characterized by a predominance of privately owned means of production, even though all have some government-owned production. Although the difference is one of degree, the impact is decidedly different between a country with 10 percent and another with 90 percent of production in the government sector. Second, their markets are very competitive. For larger economies, such as Japan and the United States, the competition is primarily among firms producing domestically. In the absence of a sufficiently large economy to sustain multiple producers, it is necessary to have international competition so that producers are encouraged to become more efficient and responsive to market needs. Third, their currencies are sound in terms of low inflation rates and convertibility, so residents have enough confidence to make savings and investments that fuel the economy. Fourth, they have private institutions to amass financial resources through savings and taxation and to make these resources available for the public and private projects to promote growth and social welfare. Fifth, they have well-functioning infrastructures (such as telecommunications, schools, and transport facilities) along with actions to protect the environment. Sixth, they provide opportunities for individuals to fulfill their goals as investors, entrepreneurs, and wage earners.[10]

In essence, none of the centrally planned economies began a process of transformation or reform with any of these conditions in place to the extent seen in the successful market economies. For example, although the educational development was high in some European HPEs, other infrastructural development, such as roads and telephone systems, was inadequate. Most of the differences were understood before the 1989 changes; however, few people in the West imagined how despoiled the Eastern European environment had become. Years of insufficient investment to clean air and water along with ill-conceived industrial policies have left a legacy that in many cases threatens a full-blown environmental disaster.[11]

Stumbling Blocks

Many factors could impede the orderly progress to becoming a successful market economy. The following discussion highlights the major hurdles.

Economic Shocks   In bringing about a market transformation, there are some negative economic consequences, at least in the short term. The basic problem is that the costs are up front, and the benefits are much later. For example, a move to increase efficiency by allowing foreign competition brings unemployment. HPEs are neither accustomed to unemployment, nor do they have the safety nets of fall-back compensation, retraining, and job-relocation assistance that were developed over a long time period in industrial countries. A deregulation of prices brings rapid inflation because the old prices were below the true market values for many of the goods being sold. When Poland deregulated most of its prices, the standard joke was, "We used to have long lines and empty shelves. Now we have no lines, full shelves, but no money to buy what's on the shelves."

Statistics may overstate the degree of hardship arising from economic shocks. The prior full-employment rates mask the fact that many employees were simply performing "make work" assignments. Although prices look lower before deregulation, before and after comparisons do not take into account prior shortages and quality differences. For example, some goods in short supply showed official prices, even though the goods may have been resold in the black market at a higher price. Furthermore, many goods with lower before than after prices could not be sold at any price. The quality or safety characteristics were so poor that no one would use them. Where central planning overstates employment and understates prices, there is a familiar joke: "We pretend to work, and they pretend to pay us."[12]

A backlash is possible from short-term economic hardships.

A reality of the economic shocks is that they are politically dangerous. Workers and consumers have had high expectations of the results of transformation—perhaps too high. To the extent that they are adversely affected by unemployment and higher prices (a lowering of real income), even in the short term, they may lose confidence in the elected political leadership and in the transformation process itself—thus slowing or preventing changes.

The most difficult prices to deregulate are those for rationed products deemed to be necessities, even though the system leads to further shortages and black-market sales. For example, the former USSR drew up a new basket of necessities in 1990 and allocated these on a subsidized basis. Each adult male's coupons could buy, among other things, 146 eggs, six and a half pounds of soap, one toothbrush, two ties, five rolls of toilet paper, twelve condoms, two pounds of chicken, and a pound of strawberry jam per year.[13]

Privatization More than 90 percent of the economy within European HPEs and China is in the state-enterprise sector. The privatization of these enterprises is extremely difficult and not likely to occur in the near future. We need only look at the privatization process within Western economies to see how slow and cumbersome the changes are. For example, Prime Minister Thatcher of the United Kingdom was hailed as the world's leading and swiftest privatizer, yet her government transferred only a few dozen state enterprises over a decade. In contrast, Poland has over 7500 state enterprises, and more than 1000 of them have more than 1000 employees.[14]

There are obstacles to privatizing state enterprises.

A major hurdle for privatization is that there are few people within the HPEs who have the necessary funds for investments. In this absence, foreign investors have sometimes purchased a share of a state enterprise, such as GE's investment of $150 million for a majority ownership of Tungsram in Hungary. But foreign investment is only a partial solution. First, it is doubtful that HPEs will allow too great a share of their economies to come under foreign control. Second, it is also doubtful that there would be sufficient foreign investment anyway, particularly given the poor condition or outdated products of many government enterprises. For instance, on a list of state companies for an investment is a maker of vacuum tubes, an item replaced by transistors in most of the world. Evidence of the difficulty comes from auctions in Poland and the Czech and Slovak Federal Republic for the sale of some enterprises to their citizens. These sales have involved only small operations, such as retail butcher shops that do not include the land on which the stores sit. It will be far more troublesome to sell the large state enterprises.

One suggestion for privatization is to give workers ownership of the enterprises where they are employed (these are sometimes referred to as employee stock ownership plans, or ESOPs), and Yugoslavia has experimented with this process. However, there are at least two problems with this approach. First, there is a question of equity, since some state enterprises are much more efficient than others, making them more likely to survive and be profitable. Second, workers would then be the directors to whom top management would be responsible. Because the workers lack any experience at making or implementing viable competitive practices, they might take steps to increase their own wages or job security at the expense of cost efficiency. Or they might feel so ill-equipped that existing state managers would perpetuate their power and autonomy without any real accountability for their actions—until it is too late. A second suggestion for privatization has been to transfer ownership of all enterprises to all citizens, who would then have a diversified portfolio of company shares that they could later sell. This approach would not yield sale revenues to the government to help pay off debts. A third suggestion is to break up giant state companies, which would then have cross-ownership in each other. As smaller entities, they may be easier to sell; however, if unsold, inefficient suppliers are perpetuated. A fourth suggestion is to encourage the development of small private enterprises, but there are short-term problems in their successful development.[15]

Soft Budgets   A **soft budget** refers to a situation in which an enterprise's excess of expenditures over earnings is compensated for by some other institution, typically the state or a state-controlled financial institution. The HPEs all have soft-budget legacies from the period when it was unthinkable that an enterprise would not survive. Even within an environment of transformation, there are pressures to continue soft-budget practices. To begin with, new managers may claim that their operating inefficiencies are due to excesses created before they took their posts. Therefore, they argue their need to continue receiving subsidies until they can make operating reversals. (Even within market economies, companies have successfully used this argument to receive indirect subsidies by limitation of import competition. A good example is the U.S. steel industry.) Second, some economists argue that soft budgets encourage enterprises to limit profits, thereby decreasing funds going as wages and dividend payments to workers and shareholders. This process reduces consumption and frees funds for growth-generating investment. Third, HPEs are burdened with many large and inefficient enterprises that they can ill-afford to let die in the "short term" for both economic and political reasons. HPEs have gone so far as to require investments by foreign automobile firms to be made in existing (inefficient) facilities for fear of economic disruptions if new facilities displace the old ones. (Again, we find examples in market economies of government support for economically significant companies when politicians fear the impact of failures and worker dislocations. Examples include U.S. past support for Chrysler, Lockheed, and Pan Am.)

When profits don't have to be made, there are few incentives for improving efficiency.

The soft budget creates a management incentive to divert efforts to make deals with authorities rather than effect efficiencies to survive. For example, during the 1980s Chinese enterprises switched to a substantial degree from measuring performance on the basis of gross output to measuring on the basis of profit. But this change took place without elimination of the soft budget within the banking system and some productive sectors. Because the banking system faced no real budget constraint, it could continue lending to enterprises regardless of their efficiencies. The continuance of the soft budget in some sectors enabled even some of those enterprises that were evaluated on profits to raise profits largely by gaining access to subsidized credit and subsidized inputs, rather than by raising sales or cutting real production costs.[16]

Human Resources   One problem plaguing many state enterprises is that they have mammoth bureaucracies that are difficult to replace. As central planning is eliminated without substituting knowledgeable owners to whom enterprise managers can report, there is little control over these managers' actions. There have already been examples in Hungary and Poland of managers who have sold output at low prices to enterprises in which they own stakes. The buying-enterprise has then sold at high prices, thus shifting profits.

HPEs are short of people who understand how to manage in a market economy.

A second problem, more acute in countries where people have no memory of market operations, is that managers have no knowledge or experience of operating without a central plan that tells them what to produce and to whom to sell. They may also lack experience in controlling their subordinates by hiring and firing them or by finding means of compensation to motivate them. Very few managers know how to understand financial statements, how to respond to market signals (such as demand changes), or how to market products where there is competition and no pent-up demand, especially in export markets to the West. Furthermore, these same managers may have a low work ethic because of their experiences with low pay and high job security. Although management training programs are being developed within HPEs, they will accommodate a very small portion of the population for the foreseeable future. Furthermore, egalitarian attitudes, especially in the CIS

and China, cause successful entrepreneurs sometimes to be viewed as speculators—a contemptuous label.[17]

Production Concentration   In the Commonwealth of Independent States
(CIS) especially, there are not only state enterprises, there are also state monopoly enterprises that produce in only one facility. For example, the Kama
River Truck factory covers nine square miles and is larger than the combined
capacity of all U.S. heavy truck manufacturing. Instead of using an automobile supply system as in Western industrial countries, every part is forged,
machined, and assembled in the same location. Table 10.3 illustrates some of
the monopolies and near-monopolies within the CIS. Like the Kama River
Truck factory, these enterprises tend to be highly vertically integrated as well;
that is, they produce most of the components they need in the one location
because they cannot assure supplies from other enterprises. In turn, these
vertically integrated facilities tend to be inefficient. (Recall that McDonald's
had to develop many of its own captive supplies because there were vertically
integrated production arrangements already in place.) Such a situation makes
it difficult to privatize and to break up existing facilities. It is also difficult for
new producers to enter the market. The sheer size of operations makes their
sale problematic. And how do you break up ownership of a single steel works
to promote competition? Potential new competitive entrants face existing
state monopolies of mammoth size, problems of gaining supplies that might
necessitate large vertically integrated operations, and difficulty in selling to
industrial customers who have long associations with existing state enterprises. To help eliminate monopolies, the CIS is planning to fine monopoly
producers. However, if prices also become deregulated as planned, the monopolies may simply pass on the cost of the fines to their customers. Overall,

*Large single-site monopo-
lies are hard to break up.*

TABLE 10.3 | MONOPOLY AND NEAR-MONOPOLY CIS* ENTERPRISES About 30 percent to 40 percent of
Soviet goods are produced by monopolies at single sites. Much of other production is in near-
monopoly situations. This table merely presents a sample.

Product	Producer and Location	% of Total Production
Sewing machines	Shveinaya, Podolsk	100
Tram rails	Integrated Steel, Kuznetsk	100
Locomotive cranes	Engineering Plant, Kirov	100
Hoists for coal mines	City Coal Machinery, Donetsk	100
Coking equipment	Kopeisk Engineering, Chelyabinsk	100
Trolley buses	Uritsky, Engels	97
Automatic washing machines	Elektrobytpribor, Kirov	90
Diesel locomotives	Industrial Association, Voroshilovgrad	95
Concrete mixers	Integrated Mill, Tuva	93

*Commonwealth of Independent States, formerly USSR.

Source: The information is selected from a more complete list in "The Best of All Monopoly Profits," *Economist,* August 11,
1990.

it is estimated that between 30 and 40 percent of the value of goods in the former Soviet Union are produced on single sites.[18]

National Heterogeneity   A nation-state is held together either through dictatorial powers or by common interests. Dictators have been replaced by democratically elected leadership in many of the HPEs. Furthermore, the common bond of fear of a Western invasion has subsided. These factors have caused ethnic and regional differences to surface as important destabilizing national elements in several countries, most notably Yugoslavia and the former USSR. In contrast, China's provinces near Hong Kong, Guangdong and Fujian, as well as some of the western provinces with large Muslim populations, are dissident, but a potent military threat keeps them under control. At one extreme, countries may split further apart, particularly where there are ethnic regions that see themselves as economically viable and where there is a different attitude about the direction or speed of economic transformation. For example, the Baltic republics in the former USSR and Slovenia and Croatia in what was Yugoslavia see themselves as able to survive without the rest of the former country. Splits could occur peacefully, such as occurred for Estonia, or by force, such as occurred for Croatia. If by force, such as through a civil war, foreign-investment properties could be at high risk and foreign trade could be disrupted. Even in a less extreme scenario, regional dissension might channel resources from investments and actions that would otherwise enhance a transformation to a market system. Furthermore, resultant splintered markets are much less desirable for Western firms to pursue.

Funds Availability[19]   There is a consensus that the transformation to a successful market economy will be very expensive. Huge capital investments will be needed for developing infrastructure, for improving the environment, and for modernizing factories. Funds will be needed for educating managers on operating within a market system. At the same time, there will be substantial consumer pressure to buy goods and services that have historically been in short supply. These pressures will limit governmental efforts to divert funds from consumer spending to capital spending as they have been diverted in the past. For example, pressure for consumer products was so great in the former Soviet Union that the government had to concede to huge importations of soap, grain, and tobacco in the early 1990s. Although some spending relief may be obtained through reductions in the military budget, the ability to reduce this budget quickly may be hampered by internal regional dissent, which may necessitate a military presence, by the need to negotiate with Western governments on bilateral or multilateral arms reductions, and by entrenched military bureaucracies that will likely resist their own loss of power. Furthermore, past development has been so distorted toward military production that resources cannot easily be used effectively for other purposes.

The ability to receive large infusions of capital from abroad is hampered in some countries by their already existing high external debts. Poland, the

---

Ethnic rivalries in some HPEs increase political risk for business.

It is uncertain if HPEs can get the vast funds needed for development.

CIS, Yugoslavia, and Hungary are already among the countries with the highest gross external debts. Two other HPEs would have been on this list a few years earlier: The German Democratic Republic, whose external debt has been taken over by the Federal Republic of Germany after their merger, and Romania, whose debt was slashed in the 1980s through extreme austerity measures taken while Nicolai Ceausescu was president. To build the trade surpluses necessary to reduce Romania's hard-currency debt, imports were restricted and exports were pushed to such an extent that people did without sufficient heat and food for almost seven years while industry was unable to improve its technology or to update machinery necessary to keep the economy growing. Although these measures have perhaps increased the foreign borrowing power of Romania as compared to other HPEs, the austerity measures have nevertheless made Romania even more dependent on additional capital than other HPEs if it is to make the transition to a successful market economy. Meanwhile, countries such as Poland and Hungary are burdened by interest payments on external debts of 5 and 7 percent of their gross national product per year. The former Soviet Union had impeccable credit ratings between the end of World War II and the late 1980s. Since then, however, its increased external debt and decreased hard-currency deposits in Western banks have raised its private borrowing costs and lowered its commercial debt ratings.

Many suggest that Western banks and governments simply write off the debts so that HPEs could start with a clean slate. The arguments are based on humanitarian concerns (i.e., that populations have suffered so long under repressive regimes) and on precedence (i.e., that German debts were forgiven a few years after the end of World War II). But questions of equity will probably prevent any massive write-off. First, benefits would primarily accrue to those countries that have either incurred large debts or have not paid debts back, whereas a country such as Romania would receive no benefits for having endured a harsh austerity program. Second, singling out HPEs would seem unfair to the large, debt-ridden LDCs in Latin America, Asia, and Africa. Third, any type of write-off could more easily be accomplished on debt to governments than on debt to private banks. Poland owed most of its external debt to other governments; thus a partial write-off for Poland in 1990 was easier than a write-off would be for Hungary, which owes most of its external debt to foreign private banks.

Others propose a massive Marshall Plan-type program for Eastern Europe. Realistically, such a program seems unlikely. The largest Western economy, the United States, has substantial balance-of-payments problems of its own and is unlikely to have the wherewithal to finance massive assistance. There are also equity problems, particularly with LDCs. In addition, it is doubtful how successful the effort might be. The great success of the Marshall Plan in Western Europe after World War II was due not only to the huge infusions of capital, but also to the fact that the efforts were established merely to bring the war-devastated economies back to where they had been five or six years earlier. Some HPEs have never been at a high developmental stage. Furthermore, in some countries central-planning regimes have been in power for so long that few people recollect successful earlier situations that should be emulated if rapid development is to take place.

FACTORS AFFECTING BUSINESS EXPANSION

The preceding section on stumbling blocks described several factors that could affect the future of business between companies in HPEs and companies in market economies. The more HPEs are economically successful, the more attention Western companies are apt to give them.

History of Internal Dependence

The combined populations of European HPEs and China make Western businesses optimistic about commercial opportunities. The combined area comprises approximately one third of the world's population, with China alone accounting for about one fifth. The CIS has a population slightly larger than the United States, and the other European HPEs have a combined population that is slightly smaller. The CIS and China rank as the world's first- and third-largest markets in terms of area. Although the large population and land mass indicate possible opportunities, they are in some ways a deterrent to expanded business with the West. Their natural resources are extremely diverse and, when coupled with the large populations, give them the potential of developing a wide variety of production. They, like the United States, might be expected to be much more nearly self-sufficient than a smaller country.

Large size means big market, but it also brings more self-sufficiency.

One of the striking features of HPEs has been their relatively small portion of world trade. The absolute amount has been smaller than might be indicated from population or income figures: They account for less than 10 percent of the world's share of imports and exports, including the trade they conduct with each other, and this share has been declining. Part of the lag in export share by these countries has been systemic to central planning and will not easily be altered until a market transformation is complete. Part has been self-imposed, as when HPEs shunned dependence on the West for political reasons and on each other for fear of delayed shipments or poor quality.[20] The result has been a shortage of people with international market knowledge needed to build higher trade dependencies.

China has conducted only about 5 percent of its trade with other HPEs. In contrast, the members of the Council for Mutual Economic Assistance (CMEA, or COMECON) (see Table 10.1 and Map 10.1) have averaged over 60 percent of their trade with each other.[21] This interchange did not use market prices for trade and perpetuated an exchange of low-quality East European machinery for Soviet raw materials. The countries began in 1991 to use

Former COMECON countries have a history of trading primarily with each other.

market prices for trade with each other and agreed to form a new association, the Organization for International Economic Cooperation. However, the members postponed the replacement of COMECON in 1991 because of differences concerning the role of the successor group. There seems little likelihood that market prices can really be ascertained for much of the machinery they manufacture or that the historical trade patterns will easily change. Personal relationships have been developed. Spare parts are needed. Eastern Europe has a sunk cost in factories that cannot be dismantled for economic or political reasons, nor are markets readily available outside the former Soviet Union. In turn, the former USSR has a large sunk cost in pipelines to deliver oil and gas to its former satellites.[22]

The Need for Two-Way Business Flows

Currency convertibility depends on a two-way business flow.

There has been much recent discussion about HPE plans for making their currencies convertible. Inevitably, the questions are "for whom?" and "for what?" For example, convertibility could be for foreigners, but not for residents; it could be for trade, but not for dividends. Regardless of the regulations or intent, business with HPEs must inevitably be two-way to succeed. If HPEs earn insufficient hard currencies, they will have insufficient hard currency for payments to foreign firms under trade, licensing, or investment agreements. As HPEs have turned toward reform or economic transformation, they have favored fixed rather than fluctuating exchange rates and have had to make large currency devaluations when unable to sustain their existing rates.

For some time, basically because of ideological differences, many people in market economies assumed that all HPE-made products were inferior, pointing to items that are in fact of low quality. The reality is that perhaps as many as 25 percent of all scientists in the world are employed in the CIS. Bulgaria and the Czech and Slovak Federal Republic have a much higher proportion of scientists and engineers in their work forces than any country in Western Europe.[23] In many technical areas HPEs are now leaders. There has been an upsurge in patent registrations from the former USSR in the United States and in sales of their technology to U.S. firms. Payload Systems was the first U.S. firm to contract to have experiments aboard what was then the Soviet space station. In 1987 the Soviets granted their first nonindustrial license to a U.S. company—from the House of Zaitzev to Tanner Companies—providing for U.S. production of high-fashion, Soviet-designed clothing aimed at affluent American women. Poland expected a hard-currency trade deficit for 1990, but instead ran a $2.5 billion surplus as state companies began seeking out export orders more vigorously than in the past.[24] HPEs could conceivably sell many products in greater abundance abroad. A factor that has apparently aided Chinese exports in recent years is that tens of millions of people of Chinese descent live outside of China. A large portion of them have family ties in China and a knowledge of market opportunities for specific Chinese products.[25] A large portion of China's trade is handled by Hong Kong–based middlemen who have such ties.

One question is what will happen to commodity prices. The CIS, Poland, Yugoslavia, and Romania have large natural resource reserves. The former Soviet Union at times has been able to mitigate its payments problems largely because of the high world prices of oil, gold, diamonds, and platinum. But the prices of these commodities fluctuate considerably. Furthermore, a study financed by the National Science Foundation of the United States focuses doubt on the former USSR's ability to take advantage of its rich storehouse of minerals. The bulk of these resources are often located in very remote areas, which makes them more expensive within the CIS than imported ones.[26] In addition, the former Soviet Union needs Western technology to exploit its own oil.

The Chinese bid on labor-intensive construction projects abroad as a means of alleviating foreign-exchange shortages. The state-run companies pay workers less than the amount they receive on contracts; additionally, workers send part of their salaries to their families in China. They have worked on such projects as highway construction in Ethiopia, the construction of a power station in Hong Kong, and the building of model farms in Algeria.[27]

In the absence of the development of sufficient foreign earnings by HPE firms, Western companies may need to take a very long-term perspective on pay-back in hard currency. Or they may need to develop hard-currency earnings from their HPE activities. Recall in the opening case that McDonald's has taken a combination of these approaches. In a survey of American, Asian, and Western European corporate chief executive officers, they saw the extraction of hard currency to be the major impediment to doing business in HPEs.[28]

Legacies of Central Planning

The historical differences in economic systems underlie current conditions that affect Western business with HPEs. The HPEs, unlike the market-driven systems of the West, did not rely much on the market to determine what to produce or what price to charge. In the former USSR, for example, 95 percent of prices were changed only twice between 1955 and 1991. Prices therefore bore little resemblance to what prices or costs would be in a market economy. Currencies were not convertible, and their values were set arbitrarily in relation to Western ones. Since the countries decided centrally what was to be produced and consumed domestically, they planned certain production to be in excess of domestic consumption and certain production to be less. Those excesses and shortages became in turn their planned exports and imports, respectively. These then were varied only on an emergency basis because of supply problems.[29] Imports were bought by large foreign trade organizations (FTOs) whose buying decisions might have little to do with whether foreign-made goods were of higher quality or lower price than domestically produced

Many prices are not set by market forces.

ones. Since they tended to buy little from the West, they were not very familiar with many of the companies that are well known in market economies.

By late 1990 the majority of consumer prices, but not labor prices, had been deregulated in Czech and Slovak, Hungary, Poland, and Yugoslavia;[30] however, most prices were still administered in other HPEs. When HPEs sold abroad, their inability to know what their costs and prices would be in a market situation made it difficult for them to sell. For primary products, such as fuels and minerals, this was less of a problem because there was usually an established world market price that could be referenced. Most CIS exports, for example, are of this type; however, Eastern European exports usually are not. The problem still manifests itself in two ways. First, COMECON countries have agreed to settle deficits with convertible currencies and to set market prices on trade with each other; however, much of the production within HPEs is still highly protected and of a quality that is not really marketable internationally except in other HPEs. HPE governmental buyers worry that the prices from other HPEs are too high. The result is that the buyers look to similar Western products to get an indication of value, which is a very cumbersome and inexact process.

Second, HPEs were formerly accused of dumping their products into Western markets. For example, the former Soviets were charged with selling such products as automobiles and trucks in the West for a fraction of their costs in order to earn foreign exchange. But since costs were not calculated the same way, it was impossible to determine whether they were sold at below what the costs would be if computed on a market basis. To the extent that prices are still administered and soft budgets prevail in HPEs, prices may still bear little resemblance to cost. Furthermore, such HPEs as China, Poland, and the CIS have greatly devalued their currencies so that their exchange rates are "more realistic." Thus far, the post-1989 euphoria has prevented new charges of HPE dumping, except for China. However, until market economies are more nearly in place in the HPEs, there are risks that Western governments will protect against HPE exports by claiming that subsidies and undervalued exchange rates create unfair competition.

In selling to the West, HPEs largely viewed exports as a necessary nuisance to pay for imports. Eastern sellers were effectively price-takers, lacking the competitive experience to obtain higher prices through such market-economy mechanisms as product differentiation. This situation is still quite prevalent. Probably the only HPE trademarks that are well known in the West are Aeroflot for air service, and Lada and Yugo for automobiles, and none of these has a quality image that commands price premiums in the West. HPE enterprises will have to compete primarily on the basis of price, and they may have difficulty competing against the low-wage countries of Southeast Asia. The lack of internal competition within HPEs also makes it difficult for their firms to react to competitive market demands when they attempt to sell in the West. For many products that they have sold, there have been reports of a lack of responsiveness to users' needs, poor maintenance, and poor after-sales support services.[31] In the absence of being able to counter this problem independently, HPE firms are turning to Western firms for assistance. For example, in 1990 the former USSR signed a five-year contract with DeBeers Consolidated Mines so that the South African company would market all of its diamonds. Another approach has been to develop cooperative ventures with Western firms which infuse production and quality improvements into existing factories and then put their own well-known trademarks on the goods for export. Two notable examples are factories to make Schwinn bicycles and Levi's jeans in Hungary.[32] The Eastern European countries also have encountered problems in selling goods in the West because of unfamiliarity with the prevalent sophisticated advertising methods. Even though these countries have relied on Western advertising agencies, the agencies have only slowly been able to convince them of the need for such things as marketing segmentation and the targeting of budgets toward key products.[33]

HPE economic figures
- Were formerly overstated
- Are now perhaps understated

Before instituting major economic reforms, HPEs set their exchange rates on their nonconvertible currencies arbitrarily, perhaps motivated by political reasons so that their statistics made them appear much wealthier than they really were. Independent assessments, such as those made by the CIA, were lower than the HPE official figures, but still much higher than they have since been calculated. For instance, the CIA had estimated the former Soviet Union's per capita gross national product at about one third and its GNP at about one half of that in the United States. These figures gave Western companies an overly optimistic picture of short-term HPE market potential for their products and services. In 1990, the former Soviet Union devalued the ruble greatly, and international agencies (the International Monetary Fund, the World Bank, the Organization for Economic Cooperation and Development, and the European Bank for Reconstruction and Development) cooperated with former Soviet agencies to estimate its economic size. The resultant estimate for the former USSR was that the GNP was only about one tenth that of the U.S. in 1989 and the per capita income only about 14 percent of that of the U.S., or about the same as Brazil. New calculations also placed Eastern European figures at less than half what they had been assumed to be.[34] Today, even state enterprises in the HPEs may report figures to central authorities that understate their performance in order to continue receiving subsidies. In turn, central authorities may undervalue exchange rates to improve trade surpluses. Therefore, the economic figures may make Western firms overly pessimistic about business opportunities in HPEs.

Decentralization of trade decisions creates new problems.

Most HPEs have liberalized trading relationships by decentralizing decision making. Whereas decisions on imports and exports used to be made by the giant national foreign trade organizations (FTOs), more decisions are now made at the regional or enterprise level. For example, in 1980 China had only a handful of FTOs that could deal with imports and exports; by 1989 the figure had risen to about 5000.[35] Previously, Western firms complained of difficulty in gaining audiences with FTO officials and lengthy negotiations once they did. With decentralization, there are new problems, such as trying to determine with which entity to make contact.[36] Once contact is made, the decision makers may be so inexperienced with Western companies that they don't know fully if they are dealing with powerful and highly reputable foreign firms or not. Furthermore, transformation brings more turnover of personnel, which aggravates inexperience. Finally, there are more uncertainties about subsequent approvals from various ministries and whether locally made concessions, such as on currency conversion, will be honored at the national level.

TRADE RESTRICTIONS

Export Controls

Export controls
• Differ according to HPE
• Differ by product
• Involve strategic control problems.

Countries maintain export controls to ensure national security, promote foreign policy objectives, and prevent the export of certain raw materials that are in short supply. While these controls may be applied to any other country, sales by industrial countries to HPEs have been most affected, especially those from the United States. Cuba, Cambodia, Mongolia, and North Korea receive practically no goods from the United States. China, on the other hand, is treated quite leniently, with few procedural requirements and restrictions on only a limited number of products that could be of strategic military importance. The other European and Asian HPEs fall somewhere in between in terms of the severity of U.S. export restrictions. These restrictions include technology exports through licensing and joint venture arrangements and vary by product as well as destination.[37] The Office of Export Control maintains a list of products for which special permission must be given before an export license is granted. The licensing requirements apply as well to controlled foreign affiliates of U.S. firms.

Many potential U.S. exporters have argued that, when permission to export certain goods is withheld, HPEs simply buy from other countries or develop technology independently. This argument is sometimes effective in obtaining a license; very often, though, it does not suffice, and groups of American companies estimate that the United States loses large amounts of export sales because of these restrictions.[38]

The United States, Canada, Japan, Australia, and the thirteen European NATO countries belong to the Coordinating Committee on Multilateral Export Controls (COCOM), which agrees not to export high-technology goods with potential military use to the Eastern bloc. There has been very little dispute on military and atomic-energy products but considerable disagreement on whether civilian sales could have military or strategic applications. The United States, for example, protested the French delivery of a sophisticated telephone exchange to the then Soviet Union. France and the former West Germany, in turn, complained of the 1984 U.S. trade liberalization with the People's Republic of China.[39] One of the biggest controversies concerned a West German contract to build the West European–Soviet pipeline.[40] As

Western European, U.S., and Japanese firms joined as subcontractors, the United States sought to have the agreement abrogated. The allies refused to do so, and the United States ultimately allowed its firms to participate. Another thorny issue has been that restricted goods (e.g., sophisticated digital computers) have been exported to countries where they can be sold legally and then reexported from those countries to nations where the sale is not allowed by the U.S. government. This led to U.S. export restrictions that worried many firms because of the greater difficulty they had in selling to countries such as Germany, Austria, and Norway. In fact, most U.S. export licenses were sought for goods to other Western countries until 1990, when the U.S. eliminated licenses for sale to allies on all but the most sensitive technologies.[41]

In 1990 COCOM eased restrictions on high-technology sales to Hungary, Poland, and Czech and Slovak but not to the extent that they eased restrictions with China in 1985. Some COCOM members also wanted the CIS to be treated more leniently; however, changes in COCOM procedures must be approved unanimously, and the United States still feared more of a strategic threat from the Soviet Union than did other COCOM countries. The United States also feared a greater likelihood of transshipment from Eastern Europe than from China to the USSR.[42] Several months later the United States barred, on security grounds, U.S. West from building a $500 million fiberoptic cable communications system across the Soviet Union, linking Japan and Europe.[43]

An emerging issue concerns possible transshipment of militarily useful technology to countries such as Iran, Iraq, Syria, and Libya, especially after the costly liberation of Kuwait from Iraq. Many observers believe that China, Eastern Europe, and the newly independent nations within the CIS are not able to monitor the end use of technologies that they export. Or, even if they can, they may be unwilling because of their need for export earnings.[44]

Export controls have also strained relationships between the United States and some other market economies. For example, a Japanese firm, Toshiba, and a Norwegian firm, Kongsberg, exported equipment to the former Soviet Union that the U.S. government thought to be militarily useful. The U.S. Congress then included economic sanctions against Toshiba and Kongsberg (i.e., restricting their sales in the United States) in a trade bill.[45]

Import Controls

Import controls
- Differ by country of origin
- Are affected by the most-favored-nation status.

In addition to virtual embargoes on goods from Vietnam, Cambodia, North Korea, Laos, and Cuba, the United States uses the 1930 tariff rates (the highest in U.S. history) on goods coming from Albania, Bulgaria, Mongolia, and Romania. The embargoes as well as the failure to grant most-favored-nation status put much HPE production at a competitive disadvantage in the U.S. market. (As of late 1990, China, Czech and Slovak, Hungary, Poland, and the former USSR did receive MFN treatment in the United States.)[46] Because of the high level of education and labor skills of many HPE populations, Western companies are interested in sourcing production in those countries. Or, they may seek markets within the HPEs but export sufficient amounts to earn foreign exchange. The lack of MFN status hampers these potentials. Furthermore, even when MFN treatment is extended, it may be taken away, thus increasing operating uncertainties. For example, the U.S. suspended Poland's MFN status in 1951, gave it back in 1960, suspended it again in 1982, and restored it again in 1987.[47] In 1990, a year after the Tiananmen Square suppression, China barely missed losing its MFN status in a U.S. Congressional vote. At the time, Nike was exporting about $100 million of shoes (mainly to the U.S.) and employing about 8000 people in China. Without MFN treatment, Nike would have been forced to shift production to Indonesia and Thailand. Mattel would have experienced a U.S. duty of 70 percent on Barbie dolls, instead of the 7.6 percent. The threat of MFN suspension for China led Reebok to abandon its Chinese production and influenced China to free 211 prisoners in an effort to prevent U.S. actions.[48]

Most HPEs are also highly protectionistic in their purchases of Western goods. When one talks about trade liberalization in the West, the context is usually one of reducing tariffs. Recent discussion of HPE trade liberalization is at an entirely different level, referring to such factors as decentralized import buying, invoicing in convertible currencies, and the lifting of quantitative restrictions.[49] Meanwhile, HPE tariffs remain high.

Because U.S. import controls are not the same for all HPEs, problems sometimes emerge if goods are transshipped from one HPE to another so that they arrive in the United States from a country for which there are few import restrictions. For example, the United States has an embargo on imports from Cuba: The United States ceased importing nickel from the former Soviet Union because of claims that Cuban nickel was reaching the United States through transshipments.[50] Given the likely continued dependence of former COMECON countries on each other, the questions of origin and destination will probably continue.

METHODS OF DOING BUSINESS WITH HPEs

Thus far we have focused on differences in doing business with HPE enterprises. Yet in spite of these differences many firms have adjusted to the nuances. The following discussion highlights ways to deal with some major concerns.

Financial Arrangements

Although balance-of-payments problems in HPEs have inhibited their ability to buy goods in the West, sales may be financed in several ways. Exports may be sold for credit, cash payment in a convertible currency, or through some type of barter arrangement. Western banks such as Dresdner, Citibank, Paribus, and Bankers Trust are now well established in the HPEs. Vneshtorbank, the CIS Foreign Trade Bank, has correspondent relations with over 1300 banks in over 100 countries and owns banks in Western Europe. Through

Sales may be financed by credit, cash, or some type of barter arrangement.

these networks, one can export by means of letters of credit or bills of exchange, which function substantially the same as the instruments used for trade with other Western countries.[51]

Many sales to HPEs are so large that long-term credit arrangements through domestic governmental agencies may be necessary. All Western industrial countries have some type of export credit insurance, which enables their exporters to raise the required credit funds from government or private sources. The United States has at times disallowed the Export-Import Bank to grant credit or credit guarantees to certain HPEs, but basically they are allowed for countries given MFN treatment. An unresolved issue at this writing is whether a state enterprise guarantee of repayment is equivalent to a state guarantee.

A Western exporter sometimes receives a cash payment in a convertible currency when selling to HPE customers. However, because of convertible currency shortages, HPEs frequently will try to pay Western firms through some type of barter or countertrade arrangement. These arrangements may be handled by the Western firm itself (internally) or by contract with another firm which will find markets for HPE products. For example, Combustion Engineering is paid in oil for its control system joint venture in the CIS.[52] When faced by the prospect of inconvertibility, a group of large U.S. firms (Johnson & Johnson, RJR Nabisco, Eastman Kodak, Mercator, and Archer-Daniels-Midland) joined in a consortium with Chevron so that some of Chevron's dollar earnings from exported oil could be used to convert the other companies' ruble earnings. Basically the consortium serves as a holding company for each firm's separate CIS joint ventures.[53]

Marketing

Consumer products presently need little marketing activity in HPEs.

A distinction needs to be made between consumer and industrial sales. For the former, brand recognition and pent-up demand often precede the Western firm's entry so that little promotion has been necessary to date.[54] In a 1990 study combining recognition and esteem to rate 400 Western trademarks in terms of brand power, CIS, Hungarian, and Polish adults all put Sony, Adidas, Ford, and Mercedes-Benz in their top-ten list. On average the Hungarians, Poles, and former Soviets recognized 250, 175, and 100 brands, respectively.[55] However, pent-up demand will not last forever; and some companies, such as American Express, Procter & Gamble, and Levi Strauss, are advertising to build brand recognition and image. Large Western advertising agencies, such as Young & Rubicam and McCann-Erickson, and market research groups, such as Gallup, have established offices in HPEs so that they will be ready when there is more than an ample supply of goods and services to sell.

Industrial sales are a different matter, since they are made to state enterprises. Occasionally, a Western firm has an industrial product or technology that is so well known or so desired by HPE enterprises and FTOs that no marketing effort is needed to secure sales. Rarely, there are also firms that manage to develop business by simply sending catalogs, price lists, and specifications. However, most firms have to develop an active approach to creating demand.

A major means of creating demand is through exhibitions at trade fairs. The fairs sometimes are general in nature and sometimes specialize in products or goods from specific countries. Some Western producers have acted as consultants, giving lectures and demonstrations to officials of research institutes in HPEs, which has led to personal contacts critical for sales. Many firms believe that they must send managers to visit HPEs at least twice a year if they are to maintain market growth.

Fiat's experience is typical for large industrial sales: Fiat signed a contract for a $1.3 billion automobile assembly plant in Poland; Fiat then set out to find subcontractors to supply most of the parts. There is usually considerable publicity attendant on the signing of large contracts, with the result that potential subcontractors may easily contact the prime contractor to solicit sales. The ultimate suppliers are often companies from a number of different countries.

Thus far this discussion has highlighted marketing opportunities for Western firms within HPEs. Because most HPE enterprises lack marketing expertise, there are also opportunities to represent them in the West. Many large Western firms and important entrepreneurs, such as PepsiCo and Armand Hammer, began promoting HPE products years ago. But other niches undoubtedly exist. For example, Steven Leber is a rock music impresario who has arranged tours for the Rolling Stones, Def Leppard, *Jesus Christ Superstar,* and other shows. He has successfully represented circuses from the former Soviet Union by arranging bookings and transportation, promoting them, and finding corporate sponsors for them.[56]

Cooperative Arrangements

Because they want to gain Western products and services with high-technology and management skill inputs and, at the same time, minimize the outflow of hard currencies, HPEs prefer arrangements by which they license Western technology, have a Western firm build and/or run the establishment for them under turnkey or management contracts, or participate in joint venture arrangements. Of particular interest are the coproduction arrangements, which involve having a Western firm provide equipment, technical input, or management for a plant owned by HPE partners in exchange for a portion of the output or output from another HPE plant. For instance, Siemens, a German equipment manufacturer, receives telephone relay equipment in Bulgaria in exchange for providing a telephone system.

Even when HPEs allow 100 percent ownership by Western foreign investors, the Western firms generally prefer joint ventures. The regulatory and bureaucratic environments within HPEs are sufficiently complex that local

Creation for demand of industrial products takes place through
- Trade fairs
- Frequent visits
- Being subcontractors

Cooperative arrangements are popular because
- HPEs conserve hard currencies
- Western firms need assistance at working with HPE bureaucracies

assistance is desirable. For example, different ministries may be able to delay actions because of their diverse control of supplies, convertible currency permits, transport, and environmental issues. There are, however, some wholly owned foreign investments, such as ones by 3M and Hilton in China.

Western companies increasingly realize the complementary nature of their resources with those of firms in HPEs. By combining these resources in other countries, companies may gain considerable economic advantages. For example, CIS, German, and Austrian firms have jointly constructed a power station in Iceland; Chrysler's joint venture with partners in Egypt assembles Belarus tractors for a CIS firm.[57]

Planning Exports to HPEs

The steps needed to develop profitable business with HPEs can be long and expensive. Recall McDonald's long negotiation process with authorities before reaching a joint venture agreement in Russia. Furthermore, there are many examples of firms that expended considerable effort without reaching their business objectives.[58] Table 10.4 outlines the major steps a U.S. manager would have to undertake to export profitably to an HPE, which is still operating close to its traditional CPE methods. Note that each step is effectively a decision point. For example, in step 1, if there are insurmountable objections within the company for doing business with HPEs, it would be fruitless to incur the costs inherent in the other steps.

LOOKING TO THE FUTURE   This chapter has differed from others in that the emphasis throughout has been on the future. Events within HPEs and between HPEs and successful market economies have been changing so rapidly that any business decisions must be made within the framework of a very uncertain future. Nevertheless, there are several questions that have not heretofore been covered that warrant some speculation. These include the emerging comparative opportunities among HPEs, the types of products and services to sell in those countries, and the comparison of companies and countries in their abilities to exploit the future opportunities.

Comparison of HPEs

Western business opinion is that opportunities are much greater in some HPEs than in others.

Western firms are more willing to expend resources where they see greater opportunities. Their perception of opportunities is thus mirrored by their expansion plans. In a 1990 survey of CEOs from the United States, Western Europe, and Japan, 34 percent included Eastern Europe and only 13 percent included the then USSR in their next five-year capital-spending plans. Within Eastern Europe, intentions were polarized by area. There was a much higher intent to exploit opportunities in Czech and Slovak, Poland, Hungary, and what was East Germany than in Yugoslavia, Romania, Bulgaria, and Al-

TABLE 10.4 | EXPORTS TO HPEs: A PLAN FOR U.S. MANAGERS* Note that each step is effectively a decision point. For example, if step 1 shows unusually high obstacles, one may decide not to proceed further.

1. Internal political obstacles
   a. If they exist, try to overcome them.
2. Validated export license
   a. Find out if one is needed.
   b. Get nonbinding opinion from the U.S. Department of Commerce on likelihood of receiving one.
3. Contact with buying agency
   a. Find out which FTO or production ministry handles product in target country from U.S. Department of Commerce or from foreign consular office.
   b. Make contact in person, through intermediary, by mail, or by phone to ascertain if proposition might be entertained.
4. Competitive situation
   a. Ascertain who your competitors are likely to be.
   b. Ascertain your competitive advantages in terms of such factors as price, quality, technology, delivery time, and payment receipt methods.
5. Counterpurchase
   a. Discover what products might be available from HPE for counterpurchase.
   b. Determine any limits for resale.
   c. Analyze if and under what terms your firm might undertake a profitable counterpurchase arrangement.
   d. Investigate internal versus external handling of arrangements.
6. Sale
   a. Negotiate an agreement.
   b. Obtain validated license, if required.
7. Growth
   a. Analyze after a year or two if continued sales look promising.
   b. Consider setting up a special operating unit in a "gateway city," such as Vienna or Hong Kong.
   c. Consider establishment of local representation in the target HPE and investigate feasibility of being granted permission by the HPE authorities.

*The authors wish to acknowledge the assistance of Paul Marer in conceptualizing these steps.

bania.[59] Unfortunately, there are no similar surveys for other HPEs; however, China seems to be perceived as a high-opportunity area. After the Tiananmen uprising, there was some "wait-and-see" attitude on the part of Western companies, but this was quickly replaced by a sharp increase in the number and value of all types of contracts between China and Western firms.[60] There is only fragmentary evidence about most other HPEs, such as Myanmar and Vietnam; however, this evidence seems to indicate that there is some interest, although not very strong, in business from the market economies.

A useful way of comparing HPEs is illustrated in Fig. 10.1. The horizontal axis rates European HPEs (except Albania) on the basis of economic development potential, and the vertical axis compares them on the likely change of economic system through reforms and transformation. The plotting closely parallels the capital spending plans for Western firms within the region, e.g., the GDR and Hungary are nearest to the desired northeast corner of the matrix and were also included in more Western investment plans. There seems

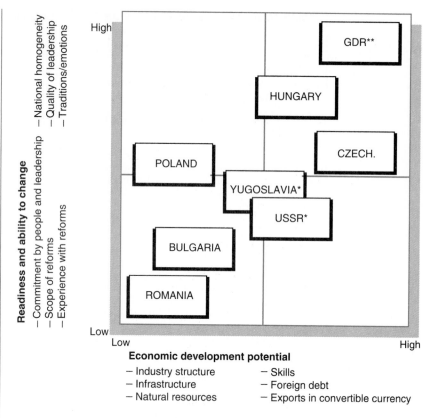

Figure 10.1
Eastern European Countries: Simplified Comparative Chances of Success
One may develop quantitative comparisons or compare countries by opinion.
The farther the country is plotted to the right, the greater is its economic
development potential. The higher it is plotted, the more likely it is that it will make
a market transformation. *Source:* Peter Kraljic, "The Economic Gap Separating East and
West," *The McKinsey Quarterly,* Spring 1990, p. 74. *Both Yugoslavia and the USSR have
subsequently split up. **The GDR is now part of Germany.

to be a near consensus that the former GDR is the area most likely to succeed.
It not only had the highest level of human and infrastructure development,
but its unification with the former West Germany will give it the capital and
resource mobility that it needs to develop rapidly.

Types of Products and Services

Because so many products and services are in short supply within the HPEs,
it is difficult to speculate where more advantages lie for Western firms. As
long as all resources enter from abroad and as long as transferees are willing
to wait long-term to repatriate their capital and earnings, almost any type of

U.S., West European, and Japanese firms have different advantages in exploiting HPE opportunities.

product and service will be welcome. However, when locally scarce resources have to be added to those brought in from abroad, HPEs will likely try to promote those projects that offer hope of economic growth, while allowing just enough expenditure on consumer goods and services to placate their consumer-products-hungry populations.

The composition of imports by HPEs from the West is an indication of their industrial emphasis. Nearly one third of imports are classified as engineering products, and the HPEs have been particularly eager to expend their resources on importing advanced machinery and equipment. From numerous examples it is obvious that HPE negotiators want to get the most advanced technology, yet they also want proven technologies. It is difficult to get both at the same time, except in mature industries where most technology transfers will probably take place. A number of Western automobile manufacturers, who see mature markets in the United States, Western Europe, and Japan, have already committed to projects in the Eastern European HPEs and in China.[61]

Of particular importance is the need for replacement machinery over the next several years. The HPEs have generally expanded the stock of equipment and machinery in order to bring additional workers into the labor force rather than increased the output of existing workers through the introduction of more labor-efficient machinery. There is a near consensus that HPEs have practically reached their limits of increasing output by simply adding to the work force. Because the participation rate in the work force is so high, housework activity is a real burden that falls, for cultural dictates, almost entirely on women, who are also working outside their homes. There would seem to be a market for any household appliances that would help alleviate this problem.

Aside from machinery for industrial and home use, it is anticipated that HPEs will have a greater need for agricultural machinery, especially machinery suitable for small- and medium-sized farms, and food-processing and distribution equipment. About one third of the CIS labor force is in agriculture, compared to only about 5 percent in the United States, yet the CIS farmer can feed many fewer people than the U.S. counterpart. The difference in productivity is due partly to natural geographic conditions, but the major culprit appears to be the lack of modern machinery. The HPEs also lag behind in the ability to preserve foods once they are produced. The lack of agricultural productivity also points to a continued need for Western agricultural products, particularly grains.

Traditionally, service firms such as banks and advertising agencies have followed their production clients abroad in order to provide them with the same types of services as at home and to help them in coordinating worldwide strategies. Service activities, including wholesaling and retailing, are poorly developed in HPEs. There is evidence that Western service firms are already entering HPEs to serve their Western clients' present and anticipated future needs.

Advantages of Companies and Countries

Company and country advantages depend, of course, on the particular products, services, and resources that they can provide. In addition, one may look at comparative opportunities by size of company, location of production facilities, and some particular operating characteristics.

Among the so-called Triad Powers (the United States, Japan, and Western Europe), Western Europe would seem to have a location advantage in trade with Eastern Europe and the Soviet Union as markets open. Furthermore, it is probable that preferential trading relationships will develop between the European Community and various Eastern European countries. Japan has a similar location advantage with China and is already the largest exporter to China. In addition, Chinese industrial purchasers rate the quality of Japanese products higher than those from the United States and higher than those from any European country except Germany.[62] U.S. production has a location advantage only with Cuba, and that market has a much smaller potential than the ones in Eastern Europe and China.

If we look at operating forms other than export-import, then the location situation is less important. U.S. firms have the greatest experience in operating plants of the size needed for the amount of output required by large Russian and Chinese markets. The U.S. is the leader in franchising. Given shortages of funds within HPEs for large operations, franchising may be an effective way to tap into HPE entrepreneurial partnerships where smaller amounts of capital are needed. Furthermore, franchising provides an upgrading of skills for local owner-managers who participate in training programs and receive operating manuals. For example, AlfaGraphics is successfully franchising printing shops in Russia, where local private individuals have sufficient resources and motivation to invest their own funds.[63] The United States also has large numbers of first- and second-generation residents from HPEs who are influential, who know a great deal about HPE markets, and who have emotional ties that could be used to develop HPE business ties.

There are several areas in which U.S. and CIS interests are complementary. One of these could involve more research collaboration, since CIS firms are strong in basic technology but weak in applying that technology to new products, an area in which U.S. firms are strong. Another is the combination of vast CIS natural resources with U.S. firms' ability to manage extraction in large projects. Still another is the CIS strength in transporting goods over long distances, which could be complemented by U.S. abilities to market such goods.

Western European firms made more earlier inroads into Eastern Europe than firms from the United States and Japan, and they show a greater willingness to invest in that area than firms from either Japan or the United States. However, their positions in China are not nearly as well developed. Because of location once again, Japan may look more to Southeast Asia and the United States to Latin America as future sources of labor-intensive components. Western European firms, however, may look more at Eastern European HPEs.

Perhaps Japan's biggest advantage is the usual willingness of Japanese managers and companies to adopt a long-term strategy. Japanese companies may, therefore, be more willing to wait as long as it takes before remitting profits and capital from their HPE endeavors. A second factor that may benefit Japanese firms is that they have less of a presence within the European Community than Western European or U.S. firms and are now targeting the EC for expansion. They therefore will not have to worry so much about the sunk cost of present facilities if they serve the EC through Eastern European production units.

Regardless of where companies are located, large firms will undoubtedly have an advantage in undertaking very large-scale HPE projects because of experience, the needed capital inputs, and the high fixed costs associated with long-term negotiations. However, smaller firms may serve as subcontractors, even on these projects. Furthermore, smaller firms may have some other advantages in the future. Their size may be more compatible with that of small private HPE enterprises that wish to develop trade or joint venture relationships with Western firms. Furthermore, smaller firms may be more flexible in their operations. For example, before McDonald's opened in Moscow, a U.S. entrepreneur with few financial resources began operating a Nathan's Famous Hot Dogs mobile unit there. From one pushcart he serves about 1000 customers a day and is very profitable. To assure supplies, he buys meat each day from the Central Market, where farmers sell from their private production at as much as seven times the price in state stores. But this way, he always has supplies. He is able to be much more flexible than a larger operation, such as McDonald's. For example, he buys whatever meat is available for the hot dogs—beef, rabbit, bear, wild boar.[64] Flexibility may thus be the key to success for small Western firms wishing to tap new HPE opportunities.

SUMMARY

- Political and economic changes within the former communist bloc have led to optimism about business therein because (a) political barriers may be lessened and (b) economic growth will enhance market potentials.

- As political relationships have varied in this century between Western countries and what are now known as HPEs, business relationships have fluctuated substantially. This has been especially true of trade between the United States and the former Soviet Union. Trade flourished when the two countries were allies but fell when animosities arose.

- Trade controls have been instituted to hurt an unfriendly country, to try to make a country change some policy, or to make a public statement of displeasure about another country's actions.

■ Not all HPEs plan to transform themselves into market economies, nor will transformation to a market economy necessarily make HPEs economically successful.

■ Regardless of the model of market economy that countries follow, the successful ones all enjoy certain conditions in common: predominance of privately owned production, producer competition, sound currencies, effective financial institutions, good infrastructures, environmental-protection interest, and opportunities for individual fulfillment.

■ Short-term economic hardships may inhibit the transformation to becoming market economies as the general population loses confidence in the changes.

■ Some of the obstacles to privatizing state enterprises are their inefficiencies, the lack of local funds and management skills to take them over, and a reluctance to allow foreign interests to take over too much of the economy.

■ Soft budgets protect state enterprises from going out of business, but they provide little incentive for effecting operating efficiencies.

■ The shortage of employees in HPEs who are trained in competitive management inhibits the transition to market-oriented operations and may leave bureaucratic managers in situations where they are not really accountable to anyone for their actions.

■ Single-site state monopolies will be difficult to sell off or break up. They are particularly present in the former USSR.

■ Regional ethnic differences have surfaced in HPEs because they are no longer suppressed dictatorially and because the common fear of the West has subsided.

■ A successful market transformation process will be very expensive; and there are uncertainties as to whether HPEs will gain access to needed funds.

■ The fact that the HPEs contain about one third of the world's population indicates a large market potential. However, the large land mass and the past desire to be as independent as possible from the West mean that the Eastern bloc is more nearly self-sufficient than other areas of the world.

■ One of the major factors inhibiting the expansion of trade between HPEs and market economies is the lack of products that can be marketed in the West in sufficient quantity to gain the exchange needed for imports.

■ Some legacies of central planning that inhibit HPEs in their international business are: the need to compete primarily on the basis of price, their lack of adequate cost or competitive price references in many cases, their unrealistic economic figures, and the lack of experience of and with new decentralized decision makers.

■ Many products that U.S. producers could sell in HPEs cannot be exported because of U.S. controls. Many potential exporters have argued that these policies result not in maintaining security, but rather in diverting purchases to non-U.S. sources.

■ When an exporter sells to an historically planned economy, it may be for credit, for cash payment, or in exchange for merchandise. All Western industrial countries have some type of export credit insurance, which helps their firms to make large sales to HPEs.

■ For sales of consumer products in HPEs, there is presently so much pent-up demand that little marketing effort is needed. For industrial product sales, two of the major means of creating demand are through exhibitions at trade fairs and by soliciting sales to other Western firms that have become major contractors for building plants and facilities in HPEs.

■ A large amount of Western business in HPEs is in the form of cooperative arrangements, such as joint ventures, licensing, and turnkey projects. Frequently, the Western firm is paid by receiving part of the merchandise, which is then sold in the West.

■ Western managers perceive much greater business opportunities in some HPEs than in others.

■ The United States, Western Europe, and Japan and companies located in each have different relative advantages for business in different HPEs.

C A S E
TAURUS HUNGARIAN RUBBER WORKS[65]

In 1989 the Hungarian government passed its Act on Transformation, which made it possible for state-owned firms to privatize. Taurus Hungarian Rubber Works' privatization had to take place in an environment of a stagnant economy and a sluggish industry. There was top management consensus that Taurus must maintain or improve its international competitiveness and become less dependent on its traditional manufacture of truck and farm tires. Between 1988 and 1990, Taurus sorted out its options.

Company Background   Before examining the options, it is useful to describe Taurus briefly. Taurus's predecessor was founded in 1882, and the company was nationalized after World War II. At various times the nationalized firm produced a variety of rubber products. In 1963 five

rubber manufacturers were merged into the present company. Purchasing, cash management, and investment were centralized and a central trade and research and development apparatus was created. Contrary to the national norm, the company used strategic planning instead of relying on centralized planning. By 1990 the company operated rubber-processing plants in five cities as well as a machine and mold factory. Taurus operated four separate divisions with an increasing emphasis on international business, and had 1989 annual sales of 20.7 billion Forints. (The exchange rate was about 50 Forints per 1 US$.) Tables 10.5 and 10.6 show 1989 performance.

The Tire division manufactured tires for commercial vehicles, with truck and farm tires accounting for about 34 and 20 percent, respectively, of the division's sales. Other products included tire retreading, inner tubes, and fork-lift truck tires. About 58 percent of the division's sales were exported, primarily to the following countries (in millions of Forints): United States,

TABLE 10.5 | SELECTED 1989 DIVISION PERFORMANCE INFORMATION (in Millions of Forints) Two divisions accounted for the bulk of 1989 activities.

Item	Division			
	Tires	Technical Rubber	Machines & Molds	Trade
Revenues	8,547	7,183	242	4,694
Assets:				
Gross fixed assets	5,519	2,787	292	—
Net fixed assets	3,016	1,120	135	—
Inventories	1,126	545	104	—
Employees	4,021	3,851	552	198

Note: Machines and molds sales includes output used in-house.

Source: Company records.

351.7; Algeria, 298.2; Czechoslovakia, 187.3; West Germany, 183.5; and Yugoslavia, 172.0. The division recently finished a World Bank-financed expansion of radial truck tire capacity. Two new lines of tires were added in 1988, another three in 1990, and six more were scheduled for the near future. The division was also developing another tire under license with a U.S. firm.

The Technical Rubber division manufactured and marketed rubber hoses, air-springs for trucks and buses, conveyor belts, waterproof sheeting, and the PALMA line of camping gear.

The PALMA camping gear and the rotary hose business have global market shares of about 15 and 40 percent, respectively. The demand for high-pressure and large-bore hoses is related closely to offshore drilling activity. The sale of air-springs was expected to increase with further acceptance of the technology. The former Soviet Union was this division's largest customer, but accounted for only about 1 percent of divisional sales. Recent sales were distributed as follows: large-bore high-pressure hoses, 7 percent; rotary hoses, 27 percent; hydraulic hoses, 15 percent; camping goods, 18 percent; waterproof sheeting,

TABLE 10.6 | TOTAL COMPANY SALES (Selected Years; in Millions of Forints) Sales in both the domestic and foreign markets increased steadily during the 1980s.

	Export	Domestic	Total
1980	2,560	7,890	10,450
1982	2,588	9,024	11,612
1984	3,704	9,381	13,085
1985	4,055	9,979	14,034
1986	4,517	11,174	15,691
1987	5,349	12,255	17,604
1988	6,843	12,056	18,899
1989	7,950	12,716	20,666

Source: 1988 Annual Report and internal company data.

14 percent; air springs, 5 percent; and conveyor belts, 14 percent.

The Machines and Molds division manufactured products used in Taurus's manufacturing process as well as by others. About 70 percent of its sales were for export, and overall sales were as follows: technical rubber molds, 24 percent; polyurethane molds, 17 percent; machines and components, 25 percent; and tire curing molds, 34 percent.

Taurus's trade division handled COMECON purchases and sales, as well as distribution functions for other firms. As of 1990, it was expected that the division would continue to serve as Taurus's purchasing agent and that it would increase its trading activities for other firms. The future of COMECON was in question.

Strategy of Strategic Alliances   Management saw that the global rubber industry had fallen from a better than average industry growth performance in the 1960–1970 period to one that was far inferior during the 1980–1987 period. Such industries as data processing, aircraft, medical equipment, and telecommunications equipment had grown much faster of late. Moreover, management was extremely aware of the increasing concentration occurring in the tire industry through the formation of joint ventures, mergers, cooperative arrangements, and acquisitions (see the Bridgestone case in Chapter 6 for more detail). At least the industry's tire segment had passed into its mature stage, and major rubber companies had responded by diversifying and attempting to find growth markets for their rubber-production capacity. Within Hungary, some other rubber manufacturers had grown faster than Taurus as they replaced their low growth lines with ones possessing greater growth potential. Table 10.7 shows market shares and Taurus's estimates for 1992.

Taurus's management recently concluded (with aid from a consulting company) that the company operated in a number of highly attractive markets and that its emphasis should be on competitive improvement of current product lines and businesses. (Product positions are shown in Fig. 10.2.)

Fundamental to Taurus's desire to be more growth oriented was its newly enunciated strategy of seeking cooperative arrangements with other firms. Now ranked thirtieth in size within the rubber industry, Taurus was facing newly formed international combinations with enormous financial strength, strong market positions, and diverse managerial assets. Given the high and growing concentration in the rubber industry and the embarkation of international cooperative relationships even among the largest firms, Taurus determined that it too should seek international cooperative arrangements. In seeking these affiliations the company would be very open and responsive to any type of reasonable alternative or combination that might be offered. Cooperative arrangements could be used to improve product or process technologies, gain

TABLE 10.7 | SHARE OF RUBBER GOODS PRODUCTION: TAURUS VERSUS OTHER HUNGARIAN MANUFACTURERS Note Taurus's diminishing market share.

	Percent of Market			
	1970	1980	1986	1992
Taurus	95	80	68	65
All others	5	20	32	35

Source: Internal company data for years 1970 to 1985 and company estimate for 1992.

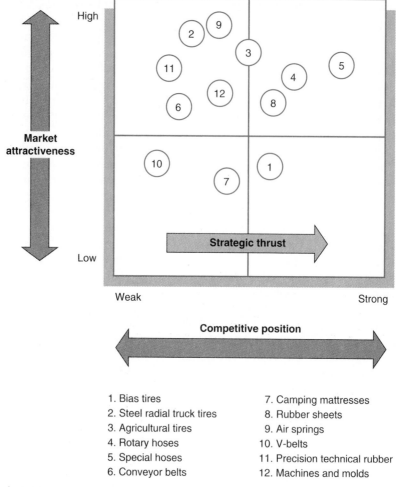

1. Bias tires
2. Steel radial truck tires
3. Agricultural tires
4. Rotary hoses
5. Special hoses
6. Conveyor belts

7. Camping mattresses
8. Rubber sheets
9. Air springs
10. V-belts
11. Precision technical rubber
12. Machines and molds

Figure 10.2
The Taurus Portfolio
The most desirable products are located toward the northeast corner of the matrix. *Source:* Company documents and consulting group's final report.

resources or efficiencies, or gain access to expanded markets. In pursuing strategic alliances, Taurus realized that its bargaining position differed greatly among the various business lines in its portfolio. These differences are shown in Table 10.8.

The problem now came to the restructuring of the company's current divisions to make them into rational and identifiable business units to other companies. For example, it might establish

a hose division and seek a joint venture partner with someone who manufactures couplings for hoses or someone who could use the same hoses in the offshore mining and drilling business.

Questions

1. How might cooperative arrangements for Taurus relate to Hungary's desire to become a successful market economy? To meeting Taurus's operating objectives?

TABLE 10.8 | COOPERATION POTENTIALS BY PRODUCT LINE Products in the second column are those where Taurus had its strongest competitive market positions and could therefore bargain more strongly with international firms.

Product Lines	Taurus's Bargaining Strength		
	Weak	Strong	Mixed
Truck tires	•		
Farm tires			•
Rotary hoses		•	
Specialty hoses			•
Hydraulic hoses	•		
Waterproofing sheets		•	
Belting	•		
Camping goods			•
Air springs			•
Machines and molds		•	
Precision goods			•

Source: Internal company report.

2. As a Western company, what would be your major concerns about cooperative arrangements with Taurus?

3. What are the benefits that Taurus might bring to a Western firm in a cooperative arrangement?

Chapter Notes

1. Jeffrey A. Tannenbaum, "Franchisers See a Future in East Bloc," *Wall Street Journal,* June 5, 1990, p. B1 ff; Erich E. Toll, "Hasabburgonya, Tejturmix and Big Mac to Go," *The Journal of Commerce,* August 24, 1988, p. 1A; Tricia A. Dreyfuss, "Negotiating the Kremlin Maze," *Business Month,* Vol. 132, November 1988, pp. 55–63; Vincent J. Schodolski, "Moscovites Stand in Line for a 'Beeg Mek' Attack," *Chicago Tribune,* February 1, 1990, Sec. 1, pp. 1–2; Bill Keller, "Of Famous Arches, Beeg Meks, and Rubles," *New York Times,* January 28, 1990, p. A1 ff; "McDonald's," *Economist,* November 18, 1989, Vol. 313, No. 7629, p. 34; Peter Gumbel, "Muscovites Queue Up at American Icon," *Wall Street Journal,* February 1, 1990, p. A12; "Big Mac in China," *Wall Street Journal,* September 10, 1990, p. A12; Don Jeffrey, "Overseas Sales Get McD Off to a Strong Start in '87," *Nation's Restaurant News,* May 11, 1987, p. 172; John F. Love, "McDonald's Behind the Arches," *Restaurant Business Magazine,* January 1, 1987, Vol. 86, No. 1, pp. 101–106; "Fast Food," *Time,* October 2, 1989, Vol. 134, No. 14, p. 83; Ann Blackman, "Moscow's Big Mak Attack," *Time,* February 5, 1990, p. 51; Jeffrey M. Hertzfeld, "Joint Ventures: Saving the Soviets from Perestroika," *Harvard Business Review,* Vol. 69, No. 1, January–February 1991, pp. 80–91.

2. Paul Marer, "Roadblocs to Economic Transformation in Central and Eastern Europe and Some Lessons of Market Economies," in Dick Clark (ed.), *United States-Soviet*

and East European Relations: Building a Congressional Cadre (Queenstown, Md.: The Aspen Institute, 1990), pp. 17–27.

3. This term was used by R.D. Schmidt, Vice Chairman of Control Data, in U.S.-USSR Trade: An American Businessman's Viewpoint," *Columbia Journal of World Business*, Vol. 18, No. 4, Winter 1983, p. 36.

4. Clyde H. Farnsworth quoting Gary C. Hufbauer, senior fellow of the Institute for International Economics, in "The Doves Capture Control of Trade," *New York Times*, October 23, 1983, sec. 3, p. 1.

5. James M. Montgomery, "The 'Cumbersome . . . Apparatus,'" in Robert Cullen (ed.), *The Post Containment Handbook: Key Issues in U.S.-Soviet Economic Relations* (Boulder, Co.: Westview Press, 1990), pp. 39–44, discusses the history of control to 1990.

6. Michael V. Forrestal and James H. Giffen, "U.S.-Soviet Trade: Political Realities and Future Potential," *Columbia Journal of World Business*, Vol. 18, No. 4, Winter 1983, pp. 29–31.

7. See James Henry Giffen, *The Legal and Practical Aspects of Trade with the Soviet Union* (New York: Praeger, 1969), pp. 139–142; Committee for Economic Development, *A New Trade Policy toward Communist Countries* (New York: Committee for Economic Development, 1972), pp. 54–59; John E. Felber, *Manual for Soviet-American Trading* (New Jersey: International Intertrade Index, 1967), pp. 7–9.

8. Economic Commission for Europe, *Economic Survey of Europe in 1986–1987* (New York: Secretariat of the Economic Commission for Europe, 1987), p. 355.

9. "Castro Laments 'Sad Events' in Other Communist Nations," *New York Times*, November 9, 1989, p. A6; Howard W. French, "Dreary Havana Flirts with Capitalism," *New York Times*, December 6, 1990, p. A4.

10. Marer, *loc. cit.*

11. *Ibid*; Peter Kraljic, "The Economic Gap Separating East and West," *The McKinsey Quarterly*, Spring 1990, pp. 62–74.

12. Charles Wolf, Jr., "Less Pain, More Gain for the East Bloc," *Wall Street Journal*, November 19, 1990, p. A14; Robert Pear, "Jobless to Soar in East, C.I.A. Says," *New York Times*, May 17, 1990, p. A6.

13. Peter Gumbel, "Soviets Change Economic Plan, Bar Price Rises," *Wall Street Journal*, July 20, 1990, p. A7; Elisabeth Rubinfein, "Central Plan or No, Moscow Believes It Still Knows Best What Ivan Needs," *Wall Street Journal*, September 20, 1990, p. A8.

14. Jeffrey Sachs, "Poland and Eastern Europe: What Is to Be Done?" in András Köves and Paul Marer (eds.), *Foreign Economic Liberalization: Transformations in Socialist and Market Economies* (Boulder, Co.: Westview Press, 1991), pp. 235–246.

15. *Ibid*; Philip Revzin, "Progress in Work," *Wall Street Journal*, April 5, 1990, p. A1 ff; Peter F. Drucker, "Junk Central Europe's Factories and Start Over," *Wall Street Journal*, July 19, 1990, p. A10; Stephen Engelberg, "First Sale of State Ownings a Disappointment in Poland," *New York Times*, January 14, 1991, p. C1 ff; "Czechoslovakia Auctions Stores to Private Buyers," *New York Times*, January 27, 1991, p. 4; Christopher Farrell and Gail Schares, "Blueprints for a Free Market in Eastern Europe," *Business Week*, February 5, 1990, pp. 88–89; Philip Revzin, "Eager Investors Flock to Hungary, Find Slim Pickings," *Wall Street Journal*, April 5, 1990, p. A18; Alan Murray, "Poland's Hope for Strong U.S. Investment May Be Misplaced, At Least in Short Run," *Wall Street Journal*, December 7, 1989, p. A10.

16. Sadao Nagaoka and Izak Atiyas, "Tightening the Soft Budget Constraint in Reforming Socialist Economies," (Washington, D.C.: The World Bank, Industry Development Division, May 1990), pp. 3–16; Dwight H. Perkins, "China's Industrial and Foreign Trade Reforms," in Köves and Marer, *op. cit.*, p. 279.

17. Sachs, *op. cit.,* pp. 238–239; Kraljic, *loc. cit.;* "Now for the Acid Test," *Euromoney,* November 1990, pp. 40–47.

18. John D. Daniels and Lee H. Radebaugh, *International Business: Environments and Operations,* 5th ed. (Reading, Mass.: Addison-Wesley, 1989), pp. 394–396; "Life in a Soviet Factory," *Economist,* December 22, 1990, pp. 21–24.

19. Most of the thoughts and information in this section were taken from Steven Greenhouse, "Evolution in Europe," *New York Times,* August 6, 1990, p. A4; Paul Marer, "East Europe's Debt Situation in Global Perspective: Utopian Versus Realistic Solutions," in H. W. Singer and Soumitra Sharma (eds.), *Growth and External Debt Management* (London: Macmillan, 1989), pp. 237–245; Igor Reichlin, Rose Brady, David Greising, and Amy Borrus, "Brother, Would You Lend Moscow a Dime?" *Business Week,* December 10, 1990, pp. 44–45; Bill Keller, "Soviet Economy: A Shattered Dream," *New York Times,* May 13, 1990, p. A1 ff; Sheryl W. Dunn, "Debt Is Squeezing Hotels in China," *New York Times,* May 28, 1990, p. 23; Peter Gumbel and Laurie Hays, "Western Suppliers Halt Deliveries to Soviets; Payment Delays Cited," *Wall Street Journal,* March 12, 1990, p. A5; Richard A. Melcher and Rose Brady, "Is the Soviet Union Becoming a Deadbeat?" *Business Week,* February 26, 1990, p. 44.

20. Daniel Franklin and Edwina Moreton, "A Little Late in Learning the Facts," *Economist,* April 20, 1985, p. 5.

21. Central Intelligence Agency, *Handbook of Economic Statistics 1986,* September 1986, pp. 98–101.

22. Barry Newman, "Beleaguered Bloc," *Wall Street Journal,* September 28, 1989, p. 1 ff; Tim Carrington, "East Bloc to Transform COMECON, Retain Economic Ties to Moscow," *Wall Street Journal,* January 10, 1990, p. A8; Peter Gumbel, "Soviets May Gain in COMECON Overhaul," *Wall Street Journal,* January 23, 1990, p. A14. "COMECON's Demise is Delayed," *Wall Street Journal,* February 26, 1991, p. A14.

23. "The Return of Central Europe," *Chicago Fed Letter,* No. 33, May 1990, pp. 1–2.

24. "U.S. Firm Plans Project on Soviet Space Station," *Wall Street Journal,* February 22, 1988, p. 6; Thomas H. Naylor, "Fashion Gives Life to Soviet Reforms," *New York Times,* September 13, 1987, p. D20; Barry Newman, "Poles Flex Unaccustomed Export Muscle," *Wall Street Journal,* September 12, 1990, p. A19; Gary McWilliams, "A Hitchhiker on Russian Rockets," *Business Week,* July 2, 1990, p. 59.

25. Perkins, *op. cit.,* p. 275.

26. Robert C. Jensen, ed., *Soviet Natural Resources in the World Economy* (Chicago: University of Chicago Press, 1983).

27. Christopher S. Wren, "China's Growing Export: Its Workers," *New York Times,* June 3, 1984, p. 3.

28. The survey was conducted jointly by the *Wall Street Journal,* Booz-Allen & Hamilton, and Nihon Keizai Shimbun and was reported in George Anders, "Going East," *Wall Street Journal,* September 21, 1990, pp. R24–25.

29. Franklyn Holzman, "Systemic Bases of the Unconventional International Trade Practices of Centrally-Planned Economies," *Columbia Journal of World Business,* Vol. 18, No. 4, Winter 1983, pp. 4–9.

30. Georg Junge and Jan de Vos, "Reform Progress in Eastern Europe," *Swiss Bank Corporation, Economic and Financial Prospects,* No. 6, 1990, pp. 6–7.

31. George D. Holliday, *East-West Technology Transfer,* Part II, "Survey of Sectoral Case Studies" (Paris: OECD, 1984), p. 75.

32. Neil Behrman, "Soviets Will Sell Diamonds to DeBeers's Swiss Arm, Borrow $1 Billion from Firm," *Wall Street Journal,* July 26, 1990, p. A2; Philip Revzin, "Progress

in Work," *Wall Street Journal,* April 5, 1990, p. A1 ff; Steven Greenhouse, "Talking Deals," *New York Times,* March 22, 1990, p. C1 ff.

33. Larissa Oleson, "Soviet Advertising Techniques in the U.S.," *Columbia Journal of World Business,* Vol. 18, No. 4. Winter 1983, pp. 63–66.

34. Robert Pear, "Jobless to Soar in East, C.I.A. Says," *New York Times,* May 17, 1990, p. A6; Hobart Rowan, "Capitalism Called Only Soviet Hope," *Washington Post,* December 22, 1990, p. A12; Paul Marer and Janos Arvay, *Historically Planned Economies: A Guide Box to Data* (Washington: World Bank, 1991).

35. Perkins, *loc. cit.*

36. Rose Brady, Peter Galuszka, and Maria Shao, "Big Deals Run into Big Trouble in the Soviet Union," *Business Week,* March 19, 1990, pp. 58–59.

37. Christine Westbrook and Alan B. Sherr, "U.S.-Soviet Joint Ventures and Export Control Policy," briefing paper No. 3 (Providence, RI: Brown University Center for Foreign Policy Development, 1990), pp. 16–18.

38. Raymond Bonner, "U.S.-Soviet Trade Bars Said to Cost $10 Billion," *New York Times,* May 25, 1984, p. D1; *Common Sense in U.S.-Soviet Trade* (Washington, D.C.: American Committee on East-West Accord, 1983).

39. Frederick Kempe and Eduardo Lachica, "COCOM Feuds over Trade to East Bloc," *Wall Street Journal,* July 17, 1984, p. 27.

40. D.A. Loeber and A. P. Friedland, "Soviet Imports of Industrial Installations under Compensation Agreements: West Europe's Siberian Pipeline Revisited," *Columbia Journal of World Business,* Vol. 18, No. 4, Winter 1983, pp. 51–62.

41. Jon Zonderman, "Policing High-Tech Exports," *New York Times,* November 27, 1983, pp. 100 + ; "U.S. Sets Trade Curb for Digital," *New York Times,* March 19, 1984, p. D1; Eduardo Lachica, "U.S. Effort to Stiffen Export Licensing Is Costly and Confusing, Industry Says," *Wall Street Journal,* March 20, 1984, p. 10; and "Export Controls," *Economist,* January 17, 1987, pp. 33–34, quoting information from a National Academy of Science publication; Eduardo Lachica, "Curbs Relaxed for Exporters of Technology," *Wall Street Journal,* June 19, 1990, p. A2; Andrew Pollack, "2 Charged in Smuggling Computer," *New York Times,* May 17, 1990, p. C11.

42. Philip Revzin, "U.S. Allies to Ease More Curbs on High-Tech Sales to East Europe," *Wall Street Journal,* February 20, 1990, p. A20. For a discussion of COCOM's voting and administrative mechanisms, see Michael Mastanduno, "What Is COCOM and How Does It Work?" in Robert Cullen (ed.), *op. cit.,* pp. 75–78.

43. Keith Bradsher, "U.S. Bars a Soviet Phone Deal," *New York Times,* June 6, 1990, p. C1 ff.

44. Walter S. Mossberg and John Walcott, "Strategic Shift," *Wall Street Journal,* August 11, 1988, p. 1 ff; Michael R. Gordon, "U.S. Is Worried that Chinese May Again Sell Missile Technology," *New York Times,* November 9, 1989, p. A4; John J. Fialka and Eduardo Lachica, "Easing of Technology Export Controls May Boost Arms Smuggling in Mideast," *Wall Street Journal,* June 19, 1990. p. A22.

45. Steven J. Dryden, Larry Armstrong, and Jonathan Kapstein, "Congress Wants Toshiba's Blood," *Business Week,* No. 3006, July 6, 1987, pp. 46–47; Clyde H. Farnsworth, "Trade Conferees in Congress Agree on Toshiba Curbs," *New York Times,* April 1, 1988, p. 1 + .

46. *Trade Between the United States and the Nonmarket Economy Countries During April–June 1990* (Washington, D.C.: United States International Trade Commission, November 1990), pp. 9–12.

47. *Ibid.,* p. 1.

48. Adi Ignatius, "Punishing China on Trade Punishes Its Free-Marketers," *Wall Street*

Journal, May 24, 1990, p. A11; Amy Borrus, Dinah Lee, and Dori Jones Yang, "The Battle of Beijing Is About to Begin—In Congress," *Business Week,* May 21, 1990, pp. 56–57; David Ignatius, "China Frees 211 Prisoners in Move Seen Aimed at Retaining Most-Favored-Nation Trade Status," *Wall Street Journal,* May 11, 1990, p. A8; Denis Fred Simon, "After Tiananmen: What Is the Future for Foreign Business in China?" *California Management Review,* Vol. 32, No. 2, Winter 1990, pp. 106–123.

49. Junge and de Vos, *loc. cit.*

50. Clyde H. Farnsworth, "U.S. Bars Soviet Nickel," *New York Times,* November 22, 1983, p. D1.

51. Paul Marer (ed.), *U.S. Financing of East-West Trade* (Bloomington: International Development Research Center, Indiana University, 1975); Igor Reichlin, John Templeman, and Györgyi Kocsis, "Where U.S. Bankers Are Running a Distant Second," *Business Week,* July 2, 1990, pp. 45–46.

52. U.S. International Trade Commission, *Analysis of Recent Trends in U.S. Countertrade* (Washington, D.C.: U.S. Government Printing Office, March 1982); Felicity Barringer, "To Russia, for Partners and Profits," *New York Times,* April 10, 1988, p. 3F +.

53. Peter Gumbel, "Group of U.S. Companies Moves Closer to Expanding Business in Soviet Union," *Wall Street Journal,* June 1, 1988, p. 21; Peter Gumbel, "U.S. Firms Flock to Moscow Despite New Impediments," *Wall Street Journal,* October 24, 1989, p. A14.

54. Mark Landler, Rose Brady, and Gail E. Schares, "Mad Ave. Takes the Perestroika Challenge," *Business Week,* March 5, 1990, p. 68; Joann S. Lublin, "Advertising," *Wall Street Journal,* November 1, 1990, p. 36.

55. Kathleen Deveny, "Brand Names Have Cachet in East Bloc," *Wall Street Journal,* June 27, 1990, p. B1.

56. Eugene Carlson, "Entrepreneur Is Ringmaster of U.S.-Soviet Promotions," *Wall Street Journal,* October 4, 1989, p. B3.

57. John Tagliabue, "Bonn Innovating in Trade with East," *New York Times,* March 19, 1984, p. D8; Tony Horowitz, "U.S.S.R. Tractors, U.S. Cars Roll out of Egyptian Plant," *Wall Street Journal,* March 28, 1988, p. 12.

58. For a good discussion on this point see Stephen Telegdy, "Doing Business in Eastern Europe: A Manager's Perspective on the Practical Aspects," in Paul Marer and Pieter Van Veen (eds.), *East European Economic Trends and East-West Trade: U.S., West and East European Perspectives* (Greenwich, CT: JAI Press, 1987), pp. 99–106.

59. Anders, *loc. cit.*

60. Dinah Lee, Lynne Curry, Pete Engardio, and Joyce Barnathan, "A Quiet Comeback: How China Broke Out of Isolation," *Business Week,* December 24, 1990, pp. 34–35.

61. Holliday, *op. cit.,* p. 65; Bradley A. Stertz and Terrence Roth, "Car-Culture Shock," *Wall Street Journal,* November 14, 1990, p. A1 ff.

62. Erdener Kaynak, "How Chinese Buyers Rate Foreign Suppliers," *Industrial Marketing Management,* Vol. 18, No. 3, August 1989, pp. 187–198.

63. Richard Poe, "Be a Franchise Czar," *Success,* September 1990, pp. 40–42.

64. Richard Poe, "Guerrilla Entrepreneurs," *Success,* September 1990, pp. 34–36; Charalambos Vlachoutsikos, "How Small- to Mid-sized U.S. Firms Can Profit from Perestroika," *California Management Review,* Vol. 31, No. 3, Spring 1989, pp. 91–112.

65. This is a condensed version of a 1990 case by Joseph Wolfe, University of Tulsa; Gyula Bosnyak, Taurus Hungarian Rubber Works, Budapest, Hungary; and János Vecsenyi, International Management Center, Budapest, Hungary, and is used with the authors' permission.

CHAPTER **11**

REGIONAL ECONOMIC INTEGRATION

Marrying is easy, but housekeeping is hard.
GERMAN PROVERB

Objectives

- To define different forms of regional economic integration.
- To describe the static and dynamic benefits of regional economic integration.
- To compare different types of regional economic integration, such as the European Community and the Canada–U.S. Free Trade Agreement.
- To describe the rationale for, and current trends in, commodity agreements.
- To discuss other bilateral and multilateral treaties affecting international business.

When the European Economic Community (EEC) was first organized in 1957, U.S. multinational enterprises (MNEs) had to change their method of servicing European markets. The large size of the U.S. market had allowed these firms to achieve economies of scale so that they could export to European countries. After the EEC was established and tariff barriers were erected to protect domestic industries, foreign firms were forced to invest in EEC countries or lose their markets. U.S. MNEs were accustomed to large-scale organizations and had the financial and managerial resources to handle the expansion.

One such example is the Ford Motor Company. Ford first began operating in Europe through its British subsidiary in 1913 and its German subsidiary in 1926. During the next several decades, however, Ford's European operations were separate operating subsidiaries reporting to Ford but not coordinating their policies in any meaningful way. This occurred for two reasons: Individual countries had: (1) different preferences and (2) unique tariff and nontariff barriers to trade. In its 1960 *Annual Report,* Ford management noted that:

> The historical patterns of trade and commerce among nations are undergoing significant changes. Trade groupings, such as the European Economic Community and the European Free Trade Association, are being established. Similar groupings are being considered in Latin America and by some of the African countries. Further changes in trade patterns have been brought about in a number of countries by government regulations that make it advantageous to manufacture locally.
>
> The Company and its subsidiaries are responding to these trends, which bear promise of increasing competition for world automobile markets, by exploring opportunities to strengthen and to expand their international operations.

As a result of the changing environment, Ford executives realized that they could begin considering Europe as one common market rather than a collection of individual markets. Shortly after the establishment of the EEC, Ford changed its management structure to include the European operations under one umbrella organization in order to exploit the economies of scale that were beginning to develop in the EEC. As noted in Map 11.1, the two large manufacturing centers in Great Britain and West Germany (eventually to be expanded to three with Spain) were to remain central to the new strategy, but they were no longer considered separate, independent operating companies. Ford decided it was best to obliterate national boundaries, even though it would be challenging because of nationalistic tendencies on the part of country management. As was noted by the West German managing director,

C A S E
INCIDENT:
FORD IN EUROPE—
THE EARLY YEARS[1]

> The pooling of the two companies cut the engineering bill in half for each company, provided economies of scale, with double the volume in terms of

Map 11.1
Ford in Europe
Ford factory truck and car sales in Europe in 1989 basically came from three locations: Germany (1,023,380), Britain (515,520), and Spain (310,481). In comparison, U.S. factory truck and car sales were 3,709,619, and Canadian truck and car sales were 326,119. In 1989, Ford market share in industry unit sales was 10.1% in Germany, 26.6% in the United Kingdom, and 8.2% in other European markets. This compares with 22.3% in the United States and 20.1% in Canada. In addition, Ford's European operations accounted for 31.5% of Ford's global employment. *Source:* Ford 1989 *Annual Report.*

purchase—commonization of purchase, common components—and provided the financial resources for a good product program at a really good price that we could still make money on.

Ford initially began developing and selling European cars rather than engineering separate cars in each market, a strategy that resulted in the Escort, Capri, and Fiesta models among others. Not only did Ford design and assemble similar automobiles throughout Europe, but it also designed common components to be used in Ford cars. To show the importance of market size in developing this plan, one Ford executive commented: "Neither the British nor the German company could have come up with the Capri separately, tooled it separately. Only with the whole volume of Europe in prospect did the Capri become a viable product development program."

As Ford continued its European expansion, it explored the possibility of having its European unit merge with Fiat in order to allow Ford's strength in northern Europe to combine with Fiat's strength in southern Europe. However, both sides were so strong and so convinced of the need for control that the proposed merger never occurred. Ford needed control to guarantee that the timing of its global strategy, which was developed in the United States, could be maintained. Fiat, on the other hand, was controlled by the Agnelli family in Italy, and loss of control to a foreign company, especially one from a country not a member of the EEC, would have been explosive politically. In addition, Fiat's management could not accept a role subordinate to Ford's management. Clearly, mergers are never easy, but cross-border mergers can often introduce unique problems.

In the late 1980s, a relatively cohesive Europe continued to be an important force in Ford's strategy. Donald E. Petersen, Chairman of Ford, was determined to globalize the company. Part of his strategy involved centralizing the development of a specific car or component wherever in the world Ford has the greatest expertise. Ford of Europe's comparative advantage with respect to the rest of the company is in the small-car market. The European company is responsible for developing a common suspension and undercarriage for compact cars that will be built and sold in the United States as well as in Europe. The growing sophistication of Ford in Europe has resulted largely from the harmonization and growth of the European Community.

No automaker other than GM is more European than Ford, even though Fiat controls Italy, Peugeot and Renault control France, and Volkswagen controls Germany. Ford of Europe has 22 plants throughout Europe and sales offices in each country in order to help tailor marketing and design strategies to local tastes. Thus Ford is poised to take advantage of increasing harmonization that is taking place in Europe.

INTRODUCTION

During the Depression of the 1930s, the world plunged into a period of isolation, trade protection, and economic chaos. Then in the mid- to late-1940s, countries felt that greater cooperation was needed to help them emerge from the wreckage of World War II. The spirit of cooperation was designed to promote economic growth and stability. This chapter discusses some of the important forms of such cooperation, such as regional economic integration and commodity agreements. The focus is on regional efforts because they tend to be more effective than global efforts. This is because global efforts tend to involve too many countries with too many divergent points of view. A major exception to this idea is the universal reaction of the U.N. to the Iraqi invasion of Kuwait. Regional groups can more easily focus on common problems. The establishment of these agreements is an important source of influence on MNEs, as Ford learned in the opening case. The agreements define the size of the market and the rules under which the firm must operate. Firms in the initial stages of expansion abroad need to be aware of the regional groups that encompass target countries. As firms proceed along the scale of multi-nationalism, they find that their organizational structure and operating strategies must conform to and take advantage of regional integration. As noted in the opening case, Ford altered its European organization soon after the formation of the EEC. This chapter explains how these regional groups affect structure and strategy.

REGIONAL ECONOMIC INTEGRATION

Economic integration abolishes economic discrimination between national economies.

During the 1950s and 1960s regional economic integration gained significant momentum. **Economic integration** can be defined as

> a process and . . . a state of affairs. Regarded as a process, it encompasses measures designed to abolish discrimination between economic units belonging to different national states; viewed as a state of affairs, it can be represented by the absence of various forms of discrimination between national economies.[2]

Since discrimination negatively affects economic activity between the countries in question, integration can be seen as valuable.

When we consider some of the major examples of economic integration, such as the **European Community (EC)**, the **European Free Trade Association (EFTA)**, the **U.S.–Canada Free Trade Agreement**, and the **Latin American Integration Association (LAIA)**, the concept of geographic proximity stands out. The major reasons that neighboring countries tend to become involved in integrative activities are:

Geographic proximity is an important reason for economic integration.

- the distances to be traversed are shorter in the case of neighboring countries;

- tastes are more likely to be similar, and distribution channels can be more easily established in adjacent economies;

- neighboring countries may have a common history, awareness of common interests, etc., and hence they may be more willing to coordinate policies.[3]

Also important are ideological and historical similarities. Cuba is a member of COMECON (the Council for Mutual Economic Assistance, an association of communist countries) because of its communist political and and economic philosophy.

Major forms of economic integration include
- Free trade area: no internal tariffs
- Customs unions: common external tariffs
- Common market: factor mobility
- Complete economic integration

There are four major forms of economic integration:

1. *Free trade area (FTA).* Tariffs are abolished among the members of the **free trade area (FTA),** but each member maintains its own external tariff against the non-FTA countries. Three examples of this form of economic integration are the U.S.-Canada Free Trade Agreement, the European Free Trade Association, and the Latin American Integration Association, a relatively loose form of free trade association that was established in 1980 with the demise of the Latin American Free Trade Association.

2. *Customs union.* In the case of a **customs union,** a common external tariff is combined with the abolition of all internal tariffs. This was the first stage of the European Community and is also descriptive of the **Andean Group,** the **Central American Common Market (CACM),** and the **Caribbean Community and Common Market (CARICOM),** three of the other major integrative groups in Latin America.

3. *Common market.* In a **common market,** all of the characteristics of a customs union are combined with the abolition of restrictions on factor mobility, such as labor and capital. This is the current state of affairs in the EC.

4. *Complete economic integration.* The **complete economic integration** stage of the economic union "presupposes the unification of monetary, fiscal, social, and countercyclical policies and requires the setting up of a supranational authority whose decisions are binding for the member states."[4] This form also implies a degree of political integration. Some would say that the institution of the European Parliament was a step in the direction of political unification of Europe, a condition nearly essential for economic integration. In addition, the establishment of a European Central Bank would help to establish uniform monetary policies in Europe.

Economic Effects of Integration

As noted in Chapter 5, the imposition of tariff and nontariff barriers disrupts the free flow of goods and therefore resource allocation. The impact of economic integration can be static or dynamic. When trade barriers are reduced, consumers tend to purchase goods with the best quality at the cheapest price. The static effect of economic integration implies that resources shift from the least efficient to the most efficient producers of goods that consumers demand. This means that trade is diverted from one country to another because of the reduction of barriers and the ability of consumers to get access to new goods. Companies that are protected in their domestic markets face real problems when the barriers are eliminated as they attempt to compete with more efficient producers.

Dynamic changes mean that there are changes in total consumption and in internal and external efficiencies as a result of growth in market size. The reduction of barriers automatically increases total demand. As resources shift to the more efficient producers, firms are able to expand output to take advantage of the larger market. This results in trade creation to take advantage of the expanded market size. This dynamic change in market size allows firms to produce goods at a cheaper price, since the fixed costs of the business can be spread out over more and more units of production.

An important dynamic effect is an increase in efficiency due to increased competition. Many firms in Europe have attempted to grow through merger and acquisition in order to achieve the size necessary to compete in the larger market.

Dynamic effect of integration: As markets grow, firms achieve production economies of scale.

Efficiency increases because of competition.

THE EUROPEAN COMMUNITY

European Evolution to Integration

World War II left a wake of economic as well as human destruction throughout Europe. To facilitate the utilization of aid provided by the Marshall Plan, a U.S. plan to provide aid to Europe after World War II, the sixteen-nation **Organization for European Economic Cooperation (OEEC),** was established in 1948 with the encouragement of the United States. Its purposes were to improve currency stability, combine economic strength, and improve trade relations. However, because the OEEC did not appear strong enough to provide the necessary economic growth, further cooperation was initiated.

According to one major school of thought championed by the French, a common market should be developed, which would: (1) result in the elimination of all restrictions to the free flow of goods, capital, and persons; (2) allow for the harmonization of economic policies; and (3) create a common external tariff. The result was the creation of the **European Economic Community (EEC)** through the Treaty of Rome in March 1957. Its members were West Germany, Belgium, the Netherlands, Luxembourg, France, and Italy. As noted in the map on page M-10, its membership has since been broadened to include the United Kingdom, Ireland, Denmark, Greece, Spain, and Portugal. It now embraces the title **European Community (EC),** which implies a form of cooperation that is broader than economic.

The OEEC was the organization of European countries established to facilitate the utilization of the Marshall Plan.

The EEC allows the economic integration of European countries leading to a free flow of resources, a harmonization of policies, and a common external tariff.

European Free Trade Association

The second major school of thought rejected the notion of total integration and favored instead a free trade area, which would allow for the elimination of all restrictions on the free flow of industrial goods among member nations and would permit each country to retain its own external tariff structure. This approach would provide the benefits of free trade among members but would

The EFTA is a free trade area that rejected the idea of total integration embraced by the EEC.

allow each country to pursue its own economic objectives with outside countries. This was especially beneficial for Great Britain, which had developed favorable trade relationships with Commonwealth countries. From the British point of view, a common external tariff would result in too much cooperation and restriction of individual sovereignty.

Following the second line of thought, the Stockholm Convention of May 1960 created the **European Free Trade Association (EFTA),** which included seven of the OEEC countries that were not partners in the EEC: Austria, Denmark, Norway, Portugal, Sweden, Switzerland, and the United Kingdom. Iceland joined the Association on March 1, 1970, and Finland, an associate member since June 1961, became a full member on January 1, 1986. Denmark, Portugal, and the United Kingdom left EFTA to become full members of the EC. Today, the EFTA is comprised of Austria, Finland, Iceland, Norway, Sweden, and Switzerland, as illustrated in Map 11.1. The original EFTA countries were initially concerned about a unified European effort in economic integration, and the major problems that eventually led them to create the EFTA were:

1. the lack of desire to harmonize social and economic policies, as would be required by the EEC;

2. the special arrangements between the United Kingdom and the Commonwealth nations; and

3. the political neutrality of Austria, Sweden, and Switzerland.

EFTA countries trade more extensively with the EC than with each other.

Nevertheless, the increasing harmonization taking place in the European Community is making it difficult for the EFTA members to maintain their separate status. Austria has formally applied to join the EC, and it is unclear what the other countries will eventually do. The six members of the EFTA have been referred to as freeloaders, desiring to share in the benefits of the EC without paying the price for entry. The EFTA has a free trade agreement with the members of the EC, but the countries don't have to contribute to the EC's costly farm and social programs.[5]

In addition, the major trading partners of the EFTA nations are the members of the EC. Over 60 percent of total EFTA imports come from the EC countries, whereas only 13 percent of EFTA imports are from EFTA countries.

Initial EEC Efforts

The European Coal and Steel Community was created in 1951 to pool the coal and steel production of the six original members of the European Economic Community. The EEC and the European Atomic Energy Community were established in 1957, with the major task of the EEC to establish a common market. Since 1967, the three communities have been supervised by the same Commission, and they became increasingly known as the European Community (EC).

The EEC was initially interested in three broad categories of activity: the free movement of goods through the elimination of tariff barriers; the free movement of persons, services, and capital; and the establishment of a common transport policy. As noted in Table 11.1, the first reduction in internal tariffs took place in 1959, and by 1968, all internal tariffs had been replaced.

The Common Agricultural Policy was established to stabilize earnings to producers and provide food for consumers.

In 1962 the Common Agricultural Policy (CAP) was established, an important element of EEC economic policy. The initial objectives of the CAP were to increase the productivity of farmers, to establish a fair standard of living for producers, to stabilize markets, to ensure food security, and to set reasonable prices for consumers. A series of tariffs and price supports were established to accomplish the goals of the CAP and to shield agricultural goods from foreign competition.

There are two major effects of the CAP, one internal and one external. Internally, a large portion of the EEC budget is used to pay price supports (subsidies) to farmers, a significant tax burden to consumers. Externally, the pricing policies and protection have led to excessive production, a reduction of imports, and an expansion of the export of subsidized goods.[6] This has been a major source of contention in GATT negotiations.

TABLE 11.1 | EUROPEAN COMMUNITY MILESTONES Two of the key milestones in the past decade that have helped the European Community come closer to its harmonization goals are the issuance of the White Paper in 1985 and the Single European Act in 1987.

1957	Treaty of Rome establishing the European Economic Community (EEC), or Common Market, signed. Original members were Belgium, France, Italy, Luxembourg, the Netherlands, and West Germany.
1959	First reduction in EEC internal tariffs.
1962	Common Agricultural Policy (CAP) established.
1967	Agreement reached on value added tax (VAT) system.
1968	All internal tariffs eliminated and a common external tariff imposed.
1973	United Kingdom, Denmark, and Ireland become members.
1979	European Parliament directly elected for the first time.
1979	European Monetary System comes into effect.
1981	Greece becomes a member.
1985	Lord Cockfield presents a White Paper to the European Commission outlining 300 steps to eliminate all remaining barriers to internal trade in goods and services. This is endorsed by the Member States and becomes Community policy.
1986	Spain and Portugal become members.
1987	Single European Act (SEA) comes into effect, improving decision-making procedures and increasing the role of the European Parliament.
1992	Target date for eliminating all trade barriers within the European Community.

Source: Ernst & Whinney, *Europe 1992: The Single Market*, p. 6.

As noted in Chapter 8, the EEC also attempted to improve the flow of capital by establishing the European Monetary System to stabilize currency values. Common accounting standards have also been established to improve the comparability of financial information and thus to enhance investment possibilities.

The EC Organizational Structure

Complexity usually breeds bureaucracy. The simpler forms of integration, such as a free trade area and customs union, usually can be managed by a coordinating committee larger than it needs to be but adequate for the job. The more complex forms of integration, however, such as the EC, have developed a very extensive bureaucracy to protect the goals and rules of the group of countries.

The key to the EC's success is the balance between common and national interests monitored and refereed through four major institutions: the Commission, the Council of Ministers, the Parliament, and the Court of Justice.

The Commission, headquartered in Brussels, Belgium, is comprised of a president, six vice presidents, and ten other members whose allegiance is to the EC rather than to an individual government, although the members are appointed by the various governments. The Commission is the EC watchdog: It is supposed to draw up policies, implement them when approved by the Council of Ministers, and ensure that treaties and laws are adhered to by member nations. It is similar to the executive branch of government, only weaker. "It studies problems and initiates measures that, if approved, it will later enforce. But it doesn't decide anything."[7]

The Council of Ministers, also headquartered in Brussels, is composed of one representative from each of the member governments. It is entrusted with making the major policy decisions for the EC, and it is the real power behind the bureaucracy.

The Parliament, headquartered in Luxembourg, is elected directly in each member country. Its representatives tend to adhere to particular political and economic views rather than to the wishes of the individual governments. Representatives of different countries with similar political leanings can form coalitions, such as Christian Democrats combining with Conservatives, to increase their power base. Figure 11.1 illustrates how the composition of the Parliament changed between the first group elected in 1979 and the group in power as of 1990. The Parliament meets annually in Strasbourg, although its committees meet in Brussels and its official address is in Luxembourg. The Parliament is not as powerful as a legislative body in a democracy, but it has veto power over the budget. In addition (as noted below), the Parliament consults in all EC legislation. However, the Council of Ministers is the real power in the EC bureaucracy, and it is the body that makes the final decision in all EC legislation. One description of the European Parliament is that it is

The Commission draws up and implements policies.

The Council of Ministers makes the policy decisions.

The Parliament advises the Commission.

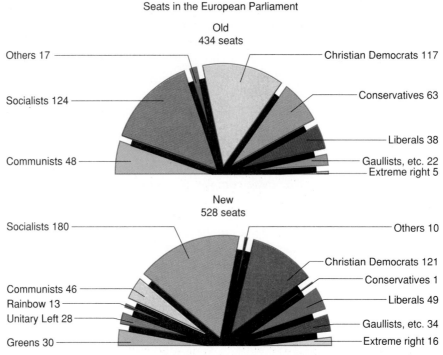

Figure 11.1
Europe from Left to Right: Composition of the European Parliament, 1979 and 1989.
The Socialists and other leftist parties have gained seats at the expense of the Christian Democrats and other conservatives, even though most European governments are conservative themselves. *Source: The Economist,* June 23, 1984, p. 32, and *Europa World Yearbook, 1990,* p. 143.

what the U.S. House of Representatives would be like if it were on wheels (because of the Brussels–Luxembourg–Strasbourg phenomenon) and if its views could be safely ignored.

The Court of Justice, also headquartered in Luxembourg, is customarily composed of one member from each country in the EC. It serves as a supreme appeals court for EC law. The Commission or member countries can bring other members to the Court for failing to meet treaty obligations. For example, the Commission brought suit against Spain in 1987 for failing to ease certification requirements on the import of computers, peripheral equipment, and other high-tech products because it considered these nontariff barriers in violation of membership in the EC.[8] Likewise, member countries, firms, or institutions can bring the Commission or Council to the Court for failure to act properly under the treaty.

The Court of Justice is an appeals court for EC law.

The legislation that is needed to open up Europe even more (known as Europe 1992 and described below) is decided by the Commission, the Parliament, and the Council of Ministers. The steps that must be followed are as follows:

1. The EC Commission makes a proposal.

2. The Parliament reviews it in first reading and may make suggestions for change.

3. The Commission revises the proposal according to Parliament's suggestions.

4. The Council of Ministers examines the proposal in first reading. It may amend it and adopt a "common position," that is, a decision to accept the proposal in principle.

5. The Parliament, within three months, examines the common-position text and can vote amendments.

6. The Commission can endorse or reject the Parliament's amendments.

7. The Council, within three months, must make a final decision. If the Commission endorses the Parliament's amendments, the Council can adopt the measure by a weighted majority vote. Any other changes in the legislation besides those agreed to by both the Parliament and the Commission must be adopted unanimously.[9]

Europe 1992

Europe 1992 involves the elimination of the remaining barriers to the free transfer of goods, services, and capital.

As noted in Table 11.2, the EC is a formidable economic bloc with 320 million people and the largest combined GNP in the world outside of the U.S.–Canada Free Trade Agreement. However, the early part of the 1980s was a difficult time for the EC. "From 1970 to 1975, gross domestic product in EC countries averaged 2.7 percent growth per year, dropping to approximately 1.4 percent annually by the 1980–1985 period. In the meantime, the United States had recorded 2.2 percent and 2.5 percent rates, respectively. In Japan, growth in the same periods averaged an impressive 7.6 percent and 3.8 percent."[10] It was evident that the elimination of tariffs was not the only solution to achieving a free flow of goods. A variety of nontariff barriers was keeping the EC from being a true common market.

Three examples illustrate how difficult it was to do business in a "unified" Europe. The first involves jam. The Dutch like to spread jam on bread for breakfast, so they like their jam smooth. The French prefer to eat jam right out of the jar, so they like their jam lumpy and fruity. The British, however, used the term "marmalade" to refer to "jam," whereas the marmalade of the Continental Europeans was nothing more than low-grade "jam" to the British. Thus the members of the EC argued for more than twenty years over what should be jam and what should be marmalade.[11]

TABLE 11.2 | COMPARATIVE DATA ON MAJOR TRADE GROUPS, THE UNITED STATES, AND JAPAN The EC and the United States dominate the world in terms of GNP, per capita GNP, and percent of world exports.

	1988 Population[a] (in Millions)	1988 GNP[b] (in Billions of U.S. Dollars)	Per Capita GNP[b] (in U.S. Dollars)	Percent of World Exports (1988)[c]
COMECON (Council of Mutual Economic Assistance)	478.7	—	—	8.0
LAIA (Latin American Integration Association)	367.7	710.962	1,933.5	3.5
EC (European Community)	324.7	4,414.27	13,594.9	39.6
ASEAN (Association of South East Asian Nations)	308.7	227.155	735.8	3.8
United States	246.3	4,886.592	19,840.0	12.0
ECOWAS (Economic Community of West African States)	183.3	63.314	345.4	.6
Japan	122.6	2,577.052	21,020.0	9.9
Andean Pact	88.2	140.661	1,594.8	.8
EFTA (European Free Trade Association)	32	643.127	19,929	6.6

[a]Data for Ivory Coast Population is from *Europa Yearbook, 1989.*

[b]Data for Ivory Coast GNP is from *Europa Yearbook, 1989.* Data shown for COMECON is for 1984; data for 1988 is unavailable.

[c]Data shown for COMECON is for 1982; data for 1988 is unavailable. Data for Brunei, Cape Verde, Gambia, Guinea-Bissau, Ivory Coast for 1988 is unavailable and not included in export percentage.

The countries included in the above groups are as follows:
COMECON: Bulgaria, Czechoslovakia, Cuba, East Germany, Hungary, Mongolia, Poland, Romania, Vietnam, and Soviet Union.
LAIA: Argentina, Bolivia, Brazil, Chile, Colombia, Ecuador, Mexico, Paraguay, Peru, Uruguay, and Venezuela.
EC: Belgium, Denmark, France, Greece, Ireland, Italy, Luxembourg, Netherlands, Portugal, Spain, United Kingdom, and West Germany.
ASEAN: Indonesia, Malaysia, Philippines, Singapore, and Thailand.
ECOWAS: Benin, Burkina, Cape Verde, Gambia, Ghana, Guinea, Guinea-Bissau, Ivory Coast, Liberia, Mali, Mauritania, Niger, Nigeria, Senegal, Sierra Leone, and Togo.
Andean Pact: Bolivia, Colombia, Ecuador, Peru, and Venezuela.
EFTA: Austria, Finland, Iceland, Norway, Sweden, and Switzerland.
Source: World Development Report, 1990 (Washington, D.C.: The World Bank, 1990).

The second example involves transportation. Even though the Europeans eliminated tariffs in 1968, they did not eliminate border guards and differences in documentation. At each border, drivers had to provide documentation averaging 35 pages, with each border requiring a different set of documents. It was estimated that in 1987 customs regulations cost companies over $6 billion in delays and red tape.[12]

The third example involves value added taxes (VAT). The major source of revenue for the EC, and 40 percent of the government revenues in France, is from the VAT. The VAT is assessed against the selling price of a product less any inputs that have already been assessed a VAT. The rates are different for different categories of products, and the rates and categories vary significantly from country to country. The standard VAT rates vary from 22 percent in Denmark to only 12 percent in Spain and Luxembourg. The rate on luxury items is 38 percent in Italy, whereas the Dutch and British do not have a VAT on luxury items. The same differences exist in excise taxes, such as on alcohol and tobacco products. The excise tax on beer in Spain is less than 3 percent of the excise tax on beer in Ireland. Several countries, such as Greece, Italy, Spain, Portugal, and Germany, do not even have an excise tax on wine.[13]

As a result of these and other issues, Jacques Delors, the President of the European Commission and, ironically, the former Socialist Finance Minister of France, decided to eliminate the remaining barriers to a free and open Europe. He appointed Lord Cockfield, a conservative British business leader, to chart a course to open Europe. Lord Cockfield identified 300 proposals that needed to be enacted to complete an internal market. As of June 1990, the total number of proposals that were to be adopted was pared down to 282, the number of proposals that had been drafted by the European Commission was 279, the number of proposals adopted by the Council of Ministers was 164, and the number of proposals incorporated in all member states was 21. Denmark and the United Kingdom had adopted 77 proposals by that time, whereas Portugal and Italy had only adopted 37 and 36 proposals, respectively.[14]

The proposals identified by Lord Cockfield and included in a 1985 White Paper to the European Commission can be divided into the following general areas:

The White Paper of 1985 identified nearly 300 proposals that needed to be adopted to eliminate barriers to European harmonization.

1. Frontier controls and formalities for goods
2. Freedom of movement and establishment for people
3. Technical and standards harmonization
4. Opening up of the public procurement markets
5. Liberalization of financial services
6. Gradual opening up of the market in information services
7. Liberalization of transport services
8. Creation of suitable conditions for industrial cooperation in the field of company law and intellectual and industrial property
9. Removal of fiscal barriers[15]

A major impediment to the implementation of the proposals was the requirement that they be adopted unanimously by the Council of Ministers. However, the **Single European Act** was established in 1987, which allowed all proposals except those relating to taxation, workers' rights, and immigration to be adopted by a system of weighted majority voting by member states (more populous countries get more votes than less populous ones).

As an example of how these proposals will solve some of the barriers to trade, let's look at the three examples of nontariff barriers that were discussed above. In the case of jam, an EC expert decided that it would be better for countries to set basic health and safety standards than to decide how much fruit and sugar had to be in jam before it could be called "jam." Several proposals were developed on issues such as food additives, food labeling, composition and special labeling requirements for particular foodstuffs, etc. In the case of border controls, there is now a one-page document that is accepted at all border crossings, significantly eliminating the delays and complexity of moving goods from country to country. France, Germany, and the Benelux countries signed an open border agreement in 1985, and those border posts are not busy. What will happen to France's 21,000 border guards when December 31, 1992, comes?[16]

Finally, taxes are probably the most difficult to harmonize. The EC has proposed that there be a normal VAT rate of 14–20 percent and a reduced rate of 4–9 percent for basic goods and services. Countries would choose their rates within the brackets.[17]

The Impact of Europe 1992—Internal and External

Internal problems to Europe 1992 include

- The potential growth of centralization and socialism
- The acceptance of key changes, like tax revision
- The possible shift of jobs from northern to southern Europe
- The elimination of small and medium firms

There are several major internal concerns about Europe 1992. The first is the spread of bureaucracy, centralization, overregulation, and socialism on the part of the free market side of the EC members, especially Britain. As former U.K. Prime Minister Margaret Thatcher said, "We haven't worked all these years to free Britain from the paralysis of socialism only to see it creep through the back door of central control and bureaucracy from Brussels."[18]

A second problem is the acceptance of key changes, such as the harmonization of the VAT. Although consumers in high-tax countries might welcome the lowering of the average VAT, consumers in low-tax countries will not appreciate the increase of the average VAT.

A third problem is the potential effect on unemployment. Although most experts believe that Europe 1992 will bring faster economic growth and the creation of jobs, local unions are not convinced. In northern Europe, in particular, unions are concerned that the free movement of capital will cause firms to seek lower costs in southern Europe.

A fourth problem is the possible elimination of small and medium-sized firms. This could occur for two different reasons. The first is elimination due to competition, since the freeing up of borders should expand the reach of large, efficient firms as they take advantage of better distribution systems. The second is the wave of mergers and acquisitions taking place as firms attempt to grow in order to compete with U.S. and Japanese rivals in Europe.

External firms are worried about a Fortress Europe.

The major external concern of Europe 1992 is often referred to as "Fortress Europe." The fear is that European regulations will favor European firms and exclude foreign, especially U.S. and Japanese, firms. While that does not seem to be the case up to this point, foreign firms are adopting a variety of strategies to reserve a place in Europe. Some large MNEs, such as Ford, Coca-Cola, and IBM, are more European than are the European firms in terms of their geographic spread, as we saw in the opening case. The medium-sized firms that are currently operating in Europe are taking part in the merger and acquisition wave to expand their size and market share. Those that are servicing Europe merely through exports are establishing offices in order to have a physical presence.[19] Those that have avoided Europe are now looking carefully at it as a market of 320 million consumers and a GNP in excess of $4 trillion.

An example of the impact of 1992 on corporate strategy, other than the Ford example in the opening incident, is that of Philips, the large Dutch electronics firm. Philips operates around Europe (as do the U.S. multinationals) by moving parts and components to different countries for final assembly and sale, as well as by centralizing the manufacture of finished goods and shipping them to distribution centers around Europe. In the pre-1992 environment, Philips management estimated that trucks spent 30 percent of their travel time waiting in customs lines. Factories could never tell when they would have components for the manufacturing process, so they carried huge inventories, averaging 23 percent of sales as compared to around 14 percent for U.S. and Japanese manufacturers. Local standards caused Philips to have large product lines. Because of the 1992 regulations that are being issued, Philips management feels that it will be able to save $300 million per year by 1992 in transportation, warehousing, and clerical costs. As local standards vanish, Philips will be able to shrink its product lines and standardize its parts and components even more, thus increasing quality and lowering costs. In one of its television plants, Philips has 70 engineers who do nothing but adjust models to local European technical requirements. These jobs will be eliminated as management eliminates different models. These are not the only jobs that will be eliminated, however. In late 1990, Philips management announced that 45,000 jobs, or about one-sixth of Philips' worldwide work force, would be eliminated by the end of 1991. In all, 1992 is expected to increase efficiency and lower costs.[20]

Europe 1992 should help firms lower transportation, storage, and product-development costs.

LATIN AMERICAN COOPERATION

Economic integration in Latin America has taken some interesting twists over the years. As Map 11.2 shows, two of the original groups, LAFTA and CARIFTA, have changed names and focus. In spite of the evolution, the initial reason for integration remains. The post–World War II strategy of import substitution to resolve balance-of-payments problems was doomed because of Latin America's small national markets. Therefore the feeling was that some form of economic cooperation was needed to enlarge the potential market

Latin America needs economic cooperation to enlarge its market size.

Latin American Integration Association
Latin American Free Trade Association (LAFTA) from 1960–1980

Members	Date of Entry	
Argentina	Jan.	1981
Bolivia	Mar.	1982
Brazil	Nov.	1981
Chile	May	1981
Colombia	May	1981
Ecuador	Mar.	1982
Mexico	Feb.	1981
Paraguay	Dec.	1980
Peru	Nov.	1981
Uruguay	Mar.	1981
Venezuela	Mar.	1982

Cartagena Agreement, Andean Group

Bolivia	Nov.	1969
Chile	Sept.	1969
	(withdrew Oct. 1976)	
Colombia	Sept.	1969
Ecuador	Nov.	1969
Peru	Oct.	1969
Venezuela	Nov.	1973

Central American Common Market (CACM)

Costa Rica	Sept.	1963
El Salvador	May	1961
Guatemala	May	1961
Honduras	Apr.	1962
	(withdrew Jan. 1971)	
Nicaragua	May	1961

Caribbean Community and Common Market (CARICOM)
Caribbean Free Trade Association (CARIFTA) from 1965–1973

Members	Date of Entry	
Antigua and Barbuda	July	1974
Bahamas	July	1983
Barbados	Aug.	1973
Belize	July	1974
Dominica	July	1974
Grenada	July	1974
Guyana	Aug.	1973
Jamaica	Aug.	1973
Montserrat	July	1974
St. Christopher and Nevis	July	1974
St. Lucia	July	1974
St. Vincent	July	1974
Trinidad and Tobago	Aug.	1973

Map legend:
- LAIA
- LAIA (Andean Group)
- CACM
- CARICOM
- Non Members

Map 11.2
Integration Systems in Latin America
The Latin American Integration Association (LAIA) covers most of Latin America, even though the most important trading partner of most Latin American countries is the United States. *Source:* "Inter-American Development Bank Predicts Renewed Push for Economic Integration in Latin America," *IMF Survey,* December 10, 1984, p. 375.

size so that national firms could achieve economies of scale and be more competitive worldwide.

A study by the **Inter-American Development Bank (IDB)** identified three types of integration in Latin America: a free trade area, a common market, and a partial economic preferences model.[21] The free trade model is best

Three basic Latin American models for economic cooperation are:
- A free trade area
- A common market (CARICOM)
- A partial economic preferences model (LAIA)

illustrated by LAFTA and CARIFTA. LAFTA was formed in 1960 during the time when the EEC was being organized, and CARIFTA was formed in 1965. However, neither of these efforts endured, the major reason for failure being that the member countries traded more with the United States than with each other, so there was not as much incentive as exists among the members of the EC.

The second model came into existence in Latin America because of the failure of the free trade area model. The **Andean Group** was formed by several members of LAFTA that were close to each other geographically, as noted in Map 11.2, and felt that it was necessary to have more than just free trade. They included a common external tariff, restrictions on the inflow of foreign investment, and the integration of economic and social policies. These measures resembled the objectives of the **Central American Common Market (CACM)** and **CARICOM.** The Andean Group decided to develop subregional industries and allocate these industries among the members of the group, which would in turn enable more even development. However, political and economic problems of the region have kept it from achieving the full benefits of integration: Less than 5 percent of its total trade is intrazonal. In 1987 the Group relaxed its restrictions on foreign investment in hopes of attracting more outside capital. In addition, its original goal of establishing regional industries has given way to assisting small and medium-sized industries in the region.

The third model, partial economic preferences, is best illustrated by the **Latin American Integration Association (LAIA),** which consists of most of the countries originally in LAFTA. By 1980 it was clear that LAFTA was not working: Only 14 percent of annual trade among members was the result of LAFTA benefits, and most of the benefits were accruing to Mexico, Brazil, and Argentina. A major goal of LAFTA was to eliminate all tariff and non-tariff barriers among countries and gradually move Latin America toward a common market. However, that program proved to be too rigid and ambitious. As a result, the LAIA was established in 1980. LAIA is much more flexible and less ambitious than LAFTA, and it gives member countries an opportunity to establish a series of bilateral agreements that may be extended to other countries if desired. This allows countries with common interests to progress faster than might be the case when disparate members have to compromise, thereby diluting the effectiveness of the agreement. However, by 1988 only 10.7 percent of the trade of LAIA countries was intrazonal. Instead of across-the-board tariff cuts, LAIA set up a more flexible regional tariff preference and other forms of economic cooperation, but it did not set a timetable for the full establishment of a common market.[22]

Only 10.7 percent of LAIA trade is intrazonal.

A more ambitious goal of regional economic integration is the "Enterprise for the Americas," a dream of U.S. President Bush to establish a free trade area that includes all of the nations of North and Latin America. As will be discussed in the case at the end of the chapter, there is an initial attempt

"Enterprise for the Americas" hopes to link together North and South America in a free trade area.

under way to establish a free trade area involving Canada, the United States, and Mexico. By the end of 1994, Brazil, Argentina, Paraguay, and Uruguay hope to eliminate all tariff barriers so that they can establish a limited free trade area. Tariffs are to be lowered by 20 percent a year until they are eventually eliminated, and the four governments also hope to eliminate exceptions to the general rule so that the tariff cuts become more widespread. It is hoped that these interim steps will pave the way to broader cooperation.

The "Enterprise of the Americas" is not an attempt to establish a European-style common market but to establish a more limited free trade area. Two things that have enhanced the possibility of such a union are first, the establishment of democratic forms of government in nearly every American country and, second, the move toward replacing state protectionism with import liberalization and the privatization of resources.[23]

CARICOM countries are rapidly establishing a common market.

The thirteen members of the Caribbean Community (CARICOM) have strengthened their cooperation by aiming to remove most of their obstacles to integration by 1991. The plan calls for the free movement of goods and capital within the region, a common external tariff, revised rules of origin, harmonization of investment incentives, coordination of policies relating to the location of trade and business, coordination of financial policies, and creation of a monetary union by 1995. The speed of change taking place in Europe and strong growth in Asia have made the CARICOM members realize that they need to move ahead quickly or be left behind.[24]

EASTERN EUROPEAN INTEGRATION

The **Council for Mutual Economic Assistance (CMEA,** or **COMECON)** was formed in 1949 to assist in the economic development of the member nations. The current members as listed in Table 11.2 and illustrated in Map 11.3 include Mongolia, Cuba, and the Socialist Republic of Vietnam, which were admitted in 1962, 1972, and 1978, respectively. Albania, an original member of COMECON, ended its affiliation in 1961, and East Germany is now a part of Germany.

Because of the rapid political and economic transformation taking place in Central and Eastern Europe, COMECON could disappear at any time. When COMECON was organized, it was interested in integrating economic activities and planning economic specialization within the region. Even though COMECON's share of total world exports was estimated at only 8 percent of the world's total in the mid-1980s, the intrazonal trade of 60 percent was the highest of any of the regional forms of integration. Table 11.2 shows that in 1988 COMECON was the most heavily populated of the re-

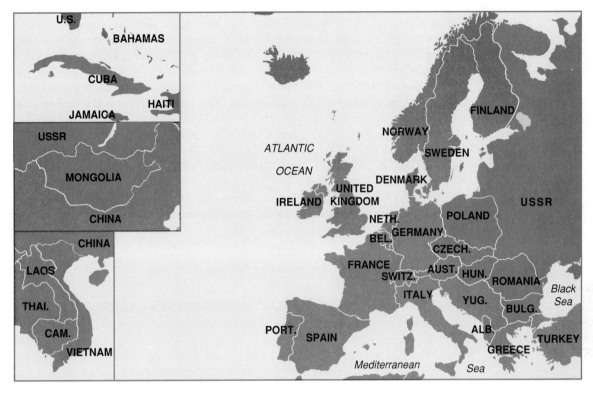

Map 11.3
Member Countries of the Council for Mutual Economic Assistance (CMEA or COMECON)
COMECON, which is in transition as the countries move from central command to market-based economic systems, is comprised of the Soviet Union and Eastern Europe, as well as Cuba, Mongolia, and Vietnam.

In COMECON the Soviet Union provides natural resources and the East Bloc countries provide finished goods.

gional groups. This is deceiving, however, because the Soviet union has 60 percent of the population and over 70 percent of the GNP of the group. No other regional economic group is so dominated economically by a single member of the group.

Trade in COMECON was based on bilateral relationships that were transacted in transferable rubles. However, these rubles could not be used to settle other accounts: for example, the surplus in one bilateral relationship could not be used to settle the deficit in another bilateral relationship. Also, the transferable rubles could not be used outside of the COMECON countries. Typically, the Soviet Union provides oil and ore to the other COMECON countries, which transform the raw materials into finished goods that are shipped back to the Soviet Union. The cheap raw materials have allowed the processing countries to be very wasteful, and thus great polluters. In addition, the low standard of production has made the Eastern European countries producers of junk.[25]

As the Soviet empire disintegrates and Eastern Europe opens to the West, the future of COMECON is uncertain. The Eastern European countries are moving to hard currencies to settle their bilateral trade, so that would tend to upset the relationships within COMECON. However, it will be very difficult to end the trading relationships abruptly. The Eastern European countries need the Soviets' raw materials, and the Soviets need the finished goods from the East Bloc. In addition, East Bloc goods will have a difficult time meeting the competitive test of the open market until they can improve quality and cost. For these reasons, COMECON members are more likely to redefine rather than dump the system.[26]

COMECON relationships are adjusting to changes in Eastern Europe.

ASIAN INTEGRATION EFFORTS

The Triad Strategy argues for a presence in Europe, North America, and Asia (primarily Japan).

It has been argued that the 1990s is the decade of the Triad Strategy.[27] Because the combined GNPs of Japan, the United States (or the United States and Canada, given that they are now involved in a free trade agreement), and the European Community are so vast, companies need to develop a Triad Strategy that includes trade and investment with all three areas. The liberalization of Eastern Europe probably will cause the economic power of the EC to expand considerably in the decade to come, and the realization of the "Enterprise of the Americas" could expand the trade and investment bases of the Americas considerably. What about regional economic integration in the Pacific Rim?

The Pacific Economic Cooperation Conference (PECC) is a forum for the discussion of common problems of the Pacific Rim countries, although it is not a regional economic bloc that is formally increasing the free flow of goods and services. The member countries are Australia, Brunei, Canada, China, Indonesia, Japan, Korea, Pacific Island nations, Malaysia, New Zealand, the Philippines, Singapore, Taiwan, Thailand, and the United States. It is interesting to note the absence of the Latin American countries that border the Pacific, India and the surrounding countries, and the Soviet Union. However, the PECC is discussing the possibility of establishing some type of permanent Pacific economic cooperation structure. The fear, of course, is the large size and influence of Japan and the United States.[28]

ASEAN has wide disparity in economic strength and is not working very aggressively.

The major form of integration in Asia is the **Association of South East Asian Nations (ASEAN),** which was organized in 1967. As noted in the map on page M-10, ASEAN, which includes Brunei, Indonesia, Malaysia, the Philippines, Singapore, and Thailand, is trying for cooperation in many areas,

including industry and trade. In industry, ASEAN countries are attempting to enter into joint projects and set up medium-sized industries in different countries. These industries would be 60 percent owned by the host country and 40 percent owned by the other members of ASEAN. The two initial projects approved and currently operating are urea (fertilizer) projects in Indonesia and Malaysia; other start-up projects were plagued by a series of problems. Nevertheless, by 1988, 15 ASEAN joint ventures had been formed, where 40 percent of the venture would be owned by private-sector companies from two or more ASEAN countries and where exports of products from the joint venture would be given preferential access to ASEAN countries.

Although ASEAN countries have not opted for a free trade area at this point, they are cooperating in reducing tariffs in a variety of areas. Their Basic Agreement on the Establishment of ASEAN Preferential Trade Arrangements was approved by GATT and has resulted in some trade liberalization. However, only 5 percent of intra-ASEAN trade consists of preferentially traded items, so the tariff-liberalization efforts have not been successful.

The Japanese, who are not members of ASEAN, have been very successful in investing in and exploiting raw materials in ASEAN nations and using them to manufacture finished goods in Japan which they re-export to the ASEAN nations. That process has created some serious tensions in ASEAN, as some have claimed that Japan is doing economically what it was not able to do militarily in World War II.[29]

A major problem with the ASEAN nations is the disparity in economic strength. In 1988 the per capita GNP of Singapore was $9,070, whereas it was only $440 in Indonesia. In addition, the involvement of the Japanese—who belong to a non-ASEAN country—is a source of contention, as mentioned above.

Japan is using the raw materials of ASEAN nations and processing them into finished goods for export back to ASEAN nations.

AFRICAN COOPERATION

Although only one form of African integration is listed in Table 11.2, several forms exist, and they are not necessarily mutually exclusive. The Ivory Coast, for example, is a member of several different organizations in Africa related to political and/or economic development. The major African groups as shown in the map on page M-10 are the **West African Economic Community** (Benin, Burkina Faso, Ivory Coast, Mali, Mauritania, Niger, and Senegal); the **Entente Council** (Burkina Faso, Benin, Ivory Coast, Niger, and Togo); the **Economic Community of West African States (ECOWAS)** (countries listed in Table 11.2); the **Organisation of African Unity** (nearly every country in Africa); and the **Southern African Development Co-ordination Conference** (Angola, Botswana, Lesotho, Malawi, Moz-

ambique, Swaziland, Tanzania, Zambia, and Zimbabwe). In addition to these specific groups, there is also an **African Development Bank.**

Clearly, there is considerable overlap among the groups. Most groups try to cooperate in some form of economic integration, although it tends to be at a fairly low level. In general the countries are so poor and economic activity is so low that there is an insignificant base for cooperation. Most African countries rely heavily on agriculture or natural resources as a major source of export revenue, so there is not much reason to lower the barriers to the primary products. Major industrial effort is fairly low level and still needs protection before opening the doors to competition, which retards the development of a free trade area. In large part, the groups also are seeking cooperation in other areas, such as transportation and other forms of infrastructure, small industrial projects, and the like.

ECOWAS is featured in Table 11.2 because it is the largest of the groups, with the exception of the Organization of African Unity (OAU), which is more a political than an economic organization. The OAU's original goals were oriented more toward the elimination of colonialism and racism in Africa than toward economic growth. The ECOWAS has four commissions: one for trade, customs, immigration, monetary, and payments; one for industry, agriculture, and natural resources; one for transport, telecommunications, and energy; and one for social and cultural affairs. Major efforts are being made to eliminate all internal tariffs and set up a common external tariff, which will make the ECOWAS a customs union in the same sense as the EC. However, it is doubtful that the ECOWAS can achieve the other types of integration accomplished by the EC. Lack of success has been attributed to the existence of so many other intergovernmental forms of cooperation, including those mentioned above, and to member governments' lack of commitment to the activities of ECOWAS.[30]

African integration is difficult because market sizes are small and resource endowments are similar.

COMMODITY AGREEMENTS

Another form of economic cooperation involves commodity agreements. Whereas the first part of the chapter focused on how countries cooperate to reduce barriers to trade, this part focuses on how countries cooperate to stabilize the price and supply of a particular commodity. Most of the developing countries traditionally have relied on the export of one or two commodities to supply the hard currencies needed for economic development. Unhappily, many short-run factors have caused price instability, leading to fluctuations in export earnings. The most important factors are:

Commodity prices fluctuate significantly due to natural forces as well as supply and demand factors.

1. natural forces such as floods, droughts, and weather;
2. relatively price-insensitive demand;

3. relatively price-insensitive supply (in the short run); and

4. business cycles in advanced industrial countries that can cause sudden changes in quantities demanded.

World commodity prices have fluctuated dramatically in recent years. Nonfuel primary commodity prices fell significantly between 1980 and 1986. By the end of 1986, both demand and supply conditions drove prices to their lowest levels since the 1930s. The major reasons for weak commodity prices were: (1) relatively low rates of economic growth in the industrial countries, leading to weak demand; (2) a reduction in the use of commodities due to structural changes in the world economy, also leading to weak demand; and (3) abundant supplies of commodities.[31]

Low rates of economic growth and abundant supplies of commodities have kept commodities' prices low in recent years.

However, prices of some commodities, especially for base, nonferrous metals, such as copper, aluminum, tin, nickel, zinc, and lead, increased significantly from 1987–1989. The major reason for the increase in prices was the fact that demand for metals was increasing faster than the growth in GNP in most consuming economies, so there was increased pressure on prices. Even though prices began to fall somewhat in 1990, they were still at higher levels than at the beginning of the 1980s.

Commodity agreements utilize buffer stocks, price ranges, and export/import quotas to attempt to keep prices relatively high.

A **commodity agreement** is an agreement between producing and consuming countries designed to stabilize prices. Some commodities, such as copper, operate in a relatively free market. Wild price fluctuations result from supply and demand as well as speculation. However, consumers and producers alike often would prefer a more stabilized pricing system that allows for predictions of future costs and earnings and thus facilitates planning. The types of commodity agreements most frequently adopted are buffer stocks, price ranges, and export/import quotas.

A buffer stock is a commodity system that utilizes stocks of commodities to regulate prices.

The **buffer stock system** provides a partially managed system monitored by a central agency. Free market forces are allowed to determine prices within a certain range, but outside of that range a central agency buys or sells the commodity to support the price. The signatory countries to the commodity agreement (those countries linked to other countries by a signed agreement) provide funds that the buffer stock manager can use to purchase commodities.

The buffer stock manager needs to be concerned on two levels about prices: the **net seller range** and the **net buyer range.** The prevailing theory is that once the price enters the "net seller" range, the buffer stock manager is required to sell the commodity in order to force the price to drop. When the price enters the low "net buyer" range, the buffer stock manager is required to buy the commodity in order to increase the price.

At one time, the tin market was managed on a buffer stock system. In the early 1980s, however, the Malaysian government began to buy tin secretly in hopes of increasing the world market price. It then began an aggressive campaign to corner the market. The fund manager was forced to

intervene in the market to defend the artificially high floor price of tin, and the fund eventually ran out of money. The result was the disintegration of the tin agreement.[32]

Price ranges can be handled in different ways. In some of the metal markets, such as zinc, lead, and platinum, prices are fixed at the smelters by producers. Although most purchases are made at the smelters, a free market with prices parallel to the smelter prices but usually at a premium or discount satisfies marginal needs. In a second approach bilateral price agreements can be negotiated between two countries to guarantee maximum and minimum prices.

Quota systems occur when producing and/or consuming countries divide total output and sales in order to keep up prices. Quota systems have been used for such products as coffee, tea, and sugar, and they are often applied in conjunction with a buffer stock system. For the quota system to work, countries must develop close ties to prevent sharp fluctuations in supply. The quota system is most effective when a single country has a large share of world production or consumption. Two of the best examples from a production standpoint are wool, which is controlled by Australians, and diamonds, which are controlled by the DeBeers Company in South Africa.

Another example of a quota system is illustrated by the International Coffee Organization (ICO). At one time, the ICO had decided to set up a quota system in which world producers would limit their exports to keep coffee prices between $1.15 and $1.55 per pound, with the quotas to be loosened or tightened as prices neared the upper or lower limit. This plan involved negotiations by producing and consuming nations alike. Two problems emerge with the quota system, however, as illustrated by the ICO: First, the quotas can be perceived as too low by some of the countries, especially those that rely on coffee as their main (and maybe only) major export cash crop. For example, whereas coffee was only 7 percent of Brazil's exports in 1988, it was 29 percent of Colombia's exports, 67 percent of El Salvador's exports, and 97 percent of Uganda's exports.[33] Second, a surplus or shortage of coffee might sabotage quantity and price controls. The quota-regulated price range of $1.15–$1.55 that existed before the breakup of the ICO is a far cry from the $3.40 per pound price that coffee carried in 1977 after the infamous Brazilian frosts.

The global quota for coffee exports was increased in 1984–1985, but the price was maintained at the same level to allow total revenues to rise for exporting countries. However, two problems faced the members of the Coffee Agreement: (1) sales to nonmembers of the Agreement were not covered, and (2) countries continued to complain about their allocations. The first point is important because of the temptation to transship coffee from a nonmenber importer to a member importer. The second problem is faced by all producer cartels, as will be seen in the discussion of OPEC later in this chapter. The quota system was temporarily suspended in 1986, largely because of

Quotas occur when producing and consuming countries divide total output and sales.

A lack of discipline on quotas broke up the International Coffee Organization, and the price of coffee fell substantially.

price increases resulting from the Brazilian drought. Some countries, notably nonmember Indonesia, held out for membership in the Organization and a reimposition of the quota system, but at significantly higher levels.[34]

On July 3, 1989, the ICO finally suspended the price and export-quota provisions, because some of the Central American countries wanted to expand their quotas, but Brazil refused to cut back on its quota in order to allow the expansion for other countries. At that time, the price range had been changed to $1.15 to $1.45, but prices fell through the floor as the agreement expired. Guatemala argued that it could sell only 50 percent of its production and had to stockpile the rest, so being able to sell all of its production at significantly lower prices would still allow it to earn more profits than under the old scheme; volume would rise and storage costs would fall. However, countries such as Uganda, Nicaragua, and El Salvador would be worse off because of the lower quality of their coffee and the lack of excess capacity.[35] By the end of 1990, coffee was still trading at below the old price range. Brazil was still not sure if it wanted a quota system, and no one expects prices to change unless there is a frost or a new agreement.

The Multifibre Arrangement

The MFA regulates the trade in textiles and garments according to a quota system.

The **Arrangement Regarding International Trade in Textiles,** more commonly known as the **Multifibre Arrangement (MFA),** originated in 1974 and has been renewed several times since then. The MFA is an agreement among the governments of over 40 countries establishing rules concerning trade in textiles and garments made of cotton, wool, and synthetic fibres. The MFA establishes rules, sanctioned by the General Agreement on Tariffs and Trade (GATT), by which quotas can be levied against producer countries. The specific arrangements are established on a bilateral basis between producer and consumer nations. The MFA initially was signed to assist the textile industries in developed countries that were facing significant foreign competition. These industries, which tend to be labor intensive, also have formed a strong political bloc in industrial countries and are exerting significant governmental influence. The MFA was directed to help the textile industries gain "breathing space" in competing with the industries in developing countries and then provide for a gradual liberalization of trade. Liberalization has not occurred, however, due to the strong political force of the developed-country industries.

Unlike the commodities agreements described earlier, which often focus on price, the MFA operates primarily on quantitative restrictions. In addition, it allows discriminatory treatment by importers against exporter nations. GATT rules require a most-favored-nation (MFN) status for countries so that all countries in the MFN category are treated similarly in terms of tariffs or quotas. The MFA, however, allows the importer countries to apply differential sanctions against exporter countries.

The major beneficiaries of the MFA are the import-competing textile industries in the developed countries as well as the quota-holding producers. Many of these producers have shifted production into higher value added products or have sold those quotas to others. Significant graft and corruption also have appeared in some of the quota-holding countries. In 1987 a U.S. garment manufacturer established an assembly facility in Mexico to take advantage of low wage rates and favorable tariff arrangements between Mexico and the United States. The manufacturer also had quotas from the Mexican government to export the product to the United States, but when the manufacturer attempted to ship the finished goods to the United States, U.S. Customs would not allow the goods to enter. Customs keeps track of the quota allotted to Mexico by product category and the value of shipments made to the United States, and when the value of shipments equals the allotted quota, other shipments are disallowed. Apparently, more quotas had been allotted by the Mexican government than were permitted under the agreement with the United States. Either someone made a mistake, or quotas were sold illegally.

According to UN estimates, the textile and garment industry is the largest employer in the developing countries. As a result, developing countries are endeavoring to loosen the MFA to allow entry of more goods to industrial countries, such as the United States, the world's largest textile importer. Quota-holding companies and the import-competing industries in the developed countries have set up strong barriers to liberalization.[36] The MFA has created significant trade friction between the producer and consumer countries. Many industrialized countries, including the United States, would like to see the MFA within GATT. However, this free trade stance is a difficult one for President Bush, because it would seriously damage textile producers in the United States.

The Organization of Petroleum Exporting Countries

In 1972 the director of the U.S. State Department's Office of Fuels & Energy boldly predicted that the average price of Middle East crude oil, then $2.25 per barrel, might rise to $5.00 or even higher by 1980. As an aside, the director mentioned that these figures would translate into higher gasoline prices, heating bills, and industrial cost.[37] This was a monumental understatement.

The **Organization of Petroleum Exporting Countries (OPEC),** as illustrated in the map on page M-10, comprises the Middle East Arab countries of Saudi Arabia, Kuwait, Qatar, the United Arab Emirates, Iraq, Libya, and Algeria; the Islamic Republic of Iran; Indonesia; Nigeria; Gabon; Venezuela; and Ecuador. OPEC's effectiveness in controlling prices and production was first illustrated by the political and economic events of 1973 and 1974,

OPEC used to be able to
control price because of
strong demand for oil and
control over production.

when the price of crude oil increased from $3.64 per barrel to $11.65 per barrel within one year. OPEC was able to accomplish this for four reasons:

1. It produced 55.5 percent of the world's oil in 1973.
2. Demand for oil was high.
3. Consuming countries were not able to supply their own needs.
4. Substitutes were not readily available.

World oil prices dropped slightly in the 1975–1978 period, but they rebounded in 1979–1980, when they peaked at about $35 per barrel.

In the early 1980s, however, OPEC's resolve began to weaken. Although oil consumption increased steadily over most of the 1970s, the oil-price rise in 1979–1980 resulted in a drop in demand for oil in the industrial countries. The major reasons for the decline in consumption were the world recession, the increase in crude-oil prices, the substitution of other fuels for oil, the effectiveness of national energy policies aimed at conservation, and the changing structure of industry and the lesser importance of energy-intensive industries.[38]

Some interesting trends developed in the oil industry. First, consumption of oil as a percentage of total energy consumption in the world declined from 48 percent to 40 percent by 1983: Natural gas, coal, hydroelectric power, and nuclear energy increased at the expense of oil. Second, the percentage of world oil consumption decreased for North America and Western Europe, whereas it increased for the centrally planned economies and the rest of the world. Finally, the output of OPEC actually decreased by 50 percent over the past decade. Part of the decrease was due to the fall in demand for oil in general, but part of it was traced to the increase in oil supplied by non-OPEC members. The major non-OPEC increases came from the USSR, Mexico, and the United Kingdom.[39] OPEC's share of production fell to 45 percent in 1980 and 30.9 percent in 1987, although it rose to 36.5 percent in 1989. In 1989 world oil production was 63.5 percent from non-OPEC countries. The USSR share of production was 19.7 percent and the U.S. share was 14 percent.[40]

OPEC's grip over prices
began to erode due to a
loss of demand and the
entrance of non-OPEC
countries producing large
amounts of oil.

Because of these trends, OPEC has been losing its grip. After successive price increases over the period 1973–1980, OPEC was forced to cut prices several times after 1983. These price cuts, along with the drop in demand, have devastated the economies of the more populous OPEC countries such as Nigeria, Indonesia, Venezuela, and Iran that need oil revenues to finance economic development. It was estimated that OPEC countries as a group suffered balance-of-payments deficits during the 1982–1985 period. Consequently, foreign-exchange reserves began to slip: Saudi Arabia's reserves, which were at $150 billion in 1982–1983, fell to less than $100 billion by early 1985.[41]

Clearly, OPEC, which had been considered the model producer cartel, was facing some serious difficulties. During the first half of 1986, prices fell

below $10 per barrel. In late 1986, OPEC was able to fashion an agreement on production quotas. The key country was Iran, which agreed to hold to a quota even if the agreement were violated by Iraq, its warring neighbor. Prices stayed at low but firmer levels during 1987, in the range of $18 per barrel. Despite OPEC's difficulties, about three quarters of the industrial world's oil reserves are held by OPEC countries. Saudi Arabia and the Persian Gulf nations hold 65 percent of the world's surplus oil production capacity, whereas OPEC as a whole holds 95 percent.[42]

By late 1987 and early 1988, OPEC began to loosen its grip even more. Prices fell to $15 per barrel in 1988, and producer countries could not agree to slow down production in order to stabilize prices. Low prices continued to devastate the U.S. oil industry, and oil exploration ceased.

However, a major problem began to develop between Iraq and Kuwait and Saudi Arabia. Prices had fallen so far in 1988 that the non-OPEC countries agreed to cut production if the OPEC countries would. However, Saudi Arabia would not go along with the plan. The Saudis felt that existing quotas should be enforced and did not want to lower production any more. In late 1988 Iran and Iraq finally agreed to the same quota, and in 1989 prices returned to about $18 per barrel. OPEC ministers agreed to increase production levels a little, but Kuwait did not want to be bound by those limits. Although oil prices had risen to slightly over $20 per barrel by mid-1990, Iraq's President Saddam Hussein attributed low world oil prices to Kuwait's quota-busting production. This was part of his motivation for invading Kuwait in August 1990 and launching war in the Middle East. Prices quickly rose to over $41 per barrel, but oil-producing countries quickly increased output to take up the slack for the embargo on Iraqi and Kuwaiti production, so prices fell to the mid-$20s by the end of 1990. Forecasts for oil prices had a peace-price of $13 per barrel and a war-price of anywhere from $70 to $100 per barrel, although post-war prices settled on around $20 per barrel. The one thing that everyone could agree on was that OPEC production would have to be cut drastically after the settlement of the Iraq-Kuwait war or prices would drop significantly. However, no one really believes that OPEC members would have either the discipline or the good will to lower production and lose revenues.[43]

The invasion of Kuwait was largely caused by Kuwait's desire to increase oil production rather than hold to its quota.

OTHER MULTILATERAL INSTITUTIONS

So far, we have discussed only a few examples of regional cooperation to provide an idea of types of cooperation and their successes and failures. It is obvious that when countries join together, they can accomplish a great deal. However, it is also obvious that nationalism and national interests play a great role in the success or failure of any form of political or economic cooperation.

In fact, nationalism usually gets in the way of successful cooperation. The best sources of information for regional groups are the *Yearbook of International Organizations* and the *Europa World Year Book*. The following are examples of three organizations that are involved in forms of cooperation that encompass more than just economic objectives.

The United Nations

Of the numerous bilateral and multilateral organizations, treaties, and agreements in existence, the United Nations (UN) is one of the most visible and extensive. Its major purposes are: (1) to maintain international peace and security; (2) to develop friendly relations among nations; (3) to achieve international cooperation in solving international problems of an economic, social, cultural or humanitarian nature; and (4) to be a center for harmonizing national efforts in these areas.

The UN has several agencies that deal with MNEs, including the Commission on Transnational Corporations and UNCTAD.

The UN comprises a Secretariat, General Assembly, Security Council, and Economic and Social Council. The Economic and Social Council is responsible for economic, social, cultural, and humanitarian facets of UN policy. This group organized a Commission on Transnational Corporations to secure effective international arrangements for the operations of transnational corporations and to further global understanding of the nature and effects of their activities. The commission has studied a variety of topics, such as transfer pricing, taxation, and international standards of accounting and reporting.

The UN has also established several regional economic commissions to study economic and technological problems of different regions of the world and recommend courses of action for resolving these problems.

A number of other bodies have been established by the UN, some dealing with issues relating to MNEs. Two such groups are the United Nations Conference on Trade and Development (UNCTAD) and the International Sea-Bed Authority. UNCTAD, as discussed in Chapter 2, has been especially active in dealing with the relationships between developing and industrial countries with respect to commodities, manufacturing, shipping, and invisibles, and financing related to trade.

The International Sea-Bed Authority, organized in October 1986 following discussions that began in 1973, is aimed at determining coastal water rights and setting policy on the exploitation of resources on the sea bed. Unfortunately, few countries have ratified the Convention.

Finally, the UN has organized a number of specialized agencies to influence the world economy: the General Agreement on Tariffs and Trade (GATT), the World Bank, the International Labor Organization, the International Monetary Fund, and the World Intellectual Property Organization. Each of these groups is discussed in greater detail elsewhere in this text.

The Organization for Economic Cooperation and Development

The OECD was established to promote economic and social welfare of member nations.

Like the UN, the Organization for Economic Cooperation and Development (OECD), as illustrated in the map on page M-10, is a multilateral form of cooperation, made up primarily of industrial countries. The OECD was organized in 1961 to assist member governments in formulating policies aimed at promoting economic and social welfare and to stimulate and harmonize members' assistance to developing countries.[44] It is comprised of 24 countries and has over 200 different committees that deal with economic issues. Three committees—the Trade Committee, the Executive Committee Special Session, and the Development Assistance Committee—deal with specific trade issues.

The Trade Committee provides a forum for considering long-range trade policies of member nations and for discussing current problems as well. The Executive Committee Special Session deals with the coordination of national economic policies. This discussion has taken on increased significance over the past few years as inflation has dropped and currencies have come under pressure owing to the fluctuating U.S. dollar. The Development Assistance Committee is concerned about the transfer of financial resources to the developing countries.

The OECD has issued a code of conduct relating to the operations of MNEs to ensure that the MNEs operate in support of economic and political objectives of the individual member nations. In addition, the OECD issued a set of guidelines dealing with MNEs' disclosure of financial and operating information.

The UN and the OECD are multilateral institutions with broader appeal than the narrower trade or economic issues described earlier in the chapter. All of these organizations, however, have an additional useful purpose: They provide a forum where nations can discuss political, economic, and social issues of mutual benefit and, it is hoped, come to a cooperative consensus.

League of Arab States

The Arab League is a political organization that is trying to mediate the crisis in Lebanon and solve the problems of the Palestinians.

A final notable group of countries is the Arab League, as illustrated in the map on page M-10. Comprised of 22 North African and Middle Eastern countries, including Palestine, the Arab League "is a voluntary association of sovereign Arab states designed to strengthen the close ties linking them and to coordinate their policies and activities and direct them toward the common good of all the Arab countries."[45] The Arab League has a variety of committees, some dealing with economic issues, but its mandate deals more with political than economic issues, and it is not attempting to establish any type of free trade area or common market. Most recently, it has attempted to mediate a solution to the crisis in Lebanon and to solve the problems of the Palestinians and the occupied territories in Israel.

The Environment

An issue that has captured the attention of the world in recent years is the environment. Pollution of the air, land, and sea clearly poses a threat to the future of the planet, and governments, corporations, and citizens are concerned about where we are and where we are heading. The opening of Central and Eastern Europe has unmasked terrible environmental damage from centrally planned economies that operated with no real thought as to the future of the environment. The growth in Mexican industries along the U.S. border has brought with it increased air, land, and water pollution. A key irritant between the U.S. and Canada is the problem of acid rain that results from air pollution in the United States. The oil spill of the *Exxon Valdez* in Alaska highlighted the potential problems of transporting oil in supertankers. The total disregard of Iraq's Sadaam Hussein for the environment was demonstrated by the detonation of oil wells and the mass spilling of oil into the Persian Gulf during the Gulf War in 1991.

People are clearly concerned about the environment. In a poll conducted frequently by the *New York Times*/CBS, the public is asked if "protecting the environment is so important that requirements and standards cannot be too high, and continuing environmental improvements must be made regardless of cost." When the question was asked in September 1981, 45 percent agreed and 42 percent disagreed. In June 1989, 79 percent agreed and only 18 percent disagreed.[46]

In a recent Conference Board study, the following issues were identified by U.S. managers as the most important:

1. Worker health and safety;
2. Clean air (pollution from stationary sources);
3. Hazardous and toxic chemical waste disposal;
4. Acid rain;
5. Toxic solid waste disposal.

In the same survey, two other issues were raised by Canadian managers: clean water (surface water contamination) and the Greenhouse effect (global warming). Clean air was ranked third by the Canadians, whereas hazardous and toxic chemical waste disposal was ranked second by both Canadian and European managers.[47]

The problem with environmental legislation is that each country is going off in its own direction, and there are significant differences in the way different countries are dealing with environmental issues. The problem is especially acute in the developing countries, where some of the worst environmental damage is taking place and where laws tend to be the most lax. As a result, companies might be tempted to locate production facilities in countries where environmental laws are weak in order to save costs.

However, many MNEs are also among the most environmentally responsible in the world as they redesign manufacturing processes to be more efficient in the use of inputs as a means of driving down costs. An example is DuPont, the U.S.-based chemical firm. DuPont voluntarily spends approximately $50 million a year on environmental projects beyond what is required by law, and its goal is zero pollution in all activities.[48] Management found that it could actually reduce costs by designing production processes to be more environmentally sound.

It is clear that corporations are responding to private environmental groups as well as self-interest in attacking environmental issues. However, global efforts are occurring in places like the United Nations as countries meet to discuss and coordinate efforts. The World Bank, for example, examines the environmental impact of each of the projects that it funds, primarily in developing countries. In June 1990, environment ministers from 93 countries agreed to phase out the production and use of chlorofluorocarbons and several other chlorine-based and bromine-based chemicals by the end of the century. In addition, a cross-national agreement was reached on ways to control the cross-border movement of hazardous wastes. Even though national efforts are important, international cooperation can also be beneficial.

LOOKING TO THE FUTURE   Regional economic integration will continue at a rapid pace. Even though nationalism will keep the European Community from becoming a United States of Europe, there will be significant economic harmonization in the years to come. However, there are a number of important problems, such as the harmonization of taxation, that will not be solved by December 31, 1992. Therefore, Europe 1992 needs to be looked at as a process, not a specific date. A key issue to watch is the potential development of one European currency, which is championed by the French and opposed by the British. Another key issue that relates to the EC is the acceptance of the Central and Eastern European countries and the place of the Soviet Union in the "European House."

Some very exciting new areas of cooperation may come out of the Americas. The closing case, which discusses a North American Common Market, illustrates some of the problems and potential benefits that will accrue to a closer Canada–United States–Mexico. At the same time, the rest of Latin America will find that economic cooperation will be essential to their continued peace and prosperity. The ability of the democratically elected governments to remain in power and to develop the democratic tradition within their countries should enhance regional cooperation.

The most unstable area for the future will be commodity prices. As those prices remain low, the exporting countries will have difficulty earning enough foreign exchange to service foreign debt and modernize. Conversely, while most of the major oil-consuming countries have cut down on oil consumption as a percentage of GNP, high oil prices can have a devastating impact on their economic growth. Although the recession of late 1990 and 1991 reduced the demand for oil and helped hold down prices, the fear was that any significant price increases would touch off an inflationary spiral that would damage economic recovery. It was estimated in 1990 that in the United States, each $1 drop in the price of a barrel of crude oil would cut the cost of gasoline by more than $2 billion per year and cut the trade deficit by $3 billion.[49] Obviously, a price increase would cause the opposite effect in the short run.

SUMMARY

- Regional economic integration emerged strongly after World War II as countries began to realize the benefits of cooperation and larger market sizes. The major types of economic integration are the free trade area, customs union, common market, economic union, and complete economic integration.

- In its most limited sense, economic integration allows countries to trade goods without tariff discrimination (i.e., free trade area). In a more complex arrangement, all factors of production are allowed to move across borders, and some degree of social, political, and economic harmonization is undertaken (i.e., complete economic integration).

- The static effects of economic integration improve the efficiency of resource allocation and affect both production and consumption. The dynamic effects involve internal and external economies that arise because of changes in growth of market sizes.

- Regional, as opposed to global, integration takes place due to the greater ease in promoting cooperation on a smaller scale, as well as to achieve the advantages of expanded market size.

- The European Community (EC) is an effective common market that has abolished most of the restrictions on factor mobility and is moving toward the status of an economic union by attempting to harmonize national economic policies to a limited extent. It includes Belgium, Denmark, France, Greece, Germany, Ireland, Italy, Luxembourg, the Netherlands, Spain, Portugal, and the United Kingdom.

- Some of the EC's major goals are: (1) abolishment of intrazonal restrictions on the movement of goods, capital, services, and labor; (2) a common external tariff; (3) a common agricultural policy; (4) harmonization of tax and legal systems; (5) a uniform policy concerning antitrust; and (6) a harmonization of national currencies.

- By December 31, 1992, the EC hopes to remove most of its remaining barriers to the free flow of goods and services.

- Other forms of economic integration have occurred in other parts of the world, notably in Latin America and among the Eastern European countries.

Various forms of free trade areas and customs unions also exist in Africa and Asia.

- Many developing countries rely on commodity exports to supply the hard currencies needed for economic development. Instability in commodity prices has resulted in fluctuations in export earnings. Commodity agreements, utilizing buffer stocks, price ranges, quotas, or combinations of the three, are often sought in the hope of stabilizing prices.

- The Multifibre Arrangement (MFA) was established to protect textile and garment manufacturers in developed countries from manufacturers in developing countries. It allowed the importing countries to establish quotas to protect domestic producers.

- The Organization of Petroleum Exporting Countries (OPEC) was successful as a producer cartel in the 1970s and effectively forced historic increases in crude-oil prices. However, the drop in demand worldwide and the entrance of major non-OPEC producers has reduced OPEC's influence. Potential war in the Middle East injected significant uncertainty into oil prices in late 1990 and early 1991 and imperiled the ability of OPEC to remain unified after the cessation of hostilities.

- The United Nations (UN) has become deeply involved in international business through the World Bank Group, the International Monetary Fund, the Commission on Transnational Corporations, and the Conference on the Law of the Sea.

- The Organization for Economic Cooperation and Development (OECD) is an association of the major industrial countries of the world whose major objective is to foster economic and social development.

- The Arab League is attempting to resolve some key disputes in the Middle East, such as the hostilities in Lebanon and the solution of the Palestinian question.

C A S E

A NORTH AMERICAN
FREE TRADE
AREA[50]

On September 26, 1990, after months of informal and often secret discussions, President Bush requested authority from the U.S. Congress to open trade talks with Mexico that were to begin formally in 1991 and to culminate in a U.S.-Mexico Free Trade Agreement. However, both the Canadians (who already have a free trade agreement with the United States) and the Americans were questioning the wisdom of such a move.

The new market would be large, as illustrated in Map 11.4, with much of its economic strength coming from the United States. In fact, the population and GNP of the free trade area would exceed that of the European Community and help offset some of Japan's strength in Asia.

It is interesting to note that the population in

Map 11.4

A North American Free Trade Area

The combined population, GNP, and intrazonal trade in North America could result in a significant regional trading block.

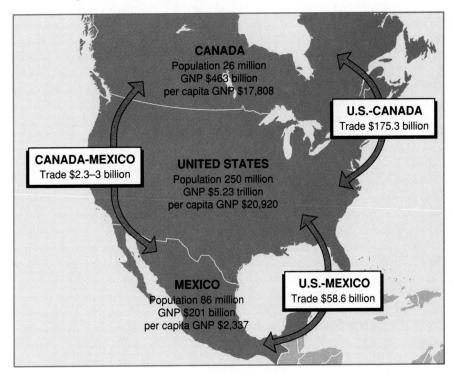

CANADA
Population 26 million
GNP $463 billion
per capita GNP $17,808

U.S.-CANADA
Trade $175.3 billion

CANADA-MEXICO
Trade $2.3–3 billion

UNITED STATES
Population 250 million
GNP $5.23 trillion
per capita GNP $20,920

MEXICO
Population 86 million
GNP $201 billion
per capita GNP $2,337

U.S.-MEXICO
Trade $58.6 billion

the United States is 69 percent of the total, whereas Germany, the largest country in the EC, is only 19 percent of the total population of the EC.

The rows of the table on page 426 represent the export of that country to the country in the corresponding column. For example, the exports from the United States to Canada in 1989 were $80.451 billion, and the U.S. imports from Canada (or Canadian exports to the United States) were $88.960 billion. Note the relatively small Canadian trade with Mexico. However, the figure shown represents 1988 data, and two-way trade between Mexico and Canada was targeted to rise to $2.6 billion in 1990.

A free trade area involving these three countries could make them totally self-sufficient in energy. In addition, manufacturers in the three countries would have unrestricted access to each other's markets. Canadian and Mexican agricultural and industrial sectors would benefit from U.S.-developed technology. The infusion of modern technology could be especially beneficial to Mexico in helping to alleviate high unemployment.

As the table on page 426 shows, the three countries already enjoy a large amount of intra-zonal trade. Trade between the United States and Canada is by far the largest bilateral trading relationship in the world, and this would likely increase in the future.

The United States-Canadian Free Trade Agreement   In the past 30 years, a variety of forms of economic cooperation have emerged between the United States and Canada. Since 1965 an Automotive Products Trade Agreement has existed between the two countries. It provides for qualified duty-free trade in specified automotive products between the United States and Canada. In the early 1980s there was discussion about developing free trade in specific sectors, such as steel and textiles, which gave way to a broader discussion of free trade. Nego-

tiations were held in 1987 to open up trade even more between the United States and Canada. The United States was concerned about the amount of governmental subsidies given Canadian businesses and also about gaining greater access to investment opportunities in Canada. The Canadians, on the other hand, sought exemption from U.S. laws protecting U.S. producers from Canadian competition. Canadians preferred dealing with an international tribunal to resolve trade disputes rather than having to deal with U.S. antidumping and countervailing duty legislation. Canadian manufacturers would be able to cut costs by an estimated 20 percent due to economies of scale that would follow from freer access to the U.S. market.

Preliminary discussions gave way to the Canada-U.S. Free Trade Agreement (FTA), which went into effect on January 1, 1989. Canadians were concerned that Canada would: (1) lose its cultural identity, (2) become too closely integrated with a violent society, (3) be hitching its wagon to a declining economic power, (4) forfeit its independence in foreign policy, and (5) be overwhelmed politically and economically by the United States. Some U.S. politicians, especially in the Midwest, worried that their states would lose production to Canada. However, the dynamic effects of the expansion of the two markets in a freer environment were expected to create an additional 750,000 jobs in the United States and 150,000 in Canada. Some experts predicted that high-volume production lines would be shifted to the United States and small-volume specialty lines would be shifted to Canada. The expansion of these two markets, with fewer trade barriers than exist currently in the EC, will result in a market that is 15 percent larger than the EC.

As mentioned above, the U.S.-Canadian trade relationship is the largest bilateral relationship in the world. Canada is the United States' largest trading partner, supplying 20 percent of U.S. imports, a just slightly smaller percentage than that of the entire European Community. The United States is Canada's largest supplier, sending across the border 70 percent of Canada's imports and receiving 78 percent of Canada's exports.

The FTA eliminates all tariffs on bilateral trade by 1998, although 73 percent of all U.S. exports to Canada were free from tariffs before the signing of the FTA. Each country retains its own external tariffs, however. In order to maintain the integrity of the bilateral relationship, the FTA established rules of origin, which means that cross-border trade must identify where the goods were produced. That keeps non-FTA goods from entering the United States through Canada and vice-versa. The FTA also expands the amount of government procurement that will be open to exporters from each country. Although there is a significant two-way flow of foreign investment—approximately $79 billion in 1988—and a large amount of services trade, the FTA liberalizes flows in both areas and allows firms from each country to gain greater market access. A new dispute-settlement mechanism was also set into place which should allow for a more efficient settlement of disputes in the future. The FTA established a Canada-U.S. Trade Commission to deal specifically with disputes arising from the application and interpretation of the FTA. The Commission can deal with any trade dispute issue except for antidumping and countervailing duty actions and financial services, but the dispute mechanism should result in actions taking no longer than eight months from start to finish to resolve.

The FTA is expected to have important ramifications as time goes on, but it is still too early to tell what the overall effects will be. Many Canadian industries are among the most efficient in the world, but many are also very inefficient. There will probably be plant closings and mergers as firms attempt to establish their market niche. Parent companies in both countries are struggling to determine how to serve both markets and whether or not to rationalize production

facilities. Canada's 25 largest corporations already control 35 percent of Canada's corporate assets, so there is some concern there that too much industrial concentration might emerge.

The Mexican Connection   Mexico has undergone some important changes in recent years. In 1986 Mexico joined GATT and began the process of dismantling tariff and nontariff barriers. Prior to that, tariffs ranged from 35 to 100 percent.

When Carlos Salinas de Gortari became President of Mexico, he decided to revolutionize the economic structure of the country so that Mexico would be better prepared to enter the twenty-first century. He cut down the size of the government bureaucracy, diversified the Mexican economy from oil, and started to privatize the economy. Then he liberalized foreign-investment rules in 1989 and renegotiated Mexico's large international debt. However, it wasn't until he made a trip to Eastern Europe that Salinas realized how much had to be done to compete with the opening of Eastern Europe as well as the exploding growth in Asia. As a result, he decided that he needed to reform even faster.

The discussions on free trade began quietly in 1990. However, they are progressing rapidly, and Canada is a formal part of the process. Mexico has much to offer both Canada and the United States. Mexico is tied with Iran as the fourth-largest oil producer in the world, after the USSR, the United States, and Saudi Arabia. However, foreign investment in the oil industry is prohibited by the Mexican constitution. In spite of that problem, Mexico's large oil reserves and production base would help to make North America relatively self-sufficient in oil.

In addition, Mexico has a huge consumer market. The population in mid-1988 was 83.7 million people, although the per capita GNP was only $1,760, which makes Mexico a lower-middle-income country. As wages continue to rise, Mexico will become a potent consumer market.

Another strength of Mexico is its low wages. The table below summarizes the hourly labor costs for Canada, the United States and Mexico, and it is easy to see why low-skill unions in Canada and the United States feel threatened by Mexico.

A TALE OF THREE COUNTRIES

Hourly labor costs, including fringe benefits, for production workers in manufacturing

	$Canadian	$U.S.		
Year	Canada	Canada	United States	Mexico
1989	$17.43	$14.72	$14.31	$2.32
1988	16.65	13.53	13.85	1.99
1987	15.85	11.95	13.40	1.57
1986	15.28	11.00	13.21	1.50
1985	14.75	10.80	12.96	2.09

Source: John Saunders, "Trade with Mexico Has Winners, Losers," *Globe and Mail,* November 14, 1990.

As the executive of a large U.S. apparel company said, "Are we going to move all U.S. production to a place where there are no employee rights or benefits? Is it right to lay off the U.S. employee who has been with the company for 20 years and go down to Mexico and hire a 16-year-old?"

Even without the FTA, there are a number of companies that have taken advantage of the low labor rates of Mexico, with mixed blessings on the U.S. economy. When Jerrold Electronics closed its plant in Kansas City, it eliminated 190 jobs that paid $9 per hour. The company relocated in Mexico, where it is paying $1 per hour. However, in an Ohio division of General Motors, workers are making parts and components that are shipped to low-cost assembly facilities in Mexico, thus keeping 8400 people employed. Thus the FTA with Mexico would allow large,

labor-intensive firms where 30 percent or more of product value comes from labor to get access to cheaper labor and parts. Foreign investment should also rise, especially in previously protected industries and possibly oil. The development of more job opportunities could also help stabilize the political situation in Mexico.

However, there are bound to be losses in low-wage jobs. Some industries, such as agriculture, might undergo painful restructuring. Mexico is the largest avocado-producing nation in the world, but it does not ship a single avocado to the United States because of protectionist legislation. Organized labor in both Canada and the United States will suffer as low-paying jobs disappear and downward pressure is put on wages. Competition will also increase, which will be good for consumers but scary for producers, and the impact on trade will be uneven—border communities will be enhanced more than those far away. Another issue surrounding the free trade talks is the concern over environmental damage. There is serious pollution in Mexico City itself and the Mexican towns bordering the United States where significant foreign investment is taking place. The concern is that an upsurge of investment in Mexico will lead to even greater environmental damage.

For a while, the Canadians were very tense about the negotiations between the U.S. and Mexico, because they felt that they were being left out. As one journalist pointed out, "The United States prefers to deal with its North American neighbors separately: bargaining for Canada's natural resources first, then for Mexico's cheap labor. To have both of its junior trading partners at the same table at the same time would only complicate matters."

Questions

1. List the benefits that would accrue to all three members of the new common market.
2. List the major economic problems that could arise from such a union.

3. Discuss the political and nationalistic ramifications of such a union.

4. How would this union compare with some of the others that we discussed in this chapter?

5. If you were a U.S. manager looking at the newly created market, what strategies might you employ to serve all three markets? What factors would you consider in making your choice?

Chapter Notes

1. The information in this incident is from the following sources: various issues of the Ford Motor Company's *Annual Reports; Forbes,* July 1, 1972, pp. 22–26; *Forbes,* April 2, 1979, pp. 44–48; Roger Cohen, "Ford-Fiat: How Their Contest of Wills Prevented a 'Perfect Marriage' in Europe," *Wall Street Journal,* November 21, 1985, p. 34; James B. Treece, *et. al.,* "Can Ford Stay on Top?" *Business Week,* September 28, 1987, pp. 78–86; Richard A. Melcher, "Ford Is Ready to Roll in the New Europe," *Business Week,* December 12, 1988, p. 60.

2. Bela Balassa, *The Theory of Economic Integration* (Homewood, Ill.: Irwin, 1961), p. 1.

3. *Ibid.,* p. 40.

4. *Ibid.,* p. 4.

5. "Twelve and Six Make What?" *Economist,* January 23, 1988, pp. 42 and 44.

6. Sanjeev Gupta, Leslie Lipschitz, and Thomas Mayer, "The Common Agricultural Policy of the EC," *Finance & Development,* June 1989, pp. 37–39.

7. Philip Revzin, "United We Stand . . . ," *Wall Street Journal,* September 22, 1989, p. R5.

8. Business International, *Business Europe,* August 10, 1987, p. 6.

9. Revzin, *op. cit.,* p. R6.

10. Ernst & Whinney, *Europe 1992: The Single Market,* September 1988, pp. 5–6.

11. E. S. Browning, "Sticky Solutions," *Wall Street Journal,* September 22, 1989, pp. R8–R9.

12. Shawn Tully, "Europe Gets Ready for 1992," *Fortune,* February 1, 1988, p. 83.

13. "Border Wars," *Economist,* July 9, 1988, pp. 19–20.

14. Grant Thornton, *ECONEWS,* Volume 3-90, p. 3.

15. Price Waterhouse, *EC Bulletin,* December 1987/January 1988, p. 1.

16. Meggan Dissly, "Hard Times at a French Customs Post," *Newsweek,* October 31, 1988, p. 10.

17. "Border Wars," *op. cit.,* p. 19.

18. Frank Comes and Jonathan Kapstein, "Reshaping Europe: 1992 and Beyond," *Business Week,* December 12, 1988, p. 50.

19. John F. Magee, "1992: Moves Americans Must Make," *Harvard Business Review,* May–June 1989, pp. 78–84.

20. Shawn Tully, "Europe Gets Ready for 1992," *Fortune,* February 1, 1988, p. 83.

21. "Inter-American Development Bank Predicts Renewed Push for Economic Integration in Latin America," *IMF Survey,* December 10, 1984, pp. 369 + .

22. *Europa World Year Book, 1990,* p. 173.

23. Thomas Kamm, "Latin America Edges Toward Free Trade," *Wall Street Journal,* November 30, 1990, p. A14.

24. Rosalind Rachid, "Caribbean Speeds Up Economic Integration," *Journal of Commerce and Commercial,* August 7, 1990, p. 3A.

25. Martin Schrenk, "Whither Comecon?" *Finance & Development,* September 1990, pp. 28–31; Barry Newman, "Beleaguered Bloc," *Wall Street Journal,* September 28, 1989, p. A1.

26. Tim Carrington, "East Bloc to Transform Comecon, Retain Economic Ties to Moscow," *Wall Street Journal,* January 10, 1990, p. A10.

27. Kenichi Ohmae, *Triad Power: The Coming Shape of Global Competition* (New York: Free Press, 1985).

28. Daniel Sneider, "Thriving Pacific Rim Nations Organize for Economic Cooperation," *Christian Science Monitor,* May 23, 1988, p. 1.

29. Donald J. Lecraw, "Trading Blocs and Trade Cooperation Among Pacific Rim Countries," paper delivered at the Academy of International Business Annual Meeting, October 1990.

30. *Europa World Year Book, 1990,* p. 134.

31. "Sustained Price Weakness Forecast for Non-Fuel Commodities," *IMF Survey,* July 13, 1987, pp. 209 + .

32. Raphael Pura, "Malaysia's Tin Scheme Stuns the Industry," *Wall Street Journal,* September 25, 1986, p. 38; and "Uncommon Fund," *Economist,* August 15, 1987, p. 55.

33. Neil Berhmann and Jose de Cordoba, "Plunging Coffee Prices Imperil Exporters," *Wall Street Journal,* July 17, 1989, p. A6.

34. "Indonesia Will Push for Seat on Board of Coffee Cartel," *Wall Street Journal,* May 26, 1987, p. 16.

35. Berhmann and de Cordoba, *op. cit.*

36. Ying-Pik Choi, Hwa Soo Chung, and Nicolas Marian, *The Multi-Fibre Arrangement in Theory and Practice* (London: Frances Pinter, 1985).

37. "The Middle East Squeeze on Oil Giants," *Business Week,* July 29, 1972, p. 56.

38. "International Oil Market Prospects," *Currency Profiles* (New York: The Henley Centre for Economic Forecasting and Manufacturers Hanover Trust Company, December 1984), p. 6.

39. *Ibid.,* pp. 6–7.

40. Business International, *Global Outlook* (New York: Business International Corporation, Third Quarter 1990), p. 8.

41. Ronald Taggiasco and William Glesgell, "OPEC Still Hasn't Faced Up to Reality," *Business Week,* February 11, 1985, p. 29.

42. Deloitte, Haskins & Sells, *DH&S Review,* June 8, 1987, p. 2.

43. James Tanner, "Looming Shock," *Wall Street Journal,* December 10, 1990, p. A1; James Tanner, "OPEC Ministers See Price Collapse if Oil Glut Occurs," *Wall Street Journal,* December 12, 1990, p. A2; *Chicago Fed Letter* (Chicago: The Federal Reserve Bank of Chicago, November 1990).

44. *Europa World Year Book, 1990,* p. 185.

45. *Europa World Year Book, 1990,* p. 174.

46. David Kirkpatrick, "Environmentalism: The New Crusade," *Fortune,* February 12, 1990, p. 46.

47. Deloitte & Touche, *Deloitte & Touche Review,* April 8, 1991, p. 3.

48. David Kirkpatrick, *ibid.,* p. 48.

49. James Tanner, "Looming Shock," *op. cit.*

50. Stephen Baker, "Mexico: A New Economic Era," *Business Week,* November 12, 1990, pp. 102+; William J. Holstein, David Woodruff, and Amy Borrus, "Is Free Trade with Mexico Good or Bad for the U.S.?" *Business Week,* November 12, 1990, pp. 112–113; Fred Blaser, "Benefits of Mexican Trade Deal," *Financial Post,* December 6, 1990; "Advantages for Canada in a North American Deal," *Globe and Mail,* October 17, 1990; Clyde H. Farnsworth, "Preliminary Trade Pact with Mexico Is Shaped," *New York Times,* October 7, 1989; Carol Goar, "Should Canada Crash U.S.-Mexico Party?" *Toronto Star,* August 7, 1990; John Saunders, "Trade with Mexico Has Winners, Losers," *Globe and Mail,* November 14, 1990; Alan Freeman, "Free-Trade Pact Creates Winners, Losers," *Wall Street Journal,* February 7, 1989, p. A14; Ann H. Hughes, "United States and Canada Form World's Largest Free Trade Area," *Business America,* January 30, 1989, pp. 2–3; Louis Kraar, "North America's New Trade Punch," *Fortune,* May 22, 1989, pp. 123–127; Earl H. Fry and Lee H. Radebaugh, eds., *Regulation of Foreign Direct Investment in Canada and the United States* (Provo, Utah: Brigham Young University, 1983); Lee H. Radebaugh and Earl H. Fry, eds., *Canada/U.S. Trade Relations* (Provo, Utah: Brigham Young University, 1984); Lee H. Radebaugh and Earl H. Fry, *The Canada/U.S. Free Trade Agreement: The Impact on Service Industries* (Provo, Utah: Brigham Young University, 1988); Edith Terry, William J. Holstein, Wendy Zellner, and Zachary Schiller, "Getting Ready for the Great North American Shakeout," *Business Week,* April 4, 1988, pp. 44–46.

CHAPTER 12

THE IMPACT OF THE MULTINATIONAL

If a little money does not go out, great money will not come in.
CHINESE PROVERB

Objectives

- To examine the conflicting objectives that MNEs face.

- To discuss problems in evaluating MNE activities.

- To evaluate the major economic impacts (balance of payments and growth) of multinational firms on donor and recipient countries.

- To introduce the major criticisms asserted about multinational firms.

- To give an overview of the major political controversies surrounding MNE activities.

Prime Minister Brian Mulroney was elected in late 1984 and soon thereafter replaced the agency formed by the eleven-year-old Foreign Investment Review Act (FIRA) with a new agency called Investment Canada. Whereas the FIRA's purpose had been to limit foreign control of the Canadian economy, Investment Canada's intent is to persuade foreign firms to invest in Canada. Investment Canada reduced substantially the number of investment applications that are subject to scrutiny: Under it, direct takeovers of Canadian firms with assets of less than C$5 million and indirect takeovers of less than C$50 million need not be examined. The old review board criterion that an investment be of "significant benefit" to Canada has been replaced with a loosely defined "net benefit" to Canada.

The birth of Investment Canada did not mark the first time Canada had changed its stance toward foreign investors. In 1972, after decades of luring foreign capital to Canada, it was estimated that of the $58 billion of total corporate assets in Canada, $43 billion, or 74 percent, were foreign-owned. No other advanced economy was so dominated by foreign ownership; such a degree of foreign control was unusual even among developing countries. The U.S. ownership was $35 billion, or about 60 percent, of the total corporate assets in Canada. (Map 12.1 shows a map of Canada.)

The evolving public opinion at that time was that foreign ownership should be restricted. This does not mean that Canada had heretofore allowed unrestricted entry of foreign firms. There were already limitations on foreign ownership in certain industries considered to be particularly sensitive to national sovereignty, including banks and other financial institutions, newspapers and magazines, broadcasting, and the uranium industry. Given these existing restrictions, what difference did it make that other firms were controlled outside of Canada? Would operations or decisions be any different than if the ownership were held by Canadians? Obviously, many Canadians thought they would be.

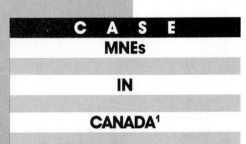

C A S E

MNEs

IN

CANADA[1]

One such allegation concerned the level of positions and type of production taking place in Canada. The Science Council, a governmental advisory board, contended that even in high-technology industries, very little research and development was being performed by the Canadian subsidiaries of foreign firms. Furthermore, very little of the production of newer sophisticated products was being done in Canada. Canadian subsidiaries depended primarily on manufacture of mature products and components. These generally had a lower profit margin and employed a higher portion of lower-skilled people than the more innovative output taking place in the MNEs' home countries. Furthermore, since the corporate headquarters of the MNEs were located abroad, Canadians in the subsidiary operations could aspire to upper-level management positions only by leaving Canada. Given the high educational level of the Canadian population and the

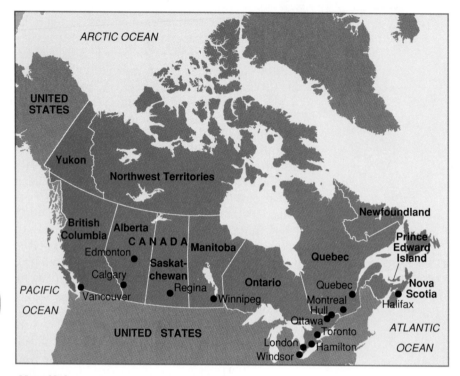

Map 12.1
Canada
More than two thirds of Canada's people live within 100 miles of the U.S. border. This map shows the Canadian provinces and the largest Canadian cities.

shrinking opportunities for advancement in Canada, there was a net flow abroad of technical and managerial persons with high skills—a so-called brain drain. Many of these workers joined the parent companies' operations, meaning that Canada then had to import the costly technical advancements that its own citizens helped to develop abroad. Many Canadians thus expected that greater Canadian control would bring increased opportunity in Canada for using their skills and would make the country less dependent on foreign technology.

There also was widespread agreement among critics of foreign ownership that in conflict situations the investors would do what was best for the home, rather than the Canadian, situation. Many observers believed that, if given a choice of exporting from Canada or the parent country, the MNEs would choose the latter. Critics were particularly upset that the U.S. government had prevented the Canadian subsidiaries of U.S. firms from exporting to China during the period before the United States opened trading relations with that country. These export limitations contributed to a drain on Canadian foreign exchange, which proved substantial because of dividend remittances to parents that exceeded the flow of foreign exchange into Canada.

Because of these contentions about foreign investment, the FIRA was passed in late 1973. It provided that any foreign takeover of an existing company would have to be screened by the Foreign Investment Review Agency, which would recommend to Parliament whether or not the investment was of "significant benefit" to Canada. The procedure applied to Canadian companies with assets of at least C$250,000 or annual sales exceeding C$3 million. A takeover would involve acquisition of 5 percent or more of the Canadian company. By the end of 1974 the law was extended to cover new investments and expansion of foreign-controlled companies into new areas of business.

The term *significant benefit* was never defined specifically: Some of the factors that were considered were the effects on employment, exports, competition, productivity, and industrial efficiency. Approval also depended on the degree of Canadian participation in a venture, although no quota of Canadian representation in the management of a company was spelled out. After Pierre Trudeau's election as Prime Minister in 1980, a ten-year National Energy Program was announced to reduce foreign ownership in the energy industry to 50 percent. This program led to the "benefit" of an 8 percent drop in foreign control of oil and gas but sparked a two-year outflow of direct and portfolio investment as many foreign investors feared a political environment that would not allow them to operate profitably. This in turn led to downward pressure on the Canadian dollar and upward pressure on Canadian interest rates.

The simultaneous occurrence of costs and benefits is one explanation for the historic disagreement within Canada on the question of foreign investment. Some critics have claimed that restrictions have not been sufficient; others have felt that controls should be eased on the foreign ownership of Canadian enterprises. Even when FIRA was passed, Premier Gerald Regan of Nova Scotia said, "We want all the foreign investment we can get." At the time, 10 percent of Nova Scotians were out of work.

While FIRA was operating, some people favored greater control, contending that FIRA had a positive impact but did not go far enough. These critics showed that although foreign firms increased their research and development (R&D) in Canada, the amount they undertook has been less than their share of the economy. The percent of GNP spent on R&D in Canada is still small in comparison with the percentage in some other industrial countries (e.g., about 60% of that in Switzerland). Critics feel that Canadian control will produce increases in R&D. They point to the Canadian takeover of de Havilland from Britain's Hawker Siddeley Group in 1974 and of Canadair from General Dynamics of the United States in 1976. With Canadian ownership and management these firms have greatly increased R&D, developed new products, increased employment, and are competing internationally. Observers believe that Canadian takeovers of other industries will lead to similar growth in Canada's technical capabilities.

Those who wanted fewer controls questioned whether Canada could fulfill its technological and capital needs if controls resulted in a lowering of direct investment flows into Canada. First, they questioned whether indigenously controlled firms would undertake in Canada the kind of R&D that foreign firms were criticized for not undertaking. These analysts have cited the fact that Northern Telecom, Canada's telecommunications giant, itself maintains an R&D facility with 500 people in the United States. Second, they have shown that technology flows more quickly, more cheaply, and with fewer restrictions between a parent and a subsidiary than by license among independent companies. In terms of restrictions, for instance, there is a high incidence of limiting output only for sale in Canada under the licensing arrangements. Among controlled operations, however, a number of investors have transferred technology so that Canada serves as the production base for worldwide sales (e.g., Westinghouse, steam turbines; Motorola, mobile radios; Honeywell, hydronic valves). In terms of capital, they pointed to a Royal Bank of Canada estimate that by the year 2000, Canada will need $1.4 trillion for energy investment alone, of which $300 billion will have to come from foreign sources. The capital-need argument became particularly pervasive as unemployment remained high during the recession in the early 1980s.

Because of these arguments Investment Canada replaced the FIRA. But how liberal has Canada become toward foreign investors? There is no definitive answer. On the one hand, Canada has permitted some very large foreign takeovers, such as the purchase of 51 percent of Hiram Walker by Britain's Allied-Lyons. On the other hand, Canadians remain worried about foreign domination, especially from the United States. Four of Canada's ten largest companies are U.S. direct investments, and in 1990 the United States illegalized the sale of goods by subsidiaries of U.S. firms to Cuba. Canadians are particularly concerned about protecting their culture, since a high percentage of English-language television and movies viewed by Canadians are from the United States. This has led the president of Investment Canada, Mr. Paul Labbé, to say, "More non-Canadian control in cultural industries is not welcome." Foreigners continue to control Canadian investments that account for about 40 percent of Canadian manufacturing employment. Recently, Canadians have questioned the value of the influx of Japanese investments, especially since the provinces have competed with incentives to attract that investment.

The ambivalence toward foreign direct investment has been further enhanced by the US-Canada Free Trade Agreement. Many Canadians fear that Canadian-controlled firms and Canadian-based production will be at a further competitive disadvantage. A particular worry is that both Canadian and non-Canadian controlled firms will choose to locate more of their production within the United States in order to avoid paying the higher Canadian social benefit taxes.

INTRODUCTION

Pressure groups push to restrict MNE movements at home and abroad.

In Canada as well as in other countries, the rapid growth of international companies has been controversial. In fact, there are powerful pressure groups in both home and host countries that have pushed their governments to implement policies restricting the movement of multinational firms. These critics are sure to play an even greater role in the future expansion of world business. This chapter examines the major contentions regarding the practices of MNEs and the main evidence supporting or refuting the contentions.

The sheer size of MNEs is an issue.
- Some are economically larger than many countries.
- Some of their executives deal directly with heads of state.

The primary criticism is that multinational firms are inadequately concerned about national societal interests because of their global bases of operations. Furthermore, the sheer size of many MNEs concerns the countries with which they come in contact. For example, the sales of General Motors, Exxon, and Mitsubishi exceed the GNP of such medium-sized economies as Argentina, Indonesia, Poland, and South Africa.[2] Large MNEs such as these have considerable power in negotiating business arrangements with nation-states that may be of greater consequence than many treaties among countries. In fact, the executives of MNEs frequently deal directly with heads of state when negotiating the terms by which they may operate.

EVALUATING THE IMPACT OF THE MNE

Trade-offs among Constituencies

Firms must satisfy
- Stockholders
- Employees
- Customers
- Society at large

A firm must satisfy different groups—stockholders, employees, customers, and society at large—if it is to survive. In the short run, the aims of each group are in conflict. Stockholders want additional sales and productivity increases, which result in higher profits to them. Employees want additional compensation. Customers want lower prices, and society at large would like to see increased corporate taxes or company involvement in social functions. In the long run, all of these aims must be achieved adequately or none will be attained at all, since each group is powerful enough to cause the demise of the organization.

Management must be aware of these various interests but serve them unevenly at any given period. At one moment, most gains may go to consumers; at another time, stockholders may benefit most. Making necessary trade-offs is a difficult task domestically. Abroad, where corporate managers are relatively unfamiliar with customs and power groups, the problem of choosing the best alternative is compounded; this is particularly true when dominant interests differ from country to country. For example, in the early 1990s General Motors faced different priorities in different parts of the world. In South Korea, much higher wage-rate increases than the global average caused its Daewoo joint venture to put more emphasis on labor savings in production while profits suffered. In much of Western Europe, society as a whole (consumers and nonconsumers alike) demanded more pollution-abatement equipment on automobiles, while wages increased only moderately. In Mexico, new legislation tied GM's growth there to employment growth in its maquiladoras, thus putting emphasis on hiring more people in labor-intensive activities. Simultaneously, GM announced that it would use a surplus 2-liter-engine production line in China, where employment, compensation, and environmental cleansing gave way to stockholder profits and consumer prices.[3]

The most cumbersome problem in overseas relationships is not so much one of trying to serve conflicting interests within countries, but rather one of handling cross-national controversies in a manner that will achieve worldwide business objectives. The international company operates in a nationalistic world. Constituencies in any given country seek to fulfill their own, rather than global, objectives. For example, labor within the United States has not been very concerned about the number of global jobs created by their employers, such as jobs created in Mexico. Instead, U.S. labor groups have lobbied only for legislation to increase the number of jobs within the United States. This complicates management's task since decisions made in one country may have repercussions in another country as well. Among the many decisions managers must make are the location of production, decision making, and research and development (R&D); the method of acquisition and operation; the markets to be served from production; the prices to charge; and the use of profits. In the opening case, for example, many Canadians were concerned about such issues. Assume that a U.S. investor has production facilities in both the United States and Canada: Which facility will export to Venezuela? Clearly, the decision will determine where the profits, taxes, employment, and capital flows will be located. Interests in either country, as well as in Venezuela, may claim that they should have jurisdiction over the sales.

Management decisions made in one country have repercussions elsewhere.

Relative and Absolute Gains or Losses

An MNE's actions may affect a wide range of economic, social, and political objectives in a given country. A positive effect on one objective, such as full employment, may be concomitant with a negative effect on another objective, such as domestic control over economic matters. In other words, there must be trade-offs. A nation finds it difficult to prioritize objectives, since it naturally wants only benefits without costs, which is seldom possible to achieve. Despite the widespread effects on various parts of the social system, much of the literature analyzing MNEs is written to attempt to isolate effects to a single given objective, sometimes because a solution is needed for a given problem, such as a balance-of-payments deficit for a country. Very often, however, proponents or opponents of an MNE choose to publicize those activities that may win support to their way of thinking.

In international transactions involving MNEs people sometimes erroneously assume that if one party gains, the other must lose. While that may happen, it is also possible that both parties will either gain or lose in economic transactions. No party would participate willingly in a cross-national transaction in the belief that the deal would harm its priorities. Controversies develop because things do not work out as anticipated, because the precedence given to the trade-offs among objectives change, and because of disagreements over the distribution of gains when it is acknowledged that both parties have benefited overall. The last problem is at the heart of most controversies. As described in the opening case, Canada has tried to encourage foreign investment but to secure more benefit from it. This was done with the FIRA and later with different approaches through Investment Canada.

The effects of an MNE's activities may be simultaneously positive for one national objective and negative for another.

In an international transaction
- Both parties may gain
- Both parties may lose
- One party may gain while the other loses

Even when both parties gain, they may disagree over the distribution of the gain.

Countries want greater share of benefits from MNE activities.

Cause-Effect Relationships

That two factors have moved in relationship to each other does not prove an interconnection between them. Yet because of the growth of MNEs, a number of events in recent years have been attributed to them. Opponents of MNEs have linked inequitable income and power distribution, environmental debasement, and societal deprivation to the growth of international firms. Proponents have linked tax revenues, employment, and exports to the presence of MNEs. The linkages are particularly prone to arise when governments consider either restricting or encouraging an inflow of foreign investment. Although the data are often accurate and convincing, it is not certain what would have happened had MNEs not operated or followed certain practices. Technological developments, competitors' actions, and governmental policies are just three of the variables that encumber a cause-effect analysis.

It is extremely hard to determine whether societal conditions are caused by MNE actions.

Individual and Aggregate Effects

One astute observer has said, "Like animals in a zoo, multinationals (and their affiliates) come in various shapes and sizes, perform distinctive functions, behave differently, and make their individual impacts on the environment."[4] Thus it is difficult to make general statements about impacts. Yet much of the literature, from the viewpoints of both protagonists and antag-

The philosophy and actions of each MNE are unique.

onists, takes isolated examples and presents them as typical. The examples chosen usually make interesting reading because of their spectacular or extreme nature, but it is dangerous to make policies based on the exceptional rather than the usual.

Some countries have tried to evaluate MNEs and their activities individually. Although this might lead to greater fairness and control, it is a cumbersome and costly process. Therefore, many countries apply policies and control mechanisms to all MNEs. Although this eliminates some of the bureaucracy, it risks throwing out some "good apples" along with the bad. With these caveats on the difficulties of evaluating MNEs in mind, this chapter will examine their economic and political impacts.

ECONOMIC IMPACT OF THE MNE

Balance-of-Payments Effects

Place in the Economic System   Of international economic relationships few topics elicit as much discussion as the balance-of-payments effect of trade and investment transactions.[5] Discussion itself often leads to incentives, prohibitions, and other types of governmental interference as countries try to regulate the capital flows that parallel trade and investment movements.

The distinction between balance-of-payments arguments and other cross-national problems is that gains are a zero sum, meaning that one country's surplus shows up as another country's deficit. If both countries were looking only at a limited time period and if both were interested only in the balance-of-payments effect of international transactions, then one country might justifiably be described as a winner at the expense of the other. In fact, objectives are not this limited. A country may be willing to endure deficits in order to achieve other aims, such as price stability or growth, or it also may be willing to forgo short-term surpluses in favor of long-term ones or vice versa.

One country's surplus is another's deficit, but long- and short-term goals are different.

Effect of Individual Direct Investment   Two extreme hypothetical examples of the impact of direct investment illustrate the need to evaluate each activity separately if a person wants to determine the effect on the balance of payments. In the first case, a foreign firm purchases a Haitian-owned company by depositing dollars in a Swiss bank for the former owners. No changes are made in management or operations, so profitability remains the same. Dividends now are remitted to the foreign owners rather than remaining in Haiti, so there is a net drain on foreign exchange for Haiti and a subsequent influx to another country. In the next case, a foreign firm purchases unemployed resources (land, labor, materials, and equipment) in Haiti that it con-

The effect of individual direct investment may be positive or negative.

verts to the production of formerly imported goods. Because of rising demand, all earnings are reinvested in Haiti, so the entire import substitution is a gain in foreign exchange.

The formula to determine effect is simple, but the figures to put in the formula are questionable.

Most investments or nonequity arrangements (such as licensing or management contracts) fall somewhere between these two simplistic and extreme examples and are not evaluated so easily, particularly when policymakers attempt to apply regulations to fit aggregate investment movements. There are numerous measurement difficulties, but guidelines are gradually emerging and are being used by both recipient and donor countries. A basic equation for making an analysis is

$$B = m + x + c - (m^1 + x^1 + c^1)$$

where

B = balance of payments effect,

m = import displacement,

m^1 = import stimulus,

x = export stimulus,

x^1 = export reduction,

c = capital inflow for other than import and export payment, and

c^1 = capital outflow for other than import and export payment.

Although the equation is simple, the problem of choosing the proper values to assign is formidable. Take the case of the **net import change** (import displacement less import stimulus) that results from the direct investment. To determine the value of m, we would need to know how much would be imported in the absence of the foreign production capability. Clearly, the amount the firm has produced and sold locally is only an indication, since the selling price and quality of products may be different from what would otherwise be imported. Furthermore, some of the local sales may have been at the expense of local competitors. The value of m^1 should include equipment, components, and materials brought in for manufacturing the product locally. It should also include estimates of import increases due to upward movements in national income caused by the capital inflow. For instance, if national income were assumed to have risen $2 million from the investment and the marginal propensity to import were calculated to be 10 percent, imports should have risen by $200,000.

The **net export effect** (export stimulus less export reduction) is particularly controversial in donor countries, since conclusions vary widely depending on the assumptions made. The argument is much like the riddle of whether the chicken or the egg came first. For example, some critics in the United States have argued that when U.S. firms develop foreign production capabilities they merely substitute for what would otherwise be produced in the United States. These critics have argued that the foreign output sometimes is a substitute for U.S. exports and sometimes imported to displace domestic output. MNEs' response to the critics has been that moves abroad are defensive; that is, restrictions of foreign governments and shifts in cost advantages make foreign production inevitable. By moving abroad, U.S. MNEs pick up business that would otherwise go to foreign firms. MNEs have argued further that the investments stimulate exports from the United States because of the purchase by foreign subsidiaries of equipment, materials, components, and complementary products. Figures show, in fact, that U.S. companies investing the most abroad are the ones whose exports are also growing most rapidly.[6] Again, we must make assumptions about the amount of these exports that could have materialized had the subsidiaries not been established.

The **net capital flow** (capital inflow less outflow for other than import and export payment) is the easiest figure to calculate because of controls at most central banks. The problem in using a given year for evaluation purposes is the time lag between the outward flow of investment funds and the inward flow of remitted earnings from the investment. Thus what appears at a given time to be a favorable or unfavorable capital flow may in fact prove to be the opposite over a longer period. The payback period (the time it takes to recoup the capital outflow) is affected by differences in company philosophy, type of industry, ability to borrow locally, the host country's balance-of-payments situation, and the perception of relative risk in the recipient country. Consequently, the capital flows may vary widely from one project to another. A further complication arises because of the possibility that international companies transfer funds in disguised forms, such as through transactions between parent and subsidiary operations at arbitrary rather than market prices, thus misstating the real consequences of the investments.

Although the equation is useful for broadly evaluating the balance-of-payments effects of investments, it should be used with caution. In addition to some of the data problems mentioned earlier, an investment movement might have some indirect effects on a country's balance of payments that are not readily quantifiable. For example, an investor might bring new technological or managerial efficiencies that are then emulated by other firms. What these other firms do may therefore affect the country's external economic relations.

Aggregate Assumptions and Responses   In spite of the formidable task of evaluating investments from a balance-of-payments standpoint, there is near consensus that, while investments are initially favorable to the recipient country and unfavorable to the donor country, the situation reverses after some time. This occurs because nearly all investors plan eventually to remit to the parent organization more than they send abroad. If the net value of the foreign investment continues to grow through retained earnings, dividend payments for a given year ultimately may exceed the total capital transfers required for the initial investment. The time period before reversal may vary

The balance-of-payments effect of direct investments usually is
- Positive initially for the recipient country and negative for the donor
- Positive later for the donor country and negative for the recipient

substantially, and there is much disagreement as to the aggregate time span needed.

In the case of U.S. firms' direct investment abroad, for example, more than half of the net value increase in recent years typically has come from the reinvestment of funds earned abroad. This means that the increase in claims on foreign assets has *not* been coming primarily from a flow of capital to the foreign operations. It also means that the return flow of funds to the United States from foreign earnings exceeds the outward flow to increase investment abroad.

From the standpoint of donor countries, restrictions on the outflow of capital improve short-term deficits, since there should be an immediate improvement in the capital account of the balance of payments. But restrictions on outflows reduce future earnings and inflows from foreign investments. Consequently, the restrictions are useful only in buying the time needed to institute other means for solving payments difficulties.

Governments also have sought to attract inflows of long-term capital as a means of developing production that will either displace imports or generate exports. This has been particularly true of LDCs. They have sought locally manufactured production in order to ease dependence on their traditional agricultural products and raw materials. The problem for recipients, then, is how to take advantage of the benefits of foreign capital while also minimizing the long-run adverse effects on their balance of payments.

Many countries have tried to ensure that the long-term negative impacts of capital outflows are minimized. Sometimes countries have required that the valuation of new foreign investment be based only on contributions of freely convertible currencies, industrial equipment, and other physical assets but not on contributions of goodwill, technology, patents, trademarks, and other intangibles. These requirements are often tied into regulations in those countries on maximum repatriation of earnings. The maximum is stated as a percentage of foreign investment value; by holding down the stated amount of investment, eventual repatriation of earnings and the investment is minimized. In this respect, governments exert greater control over the prices of equipment brought in, especially when the investor is also the equipment supplier, so that the investment value is not overstated. Governments also are often interested in receiving part of the capital contribution in the form of loans and in local holdings of equity so that the future outward capital flow is reduced and has an upward limit.

Growth and Employment Effects

Unlike balance of payments, the growth and employment effects of MNEs are not necessarily a zero-sum game among countries. Early economists assumed that production factors were at full employment; consequently, a movement of any of these factors abroad would result in an increase in output abroad and a decrease at home. Even if this assumption were true, the gains in

Donors and recipients set policies to try to improve short- or long-term effects.
- Donors set outflow restrictions.
- Recipients set repatriation restrictions, asset valuation control, and conversion to debt as opposed to equity.

Growth and employment effects are not a zero-sum game because
- MNEs may use unemployed or underemployed resources

• The healthiest domestic
firms own the bulk of
foreign direct invest-
ment

the recipient country might be greater or less than the losses in the donor country.

The argument that both the donor and the recipient country may gain from direct investment is premised partly on the assumption that resources are not necessarily fully employed and partly on the industry-specific and complementary nature of capital and technology. A farm-machinery manufacturer may, for example, be producing maximally for its domestic and export market. This firm may not move easily into other product lines or use its financial resources to effect domestic productivity increases. By participating in the establishment of a foreign production facility the firm may be able to develop foreign sales without decreasing the employment of resources domestically. In fact, the firm may hire additional domestic personnel to manage the international operations. The firm may receive dividends and royalties from its capital and technology being used abroad, thus further increasing domestic income. The foreign facility may even stimulate export sales because of a need for components and replacement parts and because of the ability of the foreign operation to sell the companies' related products.

Donor Country Losses

Home-country labor
claims that jobs are
exported through direct
investment.

Donor Country Losses   As the largest donor country for foreign licensing and direct investment, U.S. policy understandably arouses some of the major critics of outward movements. One such critic is organized labor, which argues that foreign production often displaces what would otherwise be U.S. production. For example, a criticism of Stanley Works' movement of some tool production abroad was that it took place at the expense of domestic factory improvement, which might have made U.S. output more competitive.[7] Critics also cite many examples of highly advanced technology, which has been at least partially developed through governmental contracts and then transferred abroad. In fact, U.S. MNEs are now moving their most advanced technologies abroad and are even, in some cases, producing abroad before they do so in the United States. An example is General Dynamics' transfer of aerospace technology to Japan to produce fighter planes. According to critics, if General Dynamics did not transfer the technology, Japan would purchase the products in the United States, thus increasing employment and output. Furthermore, they argue that the technology transfer (mainly to Mitsubishi) will speed the process for Japan's seizing control of future global aircraft and electronics sales. On the other hand, Japan might have developed the technology itself had General Dynamics not made the sale, even though this would have delayed Japan's acquisition of aircraft.[8] Although the cases cited are few and may not be typical, there may nevertheless be instances of donor-country losses and simultaneous gains to recipient countries.

Recipient countries may
gain through
• More optimum use of
production factors

Recipient Country Gains   Most observers agree that an inflow of foreign resources by international firms can initiate increased local development through a more optimum combination of production factors and the utilization or upgrading of idle resources. The most common types of resource

- Utilization of idle
  resources
- Upgrade of resource
  quality

transmission are capital and technology, which investors may transfer simultaneously. A firm is motivated to move these resources because of the higher potential return in an area of shortage than in an area of abundance.

International firms may enable idle resources to be used. The mere existence of resources is no guarantee they will contribute to output. Oil production, for instance, requires not only the underground deposits, but also the knowledge of where to find them and the capital equipment to bring the oil to the surface. Production is useless without markets and transport facilities, which an international investor may be able to supply. The access to foreign markets, particularly the investor's home market, may be particularly important to developing countries that lack the knowledge and resources necessary to sell there. An example is the sale of Mexican asparagus in the United States under the recognized Green Giant label. U.S. consumers associate the brand with known quality; it might be prohibitively expensive for Mexican producers to gain the same brand recognition on their own.[9] Another less tangible aspect of this relationship may lead to greater resource utilization: Through exposure to new consumer products, the local labor force may develop new wants, encouraging them to work longer and harder to acquire the new goods and services.

The upgrading of resources by the international firm may be brought about through the education of local personnel to utilize equipment, technology, and modern production methods. Even such seemingly minor programs as those promoting on-the-job safety may result in a reduction of lost worker time and machine down time. The transference of work skills increases efficiency, thereby freeing time for other activities.

Recipient countries may
lose if MNE investments

- Merely replace local
  firms
- Take the best resources
- Destroy local entrepreneurship

Recipient Country Losses   Some critics have claimed that there are examples in which MNEs have made investments that domestic firms otherwise would have undertaken. The result may be the displacement of local entrepreneurship or the bidding up of prices without additional output.

Observers argue, for example, that by its ability to raise funds in various countries, the foreign firm can reduce its capital cost vis-à-vis local firms and apply the savings either to attracting the best personnel or to enticing customers from competitors through added promotional efforts. However, evidence of these arguments is inconclusive. Frequently, international firms do pay higher salaries and spend more on promotion than local firms; however, it is uncertain whether this results from external advantages or a required added cost of attracting workers and customers when entering new markets. Added compensation and promotion costs may negate any external cost advantages from access to cheap foreign capital. Additionally, in many instances, the local competition also has access to cheap capital.

Critics also contend that foreign investment destroys local entrepreneurship drives, which have an important effect on development. Since expectation of success is necessary for the inauguration of entrepreneurial activity, the collapse of small cottage industries when confronted with the consolidation efforts of large foreign enterprises may make the local population feel incapable of competing. However, the presence of multinational firms may either increase or decrease the level of competition in host-country markets.[10]

First, the foreign firm may itself serve as a role model that local talent can imitate. Furthermore, foreign enterprises buy many services, goods, and supplies locally and may thus stimulate local entrepreneurship. For example, the Bougainville Copper Limited (BCL) in Papua New Guinea established a development foundation to help set up new businesses. BCL has used local sources of goods and services and has contracted out many things that had formerly been done by company personnel.[11] In fact, the real entrepreneur will find areas in which to compete; consequently, in any country there are success stories that can be emulated.

Finally, it is frequently contended that the international firm absorbs local capital, either by borrowing locally or by receipt of investment incentives. This raises the cost of funds and/or makes insufficient funds available to local firms. Although subsidiaries have borrowed heavily in local markets and have exploited investment incentives, this link to the ability of local firms to finance expansion is unclear. In order for international firms to have a noticeable effect on the ability of local firms to secure capital, the amount of funds diverted to foreign investors would have to be larger in relation to the size of the capital market than is probably the case. Furthermore, there are few examples of international firms that acquire all resources locally; thus the additional resources brought in should usually yield a gain for the economy.

Host countries have at times not only prohibited the entry of foreign companies that were believed to inhibit local firms, but they have also restricted local borrowing and have provided incentives for firms to locate in depressed areas where resources are idle rather than scarce.

Of particular concern to many countries are foreign investments involving the purchase of local companies. The employment effects continue to be debated because of assumptions about what would have happened had the acquisition not taken place, particularly when the takeover is of a company that is not doing well. Consider Bridgestone's acquisition of Firestone. Firestone was already laying off workers, and Bridgestone reduced employment more through its restructuring. However, Bridgestone invested heavily to make the company competitive. It is impossible to say for certain whether there was more or less employment because of the acquisition. For this reason, the employment effects of recent foreign direct investment in the United States have been evaluated as both negative and positive.[12] Canada's Foreign Investment Review Act and its Investment Canada Act, discussed in the opening case of this chapter, typify the policies of many countries in that they treat acquisitions more carefully than foreign investments started from scratch.

General Conclusions   Clearly, not all MNE activities will have the same effect on growth in either the home or host country, nor are the effects easily determined. While there are dangers in attempting to categorize, the following generalizations are helpful in understanding the circumstances under which foreign investment is most likely to have a positive impact on the host country.[13]

Direct investment more likely generates growth

- In LDCs
- When product or process is highly differentiated
- When foreign firms have access to scarce resources
- When investment is in the more advanced of the developing countries

1. *Developed versus LDCs.* Developed areas such as Western Europe or Canada are more likely than LDCs to have domestic firms capable of undertaking investments similar to those in which foreign investors engage. Foreign investment in developed countries is therefore more likely to be merely a substitute for domestic investment, thus yielding less growth than in developing countries.

2. *The degree of product sophistication.* When the foreign investor undertakes production of highly differentiated products or process technologies, it is less likely that local firms in the host country could undertake similar production on their own. The differentiation may derive from product style, quality, or brand name in addition to technology.

3. *Access to resources.* When the foreign investor has access to resources that firms in the host country cannot easily acquire, it is more likely to generate growth rather than just to substitute for what local firms would otherwise do. Some of the resources would be capital, management skills, and access to external markets.

4. *Degree of development of a developing country.* Foreign investors are more likely to transfer technology and serve as role models for growth in the more economically advanced of the developing countries. In the least developed LDCs, the investment may have a negative impact on growth if the investment merely exploits cheap labor that would otherwise be subsisting.[14]

POLITICAL AND LEGAL IMPACT OF THE MNE

Nation-states are concerned that

- MNEs are a foreign policy instrument of their home government
- MNEs are independent of any government
- MNEs are pawns of the host government

Because of the size of many MNEs, there is much concern that they will undermine through political means the sovereignty of nation-states. The foremost concern is that the MNE will be used as a foreign policy instrument of its home government.[15] Since the home countries for nearly all MNEs are industrial countries, it is understandable that this concern is taken most seriously in LDCs, although it is not restricted to them. Two other sovereignty questions are raised less frequently. One is that the MNE may become independent of both the home and the host country, thus making it difficult for either country to take actions considered to be in the best societal interest. The other is that the MNE might become so dependent on foreign operations that a host country can then use it as a foreign policy instrument against the home or another country.

Extraterritoriality

Extraterritoriality occurs when governments apply their laws to companies' foreign operations.

When governments extend the application of their laws to the foreign operations of companies, the term used to describe the situation is **extraterritoriality.** Host countries generally abhor these situations, since they weaken the host country's sovereignty over local business practices. Companies likewise fear situations in which the home and foreign laws conflict, since settlement inevitably must be between governmental offices, with companies caught in the middle. Laws need not be in complete conflict for extraterritoriality to exist. Laws requiring companies to remit earnings or to pay taxes at home on foreign earnings certainly have affected foreign expansion and local governments' control over the expansion. French firms (such as Moët-Hennessy, Piper-Heidsieck, Tattinger, and Mouton-Rothschild) are prevented by French law from using the term *champagne* for the sparkling wine they produce in California.[16]

Although extraterritoriality may result from legal differences between any two countries, the United States has been most criticized for attempting to control its firms abroad. The criticism toward U.S. policies is due largely to U.S. firms' ownership of more direct investment than firms from any other country. But the U.S. government has probably gone to further lengths than governments in any other industrial country to control the actions of its firms abroad.

Trade Restrictions   At the forefront of criticism has been the U.S. government's attempt to apply its Trading with the Enemy Act to the foreign affiliates of U.S. firms to keep them from selling to certain unfriendly countries. This puts subsidiaries in such countries as France and Canada in a dilemma because the laws in those countries require that the sales be made.[17] More recently, a number of countries have agreed to prohibit shipments of certain goods to South Africa because of its racial policies. The same racial policies have led many states and institutions within the United States to hold only "South Africa-free" stocks within their portfolios, which has contributed directly to divestment of South African investments by U.S. MNEs. Through a series of presidential orders, foreign affiliates of U.S. firms have been prevented from making sales to such countries as South Africa, Libya, and Nicaragua, even though the orders violate the laws of some of the countries where the affiliates are operating. The Cuban situation has been a particularly thorny issue between Canada and the United States. Throughout most of the 1980s, the United States permitted foreign subsidiaries to sell to Cuba; however, legislation in 1990 changed this. The result was adverse Canadian opinion, which led to discussions on whether FDI from the U.S. should be limited and whether the free-trade agreement with the U.S. should be rethought. U.S. firms' subsidiaries also are restricted from participating in the Arab boycott of Israel, even though the boycott is a foreign policy instrument of the countries where the subsidiaries are located.[18]

Antitrust   A second area of criticism has been the case of antitrust action. The United States has at various times delayed its companies from acquiring facilities in foreign countries (e.g., Gillette's purchase of Braun in Germany), prevented its firms from acquiring facilities in the United States when taking over a company abroad (e.g., Gillette's purchase of a division of Sweden's Stora Kopparbergs Bergslags could not include that division's Wilkinson Sword subsidiary in the U.S.), forced firms to sell their interest in foreign operations (e.g., Alcoa's spin-off of Alcan), and restricted entry of goods produced by foreign combines in which U.S. firms participated (e.g., Swiss watches and parts).[19] The policies for which firms have been restrained have been legal in the countries where the actions took place. The Canadian cabinet, the British House of Lords, and the Australian parliament even enacted laws that forbade Gulf Oil, Rio Tinto Zinc, and Westinghouse from supplying information to the U.S. Justice Department about their participation in a uranium cartel outside the United States. The Canadian government was particularly outraged because it had been one of the principal organizers of the cartel.[20] From a reverse standpoint, the United States objected to the European Community's (EC) antitrust prosecution of IBM because it felt the EC did not have jurisdiction.

One of the cumbersome problems for U.S. firms has been the U.S. Justice Department's ambiguity regarding their associations abroad. This has been partially mitigated with publications on foreign merger guidelines, including case situations on how antitrust enforcement principles would be applied.[21] Included in the associations that might be subject to challenge are the participation in cartels to set prices or production quotas, the granting of exclusive distributorships abroad, and the forming of joint research and/or manufacturing operations in foreign countries. The United States also has signed a number of bilateral treaties with other industrialized countries so that they consult with each other on restrictive business practices.

Emerging Ethical Standards   There are a number of areas in which legal differences among countries enable or even require firms to operate differently among these countries. When home-country constituents hold ethical or moral values that vary greatly from those abroad, there has been a growing debate over whether home-country governments should regulate their MNEs in order to institute those values abroad. As in most ethical and value controversies, the arguments are frequently highly emotional. A number of these issues may lead to future extraterritorial application, such as requiring MNEs either to follow home country racial policies or to terminate operations in South Africa if South Africa does not move more quickly to dismantle its apartheid laws.

Frequently, regulations in a foreign country are less stringent than those at home because (1) the foreign country has not yet faced certain problems, (2) it is less sophisticated at anticipating the adverse effects of certain policies, or (3) it believes that the gains outweigh the adversities. A growing controversy in the United States concerns whether products withdrawn from U.S. sales because of hazardous effects can be exported for sale abroad. On one hand, people argue that the standards are designed for the United States and should not be imposed on other countries, which can freely block the entry of hazardous products. On the other hand, critics maintain that there is no biological or ethical reason for treating people differently on safety issues, and that "Made in America" should be a sign of quality and not a warning.[22] Pharmaceutical firms have been criticized for conducting tests on humans abroad that were not allowed in the United States and for selling items abroad that were not yet approved by the U.S. Food and Drug Administration. Closely related to this has been criticism for promoting dangerous products abroad that are, nevertheless, sold legally in the United States. At the forefront has been the controversy over U.S. tobacco exports to LDCs, where it is alleged that uneducated consumers are not aware of the dangers.[23]

Firms also have been faulted for being too cautious in what they do abroad. For example, the U.S. State Department criticized Eli Lilly & Co.'s refusal to sell its herbicide, tebuthiuron, to the United States government to use for eradication of coca plants in Peru. Lilly was concerned that the product was considered too potent to use on U.S. cropland, had not been tested in Peruvian soil conditions, and was still being tested as to health effects.[24] Similarly, the U.S. Defense Department criticized the German firm, Bayer, for refusing to let its U.S. subsidiary sell the U.S. Army chemicals that could be used to make poison gas.[25] These situations involve not only the possible problems of extraterritoriality already discussed, but also the question of whether home-country governments or international firms should try to impose their own standards on other countries.

Key Sector Control

Political concerns include
- Fear of influence or disruption of local politics
- Foreign control of sensitive sectors of the local economy

Closely related to the extraterritoriality concept is the fear that if foreign ownership dominates key industries, then decisions made outside of the country may have extremely adverse effects on the local economy or may exert an influence on local politics. This suggests two questions: (1) Are the important decisions actually made outside the host countries? (2) If so, are these decisions any different from those that would be made by local companies?

There are many examples of business decisions that can and have been made centrally, such as what, where, and how much to produce and sell and at what prices. These decisions might cause different rates of expansion in different countries and possible plant closings with pursuant employment disruption. Furthermore, by withholding resources or accepting strikes the international firm may affect other local industries adversely as well.

Some observers argue that governments generally have more control over companies that are headquartered in their own countries than they have over a subsidiary of a foreign firm. Since home-country operations usually comprise the largest single portion of activity for companies, they will generally go to greater lengths to protect their home position than their foreign ones. Furthermore, since virtually all board members, upper-level corporate officers, and stockholders are home-country nationals, the firm will tend to favor home-country objectives more than foreign-country objectives in conflict situations.

Political fears are based on the beliefs that international companies may serve as instruments of foreign policy for their home governments and that they also may be powerful enough to disrupt or influence local politics. The former fear is largely a carryover from colonial periods, when such firms as Levant and the British East India Company very often acted as the political arm of their home governments. This fear has resurfaced in the case of Japanese investment in the United States. Critics have pointed out that the Japanese government and Japanese firms lobby strongly to affect U.S. governmental policy. Together they spend more than all political parties spend for House and Senate elections, and more than the five most influential U.S. business organizations combined.[26]

There is also fear that powerful foreign firms, by withholding resources at the request of the home government, might influence the political process. In the mid-1970s, for example, the U.S. State Department requested that Gulf Oil suspend its Angolan operations in an effort to weaken Soviet-backed factions that were taking control of the government. Several months later Gulf received State Department permission to deal directly with the leftist government in order to resume operations. In the mid-1980s, the story was repeated for other U.S. firms operating in Libya and Nicaragua. Then in 1988 the U.S. government urged U.S. firms not to pay taxes or debts to the Panamanian government, because of its alleged drug dealings.[27] Not only newly emerging nations have been concerned. The French and British, for example, are anxious because if U.S. computer companies were to withhold output, they could create virtual havoc in the companies, research laboratories, and governmental offices that depend on them.

Aside from establishing policies that generally restrict the entry of foreign investment, countries have selectively prevented foreign domination of a so-called **key industry,** one that might affect a very large segment of the economy by virtue of its size or influence on other sectors. The nationalization of foreign-owned mining, utility, and transportation companies is an example of such protection. In other cases, the government has required management by local personnel in order to ensure that the entities can survive, if necessary, without foreign domination. Some sensitive areas, such as radio and television transmission stations in the United States, are simply off limits for foreign investment. In the United States since 1989, the President can halt any foreign investment that endangers national security, and national security is not defined in the legislation. The first use of the legislation prevented a Japanese firm, Tokuyama Soda Company, from acquiring General Ceramics.[28] In a few cases, governments have supported the development of competitive local firms, such as consortia of computer manufacturers (e.g., ICL in Britain, Telefunken and Nixdorf in Germany, and Siemens, CII, and Philips in Germany and the Netherlands) and consortia of aircraft producers (e.g., Messerschmitt-Boelkow-Blohm in Germany, British Aerospace in Britain, Aeritalia in Italy, and Construcciones Aeronautics in Spain to ward off foreign domination.[29]

State-owned Enterprises   When the foreign MNE is also a state-owned enterprise, the political concern about home-country control of these enterprises is different only in degree from other MNEs. Both may in time of conflict give in to the home-country interests; however, the state enterprise may be more prone to do so and do so more quickly. Home-government officials may be able to influence these firms more easily. Renault, for example, did not hesitate to transfer production from Spain to France in order to avoid employment reductions in the home country whereas a private French MNE may not have come to this decision as easily.[30]

MNE Independence

The discussion thus far has centered on the fear that international firms are unduly influenced by their home governments. Many observers also fear that these companies can, by playing one country against another, avoid coming under almost any unfavorable restrictions. For instance, if they do not like the wage rates, union laws, fair-employment requirements, or pollution and safety codes in one country, they can move elsewhere or at least threaten to do so. In addition, they can develop structures to minimize their payment of taxes anywhere. This ability to play off one country against another is more likely to be evident when negotiating initial permission to operate in a country and among countries within a regional trade agreement. For example, France has become less bureaucratic in approving FDI entries, a change that was implemented after an experience in which General Motors opened a plant in Spain to export to France after France had refused the GM entry.[31] However, the fact that, once operating, companies are generally reluctant to abandon fixed assets in one country to move abroad indicates that these charges are probably exaggerated. Furthermore, the country from which a firm moves can usually restrict the importation of the goods produced abroad under the more favorable conditions.

International firms can play one country against another but are reluctant to abandon fixed resources.

Host-Country Captives

Critics have made allegations that MNEs may become so dependent on foreign operations that they begin to try to influence their home government to adopt policies favorable to the foreign countries although those policies may not be in the best interests of the home government. Such assertions are difficult to support because there is always disagreement on what policy will lead to the "best interests." However, there are certainly many examples of lobbying efforts by MNEs seeking the adoption of policies that are more palatable to the people abroad with whom they are doing business. For instance, MNEs have lobbied for different U.S. treatment toward governments in Angola, Nicaragua, and South Africa.

Political Involvement

Historically foreign firms exerted a great influence on local politics.

There is concern that the foreign firm will meddle in local politics to foster its own objectives rather than local ones. As recently as 1949, an association of six European firms handled 66 percent of Nigeria's imports and 70 percent of its exports; other European firms had a virtual monopoly on shipping and banking. Because of this economic power, the foreign companies, through forced regulations, forbade Nigerian competition and employment except in the more menial and lower-paying activities. Despite the headline examples, such as the discovery in 1972 of offers by ITT to support a group that planned to overthrow the Chilean government, most evidence shows that international firms have avoided local political involvement in recent years. Even in the ITT situation, the argument could be made that the action was no different than that taken by many locally controlled firms facing nationalization. Nevertheless, such instances kindle fears of a return to earlier periods when some foreign investors did manage to pick local leadership supportive of their firm's activities, regardless of the effect on the local population.

Bribery

Extent   No discussion of the impact of MNEs would be complete without mentioning the disclosures in the 1970s of payments to governmental officials variously described as "scandalous," "improper," "extorted," "unauthorized," "questionable," and "illegal." Inquiries by the Securities and Exchange Commission (SEC) revealed that such payments amounted to several hundred million dollars.[32]

Payments to government officials have been widespread
- To secure business from competitors
- To facilitate services
- To assure safety

While much of the criticism has been vented against MNEs (especially those from the United States), it is interesting to note how widespread the practice has been. The investigations showed that officials in industrial as well as developing countries, foreign as well as U.S. nationals, communists as well as noncommunists, have all participated in bribery.[33] Bribery is commonplace in many countries, and international firms have conformed.

Motives   By far the biggest motive for the outlays was to secure business that otherwise might not be forthcoming at all or to obtain it at the expense of competitors. Payments were mainly for governmental contract sales, and some of the higher fees were in the area of aerospace. Second in importance were expenditures to facilitate governmental services that firms were entitled to receive but that officials otherwise would have delayed. Such services included product registrations, construction permits, and import clearances. Some firms acknowledged payments in order to reduce tax liabilities, and one (General Tire) paid to keep a competitor from operating in a specific country (Morocco). A group of rubber companies made payments through the Chamber of Rubber Manufacturers in Mexico to get the government to approve price increases that were controlled. Some companies reported payments because of extortion: These included Mobil's payments to forgo the closing of its Italian refinery and expenditures by Boise Cascade, IBM, and Gillette to protect the safety of their employees. Some of the payments were contributions to political parties, a practice that is legal in certain foreign countries but not allowed in the United States.

Methods   Most payments were in cash, but in some cases they included products made by the company, such as ITT's gift of a color television set to the managing director of Belgium's state telephone system. Some payments were made directly to governmental officials by the firms; however, most involved the use of intermediaries and/or organizations in third countries. The methods were diverse: For instance, a person influential in a purchasing decision or a relative of that person was sometimes put on the firm's payroll as a consultant; in other cases, that person was paid as a middleman at a fee that exceeded normal commissions. Another common practice was to overcharge a middleman or governmental agency and rebate the overcharge to an individual, usually in a foreign country, in order to evade taxes or exchange control. One firm (Pullman) even used its auditor to effect payment to a governmental official.

Some Consequences   Bribery scandals resulted in the replacement of chiefs of state in Honduras, Japan, and Italy. Prince Bernhard of the Netherlands resigned all his public functions after charges that he had accepted a $1.1 million payoff. Officials were jailed in a number of countries, such as Venezuela, Iran, and Pakistan. Sri Lanka canceled orders for Lockheed aircraft because of that firm's scandals elsewhere. Many observers contend that these disclosures helped the political parties in many countries that opposed large defense outlays.

Foreign Corrupt Practices Act   In 1977 the United States passed controversial legislation making certain payments to foreign officials illegal. Part of the controversy surrounding this legislation has been due to its vagueness and seeming inconsistencies. The vagueness stemmed from the fact that two different U.S. agencies could prosecute firms; however, the Justice Department since has published its interpretations of the laws and the Securities and Exchange Commission (SEC) has ceded its enforcement to the Justice Depart-

The present legislation is controversial because

- *Some payments are legal to expedite compliance with law, but others are not*

- Extraterritoriality issues emerge
- Business may be lost

ment.[34] One of the seeming inconsistencies is that it is perfectly legal to make payments to people to expedite their compliance with the law but illegal to make payments to other governmental officials who are not directly responsible for carrying out the law. For example, a $10,000 payment to a customs official to clear legally permissible merchandise would be legal, but even a small payment to a governmental minister to influence the customs official would be illegal.[35] The reason for allowing the expediting payments is that in many countries governmental officials will delay compliance of laws indefinitely until they do receive payments, although these payments may themselves be illegal in the country where they are paid.

Some of the objections are more fundamental. For the United States to impose its standards on its firms operating in other countries may be viewed in some cases as just another extraterritorial infringement. In fact, it may be viewed as a double standard in that U.S. governmental aid frequently is given as a bribe, with the understanding that the recipient country will grant political concessions in return. Furthermore, there is little effort to blame donors or suspend these government-to-government programs when it is discovered that officials in recipient countries have siphoned off aid funds for themselves.

Although the actions of U.S. MNEs have been highly publicized, U.S. MNEs did not invent bribery. At present there are still at least two unknowns: (1) to what extent do domestic firms and MNEs of other countries engage in the activities for which U.S. MNEs have been criticized? and (2) to what extent is business lost to those other firms as U.S. MNEs are heavily regulated in their activities abroad?

OPERATIONAL IMPACT OF INTERNATIONAL BUSINESS ACTIVITIES

The relationship between international firms and societies has generated so many allegations and controversies that it is impossible to examine all of them in this chapter. A number of them deal not so much with whether international business should take place but rather with some specific practices. These latter allegations apply to specific operational areas of management and can, fortunately, be examined in later chapters of the text. They are no less important than the overall areas discussed in this chapter and are listed as follows to illustrate the wide range of criticisms:

1. In transferring technology to LDCs, prices are set too high and sales are restricted too stringently (Chapter 15).

2. If a country attempts regulation, MNEs merely divest and move where regulations are less stringent (Chapter 16).

3. The centralization and control of key functions by MNEs in their home countries perpetuate a neocolonial dependence of LDCs (Chapter 17).

4. Sensitive information about countries is disseminated internationally by MNEs' global intelligence networks (Chapter 17).

5. MNEs introduce superfluous products that do not contribute to social needs and perpetuate class distinctions (Chapter 18).

6. MNEs avoid paying taxes (Chapter 19).

7. Through artificial transfer pricing, MNEs undermine attempts by governments to manage their economic affairs (Chapter 20).

8. The best jobs are given to citizens of the nation in which MNEs have their headquarters (Chapter 21).

9. Inappropriate technology is introduced by MNEs to LDCs (Chapter 21).

10. National labor interests are undermined because of the global activities of MNEs (Chapter 21).

LOOKING TO THE FUTURE   As long as there is nationalism, societies will compete to try to garner a larger share of the benefits from international companies. In the short term, most countries will probably welcome FDI. Debt problems limit the ability of LDCs and historically planned economies to access sufficient capital, except through investment inflows. Budget-deficit problems will likely make the United States take a positive stance toward receipt of FDI. The European Community will likely welcome investment inflows to attain the growth predicted from its unification. However, in the longer term, FDI may be less welcome. Historically, the attitudes toward foreign direct investment have tended to vary over time, with a tendency toward more FDI restrictions when economies are thriving. Yet, there is the possibility that if rapid growth does not occur in some of the LDCs and historically planned economies after receipt of substantial foreign investment, they may learn to regard as models such countries as Japan and South Korea, which have grown rapidly without much FDI.

The locus of MNE control will continue to be questioned. Some MNEs now have so many nationalities represented in their top management ranks (such as Nestlé, SKF, ABB, ICI, CPC, Coca-Cola, and Heinz) that it is difficult to accuse them of following home-country interests. However, their internationalization opens them to the criticism of acting in their own, rather than national, interests. Some other MNEs have few shares held outside their home countries and include practically no foreigners in high-level corporate positions. These include Sandoz, Volvo, Michelin, Matsushita, and United Technologies.[36]

SUMMARY   ■ Management must understand the need to compromise and satisfy the conflicting interests of stockholders, employees, customers, and society at large. Internationally, the problem is more complex because the relative strength of competing groups will vary by country. Furthermore, the satisfaction of interests in one country may cause dissatisfaction in another country.

■ The effects of MNEs are difficult to evaluate because of conflicting influences on different societal objectives, intervening variables that obscure cause-effect relationships, and the differences among MNE practices. Countries are interested not only in their absolute gains or losses, but also in their performance relative to other countries.

■ Since a balance-of-payments surplus in one country must result in a deficit elsewhere, trade and investment transactions have been scrutinized closely for their effects. However, countries often are willing to accept short-term deficits in favor of a long-term surplus or to achieve other economic gains.

■ The basic effects on the balance of payments of a foreign investment theoretically can be determined, but there are disagreements about many assumptions that must be made concerning the relationship to trade. Projects are so different that it is difficult to generalize and set effective policies to apply to large groups of investors.

■ Governments have attempted to use investment to improve their own balance-of-payments positions by such devices as regulation of capital flows, requirements of partial local ownership, limitation of local borrowing by foreign investors, and stipulations that a part of capital inflows be in the form of loans rather than equity.

■ The growth and employment effects of MNEs do not necessarily benefit one country at the expense of another. Much of the effect is due to the relative employment of resources with and/or without the MNE's activities.

■ MNEs may contribute to growth and employment by enabling idle resources to be used, by using resources more efficiently, and by upgrading the quality of resources.

■ Among the factors affecting growth and employment results are the location where MNEs operate, the product sophistication, the competitiveness of local firms, governmental policies, and the degree of product differentiation.

■ The political concerns about MNEs center around the possibilities that they might be used as foreign policy instruments of home or host governments or that they avoid the control of any government.

■ Extraterritoriality is the application of home-country laws to the operations of companies abroad. This sometimes leads to conflicts with host countries and may put the international firm in the untenable position of having to violate the laws of one country or the other.

■ Countries are most fearful of foreign control of key sectors in their economies since decisions made abroad may be disruptive to the local economic and political stability. Furthermore, foreigners then may have enough power to adversely affect local sovereignty. There have been numerous moves to restrict foreign ownership in these sectors.

C A S E
FOREIGN REAL-ESTATE
HOLDINGS IN THE
UNITED STATES[37]

In comparison with other countries, the United States has been relatively free of restrictions on foreign investors. There are few industries, primarily certain types of transportation and communication, in which foreign control is prohibited. These prohibitions have been based on the sensitivity of these areas in informing the public and moving essential commodities in time of crisis. Historically, the only period in which there was a widespread concern about foreign ownership was in the late 1800s, when temporary prohibitions were placed on foreign ownership of agricultural land. This history does not mean that direct investment cannot be prohibited. In 1987, for example, the U.S. Commerce and Defense Departments mustered sufficient complaints about national security that Fujitsu (Japan) cancelled its bid to acquire Fairchild Semiconductor. In 1989 the United States passed legislation to prevent takeovers that would have adverse effects on security. The United States has also been a relatively safe place for investments. The only confiscations have been of properties held by interests from enemy countries during the two world wars and the seizure of Iranian assets during the hostage crisis. More recently, the use of Libyan and Kuwaiti assets was frozen, but not expropriated. (One may argue that the Revolutionary War was a confiscation of thirteen English investments.) No wars have been fought on U.S. land for over one hundred years; thus the loss of property through political unrest has been negligible.

After World War II, direct investment flows were almost all out of the United States as U.S. companies took advantage of a strong dollar and a welcome by foreign governments to establish foreign facilities and position themselves well during the pursuant growth period. Foreign firms simply lacked the resources to make the equivalent reverse flows to the United States. In the late 1960s the U.S. Department of Commerce established offices to lure investors to the United States, and several states began including foreign firms as part of their industrial promotion efforts. Although direct investment into the United States accelerated, the movement went largely unnoticed by the general public. One of the reasons was that no approval by U.S. authorities was necessary before the establishment of an investment. Furthermore, it was not even necessary to register anywhere that a foreign investment had been made. Many of the investors maintained a low profile and were not known, even by governmental officials, to be foreign investors.

The Arab oil embargo of 1973 and publicity attendant on the substantial influx of direct investment to the United States during the next few years led to Congress's adoption of the International Investment Survey Act of 1976. Although studies were carried out to assess the nature of direct investment in the United States, and although a number of bills have been introduced to restrict foreign ownership, the United States basically has maintained an open-door policy. Subsequent legislation requiring a foreign direct investor to report the establishment of a new U.S. business or acquisition of an interest in an existing U.S. business became effective in 1979. This has not been enough to assure people who are concerned about the foreign influx. The purchase of Rockefeller Center by Mitsubishi bolstered U.S. nationalistic feelings. A 1988 poll showed that 78 percent of people in the United States favor "a law to limit the extent of foreign investment in American business and real estate."

Some of the criticism about foreign investment in the United States is in response to the more stringent control of investment in other countries. The attitude is one of "why don't we treat them as harshly as they treat us?" Much of

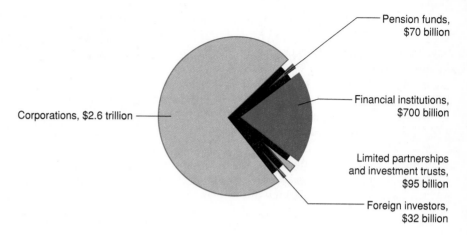

Pension funds,
$70 billion

Financial institutions,
$700 billion

Corporations, $2.6 trillion

Limited partnerships
and investment trusts,
$95 billion

Foreign investors,
$32 billion

Figure 12.1
U.S. Real Estate: Who Invests
Ownership of commercial real estate in the United States in 1989, including
property owned by government or religious organizations or directly by private
individuals. *Source:* The Roulac Group of Deloitte & Touche, "Real Estate Capital Flows,"
San Francisco, 1990.

the concern, though, has focused on specific key sectors deemed vital to the national interest, including banking, food, computers, high technology, oil, and coal. One of the areas that has been singled out is real estate, especially agricultural and residential land.

The Agricultural Foreign Investment Disclosure Act of 1978 now requires the reporting of agriculture land transfer to foreigners. The interest in real estate has evolved for a number of reasons. To begin with, it is a sector with an historical emotional tie among Americans: The country was largely settled by landless persons who were able to better themselves economically because of the availability of free or cheap land. Any threat of foreign control has been viewed negatively. Even with the so-called decline of the western frontier, Americans have placed a high priority on relatively cheap agricultural products and on housing. Numerous reports have alleged that large foreign real-estate purchases tended to inflate prices, especially in Hawaii because of Japanese investment. Many

Americans have feared that the rising prices will put land out of reach of the average American. There also has been fear that agricultural output will flow abroad rather than be sold to Americans.

But how widespread is foreign ownership? Figure 12.1 shows that only about 1 percent of U.S. real estate is foreign-owned. The U.S. Department of Agriculture estimates that less than one-half of 1 percent of American farmland is owned by foreign investors. Much of this has been acquired by foreign paper companies such as Bowater of Britain and Abitibi of Canada. Considerable publicity also has been given to foreign purchases of housing and office buildings in Miami, Honolulu, and Los Angeles, three areas in which foreign purchasers have been very active. The movement of funds (capital flight) from developing countries, particularly from corrupt dictatorships, has been massive as people have feared a risk in keeping their money in LDCs. Although no federal restrictions have been enacted, 20 of the 50 states have restrictions on ownership of property by aliens. Only three states (Iowa, Missouri, and Minnesota) have singled out agricultural property for special treatment. This was done in the late 1970s because of fear that foreign purchases would cause agricultural land prices to jump. In fact, in the 1980s the prices plummeted. Furthermore, in 1989 Japanese property investment in the United States fell 11 percent and purchases of U.S. office buildings fell 60 percent. By the 1990s U.S. land owners, real-estate brokers, and investment bankers were seeking out foreign buyers.

Questions

1. In the interests of the United States, should restrictions be placed on the foreign acquisition of real estate?
2. If restrictions were to be put in place, what should be restricted (e.g., type of land, nationality of purchaser, use of land, size of holdings)?
3. Should foreign ownership be restricted in sectors other than real estate?
4. What are the likely consequences if the United States does or does not place new limitations on foreign investment?

Chapter Notes

1. Data for the case were taken from "Limits Proposed to Canada Operations," *Wall Street Journal*, February 4, 1972, p. 8; "Canadian Brain Drain," *Wall Street Journal*, May 22, 1973, p. 1; "Canada Passes Law to Screen Investments Made There by Foreigners Starting in '74," *Wall Street Journal*, December 14, 1973, p. 21; Mitchell C. Lynch, "Canada to Tighten Foreign Ownership Rein Further as Economic, Job Pictures Improve," *Wall Street Journal*, May 4, 1973, p. 24; Edward Carrigan, "Canada Must Control Own Industry if It's to Progress," *Citizen* (Ottawa), June 27, 1980, p. 6; John Urquhart, "Canada Drive," *Wall Street Journal*, February 18, 1981, p. 1 ff; Herbert E. Meyer, "Trudeau's War on U.S. Business," *Fortune*, April 6, 1981, pp. 74–82; Harold Crookell, "The Future of U.S. Direct Investment in Canada," *Business Quarterly*, Vol. 48, No. 2, Summer 1983, pp. 22–28; "Canada Takes 'Positive' Step to Attract Foreign Investment," *American Banker*, January 2, 1985, p. 2; "Investment Canada: Invitation to Foreign Capital," *Mergers & Acquisitions*, Vol. 20, No. 4, March–April 1986, pp. 84–85; "America's Half-Open Door," *Economist*, Vol. 302, No. 7481, January 17, 1987, p. 66; John Urquhart and Peggy Berkowitz, "Northern Angst," *Wall Street Journal*, September 22, 1987, p. 1 +; D. J. Daly and D. C. MacCharles, *Canadian Manufactured Exports: Constraints and Opportunities* (Montreal: The Institute on Research on Public Policy, 1986); Brian Milner and Elizabeth Moore, "Auto Makers Masterful at Game of Incentives," *Globe & Mail* (Toronto), August 26, 1989, p. B16; United Nations Centre on Transnational Corporations, *Transnational Corporations in World Development* (New York: United Nations, 1988), pp. 213, 257.

2. For country data see *The World Bank Atlas, 1989* (Washington, D.C.: The World Bank, 1989); and for company data see "The World's 100 Largest Public Companies," *Wall Street Journal*, September 23, 1988, p. 18R.

3. Most of the examples were taken from *General Motors Public Interest Report 1990* (Detroit: General Motors Corp., May 15, 1990).

4. John H. Dunning, "The Future of Multinational Enterprise," *Lloyds Bank Review*, July 1974, p. 16.

5. The following discussion draws on problems reported in several studies that attempted to assess the balance-of-payments effects of direct investments. For a good example of opposing arguments and conclusions, see Richard Bernal, "Foreign Investment and Development in Jamaica," *Inter-American Economic Affairs,* Vol. 38, No. 2, Autumn 1984, pp. 3–21; and Ciaran O'Faircheallaigh, "Foreign Investment and Development in Less Developed Countries," *Inter-American Economic Affairs,* Vol. 39, No. 2, Autumn 1985, pp. 27–35.

6. Masaaki Kotabe, "Assessing the Shift in Global Market Share of U.S. Multinationals," *International Marketing Review,* Vol. 6, No. 5, 1989, pp. 54–69.

7. Louis Uchitelle, "The Stanley Works Goes Global," *New York Times,* July 23, 1983, p. F1 ff.

8. Stephen Kreider Yoder, "U.S. Defense Chief Approves an Accord with Japan for Joint Production of Jet," *Wall Street Journal,* June 6, 1988, p. 10; and Eduardo Lachica, "Politics & Policy," *Wall Street Journal,* April 10, 1989, p. A14.

9. David M. Henneberry, "U.S. Foreign Direct Investment in the Developing Nations: A Taxonomy of Host-Country Policy Issues," *Agribusiness,* Vol. 2, No. 1, 1986, p. 97.

10. Emilio Paguolatos, "Foreign Direct Investment in U.S. Food and Tobacco Manufacturing and Domestic Economic Performance," *American Journal of Agricultural Economics,* Vol. 65, No. 2, May 1983, pp. 405–412.

11. O'Faircheallaigh, *op. cit.,* p. 31.

12. See, for example, Thomas Omestad, "Selling Off America," *Foreign Policy,* No. 76, Fall 1989, pp. 119–140; "Foreign Investment in the United States," Hearing before the Subcommittee on Economic Stabilization of the Committee on Banking, Finance and Urban Affairs, House of Representatives, Serial No. 101–65 (Washington: U.S. Government Printing Office, 1989), pp. 21–23; and Edward M. Graham and Paul R. Krugman, *Foreign Direct Investment in the United States* (Washington: Institute for International Economics, 1990).

13. U.S. Department of Commerce, *The Multinational Corporation: Studies on U.S. Foreign Investment,* Vol. 1 (Washington, D.C., 1972), p. 61.

14. Jonghoe Yang and Russell A. Stone, "Investment Dependence, Economic Growth, and Status in the World System: A Test of 'Dependent Development,'" *Studies in Comparative International Development,* Vol. 20, No. 1, Spring 1985, pp. 98–120.

15. For a good discussion of various means of gaining political objectives through economic dependency, see Adrienne Armstrong, "The Political Consequences of Economic Dependence," *Journal of Conflict Resolution,* Vol. 25, No. 3, September 1981, pp. 401–428.

16. Frank J. Prial, "Wines of America: A Rich Harvest for Foreign Investors," *New York Times,* June 8, 1988, p. 15 ff.

17. "Review & Outlook: Exporting Leadership," *Wall Street Journal,* April 9, 1984, p. 28, gives recent examples of disagreements.

18. See, for example, "Anti-Boycott Charges Are Settled by Fines for Nine Companies," *Wall Street Journal,* October 13, 1983, p. 16; and Elizabeth Weiner and Laurence J. Tell, "Out of South Africa: Divestment Hits a Snag," *Business Week,* July 6, 1987, p. 53.

19. These are but a few of the types of antitrust actions. See J. Townsend, "Extraterritorial Antitrust Revisited—Half a Century of Change." Paper presented at the Academy of International Business, San Francisco, December 1983; and "U.S. Seeks to

Block Gillette's Purchase of Wilkinson Assets," *Wall Street Journal,* January 11, 1990, p. B6.

20. "Extraterritorial Trouble," *Wall Street Journal,* December 20, 1979, p. 7; and "Down under with the U.S. Courts," *Wall Street Journal,* May 1, 1981, p. 24.

21. Eleanor M. Fox, "Updating the Antitrust Guide on International Operations—A Greener Light for Export and Investment Abroad," *Vanderbilt Journal of Transnational Law,* Vol. 15, Fall 1982, pp. 713–766.

22. Irvin Molotsky, "Exporting Products Recalled in the U.S.," *New York Times,* April 3, 1984, p. A17; Keith Schneider, "Pesticide Makers Fight Export Curb," *New York Times,* August 26, 1990, p. A17.

23. Paul Magnusson, "Uncle Sam Shouldn't Be a Traveling Salesman for Tobacco," *Business Week,* October 9, 1989, p. 61; Philip J. Hilts, "Health Department Backs Away on Criticism of Tobacco Exports," *New York Times,* May 18, 1990, p. A1 ff.

24. "Lilly Won't Sell Herbicide to U.S. for Anti-Coca Use," *Wall Street Journal,* May 25, 1988, p. 36.

25. "Bayer Refuses to Sell U.S. a Chemical for Poison Gas," *Wall Street Journal,* March 29, 1990, p. A11.

26. Pat Choate, "Political Advantage: Japan's Campaign for America," *Harvard Business Review,* Vol. 68, No. 5, September–October 1990, pp. 87–103.

27. "Gulf Oil Seeks Talks to Resume Operations under Angola Regime," *Wall Street Journal,* February 24, 1976, p. 17; Rose Gutfeld, "U.S. Urges Firms Not to Pay Taxes, Debts to Noriega," *Wall Street Journal,* April 1, 1988, p. 30.

28. Clyde H. Farnsworth, "U.S. Stops Japanese Acquisition," *New York Times,* April 18, 1989, p. D1 ff.

29. Tim Carrington, "Europe's Plan to Build New Fighter Plane Puts Western Firms on Cutthroat Course," *Wall Street Journal,* May 23, 1988, p. 10.

30. Renato Mazzolini, "Government Policies and Government Controlled Enterprises," *Columbia Journal of World Business,* Fall 1980, pp. 47–54.

31. E. S. Browning, "France Now Tries to Offer Welcome to Japanese Firms," *Wall Street Journal,* April 20, 1989, p. C15.

32. "Questionable Payments Total Put at $412 Million," *Wall Street Journal,* January 21, 1977, p. 2.

33. See, for example, Richard H. Heindel, "American Business Bribery Shakes the World—Can Americans Remake It?" *Intellect,* April 1977, p. 313.

34. Jerry Landauer, "Agency Will Define Corrupt Acts Abroad by U.S. Businesses," *Wall Street Journal,* September 21, 1979, p. 23; Stan Crock, "SEC to Clarify Ban on Foreign Payoffs, Would Cede Power to Justice Department," *Wall Street Journal,* June 16, 1981, p. 10.

35. John S. Estey and David W. Marston, "Pitfalls (and Loopholes) in the Foreign Bribery Law," *Fortune,* October 9, 1978, pp. 182–188.

36. William J. Holstein, Stanley Reed, Jonathan Kapstein, Todd Vogel, and Joseph Weber, "The Stateless Corporation," *Business Week,* May 14, 1990, p. 103.

37. Data for the case were taken primarily from "Foreign Share of Farms, 0.5%," *New York Times,* January 28, 1980, p. D1; *International Report,* International Chamber of Commerce, August 29, 1980, p. 3; *International Report,* July 25, 1979, p. 3; "Overview of Restrictions on Foreign Ownership of Agricultural Land in the United States," unpublished report of the law offices of Dechert Price & Rhoads, submitted to the International Business Forum of Pennsylvania Briefing Courses, 1980; Cindy Skrzycki and

Maureen Walsh, "America on the Auction Block," *U.S. News & World Report,* Vol. 102, No. 12, March 30, 1987, pp. 56–58; Pat Houston, "Buy Your North 40 While It's Dirt-Cheap," *Business Week,* No. 2995, April 20, 1987, p. 92; Martin Tolchin and Susan Tolchin, "Foreign Money, U.S. Fears," *New York Times Magazine,* December 13, 1987, pp. 63–68; Walter S. Mossberg, "Most Americans Favor Laws to Limit Foreign Investment in U.S., Poll Finds," *Wall Street Journal,* March 8, 1988, p. 28; Cynthia F. Mitchell, "Buying America," *Wall Street Journal,* April 28, 1988, p. 1; Elisabeth Rubinfien, "The Price Is Right," *Wall Street Journal,* June 15, 1988, p. 1+; Joan Lebow, "The Flow of Money into Real Estate," *Wall Street Journal,* July 24, 1989, p. B1; "Is U.S. Real Estate Leaving the Japanese Cold?" *Business Week,* July 23, 1990, p. 20.

CHAPTER **13**

INTERNATIONAL BUSINESS DIPLOMACY

Without trouble there is no profit.
AFRICAN (HAUSA) PROVERB

Objectives

- To show the complementarity of interests between nation-states and multinational firms.

- To illustrate negotiations between business and government in an international context.

- To trace the changing involvements of home-country governments in the settlement of MNE disputes with host governments.

- To highlight the collective means by which firms and/or governments may seek to strengthen their positions vis-à-vis one another.

- To clarify the role of external relations in international business-governmental conflicts.

- To explain the position of firms and governments in the uneven global enforcement of intellectual property rights.

Saudi Arabia has one quarter of the world's known reserves and is the largest exporter and second-largest producer (after the former Soviet Union) of petroleum. By the early 1990s one company, Aramco, accounted for over 90 percent of the Saudi production and more than double the output of the two next-largest oil firms in the world, Royal Dutch Shell and Exxon. Aramco's ownership, policies, and division of earnings from the outset have depended on interactions among: (1) the private oil companies participating in Aramco, (2) the U.S. government, and (3) the Saudi government. As the objectives and power of these three parties have evolved, so have the operations of Aramco. To understand these changing relationships, we will review some events that preceded Aramco's first oil output in 1939.

U.S. policy toward U.S. oil firms historically has seemed contradictory because governmental objectives have involved trade-offs as well as changing priorities among the objectives. U.S. objectives have included preventing domestic monopolistic practices by oil firms, ensuring sufficient and cheap oil supplies for U.S. needs, and strengthening the U.S. political position in strategic areas worldwide. On the one hand, U.S. action dismembered the Standard Oil Trust in order to stimulate domestic competition; on the other hand, the U.S. government allowed, even encouraged, joint actions abroad by oil firms when those actions would help achieve the latter two objectives.

At least as far back as 1920 the United States realized that in the long run its domestic oil supplies would be insufficient. In the short term, though, worldwide oil supplies could not easily be sold as rapidly as they could be produced. In this environment, U.S. oil firms were in a position to serve both U.S. and Middle East interests. In the 1920s and 1930s the U.S. government wanted U.S. oil companies to gain concessions in the Middle East with the result that "representatives of the industry were called to Washington and told to go out and get it." Concessions would help assure a long-term U.S. supply, and an American presence would weaken the relative positions of the British and the French. The U.S. firms were welcomed in the Middle East as competitors to Shell Oil Company, British Petroleum (BP), and Compagnie Française des Pètroles (CFP) from Britain and France. They also were welcomed because they offered some sales in the United States that would otherwise be impossible.

CASE
ARAMCO[1]

During the 1920s and 1930s some of the U.S. oil companies also made secret arrangements abroad that proved unpopular with the U.S. public. For example, Exxon (formerly called Esso, or Standard Oil of New Jersey) agreed with BP and Shell to a system of world prices based on the U.S. price of oil. Exxon's chief executive was forced to resign in 1942 after exposure of his restrictive agreements with the I. G. Farben Company, a major participant in Hitler's World War II efforts. In situations such as these, the oil companies were not acting as instruments of American foreign policy as they were originally conceived to do; instead, they were acting independently of any government. Later they were accused of becoming captive to Middle Eastern Arab policies.

The first two companies to participate in Saudi Arabian oil production were Socal (Standard Oil of California) and Texaco, which formed a joint venture and negotiated large concessions. The U.S. government had no representatives in Saudi Arabia at this time, and the two companies conducted some quasi-official diplomacy that continued throughout World War II. They organized construction of a pipeline to the Mediterranean in 1945 and received permission from the U.S. government to use steel, which was in very scarce supply. In 1948 Exxon and Mobil joined the original Socal and Texaco in what became known as Aramco. Mobil owned 10 percent, and each of the others held a 30 percent interest.

These four firms, along with three others (Gulf, Shell, and BP), were known as the Seven Sisters. Before the 1970s they collectively controlled such a large share of the world's oil from multiple sources that they were nearly invulnerable to the actions of any single country. By 1950 the United States was entrenched in the cold war, and although it held military supremacy over the former Soviet Union, the Truman Administration wished to maintain cordial relationships with strategic countries. When King ibn-Saud demanded substantial revenue increases from Aramco, the U.S. government became directly involved in the negotiations. A plan was devised in 1951 whereby the oil companies would maintain their ownership but would pay 50 percent of Aramco's profits as taxes to Saudi Arabia. The companies then could deduct those taxes from their U.S. tax obligations so that, in effect, the increase in revenue to Saudi Arabia was entirely at the expense of the U.S. Treasury.

In 1952 Saudi Arabia learned from Iran's experience what might happen if demands on Aramco were pushed further. Iran expelled Shah Reza Pahlevi and nationalized British oil holdings. All major oil companies boycotted Iranian oil and brought the Mossadegh government to the brink of economic collapse. With CIA support, the Shah returned, and the Seven Sisters shared in 95 percent of the ownership of the new Iranian oil company.

Both Presidents Eisenhower and Kennedy proclaimed the importance to U.S. foreign policy of the oil firms' Middle East activities and intervened to prevent antitrust action against them in their joint dealings abroad. In addition to preventing Soviet entry in the Middle East, the United States was able to sidestep certain Arab-Israeli conflicts by being publicly pro-Israel and having the Aramco partners perform most of the direct interactions with Saudi Arabia. Saudi Arabia was unhappy with U.S. policies toward Israel but could not influence them.

When the Seven Sisters gained 95 percent of the Iranian oil holdings, the other 5 percent went to smaller independent U.S. companies that previously had depended on the Seven Sisters for supplies. This marked the beginning of greater competition among distributors; it also meant that countries could make agreements with the independents to gain a greater portion of the spoils. Yet as late as 1960 the producing countries were still unable to prevent the major firms from unilaterally abrogating concessions by reducing the price they paid for oil. This price decrease, which reduced government revenues of petroleum exporting countries, led to a meeting in Caracas of five governments and the resultant formation of the Organization of Petroleum Exporting Countries (OPEC). OPEC's purposes were to prevent companies from unilaterally lowering prices, to gain a greater share of revenues, and to move toward domestic rather than foreign ownership of the assets. Still, in the early 1960s OPEC lacked the power to flex its muscles.

In the 1960s three new trends weakened the Seven Sisters and strengthened Saudi Arabia's position in Aramco. First, there was continued emergence of other oil companies that made concessions in countries previously not among the major suppliers, such as Occidental in Libya, ENI in the former Soviet Union, and CFP in Algeria. These smaller companies lacked the Seven Sisters' diversification of supplies and thus were less able to move to other supply sources if a country tried to change the terms of agreement unilaterally.

Second, because of rapidly expanding industrial economies, oil demand was growing faster than supply; the earlier oil glut was quickly becoming an oil squeeze. Not even the Seven Sisters could afford any longer to boycott major supplier countries as they had earlier boycotted Iran.

Third, there was a lessened threat of military intervention to protect oil investors. The failure of the United States to support the abortive efforts of the British and French to prevent the Egyptian takeover of the Suez Canal demonstrated that the major Western powers were unlikely to unify their efforts. Although it had invaded Lebanon successfully in 1958, the United States was less prone to intervene again in the Middle East because the Soviet Union had grown stronger since 1958, thus presenting a greater risk of a major war resulting from intervention. The United States also was increasing its military involvement in an unpopular war in Vietnam, so it was less able to lend military support to its oil firms in the Middle East.

In 1970 Muammar el-Qaddafi of Libya demanded increased prices from Occidental. Since Occidental was almost completely dependent on Libya for crude, the company relented. Qaddafi then confronted the major firms that no longer had sufficient alternative supplies and gained concessions from them as well. Libya's success was noted in other countries, which used OPEC to further strengthen their negotiating positions by dealing collectively with the oil firms. The Teheran Agreement of 1971 immediately increased prices. The embargo by Arab OPEC members in 1973 demonstrated that they had sufficient power to impose further economic demands and to

cause Western powers to modify their political positions, particularly in relation to Israel. OPEC now had eleven members and controlled about 93
percent of the world's oil exports.

As the largest OPEC producer, Saudi Arabia has been able to utilize its
new-found strengths in several ways. Between 1972 and 1980 the government of Saudi Arabia bought a 100 percent ownership in Aramco operations. As smaller firms gained a larger share of the world oil sales and as
national governments in Sweden, the former West Germany, Japan, and
France began buying directly from oil-producing countries, Saudi Arabia
has increased the number of customers for its crude from the original four
Aramco partners.

How has Aramco's government-owned status affected Exxon, Texaco,
Socal, and Mobil's operations in Saudi Arabia? The companies have been
able to exploit their many assets successfully in order to maintain a profitable presence vis-à-vis Saudi Arabia. They have realized that Saudi Arabia's
increased oil revenues enable the Saudis to be a lucrative customer; they
also know that Saudi Arabia is closely allied to the West, particularly the
United States, on whom it depends for technical and defense assistance.

The four oil companies continue to help manage the Saudi oil industry
because they can make contributions that the Saudis cannot acquire easily
from other sources. As the major employer before government purchase
into Aramco, the American partners had demonstrated an ability to attract
qualified personnel from abroad, to train Saudis, and to run an efficient operation. As Aramco has expanded and moved into new activities, the oil
firms have been able to continue these efforts through lucrative contract arrangements. For example, in 1990 Mobil was a joint venture partner in a
refinery and a petrochemical complex with the Saudi government, each
worth over $1 billion. By 1991 about 12,000 (one quarter) of Aramco's em-
ployees were non-Saudi workers, but foreigners had been replaced in nearly
all top managerial positions. There was a near consensus that foreigners
would be needed in increasingly technical positions, such as in finding and
extracting oil, but engineering firms, such as Bechtel and Fluor, were competing with the oil firms for major contracts.

The oil firms' contributions to Aramco's success thus include some continued day-to-day management, the contracting of foreign workers, the infusion of technology, the training of Saudi personnel, and the marketing of
crude oil exports when sales are not made directly to a foreign government.
The marketing contribution took on more importance in the late 1980s,
when there was a glut brought about by new supplies (e.g., from Mexico)
and decreased demand. To ensure future sales, in 1988 Aramco entered a
joint venture by buying a 50 percent interest in Texaco's refining assets and
marketing system in 23 U.S. states. However, in 1990 Saudi Arabia's future
ability to supply petroleum was brought into question when Iraq occupied
Kuwait and amassed its armed forces on the Saudi Arabian border. The

threat to Saudi oil supplies was an important factor in the U.S. decision to push for the United Nations' 1991 liberation of Kuwait.

The oil firms also have been important in molding U.S. foreign policy through lobbying and advertising campaigns that proclaim, "We would like to suggest that there is only one realistic possibility: that the United States adopt a neutral position on the Arab-Israeli dispute and a pro-American rather than a pro-Israel policy in the Middle East." Given these contributions to Saudi Arabia, the oil companies have been able to sell their Aramco interest at prices reported to be above the net book value of assets. They have successfully secured a continued source of crude oil, although sometimes at a contract price above the world spot price, and have profited from management and technical contracts.

In the aftermath of Kuwait's liberation, the future strength of the Seven Sisters is in question. The destruction of oil facilities in Iraq and Kuwait may make consumers (including the oil firms) even more dependent on Saudi oil, thus strengthening the Saudi government's power in relationship to consumers. But there was no shortage of world oil during the war with Iraq. At the same time, the growing dependence of Saudi Arabia on U.S. military assistance might lead to more government-to-government negotiations, thus bypassing the Seven Sisters.

INTRODUCTION

The operating terms of international firms

- Are influenced by home and host governments
- Shift as priorities shift and as strengths of parties change

The Aramco case illustrates that the terms under which companies operate abroad are greatly influenced by both home- and host-country policies and that the terms change over time as governmental priorities shift and the relative strengths of the parties evolve. The relative strengths were shown to be affected by such factors as competitive changes, the resources that parties have at their disposal, validating public opinion, and joint efforts with other parties.

As discussed in Chapter 12, companies' foreign operations may have diverse effects on home and host countries, but there is substantial disagreement as to what these effects are and how to deal with them. There is, however, agreement on the point that governments and businesses frequently attempt to follow conflicting courses. In fact, a discord, if carried to the extreme, may result in a cessation of the particular business-government relationship, as either (1) firms refuse to operate in the locale, or (2) governments refuse to grant original or continued operating permission. Short of the extreme are practices that, although not deemed ideal by either party, nevertheless are sufficiently satisfactory to permit an evolving relationship. This chapter examines the means by which international businesses and governments attempt to improve their own positions vis-à-vis one another.

NEEDS AND ALTERNATIVES FOR FULFILLMENT ▮▮▮▮▮▮▮▮▮

Nature of Assets

Investor firms and host countries have mutually useful assets.

The international firm and the host country each may control assets that are useful to the other. There is thus an inducement to agree on the establishment of operations and to ensure that the operations continue functioning. The foreign firm may be able to bring in locally scarce resources in the form of capital, management talent, raw materials, and technology. These resources, in turn, may be used to foster local growth, employment, and balance-of-payments objectives. The foreign investor also may have access to or control of foreign markets through the ownership of the facilities that make import purchases. International firms may use these multiple facilities to contribute positively to the export development of countries in which they do business. They also may negatively affect the exports of domestic firms by denying them sales access to their operating facilities in other countries, by aggressively competing with them, or by pressuring home-country governments to erect barriers to the importation of foreign-made production. Finally, MNEs may be able to take on commercial risks that governments otherwise might have to undertake with funds borrowed in international markets.

Countries likewise have assets to offer foreign investors. First, they offer access to their own markets, which may be available only through the establishment of local production. The country also offers unique resources in the form of land needed for agricultural production, raw materials, port facilities, cheap or specialized labor, and reasonable interest rates on funds. In fact, the acquisition of some of these resources may be a requirement for the company to maintain a viable competitive position elsewhere in the world.

Strengths of the Parties

Alternative sources for acquiring resources affect company/country bargaining strengths.

If either a company or country has assets that the other strongly wishes to acquire and if there are few (if any) alternatives for acquiring them, negotiated concessions may be very one sided. For example, when a few large oil companies dominated the extraction, processing, shipment, and final sale of an oversupply of petroleum, developing countries with oil deposits could do little but accept the terms that the oil firms offered. If a government refused, a firm easily could find another country that would accept a similar proposal. As the supply of petroleum diminished and petroleum-producing countries found alternative means for exploiting their resources, the terms of the concessions gradually evolved more in favor of the oil-producing countries. But shifts are not always in favor of countries: Mexico, for example, was such a growing economy during the 1970s that it could require foreign firms to accept a minority position when establishing operations. However, in the 1980s oil prices plummeted and capital left Mexico because of fear of the slipping economy. Mexico loosened its regulations to allow majority and even 100 percent foreign ownership. As expected, there are vast differences in bargaining strength among countries, among industries, and among firms.

The strongest company bargaining assets include

- Technology
- Product differentiation
- Ability to export output
- Local product diversity

Company Bargaining Strength   Although companies have a variety of assets that they can contribute to their foreign operations, some assets have traditionally put them into better bargaining positions than others. Retailers traditionally had more difficulty gaining operating permission than manufacturers, especially in developing countries, because local governments believed (sometimes falsely) that local people can do equally well in retailing but that foreign help is needed in manufacturing. However, there has been a spurt in foreign retailing investment during the last few years. Foreign ownership in such areas as agriculture and extractive industries is not very welcome in many countries because of historical foreign domination of these sectors and belief that the land and subsoil are public resources.

The bargain struck between the foreign investor and the host country is influenced by the resources brought in by the investor and the number of firms offering similar resources.[2] Foreign investors are more likely to be able to gain a high percentage of ownership in foreign operations when they have few competitors and when they control certain types of assets. One of these assets is technology. IBM, for example, has been allowed 100 percent ownership in a number of countries because of the local need for its unique technology, whereas other firms were refused. Another asset is the control of a well-known branded product. Coca-Cola, for example, apparently has been able to gain local consumer allies who believe its differentiated products are superior. A third asset is the ability to export output from the foreign investment, especially when exports go to other entities controlled by the parent. These investments gain foreign exchange that might otherwise not be forthcoming. General Motors, for example, has been allowed 100 percent ownership of its Mexican maquiladora operations but shares ownership in its other manufacturing facilities serving Mexican consumers. Finally, the greater the product diversity, the more foreign ownership allowed. This is probably because a variety of products offers a greater future opportunity to save foreign exchange through import substitution.

Surprisingly, the amount of capital needed to set up operations has not usually affected investors' bargaining power. At least two factors have influenced this: (1) a large investment may be examined much more closely than a small one because of the potential impact (positive or negative) it might have on the economy (i.e., the host country wants the benefits of the capital inflow but is leery of being so dependent on foreign ownership); (2) the government may be more prone to borrow funds externally to invest in large enterprises. However, the ability to contribute large amounts of capital may improve future bargaining strengths of companies. As many Third World countries have encountered debt-servicing problems since the mid-1980s, they must depend more on direct investment for their future capital needs. Yet the size of the potential investor may be a factor inasmuch as governments may not wish to commit resources to negotiation with firms that are too small to make a substantial impact. For example, Nigeria will negotiate the barter of oil for imports, but only with firms whose sales are at least U.S. $100 million per year.[3]

Country Bargaining Strength   Generally speaking, firms prefer to establish investments in highly developed countries, which offer large markets and a high degree of stability. On a national basis, countries such as the United States, Canada, and Germany make few concessions to foreign investors; they are large recipients of investment without having to make special arrangements. In all three of these countries, however, there are differences in treatment between advanced and depressed areas.

Home-Country Needs

Thus far we have implied that terms of operations are highly dependent on the interplay of needs between the MNE and the host country. Although this is true, it overlooks the role of the home country. Although concerns vary widely among home countries, the home country seldom takes a neutral position in the relationship. Like the host government, the home-country government is interested in achieving certain economic objectives (such as tax receipts and full employment) and may give incentives to or place constraints on the foreign expansion of its firms in order to gain what it sees as its due share of the rewards from transactions. The home government has direct political interests with the host government that temper its position as well.[4]

The influence of home governments is illustrated by the efforts made when France was selling off interests in its government-owned companies during the mid-1980s. The U.S. government interceded to pressure the French government to accept AT&T's bid to take over CGCT, the French government-owned switchmaker, by threatening to bar U.S. government purchases of French equipment. Chancellor Helmut Kohl of Germany personally lobbied French Prime Minister Jacques Chirac on behalf of Siemen's bid for CGCT. Caught between two powers, the French government accepted the bid of a Swedish firm, Ericsson.[5]

Other External Pressures

The complementary nature of the assets that international firms and countries control would seem, at first, to dictate a mutual interest in finding means to ensure that mutual benefits are developed. While there are pressures to do this, there are other constraints as well, particularly on governmental decision makers, who may have to act in ways not in the best interest of their country. Pressure may come from local companies with which the foreign investor is presently or potentially competing, from political opponents who seize the "external" issue as a means of inciting an unsophisticated population against present political leadership, or from critics who reason that more benefits may accrue to the country through alternative means. Managers also may face pressures from stockholders, workers, consumers, governmental officials, suppliers, and other interest groups outside the country who are concerned with their own interests rather than the achievement of worldwide corporate objectives. These stresses may result in a business–host-country relationship quite different from what might be expected on a purely economic basis. Each party should understand the types and strengths of these external groups, since they affect the extent to which either side may be able to give in on issues under discussion.

NEGOTIATIONS IN INTERNATIONAL BUSINESS

Terms for investments and licensing are often two-tiered.

Increasingly, negotiations are used as a means of deciding the terms by which a company may function or terminate operations in a foreign country. At one time these negotiations prevailed only for direct investments; more recently, however, they have sometimes been extended to other operating arrangements, such as licensing agreements, debt repayment, and large-scale export sales. Although the following discussions highlight investment negotiations, most of the points apply to other forms of operations as well. The negotiation process often leads to two-tiered bargaining: An MNE must first come to an agreement with a local firm in order to purchase an interest in it, sell technology or products to it, or loan money to it; once that accordance is set, a governmental agency may approve, disapprove, or propose an entirely different set of terms. Even when the government is not directly involved in a negotiation, its needs may be taken into consideration by the participants.

Bargaining Process

Acceptance Zones   Before becoming involved in overseas negotiations, a manager usually will have some experience in a domestic bargaining process that is somewhat similar to that in the foreign sphere. For example, collective-bargaining negotiations with labor, as well as agreements to acquire or merge facilities with another firm, usually start with an array of proposals from both sides, just as in negotiations with a foreign country. The total package of proposals undoubtedly includes provisions on which one side or the other is willing either to give up entirely or to compromise. These are used as bargaining tokens, permitting each side to claim that it is reluctantly giving in on some point in exchange for compromise on the part of the other, as well as face-saving devices, which allow either side to report to interested parties that

In the bargaining process, agreement occurs only if there are overlapping acceptance zones.

it managed to extract concessions. On certain other points, it is unlikely that compromise can be reached.

As in a domestic situation, the foreign negotiation will rely partly on other recent negotiations, which serve as models. The domestic model, such as on whether to give a group of workers an additional holiday, may be the economy as a whole, the industry, the local area, or recent company experience elsewhere. Abroad, what has transpired recently between other companies and the government or between similar types of companies or the same firm in similar countries may serve as a common reference, and negotiations are not likely to stray too far from established precedent. Finally, there are zones of acceptance and nonacceptance on the proposals presented. If the acceptance zones overlap, there is a possibility of a resulting agreement. If there are no overlapping zones, there is no hope for positive negotiations. For example, if General Motors insisted on 100 percent ownership in Japan and the Japanese insisted on 51 percent local ownership, there would be no zone in which to negotiate. If, on the other hand, Chrysler insisted on a "controlling" interest in Mexico but would take as much as it could get, and the Mexicans required "substantial" local capital and wanted to maximize it, there would probably be a wide zone of ownership that would be acceptable to both parties. Assume that Chrysler is willing to go as low as 25 percent and the Mexican government will let Chrysler go as high as 90 percent, the acceptance zone is 25–90 percent for Chrysler's ownership. The final decision will be based on the negotiating ability of each company, their strengths, and other concessions that each makes in the process. Since each side can only speculate on how far the other is willing to go, the exact amount of ownership may fall anywhere within the overlapping acceptance range. Even after an agreement is reached, it is uncertain whether the maximum concessions have been extracted from the other party.

Provisions   The major difference in investment negotiations abroad and the domestic experience is a matter of degree. Negotiations may continue over a much longer period of time abroad and may include many provisions unheard of in the home country, such as a negotiated tax rate. Likewise, governments vary widely in their attitudes toward foreign investors; therefore, their negotiating agendas also vary widely.

Most countries in recent years have given incentives to attract foreign investors. These incentives are usually available to local firms as well; however, local firms often may lack the resources to be in a strong bargaining position. For example, when the Hyster Corporation announced that it would build a $100 million factory in Europe, the company was wooed by representatives of various European governments. The company finally decided on Ireland, whose government agreed to pay for employee training, made an R&D grant, and set a maximum income tax rate of only 10 percent until the year 2000.[6] Other recent incentives have included tax holidays, accelerated depreciation, low-interest loans, loan guarantees, subsidized energy and transportation, and the construction of rail spurs and roads. Governments also provide indirect incentives, such as the presence of a trained labor force that is likely to accept employers' work conditions tranquilly.

When companies negotiate to gain concessions from a foreign government, they should understand some of the problems that the incentives might bring. First, companies may encounter more domestic labor problems because of claims that they are exporting jobs in order to gain access to cheap labor. Second, the output from the foreign facility may be subject to claims of dumping because of the subsidies given by the host government (e.g., Toyota forgoing British governmental assistance for fear that other EC countries would not as readily allow its sales). Third, it may be more difficult to evaluate management performance in the subsidized operation.[7] Finally, it should be noted that there is always a risk that promises will be broken as situations change.

Negotiations are seldom a one-way street; companies agree to many different performance requirements. Those requirements on foreign investment that companies find most troublesome are foreign-exchange deposits to cover the cost of imports and capital repatriation, limits on payments for services, requirements to create a certain amount of jobs or exports, provisions to reduce the amount of equity held in the subsidiaries, and price controls. Requirements considered less bothersome include minimum local inputs into products manufactured, limits on the use of expatriate personnel and on old or reconditioned equipment, control on prices for goods imported or exported to controlled entities of the parent firms, and demands to enter into joint ventures.[8]

Renegotiations

Agreements evolve after operations begin; the company position is usually—but not always—stronger before entry.

For early foreign investments in developing countries it was common to obtain concessions on fixed terms for a long period of time or to expect that the original terms would not change. (These early investments were largely made in the commodity and utility sectors.) This type of expectation has almost ceased to exist. Not only may the terms of operations be bargained before setting up operations, but the same terms also may be rebargained any time after operations are under way.

Generally, a company's best bargaining position exists before it begins the specific operations in a foreign country. Once the capital and technology have been imported and local nationals have been trained to direct operations, the foreign firm is much less needed than before.[9] Furthermore, the company now has assets that are not easily moved to more favorable locales. The result is that the host government may be in a better position to extract additional concessions from the company. For instance, after Peru had already received loans from Britain's Midland Bank, it was in a much stronger position to renegotiate the repayment in the form of copper and other raw materials, rather than cash.[10] However, a company that is aware of and responsive to the changing needs and desires of the local economy can maintain or even improve its bargaining position by offering the infusion of additional resources that the country needs. One tactic is to promise to bring in (or withhold) the latest technology developed abroad. Another is to use plant expansion or export markets as bargaining weapons. A host government also may be restrained from pushing too hard against established companies for fear this will make the country less attractive to other firms with which the government would like to do business.

Still another renegotiation tactic is to offer quick compliance with something a government wants badly in exchange for other concessions. For example, Chesebrough-Ponds reduced its wholly owned Indian operation to a 40 percent equity holding. Since "Indianization" was the prime governmental interest, Chesebrough-Ponds was able to get new licenses to expand.[11]

A specific type of renegotiation that has been growing in importance is the valuation of company properties that have come under governmental ownership. The shift may be gradual, as in the case of the Saudi Arabian increased ownership in Aramco, or immediate, as in Libya's nationalization of Exxon and Mobil holdings. In either type of situation the amount of funds to be received by the foreign investor may depend on the negotiated valuation.

The Chilean nationalization of the ITT telephone company illustrates some of the price issues that can arise.[12] The Chilean government offered about one third of the book value of the properties, based on the argument that the equipment was run-down, causing customers to complain about service. ITT countered that the book value understated the true value because a high return on assets had been earned and could be expected to continue in the future. The government responded by saying that the return on assets was due to the rates charged to customers in the monopoly industry rather than to the equipment value. Each party proposed outside appraisal of the value, but each wanted to select appraisers and valuation criteria favorable to its position.

Behavioral Characteristics Affecting Outcome

Misunderstandings may result from differences in
- Nationalities
- Professions
- Languages

In negotiations involving people from different countries, there is a strong possibility of misunderstandings due to cross-country cultural variances as well as possible language differences. Since the individuals involved may react on the basis of how they think their own performances are being evaluated, the direction of negotiations involving company managers on one side and government officials on the other side may be uncertain from the start since the background and expertise of governmental officials may be quite distinct from that of businesspeople. Finally, it is always possible that one side or the other wishes to terminate bargaining but is hesitant to do so for fear of alienating future relationships.

Some cultural differences among negotiators are evident:

- Some negotiators are decision makers; some are not.
- Some take a pragmatic view; others take a holistic view.
- Some use gifts and flattery.
- Some expressions do not translate well.

Cultural Factors   Back in the 1930s Will Rogers quipped, "America has never lost a war and never won a conference." Many participants and observers agree with this assessment of Americans in business negotiations abroad. Much of the problem stems from cultural differences that lead to misunderstandings and mistrust across the conference table. Although we cannot delineate all the possible cultural differences, Table 13.1 illustrates some usual differences among negotiators from Japan, the United States, and Latin America. A few differences are sufficiently important to U.S. negotiators to warrant mention. U.S. negotiators are more apt to have the power to make decisions than their counterpart negotiators from some other countries; they lose confidence when other negotiators have to keep checking at the head office. U.S. negotiators want to get to the heart of the matter quickly, whereas some others feel they must spend more time to develop rapport and trust before addressing business details. Americans attempt to separate the issues into pragmatic categories (getting closure on items in a linear fashion), whereas some nationalities view the negotiations holistically.[13] U.S. executives often find it very difficult to know how to establish rapport with foreign negotiators through culturally and legally acceptable gifts or through the flattery of asking their advice and opinion.

There may be a problem finding words to express the exact meaning in another language, requiring occasional pauses while translators resort to dictionaries. Furthermore, facial reactions differ by culture and, even if understood, are difficult to judge because of the time lag between the original spoken statement and receipt of the statement in a second language. Since English is so widely understood worldwide, people with a different native language may understand quite well most of the comments and discussions in English, giving them the opportunity to eavesdrop on confidential comments and to reflect on possible responses while remarks are being translated into their language. The degree of precision in language desired by both groups also may be complicated by cultural factors. Furthermore, evidence exists that cultural factors influence whether or not interpreters are acceptable. For example, Saudi managers generally prefer to negotiate in English, even if their English is not very good. When translators are used, it is usually preferable for each side to have its own. Good interpreters also help to brief their teams on cultural factors affecting the negotiation process.

The importance of these factors may change during renegotiations because the parties get to know each other. If the relationship has been amicable, this quality is apt to be carried over. However, if the past relationship has been hostile, the renegotiation may be surrounded by even more suspicion and obstruction than existed during the original process.[14]

Business and governmental officials may mistrust each other and may not understand each other's objectives.

Personal Conflict of Negotiators   Governmental and business negotiators may start with mutual mistrust due to historic animosity or to the different status of their professional positions. The investors may come armed with business and economic data that are not well understood by governmental

TABLE 13.1 | NEGOTIATION STYLES FROM A CROSS-CULTURAL PERSPECTIVE
Negotiators from Japan, North America (Canada and the United States), and Latin America are all influenced by their own backgrounds and cultures; consequently, some misinterpretations may develop in international negotiations.

Japanese	North American	Latin American
Emotional sensitivity highly valued	Emotional sensitivity not highly valued	Emotional sensitivity valued
Hiding of emotions	Dealing straightforwardly or impersonally	Emotionally passionate
Subtle power plays; conciliation	Litigation; not as much conciliation	Great power plays; use of weakness
Loyalty to employer; employer taking care of employees	Lack of commitment to employer; breaking of ties by either if necessary	Loyalty to employer (who is often family)
Group decision-making by consensus	Teamwork provides input to a decision maker	Decisions come down from one individual
Face-saving crucial; decisions often made on basis of saving someone from embarrassment	Decisions made on a cost-benefit basis; face-saving does not always matter	Face-saving crucial in decision making to preserve honor, dignity
Decision makers openly influenced by special interests	Decision makers influenced by special interests but often not considered ethical	Execution of special interests of decision maker expected, condoned
Not argumentative; quiet when right	Argumentative when right or wrong, but impersonal	Argumentative when right or wrong; passionate
What is down in writing must be accurate, valid	Great importance given to documentation as evidential proof	Impatient with documentation, seen as obstacle to understanding general principles
Step-by-step approach to decision making	Methodically organized decision making	Impulsive, spontaneous decision making
Good of group is the ultimate aim	Profit motive or good of individual ultimate aim	What is good for group is good for the individual
Cultivate a good emotional social setting for decision making; get to know decision makers	Decision making impersonal; avoid involvements, conflict of interest	Personalism necessary for good decision making

officials, who may counter with sovereignty considerations that are nearly incomprehensible to the businessperson. Thus it may take considerable time before each understands and empathizes with the other's point of view. Even then, there is a possibility that neither will attempt to develop a type of relationship designed to assure the achievement of long-run objectives: They may see their rewards as dependent on immediate results and perhaps not expect to be closely connected with longer-run problems.

The viewpoint discrepancy has been particularly noted as many LDCs have attempted to sell state-owned enterprises (SOEs) to foreign investors. The managers within the SOEs are suspicious of MNEs, fearful of foreign domination, and insecure about the maintenance of their own jobs if the SOE is privatized.[15]

Negotiators should find a means to reinstitute future contacts.

Termination of Negotiations   For a variety of reasons, one or both parties may wish to terminate serious consideration of proposals. The method of cessation may be extremely important as it may affect the negotiators' positions vis-à-vis their superiors and the future transactions between the given country and firm, the company in other parts of the world, and the country with other foreign firms. Since termination is an admission of failure to achieve the objectives originally set forth, negotiators of organizations are prone to place blame publicly on others in order to save face themselves.[16] Statements by company officials may make it harder for the country to deal with other foreign firms. Statements by governmental officials might make it more difficult for the company to negotiate and operate in other countries. For fear of adverse consequences from terminations, negotiations sometimes drag out until a proposal eventually dies unnoticed. Although termination is stressful, the parties should attempt to find means whereby each can save face and to avoid publicity as much as possible when talks are terminating.

Simulation can be used to anticipate others' approach, but it is hard to simulate stress situations.

Choice of negotiators depends on
- The importance of the deal
- The functions involved

Preparation for Negotiations   Role-playing is a valuable technique for training negotiators for projects requiring approval of a foreign government. By practicing their own roles and those of the government's negotiator and researching the culture and history of the country to determine its attitudes toward foreign companies, business executives may be much better able to anticipate responses and plan their own actions.

The use of simulation presupposes that an MNE knows who will be doing the negotiations. The choice of negotiators will depend in part on the importance of the project, the functional areas being considered, and the level of government involved. Commonly, MNEs use a team approach so that persons with legal, financial, and operations responsibility are involved in the decision making; one or more of these aspects might be altered as the need arises. Furthermore, it is also common to use people at different organizational levels at different negotiating points. One factor that is not easily simulated is the possible stress effect of being abroad and away from family and co-workers for an extended period. The location of negotiations may thus give one side or the other an advantage in reaching the final agreement.

HOME-COUNTRY INVOLVEMENT IN ASSET PROTECTION

The Historical Background

In the nineteenth century the home country ensured through military force and coercion that prompt, adequate, and effective compensation would be received for investors in cases of expropriation, a concept known as the **international standard of fair dealing.**[17] The host countries had little to say about this standard. As late as the period between the two world wars, the United States on several occasions sent troops into Latin America to protect investors' property. The 1917 Soviet confiscations without compensation of Russian and foreign private investment led the way to noncoercive interference by home countries in cases of expropriation. In conferences attended by developing countries at The Hague in 1930 and at Montevideo in 1933, participants concluded a treaty stating that "foreigners may not claim rights other or more extensive than nationals."[18] On the basis of this doctrine, Mexico used its own courts in 1938 to settle disputes arising from expropriation of foreign agricultural properties in 1915.[19] This same doctrine formed the precedent for later settlements and, in the absence of specific treaties, remains largely in effect today.

Except for the abortive attempt by British, French, and Israeli forces to prevent Egypt's takeover of the Suez Canal, there has been no major attempt since World War II at direct military intervention to protect property of home-country citizens. (There have been, however, threatened or actual troop movements by large powers to developing countries during this period. Property protection possibly was a surreptitious factor in the movements.) The concept of nonintervention has been strengthened by a series of UN resolutions. A secondary factor has been that most expropriations have been selective rather than general, that is, involving a few rather than all foreign firms. In these cases it is thought that intervention might lead to further takeovers and jeopardize settlements for affected foreign firms.

The Use of Bilateral Agreements

Bilateral agreements improve climates for investments abroad, but they
- Usually lack settlement mechanisms
- Do not protect against gradual changes

To improve the foreign investment climates for their investors, many industrial countries have established bilateral treaties with foreign governments, often as a result of long and difficult negotiations. Although these agreements differ in detail, they generally provide for home-country insurance to investors to cover losses from expropriation, civil war, and currency devaluation or control and to exporters to cover losses from nonpayment in a convertible currency. The recipient country, by approving a contract, agrees to settle payment on a government-to-government basis. In other words, Gillette could insure its Chinese investment against expropriation because of the bilateral agreement between the United States and the People's Republic of China. If China expropriated Gillette's facilities, the U.S. government would pay Gillette and then seek settlement with China. Other types of bilateral agreements include treaties of friendship, commerce, and navigation as well as prevention of double taxation. All these efforts help promote factor mobility for MNEs.

A major problem with these agreements to protect foreign investments is that they do not normally provide a mechanism for settlement. The host governments simply may lack the financial resources to settle in an appropriate currency, for example. Even if they have the resources, it is unclear whether the amount of payment should be settled in local courts, in external courts, or through negotiations. Many recipient countries resist treaties because they imply the abrogation of sovereignty over business activities conducted within their borders and provide more protection for alien property than for that of their own citizens.[20] Another problem is that the agreements do not protect against gradual changes in operating rules, which can reduce substantially the profit of foreign operations. Revere Copper and Brass, for example, was forced by Jamaica to make payments greater than those provided by the original investment agreement. The result was an operating loss that the investment insurance did not cover.[21]

Home-Country Aid as a Weapon

Home countries may improve terms for their investors by

• Suspending aid to countries that nationalize property
• Offering aid in exchange for better investor treatment

Home countries have used the promise of aid or the threat to withhold it as a means of effectively extracting from host governments terms that are more acceptable to their investors. The Hickenlooper Amendment of 1961, in response to Brazilian nationalizations, provides for the suspension of aid to any country that nationalizes properties of U.S. citizens or that has moved to nullify existing contracts and fails within a "reasonable" period of time to take appropriate steps for settlement. The Hickenlooper Amendment has been officially used only once—after Ceylon (now Sri Lanka) nationalized certain Esso and Caltex properties in 1962. Ceylon countered by expropriating additional assets of the same companies. However, in the elections of 1965, the opposition party, which promised to settle the dispute, was elected. One day after the new government took office, a settlement was worked out. The effectiveness of the amendment in the Sri Lankan situation as well as in the other instances is difficult to assess. In several cases, aid has been reduced after takeovers, and the consequences have varied.

Rather than withholding aid and loans, home governments have promised that one or both would be made available if conflict is either avoided or resolved on terms more acceptable to the home-country foreign investors. Perhaps the best-known example of this was an accord in which France agreed to give Algeria economic aid over five years in exchange for continued operations by French enterprises in Algeria.[22]

The use of aid and loans, either as a means of averting takeovers of properties by foreign investors or as a force in settling valuation disputes, certainly may be an effective weapon at times, especially since a country may depend heavily on funds from foreign governments and international agencies as either a supplement for or an alternative to foreign private investment. However, the problems are numerous: From the host-country viewpoint, threats or promises from a foreign country may put leaders in a position where they appear to be manipulated by foreign powers, possibly forcing them to become even more adamant as public opinion becomes increasingly antiforeign. On the home-country side, governments may be inconsistent in their application of financial weapons, since their concerns are primarily with political alliances and concessions rather than with the properties of a few of their citizens. They thus may be willing to give aid in exchange for favorable votes on a UN resolution, or for permission to locate foreign military bases, or simply through fear that public opinion would shift against the country trying to "buy" favorable treatment for its companies. A further problem may occur when home-country taxpayers object to their payments going abroad in order to assure the safety and continued profitability of the investments of a few of their fellow citizens.

Before a home government comes to the assistance of its firms abroad, it must consider several objectives and possible consequences. This is well illustrated by one of the leading authorities on multinational firms:

> When Exxon's Peruvian subsidiary, the International Petroleum Company, was threatened with expropriations in Peru, . . . U.S. policymakers had to ask many thorny questions before they could decide how to react. Would a U.S. response hurt American fishing interests operating off the Peruvian shores? Would it push the Peruvian government to choose French planes for its air force? Would it precipitate a clamp-down on the 600 other American firms then operating in Peru? Would it lead Peru to vote against a variety of U.S. projects in United Nations organizations and elsewhere?[23]

MULTILATERAL SETTLEMENTS

Multilateral settlements of disputes may be handled by a neutral country or group or courts in third countries.

When international firms or home governments are unable to reach agreement with a host country, they may agree to have a third party settle the dispute. In cases of trade disputes, the International Chamber of Commerce in Paris, the Swedish Chamber of Commerce, and specialized commodity associations in London frequently are asked to assist the parties. Since the trade transactions are generally among private groups, the disputes do not create the type of widespread emotional environment often attendant upon foreign investment disputes.

Examples of active involvement by third parties in settling investment questions are extremely rare, for such involvement requires a relinquishment of sovereignty by host governments over activities within their own borders. Among the notable uses of external organizations have been the World Bank's agreement to arbitrate the compensation and to act as transfer agent for payments involving the Suez Canal nationalization. Another involved a World Bank nonbinding arbitral award that was accepted by both French bondholders and the City of Tokyo.[24] The International Center for Settlement of Investment Disputes operates under the auspices of the World Bank and provides a formal organization for parties wishing to submit their disputes. However, both parties must agree to its use, and countries have been reluctant to do so. In 1974 Jamaica refused to use the center after seizing foreign bauxite holdings, although the investors and the Jamaican government had agreed in earlier years to use the center in case of disputes. As yet there is no effective means of imposing international law on nations; however, as a result of the center's failure to offer potential investors sufficient confidence about LDCs, the World Bank established the Multilateral Investment Guarantee Agency in 1988. This agency offers insurance against expropriations, war, and civil disturbances.[25]

A notable example of multilateral settlement involved claims between the United States and Iran. This situation differed from many other attempted settlements inasmuch as each country had large amounts of investments in the other's territory. In fact, when the two governments froze each other's assets, Iran had substantially more invested in the United States than the United States had in Iran. The two countries agreed to appoint three arbitrators each to an international tribunal at The Hague, and those six selected three more. Part of the assets that the United States had held were set aside for the payment of arbitrated claims.[26]

In limited cases, courts in third countries may be used by international firms or by governments as leverage. In 1972 Kennecott Copper, whose investments in Chile had been nationalized, successfully contested in French courts payment from French importers to the Chilean government on the grounds that Kennecott still owned the operations.[27] In 1987 Britain's High Court ruled that the Libyan government could withdraw $292 million from the London facility of Bankers Trust, even though $161 million of this was on deposit in New York and the U.S. government had frozen Libyan assets in U.S. banks at home and abroad.[28]

After expropriation of their Libyan facilities, California Standard, Texaco, and Arco placed notices in the leading newspapers and periodicals of the major oil-consuming countries warning that they might file lawsuits against purchasers of Libyan oil that the oil firms claimed for themselves. They also had arbitrators appointed by the International Court of Justice at The Hague who ruled in the firms' favor and set an amount of compensation.[29] A problem with the International Court of Justice (the World Court) is that there have been many examples of countries failing to consent to judgments. As a result, the Court handles few cases.[30]

CONSORTIUM APPROACHES

In a consortium, companies or countries join together to strengthen their bargaining positions (e.g., OPEC, oil firms, ANCOM, Arab boycott, codes of conduct, joint-organization production).

As mentioned earlier, a company may at times be able to play one country against another, or a government may be able to do the same with international firms. When in a relatively weak position, companies or countries may be able to join together in a **consortium** to present a united front when dealing with the previously more powerful entity.

Petroleum

The Aramco case at the beginning of the chapter offers a good example of how companies have banded together on one side and countries have joined forces on the other side. The unity has strengthened both sides and at different points has helped to give advantages to one over the other.

ANCOM

ANCOM, as discussed in Chapter 11, sought a common policy toward foreign capital, trademarks, patents, licenses, and royalties. By unifying the policy the aims were to limit the role of MNEs and to prevent them from serving all the member countries by locating in a country with less stringent regulations. This attempt to get ANCOM members to adhere to the common stance has been less than successful; nevertheless it contrasts to the approach of the European Community, which has not had a common policy. When France wished to restrict the growth of MNE penetration within its market by withholding ownership permission, that country was helpless. MNEs could serve the French market through production in Belgium, Ireland, or Spain, where they were welcome.

Arab Boycott

The Arab boycott is a loose arrangement whereby Arab countries may cease business with firms doing business with Israel.

In the Arab boycott efforts have been made to weaken Israel by boycotting purchases of Israeli goods and by refusing to do business with firms that sell strategic tools and certain resources to Israel.[31] This is a loose agreement among participants rather than a highly structured agreement; the looseness of the boycott is in some ways a strength in that it has allowed Arab countries to buy from some firms selling to Israel when they desperately needed the goods themselves. The prevention of trade between Israel and Arab states is not an unusual type of practice, nor does it have much impact on MNEs. What is different about this arrangement is that it often forces MNEs headquartered in other countries to make a choice of selling either in the Arab countries or in Israel, but not in both. (China at times has also retaliated by disallowing certain business with a given country whose firms did sensitive business with Taiwan.) By banding together, the Arab countries represent a very formidable market. Although it is impossible to measure the precise impact of the boycott activities, the big difference in market size undoubtedly has caused many MNEs to think twice about doing business with Israel.

A second distinguishing feature is the nature of a so-called **secondary boycott.** For example, Ford Motor Company is boycotted by the Arab League. Ford was involved in negotiating a joint venture in the United States with Toyota; however, Saudi Arabia threatened retaliation against any firm that concluded a joint venture or production-licensing agreement with Ford. Since Saudi Arabia was the world's second-largest importer of Japanese cars, the Saudi warning had to be considered seriously.[32] Toyota subsequently broke off the negotiations with Ford but did not indicate that the threatened boycott was a factor in the decision.

A third distinguishing feature for U.S. firms is that they are prohibited by the U.S. Export Administration Act from providing information on their directors when registering operations in Arab countries. Both Sara Lee and Safeway Stores received fines for breaking this law, even though the information they provided was available from public sources.[33] A fourth feature is that U.S. firms are prohibited from terminating Israeli business in order to do business in Arab countries, which brings up questions of motives. For example, Baxter International, a company blacklisted by the Arab League, divested from Israel and signed a joint venture agreement in Syria a year later. Baxter officials claim the Israeli move was made simply because of inadequate financial performance; however, critics have contended that the motive was to gain the ability to operate in Arab countries.[34]

Codes of Conduct

Collective attitudes toward MNE activities are
- Clarified by a number of organizations
- Usually fairly vague
- Involve voluntary compliance
- May make it easier for countries to legislate

The first widespread attempt to regulate direct investment on a multilateral basis was made in 1929 by the League of Nations. At that time the attention was on foreign exploitation of the tropical commodity industry. Proposals were discarded quickly, however, with the onset of the Great Depression. Since World War II there have been several attempts to form agreements that would deal in part with the relationship between foreign investors and governments. Among these were the International Trade Organization (ITO) of 1948, which never became operative, attempts in 1951 by the UN Economic and Social Council (ECOSOC) to regulate antitrust, and the 1961 Code for Liberalization of Capital Movements established by the Organization for Economic Cooperation and Development (OECD).[35] None appears to have had much effect on MNE operations.

In 1975 the newly created Center on Transnational Corporations first met at the United Nations as a result of complaints issued by a large group of poor countries. (The so-called "Group of 77" now comprises more than 100 LDCs.) The Center provides for the collection of information on MNE activities, is a forum for publicizing common complaints, and has considered the adoption of several codes of conduct for the activities of MNEs. Meanwhile, the OECD, which is composed of industrial countries, approved its own code in 1976. The codes considered by the Group of 77, as well as the code set by the OECD, are necessarily vague so that consensus may be reached among various nations as well as among groups within the nations. The codes are also voluntary; thus adoption does not guarantee enforcement. The codes may, however, clarify a collective attitude toward specific practices of MNEs that could make it easier to pass restrictive legislation at the national level without fear that the legislation will be greatly out of step with external public opinion.[36]

Joint Company Activities

Joint company activities are used by countries to strengthen national capabilities vis-à-vis strong foreign competitors and
- To spread risk
- To deal more strongly with governments

To counter production dominance by foreign firms, countries have fostered consolidation among their own manufacturers. They have given governmental assistance to R&D and preferred their own firms in governmental contracts. Two of the most notable efforts have been the development of a consortium in Europe to compete against Boeing in aircraft production and the development of various cooperative arrangements in Europe to counter IBM's dominance. Other European cross-national efforts have occurred in such fields as consumer appliances, medical electronics, telecommunications, and television. Two of the more notable efforts have been the EC's Esprit program of $5 billion to fund electronics research and the Eureka program involving about 1600 companies, 99 percent of them European, to develop a wide range of technologies.[37]

Another approach has been for two or more firms from different countries to band together, not so much to strengthen the initial negotiating terms, but rather to improve their positions in possible later negotiations. By investing a smaller amount in a given locality, each firm can invest in more countries, thus reducing the impact of loss in one. Furthermore, a host government may be more hesitant to deal simultaneously with more than one home government in conflict situations.

Companies also may band together to exert pressure on a government to take action against a competitor. For example, when IBM proposed an exemption of shared ownership for a new Mexican venture, 43 computer-related firms, including Hewlett-Packard and Apple, successfully joined to advertise and to lobby so that IBM would not be treated preferentially.[38]

EXTERNAL RELATIONS APPROACHES

The Need by Countries

Through external relations, countries try to attract investors by making themselves known and expressing their viewpoint when controversies with MNEs arise.

Countries that wish to attract more foreign investment sometimes have found either that they are inadequately known to investors or that investors have false impressions of the business possibilities within their borders. Some potential investments thus are overlooked rather than rejected. An investment in a small country such as Mauritius may not be undertaken simply because the investment decision makers do not turn their thoughts to that country.

Satellite television transmission now makes it commonplace for us to watch events as they unfold in other countries. Transportation and communication advances and government-to-government accords have contributed to our increasing dependence on foreign products and markets. As this dependence grows, updated maps are a valuable tool. They can show the locations of population, economic wealth, production, and markets; portray certain commonalities and differences among areas; and illustrate barriers that might inhibit trade. In spite of the usefulness of maps, a substantial number of people worldwide have a poor knowledge of how to interpret information on maps and even how to find the location of events that affect their lives.

We urge you to use the following maps to locate the areas you study in order to build your geographical awareness. Such an awareness will help you identify viable international alternatives when you are a business decision maker.

Map 1 World View 1992   M2

Map 2 Africa   M4

Map 3 Asia   M5

Map 4 Europe   M6

Map 5 North America   M7

Map 6 Oceania   M8

Map 7 South America   M9

Map 8 International Groupings   M10

Map 9 GNP Per Capita   M12

Map 10 Population Density   M13

Map 11 Foreign Debt   M14

Map 12 Language   M15

Map 13 Major Religions   M16

ARCTIC OCEAN

A

B

SWEDEN
FINLAND
NORWAY

UNION OF SOVIET SOCIALIST REPUBLICS

C

DENMARK

EUROPE

ASIA

NETH.
GER. POLAND
BEL.—LUX. CZECH.
FRANCE AUST. HUN.
SWITZ.
ROMANIA
YUG.
BUL.
ITALY ALB.
GREECE
TURKEY
CYPRUS

MONGOLIA

D

N. KOREA
S. KOREA
JAPAN

TUNISIA
LEBANON SYRIA
ISRAEL
JORDAN
IRAQ
IRAN
AFGHANISTAN
CHINA

E

ALGERIA
LIBYA
EGYPT
KUWAIT
QATAR
SAUDI
ARABIA
UAE
OMAN
PAKISTAN
NEPAL
BHUTAN
INDIA
MYANMAR
BANGLADESH
TAIWAN
HONG KONG

Tropic of Cancer

NIGER
CHAD
SUDAN

AFRICA

F

NIGERIA
BENIN
TOGO
CENTRAL
AFRICAN REP.
REP. OF YEMEN
DJIBOUTI
ETHIOPIA
SOMALIA
THAILAND
LAOS
VIETNAM
PHILIPPINES

PACIFIC

OCEAN

CAMEROON
EQ.
GUINEA
GABON
CONGO
RWANDA
ZAIRE
BURUNDI
UGANDA
KENYA
TANZANIA
SRI LANKA
CAMBODIA
BRUNEI
MALAYSIA
SINGAPORE

PAPUA
NEW GUINEA

Equator

SOLOMON ISLANDS

G

ANGOLA
ZAMBIA
MALAWI
INDONESIA

INDIAN

ZIMBABWE
MADAGASCAR
NAMIBIA
BOTSWANA
MOZAMBIQUE

OCEAN

AUSTRALIA

Tropic of Capricorn

H

SOUTH
AFRICA
SWAZILAND
LESOTHO

NEW
ZEALAND

TASMANIA

I

M3

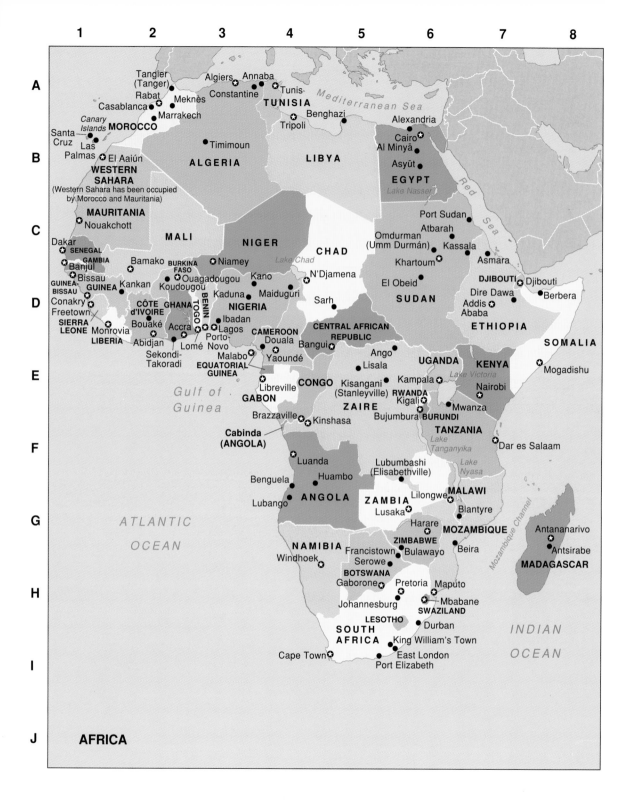

AFRICA

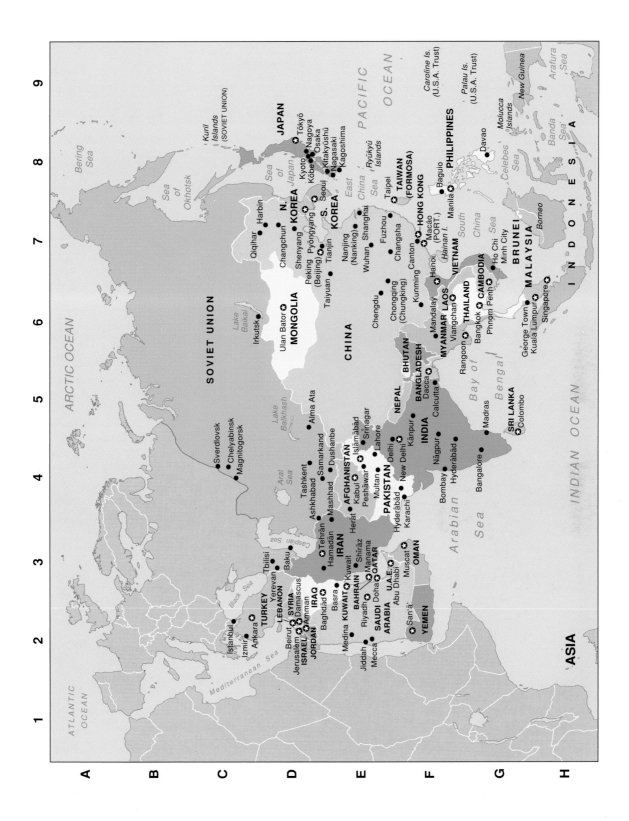

M5

EUROPE

M6

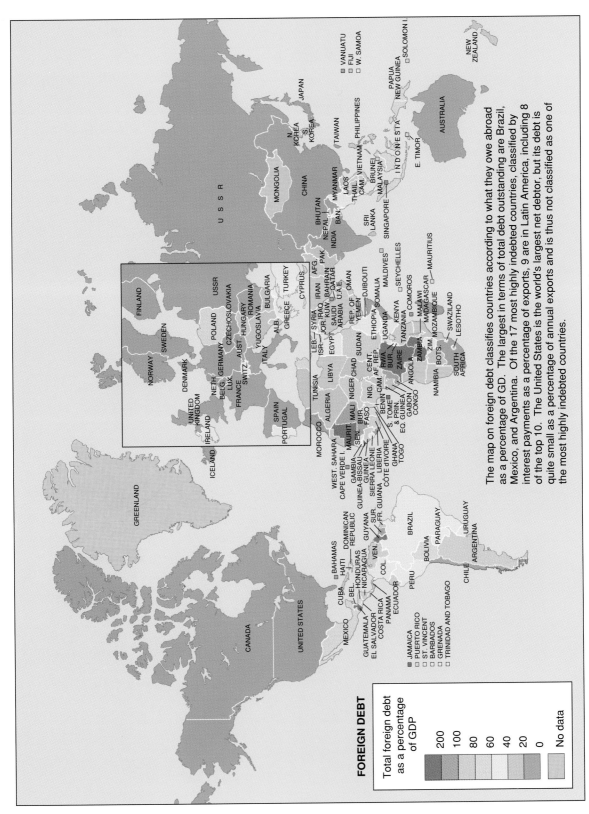

FOREIGN DEBT

Total foreign debt
as a percentage
of GDP

200
100
80
60
40
20
0

No data

The map on foreign debt classifies countries according to what they owe abroad as a percentage of GD. The largest in terms of total debt outstanding are Brazil, Mexico, and Argentina. Of the 17 most highly indebted countries, classified by interest payments as a percentage of exports, 9 are in Latin America, including 8 of the top 10. The United States is the world's largest net debtor, but its debt is quite small as a percentage of annual exports and is thus not classified as one of the most highly indebted countries.

Source: *The Economist World Atlas and Almanac;* The Economist Books/Prentice-Hall Press, pp. 84-85.   Reprinted by permission.

M14

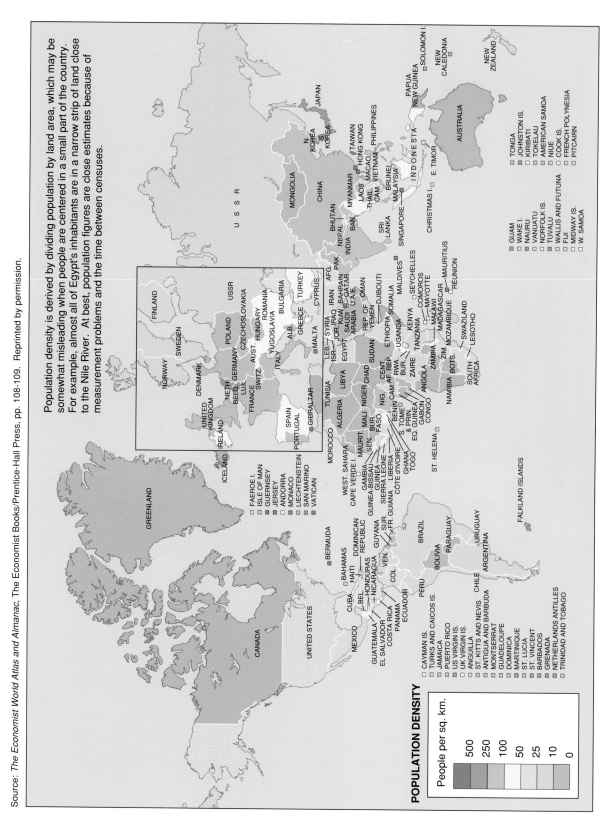

Source: *The Economist World Atlas and Almanac,* The Economist Books/Prentice-Hall Press, pp. 108–109.   Reprinted by permission.

Population density is derived by dividing population by land area, which may be somewhat misleading when people are centered in a small part of the country. For example, almost all of Egypt's inhabitants are in a narrow strip of land close to the Nile River. At best, population figures are close estimates because of measurement problems and the time between censuses.

POPULATION DENSITY

People per sq. km.

500
250
100
50
25
10
0

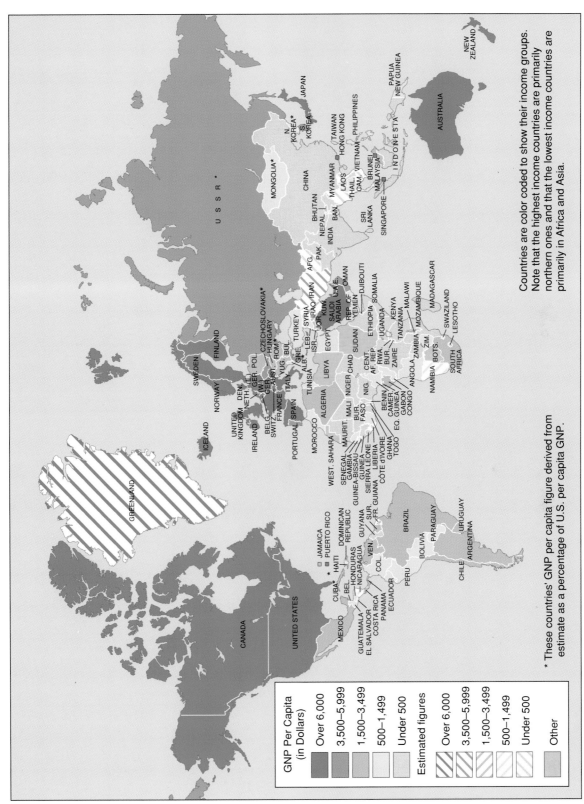

Countries are color coded to show their income groups.
Note that the highest income countries are primarily
northern ones and that the lowest income countries are
primarily in Africa and Asia.

* These countries' GNP per capita figure derived from
estimate as a percentage of U.S. per capita GNP.

GNP Per Capita
(in Dollars)

Over 6,000
3,500–5,999
1,500–3,499
500–1,499
Under 500

Estimated figures

Over 6,000
3,500–5,999
1,500–3,499
500–1,499
Under 500
Other

Source: *The World Bank Atlas, 1990* and Raul Marer and Janos Arnay, "Historically Planned Economies: A Guide Box to Data," Washington: World Bank, 1991.

THE NORTHERN HEMISPHERE–DEFENSE

NATO North Atlantic Treaty Organization

PACIFIC BASIN

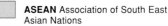

ASEAN Association of South East Asian Nations

AFRICA

OAU *non*-members of the Organization for African Unity

Franc Zone currency linked to the French Franc

SADCC Southern Africa Development Coordination Conference

PTA Preferential Trade Area for Eastern and Southern Africa

ECOWAS Economic Community of West African States

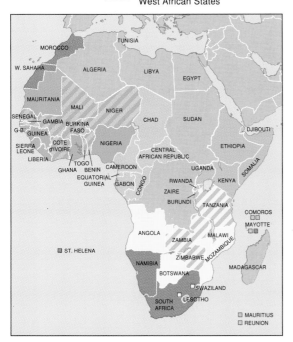

LATIN AMERICA AND CARIBBEAN

ALADI Asociación Latinoamericana de Integración

Andean Pact

CARICOM Caribbean Community and Common Market

Organization of River Plate Basin Countries

Prentice-Hall Press, pp. 100–101. Reprinted by permission.

M11

INTERNATIONAL GROUPINGS

Countries that have only partial membership, such as observer status, are not marked; neither are dependencies, and other non-sovereign states.

WORLD

UN *non*-members of the United Nations

OECD Organization for Economic Cooperation and Development

OPEC Organization of the Petroleum Exporting Countries

Commonwealth

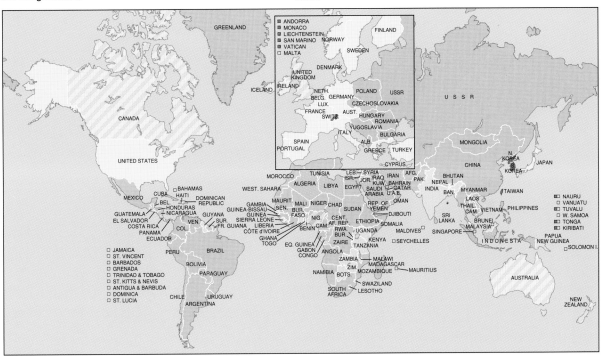

EUROPE–TRADE

EC European Community

COMECON Council for Mutual Economic Assistance; Cuba, Mongolia and Vietnam are also members

EFTA European Free Trade Association

MIDDLE EAST

OAPEC Organization of Arab Petroleum Exporting Countries

Gulf Cooperation Council

The Arab League

Egypt rejoined OAPEC and The Arab League in mid-1989

Source: *The Economist World Atlas and Almanac*, The Economist Books/

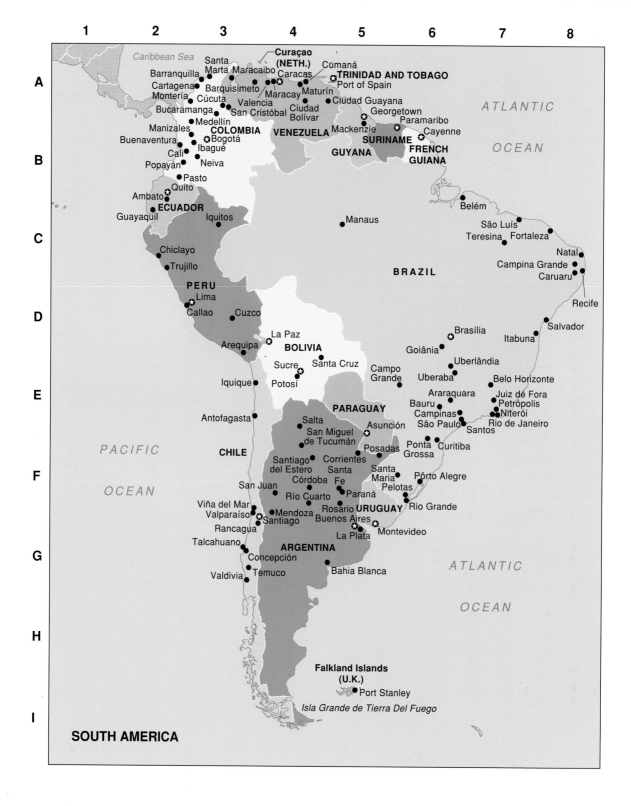

SOUTH AMERICA

M9

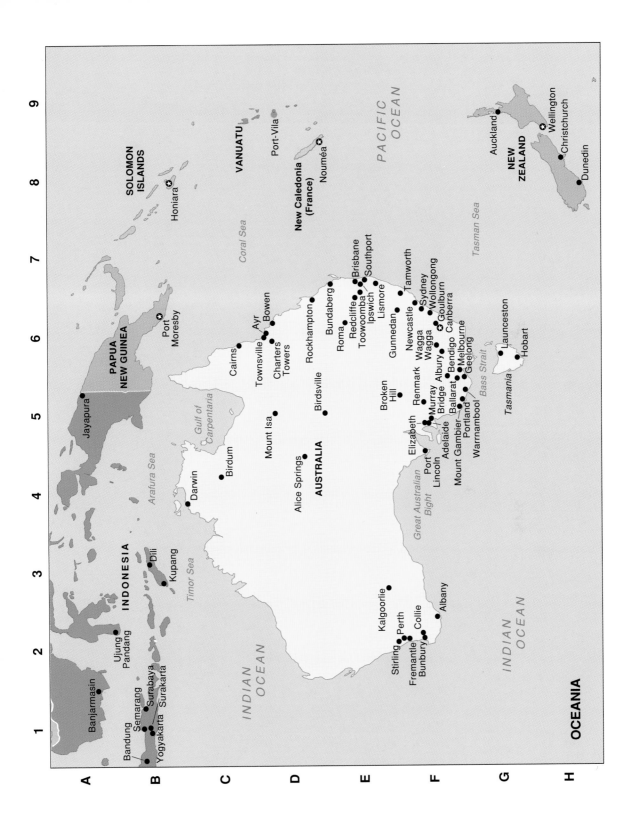

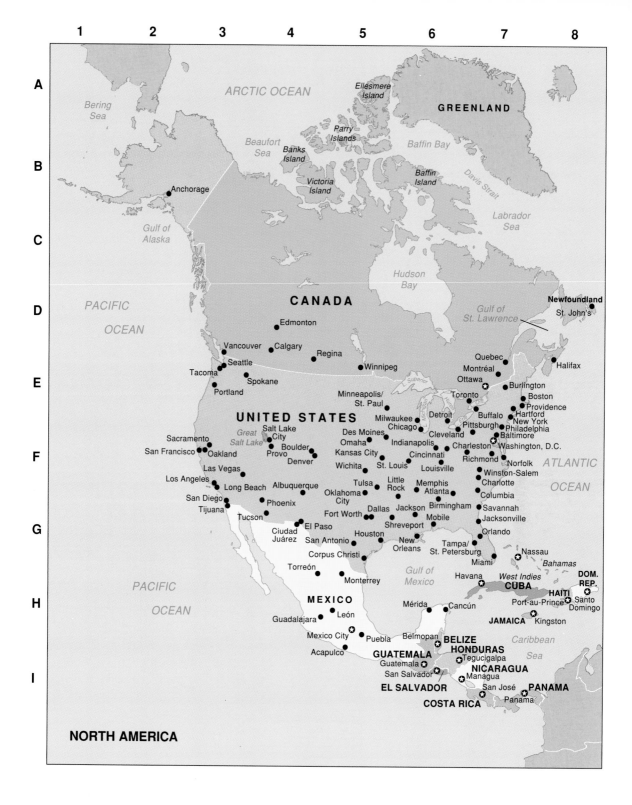

NORTH AMERICA

M7

Source: *The Economist World Atlas and Almanac*, The Economist Books/Prentice-Hall Press, pp. 116-117. Reprinted by permission.

Although hundreds of languages are spoken globally, a few dominate. This map shows the 11 primary ones. Note that English, French, or Spanish is spoken prevalently in over half the countries of the world. Some other languages, such as Mandarin and Russian, are not spoken prevalently in multiple countries but, nevertheless, are important in terms of the number of native speakers.

LANGUAGE

- Mandarin
- English
- Hindi
- Russian
- Spanish
- Portuguese
- Japanese
- Arabic
- French
- German
- Other

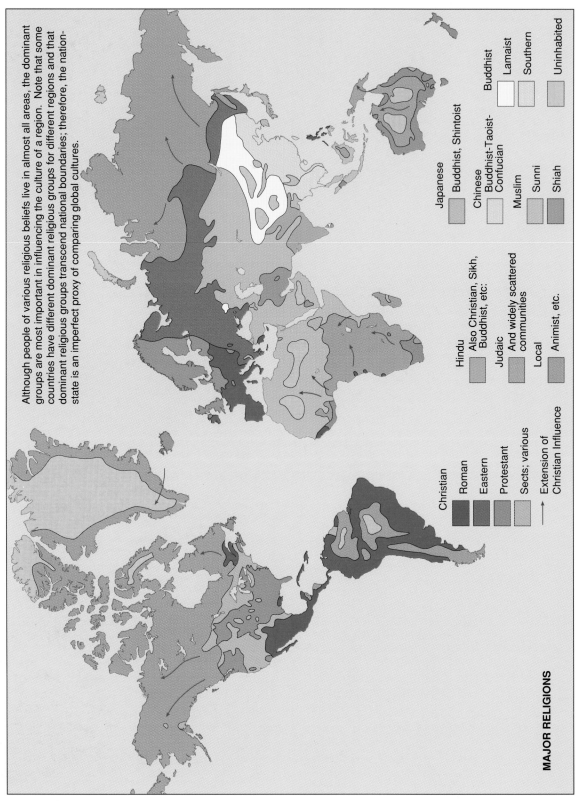

Although people of various religious beliefs live in almost all areas, the dominant groups are most important in influencing the culture of a region. Note that some countries have different dominant religious groups for different regions and that dominant religious groups transcend national boundaries; therefore, the nation-state is an imperfect proxy for comparing global cultures.

MAJOR RELIGIONS

Christian
- Roman
- Eastern
- Protestant
- Sects; various
- → Extension of Christian Influence

Hindu
- Also Christian, Sikh, Buddhist, etc:

Judaic
- And widely scattered communities

Local
- Animist, etc.

Japanese
- Buddhist, Shintoist

Chinese
- Buddhist-Taoist-Confucian

Muslim
- Sunni
- Shiah

Buddhist
- Lamaist
- Southern

Uninhabited

Source: © Bartholomew 1990. Extract from *The Times Atlas of the World*, 8th Comprehensive Edition. Used by permission.

Other countries may be victims of publicity attendant on conditions in neighboring countries. For example, there is a tendency to stereotype African or Latin American nations. Investment flows to Costa Rica thus may suffer because of a war between El Salvador and Honduras, anti-U.S. sentiment in Nicaragua, nationalization programs in Peru, or political unrest in Guatemala.

To overcome either bad publicity or no publicity at all, many countries have established public-relations programs abroad. Their activities are extremely varied: Some include participation in world fairs and exhibits so that the country becomes better known. Some advertise to provide data on the economy. Some organize conferences abroad to explain their attractiveness; for example, Vietnam, Laos, and Cambodia held a conference to explain their changed attitude toward foreign investors.[39] It is common to see full-page advertisements in the *Wall Street Journal* on such subjects as "Reasons to Invest in the Dominican Republic." In order to become better known, Morocco waged a campaign using advertisements with the slogan "Invest in Morocco. It may never have crossed your mind." Countries also have used advertising media to overcome the problems of adverse publicity.

Company Approaches

Companies publicize good-citizenship activities, pointing out when
- Business conduct satisfies social objectives
- Nonbusiness functions help society

Many firms strongly believe that by acting as a good corporate citizen abroad they will remove local animosities and concern that might affect their short- or long-term competitive ability. Some have even gone so far as to set their own published codes of conduct. The behavior itself may not be sufficient, however, since employees, governmental officials, consumers, and other groups may not know or understand what the company is doing. W. R. Grace's chairman, J. Peter Grace, said, "No matter how responsibly a corporation behaves, it will be viewed with skepticism unless it effectively communicates its activities, its plans, and its goals to its many publics."[40]

Because of conflicting pressures on the international firm from different groups, the investor can almost always be accused of bad behavior by someone. For instance, if the company offers higher wages, it may be accused of monopolistic practices and aiding inflation by attracting workers from competitors. If it pays only the going wage, it may be accused of exploiting the workers. By understanding the relative power of competing groups served by the firm, management may at least be able to emphasize practices that benefit most of the groups that are in a position to help or hurt the firm in a substantial way. A good rule for serving a given group is to try to maximize benefits without excessively disrupting the local situation. Within any given economy there usually is a range of prices, wages, and returns on investment. The international company thus may be able to be among the leaders (e.g., have wage rates or investment returns among the top quarter of firms) without being accused of disruptive practices, while still satisfying the groups directly involved.

Management should avoid public confrontation whenever possible, because this confrontation may force opponents to become more adamant in their views. When government accusations against a foreign company in India were leaked to the press, the company countered by refuting the charges in newspaper advertisements, a tactic that merely served to challenge authority and publicly tarnish the government's credentials. Conversely, in response to newspaper criticism about a U.S. pharmaceutical firm's labeling in Europe, the company decided to work with the Health Ministry, since criticisms affected not only the company but also the ministry's supervision of the matter. By jointly answering the charges, the firm maintained rapport with the ministry, its major regulator and consumer.[41]

Saint Augustine recounted that in his youth he used to pray, "Give me chastity and continence, but not yet." Like Saint Augustine, many companies try to put their efforts off as long as possible. As in the above examples, much of a company's public-relations effort is defensive—that is, it occurs in response to public criticism. Once a company is on the defensive, however, these efforts may be too little, too late. Gulf & Western, for example, reacted to adverse criticism, primarily in the United States, about its labor-relations practices in the Dominican Republic by committing $100 million over a ten-year period to improve worker welfare through such initiatives as housing construction and education programs. Several years later, however, the criticism had not subsided measurably, and Gulf & Western announced it would cease operations in the Dominican Republic.[42]

Firms should organize means to increase the number of local supporters and dampen potential criticism. Opinion surveys of such interested parties as customers and workers can be conducted through various means so as to allay misconceptions, anticipate criticism, and thereby head off potentially more damaging accusations. Many MNEs use advocacy publicity at home and abroad in an aggressive effort to win support for their international activities.[43] Mobil, for example, has used newspaper and magazine advertisements to support its international vertical integration. Both Rohm and Haas and Caterpillar have made films to support the positive effects their activities have on home- and host-country societies. MNEs have also set systematic means to identify and react to external conditions that may adversely affect their operations abroad.[44]

While it may not always be possible to dispel criticism, the international firm can do several things to mitigate it. One method is to consider those things that are important to people in the host country, or it may be something as fundamental as having the new manager continue a policy initiated by previous domestic management. On the question of what to centralize and what to decentralize, there is much to be said for permitting the local manager to determine policies concerning local customs and social matters. On such sensitive issues as employment and worker output, changes should be made only after consultation regarding the attitudes of locally interested parties. Headquarters personnel also may serve a useful public-relations function on the local scene. Since they have higher status than local managers, they may sometimes be better received by higher governmental authorities.

Allies Through Participation

The MNE might increase the number of local proponents through
- Ownership sharing
- Avoiding direct confrontation
- Local management
- Local R&D

The foreign company also may foster local participation designed both to reduce the image of foreignness and to develop local proponents whose personal objectives may be fulfilled by the foreign investor's continued operations. The parent company can follow a policy that involves its subsidiary in purchasing local supplies and raw materials whenever possible. It might be feasible for the local subsidiary to subcontract part of its assembly operations. In the case of purchasing component parts or subcontracting, it may be possible for the parent or the subsidiary to make a loan or give technical assistance to help the local supplier initiate or expand a plant. If it is economically reasonable, R&D activities may be undertaken within the host country.

Another possibility for local participation would be a stock-option plan for country nationals employed by the subsidiary, a practice that some firms have followed even in some LDCs. A company interested in improving its image in the host country also may establish a specific program for gradually replacing home-country personnel with local nationals. If local union officials are informed directly by management of possible company actions, they may cooperate with management rather than confront it.

If carried to extremes, local participation can mean that the host country becomes less dependent on the foreign firm. The company strategy might be to hold out on some resources so that the company is needed. For instance, a centralized R&D laboratory might be in charge of new product development, whereas the local R&D facility can handle the adaptations for local market and production conditions.

Some companies have taken on additional social functions to build support. For example, Dow Chemical financed a kindergarten in Chile, Citibank participated in a reforestation program in the Philippines, and McDonald's sponsored a telethon in Australia to raise funds for disabled children. Johnson and Johnson sends Kenyans abroad to study nursing. General Motors publishes a public-interest report to publicize its involvement in a wide array of activities, such as an overseas fellowship program, support for cancer research, AIDS education, and global celebration of Earth Day.[45]

Firms sometimes have been permitted greater latitude in their operations when they have agreed to invest in priority operations outside their normal line of business. These have been negotiated accords, such as a mining firm's agreement to lay out two plantations in Nigeria in exchange for relative freedom in operating its mining venture.[46]

Good corporate citizenship and the attendant publicity may not be enough to guarantee the continued conduct of business activity. If public opinion is directed against foreign private ownership in general, such as in the Cuban expropriations, all foreign firms lose out. If a firm is doing business as a key firm in a key sector, criticisms may come simultaneously from so many directions that the company defense gradually loses strength. Even in these exceptional situations, an investor's external affairs department may identify problem areas. If this is done sufficiently in advance, the company may forestall adverse actions and establish policies to prevent or minimize losses, such as decreasing new-parent obligations, selling ownership to local governments or private investors, and shifting into less visible types of local enterprises.

On occasion, an MNE may find it advantageous to be uncompromising in its dealings with a government, even when the adversary positions are reported publicly. The firm may assess its bargaining position as being sufficiently strong to afford to be adamant, or it may perceive that compromises will weaken its position in other countries. Even in these instances, however, the MNE should attempt to keep the government from losing face. Gulf & Western, for example, negotiated for five years with the Thai government for a zinc mine and refinery without coming to an agreement. Then the firm closed its office in Bangkok, which was widely reported as an effort to bully the government into accepting terms. Within a week, the Thai government did accept an agreement, but Gulf & Western announced that the office closing was simply a cost-reduction measure during a transition period.[47]

PROTECTION OF INTELLECTUAL PROPERTY RIGHTS

International treaties and agreements help safeguard patents, trademarks, and copyrights.

Most of the discussion in this chapter has centered on direct investment; however, one of the key business-government and government-to-government conflicts of recent years has involved intellectual property rights, sometimes referred to as intangible assets. The poet and essayist Ralph Waldo Emerson said, "If a man can write a better book, preach a better sermon, or make a better mousetrap than his neighbor, though he builds his house in the woods, the world will make a beaten path to his door." But if someone else gets hold of the design for the same book, sermon, or mousetrap the number of people beating the way on any single path will be divided. Some of the most valuable assets that businesses have are their intangibles, such as patents, trademarks, and copyrights, and millions of dollars can be spent in their development. Improper protection of these assets could lead to limited profitability by the parties that invested in developing the intangible. Given the different attitudes countries have toward property rights, adequate international protection of a firm's intangibles can only come about through international cooperation. Most countries have legal procedures for registering patents, trademarks, and copyrights, but it takes time for an MNE to duplicate the application process in every country in which it operates, which is why international treaties can be so important.

Patents

The first major attempt to achieve cross-national cooperation was the Paris Convention, initiated in 1883 and periodically revised. This convention gave rise to the International Bureau for the Protection of Industrial Property Rights (BIRPI) and involved the protection of patents, trademarks, and other property rights. The general idea behind the Paris Convention was that a nation would grant to foreigners who are members of the Convention the same status accorded its own citizens in the protection of property rights. A second major provision of the Paris Convention was that a registration in one country has a grace period of protection before filing in other member countries. The Inter-American Conference of 1910 on Inventions, Patents, Designs, and Models was initiated among the United States and Latin American countries to accomplish the same objectives as the Paris Convention.

The three most important contemporary cross-national patent agreements are the Patent Cooperation Treaty (PCT) of the World Intellectual Property Organization (WIPO), the European Patent Convention (EPC), and the EEC Patent Convention.[48] The PCT and EPC allow firms to make a uniform patent search and application, which is then passed on to all signatory countries.

Patent-infringement battles are both costly and complex, and they may take years to settle. The major problems on the international level are the rapid development of technology and the different patent rules and regulations in different countries.[49] Companies are forced to change their patents from country to country to meet local needs, and patent infringement is often difficult to prove. For example, a company in Italy, where there is no patent protection on pharmaceuticals, could manufacture a drug patented by a firm in the United States and sell it anywhere in the world. If the U.S. firm were to bring suit, it would have to prove patent infringement but would have difficulty getting the proof in Italy. Owing to the high costs of patent-infringement suits, many firms are attempting to settle out of court. Another problem is that the duration of patent protection varies among countries. For example, Canada has a shorter protection period on drugs than the United States has; thus Canadian producers may export generic drugs to compete against U.S. firms elsewhere in the world.

Trademarks

Companies may spend millions of dollars to develop brand names. If the brand names are not protected by a trademark, then other companies may produce under the same brand name. Even if the names have a trademark, they may become generic and thus enter the public domain. "Yo-yo" is actually a foreign trademark that has become generic in the United States; although "Ping-Pong" is a registered trademark in the United States, it has become generic in China and is used in place of "table tennis." Since the Japanese have no name for vulcanized rubber, they use "goodyear" to identify the product. One development in cross-national cooperation for trademark protection is the Trademark Registration Treaty, commonly known as the Vienna Convention. The United States, the United Kingdom, Germany, and Italy were among the industrialized countries that signed initially.

Some countries require the use of a trademark before an application of registration can be filed. Codified-law countries (those using statutory law rather than common law) traditionally have not recognized use as a precondition to registration or as a valid protection against infringement. According to the Vienna Convention, a country may not require the use of a mark as a prerequisite to obtain or maintain registration until three years after its international registration. Once the mark has been registered internationally, each country must accept it or provide grounds for refusal within fifteen months so that the firm will have sufficient time to act before its three-year period is completed.

Copyrights

Most large publishing and recording companies have extensive foreign interests and can be influenced easily by foreign competition. If there were no international copyright laws, it would be feasible for a foreign producer to copy a book or tape and then distribute it at cut-rate prices in the country where it was first produced. The Universal Copyright Convention (UCC), the major cross-national agreement, honors the copyright laws of the signatory states.

Piracy

Not all countries are members of the various agreements to protect intangible property rights. Of those that are, some enforce the agreements haphazardly. Many countries simply do not place a high priority on tracking down or prosecuting people who violate these property rights, preferring to focus their police efforts on crimes they consider more serious. Disagreement on the protection of property rights was a major factor in the inability of GATT's Uruguay Round to reach agreement by its 1990 target date. Many LDCs have resisted agreement on protection because payments almost always go to firms headquartered in industrial countries.

The cost to companies that depend on a well-known trademark to merchandise their goods has become enormous. Cashing in on massive advertising by placing well-known trademarked labels on copies of products is tempting for some companies. This has occurred with almost every type of goods—fake labels even go on merchandise that the copied companies do not make, such as the Jordache label on disco bags and caps.

What about consumers? Sometimes they get good-quality merchandise with a prestige label for a fraction of what the legitimate product would have cost. Some firms have even contracted counterfeiters to be legitimate suppliers. Often, though, shoddy or even dangerous merchandise is substituted for the original, legitimate goods. In Britain defective brake parts turned up in military aircraft, and in the United States twelve people died from counterfeit tranquilizers.[50]

Sales also are lost when products are copied, although the copier does not use someone else's trademark, such as in the copying of books, tapes, and software.[51] When the drug company Pfizer introduced Feldene, an antiarthritic drug, to Argentina, five Argentine firms were already selling generic copies in the market.[52]

Various associations of manufacturers have sprung up worldwide to deal collectively with the problem of piracy. Among the deterrents that have been proposed are greater border surveillance, criminal penalties for dealing in counterfeit goods, and the cessation of aid to countries that do not join and adhere to international agreements. Companies such as Apple Computer and Union Carbide are also successfully tracking down infringers on their own and bringing cases against them, but it is difficult to prove infringement when slight changes are made in trademarks or product models. Other companies are using high technology, such as holographic images and magnetic or microship tags, to identify the genuine products. This has cost them millions of dollars in payments for detecting devices.[53] Vuiton, a French luggage manufacturer, is fighting with a withdrawal strategy—selling registered and numbered goods only in company-owned retail outlets. Still other firms are warning the public of imitations and advising on how to discern the genuine product.[54]

LOOKING TO THE FUTURE   Probably the most significant factor affecting a possible change in business-government diplomacy is the ebbing of the cold war, which had pitted the Eastern and Western blocs against each other for nearly half a century. Governments had been prone to influence business activities because of political-military objectives, sometimes protecting their national companies so that they would gain spheres of influence abroad and sometimes withholding support for fear that a neutral nation might otherwise be prone to lend more support to the other bloc. But political schisms are not yet a thing of the past, and thus managers must continue to contend with cross-national animosities when planning their own international expansion strategies.

National economic rivalries with new alignments may well replace some of the political-military rivalries of the recent past. For instance, a new economic rivalry between Europe and North America may become as intense as the old political rivalry between the communist and noncommunist blocs. Companies may thus be no less subjected to having to satisfy national interests in their operations. During the short term, it appears that most countries will welcome foreign firms' operations or at least take a laissez-faire attitude toward them because of a belief that, on balance, they serve their national economic interests. But there are likely to be many exceptions. One involves countries such as India and South Korea, which have traditionally not welcomed wholly owned foreign operations. Another involves the privatization of state-owned enterprises, for which prospective buyers must negotiate on much more than the price. Still another involves the countries transforming from centrally planned to market economies, where negotiations are apt to be very long and complex. Furthermore, historically there have been broad swings in host-country attitudes toward foreign ownership. The present welcome to FDI could easily reverse, particularly if governments feel that their own constituencies are not receiving a just share of global economic benefits. Regardless of the direction of swings in national policies, companies are likely to face ever-more sophisticated government officials when they negotiate their operating terms abroad.

It is probably safe to say that companies headquartered in different countries will continue to become more entwined through joint ventures, licensing, contract buying, and other arrangements. Many of these companies will likewise continue to depend more on sales and production outside their home countries, while simultaneously bringing in more shareholders and top managers from abroad. These activities may strengthen their positions vis-à-vis governments as a whole, but they may weaken their positions with their home-governmental officials, who no longer see them as representing a national interest.

Government-to-government cooperation to deal with international firms is apt to move slowly, at least on a global scale. There are simply too many divergent interests among countries, which tend to divide them on different issues based on economic development levels, product-specific interests, and regional viewpoints. One such issue is the protection of intangibles, which pits the interests of industrial countries that create most of the patents, trademarks, and copyrights against the interests of many LDCs that do not want to pay for their use. In such instances, we may see more linkages to other areas in overall economic policy, such as the cessation of trade preferences for countries that do not protect intangible property rights. We may see more attempts by small groups of countries to band together to unify or coordinate policies toward international firms, such as by countries operating in trading blocs.

SUMMARY

- Although host countries and international firms may hold resources that, if combined, should achieve objectives for both, conflict may cause one or both parties to withhold resources, thus preventing the full functioning of international business activities.

- Both the managers of international firms and the host-country governmental officials must respond to interest groups that may see different advantages or no advantage at all to the business-government relationship. Therefore, the final outcome of the relationship may not be the one expected from a purely economic viewpoint.

- Negotiations increasingly are used to determine the terms under which a company may operate in a foreign country. This negotiating process is similar to the domestic processes of company acquisition and collective bargaining. The major differences in the international sphere are the much larger number of provisions, the general lack of a fixed time duration for an agreement, and the need to agree on company property values in cases of nationalization.

■ The terms under which an international firm may be permitted to operate in a given country will be determined to a great extent by the relative degree to which the company needs the country and vice versa. As the relative needs evolve over time, new terms of operation will reflect the shift in bargaining strength.

■ Generally, a company's best bargaining position is before it begins operation. Once resources are committed to the foreign operation, the firm may not move elsewhere easily.

■ Since negotiations are conducted largely between parties whose cultures, educational backgrounds, and expectations differ, it is very difficult for negotiators to understand sentiments and present convincing arguments. Negotiation simulation offers a means of anticipating responses and planning an approach to the actual bargaining.

■ Historically, developed countries ensured through military intervention and coercion that the terms agreed upon between their investors and recipient countries would be carried out. The East-West political schism and a series of international resolutions have caused the near demise of these methods for settling disputes. The promise of giving or withholding aid has been used more recently by developed countries as a device for influencing host governments.

■ A number of bilateral treaties have been established whereby host countries agree to compensate investors for losses from expropriation, civil war, and currency devaluation or control. These agreements are not often clear about the mechanism or place of settlement for the losses.

■ Although international organizations or groups in third countries are frequently used to arbitrate trade disputes among individuals from more than one country, this method has been used very rarely to settle investment disputes, because governments are reluctant to relinquish sovereignty over matters occurring within their borders.

■ To prevent companies from playing one country against another or vice versa, groups of governments or companies occasionally have banded together to present a unified front in order to improve the terms received.

■ External relations may be used by both companies and countries to develop a good image, overcome a bad one, and create useful proponents for their positions. If successful, this strategy may result in better terms of operation for either side.

■ International agreements have been made to protect important intangible assets such as patents, trademarks, and copyrights. Since millions of dollars are often spent in the development of these assets, worldwide protection is a necessity.

■ One of the big problems for firms with intangible assets in recent years has been the pirating of the assets in countries that have not signed international agreements or do not actively enforce their laws on the asset protection.

C   A   S   E
PEPSICO IN INDIA[55]

In 1989 PepsiCo chairman D. Wayne Calloway said, "We are still basically an American company with offshore interests. As the nineties progress, that's going to change. We'll be a truly global consumer products company." The company's Indian snack-food and soft-drink joint venture, which began production in 1990, was a key part of that strategy. But in the first year of operation, the joint venture's managing director announced "losses of millions of dollars" because of delays in setting up production.

The Global Competitive Situation   Two companies, Coca-Cola and PepsiCo, have dominated the global market for soft drinks. The United States has been the biggest market, with per capita consumption of about 700 bottles per year. Analysts agree that this consumption figure is so large that almost all company soft-drink growth must come by building market share rather than getting people to increase their consumption. Even so, the companies have promoted breakfast sales and have added soft-drink versions to try to increase consumption. The fierce competition within the United States has resulted in industry returns on assets and sales of less than half what they have been abroad. Within the United States in 1990 the two companies were close rivals; Coca-Cola and PepsiCo held about 40 and 32 percent of the market, respectively. But in terms of total global sales, Coca-Cola's 47 percent share was more than double that of PepsiCo's; consequently, Coca-Cola has been much stronger where profits are

higher and where sales growth is expected to be much faster. For example, per capita consumption outside the United States is only about 14 percent of the U.S. per capita consumption; thus there is much more room to grow. In 1989 Coca-Cola earned almost 80 percent of its profits outside the United States as opposed to only 15 percent for PepsiCo.

Players other than Coca-Cola and PepsiCo are small globally in comparison; however, some have large shares in specific country or regional markets, such as Cadbury Schweppes in the United Kingdom.

In the soft-drink industry it is generally conceded that there is a tremendous advantage in being first into a market. Not only is brand loyalty built up fast and difficult to change, but the early entrants gain the best bottlers/distributors. Coca-Cola preceded PepsiCo into Western Europe, Latin America, and Japan, and PepsiCo has had an up-hill battle building market share in those areas. In the late 1980s PepsiCo sponsored Michael Jackson and Madonna concerts abroad, but has clearly had problems combatting Coca-Cola. For example, PepsiCo actually lost market share in France during the late 1980s; and when PepsiCo started doing well in the United Kingdom, Coca-Cola stole the bottler/distributor Cadbury Schweppes away from PepsiCo. Yet PepsiCo beat Coca-Cola into the former Soviet Union in 1974 and dominates that market.

Because of the realization of the first-in advantage, PepsiCo has pushed hard in recent years to enter markets where Coca-Cola is not dominant, such as entering Myanmar ahead of Coca-Cola in 1990.

Indian Market Potential   PepsiCo had been in the Indian market during the mid-1950s but pulled out because of lack of profitability. Coca-Cola had operated in India for 27 years but left in 1977 because of disagreements with the Indian government. Coca-Cola's departure created an opportunity for PepsiCo; however, PepsiCo did not begin its three years of formal negotiations with the government of India until 1985. After Coke's departure an Indian firm, Parle Exports, became the dominant supplier in India with its soft drink, Thums Up. By 1988 Parle Exports was estimated to have sales of about $150 million per year, which comprised between 60 and 70 percent of the market. Parle Exports was also exporting a mango pulp drink, Maaza Mango, to various markets, including the United States.

The Indian market for soft drinks has been growing rapidly. When Coca-Cola departed, annual soft-drink sales were a little over a half billion bottles a year. By 1990 they were about 3 billion bottles a year and were expected to quadruple during the 1990s. India's population growth was expected to make that country surpass China as the most populated in the world. Furthermore, India had a much larger middle class than China, which was estimated to be about 150 million people when PepsiCo entered formal negotiations with the Indian government. Additionally, many observers have predicted that India will eventually become an economic giant, thus growing incomes should support more sales.

Another indication of market potential was that India's per capita consumption of soft drinks was estimated to be only 3 bottles per year in 1989 as compared to 13 bottles per year in neighboring Pakistan. Coca-Cola was selling 122 bottles per capita per year in Latin America, also a low-income area.

Indian Attitude Toward Foreign Investment   The attitude was summed up by India's president of the Associated Chambers of Commerce and Industry of India, who said, "The basic thing is that most of our people, in all political parties, have no concept of how the world is moving. My political friends think it's the seventeenth century and that every investment, like the East India Company, is going to come into India and take over." His reference was to the long domination of India by interests from Britain, France, and Portugal, which took out great wealth without returning noticeable benefit to the Indian economy.

India has approved foreign investment on a case-by-case basis with approval necessary at the highest governmental level. By the time PepsiCo began its negotiations, the maximum foreign equity holding was only 40 percent of an Indian enterprise. Furthermore, foreign firms were required to develop exports to compensate for imported equipment and components and for dividend payments.

Because of the political sensitivity to foreign investment, negotiations tended to be long and usually were public. Furthermore, little action was apt to be taken during election periods as politicians were afraid of adverse reaction if they were to support the entry of foreign firms. For example, when PepsiCo began its negotiations Gillette had recently been granted approval on an investment. Gillette had been lured because India has the highest unit razor-blade sales of any country in the world. Gillette spent seven years negotiating during two changes of government and finally settled on a 24 percent equity holding, an agreement to export 25 percent of its output, and the nonuse of the Gillette name on its products. The name issue has been important to Indian authorities because of (1) a belief that many consumers will think wrongly that a foreign-associated product is better and (2) that a locally associated brand name will give greater continuity in case the foreign investor leaves the market on its own or by the government's decision.

Coca-Cola and IBM both departed India at about the same time because of the strict operating restrictions that had come about after their initial entry. Coca-Cola objected to three governmental demands: that it reduce its equity holding from 100 to 40 percent, that it divulge its formula, and that it use dual trademarks so that Indian consumers would familiarize themselves with a local logo. Coca-Cola was particularly adamant about the latter two directives. It had always relied on the mystique of a secret formula for its promotion, and it feared an expropriation once the new trademark became accepted.

There has also been a pervading feeling among non-Indian firms that Indian competitors can and do use a great deal of pull to prevent foreign competition. Officially, one is told that applications have simply run into "political difficulties," but behind the scenes Indian business leaders align themselves with Indian political leaders. For example, when Coca-Cola was given its directives in 1977, Ramesh Chauhan, the head of Parle Exports was an ally of Prime Minister Moraji Desai while Coca-Cola executives were close to Indira Gandhi, the head of the opposition party.

The Negotiations   PepsiCo first negotiated a contingent joint venture arrangement with two Indian entities, which it felt could ease the negotiation process. One of these was a division of Tata Industries, perhaps India's most powerful private company. The second was a government-owned company, Punjab Agro Industries, which could give the appearance that the public interest would be served in the venture.

Although the initial investment was only $15 million, any approval had to be made at the cabinet level. There were twenty parliamentary debates about the proposed investment over a three-year period.

PepsiCo and its partners proposed that the new company be located in the politically volatile state of Punjab (see Map 13.1), where they enlisted the support of Sikh leaders who lobbied publicly in their behalf. They claimed that Sikh terrorism might be subdued by providing jobs and help to Punjabi farmers. The partners estimated that 25,000 jobs would be created in the Punjab and another 25,000 elsewhere because of the investment.

Their second argument was that even the

former Soviet Union and China had allowed entry of foreign soft-drink producers, thus putting India out of step even with other socialist countries. Their third argument was that new technology and know-how would prevent some of the wastage of Punjabi fruits, estimated to be about 30 percent. Finally, they contended that the lack of competition with foreign firms had kept prices and margins artificially high so that there was little incentive for local firms to grow and distribute widely. Competitive soft-drink sales were limited primarily to the largest cities.

Opponents contended that foreign capital and imports should be restricted to high-technology areas where India lacked expertise, that the venture's proposal to process foods (potato chips, corn chips, fruit drinks, and sauces) would simply displace what could be made in the home, and that imported equipment would hurt India's balance of payments. Journalists widely reported that PepsiCo had a CIA connection aimed at undermining India's independence.

Meanwhile, another U.S.-based company, Double-Cola, had successfully terminated a secret six-year negotiation in 1987. The agreement called for them to open three bottling plants immediately and another twenty-seven later on. Double-Cola apparently had an advantage in that it was controlled by nonresident Indians in London, and the Indian Prime Minister, Rajiv Gandhi, wanted to lure investment from Indians living overseas. Double-Cola also promised to use Indian raw materials and to reinvest profits in India.

The agreement with the PepsiCo group was signed in 1988 and included the following provisions for the venture's scheduled commencement of operations in 1990: (1) the company would export five times the value of its imports, an amount of about $150 million over the first ten-year period of operations; (2) soft drink sales would not exceed 25 percent of the joint venture's sales; (3) PepsiCo would limit its ownership to 39.9 percent; (4) 75 percent of concentrate would be exported; (5) an agricultural research center would be established; (6)

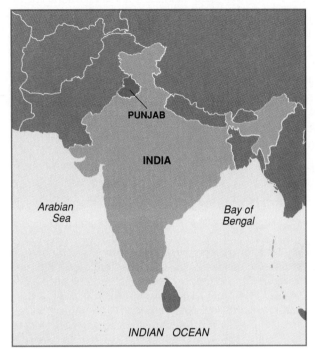

Map 13.1
India
PepsiCo's major Indian production facilities are in the state of Punjab.

the company could sell Pepsi Era, 7-Up Era, and Marinda Era; and (7) fruit- and vegetable-processing plants would be set up.

Aftermath and Renegotiation   Once PepsiCo's venture was approved, Coca-Cola made an application to reenter the Indian market through production within an export processing zone, which would permit 25 percent of output to be sold within India rather than in export markets. This was a threat to PepsiCo inasmuch as the Coca-Cola name was still well-remembered in India, and cans of Coke were even smuggled in from Nepal. But after sixteen months, Coca-Cola's application was denied, leading a Coca-Cola official to say that India "doesn't follow its own rules."

In late 1989 a new prime minister, V. P. Singh, took power in a minority government. As finance minister in the mid-1980s he had promoted liberalization of foreign investment. However, after taking power he almost immediately made conflicting statements about foreign investment. In early 1990 the venture began production of snack foods and announced that soft-drink production would begin by summer. Prime Minister Singh announced that the government would have to reexamine the PepsiCo agreement.

Several things then happened in quick succession. First, the U.S. government, without public reference to PepsiCo, announced that it might impose trade sanctions against India under its Super 301 legislation. The threat was made because of India's strict foreign investment regulations. Indian governmental officials and the joint venture's management then met secretly. Subsequently, PepsiCo agreed to place a new logo, Lehar, above the Pepsi insignia. Pepsi also lobbied publicly against Super 301 sanctions against India, and the U.S. government backed down on its threats. The partners announced that they would invest about $1 billion in the venture during the 1990s. The Minister of Food Processing Industries announced tax breaks for food processors.

Questions

1. Did PepsiCo give too many concessions to enter the Indian market? Could the company have negotiated better terms?
2. In light of later events, should Coca-Cola have abandoned the Indian market in 1977?
3. From an Indian standpoint, evaluate the government's restrictions on direct investment.
4. What behavioral factor might affect negotiations between teams from the United States and India?

Chapter Notes

1. Data for the case were taken from Louis Morano, "Multinationals and Nation-States: The Case of Aramco," *Orbis,* Summer, 1979, pp. 447–468; "Oil New Power Structure," *Business Week,* December 24, 1979, pp. 82–88; "Saudi Takeover of Aramco Looms," *Wall Street Journal,* August 6, 1980, p. 21; Ted D'Affisio, "Aramco Long-Term Contract with Saudis May Pressure Oil Company Earnings," *The Oil Daily,* February 9, 1987, p. 3; "Saudis Reportedly Map Changes for Aramco," *New York Times,* May 10, 1988, p. 34; "Arabian Might," *Economist,* December 24, 1988, p. 79; "Aramco Has Been the Bridge Between Two Nations," *The Oil Daily,* September 18, 1989, p. B-19; Andrew Pollack, "Saudi Stake of U.S. Companies," *New York Times,* August 21, 1990, p. C1 ff; John J. Fialka, "In a Saudi Oil Colony, Workers Live in Fear—Or So They Hear," *Wall Street Journal,* August 31, 1990, p. A8; Gene G. Marcial, "If a Shooting War Breaks Out, Fluor Will Win," *Business Week,* December 10, 1990, p. 209; John Rossant and Robert Buderi, "Aramco Toughs It Out." *Business Week,* February 4, 1991, p. 44.

2. Nathan Fagre and Louis T. Wells, Jr., "Bargaining Power of Multinationals and Host Governments," *Journal of International Business Studies,* Vol. 8, No. 2, Fall 1982, pp. 9–23, studied ownership percentages of foreign investors in Latin America.

3. Masaaki Kotabe, "Creating Countertrade Opportunities in Financially Distressed Developing Countries: Framework and Nigerian Example," *International Marketing Review,* Vol. 6, No. 5, 1989, pp. 36–49.

4. Many of these conflicts are discussed in "The Multinationals: An Urgent Need for New Ties to Government," *Business Week,* March 12, 1979, pp. 74–82; John C. Banks, "Negotiating International Mining Agreements: Win-Win Versus Win-Lose Bargaining," *Columbia Journal of World Business,* Winter 1987, pp. 67–71.

5. Thane Peterson, Frank J. Comes, Jonathan Kapstein, Steven J. Dryden, and John J. Keller, "The Swedes Give AT&T and the U.S. Painful Black Eyes," *Business Week,* No. 2997, May 4, 1987, pp. 44–45. For a discussion of U.S. government efforts to persuade Japan to remove its barriers to direct investment, see Marcus W. Brauchli, "U.S. to Prod Tokyo on Easing Investment," *Wall Street Journal,* November 2, 1989, p. A18.

6. Niles Howard, "The World Woos U.S. Business," *Dun's Business Month,* Vol. 120, No. 5, November 1982, pp. 38–45. For effects on locational patterns, see Raymond Vernon, "Multinationals Are Mushrooming," *Challenge,* Vol. 29, No. 2, May–June 1986, pp. 43–44. For examples of competition among the states in the United States,

see Martin Tolchin and Susan Tolchin, "The States' Global Hustlers," *Across the Board,* Vol. 25, No. 4, April 1988, pp. 14–22.

7. Robert Weigand, "International Investments: Weighing the Incentives," *Harvard Business Review,* Vol. 61, No. 4, July–August 1983, pp. 146–152; Stephen E. Guisinger, "Do Performance Requirements and Investment Incentives Work?" *The World Economy,* Vol. 9, No. 1, March 1986, pp. 79–96; Joann S. Lublin, "Toyota Spurns British Aid for Auto Plant," *Wall Street Journal,* April 18, 1989, p. A22.

8. R. Hal Mason, "Investment Incentives and Performance Requirements: A Case Study of Food Manufacturing," a paper presented to the Academy of International Business, San Francisco, December 29, 1983, which was a summary of a larger report submitted to the World Bank.

9. William A. Stoever, "Renegotiations: The Cutting Edge of Relations between MNCs and LDCs," *Columbia Journal of World Business,* Spring 1979, pp. 6–7.

10. Eric Berg, "Peru to Pay Part of Debt in Goods," *New York Times,* September 17, 1987, p. 25 + .

11. Dennis J. Encarnation and Suchil Vachani, "Foreign Ownership: When Hosts Change the Rules," *Harvard Business Review,* Vol. 63, No. 5, September–October 1985, pp. 152–160.

12. Stoever, *op. cit.*

13. These and other differences are noted in John L. Graham and Roy A. Herberger, Jr., "Negotiators Abroad—Don't Shoot from the Hip," *Harvard Business Review,* Vol. 61, No. 4, July–August 1983, pp. 160–168.

14. Stoever, *op. cit.,* pp. 12–13.

15. William A. Stoever, "Why State Corporations in Developing Countries Have Failed to Attract Foreign Investment," *International Marketing Review,* Vol. 6, No. 3, 1989, pp. 62–77.

16. Ashok Kapoor, *International Business Negotiations: A Study in India* (New University Press, 1970), p. 284.

17. George Schwarzenberger, "The Protection of British Property Abroad," *Current Legal Problems,* Vol. 5, 1952, pp. 295–299; Oliver J. Lissitzyn, *International Law Today and Tomorrow* (Dobbs Ferry, N.Y.: Oceana Publications, 1965), p. 77; and Gillis Wetter, "Diplomatic Assistance to Private Investment," *University of Chicago Law Review,* Vol. 29, 1962, p. 275.

18. Ian Brownlie, *Principles of Public International Law* (Oxford, England: Oxford University Press, 1966), pp. 435–436.

19. Green H. Hackworth, *Digest of International Law* (Washington, D.C.: U.S. Government Printing Office, 1942), pp. 655–661.

20. David R. Mummery, *The Protection of International Private Investment* (New York: Praeger Publishers, 1968), p. 49.

21. "OPIC Contends Levy Against Revere Copper Wasn't Expropriation," *Wall Street Journal,* June 15, 1977, p. 35.

22. Mummery, *op. cit.,* p. 98.

23. Raymond Vernon, "The Multinationals: No Strings Attached," *Foreign Policy,* Winter 1978–1979, p. 126.

24. Mummery, *op. cit.,* p. 74.

25. "New World Bank Agency for Investments Sets Debut," *Wall Street Journal,* April 13, 1988, p. 20; "World Bank Agency Reinsures GE Project," *Wall Street Journal,* June 6, 1990, p. A16; Ibrahim F. I. Shihata, "Encouraging International Corporate Investment: The Role of the Multilateral Investment Guarantee Agency," *Columbia Journal of World Business,* Spring 1988, pp. 11–18.

26. William A. Stoever, "Issues Emerging in Iranian Claims Negotiations," *Wall Street Journal,* May 7, 1981, p. 26; James B. Stewart and Peter Truell, "U.S. Firms Win Some, Lose Some at Tribunal Arbitrating $5 Billion in Claims Against Iran," *Wall Street Journal,* November 15, 1984, p. 38; Gerald F. Seib, "Administration Rejects Iranian Overture to Link Hostage Talks and Frozen Assets," *Wall Street Journal,* August 9, 1989, p. A5.

27. "Chile Halts Shipments to France of Copper from El Teniente Mines," *Wall Street Journal,* October 17, 1972, p. 12.

28. John Marcom, Jr., "U.K. Court Says U.S. Bank Owes Money to Libya," *Wall Street Journal,* September 3, 1987, p. 12.

29. "Arco Unit Awarded Payment from Libya's Takeover of Assets," *Wall Street Journal,* April 4, 1977, p. 4; and "California Standard, Texaco Win Ruling Against Libya Takeover of Oil Holdings," *Wall Street Journal,* March 3, 1977, p. 4.

30. Burton Yale Pines, "Hollow Chambers of the World Court," *Wall Street Journal,* April 12, 1984, p. 30.

31. For further discussions of the subject, see Jack G. Kaikati, "The Challenge of the Arab Boycott," *Sloan Management Review,* Winter 1977, pp. 83–100; Dan S. Chill, *The Arab Boycott of Israel* (New York: Praeger Publishers, 1976).

32. "Saudis Warn Toyota on Ford," *New York Times,* June 24, 1981, p. D5.

33. "Sara Lee Corp. Agrees to $725,000 Payment in Anti-Boycott Case," *Wall Street Journal,* August 8, 1988, p. 4.

34. Sue Shellenbarger, "Off the Blacklist," *Wall Street Journal,* May 1, 1990, p. A1 ff.

35. Don Wallace, Jr., *International Regulation of Multinational Corporations* (New York: Praeger Publishers, 1976), pp. 5–26.

36. For a discussion of how codes may presage national regulations, see Richard L. Rowan and Duncan C. Campbell, "The Attempt to Regulate Industrial Relations through International Codes of Conduct," *Columbia Journal of World Business,* Vol. 18, No. 2, Summer 1983, pp. 64–80.

37. Thane Peterson, "Can Europe Catch Up in the High-Tech Race?" *Business Week,* October 23, 1989, pp. 142 ff.

38. Charles T. Crespy, "Global Marketing Is the New Public Relations Challenge," *Public Relations Quarterly,* Vol. 31, No. 2, Summer 1986, pp. 5–8.

39. Helen White, "Indochina Is Wooing Outside Investment," *Wall Street Journal,* May 2, 1989, p. A12; Barry Wain, "Vietnam Luring Hardy Foreign Investors," *Wall Street Journal,* July 12, 1989, p. A12.

40. "Corporate Citizenship: Outstanding Examples Worldwide," *Top Management Report,* 1979, p. 2.

41. Ashok Kapoor and J. J. Boddewyn, *International Business-Government Relations: U.S. Corporate Experience in Asia and Western Europe* (New York: American Management Association, 1973), p. 32.

42. Belmont F. Haydel, "Case Study of a Social Responsibility Program: Gulf & Western Industries, Inc., in the Dominican Republic in Employee Health, Housing, Education, Sports, and General Welfare, and Other Assistance to the Dominican Republic," paper presented to the Academy of International Business, New York, October 7, 1983; Pamela G. Hollie, "G. & W. to Sell Dominican Holdings," *New York Times,* June 13, 1984, p. D1.

43. For a discussion of the advertising part of the promotion, see S. Prakash Sethi, "Advocacy Advertising and the Multinational Corporation," *Columbia Journal of World Business,* Fall 1977, pp. 32–46.

44. Douglas Nigh and Philip L. Cochran, "Issues Management and the Multinational Enterprise," *Management International Review*, Vol. 27, No. 1, 1987, pp. 4–12; Richard E. Wokutch, "Corporate Social Responsibility Japanese Style," *Academy of Management Executive*, Vol. 4, No. 2, 1990, pp. 56–74.

45. "Corporate Citizenship: Outstanding Examples Worldwide," *Top Management Report*, 1979, p. 2; Belmont F. Haydel, "Description and Analysis of Johnson & Johnson's Strategic Management Process of Its Live for Life Program," paper presented at the Academy of International Business Northeast Annual Meeting, Baltimore, Maryland, June 5, 1989; "General Motors Public Interest Report 1990," Detroit, May 15, 1990; Michael Schroeder and Jonathan Kapstein, "Charity Doesn't Begin at Home Anymore," *Business Week*, February 25, 1991, p. 91.

46. Frans G. J. Derkinderen, "Transnational Business Latitude in Developing Countries," *Management International Review*, Vol. 22, No. 4, 1982, p. 58.

47. "Thailand Zinc Talks by Gulf and Western Unit Run into Snag," *Wall Street Journal*, February 25, 1977, p. 22; "Gulf and Western Thailand Unit Accepts Plan for $90 Million Zinc Mine, Refinery," *Wall Street Journal*, March 2, 1977, p. 12.

48. William T. Ryan and Doria Bonham-Yeaman, "International Patent Cooperation," *Columbia Journal of World Business*, Vol. 17, No. 4, Winter 1982, pp. 63–66.

49. Thomas J. Maronick, "European Patent Laws and Decisions: Implications for Multinational Marketing Strategy," *International Marketing Review*, Vol. 5, No. 2, Summer 1988, pp. 20–30.

50. Paul Lewis, "Counterfeiting of Goods Rises," *New York Times*, October 10, 1983, p. D9; "U.S. Says Counterfeits Cost Concerns Billions of Dollars in Lost Sales," *Wall Street Journal*, February 27, 1984, p. 35.

51. See, for example, Steven Erlanger, "Thailand, Where Pirated Tapes Are Everywhere and Profitable," *New York Times*, November 27, 1990, pp. B1–B2.

52. Michael G. Harvey and Ilkka A. Ronkainen, "International Counterfeiters: Marketing Success without the Cost and the Risk," *Columbia Journal of World Business*, Vol. 20, No. 3, Fall 1985, p. 39.

53. Louis Kraar, "Fighting the Fakes from Taiwan," *Fortune*, Vol. 107, No. 11, May 30, 1983, pp.114–116; "Two Who Smuggled Counterfeit Computers Get Prison and Fines," *Wall Street Journal*, May 1, 1984, p. 62; Todd Mason, "How High Tech Foils the Counterfeiters," *Business Week*, May 20, 1985, p. 119.

54. Harvey and Ronkainen, *op. cit.*, p. 43.

55. Data for the case were taken from Sheila Tefft, Cheryl Debes, and Dean Foust, "The Mouse That Roared at Pepsi," *Business Week*, September 7, 1987, p. 42; Subrata N. Chakravarty, "How Pepsi Broke into India," *Forbes*, November 27, 1989, pp. 43–44; Lincoln Kaye, "Pepping Up the Punjab," *Far Eastern Economic Review*, October 27, 1988, pp. 77–78; Steven R. Weisman, "Pepsi Sets Off a Cola War in India," *New York Times*, March 21, 1988, p. 28; Anthony Spaeth, "India Beckons—and Frustrates," *Wall Street Journal*, September 22, 1989, pp. R23–R25; Anthony Ramirez, "It's Only Soft Drinks at Coca Cola," *New York Times*, May 21, 1990, p. C1 ff; Barbara Crossette, "After Long Fight, Pepsi Enters India," *New York Times*, May 24, 1990, p. C2; Michael J. McCarthy, "India Gives Final Approval to Pepsi's Plans," *Wall Street Journal*, May 24, 1990, p. A5; Anthony Spaeth, "Political Turbulence in India Raises Questions About the Country's Economy," *Wall Street Journal*, August 8, 1990, p. A8; Anthony Spaeth and Ajay Singh, "India Rejects Coca-Cola's Bid to Sell Soft Drinks, Giving Pepsi an Advantage," *Wall Street Journal*, March 16, 1990, p. B5; "Losses at PepsiCo Venture in India," *New York Times*, February 16, 1991, p. 33.

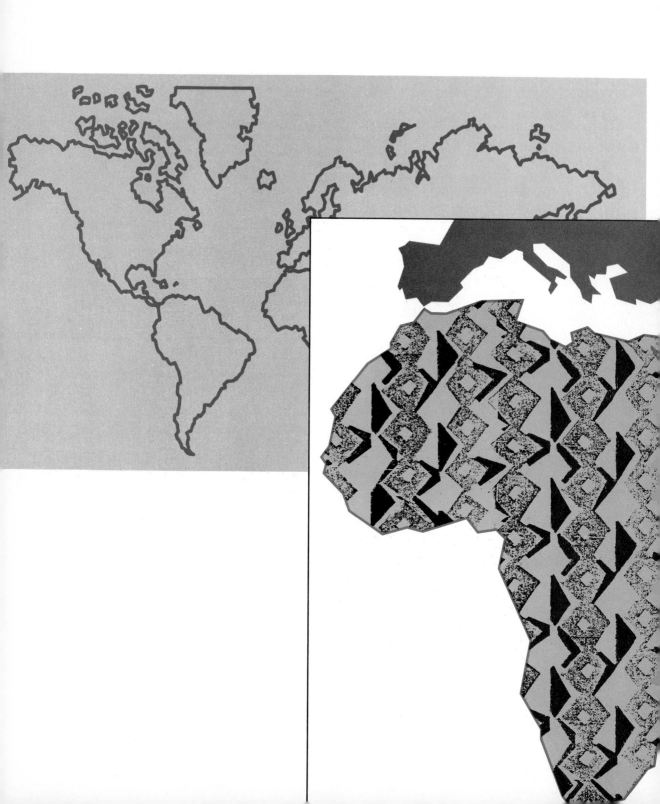

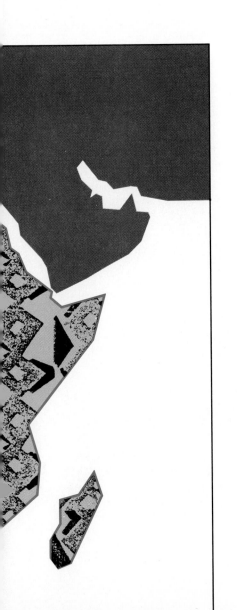

PART 6
CORPORATE POLICY AND STRATEGY

Whether a firm is heavily engaged in foreign markets or supply sources or is merely in the initial process of developing them, many interrelated alternatives must be considered. In this part we will discuss those operational alternatives that normally transcend decision making within functional disciplines. These alternatives include where to go, what form the foreign operations should take, and how to organize the corporate structure to accommodate the international operations.

Chapter 14 discusses the different strategic dimensions of global production and import/export operations. This discussion includes means of effecting off-shore manufacturing, an examination of factors favoring export operations, and a description of institutions to assist in exporting.

Chapter 15 examines some of the major means and activities by which foreign involvement may be undertaken. The chapter first examines factors that should be considered when deciding how to conduct international business, and then, it describes the major operating forms.

Chapter 16 discusses methods of comparing countries when choices have to be made in terms of where to go to sell or produce. The emphasis is on the geographic allocation of resources in terms of amount and sequence of expansion.

Chapter 17 elaborates strategies that top management can follow to make the necessary changes for foreign operations while concurrently maintaining order and control for the organization as a whole and includes a discussion of decisions, location, organization structure, and means for planning and control.

CHAPTER 14

GLOBAL SOURCING, PRODUCTION, AND EXPORT STRATEGIES

Right mixture makes good mortar.
ENGLISH PROVERB

Objectives

- To gain an overview of the different dimensions of a global production strategy.

- To describe the major differences in ways that firms can source materials and components and manufacture and assemble products for international use.

- To identify the key elements of import and export strategies.

- To understand the role of the government in the mechanics of trade, especially export promotion.

After 18 months of residing in the United States, John Robertson, a New Zealander, glances frequently at a map of the United States on his wall, wondering when he will get the time and resources to travel into the various metropolitan areas of the central, southern, and eastern states. Through such travel, he believes he can gain an improved appreciation of the characteristics of the markets for fresh-cut flowers, an item that he began importing into the United States from New Zealand during his summer "vacation" from school.

In August 1981, John and his family left New Zealand (see Map 14.1) for Seattle so that he could study for his MBA degree at the University of Washington. A month earlier, he had resigned from his job and leased their house and small farm. On completion of the degree, the Robertsons intended to return to New Zealand where John would seek employment in a senior management position with a company involved in exporting.

New Zealand is a country the size of Oregon, with a population of 3 million. The relatively small size of its population base coupled with its distance from world markets presents a barrier to its ability to establish an industrial base competitive with those of the leading world industrial nations. Therefore, New Zealand is highly dependent on world trade, importing fuel and manufacturing products and gaining most of its foreign exchange through exports of agricultural produce. Its f.o.b. (free on board, excludes international shipping cost) exports average around 22 percent of gross domestic product, compared with the U.S. figure of 8 percent. In order to hold its place in the world economy, New Zealand lobbies hard to remove the restrictions imposed on imported agricultural products by the EEC, Japan, and the United States. Alongside this campaign, efforts are being made to diversify into horticultural products like fresh flowers and fruit.

C A S E
SUNSET FLOWERS
OF
NEW ZEALAND, LTD.[1]

Immediately prior to leaving New Zealand, John had been employed for almost four years as the financial manager of a company involved in growing, wholesaling, and exporting live ornamental trees and shrubs. The company used agents to sell its product on world markets, including two based in the United States, one in Japan, and one in Europe. The agents were paid retainers and typically provided services for several export companies. The experience gained from working for this company provided John with a background in the procedures necessary for exporting and an insight into the problems that exporters face when trying to compete in foreign markets where control over representation is hindered by distance and lack of knowledge of business procedures.

It was while working for this company that John was introduced to cut-flower products. The Robertsons raised enough money to purchase a farm and then became acquainted with their neighbors, the Pratts, who were first-class horticulturalists. The Pratts had developed a new variety of the Leucadendron plant that yielded a beautiful, red leaflike flower that the Robertsons and Pratts felt could be exported successfully.

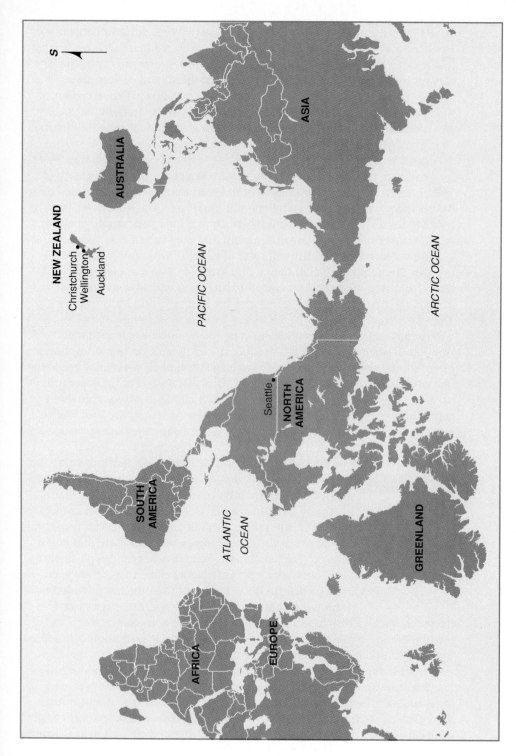

Map 14.1

New Zealanders' View of the World

New Zealand, an industrial country that is a member of the OECD, is one of two OECD countries in the Southern Hemisphere. The obvious distance from New Zealand to major world markets, such as the United States, is an important barrier that needs to be overcome by an exporter such as Sunset Flowers of New Zealand, Ltd.

During the first year of production, the Robertsons and Pratts, in a new entrepreneurial venture, exported their yield through an established export company whose principal line of business involved exporting fresh fruit and vegetables. The company had a large market share of this business and had assumed a significant share of the exports of New Zealand cut flowers. The New Zealand cut-flower export industry was small and, with the exception of a trade in orchids, immature. Export companies provided the many part-time cut-flower growers with the marketing infrastructure that they themselves were unable to put together.

As the harvesting season progressed, the returns paid to the Pratts by the exporter declined, until they reached a point where production levels of 10,000 stems or fewer became only marginally profitable. Gary and John met with the export company to discuss the trends. The company explained that price was a function of volume, and that the lower prices were a result of the increased volumes of cut flowers being placed on the world markets. Export market returns were substantiated by documentation.

Gary and John were not convinced by the explanation. However, they knew little about world markets for fresh-cut flowers, and they could only speculate as to the reasons for the price movements. As there were no other established flower export houses to turn to, the only way to research the matter seemed to be to do so themselves. As John was going to be in the United States for his MBA studies, an opportunity presented itself for him to carry out some research there.

During his first semester of school, John didn't have much time to do any research. At the end of the winter quarter of 1982, when he picked up a sample cart of Leucadendron flowers consigned by Gary to him at Sea-Tac Airport, his ideas on how to approach the market were not defined. He took the flowers home and, on inspection, found that they had kept well in transit and that their quality was good.

In the six days remaining before school began again, John felt that he should concentrate his efforts on gaining and assembling information concerning the production and shipping costs associated with the product, production forecasts, import procedures, the basic structure of the U.S. cut-flower industry, and market reaction to the Leucadendron.

When picking up the samples from the airport, John had been told by airline officials that he would have to engage the services of a customs broker if he was going to undertake imports of invoice value greater than $250.00. Presuming such brokers to be the experts on procedures required to import, he called to make an appointment with one. The broker was most helpful. John was told that imported cut flowers were required to be inspected by U.S.D.A. on arrival. Once given clearance, duty was assessed at the rate of 8 percent on f.o.b. value. The broker would arrange for these clearances through U.S.D.A. and U.S. Customs. The broker charges a fee for such services, which is fixed for shipments regardless of size but which will vary among brokers. The broker with whom the meeting was held charged

$50.00 per shipment. If John wanted, the broker would arrange for freight forwarding companies to arrange for transportation to foreign markets.

As John prepared his market strategy, he consulted numerous U.S. publications that helped him get a feel for the U.S. market. In addition, he asked Gary to mail him a copy of a market-research publication funded by the New Zealand Export-Import Corporation that included research on the U.S. flower market. From that publication, he found that the major agricultural exports from New Zealand in order of importance were kiwi fruit, apples, berryfruit, processed kiwi fruit, flowers and plants, squash, frozen vegetables, onions, and other products.

John finally contacted a Seattle wholesaler who was willing to place a large order for flowers, providing John would give him exclusive rights to distribute the flowers in Washington State. While John was pleased with the reaction from the wholesaler, he was aware that he had made the approach with insufficient preparation. Had he underpriced the product? Was the credit of the firm sound? Are "exclusive rights" typically given in this industry, and should he have conceded them? Was the reaction one that is normal when a new product is shown to a market, and will repeat orders be placed? In addition to these market-related issues, there were administrative and organizational issues to consider. What should be his role in the marketing chain? Should he act as an agent taking a commission or buy from Gary and resell the product? What form of organization should he establish?

INTRODUCTION

As the Sunset Flowers case demonstrates, there is more to export profitability than a good idea. Once an entrepreneur has identified a product, he needs to determine if there is a market somewhere, a process that involves a significant amount of market research, which may or may not be supported by the home country government. Then the entrepreneur needs to develop a production strategy, prepare the goods for market, determine the best strategy for getting the goods transported to market, sell the product, and receive payment.

All of these steps require careful planning and preparation. The production strategy for Sunset Flowers was relatively easy, because all production took place in New Zealand. In the case of industrial products, the strategy can be very complex as different countries are evaluated, using labor costs and so on, as possible production sites.

Sunset Flowers also demonstrates that a firm has limits of ability. Freight forwarders are used to move goods from one country to another, and banks are needed to collect payment. Thus export, as well as import, strategies require the utilization of experts to move ideas to finished products to final sales.

In a study of European and Japanese MNEs, for example, it was found that the MNEs use a mix of sourcing strategies simultaneously when marketing the product in the United States. Fifty-nine percent of the firms reported using a single sourcing strategy. All of the product was either exported from the home country or manufactured in the United States for the U.S. market. Japanese firms were more likely to export to the United States, whereas European firms were more likely to manufacture in the United States. Some of the European firms used production facilities in other European countries—and in some cases, Japan and Canada—to service the U.S. market. In this study, firms did not service the U.S. market from production facilities in developing countries.[2]

European firms tend to service foreign markets through investment in that market.

Japanese firms tend to service foreign markets through exports.

Global Sourcing and Production Strategies

Most firms have the option of where they want to source (locate) production for worldwide sales. As is the case in industries such as automobiles, for any given market the MNE can manufacture the product itself, or it can buy the product from someone else. If it decides to manufacture the product itself, it can either manufacture it in the local market or manufacture it in another country and import it into the market.

Corporate options include:
- Buy versus manufacture
- Manufacture in domestic or foreign plants
- Sell products at home or in foreign markets

Obviously, the true MNE is involved in fairly sophisticated forms of production sharing, in which it may produce and/or assemble components in one or several countries for markets all over the world. In its simplest form, the MNE might manufacture goods in the home country and export them to final markets. Or the MNE could establish production in different countries to service those particular markets. However, the past decade has shown an increase in intermediate goods, such as components, being produced in many countries and shipped to other countries for assembly and sale. The production and exporting functions are much more complex than they used to be under the simpler forms.

Global Sourcing and Production Alternatives

For each particular market being serviced by an MNE, the idea of global sourcing implies that firms need to determine where parts and components will be manufactured and where the final products will be assembled.

Firms develop competitive advantage by integrating operations across borders.

Historically, firms tended to operate on a country-by-country basis. However, as firms have become more global in orientation, they have found that they can develop a definite competitive advantage by coordinating and integrating their operations across national borders.[3]

From an international standpoint, this global production and sourcing strategy can be better understood by looking at Fig. 14.1, which illustrates the basic options available by country (the home country or any foreign country) and by stage in the production process (sourcing of components and sale of products).

For example, one of Ford Motor Company's strategies is to assemble cars in Hermosillo, Mexico, and ship them into the United States. The cars are

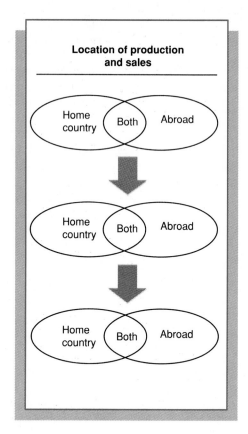

Figure 14.1
Global Sourcing and Production Strategy
Companies have many possibilities to source raw materials and assemble them into final goods to service markets worldwide. For example, a U.S. firm could source components in the United States, assemble them in Mexico, and sell them back in the United States or in other countries.

designed by the Japanese company Toyo Kogyo Co. (Mazda) and use some Japanese parts. Ford can purchase components manufactured in Japan and ship them to the United States for final assembly and sale in the U.S. market, or it can have the Japanese- and U.S.-made components shipped to Mexico for final assembly and sale in the United States and Mexico. In the case of Mexican assembly, some of the components would come from the United States, some from Japan, and a small percentage from Mexico. If the components are manufactured in Japan, many of the raw materials were probably imported.

An expansion of Fig. 14.1 would show 64 different combinations for manufacturing components and assembling them into final products for different markets. This expanded model would account for the facts that components can be manufactured internally to the firm or purchased from external (unrelated) manufacturers and that final assembly can also be done internal to the firm or by external firms. Manufacture of components and final assembly may take place in the home country of the firm, the country where the firm is trying to sell the product, a developed third country, or a developing third country.[4]

The study of Japanese and European MNEs mentioned in the introduction revealed different sourcing strategies. First, major components were generally sourced from the same location as the final assembly. Second, in the case of manufacturing in the United States, Japanese firms are more likely to source components from their home country than European firms. Third, components can be sourced from various locations. In the case of one Japanese firm in the study, 17 percent of the components came from Japan, 7 percent from European countries, 8 percent from developing countries, and the rest from the United States. Obviously, this multiple sourcing requires a high level of coordination between the parent company and related companies around the world.[5]

GLOBAL SOURCING

Before components can be manufactured, raw materials must be procured. The least complicated way of sourcing inputs is through domestic sources. Using domestic sources allows the firm to avoid problems such as language, distance, currency, wars and insurrections, strikes, political problems, tariffs, and more complicated transportation channels, to name a few. For many firms, however, domestic sources may be unavailable or more expensive than foreign sources. For a country such as Japan foreign procurement can be critical, since nearly all of its uranium, bauxite, nickel, crude oil, iron ore, copper, and coking coal and approximately 30 percent of its agricultural products are purchased from abroad. Japanese trading companies such as Mitsubishi came into being to acquire the raw materials necessary to fuel the manufacturing process.

Whether raw materials are available domestically or not, firms must devise global sourcing strategies that take changing world economic events into account. The strong dollar from 1980 to 1985 contributed to U.S. firms' stepped-up outsourcing, that is, sourcing production outside of the corporate organization or outside of the country. For example, if Ford buys components from a non-released firm or if it produces components in its plants in Brazil for assembly in the United States, it is practicing outsourcing. It would seem to follow that a weakening of the dollar during the latter half of the 1980s would have driven sourcing back on shore, but the situation is more complex than that. A 1987 survey of 107 major U.S.-based manufacturers revealed that foreign sourcing as a percentage of total purchases by U.S. firms increased from 8 percent in 1980 to 15 percent in 1985–1986. There seems to

Foreign sourcing has increased as a percentage of total purchases by U.S. firms.

be a difference of opinion in the report, however, over whether this share of foreign purchases will increase over the next decade.

The major reasons for outsourcing tend to be lower costs and improved quality. Many manufacturing firms find that materials costs are a significant percentage of total costs of manufacturing, and that nonmaterials costs as a percentage of total cost are falling. That would imply that firms need to continue to search for the most economic source of supply of materials.

In spite of the benefits of sourcing abroad, firms find that they face a variety of problems, such as the length of supply lines, inventory levels, and currency fluctuations. In addition, many firms have noted improvements in quality, design, and cost of U.S. producers as key reasons to return to the domestic market. Nearly half of the firms in the 1987 survey said that they had decided to return to the domestic market for some of their purchases;[6] however, many domestic suppliers disappeared in the early 1980s when their customers moved abroad to take advantage of cheaper sources of supply.

The Import Strategy

There are two different types of considerations for potential importers: procedural and strategic. Procedural considerations relate more to the rules and regulations of the customs office of a country. This was a key concern to John Robertson in the Sunset Flowers case, because he needed to determine the regulations for importing flowers from New Zealand to the United States.

Importation requires a certain degree of expertise in dealing with institutions and documentation that a firm may prefer to avoid. As a result, the importer may wish to work through an **import broker,** as John Robertson did. The broker obtains various government permissions and other clearances before forwarding necessary paperwork, such as a **bill of lading,** to the carrier that is to deliver the goods from the dock to the importer. The bill of lading serves as

- a receipt for goods delivered to the common carrier for transportation,
- a contract for the services to be rendered by the carrier, and
- a document of title.[7]

The strategic considerations are more critical in the long run. In the case of the U.S. auto industry, the strong U.S. dollar in the early 1980s forced GM and other auto companies to consider sourcing more of their purchases abroad. They felt that they needed to do this to help achieve cost parity in competing with foreign manufacturers. Although it is easy to say that a company chooses a foreign over a domestic supplier because of a cheaper price, the reasons given for foreign sourcing are more complex than that.

Domestic companies often choose foreign goods over domestic ones for nine basic reasons: price; quality; unavailability of items domestically; faster delivery and continuity of supply; better technical service; more advanced

Margin notes:

Outsourcing is done to achieve lower cost and better quality.

Major risks of outsourcing include
- Length of supply lines
- Inventory levels
- Currency fluctuations

Procedural issues involve the rules and regulations for imports.

An import broker is a specialist in import institutions and documentation.

The major reasons firms choose foreign over domestic supplies include
- Price, quality

- Faster delivery, better service
- Better technology
- Part of the corporate group

technology; a marketing tool (especially in conjunction with offset, where firms are required to import products from a country in order to be able to sell to consumers in that country); a tie-in with foreign subsidiaries (such as when GM decides to buy parts produced by its foreign operations in Korea or Japan); and competitive clout (to convince local suppliers to keep their prices low).[8]

In particular, the import of goods from related foreign operations is a key strategic issue. Part of the strategic advantage of the firm is its ability to recognize when it can capture more profits by establishing production facilities abroad to service local assembly or markets rather than subcontract these functions to outside firms. In 1986 almost 36 percent of U.S. imports and exports were transactions between U.S. firms and their foreign affiliates or parents. In a study of intrafirm transactions, it was found that the most important factor that caused firms to import intrafirm products was the technological intensity of the products; that is, the more technologically intense the product, the more likely the firm was to become involved in intrafirm transactions rather than to subcontract or purchase from the outside.[9]

Major problems with using foreign suppliers include

- Hard to evaluate foreign suppliers
- Delivery time
- Long distances for relationships
- Legal, political, economic, and cultural problems

In spite of the benefits, a number of problems can result from using foreign suppliers: location and evaluation of reputable vendors abroad; lead/delivery time; difficulty of expediting delivery and direct contact with foreign personnel; political and labor problems; currency fluctuations; payment methods; quality of merchandise; rejects and the problem of returns; tariffs and duties; paperwork costs due to the extra documentation needed to clear goods from customs; legal problems; transportation; language; and cultural and social customs.[10] Many of these problems are more problematic with purchases from external firms, because intrafirm transactions imply more control over quality of merchandise. However, problems that relate to the importing process, such as foreign exchange and customs documentation, are common to both types of sourcing.

The relative importance of the factors that companies must consider in developing a foreign sourcing strategy varies from industry to industry and country to country. But in some MNEs, such as electronics, instruments, and automotive, a wide variety of factors other than cost have influenced sourcing decisions in recent years.

Companies need to balance low labor cost with quality and reliability in supply.

The movement toward just-in-time inventory management (receiving components just as they need to enter the manufacturing process) has forced firms to focus more on quality, prompt delivery, low incidence of defects, and strong technical capacity.[11] In some cases, this works against the selection of traditionally low-cost labor areas and forces firms to look to countries that can provide quality and reliability. Sourcing in countries such as Japan and Germany can solve the quality and reliability problems, but the strength of their currencies against the dollar during the latter half of the 1980s made them prohibitively expensive as a source of U.S. supply. As a result, firms are looking more to the NICs, such as Brazil and South Korea. As these countries increase their technical capability, they can combine cost factors with reliability to result in a strong source of supply.

The Role of Customs Agencies

The major roles of Customs are collecting fees and enforcing laws.

When importing goods into any country, a firm must be totally familiar with the governmental customs operations. The primary duties of the U.S. Customs Service, for example, "include the assessment and collection of all duties, taxes, and fees on imported merchandise, the enforcement of customs and related laws, and the administration of certain navigation laws and treaties." As a major enforcement organization, it "combats smuggling and frauds on the revenue and enforces the regulations of numerous other Federal agencies at ports of entry and along the land and sea borders of the United States."[12] The importer needs to know how to clear goods, what duties must be paid, and what special laws exist.

Customs needs to determine the tariff classification of each import.

On the procedural side, when merchandise reaches the port of entry—Sea-Tac Airport, in the case of Sunset Flowers—the importer needs to file documents with Customs in which a tentative value and tariff classification are assigned to the merchandise. There are over 10,000 different tariff classifications, and approximately 60 percent of them are subject to interpretation; that is, more than one classification could be chosen for a particular piece of merchandise. Then Customs examines the merchandise to determine if there are any restrictions on the import of the items. After the examination, the duty can be paid and the merchandise released. The amount of the duty to be paid depends on the product's country of origin, the type of product, and other factors.[13]

Import brokers help firms clear Customs.

The broker or other import consultant can help an importer minimize import duties by:

- Valuing products to qualify for more favorable duty treatment. Different product categories have different duties. For example, finished goods typically have a higher duty than do parts and components.

- Qualifying for duty refunds through "drawback" provisions. Some exporters use imported parts and components on which they paid an import duty in their manufacturing process. The "drawback" provision allows them to apply for a refund of 99 percent of the duty paid on the imported goods, as long as they are used in the manufacture of goods that are exported.

- Deferring duties by using bonded warehouses and foreign trade zones. Companies do not have to pay duties on imports stored in bonded warehouses and foreign trade zones until they are removed for sale or use in a manufacturing process. That allows the companies to store the goods but not have to pay the duties right away.

- Limiting liability by properly marking an import's country of origin. Since governments attach duties on imports based on the nature of the product as well as the country of origin, it is possible to get a lower duty on an import by ensuring that the country of origin of the import is accurate.[14]

Sometimes goods are imported and immediately exported or assembled into an intermediate or final product and exported. Such action may allow the firm to get a total or partial refund (drawback) of any import duties.

Foreign Trade Zones

Foreign trade zones are special zones designated by the government where tariffs can be delayed or avoided.

In recent years, **foreign trade zones (FTZs)** have become more popular as an intermediate step in the process between import and final use. Oftentimes, the final use is for export; however, the zones are also good for making use of foreign sourcing.

> FTZs, established by federal grants [in the United States] primarily to state and local government agencies, provide areas where domestic and imported merchandise can be stored, inspected, and manufactured free from formal customs procedures until the goods leave the zones. The intended purpose of the zones is to encourage the domestic location of firms by affording them opportunities to defer duties, pay less duties, or to avoid certain duties completely.[15]

FTZs have been used in the United States primarily as a means of providing greater flexibility as to when and how customs duties are to be paid. However, their use in export business has been climbing. In the United States, FTZs used for exports are in one of the following categories:

- Foreign goods transshipped through U.S. zones to third countries.
- Foreign goods processed in zones, then transshipped abroad.
- Foreign goods processed or assembled in U.S. zones with some domestic materials and parts, then reexported.
- Goods produced in zones wholly of foreign content and exported.
- Goods produced in zones from a combination of domestic and foreign materials and components then exported.
- Domestic goods moved into a zone to achieve export status prior to their actual exportation.[16]

In 1975 there were only 27 general-purpose zones and subzones for individual plants. By 1991 the number of zones had increased to 176. Imports flowing through zones increased significantly during that same time period.[17]

An example of how a foreign trade zone can be used is a Coastal Corp. subsidiary that refines imported oil in Texas at a foreign trade subzone. If the subsidiary exports refined oil products, it pays no duty at all. If it sells the products domestically, it saves over $250,000 a year in interest on duties postponed until the products leave the zone.[18] Smith Corona used an FTZ facility to import parts into the United States for its typewriter-manufacturing facilities. After the parts were manufactured into typewriters in the zone, they would be imported officially into the United States at a zero duty due to a ruling in the customs code that applied to the unassembled parts but not to the parts in the final product.[19]

INTERNATIONAL MANUFACTURE

Once the manufacturer has decided on the source of raw materials and components, it must determine where the components are to be manufactured and where the final goods are to be assembled. This judgment depends on complex factors, such as the cost of transportation, duties on components versus finished goods, the need to be close to the market, foreign-exchange risk, economies of scale in the production process, technological requirements, and national image. In addition, the firm's decision where specifically in a country to manufacture is a function of external factors (such as market size and local government incentives) and internal strategic factors (such as the relative importance of product lines, location of markets, importance of cost, the improvement over time of knowledge of the country, and the perceptions of changes in risks).[20]

A firm may choose one of many manufacturing systems. It may try to serve all markets from one single plant. However, transportation charges and tariffs may render this system infeasible. In addition, the scale of production may be so large that the marginal cost of production might be higher than in smaller plant sizes that are used to achieve economies of scale. Firms also can specialize production by product or processes so that a particular plant produces a product or range of products or produces all products using a particular process and services all markets (rationalization). Or it could have several plants specializing in the same product or process so that the firm has a larger geographical spread. The process of manufacturing interchange involves plants producing a range of components and interchanging them so that all plants assemble the finished product for the local market. Obviously, there is no best way to set up the production process. For a particular product or line of products a firm may use a single-plant strategy and depend on exports to serve world markets. This would be essentially a worldwide product and production strategy. For other products or groups of products a multiplant strategy such as rationalization or manufacturing interchange might be best.

Figure 14.2 illustrates how Ford Motor Company has used global sourcing of components and manufacturing interchange to produce the Ford Escort. Components are manufactured in Ford plants in fifteen different countries, and assembly takes place in Ford plants in the United Kingdom and Germany.

Production possibilities include
- Single plant
- Multiple plants
- Manufacturing interchange (various assembly locations using common components)
- Rationalization (specialization by product or process)

Offshore Manufacturing

Offshore manufacturing outside of the United States is done in low-cost locations for importing into the United States and other markets.

In recent years, offshore manufacturing (manufacturing outside of the borders of a particular country) has provided a useful alternative to giving up the domestic market to low-cost foreign competitors. Offshore manufacturing escalated sharply in the 1960s and 1970s in the electronics industry worldwide as one firm after another set up production facilities in the Far East, principally in Taiwan and Singapore. Those locations were chosen because of low labor costs, the availability of cheap materials and components, and prox-

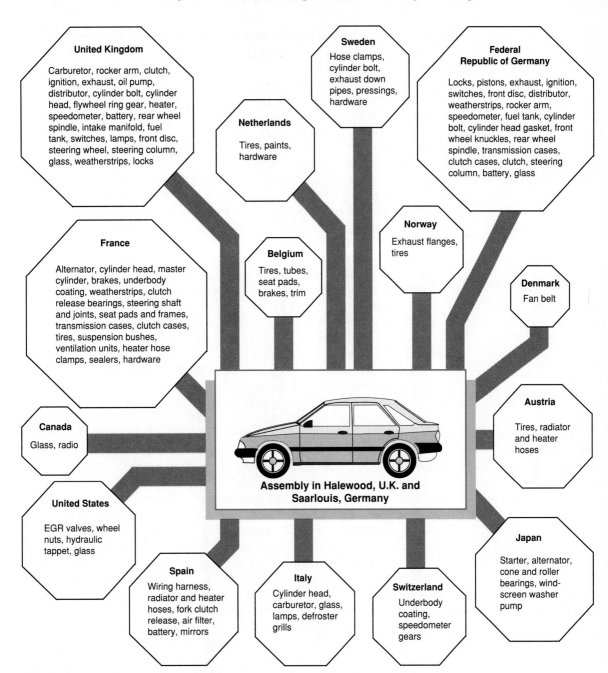

Figure 14.2
Global Manufacturing: The Component and Manufacturing Network for the Ford Escort (Europe) *Source: World Development Report 1987* (New York: Oxford University Press, 1987), p. 39.

imity to markets. Now these countries are beginning to give way to the newer "low-cost" countries of Asia (Indonesia, Thailand, Malaysia, Vietnam, and Bangladesh) and Latin America.

Maquiladora Industry   Mexico has become one of the newest centers for offshore production for U.S. firms through the **maquiladora industry.** The Mexican government estimates that the industry, which already earns more foreign exchange than any industry in Mexico except oil, could employ 1 million people by the year 2000. There are currently nearly 500,000 people employed in maquiladoras.[21] Under the maquiladora concept, U.S.-sourced components are shipped to Mexico duty free, assembled by Mexican workers, and reexported to the United States or other foreign markets under favorable tariff provisions. U.S. duties are levied on the imports only to the extent of the value added in Mexico. Since labor is so cheap, the value added is not great. Approximately 97 percent of the components are made in the United States, and the maquiladora concept is especially beneficial for firms where 30 percent or more of the product cost is labor. This industry allows U.S. firms to assemble products more cheaply than would have been possible in the United States and provides employment for Mexicans.[22] Map 14.2 identifies the major locations for the maquiladora industry and compares wage rates for Mexico and some other key countries. The maquiladora wage rates vary depending on the industry, but the average hourly labor rate plus benefits in 1988 ranged from $0.75 for the processing of food and related products to $1.15 for the manufacturing of machinery and equipment.[23]

There are approximately 1500 maquiladoras in Mexico, most of which are owned by U.S. firms. However, Japanese firms are also investing significant capital in Mexico for assembly and export into the United States. It was estimated in 1990 that 65 of the maquiladoras were owned by the Japanese.[24]

Many firms are combining the maquiladora concept with free trade zones being established by the Caribbean Basin countries. Some of the countries being used most frequently are Costa Rica, the Dominican Republic, El Salvador, Guatemala, Haiti, Honduras, Jamaica, Panama, and Puerto Rico. The major attractions of these countries are low labor costs, tax incentives, tariff concessions, and access to U.S. markets through specially negotiated agreements or provisions in the U.S. tariff schedule. In Jamaica during the mid-1980s, for example, the minimum salary for skilled workers was $16 per week, investors were exempted from sales and profit taxes, some imports and exports were duty free, and there was free repatriation of profits.[25]

There are, on the other hand, problems with the maquiladora plants. Many complain that the plants are little more than foreign enclaves on Mexican soil. Given that the firms import 97 percent of the components, the value added in Mexico is practically nothing. Because the goods are produced for export rather than domestic consumption, local consumers do not benefit from the production. In addition, the growth in employment, as noted in Fig. 14.3, has created serious social problems along the border. People are streaming to the border for jobs, because the jobless rate in the border area prior to

---

Maquiladora: A Mexican operation where U.S.-source components are shipped to Mexico duty free for assembly and reexport to the United States.

Maquiladoras work because their wage rates are low compared with competitive nations.

The problems of maquiladoras include

- *Pollution*
- *Social problems due to population growth*
- *Enclaves of foreign firms*

Where the Cheap Labor Is		
	1988	1989
Mexico	$0.88	na
Taiwan	2.82	3.53
Korea	2.50	3.57
Singapore	2.67	3.09
Hong Kong	2.40	2.79
Japan	12.80	12.63
United States	13.85	14.31

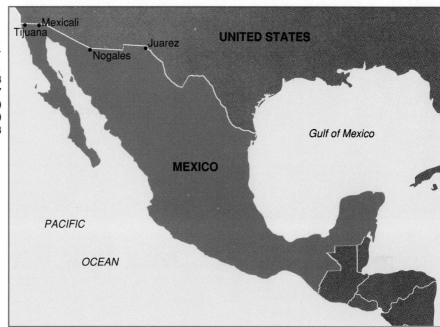

Map 14.2
Locations for Maquiladoras and Comparative Wages
Major locations for maquiladora industries are in Tijuana, Mexicali, Nogales, and Juarez. The cheap hourly wages compared with those of other countries make Mexico an attractive location for foreign investment.

the establishment of the maquiladoras was close to 40 percent, and there is not enough infrastructure to handle this influx. Living conditions are poor, and there are charges of severe environmental degradation, which the lax environmental standards have done nothing to impede, and the largest component of the labor force is women.[26]

In the future, the proposed free trade area comprised of Canada, the United States, and Mexico (discussed in Chapter 11) may change the nature of the maquiladora industry. A key condition behind the maquiladora concept is the existence of tariffs on trade between the United States and Mexico and the fact that those tariffs are relaxed on maquiladora transactions. If there were no tariff barriers between the United States and Mexico, there would still be investment in border industries, but there would be no need to remain there exclusively. Other investment could take place in Mexico and still take advantage of good labor rates.

Inventory Control

The greater the interchange of products and components, the more difficult the inventory-control process. The problems of distance and time and the

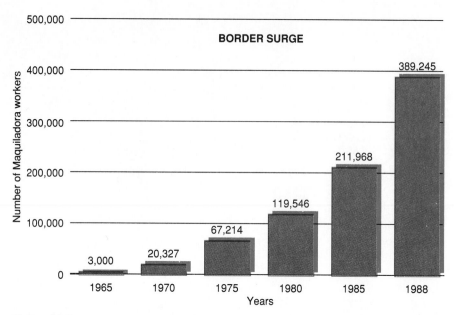

Figure 14.3
Trends in Maquiladora Employment
There has been a significant increase in employment in the maquiladora industry, up to nearly 400,000 by the end of 1988 and slightly less than 500,000 by the end of 1989. *Source:* Sonia Nararlo, "Boom and Despair," *The Wall Street Journal,* September 22, 1989, p. R27.

uncertainty of the international political and economic environment can make it difficult to determine correct reorder points. For example, if a manufacturer in a country with a weak currency regularly imports inventory from a country with a strong currency, management may wish to stockpile inventory in anticipation of a devaluation despite large carrying costs and the risk of damage or pilferage. Also, the firm may wish to stockpile inventory in anticipation of political chaos or legislation slowing down imports. Rapidly changing international events can ruin a smoothly running inventory-control system.

In recent years a lot of press has been given to the concept of just-in-time inventory management, a system that the Japanese have fine tuned. **Just-in-time (JIT)** manufacturing systems are becoming increasingly popular among U.S. manufacturers as a part of total quality control.

The concept behind JIT is that raw materials, parts, and components must be delivered to the production process just in time to be used. As a result, firms do not carry large inventories, thereby saving financing and storage costs. This means that parts must have few defects and must arrive on time to be used. Foreign sourcing can create big risks for JIT, since interruptions in the supply line can cause havoc. JIT implies that inventories need to be small, but foreign sourcing almost always requires large inventory levels

Just-in-time (JIT):
• Delivers input to production just as they are needed
• Lowers costs through higher quality and lower storage costs

Several international factors complicate JIT for firms with foreign suppliers.

in order to counteract the risk. As stated earlier, the basic idea of JIT is to produce the items needed just in time to be used or sold. In order for companies in other countries to implement such a system, the following modifications in manufacturing systems and production processes have been suggested: smooth and stable production schedules, more flexibility in manufacturing, higher quality of inputs and throughputs, better cooperation between workers and management, the development of relationships with dependable suppliers, greater concentration geographically for suppliers and manufacturers, more appropriate plant configuration, and strong management commitment and support.[27]

Thus JIT is an important dimension to the overall offshore manufacturing strategy. Firms attempt to drive down costs by producing offshore as well as by applying JIT systems to reduce storage space and carrying costs of inventory. The key is to solve the problems of combining offshore manufacturing with JIT in order to utilize both strategies in order to become more competitive.

EXPORT STRATEGY

In the discussion of global sourcing, we noted that demand in a country can be satisfied by goods produced in that country or abroad, and that domestic production can use a combination of domestic and foreign components. At this point, we need to look at how domestic production can satisfy foreign consumption through exports. In some cases, goods are shipped to foreign consumers independent of the exporter. In other cases, parts and components are exported to company-owned plants in foreign locations for final assembly and sale. Caterpillar, for example, adopted a strategy after World War II of manufacturing key components in its domestic plants and shipping them around the world for final assembly, which allowed them to maintain tight quality control. Thus the export strategy also is part of the larger sourcing and manufacturing strategy of the MNE as well as a sales strategy for servicing final markets around the world.

Exports take place for a number of good reasons. Raw materials must be exported to the manufacturer, components need to be exported to the assembly operation, and, as illustrated in the Sunset Flowers case, finished goods need to be exported to foreign distributors and consumers. Sometimes this process occurs within the confines of a vertically integrated company so that the exporter can sell directly to the next level through an intracompany transaction. However, the sale may be to an outsider; in that case, the exporter may decide to sell directly to the buyer or indirectly through an intermediary.

Factors Favoring Exportation

The most common means by which firms begin international activity is through exportation. Even firms with sizable foreign contractual arrangements and investments usually continue to export to achieve their overall objectives.

Exporting
- Expands sales
- Achieves economies of scale in production
- Is less risky than foreign direct investment
- Allows the company to diversify production locations

The major reason firms get involved in exporting is to increase sales revenues. Firms that are capital and research intensive, such as biotechnology and pharmaceuticals, need to export in order to spread their capital base over a larger volume of sales. Export sales also may be a means of alleviating excess capacity in the domestic market. Some firms export rather than invest abroad because of the perceived high risk in foreign environments. Finally, many firms export to a variety of different markets as a diversification strategy. Since economic growth is not the same in every market, broadly based exports allow a firm to take advantage of strong growth in one market to offset weak growth in another.

Building an Export Strategy

Many firms enter into exporting by accident rather than by design. When that happens, firms tend to encounter a number of unforeseen problems. In addition, the firm may never get a chance to see how important exports could be. That is why it is important to develop a good export strategy. Before developing the strategy, however, the firm must understand some of the major problems that firms face in exporting.

Potential Pitfalls   Aside from problems that are common to international business in general and are not unique to exporting, such as language and other culturally related factors, 10 mistakes are frequently made by firms new to exporting:

1. Failure to obtain qualified export counseling and to develop a master international marketing plan before starting an export business.
2. Insufficient commitment by top management to overcome the initial difficulties and financial requirements of exporting.
3. Insufficient care in selecting overseas agents or distributors.
4. Chasing orders from around the world instead of establishing a basis of profitable operations and orderly growth.
5. Neglecting export business when the U.S. market booms.
6. Failure to treat international distributors on an equal basis with domestic counterparts.
7. Unwillingness to modify products to meet other countries' regulations or cultural preferences.
8. Failure to print service, sales, and warranty messages in locally understood languages.
9. Failure to consider use of an export management company or other marketing intermediary when the firm does not have the personnel to handle specialized export functions.

10. Failure to consider licensing or joint venture agreements. This factor is especially critical in countries that have import restrictions.[28]

Another problem faced by exporters relates to the changing nature of governmental policy. Although the government can provide incentives for firms, it also can withdraw those incentives at any time. The budget cuts in the United States in the late 1980s and early 1990s created a real problem for some of the U.S. government agencies supposed to provide export services. A shortage of personnel made it difficult for them to do a good job.

Export strategy means that a firm must
- Assess export potential
- Get expert counseling
- Select market or markets
- Set goals and get product to market

Strategy Design   The design of a strategy involves a series of steps. First, a firm must assess its export potential. This involves taking a look at opportunities and resources. It would not be smart to make commitments to export if the firm did not have the production capacity to deliver the product.

Next, the firm must obtain expert counseling. For U.S. firms the best place to start is with the International Trade Administration (ITA) office of the U.S. Department of Commerce in the exporter's area. Such assistance is invaluable in helping the exporter get started. In the opening case, for example, Robertson used a lot of information provided by the U.S. government to learn about the U.S. market, and Pratt acquired a market research publication funded by the New Zealand Export-Import Corporation that included research on the U.S. flower market. In addition, the Small Business Administration can be useful in helping the firm to develop an export business plan and secure financing. As the export plan increases in scale, the exporter probably will want to secure specialized assistance from banks, lawyers, freight forwarders, export management companies, export trading companies, and others.

The next important step is to select a market or markets. This step often occurs by default if the exporter is responding to requests from abroad that result from trade shows, advertisements, or articles in trade publications. However, the firm must pick a market or markets in which to concentrate a push strategy. It should learn how to deal with foreign consumers. Because of differences in national markets, it is best to focus on a few key markets rather than try to develop global expertise all at once.

Once the markets have been targeted and the decision has been made to expend company resources in the export effort, the firm should formulate an export strategy, which usually involves dealing with the following four factors: (1) export objectives, both immediate and long term; (2) specific tactics that the firm will use; (3) a schedule of activities and deadlines that will help the firm achieve its objectives; and (4) the allocation of resources to accomplish the different activities.

Finally, the firm needs to determine how it will get the goods to market. The key in the export plan is to approach exporting from an organized point of view rather than just to sit back and let it happen.

Export Functions and Facilitating Intermediaries

A company engaged in exportation or planning to export must decide whether certain essential activities are to be handled by its own staff or through contracts with other firms. The following functions must be carried out:

1. stimulate sales, obtain orders, and do market research;

2. make credit investigations and perform payment-collection activities;

3. handle foreign traffic and shipping functions; and

4. function as support for the overall sales, distribution, and advertising staff of the firm.

Use external specialists to get goods to market.

Nearly all firms can benefit at one time or another from using the services of an intermediary organization that will assume some or all of these functions. A variety of different intermediaries can facilitate exports. Some of them act as agents on behalf of the exporter, and others actually take title to the goods and sell them abroad. In addition, some of them are involved in certain specialized aspects of the export process, such as the freight forwarder who is responsible for moving the products from the domestic to the foreign market.

Because of the cost of these different services and the expertise required, most firms tend to use specialists initially. They may develop in-house capability later on, but external specialists are useful at first to perform functions such as the preparation of export documents, the preparation of customs documents in the importing country, the identification of the best mode of export transportation, and the like. When a firm is deciding whether to market a product directly through its own staff or indirectly through external organizations, it needs to consider the size of the firm, the nature of the products, previous export experience and expertise, and business conditions in the selected overseas markets.[29]

Direct selling involves sales representatives, agents, distributors, or retailers.

Direct Selling   **Direct selling** is undertaken to give the exporter greater control over the marketing function and to earn higher profits. When selling direct, the manufacturer normally sells directly to the foreign market. The manufacturer may sell to a sales representative or agent who operates on a commission basis or to a foreign distributor who takes title to the product and earns a profit on the final sale to the consumer. Foreign retailers are outlets for consumer goods primarily and can be serviced by company traveling salespeople or by catalogs or trade fairs. Sales of products manufactured to specification, however, are made directly to the end user. This is a more common practice in industrial marketing than in consumer marketing.

If a firm decides to export directly rather than work through an intermediary, it must set up a solid organization. Firms can organize in a number of ways, from setting up a separate international division, to a separate international company, to a full integration of international and domestic activities. Whatever the form, there is commonly an international sales force separate from the domestic force. In the case of Sunset Flowers, John Robertson eventually became the sales force in the United States and sold the product to a wholesaler, who performed the role of a distributor.

Indirect Selling   **Indirect selling** implies that the manufacturer deals through another domestic firm before entering the international marketplace. The domestic firm may act as a **commission agent** for the manufacturer and not take title. The commission agent usually acts in behalf of the foreign buyer and tries to find an export product at the cheapest price. The agent is paid a commission by the foreign purchasing agent. The exporter may also choose to purchase the product from the manufacturer and sell the merchandise abroad. The latter option is common for the **export management company (EMC).**

Although EMCs originally operated on a commission basis and assumed no risks, they now operate largely on a buy-and-sell basis and provide financing for export shipments. The primary function of the EMC is to obtain orders for its clients' products through the selection of appropriate markets, distribution channels, and promotion campaigns. The EMC collects, analyzes, and furnishes credit information and advice regarding foreign accounts and payment terms. Other services the EMC may handle include documentation; arrangement of transportation (including the consolidation of shipments to reduce costs); arrangement of patent and trademark protection in foreign countries; and counseling and assistance in establishing alternative forms of doing business, such as licensing or joint ventures.[30]

EMCs, which can deal in imports as well as exports, operate on a contractual basis, usually for two to five years, and provide exclusive representation in a well-defined overseas territory. The contract specifies pricing, credit and financial policies, promotional services, and the payment basis. EMCs usually concentrate on complementary and noncompetitive products so that they can present a more complete product line to a limited number of importers. There are over 2000 EMCs in the United States, and most of them are small operations. As a result, they tend to specialize by product, function, or market area. Although EMCs perform an important function for firms that need the export expertise, the manufacturer may lose control over foreign sales. Thus the manufacturer needs to balance the desire for control with the cost of performing the export functions directly.[31] Sunset Flowers initially worked through an EMC that apparently took title to the flowers and paid Pratt and Robertson a return based on the prevailing market price and the volume sold.

Export Trading Companies   In the fall of 1982 the U.S. government enacted the Export Trading Company Act, legislation that removed some of the antitrust obstacles to the creation of **export trading companies** in the United States. It was hoped that these ETCs, which are a form of indirect selling that a manufacturer can utilize, would lead to greater exports of U.S. goods and services. ETCs are similar to EMCs, but they tend to provide a

Commission agents work for the buyer.

EMCs buy domestic merchandise for foreign distribution or act as an agent for the manufacturer.

ETCs can be formed by
- *Competitors and be exempt from antitrust legislation*

- State and local governments
- Money center banks
- Major corporations

broader range of services and often take title to goods, whereas EMCs tend to act as agents. However, the two are very similar. There are four major types of ETCs: newly formed ETCs that received antitrust certification, ETCs organized by state and local governments, ETCs created by commercial banks, and ETCs initially organized by U.S. companies to handle their own exports.

The first category involves business enterprises that would like to cooperate for foreign sales but have difficulty cooperating for domestic sales because of antitrust concerns. The government set strict guidelines on how firms would qualify for exemption from antitrust considerations: Cooperation must not lessen competition in the United States.

One example of ETCs organized by state and local governments is the Port Authority of New York and New Jersey. Their ETC, known as XPORT, is courting smaller firms with high-technology products that have an export potential.

Most of the large money center banks have applied for permission to establish ETCs. These applications must be approved by the Federal Reserve Board before the bank can start export operations. Many of the banks are concentrating on customers in their geographical market and in parts of the world where they already have a good banking network.

Some major corporations, such as Control Data, have also set up ETCs. Initially, they were designed to handle the firm's own business, but they are now expanding to include products produced by other companies as well. In the case of Control Data, its ETC first was established to handle countertrade agreements for sales of products to Eastern European countries as well as developing countries. Then the ETC of Control Data aggressively sought products of other companies. However, the ETC concept has not really taken hold in the United States. The ETC concept has worked well for undifferentiated products, such as agricultural products, but ETCs have not been successful for differentiated products that require significant individual attention.

Japanese Trading Companies   ETCs are essentially new, untested trading companies. When one thinks of trading companies, the giants such as Mitsui, Marubeni, and Mitsubishi of Japan come to mind. The **sogo shosha,** the Japanese equivalent word for trading company, can trace their roots back to the late 1800s, when Japan embarked on an aggressive modernization process. At that time, the trading companies were referred to as zaibatsu, large, family-owned businesses that were comprised of a series of financial and manufacturing companies usually held together by a large holding company. These zaibatsu were very powerful, so General Douglas MacArthur broke them up after World War II and made many of their activities illegal.

The sogo shosha initially took the primary role of acquiring raw materials for the industrialization process and then finding external markets for goods. Although there are more than 6000 trading companies in Japan, the sixteen major sogo shosha control more than a majority of Japan's exports and imports. In addition, their annual sales are slightly greater than one third of Japan's GNP, a tremendous economic concentration.[32] Table 14.1 illustrates

TABLE 14.1 | FIFTEEN LARGEST WORLD CORPORATIONS IN SALES Six of the top ten firms in the world as measured in sales are Japanese trading companies.

	Sales (in Billions of U.S. dollars)
1. Mitsui	$128.0
2. Marubeni	123.2
3. Mitsubishi	121.5
4. General Motors	110.0
5. C. Itoh	104.7
6. Sumitomo	97.3
7. Exxon*	95.2
8. Royal Dutch/Shell†	85.4
9. Ford	82.9
10. Nissho Iwai	75.1
11. IBM	62.7
12. Mobil*	56.2
13. General Electric	54.6
14. Sears Roebuck	53.8
15. Toyota Motor	52.6

*Includes excise taxes

†Excludes excise taxes

Source: "The Wall Fell Down, and the Continent Took Off," *Business Week,* July 16, 1990, p. 111.

> Japanese trading companies are the largest in the world in terms of sales.

the sheer size of the sogo shosha relative to other large firms in the world. Of the fifteen largest companies in the world in terms of sales, six of the top ten are Japanese trading companies. They generate tremendous sales volumes, even though they are not very profitable and their global ranking in terms of market value is not significant. For example, of the top 100 firms in the world in terms of market value, only one Japanese trading firm is listed—Mitsubishi Corp. at number 76. It may be smaller than Mitsui in terms of sales, but it is larger in terms of market value. Even in Japan, only four trading firms are in the top 100 in terms of market value, even though those four are larger in terms of sales volume than any other Japanese corporation.[33]

When the sogo shosha were first organized after WWII, their primary functions were handling paperwork for import and export transactions, financing imports and exports, and providing transportation and storage services. However, their operations expanded significantly to include investing in production and processing facilities, establishing fully integrated sales systems for certain products, expanding marketing activities, and developing large bases for the integrated processing of raw materials.[34]

Most of the sogo shosha are also part of a larger corporate relationship,

Japanese trading companies are part of bank-centered keiretsu or industrial-group keiretsu.

called a **keiretsu.** Several of the sogo shosha are involved in bank-centered keiretsu, such as Mitsubishi, Mitsui, and Sumitomo. Others are industrial-group keiretsu. The keiretsu relationships imply that one company agrees to become a shareholder in another in order to build a long-term and very close business relationship. The Mitsubishi group involves over 150 companies with a total market capitalization of 11 percent of the Tokyo Stock Exchange. The cross-shareholding in the Mitsubishi Group equaled 26.9 percent of all shares in 1988. Mitsubishi Corporation, the trading arm of the Mitsubishi Group, has the advantage of working with very powerful financial and industrial partners. For example, Mitsubishi Estate purchased 57.6 percent of Rockefeller Center, Mitsubishi Corporation bought control of Aristech Chemical and later sold pieces to four of its fellow group members, Mitsubishi Trust & Banking was the main lender in the purchase of the Pebble Beach golf course, and four Mitsubishi companies have been discussing global joint ventures with Daimler-Benz.[35]

An example of how a sogo shosha can help a client involves Marubeni and Bridgestone Tire. Marubeni is the second-largest trading company in Japan in terms of sales revenues (and also second-largest in the world in sales revenues). For years, Marubeni supplied Bridgestone with carbon black used in the manufacture of tires. The business had been modest, but Bridgestone was a valued client. One day, Yasushi Kawahara, the manager in charge of the Bridgestone account, received a request for help in building a unique test track for Bridgestone tires that would mirror Belgian road conditions.

Bridgestone could not solve the problem because it lacked staff in Belgium, but Marubeni did have the needed resources. Kawahara contacted one of his staff in Brussels, who hunted around until he found cobblestones that met the proper specifications. The shipment was prepared to meet export requirements in Belgium and import requirements in Japan, areas in which Marubeni had expertise. Finally, 100,000 stones were shipped to Japan and used to build the test track.

Because Bridgestone was an old and valued client, Kawahara did not price the transaction to earn a significant profit. However, he was able to develop a thriving and profitable cobblestone business for other Japanese auto and tire companies trying to emulate Bridgestone's project.[36]

The sogo shosha faced a variety of challenges in the decade of the 1980s, many of which have been brought on by changes in the domestic Japanese economy as well as the international economy. Their role in trade financing, for example, is being disputed by the banks, which have become more internationally oriented than they used to be. Many of the marketing functions are being questioned by the manufacturers themselves. The transition appears as follows:

Firms turn away from trading companies if markets are large, technology is complex, or marketing requirements are specific.

1. The larger and more significant the market, the sooner the manufacturer turns away from the sogo shosha (e.g., C. Itoh still handles auto marketing for Toyota in Saudi Arabia, a small market).

2. The more complex the technology involved, the sooner the manufacturer

turns away from the sogo shosha (because of the difficulty of the sogo shosha dealing with the technical requirements of the product).

3. The more specific and involved the marketing and service requirements are, the sooner the manufacturer turns away from the sogo shosha.[37]

Finally, the sogo shosha are beginning to get more involved in foreign investment. The Japanese have historically preferred to sell abroad through exports rather than through direct investment, as has been the strategy of U.S. companies. However, the nature of the international marketplace is causing the trading firms to consider more direct investment because many of the client firms have their own manufacturing niches and have decided to expand these operations abroad.[38] This not only illustrates a change in locational strategy but also shows how the trading companies have diversified their revenue base. As mentioned earlier, Mitsubishi Estate purchased a controlling interest in the Rockefeller Center, and Mitsubishi Corporation purchased a controlling interest in Aristech Chemical in the United States. Four Mitsubishi companies have begun discussions with Daimler-Benz to develop a number of strategic alliances in Europe.

Foreign Freight Forwarders   As was mentioned in the international sourcing section of this chapter, dealing in ocean transportation involves a number of different institutions and documentation with which the typical exporter does not have expertise. This is true even if the manufacturer is exporting components to a foreign subsidiary controlled by a common parent corporation. Commonly the services of a **foreign freight forwarder** are employed. Even export management companies and other types of trading companies often use foreign freight forwarders for their specialized services.

A foreign freight forwarder is an export/import specialist dealing in the movement of goods from producer to consumer.

The foreign freight forwarder is the largest export intermediary in terms of value and weight handled; however, the services offered are more limited than those offered by an EMC. Once a foreign sale has been made, the freight forwarder acts on behalf of the exporter in recommending the best routing and means of transportation based on space availability, speed, and cost. The forwarder secures such space and necessary storage, reviews the letter of credit, obtains export licenses, and prepares necessary shipping documents. Other services that may be provided include advice on packing and labeling, purchase of transport insurance, and repacking shipments damaged en route.

The freight forwarder usually is paid by the exporter on a percentage of the shipment value, with a minimum charge dependent on the number of services provided. In addition, the forwarder receives a brokerage fee from the carrier. The use of a freight forwarder still is usually less costly than providing the service internally, since most firms find it difficult both to utilize a traffic department full-time and to keep up with shipping regulations. The forwarder can get space because of its close relationship with carriers and can consolidate shipments in order to obtain lower rates.

Governmental Role in Exporting

Governments play a variety of roles in the export process, some of which support exporting and others that appear to retard it. For example, government regulations designed to keep high-tech products from aiding the Soviet military retard high-tech exports of U.S. companies. The **International Trade Administration (ITA)** of the U.S. Department of Commerce offers a variety of services to firms. There are offices in every state where trade specialists can help firms develop export strategy and gain access to commercial officers overseas as well as to a variety of data services. The ITA also sponsors and promotes trade shows.

Governments provide information, specialists, and financing.

Eximbank   A major federal source of assistance to U.S. exporters is the **Export-Import Bank (Eximbank).** The Eximbank is the oldest federal agency specializing in foreign lending. As a fully owned government corporation, it has been in existence since 1934, with the specific objective of financing U.S. foreign trade. The Eximbank provides assistance in the form of loans, guarantees, and insurance.[39]

The loans can be made directly to foreign buyers of U.S. exports or to intermediary parties that provide loans to foreign buyers of U.S. exports. The guarantee program is designed to provide security for firms that provide loans to purchasers of U.S. exports. Guarantees can be for political and commercial risks, but they are also available for political risk only.

Another way that an exporter can reduce risk is through the **Foreign Credit Insurance Association (FCIA).** An exporter that secures a policy with the FCIA is insured against loss resulting from failure of the exporter's customers to pay because of commercial or political reasons. Political risks include currency inconvertibility, expropriation, cancellation of import licenses, or other actions taken by foreign governments that prevent payment by the buyer. Also, the policyholder can arrange favorable financing of export receivables because of the security brought about by the insurance.

As mentioned in the opening case, other governments provide significant export assistance to their firms. Some of the assistance is in the form of data gathering, such as the marketing report developed by the New Zealand Export-Import Corporation. Other forms of assistance involve developing trading contacts, finding distributorships, and arranging low-cost financial support for exports. This latter area is especially sensitive politically when governments subsidize loans to the point that interest rates are substantially below market rates. However, these forms of assistance are considered to be very important in promoting the expansion of exports, thus jobs in a country.

LOOKING TO THE FUTURE   As global competition increases and trade barriers continue to fall, it will be increasingly important for firms to drive down costs as much as possible. This means that global firms will need to continue to develop the cheapest sources of supply that they can. Outsourcing as a means of finding components at the cheapest price will continue, and firms that rely on cheap labor as an important part of the production process will continue to look for low-cost production locations, such as Mexico for U.S. firms. In addition, firms will continue to implement the concept of total quality control in order to make their production operations more efficient and effective. The use of concepts such as JIT will enhance the quality and productivity of manufacturing operations.

In spite of the move to invest offshore in order to be closer to the market, firms will continue to export. During the late 1980s when the dollar was weak, exports were an important source of strength for the U.S. economy. Both federal and state governments realized the benefits in employment of having a strong export economy. However, federal and state budget deficits will make it difficult to provide more financial assistance for exports. This will place even greater emphasis on exchange rate management. A weaker currency will benefit exports, so monetary authorities will constantly keep an eye on their policies to balance the domestic and foreign imports of their decisions. The desire to keep interest rates high in order to control inflation also maintains strong exchange rates and therefore hurts exports.

As firms realize the importance of exports as a source of relatively easy profits in comparison with foreign investment, they will attempt to be more competitive in global markets. However, it is doubtful that new institutional forms will arise to service those exports. Existing forms, such as freight forwarders and EMCs, will continue to thrive, because they offer flexibility to the exporter by not having to incur large in-house overhead to service exports. Their services will be very much in demand.

SUMMARY

- A global production strategy involves the storage and movement of goods from the source of raw materials to the production of components, to the assembly of goods, to the distribution to consumers.

- The international firm differs from the domestic one in that goods in intermediate or final form may move from country to country rather than remain in one particular country.

- International sourcing of goods—primarily in the area of purchasing—differs from domestic sourcing in terms of language, distance, currency, wars and insurrections, strikes, political problems, and tariffs.

- Foreign sourcing is often undertaken to obtain lower costs and high quality. However, U.S. firms are beginning to compete with foreign firms in both dimensions.

- Firms must be involved in procedural as well as strategic decisions in order to import successfully. Familiarity with customs procedures is necessary and firms often require the help of specialists.

- Foreign trade zones (FTZs), long popular outside of the United States, are being used increasingly as a place to import and assemble goods for domestic consumption as well as final export.

- Manufacturing strategies include servicing the world from one production facility or from many by using multiple plants that specialize in products or processes or by interchanging components for eventual assembly.

- Many firms are using offshore manufacturing centers to take advantage of cheap labor and materials. Then the finished goods are sold in the local market, shipped to the United States, or sold in third-country markets.

- The Japanese have perfected the concept of just-in-time (JIT) inventory management, which means that inventory shipments are planned to coincide as closely as possible with their use. This cuts down the size of inventories held and therefore the carrying costs. JIT is being used increasingly by U.S. firms and is having a dramatic impact on sourcing decisions for raw materials and components in the manufacturing process.

- Firms new to exporting (and also some experienced exporters) often make lots of mistakes. One way to avoid making those mistakes is to develop a comprehensive export strategy that includes an analysis of the firm's resources as well as market opportunities.

- Exporters may deal directly with agents or distributors in a foreign country or indirectly by using export management companies or other types of trading companies.

- Trading companies, such as the Japanese sogo shosha, can perform many of the functions that manufacturers lack the expertise to do. In addition, exporters can use the services of other specialists, such as freight forwarders, to facilitate exports.

- Governments provide a variety of services for exporters. The U.S. government operates through the International Trade Administration (ITA) of the U.S. Department of Commerce.

C A S E
BLACK & DECKER[40]

Black & Decker (B&D), once known almost exclusively as a manufacturer of power tools for professionals, is now involved in "the manufacturing, marketing, and servicing of a wide range of power tools, household products, and other labor-saving devices generally used in and around the home and by professional users." In the 1970s, before broadening its base to include a larger segment of the household market, B&D was flying high. It had captured a large share of the world's power-tool market, and financial analysts were betting strongly on B&D's future.

By 1981, however, the picture began to change. Earnings had begun to slip, and a worldwide recession caused a significant downturn in the power-tools segment of B&D's business, its bread and butter. Other events in the world economy added to B&D's problems. A strong U.S. dollar eroded B&D's competitive position in export markets and made B&D vulnerable to competition from abroad.

While these events were taking place, Japan's Makita Electric Works Ltd. and Germany's Bosch began to erode B&D's market share. Makita adopted a global strategy for its products that allowed it to become the lowest-cost producer in the world. It decided that consumers in different countries really did not need significantly different products; then it combined its cost advantage with aggressive marketing, took advantage of the relatively weak yen compared with the U.S. dollar and B&D's mistakes to make serious inroads in the power-tools market. By the late 1970s and early 1980s, Makita was able to nearly equal B&D's 20 percent market share in professional tools worldwide.

B&D's problems were partly a result of its own strategy. By 1982, B&D operated twenty-five manufacturing plants in thirteen countries on six continents. It had three operating groups as well as the headquarters in Maryland. Each group had its own staff, which led to duplication and overstaffing. In addition, individual B&D companies, such as B&D of West Germany, operated autonomously in each of the more than fifty countries where B&D sells and services products. The company's philosophy had been to let each country adapt products and product lines to fit the unique characteristics of each market. The Italian firm produced power tools for Italians, the British subsidiary made power tools for Britons, and so on.

As a result, countries did not communicate well with each other. Successful products in one country often took years to introduce in others. For example, the highly successful Dustbuster, which was introduced in the United States in the late 1970s, was not introduced in Australia until 1983. When efforts were made to introduce B&D home products into European markets, the European managers refused to comply. Even though sales were stagnating, B&D held a large percentage of the power-tools market in the early 1980s—over 50 percent on the Continent and 80 percent in the United Kingdom. European managers felt that home appliances and products were uniquely American and would not do well outside of the United States.

In order to meet the tailor-made specifications of different markets, design centers were not being used efficiently. At one point, 8 design centers around the world had produced 260 different motors, even though the firm needed fewer than 10 different models. Plant capacity utilization was low, employment levels were high, and output per employee was unacceptable.

For several years, B&D split its consumer and professional tools into two different groups. Because each group did not work together to develop new product lines, Makita was able to spot a market niche that it could exploit, the mid-priced tools. In addition, B&D had begun to stagnate in new product development. It appeared that the company had decided to concentrate on its top lines and sell them aggressively.

As B&D moved into the mid-1980s, management realized that something had to be done. One area where the Japanese had not made significant inroads was the housewares and small-appliances market. Japanese consumers were not fond of those items, so Makita and other competitors had not established a strong home market to use as an export base. B&D was having trouble introducing its own line of housewares because of its image as a power-tool manufacturer. As a result, B&D acquired the small-appliances division of General Electric in 1984 to give it more shelf space in housewares and also a large enough line of products to provide economies of scale in manufacturing.

In April 1989 B&D acquired Emhart Corporation, the world-wide manufacturer of such leading brands as Kwikset door locks and hardware, Price Pfister faucets, True Temper lawn and garden products, Molly bolts, POP rivets, and other consumer and commercial products. The debt incurred to acquire Emhart was creating problems for B&D as management looked for ways to cut costs and service the debt.

Questions

1. What are the major reasons behind Black & Decker's current competitive dilemma?
2. What should it do to solve its problems?

Chapter Notes

1. This case is adapted from Harry R. Knudson, "Sunset Flowers of New Zealand, Ltd.," *Journal of Management Case Studies,* Winter 1985, Volume 1, No. 4.

2. Masaaki Kotabe and Glenn S. Omura, "Sourcing Strategies of European and Japanese Multinationals: A Comparison," *Journal of International Business Studies,* Spring 1989, pp.113–117.

3. Michael E. Porter, ed., *Competition in Global Industries* (Boston: Harvard Business School Press, 1986).

4. Kotabe and Omura, *op. cit.,* pp. 120–122.

5. *Ibid.,* pp. 122–124, 126.

6. "U.S. MNCs Increase Global Sourcing Despite Contrary Trends," *Business International,* September 21, 1987, p. 302. This information is from a report, "Global Sourcing as a Corporate Strategy—1987," issued by the Washington-based Machinery & Allied Products Institute.

7. Philadelphia National Bank, *International Trade Procedures* (Philadelphia, 1977), p. 30.

8. Michael Leenders, Harold E. Fearcon, and Wilbur B. England, *Purchasing and Materials Management* (Homewood, Ill.: Irwin, 1985), pp. 350–353.

9. Kang Rae Cho, "The Role of Product-Specific Factors in Intra-Firm Trade of U.S. Manufacturing Multinational Corporations," *Journal of International Business Studies,* Second Quarter 1990, pp. 319–330.

10. *Ibid.,* pp. 353–358.

11. "MNCs Adapt to Weak Dollar with Sourcing Strategies for Enhanced Flexibility," *Business International,* April 6, 1987, p. 105.

12. Department of the Treasury, *Importing into the United States* (Washington, D.C.: Superintendent of Documents, U.S. Government Printing Office, May 1984), p. 28.

13. Robert P. Schaffer, "Maximize Your Import Profits . . . Minimize Your Customs Duties," *Review* (New York: Price Waterhouse).

14. Robert P. Schaffer, *op. cit.*

15. *Ibid.*

16. John J. DaPonte, Jr., "Foreign-Trade Zones and Exports," *American Export Bulletin,* April 1978.

17. Ken Slocum, "Foreign-Trade Zones Aid Many Companies but Stir up Criticism," *The Wall Street Journal,* September 30, 1987, p. 1.

18. *Ibid.,* p. 31.

19. *Ibid.*

20. Paul M. Swamidass, "A Comparison of the Plant Location Strategies of Foreign and Domestic Manufacturers in the U.S.," *Journal of International Business Studies,* Second Quarter 1990, p. 302.

21. Stephen Baker, "Mexico: A New Economic Era," *Business Week,* November 12, 1990, p. 105.

22. Roger Turner, "Mexico's In-Bond Industry Continues Its Dynamic Growth," *Business America,* November 26, 1984, p. 26.

23. John Saudners, "Trade With Mexico Has Winners, Losers," *The Globe and Mail,* November 14, 1990.

24. *Ibid.,* p. 108.

25. "Caribbean Basic FTZs Offer Low-Cost Production and Entries to New Markets," *Business Latin America,* February 2, 1987, pp. 35–37.

26. Sonia Nazario, "Boom and Despair," *The Wall Street Journal,* September 22, 1989, p. R26.

27. G. H. Manoochehri, "Crucial Requirements for Effective Application of Just-in-Time System," unpublished paper, California State University, Fullerton, 1984.

28. "Ten Most Common Mistakes of New-to-Export Ventures," *Business America*, April 16, 1984, p. 9.

29. TransNational, Inc., *A Basic Guide to Exporting* (Washington, D.C.: U.S. Department of Commerce, September 1986), p. 17.

30. Philip MacDonald, *Practical Exporting and Importing*, 2nd ed. (New York: Ronald Press, 1959), pp. 30–40; TransNational, Inc., *A Basic Guide to Exporting*, p. 17.

31. "Basic Question: To Export Yourself or To Hire Someone To Do It for You?" *Business America*, April 27, 1987, pp. 14–17.

32. Charles E. Cobb, Jr., "Export Trading Companies: Five Years of Bringing U.S. Exporters Together," *Business America*, October 12, 1987, pp. 2–9.

33. Joan Warner, "The Wall Fell Down, and the Continent Took Off," *Business Week*, July 16, 1990, pp. 111+.

34. Marubeni Corporation, *The Unique World of the Sogo Shosha* (Tokyo: Marubeni Corporation, 1978), p. 14.

35. Tony Shale, "Reawakening the Sleeping Giant," *Euromoney*, November 1990, pp. 16 and 18.

36. Marubeni Corporation, *The Japanese Edge* (Tokyo: Marubeni Corporation, 1981), pp. 85–93.

37. Kichiro Hayashi and Stefan H. Robock, "The Uncertain Future of the Japanese General Trading Companies," *Kajian Ekonomi Malaysia*, December 1982, p. 61.

38. Masaaki Kotabe, "Changing Roles of the Sogo Shoshas, the Manufacturing Firms, and the MITI in the Context of the Japanese 'Trade of Die' Mentality," *Columbia Journal of World Business*, Fall 1984, pp. 33–42.

39. Susan Rodes, "U.S. Export-Import Bank Changes with World Trading Environment," *Business America*, November 9, 1987, pp. 2–9.

40. Sources for case are various issues of the Black and Decker *Annual Report*; Bill Saporito, "Black and Decker's Gamble on 'Globalization,'" *Fortune*, May 14, 1984, pp. 40–42, 44, 48; Christopher S. Eklund, "How Black and Decker Got Back in the Black," *Business Week*, July 13, 1987, pp. 86–90; "How Black and Decker Forged a Winning Brand Transfer Strategy," *Business International*, July 20, 1987, pp. 225–227; Mary Lu Carnevale, "Black & Decker Goes to Full-Court Press," *The Wall Street Journal*, November 10, 1988, p. A8; Stuart Flack, "All Leverage Is Not Created Equal," *Forbes*, March 19, 1990, p. 39.

CHAPTER **15**

STRATEGIC ALLIANCES

*When one party is willing, the match is
half made.*
AMERICAN PROVERB

Objectives

- To explain the major motives that should guide firms in their choice of form for global business activities.

- To differentiate the major operational forms by which firms may tap the potential of international business.

- To describe the considerations that firms should explore when entering into contractual international arrangements with other companies.

- To emphasize that multiple forms of international operations may exist simultaneously and that firms must develop means by which to coordinate these diverse activities.

By 1973 Mexican import restrictions had enticed most of the world's largest multinational manufacturers to establish facilities there to produce goods that Mexico otherwise might have imported. At that time the government sought to counter foreign control by setting restrictions on foreign equity in new ventures and on the expansion of existing investments with large foreign ownership.

At that time, one of the largest Mexican-owned firms was a family enterprise in Monterrey controlled by the Garza and Sada families (see Map 15.1). This firm had been affected only slightly by foreign competition because its major lines of business, steel, beer, and banking, were products and services not easily imported into Mexico because of import restrictions on steel and the need of the others (usually) to locate near customers. There were also prohibitions against foreign ownership in these sectors. Although the Garza and Sada families were relatively immune from foreign competition, the outlook was for slow growth.

The Garza-Sada families saw in the 1973 Mexicanization laws the opportunity to diversify into growth industries that foreigners would henceforth find more difficult to control. They reasoned that they might be able to buy some subsidiaries of foreign companies from firms unwilling to accept a minority ownership. They also reasoned that they were in a good position to share in cooperative arrangements with foreign firms that sought business activities involving Mexico. The owners felt that to capitalize on these possibilities, they would be better off to shed the family image. Additional shares could raise capital, and good professional management could be attracted to the company. In 1974 they divided the enterprise into four different companies and went public by issuing shares in each of them.

One of the firms that emerged from the 1974 split was Grupo Industrial

C A S E
GRUPO INDUSTRIAL ALFA[1]

Alfa, which inherited the steel facilities and several smaller businesses. At the time of the split, Alfa's assets were estimated at $315 million (U.S.), of which 75 percent was in steel. Management of the new company, with help from some of the top international consulting groups, agreed that diversification should be based on the objectives of minimizing cyclical changes in earnings, getting into growth industries, and utilizing resources for which Mexico had advantages.

During the 1974–1976 period, Alfa expanded much less than had been anticipated but did manage to acquire the television production facilities of three U.S. brands: Philco, Magnavox, and Admiral. Through these acquisitions Alfa got 35 percent of Mexico's market for television sets as well as the continued use of the three trade names for sales in Mexico.

Alfa subsequently became Mexico's largest private company. By 1980 it had assets of $1.9 billion, sales representing 1.2 percent of Mexico's gross domestic product, 157 subsidiaries, and 49,000 employees. Two events ex-

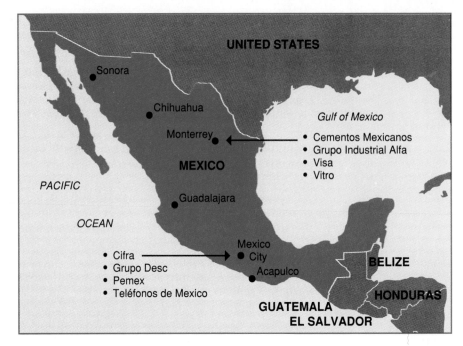

Map 15.1
Mexico
Note that the largest Mexican companies are headquartered in either the Mexico City or Monterrey areas.

ternal to Alfa contributed to the growth: The first was the discovery of huge oil and natural gas reserves in Mexico; the second was the election of a pro–private-enterprise president, José Lopez Portillo. Lopez Portillo offered many incentives for industry, including nearly free energy. Suddenly there was a rush among foreign firms to find ways of expanding their business in Mexico; almost any such expansion had to involve Mexicans. In addition to being Mexico's largest private firm, Alfa had good profitability and its management had a good reputation, so it was in an excellent position to acquire the foreign resources that it wanted. In fact, its biggest problem was in how to choose among the many opportunities.

Alfa established numerous Mexican companies in which it owned a majority interest with a foreign partner holding a minority. The foreign partners came from a number of countries, including Japan (Hitachi, electric motors; Yamaha, motorcycles), Canada (International Nickel, nonferrous metal exploration), the Netherlands (AKZO, artificial fibers), and the former West Germany (BASF, petrochemicals). For two U.S. firms, the joint venture operations involved substantial departures from prior policies. Ford's 25 percent interest in a plant making aluminum cylinder heads for the U.S. and Canadian auto markets was the first minority interest Ford had ever taken in a joint venture. DuPont had taken minority interests before accepting 49 percent to Alfa's 51 percent. However, DuPont had always handled the management of the ventures. In the Mexican synthetic fibers joint venture, Alfa did the managing; the company's policy was to import technology but to maintain management control.

In many of the above situations the Mexican output has used the trademark developed by the foreign partner, which has helped in gaining Mexican consumer acceptance. In 1979 Alfa bought 100 percent of Massey-Ferguson's tractor operation in Mexico, paying the Canadian company a royalty fee for the use of the Massey-Ferguson trade name.

In the aluminum cylinder head joint venture just described, it was not a captive Mexican market that attracted Ford; rather, it was lower production costs so as to supply the American and Canadian markets. In addition to cheap energy, Mexico had offered an abundance of cheap labor and no taxes on reinvested earnings. The motors built under the Hitachi brand name have been produced in Mexico for 25 percent below the Japanese cost. And Alfa itself has become interested in export markets: A sales arrangement was established by which the Mitsui Trading Company of Japan handles exports of Alfa's polyester chemicals abroad. Alfa opened discussions about Mexican television production with several Japanese firms in order to use known Japanese brands to penetrate the U.S. market. Because of prior contractual arrangements, Alfa could not export its "American" brands (Philco, Magnavox, and Admiral) to the United States.

Alfa developed a method of producing steel by direct reduction, thus bypassing the high capital cost of blast furnaces. To transfer this patented technology to new plants in other countries would require substantial on-site personnel and construction assistance. Alfa lacked personnel that could be spared as well as foreign construction experience. Alfa has transferred its know-how to four foreign engineering firms: Germany's GHH-Sterkrade, Japan's Kawasaki Heavy Industries, and the United States' Pullman Swindell and Dravo. Those firms have in turn acted as agents on behalf of Alfa and have constructed steel plants in such countries as Brazil, Venezuela, Indonesia, Iran, Iraq, and Zambia. Alfa receives fees for the use of the technology in foreign mills, and the engineering firms receive fees for building the plants in what are known as turnkey projects.

In order for Alfa to expand and maintain management control during the 1976–1980 period, it had to borrow and recruit managers outside of Mexico. Alfa ended up with debt of almost $3 billion from over 130 different banks; about 75 percent of this was payable in U.S. dollars. Alfa also had to pay highly to attract managers with the backgrounds it wanted. Then oil prices plummeted, and the Mexican peso devalued. By 1981 Alfa was losing so much money that it had to receive Mexican government aid of U.S. $680 million to keep afloat. Between 1980 and 1985, Alfa had to shut down 40 of its subsidiaries and reduce the number of its employees by almost 19,000. Meanwhile, many of the foreign firms that had made agreements with Alfa in the 1970s found that their expected Mexican expansion (via Alfa) had been put on hold. These included, for example, BASF's and Hercules' joint ventures with Alfa. Alfa simply lacked the resources to carry out so many agreements with so many different foreign companies.

By 1987 foreign banks had converted a part of Alfa's debt into a 27 percent stake in the company rather than have loans default. But by 1989 Mexico's economy and Alfa's financial situation had turned around to such an extent that Alfa was able to buy back the foreign banks' ownership, an event hailed in the Mexican press as the "Mexicanization" of Alfa. At this time, Alfa's management felt that the company must concentrate on core businesses that could compete internationally, a move that might necessitate new alliances with foreign firms outside Mexico. An Alfa vice president said, "Our plans from the seventies and early eighties must be thrown away, burned."

INTRODUCTION   International business may be conducted in a variety of ways. The truly experienced firm with a full global orientation usually makes use of most of the forms available, selecting them according to specific product or foreign operating characteristics.

The preceding case illustrates the use of several different methods of exploiting international opportunities. Alfa made joint ventures with foreign firms, engaged in the acquisition and sale of process and product technology through licensing and turnkey contracts, and paid for goodwill (the favor a company has acquired beyond its tangible assets) by gaining the use of trademarks through licensing agreements.

This chapter discusses the most common means by which companies commit resources to the foreign sector, methods prompted either by their own desire or by external pressures that force them to accept certain parameters. The chapter also covers the problems of control when one company enters an agreement that makes another company responsible for handling its business objectives. For example, BASF and Hercules both lost control of their Mexican expansion plans when Alfa became unable to comply with the agreed-upon plans. Two forms—trade and direct investment—will be discussed only peripherally in this chapter, since they were handled in Chapters 4, 6, and 14. However, one form of direct investment, shared ownership, will be covered in this chapter as it parallels the other strategic alliances considered here.

SOME VARIABLES AFFECTING CHOICE

Choice of form may necessitate trade-offs among objectives.

In terms of resources, the modes of foreign operations differ in terms of both the amount a firm commits to foreign operations and the proportion of the resources that is located at home rather than abroad. Exports may, for example, result in a lower additional resource commitment than direct foreign investment if there is domestic excess capacity. If a firm must increase capacity, then this increase may take place by investing the resources either at home or abroad. The former involves a substantial commitment to foreign operations, although the assets are not in a foreign location. In exporting, in direct investment, and in some of the other forms of foreign operations, a firm may be able to reduce its total resource commitment by making contracts with other companies to conduct activities on its behalf or by sharing ownership in international business endeavors. Before examining these other operational forms it is useful to discuss some of the major factors that firms should consider when selecting a form of operation in a given market. We will cover them more intensively when we discuss specific operational modes.

Factors influencing choice include legal, cost, experience, competition, risk, control, and nature of assets.

Throughout this discussion, keep in mind that there are trade-offs. For example, a decision to own 100 percent of a foreign subsidiary will normally increase the parent's fulfillment of the objective of controlling decisions; however, it may simultaneously reduce the parent's fulfillment of the objective of minimizing exposure to political risk.[2]

Legal Conditions

Legal factors may be
- Direct prohibitions against certain forms
- Indirect (e.g., affecting profitability)

As was indicated in the case on Grupo Industrial Alfa, a firm may be constrained in its choice of operating mode regardless of its preferences. Some of the foreign firms discussed, such as Ford, may have preferred a wholly owned Mexican operation but were not legally permitted. In addition to the outright prohibition of certain operating forms, other legal means may influence the choice. These include differences in tax rates, differences in the maximum funds that can be remitted, actual or possible enforcement of antitrust provisions, and stipulations on the circumstances in which a proprietary asset will be in the public domain and available for others to use.

Cost

Sometimes it is cheaper to get another firm to handle work
- Especially at small volume
- Especially if the other firm has excess capacity

In order to produce or sell abroad, certain fixed costs must be incurred, so that at a small volume of business it may be cheaper for a firm to contract the work to someone else than to handle it internally. A specialist can spread the fixed costs over services to more than one firm. If business increases enough, a firm may be able to handle the activities more cheaply itself than by buying outside services. Firms should therefore periodically reappraise the question of internal versus external handling of their varied operations.

Another reason that the external contracting of operations may be lower in cost is that another firm may have excess production or sales capacity that can be easily utilized. This utilization also may reduce start-up time and thus result in an earlier cash flow. Furthermore, the contracted firm may have environmental-specific knowledge, such as how to deal with Mexican regulations and labor, that would be expensive for the contracting firm to gain on its own.

Cooperative ventures may, however, increase operating costs. There are additional expenses to negotiate with another firm. There are usually added headquarters, costs of ongoing relationships with another firm. There may be additional control costs as reports must comply to the needs of more than one firm.

Experience

With more experience, companies take on more direct involvement abroad.

In their early stages of international development few companies are willing to expend a large portion of their resources on foreign operations; they may not even have sufficient resources to expand abroad rapidly. As a result, they usually move through stages of increased levels of international involvement. In the early stages they attempt to conserve their own scarce resources and to maximize the portion of the resources that are at home rather than abroad. This leads them to operational forms that transfer the burden of foreign commitment to outsiders. As the firms and their foreign activities grow, they will tend to view the foreign portion of their business differently. Then there is a movement toward the internal handling of more operations and locating a larger portion of resources abroad.[3]

Competition

Firms have more choice of form when there is less likelihood of competition.

When a firm has a desired, unique, difficult-to-duplicate resource, that firm is in a good position to choose the operating form that it would most like to utilize. When there are competitive possibilities, a firm may have to settle on a form that is lower on its priority list; otherwise, a competitor may preempt the market. The possibility of competition also may lead to a strategy of rapid international expansion, which may be possible (because of limited resources) only by developing external arrangements with other firms.

Minimization of competition in given markets also may be achieved through cooperative arrangements that exclude entry, share resources, or divide output. The effectiveness will depend in part on the type of mode selected as well as the permissiveness of governmental authorities to the specific agreement.

Risk

The higher the perceived risk, usually the greater the desire to operate with strategic alliances.

There are many types of risk. However, the possibility of political or economic changes affecting the safety of assets and their earnings is often at the forefront of management's concern in foreign operations. One way of minimizing loss from the seizure of assets in foreign operations is to minimize the base of assets located abroad. This may dictate external arrangements so that the asset base is shared by others. This move might also make a government less willing to move against an operation for fear of encountering opposition from more than one firm.

External forms allow for greater spreading of assets among countries.

One way of spreading risk is to place operations in a number of different countries. This strategy reduces the chance that all foreign assets will simultaneously be subject to such adversities as confiscation, exchange control, or even a slowing of sales caused by a local recession. The maximum losses as well as the year-to-year changes in consolidated earnings thus may be minimized. For companies that have not yet attained widespread international operations, operational forms that minimize their own resource expenditures may permit a more rapid dispersion of operations. These forms will be less appealing for companies whose activities are already widely extended or who have ample resources to so extend.

Control

Internal handling usually means more control and no sharing of profits.

The more a firm deals externally, the more likely it will lose control over decisions that may affect its global optimization, including where output will be expanded, new product directions, and quality. External arrangements also imply the sharing of revenues, a serious consideration in undertakings with high potential profits. They also risk giving information more rapidly to potential competitors. Some analysts suggest that the loss of control over flexibility, revenues, and competition has been the most important variable guiding firms' priorities for a mode of operation.[4]

Product Complexity

There are costs associated with the transfer of technology to another entity. Usually it is cheaper to transfer within the existing corporate family, such as from parent to subsidiary, rather than to another company. The cost difference is especially important when the technology is complex because subsidiary personnel are apt to be more familiar with approaches that the firm is using. For this reason, it has been noted that the higher the level of technology, the more likely a company will expand abroad with its own facilities rather than contracting with another firm to produce abroad on its behalf.[5]

Prior Expansion of the Company

When a company already has operations in place within a foreign country, some of the advantages of contracting an external firm to handle production are no longer as prevalent. In other words, the company knows how to operate within the foreign country and may have excess capacity that can be used to add new production. Much depends, however, on whether the existing foreign operation is in a line of business that is closely related to the product or service that is being transferred abroad. When there is similarity, such as a new type of office equipment in a company that already produces office equipment, there is the highest probability that the new production will be handled internally. In highly diversified companies, the existing foreign facility may be producing goods so dissimilar to what is being transferred that it is easier to deal with an experienced external company.

Similarity of Country

The degree of similarity among countries is a two-edged sword. On the one hand, management is more confident of its ability to operate in those foreign countries that it perceives to be similar to its home environment. U.S. companies, for example, are much more apt to handle operations internally in other English-speaking countries than in countries where the language is different. On the other hand, language and cultural differences impede communications and increase coordination costs among firms, especially if technology is being transferred. In these situations there may be a need to make some level of foreign direct investment so that personnel are more likely to move to the foreign locale to facilitate cross-national information flows.[6]

LICENSING

MNEs want return from intangible assets.

Under a **licensing agreement** a firm (the licensor) grants rights on intangible property to another firm (the licensee) for a specified period of time, and the licensee ordinarily pays a royalty to the licensor in exchange. The rights may be exclusive or nonexclusive. The U.S. Internal Revenue Service (IRS) classifies intangible property into five categories:

Licensing agreements may be
- Exclusive or nonexclusive
- Used for patents, trademarks, know-how, or copyrights

1. patents, inventions, formulas, processes, designs, patterns;
2. copyrights, literary, musical, or artistic compositions;
3. trademarks, trade names, brand names;
4. franchises, licenses, contracts; and
5. methods, programs, procedures, systems, etc.

Usually, the licensor is obliged to furnish technical information and assistance and the licensee to exploit the rights effectively and to pay compensation to the licensor.

Economic Motives

Licensing can have economic motives, such as faster start-up, lower cost, and access to additional resources.

Frequently, a new product or process may affect only part of a firm's total output and only for a limited period of time. The sales volume may not be large enough to warrant the establishment of overseas manufacturing and sales facilities. Furthermore, during the period of acquiring operations there is a risk that competitors will develop improvements that negate the firm's advantages. As discussed earlier, a firm that is already operating abroad may be able to produce and sell at a lower cost and with less start-up time. Risk of operating facilities and holding inventories is reduced for the licensor. The licensee may find that the cost of the arrangement is less than if the development were accomplished internally. For industries in which technological changes are frequent and affect many different products, such as chemicals and electrical goods, firms in various countries often exchange technology rather than compete with each other on every product in every market, an arrangement known as **cross-licensing.**

Cross-licensing may violate antitrust regulations if it results in the restriction of entry into a market by one of the parties. The regulations in this respect are extremely complex, and good legal assistance is necessary for any type of agreement. Another cross-licensing problem is that some of the parties may produce more innovations than others. American Home Products participated in pharmaceutical arrangements with several foreign drug makers that later terminated the arrangements because American Home produced few important drugs on its own.[7]

Even without a cross-licensing arrangement, a licensor may learn from the licensee. For example, Black & Decker's Heli-Coil, a fastener technology, was licensed abroad, and information on the foreign applications and testing were valuable for marketing Heli-Coil in the United States.[8]

A second economic motive concerns the resources a firm has at its disposal, a particular consideration for small firms. But large firms may also be constrained. Chrysler, for example, has insufficient resources to establish its own facilities everywhere that overseas production is necessary for Jeep sales. For some of the largest markets, such as India and Australia, Chrysler has subsidiaries. For some smaller markets, such as Sri Lanka and Pakistan, licensing arrangements are used.

Strategic Motives

Licensing can give return on products not fitting the firm's strategic priority.

Large diversified firms are constantly reevaluating and altering their product lines to put their efforts where their major strengths best complement their assessment of high-profit businesses. This may leave them with products or technologies that they themselves do not wish to exploit but which may be profitably transferred to other firms. Because it does not fit into GE's major lines of business, the company has marketed to other firms its development of a microorganism that destroys spilled oil by digesting it.[9] Or firms may license trademarks. Neither Chrysler nor Coca-Cola wish to be in the clothing business, but Murjani Merchandising has licensed the Jeep and Coca-Cola logos, which are valuable in selling a variety of merchandise.[10] However, the limited time frame for a licensing arrangement may allow licensor firms to move to a different operating form if the particular technology or trademark use is later deemed to be of strategic importance.[11]

Political and Legal Motives

Licensing hinders nonassociated firms from usurping the asset.

Aside from licensing because of restrictions on trade or foreign ownership, licensing may also be a means of protecting an asset. This may come about for two reasons. First, many countries provide very little de facto protection for a foreign property right such as a trademark, patent, or copyright unless authorities are prodded consistently. To prevent the so-called pirating of these proprietary assets, companies sometimes have made licensing agreements with local firms, which then monitor to ensure that no one else uses the asset locally. Second, some countries provide protection only if the internationally registered asset is exploited locally within a specified period of time. If a firm does not use the registration within the country during the specified period, then whoever does so first will have the right to it. Mexico is one such country: In Mexico City, Gucci, Chemise La Coste, and Cartier shops unrelated to the European houses are in close proximity. The Cartier shop copies a Cartier watch dial, bracelet, presentation box, and storefront to the smallest detail, but it puts cheap movements and poor-quality gold filling in the watches. This has hurt Cartier's reputation among unsuspecting buyers, who then refuse to buy in the authentic stores in New York and Paris. Had Cartier licensed the use of its name in Mexico early on, it might have preempted the nonassociated use of the name there. Instead, the real Cartier has opened a shop close to the bogus one in an attempt to educate and steer clients to its legitimate products.[12]

A firm that doesn't license may find that another firm can exclude its market entry at a later date or can compete in certain areas of the world through exploitation of the asset, such as in the situations described in Mexico. Western Electric has a liberal licensing policy in order to avoid patent litigation.

Problems and Provisions

Hardly any aspect of international business has been as controversial in recent years as licensing. Given the fact that virtually all royalties are paid to organizations in industrial countries, it is perhaps inevitable that groups within

LDCs have criticized the amounts and methods of payment. Since MNEs view their technologies and trademarks as integral parts of their asset bases, it is perhaps just as inevitable that they are skeptical about transferring their use to other organizations. The following discussion highlights the major concerns of licensors, licensees, and host governments that might be incorporated into a formal agreement.

Asset transference can create control problems, such as

- License inadequately worked
- Poor quality
- Development of competitor

Control and Competition   By transferring rights to another firm the owner undoubtedly loses some control over the asset. There are a host of potential problems with the lack of control that should be settled in the original licensing agreement. Provisions should be made for the termination of the agreement if the parties do not adhere to the directives. The agreement should specify the methods of testing of quality, the obligations of each party concerning expenditures on sales development, and the geographic limitations on the use of the asset. Without these provisions the license may be inadequately worked, the two parties may find themselves in competition with each other, or a poor-quality product in one country may jeopardize product image and sales elsewhere. A good example of the dangers of lack of specification is the case of Oleg Cassini, Inc., which sued the U.S. subsidiary (Jovan) of the Beecham Group from the United Kingdom. Cassini had licensed Jovan to promote and extend sales throughout the world of various Cassini fragrances, cosmetics, and beauty aids. Then Jovan introduced Diane Von Furstenberg products instead and denied Cassini the right to license the Cassini name to other firms. The case was settled when Jovan agreed to market the Cassini products; however, their sales of the products through discount stores won Cassini an award in a later suit because of image injury.[13]

Some firms have well-known trademarked names that they license abroad for the production of some products that they have never produced nor have had expertise with themselves. The Pierre Cardin label, for example, is used by over 800 licensees in 93 countries to produce hundreds of different products, from clothing to sheets and from clocks to deodorants. Monitoring and maintaining control of so much diversity is very difficult. Two U.S. firms, Saks Fifth Avenue and Eagle Shirtmakers, dropped arrangements with Pierre Cardin-labeled products because the lack of policing for quality on some licensees' products adversely affected the image of others.[14]

Depending on the nature of the asset, either the licensor or the licensee stands the risk of developing a future competitor after the agreement expires. If a brand or trademark is involved, the licensee may develop consumer preferences and have to turn the market over to the licensor. If know-how or patents are involved, the licensee may be able to exploit the assets long after the agreement is terminated. Even before an agreement is terminated, the two parties may come into competition with each other because one has made improvements on the licensed technology that make the original patents obsolete. Therefore, it has become common for firms to make provisions in the original contract for the possible use and sharing of superseding technology built on knowledge from the original transfer.

In licensing agreements,
- Seller does not want to give information without payment assurance
- Buyer does not want to pay without evaluating information

Secrecy   The value of many technologies would diminish if they were widely known or understood. Provisions that a licensee will not divulge this information historically have been included in agreements. Some licensors have, in addition, held onto the ownership and production of specific components so that licensees will not have the full knowledge or capability to produce an exact copy of the product.

Secrecy arises as a problem for negotiating agreements to transfer process technology. Many times a firm has developed techniques that it has not yet used commercially but that it wishes to sell. A buyer is reluctant to "buy a pig in a poke," but a licensor who shows the potential licensee the process risks having the process used without payment. It has become common to set up preagreements in order to protect all parties.

An area of growing controversy is the degree of secrecy in the financial terms of licensing agreements. Within some countries, for example, governmental agencies now must approve royalty contracts once the contracts have been negotiated by the parties involved. Sometimes these authorities consult with their counterparts in other countries regarding similar agreements in order to improve their negotiations with MNEs. Many MNEs object to this procedure because they believe that contract terms are proprietary information of competitive importance and that market conditions usually dictate the need for very different terms in different countries.

Stage of Technology Development   Technology may be old or new, obsolete or still in use at home, when transferred to a foreign firm.[15] For example, Crown, Cork, and Seal held on to its three-piece can manufacturing technology until it developed two-piece technology, whereupon the older technology was licensed to LDCs. United Technology transferred the same elevator technology it had been using in the United States to the People's Republic of China. Many other companies transfer technology at an early or even a developmental stage so that products are introduced almost simultaneously in different markets. On the one hand, new technology may be worth more to a licensee because it may have a longer life of use. On the other hand, newer technology, particularly in the development phase, may be worth less because of its more uncertain value in the market.

Figure 15.1
Determinants of Compensation in International Technology Licensing
The upper left-hand box shows factors in the agreement that can affect the value of technology to the licensee. The upper right-hand box shows factors external to negotiations that can affect pricing. The bottom portion shows a bargaining range based on estimates by the licensor and licensee. *Source:* Kang Rae Cho, "Issues of Compensation in International Technology Licensing," *Management International Review,* Vol. 28, No. 2, 1988, p. 76.

Agreement-specific Factors

* Market restrictions
  (including exports)
* Exclusivity of the license
* Limits on production size
* Product quality requirements
* Grantback provisions
* Tie-in provisions
* Duration of the agreement
* Age of the technology
* Duration of the patent
* Other constraints on the use of technology

Environment-specific Factors

* Government (of both licensor and licensee)
  regulations on licensing
* Level of competition in the licensee's
  product market
* Level of competition among alternative
  suppliers of similar technology
* Political and business risk in the
  licensee country
* Product and industry norms
* Technology absorptive capacity of
  the licensee country

Licensor's Offer Price

Upper limit: Smaller of
  (1) estimate of licensee's
      incremental profits
      from use of technology;
          or
  (2) estimate of licensee's
      costs of obtaining same
      or similar technology
      from alternative sources.

Lower limit:
  Estimate of direct transfer
  costs, opportunity costs, and
  R & D costs.

zero price

Bargaining
Range

Licensee's Bid Price

Upper limit: Smaller of
  (1) estimate of incremental
      profits from use of
      technology;
          or
  (2) estimate of costs of
      developing same or
      similar technology;
          or
  (3) estimate of costs of
      obtaining same or
      similar technology from
      best alternative source.

Lower limit:
  Estimate of licensor's direct
  transfer costs.

Licensing payments vary by
- Fixed fee versus usage
- Value to the licensee
- Regulatory and competitive factors
- Negotiating ability of parties

Payment   There is a wide variation in the amount and type of payment under licensing arrangements, and each contract tends to be negotiated very much on its own merits. Figure 15.1 illustrates the major factors determining the amount of payment. The upper left-hand box, agreement-specific factors, illustrates negotiated clauses that may affect the value to the licensee. For example, the value will be greater if potential sales are high, such as with exclusive worldwide rights for a long period of time before the asset becomes obsolete. The upper right-hand box, environmental-specific factors, lists other conditions that may affect the value. For example, the amount the licensee might pay could be low if its government sets upper payment limits or if other firms are vying to sell similar technology. Since neither the licensor nor the licensee can be sure of the price the other is willing to accept, the bottom of Fig. 15.1 illustrates the bargaining range based on their expectations.

Many LDC governments set price controls on what licensees pay or insist on prohibitions of restrictions.[16] One of the thorny issues on sales restrictions as seen by LDCs is that licensees are usually prevented by contract from exporting; thus small-scale production may cause high full costs to the consumers. MNEs have countered that extending sales territories would necessitate high royalties because MNEs could not sell exclusive rights to parties in other countries. They also have argued that the development of process technologies for small-scale production would often be too costly but is done when economically feasible.

Taxes may be assessed differently depending on the methods of arranging payments under the agreement, for example as income or as a capital gain. If the taxes on capital gains are different from those on income, the after-tax receipts will be different. Payment schedules also may be deferred in order to defer the payment of taxes. Fees to be paid for the use of an asset may be made in a lump sum, on a percentage of sales value, on a specific rate applied to usage, or on some combination of these methods.

It is common to negotiate a "front-end" payment to cover the cost of transfer and to follow this with another set of fees based on actual or projected usage. The reason for this is the realization that few technologies may be moved abroad simply by transferring publications and reports. The negotiation process is itself expensive and must be followed by engineering, consultation, and adaptation. The early stages of production usually are characterized by low quality and low productivity.[17] The substantial costs in the transfer process increasingly are charged to the licensee so that the licensor is motivated to assure a smooth adaptation.

Sales to controlled entities are common because they
- Are separate legal entities
- Protect value when ownership is shared

Sales to Controlled Entities   Many licenses are given to companies connected in ownership with the licensor. A license may be needed to transfer technology abroad because operations in a foreign country, even if 100 percent owned by the parent, usually are separate firms from a legal standpoint. When there is a present or potential shared ownership, a separate licensing

• Provide a way to avert payment or exchange limitations

arrangement also may be a means of compensating for contributions beyond the mere investment in capital and managerial resources.

The price at which MNEs sell to foreign operations they control is very controversial. Since much of what is transferred among controlled entities of a multinational company is unique to that company, it is highly difficult to estimate what the competitive price would be if the company were selling the same thing to a noncontrolled entity. Yet by altering the price of product, components, patents, and so on, MNEs effectively may transfer more of their profits from one country to another. Critics in donor countries have contended that too little is charged, and thus profits are transferred to low-tax countries. LDCs with low tax rates have contended the opposite, arguing that MNEs have artificially minimized their profits in LDCs in order either to move funds to countries with a stronger currency or to gain certain host-governmental concessions.[18] Obviously, MNEs cannot be shifting profits simultaneously to both the home and the host country; nevertheless, the criticisms have made it more difficult for MNEs to establish licensing contracts with their controlled affiliates. Tax authorities in home countries ask for pricing justifications. Governmental authorities in LDCs are increasingly approving transfers on a case-by-case basis.

Positioning the Licensing Unit[19]

Where the responsibility for licensing is handled typically in organizations depends on the motives for licensing. When licensing is an integral part of a company's growth and diversification objectives, a separate licensing department is likely to be in charge of buying and selling. In multidivisional firms there may be more than one of these departments. When the strategy is primarily the safeguarding of existing activities, licensing is apt to be a part of the legal or patents department. When a company combines the above two objectives, it tends to attach licensing to the R&D department.

FRANCHISING

Franchising includes provision of a trademark and continual infusion of necessary assets.

Franchising is essentially a way of doing business in which the franchisor gives an independent franchisee the use of a trademark that is an essential asset for the franchisee's business and in which the franchisor more than nominally assists on a continuing basis in the operation of the business. In many cases the franchisor also provides supplies.[20] For instance, Holiday Inn grants to franchisees the goodwill of the Holiday Inn name and the support service to get started, such as appraisal of a proposed motel site. As part of the continued relationship, Holiday Inn offers reservations services and training programs to help ensure the success of the venture. In a sense the franchisor and franchisee act almost like a vertically integrated firm because the

Many types of products
and countries are in-
volved in franchising.

parties are interdependent and each produces part of the product or service
that ultimately reaches the consumer.

Franchising goes back at least as far as the nineteenth century and is most
associated with the United States, where one third of retail sales are handled
that way. About three quarters of the sales are in three areas: car and truck
dealerships, gasoline service stations, and soft-drink bottling. Between 1971
and 1986 the number of U.S. international franchisors grew from 156 to 354,
and their number of outlets in foreign countries grew from a little over 3000
to more than 31,000.[21] Although they are located in all regions of the world,
Map 15.2 shows that only four countries (Canada, Japan, the United Kingdom, and Australia) account for about two thirds of the outlets. The fastest
growth areas of U.S. firms have been in food and business services.

Not all franchising is by U.S. firms, and foreign-owned franchise operations are growing rapidly in the United States. Pronuptia, a French bridal
wear franchisor, and such food franchisors as Wimpy's and Bake 'N' Take
from the United Kingdom and Wienerwald from Germany have been among
some of the earliest and most successful abroad. There has also been a surge
of foreign acquisition of franchisors based in the United States.[22] Burger King,

Map 15.2

International Franchising by U.S. Firms
Arrows point to the location of outlets by U.S. franchisors. *Source: Franchising in the
Economy 1986–1988.* Washington, U.S. Department of Commerce, 1988, giving data for
1986.

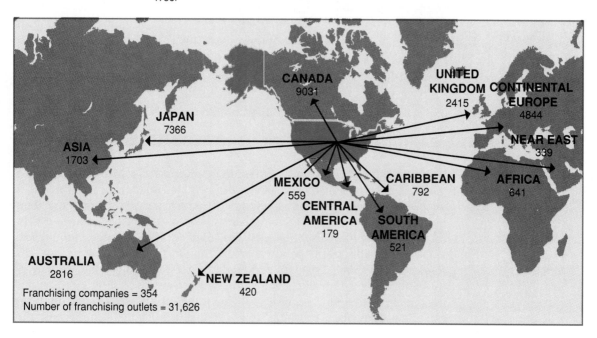

Hardees, Holiday Inn, Howard Johnson's, Baskin-Robbins, Meineke Discount Mufflers, and Great American Cookie are U.S. franchisors that have been acquired by non-U.S. firms.

Organization

The most common means (almost 60 percent) by which a franchisor penetrates a foreign country is by setting up a master franchise and giving that organization (usually local) the rights for the country or region.[23] The master franchisee may then open outlets on its own or develop subfranchisees. Royalty payments by the subfranchisees are made to the master franchisee, who then remits some predetermined percentage to the franchisor. As an example, McDonald's very successful Japanese operations are handled this way.

In about 20 percent of cases, franchisors enter by dealing directly with individual franchisees abroad. This is sometimes difficult because the franchisor may be insufficiently known to convince many local people to make investments. It is therefore common to enter with some company-owned outlets that serve as a showcase to attract franchisees.

In the case of Great American Cookie's U.K. entry, the company arranged a line of credit of $10 million with a U.K. bank in advance of seeking partners. This money was used to finance franchisees who had to put up only 10 percent.[24]

Operational Modifications

Securing good locations can be a major problem.[25] Finding suppliers can be an added problem and expense: For example, McDonald's had to invest to build a plant to make hamburger buns in the United Kingdom, and it had to help farmers develop potato production in Thailand.[26] Another concern in foreign franchise expansion has been governmental or legal restrictions that make it difficult to gain satisfactory operating permission.

Franchisors face a dilemma:
- The more standardization, the less acceptance in foreign country
- The more adjustment to foreign country, the less the franchiser is needed

Many franchise failures abroad are due to not developing enough domestic penetration first; thus they lack sufficient management depth and cash. A dilemma for successful domestic franchisors is that their success at home has been largely due to three factors: (1) product and service standardization, (2) high identification through promotion, and (3) effective cost controls. When entering many foreign countries, various restraints may make it difficult to conform to home-country methods. Yet the more adjustments that are made to the host-country's nuances, the less a franchisor has to offer a potential franchisee. The success of franchisors in Japan has been due in great part to enthusiastic assimilation of Western innovations, so firms such as McDonald's have been able to copy their U.S. outlets almost intact. Yet such food franchisors as Dunkin' Donuts and Perkits Yogurt fared poorly in the

U.K. The reason was that it was too difficult to change certain British eating habits; yet if firms offered menus that were more acceptable to the British, there would be nothing different to offer a franchisee. Even in countries where franchises have been successful, it usually has been necessary to make some operating adjustments. For example, Kentucky Fried Chicken in Japan had to redesign its equipment and stores to save space because of the higher cost of rent. It eliminated mashed potatoes and put less sugar in its cole slaw because of Japanese tastes. Pizza Hut alters its toppings by country, and in Saudi Arabia it must have two dining rooms—one for single men and one for families. McDonald's changed the pronunciation of its name in Japan to "MaKudonaldo" and substituted Donald for Ronald McDonald because of pronunciation difficulties in Japanese.[27]

Contract Problems

Some of the problems that plague franchising agreements are no different from those in licensing agreements. Contracts must be spelled out in detail, but if courts must rule on disagreements, both parties are apt to lose something in the settlement. A good example was when McDonald's granted a license for up to 166 stores in France to Raymond Dayan at less than its normal fee because of doubts that the French would ever take to fast-food restaurants. Dayan, with the help of McDonald's, found very good Paris locations for fourteen stores, which he opened over a period of several years. He was very successful, but McDonald's had the right to revoke the franchise agreement if its inspection found that the stores were not up to its level of cleanliness. The agreement was cancelled on these grounds, leading to a court case. Dayan claimed that McDonald's action was simply a ruse to make him pay McDonald's usual rate. He lost out on further expansion with the McDonald's trademark; but McDonald's lost something too. When Dayan took down the McDonald's signs, he immediately replaced them with signs saying O'Keefe's Hamburgers; and he had the clientele, the know-how, and the best locations in Paris.[28] These stores were later sold to the French firm Quick, the largest fast-food chain in France.

MANAGEMENT CONTRACTS

Management contracts are used primarily when
- The owned operation has been expropriated
- The firm manages a new facility

One of the most important assets a firm may have at its disposal is management talent. Despite huge endowments of capital and technology, many governmental enterprises in LDCs encounter difficulties because of inadequately trained management. The transmission of management internationally has depended largely on foreign investments that deploy expatriate managers and

- The firm manages an operation in trouble

specialists to foreign countries. **Management contracts** offer a means through which a firm may use part of its management personnel to assist a firm in a foreign country in general or specialized management functions for a specified period of time for a fee.

Management contracts are established in three types of situations. The first is when a foreign investment has been expropriated by a foreign government and the former owner is invited to continue supervising the operations until local management is trained. In this case the management structure may remain substantially the same, although board membership changes. A good example of this is the case on Aramco at the beginning of Chapter 13. After the Saudi Arabian government took over the ownership, the former owners continued to supply management. Some advantages of entering into contracts in this type of situation are that this may: (1) facilitate getting resources out of the country in addition to those agreed upon in the expropriation discussions, (2) ingratiate the firm with local authorities so that future business operations are possible, and (3) ensure continued access to raw materials or other resources needed from the country. The second type of management contract is when a firm is asked to manage a new venture, in which case it may sell much of its own equipment to the facility. The third situation occurs when a foreign firm is invited in to manage an existing operation more efficiently.

From the standpoint of the recipient country, the need to receive direct investment as a means of gaining management assistance is removed. From the standpoint of the firm providing management, contracts are appropriate in order to avoid the risk of capital asset loss, when returns on investment are too low and capital outlays are too high. A management contract may also serve as a means of gaining foreign experience for the supplier, thus increasing its capacity to internationalize. For example, Ansett Transport Industries of Australia developed contracts to operate Air Vanuatu for the government of Vanuatu. This led to other management contracts in the South Pacific, which in turn led to Ansett equity interests in Transcorp Airways (Hong Kong), Ansett New Zealand (New Zealand), Air Norway (Norway), Ladeco (Chile), and America West (United States).[29]

The contracts do have potential problems, not the least of which is the training of future competitors. Additionally, if the firm has differences of opinion on policy, incurs start-up inefficiencies, or does not train local managers quickly, bad feelings may result. Although the contractor has the responsibility for managing, it may frequently lack the ability to control the employees, particularly in government-owned facilities. Holiday Inn's ten-year contract in Tibet is an example. The management was precluded from giving incentives to or disciplining its staff; consequently, there was little that could be done when waiters and waitresses took their lunch breaks all together when guests showed up for lunch.[30] Contracts usually are drawn to cover three to five years, and fixed fees or fees based on volume rather than profits are most common.

_____ **TURNKEY OPERATIONS** ▮▮▮▮▮▮▮▮▮▮▮▮▮▮▮▮▮▮▮▮▮▮

Turnkey operations
- Most commonly are construction firms
- May develop future competitors

Turnkey projects involve a contract for construction of operating facilities that are transferred for a fee to the owner when the facilities are ready to commence operations. Firms performing turnkey operations are frequently industrial equipment manufacturers that supply some of their own equipment for the project. Most commonly, they are construction firms. In addition, they may be consulting firms or manufacturers that do not find an investment on their own behalf in the country to be feasible.

The customer for a turnkey operation is very often a governmental agency that has decreed that a given product must be produced locally and under its auspices. As in the case of the management contract, a firm building a turnkey facility may be developing a future competitor. Yet many firms have chosen to perform design and construction duties, particularly where there are restrictions on foreign ownership. In recent years, most of the large projects have been in oil-exporting countries, which are moving rapidly toward infrastructure development and industrialization. Of course, not all turnkey projects are developing potential competitors. Projects to build airports and port facilities, for example, do not lend themselves to competition.

The size of these contracts is one of the things setting this business apart from most other international business operations. Most of the contracts are for hundreds of millions of dollars, and many are for several billion, which means that a few very large firms account for most of the international market. Smaller firms are largely excluded from direct contracts, such as in the rebuilding of Kuwait after the liberation from Iraq, or serve as subcontractors for primary turnkey suppliers. One firm, Kellogg Rust, accounts for a significant share of the international market and of the U.S. portion of that market.[31] This also has meant hiring executives with top-level governmental contacts abroad who can gain entry with the right decision makers to negotiate their proposals in foreign countries.

Pullman-Kellogg, for example, secured a large fertilizer plant contract in Nigeria by sending Andrew Young, a former UN ambassador who enjoys immense personal prestige in Africa, to negotiate the contract.[32] The nature of the large-scale government contracts also has placed great importance on ceremony, such as opening a facility on a country's independence day or getting a head of state to inaugurate a facility in order to build goodwill for future contracts. Although public relations is important, it takes much more to sell contracts of such magnitude. The U.S. Department of Commerce lists the following four factors in order of importance:

1. price,
2. export financing,
3. managerial and technological quality, and
4. experience and reputation.[33]

Payment for a turnkey operation usually is in stages, as a project develops. It is common for 10 to 25 percent to be made as a down payment, another 50 to 65 percent to be paid as the contract progresses, and the remainder to be paid once the facility actually is operating in accordance with the contract. Because of the usual long time periods between conception and completion, the company performing turnkey operations is exposed to possible currency fluctuations for an extended period of time and should be covered, if possible, by escalation clauses or cost-plus contracts. Since the final payment is made only if the facility is operating satisfactorily, it is important to specify very precisely what constitutes "satisfactorily." For this reason, many firms insist on performing a feasibility study as part of the turnkey contract in order not to build something that, although desired by local governmental authorities, nevertheless may be too large or inefficient. Although the facility may be built exactly as desired, its inefficiency could create legal problems that hold up final payment.

Many of the turnkey contracts are in remote areas, thus necessitating massive housing construction and importation of personnel. They may involve building an entire infrastructure under the most adverse geographic conditions.

If a firm holds a monopoly on certain assets or resources, it will be difficult for other companies to be competitive in building facilities. As the production process becomes known, however, the number of competitors for performing turnkey operations increases. The president of an international consulting engineering firm has listed five stages for developing countries:

1. expatriates do all the work,
2. local subcontractors develop,
3. small local contractors start up,
4. local contractors take over local work, and
5. local contractors go abroad.[34]

This series of changes has pushed U.S. firms' involvement in recent years to the high-technology end of the spectrum, whereas firms from such countries as India, Korea, and Turkey can compete better for conventional projects where low labor costs are important.[35]

CUSTOM CONTRACTS

Contract arrangements
- Sometimes have advantages similar to vertical integration
- May spread risk and developmental costs

Companies that at one time would have integrated vertically by making direct investments for the extraction of raw materials in foreign countries now are experiencing increased desire for local ownership of the extractive process. Since the local owners frequently continue to need certain resources the foreign firms hold, contracts may be established whereby raw materials are traded for the assets held by foreign firms. For example, as the Saudi Arabian government increased its ownership share of Aramco, it still needed management and exploration assistance, which was traded for commitments of preferred status for oil sales. On the basis of this precedent, several other oil-producing countries have made arrangements whereby the oil firms take all exploration and development risks in exchange for a share of the oil produced.

One of the fastest growth areas for contract arrangements has been for projects that are too large for any single company to handle. This has been apparent in the development of new aircraft and weapons systems. From the inception of a project, companies from different countries frequently agree to take on the high cost and high risk of developmental work for different components needed in the final product; afterward a lead company buys the components from the firms that did a part of the developmental work.

The major aluminum producers have developed swap contracts whereby they can save transport costs. They are all vertically integrated firms, but not in each country where they operate. Alcan might give Pechiney semiprocessed alumina in Canada in exchange for the same amount of semiprocessed alumina delivered to Alcan in France.

Many contracts have developed among airlines in different countries that lack routes, resources, or enough customers to handle expansion independently. For example, Pan Am and Aeroflot shared a route between New York and Moscow, with each company supplying part of the crew. USAir and Air France have agreed to allocate space to each other on certain international flights, to do some joint advertising and promotion, and to share some terminal facilities. The airlines of the Cook Islands and Western Samoa share aircraft by painting the Cook Islands' colors on one side and Polynesia's on the other.[36]

IMPROVING ACCESS TO FOREIGN TECHNOLOGY

Access to foreign technology may improve a firm's domestic and international competitiveness.

In most of the aforementioned operational forms (licensing, franchising, management contracts, turnkey operations, and other contractual arrangements) an organization in one country may gain access to scientific or managerial technology from an organization in another country. By gaining these assets a firm may be in a much better position to compete domestically and internationally. Because of the competitive implications, it is not surprising that many firms are establishing mechanisms whereby they may increase the likelihood of gaining advantages before their competitors.

One of the most commonly used mechanisms is to establish company units to monitor journals and technical conferences. This is not sufficient because very few patent descriptions ever appear in other than the voluminous patent-office publications from each different country; therefore, firms must familiarize themselves with these publications as well. There are now firms that sell data bases of information they clip from thousands of periodicals in multiple languages.[37] This combined monitoring helps assure that the company learns of new developments, thereby enabling decision makers to decide whether to ignore the innovations, to try to counteract them through in-house developments, or to establish an operational link with the individuals or organizations that are apparently leading the field. A second mechanism is to develop formal links with academic and other research organizations at home and abroad so as to determine possible breakthroughs before they are publicized in professional journals. A third means is to increase visibility through participation in trade fairs, the distribution of brochures, and contacts with technical acquisition consultants. This visibility may encourage innovators to think of a particular firm rather than another when they seek out clients. A fourth means is to establish cooperative research projects with foreign firms, thereby gaining scale benefits and the use of personnel from other organizations. Finally, a company may set up part of its R&D activities in foreign countries in order to utilize foreign talent that would not likely emigrate to the company's home country.[38]

SHARED OWNERSHIP

When a firm does take an ownership in foreign operations, it may own the entire stock or it may share the ownership. There are various types of ownership sharing, just as there are several reasons for selecting an equity amount.

The Argument for 100 Percent Ownership

One hundred percent ownership is
- Easier to control
- Has no sharing of profits

Most businesspeople would prefer to have a 100 percent interest in foreign operations in order to ensure control and to prevent the dilution of profits. As long as there are no other stockholders, corporate management has a greater freedom to enact measures that, although not in the best interest of the particular operations, are in the best interest of the company as a whole. With other stockholders, the parent firm has much less freedom of action, since even minority stockholders may become very vocal to their governments about practices that are not in the best interest of subsidiaries. In fact, most countries have legislation to protect minority stockholders. Freuhauf-France, for example, received export orders that, although in the best interest of that subsidiary, were not considered by its U.S. majority owners to be in the best interests of Freuhauf's worldwide operations. When Freuhauf-France did not fulfill the export orders, the minority stockholders contested the action in French courts. This left the majority stockholders with the options of either filling the export order or paying damages to the minority holders.[39]

Even when the majority owners act in what they consider to be the best interest of the local company, there may be conflicts with local stockholders because of different opinions as to what businesses should be doing. Some points of possible conflict are dividend pay-out versus the retention of earnings, the degree of public disclosure of activities, and the degree of cooperation with various governmental agencies.

The argument against diluting profits is simple: Many firms contend that if they own all the resources necessary for the successful foreign operation and are willing to contribute these resources, they should not have to share ownership.

Reasons for Shared-Ownership Arrangements

Internal reasons for partial ownership are
- Faster geographic spread
- R&D over a larger base
- To complement resources

In spite of the advantages to owning 100 percent in a foreign facility, ownership sharing is popular.[40] The reasons for this are undoubtedly a combination of outside pressures and internal willingness to take partial ownership abroad.

From an internal standpoint, there has been a need to bring outside resources into foreign operations. By sharing ownership in some existing foreign operations, many firms have been able to spread geographically at a faster rate. This has prevented competitors from gaining dominant market shares and also allowed maximum sales expansion, which helps to spread such relatively fixed costs as R&D to a larger sales base.

Governments pressure for sharing
- Because they want local control
- But they treat industries differently

Externally, there have been increased pressures by many countries for ownership sharing with local shareholders, as countries feel this policy will enhance their economic or political objectives. In addition, many companies feel that by bringing local capital into the organization they take on a local character that decreases governmental and societal criticism (thus reducing the risk of nationalization or expropriation) and may bring captive sales to the participating shareholders. Some industries share ownership much more than others, especially those for which a high capital outlay is necessary for making the investment. The higher capital outlay in these large investments necessitates additional outside resources. Furthermore, local governments exert greater pressure for ownership sharing on those firms having the most significant impact on the economy.

A major reason for sharing ownership abroad is to gain more assured synergy among the assets held by two or more organizations in different countries. For example, Whirlpool has appliance technology and the Mexican firm Vitro has skills to manage a labor force, which the two companies put together for making washing machines in Mexico. Or they may combine certain resources to combat larger and more powerful competitors. For example, Volvo's 20 percent interest in Renault and Renault's 25 percent interest in Volvo's car subsidiary enhance their joint development and production of technically advanced components at low cost so that they can better compete against larger auto firms, such as General Motors and Volkswagen.[41] Almost any type of asset can be combined. For instance, one firm has manufacturing capabilities; another has distribution. The two may have research capabilities that complement each other. But why share in ownership instead of setting nonequity contract arrangements? Simply, a shared ownership of even a minority amount adds some assurance of say-so over the operation. For example, SAS acquired a 9.9 percent interest in Texas Air, Continental's parent. There are considerable synergies between SAS and Continental that Texas Air cannot easily nullify because SAS has a board seat on Texas Air.[42]

Equity as a Control Mechanism

The problem of deciding how much equity is necessary for control is cumbersome. With a few exceptions, the larger the percentage of equity held, the more likely it is that the owner of this equity will control the decisions and policies of the enterprise. Many firms are willing to share ownership but usually will specify whether the sharing is to be with or without control. If, for example, a firm takes only a minority holding in its foreign operations, ordinarily it can still control policies and decisions if the remaining ownership is widely fragmented. After the 1973 Mexicanization law discussed in the Grupo Industrial Alfa case, many foreign firms sought to maintain management control in spite of minority equity positions by selling 51 percent of their shares to a broad ownership market through the Mexican stock exchange. BASF, a German chemical company, maintained management control by transferring a majority interest in its pharmaceutical company to Bancomer, a big Mexican bank. The bank was simply interested in diversifying its investment holdings and had no desire to manage.[43] Another possibility is to divide profits on the basis of shares but to give voting rights only to one class of shareholders. Still another is to stipulate that your own directors will appoint management and key officers.[44]

When no one company has control, the operation may lack a significant direction. In discussing the problems of a company that was jointly owned by a U.S. and a Japanese firm, a Sterling Drug spokesman said, "You must decide right off the bat whether you'll control it or will put confidence in the Japanese organization."[45] This opinion is supported by studies showing that when two or more partners attempt to share in the management of an operation, there is a much higher incidence of failure than when one parent dominates.[46]

Joint Ventures

Joint ventures
- Need not be fifty-fifty
- There may be various combinations of ownership

A type of ownership sharing very popular among international companies is the joint venture, which occurs when a company is owned by more than one organization. Although it is formed usually for the achievement of a limited objective, it may continue to operate indefinitely as the objective is redefined. Joint ventures are sometimes thought of as fifty-fifty companies, but often more than two organizations participate in the ownership. Furthermore, one organization may frequently control more than 50 percent of the venture. The type of legal organization may be a partnership, corporation, or some other form of organization permitted in the country of operation. When more than two organizations participate, the resultant joint venture is sometimes referred to as a **consortium.**

Almost every conceivable combination of partners may exist in joint ventures. They may include, for example, two firms from the same country joining together in a foreign market, such as Standard Oil-California and International Minerals and Chemicals in India. They may involve a foreign company joining with a local company, such as Sears Roebuck and Simpsons in Canada. Companies from two or more countries may establish a joint venture in a third country—for example, Alcan (Canadian) and Pechiney (French) in Argentina. The ventures may be formed between a private company and a local government (sometimes called mixed ventures), such as Philips (Dutch) with the Indonesian government. Even some government-controlled companies have had joint ventures abroad, such as Dutch State Mines with Pittsburgh Plate Glass in the United States. The more firms are involved in the ownership, the more complex the ownership arrangement is. For example, Australia Aluminum is owned by two U.S companies (American Metal Climax and Anaconda), two Japanese companies (Sumitomo Chemical Company and Showa Denko), one Dutch company (Holland Aluminum), and one German company (Vereinigte Aluminum Werke).

The arguments for and against the sharing of ownership apply as well to joint ventures. Certain types of firms have a greater tolerance for joint ventures than others.[47] Firms with higher tolerance include those that are new at foreign operations and those with decentralized decision making domestically, very often the multiproduct companies. Since the latter firms are accustomed to extending control downward in their organizations, it is an easier transition to do the same thing internationally.

Many joint ventures break up, primarily because the parties evolve different objectives for them. For instance, one partner may want to reinvest earnings for growth and the other partner may want to receive dividends. Another problem is that one partner may offer much closer management attention to the venture than the other. If things go wrong, the more active partner blames the less active partner for its lack of attention, and the less active partner blames the more active one for making poor decisions.[48] Furthermore, partners may be suspicious that their partners are taking more from the venture (particularly technology) than they are. Therefore, the choice of joint venture partner is crucial, particularly if one is forced into a shared-ownership arrangement because of governmental regulations. For this reason many firms will develop joint ventures only after they have had long-term positive experiences with the other company through distributorship, licensing, or other contract arrangements. Compatibility of corporate cultures is also important in cementing relationships.[49]

MANAGING FOREIGN ARRANGEMENTS

Contracts with Other Firms

When contracting another firm, a firm must
- Still monitor performance
- Assess whether to take over operations itself
- Work out conflicts and disputes

Even though a company may find it beneficial to rely on other firms at home or abroad to carry out part or all of its foreign business functions, management is not relieved of the responsibility for these functions. Periodically management must assess whether the functions should be carried out internally. Great care should be taken to ensure that the best firms are involved and that they are performing the jobs of making, selling, or servicing the product adequately.

We have already referred to the major reason for getting other companies to perform functions overseas. If an outside firm can perform the same functions (assuming the same quality) at a cheaper rate, a company should give little consideration to taking on the duties itself. If it can do them more cheaply itself, there may still be justification for getting someone else to do the work. Every company has limited resources, which it should use to the best advantage. If the resources can be used to a better advantage in other activities, then it will pay the firm to commit those resources to activities with a higher return and get someone else to commit resources to the pursuit of other business, which should yield a return to both firms. Three subjective factors also enter into the analysis: (1) Management may not feel capable of doing as good a job as an outside firm, (2) management also may feel that the commitment of resources abroad would incur too large a risk for the firm, (3) management may feel that competitive risks increase when activities are not under its own control. Because situations change, decisions should be reexamined from time to time.

In choosing a firm to handle overseas business, management should consider the firm's professional qualifications, personal attributes, and motivation. Unfortunately, there is no way of precisely measuring these factors, nor is there a magic formula for weighing one qualification against another. The proven ability to handle similar business is one key professional attribute. Another is the importance the other firm places on its reputation.

Many possible conflicts can develop between the companies. Although any agreement should specify provisions for termination and should include means to settle disputes, these are costly and cumbersome means of achieving objectives. If possible, it is much better for both parties to settle disagreements on a personal basis. The ability to develop a rapport with the management of another firm is thus an important consideration in choosing a representative.

Management also should estimate potential sales, determine whether quality standards are being met, and assess servicing requirements in order to check whether the other firm is doing an adequate job. Goals should be set mutually so that both parties understand what is expected, and the expectations should be spelled out in the contractual agreements.

Multiple Forms

The same firm usually will use different forms simultaneously.

Most firms move through stages of increased involvement. Exporting usually precedes foreign production, and contracting for another firm to handle foreign business generally precedes handling it internally. A firm may be at different stages for different products and for different markets. A firm also may feel that differences in country characteristics necessitate diverse forms of involvement. Because of the multiproduct nature of most companies, diverse stages may accompany the varied products sold in the same country.

Tension may develop internally as a firm's international operations change and grow. For instance, a move from exporting to foreign production may reduce the size of a domestic product division. Various profit centers may all think they have rights to the sales in a country the firm is about to penetrate. Legal, technical, and marketing personnel may have entirely different perspectives on contractual agreements. Under these circumstances a team approach to evaluate decisions and performance may work. A firm also must develop means of evaluating performance by separating those things that are controllable and noncontrollable by personnel in different profit centers.

LOOKING TO THE FUTURE

As more businesses are becoming international, competition is becoming more global and more interrelated. Thus, what happens competitively in one country is more likely to affect competitive viability in other countries as well. To expand more rapidly to meet this challenge, firms are increasingly turning to alliances with other firms. At one extreme there are international mergers and acquisitions. The alliances discussed in this chapter might be considered half-way houses toward full merger and acquisition. It is safe to say that they will continue to accelerate because firms lack the internal resources to do everything alone as they compete internationally. These alliances will bring both opportunities and potential problems as companies move simultaneously to new-country environments and to contractual arrangements with new companies. Furthermore, the additional operating alternatives may strain the decision-making and control processes.

SUMMARY

- The forms of foreign involvement differ in terms of internal as opposed to external handling of activities and in terms of the proportion of resources committed at home rather than abroad.
- Although the mode employed for foreign operations should be examined in terms of a firm's strategic objectives, the choice often will involve a trade-off among objectives.
- Among the factors that will influence the choice of operating mode are legal conditions, the firm's experience, competitive factors, political and economic risk, and the nature of the assets to be exploited.

- Licensing is granting another firm the use of some rights, such as patents, trademarks, or know-how, usually for a fee. It is a means of establishing foreign production that may minimize capital outlays, prevent the free use of assets by other firms, allow the receipt of assets from other firms in return, and allow for income in some markets where exportation or investment are not feasible.

- Among the major controversies concerning the terms of licensing agreements are the control of use of assets as they may affect future competitive relationships, the secrecy of technology and contract terms, the method and amount of payment, and how to treat transfers to a firm's controlled foreign facilities.

- Franchising differs from licensing in that a trademark is an essential asset for the franchisee's business *and* the franchisor assists in the operation of the business on a continuing basis.

- Management contracts are a means of securing income with little capital outlay. They are usually used for expropriated properties in LDCs, for new operations, and for facilities with operating problems.

- Turnkey operations involve a contract for construction of operating facilities owned by someone else. In recent years, most of these have been very large and diverse, thus necessitating specialized skills and abilities to deal with top-level governmental authorities.

- In the absence of control of vertical operations through ownership, firms are increasingly achieving similar objectives through long-term contract and output-sharing arrangements.

- Companies usually want to own 100 percent of their foreign operations, if possible, in order to secure control and prevent the dilution of profits. However, sharing ownership is widespread because host countries want local participation and because rapid foreign expansion has necessitated that firms bring in outside resources.

- Joint ventures are a special type of ownership sharing in which equity is owned by a few organizations rather than the public at large. There are various combinations of ownership, including government and private, same or different nationalities, and two or several organizations participating.

- Jointly owned operations are often motivated by the complementary resources firms have at their disposal.

- Contracting foreign business does not negate management's responsibility to ensure that company resources are being worked adequately. This involves constantly assessing the work of the outsiders and evaluating new alternatives.

- Firms may use different forms for their foreign operations in different countries or for different products. As diversity increases, the task of coordinating and managing the foreign operations becomes more complex.

C A S E
NPC[50]

In 1974 the Northern Petrochemical Company (NPC), a subsidiary of Northern National Gas (now named Internorth), decided to get into polypropylene production. The decision was based on an analysis of NPC's production capabilities and on a forecast of future market demand.

From a production standpoint, NPC was already making propylene, which is a precursor of and building block for polypropylene. The parent company could supply many of the raw materials for the new product. From a market standpoint, NPC estimated that, since the introduction of polypropylene in the early 1960s, the compound growth rate of sales had been somewhere between 15 and 20 percent. The firm also estimated that future growth would be even more rapid because of high benzene prices and possible shortages, which would depress sales of polystyrene. In many cases polypropylene could substitute for polystyrene. The polypropylene market could be divided into two segments depending on the properties put into the product. The first, homopolymer, comprised 85 percent of the market and was used for such applications as carpet backing, packaging film, appliance moldings, and fibers; the second, copolymer, included products such as battery cases, luggage, and high-clarity bottles. The copolymer sector was of most interest to NPC because this was a newer technical area in which they could expect growth and less entrenched competition.

NPC felt that further inroads for sales were possible as continued performance and cost-effectiveness were improved. One possibility would be in automotive-component fabrication. An entry into polypropylene production would necessitate a continued commitment to R&D in order to improve both product and process technology. NPC was willing to invest over $100 million in the project but lacked the technical capabilities. To use its own R&D efforts would greatly delay market entry. It also would mean risking legal complications because already there were numerous patent-infringement cases pending: Producing companies claimed that others had copied various aspects of their technology.

The total sales for Northern Natural Gas were approximately $1 billion for 1974, of which about 20 percent were accounted for by the NPC subsidiary. About 62 percent of Northern's sales was of natural gas to customers in the United States and Canada. The NPC petrochemical subsidiary was growing faster than the rest of the company and had had successes in such products as antifreeze and LDPE resins. The technology for the resins had been licensed from another firm after NPC had identified markets for use in trash-can liners and leaf bags. A commercial success with technology developed externally therefore had been demonstrated.

NPC next set out to find a firm from which it could gain the use of polypropylene technology on acceptable terms. Of the nine producers in the United States, only three were believed to be in an advanced stage of copolymer development. The first of these was Hercules, which dominated the entire polypropylene market. Hercules was interested because some of its customers wanted a secondary supply source in case of supply problems. NPC felt that such an arrangement was incompatible with its strategy, since it would inevitably place NPC in Hercules' shadow. NPC next contacted the Rexene Division of Dart Industries. Rexene rejected outright any sharing of its technology because it did not want another competitor in the market. No agreement could be reached with Phillips Petroleum for two reasons: Phillips had not yet commercialized the aspect of production that NPC considered critical; furthermore, Phillips was not enthusiastic about creating another competitor.

Having exhausted domestic possibilities, NPC turned abroad. Identification of possible companies was more difficult because many of those companies were believed to have a bigger lag between product development work and commercial introduction of the products. In other words, management could not depend on looking at what was currently being sold to find all the firms with a current capability. Because of market differences, some of the European and Japanese producers had been known to hold on to a development for several years before commercializing it.

After some preliminary inquiries, five firms from four countries were identified as possibilities: Tokuyama Soda and Mitsubishi Petrochemical from Japan, Solvay from Belgium, Montedison from Italy, and BASF from Germany. NPC contacted all of these companies and learned that none had fully commercialized advanced copolymer production. In order to proceed to some possible agreement, each firm had to share with NPC its R&D data and to make special plant test runs to satisfy requests for further information. Interestingly, each had a very different approach to making the same product.

If NPC were to proceed to negotiations, it must choose the company and method most likely to reach the desired end results. NPC decided that BASF offered the best potential since it was and remains one of the giants among chemical companies with 1974 sales in excess of $8 billion. About 55 percent of BASF's sales were outside of Germany; its 1973 sales in the United States were $523 million. In addition to exporting to the U.S. market, BASF had substantial U.S. investments, the most notable of which were Wyandotte Chemical, which it fully owned, and a joint venture with Dow Chemical called Dow Badische. Increases in U.S. investment had been running between $45 million and $55 million per year. This was expected to go to $90 million beginning in 1975.

The chairman of BASF, Dr. Matthias Seefelder, announced that he expected no growth in the German market for 1975 because of a reluctance on the part of consumers to buy. This would make it more difficult to continue to infuse German funds into the U.S. operations,

which were saddled with uncompetitive soda ash and chlorine plants. Given the cash-flow problem, it was hard for BASF to make commitments for market development of new products. Dr. Seefelder also indicated that the company's main specialties (plastics, synthetic fibers, and dyestuffs) were encountering difficulties and that it would be necessary to give greater attention to other products that BASF had already developed. A strong German mark was making German products expensive abroad, thus jeopardizing exports.

The early stages of negotiations between the two companies left the parties in opposition as to which technology BASF would share with NPC, provided an agreement on other points could be reached. BASF was willing to sell the technology that it had developed already but was not yet willing to make a commitment to continue copolymer research, which was not now a high priority for them because of their expectation of not being able to get substantial near-term sales in Europe. Nor was BASF yet willing to commit itself to sharing the future technology if and when it was developed. NPC wanted more than the pilot plant advancements and was in a position of having to convince BASF to alter its position if an agreement were to be reached that met NPC's original expectations.

Questions

1. How likely is it that the two firms will come to a mutual agreement?
2. What type of agreement and operating form (e.g., contract sales, licensing, management contract, turnkey, joint venture) would be in the best interest of NPC? Of BASF?
3. What should NPC do if BASF won't share technology beyond the pilot plant stage?
4. What risks have the firms already incurred by going this far in their discussions?
5. NPC was seeking to obtain technology. How might a search process have differed if NPC had been trying to sell a technology?

Chapter Notes

1. Data for the case were taken from James Flanigan, "The Strategy," *Forbes,* October 29, 1979, pp. 42–52; "Dravo Agrees to Market Type of Plant for Grupo," *Wall Street Journal,* September 23, 1980, p. 38; Hugh O'Shaughnessy, "A Hive of Private Enterprise," *Financial Times,* May 4, 1979, p. 34; Christopher Lorenz, "A Front-Runner in Mexican Industry," *Financial Times,* June 1, 1979, p. 16; "Mexico: Exporting a Cheaper Way of Making Steel," *Business Week,* June 11, 1979, p. 53; Alan M. Field, "After the Fall," *Fortune,* Vol. 135, No. 8, April 22, 1985, pp. 93–95; Keith Bradsher, "Back from the Brink, Mexico's Giant Alfa Slims Down for Hard Times," *International Management,* Vol. 41, No. 9, September 1986, pp. 65–66; Matt Moffett, "Monterrey Sides with Mexican President," *Wall Street Journal,* May 22, 1989, p. A8; Stephen Baker, "Mexico's Giants March North," *Business Week,* November 13, 1989, pp. 63–64.

2. For a discussion of the many trade-offs, see James D. Goodnow, "Individual Product: Market Transactional Mode of Entry Strategies—Some Eclectic Decision-Making Formats," paper presented at Academy of International Business meetings in New Orleans, October 24, 1980. For a discussion of the many motives for alliances with foreign firms, see Farok J. Contractor and Peter Lorange, "Why Should Firms Cooperate? The Strategy and Economics Basis for Cooperative Ventures," in Farok J. Contractor and Peter Lorange (eds.), *Cooperative Strategies in International Business* (Lexington, Mass.: D. C. Health, 1988), pp. 3–28.

3. Ian H. Giddy and Stephen Young, "Do New Forms of Multinational Enterprise Require New Theories?" Working paper, No. 322A, Columbia University Graduate School of Business, April 1980; also, R. T. Carstairs and L. S. Welch, "Licensing and the Internationalization of Smaller Companies: Some Australian Evidence," *Management International Review,* Vol. 22, No. 3, 1982, pp. 33–44, found that firms typically export before licensing, which in turn precedes direct investment.

4. Ian H. Giddy and Alan M. Rugman, "A Model of Trade, Foreign Direct Investment and Licensing," Working paper, No. 274A, Columbia University Graduate School of Business, December 1979.

5. Leo Sleuwaegen, "Monopolistic Advantages and the International Operations of Firms: Disaggregated Evidence from U.S. Based Multinationals," *Journal of International Business Studies,* Vol. 16, No. 3, Fall 1985, pp. 125–133; W. H. Davidson and D. G. McFetridge, "Key Characteristics in the Choice of International Technology Transfer Mode," *Journal of International Business Studies,* Vol. 16, No. 2, Summer 1985, pp. 5–21, found evidence for this point as well as those that follow in this discussion.

6. Peter J. Buckley and Mark C. Casson, "Multinational Enterprises in LDCs: Cultural and Economic Interaction," in Peter J. Buckley and Jeremy Clegg (eds.), *Multinational Enterprises in Less Developed Countries* (London: Macmillan, 1990); Jeremy Clegg, "The Determinants of Aggregate International Licensing Behaviour: Evidence from Five Countries," *Management International Review,* Vol. 30, No. 3, 1990, pp. 231–251.

7. "American Home Plans Drug Venture in U.S. with French Company," *Wall Street Journal,* June 3, 1981, p. 54.

8. Jeffrey A. Tannenbaum, "Licensing May Be Quickest Route to Foreign Markets," *Wall Street Journal,* September 14, 1990, p. B2.

9. David Ford and Chris Ryan, "Taking Technology to Market," *Harvard Business Review,* March–April 1981, p. 118.

10. Gregory A. Patterson, "Chrysler Signs Licensing Pact for Jeep Name," *Wall Street Journal,* August 30, 1988, p. 24.

11. Richard N. Osborn and C. Christopher Baughn, "Forms of Interorganizational

Governance for Multinational Alliances," *Academy of Management Journal,* September 1990, pp. 503–519.

12. Alan Riding, "Cartier's Mexican Look-Alike," *New York Times,* October 17, 1980, p. D1+; Michael G. Harvey and Ilkka A. Ronkainen, "International Counterfeiters: Marketing Success without the Cost and the Risk," *Columbia Journal of World Business,* Vol. 20, No. 3, Fall 1985, pp. 37–45.

13. "Oleg Cassini Inc. Sues Firm Over Licensing," *Wall Street Journal,* March 28, 1984, p. 5; "Cassini Awarded $16 Million in Fragrance Line Squabble," *Wall Street Journal,* June 2, 1988, p. 28.

14. William H. Meyers, *New York Times Magazine,* May 3, 1987, pp. 33–35+.

15. Robert T. Keller and Ravi R. Chinta, "International Technology Transfer: Strategies for Success," *Academy of Management Executive,* Vol. 4, No. 2, 1990, pp. 33–43.

16. Kang Rae Cho, "Issues of Compensation in International Technology Licensing," *Management International Review,* Vol. 28, No. 2, 1988, pp. 70–79; Keller and Chinta, *loc. cit.*

17. Edwin Mansfield, "International Technology Transfer: Forms, Resource Requirements, and Policies," *American Economic Review,* May 1975, pp. 372–382.

18. Thomas Horst, "American Multinationals and the U.S. Economy," *American Economic Review,* May 1976, pp. 150–152; Claudio V. Vaitsos, *Intercountry Income Distribution and Transnational Enterprises* (Oxford: Clarendon Press, 1974); P. Streeten, "Theory of Development Policy," in *Economic Analysis and the Multinational Enterprise,* J. H. Dunning, ed. (London: Allen and Unwin, 1974); G. F. Kopits, "Intrafirm Royalties Crossing Frontiers and Transfer Pricing Behavior," *The Economic Journal,* December 1976; and Donald R. Lessard, "Transfer Prices, Taxes, and Financial Markets: Implications of Internal Financial Transfers within the Multinational Firm," paper presented for the New York University Conference on Economic Issues of Multinational Firms, November 4, 1976.

19. This is taken from D. W. Fewkes, "Positioning the Licensing Unit," *les Nouvelles,* March 1979, pp. 28–33.

20. Jerry H. Opack, "Likenesses of Licensing, Franchising," *les Nouvelles,* June 1977, pp. 102–105.

21. A. Kostecka, *Franchising in the Economy 1986–1988* (Washington: U.S. Department of Commerce, February 1988), pp. 8–10.

22. Mike Connelly, "U.S. Franchising Grows Attractive to Foreign Firms," *Wall Street Journal,* December 22, 1988, p. B2; Jeffrey A. Tannenbaum, "Foreign Franchisers in U.S. on the Rise," *Wall Street Journal,* June 11, 1990, p. B2.

23. Peng S. Chan and Robert T. Justis, "Franchise Management in East Asia," *Academy of Management Executive,* Vol. 4, No. 2, 1990, pp. 75–85.

24. Michael Selz, "Europe Offers Expanding Opportunities to Franchisers," *Wall Street Journal,* July 20, 1990, p. B2.

25. Joann Lublin, "U.S. Franchisers Learn Britain Isn't Easy," *Wall Street Journal,* August 16, 1988, p. 20.

26. Kathleen Deveny, John Pluenneke, Dori Jones Yang, Mark Maremont, and Robert Black, "McWorld," *Business Week,* No. 2968, October 13, 1986, pp. 78–86.

27. Chan and Justis, *loc. cit.*

28. "Judge Revokes License of Paris McDonald's," *International Herald Tribune* (Zurich), September 11–12, 1982, p. 14; Steven Greenhouse, "McDonald's Tries Paris, Again," *New York Times,* June 12, 1988, p. 1F+.

29. Lawrence S. Welch and Anubis Pacifico, "Management Contracts: A Role in Internationalisation?" *International Marketing Review,* Vol. 7, No. 4, 1990, pp. 64–74.

30. Nicholas D. Kristof, "A Not-So-Grand Hotel: A Tibet Horror Story," *New York Times,* September 25, 1990, p. A4.

31. Jeanne Saddler and John R. Emshwiller, "Small U.S. Firms Frozen Out of Kuwait Rebuild Effort," *Wall Street Journal,* March 8, 1991, p. B2. "Where Top 250 Found Business in 1984," *Engineering News Record,* July 18, 1985, pp. 41–53.

32. "Nigeria," *Business Week,* October 1, 1979, p. 60.

33. *A Competitive Assessment of the U.S. International Construction Industry* (Washington: U.S. Department of Commerce, International Trade Administration, July 1984).

34. Louis Berger, "The Construction Scene in Southeast Asia: Who's Getting the Business?" *Worldwide P & I Planning,* January–February 1974, p. 13.

35. Joan Gray, "International Construction," *Financial Times,* April 12, 1985, pp. 13–17.

36. Welch and Pacifico, *loc. cit.,* "USAir, Air France Plan Links Between Businesses," *Wall Street Journal,* September 25, 1990, p. C12.

37. F. A. Sviridov, ed., *The Role of Patent Information in the Transfer of Technology* (New York: Pergamon, 1981), p. 137; Shlomo Maital, "Wanted: Technology Detectives," *Across the Board,* Vol. 26, No. 9, September 1989, pp. 7–9.

38. Robert Ronstadt and Robert J. Kramer, "Getting the Most out of Innovation Abroad," *Harvard Business Review,* Vol. 60, No. 2, March–April 1982, pp. 94–99, and Beth Karlin and George Anders, "Importing Science," *Wall Street Journal,* October 5, 1983, p. 1+.

39. Carl H. Fulda and Warren F. Schwartz, *Regulation of International Trade and Investment* (Mineola, N.Y.: The Foundation Press, 1979), pp. 776–782.

40. Stephen J. Kobrin, "Trends in Ownership of American Manufacturing Subsidiaries in Developing Countries: An Inter-industry Analysis," *Management International Review,* Special Issue 1988, pp. 73–84.

41. Louis Uchitelle, "Mexico's Plan for Industrial Might," *New York Times,* September 25, 1990, p. C2; E. S. Browning, "Renault, Volvo Agree to Enter into Alliance," *Wall Street Journal,* February 26, 1990, p. A3.

42. Steven Prokesch, "S.A.S. Builds on Global Alliances," *New York Times,* November 20, 1989, p. 27 ff.

43. George Getschow, "Foreign Investment in Mexico Swells," *Wall Street Journal,* May 1981, p. 34.

44. R. Duane Hall, "International Joint Ventures: An Alternative to Foreign Acquisitions," *Journal of Buyout and Acquisitions,* Vol. 4, No. 2, March–April 1986, pp. 39–45.

45. Mike Tharp, "Uneasy Partners," *Wall Street Journal,* November 8, 1976, p. 28.

46. J. Peter Killing, "How to Make a Global Joint Venture Work," *Harvard Business Review,* Vol. 60, No. 3, May–June 1982, pp. 120–127.

47. Lawrence G. Franko, *Joint Venture Survival in Multinational Corporations* (New York: Praeger, 1971); Richard H. Holton, "Making International Joint Ventures Work," in *The Management of Headquarters-Subsidiary Relationships in Multinational Corporations,* Lars Otterbeck, ed. (London: Cower, Aldershot, 1981), pp. 255–267.

48. Yumiko Ono, "Borden's Messy Split with Firm in Japan Points Up Perils of Partnerships There," *Wall Street Journal,* February 21, 1991, p. B1 ff; Henry W. Lane and Paul W. Beamish, "Cross-Cultural Cooperative Behavior in Joint Ventures in LDCs," *Management International Review,* Vol. 30, special issue, 1990, pp. 87–102.

49. John D. Daniels and Sharon L. Magill, "The Utilization of International Joint Ventures by United States Firms in High Technology Industries," *Journal of High Technology Management Research,* Vol. 2, No. 1, 1991, pp. 113–131.

50. Data for the case were taken from Ellen Lentz, "Chemical-Group Profits Surge in West Germany," *New York Times,* December 2, 1974, pp. 53–54; Paul Kemezis, "West German Chemical Giants Plan Additional Expansion in U.S.," *New York Times,* February 10, 1975, pp. 39–40; Northern Natural Gas Company, *Annual Report,* 1974; Lou Potempa, "Business Technology Choice," *les Nouvelles,* March 1979, pp. 24–27; Steven P. Galante, "How Foreigners Botch Their U.S. Investments," *Wall Street Journal,* June 6, 1984, p. 32.

CHAPTER **16**

COUNTRY EVALUATION AND SELECTION

If the profits are great, the risks are great.
CHINESE PROVERB

Objectives

- To discuss strategies firms should develop for sequencing their penetration of countries and for committing their resources.

- To explain how clues from the environmental climate can help limit geographic alternatives.

- To examine the major variables that firms should consider when deciding whether and where to expand abroad.

- To describe some simplifying tools for firms' decisions on global geographic strategy.

- To introduce how final investment, reinvestment, and divestment decisions are made.

ord is a large company by any standard. Its 1989 sales of $96.1 billion made it one of the five largest industrial firms in the United States and one of the ten largest in the world. It is also the world's second-largest automobile company, holding about 14 percent of the worldwide market in 1989. Ford is also highly involved internationally. The company began operations in 1903 and exported the sixth car it built. By 1911 the company boasted that a man could drive around the world and stop every night at a garage handling Ford parts. By 1930 Ford was manufacturing or assembling automobiles in twenty foreign countries and had sales branches in another ten. In 1989 about 41 percent of Ford's car and truck vehicles were produced and sold outside of the United States, up from 35 percent three years earlier. Yet as large and internationally involved as Ford is, it must allocate its limited financial and human resources to maintain emphasis on those markets and production locations that are most compatible with corporate expectations and objectives.

Although foreign expansion was a stated objective at Ford's first annual meeting, the company initially was passive about where the emphasis would be. Ford's first foreign sales branches and assembly operations, such as in Canada, England, and France, were established because people in those countries made proposals to Ford.

Ford also made international expansion decisions on a highly decentralized basis. Much of the European expansion was handled through the English operation and the British Commonwealth sales through the Canadian company. Where sales grew most rapidly (e.g., in Argentina, Uruguay, and Brazil) Ford established assembly operations in order to save on transportation costs by limiting the bulk of shipments. Much of Ford's early expansion, therefore, was not based on scanning the globe to choose the best locations. Instead, Ford took advantage of opportunities as they came along.

Ford's pattern of international activities also has been influenced by policies that the company's management considered essential. One of these policies stated that Ford would not manufacture or assemble anywhere without a controlling interest. The concept of control in Ford's case went beyond that of voting shares. In 1930, for example, a Ford group inspected potential production sites in China and reported back to Henry Ford that the title for any Ford purchase of land in China would have to be in the name of a Chinese citizen because a foreigner can't own land in China. Henry Ford's response was simply, "No." In the 1950s and 1960s Ford extended this concept of control to the point that nothing short of 100 percent ownership was acceptable. This further influenced Ford's geographic area of emphasis, causing Ford to expend resources to buy out a minority interest in the British company. It also meant abandoning production in India and Spain in 1954 (Ford recommended Spanish production in 1976 and no longer adheres to

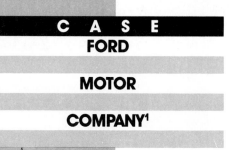

C A S E

FORD

MOTOR

COMPANY[1]

the 100 percent policy) because the governments of those countries insisted on sharing ownership.

Political conditions also have helped to forge Ford's foreign investment pattern. For example, during World War II the French facility was bombed and was not replaced. Assembly facilities were seized by communist governments in Hungary and Romania in 1946. Not until 1977, however, did Ford establish a separate department to evaluate the external political environment. Changes in governmental regulations often have caused Ford to commit a high proportion of its resources to a given area during a given period. This occurred, for example, when Mexico required a higher portion of local content in vehicles, thus forcing Ford to increase its Mexican investment or lose sales there.

Despite the extended and heavy commitment to foreign operations, Ford's production and sales are highly concentrated in a few countries. Even though Ford sells in over 200 countries and territories, Fig. 16.1 shows that about 80 percent of Ford's unit car and truck sales are in just four countries. These same four countries comprise only about 49 percent of world demand. Because of the heavier commitments in some countries than in others, Ford's competitive position is much stronger in some markets than in others. In the United Kingdom and Canada, where Ford has large investments, its market share in 1989 was 27 percent and 23 percent, re-

Figure 16.1
World Vehicle Unit Sales in Percentages by Markets: Ford versus All Manufacturers, 1989
The figure shows that Ford is much more dependent on unit sales in the United States, Canada, Germany, and the United Kingdom than automobile producers as a whole.

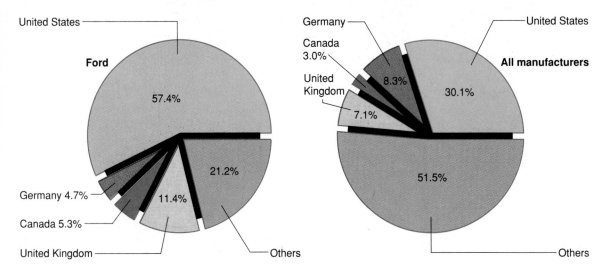

spectively. But in Europe outside the United Kingdom, the market share was only 8.5 percent.

One result of Ford's international commitment is that the dependence on multiple markets and facilities has minimized year-to-year sales and profit fluctuations. This has occurred because demand and price levels may move differently in various countries. From 1981 to 1982, for example, Ford's U.S. vehicle production fell by 91.6 thousand. This was largely made up by a 64.9 thousand increase in EC output. In 1980 Ford lost over $2 billion in the United States, earned $775 million in Britain, and lost $200 million elsewhere in the world. Between 1988 and 1989 Ford's North American net income fell by $1.4 billion; whereas its net income elsewhere in the world was almost steady. This points out not only the positive effect of geographic diversification on the smoothing of earnings, but also the importance of shifting resources in order to exploit areas of greatest profit potential.

With huge amounts of fixed assets already in place, Ford cannot easily abandon countries and then pick them up again. It can, however, compare the attractiveness of each country with actual and potential Ford operations and move toward greater emphasis on those countries with the most promising outlooks. Ford does this separately for each of its major product groups because different market conditions may affect each product group differently.

One of the tools that Ford uses to aid decision makers in choosing where to emphasize their marketing efforts is a country-comparison matrix. Ford staff members rank countries on one axis in terms of how attractive the country appears for sales of a specific type of product being considered, for example, tractors, trucks, or automobiles. On the other axis the same staff members rank the countries in terms of Ford's competitive capabilities for the specific markets. The resultant plotting helps the decision makers to narrow their major focus primarily to the areas of the world that both look attractive and seem to offer the best fit with Ford's unique capabilities. This is by no means the end of the evaluation process. The exercise does, however, enable the decision makers to concentrate on more detailed analyses of a manageable list of alternatives. It also allows them to progress to interrelated decisions, such as where to locate production facilities for the chosen markets.

INTRODUCTION

In its early stages, international expansion tends to be passive.

Ford's pattern of international expansion is typical of many firms as they become more heavily involved abroad. In the early stages, companies may lack the experience and expertise to devise strategies for sequencing countries in the most advantageous way. Instead, they respond to opportunities that become apparent to them, and many of these turn out to be highly advantageous. As they gain more international experience, however, they come to

Later expansion cannot take advantage of all opportunities.

realize that they seldom have enough resources to take advantage of all the opportunities. They see that the commitment of human, technical, and financial resources to one locale may mean forgoing projects in other areas. Consequently, foreign operations become an integral part of companies' decisions on how to allocate resources.

Choosing Geographic Sites

In choosing geographic sites, a company must decide
- Where to sell
- Where to produce

There are two interrelated questions concerning geographic areas of emphasis: (1) Which markets should be served? (2) Where should production be located to serve these markets? Frequently the answer to these two questions will be the same, particularly if transportation costs or governmental regulations require local production for serving the chosen market. In other cases, however, the sales and production may be in different countries. For example, Ford serves the French market in vehicles produced primarily in its German production facilities.

The market and production location decisions may be highly interdependent for other reasons as well. For example, a company may have excess production capacity already in place that will influence its relative capabilities of serving different country markets, or a firm may find a given market very attractive but forgo sales there because of an unwillingness to invest in needed production locations.

A firm's international objectives should not be substantially different from those that guide domestic actions. Any foreign operations should complement domestic ones, and vice versa, so that fulfillment of overall company goals is enhanced. Because of each firm's uniqueness, the decisions of where to sell and produce can be quite variable. Firms seeking foreign markets, for example, will have different considerations from those that view foreign operations as a means of acquiring scarce or cheaper resources. Furthermore, even if the objectives and situations were similar, differences in patterns would remain because of varying assumptions about such unknown factors as future costs and prices, reactions of competitors, technology, and a host of other internal and external constraints.

Overall Geographic Strategy

The determination of an overall geographic strategy must be dynamic because conditions change, and results do not always conform to expectations. A plan must therefore be flexible enough to let a company: (1) respond to new opportunities and (2) withdraw from less profitable activities. Unfortunately, there is little agreement on a comprehensive theory or technique for optimizing the allocation of resources among countries. Nevertheless, a number of approaches frequently are used.

A firm may expand its international sales by marketing more of its existing product line, by adding products to its line, or by some combination of the two. In this chapter we will assume, for the most part, that the company has decided on its product line or product portfolio. Companies frequently alter their product characteristics to satisfy foreign consumers. But nearly all firms begin with the question "Where can we sell more of our communications equipment?" rather than "What new product can we make in order to maximize sales in the Greek market?"[2]

SCANNING FOR ALTERNATIVES

Without scanning, a company
- May overlook opportunities
- May examine too many possibilities

In the opening case, Ford used scanning techniques so that decision makers could perform a much more detailed analysis among a manageable number of geographic alternatives that looked most promising. This is a useful exercise because otherwise a company might consider too few or too many possibilities.

Risk of Overlooking Opportunities

As a company tries to optimize its sales or minimize its costs, it easily can overlook or disregard some promising options. Rather than being rejected, potential projects in many countries may not be carried out simply because managers never think of them. A U.S. manager pondering foreign operations may consider countries such as Canada, Japan, and Germany while overlooking some very small countries that actually may offer better opportunities.

Even if they are considered, certain locales may be eliminated almost immediately before they are sufficiently examined for expansion possibilities. Whole groups of countries are sometimes lumped together and rejected. For instance, Zambia might not be considered because "Africa is too risky."[3] Or a country may or may not be eliminated because of conditions in a nearby country. For instance, apprehension toward investment in Latin America increased after the Cuban revolution, but other Mid-East areas were not negatively affected by the Iranian Revolution or the Iran-Iraq war.[4]

Risk of Examining Too Many

A detailed analysis of every alternative might result in maximized sales or the pinpointing of a least-cost location; however, the cost of so many studies would erode profits. For a company with 1000 products that might locate in any of 100 countries, there are 100,000 different situations to be analyzed. Within each of these situations are other alternatives as well, such as whether to export or to set up a foreign production unit. If there are conditions that would greatly enhance the probability of making or not making an investment, a firm should examine those first, before completing a more detailed feasibility study.

The Environmental Climate

In the Ford case at the beginning of the chapter, certain potential investments were discarded because Ford could not gain sufficient control of the operation. Decision makers' perceptions of environmental climate will determine whether a detailed feasibility study will be undertaken and the terms under which a project will or will not be initiated. The **environmental climate** refers to those external conditions in host countries that could significantly affect the success or failure of a foreign business enterprise. Certain variables are commonly considered important in many firms' foreign expansion decisions. The environmental analysis is key in limiting alternatives to a manageable number.

INFLUENTIAL VARIABLES

Examining key indicators helps firms
- Determine the order of entry
- Set the allocation rate among countries

The following discussion highlights the factors mentioned most often as influencing where sales and production emphasis will be placed. Some of the variables are more important for the sales-allocation decision; others are more important for the production-location decision. Some, of course, affect both decisions, especially when foreign investment is necessary for serving a given foreign market.

The ranking, or prioritizing, of countries is useful for aiding decision makers in (1) determining the order of entry into potential markets and (2) setting the allocation and rate of expansion among the different markets. The former determination assumes that a firm cannot or does not want to go everywhere at once; consequently, it chooses to allocate its resources first to those more desirable locations. The latter assumes that a firm already is selling or producing in many locales, perhaps even in all that are feasible, but wishes to decide how much of its effort should be expended in one country rather than another.

Market Size

Expectation of sales growth is probably the major attraction of a potential location.

The importance of sales potential cannot be overlooked when comparing countries as markets or as production locations. Sales probably are the most important variable in ascertaining which locations will be considered and whether an investment will be made. The assumption, of course, is that sales will be made at a price above cost; consequently, where there are sales, there will be profit.

As was the situation in the Ford case, many firms begin sales to an area very passively. They may appoint an intermediate firm to promote sales for them or a licensee to produce on their behalf; if there is a demonstrated increase in sales, the company may consider investing more of its own resources. The generation of exports to a given country is an indication that sales may be made from production located in that country as well. As long as there is no threat to export sales, however, there is little to motivate a firm to shift to production abroad.

In some cases a firm may obtain past and current sales figures on a country-to-country basis for the type product that the company would like to sell; in many cases, however, such figures are unavailable. Regardless, management must make projections about what will happen to future sales. Such data as GNP, per capita income, growth rates, size of the middle class, and level of industrialization often are used as broad indicators of market size and opportunity. Then, groups of countries may be broken down even further by such variables as the dependence on private versus government spending or inflation rates.[5]

The triad market of the United States, Japan, and Western Europe accounts for about half of the world's total consumption and an even higher proportion of purchases for such products as computers, consumer electronics, and machine tools.[6] It is not surprising therefore that most international firms expend a major part of their efforts on these areas.

Ease of Operations/Compatibility

Geographic, Language, and Market Similarities   Recall in the Ford case at the beginning of the chapter that earnings and vehicle sales were smoothed because of operations in various parts of the world. Because investors generally prefer smoother performance patterns, they are even willing to pay more for assets in internationally diversified firms.[7] Therefore, it might seem that companies would seek to go first to those countries whose economies are least correlated with that of the home country. For example, economic cycles in the United States have marked differences from those in major Latin American countries so one might expect U.S. companies to be motivated to smooth earnings by investing heavily in Latin America.[8] Evidence, however, suggests the contrary, whether companies go abroad in related or unrelated operations in terms of marketing systems, production technologies, or vertical or horizontal products.[9]

Regardless of the industry involved, U.S. firms usually make their first direct investment in Canada; the United Kingdom and Mexico alternate for the second and third positions; and Germany, France, and Australia have most of the fourth, fifth, and sixth positions.[10] This fairly remarkable similarity in patterns among dissimilar industries seems due to the fact that decision makers perceive a greater ease of operations in those countries that are near the home country. Canada and Mexico rank high because of their geographic proximity, which makes it easier and cheaper for U.S. firms to control these foreign subsidiaries. The common language helps to explain the appeal of Canada, the United Kingdom, and Australia to investors. Managers feel more comfortable in operating at early stages of international expansion in their

Companies are highly attracted to countries
- Located nearby
- That share the same language
- That have large populations and high per capita incomes

own language and in similar legal systems evolving from British law. The language and cultural similarities may also lower operating costs and risks. Finally, market similarity tends to exert a considerable influence on the early location of foreign operations. All the leading countries except Mexico have high per capita incomes, and all except Canada and Australia have large populations. Once companies have sequenced their market entries, they may grow at different rates within those markets.

Since the United States, Japan, and Western Europe share many economic and demographic conditions, firms from those areas place their relative emphasis on these areas as well.[11]

Red Tape   One of the things that companies frequently try to factor into their comparison of country-by-country opportunities is the degree of red tape necessary to operate in a given country. Red tape includes such things as the degree of difficulty in getting permission to bring in expatriate personnel, to obtain licenses to produce and sell certain goods, and to satisfy governmental agencies on such matters as taxes, labor conditions, and environmental conditions. Red tape is not directly measurable; therefore, firms commonly have people familiar with operating conditions in a group of countries rate them as high, medium, or low on this factor.

Fit with Company Capabilities and Policies   After the alternatives are pared to a reasonable number, firms must prepare much more detailed feasibility studies, which are expensive. Firms very often become committed to locations that are far from optimal for them because the more time and money they invest in examining an alternative, the more likely they are to accept that project regardless of its merits.[12] Companies first should examine very carefully their motives for considering a commitment. The project manager should have broad experience so that a corporate point of view is maintained. The feasibility study should have from the start a series of clear-cut decision points so that sufficient information is gathered at each stage and so that, if a study is unlikely to result in an investment, it may be terminated before it becomes too costly.

One way to make the surveys more manageable is to ensure that proposals fit the organization's general framework. These proposals, if presented to management decision makers, will have a higher probability of acceptance.[13] For example, consideration may be limited to locales where such variables as product and plant size will be within the experience of present managers. In fact, so many guidelines and policies may be set up that very few possibilities are investigated for final feasibility. From a policy standpoint, management may find it useful to ensure that its proposal group includes personnel with backgrounds in each functional area—marketing, finance, personnel, engineering, and production. While various factors might cause ultimate decision makers to reject a proposal once a feasibility study is completed, two factors stand out as sufficiently important to sway large numbers

The negative attraction of countries is not directly measurable.

There is best acceptance of a proposal when a location has
- *Size, technology, and other factors familiar to company personnel*
- *High percentage of ownership*
- *Easily remitted profit*

of organizations. These are restrictions on the percentage of ownership that can be held and the maximum allowed remittance of profits.[14]

Another consideration is the local availability of resources in relationship to the company's needs. Most foreign operations require combining imported resources with local inputs, which may severely restrict the feasibility of given locales. The international company may, for example, need to find local personnel who are sufficiently knowledgeable about the type of technology being brought in. Or the international firm may need to add local capital to what it is willing to bring in. If local equity markets are poorly developed and local borrowing is very expensive, the company may consider locating in a different country.

The fit for a particular country is important. Take marketing capabilities, for example. Assume that a company already has developed a product in one country that has been marketed successfully through mass advertising methods. Normally it is far easier and less costly to move that product into a country where product alterations are minimal or unnecessary and where there are few advertising restrictions.

Costs and Resource Availabilities

Costs—especially labor costs—are an important factor in the production-location decision.

So far the discussion has centered on market-seeking operations. Companies are engaged internationally in the pursuit of foreign resources as well. If this is a resource to be transferred, such as a raw material or technology, the analysis is somewhat simpler than for a resource that will be used in producing a product or component abroad for export into other markets. Eventually a firm must examine the costs of labor, raw material inputs, capital, taxes, and transfer costs in relation to productivity to approximate a least-cost location. Before all of this information is collected within a final feasibility study, there are indicators that will aid decision makers in narrowing the alternatives to be considered.

Employee compensation is the most important cost of manufacturing abroad for most companies, accounting for over 60 percent of costs besides taxes.[15] In most cases, therefore, current labor costs, trends in the costs, and unemployment rates are useful ways to approximate cost differences among countries. Labor, though, is not a homogeneous commodity. If the country lacks the specific skill levels required, the company may have to go through an expensive alternative to use the labor, such as training, redesigning production, or adding supervision. If the country already turns out competitive products embodying inputs that are similar to those required in the production being considered, labor costs most likely will be sufficiently low in the planned operation.

Any other important costs should be added into the analysis. If precise data are unavailable, useful proxies on operating conditions may be used, such as the degree of infrastructure development and the openness to imported components.

Firms should consider different ways to produce the same product.

The continual development of new production technologies makes cost comparison among countries more difficult. With increases in the number of ways the same product can be made, a firm must compare, for example, the cost of producing by using a large labor input in Malaysia with the use of robotics in the United States.[16]

RETURN ON INVESTMENT: COUNTRY COMPARISON CONSIDERATIONS

Is a projected rate of return of 9 percent in Nigeria the same as a 9 percent rate in France? Should return on investment be calculated on the basis of the entire earnings of a foreign subsidiary or just on the earnings that can be remitted to the parent? Does it make sense to accept a low return in one country if this will help the firm's competitive position elsewhere? Is it ever rational to invest in a country with an uncertain political and economic future? These are but a few of the unresolved questions that firms must debate when making international capital budgeting decisions.

Risk and Uncertainty

Most investors prefer certainty to uncertainty.

Given the same expected return, most decision makers prefer a more certain to a less certain outcome. An estimated rate of **return on investment (ROI)** is calculated by averaging the various returns deemed possible for investments. Table 16.1 shows that two identical projected ROIs may have very different certainties of achievement as well as differing probabilities around the expected return. In the table, the certainty of the 10 percent projected ROI for investment B is higher than for investment A. Furthermore, the probability of earning at least 10 percent is also higher (70 percent versus 65 per-

TABLE 16.1 | **COMPARISON OF ROI CERTAINTY** To determine the estimated ROI, (1) multiply each ROI as percentage by its probability to derive a weighted value and (2) add the weighted values.

		Investment A		Investment B	
	ROI as percentage	Probability	Weighted value	Probability	Weighted value
	0	.15	0	0	0
	5	.20	1.0	.30	1.5
	10	.30	3.0	.40	4.0
	15	.20	3.0	.30	4.5
	20	.15	3.0	0	.0
Estimated ROI			10.0%		10.0%

cent) for that alternative. Experience shows that most, but not all, investors would choose alternative B over alternative A. In fact, as uncertainty increases, investors may require a higher estimated ROI.

Often it is possible to reduce risk or uncertainty, such as by insuring against the possibility of nonconvertibility of funds. However, any such actions are apt to be costly for the firm. In the first process of scanning to develop a manageable number of alternatives, it is useful to give some weight to the elements of risk and uncertainty. At a later and more detailed stage of feasibility study, management should determine whether the degree of risk is acceptable or not without the incurring of additional costs. If it is not, then management would need to calculate an ROI that includes expenditures to increase the outcome certainty of the operation.[17]

Investors try to outguess competitors.

National boundaries play a role in the degree of certainty of return that investors perceive for alternative investments. As long as the investors are conducting business entirely within one country, the alternative investment projects fall within similar political and economic environments. Furthermore, the experience of having already operated within that country, as well as operating abroad in general, increases the probability that the company will make accurate assessments of consumer, competitor, and governmental actions.[18] This is consistent with our earlier description of how firms generally go first to those foreign environments that they perceive to be more similar to the home country. It also helps to explain the fact that reinvestments or expanded investments within a country where the company has extensive operations often are evaluated very differently than proposed moves into a country. (The reinvestment decision will be discussed later in the chapter.)

Multidomestic versus Global Strategies

The comparison of rates of return among countries as a means of making geographic capital budgeting decisions is most appropriate when operations in one country have little effect elsewhere. In such a situation, a company may effectively allocate resources among countries from the highest to lowest expected ROI, accounting of course for risk and uncertainty. But as we will show later in this chapter, it is not easy to separate the operating results in one country from those in other countries.

If a firm faces the same competitors in different markets, it may be appropriate to take a low ROI or even a negative one in some markets in order to counteract what would otherwise be a competitor's advantage. Although this strategy may overcrowd the market and lower profits for all firms in some markets, it nevertheless prevents any one company from making a high profit that it can use for advantages elsewhere in the world. For example, Caterpillar established a joint venture with Mitsubishi in Japan, the home market of Komatsu, Caterpillar's major global competitor. This move lowered Komatsu's profits within the Japanese market, which had been accounting for 80 percent of its worldwide cash flow.[19]

Competitive Risk

We have explained that one of the reasons for using nonequity arrangements is to spread business to many markets rapidly when a firm perceives that its innovative advantage may be short-lived. Even when the firm assesses that it has a substantial competitive lead time, this may vary in different markets. One of the strategies to take advantage of temporary monopoly advantages is known as the **imitation lag,** which holds that a company should move first to those countries most likely to develop local production themselves and later to other countries.[20] Local technology and high international freight costs generally result in a more rapid move to local production. If technology is available, local producers may start manufacturing well before foreign companies are willing to sell the technology. If freight costs are high for exports to the country, a local producer may, despite inefficiencies, be able to gain an advantage in cost over imported goods.

Firms also may develop strategies to find countries where there is least likely to be significant competition. When Japanese automobile producers first began selling in the European market, they shied away from countries with established national producers, such as France and the former West Germany. Instead, they targeted smaller countries, such as Denmark and Portugal, where they were able to gain significant market shares before the producers in larger European countries were able to react to them. L. M. Ericsson, the Swedish telephone-equipment producer, has developed technology aimed at the needs of small countries, partially because this fits its home market and partially because its competitors have concentrated their efforts more on the larger markets.[21] Ericsson has taken this strategy a step further by putting most of its developing country investments in those nations that lack colonial ties to Europe because its major competitors have long-standing distributional advantages and the support of the home government where there were colonial relationships.

Monetary Risk

If the firm's expansion is via direct investment, access to and the exchange rate on the invested capital and its earnings are key considerations. The concept of **liquidity preference** is a common theory to help explain capital budgeting decisions in general and can be applied to the international expansion decision.

Investors usually want some of their holdings to be in highly liquid assets, on which they are willing to take a lower return. Part of the liquidity need is for near-term payments, such as dividends; part is for unexpected contingencies, such as to purchase stockpile materials if a strike threatens supply; and part is so that funds may be shifted to even more profitable opportunities, such as purchasing materials at a discount during a temporary price depression.

There are some differences in liquidity by country of investment. One is the local availability of buyers for equity that one owns so that the funds may be used for other types of expansion endeavors. The ability to find buyers varies substantially among countries, depending largely on the existence of a local capital market.

Assuming that a foreign investor does find a local purchaser, chances are the intent is to use the funds in another country. If the funds are not convertible, then the foreign investor will be forced to spend them in the host country. Of more pressing concern for most investors is the ability to convert earnings from operations abroad, since earnings generally are used not only for expansion but also for dividend payment to stockholders in the home country. The ability to convert varies substantially among countries, and so does the cost of convertibility. It is not surprising that most investors are willing to accept a lower projected ROI for projects in countries with strong currencies than they are in countries with weak currencies.[22]

Political Risk

Political risk may come from wars and insurrections, takeover of property, and changes in rules.

One of the major concerns of international firms is that the political climate will change in such a way that their operating position deteriorates. Political actions that may affect company operations adversely are governmental takeovers of property, either with or without compensation; through operational restrictions that impede the ability of the firm to take actions it would otherwise have taken; and damage to property or personnel. These types of risks were illustrated in the opening case of this chapter. Ford's operation in Hungary was taken over by the government; the one in Mexico was given very different operating requirements; and the one in France was bombed.

The following discussion centers on only one type of political risk—the governmental takeover of foreign facilities—because the methods to evaluate this type of risk are not fundamentally different from those used to make other political-risk predictions. Three approaches to predict political risk will be discussed here: the analysis of past patterns, the use of expert opinion, and the building of models based on instability measurements.

Management can make predictions based on past patterns.

Analysis of Past Patterns   Firms cannot help but be influenced by what has been happening within a country. There are many dangers in predicting political risk on the basis of past patterns, though. Political situations in specific countries may change rapidly for the better or worse as far as foreign investors are concerned. However, the historical evolution is indicative of the broad climate for operations. Studies that have examined large numbers of government takeovers in the post–World War II period give some clues about what to expect.[23]

Almost all of the takeovers were in LDCs, with Latin American countries accounting for about half. In terms of percentage of investments affected, however, Africa and the Middle East were riskier, whereas Asia was the lowest risk area by all measurements. Even these regional categories obscure country-by-country differences. Approximately fifty countries had no takeovers, and three alone (Argentina, Chile, and Peru) accounted for about one third of the takeovers.

Governmental takeovers, except in a few countries, have been highly selective and have usually involved land, natural resources, financial institutions, and utilities.[24] Since the early 1970s, however, manufacturing investments have been the most vulnerable. The selectivity is illustrated by the experience of investors in Peru: Cerro's mining interests and ITT's telephone company were nationalized; however, Cerro's manufacturing companies and ITT's hotel were not. Even among manufacturing industries, there are differences. Those most likely to be nationalized are the ones that may have a substantial and visible widespread effect on a given country because of their size, monopoly position, necessity for national defense, or because other industries depend on them.

Both among and within industries there are variances in local need for foreign resources. Companies that hold assets badly needed in a given country and for which that country has little alternative source are much less vulnerable to political actions. This emphasizes the need for internal assessment in order to design types and places for foreign operations that minimize the risk of governmental control. Thus far, firms with a high technological input that produce a large amount of component parts outside the countries where investments are made have been less prone to takeovers.[25]

The takeover of assets does not necessarily mean a full loss to investors. In fact, most takeovers have been preceded by a formal declaration of intent by the government with a subsequent legal process to determine compensation to the foreign investor. In addition to the book value of assets, some other factors must be considered when determining the adequacy of compensation. First, the compensation may earn a different return when invested elsewhere. Second, other agreements (such as purchase and management contracts) may create additional benefits for the former investor. For example, the Saudi Arabian purchase price to the four U.S. oil partners in Aramco was only part of the total package. The oil companies have continued to receive other financial benefits from Aramco operations through contracts for petroleum, management services, and exploration. Although investors receive compensation in more than 90 percent of takeovers, it is difficult to determine how adequate the compensation is.

Firms should
- Examine views of governmental decision makers
- Get a cross-section of opinions
- Use expert analysts

Opinion Analysis   A second approach for political risk analysis is to analyze the opinions of knowledgeable people about the situation in a country.[26] In this approach one attempts to ascertain the evolving opinions of people who may influence future political events affecting business. The first step involves reading statements made by political leaders both in and out of office to determine their philosophies on business in general, foreign input to business, the means of effecting economic changes, and their feelings toward given foreign countries. Although published statements are readily available, they may appear too late for a firm to have time to react.

Management should analyze the context of statements to determine whether they express true intentions or were made merely to appease particular interest groups or social strata. It is not uncommon, for example, for political leaders to make emotional appeals to the poor based on allegations that foreign business is draining wealth from the country while, at the same time, these leaders quietly negotiate entry and give incentives to new foreign firms. Examination of investment plans offers further insights to the political climate.

Visits to the country in order to "listen" are very important for firms in determining opinions and attitudes. Embassy officials and other foreign and local businesspeople are useful for obtaining opinions as to the probability and direction of change. Journalists, academicians, middle-level local governmental authorities, and labor leaders usually reveal their own attitudes, which often reflect changing political conditions that may affect the business sector.

A more systematic method of relying on opinions is to use a panel of analysts with experience in a country and have them rate categories of political conditions over different time frames. For example, they might rate a country in terms of the fractionalization of political parties that could lead to disruptive changes in government at the present time as well as for future periods, such as one, five, and ten years. A firm may commission this rating individually, or it may rely on commercially available risk-assessment services.[27]

Instability Assessment   A third method being used to predict political risk is to build models based on instability measurements. The greater the political instability, the greater the possibility of change in the political climate. Although political instability has been found to be one of the major concerns of businesspeople, it is difficult to reach a consensus as to what constitutes dangerous instability or how such instability can be predicted. The lack of consensus is illustrated by the diverse reaction of companies to the same political situations. For example, in the late 1980s Peru had an inflation rate of over 4000 percent, guerrilla warfare, political assassinations, and a fall in industrial output; yet many foreign firms perceived the time to be opportune to invest in Peru.[28] Then there are other uncertainties, such as the time lag necessary between a political event and an investor's ability to react. Furthermore, similar symptoms of social unrest may result in different political consequences in different countries. For instance, an antiregime demonstration occurring in Iran may have different political consequences on investors than one in Mexico.[29] Political parties may change rapidly at times with little effect on business; on the other hand, sweeping changes for business may occur without a change in government. Nevertheless, there are services that measure and weight different types of political stability, differentiating, for example, among

Political instability does not always affect business.

institutionally prescribed elections, the fall of a cabinet, the outlawing of significant groups, the execution of a significant political figure, the assassination of a chief of state, a coup d'état accompanied by a mild amount of violence, and a civil war.[30] Rather than political stability itself, the direction of change in government seems to be very important; takeovers have occurred most frequently within three years after a leftist government took office.[31]

One theory, which has been used in predictive models, is that frustration—the difference between the level of aspirations and the level of welfare and expectations—develops and that foreign investment is a scapegoat when a country's frustration level is high.[32] Since frustration, aspiration, welfare, and expectations cannot be measured directly, it is necessary to use substitutes for these. For example, a growth in urbanization, literacy, radios per capita, and labor unionization are all measurable indicators of growth in aspirations; such variables as infant survival rate, caloric consumption, hospital beds per capita, piped water supply per capita, and per capita income are measurable indicators of welfare. Variables such as the change in per capita income and in gross investment rates are indicators of expectations. This approach to predicting actions toward foreign investors has considerable possibilities, since it predicts future trends rather than looking to the past and is predicated on a lead time that might be sufficient for management to adjust operations in order to minimize losses.

SOME TOOLS FOR COMPARING COUNTRIES ▰▰▰▰▰▰

Environmental Scanning

The preceding discussions dealt with indicators of opportunity and risk. But do firms generally seek out information? What information do they deem most important? Where do they get their information? Between the mid-1970s and the late 1980s, international companies became much more sophisticated in their **environmental scanning,** the systematic assessment of external conditions that might affect their operations. A majority of international firms now employ at least one executive continuously to conduct environmental scanning, and the most sophisticated of these tie the scanning to the planning process and integrate information on a worldwide basis. Companies are most likely to seek economic and competitive information in their scanning process, and they depend heavily on managers based abroad to supply them with information. Their primary concerns are with profit repatriation and devaluation.[33]

Grids are tools that
● May depict acceptable or unacceptable conditions

Grids

A grid may be used to compare countries on whatever factors are deemed important. Table 16.2 is an example of a grid with information placed into three major categories. Certain countries may be eliminated immediately

TABLE 16.2 | SIMPLIFIED GRID TO COMPARE COUNTRIES FOR MARKET PENETRATION Decision makers may choose which variables to include in the grid, thus this table is merely an example. Note also that decision makers may weight some variables as more important than others. In the above example, country I is immediately eliminated because the company will go only where 100 percent ownership is permitted. Countries II and IV are estimated to have the highest return; and countries I and II are estimated to have the lowest risk.

Variables	Weight	Countries				
		I	II	III	IV	V
1. Acceptable (A), Unacceptable (U) factors						
a. Allows 100 percent ownership	—	U	A	A	A	A
b. Allows licensing to majority-owned subsidiary	—	A	A	A	A	A
2. Return (higher number = preferred rating)						
a. Size of investment needed	0–5	—	4	3	3	3
b. Direct costs	0–3	—	3	1	2	2
c. Tax rate	0–2	—	2	1	2	2
d. Market size, present	0–4	—	3	2	4	1
e. Market size, 3–10 years	0–3	—	2	1	3	1
f. Market share, immediate potential, 0–2 years	0–2	—	2	1	2	1
g. Market share, 3–10 years	0–2	—	2	1	2	0
Total			18	10	18	10
3. Risk (lower number = preferred rating)						
a. Market loss, 3–10 years (if no present penetration)	0–4	—	2	1	3	2
b. Exchange problems	0–3	—	0	0	3	3
c. Political unrest potential	0–3	—	0	1	2	3
d. Business laws, present	0–4	—	1	0	4	3
e. Business laws, 3–10 years	0–2	—	0	1	2	2
Total			3	3	14	13

● Rank countries by important variables

from consideration because of characteristics decision makers find unacceptable. These are in the first category of variables, where country I can be eliminated. Values and weights are assigned to items so that a country may be ranked according to attributes that are important to the decision maker. In the same table, for example, country II is graphically pinpointed as a high return–low risk, country III as a low return–low risk, country IV as a high return–high risk, and country V as a low return–high risk.[34]

Both the variables and the weights should vary by product and company, depending on the firm's internal situation and consequent objectives. The grid technique is useful even when comparative analysis is not made because a company may be able to set a minimum score necessary for either investing additional resources or committing further funds to a more detailed feasibility study. Grids do tend to get cumbersome, however, as the number of variables increases. Furthermore, while they are useful in ranking, they often obscure interrelationships among countries.

Opportunity-Risk Matrix

With an opportunity-risk matrix, a firm can
- Decide on indicators and weight them
- Evaluate each country by weighted indicators

One way of showing more clearly the summary of data that could be included on a grid is to plot risk on one axis and opportunity on the other, a technique used by many companies, such as Borg-Warner.[35] Figure 16.2 is an example that is simplified to include only six countries. The grid shows that the company has current operations in four of the countries (all except countries A

Figure 16.2
Opportunity-Risk Matrix
Countries above the dashed line have less risk and those to the right of the dashed line have greater opportunity than the current world average. The dotted lines represent a projection of the world average for these variables in the future. Country D currently has greater than average risk; in the future it will move to have less risk than the projected world average.

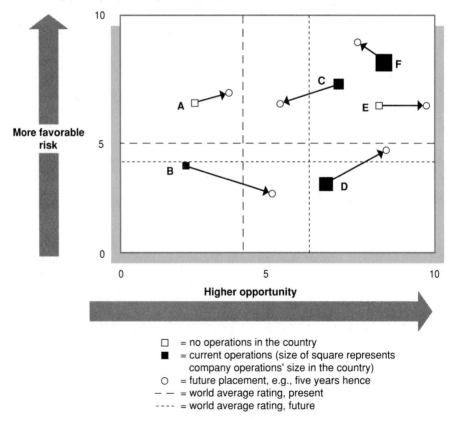

- Plot to see relative placements
- Plot size of operations differently
- Plot expected movements

and E). Of the two nonexploited countries, country A has low risk but low opportunity and country E has low risk and high opportunity. If resources are to be spent in a new area, country E appears to be a better bet than country A. In the other four countries there are large commitments in country F, medium in countries C and D, and small in country B. In the future time horizon being examined, it appears that country F will have low risk along with high opportunity. The situation in country D is expected to improve during the studied period. Country C's situation is deteriorating, and country B's is mixed (it has better opportunity but more risk). Note that the world averages being used for comparison also shift during the period under consideration. The importance of the matrix is to reflect the placement of a country *relative* to other countries.

But how are values plotted on such a matrix? It is up to the company to determine what factors are good indicators of risk and opportunity; these factors then must be weighted to reflect their importance. For instance, on the risk axis the company may give 40 percent (.4) of the weight to expropriation risk, 25 percent (.25) to foreign-exchange controls, 20 percent (.2) to civil disturbances and terrorism, and 15 percent (.15) to exchange-rate change: This makes a total allocation of 100 percent. Each country then would be rated on a scale of 1 to 10 for each of the variables, with 10 indicating the best score and 1 indicating the worst. The score on each item is multiplied by the weight allocated for the variable. For instance, if country A were given a rating of 8 on the expropriation-risk variable, the 8 would be multiplied by .4 for a score of 3.2. All of country A's risk-variable scores are then summed to give the placement of country A on the risk axis. Management would follow a similar procedure to find the plot location on the opportunity axis. Once the scores are determined for each country, management can determine the average score for risk and the average score for opportunity, thereby dividing the matrix into quadrants.

A key element of the sample matrix, and one that is not always included in practice, is the projection of the future country location. The utility of such a placement is obvious if the projections are realistic. Therefore, it is useful to have forecasts made by people who are not only knowledgeable about the countries but also knowledgeable about forecasting methods.

Country Attractiveness–Company Strength Matrix

The attractiveness-strength matrix highlights the fit of company's product to country.

Another commonly used matrix approach has been devised to highlight a company's specific product advantage on a country-by-country basis. This was briefly explained in the case on Ford. For its tractor operations, for example, Ford uses this type of matrix. On the country attractiveness scale, countries are ranked from highest to lowest attractiveness for tractors specifically; on the other scale, Ford ranks its competitive strength in tractors by country. The method of performing the ranking is the same as for the opportunity-risk matrix. Ford's weighted scale for country attractiveness includes such variables as market size, market growth, price controls, red tape, requirements for local content and exports, inflation, trade balance, and political stability. Ford's competitive strength weighted scale includes market share, market-share position, its product fit for the needs of the country, absolute profit per unit, percentage profit on cost, quality of Ford's distribution in comparison with competitors, and the fit of Ford's promotion program for the country in comparison with competitors.[36]

Figure 16.3 illustrates this type of matrix for market expansion before countries are plotted into their positions. The company should attempt to concentrate its activities in the countries that appear in the top left-hand corner of the matrix and to take as much equity as possible in investments there. In this position country attractiveness is the highest *and* the firm has the best competitive capabilities to exploit the opportunities. In the top right-hand corner, the country attractiveness is also high, but the company has a weak competitive strength for that market—perhaps because it lacks the right product. If it is not too costly, the company might attempt to gain greater domination in those markets by remedying its competitive weakness. Otherwise, it might consider either **divestment** (reducing its investment) or strengthening the position through joint venture operations with another firm whose assets are complementary. Investments ordinarily should not be made in

Figure 16.3
Country Attractiveness—Company Strength Matrix
Although countries are not plotted on this matrix, those that would appear closest to the northwest corner are the most desirable for operations and those closest to the southeast are the least desirable.

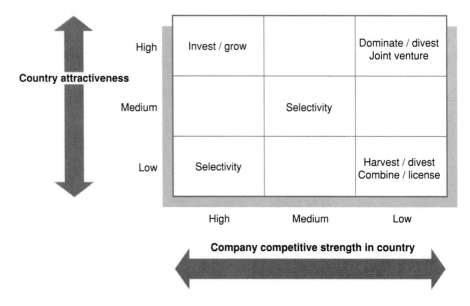

areas in the bottom right-hand corner, and divestment should be attempted. Income may be "harvested" by pulling out all possible cash that can be generated while, at the same time, not replacing depreciated facilities. Licensing still offers potential because it may generate some income without having to make investment outlays. In other areas the company must analyze situations selectively in order to decide which approach to take. These are marginal areas which require specific judgment.

DIVERSIFICATION VERSUS CONCENTRATION STRATEGIES

Strategies for ultimately reaching high commitment in many countries include

- Diversification—go to many fast and then build up slowly in each
- Concentration—go to one or a few and build up fast before going to another
- A hybrid of the two

Ultimately, a firm may gain a sizable presence and commitment in most countries of the world; however, there are different paths to reach that position. At one extreme, in a **diversification strategy** the company may move rapidly into most foreign markets, gradually increasing its commitments within each of them. This could be done, for example, through a liberal licensing policy for a given product so that there are sufficient resources for this initial widespread expansion. The company eventually may increase its involvement by internalizing activities that it initially had contracted to other firms. At the other extreme, in a **concentration strategy** the company might move only to one or a few foreign countries until it developed a very strong involvement and competitive position there. There are, of course, hybrids of these two strategies: for example, moving rapidly to most markets but increasing the commitment in only a few. The following discussion centers on those major variables a firm should consider when deciding whether to use a diversification or concentration strategy.[37] (See Table 16.3.)

Sales Response Function

An increasing sales response rate favors concentration, whereas a decreasing sales rate favors diversification.

The **sales response function** refers to the amount of sales created at different levels of marketing expenditures. If, for example, the first $100,000 of marketing expenditure in a given country yielded $1 million of sales, the next $100,000 yielded $800,000, and the third yielded $600,000, this would be a decreasing response. On the other hand, if the first $100,000 in a country yielded $600,000, the second yielded $800,000, and the third yielded $1 million, it would be an increasing response. There are products that follow each pattern over similar expenditure levels. If the company had $300,000 to spend on a marketing program for which there is the same decreasing response in each country, the company would create more sales by spreading entry over three countries. This would yield $3 million ($1M. + 1M. + 1M.), whereas a concentration on one country would yield only $2.4 million ($1M. + 0.8M. + 0.6 M.). If the same $300,000 were spent on a product with an increasing response, however, a concentration strategy would yield better results: $2.4 million ($0.6M. + 0.8 + 1M.) as opposed to $1.8 million ($0.6M. + 0.6M. + 0.6M.).

TABLE 16.3 | PRODUCT MARKET FACTORS AFFECTING CHOICE BETWEEN DIVERSIFICATION AND CONCENTRATION STRATEGIES If the "right" conditions exist under the column "prefer diversification," a company will likely benefit by moving rapidly into many countries simultaneously; otherwise the company might move to just one or a few foreign countries until a substantial presence is developed therein.

Product/Market Factor	Prefer Diversification If:	Prefer Concentration If:
1. Sales response function*	Decreasing	Increasing
2. Growth rate of each market	Low	High
3. Sales stability in each market	Low	High
4. Competitive lead time	Short	Long
5. Spillover effects	High	Low
6. Need for product adaptation	Low	High
7. Need for communication adaptation	Low	High
8. Economies of scale in distribution	Low	High
9. Program control requirements	Low	High
10. Extent of constraints	Low	High

*The terms used in the original article for "decreasing" and "increasing" were "concave" and "S curve," respectively.

Source: Igal Ayal and Jehiel Zif, "Marketing Expansion Strategies in Multinational Marketing," *Journal of Marketing,* Vol. 43, Spring 1979, p. 89. Reprinted by permission of the American Marketing Association.

Growth Rate in Each Market

Fast growth favors concentration because companies must use resources to maintain market share.

When the growth rate in each market is high, it is usually preferable for a firm to concentrate on a few markets because it will cost a great deal to maintain market share, and costs per unit are typically lower for the market-share leader. Slower growth in each market may allow the company to have enough resources to build and maintain a market share in a number of different countries.

Sales Stability in Each Market

International diversification has been shown to have an even stronger relationship to profit stability than product diversification.[38] Recall the Ford case at the beginning of the chapter and the earlier description of how earnings and sales are smoothed because of operations in various parts of the world. This is because there are leads and lags in the business cycles. Additionally, a company whose assets and earnings base are in a variety of countries will be less affected by occurrences within a single nation. A strike or expropriation therefore will affect earnings from only a small portion of total corporate assets. Currency devaluations in some countries may be offset by revaluations in other countries.

The more stable sales and profits are within a single market, the less need there is for a diversification strategy. Likewise, the more interrelated markets are, the less smoothing is achieved by selling in each. For example, Ford would seemingly get less of a smoothing effect between France and Germany (because their economies are so interrelated through the EC) than between either of those two countries and the United States.[39]

Competitive Lead Time

The longer the lead time, the more the firm can use a concentration strategy.

We have shown that one of the reasons for using nonequity arrangements as a means of serving foreign markets is to beat competitors into the market. The use of these external arrangements helps the companies to spread into more markets than if they were to use only their own resources. If a company assesses that it has a long lead time before competitors can likely copy or supersede its advantages, then it may be able to maintain control of the expansion by following a concentration strategy and still beat competitors into other markets.

Spillover Effects

Spillover effects refer to situations whereby the marketing program in one country results in awareness of the product in other countries. This can happen, for example, if the product is advertised through media viewed on a cross-national basis. In such situations a diversification strategy has advantages because additional customers may be reached with little additional incremental cost.

Need for Product, Communications, and Distribution Adaptation

Adaptation means additional costs for the firm because it is
- Hard to spread to many markets
- Hard to gain economies of scale through diversification

Products and the marketing of them may have to be altered for sale in foreign markets. The adaptation process is often costly and, if so, may lead to two factors that favor a concentration strategy: First, the additional costs may limit the resources the firm has for expansion in many different markets; second, the fixed costs incurred for adaptation cannot be as easily spread over sales in other countries as a means of reducing total unit costs.

Program Control Requirements

Diversification often implies external arrangements that may cause control to be lost.

The more necessary it is that the company control what is happening in the foreign country where the product is being sold, the more likely that it should develop a concentration strategy. This is because more of the firm's resources will need to be used to maintain that control. The need for more control could come about for a number of reasons, including fear that an external arrangement will create a competitor or the need for highly technical assistance to customers.

Extent of Constraints

Constraints limit resources for going to many places simultaneously.

Constraints on what a firm can do may come about internally or externally. In resource availability, for example, the higher the constraints, the more likely a concentration strategy is. Assume that the key resource for introducing a new product into the foreign markets is the availability of certain specialized technical personnel. If there is a shortage of these personnel both within and outside the company, the company will be constrained in the number of countries to which it can expand rapidly. Or if there are constraints in where they can be moved, the company may find it difficult to expand into many different markets rapidly.

INVESTMENT PROPOSAL EVALUATION

Internal and accounting rates of return are the most popular measurements for precise projections.

Thus far we have examined comparative opportunities on a very broad basis. At some point it is necessary for firms to do a much more detailed analysis of specific projects and proposals in order to make allocation decisions. Firms use a variety of financial criteria to evaluate foreign investments, internal rate of return and accounting rate of return being the measurements most frequently used.[40]

Measurement Problems

The derivation of meaningful rate-of-return figures is no easy task when foreign operations are concerned. Profit figures from individual operations may obscure the real impact those operations have on overall company activities. For example, if a U.S. company were to establish an assembly operation in Australia, this assembly operation could either increase or decrease exports from the United States. Management would have to make assumptions about the changed profits in the United States and elsewhere as a result of the Australian project. Or perhaps by building a plant in Brazil to supply components to Volkswagen of Brazil, the investor increases the possibility of selling to Volkswagen in other countries.

The preceding discussion assumes that, although overall company returns are difficult to calculate, those for the operating subsidiary are fairly easily ascertained, but this is not the case. A substantial portion of the sales and purchases of foreign subsidiaries may be with units of the same parent company. The prices charged on these transactions will affect the relative profitability of one unit vis-à-vis another. Furthermore, the base on which to estimate the net value of the foreign investment may not be realistically stated, particularly if part of the net value is based on exported capital equipment that is both obsolete at home and useless except where being shipped. By stating a high value, the company may be permitted to repatriate a larger portion of its earnings.

Noncomparative Decision Making

Most proposals are decided on a go-no-go basis if they meet minimum acceptance criteria.

Because of the limited resources firms have at their disposal, it might seem that companies maintain a storehouse of foreign investment proposals that may be ranked on the basis of some predetermined criteria. If this were so, management could simply start allocating resources to the top-ranked proposal and continue down the list until no further investments were possible. This is seldom the case, however. About three quarters of final investment proposals are evaluated separately, and a decision is made on what is commonly known as a **go-no-go decision.**[41] This decision is usually made on the basis that the project meets some minimum-threshold criteria. Of course, before this there is a good deal of weeding out of possible projects at various scanning and decision points along the way.

One of the major factors restricting firms from comparing investment opportunities is cost. Clearly, most firms cannot afford to conduct very many investigations simultaneously. Another factor inhibiting comparison of investment opportunities is that feasibility studies are apt to be in various stages of completion at a given time. Assume that the investigation process has been finished for a possible project in Australia but that ongoing research is being conducted for New Zealand, Japan, and Indonesia. Can the company afford to wait until the results from all the surveys are completed? The answer is probably not. The time interval between completions probably would invalidate much of the earlier results, requiring an updating, added expense, and further delays.

There are other time-inhibiting problems as well. Frequently, governmental regulations may require a decision within a given period of time. Another external limitation may be imposed by other companies that have made partnership proposals. If no answer is forthcoming in a short period of time, a proposal may be made to a different potential partner.

Finally, few companies can afford to let resources lie idle or to be employed for a low rate of return during a waiting period. They must answer to both stockholders and employees. This applies not only to financial resources but also to such resources as technical competence, since the lead time over competitors is reduced when a company holds off a decision.

Reinvestment Decisions

A company may have to make new commitments to maintain competitiveness.

Most of the net value of foreign investment has come from the reinvestment of earnings abroad rather than from new international capital transfers. The decisions to replace depreciated assets or to add to the existing stock of capital from retained earnings in a foreign country are somewhat different from original investment decisions. Once committed to a given locale, a firm may find that there is no option to move a substantial portion of the earnings elsewhere because to do so would endanger the continued successful operation of the given foreign facility. For example, the failure to expand might result in a falling market share and a higher unit cost than that of competitors.

Aside from competitive factors, a company may need several years of almost total reinvestment as well as allocation of new funds to one area in order to meet its objectives. Over a period of time, the earnings may be used to expand the product line further, integrate production, and expand the market served from present output. A further factor for treating reinvestment decisions differently is that once there are experienced personnel within a given country, they may be the best judges of what is needed for their countries; therefore, certain investment decisions may be delegated to them.

DIVESTMENT DECISIONS

Firms must decide how to get out of operations if
- They do not fit the overall strategy
- There are better alternative opportunities

Managers are less apt to propose divestments than investments.

In much of the preceding discussions we showed that firms should consider decreasing their commitments to certain areas in order to free resources for a better fit with corporate objectives. It is now common to read that a firm is terminating its ownership in an investment in a foreign country, usually involving the sale of operations that have poor performance prospects compared to alternative opportunities.

Studies of the divestment experience conclude that most firms might have fared better had they been more experienced and developed divestment specialists. There has been a tendency to wait too long by trying expensive means of improving performance. Local managers, who fear loss of their own positions if the MNE abandons an operation, propose additional capital expenditures. In fact, this question of who has something to gain or lose is a factor that sets apart decisions to invest from decisions to divest. Both types of decisions should be highly interrelated and geared to the company's strategic thrust. The idea for investment projects typically originates with middle managers or with managers already employed in foreign subsidiary operations who are enthusiastic about collecting information to accompany a proposal as it moves upward in the organization. After all, the evaluation and employment of these people depend on growth. They have no such compulsion to propose divestments. These proposals typically originate at the top of the organization after upper management has tried most remedies for saving the operations.[42]

Divestments may occur by selling or simply closing facilities. The option of selling is usually preferred because the divesting firm receives some compensation. But if a firm considers divesting because the outlook for the country's political-economic future is poor, there may be few potential buyers except at very low prices. In such situations, there may be a tendency to try to delay divestment in hope that the situation improves. If the situation does improve, the firms that waited out the situation are generally in a better position to regain markets and profits than firms that forsook their operations in the country. For example, many international firms divested their South African operations during the late 1980s primarily because South Africa's policy of apartheid caused political unrest within South Africa, trade embargoes by foreign investors' home country governments, and consumer pressure outside South Africa to divest. As more firms attempted to divest, there were fewer buyers (usually wealthy white South Africans) who were able to buy facilities even at lower prices. By the early 1990s, the dissolution of apartheid laws brought a renewed positive outlook to South Africa's future. Firms that remained in South Africa during the turmoil of the 1980s (such as Hoechst, Crown Cork & Seal, and Johnson Matthey) were able to move much faster in the early 1990s at increasing their South African business than firms that had abandoned the market.[43]

A firm cannot always simply abandon an investment either. Governments frequently require performance contracts that make a loss from divestment greater than the net value of the direct investment. Furthermore, many large multinational firms fear adverse international publicity and difficulty of reentering a market if they do not sever relations with a foreign government on amicable terms. During the early 1990s, several foreign investors (including Occidental Petroleum and Email and Elders) sought to take losses and leave the Chinese market, but the Chinese government made their departures slow and expensive.[44]

LOOKING TO THE FUTURE   International geographic expansion is a two-tiered consideration: How much of a firm's sales and production should be outside its home country? Of that outside, how should sales and production be allocated among countries? As yet there is no comprehensive model to answer these questions, and perhaps differences among companies and dynamic environmental conditions make such a model impractical. Meanwhile, companies are simply apt to place more emphasis on certain areas of the world than on other areas as they see opportunities evolving. Typical of this was a prediction by Procter & Gamble's CEO in 1989 that more than half of P&G's sales would flow from outside the United States within the next few years, up from just 27 percent in 1985, while sales would grow more rapidly in the Far East than elsewhere.[45]

For large U.S. firms, an intriguing question is whether they are approaching an optimum ratio between domestic and foreign operations. Some data suggest that they are.[46] For about a three-decade period beginning in the early 1950s, most large U.S. firms seemed to embrace a concept that "more is better" when it came to international business. This emphasis was perhaps inevitable inasmuch as most firms were starting from such a low base of international dependence. Yet the advantage of "more is better" should hold only until a firm reaches some optimum combination of domestic to foreign operations. Otherwise companies would continue to improve their performance until they had no domestic operations at all—not a logical situation. If some companies are approaching their optimum position, we should expect those companies to grow domestically and internationally at about the same rate in the future.

The need to allocate among opportunities because of insufficient resources is liable to play an even more important role in the near future. The opening up of Eastern bloc economies, the global move toward privatization, and the more liberal allowance of majority ownership have combined to create more opportunities from which to choose. At the same time companies have not increased their resource bases concomitantly to take advantage of all these new opportunities. Furthermore, the problems of many companies in the late 1980s and early 1990s that had overextended their debt positions, particularly with leveraged buy-outs, might further inhibit their unrestricted international expansion.

Data availability should continue to improve so that global environmental scanning will assume an ever greater importance. The need for information will be important, because of competitors going global and because of economic and political volatility. However, the information explosion will present new challenges in timely analyses that may necessitate an even greater reliance on tools that reduce alternatives under consideration.

SUMMARY

- Because companies do not have sufficient resources to exploit all opportunities apparent to them, two of the major considerations facing firms are (1) which markets to serve and (2) where to locate the production to serve those markets.

- The market- and production-location decisions are often highly interdependent because of requirements that markets be served from local production, because firms seek nearby outlets for excess capacity, and because firms may be unwilling to invest in those production locations necessary to serve a desired market.

- Scanning techniques are useful to aid decision makers in considering alternatives that might otherwise have been overlooked. They also help limit the final detailed feasibility studies to a manageable and promising number.

- The prioritizing of countries is useful for determining the order of entry into potential markets and in setting the allocation and rate of expansion among different markets.

- Because each company has unique competitive capabilities and objectives, the makeup of factors affecting each geographic expansion pattern will be slightly different for each. Nevertheless, certain variables have been shown to influence most firms, including the relative size of country markets, the ease of operating in the specific foreign countries, the availability and cost of resources, and the perceived relative risk and uncertainty of operations in one country versus another.

- Some tools frequently used to compare opportunities in various countries are grids that rate country projects according to a number of separate dimensions and matrices on which firms may project one attribute on a vertical axis and another on the horizontal axis, such as risk and opportunity or country attractiveness and company capability.

- By using a similar amount of internal resources a firm may choose initially to move rapidly into many foreign markets with only a small commitment in each (a diversification strategy) or to make a strong involvement and commitment in one or a few locations (a concentration strategy).

- The major variables to consider when deciding whether to diversify or concentrate are the response of sales to incremental increases in marketing expenditures, the growth rate and sales stability in each market, the expected lead time over competitors, the degree of need for product and marketing adaptation in different countries, the need to maintain control of the expansion program, and the internal and external constraints facing the company.

- ROI figures alone do not reveal the full impact a specific foreign investment may have on total corporate performance. Firms must assess such factors as effects on earnings in other countries as well as what advantages competitors would gain in the absence of the investment.

- Rather than ranking investment alternatives, once a feasibility study is complete, most investors set some minimum criteria and either accept or reject a foreign project on that basis. The reason for this type of decision is that feasibility analyses seldom are finished simultaneously, and there are pressures to act quickly.

- Reinvestment decisions normally are treated separately from new investment decisions because a reinvestment may be necessary to protect the viability of existing resources and because there are people on location who can better judge the worthiness of proposals.

- Firms must develop strategies for where new investments will be made and devise the means to deemphasize certain areas and to divest if necessary.

C A S E
MITSUI IN IRAN[47]

In 1989 Mitsui and the Iran National Petrochemical Industries Company (IRNA) announced the dissolution of a joint venture, the Iran-Japan Petrochemical Company (IJPC), at Bandar Khomeini, Iran (see Map 16.1). The joint venture agreement was signed in 1971. Planning for the project began in 1973 and construction in 1976. A Mitsui-led group of five Japanese firms owned 50 percent of the venture, with the remainder held by IRNA, an Iranian government company. At the time of the disso-lution, the two companies had invested about $5 billion. The agreed-upon abandonment of the project allowed Mitsui to claim about $1.25 billion in risk insurance from the Japanese government.

Work on the project had been suspended several times. The Iranian revolution first brought work to a halt in March 1979, when it was estimated that completion would be within six months. Construction resumed in the summer of 1980 but was halted again in October because of Iraqi attacks. Although the project escaped extensive damage from the attacks, the facilities were to have depended on naphtha supplies from a refinery in Abadan that was almost totally destroyed. During these early years of construction,

Map 16.1
Southern Iran and Neighboring Areas
Note the nearness to Iraq of Bandar Khomeini, the site of the joint venture, and Abadan, the source of naphtha supplies.

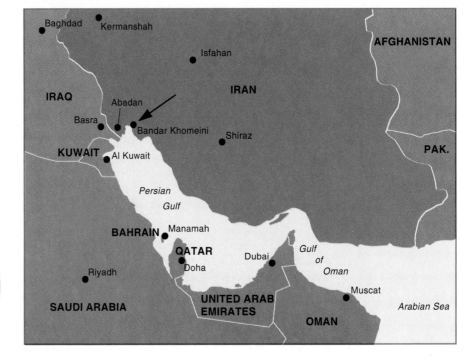

Mitsui was called upon on several occasions to add as much as $60 million to the project. In 1981 Mitsui finally stopped work because it feared the plant would become a "bottomless pit." This led to two years of exhaustive and sharp negotiations and exchanges between Mitsui and the Iranian government. By the end of 1983 the Iranian government agreed to put up some additional funds, provided that the future ownership share would be adjusted to reflect the capital contribution and assuming that Mitsui would send a survey team of 100 engineers and experts to the site to get the project rolling again. Work did resume but stopped again in 1984 after further Iraqi attacks. Late that same year construction began anew, when the completion was estimated to be in three and a half years at a project cost in excess of $4 billion as compared with the original budget of $500 million. Then in 1987 Iraq attacked again, and the Iranian government put the site off limits to representatives of Mitsui or the Japanese government.

The scope of the project was significant for Mitsui, Iran, and Japan. If completed, it would be the largest foreign investment anywhere in the world by Japanese interests. For Mitsui, the Iranian venture was a substantial portion of its total investment and even more significant in terms of its foreign assets. At the time of becoming involved in Iran, Mitsui was at an early stage of developing foreign production with only new smaller projects for Chinese coal development and for natural gas in Southeast Asia and Canada.

Meanwhile, Iran put a very high priority on completion of the facility. Of the Shah's dozen or so billion-dollar projects, it was the only one that continued under the regime of Khomeini. Iranian governmental officials indicated that Mitsui's decisions on its future participation would affect Iran's overall economic relations with Japan. The Iranian prime minister told a Japanese government survey team in Tehran that the Iranian government would ensure stable supplies of crude oil to Japan if the project was completed. The question of oil supplies was a very sensitive issue because of Japan's dependence on foreign sources for over 99 percent of its needs. Japan depended more on Iran than on any other single oil source, but Japan also was dependent on Iraq. An official of Japan's Ministry of International Trade and Industry said, "The project will decide the destiny of the fiduciary relations between Japan and the Middle East and eventually, the destiny of Japan's energy security."

Mitsui insured against war damage with the Japanese government's export insurance program. This insurance covered the cost of equipment that originated in Japan as well as losses caused by discontinuation of work, but it was originally due to expire in 1987. Prior to the expiration, Mitsui could apply for the war loss; however, without the ability to inspect the site, settlement could be much less than the damage. This would also mean abandoning ownership in the project. Alternatively, Mitsui could apply for discontinuation of work for six months at an even lower settlement, but keeping its asset ownership. Finally, Mitsui could stall for settlement; however, if the site were to be attacked after the insurance expired but before inspection, it could be claimed that the insurance would not cover the damage. In the meantime, the Japanese government wanted Mitsui to withhold claims because of its relationship with Iran and because the claims could wipe out Japan's export insurance program. Furthermore, a payment to Mitsui for withdrawal required an agreement between the governments of Iran and Japan, and Iran still wanted to see the project completed. Given the interest of Iran and Japan, Mitsui was able to negotiate an insurance extension until the end of 1989.

In 1988 Iran and Iraq agreed to a cease-fire. After inspecting the facility, Mitsui refused to invest any more money. Mitsui claimed that the damage from bombing and corrosion would require at least the same amount of investment expenditures as had been incurred up until that

time. These costs would make the plant uneco-
nomical. The Iranian view was that the project
could be completed for only 35 percent of the
original cost. This disagreement led to nearly
two years of negotiations on the terms of cancellation and how to divide the losses incurred on
the project.

After agreement was reached between Mitsui
and Iran, the Iranian government negotiated
with Hyundai and Daewoo from Korea to put $2
billion into the Bandar Khomeini project. This
was part of a larger deal in which the two companies would build tankers for Iran to be paid
for with crude oil.

Meanwhile a Mitsui publication said, "The
experience that we have gained through this
project (IJPC) will be put to full use in our future business activities." The same report indi-

cated that the plan is "to make Mitsui a truly
global enterprise" with Europe and Asia the current "major focuses of our globalization policy."

Questions

1. What might Mitsui have done to prevent the
   Iranian losses?
2. Should Mitsui have sought an insurance settlement in 1987 rather than getting an extension of coverage?
3. Where should firms, such as Mitsui, be putting their geographic emphasis during the
   1990s? What tools could help them decide?
4. Evaluate the risks/opportunities for Hyundai
   and Daewoo by their participation in the
   Bandar Khomeini project, in which Mitsui
   had previously participated.

Chapter Notes

1. Data for the case were taken from "Ford in Britain," *Economist,* February 28,
1981, pp. 66–67; Gilbert D. Harrell and Richard O. Kiefer, *MSU Business Topics,* Winter
1981, pp. 5–15; Mira Wilkins and Frank Ernest Hill, *American Business Abroad: Ford
on Six Continents* (Detroit: Wayne State University Press, 1964); Alan Nevins, *Ford:
Expansion and Challenge: 1915–33,* Vol. II (New York: Charles Scribner's Sons, 1957);
"Ford Annual Report 1989," "How Safe Is It to Invest Abroad?" *International Management,* October 1979, pp. 67–70; Steven Prokesch, "Can Europe Save Ford's Future:
Again?" *New York Times,* October 28, 1990, p. F1 ff; "Ford Around the World," Ford
International Public Affairs, Dearborn, Michigan, October 1990.

2. Karen B. Hisey and Richard E. Caves, "Diversification Strategy and Choice of
Country: Diversifying Acquisitions Abroad by U.S. Multinationals, 1978–1980," *Journal of International Business Studies,* Summer 1985, p. 52, show that between 70 and
85 percent of foreign acquisitions have been in related businesses.

3. Yair Aharoni, *The Foreign Investment Decision Process* (Boston: Harvard University
Graduate School of Business, 1966), pp. 52–53.

4. K. Fatehi-Sedeh and M. H. Safizadeh, "The Association Between Political Instability and Flow of Foreign Direct Investment," *Management International Review,* Vol.
29, No. 4, 1989, pp. 4–13.

5. For a good discussion, see Ellen Day, Richard J. Fox, and Sandra M. Huszagh,
"Segmenting the Global Market for Industrial Goods: Issues and Implications," *International Marketing Review,* Vol. 5, No. 3, Autumn 1988, pp. 14–27.

6. Kenichi Ohmae, "Becoming a Triad Power: The New Global Corporation," *International Marketing Review,* Autumn 1986, pp. 36–49; Richard L. Hudson, "IBM, Other
U.S. Computer Makers Face Challenge from the Japanese in Europe," *Wall Street Journal,* August 13, 1990, p. B1 ff.

7. Raj Aggarwal, "Investment Performance of U.S.-Based Companies: Comments and a Perspective on International Diversification of Real Assets," *Journal of International Business Studies,* Spring–Summer 1980, pp. 98–104; Rolf Buhner, "Assessing International Diversification of West German Corporations," *Strategic Management Journal,* Vol. 8, January–February, 1987, pp. 25–37.

8. Y. M. Geyikdagi and N. V. Geyikdagi, "International Diversification in Latin America and the Industrialized Countries," *Management International Review,* Vol. 29, No. 3, 1989, pp. 62–71.

9. Hisey and Caves, *op. cit.,* pp. 58–62.

10. Irving B. Kravis and Robert E. Lipsey, "The Location of Overseas Production and Production for Export by U.S. Multinational Firms," *Journal of International Economics,* Vol. 12, May 1982, pp. 201–223.

11. Ohmae, *loc. cit.*

12. Rodman L. Drake and Allan J. Prager, "Floundering with Foreign Investment Planning," *Columbia Journal of World Business,* Summer 1977, pp. 66–77.

13. Aharoni, *op. cit.,* pp. 54–56.

14. These were found in studies of reactions to the Ancom investment code by Robert E. Grosse, *Foreign Investment Codes and the Location of Direct Investment* (New York: Praeger, 1980), pp. 122–123.

15. Kravis and Lipsey, *op. cit.,* p. 212.

16. Alan Marshall, "International Facility Planning in Emerging Industries," *Industrial Development,* May–June 1983, pp. 23–25.

17. See, for example, Briance Mascarenhas, "Coping With Uncertainty in International Business," *Journal of International Business Studies,* Vol. 13, No. 2, Fall 1982, pp. 87–98; Philip J. Stein, "Should Your Firm Invest in Political Risk Insurance?" *Financial Executive,* March 1983, pp. 18–22; Pravin Banker, "You're the Best Judge of Foreign Risks," *Harvard Business Review,* Vol. 61, No. 2, March–April, 1983, pp. 157–165.

18. For an analysis of the importance of these variables in the decision-making process, see Joseph La Palombara and Stephen Blank, *Multinational Corporations in Comparative Perspective* (New York: The Conference Board, 1977), pp. x–xii.

19. Craig M. Watson, "Counter-Competition Abroad to Protect Home Markets," *Harvard Business Review,* January–February 1982, p. 40.

20. Robert B. Stobaugh, Jr., "Where in the World Should We Put that Plant?" *Harvard Business Review,* January–February 1969, pp. 132–134.

21. For more information on the Ericsson strategy, see Thomas Hout, Michael E. Porter, and Eileen Rudden, "How Global Companies Win Out," *Harvard Business Review,* September–October 1982, p. 102.

22. Marie E. Wicks Kelly and George C. Philippatos, "Comparative Analysis of the Foreign Investment Evaluation Practices by U.S. Based Manufacturing Multinational Companies," *Journal of International Business Studies,* Vol. 13, No. 3, Winter 1982, p. 39.

23. Robert G. Hawkins, Norman Mintz, and Michael Provissiero, "Government Takeovers of U.S. Foreign Affiliates," *Journal of International Business Studies,* Spring 1976, pp. 3–16; David G. Bradley, "Managing against Expropriation," *Harvard Business Review,* July–August 1977, pp. 75–83.

24. See, for example, U.S. Department of State, Bureau of Intelligence and Research, *Nationalization, Expropriation, and Other Takings of United States and Certain Foreign Property since 1960* (Washington, D.C., 1971); J. F. Truitt, "Expropriation of Foreign Investment: Summary of the Post–World War II Experience of American and British

Investors in the Less-Developed Countries," *Journal of International Business Studies,* Fall 1970, pp. 21–34.

25. Bradley, "Managing against Expropriation," pp. 81–82, noted this for takeovers by Allende and Velasco in Chile and Peru.

26. Lee C. Nehrt, "The Political Climate for Private Investment: Analysis Will Reduce Uncertainty," *Business Horizons,* June 1972, pp. 52–55; Herbert Cahn, "The Political Exposure Problem: An Often Overlooked Investment Decision," *Worldwide P & I Planning,* May–June 1972, pp. 20–22.

27. See, for example, F. T. Haner, "Rating Investment Risks Abroad," *Business Horizons,* April 1979, pp. 18–23; "As the World Twirls: BI's Ratings Show New Risks vs. Opportunities," *Business International,* April 15, 1983, pp. 113–115; and Carmen D. Chase, James L. Kuhle, and Carl H. Walther, "The Relevance of Political Risk in Direct Foreign Investment," *Management International Review,* Vol. 28, No. 3, 1988, pp. 31–38.

28. Jonathan Kavanaugh, "Peruvian Promise Lures Investors," *Euromoney,* September 1989, pp. 239–240.

29. Douglas Nigh, "The Effect of Political Events on United States Direct Foreign Investment: A Pooled Time-Series Cross Sectional Analysis," *Journal of International Business Studies,* Vol. 16, No. 1, 1985, pp. 1–17; S. Desta, "Assessing Political Risk in Less Developed Countries," *The Journal of Business Strategies,* Vol. 5, No. 5, 1985, pp. 40–53; Thomas L. Brewer, "Instability in Developing and Industrial Countries: Methodological and Theoretical Issues," *Journal of Comparative Economics,* Vol. 11, 1987, pp. 120–123; Fatehi-Sedeh and Safizadeh, *op. cit.*

30. Ivo K. Feirabend and Rosalind L. Feirabend, "Aggressive Behavior in Politics: A Cross-National Study," *Journal of Conflict Resolution,* Fall 1966, pp. 249–271.

31. Hawkins et al., "Government Takeovers of U.S. Foreign Affiliates," p. 7.

32. Harold Knudsen, "Explaining the National Propensity to Expropriate: An Ecological Approach," *Journal of International Business Studies,* Spring 1974, pp. 51–69.

33. John F. Preble, Pradeep A. Rau, and Arie Reichel, "The Environmental Scanning Practices of U.S. Multinationals in the Late 1980's," *Management International Review,* Vol. 28, No. 4, 1988, pp. 4–14.

34. This classification scheme is adapted from Carl Noble and Virgil Thornhill, "Institutionalization of Management Science in the Multinational Firm," *Columbia Journal of World Business,* Fall 1977, pp. 13–15.

35. The incorporation of risk and opportunity are considered essential elements in any portfolio analysis. Yoram Wind and Susan Douglas, "International Portfolio Analysis and Strategy: The Challenge of the 80s," *Journal of International Business Studies,* Vol. 12, No. 2, Fall 1981, pp. 72–73; "How Borg-Warner Uses Country-Risk Assessment as a Planning Element," *Business International,* November 9, 1979, pp. 353–356.

36. Harrell and Kiefer, *loc. cit.*

37. Igal Ayal and Jehiel Zif, "Market Expansion Strategies in Multinational Marketing," *Journal of Marketing,* Vol. 43, Spring 1979, pp. 84–94.

38. Joseph C. Miller and Bernard Pras, "The Effects of Multinational and Export Diversification on the Profit Stability of U.S. Corporations," *Southern Economic Journal,* Vol. 46, No. 3, 1980, pp. 792–805.

39. *Ibid.,* p. 804.

40. Kelly and Philippatos, *loc. cit.,* p. 32.

41. *Ibid.*

42. Jean J. Boddewyn, "Foreign and Domestic Divestment and Investment Decisions: Like or Unlike?" *Journal of International Business Studies*, Vol. 14, No. 3, Winter 1983, p. 28.

43. Elizabeth Weiner and Mark Maremont, "Business Gets Ready to March Back to Pretoria," *Business Week*, February 25, 1991, p. 53.

44. Julia Leung, "For China's Foreign Investors, the Door Marked 'Exit' Can Be a Tight Squeeze," *Wall Street Journal*, March 12, 1991, p. A14.

45. Keith H. Hammonds, citing John G. Smale, "P&G's Worldly New Boss Wants a More Worldly Company," *Business Week*, October 30, 1989, pp. 40–42.

46. John D. Daniels and Jeffrey Bracker, "Profit Performance: Do Foreign Operations Make a Difference?" *Management International Review*, Vol. 29, No. 1, 1989, pp. 46–56.

47. Atsuko Chiba, "Mitsui Led Group Must Pay More Money or Pull Out of Iran Petrochemical Project," *Wall Street Journal*, November 25, 1980, p. 30; "Mitsui Halts Iran Plant's Start-up," *New York Times*, April 24, 1981, p. D1; Youssef M. Ibrahim, "Japan Threatened by Iran-Iraq War," *Wall Street Journal*, November 8, 1983; Suleiman K. Kassicieh and Jamal R. Nassar, "Revolution and War in the Persian Gulf: The Effect on MNCs," *California Management Review*, Vol. 26, No. 1, Fall 1983, pp. 88–99; "Construction to Resume on War-Damaged Plant," *Journal of Commerce*, July 11, 1984, p. 22B; and "Japan Foreign Minister to Visit Iran to Query on Gulf Safety, Mitsui's Complex," *Oilgram News*, June 5, 1987, p. 2; "Mitsui in Fiscal 1990," *Mitsui Trade News*, September–October 1990, pp. 2–3; Roger Vielvoye, "Bandar Khomeini Project," *Oil & Gas Journal*, August 28, 1989, p. 31; "Iran Said to Seek Replacement for Mitsui to Rebuild Bandar Khomeini Plant," *Platt's Oilgram News*, June 14, 1989, p. 2.

CHAPTER 17

CONTROL

Form your plans before sunrise.
INDIAN-TAMIL PROVERB

Objectives

- To explain the special challenges of foreign operations.

- To indicate the advantages and disadvantages of decision making at the headquarters and foreign subsidiary locations.

- To describe the alternative organizational structures for international operations.

- To highlight both the importance of and the methods for global planning, reporting, and evaluating.

- To give an overview of some specific control considerations affecting international firms, such as the handling of acquisitions, the choice of headquarters location, and the legal structure of the foreign facility.

The former managing director of Nestlé, Pierre Liotard-Vogt, said, "Perhaps we are the only real multinational company existing." Although this may be something of an exaggeration, it is difficult to find other companies with such a high dependence on foreign involvement. The Swiss-based company, one of the 50 largest industrials in the world, was international from the start. Nestlé was formed by a 1905 merger between an American-owned and a German-owned firm. About 98 percent of Nestlé's sales are outside of Switzerland, and about half of the top management at the Vevey headquarters is non-Swiss. A Frenchman, an Italian, a German, and a Swiss who took out American citizenship have at various times held the position of chief executive officer. Map 17.1 shows Nestlé's factories by country. The one area in which the company is still primarily Swiss is in ownership. Until 1988, two thirds of the shares were registered and could be bought only by other Swiss. With the 1988 change, Nestlé expects that eventually Swiss owners will be in a minority. The earlier ownership identification with neutral Switzerland, a country that never colonized, allowed the company to do business where some of its worldwide rivals were restricted, such as in Chile under Allende, in Cuba, and in Vietnam. The 1988 change in ownership restrictions was in response to criticism about Swiss companies' takeovers abroad, particularly unfriendly ones.

In 1989 Nestlé's sales from 421 factories around the world were more than $32 billion. About 46 percent of the company's sales were in Europe, 27 percent in North America, and 27 percent elsewhere. With such a geographic spread of operations, Nestlé maintains clear-cut policies on where decisions will be made and what roles corporate and country managers will play.

A major responsibility of Nestlé's corporate management is to give strategic direction to the firm. To do this, the corporate management decides in which geographic areas and to which products it plans to allocate efforts. For instance, in the early 1980s Nestlé became less dependent on chocolate and Third World countries by placing more emphasis on culinary products and on the North American market. To maintain this control, Nestlé's headquarters staff handles all acquisition decisions as well as decisions as to which products will be researched at the centralized facilities in Switzerland. To support these functions, each geographic area is expected to provide a positive cash flow to the parent. In fact, Nestlé tries to move almost all cash to Switzerland where a specialized staff decides in which currencies it will be held and to what countries it may be transferred.

Headquarters also researches commodity situations and mandates purchase amounts and prices, such as requiring that all overseas companies contract a supply of green coffee for, say, three to six months at some maximum price. Because of a heavy dependence on the introduction of new

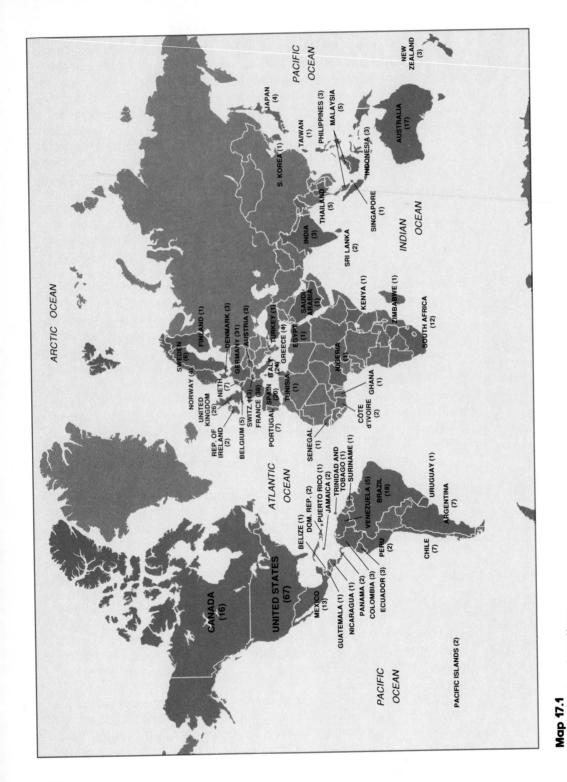

Map 17.1
Nestlé Factory Locations
Note that Nestlé's manufacturing is located in 60 different countries. Source: Nestlé Annual Report, 1989, pp. 28–29.

products that may take several years to become profitable, the company must ensure that the more established products remain sufficiently profitable for generating needed funds. If a new product does not become profitable within a reasonable period of time, such as its mineral water in Brazil, or if it has run its cycle of profitability, such as its Libby's vegetable canning operations, or if its development potential seems low, such as Beech-Nut's baby food, the management in Switzerland decides to divest the business. Other divestments occur because certain activities of acquired firms do not fit the corporate development strategy, such as the spin-off of a printing and packaging business that was part of the acquired Buitoni-Perugina operations.

The budget that originates from the country area level is the main means used to ensure that each area carries its share within the corporation. Budgets are set up on an annual basis, revised quarterly, and subject to approval in Switzerland. Actual performance reports are sent to Switzerland monthly where they are compared with budgets and the previous year's performance. The market head must explain any deviations satisfactorily or headquarters personnel will intervene. Another corporate function is to serve as a source for information: The successes, failures, and general experiences of product programs in one country are passed on to managers in other countries. Information on the success of a white chocolate bar in New Zealand and on a line of Lean Cuisine frozen food in the United States was disseminated this way.

In spite of the centralized directives described above, Nestlé's area managers have a great deal of discretion in certain matters, especially marketing. Product research is centralized so that duplication of efforts is kept to a minimum. When a new product is developed, the corporate management offers it to the subsidiaries and may urge initial trials. However, they will not force the subsidiaries to launch a new product if the subsidiary managements do not find it acceptable. If the product is introduced, local management is fairly free to adapt it as long as corporate management does not find the changes harmful. One of Nestlé's best selling products, Nescafé instant coffee, is blended and colored slightly differently from country to country.

In addition to budgets and reports, Nestlé relies heavily on information-gathering visits to the local operations. Several things are done to try to bring corporate and country management closer together. One is to alternate people between jobs in the field and jobs at headquarters; another is the scheduling of meetings and training programs to bring large groups of managers together; still another is to ensure that top management can converse with area management in at least French and English and preferably in German and Spanish as well. The compensation system and management style are established purposely to limit turnover among employees. The combination of these various methods contributes to many long-term interactions designed to break down barriers between headquarters and the field.

The method of making decisions at headquarters has not remained the same. During the 1980s Nestlé became more decentralized, largely because of the management philosophy of Helmut Maucher, who became managing director in 1982. When he took over, three levels of management approval were necessary even to put out a press release. He reduced the corporate staff, pushed more authority down to the operating level, and replaced 25-page monthly reports with a one-page reporting form. At one point Nestlé sought to balance functional, area, and product viewpoints by putting different people in charge of each activity at headquarters. This meant that the person in charge of each activity would have to agree before a decision could be made, which sometimes meant a slow process. This structure was abandoned in the mid-1980s in order to slim down the corporate staff and speed decision making. This was replaced with a board of general managers, primarily representing the zones into which Nestlé divides the world.

Many company actions necessitate new decisions on where control will be vested. Nestlé's policy of expanding largely through acquisition of existing firms is one type of action that has resulted in situations not quite fitting the established lines of responsibility. The acquisition policy is premised on the belief that it is more prudent to enter an already highly competitive market by buying an existing firm and infusing resources into it. Since acquired firms are unlikely to have the exact product and geographic basis to fit Nestlé's structure, these operations must be accommodated.

For example, Nestlé acquired Libby, McNeill & Libby, a U.S. company with substantial international operations including a subsidiary in the United Kingdom. Nestlé had to iron out not only how Libby, McNeill & Libby would relate to Nestlé's existing U.S. operations, but also whether the U.K. subsidiary should continue to report to Libby or to Nestlé's European operations. (There was a gradual transition whereby the subsidiary eventually reported to the European division.) Fifteen years later, in 1985, the Libby, McNeill & Libby production facilities and distribution center were closed; however, two other Nestlé divisions took on the manufacture and sale of products using the Libby name. In another case, the acquisition of Stouffer Foods put Nestlé into hotel ownership for the first time. Because Stouffer had been highly profitable and because the Swiss headquarters management lacked hotel experience, many more decisions were initially made at the subsidiary level than would normally be the case.

A notable Nestlé acquisition was the U.S. company Carnation for $3 billion, the largest nonoil merger in history. This was eclipsed by the nearly $4 billion acquisition of the British firm Rowntree, the creator of KitKat and other candy bars. U.S. acquisitions reported directly to Switzerland until 1981, when Nestlé named a head of North American operations for the first time. This move was designed to consolidate much of the U.S. operations. The managing director of Nestlé worldwide supported this so that he could spend time on strategic planning instead of supervising day-to-day operations. Carnation, acquired in 1985, initially reported directly to Switzerland,

and its foreign operations were acquired by local Nestlé organizations. In 1990 Carnation became consolidated with other U.S. food businesses in a move to save overhead expenses and to gain advantages of scale in combating such U.S. rivals as Kraft General Foods and Con-Agra.

Competitive factors have influenced Nestlé's decisions on where to place emphasis. For example, the rapid growth strategy in the United States has been based partially on the realization that the company must maintain a certain size relative to its competitors (which have been growing internally and through acquisition). This size helps in dealing with the few large supermarket chains that account for most of Nestlé's sales.

Another factor that has influenced decision-making authority has been a need to share subsidiary ownership of some facilities because of host-country requirements, as in Malaysia. This in turn has reduced the flexibility of corporate decision making.

INTRODUCTION

Control questions facing all companies include:

- Where are decisions made?
- How can the firm optimize globally?
- How should country units report to headquarters?

International companies take a wide variety of approaches in managing their foreign operations. Many of the problems that they face are nevertheless very similar. The Nestlé case illustrates concerns shared by all international companies: where decisions should be made, how country operations should report to headquarters, and how to optimize on a global basis. Behind each of those concerns is a more basic one—that of control. The subject of this chapter—control—is much broader than the ownership of sufficient voting shares to direct company policies. **Control** is the planning, implementation, evaluation, and correction of performance in order to ensure that organizational objectives are achieved. Several factors make the control process more difficult internationally:

Foreign control is usually more difficult because of

- Distance: it takes more time and expense to communicate
- Diversity: country differences make it hard to compare
- Uncontrollables: more outside stockholders and governmental dictates
- Degree of certainty: data problems, rapid changes

1. *Distance.* The geographic and cultural distance separating countries will increase the time, expense, and possibility of error in cross-national communications. Inquiries and control systems may not be fully understood by subsidiary managers, and the time and expense of gaining verification may very well hinder the functioning of the control systems.

2. *Diversity.* Throughout most of the text, we have shown the need for firms to adjust operations to the unique situations encountered in each country in which the international firm has operations. When market size, type of competition, product, labor cost, currency, and a host of other factors differentiate operations from one country to another, the task of evaluating performances or setting standards to correct or improve business functions is extremely complicated.

3. *Uncontrollables.* Performance evaluation is of little importance to control unless there is some means of attaining corrective action. The fact that many foreign operations must contend (1) with the dictates of outside stockholders, whose objectives may be somewhat different from those of

the parent; and (2) with governmental regulations over which the firm has no short-term influence for change means that effective corrective action may be minimal.[2]

4. *Degree of certainty.* Control implies setting goals and developing plans to meet the goals. Economic and industry data are much less complete and accurate for some countries than for others. Furthermore, political and economic conditions are subject to rapid change in some locales. These situations impede the setting of plans, especially long-range ones, and reduce the certainty of results from the implementation of the plans.

Although these factors make control more difficult in the international context, companies follow procedural and structural practices in an effort to ensure that foreign operations comply with overall corporate goals and philosophies. This chapter discusses seven aspects of the international control process: (1) location of decision making, (2) organizational structure, (3) planning, (4) business research, (5) corporate culture, (6) reporting techniques, and (7) special situations.

LOCATION OF DECISION MAKING

Centralization implies higher-level decision making, especially above the country level.

Any firm must determine where decisions will be made on such diverse questions as product policy, the acquisition of funds, and placement of liquid assets. The higher the level within the organization decisions are made, the more they are considered to be **centralized;** the lower the level, the more they are **decentralized.** The centralization-decentralization question may be addressed either from the standpoint of the company as a whole or from some part of it, such as within a particular subsidiary operation. This discussion will not cover the latter; rather, it will highlight the relationship of the country-level operations to other parts of the international company, such as headquarters, regional offices, or other subsidiaries. For purposes of this discussion, decisions made at the foreign subsidiary level are considered to be decentralized, whereas decisions made above the foreign subsidiary level are considered centralized. There are opposing pressures for centralization and decentralization; consequently, policies must be adapted to the firm's unique situation.

Complete centralization and decentralization may be thought of as the extremes. In actuality, companies neither centralize nor decentralize all decisions; instead, they vary policies according to the type of question and the particular circumstances involved. The location of decision making may vary within the same company by product, by function, and by country. In addition, actual decision making is seldom as asymmetrical as it may appear on the surface. In other words, although a manager may have decision-making authority, that manager may consult and reach consensus with other managers before exercising the authority. In spite of these differences and subtleties, the following section focuses on the rationale for locating decision control at either the corporate or the subsidiary level. Once these motivations are clear, it is easier to comprehend such elements as organization structure, planning, and evaluation, which parallel the basic centralization or decentralization philosophy.

Corporate Efficiency Factors

Firms must consider how long it takes to get help from headquarters in relation to how rapidly a decision must be made.

Cost and Expediency   Although corporate personnel may be more experienced in advising or actually making certain decisions, the time and expense involved in centralization may not justify the so-called better advice. Many decisions cannot be put off. Some headquarters' decisions could not effectively be made without face-to-face communication with subsidiary managers or on-the-spot observation. Bringing in corporate personnel may not be warranted.

The distance of foreign operations from headquarters is also a factor to consider. For U.S. subsidiaries in either Canada or Mexico, the time and cost of communications with the parent are low in comparison with subsidiaries located in a more remote country such as the Philippines. The Philippine manager may be forced to make decisions on matters for which the Canadian and Mexican managers get corporate assistance.[3] However, with advances in communications and transportation, the distance factor is becoming less important.

Decisions on moving goods or other resources internationally are more likely to be made centrally.

Resource Transference   Both product and production factors may be moved from a company's operations in one country to its facilities in another. The movement may be in the best interest of corporate goals, although individual subsidiaries may not do as well if resources are transferred. Decisions involving these relationships usually are made centrally because they require information from all operating units and the ability to mesh the various data to achieve overall corporate objectives. These relationships may involve many different types of decisions, but a few examples should suffice to explain the need for centralization.

Frequently, corporate profits may be improved by moving production factors—capital, personnel, or technology—from one subsidiary to another. Without some central control point, reports would have to be disseminated from every unit to every other unit to determine the resource from one locale that could be used elsewhere. Similarly, if exports among subsidiaries are needed to maintain a continual production flow (e.g., vertical integration or interdependent components needed in the company's end product), centralized control may be required to assure this flow. Another centralized decision may be exports to nonaffiliated companies that involve jurisdictional questions. For example, if a firm has manufacturing facilities in the United States, Venezuela, and Germany, which facility will export to South Africa? By answering that question centrally, the firm may avoid price competition among the subsidiaries that could result in reduced corporate income. Furthermore, a number of different factors can be considered, including production costs, transportation costs, tax rates, exchange controls, and capacity utilization.

What is best for the company globally may not be best for the country unit.

Economies and Interrelationships Through Standardization   Even though worldwide uniformity of products, purchases, methods, and policies may not be best for an individual operation, the overall gain may be more than sufficient to overcome the individual country losses. Standardization of machinery used in the production process, for example, may result in a more favorable purchasing price for the firm as a whole because of quantity discounts. This also may bring savings in the training of mechanics, in maintaining manuals, and in carrying inventories of spare parts. The firm may consider economies in almost any type of corporate activity, such as advertising programs, R&D, and purchase of group insurance. Uniformity of products also gives a firm greater flexibility in filling orders when supply problems arise because of strikes, disasters, or sudden increases in demand. Production can simply be expanded in one country to meet shortages elsewhere.

Another argument for adhering to like policies globally is to ensure that foreign operations do not veer so drastically from the overall line or method of business that control is completely lost. If units in different countries alter products, policies, and methods even gradually but in different directions, the eventual diversity may be so great that economies are no longer possible and the personnel, products, and ideas can no longer be interchanged easily.

Increasingly, the people with whom a firm must deal (governmental officials, employees, suppliers, consumers, and the general public) are aware of what that firm does in other countries where it operates. Concessions that have been easily granted in one country may then be demanded in other countries, where they are not afforded as easily. Suppose that, for public-relations purposes, the management in one country decided to give preferential prices to the government and established a profit-sharing plan for employees. If the governmental officials and employees in a second country were to ask for similar treatment, the result may be reduced profits through compliance or poor public relations through noncompliance.

Even internal pricing and product decisions can affect demand in other countries. With the growing mobility of consumers, especially industrial consumers, a good or bad experience with a product in one country may eventually affect sales elsewhere. This is especially true if industrial consumers themselves want uniformity in their end products. If prices differ substantially among countries, consumers even may find that they can import more cheaply than they can buy locally.

Global Competitive Strategies   A company needs to determine whether it is better off trying to emphasize country-by-country competitive positions or an integrated global position. In addition to the question of standardized versus differentiated products among countries, the firm must consider a number of other factors. One is whether large-scale production of components and finished goods can be exported so that costs can be reduced to buyers in various countries. The nature of the production process, transportation costs, and government import restrictions all affect the production integration advantages.

The present and potential existence of global customers and/or competitors also may dictate decisions to improve global performance at the expense of a particular country's operations. Price concessions to an automobile manufacturer in Brazil, for example, may help gain business for the supplier in other countries where the buyer manufactures automobiles. A company also may attack a competitor by producing and selling where that competitor gains its major resources to compete globally.

Competence Arguments

Since a condition for delegating authority is the belief that those selected will act responsibly, the perception of local managers' competence will determine to a great extent the courses of action they can pursue. Although there are rational factors affecting the belief of relative capability, it has been noted that too often unrealistic attitudes lead to excessive control delegated to either the corporate or the subsidiary managers. Unrealistic attitudes include, say, a belief that only the on-the-spot person knows the situation well enough to make a decision or a perception that corporate managers are the only individuals capable of handling decisions.

Caliber and Local Conditions   Since the local management is usually in a much better position to know what will and will not work locally, they are normally given greater latitude when local conditions are perceived as being significantly different from conditions in the home country. For example, the corporate managers of a U.S. company will probably feel more competent about dictating practices to a Canadian subsidiary than to a Mexican subsidiary, since the former is presumed to parallel successful U.S. operations more closely. Yet local conditions may be more important for some functions than others. Nestlé, for example, decentralizes most of its marketing decisions because they need to be adjusted to local needs; however, foreign-exchange decisions are centralized because of the importance of examining global conditions.

Other things would seem to dictate different approaches to local managers. Factors that would appear to favor decentralization include: when the local management team is large rather than lean, when local managers have worked a long time with the company, and when they have developed a successful track record. These factors seem to favor altering the location of decision making among country operations in different countries.[4]

The more different the foreign environment is from the home country, the more delegation occurs. The more confidence there is in foreign managers, the more delegation occurs.

The more uniform the
product is globally, the
more centralization
occurs.

Product Factors   The product itself may determine the relative competence of the centralized staff versus the local managers. For technically sophisticated products there is usually little need for local adaptations; consequently, at least for marketing policy, decisions may be made that apply to a very broad spectrum of countries. A good contrast is between Nestlé's food products, which depend on geographic differentiation, and G.E.'s power generation and jet engine businesses, which are big-ticket products that require very little adaptation to local needs. The former lend themselves much more to decentralization than the latter. Also, many products are first introduced in the largest market, and then later they are introduced to smaller markets when the country of original entry is in a later stage of the product life cycle. In such instances the centralized staff often asserts control in order to ensure that the same mistakes are not repeated in more than one country. If product technology changes rapidly, there is usually a much greater need for headquarters involvement than if the product technology remains stable for a long period of time.

The larger the total foreign operations are, the more likely headquarters has specialized staff with international expertise. The larger the operations are in a given country, the more likely that country has specialized staff.

Time and Size Variables   Usually, the longer a company operates in overseas markets, the larger its foreign sales and the greater experience it has in dealing with foreign problems. The size of total foreign operations as well as the size of operations in individual foreign countries both exert influence on the location of decision making. Increased centralization is feasible when a corporate staff that is large enough and qualified enough has developed. The company with very limited foreign operations cannot afford this centralized expertise and must therefore delegate decisions to the operating managers abroad. However, if the specific foreign country operation is very large, such as Nestlé's U.S. subsidiary, then that operation can afford to have its own specialized staff personnel and may be treated differently than smaller country operations, such as Nestlé's subsidiary in Belize.

More important decisions are made at headquarters.

Importance of the Decision   Any discussion of location of authority must consider the importance of the particular decisions. The question sometimes asked is, "How much can be lost through a bad decision?" The greater the potential loss, the higher in the organization the level of control usually is. In the case of marketing decisions, for example, local autonomy over product design is not nearly as prevalent as over advertising, pricing, and distribution. Product design generally necessitates a considerably larger capital outlay than the other functions; consequently, the potential loss through a wrong decision is higher. Furthermore, advertising approaches, pricing, and distribution decisions may be more easily reversed if an error in judgment is made. Rather than delineation of the type of decision that can be made at the subsidiary level, limits may be set instead on expenditure amount, thus allowing local autonomy on small outlays while requiring corporate approval on larger transactions.

Decentralization Considerations

Using Subsidiaries Effectively   The development of standardized practices
does not suggest that headquarters should generate all the information necessary for decision making. In fact, if the subsidiaries' viewpoints are ignored,
the company may not develop the best types of cross-national or standardized
programs. Furthermore, good local managers may gravitate to other firms
where they feel they can play a more important role. Procter & Gamble
(P&G), for example, had allowed its European country operations nearly total
autonomy in adapting technology, products, and marketing approaches. In
order to capture Europewide scale economies, P&G put one office in charge
of the strategy for all of Europe, ignoring local knowledge, underutilizing
subsidiary strength, and demotivating subsidiary managers. P&G has since
moved to greater standardization with other brand-management activities;
however, this has been led by teams representing the subsidiary operations.
In another case, EMI, a U.K.-based company, used feedback only from the
U.K. market to determine how its central laboratory would seek to improve
its CAT scanners—through better image resolution. This ignored the larger
U.S. market, where a different improvement, shorter scan times, was preferred. When GE came out with a shorter scan time, it captured the U.S.
market and got better scale economies than EMI. EMI started losing money
and had to accept a takeover bid.[5]

National Rather Than International Strategies   Although the development of a global strategy offers many advantages, there are circumstances in
which subsidiaries cannot reasonably be brought into this scheme. This occurs, for example, in products associated with uniquely national taste preferences.[6] In other situations, subsidiaries may be prevented from being a full
part of a global network because governmental protectionism isolates them
from competitive threats.[7] In such situations, corporate strategic control may
be less appropriate than national control.

Local Performance Considerations   Although some decisions clearly can
be made efficiently at the corporate level, this technical efficiency must be
weighed against morale problems created when responsibility is taken away
from the local management team. When local managers are prevented from
acting in the best interest of their own operation, they tend to think, "I could
have done better, but corporate management would not let me." These managers may lose commitment to their jobs and may not gain the experience
needed to move into jobs of even greater responsibility. Lack of commitment
may be overcome through development of a reward system that does not
penalize managers for decisions that are outside of their control. In fact, a
compensation system that rewards local managers partially on the basis of
the corporation's total worldwide performance may enhance the development of global thinking at each country level.

LDCs argue that centralization keeps them subservient.

Dependency   Many critics within the LDCs have contended that the centralization of decision making by MNEs is leading to an ever-increasing movement of management and technical functions to the home country, leaving the menial and low-skilled jobs in the LDCs. The critics recall colonial eras in which their own people were forbidden responsible positions and were dependent on the colonial powers for the control of their destinies.[8] They have been particularly disparaging about the facts that very little R&D by MNEs is done outside of their home countries and that of that portion, almost all is done in other industrial countries.[9]

This presents dilemmas for MNEs. There are some potent arguments for centralizing most R&D in home countries, such as the availability of large numbers of people to work directly for the company, the proximity to private research organizations and universities doing related work, and the general advantages of centralized authority for less duplication of efforts.

Recall that in the Nestlé case new product R&D was done in Switzerland to reduce duplication and to be close to the strategic planners who projected product needs further into the future than could country managers, who were more concerned with day-to-day operations. Nestlé did allow country areas the freedom to conduct adaptive R&D but controlled this carefully by requiring corporate approval of the adaptations. Thus even when the corporation allows adaptive or new product R&D to be carried out abroad, the corporate management may exert substantial influence on it. MNEs with substantial R&D outside the home country seldom allow the foreign affiliate complete autonomy. The corporate management may allocate budgets, approve plans, and offer suggestions. At the same time there may be substantial input from affiliates for R&D conducted centrally.[10]

By giving groups of overseas employees a great deal of autonomy in certain areas, an international company may be able to attract a high calibre of personnel who might not wish to work in the firm's home country. For example, IBM scientists at its small Zurich laboratory won the Nobel prize for physics in two consecutive years. There are many ways that certain subsidiaries may be given autonomy over certain activities, such as the development of a specific product, a specific technology, or the conduct of certain market testing.

Decentralization
- Is more likely on adaptive R&D
- May attract highly skilled foreigners

ORGANIZATIONAL STRUCTURE

As a firm develops international business activities, its corporate structure must adapt to the changing environment in order to accommodate foreign operations effectively. The organizational structure that emerges will depend on many factors, including the location and type of foreign facilities, the impact of international operations on total corporate performance, the nature of assets employed in pursuit of business abroad, and the time horizons for achieving international and total corporate goals.

Firms must establish legal and organizational structures at home and abroad to meet company objectives. Within each foreign country these arrangements may differ because of the unique nature of activities and environmental requirements. Layered above the country organizations are additional structures that coordinate activities in more than one country. The form, method, and location of operational units at home and abroad will affect taxes, expenses, and control. Consequently, organizational structure has an important effect on the fulfillment of corporate objectives.

Level of Importance

The more important the foreign operations, the higher they report in the structure.

The more important the specific foreign operations are to total corporate performance, the higher the corporate level to which these units should report. The organizational structure or reporting system therefore should change over time to parallel a company's increased involvement in foreign activities.

At one end of the spectrum is the firm that merely exports temporary surpluses through a middleman who takes title and handles all the export details. Clearly, in this situation few people in the firm are concerned with the conduct of the business. Since no personnel are either overseas or engaged in the export arrangement, there is no need for the firm to devise new personnel policies or training programs. Because the title to goods changes hands in the home country, there are no foreign legal or tax matters to consider. Also, since payment is effected in the home currency, there are no problems of transferring funds or evaluating country-by-country performance. Finally, because no attempt is made to increase foreign sales, the firm does not require new marketing programs. The entire operation is apt to be so insignificant to total corporate performance that top-level management is concerned very little with such transactions. The duties may be handled by anyone in the organization who knows enough and has time to discern whether or not orders can be filled. In this situation, foreign activities should be handled at a low level in the corporate hierarchy.

At the other end of the spectrum is the firm that has passed through intermediate stages and now owns and manages foreign manufacturing and sales facilities. Every functional and advisory group within the company undoubtedly will be involved in the establishment and direction of the facilities. Since sales, investments, and profits are now a more significant part of the corporate total, people very high in the corporate hierarchy are affected by the foreign operations.

Integrated Versus Separate
International Activities

All of a company's international activities may be grouped together (e.g., international department or division) or gathered by the product, function, or geographic structure the company relies on domestically. Figure 17.1 shows

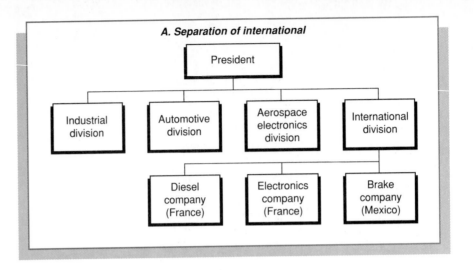

A. Separation of international

- President
  - Industrial division
  - Automotive division
  - Aerospace electronics division
  - International division
    - Diesel company (France)
    - Electronics company (France)
    - Brake company (Mexico)

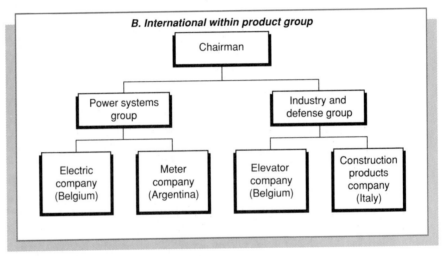

B. International within product group

- Chairman
  - Power systems group
    - Electric company (Belgium)
    - Meter company (Argentina)
  - Industry and defense group
    - Elevator company (Belgium)
    - Construction products company (Italy)

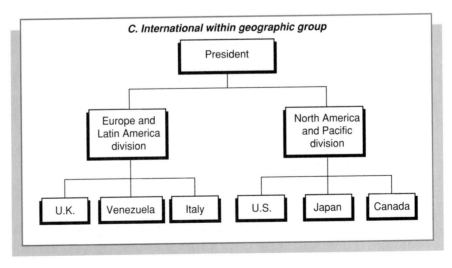

C. International within geographic group

- President
  - Europe and Latin America division
    - U.K.
    - Venezuela
    - Italy
  - North America and Pacific division
    - U.S.
    - Japan
    - Canada

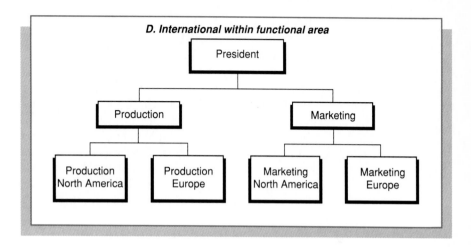

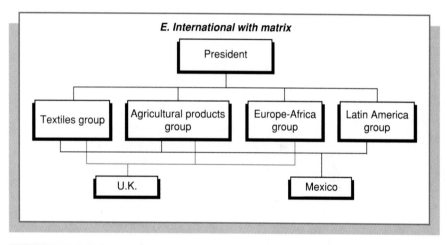

Figure 17.1
Placement of International Activities within the Organizational Structure
Although most companies have structures that are somewhat mixed, this figure
shows a simplified example of handling the major thrust of foreign operations in
the five most prevalently used archetypes.

simplified examples of different approaches to the placement of foreign activity within the organizational structure; most companies broadly fit one of these categories.

International division
- Creates critical international mass
- May have problems getting resources from domestic divisions

International Division   The separation of international activities allows for specialized personnel to handle such diverse matters as export documentation, foreign-exchange transactions, and relations with foreign governments. By combining all international operations, the international activities constitute a large enough critical mass to wield power within the organization. When separated among product or functional units, these activities may be so small in comparison to domestic business that the firm gives little attention to their development. On the other hand, this separation may necessitate dependence of the international division on the domestic divisions for product, personnel, technology, and other resources. Since managers in the domestic divisions are evaluated against domestic performance standards, they may withhold their best resources from the international group in order to improve their own performance.

Part A of Fig. 17.1 is an example of separating international operations, as used by such firms as Campbell Soup.[11] Although this structure is not popular among European multinational firms, it is very common among those based in the United States.[12] One of the apparent causes for the difference is that U.S. firms are typically much more dependent on the domestic market than are European firms; therefore, the international division allows U.S. firms to gain the "critical mass" discussed above.

Worldwide product division is popular among diverse product firms.

Product Division   Parts B, C, and D in Fig. 17.1 are types of international operations that are integrated rather than handled separately. The product organization (B) is particularly popular among companies that operate within highly diverse product groups, especially those that have become diverse primarily through acquisitions, such as Motorola. Since the product groups may have little in common, even domestically, the groups may be highly independent of each other. Note that different subsidiaries within the same foreign country will report to different groups at headquarters.

Area division is popular when foreign operations are large and are not dominated by a single country or region.

Geographic (Area) Division   The geographic organization, part C in Fig. 17.1, is used primarily by firms with very large foreign operations, not dominated by a single country or area. This structure is found more commonly among European MNEs, such as Nestlé, than among U.S. MNEs because of the dominance of the U.S. domestic market. Recall that Nestlé can use this structure because no one region dominates its operations.

Functional division is popular among extractive companies.

Functional   The functional organization, part D in Fig. 17.1, is popular among extractive companies (such as oil or bauxite extraction) because of their very homogenous products for which production and marketing methods are relatively undifferentiated from one country to another. For example, it is used by Exxon.

A matrix organization gives product, function, and area an even focus.

Matrix   Because of the problems inherent in either integrating or separating foreign operations, some firms, such as Dow Chemical, are moving toward matrix organizations, part E in Fig. 17.1. In these organizations a subsidiary reports to more than one group (product, function, or area). The theory is that, since each group shares responsibility over foreign operations, each group will depend on the others. The groups will become more interdependent, will exchange information, and will ultimately take strategic global perspectives as they seek to exchange resources with other groups. For example, product group managers must compete so that R&D personnel responsible to a functional group are assigned to the development of technologies that fall within their product domain. The same product group managers must compete as well to see that area managers put sufficient emphasis on their lines. Not only are product groups competing, the functional and geographic areas also must strive to draw upon resources held by others in the matrix.

Although a matrix form requires that all major perspectives be represented in strategic decision making, this form of organization is not without drawbacks. One of the problems is that groups and coalitions inevitably compete for scarce resources, and a management decision must be made above the group level on how to allocate the resources when lower-level managers fail to reach an agreement. Such elements as faith in a specific executive or business group may result in more decisions being made in their favor.[13] As others in the organization see this occurring, they may perceive that the locus of relative power lies with a certain individual or group, which may lead managers in turn to divert most of their energies toward the activities that are perceived as most likely to be accepted, thus perpetuating the difference in relative power. This may not represent the areas that would be the firm's best strategic choices on a global basis. Consequently, some of the advantages sought in a matrix organization may be diminished because of these interpersonal relationships. A number of alternatives may help to alleviate this problem, including the transfer of individuals among groups and the development of additional reporting and control systems reflecting each of the three groups (product, function, and area) on a global basis. However, these alternatives are not without costs.

Dynamic Nature of Structures

Companies' structures are apt to change as their business evolves. For example, as product lines become more diverse the overall organization is apt to shift from a functional to a product structure. Likewise, international business growth may necessitate structural changes. When the company is merely exporting, an export department attached to a product or functional division may suffice. But if international operations continue to grow and be conducted by overseas production in addition to exports, a department may no longer be sufficient. Perhaps an international division replaces the department. Or perhaps each product division takes on worldwide responsibility for its own products. Since most companies prefer that their divisions be of a similar size, it may be necessary to break up an international division, such as among areas, if it becomes too large relative to domestic divisions. For example, in the Nestlé case it would be hard to imagine a single international division handling over 95 percent of the sales.

Because of growth dynamics, companies seldom, if ever, have all their activities corresponding to the simplified structures we have described. Most, therefore, have certain elements of a mixed structure. A recent acquisition, for example, might report differently to headquarters until it can be consolidated efficiently within existing divisions. Or circumstances for a particular country, product, or function might necessitate its unique handling apart from the overall structure.

Coordinating Mechanisms

Rather than changing overall structure, many companies are finding mechanisms to pull product, function, and area together.

Because all of the organizational structures just described have advantages and disadvantages, companies in recent years have developed organizational mechanisms to pull together some of the diverse functional, geographic (including international), and product perspectives without abandoning their existing structures. These have included the strengthening of corporate staffs (groups of advisory personnel) so that people with line responsibilities (decision making authority) are required to listen to different viewpoints (whether they take advice or not); the use of more management rotation, such as between line and staff and domestic and international, in order to break down parochial views; the placement of international and domestic personnel in closer proximity to each other; and the establishment of liaisons among subsidiaries within the same country so that different product groups can get combined action on a given issue. Companies also use staff departments (e.g., legal or personnel) to centralize functions common to more than one subsidiary. At Heinz, for instance, one expatriate-transfer-and-compensation policy is used by all the geographic divisions, thus minimizing the duplication of effort.[14]

Hetarchies

Because of the increase in alliances among companies, much of the control must come from negotiation and persuasion rather than from authority of superiors over subordinates.

Companies have traditionally been organized in **hierarchies,** which are characterized by superior-subordinate relationships. However, many companies now depend heavily on alliances with other firms where it is not clear-cut that one company is the superior and the other the subordinate in the relationship. Therefore, the management of the alliances is among so-called equals, a situation known as a **hetarchy.**[15] Corning epitomizes this situation in that about half of its earnings come from alliances, especially joint ventures. There are formal linkages among the alliance partners; however, management at Corning's headquarters must serve as brokers, conflict negotiators, and facilitators rather than exerting direct authority over the alliances.[16]

Many Japanese companies are linked similarly in what is known as a **keiretsu,** whereby each company owns a small percentage of other companies in the group. For example, the Mitsubishi group consists of 28 core companies in which no single company predominates. The business activities are extremely diverse, ranging from mining to real estate and credit cards to tuna canning.[17] Typically within a keiretsu the core companies will buy and sell with each other only if and to the extent that the transactions make business sense. However, interlocking directorships and high levels of personal relationships among managers in core companies build common interests that do not depend on formal controls. The relationships encourage individual companies to undertake long-term and high-risk investments because other members of the keiretsu feel morally obligated to support a core company that has financial problems.

Locating International and Regional Headquarters

Locating headquarters staff in an "international" center
- Saves travel time
- Provides access to international services

Once a company develops substantial foreign operations, there may be advantages to shifting part of the headquarters staff to a new location.[18] One reason is to minimize communications and travel expense and time between the staff group and the foreign operations. Another is to be near specialized private and public institutions such as banks, factoring firms, insurance groups, public accountants, freight forwarders, customs brokers, and consular offices, which handle certain international functions. Finally, firms need to hire bilingual or multilingual personnel as well as export documentation people. The international transportation, institutions, and specialized personnel are concentrated in a few locales. For this reason, New York is by far the most popular international headquarters location for U.S. companies that maintain corporate headquarters elsewhere. If foreign operations are sufficient, staff may be segmented on a regional basis. Many U.S. firms maintain Latin American regional offices in the Miami area, and many have a European headquarters somewhere in Europe.

As transportation and communications have become faster and cheaper, some of the advantages of locating an international group apart from headquarters have lessened. This, when coupled with moves to seek greater integration of international and domestic operations, has meant that more of the international operations are being relocated near the corporate headquarters.

PLANNING

Firms must mesh objectives with internal and external constraints and set means to implement, monitor, and correct.

Throughout this text we have emphasized the firm's need to adapt its unique resources and objectives to the different and changing foreign situations. This is the essence of **planning.** Without planning, it is only by luck that a company picks the best order and method of expansion by country. Without planning, it is again by chance that a company sets policies and practices in a given locale that result in the desired performance. Since planning has been both implicitly and explicitly discussed already, this section presents merely an overview of the process.

The Planning Loop

Figure 17.2 indicates that planning must involve the meshing of objectives with the internal and external environment. The details in each planning section include items discussed in the environmental and operational sections of this text. Note that the first step (A) is the development of a long-term strategic intent, an objective that will hold the organization together over a long period of time while building an ever-increasing global competitive viability.[19] Although few firms start with such a vision, most develop them en route to significant international positions. Some, such as Honda and Canon, developed such intents long before it seemed they would ever have the capabilities to become important competitors. The next step (B) is a self-analysis of internal resources and constraints on the total corporation along with the environmental factors that affect each company differently. Only by taking this second step can a firm set the overall rationale for its international activities (step C). For instance, a company faced with rising domestic costs and expanded competition from imports may validly pursue one of several objectives, such as cost reduction, acquisition of resources the competition needs, or diversification into new markets or products. The analysis of the internal resources will help to determine which of these objectives is feasible and most important within a foreseeable planning period and will aid in selecting alternatives.

Since each country in which the firm is operating or contemplating operations also is unique, the local analysis (step D) also will have to be made before the final alternatives (step E) can be examined fully. For instance, local marketing factors will determine which product strategies can be considered. Priorities must be set among alternatives so that programs may be easily added or deleted to implement means of attaining target results (step F) as resource availability or situations change. A company may, for example, pre-

Figure 17.2
International Planning Process
The figure shows the setting of a firm's long-term strategic intent, followed in the loop by short- and medium-term steps necessary to achieve the intent.

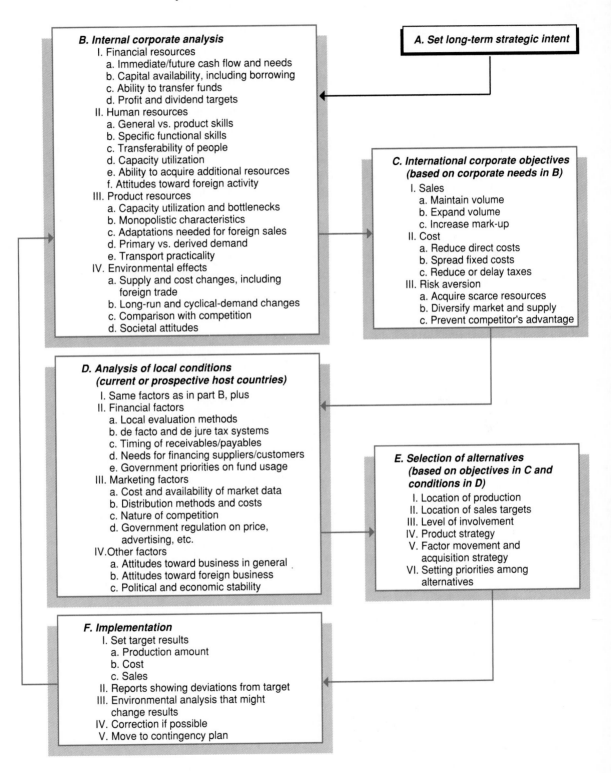

B. Internal corporate analysis
  I. Financial resources
    a. Immediate/future cash flow and needs
    b. Capital availability, including borrowing
    c. Ability to transfer funds
    d. Profit and dividend targets
  II. Human resources
    a. General vs. product skills
    b. Specific functional skills
    c. Transferability of people
    d. Capacity utilization
    e. Ability to acquire additional resources
    f. Attitudes toward foreign activity
  III. Product resources
    a. Capacity utilization and bottlenecks
    b. Monopolistic characteristics
    c. Adaptations needed for foreign sales
    d. Primary vs. derived demand
    e. Transport practicality
  IV. Environmental effects
    a. Supply and cost changes, including
      foreign trade
    b. Long-run and cyclical-demand changes
    c. Comparison with competition
    d. Societal attitudes

A. Set long-term strategic intent

C. International corporate objectives
(based on corporate needs in B)
  I. Sales
    a. Maintain volume
    b. Expand volume
    c. Increase mark-up
  II. Cost
    a. Reduce direct costs
    b. Spread fixed costs
    c. Reduce or delay taxes
  III. Risk aversion
    a. Acquire scarce resources
    b. Diversify market and supply
    c. Prevent competitor's advantage

D. Analysis of local conditions
(current or prospective host countries)
  I. Same factors as in part B, plus
  II. Financial factors
    a. Local evaluation methods
    b. de facto and de jure tax systems
    c. Timing of receivables/payables
    d. Needs for financing suppliers/customers
    e. Government priorities on fund usage
  III. Marketing factors
    a. Cost and availability of market data
    b. Distribution methods and costs
    c. Nature of competition
    d. Government regulation on price,
      advertising, etc.
  IV. Other factors
    a. Attitudes toward business in general
    b. Attitudes toward foreign business
    c. Political and economic stability

E. Selection of alternatives
(based on objectives in C and
conditions in D)
  I. Location of production
  II. Location of sales targets
  III. Level of involvement
  IV. Product strategy
  V. Factor movement and
    acquisition strategy
  VI. Setting priorities among
    alternatives

F. Implementation
  I. Set target results
    a. Production amount
    b. Cost
    c. Sales
  II. Reports showing deviations from target
  III. Environmental analysis that might
    change results
  IV. Correction if possible
  V. Move to contingency plan

fer and plan to remit dividends from one of its foreign subsidiaries back to the parent; however, this may not be possible. Management also should consider what it will do with earnings if exchange controls are put into effect. Furthermore, what alternatives will then exist for the parent, which has to do without the funds? It may be necessary to borrow more at home, remit more from other subsidiaries, forgo domestic expansion, or forgo domestic dividends. Without priorities, the firm may have to make hurried decisions to fulfill company objectives even partially.

Finally, very specific objectives should be set for each operating unit, along with ways of measuring both deviations from the plan and conditions that may cause a digression. Through timely evaluation, management may take corrective actions or at least move to contingency means to achieve the objectives. Note that there must be a constant loop from step F to step B to ensure that the company is making decisions based on currently relevant situations. Evaluation methods are discussed later in the chapter.

A distinction must be made between operating plans and strategic plans. Strategic plans are longer term and akin to step A, the strategic intent. They involve major commitments, such as the businesses the company will be in and where, and are less subject to reevaluation. Operating plans involve short-term objectives and means to carry them out. The relevant time horizon for operating plans is not clear-cut. For example, the chairman of Unilever pointed out the short-term needs for Unilever's consumer products (3 to 5 years) as compared with much longer needs for a project, such as the Anglo-French Channel Tunnel.[20] Although input for a strategic plan may come from all parts of the organization, only at the corporate level can allocations be made to implement overall planned changes in geographic and product policies. Also, it is usual for members of the corporate staff to be the primary people concerned with making strategic plans, since they have information on the firm's worldwide activities, competition, and trends.

Uncertainties and Planning

The firm's international operations have more complexity and uncertainty than the domestic ones.

The greater the amount of uncertainty, the more difficult it is to plan. It is generally agreed that operations in the international sphere involve more uncertainty than those in the domestic one because of the greater complexity of international operations. One type of complexity is caused by the increase in the number of operating environments (e.g., having to evaluate many subsidiaries); another is due to different requirements for different markets in terms of task, because of different products and how they are made within each of the subsidiaries.[21]

Generally, we would expect that greater complexity and uncertainty would lead to greater need and use for information. However, there is substantial evidence that the higher the uncertainty, the lower the amount of environmental scanning to collect information.[22] This may be because of the relative inaccessibility of accurate information internationally.

_____ **BUSINESS RESEARCH** ▆▆▆▆▆▆▆▆▆▆▆▆▆▆▆▆▆

Information is needed at all levels of control.

Business research is undertaken to reduce uncertainties in the decision process, to expand or narrow the alternatives under consideration, and to assess the merits of existing programs. The reduction of uncertainty would include attempts to answer such questions as: Is there a market for the product? Can qualified personnel be hired? Will the economic and political climate allow for a reasonable certainty of operations? Alternatives may be expanding by asking, Where are possible new sources of funds or sales? or narrowed by ascertaining, Where among the alternatives would operating costs be lowest? Evaluation and control are improved by assessing present and past performance: Is the distributor servicing sufficient accounts? What is our market share? Clearly, there is a myriad of details that, if ascertained, would be useful in meeting the firm's objectives.

How Much Research?

Companies should compare cost of information versus value.

A company can seldom if ever gain all of the information its managers would like. This is due partially to time constraints, since markets or raw materials may need to be secured before competitors gain control of them. Furthermore, contracts that call for bids or proposals usually have deadlines. The cost of information is another factor. The greater area to be considered by a multinational company, of course, compounds the number of alternatives and complexities. Therefore, it is useful to limit extensive information gathering to those projects that seemingly have the highest potential. One method is to estimate the costs of data collection along with the probable payoff from the data in terms of revenue gains or cost savings. In this way a company may prioritize research projects on the basis of expected return from the costs of the collection.

Problems in Data

The lack, obsolescence, and inaccuracy of data on many countries make much research difficult and expensive to undertake. In some countries, such as the United States, the government collects very detailed demographic and purchasing data, which are available very cheaply to any firm or individual. (But in the United States, some economists estimate that GNP figures may be understated by as much as 15 percent, and the 1990 census has been challenged by city and state officials who claim their populations have been undercounted.)[23] Using samples based on available information, a firm can draw fairly accurate inferences concerning market-segment sizes and locations, at least within broad categories. Also in the United States, the fact that so many firms are publicly owned and are frequently required to disclose considerable operating information is an advantage in learning competitors' strengths and weaknesses. Furthermore, firms may rely on a multitude of behavioral studies dealing with U.S. consumer preferences and experience. With this available information a firm can devise questionnaires or test-market with a selected sample so that responses should reflect the behavior of the larger target group to whom the company plans to sell. Contrast this situation to that in a country whose basic census, national income accounts, and foreign trade figures are suspect and where no data are collected on consumer expenditures. In such countries, business is conducted in a veil of secrecy, consumer buying behavior is speculated upon, and middlemen are reluctant to answer questions. Here, expensive primary research may be required before meaningful samples and questions can be developed. (Reasons for some of the problems in international data are discussed in the Appendix at the end of this chapter.)

External Sources of Information

Specificity and cost of information vary by source.

The number of organizations as well as publications that deal in whole or in part with information on international business is too large to explore in depth here. But in general the main sources are firms that make a living from supplying information, firms that would like to supply services connected with the conduct of international business, governmental agencies, and international organizations.

Individualized Reports   In almost any country there are market-research and business consulting firms that will conduct studies for a fee. Naturally, the quality and cost of these studies vary widely. Generally, this is the most costly information source because the individualized nature of the study restricts proration among a number of firms. However, the fact that the client can specify the information wanted often makes the expense worthwhile.

Specialized Studies   Some research organizations prepare fairly specific studies and then sell them to any interested firm at a cost much lower than for individualized studies. The studies sometimes are printed as directories of firms operating in a given locale, perhaps with financial or other information about the firms. Or they may also be about business in certain locales of the world, such as Brazil; forms of business, such as licensing; or specific products, such as baby food. They may combine any of these elements as well: For example, a title could well be "The Market for Imported Auto Parts in Germany."

Service Firms   Most firms that serve international clients, such as banks, transportation agencies, and accounting firms, publish reports that are available to potential clients. These reports usually are geared toward either the conduct of business in a given area or some specific subject of general interest, such as tax or trademark legislation. Since these are intended to reach a wide market of firms, they usually lack the specificity a firm would like for making a final decision, but much of the data give useful background information.

Some of these organizations also are helpful in giving informal opinions about such things as the reputation of possible business associates and the names of people to contact. Management also may discern useful information from other companies operating in a given locale.

Governmental Agencies   Governments are another source of information. Statistical reports on many topics vary in the quantity and quality from country to country. When a government or governmental agency has an interest in stimulating foreign business activity, the amount and type of information may be substantial. For example, the U.S. Department of Commerce not only compiles such basic data as news and regulations on individual countries, but also will help set up appointments with businesspeople in foreign countries.

International Organizations and Agencies   Numerous organizations and agencies are supported by more than one country, such as the United Nations, the International Monetary Fund, the Organization for Economic Cooperation and Development, and the European Community. All of these organizations have large research staffs that compile basic statistics as well as reports and recommendations concerning common trends and problems. Many of the international development banks will even help finance investment-feasibility studies.

Trade Associations   Many product lines have trade associations that collect, evaluate, and disseminate a wide variety of data dealing with technical and competitive factors in the industry. Much of this information is available in their trade journals, whereas other data may or may not be made available to nonmembers.

Information Service Companies   A number of companies have information-retrieval services that typically maintain data bases from hundreds of different sources, including many of those just described. For a fee, or sometimes free at public libraries, a firm can access these computerized data and arrange for an immediate printout of studies of interest.

Internal Generation

International firms themselves may have to conduct many studies abroad. Sometimes the research may consist of no more than observing keenly and asking many questions. Investigators can see what kind of merchandise is available, who is buying and where, and uncover the hidden distribution points and competition. In some countries, for example, the competition for ready-made clothes may be from seamstresses in private homes rather than from retailers. The competition for vacuum cleaners may be in the form of servants who clean with mops rather than from other electrical-appliance manufacturers. Surreptitiously sold contraband may compete with locally produced goods. Traditional analysis would not reveal such matters. In many countries, even bankers have to rely more on clients' reputations than on their financial statements. Shrewd questioning may yield very interesting results.

Firms frequently set certain minimum criteria on which to base a decision. If a company regards a total market of 35 million as satisfactory, it is fruitless to spend the time and money on determining where within a range of 90 to 100 million the market actually lies.

Often a firm must be extremely imaginative, extremely observant, or both. A soft-drink manufacturer wanted to determine the market share it held vis-à-vis its competitors in Mexico. Attempts to make estimates from the points of distribution as management would do at home were futile because of the extremely widespread distribution. The manufacturer hit upon two alternatives, both of which turned out to be feasible: The manufacturer of bottle caps was willing to reveal how many caps were sold to each client, and customs supplied data on the volume of imports of soft-drink concentrate used by each of the competitors.

CORPORATE CULTURE

People trained at head-quarters are more likely to think like headquarters personnel.

Any corporation has certain common values its employees share. These constitute the **corporate culture** and form a control mechanism that is implicit and that helps enforce the explicit bureaucratic control mechanisms that the firm has in place.[24] International firms have more difficulty relying on the corporate culture for control because managers from different countries may have different norms pertaining to the management of operations and little or no exposure to the values and attitudes prevalent at corporate headquarters. Nevertheless, many firms seek to promote a worldwide corporate culture by bringing managers from different countries into closer contact with each other. Frequent transfers of managers among foreign operations develops increased knowledge of and commitment to a common set of values and objectives so that fewer procedures, less hierarchical communication, and less surveillance are needed.[25] For example, the 3M Company not only brought managers together from different countries for training, it also developed training teams from different countries so that there would be a hybrid of national viewpoints. Iveco, Europe's second-largest truck manufacturer formed through a merger of Italian, French, and German companies, has concluded that a common culture cannot easily be developed with older, entrenched managers. The company is trying to combine the best from the three countries over time by hiring graduates from throughout Europe and moving them to all three countries before assignment to corporate headquarters.[26]

The degree of control imposed by corporate headquarters on the selection of top managers for foreign subsidiaries may dictate to a great extent how much formal control over the subsidiaries' operations the corporate personnel feel is necessary. The use of parent-country nationals in the subsidiary management, or even determining the standards of selection and training, may be perceived as a means of assuring primary loyalty to the corporate rather than the subsidiary culture.[27] This may be effective even if the operations are only partially owned or when the parent requires long-range planning from the subsidiaries.[28]

REPORTS

Need for Reports

Reports must be timely in order to allow firms to respond to them.

Headquarters needs timely reports from all operating units of an international firm so that management can allocate resources properly, correct plans, and reward personnel. First, the decisions on the use of capital, personnel, and technology are almost continuous; consequently, reports must be frequent and must show recent situations so that these resources are put to best use. Second, plans need to be updated in order to be realistic and to assure that there is a high probability of meeting desired objectives. Feedback on both results and conditions that might affect results are essential so that corrective action, whether in the form of new strategies to meet objectives or in the form of altered objectives, may be undertaken. Finally, reports are needed in order to evaluate the performance of personnel in the various operating units of the company. Not only will comparison of performance aid in determining who will receive the rewards of monetary compensation and advancement, but it also will help stimulate personnel to improve their own areas of weakness.

The use of written reports is more important in an international than in a domestic setting because subsidiary managers have much less personal and oral contact with line and staff personnel above them. Thus corporate managers miss out on much of the informal communication that can tell them about the performance of the foreign operations.

Types of Systems

Reporting systems are intended first to evaluate operating units and second to evaluate management in units.

Most international firms use reporting systems for foreign operations that are similar to those they use domestically.[29] There are several reasons for this. If the systems have been effective domestically, management often believes that they will be effective internationally as well—particularly if home-country management considers its know-how superior to that of its subsidiaries abroad. Next, there are economies through carrying over the same types of reports—the need to establish new types of reporting mechanisms is eliminated, and corporate management is already familiar with the system. Finally, like reports presumably allow management to compare one operation against another and consolidate the reports without as much fear that they have added "apples to oranges."

The main purpose of MNEs' reporting systems is to assure adequate profitability by identifying deviations from plans that would indicate possible problem areas. This focus may be on short-term performance or on longer-term indicators that match the strategic thrust of the organization. The emphasis is on the evaluation of the subsidiary rather than the evaluation of the subsidiary manager, although the profitability of the foreign unit is one of the important ingredients in the managerial evaluation.[30]

Not all information exchange is by formalized reports. Within many MNEs, certain members of the corporate staff travel much of their time in order to visit with subsidiaries. Although this may do much to alleviate misunderstandings, there are some inherent dangers if visits are not done properly. If, on one hand, corporate personnel visit the tropical subsidiaries only when there are blizzards at home, the personnel abroad may perceive the trips as mere boondoggles. If, on the other hand, subsidiary managers offer too many social activities and not enough analysis of operations, the corporate staff members may consider the trips a waste of time. Also, if visitors come only when the corporate level is upset about foreign operations, the overseas managers may always be overly defensive.

Reporting Problems

Firms should evaluate managers on things they can control, but there is disagreement concerning what is in their control.

Management Versus Subsidiary Performance   There is general agreement that subsidiaries should be evaluated separately from the management within subsidiaries. This is so that managers are not penalized for conditions and occurrences outside their control. Beyond this agreement, however, there is a good deal of difference among firms in what they do and do not include in the managerial performance evaluation. For instance, some firms hold managers abroad responsible for gains or losses in currency translation whereas others do not. Most firms deduct interest expenses before measuring the profitability of foreign operations whereas many do not.[31] These are examples of environmental factors that some, but not all, companies consider to be outside the control of the local managers.

Another area of noncontrollables is when centralized decisions are made that will optimize the performance of the total corporation. A particular subsidiary may not do as well as if it had been left to operate independently. In fact, the normal profit center records may well obscure the importance that the subsidiary plays within the total corporate entity.

It is hard to compare countries through standard operating ratios.

Cost and Accounting Comparability   Different affiliate cost structures may prevent a meaningful comparison of operating results. For example, the percentage of direct labor to sales in one country may reasonably be much higher than in a subsidiary in another country if the former has low labor and high capital costs in relation to the latter. Different accounting practices can also create problems. Most international firms keep one set of books that are consistent with parent principles and another set to meet local reporting requirements.

Country Risk   When evaluating foreign investment possibilities, most companies set a higher minimum return to invest in high-risk countries. Having done this, firms logically would expect the performance within the high-risk countries to reflect the expected higher return. Most companies agree that such an analysis would be useful; however, they also agree that they know of no reasonable means of incorporating country risk into the performance evaluation. They feel that the incorporation would penalize managers in risky countries and make them responsible for something outside their control.[32]

Firms want higher return in high-risk countries but risks may be outside management's control.

Evaluative Measurements

A system that relies on a combination of measurements is more reliable.

Multiple Measurements   Every evaluation measurement has shortcomings when applied internationally. Consequently, a system that relies on a number of different indicators may be preferable to one that relies too heavily on one measurement. Financial criteria tend to dominate the evaluation of foreign operations and their managers. Although many different criteria are used, the most important ones for evaluating the operations are budget compared with profit, budget compared with sales, and return on investment. The most common financial criteria for management appraisal are budget compared to profit, budget compared to sales, and return on sales. Many nonfinancial criteria also are employed. The only one commonly given much weight in subsidiary evaluation is market-share increase. Several nonfinancial criteria are important for evaluating the managers, though. These include market-share increase, quality control, and relationship with the host government.[33]

Firms must evaluate results in relation to budgets.

Budget Concept   One way of overcoming the problems of evaluating performance is by looking at the budget, which can help the MNE differentiate between the worth of the subsidiary and the performance of subsidiary management. The budget should include the goals for each subsidiary that will help the MNE achieve an overall objective. As long as the subsidiary manager is working toward a budgeted goal rather than a measure such as return on investment, there will be fewer problems in dealing with inflation, exchange-rate changes, and transfer prices.

Planning Information Acquisitions

Management should reevaluate information needs periodically to keep costs down and should assure that information is being used.

Thus far the discussion has centered on information needed to evaluate subsidiary and subsidiary management performance. Although this information is crucial, corporate management requires additional data. The information needs may be categorized as follows:

1. information generated for centralized coordination, such as subsidiary cash balances and needs;

2. information relating to external conditions, such as analyses of local political and economic conditions;

3. information for feedback from parent to local subsidiaries, such as R&D
   breakthroughs;

4. lateral information between related subsidiaries; and

5. external reporting needs.[34]

Since information needs are so broad, two problems for firms are (1) the cost of information relative to its value and (2) "information glut," which refers to redundancy. One technique used by some firms is Planned Information Acquisition Analysis (PIAA), which involves a periodic reevaluation of each new document or service the firm uses.[35] By comparing the number of times sources have been retrieved and found relevant, the firm may limit acquisition to those items most valuable to the firm.

Local needs and differences in data processing create problems of compatibility.

Compatibility   Another problem is the compatibility of information needed by the subsidiary and by corporate management. Even when different subsidiaries are trying to solve similar problems, their information needs may differ vastly. Consequently, corporate management may be faced with the dilemma of comparing unlike data or requiring different or additional data, which may be expensive. An approach that has been instituted by some firms is to allow diversity but to send copies and analyses to centralized data banks. For many corporate needs, standardization is not necessary, but standardization of coding is so that centralized personnel may compare the performance of subsidiary projects and suggest more refined models for local use.

Aside from the problem of data or coding uniformity, a major obstacle to the on-time retrieval of comparable information is the diversity from country to country in a company's approach to data processing, especially in terms of equipment and software packages. Uniformity of approach is hampered by substantial cost differences in personnel, hardware, and data communications.[36]

Information centers may permit a choice between centralization or decentralization.

Information Centers   With the expansion of multinational telecommunications and computer linkages, managers throughout the world now can share information almost instantaneously. On the one hand, this may permit more centralization, since truly global implications of policies may be examined. On the other hand, managers in foreign locations may become more autonomous because of the greater amount of information at their disposal.

Many countries are restricting data flows
● *To preserve personal privacy*
● *To provide economic protection*

Restrictions on Data Flows   Many countries have passed or are considering legislation that directly or indirectly affects the flow of data internationally. These laws have been enacted for three primary reasons. First, there is concern about individual privacy, particularly that the development and transmission of personnel data might give the company an undue advantage over

● Because of strategic implications

the individual. The second concern is economic; for example, local jobs will be lost if data processing and analysis are done abroad, and resource transmission will occur without payment to the country that created the resource. The third concern is that corporate networks may be used to pirate military and commercial data to be sent abroad.[37] Although most MNEs consider data flow restrictions to be more of a potential than a present problem, certain regulations already create barriers for them.[38] Such restrictions make it more difficult for the international company to maintain centralized personnel records, which assist in making international transfers. For example, Burroughs was unable to transfer its personnel records from Germany to other locations. Some legislation requires local purchases (such as for data-processing equipment, materials, or services), and other that the local subsidiary maintain copies of and monitor anything transmitted. Companies are concerned about additional costs and the possibility that proprietary information may fall into the hands of competitors.

CONTROL IN SPECIAL SITUATIONS

Acquisitions

An acquired firm is usually not a complete fit with the existing organization.

As was noted in the Nestlé case, a policy of expansion through acquisition may create some specific control problems. In the Nestlé situation, some of the U.S. acquisitions resulted in overlapping geographic responsibilities as well as new lines of business with which corporate management had no experience. Another type of problem is that the existing management in the acquired firm is probably accustomed to a great deal of autonomy. Attempts to centralize certain decision-making procedures or to change operating methods may result in distrust, apprehension, and reluctance to change. This is especially true when a firm acquires another firm in a foreign country. Resistance may come not only from the personnel, but also from governmental authorities. Authorities may use a variety of discretionary means to ensure that decision making remains vested within the country.

Moving from National to Global Strategies

It is difficult to remove control from local operations when their managers are accustomed to a great deal of autonomy. This is a particular problem for companies that attempt to move from a country-to-country to a global strategy. Within Europe, for example, many U.S. firms owned very independent operations for decades in the United Kingdom, France, and the former West Germany. These firms have often faced difficult obstacles to the integration of these operations because the country managers perceive personal and operating disadvantages through such moves.

Branch Versus Subsidiary

There are tax and liability implications for branches versus subsidiaries.

When establishing a foreign operation, management may often have to decide between making that operation a branch or a subsidiary. A foreign **branch** is legally not a separate entity from the parent; therefore, branch operations are possible only if the parent owns 100 percent. A **subsidiary,** on the other hand, is legally a separate company, even though the parent may own all of the voting stock. Because of the legal separateness of the subsidiary, it is generally concluded that liability is limited to the assets of that subsidiary. Creditors or winners of legal suits therefore may not have access to other resources owned by the parent. This limited-liability concept is a major factor in the choice of the subsidiary form, since otherwise claims against a firm for its actions in one country may be settled by courts in another. There is some evidence that the subsidiary concept will not suffice in future liability disputes. Union Carbide has had to settle with the government of India over damages in the Bhopal accident for $470 million, an amount far in excess of Union Carbide's 50.9 percent investment value in the Indian joint venture.[39]

Because subsidiaries are separate companies, a question arises concerning the nature of the decisions the parent may be allowed to dictate. Generally, this does not present a problem; however, U.S. courts ruled that Timken was in effect conspiring with another company to prevent competition when Timken dictated which markets its Canadian subsidiary could serve. Another factor related to control is public disclosure: Generally, the greater the control vested by the owners, the greater the secrecy that can be maintained. In this respect, branches are usually subject to less public disclosure because they are not covered by tight local corporate restrictions.

From these examples it should be clear that there are conflicting control advantages to either the branch or the subsidiary form that should be considered when choosing the legal form of foreign operations. In addition, each form has different tax advantages and implications. Furthermore, each may have different initiation and operating costs as well as abilities to raise capital.

Comparison of Legal Forms

Each legal form has different operating restrictions.

A firm establishing a subsidiary in a foreign country usually has a number of alternative legal forms from which to choose. The variety of these forms is too numerous to list in detail; however, some distinctions warrant mentioning. In addition to differences in liability, forms vary in terms of ability to transfer ownership, the number of stockholders required, the percentage of foreigners who can serve on the board of directors, the amount of required public disclosure, whether equity may be acquired by noncapital contributions, the types of businesses (products) eligible, and minimum capital required. Before making a decision an international firm should analyze all of these differences in terms of its corporate objectives. The nomenclature "Inc." in the United States is roughly equivalent to "S.A." in most Romance language countries, "A.G." in Germany and Switzerland, "KK" in Japan, "AB" in Sweden, and "NV" in the Netherlands. The term "PLC" is used in the United Kingdom when companies list their securities, but "Ltd." may be used for privately held companies. There are, however, subtle differences from country to country.

Minority Control

Minority control is usually harder, but there are mechanisms that can work.

As we have already discussed, a greater share of equity usually gives a firm a better chance of controlling an operation; however, it is not always possible to gain more than 50 percent of the ownership in a foreign enterprise. Aside from the dispersion of stock not held by the foreign investor, there are several other means of gaining control with only a minority interest. One is to maintain control over some asset needed by the operation abroad, such as patents, brand name, or raw materials. This in fact is a motive for setting separate licensing, franchising, or management contract agreements with the foreign subsidiary.

Another means to gain control is to set up administrative devices. One such device is to separate equity into voting and nonvoting stock so that the minority foreign investor has a majority of the voting stock. Another is to make a side agreement with a majority holder for an operating committee in which the minority foreign investor has majority representation.

Nonequity Forms

As form of operations evolves so must structure.

The use of multiple operating forms (e.g., export, license, joint venture) and the move from one to another may create the need to change areas of responsibility in the organization. Or it may mean that departments in the organization are not equally involved with all forms. For example, the legal department may have little day-to-day responsibility with exports but a great deal with licensing to the same foreign market. Organizational mechanisms, such as the planned sharing of information or joint committees, are useful to ensure that the activities complement each other. Also it is useful for the firm to plan organizational change to minimize obstacles when responsibilities shift from one group to another.

A further consideration is the importance of the nonequity operation to the firm's overall operations. For example, if a firm contracts only one supplier for an essential component, the contract will likely be controlled more closely and from higher in the organization than contracts of less strategic dependence.

LOOKING TO THE FUTURE As overseas sales and profits as a percentage of sales and profits become more important, there will likely be a decline in the autonomous power of subsidiary managers. Their power base will likely erode as greater centralized control of product, marketing, and financial planning is necessary to bring about needed synergy among firms' operating units world-wide. This centralizing tendency, within the framework of strong, capable local management, assumes (1) that trade barriers continue to decline; (2) that it becomes economically feasible, to an ever greater degree, to organize the exchange of products, components, and factors of production on a coun-try-by-country basis; and (3) that companies will increasingly need to re-spond to global competitors and more-homogeneous consumer wants.

Although control within MNEs will continue to be problematic, a grow-ing challenge will be the control of relationships with other companies as MNEs develop more alliances for which most traditional control mechanisms are not applicable.

On the one hand, centralized control may become easier because of the faster access to information from abroad. On the other hand, this may be somewhat negated by companies' limited abilities to process increased infor-mation, particularly with increases in their geographic spread of activities, their product diversity, and their competitive rivalries.

SUMMARY

■ Control is more difficult internationally because of (1) the geographic and cultural distance separating countries, (2) the need for diversity among lo-cales in methods of operating, (3) the larger amount of uncontrollables abroad, and (4) the higher uncertainty due to data problems and rapid change.

■ Whether decisions are made at the subsidiary level or by managers above the subsidiary should depend on the relative competence of individuals at the two levels, the cost of decision making at each level, and the effects the de-cisions will have on total corporate performance.

■ Even though worldwide uniformity of policies and other centralized decisions may not be best for an individual operation, the overall company gain may be more than enough to overcome the individual country losses. When top management prevents subsidiary managers from doing their best job, how-ever, they should consider the consequences for employee morale.

■ Many critics within LDCs have argued that centralization of key decision making within MNEs continues the dependency that they had in colonial periods, and they are pressuring for increased control at their level.

■ As a firm develops international business activities, the corporate structure must encompass a means for foreign operations to report. The more impor-tant the foreign operations, the higher up in the hierarchy they should report.

■ Whether a company separates or integrates the international activities, there is usually a need to develop some means by which (1) to prevent costly du-plication and (2) to ensure that domestic managers do not withhold the best resources from the international operations.

■ International or regional headquarters may be located away from corporate headquarters in order to save transport costs and gain access to specialized international talents.

■ Good planning should include environmental analysis, strategies, and contingency strategies with inputs from both top-level and subsidiary managers.

■ The amount, accuracy, and timeliness of published data vary substantially from one country to another. A researcher should be particularly aware of varied definitions, collection methods, base years for reports, and misleading responses.

■ Sources of published data on international business include consulting firms, governmental agencies, supranational agencies, and organizations that serve international business accounts. The cost and specificity of these publications vary widely.

■ The corporate culture constitutes an implicit control mechanism. Although it is more difficult in international companies because norms of values differ among countries, bringing managers together enhances the common culture.

■ Timely reports are essential for control so that resources can be allocated properly, plans can be corrected, and personnel can be evaluated and rewarded.

■ International reporting systems are similar to those used domestically because home-country management is familiar with them and because uniformity makes it easier to compare different operations.

■ The evaluation of subsidiaries and their managers are separate processes; however, some of the same inputs, including financial and nonfinancial criteria, may be used for both.

■ Two of the growing difficulties in getting timely and comparable reports from foreign operating units are the incompatibility of data-processing systems among countries and the restrictions placed on the cross-national flow of data.

■ Some situations that raise special control problems include acquired operations, operations with historical autonomy, the legal status of foreign operations, the legal organization form allowed in the specific country, and operations with shared ownership and nonequity arrangements.

C A S E
WESTINGHOUSE[40]

In 1980, during a major organizational change at Westinghouse, the company's vice chairman, Douglas Danforth, announced that he wanted the company's sales from abroad, which were then 27 percent, to be increased to 35 percent by 1984. Seventeen countries were identified as having the highest potential, and they were given emphasis in implementing this target. In light of past international growth, the 35 percent figure seemed reachable. However, Westinghouse's dependence on foreign sales declined during the 1980s, and by 1989 they were only 18 percent. To understand the relationship between Westinghouse's international goals and its organization of international operations, it is useful to look back at some significant changes over the past two and a half decades.

In 1969 Westinghouse's top management noted with concern that its chief rival, GE, gained 25 percent of its sales abroad, compared to only 8 percent by Westinghouse. Top management was determined to compete more vigorously against GE in foreign markets. At that time, Westinghouse had a separate operation, Westinghouse Electric International Company, located in New York, away from corporate headquarters in Pittsburgh. Between 1969 and 1971 overseas volume increased to 15 percent of sales, and the chairman, Donald C. Burnham, said, "I've set a goal that 30 percent of our business will be outside the United States. I hope to get there and then set a bigger goal." The spurt in foreign sales was largely the result of the aggressive pursuit of overseas acquisitions. This marked a substantial change in foreign operating practice, inasmuch as Westinghouse had depended almost entirely on exports and licensing agreements for its foreign sales since World War I, when its three European subsidiaries were confiscated.

From 1969 to 1971 the International Company operated alongside four other Westinghouse divisions. These were operated as companies that were each in charge of a group of diverse products. A major complaint of the International Company was that the four other companies tended to view foreign operations as merely an appendage to which they were unwilling to give sufficient technical or even product assistance. Since the International Company had to depend on the product groups for anything that it was going to export, there were problems gaining continued assurance of supplies. The product companies were willing to divert output abroad when they had surplus production but were reluctant to do so when there were shortages, largely because the International Company, not the product company, got credit for the sales and profits. Likewise, the product groups were reluctant to lend their best personnel to the International Company to assist in exportation of highly technical orders or to lend support to production from foreign licensing and subsidiaries.

Partially resulting from these complaints, Westinghouse eliminated its international division in 1971. The four product-based companies were then put in charge of worldwide control of production and sale of their goods. (Westinghouse produces more than 8000 different products, including such diversities as real-estate finance, nuclear fuel, television production, electronics systems, and soft-drink bottling.) The philosophy was that, because of their access to product technology, the people in those divisions would be better able to sell than was the disbanded company. Second, since they would now be evaluated on their foreign successes, they would be willing to divert resources to international development. Another factor that affected the decision to move from an international division to a worldwide product organization was that GE had made a similar move with apparent success a few years earlier.

When responsibilities were shifted to the domestic division, many of the managers from the formerly New York-based International Company did not conceal their belief that "those unsophisticated hicks back in Steeltown couldn't be trusted to find U.S. consulates abroad, let alone customers." Although management in each of the four product companies was free to pursue foreign business or not, each chose to do so, at least for some of their products. Between 1971 and 1976 foreign sales grew to 31 percent of the Westinghouse total. During this five-year period, product diversity continued to grow. Product emphasis was further accentuated in 1976, when the company was reorganized into 37 operating groups known as business units. Each unit was given a great deal of autonomy, including a free hand abroad.

From 1976 through 1978 foreign sales of Westinghouse fell to 24 percent of its total. The extension of responsibility by product units further complicated cooperation among units and created problems of duplication in foreign markets. For instance, a company salesperson called on a Saudi businessman who pulled out business cards from salespeople who had visited him from 24 other business units. His question was, "Who speaks for Westinghouse?" In another situation, different units had established subsidiaries in the same country. One had excess cash, whereas another was borrowing locally at an exorbitant rate. In many cases, large projects required the ultimate cooperation among business units to carry out different parts. At times, units could not agree in time to assemble a package and lost out to foreign competitors such as Brown, Boveri from Switzerland and Hitachi from Japan. In a case in Brazil, three different sales groups were calling on the same customer for the same job.

By 1978, Douglas Danforth was the vice chairman and chief operating officer of Westinghouse. He was highly interested in international expansion, not only because he expected greater sales and growth there, but also because he had previously worked in the Mexican and Canadian subsidiaries. In early 1979 he enlisted a Westinghouse executive to head an exhaustive study of the firm's international operations and to make a recommendation within 90 days. The study group interviewed Westinghouse personnel in the United States and abroad; it also determined how other firms were handling their international operations. The recommendation was to move gradually to a matrix system by 1983 with a head of international operations. The international operations then were to be organized along geographic lines including three regions. This plan was adopted. The number of international regions increased to five during the 1980s. To get a consensus among the people in charge of product and geographic areas was a major de-

parture from Westinghouse's product orientation. Danforth told the company's top 220 managers that "Some of you will adjust and survive, and some of you won't."

To carry out the planned growth, Westinghouse has had to mesh country unit plans with product unit plans. In other words, if a product unit wants switchgear in Brazil increased by 40 percent and the Brazilian country manager wants to increase it by 50 percent, they must either work out an agreement or defer the decision upward in the organization to the next higher product and geographic heads. Disagreements can effectively go as high as the top-level operating committee, which consists of the chairman, vice chairman, three presidents of product groups, the top financial officer, and the president of the international group.

During the late 1980s two major changes took place at Westinghouse. First, the company continually divested itself of products and services, such as consumer products, that were not currently yielding a high return. This made Westinghouse one of the 1980s' leaders in earnings-per-share growth, but led some analysts to conclude that the company was dumping business from which global competitors could profit. For example, its elevator operation had never pushed hard internationally and was earning poorly in the mature North American market. After selling it to the Schindler Group from Switzerland, sales rose 50 percent in the first half of 1989.

The second big change was a growing dependence on alliances with non–U.S.-based firms. Two involved joint ventures with the Swedish-Swiss firm Asea Brown Boveri, one for steam turbines and generators and another for equipment for energy transmission and generation. These involved the sell-off to Asea Brown Boveri of 45 percent of the former 100 percent Westinghouse ownership in these businesses, which were a significant part of the total Westinghouse sales. Another involved a start-up venture with Siemens from Germany to produce automation products. Westinghouse and Siemens are also planning to create other joint ventures to produce industrial circuit breakers and control equipment. In another case, Westinghouse sold its small and medium motor businesses, which were noncompetitive with cheaper imports, and then formed a joint venture with a Taiwanese manufacturer to produce motors.

Questions

1. What have been the major organizational problems inhibiting the international growth of Westinghouse?

2. What organizational characteristics may affect the successful implementation of the matrix management at Westinghouse?

3. How can a firm such as Westinghouse go about implementing a goal to increase the percentage of its sales accounted for by foreign operations?

4. How does the increased reliance on alliances relate to the Westinghouse international strategy and structure?

5. Do you believe Westinghouse has a long-term strategic intent? If so, what is it, and what do you think it should be?

Chapter Notes

1. Data for the case were taken from "Nestlé Centralizing to Win a Bigger Payoff from the U.S.," *Business Week,* February 2, 1981, pp. 56–58; "Nestlé—At Home Abroad: An Interview with Pierre Liotard-Vogt," *Harvard Business Review,* November 1976, pp. 80–88; Robert Ball, "A Shopkeeper Shakes Up Nestlé," *Fortune,* Vol. 106, No. 13, December 27, 1982, pp. 103–106; Damon Darlin, "Nestlé Hopes to Bring Its Other U.S. Units Up to Level of Its Stouffer Corp. Subsidiary," *Wall Street Journal,* March 15, 1984, p. 33; "Nestlé to Close Libby Units," *New York Times,* September 26, 1985, p. D5; Graham Turner, "Inside Europe's Giant Companies: Nestlé Finds a Better Formula," *Long Range Planning,* Vol. 19, No. 3, June 1986, pp. 12–19; John Carson-Parker, "Cash-Rich Nestlé Has Global Sweet Tooth," *Chief Executive,* March–April 1989, pp.26–29; Mark Alpert and Aimety Dunlap Smith, "Nestlé Shows How to Gobble Markets," *Fortune,* Vol. 119, January 16, 1989, pp. 74–78; Daniel F. Cuff, "Head of Carnation Gets New U.S. Nestlé Post," *New York Times,* November 12, 1990, p. C4; and "Nestlé Annual Report 1989;" Zachary Schiller and Lois Therrien, "Nestlé's Crunch in the U.S." *Business Week,* December 24, 1990, pp. 24–25.

2. For a good discussion of the difficulty of observing foreign environmental changes and subsequent control of them, see William R. Fannin and Arvin F. Rodrigues, "National or Global?—Control vs. Flexibility," *Long Range Planning,* Vol. 19, No. 5, October 1986, pp. 84–88.

3. For a discussion of the distance factor, see Jacques Picard, "How European Companies Control Marketing Decisions Abroad," *Columbia Journal of World Business,* Summer 1977, pp. 113–121. Also Robert L. Drake and Lee M. Caudill, "Management of the Large Multinational: Trends and Future Challenges," *Business Horizons,* May–June 1981, p. 84, found that Canadian subsidiaries of U.S. firms did not have the same degree of autonomy as subsidiaries in other countries because of their closeness to corporate headquarters.

4. Donna G. Goehle, *Decision Making in Multinational Corporations* (Ann Arbor: University Research Press, 1980).

5. Christopher A. Bartlett and Sumantra Ghoshal, "Tap Your Subsidiaries for Global

Reach," *Harvard Business Review*, Vol. 64, No. 6, November–December 1986, pp. 87–94.

6. James Leontiades, "Going Global—Global Strategies vs. National Strategies," *Long Range Planning*, Vol. 19, No. 6, December 1986, pp. 98–100, discusses how national strategies may be more appropriate in given circumstances.

7. Yves Doz and C. K. Prahalad, "Controlled Variety: A Challenge for Human Resource Management in the MNC," *Human Resource Management*, Vol. 25, No. 1, Spring 1986, p. 57.

8. Among the many treatments of this subject are Osvaldo Sunkel,"Big Business and 'Dependencia': A Latin American View," *Foreign Affairs*, April 1972, pp. 517–531, Benjamin J. Cohen, *The Question of Imperialism—The Political Economy of Dominance and Dependence* (New York: Basic Books, 1973).

9. Robert D. Pearce, "Host Countries and the R&D of Multinationals: Issues and Evidence," Reading, England: University of Reading Discussion Papers in International Investment and Business Studies, No. 101, January 1987.

10. William A. Fischer and Jack N. Behrman, "The Coordination of Foreign R&D Activities by Transnational Corporations," *Journal of International Business Studies*, Winter 1979, pp. 28–35.

11. We wish to acknowledge Allen Morrison for supplying examples of firms he has found in his research that are using the different types of structures. See K. Roth, D. Schweiger, and A. J. Morrison, "Global Strategy Implementation at the Business Unit Level: Structural Mechanisms and Organization Global Capacity," *Journal of International Business Studies*, Forthcoming 1991.

12. W. G. Egelhoff, "Strategy and Structure in Multinational Corporations: An Information Processing Approach," *Administrative Science Quarterly*, Vol. 27, 1982, pp. 435–458; John D. Daniels, Robert A. Pitts, and Marietta J. Tretter, "Strategy and Structure of U.S. Multinationals: An Exploratory Study," *Academy of Management Journal*, Vol. 27, No. 2, June 1984, pp. 292–307.

13. C. K. Prahalad,"Strategic Choices in Diversified MNCs," *Harvard Business Review*, July–August 1976, pp.67–78, explores in depth the problems inherent to the locus of relative power.

14. C. A. Bartlett, "MNCs: Get off the Reorganization Merry-Go-Round," *Harvard Business Review*, Vol. 61, No. 2, 1983, pp. 138–146; Robert A. Pitts and John D. Daniels, "Aftermath of the Matrix Mania," *Columbia Journal of World Business*, Vol. 19, No. 2, Summer 1984, pp. 48–54.

15. Ian D. Turner, "Strategy and Organization," *Management Update: Supplement to the Journal of General Management*, Summer 1989, pp. 1–8; Gunnar Hedlund, "The Hypermodern MNC—A Hetarchy?" *Human Resource Management*, Spring 1986, pp. 9–35.

16. James R. Houghton, "A Chairman Reflects: The Age of the Hierarchy Is Over," *New York Times*, September 24, 1989, p. C2.

17. William J. Holstein, James Treece, Stan Crock, and Larry Armstrong, "Mighty Mitsubishi Is on the Move," *Business Week*, September 24, 1990, pp. 98–107.

18. For an extensive discussion of various approaches to regional groupings, see Daniel Van Den Bulcke and Marie-Anne Van Pachterbeke, *European Headquarters of American Multinational Enterprises in Brussels and Belgium* (Brussels: Institut Catholique des Hautes Études Commerciales), 1984; and John D. Daniels, "Approaches to European Regional Management by Large U.S. Multinational Firms," *Management International Review*, Vol. 2, 1986, pp. 27–42.

19. Gary Hamel and C. K. Prahalad, "Strategic Intent," *Harvard Business Review,* May–June 1989, pp. 63–76.

20. F. A. Maljers, "Strategic Planning and Intuition in Unilever," *Long Range Planning,* Vol. 23, No. 2, 1990, pp. 63–68.

21. B. Mascarenhas, "Coping with Uncertainty in International Business," *Journal of International Business Studies,* Fall 1982, pp. 87–98; Egelhoff, *loc. cit.*

22. M. J. Culnan, "Environmental Scanning: The Effects of Task Complexity and Source Accessibility on Information Gathering Behavior," *Decision Sciences,* No. 14, 1983, pp. 194–206; N. R. Boulton, W. M. Lindsay, S. G. Franklin, and L. W. Rue, "Strategic Planning: Determining the Impact of Environmental Characteristics and Uncertainty," *Academy of Management Journal,* Vol. 25, No. 3, 1982, pp. 500–509.

23. "The Underground Economy's Hidden Force," *Business Week,* April 5, 1982, pp. 66–67.

24. See B. R. Balliga and A. M. Jeager, "Multinational Corporations: Control Systems and Delegation Issues," *Journal of International Business Studies,* Vol. 15, No. 2, Summer 1984, pp. 25–40; and Vladimir Pucik and Jan Hack Katz, "Information Control, and Human Resource Management in Multinational Firms," *Human Resource Management,* Vol. 25, No. 1, Spring 1986, pp. 121–132.

25. Anders Edström and Jay R. Galbraith, "Transfer of Managers as Coordination and Control Strategy in Multinational Organizations," *Administrative Science Quarterly,* June 1977, p. 251.

26. Benton Randolph, "When Going Global Isn't Enough," *Training,* Vol. 27, No. 8, August 1990, pp. 47–51; Matthew Lynn, "The Industrial Ideals of Iveco," *Business,* April 1990, pp. 92–96.

27. Samir M. Youssef, "Contextual Factors Influencing Control Strategy of Multinational Corporations," *Academy of Management Journal,* March 1975, pp. 136–145.

28. A. B. Sim, "Decentralized Management of Subsidiaries and Their Performance," *Management International Review,* No. 2, 1977, pp. 47–49.

29. David F. Hawkins, "Controlling Foreign Operations," *Financial Executive,* February 1965; V. Mauriel, "Evaluation and Control of Overseas Operations," *Management Accounting,* May 1969; and J. M. McInnes, "Financial Control Systems for Multinational Operations: An Empirical Investigation," *Journal of International Business Studies,* Fall 1971, pp. 11–28.

30. Frederick D. S. Choi and I. James Czechowicz, "Assessing Foreign Subsidiary Performance: A Multinational Comparison," *Management International Review,* Vol. 23, No. 4, 1983, p. 15.

31. *Ibid.,* pp. 18–20.

32. *Ibid.,* p. 22.

33. *Ibid.,* pp. 16–17.

34. George M. Scott, *An Introduction to Financial Control and Reporting in Multinational Enterprises* (Austin: Bureau of Business Research, Graduate School of Business, The University of Texas at Austin, 1973), pp. 77–79.

35. J. Alex Murray, "Intelligence Systems of the MNCs," *Columbia Journal of World Business,* September–October 1972, pp. 63–71.

36. Martin D. J. Buss, "Managing International Information Systems," *Harvard Business Review,* Vol. 60, No. 5, September–October 1982, pp. 153–162.

37. The information in this section is taken from Saeed Samiee, "Transnational Data Flow Constraints: A New Challenge for Multinational Corporations," *Journal of International Business Studies,* Vol. 15, No. 1, Spring–Summer 1984, pp. 141–150.

38. M. J. Kane and David A. Ricks, "Is Transnational Data Flow Regulation a Problem?" *Journal of International Business Studies*, Vol. 19, No. 3, 1988, pp. 477–483; Rakesh B. Sambharya and Arvind Phatak, "The Effect of Transborder Data Flow Restrictions on American Multinational Corporations," *Management International Review*, Vol. 30, No. 3, 1990, pp. 267–289.

39. Sanjoy Hazarika, "Bhopal Payments Set at $470 Million for Union Carbide," *New York Times*, February 15, 1989, p. 1 ff; "India Seeks to Reopen Bhopal Case," *New York Times*, January 22, 1990, p. C1 FF.

40. Data for the case were taken primarily from Hugh D. Menzies, "Westinghouse Takes Aim at the World," *Fortune*, January 14, 1980, pp. 48–53; other background information may be found in "Westinghouse's Third Big Step Is Overseas," *Business Week*, October 2, 1971, pp. 64–67; in several issues of Westinghouse's Annual Report; Thomas H. Naylor, "The International Strategy Matrix," *Columbia Journal of World Business*, Vol. 20, No. 2, Summer 1985, pp. 17–18; Gregory Stricharchuk, "Westinghouse Relies on Ruthlessly Rational Pruning," *Wall Street Journal*, January 24, 1990, p. A6; and "Expansion Through Alliances," *Mergers & Acquisitions*, July–August 1988, p. 15.

APPENDIX:
PROBLEMS OF INTERNATIONAL DATA

Reasons for Inaccuracies   For the most part, incomplete or inaccurate published data result from the inability of many governments to collect the needed details. Poor countries may have such limited resources that other projects necessarily receive priority in the national budget. Why collect precise figures on the literacy rate, governments of poor countries reason, when the same outlay may be used to build schools to improve that rate?

Inaccuracies result from
- Lack of ability to collect data
- Purposeful misleading

Education affects the competence of governmental officials to maintain and analyze accurate records. Economic factors likewise hamper the retrieval and analysis of records, since hand calculations may be used extensively instead of electronic data-processing systems. The result may be information that is years old before it is made public. Finally, cultural factors affect responses. Mistrust of how the data will be used may lead respondents to give erroneous information—particularly if questions probe financial details.

Of equal concern to the researcher is the publication of information designed to persuade the businessperson to follow a certain course of action. While perhaps not purposefully publishing false statements, many governmental and private organizations may be so selective as to create false impressions. Therefore, it is useful for firms to consider carefully the source of such material in the light of possible motives or biases.

Not all of the inaccuracies, however, are due to the collection and dissemination procedures of governments. A large proportion of the studies by academics that purport to describe business practices either by domestic firms in different countries or by international firms abroad are not necessarily accurate. Broad generalizations are frequently drawn on the basis of too few observations, nonrepresentative samples, and poorly designed questionnaires. There is a tendency for academic researchers to describe the unusual because it may make more interesting reading than the typical.

People's desire and ability to cover up data on themselves may distort published figures substantially. Part of the cover-up is attributable to unrecorded criminal activity. Economic data on Colombia, for example, do not include cocaine revenue, yet it is estimated that the export earnings from cocaine exceed all other Colombian exports combined.[1] In the United States, illegal income from such activities as drug trade, bribery, and prostitution amounts to over $100 billion a year. As much as 25 percent of the GNP in Italy and 30 percent in Israel goes unreported because of tax evasion.[2] The following illustrates the plight of Argentina:

> Last year [1986], only 130,000 out of 3 million people who were supposed to pay the three main taxes actually did. When tax agents hit the streets in search of evaders, they found that 40 percent of the people registered had declared false addresses, including one who claimed to live in the middle of the River Plate, another in a church and a third in a soccer stadium.[3]

Comparability problems include
- Collection methods, definitions, differences in base years
- Distortions in currency translations

Comparability Problems   One important variable when contrasting data from different countries is the year in which collection was made. Censuses, output figures, trade statistics, and base year calculations are published for different periods in different countries; thus it may be necessary for the researcher to make estimates of current figures based on projected growth rates.

There are also numerous definitional differences among countries; for example, a category as seemingly basic as *family income* might represent quite different things. Not only does the average number of children per family vary across national lines, but such relatives as grandparents, uncles, and cousins also may be included in the definition. In some places *literacy* is defined by some minimum of formal schooling, in others by certain specified standards, and in still others as simply the ability to read and write one's name. Furthermore, percentages may be published in terms of adult population (with different ages used for adulthood) or total population. Another definitional difference concerns accounting rules such as *depreciation,* which can substantially alter the comparability of net national product figures among countries. Accounting differences have also led to debates on whether Japan has a higher savings rate than the United States.[4]

Countries differ in how they measure *investment inflows.* Some governments record the number of foreign investment projects, some record the value of investments in their own local currency, and still others use value in U.S. dollars or another major international currency. Where value of investments is used, another question is how much of the total value is recorded as "foreign investment." Some governments record the total value of the project, regardless of what portion may be locally owned or financed; some record the value of foreign capital put in; and some the percentage of the project owned by foreign interests.[5]

National income and per capita income figures are particularly difficult to compare because of differences in the dispersion of the income. A country with a large middle class will have consumption patterns quite distinct from those in a country where large portions of the population are excluded from the money economy. For instance, in Benin, a West African country, at least half the population effectively earns nothing, which means that the per capita income of the remaining group is at least double what the published figure shows for the country as a whole. Those outside the money economy obviously have consumption patterns that are greater than zero, since they may grow agricultural products and produce other goods, which they consume or barter. The extent to which people in one country produce for their own consumption (e.g., grow vegetables, bake bread, sew clothes, cut hair) will distort comparisons with other countries that follow different patterns.

A further problem concerns exchange rates, which must be used to convert country data to some common currency. A 10 percent appreciation of the Japanese yen in relation to the U.S. dollar will result in a 10 percent increase in per capita income of Japanese residents when figures are reflected in dollars. Does this mean that the Japanese are suddenly 10 percent richer? Obviously not, since their yen income, which they use for about 85 percent of their purchases in the Japanese economy, is unchanged and buys no more. Even without the changes in exchange rates, it is difficult to compare purchasing power and living standards, since costs are so affected by climate and habit. Exchange rates constitute a very imperfect means of comparing national data.[6]

Appendix Notes

1. Peter Nares, "Getting a Fix on Colombia's Largest Export," *Wall Street Journal,* November 25, 1983, p. 13.
2. "The Underground Economy's Hidden Force," *Business Week,* April 5, 1982, p. 65.
3. Maria E. Estenssoro, "When an Economy Goes Underground," *New York Times,* July 26, 1987, p. F3.
4. Keniche Ohmae, "Americans and Japanese Save About the Same," *Wall Street Journal,* June 14, 1988, p. 30.
5. William A. Stoever, "Methodological Problems in Assessing Developing Country Policy toward Foreign Manufacturing Investment," *Management International Review,* Vol. 29, No. 4, 1989, p. 71.
6. Steven Greenhouse, "Comparing Wealth as Money Fluctuates," *New York Times,* August 23, 1987, p. E3, discusses the problem of comparing purchasing power.

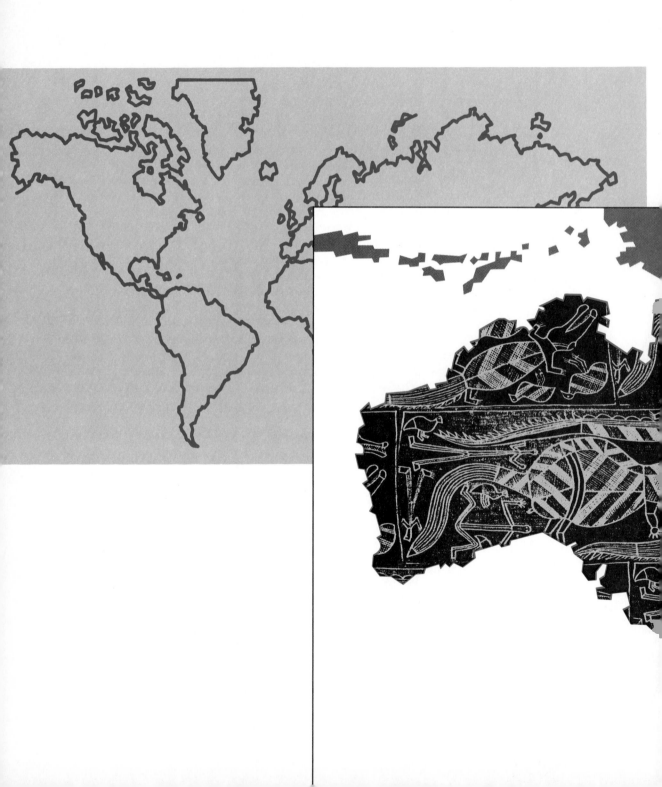

PART 7

FUNCTIONAL MANAGEMENT, OPERATIONS, AND CONCERNS

In the preceding part we discussed those alternatives that normally transcend decision making within functional disciplines. In this part we will examine concerns of a more functional orientation. This does not imply that these are of less importance. In fact, they are essential considerations within the firm's global implementation of strategy.

Chapter 18 emphasizes the uniqueness of each company, product, and country in international marketing. The chapter discusses means for estimating the market size abroad, then analyzes the conflicting advantages for standardization and differentiation of product, price, promotion, brand, and distribution.

Chapter 19 discusses the problems of accounting and tax when legal systems, exchange rates, and inflationary conditions vary among countries. The chapter first examines the factors influencing the differences in accounting methods among countries, moves to the handling of transactions in foreign currencies (including the translation of statements), and describes tax differences faced by a firm operating internationally.

Chapter 20 examines the organization of the international finance function, the securement and management of funds internationally, the method of financing international trade, the transfer of currencies, and the handling of inflation and exchange rate risks.

Chapter 21 deliberates "people problems"—emphasizing management personnel and labor. The discussion includes the effect of different labor markets, mobility problems, management syles, nationalism, and corporate objectives on selection, training, managing, and compensating.

CHAPTER **18**

MARKETING

May both seller and buyer see the benefit.
TURKISH PROVERB

Objectives

- To postulate the valid marketing philosophies for different firms in varying circumstances.

- To introduce techniques for assessing market sizes for given countries.

- To contrast practices of standardized versus differentiated programs for each country where sales are made.

- To emphasize how environmental differences complicate the management of marketing worldwide.

- To discuss the major international considerations within each of the marketing functions: product, pricing, promotion, branding, and distribution.

Great Britain often has been called a nation of shopkeepers, and Marks & Spencer (M & S) is undoubtedly the shopkeeping leader. With several hundred stores in the United Kingdom, M & S is its largest retailer, and the Marble Arch store in London is in the Guinness Book of Records as the store that takes in more revenue per square foot than any other in the world.

Soft goods (clothes and household textiles) account for about two thirds of the sales, and it is estimated that M & S has about 16 percent of the retail clothing sales in the United Kingdom. For some specific clothing items, M & S supplies over half the British market. M & S added food lines to its stores and became the largest and most profitable food retailer in Britain.

How has M & S become so dominant in the British market? The operations were begun in 1884 by a Polish immigrant who believed in selling durable merchandise at a moderate price. Since then, this philosophy has endured. M & S has merchandise made to its specifications. Because of its vast buying power, it can get producers to make cost-cutting investments and to compete by offering low prices on merchandise to be sold under M & S's St. Michael trademark. Because M & S is so well known, it has no need for many of the costly marketing expenses that other stores must undertake. There is practically no advertising, and stores are decorated austerely. There is very little personal service and no dressing rooms or public bathrooms. Customers receive no sales slips for small purchases, but merchandise is returned easily.

Another practice that has paid off for M & S in its home market has been to appeal to the nationalistic attitudes of its clientele. M & S has promoted heavily the fact that about 90 percent of the clothing it sells originates in the United Kingdom. This claim was challenged by the Transport & General Workers Union, and the company admitted in 1989 that the percentage had fallen to 87 percent and would likely fall further as its U.K. suppliers move more of their production abroad. M & S has managed to develop an image that is as British as bed and breakfast or fish and chips. Foreign visitors to England usually do not feel that they have sopped up the local atmosphere without a visit to one of the M & S stores. One of the stores has had to put its warning signs to shoplifters in five languages.

M & S has experienced foreseeable barriers to continued growth in the U.K. market. Not the least of the problems has been its high market share. Being already so dominant, M & S would have to add new products or appeal to new market segments to maintain its growth rate. In the late 1970s the company moved into higher-priced clothes by using finer materials for its traditional styles, such as silk blouses and cashmere coats. At the same

C A S E
MARKS
&
SPENCER[1]

time, the company hoped to cash in on publicity surrounding the fact that Margaret Thatcher had bought her suits at M & S before becoming prime minister. This initiative was disastrous: The Harrods-type customer did not switch to M & S, and many M & S customers traded down to even cheaper retailers. As a result, M & S dropped its higher-priced lines, but in 1980 M & S unit sales fell for the first time. By the mid-1980s M & S began again to target a more fashion-conscious market, this time with lines that moved away from its traditional styles. Because the merchandise needed for the fashion-conscious market changes rapidly, M & S had to get supplies within one week from the placement of orders instead of allowing up to fourteen weeks, which had been the custom. Although this move offered hope in Britain, an M & S executive summed up the emerging problems by saying, "Because the company is near saturation in the U.K., its growth must be overseas."

The foreign operations of M & S have been slow to achieve success. When Britain joined the EC, management saw an opportunity to expand on the continent because clothing from M & S suppliers could then enter other common market countries without tariffs. Paris and Brussels were selected as the first locations for stores. Before opening stores in 1975 the company sent a team of observers to Paris for 18 months so that product differences could be targeted to the French-speaking customers.

The team found substantial differences. One was in sizes: They noted that "French girls always seem to wear a size less than they need with everything obviously relying on the buttons, while we [English] go for a half size too large." French women wanted skirts that were longer than the English preference. French men wanted single instead of double back vents in their jackets, sweaters in a variety of colors (including pastels), and jackets and slacks rather than suits. None of these men's preferences were the norm in the United Kingdom. All of these differences had implications for the merchandise mix and the establishment of supplies.

In spite of the substantial research on product, the company was not well received initially. Many fewer people entered the stores than had been anticipated. M & S management believed that, since they were so well known in Britain and since so many foreign tourists visited London stores, their reputation had preceded them. Belatedly, they learned that only 3 percent of the French had even heard of M & S or St. Michael before the continental stores were opened. Store locations exacerbated the situation: M & S management wanted their first stores to be "flagships" and therefore sought to locate them on the most popular shopping streets. Since store space was at a premium on those streets, they had to settle for a spot in Paris where most pedestrian traffic preferred the other side of the street. In Brussels they accepted a store with a very small frontage that did not give an impression of a vast amount of merchandise on the inside. To get people to visit the stores, M & S had to depend much more heavily on advertising than the firm did in the United Kingdom. This was an added expense that made it difficult to keep prices low.

Another factor influencing costs was that M & S's continental stores lacked the kind of buying power that its stores in Britain enjoyed. Initially the company contracted nearly 80 percent of its merchandise from continental sources unwilling to treat M & S any more favorably than other department stores and retail chains already in the market. Most of the remaining merchandise came from the United Kingdom, where M & S had buying clout. Because much of the clothing was made to specifications to meet the French and Belgian needs (e.g., stronger buttons, single vent jackets, and pastel sweaters), the British producers had to make these items in short production runs. As initial large sales did not materialize, the U.K. manufacturers were reluctant to keep markups very low. Even when merchandise prices were kept low, M & S found the French highly suspicious of bargains.

An additional problem was that when potential customers went into the new stores, they were unaccustomed to the starkness and lack of service. A French fashion writer summed up the customer reaction to the Paris store as "not madly joyful unless of course one is as impervious to English shopping as one is to English cooking."

To bring customers into its Paris store, M & S has had to make operating adjustments. The primary change surprisingly has been in merchandise, the area where M & S had done so much preliminary research. In trying to copy what the continentals were offering in merchandise, M & S simply could not get a more durable product to customers at a sufficiently cheaper price to attract a mass clientele. However, it discerned fairly quickly that there was a small market segment willing to buy the more English-type merchandise for which M & S could exert its buying power. M & S now buys only 10 percent of its merchandise from continental sources and has differentiated itself from local competitors by capitalizing on its "Englishness." It now concentrates on such items as tan and navy blue sweaters, biscuits, English beer, and even a quiche Lorraine made in the United Kingdom. In deference to French tastes, M & S has carpeted its Paris store.

Not surprisingly, a large portion of the early customers turned out to be Britishers living in France, but this gradually changed. Parisians learned to like wandering through wide aisles with shopping carts before paying for all merchandise at one cash register. One Paris store now sells more per square meter than any other department store in France, and about 90 percent of its business is to Parisians.

In entering the Canadian market, M & S assumed that the "Englishness" would be a greater advantage there than on the continent. M & S quickly expanded to 60 stores in Canada in order to get nationwide distribution. However, Canadians found the merchandise to be dull, the stores to be "cold and clinical," and they did not like finding food next to clothing.

Most stores were placed in downtown locations, as is the custom in the United Kingdom. The Canadians were increasingly turning to suburban shopping centers, and only the M & S stores in those centers began to earn an early profit.

In 1979, after eight years of Canadian operations, M & S finally made an overall small profit in Canada, but this was short-lived; losses returned the next year. In deference to Canadian tastes, M & S has added fitting rooms, wood paneling, mirrors, partitions between departments, and wall-to-wall carpeting. There are still complaints about the merchandise, however. A former supplier opined that the British management did things "because that's the way they did it in England." This included the placement of bigger sleeves on clothing and the avoidance of livelier colors of clothing and of advertising. While Canadian stores carrying the Marks & Spencer logo have floundered, M & S has acquired two other Canadian clothing chains, D'Allaird's and Peoples. These acquisitions have kept their Canadian marketing programs and have been profitable. When M & S first entered Canada with its own brand of stores, management had hoped that the operations would serve as a springboard for entry into the U.S. market. In late 1986 it announced that the D'Allaird's chain had signed leases for sites at shopping malls in three cities in New York. In 1987 M & S appointed a top-level team to conduct an in-depth study of the U.S. marketplace to set up stores under the M & S name. One of the firm's executives said, "There is nothing like M & S in the United States, and we believe there could be good potential for us."

Instead, M & S concluded that the Canadian approach of copying the British formula would be a mistake; therefore, the company sought compatible U.S. acquisitions. The first, Brooks Brothers in 1988, seemed incongruous inasmuch as Brooks Brothers had a dignified image, much personal service, and expensive clothes. At first M & S announced that it would not change the Brooks Brothers' successful and profitable merchandising. But fairly quickly, M & S began trying to increase sales by changing some practices to bring less affluent customers into the stores as well. The company reduced the amount of personnel, began replacing glass display cases with open displays, ran six-week sales instead of the customary one-week ones, and decreased the number of sizes of casual coats by offering them simply as small, medium, large, and extra-large. During the first two years the results of the changes were disastrous as sales and profits declined. In 1991 Brooks Brothers announced it would try to turn its position around by offering higher commissions to sales personnel. John Weitz, a British designer, recommended that Brooks Brothers license its name to manufacturers so that the traditional suits could be sold elsewhere, while Brooks Brothers moved to less conservative styling in its own stores.

In 1988 M & S also bought Kings, a 16-store food chain in New Jersey. This acquisition has seemed compatible since Kings and M & S share an operating philosophy of emphasizing perishables and upscale prepared foods.

Existing management stayed on to provide U.S. marketing expertise; and M & S began the following year to introduce its St. Michael chilled prepared food lines into the stores, while advertising them heavily and providing discount coupons in local newspapers. The U.S. introduction began with only 18 items, prepared in Kings' stores, as compared with more than 2000 items in the U.K., all prepared in central kitchens. Some of the U.S. items, such as chili con carne, are different from those in the U.K. Because of vast distances, the U.K. concept of overnight delivery from central kitchens is not practical for the U.S.; consequently, in-store preparation creates additional potential problems of cost and quality control if M & S follows its planned strategy of building a significant U.S. food presence.

INTRODUCTION

Domestic and international marketing principles are the same, but

- Managers often overlook foreign environmental differences
- Managers often interpret foreign information incorrectly

Global versus national programs

- Are not an either/or decision
- May take degrees of one versus the other

The M & S case points out many of the problems a firm may face internationally. Although the company did substantial research before it began its international operations, it still faced unexpected problems that inhibited rapid sales growth. Marketing principles are no different in the international arena; however, environmental differences often cause managers either to overlook important variables or to misinterpret information.[2] M & S made mistakes in terms of such important marketing variables as the target market segment, the merchandise mix, promotional needs, the degree to which products would need to be altered for the markets, and distributional differences.

This chapter examines alternative approaches to the analysis of market potential among different countries and the selection of product, pricing, promotion, branding, and distribution strategies in international marketing. Within these areas, emphasis will be placed on whether firms should follow global as opposed to national marketing programs. The global versus national approaches may be viewed at opposite ends of a spectrum, with the possibility of moving differently along that spectrum for any specific marketing program or decision. The following discussion highlights the circumstances that might enhance movements toward one end or the other of the spectrum.

MARKET SIZE ANALYSIS

Broad scanning techniques

- Limit detailed analysis to the most promising possibilities
- Are good for LDCs where precise data are less available

We have explained the importance of market potential in determining a company's allocational efforts among different countries and have discussed some common variables used as broad indicators for comparing countries' market potentials. The following section covers some techniques that can be used to estimate the size of potential markets. These are merely tools to help management estimate market potential, thus helping in the decision of which markets to emphasize.[3]

To determine the potential demand for a given company, management usually must first estimate the possible sales of the category of products for all companies and then estimate its own market-share potential. For advanced countries, there usually are consumption figures and trained market-research personnel, so costly and detailed research studies are feasible. For many LDCs, however, it may be useful to develop inexpensive forecasting methods based on readily available data. Regardless of whether a firm is dealing with industrial or poor countries, there are different informational needs depending on the precision of data required and the commitments that firms have already made in markets. For example, a firm may first scan a large number of potential markets fairly inexpensively by using published data. Only those markets that appear most promising will then be analyzed more closely, such as by test marketing in those areas.

Total Market Potential

Existing Consumption Patterns   **Input-output** is a tool used widely in national economic planning to show the resources utilized by different industries for a given output as well as the interdependence of economic sectors. Through the use of tables showing all sectors on both the vertical and horizontal axes, the production (output) of one is shown as the demand (input) of another. For instance, steel output becomes an input to the automobile industry, households, government, foreign sector, and even to the steel industry itself. Many countries now publish input-output tables. By comparing these with economic projections for an economy as a whole or with plans for production changes in a given industry, management can project the total volume of sales changes for a given type of product as well as the purchases by each sector. The three major shortcomings of this method are: (1) For many countries, the data contained within the input-output tables and in plans or projections of economic changes are too sparse; (2) there is a questionable assumption that the relationships among sectors and resources are fixed; and (3) the tables may be many years old before they are published and readily available.

Input-output shows the relationship of one economic sector to another.

Data on Other Countries   The amount of sales of a product in one country may be based on the same conditions that could determine sales in other countries. For example, as incomes change, the demand for a product may change on the basis of that income change. For instance, Japanese consumption of beef, sugar, hard liquor, and dairy products grew between 1970 and 1990 as per capita income increased—closely paralleling what had occurred in the United States at an earlier period.[4] Management thus may collect data on the consumption of a given product in countries with different per capita GNPs and then project sales at different income levels by plotting a path through which average demand changes as incomes change (see Fig. 18.1).

Data assume one country will follow a pattern similar to that of another country.

Reasonably good fits for many products have been found by using this method. However, for some products the analysis breaks down in some coun-

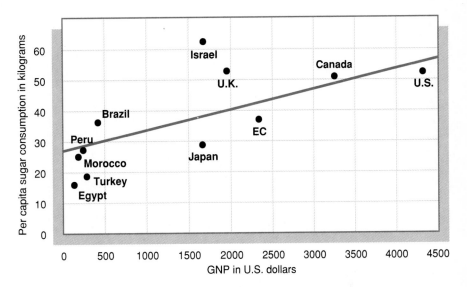

Figure 18.1
Sugar Consumption and Per Capita GNP for Selected Countries: 1970
By plotting countries for which data are available to relate sugar consumption
and GNP, one is able to construct a line to estimate consumption for countries
where there are data on GNP, but not on sugar intake. *Source: UN Statistical
Yearbook, 1972.*

tries because other variables affect demand. For instance, the consumption of
cars in Switzerland is lower than income would predict because of the public
transportation system, difficult terrain, and high import duties.[5] A further
problem is that this method is static. With changes in technology and prices,
a country may change its consumption pattern much earlier or later than
would be indicated by looking at a group of countries in only one time period.

*Time series projects future
by past trends.*

Time-Series Data   Sometimes sales follow a pattern over a historical period.
If this is the case and data are available over a period of time, a firm may be
able to make future projections based on past values.[6] Figure 18.2 illustrates
sugar consumption in the United States based on time-series data. This
contrasts with projections of sugar consumption in Fig. 18.1 based on cross-
national data. The use of time-series and cross-national data also may be
combined. Such analyses within an economy are useful for predicting total
demand and for identifying the economic sectors generating this demand.

*As percentage of income
changes, product demand
may change by a different
percentage.*

Income Elasticity   A common predictive means is to divide the percentage
of change in product demand by the percentage of change in income. If the
resultant answer is greater than 1, the demand for the product is considered
elastic (or sales are likely to increase or decrease by a percentage that is

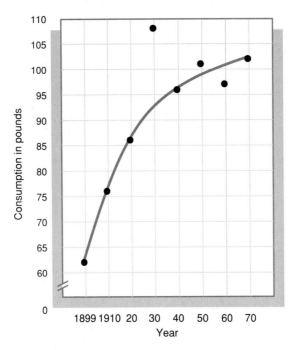

Figure 18.2
Per Capita Sugar Consumption of the United States: 1899–1970
By plotting per capita sugar consumption over time, one may extrapolate the trend to make estimates about the future. *Source: Statistical Abstract of the United States, Supplement: 1957* and *Statistical Abstract: 1972.*

greater than the percentage change in income); if the number is less than 1, demand is inelastic (or sales are likely to increase or decrease by a percentage that is less than the percentage change in income). Demand for necessities, such as food, is relatively less elastic than demand for discretionary products, such as automobiles. In other words, upward or downward movements in income ordinarily would affect automobile sales more than food sales. This concept is useful in estimating the expenditures for countries at different levels of income. For instance, people in the United States spend a lower percentage of personal income on food than do South Koreans. The difference is due not to relative appetites but rather to income differences that allow people in the United States to spend more on other types of purchases. Since a large portion of people in South Korea are poor, a change in income levels affects food consumption much more than in a higher-income country.[7] An elasticity of 1.5 would mean that a percentage change in income would result in 1.5 times that percentage change in the demand for the specific product.

As is true with any method of demand projection, income-elasticity measurements must be approached with caution, especially if a firm is making projections in one country based on demand analysis in another. Price differences and taste affect consumers' demand as well. Italy consumes a much higher quantity of fruits and vegetables than Norway, even though Norway's income is higher, because of price differences. Denmark and Switzerland have very similar per capita incomes, but per capita consumption of frozen food is much higher in Denmark because of the Danes' great penchant for convenience.[8]

Demand is related to some economic or other indicator.

Regression   Regression is an important means of refining data and making predictions by uncovering relationships between variables. By using data based on the historical relationship between demand for a given product and economic or other indicators, or between demand and some indicators in a given time period, a firm may construct a regression equation that shows the demand (the dependent variable) based on a level of the indicators (the independent variables). This technique allows an amount of consumption that is not directly attributable to changes in the indicators to be taken into consideration and allows for the determination of the degree of correlation between the independent and dependent variables. Regression analysis can thus be used to predict demand from changes in related indicators.

Gap Analysis

The difference between total market potential and companies' sales is made up of gaps:

- Usage: less product sold by all competitors than potential
- Competitive: "head-to-head" competition
- Product line: company lacks some product variations
- Distribution: company misses geographic or intensity coverage

The tools just described may give an estimation of the market potential for a given product. Once this rough determination is made, a firm must calculate how well it is doing within each of the markets. A useful tool for scanning markets and comparing countries in this respect is **gap analysis.**[9] When a company's sales are lower than the estimated market potential for a given type of product, there is a company potential for increased sales, which may be due to a usage, competitive, product line, or distribution gap.

The two largest Swiss chocolate companies, Nestlé and Interfood, have found in recent years very different types of gaps in different countries.[10] This has led them to emphasize different types of marketing programs among nations. In some markets they have found substantial usage gaps; in other words, less chocolate is being consumed than would be expected on the basis of population and income levels. This has led the two companies to try to increase primary demand in those areas for chocolate in general. Industry specialists estimated, for example, that in many countries more than 80 percent of the population have never tasted a chocolate bar. They project, consequently, that if more people can be persuaded to try chocolate bars, the companies' sales should increase with the market increase.

The U.S. market comprises another type of usage gap. Nearly everyone in this market has tried most chocolate products, but per capita consumption has fallen because of increasing concern about calories, nutrition, and health. To increase chocolate consumption in general, Nestlé for a short time promoted chocolate as an energy source for the sports-minded. The building of consumption in general is most useful when one is the leader in the market; thus Nestlé, with U.S. chocolate sales below Mars and Hershey, benefitted its competitors during the short-lived campaign. In some hot climates the companies have found that they have product-line gaps in terms of the market for sweetened products. By working on new products, such as chocolate products that melt less easily, they may be able to garner a larger share of the present market for sweetened products. They also have found chocolate products with which they do not compete directly. There are also some markets, such as Japan, where they have not yet achieved a sufficient distribution to reach their sales potentials; therefore, Nestlé formed a joint venture with a Japanese cake and candy maker, Fujiya, to make Kit Kats and gain more distribution.[11] Finally, there are competitive gaps, sales by competitors of products through distribution similar to one's own products and distribution. For example, in markets such as France and Germany Nestlé and Interfood feel that most of the potential market demand is being fulfilled but that there is a competitive gap; that is, they might increase sales there but only at the expense of competitors.

Product Policy

The Philosophies   International marketing philosophies may be categorized as:

1. we sell what we make,

2. we make what we sell, and

3. we adapt what we make to the needs of foreign consumers.

This frame of reference is useful for understanding the varied approaches firms may validly take in international product policy decisions.

We Sell What We Make   For some products, particularly raw materials and agricultural commodities, there is little need or possibility of product differentiation from one country to another. Although this is one approach within the philosophy of "we sell what we make," this idea better describes the firm that develops a product for one market and then attempts to sell the product abroad—as it is. There are three circumstances under which this approach may be valid:

1. passive exports, particularly those that serve as an appendage to the domestic market;

2. the existence of foreign-market segments or niches that may resemble the market for which the product is aimed initially; and

3. situations in which product standardization may so lower prices that a large group of consumers from many countries are willing to forgo cer-

tain nationally differentiated product characteristics in order to get lower prices.

Passive sales occur when
- Advertising spills over
- Foreign buyers seek new products

Many firms begin selling abroad very passively. Sometimes for unknown reasons, requests for information on products or even actual orders simply arrive from abroad. Foreign products are discovered through numerous channels, including new developments reported in scientific and trade journals with international circulation, advertising that spills across national boundaries, and demonstrations of products that consumers have bought in one country and transferred abroad. Finally, many firms send buyers abroad or actively search for new products. At this point firms do very little if any real adaptation to what consumers abroad might prefer, which suffices for many companies that view foreign sales as an appendage to domestic sales. This same type of company frequently exports only if it has excess inventory for the domestic market. In fact, fixed costs are sometimes covered from domestic sales so that lower prices are offered on exports as a means of liquidating inventories without disrupting the domestic market.[12]

The domestic, unaltered product may have appeal abroad.

A company may develop a product aimed at achieving a large share of its domestic market, yet find that there are market segments abroad willing to buy the same product. Sometimes the product may have a universal appeal, such as French champagne. In other situations, the company may be able to target to a mass market at home, but to a small niche within foreign locations, such as U.S. bourbon production.[13] Another situation involves sales to countries for which the total market potential is assessed to be small regardless of whether changes are geared to unique consumer needs. In small developing countries, particularly, international firms are apt to make few changes because the market size does not justify the expense to them and because competitors are apt to be other international firms that do not make product alterations. Firms may not even adjust electrical voltage and plugs to local standards, leaving the job of conversion to local purchasers. The greatest ability to sell the same product in more than one country occurs when consumer characteristics are similar and when there is a great deal of spillover in product information, such as between the United States and Canada. Improvements in international communications and transportation are increasingly extending the spillover effects to more distant countries so that there are more opportunities to aim the same products to groups of similar consumers in a number of different countries.

Standardization usually reduces costs.

Whether a firm is exporting or has foreign production facilities, it may cut costs substantially by standardizing its products. This usually is done on the basis of the home-country experience, since costs associated with product development, promotional programs, and distributional expertise already have been expended there. But for companies with foreign operating facilities in place, the standardized product may first have been developed abroad, such as Whiskas, a cat food that Mars first developed outside the United

States.[14] The transference to more than one country allows for economies as the outlays are spread over a larger volume of output.

We Make What We Sell   In a firm that operates according to the dictum described in the previous section, management is usually guided by such questions as: "Should we send some exports abroad?" "Where can we sell some more of product X?" In other words, the product is held constant, and the location of sales is varied. The type of strategy to be described in this section is one that asks, "What can we sell in country A?" In this case the country is held constant, and the product is varied.

Sometimes a firm wants to penetrate markets in a given country because of the country's size, growth potential, proximity to home operations, currency or political stability, or a host of other reasons. The extreme of this approach would be for a company to move to completely unrelated products. This is not a common strategy, but there are examples: Henkel of Germany wished to diversify into the United States in order to counter an expected sluggish market at home, but management felt that it would be difficult to compete in the United States in its major product lines, detergents and cosmetics. Thus Henkel chose instead to buy the chemical division of General Mills.[15]

This reactive attitude to consumers does not necessarily mean that a firm has to forgo the economies of standardization. A company may well do market research in a number of countries in order to develop and aim a product at a global market segment. Canon's development of a 35-millimeter automatic camera is an example. Instead of merely trying to transfer sales of a domestic product abroad, the firm designs a product to fit some global market segment, which may mean changing what is sold domestically to correspond to the international standard. The possibilities of global products for industrial users may be large as well because the purchasers are apt to be technically trained decision makers. SKF, for example, introduced a line of 20,000 ball bearings to replace 50,000 on a worldwide basis.[16]

As in the preceding philosophy, a firm following a "make-what-we-sell" approach may do so passively. Increasingly there are examples of purchasing agents who set specifications and then seek out contracts for the foreign manufacture of components or finished products. For example, S. T. King, a Hong Kong company, makes clothing to the specifications of firms such as Calvin Klein. In responding, a firm may make a product that is quite different from what it sells within its home market. In such a situation, the producer is less concerned about choosing the product characteristics than about the pricing and distribution aspects of what it is marketing abroad.

We Adapt What We Make to the Needs of Foreign Consumers   Most firms that are committed to continual rather than sporadic foreign sales adopt a strategy that combines the production and consumer orientations just described. Refusal to make changes for the needs of foreign markets means that too many sales may be lost, especially if there are aggressive competitors willing to make desired adaptations. Yet expertise concerning a type of product may be very important, and companies want the foreign operations to be compatible with their product understanding. Product changes are common but tend to occur in degree. Thus a company accustomed to manufacturing electric typewriters is more apt to move into the production of manual typewriters or personal computers than tires or detergents. The latter products ordinarily would be too far from the management's area of expertise.

Reasons for Product Alteration

Legal Factors   Direct legal requirements are the most obvious reason for altering products for foreign markets, since without adhering to the regulations the company will not get permission to operate. The exact requirements vary widely by country but are usually meant to protect people who come into contact with a given product or service. Pharmaceuticals and foods are particularly subject to regulations concerning purity, testing, and the labeling of contents. Cars sold in the United States must conform to safety and pollution standards not found in many other countries.

Legal factors are usually related to safety or health protection.

When foreign legal requirements are less stringent than those at home, a firm then may not be compelled legally to alter its products for sales in the foreign country. However, the firm will have to weigh such questions as whether foreign sales will be lost if high domestic standards are used abroad and whether there will be domestic ill will if those standards are not used. Firms have been criticized in recent years for selling abroad, especially in LDCs, such products as toys, automobiles, contraceptives, and pharmaceuticals that did not meet home-country safety or quality standards.[17]

A recurring question is to what extent it is possible to arrive at international product standards to eliminate some of the seemingly wasteful product alterations from country to country. Although there has been some progress, such as agreement on the sprocket dimensions on movie film, other things (railroad gauges and electrical socket shapes, for instance) continue to vary. In reality, there is both consumer and economic resistance. The conversion to the metric system on beverages, for example, meant that U.S. consumers had to learn that 236.58 milliliters is the same as the 8-fluid-ounce soft drinks to which they were accustomed. In an economic sense the changeover was more costly than simply educating people and relabeling. Containers had to be redesigned and production had to be retooled so that dimensions would be in even numbers. Even for new products or those still in a developmental stage, such as high-definition television (HDTV), countries seldom reach agreement because they wish to protect the investments already made by their home-based companies.[18] At best, international standards will come very slowly.

Less apparent are the indirect legal requirements that may affect product content or demand. In some countries it may be difficult or prohibitively expensive to import certain raw materials or components, thus forcing a firm to construct an end product with local substitutes that may alter the final product substantially. Or legal requirements, such as high taxes on heavy automobiles, may shift sales to smaller models, thus altering demand indirectly for tire sales and gasoline octanes.

Examination of cultural differences may pinpoint possible problem areas.

Cultural Factors   Consumer buying behavior is complex. It is difficult to determine in advance if the introduction of new or different products will meet with acceptance. Some U.S. food franchisers, such as McDonald's, have been highly successful in Japan by duplicating most of their U.S. product and distribution—an acceptance attributed to the "enthusiastic assimilation" by the Japanese of Western ways. In contrast, McDonald's found it necessary to provide cheese curds and hot gravy for french fries in seemingly more similar Canada (Quebec) to create a dish called *poutine*.[19] Furthermore, Western cosmetic firms have been able to garner only small shares of the Japanese cosmetics market. Cultural factors render some Western products unsuited to the Japanese market: Perfume is hardly used in Japan, suntans are considered ugly, and bath oil is impractical in home showers or in communal baths.[20] In another case, Armstrong World Industries had heard so much about the so-called world car that it reasoned there must be a market for a world gasket. Management found though that consumer and therefore industrial requirements were very different. For example, U.S. car owners are not bothered by an occasional drop of oil on the garage floor, whereas Japanese car owners will complain to the manufacturer.[21]

Personal incomes and infrastructures affect product demand.

Economic Factors   If consumers in a foreign country lack sufficient income, they may not be able to buy in sufficient quantity the same product the international firm sells in its home market. The company therefore may have to design a cheaper model or perhaps sell a product with characteristics similar to those sold in the home market at an earlier period. National Cash Register has designed crank-operated machines to sell in some LDCs. Where incomes are low, consumers may buy many personal items in smaller quantities, such as one aspirin, one piece of chewing gum, or one cigarette, which usually necessitates new types of packaging.

Even if a market segment has sufficient income for purchasing the same product the firm sells at home, the general level of the economy may be such that products have to be altered. The type of infrastructure (e.g., roads and utilities) in a country may determine the necessary structural composition and tolerances of products. Factory managers will have to consider the low educational levels of machine operators when planning equipment purchases, which may result in product simplification.

LDC Criticisms   Within LDCs, labor-saving industrial equipment and luxury goods are criticized for contributing to unemployment problems and to the enhancement of elitist class distinctions. Therefore, MNEs are being increasingly pressured to justify their contributions or to design and sell products that are perceived to be more in line with the needs of LDCs.[22] The question of luxury or superfluous products has been largely answered by MNEs through showing the positive side effects of seemingly unnecessary products. For example, soft-drink manufacturers have argued that they are responsible for the establishment of sanitary bottling operations, which are essential for other industries, such as pharmaceuticals.

Cost of Alteration

Some products save costs more than others through standardization.

Cost savings through uniformity may apply to any part of the marketing program; however, product standardization is the area where the greatest savings are possible. If a firm is exporting, longer production runs from a centralized output may result in substantial economies of scale. Total inventories also may be lowered, since domestic and foreign sales come from the same backlog. Even if different production centers in different countries are involved, a standardized approach ordinarily reduces product development costs and should lead to easier and more comparable cost controls. Output in different countries also may be exported to substitute for domestic production when local manufacturing units cannot fill orders, as in periods of unusual demand or during strikes.

There is a wide variance in cost-saving possibilities, though. For example, a production that has a need for a high fixed-capital input (e.g., automobile manufacture) can gain more through long production runs than one with a high proportion of variable to fixed costs (e.g., pharmaceuticals). If a company must produce abroad in order to serve the foreign market, some of the economies of product standardization, such as from long runs or inventory centralization, will be lost anyway. In this situation, there is less cost pressure to maintain uniformity.

Furthermore, some changes are cheap to effect, yet have an important influence on demand. One such area is packaging, which is the most common alteration made by exporters.[23] In Panama, Aunt Jemima Pancake Mix and Ritz Crackers are sold in cans rather than in boxes because of the high humidity—a low-cost change with a high potential payoff. Before making a decision a firm should always compare the cost of alteration with the cost of lost sales if no alteration is made.

One strategy a firm can use for compromising between uniformity and diversity is to standardize many components while changing the end characteristics. Coca-Cola, for example, exports concentrates to bottling plants all over the world; then carbonation, color, and sugar are added to conform with local preferences.[24] This type of change is practically costless, since standardization is achieved for the concentrate process and the finished product cannot feasibly be exported. Even when end products appear to be quite different, the standardization of many components is possible. Another strategy is to make product changes less frequently in small markets to spread the fixed costs associated with production over a larger amount of sales.

Extent and Mix of the Product Line

Narrowing of line allows for concentration of efforts.

Broadening may gain distribution economies.

Most companies produce multiple products. It is doubtful that all of these products would generate sufficient sales in a given foreign locale to justify the expenditures to penetrate the markets. Even if those that would did, a company may offer only a portion—such as some products at home that are not sold abroad or vice versa. Instead of offering as many models and options as in the United States, GM in Mexico produces and sells a much more limited variety, which reduces the amount of capital investment for production and spare parts, allowing sales activity to concentrate on fewer products. In other words, a firm may narrow its efforts to a few segments of a given market.

A firm also must consider whether any new products need to be added to the line for sale in certain countries. Two primary considerations in reaching these decisions are the possible effects on sales and the relative cost of having one product as opposed to a family of products. Sometimes a firm finds that it must produce and sell some unpopular items if it is to sell the more popular ones, such as sherry glasses to match the crystal wine and water glasses. The manufacturer may be forced to go to a few short production runs in order to gain the mass market on other products. If a firm must set up some foreign production if it is to sell in the foreign market, it may be able to produce locally those products in its line with a longer production run and import the other products needed to help sell the local production.

If the foreign market is small in relation to the domestic market, selling costs per unit may be high because of the fixed costs associated with selling. When faced with a situation such as this, the firm can follow a strategy of broadening the product line to be handled. This may be done by grouping sales of several manufacturers or by developing new products for the local market that the same salesperson can handle.[25] Coca-Cola, for instance, has added a line of bar mixes in South Africa, a lemonade in Australia, a mango drink in Pakistan, a tomato juice in Belgium, and some mixed juice–based drinks in Mexico and Indonesia.

Product Life Cycle Considerations

Product life cycles may differ by country in
- Time of introduction
- Shape of growth curve

There may be differences among countries in either the shape or the length of the product life cycle. Thus a manufacturer who faces declining sales in one country may be able to find a foreign market that will have growing or at least sustained sales for a product. For example, cellular phone producers, such as Ericsson and Motorola, faced falling demand growth in industrial countries during the late 1980s but found that sales in some developing countries were just entering a rapid growth stage. Mattel found that its Cheerful

Tearful Doll had a much longer sales life span in the former West Germany than in the United States.[26]

----------------------------------- **PRICING** ▋▋▋▋▋▋▋▋▋▋▋▋▋▋▋▋▋▋▋▋▋▋▋▋▋▋

Firms generally place only product above price when ranking the importance of marketing-program variables.[27] A price needs to be high enough to guarantee the proper flow of funds to carry on the other activities that bridge the gap between production and consumption. The proper price will not only assure short-term profits, but will also allow the firm to have the resources to build its other elements within the marketing mix that are necessary to achieve long-term competitive viability. Pricing in the international context is more complex than in the domestic arena because of:

1. a different degree of governmental intervention,
2. a greater diversity of markets,
3. price escalation in exporting,
4. the changing relative value of currencies,
5. differences in fixed versus variable pricing practices, and
6. strategies to counter international competitors.

Governmental Intervention

Government price controls
- May set minimum or maximum prices
- May prohibit certain competitive price practices

Every country has laws that affect the prices of goods at the consumer level, but these laws may affect different products in different ways at different times. Restrictions may prevent firms from using the strategies they consider optimal in achieving their ends. A governmental price control may set either maximum or minimum levels to be charged to the consumer. Controls against lowering prices usually are intended to prevent firms from eliminating competitors in order to gain monopoly positions. An example of this type of control would be Germany's Unfair Competition Law, which has been interpreted by the German courts to prohibit such items as coupons, boxtops, and giveaway articles unless these will remain a consistent policy of the company throughout the years. A firm accustomed to relying on such devices as a means of increasing its sales at home must develop new methods in Germany consistent with the German laws. Many countries set maximum prices on many products: If costs rise, profit margins necessarily contract, sometimes resulting in an unwillingness of producers to continue selling. For example, in 1988 Procter & Gamble and some of its suppliers were hard hit by price controls in Venezuela. Although P&G was willing to wait out the situation while negotiating with governmental authorities, its phosphate suppliers could not afford to sell P&G the materials needed for detergents. Therefore, P&G was forced to suspend operations.[28] Or price controls may force firms to lower the quality of a product, in which case they may consider changing the brand name in order to reintroduce the higher-quality product at a later date.

Another type of control that reduces discretionary pricing is directed specifically at imports. The General Agreement on Tariffs and Trade (GATT) has a provision, the Antidumping Code, that permits countries to establish restrictions against imports that come in below the price to consumers in the exporting country. The provision makes it more difficult for firms to differentiate markets through price.

A firm might wish to export abroad at a lower price than that charged at home for several reasons. One might be to test sales in the foreign market. Assume that a firm finds that it cannot export to a given country because tariffs or transportation costs make the price to foreign consumers prohibitively high, but some preliminary calculations show that by establishing foreign production, prices may be reduced substantially to the foreign consumer. Before committing resources to produce overseas, management may wish to test the market by exporting so that goods may be sold at the price that would be charged if they were produced in the local market. If sales do not materialize, management will know that factors other than price may be preventing product sales. If sales do materialize, management may go ahead and establish an investment or make a second round of exports to determine whether repeat sales develop. For example, before completing a $55 million frozen-food plant to make Lean Cuisine products in the U.K., Nestlé tested the market by exporting from Canada a year in advance.[29] The shipping of such dishes as spaghetti bolognese in refrigerated ships and the payment of customs duties made export costs much higher than the U.K. selling prices; however, Nestlé incurred a small cost in relation to the information gained and the amount of eventual commitment. Other reasons for charging different prices in different countries involve competitive and demand factors. For example, a firm may feel that prices can be kept high in the domestic market by restricting supply to that market. Excess production then can be sold abroad at a lower price as the sales price makes some contribution to overhead.

Greater Diversity of Markets

Consumers in some countries simply like certain products more and are willing to pay more for them.

Although there are numerous ways for a firm to segment the domestic market and to charge differently in each segment, the country-to-country variations create even greater natural segments. Few sea urchins can be sold in the United States, for example, at any price, yet they are exported to Japan, where they are considered delicacies. In some countries a firm may have many competitors and thus little discretion on its prices, whereas in others it may have a near monopoly due either to the stage in the product life cycle or to government-granted manufacturing rights not held by competitors. In near-monopoly situations the firm may exercise considerable pricing discretion, such as using skimming, penetration, or cost-plus strategies.

Another factor differentiating pricing possibilities is that country-of-origin stereotypes differ among countries. For example, in comparing consumer perceptions for automobiles with their objective ratings, German cars seem overrated by American consumers in relation to U.S.-made cars, yet Japanese consumers overrate Japanese cars in relation to German ones. In effect, German producers may be able to charge a higher margin above their American competitors in the United States than they can with their Japanese competitors in Japan. Yet any competitor who responds to adverse stereotypes by lowering prices to increase sales actually may reduce the product image even further.[30] This could occur, for example, if the German automobile producers were to lower their prices in the Japanese market where consumers often equate price with quality.

Cash versus credit buying affects demand.

The total cost that a consumer may pay for a product will be more than the sales price if there are additional charges because of buying on credit. How consumers view these additional charges may thus affect total demand as well as the sales price they are willing to pay. The tax treatment of interest payments as well as attitudes toward being in debt affect whether consumers will pay in cash or by credit. The Japanese, for example, have been much more reluctant to rely on consumer credit than Americans. In selling to Japanese consumers, therefore, it is less possible than in the United States to use credit payments as a means of receiving revenue from the sale of goods.

Price Escalation in Exporting

Price generally goes up by more than transport and duty costs.

If standard markups are used within the distribution channels, lengthening the channels or adding expenses somewhere within the system will increase the price to the consumer by a greater amount than the initial increase. Assume that the markup is 50 percent and that a product costs $1.00 to produce. The price of the product would then be $1.50. If the cost of the production were to increase by $.20 to $1.20, the markup of 50 percent would then make the price of the product $1.80 instead of merely $1.70. In export sales, two things happen to escalate the price of goods to the consumer: First, channels of distribution are usually longer because of greater distances and because of the need to engage organizations that know export procedures and/or selling in the foreign market; second, tariffs are an additional cost that may be passed on to consumers in an escalated form.

There are several implications of price escalation. Many seemingly exportable products turn out to be noncompetitive abroad. Furthermore, to become competitive in exporting, a firm may have to sell its product to middlemen at a lower price to lessen the amount of escalation.

Currency Value and Price Changes

Pricing decisions must consider replacement cost.

For firms accustomed to operating with one relatively stable currency, pricing in highly volatile currencies can be extremely troublesome. Pricing decisions should be made to assure that sufficient funds are received to replace the inventory that has been sold and still make a profit. If this is not done, a firm may be making a "paper profit" while liquidating itself. In other words, what shows as a profit may result from failure to adjust for inflation while the merchandise is in stock. In addition to the effect of inflation on prices, a company also must consider that its income taxes may be based on the paper profits rather than on real profits. Table 18.1 illustrates a pricing plan to make a target profit (after taxes) of 30 percent on replacement cost. If the firm does not use a procedure similar to this one, it may quickly lack sufficient funds to operate. The longer the collection period, the more important it is for the firm to use a graduated pricing model. Because of Peruvian inflation in the late 1980s, Procter & Gamble had to raise its detergent prices 20 to 30 percent every two weeks. Meanwhile, P&G eliminated its 60-day free credit to retailers and instituted interest on 15- to 30-day payments.[31]

Two other pricing problems that occur because of inflationary conditions are: (1) the receipt of funds in a foreign currency that, when converted, will buy less of the firm's own currency than had been expected and (2) the constant readjustment of prices necessary to compensate for cost changes. In the first case the firm can sometimes (depending on competitive factors and governmental regulations) specify in sales contracts an equivalency in some hard

TABLE 18.1 | EFFECT OF TAX AND INFLATION ON PRICING The pricing structure for sales or collections at the end of the year is calculated as follows: Replacement cost is cost plus inflation until collection, or $1000 + 0.36 (1000) = 1360$; income after taxes is profit goal times replacement cost, or $0.30 (1360) = 408$. Since income after taxes is 60 percent of taxable income, taxable income may be calculated by $408 \div 0.6$ or 680; tax is $0.4 (680) = 272$; sales price is original cost (1000) plus taxable income (680); markup on replacement is sales price (1680) less replacement cost (1360), or 320.

Assume: Cost at beginning of 1000
     36% inflation
     40% tax rate
     30% profit goal on replacement cost
     after taxes

If Sold and Collected at Beginning of Year		If Sold and Collected at End of Year	
Cost	1,000	Replacement cost	1,360
Markup	500	Markup on replacement	320
Sale prices	1,500	Sales price	1,680
− Cost	1,000	− Original cost	1,000
Taxable income	500	Taxable income	680
Tax @ 40%	200	Tax @ 40%	272
Income after taxes	300	Income after taxes	408

currency. For example, a sale of equipment from a U.S. manufacturer to a company in Uruguay may specify that payment be made in dollars or pesos at an equivalent price, in terms of dollars, at the time that payment is effected.

When it is necessary to change prices frequently because of inflationary conditions, it becomes more difficult to quote prices in letters or catalogues. Constant price rises even may hamper what would otherwise be a preferred distribution method. Vending machine sales, for example, make price increases difficult to effect because of the need to change machines in the process and to come up with coins or tokens that correspond to the percentage increase in price desired.

Currency value changes also affect pricing decisions for any product with potential foreign competition. For example, when the U.S. dollar becomes stronger, non–U.S.-made goods can be sold more cheaply in the U.S. market. In such a situation, U.S. producers may have to accept a lower margin in order to be competitive. When the dollar weakens, on the other hand, foreign producers may have to adjust their margins downward in order to remain competitive.

When companies sell similar goods in more than one country, price differences between the countries must not exceed by much the cost of bringing the goods in from a lower-priced country, or spillover in buying will occur. Soft-drink manufacturers can easily vary their prices by a large percentage from country to country, since the cost of transportation would render large-scale movements across borders impractical. However, consumers feasibly could buy abroad and import higher-priced items, such as cameras. For example, importers in the United States and France paid yen to buy Japanese cameras; consequently, the imported price in yen was the same in both France and the United States. But then the franc cheapened in relation to the dollar, so some U.S. dealers scurried to buy inventories located in France rather than buying from the official distributor. U.S. dealers could buy the Olympus OM-10 for $224.95 through the official distributor or for $152 from inventories already in France. Such movements, usually referred to as the gray market, could undermine the longer-term viability of the distributorship system or upset the capacity utilization balance among plants, so camera manufacturers cut camera export prices to the United States to prevent such product arbitrage from taking place. However, some companies take advantage of currency swings by switching exports from one location to another; for example, GAF does this with butane diol, a raw material used in plastic.[32]

Fixed versus Variable Pricing

There are country-to-country differences in
- Whether manufacturers set prices

There is substantial variation from country to country in the extent to which manufacturers can or must set prices at the retail level. For instance, in Venezuela most consumer products must have prices printed on the label, whereas in Chile it is illegal for manufacturers either to suggest retail prices

• Whether prices are fixed or bargained in stores
• What type of establishment has bargaining

or to put prices on labels.[33] There is also a substantial variation in whether consumers bargain in order to settle upon an agreed price. For instance, bargaining takes place in about 60 percent of the stores in India and Kenya but in less than 5 percent in the People's Republic of China and South Africa. Bargaining is much more prevalent in purchases from street vendors in India than in Singapore, whereas bargaining in high-priced specialty stores is more frequent in Singapore than in India.[34]

Countering International Competitors

As long as a firm faces local competitors that lack resources to expand internationally, pricing decisions in one locale will have little potential impact elsewhere. However, firms are increasingly facing the same potential competitors in more than one location, and in these cases pricing decisions must be examined in terms of global competitive strategy. For example, Procter & Gamble was concerned about the possible U.S. entry of the large Japanese consumer-products firm Kao. By selling detergent at a low price in the Japanese market, Procter & Gamble was able to force Kao to freeze its prices for 12 years below those of P&G.[35] This move affected a much larger portion of Kao's profits than P&G's, thus greatly delaying a Kao entry into the United States.

A firm may also face the same industrial consumer in more than one market; therefore, the paint price to Toyota in Mexico may well affect the ability to sell to Toyota in other countries as well.

PROMOTION

Promotion is the process of presenting messages intended to help sell a product or service. The types and direction of messages and the method of presentation may be extremely diverse, depending on the company, product, or country of operation.

The Push-Pull Mix

Push is more likely when
• Self-service is not predominant
• Product price is a high portion of income
• Advertising is restricted

Promotion may be categorized as **push,** which involves direct selling techniques, or **pull,** which relies on mass media. An example of the former would be door-to-door selling of encyclopedias; an example of the latter would be magazine advertisements for a brand of cigarettes. Most firms use combinations of the two strategies. For each product in each country a company must determine its total promotional budget as well as the mix of the budget between push and pull.

Several factors necessitate differences between push and pull among countries: (1) the type of distribution system, (2) the cost and availability of media to reach target markets, (3) consumer attitudes toward sources of information, and (4) price of the product relative to incomes.

Generally, the more tightly controlled the distribution system, the more likely a firm is to emphasize a push strategy because a greater effort is required to get distributors to handle a product. This is true, for example, in Belgium where distributors are small and highly fragmented, thus forcing firms to concentrate on making their goods available.[36] Another distribution factor affecting promotion is the amount of contact between salespeople and consumers. In a self-service situation, where customers lack the opportunity of asking sales personnel their opinions on products, it becomes more important for the firm to advertise through mass media or at the point of purchase.

Because of diverse national environments, promotional problems are extremely varied. In India, for example, the large number of languages, low literacy rate, and lack of reliable media information make it very difficult and expensive to reach the mass market in the country as a whole. Governmental regulations pose an even greater barrier in many countries. For example, Scandinavian television has long refused to accept commercials. A less obvious effect of government on the promotional mix is the direct or indirect tax many countries put on advertising.

France and the United States present an interesting contrast of cultural factors affecting the push-pull mix.[37] U.S. housewives spend more time watching television and reading magazines, and they rely more on friends and advertising before purchasing a new product. French housewives spend more time shopping, examining items on shelves, and listening to the opinions of retailers. It has therefore been easier to presell the U.S. housewives, whereas discounts to distributors and point-of-purchase displays have been more important in France.

Finally, the involvement of consumers before making a purchase decision varies by country. One factor is economics; thus, the price of the product relative to the income of consumers is important in the promotional mix. The more critical the purchase is in relation to income, the more time and information the customer usually will want in order to make a decision. Information is best conveyed in a personal selling situation where two-way communication is fostered. In LDCs, more products will usually have to be pushed. But there are cultural factors as well. The Chinese are poorer than the French, but motion picture attendance has to be pushed less to them. The Chinese see more films than the French and become less involved in deciding to attend films than the French.[38]

Standardization of Advertising Programs

Advantages of standard-
ized advertising include

- Some cost savings
- Better quality at local level
- Rapid entry to different countries

Just as there are possible economies in standardizing products worldwide, there are economies in using the same advertising programs as much as possible, such as on a global basis or among a group of countries with shared consumer attributes. Although these economies are not as great as those found for product standardization, they may nevertheless be significant. McCann-Erickson claims to have saved $90 million in production costs for Coca-Cola by carrying over certain elements of its advertising program on a global basis over a twenty-year period. Some savings occur in hidden costs of executive time spent in supervising advertising campaigns as well.[39] In addition to cost, standardization takes place to improve the quality of advertising at the local level where local agencies may lack expertise. A second reason is so that internationally mobile consumers are not confused by the image the company tries to project. A third reason for standardization is to speed the entry of products into different countries.[40]

Standardized advertising usually means a program that is recognizable from market to market rather than one that is identical in each. Some problems in complete standardization relate to translation, legality, and message needs. Because of these problems, truly multinational campaigns have been rare; rather, there are degrees of similarity. For example, Coca-Cola's print advertisements for the United States and France used the same concept of "refreshment" and both showed young people who had been playing sports. For the United States the slogan was "Coke is it!" and showed a baseball player in action. For France the slogan was "Un Coca-Cola pour un sourire" (A Coca-Cola for a smile) and showed soccer players.

Translation   Obviously, if a firm is going to sell in a country with a different language, messages will almost always have to be translated into that language. The most visible problem is dubbing, which never quite corresponds to lip movements. One approach is to use actors who do not speak, while using a voice and/or print overlay in each language where the ad is used. On the surface, a message translation would seem to be an easy project; however, some things, particularly plays on words, simply don't translate. One example would be the very successful ad for Kellogg's in the United States: "What are you eating? Nut n' Honey." Furthermore, the number of ludicrous but costly mistakes firms have made attest to translation difficulties. Sometimes what is an acceptable word or direct translation in one place is obscene, misleading, or meaningless in another. One firm described itself as an "old friend" of China, but used the character for "old" that meant former instead of long-term.[41] Even within the same language words can mean different things in different countries. For example, United Airlines showed Paul Hogan, star of the *Crocodile Dundee* films, in the Australian Outback on the cover of its in-flight magazine. The caption, "Paul Hogan Camps It Up," meant "flaunts his homosexuality" in Australian slang.[42]

Levi Strauss, which does not attempt to standardize its ads internationally, nevertheless emphasizes its U.S. image in many locales, such as showing James Dean in its Japanese ads and Iowa teenagers in its Indonesian ads. What sets Levi's ad image apart is that most dialogue is in English, even though the language of the country is not.[43]

Legality   What is allowed legally in one place may not be allowed elsewhere. The basic reasons for the differences are national differences in views on consumer protection, competitive protection, promotion of civil rights, standards of morality, and nationalism.[44] A few examples illustrate the vast differences that exist. In terms of protection, policies differ on the amount of deception permitted, what can be advertised to children, whether warnings must be given of possible harmful effects, and the degree to which ingredients must be listed. The United Kingdom and the United States allow direct comparisons of competitive brands (e.g., Pepsi versus Coca-Cola), whereas the Philippines prohibits them. Only a few countries regulate sexism in advertising. In terms of morality and good taste, advertising of some products (e.g., contraceptives and feminine-hygiene products) has been restricted in some locales. Elsewhere, restrictions have been placed on ads that might prompt children to misbehave or people to break laws (e.g., advertising that cars can go faster than the speed limit) and those that show barely clad women. The nationalism issue has arisen in several countries that restrict the use of foreign words, models, or themes in advertisements.

A number of countries restrict the entry of foreign-produced films, tapes, mats, and other advertising materials through import duties, quotas, or embargoes. In addition, union contracts sometimes disallow the use of foreign actors or crews in ads, thus forcing local production.[45]

Message Needs   Because of competitive differences among countries, a universal theme may not be appropriate everywhere. Recall from the discussions of gap analysis and product life cycles how conditions vary. For example, American Express's U.S. campaign of "Do You Know Me?" aimed at gaining market share from other credit cards. However, in Europe the company needed to build credit-card usage.[46]

Content analysis is a way to compare messages by counting the number of times that preselected words, phrases, or pictures appear in a particular medium. Optical scanners now allow easy tabulation and indicate that ads differ among countries apparently because of consumer expectations. For example, Japanese ads tend to be more informative than those in the United States.[47]

LDC Criticism

Critics argue that MNE advertising leads to superfluous and dangerous product consumption in LDCs.

Related to arguments that MNEs introduce superfluous products that consumers in LDCs cannot afford is the assertion that advertising for these products has led to their acceptance by people who are not equipped to understand the product implications or their needs.

The most famous case involved sales of infant formula to developing countries. Infant mortality increased in the poor countries because the rate of bottle feeding increased over breast feeding. Because of low incomes and poor education, mothers frequently overdiluted formula so that it was no longer nutritious and gave it to their babies in unhygienic conditions. Critics argued that the increased bottle feeding resulted from heavy promotion of formula by such firms as Nestlé, Bristol-Meyers, and American Home Products. The firms, in contrast, claimed that increased bottle feeding was due to factors other than promotion of formula—specifically, the firms cited the rise in the number of working mothers and a general trend toward providing fewer products and services that were made in the home. The promotion, they argued, got people to give up their "home brews" in favor of the most nutritious breast milk substitute available. The World Health Organization overwhelmingly passed a voluntary code for restricting formula promotion in developing countries. The company most hit by criticism was Nestlé because it had the largest market share in developing countries and because it was easy to organize a boycott against Nestlé because of its name-identified products. In 1984 the company agreed to prohibit advertising that would discourage breast feeding, to limit free formula supplies at hospitals, and to ban personal gifts to health officials. However, in 1989 a coalition of critics organized another boycott of Nestlé over the same issue.[48]

BRANDING

There are four major branding decisions that MNEs make: brand versus no brand, manufacturer's brand versus private brand, one brand versus multiple brands, and worldwide brand versus local brands.[49] Only the last decision is substantially affected by the international environment.

Some firms, such as Coca-Cola, have opted to use the same brand and logo globally. This gives instant recognition and may save some expense in promotion. Some others, such as Nestlé's Nestea and Nescafé, have associated many of their products under the same family of brands in order to share in the goodwill that the company has developed. Yet, there are a number of problems in trying to use uniform brands internationally.

Language Factors

One problem is that names may carry a different association in another language. GM thought that its model Nova could easily be called the same in Latin America, since it means "star" in Spanish. However, people started pronouncing it "no va," which is the Spanish translation for "it does not go." Coca-Cola tries to use global branding wherever possible, but discovered that the term "diet" in Diet Coke had a connotation of illness in Germany and Italy; consequently, the brand has become Coca-Cola Light outside the United States. Mars hesitated for years to change the name of its Marathon candy bar in Britain to Snickers in order to create an internationally known brand because of the close pronunciation to knickers, a British term for women's underwear.[50]

Pronunciation presents another problem in that languages and alphabets may lack some of the sounds of a brand from another country, or the pronunciation may have a different meaning. McDonald's uses Donald

McDonald in Japan because of the difficulty Japanese have in pronouncing the letter R. Marcel Bich dropped the H from his name when branding pens because of the fear of mispronunciation in English. Perrier's popular French soft drink, Pschitt, has an unappetizing meaning when pronounced in English.

Unilever has successfully translated a brand name for its fabric softener, while leaving its brand symbol, a baby bear, intact on the packaging. "Snuggle" in the United States is "Kuschelweich" in Germany, "Cajoline" in France, "Coccolino" in Italy, and "Mimosin" in Spain. But "Snuggle" did not quite convey the same meaning in English-language speaking Australia, where Unilever uses "Huggy."[51]

Acquisitions

Much of international expansion is through acquisition of companies in foreign countries that already have branded products. When Nestlé acquired Carnation, the Carnation name was so well known in the United States that it was kept as an addition to the canned-milk brands that Nestlé promotes elsewhere. Yet Bic Pens acquired Waterman Pens as its entry into the U.S. market in order to gain the benefit of the Waterman name; however, when the name turned out to have less value than anticipated the Bic name was adopted in the United States as well. Brand-name acquisitions may bring global bad will to the acquirer, even though there is local goodwill where the brand is used. Colgate-Palmolive acquired half ownership in Hawley & Hazel, a Hong Kong firm with a leading market share for toothpaste in several Asian countries. The brand was Darkie, and the logo showed a black minstrellike figure in a silk top hat, which was offensive to many Colgate-Palmolive customers. Subsequently, the company changed the brand to Darlie and put a man of ambiguous race under the top hat.[52] Sunbeam has continued use of acquired brand names in Italy (Rowenta, Oster, Cadillac, Aircap, and Stewart) because they are well known and enjoy goodwill; however, Sunbeam has found that by stretching the promotional budget over so many brands, promotions are not as effective as they might be.[53]

Nationality Images

Images of products are affected by where they are made.

Firms should consider whether to create a local or a foreign image for their products. Certain countries, particularly developed ones, tend to have a higher-quality image for their products than do other countries. But images can change. Consider that various Korean firms sold abroad under private labels or under contract with well-known companies for many years. Some of these companies are now emphasizing their own trade names and the quality of Korean products, such as Samsung.[54]

There also are image differences concerning specific products from specific countries. The French firm BSN-Gervais Dannone brews the largest-selling bottled beer in Europe, and the firm's director general frankly admits that the Kroenenbourg trademark "sounds German."[55]

Generic and Near-Generic Names

If a brand name is used for a class of product, the firm may lose the trademark.

Companies want their product names to become household words but not so much so that trademarked names can be used by competitors to describe similar products. In the United States, the names Xerox and Kleenex are nearly synonymous with copiers and paper tissues, respectively, but have remained proprietary brands. Some other names, such as cellophane, linoleum, and cornish hens have become generic, or available for anyone to use.

Internationally, producers sometimes face substantial differences among countries that may either help or frustrate their sales. Roquefort cheese and champagne are proprietary names in France but generic in the United States, a situation that impairs French export sales of those products. A factor impeding international sales of U.S., Canadian, Irish, and Japanese whiskies is the fact that in much of the world whisky is a synonym for Scotch whisky.

DISTRIBUTION

Firms may have to devise ways to help distributors so they give attention to their products.

A company may accurately assess market potential, design products or services for that market, and promote to likely consumers; however, it will have little likelihood of reaching its sales potential if the goods or services are not conveniently available to customers. This includes getting goods to where people want to buy them. For example, does a man prefer to buy hair dressing in a grocery store, barber shop, drugstore, or some other type of outlet?

Distribution is the course—physical path or legal title—that goods take between production and consumption. In international marketing, a producer must decide on the method of distribution among countries as well as the method of distribution within the foreign country of sale. We have already discussed many considerations for distribution, including the channels of distribution to move goods among countries, how the title to goods gets transferred, and the forms of operations for foreign-market penetration. This section does not repeat these aspects of distribution; rather, it discusses distributional differences and conditions within foreign countries that an international marketer should understand.

Difficult Standardization

Distribution reflects different country environments:
- *It may vary substantially among countries.*
- *It is difficult to change.*

Different Systems   Within the marketing mix, distribution is one of the most difficult functions to standardize internationally for several reasons. First, all countries have their own distribution systems. These are usually difficult to change because they have evolved over time and reflect countries' cultural, economic, and legal environments. Such factors as the attitudes toward owning one's own store, the cost of paying retail workers, labor legislation affecting chains and individually owned stores differently, legislation restricting the size of stores, the trust that owners have in their employees, the efficacy of the postal system, and the financial ability to carry large inventories are but a few of the factors that influence how goods will be distributed in a given country. Table 18.2, for example, shows factors that help to explain why supermarkets are different between Hong Kong and the United States—that is, in Hong Kong they carry a higher proportion of fresh goods, are smaller, sell smaller quantities per customer, and are located more closely to each other.

A few other examples should illustrate how different the distribution norms are. Finland, for example, has few stores per capita because of the predominance of general-line retailers, whereas Italian distribution is characterized by a very fragmented retail and wholesale structure. In the Netherlands buyers' cooperatives deal directly with manufacturers. In Japan there are cash-and-carry wholesalers for retailers who do not need financing or delivery. Mail-order sales are very important in Germany; however, Portugal has offered little as a market for mail-order development.

How do these differences affect companies' marketing activities? One soft-drink company, for example, has targeted most of its European sales through grocery stores; however, the method of getting its soft drinks to those stores has varied widely. For the United Kingdom there is one national distributor who has been able to gain sufficient coverage and shelf space so that the soft-drink firm can concentrate on other aspects of its marketing mix. For France a single distributor has been able to get good coverage in the larger

TABLE 18.2 | SOCIOCULTURAL ELEMENTS OF SUPERMARKET TECHNOLOGY IN THE UNITED STATES AND HONG KONG Different conditions (columns 2 and 3) in respect to sociocultural elements (column 1) have caused supermarkets in Hong Kong to sell a high proportion of fresh foods, to handle customers more frequently, to sell in low quantities, and to be located more closely to competitors.

Sociocultural Elements	United States	Hong Kong
Dietary habits	Like meats Used to frozen foods	Like seafood and meats Used to fresh foods
Shopping patterns	Objective to save time Infrequent	Objective to preserve freshness of food More frequent
Living conditions	Better conditions Spacious	Conditions not as good Crowded
Size of refrigerator	Bigger	Smaller
Availability of car	More available	Less available
Population density	Less dense	Very dense
Urbanization	Low	High

Source: Suk-ching Ho and Ho-fuk Lau, "Development of Supermarket Technology: The Incomplete Transfer Phenomenon," *International Marketing Review,* Vol. 5, No. 1, 1988, p. 27.

supermarkets, but not in the smaller ones; consequently, the soft-drink firm has been exploring how to get secondary distribution without upsetting the relationship with the primary distributor. Within the Norwegian market there are regional distributors, thus the soft-drink firm is challenged in getting them to cooperate sufficiently to enable national promotion campaigns to be effective. Within Belgium the company could find no acceptable distributor, so it has had to take on the functions itself.[56]

Most distributors are national rather than international.

Domestic Rather Than International Distributors   Whereas most large advertising and public-relations firms have become international, few wholesalers and retailers have expanded their services abroad. For advertising and public-relations firms, this has been an advantage in developing various degrees of global programs. For wholesalers and retailers, there has, of course, been some international movement (in fact, a substantial amount since the late 1980s such as Carrefours from France), but mostly companies that are marketing abroad must rely on the services of locally controlled distributors. It is extremely difficult, especially if initial sales expectations are not very high, to get these distributors to alter their accustomed practices to adhere to some practice that the producer wishes to standardize globally.

Choosing Distributors and Channels

Internal Handling   At a low level of sales it is usually more economical to handle distribution through a contract with another company, but a firm may lose a certain amount of control this way. If a company does use external distributors, management should reassess periodically whether sales have grown to the point that they can be handled effectively internally.

Distribution may be handled internally
• At high volume
• When there is a need to deal directly with the customer due to the nature of the product
• When the customer is global
• To gain a competitive advantage

In addition to a high volume of sales, some other circumstances are conducive to the internal handling of distribution. One of these involves the nature of the product. When the product has any of the characteristics of high price, high technology, and need for complex after-sales servicing (such as aircraft), the producer will probably have to get involved in dealing directly with the buyer. In such a situation, the producer nevertheless may use some type of distributor within the foreign country who will serve to identify sales leads. A second situation is when the firm is dealing with global customers, such as an auto-parts manufacturer who sells original equipment to the same automobile manufacturers in more than one country; such sales may go directly from the producer to the global customer. A third situation is when the company views its main competitive advantage to be in its distribution methods, such as some food franchisers. Eventually they may franchise abroad but maintain their own distribution outlet as well to serve as a "flagship." Amway is an example of a firm that has successfully transferred its house-to-house distribution methods from the U.S. to the Japanese market under its own control.[57]

Distributor Qualifications   When using external channels of distribution, a company usually can choose from a number of alternatives. Four common criteria for selection include (1) financial strength; (2) good connections, (3) other business commitments; and (4) personnel, facilities, and equipment. The first is important because of the potential long-term viability of the relationship as well as for assurance that money can be put into such things as the maintenance of sufficient inventory. The second is particularly important if sales must be directed to certain types of buyers, such as government procurement agencies. The third concerns whether the potential distributor has time for a firm's product and whether competitive or complementary products now are handled. Fourth, the current status of personnel, facilities, and equipment indicates not only ability to deal with the product, but also how quickly start-up is feasible.

Some evaluative criteria for distributors include
• Financial capability
• Connections with customers
• Fit with a firm's product
• Other resources

Spare Parts and Repair   Consumers are reluctant to buy products requiring future spare parts and service unless they feel assured that these will be readily available in good quality and at a reasonable price. The more complex and expensive the product, the more important after-sales servicing is. In the 1950s, for example, some European automobile producers entered the U.S. market without ample consideration of this factor. After the European firms made some initial sales, customer "horror stories" followed, such as waiting weeks or months for parts and finding no trained mechanics. Sales dried up as a result. Volkswagen entered later and successfully invested heavily in parts depots and training as well as promotion. Where after-sales servicing is important, it may be necessary for firms to invest in service centers for groups of distributors who serve as intermediaries between producers and consumers. At the same time, sales of parts and service sometimes may be as high as sales of the original product.

Spare parts and service are important for sales.

Gaining Distribution   Firms must do more than evaluate potential distributors. They also must choose which firms and products will get their emphasis. Both wholesalers and retailers have limited storage facilities, display space, money to pay for inventories, and transportation and personnel to move and sell merchandise; therefore, they try to carry only those products with the greatest potential profits. If a firm is new to a country and wishes to introduce products that some competitors are already selling, it may be difficult to convince distributors to handle the new brands. Even established firms sometimes may find it hard to gain distribution for their new products, although they have the dual advantage of being known and being able to use existing profitable lines as "bait" for the new merchandise.

If a firm wishes to use existing distribution channels, it may need to develop incentives for those distributors to handle the product. Firms must analyze competitive conditions carefully in order to offer effective incentives. They may need to identify problems of distributors in order to gain loyalty by offering assistance. For example, Coca-Cola has held seminars for mom-and-

Distributors choose what they will handle. Firms
• May need to give incentives
• May use successful products as bait for new ones
• Must convince distributors that product and firm are viable

pop stores abroad on how to operate more efficiently and compete with larger distributors.[58] Firms may turn to several other distribution possibilities, including offering higher margins, after-sales servicing, and promotional support, which may be offered on either a permanent or an introductory basis. The type of incentive to be offered should depend as well on the comparative costs within each market. In the final analysis, incentives will be of little help unless the distributors believe that a firm's products are viable. The company therefore must sell both itself as a reliable firm and its products to the distributors.

Distribution Segmentation

A firm may enter a market gradually by limiting geographic coverage and emphasizing only certain types of middlemen.

Many products and markets lend themselves to gradual development or to different distributional strategies in different areas. In many cases geographic barriers divide countries into very distinct markets; for example, Colombia is divided by mountain ranges and Australia by a desert. In other countries, such as Zimbabwe and Zaire, very little wealth or few potential sales may lie outside the large metropolitan areas. In still others, advertising and distribution may be handled effectively on a regional basis. For example, when Kikkoman first began selling soy sauce in the United States, the company could not find middlemen willing and able to get the sauce onto the shelves of supermarket chains nationally, nor did Kikkoman have the resources to bypass the middlemen. However, the firm was able to target its first sales to the San Francisco area, where the product was already well known to much of the large Japanese-American population. Through a local food broker Kikkoman gained access to distribution in neighborhoods with a large Asian population. By advertising the product to the general public on television and by showing sales results from the initial distribution, the company was able to gain distribution in other neighborhoods as well. Two years later, Kikkoman moved into Los Angeles, where it continued to expand gradually over the next seventeen years, using food brokers in all cases, until it achieved national distribution and over 50 percent of the soy-sauce market. It is not uncommon for a firm to use one type of middleman in one area and another elsewhere.

Hidden Costs

When companies consider launching products in foreign markets, they must consider what final consumer prices will be in order to estimate sales potential. Because of different national distribution systems, the cost of getting products to consumers varies widely from one country to another. Three of the areas that often contribute to cost differences in distribution are (1) the number of levels in the distribution system, (2) retail inefficiencies, and (3) inventory stock-outs.

Many countries have small multitiered wholesalers who sell to each other before the product reaches the retail level. This sometimes occurs because wholesalers are too small to cover more than a small geographic area, thus national wholesalers sell to regional ones, who sell to local ones, and so on. Japan is an example of a market in which there are about the same number of wholesalers as in the United States despite the much smaller geographic area and population. Because each intermediary adds a markup, the product prices are driven up.[59]

Because of low labor costs and a basic distrust by owners of all but family employees, it is common to find retail practices, particularly in developing countries, that raise the price of merchandise to the shopper. A typical situation is counter rather than self-service: A customer waits to be served and shown merchandise. If the customer decides to purchase what is shown, the customer is given an invoice to take to a cashier's line in order to pay. Once the invoice is stamped as paid, the customer must go to another line to pick up the merchandise after presenting the stamped invoice. This procedure is followed for purchases as small as a pencil. The use of the added personnel adds to the cost of retailing, and the added time that people must be in the store means that fewer people can be served in the given space.

Where retailers are typically small, such as grocers in Spain, there is little space to store inventory. Wholesalers must incur the cost of making small deliveries to many more establishments and may sometimes have to visit each retailer more frequently because of stock outages.

LOOKING TO THE FUTURE   One of the trends that is most likely to have an impact on the future of international marketing is the continued growth in transportation and communications, which gives rise to the global awareness of products and life-styles. Thus a continued trend toward standardized marketing programs on a worldwide basis is likely. This does not, however, mean that international firms will be able to narrow their product lines or promotional activities. Instead, they may have to differentiate further in order to satisfy people's needs according to demographic, sociographic, and psychographic variables that cut across national boundaries. For example, companies may well find themselves defining a market segment as finely as "females, age 26 to 30, working, unmarried, three to four years of college, high achievement motivation, church members, and low dogmatic personalities." As discretionary income increases, not only do exotic products become so commonplace that they lose their attractiveness, but also more products and services compete with each other (e.g., cars, travel, jewelry, and furniture competing for the same discretionary spending) so that increased segmentation is likely to be necessary.

Greater standardization also should not suggest that companies can disregard national differences. As firms from industrial countries have embraced the concept of more global standardization, there is some evidence that they are losing market niches to firms from NICs that are more willing to make adaptations.

Most projections are that disparities between the "haves" and "have-nots" will grow rather than diminish in the foreseeable future, both within and among countries. This is likely to mean a simultaneous growth in affluent and poor market segments. The global affluent sector will have the means of purchasing more goods and services and will not be likely to forego purchases because of antimaterialistic sentiments. Because of the growing education of this sector, more people will be knowledgeable about slight differences in the end utility of products. It will be less possible to segment along national lines to reach these consumers.

The rise in affluence and leisure of the "haves" will probably result in changes in the composition of expenditure. As these people take at least a part of productivity increases in the form of leisure, they will spend a proportionately larger amount of their incomes on entertainment, sports clothes and equipment, organization memberships, and travel. A further change will likely be a greater share of expenditures on services in relation to products.

At the other extreme will be growing numbers of poor people who will have little disposable income to spend on nonnecessities. MNEs will face increasing pressures to develop standardized products to fit the needs of these people and to produce goods by labor-intensive methods so as to employ more people. This will create operational problems because of conflicting competitive pressures to differentiate products and to cut costs through capital-intensive methods.

What products and services are likely to be major growth markets? It is generally agreed that the generation and storage of information will continue to be one of the major growth areas during the next few decades. In addition, it is probable that companies making breakthroughs in process technologies to improve productivity, such as through lasers, optics, and robotics, and those making breakthroughs in energy conservation, such as solar photovoltaics, fuel cells, and coal conversion, will be among the market-growth leaders.

SUMMARY

- Although the principles of selling abroad are the same as those in the home country, the international businessperson must deal with a less familiar environment, which may be subject to rapid change.

- Some methods for broadly assessing foreign demand for products are analysis of consumption patterns, estimates based on what has happened in other countries, studies of historical trends, income elasticity, regression, and gap analysis. Some problems with these tools include taste and technology changes that render past observations and observations in other countries invalid for specific countries.

- A standardized approach to marketing implies maximum uniformity in products and programs among the countries of operation. Although this will minimize· expenses, most firms make changes to fit country needs in order to increase the volume of sales.

■ A variety of legal and other environmental conditions may call for alteration of products in order to capture foreign demand. In addition to determining when products should be altered, businesspeople also must decide how many and which products to sell abroad.

■ Because of different demand characteristics, a product may be in a growth stage in one country and a mature, or declining, stage in another. Firms can usually exert more control over pricing during the growth stage.

■ Governmental regulations may directly or indirectly affect the prices companies charge. International pricing is further complicated because of changes in the values of currencies, differences in product preferences, and variations in fixed prices versus bargaining.

■ For each product in each country a company must determine not only its promotional budget, but also the mix of the budget between push and pull. The relationship between push and pull promotions should depend on the distribution system, cost and availability of media, consumer attitudes, and the product price relative to incomes.

■ Some major problems for standardizing advertising in different countries involve translation, legality, and message needs.

■ Global branding is hampered by language differences, expansion by acquisition, national images, and laws concerning generic names.

■ Distribution channels vary substantially among countries. These differences may affect not only the relative costs of operating, but also the ease of making initial sales.

C   A   S   E
SOURCE
PERRIER[60]

During the strong-dollar era of the 1950s–1960s, when hordes of tourists flocked to France from the United States, one of their concerns was the purity of French tap water. When purchasing the alternative, bottled water, they complained about those with bubbles. At that time, the probability that, by 1980, Americans would be importing from France over $65 million per year of Perrier's naturally carbonated water seemed

very remote. Yet there had been an earlier market for French water in the United States: One of the earliest customers was Benjamin Franklin, who, after returning from being ambassador in Paris, imported his drinking water. Near the turn of the century, Perrier set up U.S. distribution; however, by 1976 sales had reached only 3.5 million bottles per year. The so-called Perrier freaks had to hunt in gourmet shops or a few bars to quench their thirsts. At over $1 for a 23-ounce bottle, the product had gained acceptance only among a small group of high-income people. Thus, it was a product with small sales and high retail margins.

By the early 1970s, Source Perrier, given its large share of the bottled-drink market, was having trouble sustaining growth in France. The company sought to increase sales by acquiring related French companies, including firms producing soft drinks, milk, chocolate, and confectionery products. In 1972 Poland Spring, a U.S. firm producing still (noncarbonated) spring water was acquired. None of these ventures fared well under Perrier's leadership.

The Chairman of Source Perrier, Gustave Levin, met Bruce Nevins, who as an executive of Levi Strauss had been instrumental in the upsurge of jeans sales. Nevins believed it would be possible to develop a mass market for a "noncaloric, chic alternative to soft drinks." The U.S. soft-drink market at that time was about $10 billion wholesale. Thus the stakes were high—so high, in fact, that Perrier sold off 70 percent of its acquisitions in 1975–1976 (including Poland Spring) to finance a U.S. marketing subsidiary. The new subsidiary, Great Waters of France, was headed by Bruce Nevins.

A number of conditions made Nevins optimistic about the possible acceptance of Perrier water by U.S. consumers. The most important of these was growing consumer diet-consciousness. Miller Brewing had had phenomenal success a few years earlier with the introduction of Lite beer. Since cyclamates had been banned in soft drinks, producers of low-calorie sodas had turned to saccharin, which many people found distasteful. Also there was no popular low-calorie drink that was considered chic. The use of the adjective "diet" simply announced that the drinker had weight problems. If people could be persuaded that Perrier tasted good, then it could become a preferred low-calorie alternative.

A second trend Nevins observed was a movement toward natural foods for health reasons. Even tap water and the 75 percent of bottled water processed from tap water had become suspect because in the process of purification, cancer-suspect chlorine derivatives were added

to water. Furthermore, certain viruses, sodium, and heavy metals still were found in most purified water and soda water. Perrier came from natural springs and contained high levels of calcium, very little sodium, and no additives. It could be promoted as a natural drink with healthy properties, even though some of the bubbles were lost when the water was removed from the springs and put back in during the bottling process.

A third factor was a growing U.S. preference for imports, apparent not only in the rising ratio of imports to gross national expenditures, but also in the acceptance of "foreignness." In terms of food, so-called gourmet restaurants, cookbooks, dinner clubs, ingredients, and wines were becoming commonplace, and French items were practically synonymous with the word gourmet. Perrier might capitalize successfully on these attitudes.

The marketing program for Great Waters of France got underway in 1977. One of the first questions was in which part of the market to position Perrier. The three trends just discussed clearly would lead to different price, promotional, and distributional strategies. In seeking the diet market segment, for example, Perrier would come face-to-face with Coca-Cola and Pepsi-Cola, which between them controlled 45 percent of the soft-drink market. These firms, along with many others, fought vigorously in the market by keeping prices fairly low, advertising heavily, and clamoring for shelf space in supermarket soft-drink sections. The difficulty of competing in this segment is evident from the experience of Schweppes, which despite establishing U.S. bottling facilities and engaging in heavy marketing outlays had failed to get even 1 percent of the market. Competing in this mass-market segment also might cause Perrier to lose the snob appeal it held among high-income buyers.

Entering the natural or health-foods segment would pit Perrier against other bottled-water producers and various tonics that contained healthful additives. This was a very small market compared with that for soft drinks. The 1976 sales of bottled water were $189 million, of which 93 percent was from purified domestic still water, which was sold largely in five-gallon containers at low prices through home or commercial delivery. Less than 20 percent of bottled water was sold in retail stores, and there was little brand identification. To expand retail sales probably would mean concentrating on gaining shelf space in the health-food sections of stores. Since bottled-water sales were determined to be much more geographically concentrated (about 50 percent in California) than soft-drink sales, it would be far easier for Perrier to target its promotion and distribution for this segment.

Source Perrier had been selling to the gourmet market for some 70 years. Undoubtedly there were usage and distribution gaps in this market. The total sales of mineral water in 1976 were only $15 million. Primary demand might be increased, and Perrier might be made more readily available through increased distribution to specialty stores and new distribution to the growing gourmet sections of supermarkets.

Perrier decided to hit the mass market by competing in the soft-drink market segment, but price was a problem. Through massive distribution, the retail price could be cut about 30 percent from what it was when the company emphasized the gourmet segment of the market; however, the price was still about 50 percent higher than the average soft-drink price, partly due to the cost of transporting water across the Atlantic. Furthermore, the price included a retail gross margin of 27.6 percent as compared to 22.6 percent on soft drinks in order to make supermarkets more willing to handle Perrier. Perrier kept its price at "rock bottom" not only to become more price competitive with domestic soft drinks, but also to dissuade other European firms from exporting to the United States. To get people to pay what was still a high price, the company had to segment the soft-drink market differently than anyone had done so far—by

aiming at an adult population and using the higher price to gain snob appeal.

Great Waters of France felt that distribution was the key to success. A sales force of 40 people, almost all of whom were formerly with soft-drink firms, was hired. Three cities (New York, San Francisco, and Los Angeles) were picked for the first expansion efforts because they had consumers with the largest penchant for imported food items. The company made a film designed to convey to distributors and supermarket chains that Perrier water had a long-term viability. The film showed that the springs had been popular as far back as 218 B.C., when Hannibal partook of the waters, and that the present firm dated back to 1903, supplied 400 million bottles a year, and outsold the leading cola in Europe by 2 to 1. Perrier sought the most aggressive distributors, including soft-drink bottlers, alcoholic-beverage distributors, and food brokers in different areas. For Perrier's success, it was essential that distributors be able to get supermarket space in the soft-drink sections, replenish stocks frequently, and set up point-of-purchase displays. One of the first distributors, Joyce Beverage Management, bought 55 trucks and hired 100 additional people to handle the Perrier account. In the introductory period, arrangements were made for secondary display stacks and in-store tastings. The company also gave cents-off coupons with purchases. Within a year, Perrier had moved from three to twenty major market areas; this was doubled in the second year.

Perrier developed 11-ounce and 6.5-ounce bottles, the latter sold in multipacks. They also developed a modern logo on the bottles, which was later replaced by the original label design, more in line with the old-world image that the firm wished to project. With initial distribution assured, it was necessary to get sufficient appeal so that the bottles on the shelves would be sold. In Europe the company could make therapeutic claims; however, U.S. law very strictly forbade this. In test marketing, Perrier tried such themes as "Formerly heavy drinkers such as Richard

Burton and Ed McMahon are now 'hooked' on Perrier" and Perrier "contains no sodium which causes heartburn."

These claims were abandoned in favor of messages emphasizing the water's qualities as a natural thirst-quencher with no calories and no additives. Initial promotion was regional, relying heavily on the print media. Groups of food and beverage writers were invited for dinners and exhibitions so that they would write about Perrier. The company sponsored marathons so that the product would be associated both with "healthiness" and "thirst-quenching." As distribution became national, Perrier switched to television spots on major networks. The advertising budget was set high. Perrier was able to maintain snob appeal by getting tidbits in gossip columns about celebrities being seen sipping Perrier in the "right places."

Sales increased rapidly to over 200 million bottles in 1980. The increase did not go unnoticed by either the media or competitors. By 1979 a bottling executive said, "Everyone with water seeping from a rock is buying glass, slapping a label on it, and marketing a new bottled water." Some of the old bottled spring water firms suddenly sought a larger share of the growing market. They promoted blind tasting comparisons to emphasize that U.S. water was just as tasty as the imports. Nestlé's Deer Park brand made a challenge with a spring water priced 35 to 40 percent below Perrier. A Chicago firm, Hincley and Schmitt, introduced Premier in a bottle with a label that unashamedly copied Perrier. Its theme was, "Let your guests think it's imported." Norton Simon's Canada Dry began repositioning its club soda to be more competitive with Perrier. A market-research group, SAMI, reported 104 brands of bottled waters in its territory.

By 1980, Bruce Nevins believed that the "U.S. market for sparkling water is in the process of maturing." Perrier's sales peaked in 1980 and began falling, largely because of competition from domestic seltzer (carbonated tap water) and domestic club soda (carbonated tap water to

which mineral salts are usually added). Sales of imported water in the United States fell from 28.1 million gallons in 1979 to 12.1 million in 1982. To combat U.S. domestic competition, Perrier repurchased Poland Spring in 1980. After buying Poland Spring in 1976 for $1 million, Poland Spring's new owners had carbonated the still water, modernized the facilities, and captured 6 percent of the bottled-water market. The reported purchase price in 1980 was $10 million. But most of the growth in bottled waters was not for spring waters, which constituted only 11 percent of the bottled-water market by 1982. Another problem was that the name Perrier was becoming practically generic as customers increasingly asked for Perrier when they simply wanted some kind of sparkling water.

In 1982 Perrier devised a new U.S. strategy, the handling of specialized imports that could be sold to market segments similar to those to which Perrier seemed to appeal. This segment was described by different Perrier officials as "aspirant people who try to improve their quality of life," as "households with incomes of $30,000 or more," and as "the same people who tend to buy better fashions, better cars, and the like." Perrier took on Lindt chocolate from Switzerland in 1982 and Bonne Maman preserves from France in 1983. Both of these firms had been selling previously in the U.S. market with annual sales of $1 million and $1.5 million before the Perrier connection. By 1984 their sales were estimated to be $15 million and $5 million, respectively. In 1985 Perrier began marketing its mineral water with traces of lemon, lime, or orange flavoring to try to shore up its U.S. water sales.

But what had appeared to be a maturing of the U.S. bottled-water market turned out to be a mere blip. By the mid-1980s industry sales were growing at between 15 and 20 percent annually, the second-fastest beverage growth just behind wine coolers. The fastest segment of that growth was for imported mineral water. But the U.S. market has continued to be fragmented. One reason is that the cost and technology to enter the market are low; thus 50 new companies started up in 1986 alone. A second reason is that transportation costs lead to regional distribution. By 1985 only Perrier was distributed nationally because it is actually cheaper to ship the water from France than to ship domestic waters across the United States by truck or rail. By 1988 several industry trends seemed apparent to Perrier's management:

1. Growth in all sectors of the bottled-water market would be robust over the next ten years, especially in geographic areas not yet accounting for a large share of the sales.

2. Big competitors increasingly would get involved. Coca-Cola, PepsiCo, Anheuser-Busch, and Japan's Suntory had all recently become involved in some aspect of the market through ownership, bottling, or distribution.

3. Because of the capital-intensive nature of distribution (e.g., cost of adding trucks), growth would be more apt to come from acquisitions by the bigger competitors than from the start-up of new firms.

4. New importers would attack Perrier through targeting specific U.S. market niches. For example, Rambosa (Sweden) targeted snooty consumers, Eau Canada Sparcal (Canada) played up its high calcium content to appeal to women fearful of developing weak bones, and Heart of Tuscany (Italy) promoted its low mineral content for therapeutic value.

As a result of these trends, Perrier reemphasized the bottled-water market in the United States as opposed to the handling of related products. This was done largely through acquisitions: Perrier acquired Calistoga in California, Oasis Water in Texas, and Zephyr Hill in Florida. It outbid major competitors to acquire Arrowhead, the market-share leader in bottled water, for an estimated $500 million. Perrier has made no attempt to connect these brands to the Perrier name.

In 1990 Perrier was hit by two unforeseen events that had a negative impact on its U.S. sales. First, due to a bottling worker's error in France, some bottles reaching the U.S. were contaminated with benzene, forcing a worldwide recall. Second, the Federal Food and Drug Administration (FDA) required two changes in Perrier's labels: The terms "naturally sparkling water" and "calorie free" had to be dropped because of carbonation added and because "calorie-free" seemed to imply that other water contains calories. Prior to the recall the Perrier brand held 5.7 percent of the U.S. bottled-water market and 44.8 percent of the imported market, but these sales fell 42 percent in 1990. Its major French competitor, BSN's non-bubbly Evian, became the number-one U.S. water import. Yet Perrier-owned brands in the United States, which held 18.2 percent of the bottled-water market, increased their sales so that overall sales went up by 3 percent in the U.S. market.

Many U.S. analysts openly questioned whether Perrier would ever regain the market share that had made it the best-selling bottled water in the United States. U.S. supermarket sales rebounded to their earlier level in the first year after the benzene-scare recall; however, sales in restaurants and bars, which had accounted for 35 percent of the Perrier brand sales in the United States, have not recovered completely. In contrast, Perrier regained its French market share (the number 2 position after BSN's Badoit for bubbly water) almost immediately after relaunching the water in 1990.

In 1991 Perrier's new chairman, Jacques Vincent, announced a long-term strategic change for Perrier. The company plans to position Perrier as a more exclusive product to be sold mainly in restaurants. Supermarket sales will focus on locally produced, less expensive brands that are not readily associated with the Perrier name. To this end, Perrier acquired Volvic and Contrex, two popular brands in Europe outside of France. Through brand diversification, Perrier expects to be able to minimize problems with any single brand.

Questions

1. Might Perrier have been better off by positioning itself in a segment other than the soft-drink market?
2. Should Perrier have tried a means other than exporting to penetrate the U.S. market?
3. What insights or useful analysis might be gained by applying the tools and concepts of this chapter to Perrier?
4. What characteristics might account for Perrier's quicker recovery in the French than in the U.S. market?
5. What options are open to Perrier in the United States?

Chapter Notes

1. Data for the case were taken from "M & S in Japan," *The Times* (London), August 7, 1978; "M & S Getting Their French Lessons Right," *The Times* (London), August 2, 1976, p.16; Sandra Salmans, "Britain: How Marks & Spencer Lost Its Spark," *New York Times*, August 31, 1980, p. F3; Barbara Crossette, "British Store Shapes Up for Parisians," *New York Times*, June 28, 1975, p. 14; "St. Michael Spreads the Gospel," *Economist*, September 1977, pp. 68–69; "Super Supermarkets," *The Accountant*, June 26, 1980, pp. 981–983; Carrie Dolan, "Marks & Spencer Finds No-Frills Policy in Retailing Suits the British Just Fine," *Wall Street Journal*, April 14, 1981, p. 35; Alan Freeman, "Marks & Spencer Canada Adheres to Parent's Principles Despite Losses," *Wall Street Journal*, August 4, 1981, p. 39; Patience Wheatcroft, "Marks Looks at Sparks," *The Times* (London), October 23, 1983, p. 53; Margaret de Miraval, "British Influence Aiding French Department Stores," *Christian Science Monitor*, July 7, 1983, p. 15; "Marks & Spencer Tries Yet Again," *Financial Times*, April 25, 1985, p. 16; Brian Oliver, "M & S Targets U.S.," *Advertising Age*, Vol. 58, No. 9, March 2, 1987, p. 46; Mina Williams, "St. Michael Chilled Foods Introduced in Kings Stores," *Supermarket News*, December 11, 1989, p. 1 ff; Andrew Collier, "Marks & Spencer to Buy More Abroad," *Women's Wear Daily*, October 6, 1989, p. 6; Stephen Dowdell, "Marks & Spencer Buys Kings in First U.S. Food Venture," *Supermarket News*, August 15, 1988, p. 1 ff; Steven Weiner, "Low Marks, Few Sparks," *Forbes*, September 18, 1989, pp. 146–147; and Isadore Barmash, "Brooks Brothers Stays the Course," *New York Times*, November 23, 1990, p. C1.

2. For a discussion of differences and similarities, see Hugh E. Kramer, "International Marketing: Methodological Excellence in Practice and Theory," *Management International Review*, Vol. 29, No. 2, 1989, pp. 59–65.

3. For a more extensive coverage of similar techniques, see Susan P. Douglas, C. Samuel Craig, and Warren J. Keegan, "Approaches to Assessing International Marketing Opportunities for Small- and Medium-sized Companies," *Columbia Journal of World Business*, Vol. 17, No. 3, Fall 1982, pp. 26–32.

4. Bill Powell and Frederick Shaw Myers, "Death by Fried Chicken," *Newsweek*, September 24, 1990, p. 36.

5. Reed Moyer, "International Market Analysis," *Journal of Marketing Research*, November 1968, pp. 357–359.

6. Houston H. Stokes and Hugh Neuburger, "The Box-Jenkins Approach—When Is It a Cost-Effective Alternative?" *Columbia Journal of World Business*, Winter 1976, pp. 78–86.

7. H. Youn Kim, "Estimating Consumer Demand in Korea," *Journal of Development Economics*, Vol. 20, No. 2, 1986, pp. 325–338.

8. Joann S. Lublin, "Slim Pickings," *Wall Street Journal*, May 15, 1990, p. A20.

9. J. A. Weber, "Comparing Growth Opportunities in the International Marketplace," *Management International Review,* No. 1, 1979, pp. 47–54.

10. "Chocolate Makers in Switzerland Try to Melt Resistance," *Wall Street Journal,* January 5, 1981, p. 14.

11. Yumiko Ono, "Japanese Treating Themselves to More Imported Chocolate," *Wall Street Journal,* January 5, 1990, p. A4.

12. Bruce Siefert and John Ford, "Are Exporting Firms Modifying Their Product, Pricing and Promotion Policies?" *International Marketing Review,* Vol. 6, No. 6, 1989, pp. 53–68, discuss these points.

13. For a discussion of niche strategy, see James Leontiades, "Going Global—Global Strategies vs. National Strategies," *Long Range Planning,* Vol. 19, No. 6, December 1986, pp. 96–104. For details on the bourbon example, see James S. Hirsch, "U.S. Liquor Makers Seek Tonic in Foreign Markets," *Wall Street Journal,* October 24, 1989, p. B1 ff.

14. Michael J. McCarthy, "More Companies Shop Abroad for New Product Ideas," *Wall Street Journal,* March 14, 1990, p. B1 ff.

15. John D. Daniels, "Combining Strategic and International Business Approaches through Growth Vector Analysis," *Management International Review,* Vol. 23, 3, 1983, p. 11.

16. John Thackray, "Much Ado about Global Marketing," *Across the Board,* April 1985, pp. 38–46; Yves L. Doz, "Managing Manufacturing Rationalization within Multinational Companies," *Columbia Journal of World Business,* Fall 1978, pp. 82–93.

17. John S. Hill and Richard R. Still, "Adapting Products to LDC Tastes," *Harvard Business Review,* Vol. 62, No. 2, March–April 1984, pp. 92–101.

18. Bob Davis, "Europe Defeats Japan's Proposal on TV Standard," *Wall Street Journal,* May 25, 1990, p. B4.

19. G. Pierre Goad, "In the U.S., They'll Probably Try Renaming It McGlop or Big Muck," *Wall Street Journal,* March 8, 1990, p. B1.

20. Andrew H. Malcolm, "On the Battlefield of Beauty," *New York Times,* May 22, 1977, p. 1.

21. William W. Locke, "The Fatal Flaw: Hidden Cultural Differences," *Business Marketing,* Vol. 7, No. 4, April 1986, p. 65 +.

22. Donald G. Howard, "Developing a Defensive Product Management Philosophy for Third World Markets," *International Marketing Review,* Vol. 5, No. 1, Spring 1988, pp. 31–40.

23. Siefert and Ford, *loc. cit.*

24. *Momentum* (an in-house magazine published by Coca-Cola), 1970, p. 17.

25. Susan P. Douglas and C. Samuel Craig, "Evolution of Global Marketing Strategy: Scale, Scope and Synergy," *Columbia Journal of World Business,* Vol. 14, No. 3, Fall 1989, p. 54.

26. Mattel, *1979 Annual Report,* p. 10; Stephen Baker, Sally Gelston, and Jonathon Kapstein, "The Third World Is Getting Cellular Fever," *Business Week,* April 16, 1990, pp. 80–81.

27. Saeed Samiee, "Pricing in Marketing Strategies of U.S.- and Foreign-Based Companies," *Journal of Business Research,* Vol. 15, No. 1, February 1987, pp. 17–30.

28. Alicia Swasy, "Foreign Formula," *Wall Street Journal,* June 15, 1990, p. A7.

29. Mark Alpert and Aimety Dunlap Smith, "Nestlé Shows How to Gobble Markets," *Fortune,* Vol. 119, January 16, 1989, p. 76.

30. Johny K. Johansson and Hans B. Thorelli, "International Product Positioning," *Journal of International Business Studies,* Vol. 16, No. 3, Fall 1985, pp. 57–75.

31. Swasy, *loc. cit.*

32. Ann Hughey, "'Gray Market' in Camera Imports Starts to Undercut Official Dealers," *Wall Street Journal,* April 1, 1982, p. 29; Douglas R. Sease, "Selling Abroad," *Wall Street Journal,* August 31, 1987, p. 1 +.

33. Hill and Still, *op. cit.,* p. 95.

34. Laurence Jacobs, Reginald Worthley, and Charles Keown, "Perceived Buyer Satisfaction and Selling Pressures versus Pricing Policy: A Comparative Study of Retailers in Ten Developing Countries," *Journal of Business Research,* Vol. 12, No. 1, March 1984, p. 67.

35. Alicia Swasy and Jeremy Mark, "Japan Brings Its Packaged Goods to U.S.," *Wall Street Journal,* January 17, 1989, p. B1.

36. Seymour Banks, "Cross-National Analysis of Advertising Expenditures: 1968–1979," *Journal of Advertising Research,* Vol. 26, No. 2, April–May 1986, p. 21.

37. Robert T. Green and Eric Langeard, "A Cross-National Comparison of Consumer Habits and Innovator Characteristics," *Journal of Marketing,* July 1975.

38. Judith I. Zaichkowsky and James H. Sood, "A Global Look at Consumer Involvement and Use of Products," *International Marketing Review,* Vol. 6, No. 1, 1989, pp. 20–34.

39. John A. Quelch and Edward J. Hoff, "Customizing Global Marketing," *Harvard Business Review,* Vol. 64, No. 3, May–June 1986, p. 62; Dennis Chase, "Global Marketing: The New Wave," *Advertising Age,* June 25, 1984, p. 49 +; Joanne Lipman, "Ad Fad," *Wall Street Journal,* May 12, 1988, p. 1 +.

40. "Multinationals Tackle Global Marketing," *Advertising Age,* June 25, 1984, p. 50.

41. Rene White, "Beyond Berlitz: How to Penetrate Foreign Markets through Effective Communications," *Public Relations Quarterly,* Vol. 31, No. 2, Summer 1986, p. 15.

42. John R. Zeeman, "What United Airlines Is Learning in the Pacific," speech before the Academy of International Business, Chicago, November 14, 1987.

43. Maria Shao, Robert Neff, and Jeffrey Ryser, "For Levi's, A Flattering Fit Overseas," *Business Week,* November 5, 1990, pp. 76–77.

44. Frank J. Prial, "Very, Very Bad, Pakistani Says as He Confiscates Lingerie Ad," *New York Times,* April 20, 1981, p. A11; Barry Newman, "Watchdogs Abroad," *Wall Street Journal,* April 8, 1980, p. 1 +; J. J. Boddewyn, "Advertising Regulation in the 1980s: The Underlying Global Forces," *Journal of Marketing,* Vol. 46, Winter 1982, pp. 27–35; Damon Darlin, "Advertising," *Wall Street Journal,* April 19, 1989, p. B1; Michael Richardson, "Malaysia TV Debate: Beyond Skin-Deep," *International Herald Tribune,* June 28, 1989, p. 5; "Breaking Britain's Speed Limit," *Wall Street Journal,* September 24, 1990, p. A10.

45. Jean J. Boddewyn, *Barriers to Trade and Investment in Advertising: Government Regulation and Industry Self-Regulation in 53 Countries* (New York: International Advertising Association, 1989).

46. John Marcom, Jr., "American Express's Ads in Europe Seek to Leap Borders," *Wall Street Journal,* April 1, 1988, p. 16.

47. David R. Wheeler, "Content Analysis: An Analytical Technique for International Marketing Research," *International Marketing Review,* Vol. 5, No. 4, Winter 1988, pp. 34–40.

48. "Boycott against Nestlé over Infant Formula to End Next Month," *Wall Street Journal,* January 27, 1984, p. 19; Alix M. Freedman, "Advertising," *Wall Street Journal,* April 25, 1989, p. B6.

49. Sak Onkvisit and John J. Shaw, "The International Dimension of Branding: Stra-

tegic Considerations and Decisions," *International Marketing Review,* Vol. 6, No. 3, 1989, pp. 22–34.

50. Steven Prokesch, "'Eurosell' Pervades the Continent," *New York Times,* May 31, 1990, p. C1 ff.

51. Shlomo Maital, "Transnational Teddies," *Across the Board,* Vol. 26, No. 10, October 1989, pp.15–18.

52. Douglas C. McGill, "Colgate Will Change Toothpaste's Name," *New York Times,* January 27, 1989, p. 25.

53. Myron M. Miller, "Sunbeam in Italy: One Success and One Failure," *International Marketing Review,* Vol. 7, No. 1, 1990, pp. 68–73.

54. "Marketing Korean as Korean," *Business Korea,* Vol. 3, No. 5, November 1985, p. 41.

55. William H. Flanagan, "Big Battle Is Brewing as French Beer Aims to Topple Heineken," *Wall Street Journal,* February 22, 1980, p. 16. For some Japanese examples, see Yumiko Ono, "Japan Eats Up 'U.S.' Food Never Tasted in America," *Wall Street Journal,* April 4, 1990, p. B1 ff.

56. John D. Daniels, "Bridging National and Global Marketing Strategies Through Regional Operations," *International Marketing Review,* Vol. 4, No. 3, Autumn 1987, pp. 29–44.

57. Yumiko Ono, "Amway Translates with Ease into Japanese," *Wall Street Journal,* September 21, 1990, p. B1 ff.

58. Michael J. McCarthy, "The Real Thing," *Wall Street Journal,* December 19, 1989, p. A1 ff; Bert Rosenbloom, "Motivating Your International Channel Partners," *Business Horizons,* Vol. 33, No. 2, March–April 1990, pp. 53–57.

59. Michael R. Czinkota, "Distribution in Japan: Problems and Changes," *Columbia Journal of World Business,* Vol. 20, No. 3, Fall 1985, p. 66.

60. Data for the case were taken from Louis Botto, "Straight from the Source," *New York Times Magazine,* June 26, 1977, pp. 68–72; Roger B. May, "French Bottler Tries to Replace U.S. Pop with a Natural Fizz," *Wall Street Journal,* April 12, 1978, p. 1 +; "Deep Chic," *Wall Street Journal,* December 7, 1979, p. 24; Carolyn Pfaff, "Perrier Fortunes Rest On Whimsical Chief," *Advertising Age,* April 14, 1980, p. 66; Peter C. DuBois, "Perrier Going Flat?" *Barron's,* May 12, 1980, p. 71; "Perrier: Putting More Sparkle into Sales," *Sales & Marketing Management,* January 1979, pp. 16–17; Bob Lederer and Martin Westerman, "How Perrier Became a Soft Drink," *Beverage World,* May 1979, pp. 37–45; "Perrier: The Astonishing Success of an Appeal to Affluent Adults," *Business Week,* January 22, 1979, pp. 64–65; "The Water Treatment," *Fortune,* January 12, 1981, p. 22; "Sales Boon for Bottled Water," *New York Times,* August 8, 1982, p. F27; Steven P. Galante, "Perrier's U.S. Marketing Know-How Put to Use for Other European Brands," *Wall Street Journal,* June 26, 1984, p. 30; Lawrence M. Fisher, "A New Zip to Bottled Water Sales," *New York Times,* May 23, 1986, p. F6; John Roussant, "Perrier's Unquenchable U.S. Thirst," *Business Week,* No. 3005, June 29, 1987, p. 46; Robert Alsop, "New Imports Aiming to Take the Fizz Out of Perrier's Sales," *Wall Street Journal,* December 24, 1987, p. 11; Anthony Ramirez, "Perrier Recall: How Damaging Is It?" *New York Times,* February 13, 1990, p. C1 ff; Barry Meier, "Perrier Will Bow to F.D.A. and Change Its Label," *New York Times,* April 19, 1990, p. C7; Alix M. Freedman, "Perrier Finds Mystique Hard to Restore," *Wall Street Journal,* December 12, 1990, p. B1 ff; Mark Landler, Lisa Driscoll, and Stewart Toy, "You Can Lead a Restaurateur to Perrier, But . . . ," *Business Week,* June 25, 1990, pp. 25–26; E. S. Browning, "Perrier Chief Serves Up New Formula," *Wall Street Journal,* February 14, 1991, pp. B1–B2.

CHAPTER **19**

MULTINATIONAL ACCOUNTING AND TAX FUNCTIONS

Even between parents and children, money matters make strangers.
JAPANESE PROVERB

Objectives

- To examine the major factors influencing the development of worldwide accounting objectives, standards, and practices.

- To explain how to account for foreign currency transactions and foreign currency financial statements.

- To show how firms must disclose financial data concerning their international operations.

- To investigate the major aspects of the taxation of foreign-source income in the United States from export activities, branches, and foreign affiliates and subsidiaries.

- To examine some of the major non-U.S. tax practices and to show how international tax treaties can alleviate some of the impact of double taxation.

- To learn what MNEs need to consider in order to plan the tax function properly.

In 1989 Daimler-Benz was the second-largest corporation in Germany in terms of market value, the forty-second-largest corporation in the world in terms of market value, and the fifth most profitable firm in the world with profits of $3.8 billion. Its primary product divisions are Mercedes-Benz, AEG (which focuses on automation systems, office and communications systems, electrotechnical systems and components, electrical consumer products, microelectronics, and transportation systems), and Deutsche Aerospace. In 1989 Daimler-Benz derived 61 percent of its sales from abroad. As illustrated in Map 19.1, Daimler-Benz lists its principal subsidiaries and affiliated companies in the annual report and provides several pieces of financial information for its major subsidiaries around the world.

Daimler-Benz stock has been listed on all German stock exchanges and the Swiss stock exchanges in Basel, Geneva, and Zurich. In 1990 Daimler-Benz stock was introduced on the London and Tokyo exchanges. Thus it must comply with the listing requirements for exchanges in all four countries.

Daimler-Benz provides some interesting information not always seen in a U.S. annual report. Consolidated sales information is provided for the period 1985–1989, as shown in Fig. 19.1. However, it is not possible to find profit and identifiable asset information as would be the case for U.S. and U.K. firms.

Management also breaks down employment into foreign and domestic operations and provides a great deal of information on the major factors causing changes in employment from year to year. Daimler-Benz also includes a value-added statement as shown in Fig. 19.2. The value-added statement separates sales revenues into different categories so that one can see how much value was added to the inputs purchased from the outside. This type of statement is seen in Europe on occasion but is totally lacking in U.S. reports.

As illustrated in Fig. 19.3, Daimler-Benz's balance sheet is very different from what one would see in the United States, but is more similar to what would be seen in the European Community. The EC directive on the format and content of financial statements has created a more uniform set of financial statements for European firms.

Daimler-Benz also does a good job of describing how world events have affected its operations. For each of its divisions, there is a discussion of the performance of the division and what the key sources of influence were. Although market demand was more a function of economic growth in export markets than in currency values in 1989, that was not the case in other years. In 1985–1987, when the dollar began its first long drop against the Deutsche mark and other hard currencies, the weak dollar was making it very difficult for Daimler-Benz to sell in the United States.

C A S E
DAIMLER-
BENZ[1]

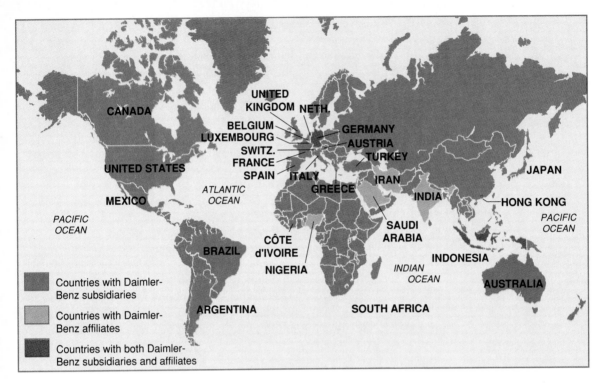

Map 19.1
The World of Daimler-Benz
Daimler-Benz has subsidiaries in 23 countries involved in manufacturing or
assembly operations, distribution, real estate and finance operations, and service
operations. It also has affiliated companies in eight countries. *Source:* Daimler-Benz,
Annual Report, 1989.

Because Daimler-Benz is a German company, the financial statements
are in Deutsche marks rather than in dollars, and the financial statements
are generated according to generally accepted accounting standards in Germany. In its notes to the financial statements, management describes the
key accounting principles and methods followed. The following statement
from the 1989 annual report illustrates the difficulties that an MNE faces as
it tries to satisfy financial statement users from around the world.

> Due to the requirements arising from its restructuring into a globally operating,
> integrated high-technology group, Daimler-Benz has brought the application of
> accounting principles more closely into line with national and international
> practice. When operating purely as an automobile company, a conservative ac-
> counting and valuation policy was applied; this, however, led to a situation
> whereby the newly structured Daimler-Benz group could no longer be appro-

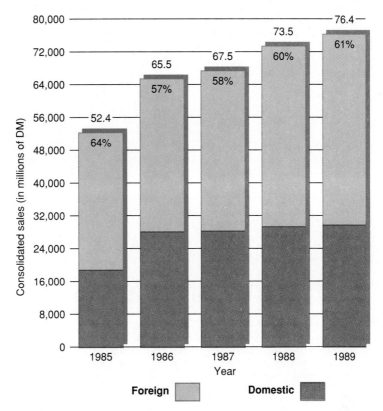

Figure 19.1
Consolidated Sales, Daimler-Benz
Foreign sales as a percentage of total sales is greater than 50 percent,
demonstrating the importance of global markets to Daimler-Benz. *Source:* Daimler-
Benz, *Annual Report, 1989,* p. 11.

priately judged in international comparison. It is for this reason that we have
made the following specific valuation changes. . . .

Management then goes on to describe the key changes in valuation
that it made for the 1989 annual report.

In 1990 Daimler-Benz announced that it was discussing different forms
of cooperation with some of the divisions of the Mitsubishi Group. The
sharing of financial information between a German and Japanese firm could
result in problems in interpreting that information, even though the Japanese accounting system was significantly influenced by the Germans in the
latter part of the nineteenth century and the early part of the twentieth
century.

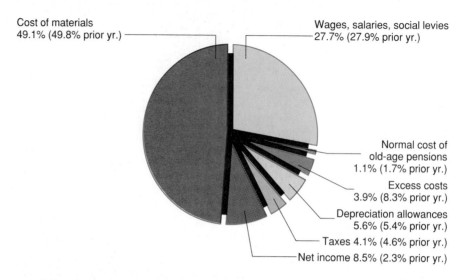

Cost of materials
49.1% (49.8% prior yr.)

Wages, salaries, social levies
27.7% (27.9% prior yr.)

Normal cost of
old-age pensions
1.1% (1.7% prior yr.)

Excess costs
3.9% (8.3% prior yr.)

Depreciation allowances
5.6% (5.4% prior yr.)

Taxes 4.1% (4.6% prior yr.)

Net income 8.5% (2.3% prior yr.)

EXPENSE STRUCTURE IN TERMS OF TOTAL OUTPUT DAIMLER-BENZ GROUP
Total output DM 80.6 billion (DM 75.6 billion last year)

Figure 19.2
Daimler-Benz Value-Added Statement
The two largest portions of the sales dollar of Daimler-Benz are the cost of
materials that are purchased from the outside and the wages and salaries that
are used to convert the materials into final products. *Source: Annual Report, 1989,
Daimler-Benz, p. 62.*

INTRODUCTION

The accountant is essential in providing information to decision makers.

The finance and accounting functions of Daimler-Benz, like those of any multinational enterprise, are very closely related. Each relies on the other in fulfilling its own responsibilities. The financial manager of any firm, whether it be domestic or international, is responsible for procuring and managing the company's financial resources. But these functions cannot be performed without the availability of adequate and timely information from the accountant.

The actual and potential flow of assets across national boundaries complicates the finance and accounting functions. The MNE must learn to cope with differing rates of inflation, changes in exchange rates, currency controls, the risk of expropriation, and different customs, levels of sophistication, and local requirements.

The international controller must be concerned about different currencies and accounting systems.

A firm's accounting or controllership function is responsible for collecting and analyzing data for internal and external users. To manage assets, the corporate treasurer needs accounting information on the nature and extent of those assets. As noted in Chapter 17, local managers and operations are usually evaluated with information provided by the controller's office. Reports

70 |

ASSETS	Notes	December 31, 1989 In Millions of D-Marks	December 31, 1988 In Millions of D-Mark
Non-Current Assets			
Intangible Assets	(1)	130	1,575
Fixed Assets	(2)	13,508	10,984
Financial Assets	(3)	1,403	1,105
Leased Vehicles	(4)	5,043	3,678
		20,084	17,342
Current Assets			
Inventories	(5)	18,726	12,923
Advance Payments Received	(6)	(6,390)	(4,538)
		12,336	8,385
Receivables	(7)	10,511	8,523
Other Assets	(8)	9,732	8,179
Marketable Securities	(9)	6,016	5,279
Cash	(10)	2,985	3,179
		41,580	33,545
Prepaid Expenses and Deferred Taxes	(11)	1,073	1,044
		62,737	51,931

STOCKHOLDERS' EQUITY AND LIABILITIES			
Stockholders' Equity	(12)		
Capital Stock	(13)	2,330	2,118
Paid-In Capital	(13)	2,114	370
Retained Earnings	(14)	11,195	7,518
Minority Interests	(15)	767	626
Unappropriated Profit of Daimler-Benz AG		560	691
		16,966	11,323
Provisions			
Provisions for Old-Age Pensions and Similar Obligations	(16)	10,086	13,624
Other Provisions	(17)	16,624	12,287
		26,710	25,911
Liabilities			
Accounts Payable Trade	(18)	5,810	4,837
Other Liabilities	(19)	12,963	9,732
		18,773	14,569
Deferred Credits		288	128
		62,737	51,931

Figure 19.3
Consolidated Balance Sheet of Daimler-Benz AG
The balance sheet of Daimler-Benz is very different from that of a U.S. company, especially in the order of liquidity. *Source: Annual Report, 1989,* Daimler-Benz, p. 70.

also must be generated for internal consideration, local governmental needs, creditors, shareholders, and prospective investors. The controller must be concerned about the impact of many different currencies and varied rates of inflation on the statements as well as be familiar with different countries' accounting systems.

FACTORS INFLUENCING THE DEVELOPMENT OF ACCOUNTING AROUND THE WORLD

Both the form and the substance of financial statements are different in foreign countries.

One of the problems that Daimler-Benz faces is that accounting systems vary around the world. This means that financial statements in France, for example, do not look the same as financial statements in the United States. Some observers argue that this is a minor matter, based in form rather than substance. In fact, however, the substance is also different, such as in Peru, where consolidation of related companies is not allowed; in Sweden, where significant inventory write-downs are allowed; and in France and Germany, where tax accounting and book accounting are essentially the same. These variations put the MNE in a difficult position because it needs to prepare and understand reports generated according to the local accounting standards as well as prepare financial statements consistent with **generally accepted accounting principles (GAAP)** in the home country in order to generate consolidated financial statements.

Accounting Objectives

The FASB sets accounting standards in the United States.

Critical users of information are creditors, stockholders, investors, and employees.

The IASC is an international private-sector body that sets accounting standards.

Accounting is basically a process of identifying, recording, and interpreting economic events, and its goals and purposes should be clearly stated in the objectives of any accounting system. The **Financial Accounting Standards Board (FASB)** in the United States stated that financial reporting should provide information useful in: (1) investment and credit decisions; (2) assessments of cash-flow prospects; and (3) evaluating enterprise resources, claims to those resources, and changes in them.[2] The users identified by the board are primarily investors and creditors, although other users might be considered important. The **International Accounting Standards Committee (IASC),** a multinational standard-setting organization comprised of professional accounting organizations from over 40 countries, includes employees as well as investors and creditors as the critical users. Also named are suppliers, customers, regulatory and taxing authorities, and many others.

Although the question has been discussed widely, there has been no consensus on whether a uniform set of accounting standards and practices exists for all classes of users worldwide or even for one class of users. To understand the different accounting principles and how they affect the MNEs' operations, we must examine some of the forces leading to the development of accounting principles internationally. Figure 19.4 shows these major factors. The top four factors deal with the nature of the enterprise and the direct users of information. The bottom four represent other major factors that affect accounting objectives, standards, and practices.

Nature of the Enterprise   Within every enterprise there are many users of information, such as managers and employees. The quantity and quality of information provided depends on the users' level of sophistication as well as

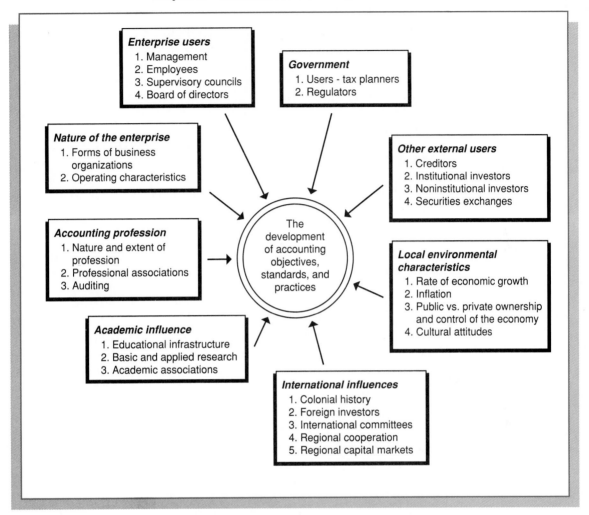

Figure 19.4
Major Domestic and Worldwide Factors Influencing the Development of Accounting Objectives, Standards, and Practices
There are several factors that influence the development of accounting objectives, standards, and practices; most of them relate to internal factors, but some of them are a result of external influences. *Source:* Lee H. Radebaugh, "Environmental Factors Influencing the Development of Accounting Objectives, Standards, and Practices—The Peruvian Case," *The International Journal of Accounting,* Fall 1975, p. 41.

on the accountants' technical competence. Managers require specialized information to assist in decision making, and this has led to the development of managerial accounting. Employees, especially in Europe, have a vested interest in the enterprise and may have an impact on the disclosure of financial data as they seek better wages and working conditions.

Government   Government is one of the most pervasive forces in the development of accounting objectives, standards, and practices. Government can be divided into two groups: users and regulators. Users are tax authorities, planning commissions, and various agencies that compile statistics for general use. Regulators, such as the Securities and Exchange Commission in the United States, respond to the perceived best interests of the general public.

The extent to which the government becomes involved in the setting of objectives, standards, and practices depends on the interaction of all the factors listed in Fig. 19.4. Where the government is an important user of information, does not feel that the accounting profession is meeting users' needs, and does not foresee much change in the near future, it will probably take a much more active role in influencing the development of accounting.

Other External Users   The major external users of information other than those mentioned above are investors and creditors. Investors can work alone or through institutions by way of pension funds, mutual funds, and other such investments. In countries where there is a small equity market, creditors tend to be an important source of financing and thus a strong influence on accounting standards and practices.

Local Environmental Characteristics   This category of factors influencing accounting is probably the broadest and perhaps the most important, including such diverse influences as cultural attitudes and the nature and state of the economy. The four factors listed in Fig. 19.4 are by no means exhaustive. Although the characteristics are referred to as "local," they are not independent of the world economy. The rates of economic growth and inflation depend on a country's major trading partners as well as on internal economic conditions.

International Influences   Many international forces that are institutional rather than environmental have influenced accounting principles worldwide. A prime example is the colonial influence of England and France during the past few centuries. Each of these countries carried their business and accounting philosophies to their colonies and instituted similar systems. The United States also has tended to do this as its economic influence has spread through direct foreign investment.

Accounting Profession   As it has done in countries such as the United States, Canada, the United Kingdom, and the Netherlands, the accounting profession itself can influence the development of accounting principles. Three aspects of the profession are important: (1) its nature and extent, (2) the existence of professional associations, and (3) the auditing function. In some countries, the profession is relatively undeveloped and has little influence on accounting. In the United States and the United Kingdom, however, the profession is quite large and well-developed, and it has a strong influence on the development of accounting standards and practices. The existence of associations, such as the American Institute of CPAs, is important, because these groups can often be a force for change. Finally, a strong profession often results in a strong auditing function. Independent external auditors are needed to verify that the financial statements adhere to accepted accounting standards and that they represent the true financial position of the firm.

Academic Influence   The academic infrastructure refers to the quality of accounting education offered as well as to the accessibility of this education. One of the typical problems in developing countries is the shortage of qualified professors in the accounting field. Since instruction in accounting is not considered a full-time profession and generally is not done at a very high level, little academic research that could introduce change in accounting practices is done.

HARMONIZATION OF DIFFERENCES

Because of the different factors that influence the establishment of accounting standards and the practice of accounting in each country, there are significant differences in the way accounting is practiced. In the opening case, we discussed the disclosure of information by Daimler-Benz, a German corporation. Germany relies on the law for the basis of its accounting standards. When German auditors audit the financial statements of German firms, they try to make sure that the firms use accounting practices that are in compliance with the law. In fact, the audit report of Daimler-Benz states the following:

> The annual accounts, which have been audited in accordance with professional standards, comply with the legal provisions. With due regard to the generally accepted accounting principles, the annual accounts give a true and fair view of the assets, liabilities, financial position and profit and loss of Daimler-Benz Aktiengesellschaft.

The reference to the legal provisions is significant. The British tend to establish their accounting standards through the private sector, so the law contains only general guidance as to the form and content of financial statements. However, the law does require that the financial statements reflect a true and fair view, so that tends to be the overriding principle in financial accounting and reporting. The Germans also have a true and fair view, but they assume that their laws are true and fair, so compliance with the law is the same as a true and fair view.

This illustrates one of the ways that accounting standards and practices differ from country to country. The major reasons why accounting standards differ are as follows:

1. Varying perceptions of the objectives of business organizations, e.g., government-owned vs. private-owned.

2. Differing views regarding the purpose of financial statements, such as the legal vs. true and fair view described above.

3. Differences in the development of the accounting profession.

4. Influence of the tax laws.

5. Legal requirements.

6. Differences in basic economic facts, such as inflation in Brazil.

7. Lack of enforceability of worldwide standards.

8. Government vs. private-sector development of standards.

9. Widespread cultural differences—language, government priorities, societal needs.

10. A strong sense of nationalism and the desire to avoid dependency on outside influences for the establishment of accounting standards.

Harmonization is possible because of the growing linkage of global capital markets and the activities of MNEs.

In spite of the reasons for differences in accounting, there are still a number of major forces leading to harmonization. The major force is the movement to an investor orientation in different countries. That implies that firms will need to provide information compatible with the needs of investors. Second, there is a global integration of capital markets taking place. Since investors can get access to investment opportunities around the world more easily and faster than ever, they need financial information that is more comparable. Third is the need on the part of MNEs to raise capital in capital markets outside of their own national markets and the desire to generate as few different financial statements as possible. Fourth is regional political and economic harmonization, such as the efforts to integrate in Europe. That harmonization has an impact on accounting as well. Finally, MNEs are pressuring for more uniform standards, not only for accessing global capital, but also for greater ease and reduced costs in their general reporting in each country and on a consolidated basis.

The European Community is harmonizing accounting in order to promote the free flow of capital.

Given these incentives, some serious efforts have been undertaken to harmonize accounting standards on a regional as well as an international level. Regionally, the most ambitious and potentially most effective efforts are taking place in the EC. The EC's Commission is empowered to set directives, which are orders to the member states to bring their laws into line with EC requirements within a certain transition period. The initial directives involved the type and format of financial statements, the measurement bases on which the financial statements should be prepared, the importance of consolidated financial statements, and the requirement that auditors ensure that the financial statements reflect a true and fair view of the operations of the firm being audited.

The International Accounting Standards Committee (IASC), organized in 1973 by the professional accounting bodies of several primarily industrial countries and Mexico, has worked toward harmonizing accounting standards. Initially, the IASC wanted to develop standards that would have rapid and broad acceptance; thus it seemed to focus mostly on improved disclosure. More recently, it has been interested in tackling some more substantive issues. It also issued an exposure draft on narrowing the options present in the earlier standards so that it could have standards that are much more precise.

The IASC has no power to enforce its standards.

The IASC must rely on goodwill for acceptance of its standards since it has no legislative mandate as does the EC. However, with over 100 professional accounting organizations representing 70 countries and more than 900,000 accountants in the IASC, a number of countries have used the standards as models for their own legislation. Singapore, for example, has adopted IASC standards successfully.

Most IASC standards have been issued after the relevant U.S. standards. Consequently, there are few major differences between IASC standards and U.S. GAAP. Apparently the presence of the United States as a founding member of the IASC has allowed it considerable input and influence in the decision-making process. Although it would be difficult to imagine an IASC standard in substantial conflict with U.S. GAAP, there were some standards being considered in 1990–1991 that would conflict with U.S. GAAP and require a decision on the part of the U.S. standard-setting community as to the role of international standards.

TRANSACTIONS IN FOREIGN CURRENCY

One of the major problems of accounting for international business is that of operating in different currencies. In addition to eliminating or minimizing foreign-exchange risk, a firm must concern itself with the proper recording and subsequent accounting of assets, liabilities, revenues, and expenses that are measured or denominated in a foreign currency. These transactions can result from the purchase and sale of goods and services as well as the borrowing and lending of foreign currency.

Recording of Transactions

Foreign currency receivables and payables give rise to gains and losses whenever the exchange rate changes.

Any time a U.S. importer is required to pay for equipment or merchandise in a foreign currency, it must trade U.S. dollars for that currency to pay the supplier. Assume that Sundance Ski Lodge buys skis from a French supplier for FF 28,000 when the exchange rate is $0.1900/FF. Sundance would record the following on its books:

Purchases	5,320	
Accounts payable		5,320
FF 28,000 @ $0.1900		

As long as Sundance pays immediately, there is no problem. But what happens if the exporter extends 30 days' credit to Sundance? The original entry would be the same as above; during the next 30 days, anything could happen. If the rate changed to $0.1800/FF, Sundance would record a final settlement as follows:

Accounts payable	5,320	
Gain on foreign exchange		280
Cash		5,040

The merchandise stays at the original value of $5320, but there is a difference between the dollar value of the account payable to the exporter ($5320) and the actual dollars that the importer must come up with in order to purchase the French francs to pay the exporter ($5040). The difference between the two accounts ($280) is the gain on foreign exchange and is recognized as income.

Transaction gains and losses must be included in income in the accounting period in which they arise.

These gains and losses arising from foreign currency transactions must be recognized at the end of each accounting period, even if the payable (in the case of a purchase) or receivable (in the case of a sale) has not been settled. For most U.S. companies this adjustment is made every month. Using the example just given, assume that the end of the month has arrived and Sundance still has not paid the French exporter. The skis continue to be valued at $5320, but the payable has to be updated to the new exchange rate of $0.1800/FF. The journal entry to record that would be:

Accounts payable	280	
Gain on foreign exchange		280

The liability would now be worth $5040. If settlement were to be made at the end of the next month and the exchange rate were to remain the same, the final entry would be:

Accounts payable	5,040	
Cash		5,040

If the U.S. firm were an exporter and anticipated receiving foreign currency, the corresponding entries (using the same information) would be:

Accounts receivable	5,320	
Sales		5,320
Cash	5,040	
Loss on foreign exchange	280	
Accounts receivable		5,320

In this case a loss results because the firm receives less cash than if it had collected its money immediately.

Correct Procedures for U.S. Firms

The procedures that U.S. firms must follow to account for foreign currency transactions are found in Financial Accounting Standards Board (FASB) Statement No. 52, "Foreign Currency Translation," which was adopted in December 1981. The FASB is the private-sector organization in the United States that establishes accounting standards. Statement 52 requires that firms record the initial transaction at the spot-exchange rate that is in effect on that date and record receivables and payables at subsequent balance-sheet dates at the spot-exchange rate on those dates. Any foreign exchange gains and losses that arise from carrying receivables or payables during a period when the exchange rate changes are taken directly to the income statement.[3] In its 1988 Annual Report, for example, Ford Motor Company stated the following: "Exchange gains and losses from transactions in a currency other than the local currency of the entity involved . . . are included in income. Changes in foreign exchange rates reduced net income by \$117 million (24 cents a share) in 1988. . . . These amounts included net transaction and translation gains before taxes of \$734 million in 1988. . . ."[4] Although some information was provided, Ford did not specifically state how much of the exchange gain was due to foreign currency transactions and how much was due to the translation of foreign currency financial statements.

TRANSLATION OF FOREIGN CURRENCY FINANCIAL STATEMENTS ▮

Translation is the process of restating foreign currency statements into U.S. dollars.

Consolidation is the process of combining financial statements of different operations into one statement.

Even though MNEs receive reports originally developed in a variety of different currencies, they eventually must end up with one set of financial statements in U.S. dollars in order to help management and investors get an aggregate view of worldwide activities in a common currency. The process of restating foreign currency financial statements into U.S. dollars is known as **translation.** The combination of all of these translated financial statements into one is known as **consolidation.**

Translation in the United States is a two-step process: The first step involves recasting the foreign currency financial statements into statements consistent with U.S. GAAP; the second step involves translating all foreign currency amounts into U.S. dollars. FASB Statement No. 52 also describes the manner in which firms must translate their foreign currency financial statements into dollars.

Translation Methods

Statement 52 allows for two methods to be used to translate financial statements: the current rate and the temporal methods. The choice of the translation method depends on the functional currency of the foreign operation. The **functional currency** is the currency of the primary economic environment in which the entity operates. If the functional currency is that of the local operating environment, the firm must use the **current rate method.** If the functional currency is the U.S. dollar, the firm must use the **temporal method.** For example, Coca-Cola states in its annual report that it distributes its products in more than 160 countries and uses approximately 40 functional currencies. In countries like Germany and Britain, the functional currency would be the Deutsche mark and the pound, respectively, because Coca-Cola's primary operating environment would be the local environment. Thus Coca-Cola would use the current rate method to translate its financial statements from Deutsche marks and pounds to dollars.

Since the current rate method is used more extensively than the temporal method, the following illustration focuses on the current rate method. The temporal method is also more complex than the current rate method and beyond the scope of this book. According to the current rate method, all assets and liabilities are translated into dollars at the exchange rate in effect on the balance-sheet date, also known as the current rate. For most U.S.-based MNEs, which tend to use a calendar year, that would be the exchange rate in effect on December 31. Capital stock is translated at the exchange rate in effect when the stock is actually issued, and retained earnings is simply the dollar accumulation of income from all prior years.

The income statement is translated into dollars by using the average exchange rate for the year. The exchange rate used to translate dividends into dollars is the rate in effect when the dividends are actually declared.

Table 19.1 shows how to translate a balance sheet using the current rate method, and Table 19.2 does the same for the income statement method. Note that the current rate (the exchange rate in effect on December 31, 1991) was $1.30, the rate in effect when capital stock was issued was $1.90, the average rate for the year was $1.40, and the rate in effect when dividends were declared was $1.42.

As noted in Table 19.2, the retained earnings balance at the end of 1990 was $11,560. The retained earnings balance for the end of the year is determined by adding net income for 1990 to the beginning retained earnings balance and subtracting dividends. That amount can then be put into the

---

The functional currency is the currency of the primary economic environment in which the entity operates.

The current rate method is used when the local currency is the functional currency.

The temporal method is used when the parent's reporting currency is the functional currency.

For the current rate method, every income statement account is multiplied by the average exchange rate.

TABLE 19.1 | BALANCE SHEET, DECEMBER 31, 1991 The balance-sheet accounts are translated at the current exchange rate, except for capital stock and net worth.

	Local currency	Current Rate Method Exchange rate	Current Rate Method Dollars
Assets			
Cash and receivables	4,000	1.30	$ 5,200
Inventory	4,500	1.30	5,850
Property, plant, and equipment (net)	14,000	1.30	18,200
	22,500		$29,250
Liabilities and Shareholders' **Equity**			
Current liabilities	5,500	1.30	$ 7,150
Notes payable	5,500	1.30	7,150
Capital stock	5,000	1.90	9,500
Retained earnings	6,500		13,650
Accumulated translated adjustment			(8,200)
	22,500		$29,250

TABLE 19.2 | INCOME STATEMENT, 1991 The income statement reflects operating income but does not include translation gains and losses.

	Local currency	Current Rate Method Exchange rate	Current Rate Method Dollars
Sales	18,000	1.40	$25,200
Expenses			
Cost of Sales	9,000	1.40	12,600
Depreciation	3,000	1.40	4,200
Other expenses	2,100	1.40	2,940
	14,100		19,740
Income before taxes	3,900		$ 5,460
Income taxes	1,900	1.40	2,660
Net income	2,000		2,800
Retained earnings (12/31/90)	5,000		11,560
	7,000		$14,360
Dividends	500	1.42	710
Retained earnings (12/31/91)	6,500		$13,650

balance sheet in Table 19.1. The only amount in the balance sheet that is not determined by translating a local currency amount into dollars is the accumulated translation adjustment, which arises because accounts from year to year are translated at different exchange rates. That amount can be determined by subtracting liabilities, capital stock, and retained earnings from total assets.

Disclosure of Foreign-Exchange Gains and Losses

We have seen that a company can experience two kinds of foreign-exchange gains and losses: those that arise from foreign currency transactions and those that arise from the translation of foreign currency financial statements into dollars. Gains and losses from foreign currency transactions are taken directly to the income statement, but a firm is not required by Statement 52 to show the amount or the location on the income statement.

According to the current rate method, the translation gain or loss is taken to stockholders' equity.

The treatment of foreign-exchange gains and losses arising from translation depends on how the firm translates its financial statements. If the current rate method is used, the translation gains and losses are taken to the balance sheet and called the accumulated translation adjustment. Table 19.3 illustrates the stockholders' equity section of the balance sheet for Ford Motor Company in 1988. As can be seen, the accumulated translation adjustment is a significant number. The change between 1987 and 1988 for Ford was very big due to the relative instability in foreign-exchange markets during that time.

In the temporal method, the translation gain or loss is taken to income.

If the temporal method is used, the translation gains and losses are taken to the income statement. That has caused a corporation's net income (and, therefore, earnings per share) to fluctuate wildly as the exchange rate changes, which is a major reason why firms prefer to use the current rate method where possible. In the case of Ford Motor Company, the notes to the financial statements mentioned transactions *and* translation gains in income in 1988, so it must have had some foreign operations that translated financial statements according to the temporal method. Since it also had foreign operations that translated financial statements according to the current rate method, it is evident that firms can use the current rate method for some operations and the temporal method for others; one does not have to use one method exclusively.

Daimler-Benz does not provide as much information about the translation of financial statements as does Ford. The translation methodology used by Daimler-Benz is different from what is required in the United States, as is the recognition of translation gains and losses. Some are taken to retained earnings, and some are recognized directly in income. In addition, Daimler-Benz does not recognize the amount of the transactions and translation gains and losses recognized in 1989.

TABLE 19.3 | STOCKHOLDERS' EQUITY, FORD MOTOR COMPANY (in millions) The stockholders' equity section of Ford Motor Company's balance sheet contains an accumulated translation adjustment account that is the result of translating the financial statements by the current rate method.

Stockholders' Equity	1988	1987
Capital stock		
Preferred stock, par value $1.00 a share	—	—
Common stock, par value $1.00 a share (453.6 and 469.8 shares issued)	453.6	469.8
Class B stock, par value $1.00 a share (37.2 and 37.7 shares issued)	37.2	37.7
Capital in excess of par value of stock	586.7	595.1
Foreign currency translation adjustments	325.0	672.6
Earnings retained for use in business	20,126.5	16,717.5
Total stockholders' equity	21,529.0	18,492.7

TAXATION

Tax planning influences profitability and cash flow.

Tax planning is crucial for any business, since it can have a profound effect on profitability and cash flow. This is especially true in international business. As complex as domestic taxation seems, it is relatively simple compared to the intricacies of international taxation. The international tax accountant must be familiar not only with the home country's tax policy relating to foreign operations, but also with the laws of each country in which the client operates.

Taxation has a strong impact on the choice of: (1) location in the initial investment decision; (2) legal form of the new enterprise, such as branch or subsidiary; (3) method of finance, such as internal versus external sourcing and debt versus equity; and (4) method of arranging prices between related entities.[5] This section of the chapter examines taxation for the firm involved in international operations. Emphasis will be placed on U.S. tax policy because of the nature and extent of U.S. foreign direct investment. As any country finds its firms generating more and more foreign-source income, it must decide on the principles of accounting for that income. Therefore, principles of taxation that U.S.-based MNEs face at home and abroad are, or could be, applicable to firms domiciled in other countries.

TAXATION OF FOREIGN-SOURCE INCOME ▮▮▮▮▮▮▮▮▮

When a domestic firm makes the decision to sell its products internationally, it can do so directly through the export of goods and services (including licensing agreements, management contracts, and so on), through foreign branch operations (a legal extension of the parent), and through foreign corporations in which the domestic firm holds an equity interest that could vary from a small percentage to complete ownership.

Export of Goods and Services

Many enterprises, such as public accounting firms, advertising agencies, banks, and management consulting firms, deal in services rather than products. Many manufacturing industries also find it easier and more profitable to sell expertise, such as patents or management services, rather than goods. Generally, payment is received in the form of royalties and fees, and this payment usually is taxed by the foreign government. Since the sale of services is made by the parent, the sale also must be included in the parent's taxable income.

Despite the large amount of foreign direct investment, U.S. firms still export a great deal of merchandise. In 1990 this export figure reached $389.3 billion.[6] Generally, the profits from these exports are taxable immediately to the parent. However, many governments have created tax incentives to encourage exports.

An FSC can be used by a U.S. exporter to shelter some of its income from taxation.

In order to gain tax advantages from exporting, a U.S. firm can set up a **Foreign Sales Corporation (FSC)** abroad, according to strict guidelines established by the IRS. If the foreign corporation qualifies as an FSC, a portion of its income is exempt from U.S. corporate income tax. Also, the law provides that any dividends distributed by the FSC to its parent company are exempt from U.S. income taxation as long as that income is foreign trade income.

The FSC must be engaged in substantial business activity.

Certain kinds of economic activity qualify for the FSC legislation: the export of merchandise as well as services such as engineering services or architectural services. Also it is important that substantial economic activity take place outside of the United States. The FSC cannot be a mailbox company in Switzerland that simply passes documents from the United States to the importing country. The FSC must engage in advertising and sales promotion, processing customer orders and arranging for delivery, transportation, the determination and transmittal of a final invoice or statement of account and the receipt of payment, and the assumption of credit risk.[7]

Foreign Branch

A foreign branch is an extension of the parent rather than an enterprise incorporated in a foreign country, as is a foreign manufacturing subsidiary.

Foreign branch income (loss) is directly included in the parent's taxable income.

Therefore, any income generated by the branch is taxable immediately to the parent, whether or not cash is remitted. One important aspect of taxation of foreign branch income is that if the branch suffers a loss, the parent is allowed to deduct that loss from its taxable income, thus reducing its overall tax liability. There is no such thing as deferral in the case of a branch, since all income or loss is immediately combined with parent income or loss. **Deferral** means that foreign-source income generally is not taxed until it is remitted to the parent company.

Deferral means that income is not taxed until it is remitted to the parent company as a dividend.

Foreign Corporations

In a CFC 50 percent of voting stock is held by U.S. shareholders.

CFC   From a tax standpoint it is critical to determine first of all whether or not the foreign subsidiary or affiliate is a **controlled foreign corporation (CFC).** A CFC is any foreign corporation in which 50 percent or more of the voting stock or value of the corporation is held by "U.S. shareholders." A U.S. **shareholder** is a U.S. person or enterprise that holds 10 percent or more of the voting stock of the subsidiary. Table 19.4 explains how this might work.

Foreign corporation A is a CFC because it meets both tests described above. This is the case when A is a wholly owned subsidiary of parent firm V in the United States. Foreign corporation B is also a CFC because U.S. persons V, W, and X are qualified "U.S. shareholders," and their share of the voting stock exceeds 50 percent. Foreign corporation C is not a CFC, because only U.S. persons V and W are qualified "U.S. shareholders," and their combined voting shares do not equal or exceed 50 percent.

Active income derives from the active conduct of a trade or business.

Once a CFC has been identified, its income must be divided into two categories: (1) active income and (2) subpart F, or passive, income. **Active income** implies that it is income derived from the active conduct of trade or business, whereas **passive income** usually results from operations in **tax-haven countries,** such as Panama, the Bahamas, the Netherlands Antilles,

TABLE 19.4 | DETERMINATION OF CONTROLLED FOREIGN CORPORATIONS A controlled foreign corporation must have U.S. shareholders holding more than 50 percent of the voting shares.

Shareholders and Their Percentage of the Voting Stock	Foreign Corporation A	Foreign Corporation B	Foreign Corporation C
U.S. person V	100%	45%	30%
U.S. person W		10	10
U.S. person X		20	8
U.S. person Y			8
Foreign person Z		25	44
Total	100%	100%	100%

Passive income is usually derived from operations in tax-haven countries.

Hong Kong, and Switzerland. In Chapter 9, we discussed the importance of offshore financial centers. Companies established in these centers are often called tax-haven subsidiaries.

A tax-haven country is one with low or no taxes on foreign-source income.

The tax-haven subsidiary sometimes has acted as a holding company for its parent of stock in foreign subsidiaries (called grandchild or second-tier subsidiaries, as illustrated in Fig. 19.5), a sales agent or distributor, an agent for the parent in licensing agreements, or an investment company. The tax-haven subsidiary is meant to concentrate cash from the parent's foreign operations into the low-tax country and to use the cash for global expansion. As long as a dividend is not declared to the parent, no U.S. tax must be paid. However, the Revenue Act of 1962 eliminated the deferral concept for tax-haven subsidiaries involved in passive rather than active investments.

Subpart F income is earned by a CFC in a tax-haven country from passive activities outside of the country.

Subpart F Income   As noted earlier, **subpart F income** is passive income, because it is not derived from the active conduct of a trade or business, such as manufacturing and selling products at market prices. Subpart F income basically is earned by CFCs in a tax-haven country from activities outside of that country. This type of income comes from the following major sources.

1. **Holding company income:** primarily dividends, interest, rents, royalties, and gains on sale of stocks.
2. **Sales income:** income from foreign sales subsidiaries that are separately incorporated from their manufacturing operations. The product is either manufactured, produced, grown, or extracted outside of and sold for use

Figure 19.5
The Tax-Haven Subsidiary Acting as a Holding Company
A parent company can shelter income from U.S. tax by utilizing a tax-haven subsidiary in low-tax countries.

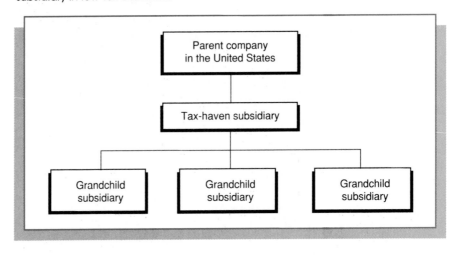

outside of the CFC's country of incorporation. Any CFC performing significant operations on the property is excluded, such as when personnel in the CFC are heavily involved in selling the product.

3. **Service income:** income from the performance of technical, managerial, or similar services for a related person and performed outside the country in which the CFC is organized.

The importance of distinguishing between a CFC and a non-CFC and subpart F and active income is in the application of the deferral principle, which is summarized in Fig. 19.6. As long as a foreign corporation is not a controlled foreign corporation, its income is not taxable to the parent until a dividend is received by the parent. Thus the income is deferred from taxation in the U.S. If the foreign corporation is a controlled foreign corporation, the deferral principle applies to the active but not to the subpart F income, which is immediately taxable to the parent.

There is an exception, however. If foreign-base company income is the lower of $1 million or 5 percent of gross income, none of it is treated as subpart F income. If foreign-base company income is subject to a tax of at least 90 percent of the U.S. tax liability, the income also is not subject to U.S. tax.

Figure 19.6
Deferral for Different Legal Forms
The three forms of foreign organization have different rules relating to the deferral principle.

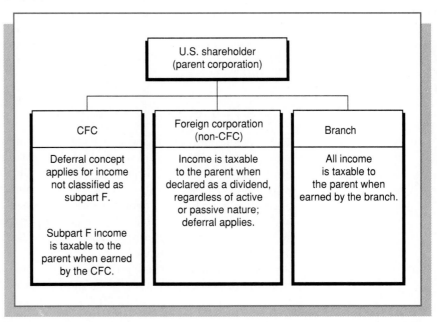

Tax Credit

The IRS allows a tax credit for corporate tax paid to another country.

Every country has a sovereign right to levy taxes on all income generated within its borders. Problems arise when firms are owned by foreigners, such as foreign corporations, or are branches of foreign corporations. This problem has been important for U.S. firms because of the magnitude of foreign direct investment.

The credit is a dollar-for-dollar reduction of the tax liability and must coincide with the recognition of income.

As was mentioned earlier, the U.S. parent is able to defer recognition of active income until a dividend is declared to the parent. Then the parent gets credit for a portion of income taxes paid. For example, if 50 percent of the income of the foreign subsidiary is distributed as a dividend to the parent, the parent can claim no more than 50 percent of the tax as a creditable tax. Branches are not allowed the deferral privilege, so their income is taxed immediately to the parent, but all branch foreign income taxes are eligible for inclusion in the tax credit. Credit also is allowed for taxes (called **withholding taxes**) paid by the parent to the foreign government on dividends paid by the foreign corporation to the parent.

Credit is subject to the upper limit of what the tax would have been in the United States.

After the firm adds up its eligible credits, it finds that it is constrained by an upper limit imposed by the IRS. The upper limit is what the firm would have paid in taxes on that income in the United States. If the foreign-source income is $1,000,000 and the applicable U.S. tax rate is 34 percent, the upper limit would be $340,000. If the tax credits exceeded the $340,000, the firm could carry the excess credits back two years and re-compute their tax burden or carry them forward five years and try to use them. If the amount were less than the upper limit, the firm would be allowed the full amount.

In reality, the computation of the tax credit is significantly more complex than that. Foreign-source income must be divided up into separate categories, or baskets: "overall" and "passive." The overall category would contain basically active income and probably generate excess credits. The passive category basically would contain subpart F income and probably use up all of its available credits with room to spare.

Taxation of U.S. Citizens Abroad

There are unique problems associated with compensating U.S. personnel working abroad. A firm usually must offer employees a significant salary to entice them to move abroad. The salary usually consists of the base salary plus additional compensation in the form of a housing allowance, a hardship allowance, an education allowance for children, a cost-of-living differential, and so on. These additional allowances can escalate an employee's salary significantly and subject it to a higher income tax in the foreign country as well as in the United States.

The U.S. policy of taxing that foreign income has changed significantly throughout history. The more lenient the tax provisions, the easier it is for a

U.S. employees working abroad can exclude $70,000 of their income from U.S. tax.

firm to send employees abroad. The Tax-Reform Act of 1986 changed the law considerably and has made it more costly for firms to send employees abroad. U.S. expatriates (that is, U.S. citizens working abroad) are allowed to exclude up to $70,000 of their foreign-source income from U.S. taxation.

An expatriate might receive a significant amount of income that could be taxed by foreign and U.S. authorities. Income taxes paid to foreign governments can be treated as a credit or deduction, similar to the treatment of corporate taxes. However, the companies sending expatriates abroad generally must make up the difference between what the expatriate would have paid in taxes in the United States and what must be paid due to the foreign assignment. The difference in tax liability is usually a result of the higher income earned by the expatriate as a result of housing allowances, hardship allowances, cost-of-living allowances, etc. That tax-equalization practice can be quite expensive for the corporation.

NON-U.S. TAX PRACTICES

Problems with different countries' tax practices are related to
- Lack of familiarity with laws
- Loose enforcement

Differences in tax practices throughout the world often cause problems for domestic firms operating overseas. Lack of familiarity with laws and customs can create confusion. In many countries, tax laws are loosely enforced, whereas in others taxes generally are negotiated between the tax collector and the taxpayer, if they are ever reported at all.

A variance among countries in GAAP can lead to differences in the determination of taxable income. This in turn could affect the cash flow required to settle tax obligations. For example, France allows companies to depreciate assets very quickly and allows additional depreciation for certain assets. In Sweden, companies can reduce the value of inventories, which tends to reduce taxable income.

In the separate entity approach, each unit is taxed when it earns income.

Taxation on corporate income is accomplished by one of two approaches in most countries: (1) the separate entity, or classical, approach and (2) the integrated system. In the **separate entity approach,** which is used in the United States, each separate unit (firm or individual) is taxed when it earns income. For example, a corporation is taxed on its earnings, and shareholders are taxed on the distribution of earnings (dividends), which results in double taxation.

An integrated system tries to avoid double taxation of corporate income through split rates or tax credits.

Most other industrial countries use an **integrated system** to eliminate double taxation. The British give a dividend credit to shareholders to shelter them from double taxation. In Germany a split-rate system is used so that a lower corporate income tax rate is applied to distributed profits since the shareholders are taxed also. The rate on retained profits is 56 percent and on distributed profits only 36 percent. A German shareholder must increase the value of the dividend by including the corporate tax that was paid, then pay the tax based on the individual tax rate. However, the shareholder is allowed to take a tax credit equal to what the corporation paid at 36 percent.

Table 19.5 illustrates some of the differences in tax rates among countries, but it is difficult to make a simple comparison. Most of those rates are subject to conditions, such as tax treaties, that will be discussed next. Japan has different tax rates, depending on the amount of capitalization and whether the income is distributed or not. Switzerland has federal tax rates ranging from 3.63 percent to 9.8 percent. However, each canton, or local government, imposes its own income tax, which ranges from 0 percent to 35 percent.[8]

Different countries also have unique systems for taxing the earnings of the foreign subsidiaries of domestic corporations. Some countries, such as France, use a territorial approach and therefore tax only domestic-source income. Other countries, such as Germany and the United Kingdom, use a global approach; that is, they tax the profits of foreign branches and the dividends received from foreign subsidiaries. The United States is the only country to tax unremitted earnings in the form of subpart F income.

Value-Added Tax

Under VAT, each firm is taxed only on the value added to the product.

The **value-added tax (VAT)** has been used since 1967 by most of the countries of Western Europe. The VAT is computed by applying a percentage rate on total sales less any purchases from other business entities. As the name implies, VAT means that each independent company is taxed only on the value added at each stage in the production process. If one company was fully

TABLE 19.5 | TAX RATES OF SELECTED COUNTRIES, 1987 (rate as percent) There is a significant difference in tax rates for domestic corporations, a branch of a foreign corporation, and withholding tax on dividends.

	Domestic Corporation	Branch of Foreign Corporation	Withholding Tax on Dividends
Brazil	35	35	25
Canada	45	45	25
France	42	42	25
West Germany	56	50	25
Hong Kong	18	18	0
Mexico	25	25	55
Singapore	33	33	0
United Kingdom	35	35	0
United States	34	34	30

Source: Ernst & Whinney, *1988 Foreign and U.S. Corporate Income and Withholding Tax Rates* (New York: Ernst & Whinney, 1988).

integrated vertically, the tax rate would apply to its net sales because it owned everything from raw materials to finished product.

The country VAT rates in Europe vary significantly despite efforts toward harmonization by the EC. The VAT does not apply to exports, since the tax is rebated (or returned) to the exporter and thus is not included in the final price to the consumer, which results in an effective stimulus for exports.

Tax Treaties: The Elimination of Double Taxation

The purpose of tax treaties is to prevent double taxation.

The primary purpose of most tax treaties is to prevent international double taxation or to provide remedies when they occur. The United States has active income tax treaties with more than 30 countries. The general pattern for withholding tax between two treaty countries is to grant reciprocal reductions on dividend withholding and to exempt royalties and sometimes interest payments from any withholding tax.

The United States has a withholding tax of 30 percent for owners of U.S. securities (individuals and corporations) who are from countries with which no tax treaties are in effect. However, interest on portfolio obligations and bank deposit interest are normally exempt from withholding. Where a tax treaty is in effect, the U.S. rate on dividends generally is reduced to 15 percent, and the tax on interest and royalties either is eliminated or reduced to a very low level.

A good example of a tax treaty is one between the United States and Canada. Canadian dividends, interest, and royalties remitted to U.S. citizens and corporations normally are subject to a 25 percent withholding tax rate by the Canadian government, but for U.S. firms they are subject to only 15 percent as a result of the tax treaty between the two countries.

Planning the Tax Function

Firms should
- *Set up a branch in early years to recognize losses*
- *Set up subsidiaries in later years to shield profits*

Since taxes affect both profits and cash flow, they must be considered in the investment as well as the operational decision process. When a U.S. parent decides to set up operations in a foreign country, it can do so through a branch or a foreign subsidiary. If the parent expects the foreign operations to operate at a loss for the initial years of operation, it should operate through a branch, since it can deduct branch losses against the current year's income at the parent's level. As the operations become profitable, the firm should switch to a foreign manufacturing subsidiary. If the deferral principle applies to the subsidiary income, then the income of the subsidiary would not be taxed until a dividend is declared.

Debt versus equity financing has tax ramifications.

Tied in with the initial investment decision as well as with continuing operations is the financing decision. Both debt and equity financing affect taxation. If parent loans are used to finance foreign operations, the repayment of principal is not taxable, but the receipt of interest income is taxable to the parent. Also, the interest expense paid by the subsidiary is generally a business expense, which reduces taxable income in the foreign country. Dividends, which are a return to equity capital, are taxable to the parent and are not a deductible business expense to the subsidiary. One reason why international finance subsidiaries are set up outside the United States is to escape withholding tax requirements.

Corporations should take advantage of tax-haven countries.

A multinational corporation aiming to maximize its cash flow worldwide should concentrate profits in a tax-haven or at least low-tax countries. This can be accomplished by carefully selecting a low-tax country for the initial investment; setting up tax-haven corporations to receive dividends; and carrying out judicious transfer pricing.

Whenever possible, the parent should utilize the 5 percent rule. If the parent has a profitable operating subsidiary in a relatively low-tax country, it can accumulate subpart F income there without worrying about U.S. taxes as long as that income does not reach 5 percent of total subsidiary income. For example, because of its low-tax status and membership in the EC, Ireland can be used both as a manufacturing center to supply the EC with goods and as a tax-haven corporation. The subpart F income provisions have complicated tax planning, but opportunities still exist.

Firms should utilize tax treaties to minimize taxes.

A judicious use of tax treaties also can be very helpful for corporations. For example, the treaty between the United States and the United Kingdom provides for a 15 percent withholding tax on dividends, whereas the treaties between the United States and the Netherlands and between the Netherlands and the United Kingdom provide for 5 percent withholding taxes under certain circumstances. In addition, the Netherlands does not tax dividends from foreign sources. This policy would allow a U.S. firm to set up a holding company in the Netherlands that would receive dividends from a U.K. subsidiary and remit them to the U.S. parent at a combined withholding tax of only 10 percent rather than 15 percent.

Tax law is very complicated, and a firm needs the counsel of an experienced lawyer. The following is a checklist that can assist a tax manager in proper tax planning.

1. Ask the respective controllers for tax projections that enumerate the items that are non–tax exempt. Likewise, timing differences due to accelerated depreciation, and so on, should be shown.

2. Work out a minimum dividend distribution plan so that at year's end the group of companies can exploit any U.S. tax concessions.

3. Find avenues for bona fide reduction of the taxable profit (accelerated depreciation, inventory write-offs, etc.).

4. Check the local company's tax declarations.

5. Examine the local tax assessments and advise management of the nondeductibility of certain items so that corrective measures can be taken.

6. Verify that unjustified tax assessments are contested.

7. Verify that all relevant papers (tax returns, etc.) and tax receipts (photocopies) are forwarded to the parent company in order to obtain foreign tax credits.

8. Ensure that U.S. management is aware of major changes in local tax legislation so that corporate policy for such matters as future investments, cash flow, dividend remittances, and minimum dividend distribution can be formed accordingly.[9]

LOOKING TO THE FUTURE   Although accounting standards differ significantly from country to country, the differences are beginning to narrow. As capital markets become increasingly integrated and as firms increasingly move to list their stock on different national stock exchanges, accounting differences will narrow. The stock exchanges will become an increasingly more important force in harmonizing accounting standards.

It is hard to predict what will happen in taxation, since tax policy is at the whim of government. Certainly tax differences among countries in the EC will narrow in the years to come. Harmonization should take place in the determination of taxable income and the tax rates themselves. MNEs will need to be more creative in their tax payments worldwide as they seek to operate in such a way as to minimize their tax liabilities.

SUMMARY

■ The MNE must cope with differing rates of inflation, changes in exchange rates, currency controls, customs, levels of sophistication, and local reporting requirements in performing its finance and accounting functions.

■ Some of the major factors that influence the development of accounting objectives, standards, and practices are the nature of the enterprise, the enterprise's users of information, governmental users and regulators, other external users (such as creditors), local environmental characteristics, international influences, academic influences, and the accounting profession.

■ There are important differences in worldwide accounting standards and practices. However, groups such as the EC and the International Accounting Standards Committee (IASC) are attempting to harmonize accounting practices and upgrade the accounting profession.

■ In translating transactions denominated in foreign currency, all accounts are recorded initially at the exchange rate in effect at the time of the transaction. At each subsequent balance-sheet date, recorded dollar balances representing cash and amounts owed by or to the enterprise that are denominated in a foreign currency are adjusted to reflect the current rate.

■ The translation of financial statements involves measuring and expressing in the parent currency and in conformity with parent country GAAP the assets, liabilities, revenues, and expenses that are measured or denominated in foreign currency.

■ According to FASB Statement No. 52, the financial statements of most foreign firms are translated into dollars by using the current rate translation method. According to that method, all balance-sheet accounts except stockholders' equity are translated into dollars at the current exchange rate in effect on the balance-sheet date. All income statement accounts are translated at the average exchange rate in effect during the period.

■ Foreign-exchange gains and losses arising from foreign currency transactions are taken to the income statement during the period in which they occur. Gains and losses arising from translating financial statements by the current rate method are taken to a separate component of stockholders' equity. Those arising from translating according to the temporal method are taken directly to the income statement.

■ International tax planning has a strong impact on the choice of location in the initial investment decision, the legal form of the new enterprise, the method of financing, and the method of setting transfer prices.

■ The Foreign Sales Corporation (FSC) is a company incorporated in a foreign country or a U.S. possession (except Puerto Rico). If it engages in substantial export services for its parent company, some of its income will be considered exempt from U.S. corporate income tax.

■ Deferral means that income earned by a subsidiary incorporated outside of the home country is taxed only when it is remitted to the parent as a dividend, not when it is earned.

■ A controlled foreign corporation must declare its subpart F income as taxable to the parent in the year it is earned, whether or not it is remitted as a dividend.

■ The tax credit allows a parent corporation to reduce its tax liability by the direct amount paid to foreign governments on dividends declared by its subsidiary to the parent as well as by the amount of the corporate income tax paid by the subsidiary to the foreign government.

■ Policies in other countries vary as to what is taxable income, how honest taxpayers are in filing returns, and how taxes are assessed. The United States taxes each separate unit (the classical approach), whereas most other industrial countries use an integrated system in which double taxation of dividends is minimized or eliminated.

■ The purpose of most tax treaties is to prevent international double taxation or to provide remedies when it occurs.

From 1886, when Atlanta pharmacist J. S. Pemberton mixed up his first batch of Coca-Cola, to 1989, when Cuban Robert C. Goizueta presided over the company as chairman and chief executive officer, Coca-Cola's worldwide revenues increased from $50 to $8.966 billion. Coke's rapid worldwide expansion has resulted in over 65 beverage trademarks worldwide and sales in 155 countries. From Fig. 19.7 we can see that Coke's international revenues in 1987 were 55 percent of total revenues. Coca-Cola's international presence has resulted in a number of interesting challenges and opportunities. In 1986 its operations were divided into three different product categories: soft drinks, entertainment, and foods.

In 1989 the soft-drinks division comprised about 18 percent of total revenues and foods comprised about 18 percent of revenues. Coca-Cola sold its entire equity interest in Columbia Pictures in November 1989. Its soft-drink business is particularly strong internationally, capturing over 40 percent of the soft-drink market in the 155 countries where it is operating and a significantly higher percentage of the market in its major markets. Coca-Cola management feels that international markets are virtually untapped and are clearly the growth area of the future.

In 1989 Coca-Cola increased its soft-drink sales to more than 48 percent of the global market. A major strength of Coca-Cola is the European Community, which accounts for 24 percent of Coke's total international gallon sales. However, Coke also has a strong presence in Latin America and Asia.

Specific information was provided in the An-

Figure 19.7
The Coca-Cola Company Geographic Segment Results
Although the United States is clearly the most important geographic area in terms of sales for Coca-Cola, the Pacific and Canada geographic segment provides a greater percentage of operating income than does any other geographic area.
Source: 1987 Coca-Cola *Annual Report.*

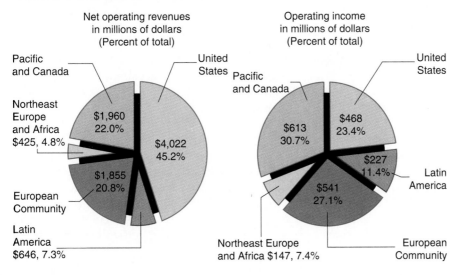

nual Report on changes in the value of the German mark, the Japanese yen, the British pound, and the Australian dollar. In 1988 other income (a category in the income statement) was reduced by $13 million due to transactions and translation losses, and in 1989 other income was increased by $20 million by transactions and translation gains.

In 1989 nearly 96 percent of operating income came from the sale of soft-drink concentrates and syrups. International sales accounted for nearly 80 percent of Coke's soft-drink operating income. International soft-drink operating income grew 13 percent in 1989, despite the effects of a U.S. dollar that strengthened approximately 6 percent against key foreign hard currencies during the year.

Coca-Cola's other major product group is not quite as international as the beverage category, but it is increasingly moving into international markets. Coke's food division is increasing its international sales, especially in Canada.

As noted earlier, Coca-Cola operates in 155 different countries; it used 40 different functional currencies to translate its financial statements from foreign currencies into U.S. dollars. The dollar is the functional currency of operations in hyperinflationary economies, such as Brazil and Mexico. Exchange effects on foreign currency transactions and translation of balance-sheet accounts in hyperinflationary countries are included in "other income" in the consolidated income statement.

In one place in its Annual Report, Coca-Cola's management noted that it had $212 million worth of 5¾ percent debt in Japanese yen, over half of which is designated as a hedge against its net investment in Japan. The 1986 Annual Report classified this as a Euroyen debt (Eurocurrency debt denominated in Japanese yen), but there was no such distinction in the 1989 Annual Report. In another place in the same report, it states that in general the company does not hedge its net investments in for-

eign operations. However, it sometimes enters into hedges to protect cash flows in foreign currencies.

An Accounting Procedures Manual   In the mid-1980s Coke management saw that its international operations were increasing significantly and that the nature of its business had changed since its last accounting manual had been written. It needed a comprehensive, easy-to-reference accounting manual to help maintain strong financial controls over operations. Management felt that a better accounting manual would help the firm acquire reliable information about units all over the world in order to help local subsidiaries operate at peak efficiency and generate corporatewide reports consistently.

A team consisting of a project manager and three senior accountants worked for eight months to develop an entirely new accounting manual. A universal chart of accounts was set up so that each account in the balance sheet and income statement would be consistent around the world. Based on the chart of accounts, definitions of each account were written and policies and procedures governing the use of each account and the flow of information into the financial statements were developed. A separate section was written describing how to translate financial statements from local currencies into U.S. dollars. Drafts of the report were given to audit, legal, and tax managers for their comments, and other field accounting managers were asked for their input before a final draft was completed.

Questions

1. Explain how the changing value of the dollar has affected sales and earnings of Coca-Cola.
2. Describe how Coca-Cola translates its financial statements into U.S. dollars. How do you think transactions and translation gains and losses are recognized in the financial statements?

3. What are some of the major problems that Coca-Cola might have confronted in writing a uniform accounting policy manual?

4. What would you recommend that management do in order to resolve some of these problems?

Chapter Notes

1. Daimler-Benz, *Annual Report, 1989;* "Global 1000," *Business Week,* July 16, 1990, p. 111+.

2. Financial Accounting Standards Board, *Statement of Financial Accounting Concepts No. 1—Objectives of Financial Reporting by Business Enterprises* (Stamford, Conn.: FASB, 1979), paragraphs 34–54.

3. Financial Accounting Standards Board, *Statement of Financial Accounting Standards No. 52: Foreign Currency Translation* (Stamford, Conn.: FASB, December 1981), pp. 6–7.

4. Ford Motor Company, *Annual Report, 1988,* p. 34.

5. Albert J. Radler, "Taxation Policy in Multinational Companies," in *The Multinational Enterprise in Transition,* A. Kapoor and Philip D. Grub, eds. (Princeton: Darwin Press, 1972), p. 30.

6. *Survey of Current Business,* March 1991, p. 34.

7. Prentice-Hall, *A Complete Guide to the Tax Reform Act of 1984* (Englewood Cliffs, N.J.: Prentice-Hall, 1984), pp. 1791–1805.

8. Ernst & Whinney, *1988 Foreign and U.S. Corporate Income and Withholding Tax Rates,* p. 21.

9. Ernst K. Briner, "International Tax Management," *Management Accounting,* February 1973, p. 50. Reprinted by permission.

10. Sources for the case were the 1989 Annual Report of the Coca-Cola Company; Timothy K. Smith and Laura Landro, "Profoundly Changed, Coca-Cola Co. Strives to Keep on Bubbling," *Wall Street Journal,* April 24, 1986, p. 1; and Andrew L. Nodar, "Coca-Cola Writes an Accounting Procedures Manual," *Management Accounting,* October 1986, pp. 52–53.

CHAPTER **20**

THE MULTINATIONAL FINANCE FUNCTION

To have money is a good thing; to have a say over the money is even better.
YIDDISH PROVERB

Objectives

- To describe the multiple facets of the finance function and show how this function fits in the organizational structure of the MNE.

- To discuss the major internal sources of funds available to the MNE and show how these funds are managed globally.

- To explain the major financial risks of inflation and exchange-rate movements.

- To compare operating strategies and forward contracts as protection against exchange-rate risks.

- To highlight some of the financial aspects of the investment decision.

Carlo De Benedetti took over as CEO of Olivetti in 1978, and turned the company, known primarily as a typewriter company, into the leading European-based office-automation company and one of the largest manufacturers of IBM-compatible computers. De Benedetti's aggressive strategy thrust Olivetti into the international marketplace and forced management to reexamine its exposure to foreign-exchange risk and determine whether or not the policies and procedures designed to protect against risk were adequate in light of its new international strategy.

The Company   When De Benedetti was offered the CEO spot at Olivetti in 1978, the company was losing $8 million a month, had a debt position in excess of liquid assets by more than $600 million, and also had a management team that was very discouraged. "We had only a few products and a local culture," recalls Elserino Piol, executive vice president for corporate strategies. "We were sort of a country-boy company." As soon as De Benedetti came on board, he instituted massive layoffs, increased the research and development budget significantly, introduced new products, and replaced most of Olivetti's top management.

By 1986 sales were $4.9 billion, and earnings were $380 million. Of Olivetti's sales, approximately 49 percent are in Italy, 32 percent in other European countries, and 18 percent in non-European countries. Olivetti struck strategic alliances with a number of MNEs, including Matsushita Electrical Industrial Co. and Toshiba. As noted by De Benedetti, "The traditional multinational approach is *dépassé* [obsolete]. Corporations with international ambitions must turn to a new strategy of agreements, alliances, and mergers with other companies."

However, Olivetti's fortunes began to wane in the late 1980s. As the Italian economy began to slow in 1989, so did the growth of Olivetti. Profits in 1989 were down 40 percent from their level in 1988, and the company's market share in Europe dropped from 9 to 8 percent. Layoffs in 1990–1991 were expected to reach 5 percent of Olivetti's labor force. De Benedetti and Managing Director Vittorio Cassoni realized that mergers or alliances would be necessary to catapult Olivetti into a solid position in Europe, but they have had trouble finding the right partner. It looked like the 1984 joint venture with American Telephone & Telegraph would do the trick, but the venture fell apart in 1989.

In spite of these failures, De Benedetti wanted to move away from the narrow niche of being a hardware manufacturer to being a firm that solves business problems through hardware and software. Olivetti entered into an arrangement with GM's Electronic Data Systems Corp. to provide computer services in Europe. Currently, Olivetti is the top computer maker in Italy, but it is struggling in Europe and the United States. Given the size and strength of the U.S. market, especially in the hardware and software industry, De Benedetti is determined to improve Olivetti's position there, even though the venture with AT&T was not successful.

The Olivetti Risk-Management Strategy   Olivetti has production and distribution facilities scattered around the world. As a result, it has tried to establish good strategies for managing foreign-exchange risk. Olivetti's strategy is developed by a committee made up of a group controller, the international treasurer, the chief economist, and a member of the operational planning department.

The first thing that the committee does is consider the relationship among three currencies: the local currency (the currency of the country where the operation is located); the currency of denomination (the currency in which a transaction actually is denominated); and the currency of determination (the currency used to determine the global price of products). The committee tries to see how fluctuation in the three currencies will affect Olivetti's competitiveness in the markets where it operates. Once a year, the committee simulates the effect of different exchange-rate scenarios on the profitability of each unit and the company as a whole.

There is a strong interrelationship between the exchange rate and the economic environment. As noted by Angelo Fornasari, Olivetti's vice president of finance: "To maintain market share and satisfactory profit levels, Olivetti must constantly consider the problems of sourcing product input, of funding in different currencies and markets, of reorienting market efforts, of seeking higher productivity levels, of shifting from one currency of invoicing (i.e., of denomination), to another, etc." Olivetti develops its economic exposure scenario three years into the future.

The hedging strategy is centralized at the corporate level so that local managers can concentrate on operating decisions. Transaction exposure is centralized, and hedging activities are carried out for the balances of transactions actually booked, as well as for forecasts of what the balances are expected to be four months into the future.

INTRODUCTION   It is February 6, 1989, and you awaken from a good night's sleep to face a bright, sunny day. After a brisk 5000 meter run, you take a shower and think about your upcoming trip to Buenos Aires, Argentina, where you will meet with the treasurer of your Argentinean subsidiary. It has been only a month since you were appointed Latin American regional treasurer of your firm, and you are eager to learn more about the Argentinean operations, which constitute a significant percentage of your region's sales and earnings.

As you sit down to breakfast you turn on the news and hear the following announcement: "Today, the government of Argentina announced an unscheduled bank holiday. It is rumored that the government is planning to move the free-market exchange rate from 16 Australs per dollar to A23:$1. Exchange markets are expected to remain extremely turbulent until the next presidential election."[2] Do you spill orange juice on your new suit, or do you relax through breakfast, confident that your operations had been covered adequately?

While the treasury function of an MNE can be exciting and challenging, it also can be filled with surprises and headaches. Among the key challenges are the acquisition and management of funds both external and internal to the firm, different means of financing imports and exports, the management of risk due to inflation and exchange-rate changes, and capital investment decisions.

Coca-Cola is a good illustration of the dimensions of the treasury function. Coca-Cola soft drinks are marketed in over 160 countries, and more than half of the company's operating income is generated outside of the United States. The treasurer reports directly to the Chief Financial Officer (CFO), as do the controller, the tax manager, and the directors of corporate data processing and corporate audit. Coca-Cola's treasurer identified his major challenges as financial risks and financing costs. Financial risks are defined as "currency transaction and translation risks, as well as property and product liability risks. The management of financing costs involves all short- and long-term borrowings companywide, as well as the company's overall cash management. . . ."[3]

Government policies, interest-rate and inflation differentials, and exchange rates are complicating factors that are not a major issue for domestic firms.

ORGANIZATION OF THE FINANCE FUNCTION

To optimize the flow of funds worldwide, the MNE must determine the proper parent-subsidiary relationship with respect to the finance function. There are three distinct patterns of parent-subsidiary relationships: (1) complete decentralization at the subsidiary level, (2) complete centralization at the parent level, and (3) varying degrees of centralization.[4] It is important to understand that the treasury function is fairly broad, and not all decisions are dealt with the same way. Some functions, such as foreign-exchange risk management, may be centralized; others, such as short-term financing decisions, may be decentralized. Thus the centralization/decentralization concept can refer to the general orientation of the treasury function or its separate components.

Types of parent-subsidiary relationships include
- Complete decentralization at subsidiary level
- Complete centralization at parent level
- Varying degrees of centralization

Decentralization—the subsidiary is independent of the parent.

In a decentralized situation the subsidiary is independent of the parent. The parent receives reports but generally issues only minor guidelines, especially when foreign sales comprise a small part of total sales and when the parent staff is relatively unfamiliar with the foreign environment.

Centralization—the parent dominates decision making.

In a centralized situation the parent staff dominates planning and decision making, whereas the subsidiary carries out orders. The idea behind this approach is that the more sophisticated parent staff understands the intricacies of moving funds across many national boundaries in order to serve the needs of the whole system at the greatest profit. Olivetti centralizes its hedging strategy at the corporate level so that management can be concerned with operating rather than foreign-exchange decisions. However, Olivetti does not centralize all of its treasury decisions.

Compromise—guidelines are passed from the parent to regional or local operations.

The third approach, varying degrees of centralization, attempts to use the best aspects of centralization and decentralization by achieving high levels of financial sophistication on both parent and subsidiary levels. Because of this expertise, the subsidiary staff is better able to act within specified guidelines. The parent staff coordinates system activities and monitors results. To maintain close proximity to foreign financial-information sources, many firms have organized regional financial decision-making centers. The parent staff continues to issue guidelines for decision making and coordinates the entire system, but the financial organization and management functions are turned over to the regional organizations.

Coca-Cola has devised a system that involves cooperation between the parent and local operations. The decision to hedge or not to hedge is a function of cooperation between the Atlanta-based centralized treasury group (Coca-Cola's world headquarters are located in Atlanta) and local management. Corporate staff makes sure that local management understands the risks and potential hedging strategies, and both groups determine the strategies that will be adopted. Although the corporate staff has the expertise, local management understands the local environment much better and can help corporate staff understand risks and design strategies. Coca-Cola has treasury service managers at headquarters that speak to the international group presidents on a weekly basis and to local operations on a daily basis. That gives the local managers direct access to treasury expertise and also helps headquarters get a better feel for the local situation.[5]

General Motors is another company that combines centralization with decentralization. GM centralizes some of the treasury functions to concentrate expertise, increase clout in financial markets, and reduce transactions costs due to centralized cash flows. However, it realizes that local expertise is necessary to understand local situations and to react quickly to events. While the corporate treasury function is located in New York, it has a European center in Brussels, and each overseas subsidiary also has its local treasurer that establishes banking relationships, etc. However, the regional or corporate treasury still provides significant input, and regional actions are subject to HQ policies and limits.[6]

INTERNAL SOURCES OF FUNDS

Funds are working capital, or current assets minus current liabilities.

If a firm wants to expand operations or needs additional working capital, it can look to outside sources or to sources within the firm. In the case of the MNE, the complexity of internal sources is magnified because of the number of related affiliates and the diversity of environments in which they operate. "Funds" can have many different definitions, and the term usually means cash. However, the term *funds* is used in a much broader sense in business and generally refers to working capital, that is, the difference between current assets and current liabilities.

Sources of internal funds include
- Loans
- Dividends
- Intercompany receivables and payables
- Investments through equity capital

Figure 20.1 illustrates a situation involving a parent firm with two foreign subsidiaries. The parent, as well as the two subsidiaries, may be increasing funds through normal operations. These funds must be used on a firmwide basis. One possible way is through loans: The parent can loan funds directly to the French subsidiary or guarantee an outside loan to the Brazilian subsidiary.

Additional equity capital from the parent is another source of funds for the subsidiary. Funds also can go from subsidiary to parent. The subsidiary could declare a dividend to the parent as a return on capital or could directly loan cash to the parent. If the subsidiary declares a dividend to the parent, the parent could lend the funds back to the subsidiary. That allows the parent to recapitalize its foreign investment in order to shift income from the subsidiary to the parent. The interest payment to the parent would be additional

Figure 20.1
Internal Sources of Working Capital
There are many ways for firms to use internal cash to fund operations around the world.

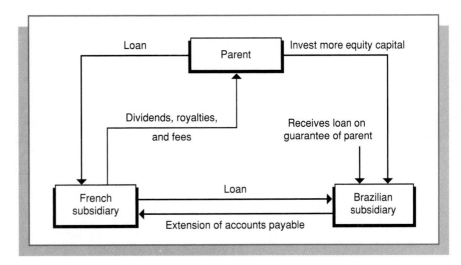

foreign-source income. A problem is that there may be a withholding tax on the interest payment, which might be viewed as a local cost of doing business. If that withholding tax is less than the tax on dividends, then local management might be happy with lower tax outflow.[7]

Sometimes governments create problems for intercompany lending. In Italy, profitable companies were able to shield income from the 36 percent corporate income tax by lending money to affiliates at low interest rates. The lender would only have to recognize the low-interest income for tax purposes, and the borrower would be able to get access to funds at low interest rates. In 1986 it was estimated that roughly 30 percent of total indebtedness of Italian companies was from intercompany financing. Non-Italian MNEs that established central Italian treasuries to move funds among related firms in Italy used the same tax-minimization scheme. Their cross-border intercompany loans were subject to a market interest rate but their Italian intercompany loans were not. In 1989, however, the Italian government moved to close this advantage by requiring that firms charge the average official discount rate for intercompany loans.[8]

Intercorporate financial links become extremely important as the MNE increases in size and complexity. Goods as well as loans can travel between subsidiaries, thereby giving rise to receivables and payables. Firms can move money between and among related entities by paying quickly (leading payments) or can accumulate funds by deferring payment (lagging payments). They can also adjust the size of the payment by arbitrarily raising or lowering the price of intercompany transactions in comparison with the market price. This strategy will be discussed more fully in the section on transfer pricing.

Government restrictions on intercompany transfers can limit the use of internal funds.

GLOBAL CASH MANAGEMENT

The problems of managing cash globally are complex. International cash management is complicated by governmental restrictions on the flow of funds, differing rates of inflation, and changes in exchange rates.

General Principles

We can discuss some general principles of international cash management without reference to the risks of inflation and exchange-rate changes. Effective cash management is one of the chief concerns of the MNE, and three questions must be raised to ensure effective cash management:

1. What are the local and corporate system needs for cash?
2. How can the cash be withdrawn from the subsidiary and centralized?
3. Once the cash has been centralized, what should be done with it?

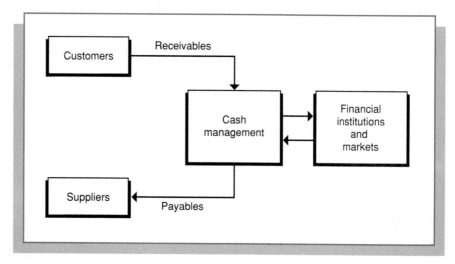

Figure 20.2

Cash-Flow Cycle

The cash-flow cycle relates the generation of cash from sales with the payment of cash for inputs in the production process.

The general cash-flow cycle that a firm must deal with is illustrated in Fig. 20.2. The MNE must collect and pay cash in its normal operational cycle, and then it must deal with financial institutions, such as commercial and investment banks, in generating and investing cash.

Before any cash is remitted to a control center, whether on a regional or a parent level, local cash needs must be properly assessed through cash budgets and forecasts. Since the cash forecast will project the excess cash available, the manager also will know how much cash can be invested for short-term profits.

A good reporting system is an important aspect of global determination of cash needs. However, there are four major reasons why foreign affiliates are often reluctant to provide good quality information to the parent: (1) language difficulties, (2) local resistance, (3) technical problems, and (4) governmental regulations.

Language problems are obvious. Local resistance is often cultural in that foreign affiliates sometimes tend to feel more independent than the parent company would prefer. Requests for information often are seen as a threat to the subsidiary's independence rather than a legitimate need.

Technical problems arise in cross-border data flows. In developing countries, there may be a lack of a good communications infrastructure. In other cases, the problem may be an incompatibility of corporate and affiliate computer systems. MNEs use a variety of different communications links to cope

Budgets and forecasts are essential in assessing a firm's cash needs.

Four barriers to intercompany sharing of information are

- *Language*
- *Local resistance, often cultural*
- *Technical problems*
- *Government regulations*

with different environments. Governmental regulations range from rules about simply transferring information to rules about actually transferring funds. Governmental requirements that certain communications links be used and that data be put in a specific format can often create delays in the transfer of information.[9]

Once local needs have been adequately provided for, the cash manager must decide whether to allow the local manager to invest the excess cash or have it remitted to a central cash pool. If the cash is centralized, the manager must find a way of making the transfer. A cash dividend is the easiest way to distribute cash, but governmental restrictions may reduce the effectiveness of this tool. Exchange controls may prevent the firm's remitting as large a dividend as it would like. In some countries, the size of the dividend may be tied to the capital invested in the local operation. The parent must develop approaches, such as revaluation of fixed assets, to increase its subsidiary's investment base. In Brazil, for example, annual average net dividends and branch profits declared (after a 25 percent withholding tax) in excess of an annual average of 12 percent of the foreign registered capital over a three-year period are subject to a supplementary tax, which ranges from 40 to 60 percent of the amount remitted.[10] Cash also can be remitted through management fees, royalties, and repayment of principal and interest on loans.

Many of the developing countries with large foreign debt, such as Brazil, have created difficulties for firms attempting to transfer money abroad. This has been because they have tried to curtail the outflow of foreign exchange. One U.S. company with large operations in Brazil used dividends, loan repayments, and sales commissions to transfer funds out of Brazil. The Brazilian operation was treated as a manufacturing facility, and all export sales were made by a sales subsidiary of the parent firm in the United States. When the manufacturing facility was established in Brazil, it was financed primarily by debt rather than equity. The parent company could get more cash out of Brazil by paying off principal and interest than it could by paying a dividend, which was subject to such large taxes. When foreign sales were made, the Brazilian manufacturer was permitted to pay a commission to the sales company in the United States, which allowed it to transmit more funds abroad. The Brazilian government constantly tried to lower the amount of the commission, whereas the parent company tried to increase the amount of the commission.

In mid-1989 the Brazilian government used administrative controls to slow down the outflow of funds from Brazilian subsidiaries to foreign parents. The government required that MNEs wanting to remit funds get high-level approval from the central bank, and MNE money managers reported that it was taking 30–45 days for bureaucrats even to look at applications. Then it might take another month to get approval. Companies like Rohm & Haas were forced to invest their unremittable cash in high-yielding financial instruments or fixed assets, such as land and buildings.[11]

Dividends are a good source of intercompany transfers, but governments often restrict the free movement of dividends.

Transfer Pricing

A transfer price is the price on inventory sold between related parties, often called intercompany transactions.

Transfer pricing is another way to move cash. A **transfer price** is the price on inventory sold between related entities. The transfer price could be market based or nonmarket based. A market-based transfer price uses the prevailing market price for exchanging products within the corporate group. A non-market-based system uses something other than an arms-length, market price. If the parent sells inventory to the subsidiary, a high transfer price would help concentrate cash in the central cash pool. The same effect would hold if the subsidiary were to sell inventory to the parent at a low transfer price.

Major determinants of transfer pricing policies are
• Legal factors
• Cash-flow requirements
• Local environmental variables

In one survey on transfer pricing policies of U.S. firms, the most important influences on transfer pricing decisions found were (1) market conditions in the foreign country, (2) competition in the foreign country, (3) reasonable profit for the foreign affiliate, (4) U.S. federal income taxes, (5) economic conditions in the foreign country, (6) import restrictions, (7) customs duties, (8) price controls, (9) taxation in the foreign country, and (10) exchange controls.[12] Management of cash flows itself was not considered important. However, when factors were grouped together according to common characteristics, influences on cash flows were rated the second most important factor grouping after the local environment.

It is difficult to rely on surveys, because it is impossible to measure the truthfulness of responses. In an area such as transfer pricing, it might be difficult for the researcher to accept all statements as true, given the sensitive nature of transfer pricing policies. In a more recent survey of transfer pricing policies, however, there are several interesting conclusions. First, it was determined that legal and size variables were the most important in determining transfer pricing policies. The legal factors were (1) compliance with U.S. tax regulations, (2) compliance with tax and customs regulations of host countries, (3) compliance with financial reporting rules and requirements, (4) and compliance with antitrust and antidumping legislation of host countries. The legal factors implied that firms tended to use market-based transfer pricing systems. Also, large firms were more likely to use market-based systems since nonmarket-based systems may lead to charges of inappropriate conduct. The researchers did not find evidence that nonmarket-based systems were used because of unstable sociocultural conditions, external economic factors (such as exchange controls, price controls, etc.), and internal economic factors (such as increased market share, the strengthening of competitive position of foreign affiliates, and performance evaluation).[13] This is an interesting conclusion, since most prior researchers would have identified those as the key variables.

One problem with making a transfer pricing decision is that multiple objectives could conflict with each other. For example, a high transfer price from parent to subsidiary would concentrate cash in the parent and also in-

Multiple objectives can complicate transfer pricing policies.

crease income because of the higher value placed on sales. However, if the corporate tax rate to the subsidiary is considerably lower than to the parent, it might be better to concentrate profits in the subsidiary to take advantage of the tax situation. This would require an opposite transfer pricing approach to that just described. Obviously, the overall impact of a transfer pricing scheme must be analyzed before a firm policy is selected.

Transfer prices are not subject to some of the same restrictions as are dividends and interest payments.

The advantage of using transfer pricing to move cash is that the cash is not subject to the withholding taxes and restrictions that dividends and royalties are. This is especially true in countries with which the United States does not have a tax treaty and where withholding taxes are relatively high. The United States has tax treaties with only about 30 countries. Arbitrary transfer pricing can create problems in performance evaluation, though. Subsidiary managers find it very difficult to be motivated in a profit-center context when they cannot control or influence pricing decisions.

The choice of currency for transfer prices is also important. A U.S. company that determines all transfer prices in dollars is essentially shifting the burden for exposure management to the affiliates. Many firms began to shift to local currency transfer prices in the mid-1980s due to the high degree of volatility in currencies and the desire of the parent company to react to that volatility on a global basis.[14]

Government tax law restricts the freedom of setting transfer prices.

An important variable, as identified in the second study summarized above, is the legal dimension. Tax law relating to transfer pricing strategies has been evolving in the United States in the past few years. The IRS prefers that MNEs apply for an Advanced Determination Ruling (ADR) before establishing a transfer pricing policy. The firm would submit a description of its policy to the IRS, which would then determine whether or not the policy is appropriate. The concern in early 1991 was that the IRS would be unreasonable in its request for backup information and that the information could leak out to competitors.[15] It was clear, however, that the IRS preferred an exact comparable transfer pricing policy, which means that companies would charge overseas subsidiaries the same price for components and products as they charge independent third parties.[16]

Surplus cash can be used to retire debt, finance new investment, or acquire financial instruments.

Once cash has been remitted to the central pool, the cash manager must decide what to do with it. Obviously, the cash manager ensures that all system needs for cash are met. Then any leftover cash can be used to retire debt in the system, to finance new ventures, or simply to earn a return through the acquisition of marketable securities worldwide.

One successful example of that strategy involves the German pharmaceutical company Bayer. In the late 1970s and early 1980s, Bayer invested billions of dollars in expansion (largely in the United States) when most other pharmaceuticals were being more cautious. That strategy seems to have paid off since Bayer is using its healthy cash flow worldwide to retire much of its investment-related liabilities. The company also used a lot of that liquidity to acquire inventory denominated in dollars as a hedge against rising prices and the rising dollar.[17]

By purchasing securities in countries other than that of corporate head-quarters a firm might be able to diversify its risk/return on investments. As world economies diverge in their growth cycles, the return on investments in strong countries could offset relatively weak returns in stagnant countries. However, as one pension fund manager pointed out, "You're dealing with the stability of foreign governments and with expropriations, [factors] we don't feel we have the ability to cope with."[18]

Multilateral Netting

Multilateral netting allows firms to reduce the amount of cash flow and move cash more quickly and efficiently.

An important cash-management strategy is netting cash flows internationally. As shown in Fig. 20.3, an MNE with operations in four European countries could have several different intercompany cash transfers resulting from loans, the sale of goods, licensing agreements, etc. There are seven different flows among the countries. However, many MNEs are establishing clearing accounts in a central location to coordinate those flows. Table 20.1 identifies the total receivables and payables for each country, along with the net position. Figure 20.4 illustrates how the subsidiaries in a net payable position would transfer funds to the central clearing account, and the manager of the clearing account would then transfer funds to the accounts of the net receiver subsidiaries. Thus there are only four transfers that need to take place.

The clearing account manager receives monthly transactions information and computes the net position of each subsidiary. Then the manager orchestrates the settlement process. The transfers would take place in the currency of the payer, and the foreign-exchange conversion would take place centrally.

Figure 20.3
Multilateral Flows
Multilateral flows in the absence of netting require each subsidiary to settle intercompany obligations.

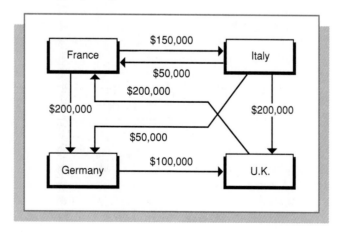

TABLE 20.1 | NET POSITIONS (in dollars) Net positions show total receivables less total payables.

	Total Receivables	Total Payables	Net Positions
France	250,000	350,000	(100,000)
Germany	250,000	100,000	150,000
Italy	150,000	300,000	(150,000)
U.K.	300,000	200,000	100,000

The major advantages of the netting process are: the savings of foreign-exchange conversion costs, since the central manager can effect large exchanges; the savings of transfer charges and commissions, once again due to the large size and smaller number of transactions; and the quicker access to the funds. It can sometimes take five days for funds to be exchanged through wire transfer, so the netting allows you to get access to the cash much faster. Electronic transfers also allow the firm to standardize and streamline payment routes and banking channels.[19]

However, there are also some problems with global netting operations. Many governments place controls on netting operations. Prior to 1989 Italy had a variety of barriers to netting operations. At that time, netting was per-

Figure 20.4
Centralized Netting
Centralized netting allows firms to transfer their net intercompany flows to a cash center, which disburses cash to net receivers.

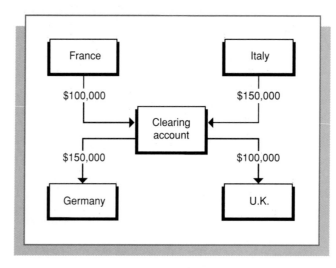

mitted only for trade transactions. Even at that, the administrative delays in gaining permission for netting operations resulted in a waiting period of several months. Mattel successfully established a netting operation in Italy in the early 1980s, but it was not allowed to pay for imports until they had cleared customs. That sometimes took up to three months after the date of invoice. In 1989 the restrictions were loosened significantly, so that the only obstacle to the establishment of a successful netting operation was convincing local management that it was a good thing to do.[20]

Coordination Centers

Regional coordination centers can be used to centralize cash-management strategies and practices.

The netting operation described above is one of the functions that a regional finance coordination center can perform. Some of the functions that the centers can perform are:

1. the centralization of financial transactions, including foreign-exchange dealing, netting, pooling, and reinvoicing;

2. centralization of administration, accounting, data processing, and the supply and collection of information;

3. advertising, insurance and reinsurance; and

4. auxiliary services (such as planning).[21]

Europe is currently a favored location for those centers as firms anticipate Europe 1992. Belgium (especially Brussels) is a popular location because it levies virtually no taxes on those operations and offers low rents and salaries in comparison with European standards.

INFLATION AND FOREIGN-EXCHANGE RISK MANAGEMENT

Major financial risks are due to inflation and exchange-rate changes.

The discussions of global cash management have focused on the flow of money for specific operating objectives. In addition, an important objective of the financial strategy of an MNE is to protect against the risks of investing abroad. The strategies that a firm adopts to protect against risk may involve the internal movement of funds as well as the use of one or more of the foreign-exchange instruments described in Chapter 7, such as options and forward contracts.

Financial managers need to assess
- Nature of financial risk
- Circumstances under which it can occur
- Implications of risk
- Defensive strategies

In examining the risk encountered in international business, it is important that firms consider the nature of the risk, the circumstances under which it can occur, the implications for the firm, and the best defense against it. Risks related to currency, commercial, and political factors are the major ones. Currency risks include both inflation and exchange-rate changes. Commercial risks involve the problems of extending and receiving credit and the difficulties of collection or payment of accounts in different currencies. Political risks are extensive and cover trade relations, expropriations, and items that could be included as currency risks.

Inflation

High inflation is often accompanied by a weak currency.

Inflation occurs in varying degrees in nearly every country in which MNEs operate. Inflation tends to erode the value of financial assets and make financial liabilities more attractive. The attractiveness of liabilities is softened somewhat by the high interest rates that often accompany loans in countries with high inflation such as Brazil and Argentina.

High rates of inflation often bring a variety of problems that influence the way an MNE operates. The most important ones are (1) accelerated depreciation or devaluation of the local currency or a maxidevaluation, (2) tighter capital controls and import restrictions, (3) scarcer credit and higher borrowing costs, (4) a buildup of accounts receivable and lengthening of collection periods, (5) price controls to help bring inflation under control, (6) economic and political chaos and labor unrest, (7) capital flight, (8) and greater difficulty in evaluating the performance of foreign subsidiaries.[22]

Price controls can be circumvented by
• Modifying product strategies
• Reintroducing products with a different brand name
• Changing packaging

Many companies faced with price controls need to get around controls through imaginative product development and pricing strategies. This may involve slight product or packaging modifications and brand-name changing in order to effect price increases. Quite frequently, MNEs are so brand-conscious that they refuse to exploit this strategy. Coca-Cola, for example, would never consider changing its product name in order to get a price increase. The importance of the brand name outweighs the advantage to be gained by changing it.

One multinational cosmetics firm operating in Brazil got around price controls by changing the container size of a brand-name product to a smaller container but listing the product at a significantly higher price. However, it would sell the product for considerably less than list price in order to attract sales. Then it could increase the price according to inflationary trends up to the upper price limit established by price-control authorities.

One of the major problems the firm faced was trying to estimate inflation correctly. If it predicted inflation at 200 percent and priced accordingly, it would be in serious trouble if inflation was actually 500 percent. It would have underpriced its products and sold them for less than the replacement cost of raw materials. On the other hand, if inflation came in at less than 200 percent, the firm ran the risk of pricing itself out of the market.

In countries with high inflation, payables need to be stretched out, receivables need to be collected quickly, and excess cash needs to be repatriated or invested.

It is evident that a firm operating in an inflationary environment needs to manage receivables and payables carefully. Receivables must be collected on a timely basis through a well-trained credit and collection department and a sophisticated and reliable reporting system.[23] Once it is collected, idle cash should be kept at a minimum. Funds should be remitted to the parent cash pool, as noted in the previous section, or invested in income-producing assets that provide a return in excess of inflation.

Exchange-Rate Changes

If all exchange rates were fixed in relation to one another, there would be no foreign-exchange risks. However, rates are not fixed, and currency values change frequently. Instead of infrequent one-way changes, currencies can fluctuate either up or down; this has especially been the case with the dollar since the mid-1980s.

A change in the exchange rate can result in three different exposures for a firm: translation exposure, transaction exposure, and economic exposure.

Translation Exposure   Foreign currency financial statements are translated into the reporting currency of the parent company (assumed to be U.S. dollars for U.S. companies) for a number of reasons, such as consolidation, performance evaluation, creditors, and taxation. Exposed accounts—those translated at the balance sheet or current exchange rate—either gain or lose command over dollars. For example, assume that a subsidiary operates in Mexico. The Mexican peso, weakened by inflation, depreciates in relation to the dollar from P3000:$1 to P3600:$1. The subsidiary's bank account of P300,000,000 would be worth only $83,333 after the depreciation instead of the $100,000 original value.

Translation exposure— as the exchange rate changes, the dollar value of the exposed asset or liability changes.

The combined effect of the exchange-rate change on all exposed assets and liabilities is a gain or a loss. If the foreign currency financial statements are translated according to the temporal method, the gains or losses are taken directly to the income statement. If the statements are translated according to the current rate method, the gains and losses are taken to a separate component of stockholders' equity. No matter which method is used for translation purposes, this gain or loss is not an immediate cash-flow effect. The cash in the bank in Mexico is only translated, not converted into dollars.

Transaction Exposure   The treasury difficulty from a transaction denominated in a foreign currency arises because the company has accounts receivable or payable in foreign currency that must be settled eventually. For example, assume that a U.S. exporter delivers merchandise to a British importer at a total price of $500,000 when the exchange rate is $1.9300/£. If the exporter receives payment in dollars, there is no immediate impact to the exporter if the dollar/sterling exchange rate changes. If payment were to be received in sterling, however, the exporter could be exposed to an exchange gain or loss.

Transaction exposure— the receivable or payable changes in value as the exchange rate changes.

For example, using the above exchange rate, the sale would be carried on the exporter's books at $500,000, but the underlying value in which the sale is denominated, as explained in the previous chapter, would be £259,067. If the rate moves to $1.9000 at the time the receivable is collected, the exporter would receive £259,067, but that would be worth $492,227 a loss of $7773. This is an actual cash-flow loss to the exporter.

Economic exposure—the
exchange rate changes
- Future cash flows
- The sourcing of parts
  and components
- The location of invest-
  ment
- The competitive posi-
  tion of the firm in different markets

Economic Exposure   Economic exposure includes such issues as the pricing of products, the source and cost of inputs, and the location of investments.

The economic impact on the firm is difficult to measure, but it is crucial to the operations of the firm in the long run. Aside from the immediate impact described earlier, there is a long-term impact that involves pricing strategies. The inventory sold to the British importer just discussed probably was sold to final users before the exchange rate fluctuated, but future sales would be affected. The following example using different exchange rates illustrates what could happen from an economic standpoint. Assume that the exchange rate before the change was $1.80:£ and after the change was $1.85:£.

If the merchandise had been invoiced in sterling, the strengthening of the sterling would have resulted in a gain of revenue to the exporter of $50. If the merchandise had been invoiced in dollars, the cost of the product to the importer in Britain would have decreased to £973. In the first case, the exporter must decide whether to reduce the price in pounds to maintain the same level of dollar revenues and (hopefully) increase market share. In the second case, the importer must decide whether to pass on the savings to consumers by reducing prices or keep the price the same and increase profit margins.

There are lots of good examples of how currency movements have affected corporate profits and strategies. In 1990 the German mark strengthened significantly against the U.S. dollar. German firms like Deutsche Airbus, which invoices its export sales of aircraft in U.S. dollars, were having a difficult time generating profits, because their costs were in high Deutsche marks, but their sales were in relatively cheap dollars. Some industries, like aircraft, operate in dollars worldwide, even though the exporters may be from other countries, such as Deutsche Airbus in Germany. German exporters that invoiced their sales in Deutsche marks were also having problems but of a different nature. Their sales prices were so high that they were losing business to exporters from other countries. For example, in September 1990, Germany exported 7.5 percent fewer goods to other EC countries than it did a year earlier, even though exports of other EC countries to Germany actually increased 10.8 percent over the prior year. Some German companies, such as Continental AG, the huge tire manufacturer, were benefitting from the strong mark. Continental AG purchased General Tire in the United States, so it is able to service its U.S. market and some global markets from cheaper U.S. production. Continental is also losing money in the United States, so the cheaper dollar makes the loss less of a problem than if the dollar were really strong.[24]

In 1990, the situation of U.S. companies in the face of a weak dollar was also mixed. Due to the weak dollar, Hurco Cos., an Indianapolis manufacturer that sells 40 to 45 percent of its machine tools and electronic controls in Europe, increased its market share (an economic impact) and raised its prices in dollars to yield greater sales revenues. However, Hurco also has found that some of its European buyers have cut back their purchases since business volume is down due to stronger local currencies and relatively weak economies. In addition, Hurco's imported parts and components have increased in cost due to the weaker dollar, a transactions impact. Thus the impact of the weak dollar is mixed.[25]

The impact of the weak dollar on Black & Decker and Coca-Cola is very different from that of Hurco. In the case of Black & Decker, the weak dollar has allowed it to sell some of the assets of Emhart Corp., one of its recent acquisitions, to foreign buyers who have relatively strong currencies. As a result, B&D has been able to eliminate some of its heavy debt. Coca-Cola, which generates 80 percent of its earnings abroad, benefits from strong foreign currencies, because those profits are translated into dollars at favorable exchange rates, helping to increase sales and profits (a translation impact). Coke management issues twice-daily updates of key currencies to its senior managers in order to assist in developing strategy. When the dollar is relatively weak, Coke tries to increase its reinvestment abroad (an economic impact).[26]

A final example of exchange-rate changes on strategy involves the Japanese auto companies. In 1986–1987, when the dollar plunged from its highs of the early 1980s, the Japanese automakers were forced to increase prices in order to make money. However, the fall of the dollar in 1990 did not seem to have the same impact. There were two reasons for that. The first is that many of them restructured their business through significant cost-cutting measures to allow them to operate at stronger yen values. In addition, some of them, like Honda, restructured their businesses to insulate them a little more from rate changes. Honda increased its U.S. manufacturing capacity so that only 25 to 30 percent of its content comes from Japan. They figure that if the dollar does not fall to below 125 to 130 yen, they can operate reasonably profitably without having to raise prices.[27]

KEY ISSUES IN FOREIGN-EXCHANGE RISK MANAGEMENT

Key strategic issues are to
- Define and measure exposure
- Establish a reporting strategy
- Adopt an exposure management strategy
- Adopt a hedging strategy

To protect assets adequately against risks from exchange-rate fluctuations, it is important for management to (1) define and measure exposure, (2) organize and implement a reporting system that monitors exposure and exchange-rate movements, (3) adopt a policy on assigning responsibility for hedging exposure, and (4) formulate a strategy for hedging exposure.

Measurement

Most MNEs will be subject to all three types of exposure described above. In order to develop a viable hedging strategy, the firm must be able to forecast

Determine the different
types of exposure that
must be monitored and
measured.
the degree of exposure in each major currency in which it operates. Because
the three types of exposure are very different from each other, the actual
exposure by currency must be kept separate. The translation exposure in Brazilian cruzeiros, for example, should be kept separate from the transaction
exposure. The reason is that the transaction exposure will result in an actual
cash flow, whereas the translation exposure may not. Thus the firm may
adopt different hedging strategies for the different types of exposure.

Forecasting Exchange Rates

Another key aspect of measurement involves forecasting exchange rates that
are applicable to the identified exposure. Estimating future exchange rates is
similar to using a crystal ball: Approaches range from gut feeling to sophis-
Forecast rate movements
using in-house or exter-
nal experts.
ticated economic models and with varying degrees of success. Whatever a
firm decides to do, its management should estimate ranges within which it
expects a currency to vary over the relevant decision period.

Some firms develop in-house capabilities to monitor exchange rates, using economists who also try to obtain a consensus of exchange-rate movements from the banks with whom they deal. Their concern is to forecast the
direction, magnitude, and timing of an exchange-rate change. Other firms
contract out this work.

Reporting System

Once the firm has decided to define and measure exposure and estimate future exchange rates, it must design, organize, and implement a reporting system that will assist in protection against risk. Because of the nature of the
problem, substantial participation from foreign operations must be combined
with effective central control. Foreign input is important in order to ensure
the quality of information being used in forecasting techniques. Since exchange rates move frequently, firms must obtain input from someone who is
Design a reporting system
that utilizes central and
local personnel.
attuned to the pulse of the country. In addition, the maximum effectiveness
of hedging techniques will depend on the cooperation of personnel in the
foreign operations.

A central control of exposure is needed to protect resources more efficiently. Each organizational unit in the firm may be able to define its exposure, but the corporation itself also has an overall exposure. To set hedging
policies on a separate-entity basis might not take into account the fact that
exposures of several entities (i.e., branches, affiliates, subsidiaries, and so on)
could offset one another.

Management should devise a uniform reporting system to be used by all
units reporting to the MNE. The report should identify the exposed accounts
the firm wants to monitor, the exposed position by currency of each account,
and the different time periods to be covered. Exposure should be separated

into translation and transaction components, with the transaction exposure identified by cash inflows and outflows over time.

The time periods to be covered depend upon the firm. One possibility is to look at long- as well as short-run flows. For example, staggered periods (thirty, sixty, and ninety days; six months, nine months, and twelve months; and two, three and four years) could be considered. The reason for the longer time frame is that operating commitments, such as plant construction and production runs, are fairly long-run decisions.[28]

Once each basic reporting unit has identified its exposure, this should be sent to the next organizational level for a preliminary consolidation. That level may be a regional headquarters (such as Latin America or Europe) or a product division. The organizational structure of the firm will determine what that level is. The preliminary consolidation allows the region or division to determine exposure by account and by currency for each time period. These reports should be routine, periodic, and standardized to ensure comparability and timeliness in formulating strategies. Final reporting should be at the corporate level. There, corporate exposure can be determined and strategies identified to reflect the best interests of the corporation as a whole.

Exposure Management Policy

It is important for management to decide at what level hedging strategies will be determined and implemented. To achieve maximum effectiveness in hedging, policies should be established at the corporate level. With a larger overview of corporate exposure and the cost and feasibility of different strategies at different levels in the firm, the corporate treasury should be able to design and implement a cost-effective program for exposure management. As a firm increases in size and complexity, it may have to decentralize some decisions in order to increase flexibility and speed of reaction to a more rapidly changing international monetary environment. However, such decentralization should stay within a well-defined policy established at the corporate level. This is the strategy that GM uses.

Centralized exposure management permits economies of scale and the specialization of experts.

Some companies, such as Eastman Kodak and Nestlé Foods, tend to run their hedging operations as profit centers and nurture in-house trading desks, whereas most MNEs are very traditional and conservative in their approach, preferring to cover exposure rather than extract huge profits. Mattel, Inc., the U.S. toymaker, straddles the line between the two approaches. Mattel combines in-house expertise with the use of an outside manager. Treasury felt that it did not have the expertise to manage exposure to take advantage of significant opportunities, so it decided to turn some of its exposure over to an outside professional foreign-exchange manager with the goal of generating profit.[29]

Another part of the management strategy has to deal with deciding which exposure will be hedged and at what level. Even though the different exposures were identified above, not all firms feel the same way about them. For example, Kodak has a cash-flow definition of exposure that largely ignores translation exposure.[30] Coca-Cola's treasurer, however, disagrees with that approach. He says that "From a treasury point of view, all exposures are current exposures."[31] The assistant treasurer of Black & Decker feels the same way. His point is that translation exposure can reduce equity and raise leverage, thus potentially affecting borrowing costs. His approach is to hedge translation exposure 100 percent.[32]

Effective management of exchange risk involves deciding which of the risks is important and then establishing a management structure that can manage the risk.

Hedging Strategies

Once a firm has identified its level of exposure and determined which exposure is critical, it can hedge, or protect, its position from exchange-rate changes. A firm can adopt numerous strategies, each with cost/benefit implications as well as operational implications. The safest position for a firm to be in is a balanced position, in which exposed assets equal exposed liabilities.

Hedging strategies can be operational or contractual.

This involves operational strategies to hedge exposure. The principal operational methods that MNEs use to protect against exposure are balance-sheet management and leads and lags in the transfer of funds. In addition, firms can enter into a number of contractual obligations to hedge exposure, such as forward-exchange contracts and currency options.

Operational strategies involve
- *Leads and lags of intercompany payments*
- *Using local debt to balance local assets*

Operational Strategies   To reduce exposure through operational strategies management must determine the working capital needs of the subsidiary. Although it might be wise to collect receivables as fast as possible in an inflationary country where the local currency is expected to depreciate, the firm must consider the competitive implications of not extending credit.

In reality, working capital management under exchange risk assumes that currency values move in one direction. A weak-currency country generally (although not always) suffers from inflation. The approach to protecting assets in the face of currency depreciation also applies to protection against inflation. Inflation erodes the purchasing power of local currency, whereas depreciation erodes the foreign currency equivalent.

In the weak-currency situation, subsidiaries' cash should be remitted to the parent as fast as possible or invested locally in something that appreciates in value, such as fixed assets. Accounts receivable should be collected as quickly as possible when they are denominated in the local currency and stretched out when denominated in a stronger currency. Liabilities should be treated in the opposite manner.

A policy for inventory is difficult to determine. If inventory is considered to be exposed, it should be kept at as low a working level as possible. However, since its value usually increases through price rises, it can be a successful hedge against inflation and exchange-rate moves. If the inventory is imported, it should be stocked before a depreciation since it will cost more local currency after the change to purchase the same amount in foreign currency. Where price controls are in effect or where there is strong competition, the subsidiary may not be able to increase the price of inventory. In this situation, inventory can be treated in the same way as cash and receivables. These principles can be reversed when an appreciation is predicted—that is, keep cash and receivables high, and liquidate debt as rapidly as possible. The safest approach is to keep the net exposed position as low as possible.

The use of debt to balance exposure is an interesting phenomenon. Many firms have adopted a "borrow locally" strategy, especially in weak-currency countries. One problem is that interest rates in weak-currency countries tend to be quite high, so there must be a trade-off between the cost of borrowing and the potential loss from exchange-rate variations. Coca-Cola, for example, has a strategy that at least half of its net exposed asset position in foreign countries is offset by foreign currency borrowings.[33] Black & Decker also uses local borrowings to hedge a net exposed asset position, but each exposure is considered on a case-by-case basis rather than automatically covering with local borrowing.[34]

Protecting against loss from transaction exposure becomes very complex. In dealing with foreign customers it is always safest for the firm to denominate the transaction in its own currency. Alternatively, it could denominate purchases in a weaker currency and sales in a stronger currency. If forced to make purchases in a strong currency and sales in a weak currency, the firm could resort to contractual measures or try to balance its inflows and outflows through more astute sales and purchasing strategies.

Leads and Lags   Another operational strategy, known as "leads and lags," is often used to protect cash flows among related entities, such as a parent and its subsidiaries. The **lead strategy** involves collecting foreign currency receivables before they are due when the foreign currency is expected to weaken and paying foreign currency payables before they are due when the foreign currency is expected to strengthen. A **lag strategy** means that a firm will delay receiving foreign currency receivables if that currency is expected to strengthen and delay payables when the currency is expected to weaken. Another way to state this is to say that a company usually leads into and lags out of a hard currency and leads out of and lags into a weak currency. For example, General Electric used a lag strategy in 1984 when the Japanese yen was relatively weak against the U.S. dollar. Because GE predicted a strengthening of the yen, it delayed remitting a yen dividend to the parent company until the yen began to strengthen.

Leads and lags are much easier to use among related entities in which a central corporate financial officer can spot the potential gains and implement a policy. There are two problems with the lead/lag strategy. First, it may not involve the movement of large blocks of funds. If there are infrequent deci-

Leads involve collecting or paying early.

Lags involve collecting or paying late.

sions involving small amounts of money, it is easy to manage the system, but as the number and frequency of transactions increase, it becomes difficult to manage. Second, as mentioned earlier in the chapter, leads and lags are often subject to governmental control since movements impact the balance of payments of a country.

Forward contracts can be used to establish a fixed exchange rate for future transactions.

Forward Exchange Contracts   In addition to the operational strategies just mentioned, a firm may resort to contractual arrangements. The most prevalent approach is the **forward contract,** a contract between a firm and a bank to deliver foreign currency at a specific exchange rate at a set date in the future.

For example, assume that a U.S. manufacturer sells goods to a British manufacturer for £1,000,000, with payment due in 90 days. The spot exchange rate is $1.9000 and the forward rate is $1.8500. In 90 days, the actual exchange rate is $1.8700. At the time of the sale, the sale is recorded on the books of the exporter at $1,900,000, and a corresponding receivable is set up for the same amount. However, the exporter is concerned about the exchange risk. The exporter can enter into a forward contract, which will guarantee that the proceeds of the receivable can be converted into dollars at a rate of $1.8500, no matter what the actual future exchange rate is. That would yield $1,850,000, or a cost of protection of $50,000. Or the firm could wait until the receivable is collected in 90 days and gamble on a better rate. Assuming an actual rate of $1.8700, the exporter would receive $1,870,000, which is not as good as the initial receivable of $1,900,000, but it is better than the forward yield of $1,850,000. However, if the dollar were to strengthen to $1.8000, the exporter would have been much better off with the forward contract.

Currency options can be utilized to assure access to foreign exchange at a specific exchange rate.

Currency Options   The foreign currency option is a relatively recent foreign-exchange instrument. It is more flexible than the forward contract because it gives the purchaser of the option the right, but not the obligation, to buy or sell a certain amount of foreign currency at a set exchange rate within a specified amount of time.

For example, assume that a U.S. exporter decided to sell merchandise to a British importer for £1,000,000 when the exchange rate was $1.9000. At the same time, the exporter went to the Philadelphia Stock Exchange and entered into an option to deliver pounds for dollars at an exchange rate of $1.9000 at an option cost of $25,000. That means that whether or not the exporter exercises the option, the right to have the option costs $25,000. When the exporter receives the £1,000,000 from the importer, a decision must be made on whether or not to exercise the option. If the exchange rate is above $1.9000, the exporter will not exercise the option, because he/she can get a better yield by converting pounds at the market rate. The only thing lost is the $25,000 cost of the option, which is like insurance. On the other hand, if the current exchange rate is below $1.9000, say $1.8000, the exporter will exercise the option and trade pounds at $1.9000. The proceeds will be $1,900,000 less the option cost of $25,000.

Historically, firms have preferred to use forward contracts when the amount and timing of the future cash flow are certain. The flexibility of options makes them useful for firms when there is high uncertainty in the amount and timing of the cash flows. Although the option can appear to be more expensive than the forward contract, especially when exchange markets are highly volatile, its flexibility can make it very useful in some cases. The option is also being used more often by corporate treasurers because of its flexibility, a move that has accelerated since the mid-1980s.

There are many other instruments that firms can use to hedge exposure, but the forward contract and the option illustrate the role contractual procedures can play.

FINANCIAL ASPECTS OF THE INVESTMENT DECISION

An MNE considering foreign investment has many financing options available. The parent company must consider the mix of debt and equity that it will use and which capital market around the world will be tapped to supply the funds. There are at least two basic reasons why the debt-equity ratio for a foreign subsidiary may differ from that of the parent. First, the attitude toward the debt-equity ratio in the host country may differ from that in the parent country. Firms in Japan and Germany, for example, tend to be more highly leveraged than their U.S. counterparts, which means that they rely much more on debt than on equity capital.

Second, different tax rates, dividend remission policies, and exchange controls may cause a firm to rely more on debt in some situations and on equity on others. The debt-equity ratio of the MNE will be a weighted average of the debt-equity ratios of all entities in the corporate structure. Japanese, German, and Swiss firms have traditionally relied on debt financing because of the relatively better availability on debt rather than equity financing and because of low interest rates. A rise in interest rates and improvement in equity markets in recent years have caused firms in those countries to consider shifting the mix of debt and equity financing.

Discounted cash flows often are used to compare and evaluate investment projects. Several aspects of capital budgeting unique to foreign project assessment follow:

1. There is a need to distinguish between total cash flows of the project and cash flows remitted to the parent company.

2. Because of differing tax systems, restrictions on financial flows, local norms, and differences in financial markets and institutions, the financing and remittance of funds to the parent firm must be recognized.

3. Different rates of national inflation can be important in changing competitive positions (and thereby cash flows) over time.

4. Foreign-exchange rate changes may alter the competitive position of a foreign affiliate.

5. Political factors can drastically reduce the value of a foreign investment.

6. The final sale value is difficult to estimate because of possible divergent market values of a project to potential purchasers from the host, parent, or third countries.[35]

The parent firm must compare the net present value or internal rate of return of a project with that of other parent projects. At the same time, it should compare the project with others available in the host country.

Management must view cash flows from two perspectives: (1) the total flows available to the local operations and (2) the cash available to the parent. The outflows to the parent are important to consider in light of the original investment made, especially if the investment was with parent funds. Finally, the firm must analyze foreign political and exchange risks. The best approach is for the firm to adjust forecasted cash outflows to different estimates representing different levels of risk.

LOOKING TO THE FUTURE   Two things are going to have a significant influence on the cash-management and hedging strategies of MNEs in the future. First is the information and technology explosion, and second is the growth and sophistication of hedging instruments (financial derivatives such as options and forwards). The information explosion will continue to allow firms to get information more quickly and cheaply than in the past. In addition, the advent of electronic data interchange (EDI) will allow firms to transfer information and money instantaneously around the world. Firms will significantly reduce the paper flow and increase the speed of delivery of information and funds, thus enabling them to manage cash much more effectively. Not only will that reduce the cost of producing information, but it will also allow firms to reduce interest and other borrowing costs as they utilize intercompany resources much more effectively.

Second, the growing number and sophistication of financial derivatives, as well as the growing expertise of providers and users of derivatives, should allow companies to identify and hedge their exposure much more effectively. Firms that previously ignored hedging certain types of exposure will find that the availability of derivatives will increase and the cost will decrease, making cover much more possible.

Also, the centralization and regionalization of cash management and exposure management will increase, not decrease, even though local treasury staff becomes much more sophisticated. The sheer volume of transactions and resulting economies argues for more, not less, centralization. The speed and sophistication of communication should allow firms to manage assets much more quickly than was the case a decade ago.

SUMMARY

- The finance, or treasury, function deals primarily with (1) the generation of funds for operating needs and expansion, (2) the management of working capital, and (3) the financial aspects of the foreign investment decision process.

- Three distinct patterns of parent-subsidiary relationships have surfaced with respect to the finance function: (1) complete decentralization at the subsidiary level, (2) complete centralization at the parent level, and (3) varying degrees of centralization.

- The major sources of internal funds for an MNE are intercompany loans, loans from parent to subsidiaries, dividends, royalties, management fees, the purchase and sale of inventory, and equity flows from the parent to subsidiaries.

- Cash management involves determining local and system needs for cash, methods of centralizing cash, and uses for cash.

- Global cash management is complicated by governmental restrictions on the flow of funds, differing rates of inflation, and changes in exchange rates. A sound global cash-management system requires timely reports from affiliates worldwide.

- Management must protect corporate assets from loss due to inflation and exchange-rate changes. Exchange rates can influence the dollar equivalent of foreign currency financial statements, the amount of cash that can be earned from foreign currency transactions, and production and marketing decisions of a firm.

- Foreign-exchange risk management involves defining and measuring exposure, setting up a good monitoring and reporting system, adopting a policy to assign responsibility for exposure management, and formulating a strategy for hedging exposure.

- Forward contracts can lock the firm into a specific exchange rate for future obligations, which could result in gains or losses, depending on what happens to the future spot rate. However, the forward contract eliminates the uncertainty for the firm.

- Foreign currency options give the purchaser the option of buying or selling foreign currency in a certain amount, at a fixed exchange rate, during a period of time in the future. It is more expensive than a forward contract but has more flexibility.

- When deciding to invest abroad, a firm must consider its optimal debt-equity ratio, evaluate local currency and investor currency rates of return, identify cash flows unique to foreign investment, calculate a multinational cost of capital, and offset foreign political and exchange risks.

HEWLETT-PACKARD IN EUROPE: A CASH-MANAGEMENT STRATEGY[36]

Hewlett-Packard (HP) is a nearly $12 billion company that designs, manufactures, and services electronic products and systems for measurement and computation. Management states in its 1989 Annual Report that "HP's basic business purpose is to provide the capabilities and support needed to help customers worldwide improve their personal and business effectiveness." The California-based company is publicly traded in the United States, as well as on the exchanges in London, Paris, Frankfurt, and Zurich.

Europe is a very important geographic region for HP. In 1989 HP derived 34.7 percent of its revenues and 26.6 percent of its profits from Europe, and 25.1 percent of its identifiable assets were in Europe. HP operates in sixteen countries in Europe, but its largest operations are in the United Kingdom, France, and Germany. HP is the third-largest U.S. computer maker after IBM and DEC, and it was also the third-largest U.S. computer maker in Europe in 1989: 37 percent of IBM's sales and 40 percent of DEC's sales were in Europe.

HP views Europe as a regional market, although the advent of Europe 1992 is causing management to change to a Pan-European orientation with operations that are going to be far more global as goods and capital move more freely.

HP has established a European headquarters in Geneva, Switzerland, and it centralizes many of its treasury functions there. The Geneva headquarters is a reinvoicing center that buys from supply factories and resells to sales companies. Its European subsidiaries purchase up to 50 percent of their inventories in dollars but bill in local currencies. HP currently sells more than 10,000 products worldwide, making different pricing and hedging strategies necessary. In addition, since many of its sales are intercompany, it must plan around IRS regulations on intercompany transactions.

Pricing Strategy   There are two key pricing issues facing HP: One of them is intercompany and the other is external. In 1990 HP management made the decision that HP would not support the Advanced Determination Ruling (ADR) procedure for any of its intercompany transactions. On the benefit side, management stated: "We have been strongly supportive of the ADR process as an attractive alternative to the current process of worldwide sporadic intercompany audits, litigation, and competent authority appeals as a means to resolve these disputes." However, management felt that the cost of an ADR would be far greater than any possible benefits.

In spite of the decision to forgo any ADRs, HP management identified several criteria that would have to be addressed in order for them to reconsider their decision:

1. The detailed economic analysis required for an ADR would have to be curtailed and abbreviated. Management estimated that the interviews, paperwork, and economics staff would cost between $750,000 and $1,000,000 for each ADR.

2. Assurances concerning the proprietary nature of the information would have to be made. HP management is concerned about two possible groups of users: competitors, who would be able to get access to the information through public disclosure laws, and other IRS agents who are currently auditing HP transfer pricing practices from prior years.

3. Assurances that tax authorities from other countries would accept an ADR and vice-versa.

On the external side, importing products in one currency and selling them in another results in one of three alternatives:

1. price for the currency swings and hope that demand carries the product;

2. lose market share but maintain profit margins;

3. keep market share and accept a lower profit margin.

HP had decided to retain profitability rather than keep market share. However, HP has also promised buyers a three-month guarantee on any prices that it quotes. That means that it is exposed to foreign-exchange gains and losses over that three-month period.

In order to hedge the exposure, HP management, during a period of a strengthening dollar, uses forward contracts for the first month and options for the next two months. The use of forwards for a short time is usually less expensive and more predictable, whereas the options are more valuable the further into the future you go. HP has a policy that options cannot cost more than 1.5 percent of the underlying exposure, so it uses that policy to try to hold down its costs. In the case of a weakening dollar, HP takes forward cover for two months and options for the third.

Cash Management   As mentioned above, HP has a Geneva headquarters that manages its cash for Europe. By acting as a purchaser and seller of HP products, the Geneva headquarters can net its cash flows more effectively. As noted by their European treasurer, "Several of our subsidiaries generate profits and excess cash. We regularly collect funds in each country and bring them back to Geneva to the in-house bank. Usually we keep the cash in dollars, our natural currency of operations, and then swap into whatever currency we need for financing the subs via the in-house bank."

HP uses a proprietary software system called HP Cash to keep track of its cash availability and needs. HP Cash is a fully integrated cash-management system. All cash information from the different subsidiaries is transferred electronically by the subs and their banks to Geneva, and the information is automatically reconciled by HP Cash. When the European Treasurer comes in each morning, he can instantly look at HP's net cash position and determine how to use the funds most effectively.

Each of the larger HP operations in Europe has its own cash installations, and they communicate with Geneva electronically through a private company network. By centralizing the cash information and cash flow, HP has been able to reduce the number of banks that it has to do business with. Bank and other legal regulations meant that they had to do business with several banks in order to get access to the credit and services they needed. Now, however, they can utilize intercompany financing much more effectively.

Questions

1. What do you think are the major factors that are driving HP's centralization strategy?

2. Identify the major foreign-exchange exposures that HP has.

3. Evaluate HP's foreign-exchange exposure strategy. What are some of the things that you would recommend HP consider as it continues to refine its exposure management strategy?

4. Discuss some of the financial considerations that HP has because of its intercompany transactions. Evaluate its response to the ADRs.

Chapter Notes   1. Sources for the case are as follows: Olivetti Annual and Extraordinary General Meeting, 1985; "How Olivetti Manages FX Risk to Protect Long-Term Profits," *Business International Money Report* (New York: Business International, November 2, 1987), pp. 349–351; William C. Symonds, Thane Peterson, John J. Keller, and Marc Frons, "Dealmaker De Benedetti," *Business Week,* August 24, 1987, pp. 42–47; John Rossant, "Can Italy Catch Up?" *Business Week,* June 11, 1990, p. 34.

2. Pablo Maas and Brad Asher, "Argentina Moves to Three FX Tiers," *Business International Money Report* (New York: Business International Corporation, February 13, 1989), p. 41. This is not an exact quote, but the information is from the above source.

3. Bill Millar, "How Coca-Cola's Treasury Manages a Giant's Global Finances," *Business International Money Report* (New York: Business International Corporation, September 25, 1989), pp. 307, 310.

4. Sidney M. Robbins and Robert B. Stobaugh, *Money in the Multinational Enterprise* (New York: Basic Books, 1973), pp. 37–48.

5. Bill Millar, *op. cit.,* p. 310.

6. Brad Asher and Tom Dolezal, "The Treasury Function at GM," *Business International Money Report* (New York: Business International Corporation, April 10, 1989), p. 107.

7. Robert K. DeCelles and Anthony G. Alexandrou, "Relaxed U.S. Interest Allocation Rules Open Up Intercompany Debt for Foreign Funding," *Business International Money Report* (New York: Business International Corporation, February 6, 1989), pp. 34–35, 39.

8. Riccardo Loi, "Nonbank Lending in Italy Is Under Attack," *Business International Money Report* (New York: Business International Corporation, February 27, 1989), pp. 57–58.

9. "Successful Global Cash Management," *Financing Foreign Operations* (New York: Business International Corporation, March 1986), pp. 1–3.

10. Ernst & Whinney, *1988 Foreign Exchange Rates and Restrictions* (New York: Ernst & Whinney, 1988), p. 30.

11. Edward Mervosh and Steven Graham, "Brazil's Squeeze on Remittances Leaves MNCs Hanging Loose," *Business International Money Report* (New York: Business International Corporation, September 4, 1989), p. 279.

12. Jane O. Burns, "Transfer Pricing Decisions in U.S. Multinational Corporations," *Journal of International Business Studies,* Vol. 11, No. 2, Fall 1980, p. 25.

13. Mohammad F. Al-Eryani, Pervaiz Alam, and Syed H. Akhter, "Transfer Pricing Determinants of U.S. Multinationals," *Journal of International Business Studies,* Third Quarter 1990, pp. 409–425.

14. Brad Asher, "What New Currency Strategies Should Treasurers Adopt Now?" *Business International Money Report,* (New York: Business International Corporation, December 7, 1987), p. 396.

15. Edward Neumann, "MNCs Start Taking IRS Surveillance of Transfer Pricing More Seriously," *Business International Money Report* (New York: Business International Corporation, May 7, 1990), p. 167.

16. Edward Neumann, "Transfer Pricing: New Rules and a Flatter Playing Field in 1991," *Business International Money Report* (New York: Business International Corporation, January 7, 1991), pp. 6–7.

17. "Bayer: Why the High Dollar Is No Headache," *Business Week,* October 29, 1984, p. 53.

18. Daniel Hertzberg, "Pension Managers Invest More Overseas, Aware of Risks but Hopeful about Profits," *Wall Street Journal,* July 2, 1981, p. 44.

19. William J. Bokos and Anne P. Clinkard, "Multilateral Netting," *Journal of Cash Management,* June/July 1983, pp. 24–34.

20. Nilly Landau, "MNCs Should Reconsider Leading, Lagging and Netting for Italian Subsidiaries," *Business International Money Report* (New York: Business International Corporation, May 29, 1989), p. 172.

21. Bill Millar, "What Is a BCC?" *Business International Money Report* (New York: Business International Corporation, March 6, 1989), p. 67.

22. "Financial Strategies in Risky Markets," *Financing Foreign Operations* (New York: Business International Corporation, January 1987), pp. 1–2.

23. "Financial Strategies in Risky Markets," *op. cit.*, pp. 2–5.

24. Terence Roth, "Germany's Export Industry Is Feeling the Pinch as Bonn Moves to Keep Mark at Record Heights," *Wall Street Journal,* December 13, 1990, p. A8.

25. "How Dollar's Plunge Aids Some Companies, Does Little for Others," *Wall Street Journal,* October 22, 1990, p. A1.

26. *Ibid.*

27. "Rise in Car Prices Isn't Now Planned by Japan's Makers," *Wall Street Journal,* October 22, 1990, p. A6.

28. Helmut Hagemann, "Anticipate Your Long-Term Foreign Exchange Risks," *Harvard Business Review,* March–April 1977, p. 82.

29. Nilly Landau, "Finding a Balance Between Opportunistic and "Safe" Hedging," *Business International Money Report* (New York: Business International Corporation, December 4, 1989), p. 387.

30. Bill Millar, "Strategic Risk: The Kodak Approach," *Business International Money Report* (New York: Business International Corporation, December 18, 1989), p. 402.

31. Bill Millar, "How Coca-Cola's Treasury Manages a Giant's Global Finances," *op. cit.,* p. 311.

32. Susan Arterian, "How Black & Decker Defines Exposure," *Business International Money Report* (New York: Business International Corporation, December 18, 1989), p. 404.

33. Bill Millar, "How Coca-Cola's Treasury Manages a Giant's Global Finances," *op. cit.,* p. 311.

34. Susan Arterian, *op. cit.,* p. 405.

35. David K. Eiteman and Arthur I. Stonehill, *Multinational Business Finance,* 5th ed. (Reading, Mass.: Addison-Wesley, 1989), pp. 520–521.

36. Marione Kazimirski, "Hewlett-Packard: Getting Finance Organized for 1992," *Business International Money Report* (New York: Business International Corporation, February 12, 1990), pp. 53–54; Edward Neumann, "Hewlett-Packard: Jousting with the IRS over Transfer Prices," *Business International Money Report* (New York: Business International Corporation, June 11, 1990), pp. 223, 226; Hewlett-Packard *Annual Report, 1989;* Marione Kazimirski, "Hewlett-Packard: A Cash Management System that Makes Banking Easier," *Business International Money Report* (New York: Business International Corporation, March 12, 1990), pp. 98–99.

CHAPTER **21**

HUMAN RESOURCE MANAGEMENT

If the leader is good, the followers will be good.
PHILIPPINE PROVERB

Objectives

- To explain the unique qualifications of international managers.

- To evaluate the specific issues that occur when managers are transferred internationally.

- To examine alternatives for recruitment, selection, training, and compensation of international managers.

- To discuss how national labor market differences can affect optimum methods of production.

- To describe diversities in labor policies and practices on a country-to-country basis.

- To highlight some major international pressures on how MNEs can deal with labor worldwide.

- To examine the effect of transnational operations on collective bargaining.

Bulgarian-born Frank P. Popoff became chief operating officer of U.S.-based Dow Chemical in 1987 when he replaced Italian-born Paul Oreffice, who became chairman of the board. Oreffice had replaced Hungarian-born Zoltan Merszei in 1979. On becoming chief of Dow, Mr. Popoff, who had once headed Dow's European division, said, "I had a lot of international experience and I think, for a company that has over 50 percent of its sales outside the U.S., that's very important." As of 1990 Dow's 22-member management committee at the top of the company included 10 who were non-U.S. born and 17 with foreign experience.

This placement of foreign-born and/or internationally experienced persons at the helm of the firm might suggest the process of multinationalization. For example, Peter Drucker, a leading management authority, stated that a truly multinational firm "demands of its management people that they think and act as international businessmen in a world in which national passions are as strong as ever." A firm whose top management includes people from various countries and with varied country experiences presumably is less likely to place the interests of one country above those of others and supposedly will have a more worldwide outlook.

Whether or not nationality or birthplace of a firm's officers indicates worldwide outlook is debatable. However, the experience of working abroad under some very different environmental conditions is very useful for grasping some of the problems that are not as prevalent in a purely domestic context. In 1980 Paul Oreffice described his foreign experience at Dow as follows:

> I would never have risen as far as I have in Dow if it hadn't been for my foreign experience. What I learned in Brazil in the 1960s influenced and advanced my career. . . . In a high-inflation country . . . the only way we could get dollars to import goods from the U.S. was to go to the exchange and bid on how many cruzieros we would pay per dollar for imported goods. . . . I learned the maintenance of margins or replacement cost pricing, which is the only way you can make sufficient profit to buy and build more plants.

In 1990 Oreffice reiterated the importance of this experience when he said:

> Our chief financial officer is Cuban, our treasurer is Brazilian, the next man at the top is Italian, and after him comes a Chilean. Native-born Americans seem to have fallen behind in Treasury simply because of the wider experience that financial people from other countries have had all over the world.

That most Dow top executives have had considerable foreign experience indicates that international operations are an integral part of Dow's total commitment. To bring about this commitment, Dow had to gain a dedication to international business from a broad spectrum of managers. The company estimates that the attitude change took about 20 years to

C A S E

DOW'S INTERNATIONAL

MANAGEMENT

DEVELOPMENT[1]

complete. Until 1954 only about 6 percent of Dow's business was abroad, and over 80 percent of that was from its one foreign subsidiary in Canada. The attitude in the late 1950s was expressed by a company historian as follows:

> As for the overseas operations, a majority of the veterans regarded them as a sideline. The foreign market was all right as a place for getting rid of surplus products, but the only truly promising market was in the United States. They questioned the idea of the company becoming too deeply involved in countries whose politics, language, culture, monetary controls, and ways of doing business were strange to them.

Some of Dow's younger managers did not share this ethnocentric attitude, but dramatic steps were needed to convert the majority of managers to an international outlook. One method employed by the company's president in 1958 was to give international responsibilities to people who were widely perceived to be destined for top-level positions in the firm. C. B. Branch, who was managing Dow's fastest growing department, was appointed head of foreign operations. Herbert "Ted" Dow Doan, who at 31 was already a member of the board of directors, went to Europe on a fact-finding mission. (Ted Doan's father and grandfather both had been Dow presidents.) Both Branch and Doan went on quickly to become presidents of Dow. Thus the importance of international operations became readily apparent to any manager in the company.

Although the discussion so far emphasizes the importance of international exposure for top-level managers in firms with global commitments, this experience is not the only international management consideration. Firms also must attract and retain high-quality personnel within each country where they operate. These are largely local personnel. To attract high-quality local personnel, Dow feels it must give people from all over the world the same opportunity to reach the top at Dow. Local needs also change as corporate strategies evolve. For instance, Dow had to hire many more non-U.S. scientists and technicians in the 1980s when the company was strengthening R&D in Europe and Asia.

Firms also must transfer people to foreign locations when qualified local managers are not readily available, or to infuse some technology to foreign subsidiaries. When Dow sends managers to foreign operations, what type of qualifications should they have? Robert Lundeen, a former Dow chairman who had served twelve years as president of the Pacific division and three years as president of the Latin American division, gave some indication of his philosophy. After speaking about the obvious technical needs, he said, "When I worked in Asia, I observed that many Americans seemed to delight in their insularity and that attitude hurts the ability of the United States to do business in foreign countries."

For many years, Dow had difficulty in convincing people to take foreign assignments because of bad experience in repatriating them to acceptable positions. Dow has reacted to this problem in three ways: (1) sending some of its best people abroad so that "everybody will want them when they come back"; (2) assigning higher-level supervisors to serve as "godfathers" by looking after the transferred employees' home-career interests; and (3) providing each transferee with a letter guaranteeing a job at the same or higher level on return from the foreign assignment.

Because many managers have difficulty in adjusting to foreign locations, Dow holds a briefing session with each prospective transferee to explain transfer policies and to provide a briefing package compiled by personnel in the host country. This is followed by a meeting of the transferee and spouse with a recently repatriated employee or spouse to explain the emotional issues involved in the early stages of the move. The couple is also given the option of attending a two-week language and orientation program.

INTRODUCTION   The preceding case highlights one firm's experience in dealing with some international aspects of its personnel policies, an experience that is more comprehensive than one finds within most other firms operating internationally.[2] Although companies have taken a variety of approaches to international human resource management, most agree on the importance of qualified personnel if they are to achieve their foreign growth and operation objectives. For instance, the Conference Board held a roundtable discussion of chief executives on how the world is changing and what, if anything, managements can do to keep change under control. The chairman of Unilever said, "The single most important issue for us has been, and will continue to be, organization and people."[3]

The need for highly qualified people to staff the organization cannot be overemphasized. Any company must determine its personnel needs, hire people to meet those needs, motivate them to perform well, and upgrade their skills so that they can move to more demanding tasks. The following summarizes the factors that make the management of international human resources different from the management of domestic resources.

1. *Different labor markets.* Each country has a different mix of available workers and a different mix of labor costs, and international companies may gain advantages by accessing these various human resource capabilities. For example, GM's Mexican upholstery operation employs low-cost production workers and IBM's Swiss R&D facility hires skilled physicists. Whether companies seek resources or markets abroad, they may produce the same product differently among countries, such as substituting hand labor for machines because of diverse labor markets.

2. *International mobility problems.* There are legal, economic, physical, and cultural barriers in moving workers to a foreign country. Yet interna-

tional firms benefit from moving people, especially when labor market differences result in shortages of needed skills. In such cases, companies often must develop special recruitment, training, compensation, and transfer practices.

3. *Management styles and practices.* Attitudes toward different management styles vary from country to country; norms among management practices and labor-management relations testify to this. These differences may strain relations between headquarters and subsidiary personnel or make a manager less effective when working abroad than at home. At the same time, the experience of working with different national practices offers some opportunities for transferring successful practices from one country to another.

4. *National orientations.* Although a company's goals may include attaining global efficiencies and competitiveness, its personnel (both labor and management) may emphasize national rather than global interests. Certain personnel practices can help overcome the national orientations, and other operating adjustments may be necessary when the nationalistic orientations prevail.

5. *Control.* Such factors as distance and diversity make it more difficult to control foreign operations than domestic ones, and personnel policies sometimes are used to gain more control over foreign operations. At the same time, distance and diversity may inhibit a company's ability to conduct personnel policies as it might prefer and cause its practices to vary from one country to another.

This chapter emphasizes these points, differentiating between managerial and labor personnel.

MANAGEMENT QUALIFICATIONS AND CHARACTERISTICS

Headquarters-Subsidiary Relationship

Management must consider country and global needs.

International management staffing is two-tiered: First, the subsidiary level must employ persons who are equipped to manage the activities within the countries where they are located; second, people at corporate and/or regional headquarters must be equipped to coordinate and control the firms' various worldwide and regional operations. These two staffing dimensions are very much related, particularly since headquarters personnel usually choose and evaluate those who direct the subsidiaries abroad. These concerns also are related in that headquarters and subsidiary personnel must both be sufficiently aware of and willing to accept trade-offs between the need to adapt to local environmental differences and the need to gain global efficiencies.

The balance of power in these trade-offs is complex, depending on such factors as the firm's philosophy (e.g., polycentric versus ethnocentric) and on how much operations in different countries may benefit from independence as opposed to interdependence. When firms have a polycentric philosophy and their foreign subsidiaries are a federation of highly independent operations, there is much less effort to impose standard practices or a corporate culture abroad than when the philosophy is ethnocentric and foreign operations are internationally interdependent.[4] Regardless of where between these extremes the international firm lies, it may face dilemmas because the technology, policy, and managerial style it has developed in one place may be only partially applicable elsewhere. International managers, at headquarters and subsidiaries, are responsible for introducing (or not introducing) practices new to a country.

Relations are affected by
- *Polycentrism versus ethnocentrism*
- *Benefits of independence*

Top-Level Duties Abroad

Subsidiary Management Although foreign subsidiaries usually are much smaller than their parents, their top-level managers often have to perform top-level management duties. This usually means being more of a generalist than specialist, more of a leader than a follower, having responsibility for a wide variety of functions, spending more time on the job, and spending a larger portion of time on external relations with the community, government, and general public as well as outside business meetings. Managers with comparable profit or cost responsibility in the home country still may be performing middle-management tasks and lack the breadth of experience necessary for a top-management position in a foreign subsidiary.

Top management in subsidiaries usually have broader duties than people with same size operation at home.

Headquarters Travel The corporate staff charged with responsibility for international business functions also must interact frequently with very high-level authorities in foreign countries. Such activities as negotiations for new or expanded plants, the sale of technology, and the assessment of monetary conditions require high levels of interaction by the corporate staff during their travels to foreign countries. In many ways their tasks are even more difficult than those of the subsidiary managers since they must be away from home for extended and indefinite periods while seeking the confidence and rapport of officials in many foreign countries rather than in just one. Even if they are not faced with the rigors of foreign travel, they may be ill at ease with the foreign aspects of their responsibilities if their rise to the corporate level has been entirely through work in domestic divisions.

Corporate staff abroad
- *Deal at top level in many countries*
- *Experience the rigors of foreign travel*
- *Face difficulties if they have risen entirely through domestic divisions*

Communications Problems of the Job

International communications are complex and more likely to be misunderstood than domestic ones.

Interpretation   International managers must communicate well to ensure that the intent of messages between the home and subsidiary operations is understood. This is somewhat complicated by the cost of overseas calls and faxes, the different time zones, and the slower delivery of mail.

Communications between managers whose native languages are different are compounded even further. Corporate communications, directives, and manuals may be translated, which takes time and expense. If not, the content may be understood perfectly abroad, but the comprehension time may be longer because people read more slowly in a second language. Likewise, because of communication problems a manager working abroad often has to work harder to do the same quality work that could be done at home with less difficulty.[5] These inherent inefficiencies are often overlooked by the parent, yet foreign subsidiary management is held responsible.

Because cultural differences color intents and perceptions of what is transmitted and received in formal communications, international managers may assume erroneously that foreigners will react the same way as their compatriots to such things as decision-making and leadership styles. This is a particular problem when various nationalities are grouped, such as on a team project. Some of these differences may be lessened through the development of a common corporate culture, but this may be of little use when managers must work internationally in the growing number of cooperative ventures that include not just different nationalities but also different firms, such as within joint ventures and licensing agreements.[6]

Use of English   English is today the international language of business because (1) so much international business is conducted by firms from and in English-speaking countries and (2) English has become the major second language worldwide. Furthermore, managers cannot be expected to learn all the languages where their firms operate. Consequently, business between Mexico and Brazil or between Italy and Saudi Arabia may be conducted in the common second language of English. Even some multinationals from Germany, Japan, the Netherlands, Switzerland, and Sweden have adopted English as their official tongue.[7]

A working knowledge of the language spoken where a manager is operating can, nevertheless, help in adapting to the foreign country as well as gaining acceptance by people there. However, even if they are fully fluent in a common language, managers should consider employing good interpreters when they are attempting serious discussions, such as negotiations with government officials.

What foreign language should a native English speaker learn who wants a successful international business career? Much depends on where one's employer does business and much on one's geographic work preference. Nevertheless, one poll of U.S. firms on the most important language from 1990 to

2010 put Spanish clearly in front with 44 percent of responses. Japanese followed at 33 percent. The only other languages receiving at least a 1 percent response were French (8), Chinese (6), German (5), and Russian (1).[8]

Isolation

International managers are isolated and have less access to staff specialists.

A foreign subsidiary manager must be able to work independently because many staff functions are eliminated abroad to reduce the cost of duplication. At headquarters a manager can easily walk to the next office or make a few telephone calls to get advice from specialists. The subsidiary manager, however, ends up relying much more heavily on personal judgment.

Headquarters personnel traveling abroad may face the same problems of isolation as foreign subsidiary managers, with additional isolation in their personal lives. Although many domestic positions require traveling, the domestic trips are apt to be of shorter duration because of the greater ease of returning home for weekends. One international executive presented this humorously:

> Often you won't be able to plan in advance when you are leaving on business or when you will return. Being present at birthdays, school plays, anniversaries, family reunions, and other events may become the exception instead of the rule. While you're away, mortgage payments will probably be due, the MasterCard bill will arrive, the furnace will fail, your child will get chicken pox, the IRS will schedule a full audit, the family car will be totaled, and your spouse will sue for divorce.[9]

FOREIGN MANAGERIAL TRANSFERS

Some Definitions

International firms commonly categorize managers as **locals** (citizens of the countries where they are working) or **expatriates** (noncitizens). The expatriate group is further categorized as **home-country** and **third-country nationals.** These are, respectively, citizens of the country where the company is headquartered and citizens neither of the country where they are working nor of the headquarters country of the firm. Locals or expatriates may be employed in the firm's home country or in the firm's foreign operations.

Expatriates: A Minority of Managers

Most managerial positions are filled by locals rather than expatriates in both headquarters or foreign subsidiary operations. The one exception is for project management in some developing countries, such as Saudi Arabia, where there is an acute shortage of qualified local candidates.

Managerial slots are difficult to fill because
• Many people don't
  want to move
• Expatriates are more
  costly
• There are legal impedi-
  ments to using expa-
  triates

Mobility   Many people, regardless of nationality, simply do not want to work in a foreign country; this is particularly true if an assignment is perceived to be permanent or very long term. In many cases companies have had to set up special operating units to employ people who will not work where the company would prefer. For instance, this has been a motive for setting up R&D labs and regional staff offices abroad when the personnel refused to move to the global headquarters country.

The cost of using expatriates is another factor firms must face in filling managerial positions. Firms typically pay for moving expenses (including customs duties on household effects), settling-in expenses (such as the cost of adapting appliances to foreign electrical systems), and storage expenses for goods not shipped abroad, since employers may balk at moving pianos, antiques, boats, and hobby equipment. Generally it is more expensive for firms to maintain expatriates than local managers after the transfer. There are legal impediments as well, such as licensing requirements that prevent the use of foreign-trained accountants and lawyers and immigration restrictions that cause delays in filling positions. Since governmental regulations and their enforcement may change drastically and quickly, firms face considerable uncertainty.

Local Competitive Needs   The greater the need for local adaptations, the more advantageous it is for firms to use local management since they presumably understand local conditions better than someone from outside the country. These needs may arise because of unique environmental conditions, barriers to imports, or the existence of strong local competitors or customers.

Locals in management
may help sales and mo-
rale.

The Local Image   Sometimes it is useful for the firm to create a local image for foreign operations, especially when there is animosity toward foreign-controlled operations. Local management may be perceived locally as "better citizens" because they presumably put local interests ahead of the companies' global objectives. This local image may play a role in employee morale as well, since many subsidiary employees prefer to work for someone from their own country.[10]

If top jobs are given only
to expatriates, it may be
hard to attract and keep
good locals.

Incentives to Local Personnel   Proponents of employing local nationals sometimes argue that the possibility of advancement provides an incentive to employees to perform well; without this incentive, it is contended, they may seek employment with other firms. Opponents argue that practices restricting the best qualified people, regardless of nationality, from positions are even more damaging to employee motivation. Anyone in the organization, they say, should have the opportunity to move up to any post, including positions in the corporate headquarters.

Expatriates may take
shorter-term perspectives.

Long-Term Objectives   Since people transferred to subsidiaries usually expect to be there for only a few years, they are often more anxious than local nationals to choose short-term projects that will materialize during their tenure in the foreign location.[11] In producing highly visible and measurable results that help satisfy personal advancement needs when the foreign assignment is terminated, they may not be best serving the longer-range corporate goals. Local nationals who stay on for a longer duration therefore may take more heed of long-term objectives because of the probability of still working there when the instituted practices are completed.

Reasons for Using Expatriates

Despite expatriate managers being a minority of total managers within international firms, there are still several hundred thousand employed worldwide.

Technical Competence   The major reason companies use expatriate employees is that they cannot find local candidates who have the technical qualifications for the job. This is partly a function of the level of development of the country; thus expatriates constitute a much smaller portion of subsidiary managers in industrial than in developing countries. It is also a function of the need to infuse new home-country developments abroad. When, for example, there is a transference of new products or new production methods, especially in start-up operations, there is usually a need for transfers of home-country personnel to subsidiaries or of subsidiary personnel to the home country until the changes are running smoothly.

There are more shortages of technically trained personnel in LDCs.

Management Development   MNEs transfer foreigners into their home country or regional operations and transfer home-country nationals abroad to train them to understand the overall corporate system.[12] In firms with specialized activities only in certain countries (extraction separated from manufacturing, for example, or basic R&D separate from applied), long-term foreign assignments may be the only means of developing a manager's integrative competence. These moves also enhance managers' ability to work in a variety of social systems and are therefore valuable training for ultimate corporate responsibility, including domestic and foreign operations.

Multicountry experience gives upward-moving managers new perspectives.

Control   MNEs use transfers and visits to subsidiaries to control the foreign operations and coordinate organizational development. These goals are accomplished because the people who are transferred are used to doing things the headquarters way and because frequent transfers let them increase their knowledge of the company's global network.[13] Likewise, foreign nationals may spend time at worldwide or regional headquarters, thereby giving a foreign perspective to the firm's global direction. Through the greater interchange brought about by moves of both home- and host-country nationals, a new hybrid corporate culture, or at least an understanding and acceptance of global corporate goals, can become a means of controlling the company's operations.[14]

People transferred from headquarters are more likely to know headquarters policies.

People transferred to headquarters learn the headquarters way.

Where there is more of a global strategy, there is a need to use more expatriates for control purposes. They are or become generally more familiar with the complexities of the business family system as a whole and tend not to see their own personal development in terms of what happens only in the country to which they are assigned.[15]

Home-Country versus Third-Country Nationals

Most advances in technology, product, and operating procedures originate in the home country and are transferred into foreign operations later. Since the use of expatriates in foreign facilities is dictated in part by a desire to infuse new methods, the personnel with recent home-country experience (usually home-country citizens) are apt to have the desired qualifications.

Third-country nationals may be more knowledge-able of
- Language
- Operating adjustments

However, third-country nationals might sometimes have more compatible technical and personal adaptive qualifications than home-country expatriates. For example, a U.S. company used U.S. personnel to design and manage a Peruvian plant until local managers could be trained. Years later, the firm decided to manufacture in Mexico with a plant more closely resembling the Peruvian operations than those in the United States in terms of size, product qualities, and factor inputs. Therefore, Spanish-speaking Peruvian managers were adaptive and were used effectively in planning, start-up, and early operating phases in Mexico.

Some Individual Considerations for Transfers

Job-ability factors are a necessary attribute.

Technical Competence   Unless the foreign assignment is clearly intended for training the expatriate, local employees will resent someone coming in from a foreign country (usually at higher compensation) who, they feel, is no more qualified than they are. The opinions of corporate-transfer decision makers, expatriate managers, and local managers all confirm that job-ability factors are the most important determinants of success in overseas assignments.[16] Although a variety of additional skills is important for success in an overseas assignment, the expatriate must know the technical necessities of the tasks as performed in the home country and be able to adapt to foreign variations, such as scaled-down plants and equipment, varying standards of productivity, lack of efficient internal distribution, nonavailability of credit, and restrictions on type of communications media selected. He or she must also be fully aware of corporate policies so that foreign decisions are compatible with global philosophies. For these reasons, managers usually have several years' work experience with a company before being offered a foreign assignment.

Adaptiveness   Although some firms rely only on technical competence criteria in the selection of expatriates, three types of adaptive skills are important for success when entering a new culture. First, there are skills needed for self-maintenance, such as stress reduction and self-confidence. Second, there are skills related to the development of satisfactory relationships with host nationals. Third, there are cognitive skills that help one to perceive correctly what is occurring within the host society.[17] When lacking any one of these, one may not be able to function effectively. At an extreme, the expatriate may leave, either through his or her own choice or by a company decision.

Estimates vary widely on the percentage of families transferred abroad who return home prematurely or perform ineffectively because of adjustment problems. Nevertheless, the costs to international firms are generally considered to be high. There are direct transfer costs and costs of lost performance because of the employee's or family's adjustment problems.[18] An international move usually means a great disruption in a family's current way of living, especially since the greatest shortage of managers is in the LDCs, and a major reason for failure in a foreign assignment is the family's inability to adjust. A move means new living and shopping habits, new school systems, and unfamiliar business practices. In addition, close friends and relatives—the personal support system—are left behind. Because some individuals do enjoy and adapt easily to a foreign way of life, it is preferable to use them if possible when transfers are necessary. Some firms maintain a specific group of international employees who are the only ones assigned abroad.

A distinction needs to be made between a foreign assignment of fixed duration and one that is open-ended. Many more people can cope with a position abroad if they know that they will return home after a specific period of time than if the assignment may turn out to be permanent.

Local Acceptance   Expatriates may encounter some acceptance problems regardless of who they are. For instance, it usually takes time for managers to gain recognition of their personal authority, and expatriates may not be there long enough to achieve this. Local employees may feel that the best jobs are given to overpaid foreigners. The expatriate may have to make unpopular decisions in order to meet global objectives. Or local management may have had experiences with expatriates who made short-term decisions and left before dealing with the longer-term implications.[19] If negative stereotypes are added to these attitudes, it may be very difficult for the expatriate to succeed. Therefore, certain individuals are often excluded from consideration for transfer: A black manager in South Africa, a Jewish manager in Libya, a very young manager in Japan, or a female manager in Saudi Arabia, for example, might encounter insurmountable problems in dealing with employees, suppliers, and customers. The U.S. Supreme Court ruled in 1991 that the federal law barring discrimination in employment does not apply to foreign operations of U.S. companies; however, there is considerable public opinion and congressional support for a new law that will extend antidiscrimination measures abroad.[20]

But do companies overreact to these acceptance problems? Take stereotypes of women, for example: They should not give orders to men, they are temperamental, their place is in the home, clients will not accept them, em-

Family adaptation is important.

Fixed-term versus open-end assignments are viewed differently.

Expatriates may meet with local prejudice.

ployees will not take them seriously, they don't have the stamina to work in harsh areas, they will not be given work permits, they don't want to upset their husbands' careers. In response to these stereotypes, firms give very few expatriate positions to women. Yet, there are women who have succeeded as expatriates, primarily in service rather than industrial products industries, in such places as Japan, Thailand, and India because they were first seen as foreigners and then as women.[21] Some suggestions have been made to improve the acceptability of women as expatriates that may be applied as well to improve the acceptability of other groups. These include the selection of very well-qualified older, midcareer women who could command more authority; the advance dissemination of information concerning the high qualifications; the placement of expatriate women in locations where there are already some local women in management positions; and the establishment of longer than normal assignments in order to develop role models of acceptance.[22]

Post-Expatriate Situations

Repatriation Problems   Problems with repatriation from foreign subsidiary assignments arise in three general areas: (1) personal finances, (2) readjustment to home-country corporate structure, and (3) readjustment to life at home. Expatriates are given many financial benefits to encourage them to accept a foreign assignment. While abroad they may live in the best neighborhoods, send their children to the best private schools, socialize with the upper class, and still save more money than before. But this higher life-style is lost on return: An estimated 50 percent increase in salary would be necessary to maintain the same standard of living in the United States that U.S. executives enjoy overseas. Returning expatriates often find that many of their peers have been promoted above them in their absence, that they now have less autonomy in the job, and that they are now "little fish in a big pond." In addition to a drop in social status on return, many families that have successfully adjusted to a foreign life-style have problems in readjusting to schools and other aspects of life in their home countries. Some suggestions for smoothing the reentry include early advice of return, maximum information on the new job, housing assistance, a reorientation program, bringing the expatriate manager back to headquarters frequently, and the use of a formal headquarters mentor who will look after the manager's interests while he or she is an expatriate.[23]

Coming home can be an adaptation in many areas:
- Financial
- Job
- Social

Career Movements   What an overseas assignment means to one's career varies widely. Studies based on the opinions of repatriated employees and of career paths of top executives illustrate that a foreign assignment is most likely to have a neutral effect on one's long-term career; however, foreign assignments have had positive or detrimental effects for significant numbers

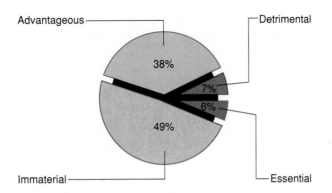

Figure 21.1
How U.S. Companies View the Career Impact of an Assignment Overseas
The figure shows the results of 56 MNEs' opinions on careers within their
companies in 1990. *Source:* Moran, Stahl & Boyer, 1990, as reported in the *New York
Times,* June 17, 1990, sec. 3, p. 1.

of former expatriates as well.[24] In addition to individual differences, differences exist by company, depending on such factors as the commitment to
foreign operations, the integration between domestic and international activities, and the communications linkages between headquarters and subsidiary
personnel. Figure 21.1 illustrates the diversity found in one study.

For companies with a very high commitment to global operations, multicountry experience may be as essential as multifunctional and multiproduct
experience in reaching upper-echelon organizational levels. The opening case
on Dow illustrates such a situation. Unilever's chairman described his firm's
situation as follows: "Most people who rise toward the top of our business
will have worked in at least two countries, probably three. They will probably
speak another language, but I think that is more a symbol of internationalism
than a necessity. And they almost certainly will have worked in different
product areas, say, in chemicals and in food. By the time they reach the critical age when management will decide if they are going to the top or not,
they are extremely well prepared."[25]

Some companies with high international commitments, nevertheless, so
separate foreign and domestic operations that the corporation functions almost as two separate companies. If the domestic business is dominant, there
may not only be little interchange of personnel, there may be little advancement of personnel with international experience to top-level positions. General Motors pointed out how career-enhancing foreign work experience was
in its organization because three of its eighteen top executives had foreign
assignment tours.[26] That 83 percent of the executives succeeded without the
foreign experience does not seem to indicate a great career enhancement from
international assignments. Nevertheless, this has not daunted GM's foreign
success: It is one of the largest U.S. exporters; its overseas production, espe-

cially in the United Kingdom and Germany, is highly competitive. Its personnel and organization policies are compatible because of its largely multidomestic strategy; nevertheless, GM in 1989 instituted a policy of sending ten U.S. mid-level managers per year abroad for three to twelve months and increased the number to twenty in 1990 (out of about 100,000 salaried U.S. domestic employees).[27]

But very few people reach the top rungs of large companies, with or without foreign work experience. Some companies, particularly those with international divisions, depend heavily on a cadre of international specialists who may either rotate between foreign locations and international headquarters assignments or spend most of their careers abroad. Although not reaching the top levels of the parent corporations, they can reach plateaus above most domestic managers in terms of compensation and responsibility. Many people with a penchant for international living do not aspire to anything different.

Within some companies, there is a high career risk through foreign assignments, regardless of corporate executives' statements to the contrary. In one candid appraisal, a Ford Motor Company vice president said, "For the vast majority of people [in middle and senior-middle management] at Ford, foreign assignments are a career negative." This may come about for two reasons. First, there may be little provision to fit someone into the domestic or headquarters organization upon repatriation. One's old office simply does not stay vacant while one is abroad for several years; thus, the repatriated employee cannot easily bump the replacement. A senior engineer working for Westinghouse in Belgium described his finding a job with Westinghouse in the U.S. as the same as when he first applied to the company while in college.[28] Second, some "out of sight, out of mind" may come into play. A General Dynamics executive said he would never have known about domestic openings if a friend had not kept him apprised of the organization's promotional pipeline.[29] Reentry is further complicated if the expatriate is on lengthy assignment where older technologies and corporate policies are practiced.

When repatriated employees have career problems, it becomes more difficult to convince other people to take foreign assignments. Some companies simply explain the career risk and compensate employees so highly that they are enticed to become expatriates anyway. To combat the problem, more companies (but still a minority) are integrating foreign assignment into career planning and are developing mentor programs to look after the expatriates' domestic interests.[30] Very few firms make written guarantees that repatriated employees will come back to jobs at least as good as the ones they left, as does Dow in the opening case. Companies don't make such a guarantee of a future position to their domestic managers either.

Foreign nationals who are transferred to headquarters sometimes confront a different problem. If the assignment is a promotion from a manager's subsidiary post rather than part of a planned rotation, then the move to headquarters may be permanent. For example, the Brazilian head of the Brazilian subsidiary may have performed so well that the MNE wants to give that manager multicountry responsibility at the corporate offices in New York or Frankfurt. Since there would be no way to go back to Brazil without taking a demotion, the Brazilian manager might turn down the transfer; otherwise, he or she would give up working in the home country permanently.

Expatriate Compensation

Firms must pay enough to entice people to move but not overpay.

If a U.S. company transfers its British finance manager, who is making $50,000 per year, to Italy where the going rate is $60,000 per year, what should the manager's salary be? Or if the Italian financial manager were to be transferred to the United Kingdom, what pay should be offered? Should the compensation be in dollars, pounds, or lira? Whose holidays should apply? Which set of fringe benefits should be used? These are but a few of the many questions that must be solved when firms move people abroad. On the one hand, the firm must try to prevent excessive costs; on the other hand, it must maintain high employee morale.

The amount and type of compensation necessary to entice a person to move to another country vary widely by person and locale. For companies with very few expatriate employees a foreign compensation package may be worked out on an individual basis. As international activities grow, a company cannot work out each movement this way. Questions of equity would be raised, since two people with different pay packages could end up in the same locale. As long as consistency is sought in transfer policy, some people inevitably will receive more than would be necessary to entice them to go abroad. Overall, the package may multiply the compensation cost in comparison with what the expatriate had been making domestically. Table 21.1 illustrates a typical package.

Cost of Living   Most people who move to another country encounter cost-of-living increases (sometimes called a goods-and-services differential), primarily because they are used to living in a certain manner that is expensive to duplicate in a new environment. Habits are difficult to change. Knowledge of the local country is a second consideration. Food and housing may be obtained at higher than the local rate because expatriates may not know the language well, where to buy, or how to bargain for reductions.

Living is more expensive abroad because
- Habits change slowly
- People don't know how and where to buy

Firms use various cost-of-living indexes and
- Increase compensation when foreign cost is higher
- Do not decrease compensation when foreign cost is lower

Most firms adjust salaries upward with a differential to account for higher costs while living abroad. When returning home, the differential is removed. When moves are to areas with a lower cost of living, firms rarely reduce the size of the employee's paycheck, since this would have a negative impact on morale; thus the expatriate may receive a windfall. Companies rely on estimates of cost-of-living differences, even though they do not fit everyone's situation perfectly. Some commonly used sources are the U.S. State Department's cost-of-living index published yearly in *Labor Developments*

TABLE 21.1 | TYPICAL FIRST-YEAR COST OF A UNITED STATES EXPATRIATE (MARRIED, TWO CHILDREN) IN TOKYO, JAPAN An expatriate's cost to the company may be several times what the cost would be for the same employee in his or her home country.

Direct Compensation Costs	
Base Salary	$100,000
Foreign-Service Premium	15,000
Goods and Services Differential	73,600
Less: U.S. Housing Norm*	(15,400)
U.S. Hypothetical Taxes	(17,200)
Company-paid Costs	
Schooling (two children)	15,000
Annual Home Leave	4,800
Housing*	150,000
Japanese Income Taxes*	84,000
Transfer/Moving Costs	38,000
Total Company Costs	**$447,800**

*Assumes company rents housing in its name and provides to expatriate. If instead, company pays housing allowance, Japanese income taxes (and total costs) will be about $65,000 higher. Note that Japanese income taxes will increase each year as some company reimbursements, most notably for taxes, become taxable.

Source: Organization Resources Counselors, Inc.

● Remove salary differential when the manager is repatriated

Abroad, the *U.N. Monthly Bulletin of Statistics,* and surveys by the *Financial Times, Business International,* and the International Monetary Fund *Staff Papers.* In using any of these indexes, firms must determine what items are included so as to adjust other expenditures separately. Some items commonly handled separately are housing, schooling, and taxes. The ultimate objective of cost-of-living adjustments is to ensure the expatriates' after-tax income will not suffer as a result of a foreign assignment. Because taxes are usually assessed on the overseas premiums in addition to the base salaries, the premiums must be adjusted even further upward if the foreign tax is higher than in the home country. In Sweden it is sometimes less expensive for expatriates to commute daily by plane from Germany rather than be subject to the Swedish personal income taxes, which are among the highest in the world. Since differences in inflation and exchange rates may quickly render surveys and indexes obsolete, it is necessary to update cost-of-living adjustments frequently.

A suggestion often made but seldom followed is that cost-of-living differentials be reduced the longer the employees are in a given country. The rationale is that, as expatriates become better assimilated, they should be able to adjust more to local purchasing habits—for example, buying vegetables from a native market instead of using imported packaged goods.

Job-Status Payment

Some employees may not accept a position abroad unless it is considered to be a promotion, and a promotion without a pay increase is considered inequitable by most people. Because expatriates compare the equity of their compensation with other managers in both the country to which they are sent and the country of which they are citizens, companies will also normally temporarily raise the salary for individuals while they are working in a country where the going rate for the job is higher than in the home country.

Foreign-Service Premiums and Hardship Allowances

There are bound to be things employees will have to do without when living abroad. Such sacrifices range from nuisance to hardship. For example, employees may miss following particular sports results, certain foods, a holiday celebration, or television in the native language. Or children may have to attend school away from home, perhaps even in another country. There is also the problem of adjusting to a new culture, which may cause adverse psychological effects and social frustrations. Given these adjustments, firms frequently give foreign-service premiums just for being posted in a foreign location; however, there has been some tendency to eliminate these in so-called world capitals where there is assumed to be little deprivation and where it is not difficult to get people to transfer.

Few would deny that living conditions in certain locations present particularly severe hardships, such as harsh climatic or health conditions or political insurrection or unrest that places the employee and family in danger. For instance, in recent years, antigovernment groups kidnapped for ransom expatriate employees of such companies as Ford, Kodak, and Owens-Illinois. In fact, the growing incidence of kidnapping and terrorism has caused firms not only to rethink their hardship allowances, but also to purchase ransom insurance and to embark on training programs to advise personnel and families of dangers and how to deal with them. Corporations have been hit by legal suits from victims' families, which have alleged that companies mishandled ransom negotiations. Firms also have been hit by shareholder suits claiming that the company should not pay ransoms.[31]

Finally, a hardship may occur because of potential changes in total family income and status. In the home country, all members of the family may be able to work. Seldom will more than the transferred employee be given permission to work in a foreign country, so if an individual is moved abroad, his or her spouse (or live-in companion) may have to give up well-paying and satisfying employment.[32] Firms realize that changes in location present various types of hardship problems and attempt to compensate their employees accordingly.

Choice of Currency   Expatriate employees' salaries are usually (but not always) paid partly in local currency and partly in the currency of the employee's home country. This allows employees to save in their home countries and often to forgo host-country taxes on the home-country portion of income. Some other factors influencing the preference for payment in home versus host currencies include whether hard currency expenditures can be charged to the local operation, whether exchange control exists, and whether the expatriate can receive more local currency by exchanging the hard currency through a free market.

Salaries are usually a mixture of home and host currency.

Remote Areas   Many large-scale international projects are in areas so remote that MNEs would get few people to transfer if the companies did not create an environment more like the one at home or make other special arrangements. Lockheed Aircraft, for example, set up its own color television broadcasting station in Saudi Arabia for its expatriates there. INCO built schools, hospitals, churches, supermarkets, a golf course, yacht club, motel, and restaurant for its expatriates in Indonesia.[33]

For their employees in remote areas, firms may have to provide more fringe benefits.

Expatriate employees in these remote areas are often handled very differently from those in other locales. To attract the large number of people necessary for construction and start-up, MNEs will usually offer fixed-term contract assignments at high salary and hire most people from outside the firm. Some are attracted to these assignments and are willing to undergo different living conditions because they can save at a rate that would be impossible at home.

MANAGEMENT RECRUITMENT AND SELECTION

College Recruitment

College recruitment is used at home and abroad, but the biggest need abroad is for higher-level managers.

International companies recruit through universities at home and abroad to find capable nationals of the countries where they have foreign facilities. This method has some drawbacks since the most acute personnel shortage in foreign facilities is for people who already have considerable experience. As the new hires gain experience, however, they may eventually move into higher-level management positions, thus decreasing the need for expatriates. These same firms also recruit home-country nationals, usually to work in their domestic operations until they have gained technical experience and know the corporate culture.

Management Inventories

Foreign personnel are not easily encompassed in inventories because

- *Foreign operations may not be wholly owned*

Some companies have centralized personnel record systems, which include home- and foreign-country nationals. These include not only the normal technical and demographic data, but also such adaptive information as foreign-language abilities, willingness to accept foreign assignments, and re-

• There may be restrictions on cross-national data flows.

sults of company-administered tests to indicate adaptiveness. There are some problems in bringing foreign managers into these systems because, if the firm owns less than 100 percent of the foreign facility, the other stockholders may complain.[34] Furthermore, restrictions on data flows among countries could inhibit future uses of centralized management inventories.

Adaptability Assessment

Since companies usually know more about their employees' technical than adaptive capabilities, they must focus on measuring adaptation abilities for foreign-transfer purposes. For example, people who have successfully adjusted to domestic transfers or have previous international experience are more likely to adapt abroad. In addition, some companies use a variety of testing mechanisms to aid in the assessment. One is the Early Identification Program (E.I.P.), which assesses an individual's match with different environments. Many other tests assess personality traits that indicate a willingness to change basic attitudes: These include the Minnesota Multiphasic Personality Inventory, the Guilford-Zimmerman Temperament Survey, and the Allport-Vernon Study of Values.[35]

A small minority of companies include spouses in tests and extensive interviews because a foreign assignment is usually more stressful for the spouse than for the transferred employee. The foreign assignment is generally an advancement for (in most cases) the husband; however, the wife must start at the bottom in developing new social relations and learning how to carry out the day-to-day management of the home. The separation from friends and family often makes the wife very lonely so that she turns to her husband for more companionship. But the husband may have less time because of his new working conditions. This may lead to marital stress which, in turn, affects work performance. Interviewers thus look not only at likely adaptiveness, but also at whether the marriage is strong enough to weather the stress and not impede performance of employment duties.[36]

Test predictability for success in foreign assignments is not very high.

Although some companies follow a rigorous procedure of selecting and training people cross-culturally for foreign assignments, the adjustment and performance of their expatriates have been mixed. Nevertheless, the evidence supports a positive relationship between vigorous procedures and adjustment and performance.[37]

The Help of Local Companies

Acquisitions and joint ventures secure staff but they may be

• Inefficient
• Hard to control

One way of attaining personnel for foreign operations is by buying an existing firm abroad and using the personnel already employed; however, firms should consider the possible efficiency problems of acquisitions. Firms also may tie in closely with local companies in the expectation that these firms will contribute personnel to the operation as well as hire new personnel. In countries such as Japan, where the labor market is tight and people are reluctant to move to new firms, the use of a local partner may be extremely important. However, if a local partner handles staffing arrangements, the employees may see their primary allegiance to that partner rather than to the foreign investor.

MANAGEMENT TRAINING

Internationalizing the Organization

Preemployment Training   In spite of a lessening need worldwide to convince managers of the advantages of taking an international perspective on business, there is still a need to train managers in business operating differences brought about by internationalization. Business schools are increasing their international offerings and requirements, but there is no consensus as to what students should learn to help prepare for international responsibilities. Two distinct approaches are (1) the conveying of knowledge specific to foreign environments and in area studies, and (2) training in interpersonal awareness and adaptability. For example, the former may tend to remove some of the fear and aggression that are aroused when dealing with the unknown. However, the understanding of a different culture does not necessarily imply a willingness to adapt to that culture. Although either approach generally helps a person adjust relative to those who lack training, there appears to be no significant difference in the effectiveness of the two approaches.[38]

Postemployment Training   Many employees may still place domestic performance objectives above global ones or feel ill-equipped to handle worldwide responsibilities as they move up in their organizations. One approach is to train those people who are about to take a foreign assignment, such as through language and orientation programs. Another is to include international business components in external or internal programs, where companies train managers regularly. External programs are offered at many universities.[39] A sampling of internal programs are those at General Mills and Celanese that include yearlong training in which foreign nationals spend time at all of the companies' domestic divisions, IBM's regional training centers in which managers from several countries are gathered for specific topics, Cummins Engine's voluntary evening language courses that any employee may take, and cultural awareness workshops at Westinghouse.[40]

Program content may emphasize adaptability rather than knowledge of another environment. The Peace Corps, for example, uses sensitivity training, which is designed to develop attitudinal flexibility. Another method is to expose trainees to subcultures within their own countries. Still another has been for a firm in one country to train employees from an unaffiliated firm in another country through on-the-job assignments.[41]

Transferees may find it difficult to know even what questions to ask, which is why the most common predeparture training takes the form of an

Margin notes:

There is an increase in international studies in universities.

Postemployment training may
- Include environment-specific information
- Include adaptiveness training
- Give on-the-job training within an unaffiliated firm abroad

informational briefing. Such factors as job design, compensation, housing, climate, education, health conditions, home sales, taxes, transport of goods, job upon repatriation, and salary distribution typically come to mind. But such things as the foreign social structure, communications links, kidnapping precautions, and legal advice on the law of domicile are seldom considered before settlement abroad.[42]

LABOR MARKET DIFFERENCES

External Reference Points

Firms should look to existing operations as reference for planning manpower needs in new operations abroad.

Typically, a company setting up a new operation in a foreign country is duplicating, perhaps on a small or slightly altered scale, a product, process, or function being performed at home. Past experience will have shown company officials what type and how many employees are needed for the size of operation being built. The company will probably have job descriptions for each category to be filled, and from past experience will know what types of people ideally fit into specific positions.

Appropriate Technology

Firms may shift labor or capital intensities if relative costs are different.

There is some danger in a firm's attempting to duplicate organizational structures and job descriptions abroad, particularly in LDCs. For one thing, labor-saving devices that are economically justifiable at home, where wage rates are high, may be more costly than labor-intensive types of production in a country with high unemployment rates and low wages. Labor-intensive methods also may ingratiate the firm with governmental officials, who must cope with unrest from the unemployed portion of the population. Because of differences in labor skills and attitudes, the firm also may find it advantageous to simplify tasks and use equipment that would be considered obsolete in a more advanced economy.

Critics have argued that MNEs have too often established capital-intensive rather than labor-intensive production methods, thus not contributing fully to the decrease needed in LDC unemployment. The term **appropriate technology** refers to that technology which best fits the factor endowment where it is used. The term usually is used to mean technology that is more labor-intensive than would be cost-efficient in an industrial country.

The evidence of whether MNEs do alter production possibilities to the extent that is cost-feasible is very mixed. On the one hand, there are undoubtedly engineering biases toward duplicating facilities with which the firm has recent experience; these are the plants built to save labor in industrialized countries. Management control systems also may place heavy emphasis on output per person, which is more relevant to production needs in industrialized countries. Likewise, many governmental authorities within the LDCs are anxious to have showcase plants to promote the message that the countries are modernizing rapidly. On the other hand, case studies point to substantial alterations by MNEs, such as replacing mechanized loading equipment with human efforts, because of local costs and availabilities.[43] As long as unemployment continues to be a major social and economic problem within LDCs, controversies will continue over the amount of labor that should be employed in the production process.

International Labor Mobility

Extent   At the same time that most developing countries have faced critical unemployment problems, many industrialized nations and the underpopulated oil producing countries have been short of workers to run their facilities. This has created a great deal of pressure for increased immigration, which in turn has been tempered by legal restrictions to minimize the economic and social problems for the countries absorbing large numbers of aliens.

There is pressure for labor to move from high unemployment and low-wage areas to places of perceived opportunities.

Reliable figures on the amount of international migration are unavailable because of the large number of illegal aliens. However, the fragmentary evidence is rather startling. For example, remittances home from workers from such countries as Jordan, the Republic of Yemen, Pakistan, and Egypt exceed the value of exports from those countries.[44]

Work-Force Stability Problem   Migrant workers in many countries, such as New Zealand's workers from Fiji and Tonga, have permission to stay for only short periods of time, such as three to six months. In many other cases, workers leave their families behind in the hope of returning home after saving sufficient money while working in the foreign country. In the mid-1970s, for example, France had a net loss in its work force as large numbers of Spanish workers returned home. In the late 1980s, the U.S. had a net loss of Korean scientists and engineers. Another uncertainty is the extent to which governmental authorities will restrict the number of foreign workers, and there are pressures in all industrial countries to expel foreign workers in order to protect job opportunities for domestic workers or to promote a more homogeneous culture. Even if cutbacks are accomplished during a slack period in the economy, so that a firm may switch to using local rather than foreign workers, a firm then may face the costly process of training workers who may leave as soon as the economy improves.

Companies are less certain of labor supply when they depend on foreign laborers because
- Countries become restrictive
- Workers return home
- Turnover necessitates more training

Employment Adjustments   The ability of multinational firms to mobilize capital, technology, and management has fed the demand for migrant workers in remote parts of the globe. To operate facilities where minerals are located or in previously unoccupied areas of oil producing countries, firms have had to bring in large numbers of skilled and unskilled workers from abroad. In doing this, MNEs have had to construct housing and infrastructure and to

MNEs must build infrastructure in remote areas.

develop social services to serve the new population. Even in populated areas, housing shortages might prevent the influx of temporary workers if a company did not make provisions.

The influx and use of workers from different countries create additional problems in the workplace.[45] In the United States during the early twentieth century, large numbers of foreign laborers were secured to work in city industries, for railroads, and in construction. It was common for each nationality group to work under the auspices of its own interpreters and to do particular types of tasks. Barracks and kitchens, provided by employers, were separate, so ethnic separation was perpetuated. Similar practices exist in parts of Western Europe today, particularly as Poles, Czechs and Slovaks, and Romanians have arrived to work from Central Europe. Some of the results are the relegation of certain nationality groups to less complex jobs owing to the language problem in training, the development of homogeneous ethnic work groups at cross-purposes with other groups in the organization, and the emergence of go-betweens who can communicate with management and labor.

LABOR COMPENSATION

Importance of Differences

Compensation policies and practices directly affect a firm's competitive viability because they influence the competitive ingredient of attracting, maintaining, and motivating personnel. Labor cost differences among countries sometimes lead to competitive advantages and motivate many firms to establish foreign production facilities. The amount of compensation people receive depends on the estimated contributions made to the business, supply and demand ("going wage") for particular skills in the area, cost of living, governmental legislation, and collective-bargaining ability. The methods of payment (salaries, wages, commissions, bonuses, and fringe benefits) depend on customs, feelings of security, taxes, and governmental requirements.

MNEs may need to pay more than local firms to entice workers from existing jobs.

International firms usually pay slightly better than their local counterparts in the lower-wage countries, but far below the salary paid for similar jobs in the highest-wage countries. Some factors leading to higher wages by international companies relate to their management philosophy and structure: For example, techniques that lead to greater efficiencies allow for higher employee compensation. The international company's management philosophy, particularly in contrast to local, family-run companies, is often to attract high-level workers by offering higher relative wages. Furthermore, when a firm first comes into a country, experienced workers may demand higher compensation because they have doubts about whether the new operation will succeed.

Fringe Benefits

Fringe benefits differ radically from one country to another. Direct-compensation figures therefore do not accurately reflect the amount a company must pay for a given job in a given country. The types of benefits that are either customary or have been required are also widely divergent. In Japan, for example, workers in large firms commonly receive such benefits as family allowances, housing loans and subsidies, lunches, children's education, and subsidized vacations, meaning that fringe benefits make up a much higher portion of total compensation than is the case in the United States. In the United Kingdom about 70 percent of automobiles are corporate-owned because of the personal tax advantages of using a company car rather than receiving income to buy a personal car. Other types of benefits such as end-of-the-year bonuses of up to three months' pay, housing, payments based on the number of children, long vacations, and profit sharing are common in many countries.

Job-Security Benefits   Firing or laying off an employee may be either impossible or very expensive in many countries, resulting in unexpectedly higher costs for a company accustomed to the economies of manipulating its employment figures. In the United States, for instance, layoffs are not only permitted but have grown to be expected when demand falls seasonally or cyclically. In many countries a firm has no legal recourse except to fire workers—and then perhaps only if the firm is closing down its operations. In Germany, for example, a fired worker may get up to eighteen months' salary. To curtail operations there, a company must come to an agreement with its unions and the government on such issues as extended benefits and the retraining and relocation of workers.

Liability for Injuries   Company, worker, or third-party neglect may lead to various types of worker or company injury. Physical injury may result from negligent driving by transport workers, faulty maintenance of equipment, and lack of safety equipment. The firm may be injured monetarily from careless handling of cash, embezzlement of funds, and breakage of product and equipment. There are widespread variances in the extent to which companies or workers are held responsible for injuries.[46] The determination of responsibility should dictate how firms handle these contingencies. The amount and allocation of expenditures for insurance, training, and safety equipment thus vary substantially by country.

How to Compare   Too often, compensation expenses are compared on a per-worker basis, which may bear little relationship to the total expense of the employment of these individuals. People's abilities and motivations vary widely; consequently, it is the output associated with cost that is important. Seemingly cheap labor actually may raise the total compensation expenditure because of the need for more supervision, added training expenses, and adjustments in the method of production.

Labor-Cost Dynamics

Relative costs change, so firms must consider
- Productivity change
- Labor rate change
- Conversion of labor rate to competitor's currency.

Differences among countries in amount and type of compensation are not static. Salaries and wages (as well as other expenditures) may rise more rapidly in one locale than another. Therefore, the relative competitiveness of operations in different countries may shift. Since it is the output associated with cost that is most important in comparing labor competitiveness, an example will illustrate shifting capabilities. Assume U.S. productivity per worker in manufacturing increased by 2.8 percent, whereas hourly compensation rates went up by 10.2 percent. The result was a unit labor cost increase of 7.2 percent (1.102 ÷ 1.028). Meanwhile, productivity in the United Kingdom increased by 5.9 percent and hourly compensation in pounds sterling by 16.2 percent, amounting to a unit cost increase of 9.7 percent (1.162 ÷ 1.059) when measured in pounds sterling. This meant that labor costs were rising more rapidly in the United Kingdom than in the United States in terms of local currencies. Because sterling fell substantially in relation to the dollar, however, the unit labor cost measured in dollars could actually have become more favorable in the United Kingdom as compared to the United States.[47]

COMPARATIVE LABOR RELATIONS

In each country where an MNE operates, it must deal with a group of workers whose approach will be affected by the sociopolitical environment of the country and by the traditions and regulations of collective bargaining.

Sociopolitical Environment

Overall attitude in a country affects how labor and management view each other and how labor will try to improve its lot.

There are striking international differences in how labor and management view each other. When there is very little mobility between the two groups, there may be little direct cooperation toward reaching an overall corporate objective. This type of separation may be enhanced if a marked class difference exists between management and labor. Certainly, much labor strife may be traced to labor's and management's perceived involvement in a class struggle, even though labor may have been gaining a greater share of total income and wealth for some time.

In such countries as the United States, Brazil, and Switzerland, labor demands are largely met through an adversary process between the directly affected management and labor.[48] The adversarial relationship in the United States has perhaps given employers an added incentive to oppose unions and set up nonunion operations. Between 1970 and 1989 the percentage of workers belonging to unions fell by about two thirds to only 16 percent, whereas union membership in the 17 major industrialized competitors of the United States rose to slightly over half of the work forces.[49] In the United States unions have little influence on how members actually vote in political elections. In contrast, labor groups in many countries vote largely in blocs, resulting in a system in which demands are met primarily through national legislation rather than collective bargaining with management. Such mechanisms as strikes or slowdowns to effect changes may also be national in scope. This implies that a company's production or ability to distribute its product may be much more dependent on the way labor perceives conditions in the country, as a whole. For example, French truckers demanded lower taxes on diesel fuel, insurance, and a subsidy to modernize French trucking. To make their demands known, the truckers set up blockades, closed off major airports, and set fire to the Paris-Lyon railway line.[50] The entire economy was affected.

The use of mediation by an impartial party to try to bring opposing sides together varies as well. In Israel it is required by law; in the United States and the United Kingdom it is voluntary. Among countries that have mediation practices, attitudes toward it are diverse; for example, there is much less enthusiasm for it in India than in the United States.[51] Not all differences are settled through either changes in legislation or through collective bargaining. Another means is the labor court or government-chosen arbitrator. For example, in Austria wages in many industries are arbitrated on a semiannual basis.[52] Settlements may be very one-sided if appointments to labor courts in a country have been made by political parties that are pro- or antilabor.

Union Structure

Union structure can be
- National versus local
- Industry versus company
- One versus several for the same company

Companies in a given country may deal with one or several different unions. A union itself may represent workers in many different industries, in many different companies within the same industry, or merely in one company. If it represents only one company, the union may represent all plants or just one plant. Although there are diversities within countries, the most prevalent relationships vary from one country to another. For example, in the United States, unions tend to be national, representing certain types of workers (e.g., airline pilots, coal miners, truck drivers, or university professors), so a company may deal with several different national unions. Each collective-bargaining process is usually characterized by a single firm on one side, rather than an association of different firms that deals with one of the unions representing a certain type of worker in all the company's plants. In Japan a union typically represents all the workers in a given company and has only very loose affiliations with unions in other companies. This allegedly explains why Japanese unions are less militant than those in most other industrialized countries: They seldom strike, and when they do, they may stop working for only a short period of time or may continue working while wearing symbolic arm bands. Because of the closer company affiliation, Japanese union leaders are hesitant to risk hurting the company's ability to compete in the world markets.[53] In Sweden the bargaining tends to be highly centralized in that employers from numerous companies in different industries deal together with a federation of trade unions. In Germany employers from associations of firms in the same industries bargain jointly with union federations.[54]

Protection from Closures and Redundancy

Worker takeover of plants has been done to publicize their plight.

In response to proposed layoffs, shifts in production location, and cessation of operations, workers in many countries have moved into plants to prevent the transfer of machinery, components, and finished goods.[55] They have even continued to produce until they ran out of raw materials and components and sold the output on the street in order to prolong their ability to occupy the plants. The results of these efforts have been mixed, sometimes preventing the plant's closing and other times not.

Notification of plant closings has been legislated in some countries.

The fact that workers will go so far to try to prevent a plant from closing indicates how important this issue is in some countries, particularly those in Western Europe where prenotification has been negotiated or legislated almost everywhere. The Western European situation is in contrast to that in Canada and the United States where fewer than one fifth of contracts require employers to give more than a week's notice of closure.[56]

Lifetime employment in Japan
- *Is a dual system*
- *Helps institute certain efficiency measures*

The lifetime-employment custom within Japan offers some contrasts to labor practices in North America and Western Europe. Within Japan some employees, usually skilled male workers in large firms, enjoy lifetime employment. In turn, these employees voluntarily switch firms less frequently than those in North America and Europe. Other workers are considered temporaries; the number of temporaries is large, constituting about 40 percent of the work force even in a large firm such as Toyota. In addition, there are many part-time workers. When business takes a downturn or when labor-saving techniques are introduced, companies keep the lifetime employees on the payroll by releasing the temporary workers, reducing the variable bonuses of lifetime employees, and transferring workers to other product divisions. Thus far, this system has enabled Japanese firms to introduce robotics more effectively than firms elsewhere because there has been little concern about job security among unionized employees. It has also helped Japanese firms to spend heavily on training because the lifetime employees have a strong moral commitment to stay with their employers. The temporary workers have tolerated the system because of the labor shortage that has existed during recent decades in Japan and because many are women who, by cultural definition, are disinclined toward adversarial behavior.[57]

Codetermination

Some firms seek labor-management cooperation through sharing in leadership.

Particularly in northern Europe, labor participates in the management of firms, a process known as **codetermination.** The most common means has been by having labor represented on the board of directors, either with or without veto power.

Despite some voluntary moves toward codetermination, most existing examples have been mandated by legislation, such as in Germany. These moves have been dictated not only by the philosophy of cooperative leadership but also the sense that labor has risks and stakes in the organization as well as shareholders. Because of a belief that the interests of blue- and white-collar workers are different, some efforts have been made to assure that each group is represented.[58] Although there were some early examples of effective blockage of investment outflows, acquisitions, and plant closures, codetermination apparently has had little or no effect on either the types of decisions reached by firms or the speed with which those decisions have been reached. One of the reasons given for the minimal effect is that workers are so divided in terms of what they want that it is hard for their representatives to take strong stances on issues. Where layoffs have been necessary, foreign workers have been given less protection than citizens.[59]

In Germany, for example, workers elect representatives to serve on the Works' Council of the firm.[60] This council makes decisions on social matters (such as the conduct of employees, hours of work, and safety) so that when disputes arise between the Works' Council and the Labor Director of the firm, they are settled by arbitration. In economic and financial matters the Works' Council is provided information and consulted in decisions, but the Council does not have the same strength because, although the shareholders and employees have an equal number of representatives, the chairman (elected by shareholders) has the tie-breaking vote.

The Works' Council and the unions have different responsibilities. For instance, collective bargaining takes place between employer associations and the unions and covers all workers within a German state or part of that state. Since the companies in the employer associations vary in size and ability to cover different possible wage rates, the negotiated annual wage rates are minimums and can be negotiated upward at the company level. But the unions are barred by law from negotiating at the company or plant level; this is the task of the Works' Council.

Quality Control Circles

To improve worker productivity, companies worldwide have experimented with a variety of means to commit workers to suggest ways to improve output. Codetermination efforts have been motivated partially by this objective, and suggestion boxes are probably the most visible symbol of the movement. Because of rapid productivity increases in Japan recently, attention naturally has focused on Japanese approaches to worker involvement. One such activity is the **quality control circle,** which involves small groups of workers meeting regularly to spot and solve problems in their areas. It is a participatory effort designed to get people to say things among their peers that as individuals they would be reluctant to communicate to managers.

Team Efforts

In some countries, particularly Japan and its investments abroad, there has been an emphasis on work teams in order to (1) foster a group cohesiveness and (2) get workers involved in multiple rather than a limited number of tasks. In terms of group cohesiveness, it is not uncommon for a portion of the compensation to be based on the group output so that peer pressure is created to reduce absenteeism and increase efforts. In terms of worker involvement in multiple tasks, workers may rotate jobs within the group to reduce boredom and to develop replacement skills when someone is not present. Practices whereby workers' groups control their own quality and repair their own equipment also have been included.[61]

INTERNATIONAL PRESSURES ON NATIONAL PRACTICES

The ILO monitors labor conditions worldwide.

In 1919 the International Labor Organization (ILO) was set up on the premise that the failure of any nation to adopt humane conditions of labor is an obstacle in the way of other nations that desire to improve conditions in their own countries. There are also several associations of unions from different countries, which support similar ideals. They include various international trade secretariats representing workers in specific industries; the International Confederation of Free Trade Unions (ICFTU), the World Federation of Trade Unions (WFTU), and the World Confederation of Labour (WCL).[62] Through these organizations' activities and the general enhancement of communications globally, people increasingly are aware of differences in labor conditions among countries. Among the newsworthy reports have been legal proscriptions against collective bargaining in Malaysia and wages below minimum standards in Indonesia. The ILO also brought attention to the prevalence of child labor in LDCs, many of whom are under ten years old and receive practically no compensation. Once these conditions have been noted, there have been varying efforts to pressure for changes through economic and political sanctions from abroad.

The most noteworthy example of efforts to effect internal changes in labor conditions involved pressures by various groups on MNEs operating in South Africa. For example, through church groups, resolutions were presented to stockholders proposing that firms cease, cut back, operate on a non-discrimination basis, or report more fully on their South African operations. These pressures led to a large exodus of foreign direct investors from South Africa in the late 1980s and the 1991 repeal of apartheid laws.

Another area influencing the labor practices of MNEs has been codes of conduct on industrial relations issued by the Organization for Economic Cooperation and Development (OECD) and the ILO. Although the OECD and ILO codes are voluntary, they may signal some transnational regulations of future MNE activities. Trade unions have been anxious to get interpretations of the guidelines and make them legally enforceable. The present complaint mechanism is slow, but it can strengthen national governments as they pressure MNEs.[63]

MULTINATIONAL OWNERSHIP AND COLLECTIVE BARGAINING[64]

MNE Advantages

There is disagreement on home-country employment effects of foreign direct investment, but labor pushes to save home-country jobs.

Job Security   It is often argued that, when the number of jobs is not growing, workers are concerned about employment stability rather than other work conditions. If MNEs have exported jobs from industrialized countries, then it should follow that labor demands in those countries have been tempered in the process. Yet it is difficult to conclude whether MNEs have increased or decreased home-country employment by making direct investments abroad.

The composition of work forces in industrial countries has moved more toward white-collar than blue-collar jobs. Although some of this internal realignment in work-force composition may be inevitable with or without MNE activities, the result is nevertheless a shrinking of *traditional* bargaining units made up of blue-collar workers.[65] The white-collar workers have been less prone to join unions in the United States than they have in other industrial countries. But even when they are organized by unions, they may not be as adverse to management as blue-collar workers are, since they may look forward to moving into management positions themselves. MNEs may rationalize international activities by setting up production facilities in countries with low wages and high unemployment while simultaneously concentrating such functions as accounting, R&D, and staff support in industrialized countries. To the extent that they do this, they are contributing to work-force composition changes that weaken the size of traditional production bargaining units in industrialized countries.

Labor may be at a disadvantage in MNE negotiations because
* *Country bargaining unit is only a small part of MNE activities*

Product and Resource Flows   If, during a strike in one country, an MNE can divert output from facilities in other countries to the consumers in the country where the strike occurs, there is less client pressure on the MNE to reach an agreement. Furthermore, since the operations in a given country usually comprise a small percentage of the MNE's total worldwide sales, prof-

MNE may continue serving customers with foreign production or resources

its, and cash flows, a strike in that country may have minimal effects on the MNE's global performance. The MNE's geographic diversification therefore is argued to be to its advantage when bargaining with labor in a given country. Some analysts contend that an MNE simply may hold out longer and be less affected in a strike situation.

MNE limitations come from capacity, legal restrictions, shared ownership, integrated production, and differentiated products.

Several factors moderate the MNE's ability to continue supplying customers in the struck country. The MNE may divert output to other markets only if it has excess capacity and only if there is a homogeneous product produced in more than one country. If these two conditions are present, the MNE would still confront the cost and trade barriers that led to the initial establishment of multiple production facilities. If the struck operation is only partially owned by the MNE, partners or even minority shareholders may be less willing and able to sustain a lengthy work stoppage. If the idle facilities normally produce components needed for integrated production elsewhere, then a strike may have much more far-reaching effects. This latter point is particularly important as firms have sought to decrease production costs through instituting just-in-time inventory systems. During a U.K. strike at Ford, Belgian facilities were shut down almost immediately because the firm needed British components; this may have speeded Ford to agree to a settlement.[66] It may therefore seem that the advantages of international diversification upon the collective-bargaining process are present, but only in limited circumstances.

Production Switching   There are documented examples of threats by MNEs to move production units to other countries if labor conditions and demands in one country result in changes in the least-cost location of production. A good case occurred when the chief executive of Hyster told employees in Scotland that the company was prepared to move two production lines from the Netherlands to Scotland and expand its Scottish operations if workers decided within 48 hours to take a 14 percent pay cut. The following morning, workers received letters saying that the company might go somewhere else unless its offer was accepted.[67]

MNE may threaten workers with moving production abroad.

Even domestic firms face threats of losing jobs to foreign operations.

Production shifts may occur because of changes in the least-cost location whether an MNE produces in both locations or not; this is particularly true as economies have become more open to imports. During a rubber strike, for example, Firestone advertised that U.S. worker demands would lead to more imports (by producers other than Firestone) of foreign-made tires. So the threat of international switches in production location is not purely the result of increased MNE activities.

Although there are circumstances in which shifts would seem more plausible when MNEs are involved, MNEs may be less likely to cause shifts in production than when national competitors are involved in various countries. The MNE, such as a Canadian-based firm with a Korean facility, must weigh the cost-saving advantages of moving its production location against the losses in terms of cutting back at existing facilities, creating bad will, and becoming vulnerable through decreased diversification. A national company, such as a Korean firm producing in Korea, may not worry nearly so much about what happens to a Canadian-owned plant in Canada when it exports to the Canadian market.

Labor claims it has disad-vantages in dealing with MNEs because
● Decision making is far away
● It is hard to get full data on MNEs' global operations

Structural Problems   Observers often contend that it is difficult for labor unions to deal with MNEs because of the complexities in the location of de-cision making and the difficulties involved in interpreting financial data. If the real decision makers are far removed from the bargaining location, such as home-country headquarters, it is often assumed that this will lead to ar-bitrarily stringent management decisions. Conceivably, the opposite might happen, particularly if the demands abroad seem low in comparison with those being made at home. In reality, labor relations tend to be very much delegated to subsidiary management.

The question of interpreting financial data of MNEs is complex because of disparities among managerial, tax, and public disclosure requirements in home and host countries. Labor has been particularly leery of the possibility of artificial transfer pricing to give the appearance that a given subsidiary is unable to meet labor demands. These concerns seem to place an overreliance on a company's ability to pay, rather than the seemingly more important going wage rates in the industry and geographic area. Although MNEs may have more complex data, at least some set of financial statements must satisfy local authorities. This set should be no more difficult to interpret than that involving a purely local firm. In terms of transfer pricing, it is very doubtful that MNEs set artificial levels to aid in collective-bargaining situations. To understate profits in one place would imply overstating elsewhere, which would negate the advantage, unless changes are made to reflect different con-tract periods. Tax authorities would not likely approve sudden price changes before contract negotiation. Furthermore, any artificial prices also would have to consider income taxes, tariffs, and opinions of minority shareholders.

Labor Responses and Initiatives

Labor might strengthen its position vis-à-vis MNEs through cross-national cooperation.

Information Sharing   The most common form of cooperation among unions in different countries is through an exchange of information. This helps them refute company claims as well as cite precedents from other coun-tries when bargaining issues seem transferable. The exchange of information is carried out by international confederations of unions representing different types of workers and ideologies, by trade secretariats composed of unions in a single industry or in a complex of related industries, and by company coun-cils that include representatives from an MNE's plants around the world.[68]

Assistance to Foreign Bargaining Units   Labor groups in one country may support their counterparts in other countries in a number of ways. These include refusing to work overtime when that output would supply the market normally served by striking workers' production, sending financial aid to workers in other countries, and presenting demands to management through other countries. Although there are examples involving these types of assistance, for now they must be classified as potential rather than actual initiatives. There are more examples of refusals to cooperate in these matters than of successful collaboration.

Simultaneous Actions   There have been a few examples of simultaneous negotiations and strikes.[69] Among the more notable have been meetings among the unions that negotiate with GE worldwide, a common strategy for unions from nine countries that represent St. Gobain, and simultaneous work stoppages in England and Italy against Dunlop-Pirelli. The concept of multinational collective bargaining seems less appealing to labor leaders now than it did in the 1970s. This is due to the relatively few successes and the national differences in terms of union structures and demands. Furthermore, there has undoubtedly been a growing nationalism of workers as their fear of foreign competition has grown.

National Approaches   Unions' conflict with MNEs has been primarily on a national basis. There is little enthusiasm on the part of workers in one country to incur costs in order to support workers in another country, since they tend to view each other as competitors. Even between the United States and Canada, where there has long been a common union membership, there has been a move among Canadian workers to form unions independent of those in the United States. One Canadian organizer summed up much of the attitude by saying, "An American union is not going to fight to protect Canadian jobs at the expense of American jobs." The logic was that international unions will adopt policies favoring the bulk of their membership, which is bound to be American in any joint Canadian-U.S. relationship.[70]

Through national legislation, workers have managed in places to acquire representation on boards of directors, to regulate the entry of foreign workers, to limit imports, and to limit foreign investment outflows. Therefore, it is probable that most regulations will be at the national rather than the international level.

LOOKING TO THE FUTURE   As capital and technology continually become more mobile, from one country to another and from one firm to another, human resource development should account increasingly for competitive differences. Consequently, the access to and retention of ever more qualified personnel should gain in importance. This does not imply a lack of employee mobility. In fact, the high-skill, high-value worker will likely be more difficult to retain in the future.[71]

From a managerial standpoint, a challenge will be to break down nationalistic barriers that impair the achievement of global corporate cultures and integrated global strategies. To accomplish these ends, more cross-national interchange will be necessary. The traditional problems of cost and governmental regulations will likely continue to impede these interchanges; however, those causes are not likely to become more acute in the future. Personal adaptation will, however, likely be an even greater problem. The head of international human resources at Campbell Soup Company said on this subject, "There is too much emphasis on executives' technical abilities and too little on their cultural skills and family situation."[72] This does not mean that technical skills will be less important for success in foreign assignments, but rather that this dimension is already well understood and taken into account. But we still know far too little about the identification and training for success in overseas assignments. Furthermore, such factors as two-career families and international terrorism may make managers even more reluctant to accept foreign assignments.

Demographers are nearly unanimous in projecting that populations will grow much faster in developing countries (China being an exception) than in industrial countries, at least up to the year 2030.[73] At the same time, in industrial countries there will be a growth of elderly people as a percentage of the population, a necessity to be educated for more years to get the so-called "better jobs," and some attempts to retire at earlier ages. Overall, these industrial-country trends indicate that there will be a smaller portion of people left to do the productive work within society and an acute shortage of personnel. Adjustments may come about in any of several ways or combinations thereof, and each way has a number of social and economic consequences. International companies must adapt their production to these changing conditions.

One reaction might be the encouragement of immigration to industrial countries from LDCs, which do not now have nor are expected to generate enough jobs for their potential workers. In the United States, Canada, and parts of Western Europe there has been a fairly long-term entry of foreign workers, both legally and illegally. During the late 1980s, both Italy and Japan had to seek foreign workers, perhaps for the first time ever. Such movements bring assimilation costs within receiving nations and, if they involve highly qualified personnel, charges of a "brain drain" from LDCs. If such movements develop, companies will have to spend more efforts on paperwork required for work permits and develop means of incorporating different groups into the work force.

Another potential reaction is a continued push toward adoption of robotics and development of further labor-saving equipment. Although this may help solve some of the shortages in industrial countries, average work-skill levels may increase so much that less-educated members of the work force may be either unemployable or forced to take less well-paying jobs in the service sector. Gaps between haves and have-nots may thus widen, and unemployment problems of LDCs will not be solved. From a company standpoint, this alternative may necessitate some shifts in technology spending, such as from natural resource saving and new product development to labor saving.

A third possibility is that the migration of industry to LDCs to tap ample supplies of labor will accelerate. While such moves enhance the international division of labor, they may amplify the distinctions between rich and poor countries and the dilemma of what to do with marginal workers in industrial countries. Companies sourcing more in LDCs will have to expend more efforts on logistics to assure that supplies flow among countries. They will also have to concern themselves more with efforts to minimize the political and monetary risks of operating in LDCs.

SUMMARY

■ Among the factors that differentiate between the tasks of international and purely domestic managers are that the international manager must know how to adapt home-country practices to foreign locales and will be more likely to deal with high-level governmental officials.

■ The top-level managers of foreign subsidiaries normally perform much broader duties than domestic managers with similar cost or profit responsibilities. They must cope with communications problems between the corporate headquarters and the subsidiaries, usually with less staff assistance.

■ MNEs usually prefer to appoint local rather than expatriate managers because: (1) The locals understand regional operating conditions; (2) this demonstrates the opportunities for local citizens and shows consideration for local interests; (3) it avoids the red tape of cross-national transfers; (4) it is usually cheaper; and (5) the locals may focus more on long-term operations and goals.

■ Firms transfer people abroad in order to infuse technical competence and home-country business practices, to control foreign operations, and to develop managers.

■ When firms transfer personnel abroad, they should consider how well the people will be accepted, how to treat them when the foreign assignment is over, and how well they will adapt.

■ When transferred abroad, an employee's compensation is usually changed because of differences in cost of living, job status, and hardship.

■ Firms frequently acquire personnel abroad by buying existing companies. They also may go into business with local firms, which take on the major staffing responsibilities.

■ Two of the major international training functions are (1) to build a global awareness among managers in general and (2) to equip managers to handle the specific situations entailed in an expatriate assignment.

■ When setting up a new operation in a foreign country, firms may use existing facilities as guides for determining labor needs. They should adjust, however, to compensate for different labor skills, costs, and availabilities.

■ For some areas of the world a substantial portion of the labor supply is imported, which creates special stability, supervision, and training problems for the companies employing them.

■ Owing to the enormous variance in fringe benefits, direct-compensation figures do not accurately reflect the amount a company must pay for a given job. In addition, job-security benefits (no layoffs, severance pay, etc.) add substantially to compensation costs.

■ Although per-worker comparisons are useful indicators of cost differences, what is relevant for international competitiveness is the output associated with total costs. The costs may shift in time, thus changing relative international competitive positions.

■ The sociopolitical environment will determine to a great extent the type of relationships between labor and management and affect the number, representation, and organization of unions among countries.

■ Codetermination and quality control circles are two types of labor participation in the management of firms. The purpose is usually to cultivate a cooperative rather than an adversarial environment.

■ In recent years there have been efforts to get firms to follow internationally accepted labor practices regardless of where they are operating or whether the practices are contrary to the norms and laws of the countries in which they are operating.

■ MNEs are often blamed for weakening the position of labor in the collective-bargaining process because of MNEs' (1) international diversification, (2) threats to export jobs, and (3) complex structures and reporting mechanisms.

■ Cooperation between labor groups in different countries is small but has on occasion been used to combat multinational firms. Strategies include information exchanges, simultaneous negotiations or strikes, and refusals to work overtime if the intent is to compensate for a striking firm in another country.

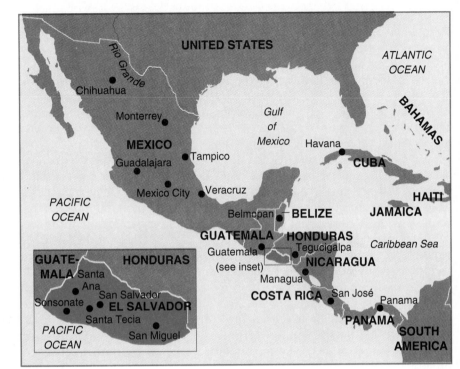

Map 21.1
Central America/El Salvador
El Salvador is the most densely populated country in Central America.

C A S E

THE OFFICE

EQUIPMENT

COMPANY

In 1992 the Office Equipment Company (OEC) had to replace its manager in San Salvador, El Salvador, because the present managing director (a U.S. national) announced suddenly that he would leave within one month. OEC manufactured a wide variety of small office equipment (such as copying machines, recording machines, mail scales, paper shredders) in eight different countries that was distributed and sold worldwide.

OEC had no manufacturing facilities in El Salvador (see Map 21.1) but had been selling and servicing there since the early 1970s. OEC had first tried selling in El Salvador through independent importers but quickly became convinced that it needed to have its own staff there to make sufficient sales. Despite political turmoil, which over the last few years had bordered on being a full-scale civil war, OEC's operation in El Salvador (with about 100 employees) had enjoyed good and improving sales and profitability.

OEC was in the process of constructing a factory in El Salvador that would begin operations in early 1993. This factory would import components for personal computer printers and assemble them locally. The government would allow up to 10 percent of the output to be sold locally, provided at least 90 percent was exported. The assembly operation would employ approximately 150 people. El Salvador offered an abundant supply of cheap labor. Furthermore, by assembling and exporting, OEC expected to be able to ward off any trade restrictions on the other office equipment it imported for sale within El Salvador. The construction of this plant was being supervised by a U.S. technical team, and a U.S. expatriate would be assigned to direct the production. This expatriate director would report directly to the United States on all production and quality-control matters but would report to the managing director in El Salvador for all other matters, such as accounting, finance, and labor relations.

The option of filling the managing director position with someone from outside the firm was alien to OEC's policy. Otherwise, the options were fairly open. OEC used a combination of home-country, host-country, and third-country nationals in top positions in foreign countries. It was not uncommon for managers to rotate among foreign and U.S. domestic locations. In fact, it was increasingly evident that international experience was an important factor in deciding who would be appointed to top corporate positions. The sales and service facility in El Salvador reported through a Latin American regional office located in Coral Gables, Florida. A committee at the regional office quickly narrowed its choice to five candidates.

Tom Zimmerman   Zimmerman had joined the firm 30 years before and was well versed in all the technical and sales aspects required in the job. He had never worked abroad for OEC but had visited various of the company's foreign facilities as part of sales teams during his career. He was considered competent in the management of the duties he had performed during the years and would retire in about four and a half

years. Neither he nor his wife spoke Spanish; their children were grown and living with their own children in the United States. Zimmerman was currently in charge of an operation about the size that the one in El Salvador would be after the factory began operating. However, that operation was being merged with another, so his present office would become redundant.

Brett Harrison   At age 40, Harrison had spent fifteen years with OEC. He was considered highly competent and capable of moving into upper-level management within the next few years. He had never been based abroad but had worked for the last three years in the Latin American regional office, and he frequently traveled to Latin America. Both he and his wife spoke Spanish adequately. Their two children, ages fourteen and fifteen, were just beginning to study Spanish. His wife was a professional as well, holding a responsible marketing position with a pharmaceutical company.

Carolyn Moyer   Moyer had joined OEC after getting her MBA from a prestigious university twelve years before. At age 37 she had already moved between staff and line positions of growing responsibility. For two years she was second in command of a product group about the size of the expanded one in El Salvador. Her performance in that post was considered excellent. Currently she worked as a member of a planning staff team. When she joined OEC, she had indicated her eventual interest in international responsibilities because of her undergraduate major in international affairs. She had expressed a recent interest in international duties because of a belief it would help her advancement. She spoke Spanish well and was not married.

Francisco Cabrera   Cabrera was currently one of the assistant managing directors in the larger Mexican operation, which produced and sold for the Mexican market. He was a Mexican citizen who had worked for OEC in Mexico for all his twelve years with the company. He held an MBA from a Mexican university and was considered to be one of the likely candidates to head the Mexican operation when the present managing director retired in seven years. He was 35, married with four children (ages two to seven). He spoke English adequately; his wife did not work outside the home and spoke no English.

Juan Moreno   At age 27 he was assistant to the present managing director in El Salvador, a position he had assumed when he joined OEC after completion of his undergraduate degree in the United States four years before. He was considered competent, especially in employee relations, but lacking in experience. He had been successful in increasing OEC's sales, an advantage being that he was well connected with the local families who could afford to buy new office equipment for their businesses. He was not married.

Questions

1. Whom should the committee choose for the assignment and why?
2. What problems might each individual encounter in the position?

3. How might OEC go about minimizing the problems that the chosen person would have in managing the El Salvador operations?
4. Calculate an estimated compensation package for each of the five candidates based on the following additional assumed information:
   a)   Present annual salaries: Zimmerman, US$70,000; Harrison, US$75,000; Moyer, US$65,000; Cabrera, M$120,000,000; Moreno, C150,000.
   b)   Exchange rates: $1 = M$3,000 (Mexican peso); $1 = C5 (El Salvador colon).
   c)   U.S. Department of State cost-of-living index: Washington, D.C. = 100; San Salvador = 93; Mexico City = 76, based on items covering 35% of income for a family of one, 40% for a family of two, 45% for a family of four, and 50% for a family of five or more.
   d)   U.S. Department of State foreign-service premiums for El Salvador: hardship = 15%; danger = 20%.
   e)   Housing allowance (nontaxable) single = US $11,300; family = US $12,400.
   f)   Schooling allowance: age 6–12 = US $5000; age 13–18 = US $9000.
   g)   Average tax rates: Mexico = 20%; U.S. = 25%; El Salvador = $30%.

Chapter Notes

1. The data for the case were taken from Edwin McDowell, "Making It in America: The Foreign-Born Executive," *New York Times*, June 1, 1980, Section 3, p. 1 +; Don Whitehead, *The Dow Story* (New York: McGraw-Hill, 1968); "Dow's Shifts in R&D Presage Overseas Work," *Chemical Week*, Vol. 128, No. 13, April 1, 1981, p. 17; "Lundeen Urges More Aid for Universities," *Chemical Marketing Reporter*, Vol. 224, No. 19, November 7, 1983, p. 3 +; John Bussey, "Dow Chemical's Popoff Named President," *Wall Street Journal*, May 15, 1987, p. 49; Paul L. Blocklyn, "Developing the International Executive," *Personnel*, Vol. 66, March 1989, pp. 44–47; and "Globesmanship," *Across the Board*, Vol. 27, No. 1, 2, January–February 1990, pp. 24–34.

2. Gary R. Oddou and Mark E. Mendenhall, "Succession Planning for the 21st Century: How Well Are We Grooming Our Future Business Leaders?" *Business Horizons,* January–February 1991, pp. 26–34.

3. "Globesmanship," *op. cit.,* p. 26, quoting Michael Angus.

4. Daniel Ondrack, "International Transfers of Managers in North American and European MNEs," *Journal of International Business Studies,* Vol. 16, No. 3, Fall 1985, pp. 1–19.

5. Bob Masterson and Bob Murphy, "Internal Cross-Cultural Management," *Training and Development Journal,* Vol. 40, No. 4, April 1986, pp. 56–60.

6. Peter Lorange, "Human Resource Management in Multinational Cooperative Ventures," *Human Resource Management,* Vol. 25, No. 1, Spring 1986, pp. 133–148; Mark N. Nelson and E. S. Browning, "GE's Culture Turns Sour at French Unit," *Wall Street Journal,* July 31, 1990, p. A10; Lynn Matthew, "The Industrial Ideals of Iveco," *Management,* April 1990, pp. 92–96.

7. Jean Ross-Skinner, "English Spoken Here," *Dun's Review,* March 1977, pp. 56–57; Urban C. Lehner, "When in Japan, Do as the Japanese Do, by Speaking English," *Wall Street Journal,* December 8, 1980, p. 1.

8. "When in Rome?" *Wall Street Journal,* September 28, 1989, p. 1.

9. David C. Waring, "Doing Business Overseas," *Cornell Enterprise,* Fall–Winter 1988, p. 29.

10. Dafna N. Izraeli, Moshe Banai, and Yoram Zeira, "Women Executives in MNC Subsidiaries," *California Management Review,* Vol. 23, No. 1, Fall 1980, pp. 53–63; Yves Doz and C. K. Prahalad, "Controlled Variety: A Challenge for Human Resource Management in the MNC," *Human Resource Management,* Vol. 25, No. 1, Spring 1986, pp. 55–71.

11. Yoram Zeira and Ehud Harari, "Structural Sources of Personnel Problems in Multinational Corporations: Third-Country Nationals," *Omega,* Vol. 5, No. 2, 1977, pp. 167–168.

12. Anders Edström and Jay R. Galbraith, "Alternative Policies for International Transfers of Managers," *Management International Review,* No. 2, 1977, pp. 13–14; Asya Pazy and Yoram Zeira, "Training Parent-Country Professionals in Host-Country Organizations," *Academy of Management Review,* Vol. 8, No. 2, 1983, pp. 262–272.

13. Anders Edström and Jay R. Galbraith, "Transfer of Managers as a Coordination and Control Strategy in Multinational Organizations," *Administrative Science Quarterly,* June 1977, pp. 248–261; A. B. Sim, "Decentralized Management of Subsidiaries and Their Performance," *Management International Review,* No. 2, 1977, p. 48.

14. Alfred Jaeger, "Organization Development and National Culture: Where's the Fit?" *Academy of Management Review,* Vol. 11, No. 1, 1986, pp. 178–190; "Globesmanship," *op. cit.,* p. 30.

15. Anders Edström and Peter Lorange, "Matching Strategy and Human Resources in Multinational Companies," *Journal of International Business Studies,* Fall 1984, pp. 125–137; Stephen J. Kobrin, "Expatriate Reduction and Strategic Control in American Multinational Corporations," *Human Resource Management,* Vol. 27, No. 1, Spring 1988, pp. 63–75; Louis Uchitelle, "Only the Bosses Are American," *New York Times,* July 24, 1989, pp. 21 ff.

16. Duerr and Greene, *The Problems Facing International Management,* p. 18; See also Richard D. Hays, "Behavioral Determinants of Success-Failure among U.S. Expatriate

Managers," *Journal of International Business Studies*, Spring 1971, pp. 40–46; Martine Gertsen, "Intercultural Competence and Expatriates," Working Paper No. 1, 1990, Copenhagen School of Economics and Business Administration, Institute of International Economics and Management; Moran, Stahl & Boyer, Inc. *International Human Research Management*. Boulder: Moran, Stahl & Boyer, Inc., 1987.

17. J. Stewart Black and Mark Mendenhall, "Cross-Cultural Training Effectiveness: A Review and a Theoretical Framework for Future Research," *Academy of Management Review*, Vol. 15, No. 1, January 1990, p. 117; Mark Mendenhall and Gary Oddou, "The Dimensions of Expatriate Acculturation: A Review," *Academy of Management Review*, Vol. 10, No. 1, January 1985, pp. 39–47.

18. Philip R. Harris and Robert L. Moran, *Managing Cultural Differences* (Houston: Gulf, 1979), p. 164; J. Stewart Black and Gregory K. Stephens, "The Influence of the Spouse on American Expatriate Adjustment and Intent to Stay in Pacific Rim Overseas Assignments," *Journal of Management*, Vol. 15, No. 4, 1989, pp. 529–530.

19. Izraeli et al., *loc. cit.*

20. Linda Greenhouse, "Court Says Rights Law Doesn't Protect U.S. Workers Abroad," *New York Times*, March 27, 1991, p. C21.

21. Mariann Jelinek and Nancy J. Adler, "Women: World Class Managers for Global Competition," *Academy of Management Executive*, Vol. II, No. 1, February 1988, pp. 11–19; Jolie Solomon, "Women, Minorities and Foreign Postings," *Wall Street Journal*, June 2, 1989, p. B1.

22. Izraeli, et al., *loc. cit.*; For some suggestions on how women may make themselves more acceptable, see Gladys L. Symons, "Coping with the Corporate Tribe: How Women in Different Cultures Experience the Managerial Role," *Journal of Management*, Vol. 12, No. 3, 1986, pp. 379–389; and Marlene L. Rossman, *The International Businesswoman*, (New York: Praeger, 1986).

23. David M. Noer, "Integrating Foreign Service Employees to Home Organization: The Godfather Approach," *Personnel Journal*, January 1974, pp. 45–50; William F. Cagney, "Executive Reentry: The Problems of Repatriation," *Personnel Journal*, September 1975, pp. 487–488; J. Alex Murray, "Repatriated Executives: Culture Shock in Reverse," *Management Review*, November 1973, pp. 43–45; Philip R. Harris, "Employees Abroad: Maintain the Corporate Connection," *Personnel Journal*, Vol. 65, No. 8, August 1986, pp. 107–110; Oddou and Mendenhall, *loc. cit.*

24. Oddou and Mendenhall, *ibid.*, found that foreign assignments helped careers in 29 percent of cases. Moran, Stahl & Boyer found advantages in 44 percent of cases, as shown in Figure 21.1.

25. "Globesmanship," *op. cit.*, p. 29, quoting Michael Angus.

26. "Fast-Trackers Fight," *Wall Street Journal*, November 8, 1988, p. 1.

27. Joann S. Lublin, "Grappling with the Expatriate Issue," *Wall Street Journal*, December 11, 1989, p. B1 ff.

28. Thomas F. O'Boyle, "Little Benefit to Careers Seen in Foreign Stints," *Wall Street Journal*, December 11, 1989, p. B4.

29. Claudia H. Deutsch, "Getting the Brightest to Go Abroad," *New York Times*, June 17, 1990, p. C1.

30. *Ibid.*

31. Sam Passow, "Manager's Journal," *Wall Street Journal*, June 18, 1984, p. 18; Rod Willis, "Corporations Vs. Terrorists," *Management Review*, Vol. 75, No. 11, November 1986, pp. 16–27; Jonathan Dahl, "Firms Warn Workers Traveling Abroad," *Wall Street*

Journal, April 10, 1989, p. B1; Don Dunn, "A Baedeker for Travel in a Tense World," *Business Week,* September 10, 1990, p. 105; David D. Medina and Carolyn Phillips, "Companies with Hostages in Persian Gulf Struggle to Help Stateside Families Cope," *Wall Street Journal,* September 26, 1990, p. B1 ff; Larry Light and Jeffrey Ryser, "The Miniboom in Kidnapping Coverage," *Business Week,* March 19, 1990, p. 100.

32. Joann S. Lublin, "More Spouses Receive Help in Job Searches When Executives Take Positions Overseas," *Wall Street Journal,* January 26, 1984, p. 35.

33. "Global Report," *Wall Street Journal,* July 11, 1977, p. 6; Barry Newman, "Mine over Matter," *Wall Street Journal,* August 25, 1977, p. 1.

34. Samir M. Youssef, "The Integration of Local Nationals into the Managerial Hierarchy of American Overseas Subsidiaries: An Exploratory Study," *Academy of Management Journal,* March 1973; p. 29: Oded Shenkar and Yoram Zeira, "Human Resources Management in International Joint Ventures: Directions for Research," *Academy of Management Review,* Vol. 12, No. 3, July 1987, pp. 546–557.

35. Rosalie L. Tung, "Selection and Training of Personnel for Overseas Assignments," *Columbia Journal of World Business,* Vol. 16, No. 1, Spring 1981, p. 72; Canadian International Development Agency (CIDA), "Going Abroad with CIDA;" Bureau of Naval Personnel, *Overseas Diplomacy: Guidelines for United States Navy: Trainer* (Washington, D.C.: U.S. Government Printing Office, 1973); M. H. Tucker, D. Raik Rossiter, and M. Uhes, *Improving the Evaluation of Peace Corps Training Activities,* Vol. 3 (Denver: Center for Research and Education, June 4, 1973); J. Stewart Black, "Workrole Transitions: A Study of American Expatriate Managers in Japan," *Journal of International Business Studies,* Vol. 19, 1988, pp. 277–294.

36. Michael G. Harvey, "The Executive Family: An Overlooked Variable in International Assignments," *Columbia Journal of World Business,* Spring 1985, pp. 84–92; Black and Stephens, *loc. cit.*

37. Black and Mendenhall, *op. cit.,* pp. 118–119; J. Stewart Black, Mark Mendenhall, and Gary Oddou, "Toward a Comprehensive Model of International Adjustment: An Integration of Multiple Theoretical Perspectives," *Academy of Management Review,* March–April 1991.

38. P. Christopher Early, "Intercultural Training for Managers: A Comparison of Documentary and Interpersonal Methods," *Academy of Management Journal,* Vol. 30, No. 4, December 1987, pp. 685–698.

39. For an example of an innovative one, see Jeremy Main, "How 21 Men Got Global in 35 Days," *Fortune,* November 6, 1989, pp. 71–79.

40. Jeffrey L. Blue and Ulrich Haynes, Jr., "Preparation for the Overseas Assignment," *Business Horizons,* June 1977, pp. 61–67; Philip R. Harris and Dorothy L. Harris, "Preventing Cross-Cultural Shock," *Management and Training,* May 1976, pp. 37–41; F. T. Murray and Alice Haller Murray, "SMR Forum: Global Managers for Global Businesses," *Sloan Management Review,* Vol. 27, No. 2, Winter 1986, pp. 75–80.

41. R. Lynn Barnes, "Across Cultures: The Peace Corps Training Model," *Training and Development Journal,* Vol. 39, No. 10, October 1985, pp. 46–49; Yoram Zeira and Asya Pazy, "Crossing National Borders to Get Trained," *Training and Development Journal,* Vol. 39, No. 10, October 1985, pp. 53–57.

42. Frank L. Acuff, "Awareness Levels of Employees Considering Overseas Relocation," *Personnel Journal,* November 1974, pp. 809–812; Kenneth Darrow and Bradley Palmquist, eds., *Trans-Cultural Study Guide* (N.P.: Volunteers in Asia, 1975, 2d ed.) lists pertinent questions to ask.

43. For a good survey of the various studies, see Peter Enderwick, *Multinational Business & Labor* (New York: St. Martin's Press, 1985), pp. 55–58.

44. R. Aggarwal and I. Khera, "Exporting Labor: The Impact of Expatriate Workers on the Home Country," *International Migration,* Vol. 25, No. 4, 1987, pp. 415–424.

45. For a discussion of business adjustments, see John D. Daniels, "International Mobility of People," *Essays in International Business,* No. 1, March 1980, pp. 3–7.

46. Felice Morgenstern, "The Civil Liability of Workers for Injury or Damage Caused in Their Employment," *International Labour Review,* May–June 1976, pp. 317–328.

47. The cited example happened in 1981. For a good discussion on the calculation of the cost dynamics, see Edwin Dean, Harry Boissevain, and James Thomas, "Productivity and Labor Costs Trends in Manufacturing, 12 Countries," *Monthly Labor Review,* Vol. 109, No. 3, March 1986, pp. 3–10.

48. Efrin Córdova, "A Comparative View of Collective Bargaining in Industrialised Countries," *International Labour Review,* July–August 1978, p. 423; and Eduardo B. Gentil, "Brazil's Labor Movement," *Wall Street Journal,* November 11, 1980, p. 34.

49. Gene Koretz, "Why Unions Thrive Abroad—But Wither in the U.S.," *Business Week,* September 10, 1990, p. 26, referring to a study by David Blanchflower and Richard Freeman for the National Bureau of Economic Research.

50. "The Europarking Lot," *Wall Street Journal,* February 24, 1984, p. 32.

51. Joseph Krislov, "Supplying Mediation Services in Five Countries: Some Current Problems," *Columbia Journal of World Business,* Vol. 18, No. 2, Summer 1983, pp. 55–63.

52. Frances Bairstow, "The Trend toward Centralized Bargaining—A Patchwork Quilt of International Diversity," *Columbia Journal of World Business,* Spring 1985, pp. 75–83.

53. Masayoshi Kanabayashi, "Japan's Unions, Anxious to Avoid Fight, Again Likely to Accept a Modest Pay Raise," *Wall Street Journal,* February 9, 1984, p. 31.

54. Bairstow, *loc. cit.*

55. Donna Bridgeman, "Worker Take-Overs," ICCH Case 9-475-093, Harvard Business School, 1975; "Bulova Watch Plant Is Occupied to Protest Closing," *Wall Street Journal,* January 19, 1976; "ICL Workers Say They Took Over Plant to Prevent Closing," *Wall Street Journal,* November 11, 1980, p. 34; Barbara Ehrenreich and Annette Fuentes, "Life on the Global Assembly Line," *Ms.,* January 1981, pp. 53–71.

56. Bennett Harrison, "The International Movement for Prenotification of Plant Closures," *Industrial Relations,* Fall 1984, pp. 387–409.

57. Mourdoukoutas and S. N. Sohng, "The Japanese Industrial System: A Study in Adjustment to Automation," *Management International Review,* Vol. 27, No. 4, 1987, pp. 46–55; John Hoerr and Wendy Zellner, "A Japanese Import That's Not Selling," *Business Week,* February 26, 1990, pp. 86–87; Masayoshi Kanabayashi, "Bucking Tradition," *Wall Street Journal,* October 11, 1988, p. 1 ff; Masayoshi Kanabayashi, "Japanese Workers Aren't All Workaholics," *Wall Street Journal,* May 8, 1989, p. A10

58. Peter F. Drucker, "The Battle Over Co-Determination," *Wall Street Journal,* August 10, 1977, p. 14; "Co-Determination Passes," *Business Europe,* March 26, 1976, pp. 99–100.

59. For early operational problems, see "Sweden: Worker Participation Becomes the Law," *Business Week,* June 21, 1976, pp. 42–46; G. McIsaac and H. Henzler, "Co-Determination: A Hidden Noose for MNCs," *Columbia Journal of World Business,* Winter 1974, pp. 67–74; M. Warner and R. Peccei, "Worker Participation and Mul-

tinationals," *Management International Review,* No. 3, 1977, pp. 93–98. For recent evidence on overall effects, see Wolfgang Scholl, "Codetermination and the Ability of Firms to Act in the Federal Republic of Germany," *International Studies of Management & Organization,* Vol. XVII, No. 2, Summer 1987, pp. 27–37; and Giuseppe Benelli, Claudio Loderer, and Thomas Lys, "Labor Participation in Corporate Policy-making Decisions: West Germany's Experience with Codetermination," *Journal of Business,* Vol. 60, No. 4, October 1987, pp. 553–575.

60. Much of the information on co-determination in Germany is taken from Trevor Bain, "German Codetermination and Employment Adjustments in the Steel and Auto Industries," *Columbia Journal of World Business,* Vol. 18, No. 2, Summer 1983, pp. 40–47.

61. For two discussions of these efforts, see Duane Kujawa, "Technology Strategy and Industrial Relations: Case Studies of Japanese Multinationals in the United States," *Journal of International Business Studies,* Vol. 14, No. 3, Winter 1983, pp. 9–22; Wolf Reitsperger, "British Employees: Responding to Japanese Management Philosophies," *Journal of Management Studies,* Vol. 23, No. 5, September 1986, pp. 563–586.

62. "Child-Worker Abuses in Third World Draw Fire of Labor Group," *Wall Street Journal,* June 8, 1988, p. 26.

63. Richard L. Rowan and Duncan C. Campbell, "The Attempt to Regulate Industrial Relations through International Codes of Conduct," *Columbia Journal of World Business,* Vol. 18, No. 2, Summer 1983, pp. 64–72.

64. Unless otherwise noted, information in this section is taken largely from the following treatises: Gerald B. J. Bomers and Richard B. Peterson, "Multinational Corporations and the Industrial Relations: The Case of West Germany and the Netherlands," *British Journal of Industrial Relations,* March 1977, pp. 45–62; Duane A. Kujawa, "Collective Bargaining and Labor Relations in Multinational Enterprise: A U.S. Policy Perspective," paper presented at New York University Conference on Economic Issues of Multinational Firms, November 1976; Duane Kujawa, "U.S. Manufacturing Investment in the Developing Countries: American Labour's Concerns and the Enterprise Environment in the Decade Ahead," *British Journal of Industrial Relations,* Vol. 19, No. 1, March 1981, pp. 38–48; Roy B. Helfgott, "American Unions and Multinational Enterprises: A Case of Misplaced Emphasis," *Columbia Journal of World Business,* Vol. 18, No. 2, Summer 1983, pp. 81–86.

65. For some figures on the decreased unionized share of work forces, see Rick Melcher, John Templeman, John Rossant, Steve Dryden, and Bob Arnold, "Europe's Unions Are Losing Their Grip," *Business Week,* November 26, 1984, pp. 80–88.

66. Richard L. Hudson, "Strike at Ford Shows Problems of New Methods," *Wall Street Journal,* February 10, 1988, p. 14; Barbara Toman, "Ford, Unions Agree on Contract Offer in Breakthrough in 9-Day U.K. Strike," *Wall Street Journal,* February 17, 1988, p. 2.

67. Barry Newman, "Border Dispute," *Wall Street Journal,* November 30, 1983, pp. 1+; See also "Ford Threatens to Move More Production Abroad," *Wall Street Journal,* April 22, 1981, p. 3.

68. Martin C. Seham, "Transnational Labor Relations: The First Steps Are Being Taken," *Law and Policy in International Business,* Vol. 6, 1974, pp. 347–354.

69. For examples, see I.A. Litvak and C. J. Maule, "The Union Response to International Corporations," *Industrial Relations,* February 1972, pp. 66–67; Duane A. Kujawa, "International Labor Relations: Trade Union Initiatives and Management Responses," *Personnel Administrator,* February 1977, p. 50.

70. Douglas Martin, "A Canadian Split on Unions," *New York Times*, March 12, 1984, p. D12.

71. For a good discussion of the changing power of employees, see Frank P. Doyle, "The Changing Workplace: People Power: The Global Human Resource Challenge for the 1990s," *Columbia Journal of World Business*, Vol. 25, Nos. 1 and 2, Spring–Summer 1990, pp. 36–45.

72. Blocklyn, *op. cit.*, p. 44, quoting Roger Herod.

73. For a short summary, see Kenneth H. Bacon, "The Outlook," *Wall Street Journal*, June 6, 1988, p. 1.

GLOSSARY

Absolute advantage: A theory first presented by Adam Smith, which holds that because different countries can produce different goods more efficiently than other countries, they should specialize in and export those things which they can produce more efficiently in exchange for those things which they cannot.

Accounting: The process of identifying, recording, and interpreting economic events.

Acquired advantage: A form of trade advantage that a country acquires through technology rather than through the availability of natural resources.

Acquired group membership: This refers to affiliations not determined by birth, such as religion, political affiliation, and associations.

Acquisition: The purchase of one company by another company.

Active income: Income derived from the active conduct of trade or business.

Administratively guided market economy: A country in which there is a great deal of cooperation among government, management, and workers to achieve growth and full employment with low job turnover on a nonmandated basis.

Ad valorem duty: A duty (tariff) assessed as a percentage of the value of the item.

Advanced Determination Ruling (ADR): A process that the U.S. Internal Revenue Service would like companies to follow in order to get permission for the transfer price that the companies use.

Advance import deposits: A type of foreign exchange control in which importers must deposit some percentage of the value of a product with authorities for a specified period of time.

African Development Bank: A development bank that provides financial assistance for African governments and enterprises.

American Depository Receipt (ADR): A negotiable certificate issued by a U.S. bank in the United States to represent the underlying shares of a foreign corporation stock held in trust at a custodian bank in the foreign country.

ANCOM: See Andean Group.

Andean Group (ANCOM): A South American economic integration group involving Venezuela, Colombia, Peru, Bolivia, and Ecuador.

Anthropology: The study of human beings in relation to physical characteristics, environment and society, and culture.

Appropriability theory: A theory to explain that firms will favor foreign direct investment over such nonequity operating forms as licensing arrangements in order that potential competitors will be less likely to gain access to proprietary information.

Appropriate technology: Technology that best fits the factor endowment; often used to mean a more labor-intensive technology than what would be cost efficient in a developing country.

Arab League: Primarily a political organization of 22 North African and Middle Eastern Arab countries.

Arbitrage: The process of buying and selling foreign exchange at a profit due to price discrepancies between or among markets.

Area division: See geographic division.

Arrangement Regarding International Trade in Textiles: An agreement among governments establishing rules on textile trade. Also known as the Multifibre Arrangement (MFA).

Ascribed group memberships: Affiliations determined by birth, such as those based on sex, family, age, caste, and ethnic, racial, or national origin.

ASEAN: See Association of South East Asian Nations.

Association of South East Asian Nations (ASEAN): An economic integration agreement among a group of Asian countries.

Autocratic: A type of leadership in which upper-level authorities have nearly unlimited power.

Back-to-back loan: A loan that involves a company in Country A with a subsidiary in Country B, and a bank in Country B with its branch in Country A.

Balance of payments: Statement which summarizes all economic transactions between a country and the rest of the world during a given period of time.

Balance-of-payments deficit: An imbalance of some specific component within the balance of payments such as on merchandise trade or the current account. A deficit implies that a country imports more than it exports.

Balance-of-payments surplus: An imbalance in the balance of payments when a country exports more than it imports.

Balance of trade: The value of a country's exports less the value of its imports. "Trade" can be defined as merchandise trade, services, unilateral transfers, or a combination of the above.

Balance-of-trade deficit: A negative term which implies that exports are less than imports.

Balance-of-trade surplus: A positive term which implies that exports are greater than imports.

Balance on goods and services: The value of a country's exports of merchandise trade and services less imports.

Bank of International Settlements (BIS): A bank in Switzerland which facilitates transactions among central banks, effectively the central banks' central bank.

Barter: The exchange of goods for goods instead of for money.

Base currency: The currency whose value is "one" when a quote is made between two currencies. For example, if the cruzeiro were trading at 2962.5 cruzeiros per dollar, the dollar would be the base currency, and the cruzeiro would be the quoted currency.

Basic balance: The net current account plus long term capital within a country's balance of payments.

Benelux countries: The countries of **Bel**gium, the **Net**herlands, and **Lux**embourg.

Bid (buy): The amount a trader is willing to pay for foreign exchange.

Bilateral agreement: An agreement between two countries.

Bill of lading: A receipt issued to a shipper by a carrier, listing the goods received for shipment.

BIRPI: See International Bureau for the Protection of Industrial Property Rights.

Black market: The foreign exchange market that lies outside the official market.

Bloc: A group of nations tied by treaty or agreement for mutual support or interest.

Body language: The way people move their bodies, touch, and walk to convey meaning to others.

Bonded warehouse: A building or part of a building used for the storage of imported merchandise. These buildings are under supervision of U.S. Customs and can be used to avoid or defer payment of customs duties.

Book value: The asset value recorded in accounting statements at historical cost, not necessarily the market value.

Booking center: An offshore financial center, the main function of which is to act as an accounting center. The booking center is used to minimize the payment of taxes. It primarily records information rather than engages in specific economic activities, such as sales or service.

Branch (foreign): A foreign operation, not a separate entity from the parent which owns it.

Brand: A class of goods identified with a particular firm by means of name, logo, or other method, usually protected with a trademark registration.

Bretton Woods: An agreement among countries to promote exchange-rate stability and to facilitate the international flow of currencies.

Broker: An institution or individual who arranges purchases and sales of securities (or currency) and receives a commission on each transaction.

Broker (in foreign exchange): Specialists who facilitate transactions in the interbank market.

Brokerage house: A financial institution that acts as a broker, dealer, and underwriter of securities.

Buffer stock system: A commodity system that utilizes stocks of commodities to regulate prices.

Bundesbank: The German central bank.

Buy-local: Legislation or practices whereby governmental authorities prefer to purchase domestically sourced goods or services over imported ones, even though the imports may be a better buy for the expenditure.

CACM: See Central American Common Market.

Canada-U.S. Free Trade Agreement: An agreement, enacted in 1989, establishing a free trade area between the United States and Canada to promote economic growth between the two countries.

Capital/asset ratio: Capital, the residual amount of ownership after liabilities, divided by the overall assets of the enterprise.

Capital market: The market for stocks and long-term debt instruments.

Caribbean Community and Common Market (CARICOM): A customs union in the Caribbean.

CARICOM: See Caribbean Community and Common Market.

Central American Common Market (CACM): A customs union in Central America.

Central bank: A governmental "bank for banks," customarily responsible for national monetary policy.

Centralized (centralization): When decision making is typically at the home office rather than the country level.

Centrally Planned Economy (CPE): See command economy.

CEO: The chief executive officer of a company.

Certificate of Deposit (CD): A time deposit with a specific future maturity date.

CHIPS: See Clearing House Interbank Payment System.

CIA: The Central Intelligence Agency, a U.S. governmental agency charged with gathering intelligence information abroad.

Civil law system: A system of law based on a very detailed set of laws that are organized into a code. Countries with a civil law system, also called a codified legal system, include Germany, France, Japan, and the U.S.S.R.

Civil liberties: The freedom to develop one's own views and attitudes.

Classical approach: See Separate entity approach.

Clearinghouse: A facility for settling transfers of funds between banks.

Clearing House Interbank Payment System (CHIPS): An international electronic check transfer system that moves money between major U.S. banks, branches of foreign banks, Edge Act corporation subsidiaries of out-of-state banks, and other institutions.

CMEA: See Council for Mutual Economic Assistance.

COCOM: See Coordinating Committee on Multilateral Export.

Code of conduct: A set of principles guiding the actions of multinational firms in their contacts with societies.

Codetermination: A situation in which both labor and management participate in the management of a firm.

Codified legal system: See Civil law system.

COMECON: See Council for Mutual Economic Assistance.

Command economy: An economy in which resources are allocated and controlled by government decision.

Commercial bank: A financial institution offering a wide variety of services, including checking accounts and business loans.

Commercial Bill of Exchange: An instrument of payment in international business which instructs the importer to forward payment to the exporter.

Commercial paper: A form of IOU backed by standby letters of credit.

The Commission: One of the four major institutions of the EC. The Commission is comprised of a president, six vice presidents, and ten other members whose allegiance is to the EC. The Commission serves as an executive branch for the EC.

Commission agent: A type of middleman who sells for commission without taking title on the goods.

Commission on Transnational Corporations: A United Nations agency that deals with Multinational Enterprises.

Commodities: Basic raw materials or agricultural products.

Commodity agreements: Agreements among countries to influence prices of commodities.

Common agricultural policy (CAP): An EC policy among member countries aimed at free trade, price supports, and modernization programs in agriculture.

Common law system: A system of law based on tradition, precedent, and custom and usage, in which the courts interpret the law based on those conventions. This is the system of law in the United Kingdom and former British colonies.

Common market: A form of regional economic integration in which countries abolish internal tariffs, use a common external tariff, and abolish restrictions on factor mobility. The term "Common Market" is also used to represent the European Community (EC).

Communism: A form of totalitarianism initially theorized by Karl Marx in which the political and economic systems are virtually inseparable.

Comparative advantage: The theory that there may still be gains from trade if a country specializes in those products that it can produce more efficiently than other products, whether or not the country has an absolute advantage or disadvantage with other countries.

Compensatory trade: Any of several different arrangements in which goods and services are bartered, either on a bilateral or multilateral basis.

Complete economic integration: A theoretical form of regional integration which presupposes the unification of monetary, fiscal, social, and counter-cyclical policies, and requires the setting up of a supranational authority whose decisions are binding for the member states.

Compound duty: A tax placed on goods traded internationally, based on value plus units.

Concentration strategy: Building up operations quickly in one or a few countries before going to another.

Confidence: The concept of foreign exchange in which during times of turmoil, people prefer to move out of currencies of risky countries and to move into currencies of more stable countries, resulting in strengthening strong currencies and weakening risky currencies.

Confirmed letter of credit: A letter of credit in which a bank in the exporter's country adds its guarantee of payment.

Consolidation: An accounting process in which financial statements of related entities, such as a parent and its subsidiaries, are added together to yield a unified set of financial statements. In the process, transactions among the related enterprises are eliminated so that the statements reflect transactions with outside parties.

Consortium: The joining together of several entities, such as firms or governments, in order to strengthen the possibility of achieving some objective.

Consortium bank: Several banks pooling resources to form another bank (the consortium bank) that engages in international transactions. The parent banks retain their separate operating identities, and the consortium bank becomes a new entity operated by the parent banks.

Consumer-directed market economy: An economy in which there is minimal government participation while growth is promoted through the mobility of production factors, including high employment turnover.

Consumer sovereignty: The freedom of consumers to influence production through choice.

Content analysis: A method of comparing messages by counting the number of times that preselected words, phrases, or pictures appear in a particular medium.

Continental terms: See European terms.

Control: The planning, implementation, evaluation, and correction of performance to ensure that organizational objectives are achieved.

Controlled Foreign Corporation (CFC): A foreign corporation in which more than 50 percent of the voting stock is owned by U.S. shareholders (taxable entities that own at least 10 percent of the voting stock of the foreign corporation).

Convertibility: The exchange without restrictions of one currency into another currency.

Convertible bonds: Bonds converted from debt to equity at the option of the investor.

Coordinating Committee on Multilateral Export (COCOM): An agreement among western industrial nations to limit militarily useful exports to communist countries.

Copyright: The right to reproduce, publish, and sell literary, musical, or artistic works.

Corporate culture: The common values for employees in a corporation which form a control mechanism that is implicit and which helps enforce other explicit control mechanisms.

Correspondent (bank): A bank in which funds are kept by another, usually foreign, bank to facilitate check clearing and other business relationships.

Correspondent relationships: Banks in different countries facilitating international financial transactions for each other's clients:

Cost of living adjustment: A compensation adjustment for expatriates when foreign living costs are more expensive than those in the home countries.

The Council of Ministers: One of the four major institutions of the EC. Comprised of one member from each country in the EC, the Council of Ministers is entrusted with making the major policy decisions for the EC.

Council for Mutual Economic Assistance (CMEA or COMECON): A regional form of economic integration that is associated with communist countries. The members are essentially those considered to be within the Soviet bloc of influence. In 1991, COMECON was finally terminated.

Countertrade: A sale involving obligations by the seller to generate foreign exchange for the buying country.

Country-similarity theory: The theory that a producer, having developed a new product in response to observed market conditions in the home market, will turn to markets that are most similar to those at home.

Country size theory: See Theory of country size.

The Court of Justice: One of the four major institutions of the EC. It is composed of one member from each country in the EC and serves as a supreme appeals court for EC law.

CPE (Centrally Planned Economy): See Command Economy.

Cross-licensing: The exchange of technology by different firms.

Cross rate: An exchange rate between two currencies computed from the exchange rate of each of those two currencies in relation to the U.S. dollar.

Culture: The specific learned norms of a society, based on attitudes, values, and beliefs.

Culture shock: A generalized trauma one experiences in a new and different culture because of having to learn new cues when one's old ones will not work.

Currency option: A relatively recent foreign exchange instrument that gives the purchaser of the option the right, but not the obligation, to buy or sell a certain amount of foreign currency at a set exchange rate within a specified amount of time.

Current-account balance: Exports minus imports of goods, services, and unilateral transfers.

Current rate method: Used for translating foreign currency financial statements into the reporting currency. The current rate method is used when the local currency is the functional currency. All assets and liabilities are translated by using the current exchange rate, also known as the exchange rate in effect on the balance sheet date. Income statement accounts are translated by the average exchange rate for the period.

Customs: Duties or taxes imposed on imported goods.

Customs union: A form of regional economic integration which eliminates tariffs among member nations and establishes common external tariffs.

Customs valuation: The value on which customs authorities charge tariffs. If values are set arbitrarily high, tariffs will also be higher and more restrictive.

Debt market: A market dealing in bonds that represent borrowing of entities.

Debt service ratio: The ratio of interest payments plus principal amortization to exports.

Debt-equity swap: A modern financing device

whereby a lender exchanges its loan for real assets.

Decentralized: Lower-level decision making in the organization. In international operations, decisions would be made at the country-operating level rather than at headquarters.

Deferral (of foreign source income):   Foreign source income generally not taxed by the parent country until it is remitted to the parent company.

Demand deposit: Accounts at a financial institution which permits the account holder to transfer funds to a third party by writing a check.

Democracy: A political system which relies on citizen participation in the decision-making process.

Democratic socialism: The belief that economics and politics are so closely connected that the voters should rely on their elected governments to control the economic system.

Demography: The statistical study of populations and their subgroups.

Dependency: The term to describe one country being too dependent on the sale of one primary commodity and/or too dependent on one country as a customer and supplier.

Depreciation: In accounting, an amount that firms may deduct as expenses to compensate for estimated decreased value of assets.

Derivatives market: Markets designed to protect underlying transactions. For example, forward contracts, futures, options, and swaps are derivatives used to hedge or protect foreign exchange transactions.

Devaluation: The value of a currency is formally reduced in relation to another currency. The foreign currency equivalent of the devalued currency falls.

Developing country: A poor country, also known as third world, less developed, or LDC.

Development bank: Banks that have available loanable funds earmarked for specific types of development projects. The loans are usually made available to developing countries, commonly for infrastructure projects.

Direct foreign investment: An operation controlled by entities in a foreign country.

Direct investment: See Direct foreign investment.

Direct quote: The number of units of the domestic currency given for one unit of foreign currency.

Direct selling: An action taken by an exporter to give greater control over the marketing function and to earn higher profits. The exporter sells directly to distributors or final consumers rather than to trading companies or other intermediaries.

Discount (in foreign exchange):   A foreign currency selling at a discount in the forward market when the forward rate is less than the spot rate, assuming that the domestic currency is quoted on a direct basis.

Distribution: The course—physical path or legal title—that goods take between production and consumption.

Diversification: A process of becoming less dependent on one or few customers or suppliers.

Diversification strategy: A term used in international business to mean that a company produces or sells in many countries to avoid relying on one particular market.

Divestment: Reduction in the amount of investment.

Double-entry accounting: The concept that each transaction has two entries of equal value to be accounted for. Debits have negative arithmetic signs while credits have positive arithmetic signs.

Dow Jones Industrial Average (DJIA):   A measure of the level of stock prices on the New York Stock Exchange (NYSE) based on the prices of thirty blue-chip industrial companies.

Dualism: Progress that is confined to certain sectors of an economy while the rest of the sectors are left in a less-developed state.

Dumping: The underpricing of exports, usually below cost or below the home country price.

Duty: A governmental tax (tariff) levied on goods shipped internationally.

Eastern bloc: A nongeographic term, referring to the centrally planned economies.

EC: See European Community.

Economic Community of West African States (ECOWAS):   A form of economic integration among certain West African countries.

Economic exposure: The foreign exchange risk in international business involved with pricing of products, the source and cost of inputs, and the location of investments.

Economic integration: The abolition of economic

discrimination between national economies, such as the establishment of the European Community.

Economics: A social science concerned chiefly with the description and analysis of the production, distribution, and consumption of goods and services.

Economic system: The system concerned with the allocation of scarce resources.

Economic union: A form of regional economic integration which combines the characteristics of a common market with some degree of harmonization of national economic policies.

Economies of scale: The lowering of cost per unit with added output because of allocation of fixed costs over more units produced.

ECU: See European Currency Unit.

Edge Act corporation: A banking corporation which allows banks to set up offices in money centers in the United States in places other than those where the bank is legally allowed to operate for the purpose of performing international banking activities.

EEC: See European Economic Community.

Effective tariff: An argument used by developing countries which states that the real (effective) tariff on the manufactured portion of their exports is higher than indicated by the published rates because the ad valorem tariff is based on the total value of the product which includes raw materials that would have had duty-free entry.

EFTA: See European Free Trade Association.

Electronic Data Interchange (EDI): The electronic movement of money and information through the use of computer and telecommunications equipment.

Embargo: A specific type of quota that prohibits all trade.

EMC: See Export Management Company.

EMS: See European Monetary System.

Entente Council: A regional economic bloc in Africa that included the nations of Benin, Burkina Faso, Côte d'Ivoire, Niger, and Togo.

Entrepôt: An country that is an import/export intermediary. For example, Hong Kong is an entrepôt for trade between China and the rest of the world.

Environmental climate: See Investment climate.

Environmental scanning: The systematic assessment of external conditions that may affect a firm's operations.

EPC: See European Patent Convention.

Equity: An ownership share, usually with voting rights, in an organization.

Equity market: A market that deals in stocks representing ownership interest in corporations. See Stock exchange.

Essential-industry argument: A protectionist argument that a particular industry is needed for security purposes.

Ethnocentrism: A belief that one's own group is superior to others; also used to describe a firm's belief that what worked at home should work abroad.

Eurobond: A bond sold in a currency other than that of the country of issue.

Eurocredit: A Eurodollar loan that has a medium-term maturity of 3–5 years.

Eurocurrency: Any currency banked outside of its home country and thus free from home government control.

Eurodebt: Debt that is denominated in a Eurocurrency.

Eurodollars: Dollars held at branches of U.S. banks or banks outside of the United States.

Euroequity market: The market for shares sold outside of national boundaries of the issuing company.

Europe 1992: Legislation enacted by the EC designed to eliminate most key barriers to trade of goods and services by December 31, 1992.

European Community (EC): A form of regional economic integration in Europe. It involves a free trade area, a customs union, and the free mobility of factors of production. In addition, the EC is working toward political and economic union.

European Currency Unit (ECU): A currency basket comprised of the currencies of the members of the EC. It is similar to the Special Drawing Right issued by the International Monetary Fund but is comprised of a different basket of currencies.

European Economic Community (EEC): See definition of European Community.

European Free Trade Association (EFTA): A form of regional economic integration involving a group of European countries which are not members of the EC. These countries have established a free trade area.

European Investment Bank: A regional development bank that offers funds for private and public industrial and infrastructure projects in Europe and to the 70 nations associated with the European Community (EC).

European Monetary System (EMS): A cooperative foreign exchange agreement involving most of the members of the EC and designed to promote exchange stability within the EC.

European Patent Convention (EPC): A European agreement allowing firms to make a uniform patent search and application which is then passed on to all signatory countries.

European terms: Currencies quoted on an indirect basis by foreign exchange traders. See Indirect quote.

Evidence account transactions: A requirement that certain contractual obligations be adhered to in international trade. It is a form of countertrade or offset trade.

Exchange rate: The price of one currency in terms of another currency.

Excise tax: A tax on various commodities within a country, such as tobacco and alcoholic beverages.

Eximbank: See Export-Import Bank.

Expatriates: Noncitizens of the countries in which they work.

Experience curve: The measurement of production-cost reductions as output increases.

Export-Import Bank (Eximbank): A U.S. federal agency specializing in foreign lending to support exports.

Export-led development: An industrialization program emphasizing industries that will have export capabilities.

Export Management Company (EMC): A firm that buys merchandise from manufacturers for international distribution or that sometimes acts as an agent for manufacturers.

Exports: Goods or services leaving a country.

Export tariff: A tax on goods leaving a country.

Export Trading Company (ETC): A trading company sanctioned by law to become involved in international commerce. The law that established the ETC in the United States was designed to

eliminate some of the antitrust barriers to cooperation.

Expropriation: The transfer of property rights in the exercise of a country's sovereignty. In other words, the taking of private property by a country.

External convertibility: See Nonresident convertibility.

Extraterritoriality: The situation in which governments extend the application of their laws to foreign operations of companies.

Factor mobility: Factors of production, such as labor and capital, moving freely across borders.

Factor-proportions theory: Differences in a country's proportionate holdings of factors of production (land, labor, and capital) which explain differences in the costs of the factors so that the best export advantages are in the production of goods which use the most abundant factors.

FASB: See Financial Accounting Standards Board.

Fatalism: A belief that events are fixed in advance so that human beings are powerless to change them.

Favorable balance of trade: Exporting more than a country imports.

FCIA: See Foreign Credit Insurance Association.

FDI: See Foreign direct investment.

The Federal Reserve ("The Fed"): The central bank of the United States.

Federal Open Market Committee (FOMC): The organization within "The Fed" that makes decisions pertaining to the buying and selling of the United States' federal government securities.

Fees: Payment for the performance of certain activities abroad.

Finance function: The function of a business that deals primarily with the generation of funds for operational needs and expansion; the management of working capital; the protection against financial and foreign exchange risk; and the financial aspects of the foreign investment decision. Also called the Treasury function.

Financial Accounting Standards Board (FASB): The private-sector organization in the United States that sets financial accounting standards.

Financial liquidity: The ability of a business to meet its debts as they come due.

Financial risk: Currency transaction and translation risks, as well as property- and product-liability risks.

FIRA: See Foreign Investment Review Act.

Firm: A business enterprise.

First world countries: Nonsocialist industrial countries.

Fiscal policy: The policies of government expenditures.

Fisher effect: The relationship between inflation and interest rates in two countries. For example, if the nominal interest rate in the home country is lower than that of the foreign country, the home country's inflation should be lower so that the real interest rates would be equal.

Fixed price: A method of selling in which price bargaining does not take place.

Flexible exchange rate: An exchange rate determined by the laws of supply and demand and with minimal governmental interference.

Floating currency: A currency whose value responds to the supply and demand for that currency.

Floating exchange rate: The same as a flexible exchange rate.

Foreign bond: A bond sold outside of the borrower's country but sold in the currency of the country of issue.

Foreign Corrupt Practices Act: A law against certain types of illegal payments by U.S. firms, e.g., bribes to foreign governmental officials.

Foreign Credit Insurance Association (FCIA):   A U.S. federal agency that insures against nonpayment on export sales.

Foreign currency swaps: One currency traded for another currency with the agreement that the transaction would be reversed at some point.

Foreign direct investment: An operation controlled by entities in a foreign country.

Foreign exchange: Currency from another country.

Foreign-exchange control: A requirement to apply to governmental authorities for permission to buy foreign currency.

Foreign freight forwarder: A firm that facilitates the movement of goods from one country to another.

Foreign investment: Direct or portfolio ownership of assets in another country.

Foreign Invest Review Act (FIRA):   A Canadian act to limit foreign control of the economy.

Foreign Sales Corporation (FSC):   A special corporation established by U.S. tax law to be used by a U.S. exporter to shelter some of its income from taxation.

Foreign trade organizations (FTO):   Agencies, organized along product lines, to handle foreign sales and purchases in most centrally planned economies.

Foreign trade zones (FTZ):   Special physical sites where the government allows firms to delay or avoid paying tariffs on imports.

Fortress Europe: The fear that European regulations related to Europe 1992 will favor European firms and exclude foreign, especially U.S. and Japanese, firms.

Forward contract: A contract between a firm or individual and a bank to deliver foreign currency at a specific exchange rate on a set date.

Forward rate: A contractually established exchange rate between a foreign exchange trader and the customer for delivery of foreign exchange on a specific date.

Four Tigers (of Asia):   A term referring to the rapidly developing countries of Hong Kong, Taiwan, Singapore, and South Korea.

Fractional reserve: An amount held by banks as a precaution. The amount is generally much lower than that loaned and reloaned to users.

Franchising: A way of doing business in which one party (the franchisor) gives an independent party (the franchisee) the use of a trademark that is an essential asset for the franchisee's business and continual assistance in the operation of the business.

Free on board (f.o.b.) exports: The exporter's quote of a price that includes all costs up to the point of shipment abroad. All other costs are assumed by the importer.

Free Trade Area (FTA):   A form of regional economic integration in which internal tariffs are abolished, but countries set their own external tariffs.

Fringe benefit: Employee benefits other than salary, wages, and cash bonuses.

FTO: See Foreign trade organization.

Full convertibility: A situation in which both residents and nonresidents can purchase unlimited amounts of any currency.

Functional currency: In translating foreign currency financial statements, the currency of the primary economic environment in which the entity operates.

Functional division: An organizational structure in which each function in foreign countries (e.g., marketing and production) report separately to counterpart functional groups at headquarters.

Functions: A means of dividing business operations according to the type of activity performed, such as between the marketing and accounting functions.

Funds: Working capital, the difference between current assets and current liabilities. A more narrow definition of funds includes only cash.

Futures contract: A contract that specifies an exchange rate in advance of the future exchange of the currency. The contract is not as flexible as the forward contract because the futures contract is for specific amounts of currency and for specific maturity dates.

Gap analysis: A tool used to estimate why a market potential for a given product is less than a company's sales in a country. The reasons may be due to a usage, competitive, product line, or distribution gap.

GATT: See General Agreement on Tariffs and Trade.

General Agreement on Tariffs and Trade (GATT):   An institution formed to provide a forum in which to promote and negotiate trade on a multilateral basis. It is specifically interested in reducing barriers to trade, of both a tariff and nontariff nature.

Generalized System of Preferences (GSP):   Preferential import restrictions given by industrial countries to developing countries.

Generally Accepted Accounting Principles (GAAP):   Those accounting standards accepted by users of statements in a particular country.

Generic: The name given to a class of products, rather than the brand of a particular company, and, therefore, not protected by a trademark.

Geographic division: An organizational structure in which a firm's operations are separated for reporting purposes into global regional areas.

Geography: A science dealing with the earth and its life, especially with the description of land, sea, air, and the distribution of plant and animal life.

Glasnost: A Russian term referring to openness in political policies.

Global cash management: The central management of cash in a multinational firm to minimize borrowing costs and to maximize returns on cash.

Global company: A company that integrates operations from different countries.

Global sourcing: A domestic firm's acquiring of raw materials, parts, and subassemblies from foreign countries to be manufactured in the domestic country.

Go-no-go decision: A basis of decision making, such as for foreign investments, which does not compare different alternative opportunities.

Goods and services differential: See Cost of living adjustment.

Government: A system of ruling, political administration, and so forth.

Grandchild Subsidiary: Also called second tier subsidiary; one that is under a tax-haven subsidiary.

Group of 7:   A group of developed countries that periodically meet to make economic decisions. This group consists of the United States, Germany, Canada, Italy, France, Japan, and the United Kingdom.

Group of 77:   A group of developing countries originally formed as a voting block in the United Nations. Later, it was expanded to more than 77 countries.

Group of 10:   A group of developed countries that periodically meet to make economic decisions. This group consists of the members of the Group of 7 plus Sweden, Switzerland, Belgium, and the Netherlands.

GSP: See Generalized System of Preferences.

Hard currency: A currency that is freely traded without many restrictions and for which there is usually strong external demand. Hard currencies are often called freely convertible currencies.

Hardship allowance: A supplement to compensate expatriates for working in dangerous or adverse conditions.

Hedge: A form of protection against an adverse movement of an exchange rate.

Hetarchy: An organizational structure in which management is in a so-called equal rather than superior-subordinate relationship. This structure is primarily used in the management of alliances among companies.

Hickenlooper Amendment: A U.S. act requiring cessation of aid to a country that nationalizes assets of U.S. citizens or has moved to abrogate contracts without taking appropriate means of settlement within a reasonable period of time.

Hierarchy: A superior-subordinate relationship that exists between and among companies.

Hierarchy of needs: A well-known motivation theory stating that there is a hierarchy of needs and that people must fulfill the lower order needs sufficiently before being motivated by the higher order needs.

High-need achiever: One who will work very hard to achieve material or career success as opposed to a person who is more concerned with developing smooth social relationships or spiritual achievements.

Historically Planned Economy (HPE): The World Bank's reference to second world countries in transition to market economies.

History: A branch of knowledge that records and explains past events.

Holding company income: Income to an enterprise from dividends, interest, rents, royalties, and gains on sale of stock.

Home country: The country in which an international firm is headquartered.

Home-country nationals: The citizens of the country in which the company is headquartered.

Hong: A Hong Kong family-controlled business empire.

Horizontal expansion: A combination of firms engaged in the same line of business.

Host country: The nonheadquartered country in which an international firm operates.

HPE: See Historically Planned Economy.

IDA: See International Development Association.

IDB: See Inter-American Development Bank.

Idealism versus pragmatism: Idealism is the condition whereby people try to settle principles before they settle small issues; pragmatism involves people approaching problem solving from the opposite direction.

Ideology: The systematic and integrated body of constructs, theories, and aims that constitute a society.

IFC: See International Finance Corporation.

ILO: See International Labor Organization.

IMF: See International Monetary Fund.

Imitation lag: One of the strategies to take advantage of temporary monopoly advantages by moving first to those countries most likely to develop competitors.

Import broker: An individual who works for an importer by obtaining various governmental permissions and other clearances before forwarding necessary paperwork to the carrier that will deliver the goods from the dock to the importer.

Import deposit requirements: The government's requiring a deposit prior to the release of foreign exchange.

Import licensing: A method of governmental control of the exchange rate, whereby all recipients, exporters, and others who receive foreign exchange are required to sell to the central bank at the official buying rate.

Imports: Goods or services entering a country.

Import substitution: An industrialization policy whereby new industrial developments emphasize products that would otherwise be imported.

Import tariff: A tax placed on goods entering a country.

In-bond industry: An industry based on the processing of imported components which can enter a country free of duty, provided that the components will be reexported.

Income elasticity: The change in product demand as incomes change.

Independence: A term referring to an extreme situation in which a country would not rely on other countries.

Indirect quote: A foreign exchange quote given in terms of the number of units of the foreign currency for one unit of the domestic currency. Also see European terms.

Indirect selling: The implication that the manufacturer deals through another domestic firm before entering the international marketplace.

Individual: A person, rather than an enterprise, who owns resources and consumes products.

Industrialization argument: A rationale for protectionism, proposing that the development of industrial output should come about even though domestic prices may not become competitive on the world market.

Infant industry argument: The logic of the infant industry argument for protection is that while initial output costs for an industry in a given country may be too high to be competitive in world markets, over a period of time, the costs will decrease sufficiently so that efficient production will be achieved.

Infrastructure: The underlying foundation of a society, such as roads, schools, and so forth, that allows it to function effectively.

Input-output: A tool widely used in national economic planning to show the resources consumed by different industries for a given output as well as for the interdependence of economic sectors.

Intangible property: See Intellectual property rights.

Integrated system: A tax system aimed at preventing double taxation of corporate income through split rates, e.g., distributed profits versus retained earnings or tax credits.

Intellectual property rights: Intangible assets, such as patents, trademarks, copyrights, and know-how.

Inter-American Development Bank (IDB): An international organization aimed at improving economic conditions in Latin America, primarily by lending for public projects.

Interbank market: The foreign exchange market among banks.

Interbank transactions: Foreign exchange transactions that take place between banks as opposed to those between banks and nonbank clients.

Interdependence: The development of mutually needed economic relations among countries

Interest arbitrage: Investing in interest-bearing instruments in foreign exchange and earning a profit due to interest rate and exchange rate differentials.

Interest rate differential: An indicator of future changes in the spot exchange rate.

Intermediation costs: The costs of establishing, maintaining, regulating, and using foreign markets.

Internalization: The self-handling of foreign operations, primarily because it is less expensive to deal within the same corporate family than to contract with an external organization.

International Accounting Standards Committee (IASC): The international private-sector organization established to set financial accounting standards that can be used worldwide.

International Bank for Reconstruction and Development (IBRD): A multi-government owned bank to promote development projects, primarily through low-interest infrastructure loans.

International Banking Facility (IBF): A domestic branch bank established for international banking and treated for regulatory purposes as a foreign branch.

International Bureau for the Protection of Industrial Property Rights (BIRPI): A multilateral agreement to protect patents, trademarks, and other property rights.

International business: All business transactions involving two or more countries. The business relationships may be private or governmental.

International Development Association (IDA): A multigovernmental association through the World Bank in which developed countries subscribe funds to lend to LDCs on liberal terms.

International division: An organizational structure in which virtually all foreign operations are segmented within the same division.

International Finance Corporation (IFC): A division of the World Bank which provides development financing for private enterprise projects in developing countries.

International Fisher Effect: The relationship between interest rates and exchange rates implying that the currency of the country with the lower interest rate will strengthen in the future.

International Labor Organization (ILO): A multilateral organization promoting the adoption of humane conditions of labor.

International law: A concept that can be so broad as to encompass any laws that influence international transactions, or so narrow as to refer only to treaties that govern the relationships between sovereign nations.

International Monetary Fund (IMF): A multigovernmental association organized to promote exchange rate stability and to facilitate the international flow of currencies.

International Monetary Market (IMM): A specialized market located in Chicago to deal in select foreign currency futures.

International Sea-Bed Authority: A United Nations group aimed at determining coastal water rights and setting policy on the exploitation of resources on the sea bed.

International standard of fair dealing: A concept that prompt, adequate, and effective compensation will be received for investors in cases of expropriation.

International Trade Administration (ITA): A branch of the U.S. Department of Commerce offering a variety of services to U.S. exporting firms.

Intrazonal trade: Trade among countries which are part of a trade agreement, such as the members of the European Community.

Investment banks (or companies): Financial institutions specializing in designing and marketing new issues of stocks and bonds.

Investment Canada: An act in Canada, the intent of which is to persuade foreign firms to invest in Canada.

Investment climate: Those external conditions in host countries that could significantly affect the success or failure of a foreign enterprise.

Invisibles: See Services.

Irrevocable letter of credit: A letter of credit that cannot be changed without consent of all parties involved.

Islamic law: A form of theocratic law based on the religious teachings of Islam. It is also called Muslim law.

JIT: See Just-in-time.

Joint venture: Two or more organizations sharing the ownership of a direct investment.

Just-in-time (JIT): A manufacturing system which decreases inventories by having components and parts delivered as they are needed in production.

Keiretsu: A linkage among certain Japanese companies, usually involving a noncontrolling interest in each other, strong high-level personal relationships among managers in the different companies, and interlocking directorships.

Key industry: An industry that might affect a very large segment of the economy by virtue of its size or influence on other sectors.

Kremlin: The government headquarters of the Soviet Union located in Moscow.

Labor market: The mix of available workers and the mix of labor costs from which firms may hire.

Labor unions: Associations of workers to promote and protect the welfare, interests, and rights of its members, primarily by collective bargaining.

Lag strategy: A foreign exchange management strategy that results in delaying payments or delaying receipts in a foreign currency. Lagged collection is typically done because the foreign currency is expected to become stronger. Lag strategy is the opposite of lead strategy.

LAIA: See Latin American Integration Association.

Laissez-faire: A concept of minimal governmental intervention in a society's economic activity.

Large corporations: Enterprises big enough to control the flow of resources.

Latin American Integration Association (LAIA): A free trade area form of regional economic integration involving most of the Latin American nations.

Law: A binding custom or practice of a community.

Lead strategy: The implication that firms would pay off foreign currency debts early and collect foreign currency receipts early. Early collection is typically done because the foreign currency is expected to weaken. Lead strategy is the opposite of lag strategy.

Learning curve: A concept used to support the infant industry argument for protection; it assumes that costs will decrease as workers and managers gain more experience.

Leontief paradox: A surprising finding by Wassily Leontief that overall U.S. exports were less capital intensive and more labor intensive than U.S. imports.

Less Developed Country (LDC): See Third world country.

Letter of credit: A precise document by which the importer's bank extends credit to the importer and agrees to pay the exporter.

Leveraged buy-outs (LBO): The borrowing of a large amount of money to buy a controlling interest of a company or the stock of a company.

LIBID: The London Inter-Bank Bid Rate, the interest rate that banks pay bank customers for deposits in the London interbank market.

LIBOR: See London Inter-Bank Offer Rate.

License: A formal or legal permission to do something specified.

Licensing agreements: Agreements whereby one firm gives rights to another for the use, usually for a fee, of such assets as trademarks, patents, copyrights, or other know-how.

Licensing arrangement (on trade): A procedure that requires potential importers or exporters to secure permission from governmental authorities before they conduct trade transactions.

Lifetime-employment: A customary Japanese situation in which groups of workers are effectively guaranteed employment with the company for their working lifetime and in which the workers seldom leave for employment opportunities with other companies.

LIFFE: See London International Financial Futures Exchange.

Liquidity preference: A common concept to help explain capital budgeting, which, when applied to international operations, means that investors are willing to take less return in order to be able to shift the resources to alternative uses.

Locals: The citizens of the country in which they work.

London Inter-Bank Offer Rate (LIBOR): The interest rate for large interbank transactions in the international banking market. It is the rate that banks charge for loans to other banks in the London interbank market.

London International Financial Futures Exchange (LIFFE): An exchange dealing in futures contracts in several major currencies.

London Stock Exchange: A stock exchange located in London and dealing in Euroequities.

Management contract: An arrangement through which one firm assists another by providing management personnel to perform general or specialized management functions for a fee.

Maquiladora industry: An industry concept developed by the Mexican government in which U.S.-source components are shipped to Mexico duty-free and are reexported to the United States. Also see In-bond industry.

Market capitalization: A common measure of the size of a stock market. The figure is computed by multiplying the total number of shares of stock listed on the stock exchange by the market price per share.

Market economy: An economic philosophy in which resources are allocated and controlled by consumers who "vote" by buying goods.

Market value: As applied to a firm as a whole, the current market value of the stock times the number of shares outstanding.

Marshall Plan: The plan implemented by the United States after World War II with the objective of rebuilding Western Europe.

Matrix: A method of plotting data on a vertical and horizontal axis, so as to compare countries in terms of risk and opportunity.

Matrix structure: An organizational structure in which foreign units report (by product, function, or area) to more than one group, each of which shares responsibility over the foreign unit.

Maxidevaluation: A major devaluation of a country's currency. This usually occurs for a currency such as the cruzeiro in Brazil where inflation is a major problem and where existing devaluations are not large enough to compensate for inflation.

Mentor: A person at headquarters who looks after the interest of an expatriate employee.

Mercantilism: An economic philosophy based on the belief that a country's wealth is dependent on its holdings of treasure, usually in the form of gold. In order to increase wealth, countries attempt to export more than they import.

Merchandise exports: Goods sent out of a country.

Merchandise imports: Goods brought into a country.

Merchandise trade balance: The net of merchandise imports and exports within a country's balance of payments.

Merger: Two companies combining their operations

to form a new company. In the case of a merger, the original companies disappear, to be replaced by the new company.

MFA: See Multifibre Arrangement.

MFN: See Most Favored Nation.

Ministry of International Trade and Industry (MITI):   The Japanese governmental ministry responsible for coordinating overall societal business directions and helping individual firms take advantage of global business opportunities.

Mixed economy: Economies characterized by different mixtures of market and command economies and public and private ownership of resources.

Mixed venture: A special type of joint venture in which a government is in partnership with a private company.

Monetary policy: Governmental policy, usually regulated by a central bank, concerned with the growth of the money supply.

Most Favored Nation (MFN):   A policy of granting a concession that is given to one country to all other countries of the world (with a few exceptions).

Multidomestic company: A way of managing international operations in which operations in each country are relatively independent of those in other countries.

Multifibre Arrangement (MFA):   See Arrangement Regarding International Trade in Textiles.

Multilateral agreement: An agreement involving more than two governments.

Multilateral institution: An institution, the leadership and membership of which are drawn from various societies.

Multilateral Investment Guarantee Agency (MIGA):   A member of the World Bank Group which encourages equity investment and other direct investment flows to developing countries by offering investors a variety of different services.

Multinational corporation: See Multinational Enterprise

Multinational Enterprise (MNE):   An integrated global philosophy encompassing both domestic and overseas operations. It is sometimes used synonymously with multinational corporation and transnational corporation.

Multiple exchange rate system: A system in which the government sets different exchange rates for different transactions.

Muslim law: See Islamic law.

Nationalism: The feeling of pride and/or ethnocentrism focused on an individual's home territory.

Nationalization: The transfer of ownership to the state.

Natural advantage: A country may have a natural advantage in the production of a product because of climatic conditions or access to certain natural resources.

Neomercantilism: Describes countries that try to run favorable balances of trade, not seek an influx of gold, in an attempt to achieve some social or political objective.

Net buyer range: The price range in which the commodity buffer stock manager must buy more of the commodity in order to keep prices from falling too low.

Net capital flow: Capital inflow less outflow, for other than import and export payment.

Net seller range: The price range in which the commodity buffer stock manager must sell more of the commodity in order to keep the price from rising too high.

Netting: The netting of cash flows internationally refers to subsidiaries in a net payable position transferring funds to the central clearing account, and the manager of the clearing account transferring funds to the accounts of the net receiver subsidiaries.

Newly Industrializing Country (NIC):   Third world countries in which the cultural and economic climate has led to a rapid rate of industrialization and growth since the 1960s.

Nikkei Index: A measure of the level of stock prices on the Tokyo Stock Exchange, based on the prices of a group of Japanese securities.

NME (nonmarket economy):   See Command economy.

Nonaccrual loan: A loan to a developing country in which principal or interest is 90 days past due or on which payment of interest or principal is deemed to be doubtful.

Nonmarket economy: See Command economy.

Nonperforming loan: Loans on which interest or principal payments are not being made.

Nonresident convertibility: The ability of a nonresident of a country to convert deposits in a bank to the currency of any other country. Also known as External convertibility.

Nontariff barriers: Barriers to imports that are not tariffs. Examples would be administrative controls, "Buy America" policies, and so forth.

Normal quote: See Direct quote.

OAU: See Organisation of African Unity.

OECD: See Organization for Economic Cooperation and Development.

OEEC: See Organization for European Economic Cooperation.

Offer Rate: The amount for which a foreign exchange trader is willing to sell foreign exchange.

Official reserves: A country's holdings of monetary gold, Special Drawing Rights, and internationally acceptable currencies.

Offset: A form of barter in which an export must be offset by some type of import transaction.

Offset trade: See Countertrade.

Offshore financial centers: Cities or countries that provide large amounts of funds in a currency other than their own.

Offshore manufacturing: Manufacturing outside the borders of a particular country.

Oligopoly: An industry in which there are few producers or sellers.

OPEC: See Organization of Petroleum Exporting Countries.

Open account: A situation in which the exporter extends credit directly to the importer.

Operational centers: Offshore financial centers that perform specific functions, such as the sale and servicing of goods.

Opinion leader: One whose acceptance of some concept is apt to be emulated by others.

Optimum tariff: A situation in which a foreign exporter lowers its prices when an import tax is placed on its products.

Option: The right to buy or sell foreign exchange within a specific period or at a specific date.

Organisation of African Unity (OAU): An organization of African nations concerned more with political than economic objectives.

Organizational structure: The reporting relationships within an organization.

Organization for Economic Cooperation and Development (OECD): A multilateral organization of industrialized and semi-industrialized countries that helps formulate social and economic policies.

Organization for European Economic Cooperation (OEEC): A sixteen-nation organization established in 1948 to facilitate the utilization of aid from the Marshall Plan. It evolved into the EEC and EFTA forms of regional economic integration.

Organization of Petroleum Exporting Countries (OPEC): An organization of petroleum exporting countries which attempt to agree on oil production and pricing policies.

Outright forward: A forward contract not connected to a spot transaction.

Outsourcing: A situation in which a domestic company uses foreign suppliers for components or finished products.

Pacific Economic Cooperation Conference (PECC): A forum for the discussion of common problems of the Pacific Rim countries.

Parallel market: A secondary currency market with currency rates different from those in the official market. Sometimes known as the black market.

Parent: A company that controls another, its subsidiary.

The Parliament: One of the four major bodies of the EC. Its representatives are elected directly in each member country.

Parliamentary government: A form of government that involves the election of representatives to form the executive branch of the government.

Par value: The benchmark value of a currency, originally in terms of gold or the U.S. dollar, now quoted in terms of Special Drawing Rights.

Passive income: Income, usually from operations in tax-haven countries, which results from investments in other countries and from sales and services income that involve buyers and sellers in other than the tax-haven country. Either the buyer or the seller must be part of the same organizational structure as the corporation that earns the passive income.

Patent cooperation treaty: A multilateral agreement to protect patents.

Peg: To fix an exchange rate to some benchmark, such as another currency.

Petrodollars: Dollars generated from the sale of oil.

Philadelphia Stock Exchange (PSE): A specialized market located in Philadelphia dealing in select foreign currency options.

Piracy: The unauthorized use of property rights, supposedly protected by patents, trademarks, or copyrights.

Planning: The meshing of objectives with internal and external constraints to set means to implement, monitor, and correct operations.

PLC: See Product life cycle theory.

Pluralistic societies: Societies in which different ideologies are held by numerous segments of society rather than one ideology adhered to by all.

Political freedom: The right to participate freely in the political process.

Political risk: Potential changes in political conditions that may cause company operating positions to deteriorate.

Political science: A discipline that helps explain the patterns of governments and their actions.

Political system: The system designed to integrate the society into a viable, functioning unit.

Polycentrism: Characteristic of an individual or organization that feels that differences in a foreign country, real and imaginary, great and small, need to be accounted for in management decisions. The differences are so overwhelming that few if any management practices can be brought into the foreign environment without significant change.

Portfolio investment: Either debt or equity, but the critical factor is that control does not follow the investment.

PPP: See Purchasing-power parity.

Pragmatism: See idealism versus pragmatism.

Premium (in foreign exchange): The difference between the spot and forward exchange rates in the forward market. A foreign currency sells at a premium when the forward rate exceeds the spot rate and when the domestic currency is quoted on a direct basis.

Pressure group: A group that tries to influence legislation or practices to foster its objectives, such as preventing certain imports.

Price escalation: The process by which the lengthening of distribution channels increases a product's price by more than the direct added costs, such as transportation, insurance, and tariffs.

Price range: In commodity agreements, the difference between what a commodity buffer stock should be bought at and what it should be sold for.

Private enterprise: A firm in which production is privately owned.

Private ownership: Individuals rather than the government own economic resources.

Privatization: A situation in which government-owned assets are sold to private individuals or groups.

Product division: An organizational structure in which different foreign operations report to different product groups at headquarters.

Production agreements: Agreements between firms in which one firm agrees to produce products for another firm. This is a strategic alliance that does not have to involve equity ownership.

Production switching: The movement of production from one country to another in response to changes in cost.

Product life cycle (PLC) theory: The theory that certain kinds of products go through a cycle consisting of four stages (introduction, growth, maturity, and decline) and that the location of production will shift internationally depending on the stage of the cycle.

Promotion: The process of presenting messages intended to help sell a product or service.

Protestant ethic: A theory that there is more economic growth when work is viewed as a means of salvation and when people prefer to transform productivity gains into additional output rather than into additional leisure.

Public ownership: The government, rather than individuals, owns the economic resources.

Pull: A promotion strategy which sells consumers before they reach the point of purchase usually by relying on mass media.

Purchasing-power parity (PPP): A theory to explain exchange rate changes based on differences in price levels in different countries.

Push: A promotion strategy which involves direct selling techniques.

Quality control circle: A production system in which small groups of workers meet regularly to spot and solve problems in their area.

Quantity controls: Government limitations on the amount of foreign currency that can be used in a specific transaction.

Quota: A limit on the quantitative amount of a product allowed to be imported into or exported out of a country.

Quota systems: A system in which producing and/or consuming countries divide total output and sales for a particular product.

Quoted currency: An exchange rate quoted by relating one currency to the other. The currency of which the numerical value is "one" is the base currency; the other currency is the quoted currency. For example, if the exchange rate between the British pound and dollar were to be quoted at $1.40 per pound, the pound would be the base currency, and the dollar would be the quoted currency.

Rationalization: See Rationalized production.

Rationalized production: Companies increasingly producing different components or different portions of their product line in different parts of the world to take advantage of varying costs of labor, capital, and raw materials.

Reciprocal quote: The reciprocal of the direct quote. Also see Indirect quote.

Regional development bank: A development bank that makes loans only to countries in particular regions, for example, a bank that loans funds only to European countries.

Regression: A statistical method showing relationships among variables.

Reinvestment: The use of retained earnings to replace depreciated assets or to add to the existing stock of capital.

Renegotiation: A process through which international firms and governments decide a change in terms for operations.

Repatriation: An expatriate's return to his or her home country.

Representative democracy: A type of government in which individual citizens elect representatives to make decisions governing the society.

Return on investment: Profits, sometimes measured before and sometimes after the payment of taxes, divided by the amount of investment.

Revaluation: A formal change in an exchange rate when the foreign currency value of the reference currency rises. A revaluation results in a strengthening of the reference currency.

ROI: See Return on investment.

Rounds: Conferences held by GATT promoting multilateral agreements to liberalize trade.

Royalties: Payment for the use of intangible assets abroad.

Sales income: Income from foreign sales subsidiaries that are incorporated separately from their manufacturing operations.

Sales response function: The amount of sales created at different levels of marketing expenditures.

SDR: See Special Drawing Rights.

SEAQ International: The London Stock Exchange's screen-based quotation system that is the leader in the trading of international equities.

Secondary boycott: The boycotting of a firm doing business with a firm being boycotted.

Second-tier subsidiaries: Subsidiaries that report to a tax-haven subsidiary.

Second world countries: Socialist countries, often referred to as historically planned economies, centrally planned economies, or communist countries.

Secular totalitarianism: A dictatorship not affiliated with any religious group or precepts.

Securities and Exchange Commission (SEC): A U.S. government federal agency that regulates securities brokers, dealers, and markets.

Separate entity approach: A tax system in which each unit is taxed when it receives income; e.g., a firm is taxed on its profits, and individuals are taxed on the dividends paid from the firm's profits.

Service income: Income from the performance of technical, managerial, or similar services for a related person and performed outside the country in which the corporation is organized.

Services: International earnings other than those on goods sent to another country. Also referred to as invisibles.

Shareholder: In terms of a controlled foreign corporation, a U.S. shareholder is a U.S. person or enterprise that holds 10 percent or more of the voting stock of the foreign corporation.

Sight draft: A bill of exchange which requires payment to be made as soon as it is presented to the party obligated to pay.

Silent language: Messages given by a host of cues other than those of formal language.

Single European Act: An act established in 1987 by the EC allowing all proposals except those relating to taxation, workers' rights, and immigration to be adopted by a system of weighted majority by member states.

Small Business Administration (SBA): An agency of the U.S. federal government to aid the formation and workings of small businesses.

Socialism: The theory of ownership and operation of the means of production by the society, wherein all members share in the work and the consumption of the products.

Social market economy: A nation characterized by heavy governmental spending and high taxation to pay for such social services as health care, education, subsidized housing for the poor, and unemployment benefits; however, the price of products is determined by supply and demand rather than by government fiat.

Society: A broad grouping of people having common traditions, institutions, and collective activities and interests. The nation-state is often used as a workable term to denote society in international business.

Society for Worldwide Interbank Financial Telecommunications (SWIFT): A telecommunications system that transfers funds instantaneously between banks internationally.

Soft budget: A situation in which an enterprise's excess of expenditures over earnings is compensated for by some other institution, typically a state-controlled financial institution.

Sogo Shosha: Japanese trading companies that import and export merchandise.

Sourcing strategy: The strategy that a firm pursues to purchase materials, components, and final products; the sourcing can be from domestic and foreign locations.

Southern African Development Coordinating Conference: A regional economic group in Africa that involves Angola, Botswana, Lesotho, Malawi, Mozambique, Swaziland, Tanzania, Zambia, and Zimbabwe.

Special Drawing Rights (SDR): A unit of account issued to governments by the International Monetary Fund.

Specific duty: A duty (tariff) assessed on the basis of a tax per unit.

Speculator: A person who takes positions in foreign exchange with the objective of earning a profit.

Spillover effects: Situations in which the marketing program in one country results in awareness of the product in other countries.

Spot exchange rate: An exchange rate quoted for immediate delivery, usually within two business days.

Spread (in the forward market): The difference between the spot rate and the forward rate.

Spread (in the spot market): The difference between the bid (buy) and offer (sell) rates quoted by the foreign exchange trader.

Stereotype: A standardized mental picture of a group representing an oversimplified opinion.

Stock exchange: A market in which equity securities are traded.

Strategic alliance: An agreement between firms that is of strategic importance to one or both firms' competitive viability.

Subcontract: A secondary contract that undertakes some or all of the obligations of another contract.

Subpart F income: In a tax-haven country, income earned by controlled foreign corporations (CFCs) from activities outside of that country. It is classified as passive income.

Subsidiary: A foreign operation that is legally separate from the parent, even if wholly owned by that parent.

Subsidies: Direct or indirect governmental assistance to companies, making them more competitive with imports.

Super 301: A clause in United States tariff legislation permitting U.S. trade negotiators to threaten more restrictive import regulations to get other countries to lower their restrictions against U.S.-made products or services.

Supranational agencies: Agencies whose membership is comprised of many different countries and which are not subject to any one country's restraint. Agencies of the European Community (EC) are examples.

Swap: A simultaneous spot and forward foreign exchange transaction.

Swap contract: An agreement by which firms deliver an equal value to each other in two or more countries, such as cruzeiros in Brazil for dollars in the United States or alumina in France for alumina in the United States. Also see foreign currency swaps.

Syndicated loans: A loan arranged by a bank involving many different banks, both foreign and domestic.

Syndication: A lead bank getting several banks involved in making a large loan to a public or private organization.

Taipan: The top manager of a Hong Kong trading company.

Tariff: A governmental tax, usually on imports, levied on goods shipped internationally. It is the most common type of trade control. See Duty.

Tax-haven countries: Countries with low income taxes or no taxes on foreign source income.

Tax-haven subsidiary: A subsidiary of a company established in a tax-haven country for the purpose of minimizing income tax.

Tax holiday: A period of time during which a government does not charge taxes to an enterprise.

Technical factors: Factors that influence exchange rates such as the release of national economic statistics, seasonal demands for a currency, and a slight strengthening of a currency following a prolonged weakness or vice versa.

Technology: The means employed to produce goods or services.

Temporal method: Translating foreign currency financial statements into the reporting currency of the parent company. It basically requires that the monetary assets and liabilities be translated at the current balance sheet exchange rate, and other assets, liabilities, and owner's equity be translated at historical exchange rates. Translation gains and losses are taken directly to the income statement. The temporal rate is used when the parent's reporting currency is the functional currency.

Terms of trade: The quantity of imports that can be bought by a given quantity of a country's exports.

Theocratic law system: A legal system based on religious precepts.

Theocratic totalitarianism: A dictatorship led by a religious group.

Theory of country size: The theory that larger countries are generally more nearly self-sufficient than smaller countries.

Third-country nationals: Citizens of neither the country where they are working nor the country where the firm is headquartered.

Third world countries: Developing countries or those not considered socialist or nonsocialist industrial countries.

Time deposit: A bank deposit with a scheduled maturity date. If the deposit is withdrawn prior to the maturity date, some interest is lost as a penalty.

Time draft: An agreement calling for payment at a later time after delivery of sale.

Time series: A statistical method of illustrating a pattern over time, such as demand for a particular product.

Totalitarianism: A political system characterized by the absence of widespread participation in decision making, restricting it to only a few individuals.

Total Quality Control (TQC): A firm's establishment of policies to reduce errors in order to increase quality of production.

Trademark: A name or logo distinguishing a company or product.

Transaction exposure: Foreign exchange risk occurring because the company has accounts receivable or accounts payable that are denominated in a foreign currency and which must be settled eventually.

Transfer price: A price charged on goods sold between entities that are related to each other through stock ownership, such as a parent and its subsidiaries or subsidiaries owned by the same parent.

Transit tariff: A tax placed on goods passing through a country.

Translation: The restatement of financial accounts from one currency to another.

Translation exposure: Foreign exchange risk that occurs because the parent company must translate foreign currency financial statements into the reporting currency of the parent company.

Transnational corporation: A company owned and managed by nationals in different countries. The term is synonymous with multinational enterprise although this text prefers the first definition.

Treasury function: See Finance function.

Triad strategy: A strategy proposing that an MNE should have a presence in Europe, the United States, and Japan.

Triangular arbitrage: The process of buying and selling foreign exchange at a profit due to price discrepancies where three different currencies are involved.

Turnkey operations: A contract for the construction of an operating facility that is transferred to the owner when the facility is ready to begin operations.

Underemployed: Refers to people working at less than their capacity.

Underwriting: The process by which a newly issued security is sold to the public.

Unfavorable balance of trade: Imports are greater than exports.

Unilateral transfer: A transfer of currency from one country to another to buy goods. The transferring country does not sell goods to the transferee country in return. An example would be foreign aid to a country devastated by earthquake or flood.

Unitary tax: A method of taxing based on a percentage of a company's worldwide operations rather than on profits in the area where the taxing authorities are located.

United Nations (UN): An international organization of nations formed to promote world peace and security. It was formed in 1945 after World War II.

United Nations Conference on Trade and Development (UNCTAD): A United Nations conference that has been especially active in dealing with the relationships between developing and industrialized countries with respect to trade.

Unit of account: A benchmark on which to base the value of payments.

Universal Copyright Convention: A multilateral agreement to protect copyrights.

Unrequited transfer: See Unilateral Transfer.

U.S.-Canada Free Trade Agreement: See Canada-U.S. Free Trade Agreement.

U.S. shareholder: For U.S. tax purposes, a person or firm owning at least 10 percent of the voting stock of a foreign subsidiary.

U.S. terms: The quotation of exchange rates using the direct method. See Direct quote.

Value-Added Tax (VAT): A tax in which each firm is taxed only on the value added to the product by that firm.

Variable price: A method of selling in which buyers and sellers negotiate the price.

VAT: See Value-Added Tax.

Vertical integration: The gaining of control of different stages in which the special drawing rights of a product move from the earliest production to the final distribution.

Water's edge concept: A variation of the unitary tax in which a state tax authority taxes a firm's state sales based on sales and earnings earned within the United States rather than on sales and earnings earned globally.

West African Economic Community: A regional economic group involving Benin, Burkina Faso, Côte d'Ivoire, Mali, Mauritania, Niger, and Senegal.

WIPO: See World Intellectual Property Organization.

Withholding taxes: Taxes paid on dividends from the subsidiary to the parent.

World Bank: See International Bank for Reconstruction and Development.

World Intellectual Property Organization (WIPO): A multilateral agreement to protect patents.

Zaibatsu: Large, Japanese family-owned businesses which existed before World War II and were comprised of a series of financial and manufacturing companies usually held together by a large holding company. After World War II, General Douglas McArthur broke up the zaibatsu and made many of their activities illegal.

Zero sum: One party's gain is another's loss.

COMPANY INDEX AND TRADEMARKS

ABB (see Asea Brown Boveri)
Abbey National Bank, 326
Abitibi, 457
Adam Opel (see Opel)
Adidas, 370
ADM (see Archer Daniels Midland)
Admiral, 227, 537, 539
AEG (see Daimler Benz), 699
Aeroflot, 365, 558
Aerolineas Argentinas, 64, 70
Airborne Accessories Corporation, 207
Aircap (see Sunbeam), 681
Air France, 558
Air Jordan (see Nike), 182
Air Norway, 555
Air Vanuatu, 555
AKZO, 538
Alcan, 317, 447, 556, 562
Alcoa, 447
Alfa (see Grupo Industrial Alfa)
Alfa Romeo, 221
Allied-Lyons, 434
AltaGraphics, 376
America West, 555
American Express, 108, 370, 679
American Home Products, 545, 679
American Metal Climax, 562
Amway, 684
Anaconda, 562
Anheuser-Busch (includes Busch Gardens), 33, 693
Ansett-New Zealand, 555
Ansett Transport Industries, 555
Apple Computer, 79, 484, 491
Aramco, 463–7, 474, 482, 555, 558, 586
Archer Daniels Midland (ADM), 370
Arco, 481
Aristech Chemical, 528–9

Armco, 195
Armstrong World Industries, 668
Arrowhead, 693
Arthur Martin, 227
Asea Brown Boveri (ABB), 454, 649
Atari, 7
AT&T, 470, 731–2
Aunt Jemima Pancake Mix, 669
Australia Aluminum, 562

Badoit (see BSN-Gervais Dannone), 693
Bake 'N' Take, 552
Banco Bilbao Viscaya, 326
Bancomer, 561
B & D (see Black & Decker)
BankAmerica, 326
Bank of Tokyo, 265, 267
Banker's Trust (includes BT Securities), 240–1, 322–4, 369, 481
Banque Nationale de Paris, 320
Barbie (see Mattel), 369
Barclays Bank, 319
BASF, 9, 538, 540, 561, 567
Baskin-Robbins, 553
Bata Ltd., 77–80
Baxter International, 483
Bayer, 448, 740
BCL (see Bougainville Copper Limited)
Bear Stearns, 328
Bechtel, 466
Beecham Group (includes Jovan), 547
Beech-Nut, 611
Beijerinvest, 227
Belarus, 372
Bethlehem Steel, 195

Bic Pens, 681
Big Mac (see McDonald's), 345–6
Black & Decker (includes Dustbuster, Heli-Coil), 532–5, 545, 747, 750–1
Boeing, 297, 484
Boise Cascade, 452
Bonne Maman, 692
Borg-Warner, 590
Bosch-Siemens, 533
Bougainville Copper Limited (BCL), 444
Bowater, 457
B.P. (see British Petroleum)
Braun, 447
Bridgestone Tire, 201, 203–4, 206, 211, 215–7, 220, 222, 381, 444, 528
Bristol-Meyers, 679
British Aerospace, 450
British East India Co., 449, 495
British Petroleum (BP), 220, 317, 463–4
Brooks Brothers, 658
Brown Boveri (see also Asea Brown Boveri), 645
BSN-Gervais Dannone (includes Badoit, Evian), 681, 693
BT Securities (see Bankers Trust)
Buitoni-Perugina, 611
Bundesbank, 274
Burger King, 552
Burroughs, 639
Busch Gardens (see Anheuser-Busch)

C. Itoh & Co. Ltd., 527–8
Cadbury Schweppes (includes Schweppes), 494, 690
Cadillac (see Sunbeam)

Cajoline (see Unilever)
California Standard (see Standard Oil of California)
Calistoga, 693
Caltex, 479
Calvin Klein, 666
Campbell Soup, 624, 794
Canada Dry (see Norton Simon), 692
Canadair, 433
Canon, 628, 666
Capri (see Ford), 390–1
Carnation, 612–3, 681
Carrefours, 684
Cartier, 546
Caterpillar Tractor, 169, 195, 293, 295–8, 304, 486, 521, 583
Cathay Pacific, 42
Celanese, 780
Cerro, 586
CFP (see Compagnie Française des Petroles)
CGCT, 470
Chase Manhattan, 247, 323
Cheerful Tearful Doll (see Mattel), 670
Chemical Bank, 305
Chemise La Coste, 546
Chesebrough-Ponds, 474
Chevron, 370
Chrysler (includes Jeep), 166–8, 190, 221, 358, 372, 472, 545–6
CII, 450
Citibank, 369, 487
Citicorp, 312, 320, 323–6
City Coal Machinery (Donetsk), 359
Coastal Corporation, 515
Coca-Cola, 7, 79, 215, 343, 403, 454, 469, 494–8, 546, 669–70, 678–80, 685, 690, 693, 695, 712, 727–9, 733–4, 747, 750–1
Coca-Cola Light (see Coca-Cola), 680
Coccolino (see Unilever), 681
Coke (see Coca-Cola)
Colgate-Palmolive (includes Darkie), 681
Columbia Pictures, 727
Combustion Engineering, 370
Compagnie Française des Petroles (CFP), 219–20, 463, 465
Con-Agra, 613
Construcciones Aeronauticas, 450
Continental AG, 746
Continental Airlines, 561
Contrex, 693
Control Data, 526
Corning, 625
CPC, 454
Cray Research, 175
Credit Agricole, 319–20
Crown Cork and Seal, 548, 599

CS First Boston, 328
Cummins Engine, 780

D'Allaird's, 658
Daewoo Corp., 167, 436, 604
Dai-Ichi Kangyo Bank, 319
Daimler Benz (includes Mercedes, AEG, and Deutsche Aerospace), 86, 221, 370, 528–9, 699–704, 707, 714, 729
Daiwa Securities, 328
Darkie (see Colgate-Palmolive), 681
Dart Industries (includes Rexene), 566
David's Cookies, 213
Dean Witter, 328
DeBeers Company, 366, 412
DEC (see Digital Equipment Corp.), 756
Deer Park (see Nestlé), 692
de Havilland, 433
Deloitte & Touche, 428, 457
Deloitte Haskins & Sells, 312, 428
Deutsche Aerospace (see Daimler Benz), 699
Deutsche Airbus, 746
Deutsche Bank, 317, 319
Diane Von Furstenberg, 547
Diet Coke (see Coca-Cola), 680
Digital Equipment Corp. (DEC), 756
Disney, Disneyland, Disneyworld (see Walt Disney Corporation)
Donald McDonald (see McDonald's of Japan), 680
Double-Cola, 496
Dow Badische, 567
Dow Chemical, 487, 567, 625, 761–3, 773–4
Dravo, 539
Dresdner Bank, 369
Duncan-Hines (see Procter & Gamble), 182
Dunkin' Donuts, 553
Dunlop-Pirelli, 793
DuPont, 420, 539
Dustbuster (see Black & Decker), 533
Dutch State Mines, 562

Eau Canada Sparcal, 693
Eagle Shirtmakers, 547
EDS (see Electronic Data Systems Corp.)
Electrolux, 9, 226–8
Electronic Data Systems Corp. (EDS), 731
Elektrobytpribor, 359
Eli Lilly & Co., 448
Email & Elders, 599
Emhart Corp., 533, 747
EMI, 619

ENESA, 185
Engineering Plant (Kirov), 359
ENI, 54, 220, 465
Ericsson Telephone (includes L. M. Ericsson), 470, 584, 670
Ernst & Whinney, 396, 427, 722, 729, 758
Escort (see Ford), 390, 516–7
Esso (see Exxon), 463, 479
Eureka, 226
Evian (see BSN-Gervais Dannone), 693
Exxon (includes ESSO, Standard Oil of New Jersey, Standard Oil Trust), 435, 463–4, 466, 474, 479, 480, 527

Facit, 227
Fairchild Camera & Instrument Corp., 334
Fairchild Semiconductor, 456
Feldene (see Pfizer)
Ferruzzi Finanziaria S.p.A., 54
Fiat, 221, 371, 391
Fiesta (see Ford), 390
Firestone, 201, 203, 444, 791
First Chicago Bank, 326
Flavorex, 207
Fletcher and Stewart, 159
Fluor, 466
Ford Motor Company (includes Capri, Escort, Fiesta), 79, 166–8, 190, 201, 221, 370, 389–92, 403, 427, 483, 509–11, 516, 527, 541, 573–9, 585, 591–2, 594, 711, 714, 729, 774, 777, 791
Freuhauf, 559
Freuhauf-France, 559
Frigidaire, 227
Fuji Bank, 319
Fujitsu, 456
Fujiya, 664

GAF, 675
Gallup, 370
GE (see General Electric)
General Ceramics, 449
General Dynamics, 433, 442, 774
General Electric (GE), 356, 527, 533, 546, 618–9, 644, 751, 793
General Mills, 7, 666, 780
General Motors (GM) (includes Nova), 79, 153, 166–8, 190, 201, 203, 205–6, 218, 221, 256, 391, 426, 435–6, 450, 458, 469, 472, 487, 512–3, 527, 560, 670, 680, 734, 749, 763, 773–4
General Tire and Rubber, 452, 746
GHH-Sterkrade, 539

Gibson, 227
Gillette, 447, 452, 479, 495
GM (see General Motors)
Goldman Sachs, 319, 323, 328
Goldstar, 74
Goodyear, 201, 204, 206
Grace (see W.R. Grace)
Granges, 227–8
Great American Cookie Co., 553
Great Waters of France (see Perrier), 690–1
Green Giant, 443
Gresham Bank Ltd., 301
Grupo Industrial Alfa (Alfa), 537–41, 561
Gucci, 546
Gulf & Western, 486, 488
Gulf Oil, 447, 464

Handy & Harman's Indiana Tube Corporation (see Indiana Tube)
Hardee's, 553
Harrod's, 656
Hawker Siddeley Group, 433
Hawley & Hazel, 681
Heart of Tuscany, 693
Hees International, 328
Heinz, 454, 624
Heli-Coil (see Black & Decker), 545
Henkel, 666
Hercules, 540, 566
Hershey, 664
Hewlett-Packard (includes HP Cash), 484, 756–7, 759
Hilton International, 372
Hincley and Schmitt (includes Premier), 692
Hiram Walker, 434
Hitachi, 175, 538–9, 645
Hoechst Chemical, 215, 599
Holiday Inn, 551, 553, 555
Holland Aluminum, 562
Honda, 156, 165, 168, 215, 218, 628, 747
Honeywell, 79, 434
Hong Kong and Shanghai Bank, 305, 325
Hoover, 227
Howard Johnson's, 553
HP Cash (see Hewlett-Packard), 757
Huggy (see Unilever), 681
Hurco Cos., 746–7
Husqvarna, 227
Hutchison Whampoa, 39
Hyster Corp., 472, 791
Hyundai, 74, 604

Iberia, 64, 70
IBM (see International Business Machines)

ICI, 454
ICL, 450
I. G. Farben, 463
INCO, 776
Indiana Tube Corp. (includes Handy & Harman), 195
Industrial Association (Voroshilovgrad), 359
Industrial Bank of Japan, 319
Inland Steel, 195
Integrated Mill (Tuva), 359
Integrated Steel, 359
Interfood, 663–4
International Business Machines (IBM), 9, 79, 403, 447, 452, 469, 484, 495, 527, 620, 731, 756, 763, 780
International Harvester, 79
International Minerals and Chemicals, 562
International Nickel, 538
International Petroleum Company, 480
Internorth (see Northern Natural Gas), 566
Investment Canada, 434
Iran-Japan Petrochemical Co., 602
Iran National Petrochemical Industries Co. (IRNA), 602
Isuzu Motors Ltd., 167–8
Itoh, 451–2, 474, 586
ITT, 451–2, 474, 586
Iveco, 634

Jardine Matheson, 39, 42
Jeep (see Chrysler), 545–6
Jerrold Electronics, 426
Johnson & Johnson, 370, 487
Johnson Matthey, 599
Jordache, 490
Jovan (see Beecham Group)
Joyce Beverage Management, 691
J.P.D.C., 220
J. P. Morgan & Co., 323, 326

Kama River Truck, 359
KAO, 676
Kawasaki Heavy Industries, 539
Kellogg Rust, 556
Kellogg's (includes Nut n' Honey), 678
Kelvinator, 227
Kennecott Copper, 481
Kenner, 7, 9, 12, 17
Kentucky Fried Chicken, 554
Kia Motors, 167
Kidder Peabody, 328
Kikkoman, 686
Kings, 658–9
KitKat (see Rowntree), 612, 664

Kleenex, 682
Kleinwort Benson, 328
Kobe Steel, 195
Kodak, 370, 749–50, 777
Kokusai Securities, 328
Komatsu Ltd., 293, 296, 298, 583
Kongsberg, 368
Kopesik Engineering, 359
Kraft General Foods, 613
Kroenenbourg, 682
Kuschelweich (see Unilever), 681

Lada, 365
Ladeco, 555
Land Rover (see Rover Group Ltd.), 182
Lean Cuisine, 611, 672
Lenox China, 31
Leonard Petroleum, 219
Levant, 447
Levi Strauss, 366, 370, 678, 690
Libby's, 611–12
Lindt, 692
Lionel Trains, 217
Lite Beer (see Miller Brewing), 690
Liz Claiborne, 169
Lloyds Bank, 305
L. M. Ericsson (see Ericsson Telephone)
Lockheed, 358, 452, 778
LSI Logic Corp., 332–6
LTV, 195
Lucasfilm, 6, 7, 9, 15, 17

Maaza Mango (see Parle Exports), 495
McCann-Erickson, 370, 677
McDonald's (includes Big Mac, Donald McDonald, Ronald McDonald), 31, 343–7, 350–1, 359, 364, 372, 377, 487, 553, 554, 668, 680
McDonnell Douglas, 253–4
McGraw-Hill, 219
McNeill & Libby, 612
Magic Chef, 227
Magnavox, 537, 539
Makita Electric Works Ltd., 533
M & S (see Marks & Spencer)
Mannesmann, 317
Manufacturers Hanover Trust, 247, 323
Marathon (see Mars), 680
Marathon Oil, 195
Marks & Spencer (M & S) (includes St. Michael), 655–9
Mars (includes Marathon, Snickers, Whiskas), 664–5, 680
Marubeni Corp., 526–8, 535
Massey-Ferguson, 539

MasterCard, 767
Matsushita Electrical Industrial Co., 454, 731
Mattel (includes Barbie Doll, Cheerful Tearful Doll), 369, 670, 695, 749
Maytag, 227
Mazda (see Toyo Kogyo), 167–8
MCA, 33
Meineke Discount Mufflers, 553
Mercator, 370
Mercedes (see Daimler-Benz), 699
Merrill Lynch, 328
Messerschmitt-Boelkow-Blohm, 450
Mesta Machine, 18
Metropolitan Life, 336
Michelin, 9, 201, 454
Midland Bank, 473
Miller Brewing (includes Lite), 690
Mimosin (see Unilever), 681
Mister Donut, 31
Mitsubishi Bank, 319, 528
Mitsubishi Corp., 167–8, 435, 442, 456, 526–9, 583, 627, 701
Mitsubishi Petrochemical, 567
Mitsui, 527–8, 602–4
Mitsui Trading Company, 253, 526, 539
Mobil, 452, 464, 466, 474, 527
Moët-Hennessy, 446
Molex, 92
Montedison, 54, 567
Moran, Stahl & Boyer, 773, 801
Morgan Grenfell, 328
Morgan Stanley & Co., 328, 336
Motorola, 434, 624, 670
Mouton-Rothschild, 446
Murjani Merchandising, 546

Naarden, 207
Nathan's Famous Hot Dogs, 377
National Australia Bank, 326
National Cash Register (NCR), 668
Nat West (Bank), 319
NCNB (Bank), 326
NCR (see National Cash Register), 668
NEC Corp., 336
Nescafé (see Nestlé), 611, 680
Nestea (see Nestlé), 680
Nestlé, 9, 454, 609–13, 617–8, 620, 624, 626, 639, 663–4, 672, 679–81, 692, 749
New Japan Securities, 328
Nihon Semiconductor Inc., 336
Nike, 182, 369
Nikko Securities, 328
Nippon Kangyo Kakumaru, 328
Nippon Koban, 195
Nippon Life Insurance, 336

Nippon Telegraph and Telephone Public Corp. (NTT), 184
Nissan, 167
Nissho Iwai Corp., 527
Nixdorf, 450
Nobel, 212
Nomura Securities, 319, 327–8, 336
Norge, 227
Northern Natural Gas (includes Internorth), 566
Northern Petrochemical Co.(NPC), 566–7
Northern Telecom, 434
Norton Simon (includes Canada Dry), 691
Nova (see General Motors), 680
NPC (see Northern Petrochemical Co.)
NRM Steel, 177
NTT (see Nippon Telegraph)
Nucor, 195
Nut n' Honey (see Kellogg's), 678

Oasis Water, 693
Occidental Petroleum, 253, 465, 599
Okasan Securities, 328
O'Keefe's Hamburgers, 554
Oleg Cassini, 547
Olivetti, 312, 731–2, 734, 757
Oltremare Industria, 159
Olympus, 675
Organization Resource Counselors, Inc., 776
Oriental Land Company, 31
Oster (see Sunbeam), 681
Owens-Illinois, 777

Paine Webber, 328
PALMA (see Taurus), 380
PanAm, 358, 558, 680
Panasonic, 218
Paribas (Bank), 326, 369
Parker Kenner, 9
Parle Exports (includes Maaza Mango, ThumsUp), 495
Parris-Rogers International (PRI), 83–5, 87, 92
Payload Systems, 363
Pechiney, 558, 562
Peoples, 658
PepsiCo (includes Pepsi-Cola, Pizza Hut), 14, 212, 250, 253, 312, 346, 371, 494–8, 554, 679, 690, 693
Pepsi-Cola (see PepsiCo)
Perkits Yogurt, 553
Perrier (includes Source Perrier, Great Waters of France, Pschitt), 180, 681, 689–94
Peugeot, 391

Pfizer (includes Feldene), 491
Philco, 537, 539
Philips, 9, 227–8, 403, 450, 562
Phillips Petroleum, 566
Pierre Cardin, 547
Piper-Heidsieck, 446
Pittsburgh Plate Glass (PPG), 562
Pizza Hut (see PepsiCo), 14
Plessey, 207
Pohang Iron & Steel, 29, 194–5
Poland Spring, 690, 692
PPG (see Pittsburgh Plate Glass), 562
Premier (see Hincley & Schmitt), 692
Prentice-Hall, 729
PRI (see Parris-Rogers International)
Price Waterhouse, 427
Procter & Gamble, 7, 182, 370, 599, 619, 671, 674, 676
Pronuptia, 552
Prudential, 336
Prudential-Bache, 328, 336
Pschitt (see Perrier), 681
Pullman (includes Swindell-Dressler), 452
Pullman-Kellogg, 556
Pullman Swindell, 539
Punjab Agro Industries, 496

Quick, 554

Rambosa, 693
Reebok, 369
Renault, 391, 450, 560
Republic Steel, 195
Revere Copper and Brass, 479
Rexene (see Dart Industries), 566
Rio Tinto Zinc, 447
Ritz Crackers, 669
RJR Nabisco, 370
Rohm and Haas, 486, 738
Ronald McDonald (see McDonald's), 554
Rover Group Ltd. (includes Land Rover), 182
Rowenta (see Sunbeam), 681
Rowntree (includes KitKat), 612, 664
Royal Bank of Canada, 434
Royal Dutch Shell (see Shell Oil)

Saab Scandia, 221
Safeway Stores, 483
St. Gobain, 793
St. Michael (see Marks & Spencer), 655–6, 659
Saks Fifth Avenue, 547
Salomon Inc., 329
SAMI, 692
Samsung, 681
Sandoz, 454
Sanwa Bank, 319

Sanyo Securities, 328
Sara Lee, 483
SAS, 561
Schindler Group, 645
Schlumberger Ltd., 317, 334
Schweppes (see Cadbury
   Schweppes), 690
Schwinn, 366
Sears Roebuck, 110, 527, 562
Security Pacific Bank, 326
S. G. Warburg, 328
Shearson Lehman Hutton, 328
Shell Oil Co. (includes Royal Dutch
   Shell), 304, 317, 463–4, 527
Showa Denko, 562
Shveinaya, 359
Siemens, 317, 371, 450, 470, 649–50
Simpsons, 562
Singer Co., 146
Skandinaviska Enskilda Banken, 326
SKF Ball Bearing, 454, 666
Smith Corona, 515
Smith Kline Beecham, 317
Snickers (see Mars), 680
Snuggle (see Unilever), 681
SOCAL (see Standard Oil of
   California)
Solvay, 567
Sony, 9, 370
Source Perrier (see Perrier)
Standard Oil of California (SOCAL),
   464, 466, 481, 562
Standard Oil of New Jersey (see
   Exxon)
Standard Oil Trust (see Exxon), 463
Stanley Works, 442
Sterling Drug, 561
Stewart (see Sunbeam), 681
S. T. King, 666
Stora Kopparbergs Bergslags, 447
Stouffer, 612
Subaru, 167
Sumitomo Bank, 319, 327
Sumitomo Chemical Company, 562
Sumitomo Corporation, 527–8
Sunbeam (includes Cadillac, Oster,
   Stewart), 681

Suntory, 693
Suzuki Motors, 182
Sveriges Riksbank, 271
Swindell-Dressler (see Pullman)
Swire Group, 39, 42, 58
Swiss Bank Corp., 336

Tanner Companies, 363
Tappan, 227
Tata Industries, 496
Tattinger, 446
Taurus Hungarian Rubber Works
   (includes PALMA), 379, 381–3
Tecnotrade, 185
Telefunken, 450
Texaco, 464, 466, 481
Texas Air, 561
Therma, 227
Thompson Newspapers, 212
3M Co., 372, 634
ThumsUp (see Parle Exports), 495
Timken, 640
Tokuyama Soda, 449, 567
Toshiba, 368, 731
Toyo Kogyo (includes Mazda), 167–
   8, 510
Toyota, 167, 203, 215, 312, 473, 483,
   527–8, 676, 787
Transcorp Airways, 555
Tungsram, 357

Unilever (includes Cajoline,
   Coccolino, Huggy, Kuschelweich,
   Mimosin, Snuggle), 212, 630,
   681, 763, 773
Union Carbide, 491, 640
Uniroyal Goodrich, 201
United Airlines, 678
United Technologies, 454, 548
Universal Studios, 33
Uritsky, 359
USAir, 558
U.S. Steel (see USX), 195
USX, 194–5

Vauxhall Motors, 205
Vereinigte Aluminum Werke, 562

Vitro, 560
Vneshtorbank, 369
Volkswagen, 181, 215, 221, 317,
   391, 560, 596, 685
Volvic, 693
Volvo, 153, 454, 560
Vuiton, 491

Wako Securities, 328
Walt Disney Corporation (includes
   Disney, Disneyland,
   Disneyworld), 5, 31–3
Warnaco, 169
Warner Communications, 7, 79
Waterman Pens, 681
Wells Fargo Bank, 326
Western Electric, 546
Westin Hotels, 206
Westinghouse, 434, 447, 643–6, 774,
   780
Westinghouse Electric International
   Co., 644
Whirlpool, 227–8, 560
Whiskas (see Mars), 665
White Consolidated Industries, 227
White-Westinghouse, 227
Widmer and Ernst, 159
Wienerwald, 552
Wilkinson Sword, 447
Wimpy's, 552
W. R. Grace (includes Grace), 485
Wyandotte Chemical, 567

Xerox, 682

Yamaha, 538
Yamaichi Securities, 328
Yasuda Fire & Marine Insurance, 216
Young & Rubicam, 370
Yugo, 365

Zanussi, 227
Zephyr Hill, 693

NAME INDEX

Acuff, Frank L., 802
Adilman, Sid, 33
Adler, Nancy J., 118, 801
Aggarwal, Raj, 605, 803
Agnelli, G., 391
Aharoni, Yair, 604–5
Akhter, Alam, 758
Akhter, Pervaiz, 758
Akhter, Syed H., 758
al Burney, Mahmud, 81, 758
Alexandrou, Anthony G., 758
Aliber, Robert Z., 231
Allende, Salvador, 609
Alpert, Mark, 646, 695
Alsop, Robert, 697
Althaus, Dudley, 230
Ambrose, Saint, 110
Amsden, Alice H., 163
Anders, George, 385, 387, 570
Andrew, John, 196
Angus, Michael, 800–1
Ansbery, Clare, 199
Aquinas-Marx, Hector, 302
Arensberg, Conrad M., 120
Arizpe, Lourdes, 121
Armstrong, Adrienne, 459
Armstrong, Larry, 386, 647
Arnett, Nick, 339
Arnold, Bob, 804
Arnold, Ulli, 163
Arterian, Susan, 759
Arvay, Janos, 386
Asher, Brad, 758
Atiyas, Izak, 384
Augustine, Saint, 486
Awata, Keiske, 336
Axebank, Albert, 34
Ayal, Igal, 594, 606

Bach, Christopher, L., 34
Bacon, Kenneth H., 805
Bain, Trevor, 804
Bairstow, Frances, 803
Baker, Stephen, 81, 229–30, 429,
    534, 568, 695
Balassa, Bela, 161, 162, 229, 427
Ball, Robert, 646
Balliga, B. R., 648
Banai, Moshe, 800
Banker, Pravin, 605
Banks, John C., 498
Banks, Seymour, 696
Barmash, Isadore, 694
Barnathan, Joyce, 387
Barnes, R. Lynn, 802
Barnett, Donald F., 199
Barone, Michael, 80
Barringer, Felicity, 387
Bartlett, Christopher A., 646–7
Bata, Tom, 77–8
Baughn, C. Christopher, 568
Beamish, Paul W., 570
Beazley, J. Ernest, 198–9
Behrman, Jack N., 647
Behrman, Neil, 385, 428
Benelli, Giuseppe, 804
Berg, Eric, 499
Berg, Gerard, 199
Berger, Joan, 197
Berger, Louis, 570
Berger, Michael, 198
Berkowitz, Peggy, 458
Bernal, Richard, 459
Bernhard, Prince, 452
Best, Chris, 198
Bhagat, Rabi S., 120
Bhagwati, Jagdish N., 229

Bich, Marcel, 681
Bieber, Owen, 196
Black, Robert, 569
Black, Stewart, 801–2
Blackman, Ann, 383
Blanchflower, David, 803
Blank, Stephen, 605
Blaser, Fred, 429
Blebtreu, Herman K., 118
Blocklyn, Paul L., 799, 805
Blue, Jeffrey L., 802
Blunt, Peter, 121
Bochner, Stephen, 120
Boddewyn, Jean J., 198, 228, 500,
    607, 696
Boeke, J. H., 119
Bogert, Carroll, 80
Boissevain, Harry, 803
Bokos, William J., 759
Bomers, Gerald B. J., 804
Bonham-Yeaman, Doria, 501
Bonner, Raymond, 386
Borrus, Amy, 385, 387, 429
Bosnyak, Gyula, 387
Botto, Louis, 697
Boulton, N. R., 648
Bovard, James, 197
Bracker, Jeffrey, 231, 607
Bradford, Hazel, 197
Bradley, David G., 605–6
Bradsher, Keith, 385–6, 568
Brady, Rose, 385–7
Brady, Simon, 338
Brainard, William C., 337
Branch, C. B., 762
Brauchli, Marcus W., 338, 498
Breskin, Ira, 81
Brewer, Thomas L., 606

Bridgeman, Donna, 803
Briner, Ernst K., 729
Briones, Rodrigo, 337
Broad, William J., 162
Brooke, James, 199
Brooks, Geraldine, 118
Browning, E. S., 427, 460, 570, 697, 800
Brownlie, Ian, 499
Bryson, Bill, 120
Buckley, Peter J., 568
Buderi, Robert, 498
Buell, Barbara, 198, 337
Buhner, Rolf, 605
Burnham, Donald C., 644
Burns, Jane O., 758
Burton, Richard, 691
Bush, George, 405, 414, 423
Buss, Martin D. J., 648
Bussey, John, 799
Buzzell, Bradley T., 162
Buzzell, Robert D., 162
Byrne, Harlan S., 299

Caeser, Claudius, 125
Cagney, William F., 801
Cahn, Herbert, 606
Calloway, D. Wayne, 494
Calvet, A. L., 228
Campbell, Duncan C., 500, 804
Carlson, Eugene, 197, 387
Carlson, Robert S., 263
Carnevale, Mary Lu, 535
Carrigan, Edward, 458
Carrington, Tim, 385, 428, 460
Carson-Parker, John, 646
Carstairs, R. T., 568
Carter, Jimmy, 351
Casse, Pierre, 476
Casson, M., 229, 568
Cassoni, Vittorio, 731
Castro, Fidel, 220–1, 354
Cattin, Philippe, 230
Caudill, Lee M., 646
Caves, Richard E., 229, 604–5
Ceausescu, Nicolai, 361
Chakravarty, Subrata N., 501
Chan, Peng S., 569
Chandler, Clay, 338
Chase, Carmen D., 606
Chase, Dennis, 696
Chauhan, Ramesh, 496
Chenery, Hollis, 162
Chiba, Atsuko, 607
Child, J. D., 121
Chill, Dan S., 500
Chinta, Ravi R., 569
Chirac, Jacques, 63, 470
Cho, Kang Rae, 534, 569

Choate, Pat, 460
Choi, Frederick D. S., 648
Choi, Ying-pik, 428
Chrystal, K. Alec, 263
Chung, Hwa Soo, 428
Clark, Dick, 383
Clark, Evert, 197
Clark, Lindley H., Jr., 198
Clarke, Angela, 83–86, 118
Clarke, Gerald, 33
Clegg, Jeremy, 568
Clinkard, Anne P., 759
Cobb, Charles E., Jr., 535
Cochran, Philip L., 501
Cockfield, Lord, 396, 401
Cohen, Benjamin J., 647
Cohon, George A., 343, 346
Collier, Andrew, 694
Collison, Robert, 81
Comes, Frank J., 427, 498
Connelly, Mike, 569
Contractor, Farok J., 568
Cordova, Efrin, 803
Corley, T. A., 229
Corrigan, Wilfred, 334–6
Craig, C. Samuel, 694–5
Crandell, Robert W., 196
Crespy, Charles T., 500
Crock, Stan, 460, 647
Crookell, Harold, 458
Crosette, Barbara, 501, 694
Cuff, Daniel F., 646
Culbertson, John M., 197
Cullen, Robert, 384, 386
Culnan, M. J., 648
Cummings, L. L., 119, 121
Curry, Lynne, 387
Czechowicz, I. James, 648
Czinkota, Michael R., 697

D'Affisio, Ted, 498
Dagg, Alexander, 196
Dahl, Jonathan, 801
Daly, D. J., 458
Danforth, Douglas, 643, 645
Daniels, Anthony, 6
Daniels, John D., 231, 385, 570, 607, 647, 695, 697, 803
DaPonte, John J., Jr., 534
Dardis, Rachel, 196
Darlin, Damon, 646, 696
Darnton, Nina, 198
Darrow, Kenneth, 802
David, Kenneth, 120
Davidson, W. H., 568
Davis, Bob, 695
Day, Ellen, 604
Dayan, Raymond, 554
De Benedetti, Carlo, 731–2

de Cordoba, José, 428
de Gaulle, Charles, 233
De Klerk, F. W., 79
de Miraval, Margaret, 694
de Silva, Colin, 161
de Villafranca, Jill, 118
de Vos, Jan, 385, 387
Dean, Edwin, 803
Dean, James, 678
Debes, Cheryl, 501
DeCelles, Robert K., 758
Def Leppard, 371
Delors, Jacques, 401
Derkinderen, Frans G. J., 501
Desai, Moraji, 496
Desta, S., 606
Deutsch, Claudia H., 801
Deveny, Kathleen, 387, 569
Diaz Alejandro, Carlos F., 230
Diebold, John, 197
Disney, Roy E., 33
Disney, Walt, 32
Dissly, Megan, 427
Diugid, Lewis H., 231
Doan, Herbert Dow, 762
Dobbs, Michael, 34
Dolan, Carrie, 694
Dolezal, Tom, 758
Dollar, David, 161
Douglas, Susan P., 606, 694–5
Dowdell, Stephen, 694
Downs, James F., 118
Doyle, Frank P., 805
Doz, Yves, 229–30, 647, 695, 800
Drake, Robert L., 646
Drake, Rodman L., 605
Dreyfack, Kenneth, 119, 230
Dreyfuss, Tricia A., 383
Driscoll, Lisa, 697
Drucker, Peter F., 196, 384, 761, 803
Dryden, Steven J., 161, 386, 498, 804
DuBois, Peter C., 697
Ducat, Vivian, 129
Duerr, Michael G., 800
Dunn, Don, 802
Dunn, Sheryl W., 385
Dunning, John H., 34, 228–9, 458, 569

Early, P. Christopher, 802
Ebenstein, William, 46
Echikson, William, 231
Edström, Anders, 648, 800
Egelhoff, W. G., 647
Ehrenreich, Barbara, 803
Einstein, Albert, 130
Eisenhower, D. D., 464
Eiteman, David K., 263, 298, 338, 759

Eklund, Chrisopher S., 535
Elliott, Karen, 118
Ellis, H., 197
el-Qaddafi, Muammar, 465
Emerson, Ralph Waldo, 488
Emshwiller, John R., 570
Encarnation, Dennis J., 499
Enderwick, Peter, 803
Eng, Maximo, 335
Engardio, Pete, 80, 387
Engel, Ernst, 18
Engelberg, Stephen, 384
England, Wilbur B., 534
Erlanger, Stephen, 501
Errunza, Vihang R., 338
Estenssoro, Maria E., 651
Estey, John S., 460

Fabrichant, Geraldine, 34
Fagre, Nathan, 498
Fannin, William R., 646
Farmer, Richard N., 80, 118
Farnsworth, Clyde H., 197–8, 384,
    386–7, 429, 460
Farrell, Christopher, 384
Fatehi-Sedeh, K., 604
Fearon, Harold E., 534
Feder, Barnaby J., 162
Feinberg, Phyllis, 34
Feirabend, Ivo K., 606
Feirabend, Rosalind L., 606
Felber, John E., 384
Feldman, Joan M., 198
Ferrieux, Emmanuelle, 120
Fewkes, D. W., 569
Fialka, John J., 299, 386, 498
Field, Alan M., 568
Finnegan, Marcus B., 568
Fischer, William A., 647
Fisher, Carrie, 6
Fisher, Irving, 276, 281
Fisher, Lawrence M., 697
Flack, Stuart, 535
Flanagan, William H., 697
Flanders, M. June, 196
Flanigan, James, 568
Flowers, Edward B., 230
Ford, David, 568
Ford, Harrison, 6
Ford, Henry, II, 573
Ford, John, 695
Forman, Craig, 338
Fornasari, Angelo, 732
Forrestal, Michael V., 384
Foust, Dean, 501
Fox, Eleanor M., 460
Fox, Richard J., 604
Franklin, Benjamin, 689
Franklin, Daniel, 385
Franklin, S. G., 648

Franko, Lawrence G., 570
Freedman, Alix M., 696–7
Freeman, Alan, 429, 694
Freeman, John R., 81
Freeman, Richard, 803
French, Howard W., 384
Friedland, A. P., 386
Friedman, Kenneth, 118
Frons, Marc, 758
Fry, Earl H., 429
Fuentes, Annette, 803
Fulda, Carl H., 570
Fullerton, Kember, 119
Furnham, Adrian, 120

Galante, Steven P., 230, 571, 697
Galbraith, Jay R., 648, 800
Galuszka, Peter, 386
Gandhi, Indira, 496
Gandhi, Rajiv, 496
Gardini, Faul, 54
Garza family, 537
Gelston, Sally, 695
Gentil, Eduardo B., 803
George, Abraham M., 337
Gertsen, Martine, 801
Getschow, George, 570
Geyikdagi, N. V., 605
Geyikdagi, Y. M., 605
Ghiselli, Edwin, 119
Ghoshal, Sumantra, 646
Giddy, Ian H., 162, 337, 568
Giffen, James Henry, 384
Glasgall, William, 326, 337
Gledhill, David, 39
Glenn, E., 120
Glesgell, William, 428
Glover, Katherine, 120
Goad, G. Pierre, 695
Goar, Carol, 429
Goehle, Donna G., 646
Goizueta, Roberto C., 727
Gomez-Mejia, Luis R., 118
Goodnow, James D., 568
Gorbachev, Mikhail S., 49
Gordon, Michael R., 386
Gosling, Peter, 120
Grace, J. Peter, 485
Graham, Edward M., 459
Graham, John L., 499
Graham, Steven, 758
Grassman, Sven, 162
Graven, Kathryn, 119
Gray, Joan, 570
Grebner, Robert M., 33
Green, Robert T., 34, 162, 696
Greene, James, 800
Greenhouse, Linda, 801
Greenhouse, Steven, 35, 385–6, 569,
    651

Greising, David, 385
Grosse, Robert E., 228, 605
Grover, Ronald, 34
Grub, Philip D., 729
Guenther, Robert, 338
Guiles, Melinda Grenier, 196
Guiness, Alec, 6, 655
Guisinger, Stephen E., 499
Gumbel, Peter, 383–5, 387
Gunders, S., 118
Gupta, Sanjeev, 427
Gupta, Udayan, 339
Gutfeld, Rose, 460

Haberler, Gottfried, 196
Haberman, Clyde, 81, 229
Hackworth, Green H., 499
Hafner, Craig R., 118
Hagemann, Helmut, 759
Hagen, Everett E., 119
Haire, Mason, 119
Hall, Dwaine R., 570
Hall, Edward T., 120
Hamel, Gary, 648
Hamill, Mark, 6
Hamilton, Alexander, 170
Hammer, Armand, 371
Hammonds, Keith H., 607
Haner, E. T., 606
Hannibal, 691
Harari, Ehud, 800
Harfoush, Samira, 118
Harmetz, Aljean, 33
Harnett, D. L., 119
Harrell, Gilbert D., 604, 606
Harris, Dorothy L., 802
Harris, Philip R., 120, 801–2
Harrison, Bennett, 803
Harvey, Michael G., 501, 569, 802
Hawkins, David F., 648
Hawkins, Robert G., 230, 605–6
Hayashi, Kichiro, 535
Haydel, Belmont F., 500–1
Haynes, Ulrich, Jr., 802
Hays, Laurie, 385
Hays, Richard D., 800
Hazarika, Sanjoy, 649
Heckscher, Eli, 140, 141, 161
Hedlund, Gunnar, 647
Heenan, David A., 81
Heindel, Richard H., 460
Hekman, Christine R., 263
Helbling, Hans H., 298
Helfgott, Roy B., 804
Helyar, John, 196
Henneberry, David M., 459
Henzler, H., 803
Herberger, Roy A., 499
Herod, Roger, 805
Hertzberg, Daniel, 758

Hertzfeld, Jeffrey M., 383
Hicks, Jonathan P., 228
Hill, Frank Ernest, 604
Hill, G. Christian, 120, 338
Hill, John S., 695–6
Hilts, Philip J., 460
Hirsch, James S., 695
Hisey, Karen H., 604–5
Ho, Suk-ching, 683
Hoerr, John, 81, 803
Hoff, Edward J., 696
Hofstede, Geert, 119
Hogan, Paul, 678
Holliday, George D., 385, 387
Hollie, Pamela G., 500
Holstein, William J., 161, 429, 460, 647
Holton, Richard H., 570
Holusha, John, 229
Holzman, Franklyn, 385
Horowitz, Tony, 120, 387
Horst, Thomas, 229, 569
Houghton, James R., 647
House, Karen Elliott, 118
Houston, Pat, 461
Hout, Thomas, 605
Howard, Donald G., 695
Howard, Niles, 498
Howenstine, Ned G., 34
Hoxha, Enver, 149
Hudson, Richard L., 604, 804
Hufbauer, Gary C., 161, 198, 384
Hughes, Ann H., 429
Hughey, Ann, 696
Hussein, Saddam, 416, 419
Huszagh, Sandra M., 604
Hymer, Stephen H., 231
Hymowitz, Carol, 199

ibn-Saud, King, 464
Ibrahim, Youssef M., 607
Ignatius, Adi, 386
Ignatius, David, 118, 187
Izraeli, Dafna N., 800–1

Jackson, Michael, 494
Jacobs, Laurence, 696
Jaeger, Alfred M., 648, 800
Jamieson, Ian, 118, 121
Jardine, William, 39
Javetski, Bill, 198, 230
Jeannet, Jean-Pierre, 163
Jefferson, David J., 34
Jeffrey, Don, 383
Jelinek, Mariann, 801
Jensen, Robert C., 385
Jeon, Bang Nam, 337
Johansson, Johny K., 695
Johnson, Bill, 196
Johnson, Robert, 231

Jolibert, Alain, 230
Jones, James Earl, 6
Jones, Kent A., 198
Jones, Ronald W., 161
Junge, Georg, 385, 387
Justis, Robert T., 569

Kaikati, Jack G., 500
Kamm, Thomas, 427
Kanabayashi, Massayoshi, 803
Kane, M. J., 649
Kapoor, Ashok, 499, 500, 729
Kapstein, Jonathan, 81, 386, 427, 460, 498, 501, 695
Karlin, Beth, 570
Ka-Shing, Li, 39
Kassicieh, Suleiman K., 607
Katona, G., 119
Katz, Jan Hack, 648
Kavanaugh, Jonathan, 606
Kawahara, Yasushi, 528
Kaye, Lincoln, 501
Kaynak, Erdener, 387
Kazimirski, Marione, 759
Kedia, Ben L., 120
Keegan, Warren J., 81, 694
Keesing, Donald, 162
Keller, Bill, 383, 385
Keller, John J., 498, 758
Keller, Paul, 337
Keller, Robert T., 569
Kelly, Kevin, 299
Kelly, Marie E. Wicks, 605–6
Kemezis, Paul, 571
Kempe, Frederick, 386
Kenen, Peter, 161
Kennedy, J. F., 464
Keown, Charles, 696
Khalid, King S. M., 83
Khera, I., 803
Khomeini, Ayatollah, 603
Khoury, Sarkis, 230
Kiefer, Richard O., 604, 606
Kierzowski, Henry, 162
Killing, J. Peter, 670
Kilpatrick, James J., 196
Kim, H. Youn, 694
Kimura, Yui, 231
Kindleberger, Charles P., 196, 231
Kirkpatrick, David, 428
Knickerbocker, Frederick, 230
Knight, Robin, 162
Knudsen, Harold, 606
Knudsen, Harry R., 534
Kobrin, Stephen J., 570, 800
Kocsis, Györgyi, 387
Koenig, Richard, 197
Kohl, Helmut, 49, 470
Kojima, K., 230
Kopits, G. F., 569

Koretz, Gene, 803
Kostecka, A., 569
Kotabe, Masaaki, 163, 229, 459, 498, 534–5
Kotlowitz, Alex, 299
Kottak, Conrad Phillip, 33
Köves, András, 384
Kraar, Louis, 429, 501
Kraljic, Peter, 384–5
Kramer, Hugh E., 694
Kramer, Robert J., 570
Kravis, Irving B., 605
Krisher, Bernard, 228–9
Krislov, Joseph, 803
Kristof, Nicholas D., 570
Krueger, Anne O., 161
Krugman, Paul, 161, 459
Kuhle, James L., 606
Kujawa, Duane, 804
Kuttner, Robert, 163

Labbe, Paul, 434
Lachica, Eduardo, 196–7, 338, 386, 459
Laderman, Jeffrey M., 338
Lall, Sanjaya, 229–30
Landau, Nilly, 759
Landauer, Jerry, 460
Landauer, Thomas K., 118
Landler, Mark, 697
Landro, Laura, 729
Lane, Henry W., 570
Langeard, Eric, 696
La Palombara, Joseph, 605
Lau, Ho-fuk, 683
Laurent, André, 121
Lauter, Geza Peter, 119
Leber, Steven, 371
Lebow, Joan, 461
Lecraw, Donald J., 428
Lederer, Bob, 697
Lee, Dinah, 387
Lee, Eve, 118
Leenders, Michael, 534
Lees, Francis A., 337
Lehner, Urban C., 119, 800
LeMoyne, James, 118
Lenin, Vladimir, 347
Lentz, Ellen, 571
Leontiades, James, 647, 695
Leontief, Wassily W., 141, 144, 161
Lessard, Donald R., 569
Lethbridge, David, 80
Letovsky, Robert, 197
Leung, Julia, 607
Levin, Doran P., 196
Levin, Gustave, 690
Levine, Jonathan B., 337
Levi-Strauss, Claude, 6
Lewis, Bernard, 120

Lewis, Paul, 81, 501
Lewis, Peter, 34
Lewis, W. Arthur, 196
Light, Larry, 802
Lin, Jia-Yeong, 196
Lincoln, James R., 119
Linder, Stefan B., 162
Lindsay, W. M., 648
Lindsey, Brink, 198
Linton, Ralph, 118
Liotard-Vogt, Pierre, 609
Lipman, Joanne, 696
Lipschitz, Leslie, 427
Lipsey, Robert E., 605
Lissitzyn, Oliver J., 499
Litka, Michael, 80
Litvak, Isiah A., 804
Locke, William W., 695
Loderer, Claudio, 804
Lodge, G. C., 163
Loeber, D. A., 386
Lohnes, Coleen, 230
Loi, Riccardo, 758
Lopez Portillo, José, 538
Lorange, Peter, 568, 800
Lorenz, Christopher, 568
Love, John F., 383
Lublin, Joann S., 34, 231, 398, 400,
    570, 694, 801–2
Lucas, George, 5, 6
Lundberg, Erik, 162
Lundeen, Robert, 762
Lutz, James M., 162
Lynch, Mitchell C., 458
Lynn, Matthew, 648
Lys, Thomas, 804

Maas, Pablo, 758
MacArthur, Douglas, 526
MacCharles, D. C., 458
MacDonald, Philip, 535
MacKay, Gillian, 33
MacLeish, Kenneth, 162
Madonna, 494
Maehr, M. L., 119
Magee, John F., 427
Magee, Stephen P., 161, 229
Magill, Sharon L., 570
Magnusson, Paul, 198, 460
Main, Jeremy, 802
Maital, Shlomo, 570, 697
Malcolm, Andrew H., 695
Maljers, F. A., 648
Mandela, Nelson, 79
Mann, Dean, 46
Manoochehri, G. H., 535
Mansfield, Edwin, 569
Marcial, Gene G., 498
Marcom, John, Jr., 35, 500, 696
Maremont, Mark, 34, 569, 607

Marer, Paul, 373, 383–7
Marian, Nicolas, 428
Mark, Jeremy, 696
Maroff, John, 197
Maronick, Thomas J., 501
Marshall, Alan, 605
Marston, David W., 460
Martin, Douglas, 805
Marx, Karl, 48, 49, 347
Mascarenhas, Briance, 229, 231, 605,
    648
Maslow, Abraham, 96, 119
Mason, R. Hal, 499
Mason, Todd, 501
Mastanduno, Michael, 386
Masterson, Bob, 800
Matheson, James, 39
Matthew, Lynn, 800
Maucher, Helmut, 612
Maule, Christopher J., 804
Mauriel, V., 648
May, Roger B., 697
Mayer, Thomas, 427
Mazzolini, Renato, 231, 460
McCaffrey, James, 118
McCarthy, Michael J., 501, 695, 697
McClelland, David C., 119
McColm, R. Bruce, 81
McDowell, Edwin, 799
McElheny, Victor K., 162
McFetridge, D.G., 568
McGill, Douglas C., 697
McInnes, J. M., 648
McIsaac, G., 803
McMahon, Ed, 692
McNamee, Mike, 298
Medina, David D., 802
Meier, Barry, 697
Melcher, Richard A., 337, 385, 427,
    804
Mendenhall, Mark E., 800–2
Mendez, José A., 199
Menzies, Hugh D., 649
Merrill, Giles, 198
Merszei, Zoltan, 761
Mervosh, Edward, 758
Meyer, Herbert E., 458
Meyers, William H., 569
Millar, Bill, 758–9
Miller, James P., 231
Miller, Joseph C., 231, 606
Miller, Myron M., 697
Milner, Brian, 458
Milner, Helen V., 198
Mintz, Norman, 605
Mitchell, Cynthia F., 461
Mitchell, Daniel J. B., 162
Mitterrand, François, 63
Moffett, Matt, 568
Mohr, Iris, 198

Molotsky, Irvin, 460
Montand, Yves, 32
Montgomery, James M., 384
Moore, Elizabeth, 458
Moran, Robert T., 120
Morano, Louis, 498
Moreton, Edwina, 385
Morgan, Theodore, 196
Morgenstern, Felice, 803
Morrison, Alan J., 647
Morrison, Ann V., 198
Mossadegh, Mohammed, 464
Mossberg, Walter S., 386, 461
Mourdoukoutas, P., 803
Moyer, Reed, 694
Mufson, Steve, 81
Mullor-Sebastian, Alicia, 162
Mulroney, Brian, 431
Mummery, David R., 499
Murdock, George P., 118
Murphy, Bob, 800
Murray, Alan, 384
Murray, Alice Haller, 802
Murray, F. T., 802
Murray, J. Alex, 648, 801
Murugasu, P., 161
Mydans, Seth, 162
Myers, Frederick Shaw, 694

Nagaoka, Sadao, 384
Nagashima, A., 230
Nagourney, Steven H., 296
Nares, Peter, 651
Nash, Manning, 120
Nassar, Jamal R., 607
Naylor, Thomas H., 649
Nazario, Sonia L., 535
Neff, Robert, 34
Nehrt, Lee C., 606
Nelson, Mark M., 197, 800
Neuburger, Hugh, 694
Neumann, Edward, 758–9
Nevins, Alan, 604
Nevins, Bruce, 690, 692
Newman, Barry, 385, 428, 696, 802,
    804
Newman, Peter C., 81
Nicholls, J. G., 119
Nickerson, David, 230
Nicolaides, Phedon, 198
Niehoff, Arthur H., 120
Nigh, Douglas, 501, 606
Nixon, Richard, 270
Noble, Carl, 606
Nodar, Andrew L., 729
Noer, David M., 801
Noga, Edward, 228

Oberg, Kalervo, 120
O'Boyle, Thomas F., 34, 198–9, 801

Ocampo, José Antonio, 162
Oddou, Gary R., 800–2
O'Faircheallaigh, Ciaran, 459
Ohlin, Bertil, 140, 141, 161, 230
Ohmae, Kenichi, 428, 604–5, 651
Oleson, Larissa, 386
Oliver, Brian, 694
Omestad, Thomas, 459
Omura, Glenn S., 229, 534
Ondrack, Daniel, 800
Onkvisit, Sak, 696
Ono, Yumiko, 34, 196, 570, 695, 697
Opack, Jerry H., 569
Oreffice, Paul, 761
O'Reilly, Brian, 230
Orr, D., 229
Osborn, Richard N., 568
O'Shaugnessy, Hugh, 568
Otten, Alan L., 231
Otterbeck, Lars, 570
Overholt, William H., 80
Owens, Cynthia, 338
Ozawa, Terutomio, 231

Pacifico, Anubis, 569–70
Paguolatos, Emilio, 459
Pahlavi, Shah Reza, 464, 603
Palmquist, Bradley, 802
Passow, Sam, 801
Patterson, Gregory A., 568
Pauly, David, 228
Pazy, Asya, 800, 802
Pear, Robert, 384, 386
Pearce, Richard D., 647
Peccei, R., 803
Pemberton, J. S., 727
Pennar, Karen, 197
Perkins, Dwight H., 384, 386
Perry, George L., 337
Petersen, Donald E., 391
Peterson, Richard B., 119, 804
Peterson, Thane, 498, 500, 758
Pfaff, Carolyn, 697
Phatak, Arvind, 649
Philippatos, George C., 605–6
Phillipps, Carolyn, 802
Picard, Jacques, 646
Pines, Burton Yale, 500
Piol, Elserino, 731
Pitts, Robert A., 647
Plattner, Marc F., 80
Pluenneke, John, 569
Poe, Richard, 387
Pollack, Andrew, 386, 498
Polo, Marco, 16, 125
Popoff, Frank P., 761
Porter, Lyman, 119
Porter, Michael E., 162, 229, 534, 605
Portillo, José Lopez (see Lopez
    Portillo)

Potempa, Lou, 571
Powell, William J., Jr., 694
Prager, Allan J., 605
Prahalad, C. K., 647–8, 800
Pras, Bernard, 231, 606
Prebisch, Raul, 196
Preble, John F., 606
Prial, Frank J., 459, 696
Pritchett, C. Herman, 46
Prokesch, Steven, 570, 604, 697
Provissiero, Michael, 605
Prowse, David, 6
Pucik, Vladimir, 648
Pura, Raphael, 428
Purushothaman, Shoba, 197

Quelch, John A., 696

Rachid, Rosalind, 428
Radebaugh, Lee H., 385, 429, 705
Radler, Albert J., 729
Rahman, M. Z., 228
Rajakarunanayake, Lucien, 161
Rajapatirana, Sarath, 161
Ramirez, Anthony, 501, 697
Randolph, Benton, 648
Rau, Pradeep A., 606
Reagan, Ronald, 351
Reaves, Lynne, 80
Reed, Stanley, 460
Regan, Gerald, 433
Rehder, Robert R., 119
Reich, Robert B., 161
Reichel, Arie, 606
Reichlin, Igor, 385, 387
Reinhold, Robert, 197
Reitsperger, Wolf, 804
Remmers, H. Lee, 263
Revzin, Philip, 384–6, 427
Reynolds, Lloyd G., 196
Reynolds, Morgan O., 196
Reyser, Jeffrey, 198
Ricardo, David, 136, 139, 140, 161
Richardson, Michael, 696
Richman, Barry M., 80, 118
Ricks, David A., 649
Riding, Alan, 569
Robbins, Sidney M., 758
Robock, Stefan H., 535
Rodes, Susan, 535
Rodrigues, Arvin F., 646
Roessler, Frieder, 198
Rogers, David, 197
Rogers, Will, 475
Rolling Stones, 371
Ronen, Simcha, 105
Ronkainen, Ilkka A., 501, 569
Ronstadt, Robert, 570
Root, Franklin R., 800
Rose, Robert L., 299

Rosenbloom, Bert, 697
Rosewicz, Barbara, 197
Rossant, John, 498, 758, 804
Rossiter, D. Raik, 802
Rossman, Marlene L., 801
Roth, K., 647
Roth, Terrence, 387, 759
Roussant, John, 697
Rout, Lawrence, 229, 263
Rowan, Hobart, 386
Rowan, Richard L., 500, 804
Rubinfien, Elisabeth, 384, 461
Rudden, Eileen, 605
Rue, L. W., 648
Rugman, Alan M., 229, 231, 568
Rundle, Rhonda L., 35
Ryan, Chris, 568
Ryan, William T., 501
Ryser, Jeffrey, 81, 696, 802

Sachs, Jeffrey, 384–5
Sada family, 537
Sadanad, Venkatraman, 230
Saddler, Jeanne, 570
Safizadeh, M. H., 604
Salinas de Gortari, Carlos, 261–2,
    425
Salmans, Sandra, 694
Sambharya, Rakesh B., 649
Samiee, Saeed, 648, 695
Sanger, David E., 80
Saporito, Bill, 535
Sarathy, Ravi, 198
Saunders, John, 426, 429, 535
Schaffer, Robert P., 534
Schares, Gail E., 80, 384, 387
Scharp, Anders, 227
Schiller, Zachary, 228, 429, 646
Schlesinger, Jacob M., 198–9
Schmidt, R. D., 384
Schmitt, Richard B., 336
Schneider, Keith, 460
Schodolski, Vincent J., 383
Scholl, Wolfgang, 804
Schooler, Robert D., 230
Schorsch, Louis, 199
Schreffler, Roger, 228
Schrenk, Martin, 428
Schroeder, Michael, 501
Schwartz, Warren F., 570
Schwarzenberger, George, 499
Schweiger, D., 647
Scott, George M., 648
Scott, J. T., 229
Sease, Douglas R., 696
Seefelder, Matthias, 567
Segall, Marshall H., 118
Seham, Martin C., 804
Seib, Gerald F., 500
Selz, Michael, 569

Seringhaus, F. H. Rolf, 197
Servern, A., 231
Sesit, Michael R., 338
Sethi, S. Prakash, 500
Shah of Iran (see Pahlavi)
Shakespeare, William, 16, 17
Shale, Tony, 535
Shao, Maria, 161, 386, 696
Sharma, Soumitra, 385
Shaw, John J., 696
Sheba, Queen of, 125
Shellenbarger, Sue, 500
Shenkar, Oded, 105, 802
Sherr, Alan B., 386
Shihata, Ibrahimn F. I., 499
Siddharthan, N. S., 229–30
Siefert, Bruce, 695
Sim, A. B., 648, 800
Simon, Denis Fred, 387
Sinbad, 125
Singer, H. W., 385
Singh, Ajay, 501
Singh, V. P., 497
Skrzycki, Cindy, 460
Sleuwaegen, Leo, 568
Slocum, Ken, 534
Smale, John G., 607
Smith, Adam, 132, 136, 140, 161
Smith, Aimety Dunlap, 646, 695
Smith, Timothy K., 729
Snape, R. H., 198
Sneider, Daniel, 428
Sohng, S. N., 803
Solomon, Jolie, 801
Solomon, King, 125
Sood, James H., 696
Spaeth, Anthony, 501
Spence, A. M., 229
Srivastava, Rejendra K., 162
Stavro, Barry, 299
Staw, B. M., 121
Stein, Herbert, 233
Stein, Philip J., 605
Stephens, Gregory K., 801–2
Stertz, Bradley A., 387
Stevens, D. J., 119
Stewart, Frances, 162
Stewart, James B., 500
Still, Richard R., 695–6
Stobaugh, Robert B., Jr., 605, 758
Stockton, William, 120
Stoever, William A., 499, 500, 651
Stokes, Houston H., 694
Stone, Russell A., 459
Stonehill, Arthur I., 263, 298, 338, 759
Streeten, Paul, 81, 162, 569
Stricharchuk, Gregory, 228, 649
Strumpel, B., 119

Sudweeks, Bryan Lorin, 338
Sultaw, Gale, 162
Sultaw, Ralph G. M., 163
Sunkel, Osvaldo, 647
Sviridov, F. A., 570
Swamidass, Paul M., 534
Swasy, Alicia, 695–6
Sweeney, Louise, 33
Swire, John, 39
Symonds, William C., 758
Symons, Gladys L., 801

Taggiasco, Ronald, 428
Tagliabue, John, 387
Tannenbaum, Jeffrey A., 383, 568–9
Tanner, James, 428
Tavlas, George S., 298
Teece, David J., 229
Tefft, Sheila, 501
Telegdy, Stephen, 387
Tell, Laurence J., 459
Tellez, Theresa, 162
Templeman, John, 198, 230, 387, 804
Templin, Neal, 198
Terpstra, Vern, 120
Terry, Edith, 429
Thackray, John, 695
Tharp, Mike, 228, 570
Thatcher, Margaret, 41, 47, 63, 83, 274, 356, 402, 656
Therrien, Lois, 646
Thomas, James, 803
Thomas, Michael J., 162
Thompson, Anne, 33
Thorelli, Hans B., 119, 120, 695
Thornhill, Virgil, 606
Thorton, Grant, 427
Thurow, Roger, 196
Ting, Wenlee, 34
Tolchin, Martin, 461, 499
Tolchin, Susan, 461, 499
Toll, Erich E., 383
Toman, Barbara, 804
Townsend, J., 459
Toy, Stewart, 34, 697
Treece, James B., 228, 427, 647
Treiman, Donald, 119
Trembly, Susan, 33
Tretter, Marietta J., 647
Triandis, Harry C., 119, 120
Trucco, Terry, 34
Trudeau, Pierre, 431
Truell, Peter, 196–7, 199, 338, 500
Truitt, J. F., 605
Truman, Harry S., 464
Tucker, M. H., 802
Tully, Sharon, 231
Tully, Shawn, 427

Tung, Rosalie L., 802
Turner, Graham, 646
Turner, Henry A., 46
Turner, Ian, 647
Turner, Roger, 535
Tyman, J. H. P., 163

Uchitelle, Louis, 231, 459, 570, 800
Uhes, M., 802
Urquhart, John, 458

Vachani, Suchil, 499
Vaitsos, Claudio V., 569
Vallely, Jean, 33
Van Den Bulcke, Daniel, 647
Van Pachterbeke, Marie-Anne, 647
Van Veen, Pieter, 387
Vecsenyi, János, 387
Verne, Jules, 16, 32
Vernon, Raymond, 161, 230, 498–9
Verzariu, Pompiliu, 254–5, 263
Vielvoye, Robert, 607
Vincent, Jacques, 693
Vineberg, Gary, 81
Viner, Jacob, 233
Vlachoutsikos, Charalambos, 387
Vogel, E. F., 163
Vogel, Todd, 460
Von Furstenberg, George M., 337

Wain, Barry, 500
Walcott, John, 386
Walker, Dean, 81
Wallace, Don, Jr., 500
Wallace, Laura, 198
Walmsley, Julian, 262, 298
Walsh, Mary Williams, 119
Walsh, Maureen, 461
Walter, Ingo, 198, 261
Walther, Carl H., 606
Waring, David C., 800
Warner, Joan, 535
Warner, M., 803
Warren, Neil, 119
Wartzman, Rick, 199
Watson, Craig M., 605
Wayne, Leslie, 196
Webber, Ross A., 119–120
Weber, J. A., 460, 695
Weber, Max, 94, 119
Weigand, Robert, 230, 499
Weiner, Elizabeth, 81, 459, 607
Weiner, Steven, 694
Weisman, Steven R., 501
Weitz, John, 658
Welch, L. S., 568–70
Wells, Louis T., Jr., 34, 498
Wesson, Robert, 80
Westbrook, Christine, 386

Westerman, Martin, 697
Wetter, Gillis, 499
Wheatcroft, Patience, 694
Wheeler, David R., 696
White, Helen, 500
White, Joseph B., 196
White, Rene, 696
White, Timothy, 33
Whitehead, Don, 799
Whiting, J. M. W., 118
Whorf, Benjamin Lee, 120
Wilkins, Mira, 604
Williams, Christine L., 119
Williams, Lorna V., 118
Williams, Mina, 694
Willis, Rod, 801

Wilson, R. J., 163
Wind, Yoram, 606
Wiseman, Paul, 338
Wokutch, Richard E., 501
Wolf, Charles, Jr., 384
Wolfe, Joseph, 387
Wolff, Carlo, 34
Woodruff, David, 230, 429
Worthley, Reginald, 696
Woytinski, E. S., 25
Woytinski, W. S., 25
Wren, Christopher S., 385
Wrubel, Robert, 34

Yang, Dori Jones, 387, 569
Yang, Jonghoe, 459

Yoder, Stephen Kreider, 459
Yoffie, David B., 198
Yoshino, M. Y., 230
Young, Andrew, 556
Young, Stephen, 568
Youssef, Samir M., 648, 802

Zahn, E., 119
Zaichkowsky, Judith I., 696
Zeeman, John R., 696
Zeira, Yoram, 800, 802
Zellner, Wendy, 429, 803
Zif, Jehiel, 594, 606
Zonderman, Jon, 386

MAP INDEX

(Map Index refers to maps in the color insert.)

Country	Map 1	Map 2	Map 3	Map 4	Map 5	Map 6	Map 7
Afghanistan	E11		E4				
Albania	E9			H6			
Algeria	E9	B3					
Angola	G9	G4					
Argentina	H6						G4
Australia	H14					D4	
Austria	D9			G5			
Bahrain			E3				
Bangladesh	F12		F5				
Belgium	D9			F4			
Belize	D9				H6		
Benin	F9	D3					
Bhutan	E13		F5				
Bolivia	G6						D4
Botswana	H10	H5					
Brazil	G6						C6
Bulgaria	E10			H7			
Burkina Faso	F8	D2					
Burundi	G10	F6					
Cambodia	F13		G6				
Cameroon	F9	D4					
Canada	D4				D4		
Central African Rep.	F9	D5					
Chad	F9	C5					
Chile	H5						F4
China	E13		E6				

Country	Map 1	Map 2	Map 3	Map 4	Map 5	Map 6	Map 7
Colombia	F5						B3
Congo Rep.	G9	E4					
Costa Rica	F5				I7		
Côte d'Ivoire	F8	D2					
Cuba	F5				H7		
Curaçao							A4
Cyprus	E10						
Czech. & Slovak Fed. Rep.	D9			F6			
Denmark	D9			E4			
Djibouti	F10	D7					
Dominican Rep.	F5				H8		
Ecuador	G5						C2
Egypt	E10	B6					
El Salvador	F5				I6		
Ethiopia	F9	D7					
Falkland Islands	I6						I5
Finland	C10			C7			
France	D9			G3			
French Guiana	F6						B6
Gabon	G9	E4					
Gambia	F8	C1					
Germany, Fed. Rep.	D9			F5			
Ghana	F8	D2					
Greece	E9			H7			
Greenland	A7				A7		
Guatemala	F4				I6		
Guinea	G9	D1					
Guinea-Bissau	F8	D1					
Guyana	F6						B5
Haiti	F5				H8		
Honduras	F5				I7		
Hong Kong	F14		F7				
Hungary	D9			G6			
Iceland	C8			B1			
India	F12		F5				
Indonesia	G14		H7			B3	
Iran	E11		E3				
Iraq	E10		D3				
Ireland	D8			E2			
Israel	E10		D2				
Italy	E9			H5			

Country	Map 1	Map 2	Map 3	Map 4	Map 5	Map 6	Map 7
Jamaica	F5				H7		
Japan	E15		D8				
Jordan	E10		D2				
Kenya	G10	E7					
Korea, North	E14		D7				
Korea, South	E14		D8				
Kuwait	E11		E3				
Laos	F13		F6				
Lebanon	E10		D2				
Lesotho	H10	H6					
Liberia	F8	D2					
Libya	E9	B4					
Luxembourg	D9			F4			
Madagascar	G11	G8					
Malawi	G10	G6					
Malaysia	F13		H6				
Mali	F8	C2					
Malta	E9			I5			
Mauritania	F8	C1					
Mexico	F4				H5		
Mongolia	D13		D6				
Morocco	E8	B2					
Mozambique	H10	G6					
Myanmar	F13		F6				
Namibia	H9	G4					
Nepal	E12		F5				
Netherlands	D9			F4			
New Zealand	H16					H8	
Nicaragua	F5				I7		
Niger	F9	C4					
Nigeria	F9	D3					
Norway	C9			C5			
Oman	F11		F3				
Pakistan	E12		E4				
Panama	F5				I8		
Papua New Guinea	G15					B6	
Paraguay	H6						E5
Peru	G5						D3
Philippines	F14		F8				
Poland	D9			F6			
Portugal	E8			H1			
Puerto Rico	F6						

Country	Map 1	Map 2	Map 3	Map 4	Map 5	Map 6	Map 7
Qatar	F11		E3				
Romania	D10			G7			
Rwanda	G10	E6					
Saudi Arabia	F9		E2				
Senegal	F8	C1					
Sierra Leone	F8	D1					
Singapore	G13		H6				
Solomon Is.	G15					B8	
Somalia	F11	D8					
South Africa	H10	H5					
Spain	E8			H2			
Sri Lanka	F12		F5				
Sudan	F10	D6					
Suriname	F6						B5
Swaziland	H10	H6					
Sweden	C9			C5			
Switzerland	D9			G4			
Syria	E10		D2				
Taiwan	F14		F8				
Tanzania	G10	F6					
Tasmania	I15					G6	
Thailand	F13		G6				
Togo	F9	D3					
Trinidad and Tobago							A5
Tunisia	E9	A4					
Turkey	E10		D2				
Uganda	G10	E6					
United Arab Emirates	F11		E3				
United Kingdom	D8			E3			
United States	E4				F4		
Uruguay	H6						E5
USSR (now CIS)	C13		C6	D8			
Vanuatu						C9	
Venezuela	F6						B4
Vietnam	F13		F7				
Western Sahara	F8	B1					
Yemen, Rep.	F11		F2				
Yugoslavia	E9			G6			
Zaire	G10	E5					
Zambia	G10	G5					
Zimbabwe	G10	G6					

SUBJECT INDEX

Absolute advantage (also see Comparative cost), 129, 132–136, 138–139
Accounting differences, 708
Accounting harmonization, 707–709
Acquired advantage, 133
Acquired group membership, 91
Acquisition, 206–207, 221, 222, 444, 608, 612–613, 639, 681
Active income, 717
Administratively guided market economy, 355
ADR (see American Depository Receipt)
Ad valorem duty, 180
Advanced Determination Ruling (ADR), 740
Advertising, 677–678
African Development Bank, 410
Age-based groups, 92–93
Agricultural Foreign Investment Disclosure Act, 457
Aid, 479–480
American Depository Receipt (ADR), 317
ANCOM, 482
Andean group, 393, 405
Anthropology, 15
Antitrust, 447
Appearance, 89
Appropriability theory, 206
Appropriate technology, 781–782
Arab boycott, 446, 482–483
Arab League (see League of Arab States)
Arbitrage, 257
Area division structure (see Geographic division structure), 623–624

Arrangement Regarding International Trade in Textiles, 413–414
Ascribed group membership, 91
Asian Development Bank, 21
Association of South East Asian Nations (ASEAN), 408–409

Back-to-back loan, 305
Balance of payments, 67–68, 174–175, 284–289, 438–441
Balance of trade (see Balance of payments, Merchandise trade balance)
Balance of trade deficit (see Deficit)
Balance of trade surplus (see Surplus)
Balance on goods and services (see Balance of payments)
Bank for International Settlements, 276, 319
Banks, 319–327
Bargaining (see Variable prices)
Barter, 253–254, 369–370
Base currency, 240
Basic balance, 287–288
Basket of currencies, 269, 271
Bid rate (foreign exchange), 240
Big Bang, 315
Bilateral agreements, 478–479
Bilateral treaties, 447
Bill of lading, 512
BIRPI (see International Bureau for the Protection of Industrial Property)
Black market, 251, 275
Blocs, 20
Body language, 102
Bonds, 310–312
Booking centers, 313

Brain drain, 432
Branch, 640
Branch (bank), 320
Branding, 680–682
Bretton Woods, 268, 270
Bribery, 451–453
Brokers (foreign exchange), 244, 247
Budget, 611, 637
Buffer stock, 411
"Buy-Local," 184
Buy-versus-build (also see Acquisitions), 221–222

CACM (see Central American Common Market)
Canada-U.S. Free Trade Agreement (see U.S.-Canada Free Trade Agreement)
Capacity, 153, 212
Capitalist, 52
Capital market (see Equity market)
Career, 772–774
Caribbean Community and Common Market (CARICOM), 393, 406
CARICOM (see Caribbean Community and Common Market)
Cartel, 447
Cash management, 736–738
Central American Common Market (CACAM), 393, 405
Central Banks, 276
Centralization, 611, 614–620
Centrally planned economy (see also Historically planned economy), 54, 58
Certificate of Deposit, 309
Change, 109–112
CHIPS (see Clearing House Interbank Payment System)

City of London, 315
Civil law, 43–44
Civil liberties, 50
Class structure, 93, 97–98
Clearing House Interbank Payment
  System (CHIPS), 323
CMEA (see COMECON)
COCOM (see Coordinating
  Committee on Multilateral
  Export Controls)
Codes of conduct, 483–484
Codetermination, 787–788
Codified law, 43–44, 490
Collective bargaining, 790–793
COMECON, 348, 362–363, 365
Command economy, 52, 54
Commercial bank (see Banks)
Commercial paper, 304
Commission agent, 525
Commodities, 150–151, 364, 410–
  416, 608
Commodity agreements, 410–416
Common Agricultural Policy (EC),
  396
Common law, 43, 490
Common market, 393
Communications, 100–102
Communism, 47–49
Company bargaining strength, 469–
  470
Comparative advantage, 129, 136–
  139
Comparative cost, 216–217
Compensation, 611, 775–778, 783
Compensatory trade, 253–255
Competence, 91, 617–618
Competition, 595
Competition (effect on operating
  form), 542, 547–548
Competitive risk, 584
Complete economic integration, 393
Composite currency, 271
Compound duty, 180
Concentration strategy, 593–596
Consolidation, 711
Consortium, 370, 450, 482, 484,
  558, 562
Consortium bank, 320–321
Consumer-directed market economy,
  354–355
Consumer sovereignty, 53
Continental terms (see European
  terms)
Contract problems, 547–548, 554
Contractual arrangements, 563
Control, 205–206, 540, 543, 547–
  548, 608–646, 764, 769–770
Controlled Foreign Corporation
  (CFC), 717–719
Convertibility, 363–364

Convertibility of foreign exchange,
  250–251
Convertible bond, 311
Cooperative arrangements, 371–372
Cooperative exchange agreements,
  273
Coordinating Committee on
  Multilateral Export Controls
  (COCOM), 367
Coordinating mechanisms, 626
Copyrights, 490, 492
Corporate culture, 634–635
Correspondent relations, 320, 369–
  370
Cost, 541, 581–582, 615–636, 669–
  670, 686–687, 785
Cost-of-living adjustment, 775–777
Council for Mutual Economic
  Assistance (CMEA or
  COMECON), 406–408
Counterfeit (see Piracy)
Countertrade, 185, 254
Country evaluation, 572–607
Country similarity theory, 129, 147–
  148, 544, 579–581
Country size (theory of), 129, 135–
  136
CPE (see Centrally planned economy,
  Historically planned economy)
Cross-licensing, 545
Cross-rate (foreign exchange), 242
Cultural adaptation, 770–771, 779
Culture, 83–118, 474–475, 668,
  682–684
Culture shock, 104
Currency value (related to price),
  673–675
Currency values (as explanation of
  direct investment), 216–217, 223
Current account balance, 286, 288
Current rate method (translation of
  financial statements), 712–714
Customers (as motive for direct
  investment), 215–216
Customs agencies, 514–515
Customs union, 393
Customs valuation, 182, 187–188

Data (see Information)
Data (problems of), 366
Data flow restrictions, 638–639
Debt, 68–70, 72, 73
  Euromarkets, 306–312
  HPE, 361–362
  Local markets, 304–306
Debt-equity swap, 70
Decentralization, 612, 614–620
Deferral (taxation), 717
Deficit, 288–289

Delivery risk, 215
Democracy, 46–47, 50, 56–57
Democratic socialism, 56–57
Dependency, 129, 148–152, 173,
  362, 620
Depreciation (see Devaluation)
Deregulation, 315–316
Derivatives, 323–324
Devaluation, 268, 270, 278–279, 290
Developed country (see First World
  country)
Developing countries (also see Less-
  developed country), 58, 62, 150,
  318, 326, 329–333
Development banks, 329–333
Direct investment, 12, 26–29, 201–
  226, 430–454
Direct quote (foreign exchange), 240
Direct selling, 524
Discount (foreign exchange), 244
Distance, 613, 627
Distribution, 682–687
Diversification, 9–10, 173
Diversification strategy, 593–596
Divestment, 446, 592, 598–599, 609
Dividends, 738
Dow Jones Industrial Average
  (DJIA), 316
Dumping, 175–176, 189, 365
Duty (see Tariff)
Dynamic effect (economic
  integration), 393–394

Eastern bloc, 346
EC (see European Community)
Economic Community of West
  African States (ECOWAS), 409–
  410
Economic environment, 52–56
Economic exposure, 746–747
Economic growth, 62–64
Economic integration, 392–394
Economic (related to marketing),
  668, 683–684
Economics, 14–15, 18
Economic shocks, 355–356
Economic system, 45
Economy of scale, 135–136, 170, 213
ECU (See European Currency Unit)
Edge Act Corporation, 321, 323
EDI (see Electronic data interchange)
EEC (See European Community)
Effective tariff, 180
EFTA (see European Free Trade
  Association)
Electronic data interchange (EDI),
  323
Embargo, 183–184
Emerging equity markets, 318, 331
Employee stock ownership plan, 357

Employment discrimination, 771–772

Employment (effect of direct investment), 441–445

EMS (see European Monetary System)

Entente Council, 409

Enterprise of the Americas, 405–406

Entrepôt, 41

Entrepreneurship, 443–444

Environment, 176–177, 330, 419–420

Environmental climate, 578

Environmental scanning, 588

EPC (see European Patent Convention)

Equity market (and securities), 314–318

Errors and omissions, 284–289

Essential-industry argument, 177–178

Ethics, (see also Value system), 103, 447–448

Ethnocentrism, 108–109, 765

Eurobond, 311

Eurocredit, 309

Eurocurrency, 308–310

Eurodebt, 304–310

Eurodollars, 309

Euroequity market, 316–317

Europe 1992, 324–325, 399–403

European Atomic Energy, 395

European Central Bank, 274

European Coal and Steel Community, 395

European Commissions, 397–399

European Community, 20, 22, 324–325, 393, 394–403

European Council of Ministers, 397–399

European Court of Justice, 398

European Currency Unit, 274, 312

European Economic Community (see European Community)

European Investment Bank, 332

European Monetary System, 273–274

European Parliament, 393, 397–398

European Patent Convention (EPC), 489

European terms (foreign exchange), 240

Evidence account transaction, 254–255

Exchange rate (also see Currency value, Foreign exchange), 239

Exchange rate changes, business implications of, 289–291

Exchange rate determinants, 276–283

Exchange rate (fixed), 268, 270, 278–279

Exchange rate (flexible), 270

Exchange rate (floating), 270, 276–278

Exchange rate forecasting, 283–289

Eximbank (see Export-Import Bank)

Expatriates, 767–770

Experience (effect on operating form), 542, 544

Experience curve, 153

Export controls, 351, 367–368, 446–448

Export-Import Bank, 370, 530

Export-led development, 174

Export management company, 525

Export restrictions, 175, 177, 183–184

Export strategy, 521–530

Export tariff, 178

Export Trading Company, 525–526

Exports, 10, 287

Exposure (foreign exchange), 745–747

Expropriation, 478–481, 585–588

External relations, 484–486

Extraterritoriality, 45, 446–448, 453

Factor mobility, 207–210

Factor proportions, 129, 140–141, 155

Family-based groups, 93

Fatalism, 99

Favorable balance of trade, 131

FDI (see Direct investment)

Fees, 11

Finance function, 733–734

Financial Accounting Standards Board (FASB), 704

Financial engineering, 323–324

Financial risk, 743–753

Financial services, 325, 327–329

FIRA (see Foreign Investment Review Act)

First World country, 21, 22, 25, 58

Fisher Effect, 281

Fixed prices, 675–676

Foreign bond, 311

Foreign branch (tax), 716–717

Foreign Corrupt Practices Act, 452–453

Foreign Credit Insurance Association (FCIA), 530

Foreign currency transactions, 709–711

Foreign Direct Investment (see Direct investment)

Foreign exchange, 239

Foreign exchange arrangements, 270–273

Independently floating, 275

Limited flexibility, 271–274

More flexible, 274–275

Other managed floating, 275

Pegged rates, 271

Foreign exchange control, 185

Foreign exchange restrictions, 251–253

Foreign exchange risk, 305–306, 709–715

Foreign exchange trading, 322

Foreign freight forwarder (see Freight forwarder)

Foreign investment, 753–754

Foreign Investment Review Act (FIRA), 431, 433–434, 437

Foreign policy, 177–178

Foreign Sales Corporation (FSC), 716

Foreign trade organization (FTO), 364, 366–367

Foreign trade zones, 515

Fortress Europe, 402

Forward contracts, 257, 322, 324, 752

Forward exchange rate, 240, 243–244, 282

Forward market (foreign exchange), 241–242, 243–244, 245

Fractional reserve, 307

Franchising, 11, 376–377, 551–554

Freedom, 50

Free Trade Agreement (United States and Canada), 45

Free Trade Area, 393

Freight forwarder, 529

Fringe benefits, 784–785

FTO (see Foreign trade organization)

Functional adjustments, 15

Functional division structure, 623–624

Funds, 735–736

Futures contract, 324

Futures in foreign exchange, 245–246

Gap analysis, 663–664

GATT (see General Agreement on Tariffs and Trade)

Gender-based groups, 92

General Agreement on Tariffs and Trade, 21, 44–45, 186–189, 191

Generalized System of Preferences, 180

Generally Accepted Accounting Principles (GAAP), 704

Generic, 682

Generic names, 489

Geographic division structure, 623–624

Geography, 13–14

Global cash management (see Cash management)
Global company, 13
Global competition, 17
Global sourcing strategies, 509–512
Global strategy, (also see Economy of scale), 583, 616–617, 619, 639, 659, 676, 687–688
God, 268, 270
Godfather (see Mentor)
Gold, 266–268
Go-no-go decision, 597–598
Grandchild subsidiary, 718
Gray market, 675
Grids, 588–590
Group affiliations, 91–93, 99–100

Hard currencies, 251
Hardship allowance, 777
Hedge, 257, 750–753
Hetarchy, 626–627
Hickenlooper Amendment, 479–480
Hierarchy of needs, 96–97
High-income economies, 58–62
High-need achiever, 95–96
Hiring, 93
Historically planned economy, 21, 22, 342–383
History, 14
Home-country (effect on FDI), 470
Home-country national, 767–770
Hong, 39
Horizontal expansion, 212
Human resources, 760–799

IBRD (see International Bank for Reconstruction and Development)
ICAO, see International Civil Aviation Organization
IDA (see International Development Association)
IDB (see Inter-American Development Bank)
Idealism, 102
Ideology (political), 45–46
IFC (see International Finance Corporation)
ILO (see International Labor Organization)
IMF (see International Monetary Fund)
Imitation lag, 584
Imports, 10, 285, 287
Import deposit (foreign exchange), 250, 252
Import licensing, 184
Import opportunities, 154
Import strategies, 512–515
Import substitution, 174, 439

Import tariff, 179
Income elasticity, 661–663
Indirect quote (foreign exchange), 240
Indirect selling, 525
Industrial countries (also see First World country), 58, 62
Industrialization (as protectionist argument), 171–174
Infant industry, 170–171
Inflation, 64–66, 279–281, 744
Information, 611, 649–651
Information centers, 638
Information sources, 632–634
Innovation, 142–144
Input-output, 660
Instability assessment, 587–588
Intangible assets (see Intellectual property rights)
Integrated system (taxation), 721–722
Intellectual property rights, 488–492
Inter-American Conference on Inventions, Patents, Designs, and Models, 489
Inter-American Development Bank (IDB), 21, 332, 404
Interbank foreign exchange transactions, 239, 244, 246
Interdependence, 149
Interest arbitrage, 257
Interest rates, 281–282
Internalization, 206
International Accounting Standards Committee (IASC), 704
International Bank for Reconstruction and Development (IBRD), 329–330
International Banking Facility, 321
International Bureau for the Protection of Industrial Property Rights (BIRPI), 489
International business motivation, 9–10 defined, 8
International Center for Settlement of Investment Disputes, 481
International Chamber of Commerce, 480
International Civil Aviation Organization, 20
International Court of Justice, 481
International Development Association (IDA), 329–331
International division structure, 623–624
International Finance Corporation (IFC), 329–331
International Fisher Effect, 281–282
International Investment Survey Act, 456

Internationalization, 206, 211
International Labor Organization (ILO), 789–790
International law, 44–45
International Monetary Fund (IMF), 20, 70, 72–73, 268–275
International Monetary Market, 248–250
International product standards, 667
International Sea-Bed Authority, 417
International standard of fair dealing, 478
International Trade Administration (ITA), 530
Intrazonal trade, 406
Inventory control, 519–521
Investment banking, 322–323
Investment Canada, 431, 437
Investment guarantee program, 478–479
Investment incentives, 173, 219, 441, 472, 473
Investment proposal evaluation, 596–598
Investments, 12
Invisibles, 11
Islam, 44
Isolation, 767

Jamaica Agreement, 270–271
Japanese trading companies, 526–529
Joint venture, 12, 466, 494–498, 561–562
Just-in-time, 520–521

Keiretsu, 528–529, 627
Key industry, 449
Key sector control, 448–450
Kremlin, 49

Labor, 781–796
Labor intensity, 364
Labor markets, 763, 781–783
Labor relations, 785–793
Lag strategy, 751
LAIA (see Latin American Integration Association)
Language, 100–102, 475, 611, 678, 680–681, 763, 766–767
Latin American Integration Association (LAIA), 393, 405
Latin American integrator, 403–406
Law (see Legal environment), 14
LDC (see Less-developed country)
LDC criticisms, 668–669, 679–680
Lead strategy, 751
League of Arab States, 418
Learning curve, 170
Legal (effect on operating form), 541, 546

Legal (related to marketing), 667–668, 671–672, 678–679
Legal environment, 43–45
Legal forms, 640–641
Legal systems, 43–44
Leontief paradox, 141
Less-developed country, 22, 23
Leveraged buy-out, 327
LIBID, 310
LIBOR (See London Inter-Bank Offered Rate)
Licensing, 544–551
Licensing (foreign exchange), 251–252, 275
Licensing agreements, 11, 184–185
Lifetime employment, 787
Limited flexibility, 271, 640
Limited liability, 640
Liquidity, 269–270
Liquidity preference, 584–585
Loans to developing countries, 323–326
Local nationals, 679
London Inter-Bank Offered Rate, 309
London International Financial Futures Exchange (LIFFE), 248, 250
London Stock Exchange, 314, 316–317
Long-term capital, 285
Low income economies, 58–62

Management contracts, 11, 554–555
Management development, 769
Management recruitment, 778–780
Management style, 764
Management training programs, 358
Manufacturing strategies, 516–521
Maquiladora, 218, 436, 469, 518–519
Market capitalization, 314
Market economy, 52–53, 56–57
Market-expansion (as motivation for direct investment), 211–217
Marketing, 370–371, 655–738
Market size, 578–579
Market size analysis, 659–664
Market transformation, 354–362
Marshall plan, 329, 361, 394
Matrix, 590–593, 623, 625
Maxidevaluation (see Devaluation)
Mentor, 763
Mercantilism, 129, 130–132
Merchandise exports (see Exports)
Merchandise imports (see Imports)
Merchandise trade balance, 286, 288
Merchant banking, 322–323
Merger and acquisition, 394
MFA (see Arrangement Regarding International Trade in Textiles)

MFN (see Most-favored-nation)
Middle-income economies, 58–62
MIGA (see Multilateral Investment Guarantee Agency)
Ministry of International Trade and Industry (MITI), 55, 56
Minority control, 641
Mixed economy, 52, 54–56
Mixed venture, 12
MNC (see Multinational corporation)
MNE (see Multinational enterprise)
Mobility, 763–764, 768, 782–783
Monetary risk, 584–585
Monopoly, 359–360
Most-favored-nation, 186–187
Motivation, 94–97
Multidomestic strategy (also see National program), 13, 583, 687–688
Multifibre Arrangement (MFA) (see Arrangement Regarding International Trade in Textiles)
Multilateral Investment Guarantee Agency (MIGA), 329, 331–332, 481
Multilateral settlement of disputes, 480–481
Multinational agreements, 20–21
Multinational corporation, 13
Multinational enterprise, 13, 73–74
Multiple exchange rates, 252
Muslim law (see Islamic law)

National heterogeneity, 360
National program, 659
Nationalism, 214
Nationality image, 681–682
Nationalization (see Expropriation)
Natural advantage, 132–133
Negotiations, 366, 435, 468–478
Neomercantilism, 129, 132
Net capital flow, 440
Net export effect, 439–440
Net seller/buyer range (buffer stock), 411
Netting, 741–743
Newly industrialized country (NIC), 22, 58
New York Stock Exchange, 314–318
Nikkei Index, 316
Nonaccrual loan, 326
Nonequity forms (also see Strategic alliance and specific types of forms), 641
Nonmarket economy (NME) (see Historically planned economy)
Nonresident convertibility, 250
Nontariff barriers, 181–185
North America Free Trade Area, 423–427

North-South dialogue, 72–73

Occupation, 97
OECD (See Organization for Economic Cooperation and Development)
OEEC (See Organization for European Economic Cooperation)
Offer Rate (foreign exchange), 240
Offset trade, 185, 254–255
Offshore financial centers, 312–314
Offshore manufacturing (see Manufacturing strategies)
OPEC (See Organization of Petroleum Exporting Countries)
Operational centers, 313
Opinion leaders, 111
Optimum-tariff, 176
Options, 324, 752–753
Options in foreign exchange, 245–246, 250
Organisation of African Unity, 409–410
Organizational structure, 551, 620–627
Organization for Economic Cooperation and Development (OECD), 418
Organization for European Economic Cooperation (OEEC), 394–395
Organization of Petroleum Exporting Countries (OPEC), 414–416, 465–466
Outright forward, 245
Outsourcing (sourcing), 509–515

Pacific Economic Cooperation Conference (PECC), 408
Parallel market (foreign exchange), 251, 275
Paris Convention, 488–489
Parliamentary government, 48
Participation, 110–111, 487–488
Par value, 268
Passive income, 717
Patent Cooperation Treaty (PCT), 489
Patents, 488–492
PCT (see Patent Cooperation Treaty)
Pegged exchange rates, 270
Perception, 102
Performance evaluation, 619, 636–639
Performance requirements, 473
Philadelphia Stock Exchange, 248, 250
Physical attributes (human), 89–90
Piracy, 490–491
Planned Information Acquisition Analysis (PIAA), 637–638

Planning, 628–630
PLC (see Product life cycle)
Pluralistic, 45–56
Political environment, 45–51, 451
Political freedom, 50
Political motives for investment, 219–220
Political rights, 50
Political risk, 350–354, 585–588
Political science, 14
Political systems, 45, 48–50
Polycentrism, 108, 765
Portfolio investment, 12, 26
Poverty, 70–71
Pragmatism, 102
Premium (foreign exchange), 244
Pressure groups, 168–170, 435, 470–471
Price escalation, 673
Price ranges (commodity agreements), 412
Pricing, 671–676
Pricing (of technology), 548–550, 556
Private enterprise, 52
Privatization, 57, 62–64, 191, 356–357, 491–492
Product alteration, 215, 553–554, 667–670
Product complexity, 543
Product differentiation, 469
Product division structure, 623–624
Product image (by nationality), 214–215
Production concentration, 359–360
Production switching, 791–792
Product life cycle, (also see Stage of technology development), 129, 219, 142–146, 670–671
Product line mix, 670
Product policy, 664–667
Product standardization (see Standardization)
Product standards, 447–448
Promotion, 676–680
Property ownership, 52, 56–57
Protectionism, 53, 165–195, 368–369
Protectionism (as motivation for direct investment), 213–214
Protestant ethic, 94
Public ownership, 52
Public relations (see External relations)
Pull, 676–677
Purchasing-power parity, 279–281
Push-pull mix, 676–677

Quality control circle, 788
Quantity controls (foreign exchange), 253

Quota, 183
Quota (IMF), 269
Quotas (commodity agreements), 412–413
Quoted currency, 240

Rationalized production, 218
Reciprocal (foreign exchange), 240
Red tape, 580
Regional development banks, 332
Regional headquarters, 627
Regression, 663
Reinvestment, 441, 598
Religion, 44
Renegotiations, 473–474
Repatriation, 772–775
Reports, 635–639
Representative democracy, 47–48
Research, 631–634, 649–651
Reserves, 269
Resource acquisition, 9
Resource allocation, 52
Resource control, 52
Resource-seeking expansion, 581–582
Resource-seeking investments, 217–220
Resource transference, 615
Retaliation, 168–170
Return on investment (ROI), 582–583
Revaluation, 268, 279
Risk (also see Political risk, Monetary risk), 543, 582–588, 637
Role-playing, 477–478
Royalties, 11, 738

Sales expansion, 9
Sales to controlled entities, 550–551
Scale economy (see Economy of scale)
Scanning, 577–593
SDR (see Special Drawing Right)
SEAQ International, 317
SEC (see Securities and Exchange Commission)
Secondary boycott, 483
Second tier subsidiaries, 718
Second World (also see Historically planned economy), 58
Securities and Exchange Commission (SEC), 317
Separate entity approach (taxation), 721
Services, 11, 139, 185, 287
Seven Sisters, 464–467
Shared-ownership arrangements, 560–561
Silent language, 101–102
Single European Act, 401

Smithsonian Agreement, 270, 273
Social market economy, 354
Social responsibility, 485–486
Socialist, 52
Society, 88
Society for Worldwide Interbank Financial Telecommunications (SWIFT), 323
Soft budget, 357–358
Sogo shosha, 526–529
Sourcing strategy, 509–511
Southern African Development Coordination Conference, 409
Spare parts, 685
Special Drawing Right, 269, 271
Specific Duty, 180
Speculators, 257
Spillover, 595
Spot exchange rate, 239–243
Spot market (foreign exchange), 240–243, 245–248
Spread (foreign exchange), 243
Stage of technology development, 548
Standardization, 616
Start-up (see Buy-versus-build)
State-owned enterprises, 450
Static effect (economic integration), 393
Stereotypes, 90, 104
Stock exchanges, 314–318
Strategic alliance, 537–567, 642
Strategic intent, 628–629
Strategic trade policy, 191
Strategy (effect on operating form), 545–546
Strategy (related to trade policy), 189–191
Subpart F income, 718–719
Subsidiary, 640
Subsidiary management, 764–765
Subsidy, 181–182
Super 301, 176
Superior-subordinate relationships, 98
Surplus, 288–289
Swaps, 70, 245, 324, 558
SWIFT (see Society for Worldwide Interbank Financial Telecommunications)
Syndication, 309, 322–323

Tariffs, 178–181
Tax agreements, 20
Tax credit, 720
Tax-haven countries, 717–718
Tax planning, 723–725
Tax treaties, 723
Taxation, 715–725
Technical competence, 770

Technology, 16, 19
Technology (accessing), 558–559
Technology transfer, 443
Temporal method (translation of financial statements), 712
Terms of trade, 173–174
Theocratic law, 44
Third-country national, 767
Third World (also see Less-developed country), 58
Time series, 661
TNC (see Transnational corporation)
Tokyo Round (see General Agreement on Tariffs and Trade)
Tokyo Stock Exchange, 314–318
Totalitarianism, 46–48, 50, 56–57
Trade barriers, 393
Trade impediments, 154–155
Trade patterns, 21–25
Trade restrictions (see Protectionism)
Trade strategies, 66–67
Trade theory, 125–158
Trademark Registration Treaty (Vienna Convention), 489–490
Trademarks, 365, 489–491
Trading company, 525–529
Trading with the Enemy Act, 446
Training, 170, 780–781
Transaction exposure, 745
Transfer pricing (also see Sales to controlled entities), 440, 739–741
Transfers, 634–635

Transit tariff, 178
Translation exposure, 745
Translation of financial statements, 711–715
Transnational corporation, 13
Transportation, 211–212
Transport cost, 135, 139
Travel, 765
Treaties, legal, 45
Triad strategy, 333
Turnkey, 556–557
Turnkey operations, 11
Two-tiered bargaining, 471

UCC (see Universal Copyright Convention)
Uncertainties, 614, 630
Uncontrollable, 613–614
UNCTAD (see United Nations Conference on Trade and Development)
Unemployment, 169–170
Unilateral transfers, 287
Union (see Labor relations, Collective bargaining)
Unit of account, 270
United Nations, 417–418
United Nations Conference on Trade and Development (UNCTAD), 22, 72–73
U.S.–Canada Free Trade Agreement, 393, 394–395, 435
U.S. terms (foreign exchange), 240

Universal Copyright Convention (UCC), 490
Unrequited transfers, 287
Uruguay Round, 490

Value-Added Tax (VAT), 400–402, 722–723
Value system, 109–110
Vanilla derivatives, 322, 324
Variable prices, 675–676
Vertical integration, 217–218
Vienna Convention (see Trademark Registration Treaty)

Wars and insurrection, 19–20
Welfare, 54, 57
West African Economic Community, 409
Wholly owned operations, 559–561
Withholding tax, 720
Women, 330
Work (importance of), 94–97
Work teams, 789
World Bank, 21, 72–73, 268, 329, 481
World Court (see International Court of Justice)

Zaibatsu, 526